AN INTRODUCTION TO
CLASSICAL
RHETORIC

For Ako, Austin, and Sarah Elizabeth

AN INTRODUCTION TO CLASSICAL RHETORIC

Essential Readings

EDITED BY JAMES D. WILLIAMS

WILEY-BLACKWELL

A John Wiley & Sons, Ltd., Publication

This edition first published 2009
Editorial material and organization © 2009 James D. Williams

Blackwell Publishing was acquired by John Wiley & Sons in February 2007. Blackwell's publishing program has been merged with Wiley's global Scientific, Technical, and Medical business to form Wiley-Blackwell.

Registered Office

John Wiley & Sons Ltd, The Atrium, Southern Gate, Chichester, West Sussex, PO19 8SQ, United Kingdom

Editorial Offices

350 Main Street, Malden, MA 02148-5020, USA

9600 Garsington Road, Oxford, OX4 2DQ, UK

The Atrium, Southern Gate, Chichester, West Sussex, PO19 8SQ, UK

For details of our global editorial offices, for customer services, and for information about how to apply for permission to reuse the copyright material in this book please see our website at www.wiley.com/wiley-blackwell.

The right of James D. Williams to be identified as the author of the editorial material in this work has been asserted in accordance with the Copyright, Designs and Patents Act 1988.

Wiley also publishes its books in a variety of electronic formats. Some content that appears in print may not be available in electronic books.

Designations used by companies to distinguish their products are often claimed as trademarks. All brand names and product names used in this book are trade names, service marks, trademarks or registered trademarks of their respective owners. The publisher is not associated with any product or vendor mentioned in this book. This publication is designed to provide accurate and authoritative information in regard to the subject matter covered. It is sold on the understanding that the publisher is not engaged in rendering professional services. If professional advice or other expert assistance is required, the services of a competent professional should be sought.

Library of Congress Cataloging-in-Publication Data

An introduction to classical rhetoric : essential readings / edited by James D. Williams.
    p. cm.
Includes bibliographical references and index.
    ISBN 978-1-4051-5860-2 (hardcover : alk. paper) – ISBN 978-1-4051-5861-9 (pbk. : alk. paper)
1.   Rhetoric, Ancient. I. Williams, James D. (James Dale), 1949–
PA3265.I58 2009
808'.00938–dc22

                                        2008055859

A catalogue record for this book is available from the British Library.

Set in 10/12pt Dante by SPi Publisher Services, Pondicherry, India
Printed and bound in Singapore by Ho Printing Singapore Pte Ltd

03   2013

Contents

Detailed Contents

Plates appear between pp. 276 and 277

Acknowledgments

Several people have contributed significantly to this book and should be acknowledged here. Jim Aune, David Zarefsky, Walter Jost, Robert Gaines, and Sharon Crowley provided useful comments and suggestions that helped shape the direction of my work. Thomas Cole gave me valuable advice regarding the use of τεχνη in reference to display texts. My assistant, Lynn Hamilton-Gamman, provided invaluable support. I could not have written this text without the help of our university librarian, Lisa Polfer, who was able to locate even the most hard-to-find texts. My colleague Nalini Rao generously advised me regarding illustrations. Irene Clark's encouragement and support stimulated me to undertake this complex project even in the face of numerous obstacles. I also must thank my wife, Ako, for patiently listening to me talk incessantly about ancient Greeks and Romans during the writing process.

Introduction

An Introduction to Classical Rhetoric: Essential Readings examines several major figures in the history of classical Greek and Roman rhetoric and offers access to some of their original writings. The text is designed to meet the needs of advanced undergraduate and beginning graduate students in communications as well as those in rhetoric and composition programs.

The rationale for the text grew out of my work in teaching the history of rhetoric, as well as from conversations with colleagues around the country who have been looking for a book that meets their needs in ways that existing texts do not. Anthologized readings are readily available, but the amount of background information in them, so crucial to contextualizing the readings, is commonly sparse. As a result, students just beginning the study of classical rhetoric find it difficult to understand the social and historical factors that influenced periods and orators. The great length of most of the works demands that the number of complete texts be limited, which further increases the need for contextualizing information. In addition, these texts often lack any pedagogical apparatus, which decreases their usefulness as learning tools.

An Introduction to Classical Rhetoric: Essential Readings addresses these issues in two ways. First, I agree with Rorty's (1984) statement that "It is useful to recreate the intellectual scene in which the dead lived their lives" (p. 50). People as well as ideas exist within a cultural framework that both grounds and defines them. Although looking specifically at Plato's works, Wolfsdorf's (1998) assessment is nevertheless relevant here: "In order to understand a historical artefact … an investigation of the artefact must be made with attention to its historical setting …. Yet remarkably few … scholars have taken great pains to understand … [Plato's] works in the light of this complex historical setting" (p. 127). One of my primary goals in *An Introduction to Classical Rhetoric*, therefore, is to provide students with the necessary historical setting – even while recognizing that a text like this cannot explore the relevant sociocultural frameworks in great detail and must necessarily engage in a certain degree of reduction and oversimplification. But within the various and fairly obvious restricting parameters, the text provides information in its general introductions to the Greek and Roman periods that will give students at least a rudimentary understanding of the complex social, cultural, economic, intellectual, and historical factors that shaped rhetoric in ways that reverberate even today. Each selection also has an introduction that locates the figure and the work in their sociocultural milieu and that, when appropriate, considers the relation of the passage to the longer work from which it came. Second, to enhance pedagogical effectiveness, reading selections are followed by study questions, suggestions for further reading, and potential writing topics designed to stimulate critical thinking and multiple perspectives on the material and to provide starting points for dialogue, writing, and research. Because theory and practice have been intertwined throughout history to such an extent that it sometimes is difficult to determine where theory ends and practice begins, the text provides guidance by identifying those works that primarily reflect theory and those that reflect practice.

Part I: Greek Rhetoric

While recognizing the uncertainty inherent in locating the origins of rhetoric, the introduction to Greek rhetoric in Part I is located within the framework of Havelock's (1986) argument that formal theories of rhetoric emerged as ancient Greece transitioned from an oral to a literate society. The text examines various social and cultural dynamics that, as far as we can determine, influenced those theories: a fascination with language in general and poetry in particular; a society affected by shifting economies, slavery, war, and class struggle; and efforts to understand such fundamental concepts as truth, justice, and what constitutes the good.

Literacy among the Greeks was lost during the dark ages that followed the collapse of the Minoan civilization. Consequently, the transmission of information, whether it be messages or history, was oral. As the dark ages ended, literacy began to reemerge until Greek societies reached the transition point to full literacy. At the core of this change was an intellectual move away from the mythico-poetic view that dominated the ancient world. Philosophy, logic, and dialectic – not poetry and myth – became the methods of choice for understanding the world, and politics and manmade law became the primary means of guiding human conduct.

One of the more interesting results was the effect on women. Throughout the Archaic Period, religion and poetry were interrelated, and women were involved in both. Enheduanna (c. 2300 BC), for example, was the high priestess of the goddess Nanna in ancient Ur, and her poems were so popular that they were being copied 500 years after her death. Sappho (c. 630 BC), although perhaps best known for her homoerotic poetry, wrote numerous verses describing women engaged in religious rites and festivals. Women, it seems, produced poetry with some degree of regularity, and there is good reason to view poetry in Greece as the precursor to rhetoric. But when public speaking designed to influence others – rhetoric – supplanted poetry, women were effectively excluded from the practice of rhetoric because in Greece they were not allowed to participate in legal matters or politics. Nevertheless, the foundation that women poets laid continued to influence rhetoric throughout both the Greek and Roman periods in complex and often subtle ways.

The Sophists were the principal teachers of poetry during the fifth century BC, and they served a pivotal role in the transition from orality to literacy. The introduction therefore analyzes the Older Sophists and their contributions to the development of rhetoric and rhetorical theory. In the process, it contextualizes the work of Plato and Aristotle by linking their theories of rhetoric to the groundwork the Sophists laid, as well as to the social forces of the time. For example, the link between democracy and rhetoric is commonly acknowledged, but we find what may be the first overt connection in 403 BC, when the Council of Thirty banned the teaching of rhetoric owing to its potential for sowing sedition. What readers discover as they move through Part I is that many of the issues debated by ancient Greek rhetoricians are still being contested today: humanism, ethics, the subjective or objective nature of reality, justice and injustice, good government, rationalism v. empiricism, and the nature of virtue.

Part II: Roman Rhetoric

The great influence Greece had on Rome has led some scholars to argue that there was no such thing as "Roman rhetoric" and that a more accurate appellation is *Greco-Roman*. Although gifted engineers and legislators, Romans seem to have had little penchant for original philosophizing or theorizing, so they borrowed copiously from the Greeks to fill their needs. Early Rome was a republic rather than a direct democracy, but it was a society in which public speaking was as important to civic life as it had been in Athens, although for different reasons. Leaders began studying Greek literature, philosophy, and rhetoric after the end of the Punic Wars not only to become more cultured but also to exercise more control over the people. The brothers Tiberius and Gaius Gacchi, who began the social revolution that eventually brought down the Republic, had studied rhetoric with two of the best teachers of the time, and Julius Caesar was highly acclaimed for his oratory and was deemed to have only one superior in this regard – Cicero.

The introduction to Part II examines the influence of Greek rhetorical theory and practice on Roman education and the practice of rhetoric. Education and practice in Rome were not always congruent, however. What was taught in the schools and the handbooks – rhetoric – often failed to match what speakers did in the assemblies and courts – oratory. The discussion therefore differentiates oratory and rhetoric in the Roman context. In addition, it explores some of the social forces that shifted Rome from republic to empire, considering how war, social turmoil, and struggle for prominence were significant factors in the development of rhetoric and oratory in Rome. Cicero (c. 106–43 BC), for example, came of age as the general Sulla was accumulating the unprecedented power that allowed him to become Rome's first dictator. Cicero's career was also dedicated to accumulating and exercising power, albeit via the path of oratory rather than the sword.

The connection between rhetoric and democracy was as evident during the Roman Period as it was during the Greek, but in quite different ways. The ruling elite viewed rhetoric with suspicion, leading the Roman Senate to ban the teaching of rhetoric and close all the schools in 161 BC. Although this move was partially motivated by strong anti-Greek sentiments among the Romans, it is clear that the Senate also was motivated by a desire to eliminate a powerful tool for social change. In the hands of demagogues like the Gracchi, rhetoric had the potential to stir the restless poor, inciting them to riots as part of the endless internal conflicts among the ruling elite. In the hands of skillful legal orators like Lucius Licinius Crassus and Cicero, it had the power to undermine Rome's traditionally rigid interpretation and application of law.

The lack of democratic forums for persuasive speech – crucial to both rhetorical practice and theory – had important consequences, especially after the transition from republic to empire. Oratory became a form of entertainment, giving rise to increased interest in questions of style. To counter the dominant style, known as Asianism, rhetoricians and orators began exploring practices of the past, specifically the work of the Greek Sophists, which led to the Second Sophistic. Meanwhile, instruction focused on steeping students in Greek culture and teaching them elaborate rules and procedures that were based on the close study of Greek texts from the fourth and fifth centuries BC. The emphasis on language as entertainment may have acted as a stimulus for a remarkable explosion of literary talent in the first two centuries of the Empire, known as the Age of Silver. During this period, the lines between rhetoric and literature blurred, and we find certain similarities with the work of the early Sophists, whose rhetoric often included poetic features.

Beginning in the sixth century BC, Thales and other Ionian philosophers had initiated an intellectual revolution when they rejected the prevalent mythic view of the world, decried belief in the supernatural, and advocated the application of empirical observation to understanding the natural laws that govern the universe. This proto-scientific approach to knowledge was very influential, and by the time of Aristotle it had led to a significant alteration in poetic allegory. No longer a device for interpreting supposedly hidden meanings related to the nature of gods and men, allegory became simply a rhetorical figure, and logic became a principal feature of speaking and writing. The emergence of Christianity, however, challenged the centuries-old tradition of reason and empiricism. Predicated on faith and belief in the supernatural, Christianity was hostile to this tradition. Early Christian leaders, men like Origen, Ambrose, and Augustine, used their rhetorical training to initiate a return to a mythic world view. Their treatises, sermons, and letters rejected knowledge that was not derived from or linked to the Bible and effectively dismantled the approach to learning and wisdom that had dominated the Classical Period. Empirical observation was replaced by faith. In the process, they created a new rhetoric, a Christian rhetoric, that was predicated on interpreting the Scriptures through allegory.

Christian leaders like Augustine had few opportunities to speak outside their churches owing to the sociopolitical environment, so they applied their rhetorical techniques to writing, which contributed greatly to what Kennedy (1980) called "secondary rhetoric," and the text examines how secondary rhetoric was linked to the end of the pagan world and the rise of Christianity. The transition created a variety of tensions for rhetoric and oratory, and the final chapter examines some of them by looking at Libanius, a pagan rhetorician, and Augustine, Bishop of Hippo. Libanius was among the leading rhetoricians of the fourth century, whereas Augustine was one of the fathers of the early Catholic Church. Each was important in his own right, and by examining them in the final chapter, the text allows readers to see how culture, ideology, education, and religion influenced the direction of rhetoric and oratory. The text considers how Augustine applied his skill to develop Church doctrine and how his reversion to ancient allegorical techniques played an important role in reinstating the mythico-poetic world view that the early Greek philosophers had sought to eliminate. In the process, he shaped biblical exegesis and established the foundational methodology for modern literary analysis.

Writing about History

Anyone writing about history faces many challenges, and two are particularly troublesome. One is the limited availability of documents that allow us to understand fully the social dimensions of a given period. The number of documents that have survived the passage of time is relatively small, which for centuries has led to speculation about the past that is difficult to support. This is especially true of early Greek history. Another challenge is understanding and interpreting those documents in their original contexts when our analyses are limited by the paucity of information and are colored by the lens of our own modernity. Barring the unlikely discovery of additional texts from these early periods, there is no way to address the first challenge. With regard to the second challenge, my interpretations are evident throughout, although in striving for objectivity I have indicated competing views to the extent possible. It is inevitable that some readers will contest my analyses, and I hope that this generates more light than heat and encourages critical thinking among students.

Perhaps even more problematic is that writing a book like this one necessarily requires a great deal of oversimplification. Many important theories, philosophies, movements, works, and secondary periods had to be excluded to keep the text to a feasible length. Doing a thorough job of exploring just the origins of formal theories of rhetoric requires a book-length treatment, and the same could be said about the relation between poetry and rhetoric and most of the other topics addressed in this work. Therefore, it is important to acknowledge at the outset that *An Introduction to Classical Rhetoric: Essential Readings* recognizes the complexities inherent in the material but does not – indeed, cannot – address them all.

A Note on Translations

The reading selections are those that are widely, but not universally, viewed as essential to an introduction to the foundations of rhetoric. Space constraints led to the exclusion of several valuable authors and texts, and there is no question in my mind that a different hand would have made different selections. To compensate for this unavoidable compromise, suggestions for further reading are included throughout.

Various translations exist for most of the texts included here, and selecting the best one in each case presented a significant challenge. In many instances, such as Gorgias' *Encomium of Helen*, the stylistic qualities of the original make translation into English difficult, and different translators focus on different features of the text. Purists might argue that translation is impossible and that those who study the history of rhetoric can understand these works fully only by reading them in their original Greek or Latin. While sympathetic to this view, I recognize that it is not congruent with the needs of the majority of students today.[1]

My choices of English translations for the readings were based on a combination of factors: reliability, accuracy, readability, and cost. As in the case of the reading selections themselves, there is no question that another hand would have made different choices. When discussing the readings and their historical contexts, I occasionally refer to related works in Greek or Latin; in these instances, I provide the original text followed by my own translation. In producing these translations, I sought to convey the substance of the original in contemporary language and structures. Some readers, preferring more literal translations, might object to this approach, arguing that it fails to capture the full flavor of the originals. Again, I am sympathetic but believe that translations that adhere too closely to the original language and structures can be overly taxing in an introductory text.

---

[1] Those who are proficient in languages other than English may want to examine the two classics in the field of Greek rhetoric: Diels and Kranz's *Die Fragmente der Vorsokratiker*, 6th ed., which was published in three volumes in 1951 and 1952, as well as Untersteiner and Battegazzore's *Sofisti, Testimonianze e frammenti IV: Antifonte, Crizia*, published in 1962.

Part I

Classical Greek Rhetoric

1

Introduction to Greek Rhetoric

Rhetoric today has many different meanings. In some cases, we use the term to designate language that is pretentious or insincere, as in the expression "empty rhetoric." In other cases, we use it to refer to a particular kind of language, as in "political rhetoric" or "campaign rhetoric." We also use it to refer to speaking effectively and persuasively, as well as to college composition courses, which often are described as courses in rhetoric. In addition, rhetoric describes a field of academic study. The sheer number of different uses of the word makes it difficult to define, and some scholars have argued that this difficulty is symptomatic of a greater problem – a pervasive decline in the value we accord language in general and rhetoric in particular. Addressing the state of rhetoric as it is embodied in composition courses, Fleming (2002), for example, argued that it is an anemic enterprise compared to the rich tradition of rhetoric in the past.

Many of us – perhaps most of us – are immersed in pedestrian language that lacks precision and persuasive force. Only when we hear the "I Have a Dream" speech of Martin Luther King or the speeches of John F. Kennedy are we reminded of how language can elevate us, move us. It often seems that effective communication is discounted because close attention to language is considered elitist. Yet there was a time when attention to language was so great that entire societies recognized rhetoric as the most important subject a person could master. In the history of Western civilization, in fact, the intense study of rhetoric lasted for more than 2,000 years. On this basis, our current period could easily be considered an anomaly.

But what about the Classical Period? How was rhetoric defined then? Close examination of the available texts indicates that even in classical times it lacked a single definition. The simplest definition, linked to Plato (c. 427–347 BC), who may have coined the term, was persuasive speech in a public forum. But he also defined rhetoric as a form of pandering that influenced the masses by telling them what they wanted to hear. It was the artificer of deception, the antagonist of truth and justice. Aristotle (c. 384–322 BC) complicated matters further by presenting several definitions in his *Art of Rhetoric:* It is an "art" (*technê*), "a counterpart to dialectic" (I. I. 1), and the ability of observing or discovering "in each case the existing means of persuasion" (I. I. 14), with the aim of securing a judgment. In all these definitions, however, one factor is consistently present – the power of language to persuade and influence others.

The Origins of Rhetoric

Today we recognize that rhetoric existed (and exists) in many forms in many societies. We may talk about Chinese rhetoric, for example, or Arabic rhetoric. Yet as far was we can tell, it was the ancient Greeks who were the first to engage in the systematic study and teaching of rhetoric and oratory. Tradition holds that the formal study of rhetoric began around 467 BC in the Greek city of Syracuse on the island of Sicily. In Book 3 of *The Art of Rhetoric*, Aristotle identified Corax and Tisias, two Sicilians, as the first teachers of rhetoric. In the standard account, Corax, after observing several trials, noticed that successful litigants used certain techniques in speaking that their adversaries did not. He used his observations to develop a "system" of rhetorical study and began teaching classes on how to win in court. Corax took on a student named Tisias, and together they supposedly went on to produce handbooks on public speaking that were very popular, especially in Athens (Enos, 1993; Kennedy, 1980), where democracy was well established and where a less systematized form of rhetoric combined to provide fertile ground for the handbooks. The handbooks did not survive the passage of time, but various sources report that their primary contribution to rhetoric was the introduction of argument based on probability. That is, in any cause of action, the paramount question was whether it was *probable* that the accused had committed the wrong. The value of this innovation can be properly understood only when one considers that direct testimony of witnesses was highly suspect in ancient Greece owing to the prevalence of rampant bribery. In most cases, a jury just could not believe witnesses.

Plato and the origin of rhetoric

Both Cole (1991) and Schiappa (1999, 2003) argued that there is no evidence to support the claim that Corax and Tisias were the first teachers of rhetoric – and more important, that the term "rhetoric" did not even exist before Plato wrote his dialogue *Gorgias* around 385 BC. In his extensive review of classical texts, Schiappa (2003) found that the term "rhetoric" (*rhêtorikê*) "does not appear in fifth- and early fourth-century texts where it would be expected to appear if the term were in common, or even in specialized, usage" (p. 41). Instead, the word used in these texts is *logos* (and its variants). On this account, Cole and Schiappa declared that Plato originated rhetoric, at least in the formal sense. From this perspective, those who came before Plato practiced a form of public speaking, but it was not rhetoric.[1]

The difference may initially appear overly subtle, but *logos* is a difficult word to define, owing to its numerous uses in ancient Greek. In many fifth-century texts, it appears as *technê orthos legein*, "the skill of speaking correctly" and as *technê logon*, "the skill of argument." According to Schiappa (2003), these terms are broader than "rhetoric," which seems to derive from *rhêtor*, the term used in the sixth and fifth centuries to designate a politician who frequently made speeches in the assembly. Schiappa argued that Plato coined the term "rhetoric," as well as the term "oratory," to shift the focus, to establish a technical vocabulary that differentiated persuasive discourse from just correct speaking: thus, *rhêtoreia* (oratory) and *rhêtorikê* (rhetoric).[2] On this account, Schiappa noted that "oratory … [was] the product of the rhetor, and rhetoric … [was] the art or skill of the rhetor" (2003, p. 40). *Logos*, on the other hand, focused on precision in language and critical thinking, not on persuasive public speaking, which was secondary. Schiappa claimed, therefore, that "It is more likely that Corax and Tisias attempted simply to teach would-be orators how to plead reasonable and hence believable cases" (2003, p. 51).

---

[1] For several decades, it has been popular to define all communication as rhetorical. Doing so may be overstating the case and confusing rhetoric with semiotics. In any event, ancient Greeks may have questioned this definition as too broad.

[2] Note that in modern Greek *rhêtoreia* and *rhêtorikê* have almost exactly the same meaning: public speaking.

Not all scholars agree with the claim that Plato coined the term "rhetoric." Pendrick (1998), for example, argued that the Sophists' broad understanding of *technê logon* did not preclude the more specific application to speeches in the courts and the assembly. In support he noted that Plato, Isocrates (c. 436–338 BC), and Aristotle attested to the existence of various handbooks on rhetoric that offered some measure of technical discussion on the skill of speaking correctly. We might consider, in this regard, the discussion of "books of rhetoric" in Plato's *Phaedrus* that provide for the division of oratory into its various parts – exordium, statement of facts, presentation of witnesses, and so on. Pendrick on this basis concluded that Cole and Schiappa's argument that Plato invented rhetoric lacks substantiation: "All our evidence indicates that even before Plato's attack on ρητορικη [rhetoric] there existed an evolving discipline concerned with the techniques of persuasive speech" (1998, p. 23).

Slavery, freedom, and democratization

If we are to locate emergent rhetoric in its social context, we must consider a number of related factors that influenced Greek social structure, attitudes, and ways of thinking. Of paramount importance is the high value the Greeks had placed on public discourse for centuries. Homer's (1991) *Iliad*, put into written form around 800 BC, provides some insight into the nature of Greek education before the sixth century. Here we find that the hero Achilles was tutored as a youth to be "a speaker of words and a doer of deeds" (9.454–455), and the work includes numerous speeches that illustrate the importance of speaking well. As Wheelock (1974) noted, "All this foreshadows the conspicuous place of … elocution and rhetoric in later Greek education" (p. 4). We therefore can safely conclude that education, public speaking, and politics developed a symbiotic relation early in Greek society. Vernant (1982) argued, therefore, that democracy and rhetoric – used now in its technical sense – were simultaneously stimulated in Athens in the middle of the seventh century BC when the ruler Draco (c. 659–601 BC) codified Athenian law, thereby setting limits on aristocratic power and laying the foundation for democracy. In this view, Draco's laws were revolutionary because they articulated a new way of governing: The sword ceased being the sole – or even the primary – means of governing the populace. Vernant also argued that after the seventh century BC, speech gained increasing importance as a means of exercising political power, in large part because increasing numbers of people were becoming literate. At the core of this argument is the astute awareness that rhetoric in the Classical Period was closely tied to politics.

Other factors to consider when exploring rhetoric's origins are the social and economic changes that began in the seventh century, when agriculture in Greece shifted from grain to olives, figs, and wine. The Greek mainland is mountainous and rugged and therefore not well suited to agriculture. The little cultivable land available was of poor quality and produced such low yields that by the fifth century BC the bulk of Athens' grain came from Euboea and the Bosporus region. The new crops were significantly more profitable than grain because they were less taxing on the soil and because they were in high demand. But they required large sums of capital owing to the fact that the trees and vines took several years to bear fruit. Thus, Patterson (1991) argued that the shifting economic base effected changes in politics and education that gave rise to rhetoric. Lack of sufficient capital for orchards and vineyards, combined with poor yields, forced many small farmers and sharecroppers off their land, and those who were displaced had no alternative but to travel to Athens in search of work. Patterson suggested that the displaced small farmers created a farm-labor shortage and that the landowners responded by relying increasingly on slave labor to tend and harvest crops.

In the ancient world, warfare and the loot it provided upon success were important parts of all economies. Warfare also offered Athens a steady supply of slaves to solve the labor crisis. But there were unforeseen consequences. Hesiod's *Works and Days*, written in the eighth century, described eloquently the value inherent in hard manual labor and how life on the farm was embedded in the very notion of human dignity. But by the fifth century, when 30 percent of Athens' population consisted of slaves, these notions had to strike many as quaint (see Martin, 1996). With slaves doing all the hard work, manual labor came to be viewed as demeaning and unbefitting a citizen.

Warfare and changing economic conditions, moreover, seem to have changed Athenians' understanding of the world and themselves. They more clearly recognized the ease with which a person's life could be turned topsy-turvy. As the number of slaves increased, Athenians gained a keen perception of life's vicissitudes and an even keener appreciation for freedom, especially as the economic plight of displaced farmers grew so extreme that large numbers were sold into slavery (often to foreign masters) to satisfy their debts. Solon's (c. 640–559 BC) decree prohibiting slaves from using the gymnasia, which they had been able to do previously, reflected a social move to differentiate more rigorously freemen from slaves. Simultaneously, Solon authorized the use of public funds to purchase the freedom of all Athenians whom necessity had put under the yoke of slavery; then he took the even more extraordinary step of discharging all debts for the lower classes and forbidding the practice of indebted slavery for citizens.

In this context, the many free but destitute displaced farmers in Athens used the threat of revolution as leverage to pry political power from the ruling oligarchs, demanding and getting restraints on the elite's power and greater roles in the political process. About 10 percent of Athenian citizens were wealthy, and by law they were required to use their wealth to erect government buildings, pay for festivals, and field armies and navies in time of war – expenditures that frequently sent families and entire clans into bankruptcy. The poor made up about 50 percent of the citizens, and the middle class made up the remaining 40 percent. The shift in the economy led to an expansion of trade, especially as Athens established its empire, which allowed some members of the middle class to become wealthy. Their wealth, in turn, led them to demand a greater voice in public affairs, thereby challenging the traditional role of the nobility. Overall, however, the middle class, like the poor, lacked the means to provide material benefits to the city, so their contributions came in the form of government service, a happy compromise, particularly after Pericles (c. 495–429 BC) used his influence as leader of Athens to secure payment for those who held government positions. The ruling elite were saved from revolution, while maintaining their general status, and the displaced received a modest stipend that enabled them to survive. The result was a movement toward democratization that accelerated when war broke out between Athens and Sparta in 431 BC. Athens depended on members of the lower and middle classes to man its large navy, and with the spark of democracy burning in their breasts, these warriors demanded and received greater participation in political decisions. Freedom took on new meaning and became one of the more discussed and analyzed topics over the next 100 years. Participation in politics, however, required skill in public speaking. In this analysis, the combination of democratization, war, and a new sense of freedom was the catalyst for rhetoric.

Missing from discussions of the socioeconomic influences on rhetoric, however, is recognition that increasingly stable political structures and more equitable distribution of resources led to increased prosperity and more leisure time for Athenian citizens.

Sources of entertainment were extremely limited, and without the burden of constant toil to put food on the table, citizens were no doubt eager to find interesting ways to spend their time. The literature on rhetoric and oratory from both the Greek and the Roman periods frequently mentions the ability of speakers to attract large crowds and to awe them with their orations. Some rhetoricians were treated like today's movie stars, celebrities whose fame and fortune were unparalleled. For us to begin to understand the role of rhetoric and oratory in the ancient world, therefore, it is important to recognize that, in addition to its important pragmatic functions, oratory served for centuries as one of the more popular forms of entertainment.

Precursors of Rhetoric

Although the above accounts of rhetoric's origins are interesting, they are not sufficiently elaborated and do not fully address the complexity of the subject. A given in the study of history is that few, if any, events spring out of nothing. The closer we look, the more obvious it becomes that everything develops from and is connected to what existed previously. This understanding makes the traditional account of rhetoric's origins involving Corax and Tisias, for example, seem suspect and leads inevitably to an obvious question: What came before? Answering this question requires us to look farther back in history.

Writing originated in about 4000 BC in Mesopotamia and spread throughout the Mediterranean in different forms. According to Maisels (1990), by the time of King Sargon (reigned c. 2334–2279 BC), every household in Sumeria included "at least one person able to read, write, and calculate" (p. 121). Around 2000 BC, writing appeared on the island of Crete, home of the Minoan civilization, in the form known as Linear A – hieroglyphics that scholars have not been able to decipher but that are decidedly non-Greek. Over the next several centuries, the Minoans had increasing contact with Greek-speaking traders from the mainland, commonly known as Mycenaeans. Little is known about the relations between the two cultures, but based on artwork and archaeological excavations, the Mycenaeans appear to have been significantly more warlike, which has led to speculation that they conquered the Minoans. In any event, by about 1500 BC, the Mycenaeans were in control of Crete and began the transfer of culture and artifacts to the mainland. In the process, they adapted Linear A to writing early Greek, which we have in the form of what is known as Linear B.

The Mycenaean civilization prospered until about 1200 BC, at which time unknown factors led to its collapse. Some scholars believe that a tribe called the Dorians, originating in what is now Macedonia, swept through Greece, defeating the Mycenaean armies and destroying cities and towns until little was left. Others attribute the collapse to a full-scale assault by seafaring warriors called the Sea People, who terrorized the entire Mediterranean, crippling the Egyptian Empire and destroying the ancient civilization of the Hittites. Still others see the end of the Mycenaean civilization as being part of a region-wide social collapse owing to rapid and drastic climate change – perhaps accompanied by the widespread destruction wreaked by bands of warriors like the Dorians and the Sea People – which caused famine on an unprecedented scale. In this account, cities and towns were depopulated as residents left in search of food and safety. What followed was a massive migration of people across the entire Mediterranean that reconfigured centuries-old cultural and social characteristics and plunged the Aegean region into a dark age. In this chaos, literacy was lost among the Greeks.

Women and poetry

The most important social institutions, however, were not lost – education and religion chief among them. Women played important roles in both. They had held significant positions in religion from the earliest days of the great civilizations. Campbell (1970) pushed the dates back even further, arguing that women's prominent place in religious rituals may have begun as early as the proto-Neolithic Period (c. 12000–8000 BC), or earlier, and that by the Neolithic Period (c. 8000–4000 BC) religion was dominated by women who were responsible for pervasive mother-goddess cults.

One of the better known examples of a woman in a powerful religious position is Enheduanna (c. 2300 BC). Although officially she was high priestess to the moon god Nanna in the Mesopotamian city of Ur, Enheduanna appears to have dedicated herself to the goddess of love and war, Inanna. As J. Roberts (2004) noted, the role of high priestess was complex, involving supervision of religious rituals (particularly those associated with harvests and child birth), support for the divine right of the king, and the composition of hymns to the gods. Enheduanna excelled in this latter task, and her poetic songs of praise are "the first known written record of a religious belief system" (Meador, 2000, p. 155). They also are among the oldest known examples of literary writing and are the earliest in which we find the writer working in the first person, writing as an individual.

The scarcity of historical artifacts and texts forces us to speculate, but it seems reasonable to assume that women held similar positions during the Mycenaean Period in Greece. We know, for example, that from at least 1400 BC the most important religious site in Greece was at Delphi, where women served as the Pythia, the oracle and priestess of Apollo.[3] When the dark ages descended and literacy was lost, however, the only way priestesses could continue to produce hymns to the gods was through oral composition. After 400 years or more, Greece began to emerge from the dark ages and entered what is referred to as the Archaic Period (c. 800–500 BC), and by then, the oral tradition was fully developed.

This tradition was based solidly on poetry, performed as song, usually accompanied by music. The poetry was not limited to hymns to the gods; it also preserved and conveyed history, morals, and social norms. We cannot determine the degree to which priestesses and other women in the temples contributed to the development of the oral tradition, but it seems likely that their role was significant. The collapse of the Roman Empire may provide a useful analogy here. During the Dark Ages that followed the Empire's collapse, the Church was one of the few institutions that survived, and its priests and monks became the custodians of knowledge. The priestesses of the Greek temples may also have taken on this task, which would explain why the (female) Muse of poetry grants divine inspiration and knowledge, thereby setting the poet apart from ordinary mortals. It also would explain why the history that was preserved involved epic stories of gods and heroes, legends and myths – and why the dead Mycenaean Period that is the subject of these tales emerged as a Golden Age.

What we know with certainty is that during the Archaic Period, women in the temples as well as those outside the priestly class frequently engaged in religious activities and festivals, in which they sang songs and recited poetry. Evidence comes from existing

---

[3] We also know that this tradition continued through both the Archaic and Classical periods. As Gould (1980) noted, "In the sacred and ritual activities of the community the active presence of women in the public world is not merely tolerated but required. As priestesses in many of the major cults of the *polis*, as *kanephoroi* [basket carriers] and *hydrophoroi* [water carriers] in the great religious processions … in mourning and at funerals, in the rituals of marriage, the participation of women is indispensable to the sacral continuity, the ordering of society" (pp. 50–51).

fragments, such as the Spartan poet Alcman's (c. 650 BC) *Partheneia*, a choral song performed publicly by young girls during their rites of initiation into womanhood. Sappho (c. 610–570 BC), the only female Greek poet from the Archaic Period whose writing has survived, wrote poems that seem to deal with the initiation rites of young girls. On this basis, some have argued that Sappho operated a school for girls that prepared them for marriage (such preparation was necessary because girls in all Greek communities other than Sparta were closely sheltered and also because they commonly wed between the ages of 13 and 15). In addition, Greek funerary vases provide a glimpse into women's role in funeral rites. As early as 750 BC, these vases depicted women mourners, and there is some evidence that a century later women's participation had become institutionalized to such an extent that the practice of hiring them as mourners was widespread (Fantham et al., 1994; Holst-Warhaft, 1992).

Social structures, however, appear to undergo a change in the seventh century, which imposed greater restrictions on women's activities. Gould (1980) offered a possible explanation when he noted that legal cases involving women reveal a "strict parallelism between the formal rules controlling the treatment of women and those that govern the transmission and inheritance of property" (p. 44). Such cases also suggest that the presence of women in public offered opportunities for seduction, which threatened both the concept of property and social stability. We see evidence of the increased restrictions under Solon's (c. 640–559 BC) leadership. He implemented a law that controlled women's dress, their travel about Athens, and their mourning and lamentation at funerals:

> He [Solon] regulated the walks, feasts, and mourning of the women, and took away everything that was either unbecoming or immodest; when they walked abroad, no more than three articles of dress were allowed them; an obol's worth of meat and drink; and no basket above a cubit high; and at night they were not to go about unless in a chariot with a torch before them. Mourners tearing themselves to raise pity, and set wailings, and at one man's funeral to lament for another, he forbade. To offer an ox at the grave was not permitted, nor to bury above three pieces of dress with the body, or visit the tombs of any besides their own family, unless at the very funeral; most of which are likewise forbidden by our laws, but this is further added in ours, that those that are convicted of extravagance in their mournings, are to be punished as soft and effeminate by the censors of women. (Plutarch, 1959, p. 97)

It is difficult to gauge accurately the effect this and other, equally restrictive, laws had on women, but the available evidence indicates that they created a society in which reputable women were largely separated from males. Homes in Athens, for instance, consisted of separate living quarters for males and females. The female quarters had only one entrance/exit, and it was accessed via the male quarters, thereby limiting freedom of movement out of and into the house. Not all households could afford slaves to do the shopping, so the *agora*, or marketplace, in Athens was divided into male and female areas to allow poorer women to shop without significant face-to-face contact with males. Most telling in the context of rhetoric, however, is the fact that Athens failed to produce a single female poet. Sparta, on the other hand, which had a significantly different social structure that gave women more freedom, produced two – Megalostrata and Cleitagora (Fantham et al., 1994).

Literacy and *Paideia*

The most esteemed poet was Homer, and the most esteemed work was *The Iliad*. Homer's works provided edification (*paideia*) on the nature of the divine, the relationship of god to man, the essence of friendship, courage, moderation, and good leadership (Robb, 1994). Indeed, poetry in general was a source of *paideia* until the early sixth century, when what we may think of as the Age of Myth began to give way to reason and logic.[4]

In his classic work on mythology, *The Masks of God*, Campbell (1970) noted that early cultures viewed the world as a richly spiritual place. Supernatural beings existed everywhere – in rivers, forests, oceans, clouds, on mountaintops. Gods and demigods controlled not only their individual domains but also the lives of men and women and had to be propitiated through ritual and sacrifice. What we think of as natural phenomena were, in early cultures, understood to be the acts of deities. Thus, in *The Iliad*, it is Apollo, not a virus, who strikes down the Greek army with the plague, and he does so in response to the prayer of his devoted priest Chryses:

"Hear me, Apollo! God of the silver bow
who strikes the walls of Chryse and Cilla
sacrosanct ... god of the plague!
If I ever roofed a shrine to please your heart,

ever burned the long rich bones of bulls and
   goats
on your holy alter, now, now bring my prayer
   to pass. (I.43–48)

Literacy appears to have brought about a cultural shift away from this mythic view, as well as its corresponding way of thinking about the world. Although writing had reemerged from the Greek dark ages between 800 and 700 BC, for perhaps 200 years only a small percentage of the population was literate (Robb, 1994). The situation began to change fairly rapidly, however, following Solon's reforms, and Greece started shifting from an oral to a literate culture. The evidence is not conclusive, but there are indications that democracy accelerated the reemergence of literacy in Athens. When Solon opened government service to those who were not members of the elite class, the entire male population required more and better education and greater skill as speakers in the governing assemblies. Athenian society was growing more complex, and complex societies are difficult to manage without literacy.

Literacy on even a modest scale required schools. As a result, education for boys moved out of the privacy of the home. According to Marrou (1982), a system of education beginning at the elementary level and proceeding through the secondary level was well established by the middle of the fifth century BC (also see Beck, 1964; Welch, 1990). Young boys typically finished their secondary education around the age of 15 or 16. We learn in Plato's *Progatoras* that families with the means continued the education of their sons by providing them with advanced training in rhetoric. On this basis, Raaflaub (1983) stated that "To go to school and to be trained in a few elementary disciplines had become fairly normal for an Athenian citizen" (p. 530). Many of the teachers in these schools seem to have come to Athens from Ionia, where education and literacy were more advanced and had been for some time.

[4] Frentz (2006) argued that the *paideia* of oral culture required an audiences' rapt attention because whatever "was forgotten was lost forever"; therefore, any "careless moment ... any lapse of concentration ... could result in lost knowledge" (p. 247). He went on to claim that Greek audiences listening to poetry "became mesmerized, drugged, 'lost' in the performance, for only this mind state could record the living history that was Greece" (p. 247). This analysis seems significantly off base. It fails to acknowledge the fact that poetry was embedded in the daily lives of Greeks. Homer's epics were not performed once in a lifetime but repeatedly, portions perhaps even daily. Furthermore, Frentz ignored the mnemonic effect of rhythm and rhyme, which enable the mind to remember long stretches of discourse after a single exposure. The modern musical provides a relevant example: Audiences commonly exit the theater singing (mentally or not) a tune they have heard but once.

We should not be surprised that the move away from *mythos* began in Ionia. Formal education affects cognition. In one of the more thorough studies of the consequences of schooling and literacy on an oral culture, Scribner and Cole (1981) reported the following: "Of all the ... [investigated] tasks, logic problems proved the most predictable and demonstrated the strongest effects of schooling. Not only did amount of school increase the number of correct answers, but it contributed to the choice of theoretical explanations, over and above correct answers" (p. 127). That is, the schooling necessary for teaching literacy – not literacy itself – improved the ability of the subjects in Scribner and Cole's study to perform logical operations correctly.[5] The change entailed the application of *formal logic*, as opposed to the informal logic of everyday life that, as Johnson-Laird (1983) noted, is based on perceptions and what is already known rather than on systematic principles of reasoning.

The Milesians

Perhaps it was the effects of schooling and literacy or the city's position as a major trade route, with the resulting confluence of ideas, but in any event, Miletus, located on the western tip of Ionia, gave birth to three innovative thinkers: Thales (c. 625–546 BC), Anaximander (c. 610–546 BC), and Anaximenes (c. 585–525 BC). These *hoi physikoi*, or "physicists," developed what may be considered a proto-scientific approach to observing and explaining natural phenomena. Consequently, they discounted the involvement of gods and strove to use formal reasoning to explain such phenomena by reducing causes and effects to basic principles, thereby adopting a monistic view of the universe. According to Aristotle (*Metaphysics*, 983), Thales believed that water was the first principle from which all things originated. Anaximander, on the other hand, proposed that the first principle was an undefined "limitlessness" (*apeiron*), or force, that gave rise to the world. Anaximenes saw air as the first principle. Through condensation, air forms moisture; further condensation converts moisture into earth. Although from our perspective these speculative notions seem primitive, they were revolutionary at the time. We can see in them an attempt to explain the world through natural processes governed by some as yet unknown natural laws. In stark contrast is the mythic view, which relies on anthropomorphized metaphor and allegory to explain natural phenomena.[6] The Greeks described a flash of lightning, for example, as Zeus hurling his thunderbolt. Storms at sea were attributed to Poseidon.

The individual ideas of these men were influential, but their approach to knowledge was more so. Over the next hundred years, efforts to understand the world using observation, reason, and logic increased. Thales, Anaximander, and Anaximenes were followed by such important intellectuals as Xenophanes of Colophon (c. 570–480 BC), Pythagoras (c. 582–507 BC), Heraclitus (c. 535–475 BC), Parmenides (c. 510 BC–?), Anaxagoras (c. 500–428 BC), Zeno (c. 490–425 BC), and Empedocles (c. 490–430 BC). Some of their ideas resonate with us today. Heraclitus, for example, remains famous for his statement on relativism: One cannot step into the same river twice. And relativism was to have a significant influence on the development of rhetoric. Pythagoras we remember for his groundbreaking work in mathematics: the Pythagorean Theorem and the discovery of irrational numbers. Zeno is well known for his paradox "proving"

---

[5] Many scholars have been confused on this issue, mistakenly identifying literacy as the cause for changes in cognition (e.g., Colby and Cole, 1976; Dillon, 1981; Goody, 1968, 1972, 1987; Greenfield, 1972; Ong, 1982).
[6] Science also relies on metaphor but without anthropomorphizing.

that the great runner Achilles cannot overtake a tortoise in a race. Efforts to account for change in a monistic universe led to the postulation of dichotomies and dualism. Anaximenes' cosmology, for example, was driven by the interaction of two opposing "forces": heat and cold. For Xenophanes, it was earth and water; for Heraclitus, fire and water. Such attempts to understand the workings of nature through agonistic contraries probably underlie Parmenides' considerably more abstract views on how to think about the world. One of the more important was his assertion that in saying what something is, we also are saying what something is not.

The spread of education meant that not only the ideas of these philosophers but also their proto-scientific approach to understanding the world were familiar to increasing numbers of people. The old myths, with their all-too-human gods committing adultery and murder, did not serve as well as they had in the past; and among many intellectuals, at least, there was the growing sense that these tales were both metaphorically inaccurate and substantially immoral. Although it would be an exaggeration to claim that Greek society became secularized as a result, there is no question that the thinking of people like Thales, Xenophanes, and Anaxagoras led to a shift away from unquestioned belief in myth to the application of reason to cosmology and, more important, human affairs (see Bryant, 1986; Burket, 1985; Den Boer, 1973; Dodds, 1951).

The Athenian Legal System

Solon not only canceled the debts that had enslaved the poor but also reformed the Athenian legal system. Prior to his reforms, justice was administered by elected magistrates called *archons*, and only members of the aristocracy were allowed to serve in this position. Recognizing the growing influence of the middle class, Solon instituted a property qualification for the archonship that allowed citizens of means to serve as magistrates even though they were not members of the nobility. This innovation had several consequences, but among the more important was that it led to additional democratic reforms that eventually eliminated the long-standing property requirement for citizenship and participation in the governing assembly (Samons, 2004). Unlike virtually all modern countries that practice democracy but that are nevertheless republics, Athens practiced direct democracy, with citizens making decisions, establishing laws, and setting policies through hands-on involvement in the political process. A simple majority vote was required to pass a measure.

As in our own judicial system, specific courts in Athens were designated for certain types of cases. The Middle Court, for example, heard misdemeanors, whereas the Areopagus and the Palladion dealt with homicides. Jury service was a duty for all male citizens (females were barred from service), and when Pericles established payment for jurors (three *oboloi* a day), it reduced the hardship of jury duty for poor citizens (*thetes*). In an attempt to attenuate rampant bribery and intimidation, Athenian juries were large, ranging from several hundred to several thousand members, depending on the court in which a case was heard. Such numbers made corruption more difficult, but they also meant that jurors could not confer to evaluate facts in evidence or to decide a case. They received tokens before each trial that they afterwards deposited to signify their verdict. Again, a simple majority determined the outcome. Trials typically consisted of two parts: the guilt phase and the penalty phase. Decisions could not be appealed.

There were no attorneys in ancient Greece, nor were there state prosecutors. Complaints of all types were brought by individual citizens. Litigants were not allowed to have someone speak for them – both prosecutor and defendant had to speak for themselves. Women were not allowed in the courts, and as Gould (1980) noted, the names of respectable women generally could not even be uttered in court; they were identified as the wife or daughter of a man whose name was given. Consequently, women who had a legal complaint were required to have a male relative bring their suit to trial. By the same token, if a woman was accused, she had to enlist the aid of a male relative to defend her in court. The concept of legal evidence as understood in the modern world did not exist in ancient Athens, although both prosecution and defense were allowed to present witness testimony. Cases therefore depended almost entirely on the speeches of the litigants, and they were carefully crafted to be persuasive. Each speech was timed via a water clock to ensure expediency and fairness.

Penalties for what today might seem minor offenses were often harsh: large fines, confiscation of property, exile, and death. Found guilty on the charge of mutilating sacred statues, Alcibiades (c. 450–404 BC) was sentenced to death; Socrates (c. 469–399 BC) received the same sentence after being found guilty of corrupting Athenian youth. A citizen who prosecuted a case unsuccessfully also was at risk of having to pay a fine. Moreover, it was quite common for a defendant to file a counterclaim against the prosecutor. Thus, for anyone engaged in a legal proceeding, the stakes were high, and many trials became literally life and death struggles. With so much riding on the effectiveness of a single speech, few litigants were willing to trust their own skills as an orator, and those who could afford to do so hired a *logographos* – a legal speech writer – to produce a speech for them.

The fears of conservatives like Plato that rhetoric would make a mockery of the legal system were not without foundation. We do not have to look all the way back to ancient Greece to see the power of rhetoric to persuade and influence large numbers of people, but if we do we find clear examples of what, from our perspective, appears to be injustice in the Athenian courts. Alcibiades and Socrates were mentioned above, but we could just as easily consider the many trials during the Peloponnesian War in which Athenian generals were tried and executed because they had lost a battle. In addition, during the fourth century BC, litigation initiated by poor complainants hoping to secure a monetary judgment against an aristocrat – or the threat of litigation to secure an out-of-court settlement – became so common that the assembly passed a law against such frivolous suits that fined the *sykophantai* who filed them. Nevertheless, it is important to note that from Solon to Alexander the Great, the Athenian legal system changed very little, suggesting that is adequately served the needs of the people, even with its notable shortcomings from our perspective.

The Sophists

By the fifth century BC, formal education in Athens and other Greek cities was fairly well established. It focused on poetry, which during the dark ages had become the repository for history, religion, ritual, culture, and morals. Poetry was the oldest subject of study in Athens. It was deemed to contain valuable lessons encompassing all facets of an honorable life. Stories of the gods and their interactions with people provided a solid foundation in religion and guidelines for worship. Not surprisingly, knowledge of poetry and the ability to produce poetry were linked to ideals of *aretê*, or personal excellence. We can see, therefore, that poetry had a different place in Greece than it has in modern society. It was part of the very substance of Greek life – for men as well as women – because its truths and moral lessons were deemed vital in educating the young and providing guidelines for proper behavior.

Initially, much of the schooling children received was provided by slaves, but as the fifth century progressed, there was a shift to better trained and more knowledgeable teachers, many of whom came from Ionia. Young men of means began looking to continue their education beyond the secondary level, and a small group of teachers emerged willing to provide it. They came to be known as *Sophists* – from the Greek word for wisdom, *sophia*.

Any definitive understanding of the Sophists probably will always be beyond us, but some general observations are possible. They were not prolific writers, and what survived the millennia consists largely of fragments embedded in the works of others who may have produced inaccurate records. Even though we refer to them as a group, the Sophists held only a few views in common, which increases the difficulty of reaching any generalizable conclusions about them. One point, however, is crucial to our understanding of Greek rhetoric: The Sophists were heirs to the proto-scientific approach to knowledge developed by the Milesians and the philosophers who followed them.

The Sophists taught grammar and poetry, and their inclination to look below the surface of things led them to construct the technical vocabulary necessary to professionalize poetry and thereby change how it was understood. This development was important because, until the mid-fifth century, poetry in Greece was entirely a performative act – song presented to a group, accompanied by music. Thus, when we use the word "poetry" in relation to ancient Greece, we must recognize that it existed as song embedded in the religious and cultural activities of the society.

The centrality of poetry in Greek social life is evident in the popularity of *symposia*, regular meetings in private residences in which men drank and sang songs: some traditional, some current and popular, and some made up on the spot. Although the circumstances in which women gathered to perform their own songs cannot be reconstructed with any certainty, it appears that they may have had similar gatherings. Given the potential for such assemblies to become drunken revels, a high value was placed on order (*kosmos*) and decorum, which when preserved were deemed to reflect the social order of the community.

The emphasis on *kosmos* suggests that *symposia* were more than drinking contests or merely a form of entertainment. We know that different occasions called for different types of song, and Ford (2002) argued that a singer was criticized if his selection did not fit the occasion. A goal of *symposia* attendees, therefore, was to perform songs that did fit (*prepei*) so that their peers would judge them as appropriate to the social and religious performative dimensions of the event, even after everyone had been drinking for hours. Plato's dialogue *Symposium* suggests that in some instances singing did not occur at all, and if it has any basis in reality, the dialogue reflects how these gatherings involved intellectual discussions that served didactic purposes.

In Ford's (2002) analysis, song could not truly take on the characteristics of poetry as we know it until the Greeks developed a formal, technical vocabulary that professionalized the discussion of verse and that separated the linguistic act from performance. According to Ford, without such a vocabulary, any critique of a song would be limited to performance and appropriateness – to the quality of voice, for example, or tone. A technical vocabulary enabled discussion of rhyme, meter, alliteration, and so on, which opened an entirely new dimension of critical analysis that shifted poetry outside the religious and morally didactic spheres that had governed performance for centuries.[7] Equally important, although often overlooked, is the likelihood that the analytical

---

[7] Note that even Greek theater was solidly rooted in religion. The term "tragedy" (*tragoidia*), for example, literally translates as "goat song" and is associated with the traditional sacrifice of a goat as part of a religious ritual.

tools the Sophists developed gave them more insight into poetry's expression of individuality, which had been evident since the work of Enheduanna around 2300 BC and which had emerged with powerful effect in Archilochus and Sappho. Jaeger (1976) examined individuality in the work of the great poet Archilochus (c. 680–645 BC) and declared: "Man's thought now becomes master of his traditional morality. ... [W]hen a poet begins to write freely of his private pleasures, it is a new step in poetry, and one which deeply influences human nature" (pp. 126–9). That is, the expression of individuality in poetry not only reflected but also reinforced the concept of a personal relationship with the gods that had begun two millennia earlier, allowing people to believe that they had more control over their lives. When the Sophists applied their study and teaching of poetry to rhetoric, they no doubt found fertile ground. Their infusion of individuality into oratory met the needs of the ambitious who sought to elevate themselves above the level prescribed by tradition, and it simultaneously fueled democracy. We may not be unjustified in concluding that poets like Enheduanna, Archilochus, and Sappho indirectly influenced rhetoric, politics, and even entire societies.

Some Sophists expanded their study of poetry to include philosophic contemplation of the world. Like the Milesians, Protagoras (c. 490–420 BC), for example, was interested in mathematics; Gorgias (c. 483–378 BC) produced a treatise on nature. We do not know when the Sophists began teaching rhetoric, but it probably was toward the middle of the fifth century BC. Nor do we know why they enlarged their curriculum. The various social changes already discussed – war, the spread of democracy, the growth of empire, and so forth – no doubt exerted considerable influence, but it seems reasonable to propose that a significant factor was their general embrace of the proto-scientific way of thinking, with its emphasis on classification, reduction to first principles, and *physis*. As Cole (1991, p. 66) stated:

> the rationalizing tradition to which the Sophistic belongs was concerned with rewriting history and mythology to meet the demands of logic, empirical observation, and Ionian "science." To those involved in it the process doubtless seemed a single, unified effort to purge traditional lore of the fabrications with which poetic fancy had encumbered it.

Charges of immorality

Although the Sophists are sometimes credited with establishing rhetorical theory (albeit rudimentary), the evidence for this is sparse. As a group, they may have developed the idea of argument from probability, but this feature of their theory/practice may have been predicated simply on the legal realities of the time. Their primary goal was pragmatic: to give their students the tools necessary to prevail in courts and governing assemblies (see Wardy, 1996). We know that their teaching of rhetoric was controversial because it was believed that they provided students with the means to defeat just arguments, which was deemed immoral, and because some charged high fees for their services, at least at the advanced level, which made them appear to be more interested in money than in truth or justice – both topics of immense concern during the fifth and fourth centuries BC. Kimball's (1986) assessment is typical in this regard: "The Sophists ... attended more to devising persuasive techniques than to finding true arguments, and this amoralism exacerbated the disintegration of the ethical tradition and led to their condemnation" (p. 17).

The charge that Sophists were immoral is widespread in the existing literature. It finds specific expression in *The Art of Rhetoric*, where Aristotle noted that Protagoras, and by implication all Sophists, made "the worse appear the better argument" (1402a).

Aristophanes' *The Clouds* provides an example of this charge in action. In the play, the main character, Strepsiades, has been driven into debt by his wastrel son. Hearing that Sophists teach students how to make the worse case seem the better, Strepsiades goes to the Thinkery, home of the city's most renowned Sophist, Socrates, to learn how to cheat his creditors. Although Socrates readily provides instruction, Strepsiades proves to be a dull student and is expelled.

Some Sophists undoubtedly adopted this position – after all, it would have a tangible appeal in many cases – but we cannot be certain that "making the worse appear the better argument" is what Protagoras wrote or meant. Schiappa (2003) argued that the phrase has been consistently mistranslated, owing to the influence of Plato and Aristotle. In his view, a more accurate translation is *"to make the weaker argument stronger."* As he noted, "Translating the fragment accordingly makes its interpretation far more comprehensive in terms of fifth-century thinking" (p. 107) – and it certainly is more congruent with the teaching and practice of rhetoric. Furthermore, if Plato's *Protagoras* even modestly reflects Sophists' views (and the assessment of many scholars is that this is one of the least biased of the dialogues), we have to conclude that they do not appear to be either immoral or amoral. Quite the opposite. Protagoras' sense of morality as presented in the dialogue, however, is different from Socrates' – or Plato's (see Poulakos, 1995).

Another factor that perhaps influenced the assessment that Sophists were immoral is the nature of their discourse. The available documents suggest that, like the Milesians, they tended toward relativism. Morality, however, is based on absolutism, and commonly it has some form of divine support. Although viewing human actions in absolute terms may be fruitful when engaged in philosophy, it has little utility in a court of law, and perhaps not even in the governing assembly, because so often human actions do not involve questions of what is absolutely right or absolutely wrong but rather what is more right and less wrong.

Sophistic relativism had manifold consequences. Relativism is ineluctably tied to individuality, and thus in advocating this view the Sophists undermined the traditional concept of the divine and placed mankind, not the gods, as the arbiters of morality and justice. In this respect, Sophistic relativism also appears as a form of humanism, as we see in this fragment from Protagoras: "Man is the measure of all things, of the things that are, that they are, and of the things that are not, that they are not." Relativism and individuality led the Sophists to understand that there are at least two sides to every case, both equally valid from the perspective of their champions even though diametrically opposed; thus, those advocating these positions think that they are obviously right and that their opponents are obviously wrong. This understanding is known as the *dissoi logoi*, or "two sides," argument, attributed to Protagoras (or in some instances Pythogoras) but reminiscent of Milesian foundational dualism: what is/what is not; hot/cold; wet/dry. Sophists believed, on this basis, that just as the philosopher will understand what is not by understanding what is, a competent rhetorician should be able to recognize and argue both sides of a topic or dispute so as to have more control over the issues, and their teaching incorporated *dissoi logoi* as practice. Given the human tendency to view the world in black and white terms, instruction in *dissoi logoi* combined with instruction in making weaker arguments stronger may have been more than sufficient evidence of the Sophists' immorality.

The role of technai

To a certain degree, the Sophists resembled the rhapsodes insofar as they led peregrinatory lives, traveling from city to city to increase the pool of potential students. They would go to the *agora* upon entering a city and give demonstration speeches that displayed their skill and eloquence. Teaching typically took place in a private residence, a situation that did not change until Plato and Isocrates opened their schools in Athens in 387 and 390 BC respectively. We have no way of knowing how long an individual Sophist would stay in a given city, but anything shorter than a year or two probably would have resulted in fairly shallow instruction.

The demand for rhetorical training was great owing to democratization and the plethora of lawsuits in which plaintiffs and defendants had to plead their own cases. Some Sophists consequently earned their living as *logographoi*. (Litigants memorized their respective orations and presented them to the jury, a task that required a prodigious memory because speeches were sometimes quite long.) The extant speeches show great attention not only to a recitation of the facts of the case but also to the speakers' characters and to argument from probability. Such speeches were expensive, for obvious reasons; yet the hot litigious atmosphere of the times meant that many men were brought to trial more than once, particularly if they were influential. Government administrators were selected from the aristocracy, and at the end of their one-year appointment, they were required to submit financial accounts (*euthynai*). Any citizen could charge the outgoing administrator with financial malfeasance, and as the tensions between rich and poor escalated, many did. Instruction in rhetoric, therefore, was a smart investment, reducing the need to hire a *logographos*. Only a small percentage of people, however, had the means to pay for advanced rhetorical training, and most likely many students could afford only a few lessons. Although Plato portrayed the Sophists as scoundrels who became rich by charging wealthy young men exorbitant fees, Isocrates gave what probably is a more accurate assessment in *Antidosis*, in which he noted that most Sophists barely made ends meet owing to the fact that they charged low fees so as to attract the widest range of pupils.

This reality, together with their wandering from city to city, necessitated that Sophists provide students some sort of relatively inexpensive pedagogical resource that would serve them when instruction was limited and the teacher might pack his bags and be gone on short notice. The available evidence suggests that many Sophists put their demonstration speeches into writing and sold them as instructional texts (*technai*). Isocrates, Plato, and Aristotle described instructional handbooks (which also were labeled *technai*) that addressed such features as structure and organization, but none have survived the passage of time. In *The Origins of Rhetoric in Ancient Greece*, Cole (1991) argued that *technai* were not theoretical but rather reflected the pragmatic orientation of the Sophists. They identified a topic or theme (*topos*), such as Helen's elopement with Paris, and illustrated several different ways of arguing the point. This structure recognized the fact that the uncertainties in the assembly or court made a memorized speech problematic. What an orator or a litigant needed was the flexibility afforded by a repertoire of arguments or argumentative approaches for the matter at hand.

Sophistic *technai* fell short of theory because they never achieved a sufficient level of generalizability. Their *topoi*, for example, were always specific and were the equivalent of case studies or exercises that offered students several possible solutions to real-life problems. Lacking any development of general principles, a given *technê* might illustrate half a dozen different argumentative approaches, but it would fail as a pedagogical tool the moment the orator was faced with the need for a seventh. Cole (1991) therefore identified the Sophists as "proto-rhetoricians" and their *technai* as "proto-rhetorical." As far as we can determine, *technê* in the sense of the formal handbook combining theory and technical matters did not appear until Aristotle produced his *Art of Rhetoric*.[8]

---

[8] We know from Book I of Aristotle's *The Art of Rhetoric* that handbooks had existed for some time, but they "provided us with only a small portion of this art" (I.1.3).

The Sophists and aretê

As is typical of many traditional societies, ancient Greek culture was rooted in the concepts of honor and the heroic. Nowhere are these intertwined concepts more visible than in *The Iliad*. Linked to both was the notion of *aretê*, which in *The Iliad* can be translated as either "excellence" or "virtue," depending on context. Although *aretê* signifies a quality (the adjectival form is *agathos*), it also can signify one's effort at striving to be the best one can be.

Aretê appears to have played an important role in the development of rhetoric, in part because the Sophists consistently claimed that they could teach it as an inherent part of rhetorical study. We can begin to understand this role by considering how the concept changed between the eighth and fourth centuries. *Aretê* in the Homeric world focused on actions and abilities associated with warfare but nevertheless included other dimensions, such as speaking. The true possessor of *aretê* displays excellence in all arenas, which explains, perhaps, why in *The Iliad* Achilles is not only the best warrior but also the best speaker. It is important to note, however, that in *The Iliad aretê* is a complex combination of extreme individuality and conservative tradition. King Agamemnon gathered the heroes of Greece to attack Troy not in the name of what today we might think of as national interests but to avenge the stain on his brother Menalaus' honor. Thousands die because Menalaus' wife, Helen, ran away with Paris, prince of Troy. The heroes on both sides do not fight indiscriminately but battle only with their peers, usually in *individual* combat to display their *aristeia*, or "finest moments." But although the *aretê* of Achilles and *The Iliad* is personal, its locus nevertheless is the self as defined by lineage as well as deeds, which explains why the introduction of each hero includes his patrilineage and his list of accomplishments.

Munn (2000) argued that the Greek's victory over the Persians in 480 BC may have been a significant factor in altering the concept of *aretê*. Victory was won when the Athenian fleet routed the Persians at Salamis, and the level of pride Athenians took from defeating the greatest empire in the world when outnumbered 10 to 1 was considerable. Heroditus (c. 484–425 BC) offered insight into one effect of the victory when he reflected on the unlikely outcome and the special love of freedom and the strength of the *demos* that made it possible. Munn therefore proposed that the defeat of the Persians and the subsequent growth of empire nurtured a sense of pride as well as manifest destiny among the Athenians, which in turn led to widespread reflection on the various factors that distinguished Athens from all other cities in the ancient world.

One result was a shift in the ideals of personal excellence or virtue to include the ideals of civic duty: An excellent man was also an excellent citizen. This change had important consequences. As Guthrie (1977) noted, "*Aretê* when used without qualification denoted those qualities of human excellence which made a man a natural leader in his community, and hitherto it had been believed to depend on certain natural or even divine gifts which were the mark of good birth and breeding" (p. 25); and then, "Any upper-class Athenian should understand the proper conduct of [political] affairs by a sort of instinct inherited from his ancestors, and be prepared to pass it on to his sons" (p. 39). In Munn's (2000) analysis, however, Athenian society, and the very concept of *aretê*, underwent a transition to a *communal identity* as a result of the Persian war. This communal identity resulted in a redefinition of *aretê* – it came to mean, first and foremost, *civic virtue*.

Attributing such a significant cultural change to one or two factors is not entirely satisfying, and Munn's (2000) assessment does not adequately take into account the spread of literacy toward the end of the fifth and beginning of the fourth centuries BC.

We no doubt should consider the Sophists' claim to teach *aretê* in the context of the Milesian influence, as well as their role as teachers of literacy, grammar, and poetry. In Schiappa (2003), we find yet another interesting perspective. He argued, for example, that rhetoric was not the principal focus of Sophistic teaching but that *logos* was – moreover, that they "were representatives of an intellectualist movement that favored abstract thinking over what Havelock has called the poetic mind" (p. 55). Their teaching was predicated on the proto-scientific principles established by the Milesians and was designed to challenge the mythico-poetic traditions of Greek society. According to Schiappa, Sophistic teaching "called for *arguing* rather than merely *telling*. The substantive challenges to traditional ways of thinking brought a new humanism of *logos*" (p. 56).

The "new humanism of *logos*" entailed a redefinition of the individual vis-à-vis society and politics, leading the Sophists, in Munn's (2000) words, to adapt "their teachings and writings to the subject of politics and to its medium in another form of artful expression: persuasive non-poetic speech" (p. 78). This redefinition may well have started with the Sophists' interest in grammar. They created the technical vocabulary necessary for describing language, giving us not only the terms for nouns, verbs, prepositions, and so forth, but also – and more important – the abstract concepts necessary for grammatical analyses that differentiate form and function and that allow for meta-linguistic taxonomies. This vocabulary enabled the study of language as an artifact separate from its performative dimension as speech act. Today, we readily recognize that we can examine any utterance in two ways – in terms of its social effects (its performative, or illocutionary, force) and in terms of its structure – but this was a novel idea in Greece, fifth-century BC. Ford (2002), for example, noted that the word *metron* was used in either the simple sense of "unit of measure" or in the ethical sense of "due measure" throughout most of the fifth century BC. Only toward the end of the fifth and then more frequently in the fourth century do we find *metron* being used to describe poetic meter. And even then this usage was novel, as illustrated "by a scene of higher education in Aristophanes' *Clouds* (first performed in 423), where understanding such matters as 'dactyls' and 'meters' (*metra*, 638) is beyond the ken of a yokel … who naturally takes *metra* as referring to bushels and pecks" (Ford, 2002, p. 18).

One of the more obvious consequences of this shift is that by enabling the separation of poetry's performative from its linguistic dimension, the Sophists were separating poetry from the religious and ethical. Another is that by developing the analytical tools necessary for examining structure, they established poetry as an object of study. With such tools, one could consider whether a poem was well formed, regardless of its effect on an audience. And the systematization of poetry had the added benefit of enhancing the Sophists' pedagogy: *Systems can be taught.*

And here we seem to find an important foundation for the development of rhetoric as well as for Munn's (2000) assessment that the Sophists adapted their teaching to "persuasive non-poetic speech." Both became systematized and professionalized. The clearest examples of the intertwined nature of this change are Aristotles' *The Art of Poetry* and *Art of Rhetoric*, which Cole (1991) characterized as "sister" works (p. 15). The formalization of poetry, in other words, provided the basis for the formalization of persuasive speaking. Once this process began, the Sophists saw abundant opportunities in other areas and applied it to examinations of the nature of truth, virtue, society, politics, and knowledge (*epistêmê*). Rather than teach one specific subject, such as rhetoric, the Sophists appear to have offered a more comprehensive education that included both practical and technical knowledge in an effort to understand the human condition. The goal – at least for some men, such as Antiphon and Isocrates – was to develop leaders who understood the contingent nature of government and society. Antiphon, for example, noted in *On Truth* that justice reflects agreements among people regarding behavior, not established truths. This represented a significant, one might even say radical, departure from traditional views, but it came to be widely embraced by Athenians and citizens in other democratic city-states. The semantics of *logos* became more philosophical, and the Sophists began to emphasize a theory of knowing, particularly as it related to the nexus of the personal and the communal. In addition, the professionalization of language and the study of poetry seem to have led to a better understanding not only of structure but also of substance. From this perspective, the systematization of poetry provided deeper immersion in the lessons to be found in both poetry and myth, including those associated with *aretê*.

In search of civic virtue

According to Munn (2000), by the early fourth century BC a new sense of community led to an expanded concept of *aretê*: "Private identity ... now openly competed with communal identity" (p. 52). The change was significant. We know that by the fourth century the *aristeia* of *The Iliad* was a thing of the past and that among the aristocracy *aretê* was generally limited to a combination of birth, wealth, and education. We also know that the meaning had shifted. In Homer, for example, *aretê* signifies both excellence and virtue, depending on context, but the emphasis is on excellence. By the fourth century, the emphasis was on virtue, especially civic virtue. In the process, notions of *aretê* changed to such a degree that the distinction became blurred, if not lost, between what Edmund Burke, writing in the eighteenth century, called *actual* and *presumptive virtue*. Members of the aristocracy *presumed* that they possessed *aretê*, yet with few opportunities to display *aristeia*, there was little evidence to support this presumption. *Aretê* could be enhanced, certainly, through success in war, politics, sports, and poetry, but the triad of personal traits was a prerequisite.

The Sophists challenged the belief that *aretê* was innate and claimed that they could teach students how to be better citizens. In doing so, they were solidly locating the new definition of *aretê* within their pedagogical tradition. As the Sophists adapted their teaching to persuasive speaking, they did not abandon poetry but rather applied their knowledge of it to rhetoric. The study of rhetoric, moreover, proved a much more effective means of supporting the claims of inculcating civic virtue, for the spread of literacy, formal logic, and scientific reasoning had shifted social perceptions of *paideia* from poetry to prose, firmly embedding rhetoric in two of society's more important institutions: government and law. The transition to a literate society immersed in politics and litigation, with success in both arenas increasingly predicated on rhetorical skill, seems to have led naturally to a fusion of the hermeneutics of poetry and persuasive non-poetic speech. For the Sophists, business was good.

The Sophists' logic appears to have been impeccable. Not everyone is blessed with the gift of song, and in a society in which song and singing are important factors, being able to teach singing more effectively will have clear benefits. Likewise, not everyone is blessed with the ability to produce poetry or persuasive speeches, so in a society that places high value on both, the rewards will be great for those who can devise a better teaching method. Moreover, students and society also benefit. Some Sophists may well have viewed their efforts to teach rhetoric as serving the public good by developing citizens who could produce and deliver the well-formed, effective speeches necessary in a deliberative democracy. Systematization was the key.

Plato's dialogues make it plain that he thought the Sophists' claims were absurd, but a moment's consideration shows that they were not. There is no question that Sophists had been teaching *aretê* for years as instructors and interpreters of poetry. Whether they were successful is irrelevant, for we must remember that Greek culture as a whole accepted the idea that hymns and familiarity with poems like *The Iliad* and *The Odyssey* instilled a full range of virtues. In addition, Plato's objections were not based on the idea that virtue cannot be taught, but rather on his disagreement regarding methods and techniques. There is no question that he believed in the teachability of *aretê*: *The Republic* can be viewed as a manifesto on how best to educate people and thereby form the perfect state, and we know that he was intimately involved in a messy coup in Syracuse that temporarily installed his student Dion in power. From Plato's *Letter VII* (see Bluck, 1947), we know that he believed, at least initially, that his instruction would enable Dion to be a wise and prudent leader.[9] Also, Plato's academy must have promised to teach *aretê*, given how important Athenians deemed civic virtue at the time. The issue was that Plato equated virtue with knowledge. Because the Sophists, in his view, taught deception and had no knowledge, they could not teach *aretê*.

Inherent in the claim that civic virtue can be taught is the implication that it had to be taught. If this assessment is correct, two explanations are possible. First, the quest for virtue may very well have been embedded in the significant social and cultural changes that began in the seventh century BC – the spread of education, literacy, and the proto-scientific approach to understanding the world – that led philosophers like Xenophanes to question religion. (If an ox could draw, Xenophanes declared, his god would look like an ox.) Our understanding today is that morality and virtue are based on the reciprocal altruism necessary for sociality. As humans transitioned to agriculture, the size of social groups expanded significantly, from the one hundred or so that characterized hunter-gatherers to villages with several hundred and towns with thousands. The need to expand the radius of trust that enables people to live and work together cooperatively increased correspondingly, but so did the likelihood of a violation of trust by individuals who derived benefits from the group without contributing to it, the so-called "freeloaders" (Aviles, 2002). According to N. Wade (2006), "Human societies long ago devised an antidote to the freeloader problem. This freeloader defense system, a major organizing principle of every society, has assumed so many other duties that its original role has been lost sight of. It is religion" (p. 163).

Religion replaces kinship in larger societies as a means of controlling cheats and liars. It establishes an in-group with bonds that resemble kinship and regulates behavior accordingly, providing an effective means of social control. The focus on *aretê*, therefore, may be viewed as a response to the decline in religious belief (at least among elites) resulting from proto-scientific reasoning and a tendency toward secularism, which has the potential to increase the level of freeloading significantly. As the Greeks began to have less faith in the traditional gods, they needed something to replace the sacred so as to maintain barriers to freeloading and thereby hinder the inevitable social damage. The emphasis on civic virtue would have served this need, in effect establishing service to the state as a new locus of belief, and the laws governing mischievous behavior would have enforced sanctions through altruistic punishment. This analysis helps us understand why punishments in Athens were so severe, especially for those found guilty of crimes against the state. Thus, religion as a form of social control can be seen as giving way to social conventions associated with civic virtue, and hence the need to teach *aretê*.

The second explanation lies in the Sophists' challenge to the idea of *aretê*'s innateness, which suggests that they were supporters of democracy (see Beck, 1964). There is little

---

[9] Dion turned out to be a thug and was soon overthrown. Plato blamed the bad outcome on Dion's limited intellect, not on his instruction.

direct evidence to support this view, however, and the indirect evidence is far from dispositive but is nevertheless interesting. Instruction in rhetoric was the equivalent of a college education, and if the tuition was high, students did not come from the lower classes, and probably the number from the middle class was limited to those from upwardly mobile families. In his dialogue *The Sophist*, Plato described Sophists as hunters "after young men of wealth and rank" (223). Even if this characterization was only partially accurate, those who received education in civic virtue were primarily (although not exclusively) members of the aristocracy and nobility.

These young men, it seems, generally did not pursue rhetorical training to become better citizens but rather to become more influential ones. A cynic therefore might propose that the claim of teaching civic virtue was merely a charade to appease critics who saw the Sophists instructing their students how, as Aristotle noted, to make "the worse appear the better argument." Another possibility is that with more critical reasoning faculties, the Sophists and others benefiting from the change to formal schooling recognized that the concept of *aretê* found in Homer could not logically apply to democracy or to empire. The communal or civic identity necessary for both requires a suppression of extreme individuality and a rechanneling of energy and commitment from personal goals to the common good (an idea later developed more fully by Aristotle in his *Politics*). Without this commitment, a political entity larger than a city is difficult, if not impossible, to sustain because the society fragments into social islands defined by kinship, ethnicity, socioeconomic status, ideology, and so forth, which fosters civil conflict. As Fukuyama (1999) and Putnam (2001) argued, social capital and a wide radius of trust are vital to political stability and social harmony.

A civic identity among the *demos* would serve the empire, and it is certain that the benefits of empire trickled down to the *demos*. The principal beneficiaries, however, were members of the aristocracy. As the empire expanded and their fortunes grew, their hubris no doubt swelled as well. Any number of events from 480 BC on demonstrate that many of Athens' elites had a distorted notion of communal identity, if they had one at all. From the realist's perspective, the Sophists' claim to teach civic virtue can be seen as a response to a pressing state of affairs: Young men of the ruling class needed to be taught civic virtue because they had so little. We might say that the louche actions of the aristocracy had subverted the presumption of *aretê* that had been their birthright from the earliest days of the Mycenaean era. Citizens of the lower and middle classes had ample reasons for entertaining this view, just as they had ample reasons for embracing the notion that civic virtue can be taught. Doing so surely would have served as an anodyne for the generations of slights and insults suffered at the hands of the aristocracy, and it would have been congruent with the political philosophy underlying democracy. In the Platonic dialogue under his name, Protagoras explains his views on the moral education of the child, noting that "all men are teachers of virtue, each one according to his ability" (328). If we can invest any historical credibility in this statement as a true reflection of Protagoras' thinking, at least one Sophist, it seems, believed that a pedagogical agenda that included civic virtue had the power to undermine the notion that *aretê* was innate among the elites, to attenuate the extreme individuality among the ruling class, to imbue them with a sense of *communitas*, or community, and to sow the seeds of *dignitas* in those who were not wealthy and privileged.

Whether the Sophists failed or succeeded in teaching civic virtue is an open question, but what is certain is that various leaders, such as Alcibiades and Cleophon, used the inclusive definition of *aretê* to their advantage. The pursuit of *aretê* among the aristocracy continued to be linked to reputation and status. On the personal level, they could cultivate reputations through athletic competitions, appearance, success as military leaders, and, *ne plus ultra*, success in politics. On the communal level, they relied on lineage and public service in the form of gifts to the city. The common people, on the other hand, had few if any opportunities for personal *aretê*. They could participate in politics and government to a limited degree, but average citizens frequently failed to speak with one voice. Moreover, important decisions often were worked out in secret among the wealthy and influential of the city. The *demos* therefore were forced to turn to those among the aristocracy willing to align themselves with the people – demagogues (from *demos*, "people," and *agogos*, "leading") – and thereby advance their own ambitions and dreams of power. Cleophon serves as an illustrative example. Having made his fortune as a manufacturer of musical instruments, he rose to political prominence by asserting that all Athenians were entitled to the privileges of the aristocracy and that these could be attained through distinguished public service. Such political rhetoric made average citizens feel good, even though the realities of life and politics made it extremely difficult for them to rise above their stations.

This analysis would explain why shared notions of civic virtue did not lead to harmonious relations between aristocrats and the common people. The opposite was true. Even as average citizens embraced the idea of communal identity, resentment among many members of the aristocracy toward the *demos* became sharper. For their part, the common people became intoxicated with their growing power and wanted more. It was the people and their leaders, for example, who, blinded by greed and a lust for booty, urged the conquest of Syracuse so as to expand the empire, ignoring completely those who advised caution and restraint.[10] Sparta was drawn into that conflict, which resulted not only in a disastrous defeat in Sicily but also the Peloponnesian War (see Kagan, 2003).

What seems obvious is that, initially, developing *aretê* among the general population may have accrued significant social capital without much cost to the ruling class. Civic virtue among the common people led them to support the empire while earning minimum wages rowing the galleys and serving in the military. However, the accrual of social capital and the leadership provided by demagogues changed the dynamics of power. A communal identity imbued average citizens with a sense of worth and a sense of recognition that, as Hegel (1956) argued, is at the core of social change, and clearly Athens became more democratic during the fourth century. It seems reasonable to conclude that the Sophists' role in shifting the concept of *aretê* influenced the spread of democratic ideals in the fifth and fourth centuries, which eventually led to the defeat of the oligarchs and their supporters in Athens. It is important to note, of course, that there is no evidence that the Sophists were aware of the effects their teaching was having on society.

War

The Peloponnesian War between Athens and Sparta began in 431 BC and brought a new level of intensity to political debates. Because the stakes were so high, the usual struggles for power and prominence became more vicious. Effective speeches in the assembly and in the courts were more important than ever. The assembly necessarily had to

---

[10] The principal opponent of the expedition was Nicias, who deliberately inflated the estimated costs and number of ships and troops required, thinking that this would dissuade the assembly. He failed. The assembly not only voted to accept his inflated estimate but also selected him to serve as co-leader of the invasion force.

make decisions on myriad details involving the conduct of the war, and in retrospect, several critical decisions were fundamentally wrong. The war went badly for Athens as a result. By 405 BC, the city was forced to discuss surrender terms. Cleophon, who championed the people, urged the assembly to hold out while seeking aid from abroad. We know from the surviving works of Lysias (c. 459–380 BC), however, that pragmatists and Spartan sympathizers among the aristocracy were ready to end the war, and when their leader, Theramenes, proposed that he could negotiate a peace treaty that would preserve the city, the assembly made yet another huge mistake: Not only was Theramenes granted full authority to negotiate a treaty, he also was sent to Sparta alone.

In *Against Agathos*, Lysias reported that Theramenes "stayed … [in Sparta] a long time, though he had left you here in a state of siege and knew that your population was in desperate straits, as owing to the war and its distresses the majority must be in want of the necessities of life" (13.11). The goal was to so enfeeble the population that they would accept peace under any conditions, and he succeeded. The terms were that Sparta would spare the city and its inhabitants, provided its protective walls to the sea be torn down, that it abandon all the holdings acquired during the empire, and that it accept the return of all those citizens who had been exiled for their support of oligarchy over democracy. The terms were nonnegotiable and seem to have been harsher than what had been offered before Theremenes' mission. Facing a huge fleet off the coast and a large army to the north, Athens was forced to surrender to Sparta in April or May of 404.

What followed was the summary execution of the most outspoken supporters of democracy. A governing Council of Thirty was formed upon the exiles' return, with Theramenes, Agathos, and Critias taking prominent roles. Critias, it is worth noting, was related to Plato, either his cousin or uncle. The Thirty's first act was to arrest and execute Cleophon. Then, concerned that resistance might be fomenting in Eleusis, just a few miles west of Athens, the Thirty, at the urging of Critias, ordered all the young men in Eleusis of military age to register for duty. Xenophon reported that approximately 300 men were thus seized, bound, and executed.

To suppress democracy further, the Thirty limited Athenian citizenship to 3,000, thereby disenfranchising most of the population, and ordered all non-citizens expelled from the city, conveniently confiscating their property in the process. At the time, the total population may have been about 120,000 (reduced by the war from about 180,000) (Domitus, 2005). Anyone who refused to leave was immediately executed. The Thirty also banned the teaching of rhetoric on the grounds that it encouraged sedition, and at least one rhetorician, Euthydemus, was executed simply owing to his reputation as a gifted speaker.

Civil war: The crucible of rhetorical theory

As the Thirty were consolidating their power through murder, intimidation, and confiscation of property, resistance was stirring. Surprisingly, it appeared first inside the Council of Thirty itself, when Theremenes suggested to his colleagues that limiting citizenship to 3,000 might be a mistake. Enraged at what he saw as opposition to the regime, Critias ordered Theremenes arrested and executed.

Expelling the majority of Athenians from the city may have satisfied an ideological agenda, but politically, it was a significant error. The exiles were no longer under the direct threat of the Thirty and began organizing via the leadership of General Thrasybulus, a hero from the war with Sparta. Within a few months, he had an army of supporters. Lysias reportedly provided the men with money and shields. Ironically, few of these troops were from the *demos*, a group that had been so beaten down by fear that they had no will to fight; instead, they were from the middle class and the aristocracy, groups that had lost the most during the reign of terror. Meanwhile, Spartan leadership had grown uncomfortable with the actions of the Thirty, a position that was exacerbated by disagreement between the two Spartan kings, Lysander and Pausanias. When conflict broke out between Thrasybulus and his men and the supporters of the Thirty, the Spartans did not intervene. After an initial skirmish at Phyle, not far from Thebes, Thrasybulus marched to Piraeus, the port of Athens, where thousands of additional exiles joined his forces. Overconfident, Critias and several other members of the Thirty marshaled the "citizens" of Athens and attacked Piraeus, only to be soundly defeated. During the battle, Critias was killed, as was Plato's brother Glaucon.

Even though the power of the Thirty was effectively broken, the civil war continued for a year. Several factors worked to end the fighting, particularly King Pausanias' decision to resolve the conflict and a desire among the exiles and supporters of the oligarchy to find a mutually acceptable compromise. It quickly became apparent that the only obstacles to peace were the surviving members of the Council of Thirty, which had been reorganized as a Board of Ten. Pausanias therefore dissolved the Board and arranged for new elections that effectively restored democracy while leaving the other terms of the peace treaty in place. Defeated politically as well as militarily, what was left of the Thirty, as well as the Ten and their supporters, exiled themselves to Eleusis toward the end of 403. The civil war was over.

The restoration of democracy in Athens did not end the conflict between the supporters of oligarchy and democracy; it simply changed the terms. For the next few years, debates raged in the assembly over the laws that should govern the city. The courts were equally busy as litigants sought to redress wrongs committed during the Thirty's reign of terror. The atrocities during 404–403 were perpetrated under the color of authority, and neither side was willing to walk that dark path again. Consequently, a commission was formed to review all laws, with the aim of determining their legitimacy. When we scrutinize extant speeches after the restoration, we see a sudden change in the nature of debate: There are fewer and fewer arguments from probability and a much more careful examination of the exact wording and meaning of laws. For the first time, we are able to find extensive citation and interpretation of written statutes in speeches presented in the assembly and in court.

Historically, Athenians had recognized two types of law: *physis* (natural law) and *nomos* (manmade law). The authority of manmade laws was based on the perception that they were related to laws of nature and therefore were rooted in fundamental truths that, although never clearly defined or explicated, were recognized by everyone. After the reign of terror, the majority of Athenians were unwilling to accept this nebulous relationship between *nomos* and *physis* because they had seen how easily it could be made to serve evil purposes. They also were skeptical of any manmade law that was not crystal clear, for they understood that even the slightest ambiguity could be manipulated. We get a sense of just how seriously Athenian courts adhered to manmade law after the restoration by looking at the speech *Against Ctesiphon*, by Aeschines (c. 390–314 BC), politician and subsequently practicing Sophist:

I have heard my own father say, for he lived to be ninety-five years old, and had shared all the toils of the city, which he often described to me in his leisure hours – well, he said that in the early days of the reestablished democracy, if any indictment for an illegal motion came into court, the word was as good as the deed. For what is more wicked than the man who speaks and does what is unlawful?

And in those days, so my father said, they gave no such hearing as is given now, but the jurors were far more severe toward the authors of illegal motions than was the accuser himself; and it frequently happened that they made the clerk stop, and told him to read to them the laws and the motion a second time; and they convicted a man of making an illegal motion, not in case he had overleaped all the laws together, but if one syllable only was contravened. (3.191–192)

Plato on Rhetoric

Plato came of age during this time of turmoil. His family, although not especially wealthy, was nevertheless part of the aristocracy and had been influential in Athenian politics for generations. As already noted, Critias was a close relative and leader of the Thirty Tyrants; Plato's brother Glaucon fought and died in support of the oligarchy. Although we must be careful not to get drawn into any nature/nurture debate, it seems undeniable that the decades-long conflict between the supporters of oligarchy and those of democracy – of which the Peloponnesian War was a part – influenced Plato during his formative years.

Brilliant, complex, and articulate, he could have entered politics but chose philosophy instead. This decision proved advantageous, for it probably saved him from execution and gave us a body of work that has influenced Western civilization for nearly 2,500 years. Only a small part of this work is related specifically to rhetoric, which Plato viewed very negatively, but it laid the foundation for the fully developed theoretical work of Aristotle.

The emphasis on justice

People and ideas exist in a context. Sometimes when writing about history, we cannot determine what the context was, but in the case of Plato we have enough information to do so. The Peloponnesian War ended when Plato was in his 20s. It was followed immediately by the Athenian civil war. When his teacher Socrates was executed in 399 BC, Plato was about 28. Throughout this period, in the governing assembly and the courts, Plato observed rhetoric in action. He saw how easily rhetoric inflamed already hot passions and social divisions. He witnessed how readily the *demos* could be persuaded to change its opinion, frequently with disastrous results, and act unjustly.

The most well-known case involves Socrates. Plato wrote four dialogues concerning the trial and execution of Socrates: *Euthyphro*, *Apology*, *Crito*, and *Phaedo*. In each of these, Socrates is characterized in the most positive terms as an innocent unjustly accused of impiety and corrupting the youths of Athens. Anyone unfamiliar with the history of the period would be led to believe that Socrates was a martyr for truth and philosophy who was executed by ignorant brutes. The charges against Socrates can be hard for us to fathom today. The Platonic dialogues portray Socrates as a teacher of young people, not a corrupter. But in *Apology* (the Greek term *apologia* means "defense"), Socrates states that he follows his own *daimon*, or god, which was not recognized by the state and therefore was deemed an act of impiety.

The second charge – corrupting the youth of Athens – was perhaps more damning because of the events immediately following the war with Sparta. The tyrant Critias was one of Socrates' students, as was the demagogue Alcibiades, one of the more fascinating figures in ancient Greece.[11] And if Socrates' association with such persons was not sufficiently serious, the jurors at his trial had to contend with other unsavory facts: Socrates had been consistently critical of democracy and had lived safely in the city during the rule of the Thirty while other citizens were being murdered or exiled; although at his trial he claimed to have disobeyed an illegal order he received from the Thirty, at no point did he offer any evidence that he opposed their tyranny or protested their crimes. We also learn from *Apology* that this was not the first time that Socrates had been accused. He had faced similar charges some years earlier, but the case was dismissed when the complainant failed to appear. Thus, the jury had yet another factor to contend with in its deliberations – Socrates' unmitigated arrogance. The previous charges had been a warning that he chose to ignore completely. And his arrogance is manifest throughout *Apology,* even though it was composed by his most devoted student. He refused to address directly the charges against him and elected instead to insult the jury, and thereby all Athenians, as loggerheads. When found guilty on both counts, he angered the jury by recommending that his punishment be a reward – free meals for life at the city's expense. Convinced at this point that Socrates was hopeless, the jury voted overwhelming to sentence him to death rather than impose some lesser penalty, such as a fine.

From what was probably Plato's perspective, however, Socrates was just being Socrates – a quarrelsome old man who had been annoying Athenians for decades but who never meant anyone any harm. The trial of Socrates from this point of view was not about facts or capital crimes, and it most certainly was not about justice. It was about the public's dislike of someone who enjoyed showing people how stupid they were. Rhetoric gave the prosecutor the means to demonize Socrates, to turn dislike into a darker emotion, and to secure the death penalty on the basis of who the defendant was rather than what he had done. Plato saw rhetoric's power to overcome reason, its power to inflame passions to such a degree that facts and truth became irrelevant. And such power is dangerous because it subverts justice.

Acknowledging this perspective and putting it in the context of his philosophy helps us understand why Plato's dialogues interpret actions and ideas in terms of justice and knowledge. His philosophy is based on *rationalism* – the belief that reason, rather than empirical observation, is the only valid source of knowledge and truth. The dialogues express the rationalist's conviction that knowledge leads to justice, whereas lack of knowledge leads to injustice. We find Socrates asserting in *Protagoras* that evil actions are the result of ignorance, not evil intent. This rubric allowed Plato to reduce the complex calculus of human behavior to a simple equation. As Candreva (2005) noted: "By making justice or *dikaiosune* the standard against which all other virtues are measured, Plato attempts to avoid the uncertainty and relativity of *doxa*" [opinion] (p. 37). In the context of Platonic rationalism, opinion – the province of rhetoric – is always in a state of flux, always capricious; knowledge, on the other hand, is the province of philosophy and is both absolute and certain. Thus, we find in the dialogues an important dualism – opinion/knowledge – that reflects a yearning for certainty in an uncertain world.

---

[11] Alcibiades – intelligent, strong, ambitious, reportedly the most handsome man in Greece, an incorrigible womanizer, brilliant commander, and superb rhetorician. His speech before the governing assembly in 415 BC led to his being appointed general of Athenian forces in yet another attempt to conquer Sicily. As soon as he set sail with his forces, his enemies accused him of sacrilege. He was tried in absentia and sentenced to death. Rather than face execution, he fled to Sparta, betraying military secrets that contributed to Athen's defeat in the campaign.

Oakeshott (1991) argued that this yearning becomes hazardous in the world of politics because of rationalism's unquestioned belief that all political problems – which is another way of saying all human problems – can be solved through the application of reason: "[T]he 'rational' solution of any problem is, in its nature, the perfect solution" (p. 10). According to Oakeshott, "the politics of perfection ... are the politics of uniformity" (p. 9). But in the sphere of human behavior, the only way to achieve even a measure of certainly and uniformity is through a radical abridgment of individuality and freedom, not through knowledge. We find the blueprint for uniformity in Plato's *Republic,* which calls for an end to individuality and freedom. It would accomplish these goals through laws, to be sure, but also through education and state-imposed class structure. From this perspective, *The Republic* represents Plato's ultimate and final response to the Sophists.

Plato's criticism of the Sophists and rhetoric may therefore be viewed as an ideological dispute between rationalism on the one hand and pragmatic realism on the other. As ideology, it transcended Plato's place and time. After a long period of quiescence, rationalism reemerged forcefully during the British Enlightenment to exert a powerful influence on Western culture. The faith that all problems – from teenage pregnancy to racism – can be solved through education and knowledge governs virtually all public policy and can be viewed as the triumph of Platonism.

Aristotle

Aristotle was born circa 384 BC in Stagira, a town in the northern part of Greece. His father, Nichomachus, was the court physician to King Amyntas of Macedonia. Although it is likely that his family expected him to become a physician, this plan was derailed by the untimely death of his father. His guardian, Proxenus, sent him to Athens at age 17 to attend Plato's academy. After completing his studies, he stayed on as a teacher for many years. Kennedy (1991) suggested that, along with other classes, Aristotle began teaching rhetoric of some kind in the late 350s: "The course seems to have been open to the general public – offered in the afternoons as a kind of extension division of the Academy and accompanied by practical exercises in speaking" (p. 5).

There is no question that Aristotle was brilliant, and it is enticing to imagine the interactions that must have transpired between Plato and his pupil. Clearly, Aristotle's intelligence was drawn to a wider range of subjects. He reportedly produced approximately 150 scientific and philosophical treatises. Only 30 survive, but they give some sense of the breadth of his interests, covering biology, zoology, psychology, physics, ethics and morals, aesthetics, politics, poetry, logic, and rhetoric. In many instances, these subjects did not exist as systematic areas of study before Aristotle. He laid the foundation for taxonomy in biology and zoology, was the first to explore psychology systematically, and established various axioms for deductive logic, such as the well-known syllogism:

Every Greek is a person.   Therefore, every Greek is mortal.
Every person is mortal.

His foundational work permeates nearly every facet of intellectual life today, and even many of his speculative conclusions remain relevant, such as his assessment in Book IV of *Physics* that time is related to movement through space.

Aristotle's intellectual pursuits were different from Plato's in numerous respects. Even a nodding acquaintance with Plato's work makes plain that his focus was much more narrow. What may not be quite so obvious is that Aristotle and his mentor had fundamentally different ideas about the source of knowledge. Plato maintained that the world we perceive is only a faint semblance of what he called the "Ideal Forms" that comprise reality. He captured the essence of this philosophy in *The Republic,* through his allegory of the cave: Like imprisoned cave dwellers whose understanding of the world is based on their view of shadows cast on the walls by the sun outside, our knowledge is merely a weak reflection of reality. Because our souls are divinely connected to the Ideal Forms, we can discover truth and acquire knowledge merely by thinking, provided we apply philosophical inquiry, or dialectic. Rhetoric necessarily fails us in this regard because it does not separate the true from the false but simply flatters us into believing that the shadows we perceive are reality, thereby keeping us happy prisoners in the cave of our own ignorance. His discussion of Forms hinges on the notion of *a priori* knowledge – that is, knowledge that is independent of experience and that therefore can be obtained only through ratiocination.

Perhaps because of his early training in biology, or perhaps owing to witnessing his father practicing medicine, Aristotle took a different approach. He based his work on collecting and categorizing data from nature and then reasoning his way to conclusions based on *observation*. Aristotle's philosophy, therefore, is an early form of *empiricism*.

These two approaches to knowledge and understanding the world still govern much of our thinking. Work in humanities – such as literature, for example – tends to focus on reflexive contemplation owing to the belief that each individual is connected to pre-existing universal truths that are inherently generalizable once they are recognized, what William Faulkner once called the "eternal verities." Work in science and social science, on the other hand, tends to be based on the collection, classification, and analysis of data, with generalizations limited to the data under consideration. We therefore can say that Aristotle advanced significantly the proto-scientific approach to knowledge that began with the Milesians, giving us the necessary foundation for science.[12]

Aristotle's divergent method of inquiry may have had a tangible consequence. When Plato died in 347 BC, Aristotle, as the Academy's outstanding student and its most successful teacher, should have been the logical choice to become the new head of the school, but Plato's nephew Speusippus was selected, instead. Aristotle's approach to knowledge may have been too radical for Plato and others associated with the Academy. His connection to the Macedonian court and the fact that he was a *metic*, or resident alien, may also have been contributing factors. At about this time, King Philip of Macedonia was striving to bring all of Greece under his control, and Athenians were bitterly opposed. In any event, Aristotle left Athens shortly after Plato's death and traveled to the city of Assos, in Asia Minor, just east of Lesbos, where he enjoyed the hospitality of King Hermeas for approximately three years. During this time, he married the niece of the king, fathered a daughter, and gathered around him a group of scholars with whom he engaged in intensive biological and zoological research – the very sort of study that Plato ignored. Soldiers of the Persian Empire attacked Assos in 344 BC, forcing Aristotle and his family to flee. They traveled first to Lesbos and then to Macedonia, where King Philip made Aristotle the court philosopher and put him in charge of educating Prince Alexander, later called The Great.

When Philip was assassinated in 336 BC, Alexander was elevated to the throne. His duties as tutor over, Aristotle returned to Athens with the aim of founding his own

---

[12] Science but not the scientific method.

school. By this time, Athens and Macedonia had signed a treaty that created a less hostile political environment than had existed a decade earlier. Although facing competition from Plato's Academy and from Isocrates' school, Aristotle established the Lyceum in 335 BC. The school flourished, and it was during this period that Aristotle is thought to have produced most of his treatises, which many believe were his lecture notes and were never intended for publication.

As Alexander proceeded to conquer the Persian Empire, there was growing unrest on the Greek mainland. He was forced to maintain a sizable army there to prevent rebellion. Headstrong and freedom-loving, most Athenians resented being under the hegemony of Macedonians, whom they classified as barbarians and contemptuously refused to recognize as Greeks (see Cartledge, 2004). In 323, after countless battles and numerous grievous wounds that would have killed a lesser man, Alexander settled in Babylon to plan a major campaign against the Arabs when he suddenly contracted a fever and died within a matter of days, at the age of 32. The Athenians immediately organized neighboring city states and attacked the Macedonian garrisons in what is known as the Lamian War. Aristotle's close association with Macedonia became a serious liability without the might of Alexander as protection, and he was forced to flee the city. He traveled to the island of Euboea only to fall ill and die in 322 BC.

As in the case of Plato, rhetoric for Aristotle was merely a side interest. We can assume that he taught rhetoric, but there is no evidence that he practiced it. His interest, in fact, appears to have been predicated on his effort to produce a comprehensive examination of human nature. Even so, his book *The Art of Rhetoric* is arguably the most influential text on the subject in history, rivaled only by Cicero's works. He based his theory on observations of public speaking as it was practiced in the assembly and the courts, on his observations of people and their behavior, and on the analysis of existing speeches produced by Sophists. Although he was neither a Sophist nor a rhetorician, the often exquisite detail of his *Rhetoric* suggests that he understood that he could do a better job of explaining the nature of the art than anyone who had previously addressed the topic, including Plato.

The Stage Is Set

Together, Plato and Aristotle set the stage for all discussions of rhetoric that followed. Although Plato's treatment of rhetoric does not reach the true level of theory because it lacks an explanatory component and its descriptive component is simplistic and biased, it nevertheless established ethical and moral criteria by which rhetoric has been judged ever since. Aristotle, on the other hand, provided a richly detailed theory that has resonated throughout history and continues to be relevant. Current textbooks on rhetoric, for example, commonly make reference to Aristotle's notions of *ethos*, *pathos*, and *logos* as rhetorical proofs. Modern theories of communication and advertising rely heavily on the notions of *ethos* and *pathos*, as well as the psychology of the audience, a point that Aristotle emphasized. Furthermore, Aristotle's *Poetics* (often referred to as *The Art of Poetry*) and *The Art of Rhetoric* may be viewed as the culmination of the Sophists' efforts to systematize the two forms of linguistic expression – and also the completed transition from an oral to a literate society. The quality of a given poem or speech was no longer limited to its performance or the effect it had on listeners but now could also be assessed on the basis of its structure. As societies changed over the centuries and occasions for oral discourse diminished or disappeared altogether, the work begun by the Sophists and completed by Aristotle took on ever growing importance.

2

Female Voices

Women and Rhetoric in Ancient Greece

The pervasive male voice in classical Greek rhetoric is troubling from our modern perspective, and for a number of years there have been efforts to recover female voices that, ostensibly, have been lost over the millennia (e.g., Bizzell and Herzberg, 2000; Enos, 2002; Fantham et al., 1994; Glenn, 1997; Henry, 1995; Lunsford, 1995). Many current scholars claim that the strongest candidate is Aspasia, and it has become popular to identify her as one of the more important rhetoricians of Classical Athens.

Aspasia was a *hetaira*, or courtesan, who arrived in Athens from Ionia around 440 BC. Unlike female citizens, whose lives were fairly well controlled by law and custom during this period, *hetairai* were free to travel from city to city, and, of course, they were free to associate with men outside their immediate families. Upon her arrival in Athens, Aspasia opened a brothel and began training young girls to be courtesans for the wealthy and influential men of the city. She reportedly caught the attention of Pericles, Athens' political leader, who subsequently divorced his wife and abandoned his two children so that he could cohabit with Aspasia. At some point they married and had a son. According to Plutarch (1959), their home became a place where politicians and intellectuals gathered regularly to discuss with Aspasia the topics of the day.[1]

Little more is known of Aspasia, even though she is mentioned in a few classical texts. In *Acharnians*, the comic playwright Aristophanes (c. 448–380 BC) accused her of using sex to influence government policy, and Cicero, writing in about 80 BC, offered a fragment from *Aspasia*, a lost work by Aeschines that supposedly depicts her engaged in a dialogue. However, the only significant contemporary account of her that has survived are about 12 lines in Plato's dialogue *Menexenus*, in which Socrates states not only that Aspasia taught him rhetoric but also that she taught Pericles how to be a fine public speaker. Noting that he was a bad student, Socrates remarks that Aspasia was always ready to pummel him for his poor memory; then he proceeds to recite verbatim a lengthy funeral speech that she had composed the previous day.[2]

Concluding from these texts that Aspasia was a practicing rhetorician seems hasty. The reasons are straightforward. Rhetoric was practiced in the public arena: at court, in

---

[1] In several extant legal cases from the period, the presentation of evidence that a woman ate and drank with males outside her immediate family was dispositive in establishing that she was a prostitute, not a wife (Gould, 1980). Note that *hetairai* were distinguished from *pornê*, or common prostitutes.

[2] Another interesting illustration of Socrates' formidable memory appears in Plato's *Ion*, in which Socrates easily matches the rhapsode Ion, an acclaimed expert on Homer, in recalling specific passages from *The Iliad* at will.

the governing assembly, at festivals, and at funerals. Women were absolutely excluded from the first two venues, and their participation in the latter two, although very important, was limited in a number of ways (see Pomeroy, 1995). Foreigners like Aspasia were, as far as we know, barred from any formal participation in religious rituals and festivals. The fragment from Aeschines' dialogue does not support Aspasia's status as a rhetorician because it seems to depict her in the role of a marriage counselor, not an orator. As for Aristophanes, his plays must be viewed through the lens of Athenian culture, not our own. Thus, the suggestion that Pericles based his political decisions on the advice of a prostitute was probably intended to portray the leader as a comic figure and was not intended as a historical account of Aspasia. We can gain a better understanding of the situation by imagining the effect on voters if they learned that the US President made political decisions on such dubious advice.

Using *Menexenus*, as many do, to affirm that Aspasia was a rhetorician also seems to slight the cultural framework in which the dialogue was produced. Plato was not a supporter of Periclian democratic reforms, and he was an opponent of rhetoric, especially the platitudinous "set-piece" rhetoric that Aspasia's funeral oration illustrates. In addition, Plato's assertion that Pericles not only learned oratory from a *hetaira* but also relied on her for many of his speeches must be viewed as a significant insult, highlighting the leader as an object of ridicule. As for the funeral oration itself, most scholars view it as simply a parody of Pericles' funeral oration in Thucydides' (c. 455–400 BC) account of the Peloponnesian War. Having Socrates declare that Aspasia also taught him rhetoric – and then having him reproduce one of her speeches as an example of bad rhetoric – seems designed as a scathing commentary on the woman, Pericles, the speech, and rhetoric in general. Also worth noting is that this structure is duplicated in *Symposium*, although the content and purpose are different. In that dialogue, Socrates declares that he was taught "the art of love" by Diotima of Mantineia, and, as in *Menexenus*, he then recalls, again from memory, a dissertation on "the being and nature of Love" that she had shared with him previously. The similarities here suggest a literary device. We know nothing about Diotima, not even whether she was a real person or merely a name Plato invented, but under the circumstances of the time, if she existed she was in all likelihood a prostitute, leading to speculation that the character of Diotima was modeled on Aspasia (something that Plato's contemporaries would know). If this was the case, then the allusion would be yet another blow against Pericles, who by inference shared his woman even with someone as notoriously poor and unkempt as Socrates.

It is important to acknowledge, however, that the disdain Aspasia experienced from such powerful men as Aristophanes and Plato was a recognition of her influence in a society that granted women few privileges. Moreover, she is among a select group of people who continue to be a topic of discussion 2,500 years after their deaths. This is a tribute to her qualities as a person. She may have been a gifted speaker and conversationalist, and we have no reason to doubt that she influenced Pericles, in the way that spouses inevitably do. But we have insufficient evidence to conclude that she was a rhetorician.

Clearly, the absence of female rhetoricians during the Classical Period does not mean that women can be excluded from discussions of rhetoric. Women had played important roles as priestesses and poets for many centuries, and it is highly likely that they contributed significantly to the preservation of history and culture after the loss of literacy during the Greek dark ages, helping to develop the oral culture that dominated Greece until literacy began to reemerge sometime between 800 and 700 BC. In addition, as we see in the works of Enheduanna and Sappho, their poetry not only expressed but also, in a sense, validated the individual. It reflected and simultaneously gave impetus to individuality, which was necessary for the development of both democracy and rhetoric, which came to characterize Western culture. Unfortunately, these more substantive issues and their relations to rhetoric have not received the level of research and exploration that they merit.

Reconstructing the extent of women's contributions in any detail is not possible here, but given the importance of poetry to the development of formal theories of rhetoric, as well as the degree to which women were involved in creating poetry, it does seem reasonable to conclude that their work served as a precursor to rhetoric, and two of the more likely representatives of this view are Enheduanna and Sappho.

Introduction to Enheduanna (c. 2300 BC)

Enheduanna was the daughter of Sargon of Akkad (c. 2334–2290 BC), a military leader who established himself as king and then sought to unite northern and southern Sumeria, which today corresponds roughly to the country of Iraq. Although the Akkadians and the Sumerians worshipped essentially the same gods, they called them by different names. One of the more important deities for the Akkadians, for example, was Ishtar – goddess of love, fertility, and war; the Sumerians worshipped the same goddess but called her Inanna. In a political move to further the unification of the two lands, Sargon installed Enheduanna as high priestess to the moon god Nanna in the temple at Ur. As high priestess, Enheduanna would have undergone a ritual "marriage" to the god. The symbolic status of this marriage was similar to more earthly marriages between nobility and heads of state and strengthened Sargon's position in the conquered territory, but it may have been unique at the time insofar as it had both political and religious implications.

Aside from routine tasks such as maintaining the temple and bestowing divine imprimatur on her father's rule, any attempt to identify Enheduanna's nonpublic duties leads to sheer speculation. But we do know that the chief role of a high priestess was to lead religious rituals, performing the sacred rites that involved propitiation through sacrifices and hymns of praise. These were public ceremonies that engaged large numbers of people, so it seems reasonable to assume that the performative function of the songs had a high priority. And yet, surprisingly, Enheduanna's surviving compositions are striking in that they are both private and personal. In fact, they are the oldest known works in which the author identifies herself and speaks in the first person.

Although innovative, the personal nature of these hymns may reflect the cultural milieu of the time. Jacobsen's (1978) classic investigation of Mesopotamian religion noted that during this period, the concept of the divine had changed from remote gods only marginally involved in human affairs to helpers with particular human interests. Their distance from people lessened considerably, and for the first time they became personal patrons who might bring succor to those in trouble. According to Jacobsen, the change allowed individuals to claim a "close personal relationship to the divine, expecting help and guidance in his personal life and personal affairs" (p. 147).

This close personal relationship is vibrant in the extant poems. Many are hymns to Nana and Inanna, praising their strength and promising everlasting devotion. Modern readers are more likely to favor the two longer works, "Lady of the Largest Heart" and "Exaltation of Inanna," which describe how during uprisings in Ur and Uruk, a rival military leader, Lugalanne, took control of the kingdom and subsequently banished Enheduanna from the temple. The poems are deeply personal and reflect Enheduanna's feelings of rage and abandonment. Driven into exile, she is scorched by the sun, blasted by the desert wind, banished among the lepers. She prays for divine intervention, however, and eventually is restored.

Reading 1

The Second Poem – Lady of the Largest Heart

Excerpt from "The Second Poem – Lady of the Largest Heart," pp. 126–36 from *Inanna, Lady of the Largest Heart: Poems of the Sumerian High Priestess Enheduanna* by Betty De Shong Meador. © 2000 by Betty De Shong Meador. Reprinted by permission of the author and the University of Texas Press.

[...]
Mistress
you outclass Enlil and An
your praiseworthy path shows forth
without YOU is no fate fixed
without YOU is no keen counsel arrived

★ ★ ★

to run   to steal away
to cool the heart   to soothe
are yours Inanna

fitful wandering
speeding by
rising   falling
reaching the fore
are yours Inanna

to smooth the traveler's road
to clear a path for the weak
are yours Inanna

to straighten the footpath
to make firm the cleft place
are yours Inanna

to destroy   to build
to lift up   to put down
are yours Inanna

to turn man into woman
woman into man
are yours Inanna

allure   ardent desire
belongings   households
are yours Inanna

wealth   brisk trading
quick profits   hoard even more
are yours Inanna

prosperous business   abundance of
money
indebtedness   ruinous loss
are yours Inanna

to teach   watch over
supervise   scrutinize

are yours Inanna

life vigor   fitting modesty
male guardian spirits
female guardian spirits
disclosing sacred spots
are yours Inanna

to worship in lowly prostration
to worship in high heaven
are yours Inanna

the word of rejection
the word of riddance
are yours Inanna

(10 to 12 lines missing)

to hand out tender mercies
restore your heart to someone
are yours Inanna

heart trembling   weakness
shivering cramps   illness
are yours Inanna

to have a husband   to have a wife
to thrive in the goodness of love
are yours Inanna

to spark a quarrel
within love's lusty delight
is yours Inanna

to be negligent
tend carefully
are yours Inanna

to build a house
construct the women's rooms
furnish them
to kiss a baby's lips
are yours Inanna
    [...]

(13 lines missing)

    [...]
to be all knowing
is yours Inanna

to build a bird's nest
safe in a sound branch
make indestructible
are yours Inanna

to lure snakes from the wasteland
terrorize the hateful
throw in chains   hold in bondage
are yours Inanna

to summon the hated
is yours Inanna

to cast lots
is yours Inanna

to gather the scattered
restore the living place
are yours Inanna

setting free
is yours Inanna

★ ★ ★

    […]
(10 lines missing)

a sorrowful wail is your song
no one can overthrow your works
your rage tramples under foot

    […]
your torch flames
heaven's four quarters
spreads splendid light in the dark
those warrior women
like a single thread
come forth from beyond the river
do common work
in devotion to you
whose hands sear them with purifying
fire

your many devoted
who will be burnt
like sun-scorched firebricks
pass before your eyes

    […]
you have realized
the Queen of Heaven and Earth
to the utmost
you hold everything
entirely in your hands

Mistress
you are splendid
no one can walk before you
you lie with great An

on an unblemished bed
    […]

you alone are sublime
praise your name

★ ★ ★

I
I am Enheduanna
High Priestess of Nanna
with single heart
I am devoted to Nanna

(20 lines missing)

I plead with you
I say STOP
the bitter hating heart and sorrow

my Lady
what day will you have mercy
how long will I cry a moaning prayer
I am yours
why do you slay me
may your heart be cooled toward me
I cry   I plead
for your attentive thoughts

may I stand before you
may your eyes shine upon me
take my measure

I
who spread over the land
the splendid brilliance
of your divinity
you allow my flesh
to know your scourging

my sorrow and bitter trial
strike my eye as treachery
tear me down from heaven
mercy   compassion   attention
returning your heart to someone
folded-hand prayer
are yours Inanna

your storm-shot torrents
drench the bare earth
moisten to life

moisture bearing light
floods the dark

O my Lady
my Queen

I unfold your splendor in all lands
I extol your glory

I will praise your course
your sweeping grandeur
forever

You
who can touch your divinity
who can match your rites

may great An
whom you love
beg your mercy

may all the great gods
soothe your temper
may you gladden
as you near
the clear blue lapis throne
of the Queen
may the high sitting-place
say to you
SIT

may your holy lying place
say to you
rest
give way
refresh

where dawn breaks
    Utu flares
may the people herald
your glorious divinity
O you who are Queen

may they declare your splendor

for you
An and Enlil
and all gods in accord
fix a great fate

to you
they give
Queenship of the Throne Room

and You
O Queen
say who of the godly sisters
is worthy of Queenship

Queen
Mistress
you are sublime
you are venerable

Inanna
you are sublime
you are venerable

my Lady
I have shown your grandeur resplendent
restore your heart to me

your great deeds are boundless
may I praise your eminence
O maiden Inanna
sweet is your praise

Reading 2

The Third Poem – The Exaltation of Inanna

Excerpt from "The Third Poem – The Exaltation of Innana," pp. 174–80 from *Inanna, Lady of the Largest Heart: Poems of the Sumerian High Priestess Enheduanna* by Betty De Shong Meador. © 2000 by Betty De Shong Meador. Reprinted by permission of the author and the University of Texas Press.

    [...]
mistress of the scheme of order
great Queen of queens
babe of a holy womb
greater than the mother who bore you
You all knowing
You wise vision
Lady of all lands
life-giver for the many
faithful Goddess
worthy of powers

to sing your praise is exalted
You of the bountiful heart
You of the radiant heart
I will sing of your cosmic powers

★ ★ ★

truly for your gain
you drew me toward
my holy quarters
I
the High Priestess

I
Enheduanna

there I raised the ritual basket
there I sang the shout of joy

but *that man* cast me among the dead
I am not allowed in my rooms
gloom falls on the day
light turns leaden
shadows close in
dreaded southstorm cloaks the sun

he wipes his spit-soaked hand
on my honey sweet mouth
my beautiful image
fades under dust

what is happening to my fate
O Suen
what is this with Lugalanne

speak to An
he will free me
tell him "Now"
he will release me

the Woman will dash his fate
that Lugalanne
the mountains the biggest floods
lie at Her feet

the Woman is as great as he
she will break the city from him
    (may her heart grow soft for me)

stand there
I
Enheduanna   Jewel of An
let me say a prayer to you
    (flow tears refreshing drink for Inanna)
    […]

he robbed An of his temple
    he does not fear Big Man An
the potent vigor of the place
does not fill him
he spoiled its allure
truly he destroyed it

haunt him
with the ghost
of her you set up as your partner

O my divine ecstatic wild cow
drive this man out
hunt him down
catch him

I
who am I
in the place which holds up
life's key elements

may An desert those rebels
who hate your Nanna
may An wreck that city
may Enlil curse its fate
may the mother not comfort
her crying child

Queen
creator of heart-soothing
that man junked
your boat of lamentation
on an alien sea

I am dying
that I must sing
this sacred song
I
even I
Nanna ignores my straits
am I to be ruined by treachery
I
even I
Ashimbabbar
neglects my case
whether he neglects me
or not
what does it matter
that man threw me out of the temple
I who served triumphant

he made me fly
like swallows swept
from their holes in the wall

he eats away at my life
I wander through thorny brush in the
mountains
he robbed me
of the true crown
of the High Priestess

he gave me
the ritual dagger of mutilation
he said
"it becomes you"
    […]

that man has not settled my claim
again and again
he throws a hateful verdict
in my face

I no longer lift my hands
from the pure sacred bed
I no longer unravel
Ningal's gifts of dreams
to anyone

I
most radiant priestess of Nanna
may you cool your heart for me
my Queen
beloved of An

PROCLAIM!
PROCLAIM!
I shall not
pay tribute to Nanna
it is of YOU
I PROCLAIM

that you are exalted as An
PROCLAIM!

that you are wide as earth
PROCLAIM!

that you crush rebellious lands
PROCLAIM!

that you shriek over the land
PROCLAIM!

that you smash heads
PROCLAIM!

that you gorge on corpses like a dog
PROCLAIM!

    [...]
that you stand victorious
PROCLAIM!

I have not said this of Nanna
I have said it of YOU
my phrases glorify YOU
    who alone are exalted
my Queen
beloved of An

I have spoken
of your tempestuous fury

★ ★ ★

I have heaped up coals in the brazier
I have washed in the sacred basin
I have readied your room in the tavern
(may your heart be cooled for me)
suffering bitter pangs
I gave birth to this exaltation
for you my Queen

what I told you in the dark of night
may the singer recount at noon

child of yours   I am a captive
bride of yours   I am a captive
it is for my sake your anger fumes
your heart finds no relief

★ ★ ★

the eminent Queen
guardian of the throne room
receives her prayer

the holy heart
of Inanna
returns to her

the day is favorable
she dresses lavishly
in woman's allure

she glows with beauty's shine
like the light of the rising moon
Nanna lifts her
into seemly view

at the sound of Ningal's prayer
the gate posts open
    Hail
    Be Well

★ ★ ★

this poem
spoken for the sacred Woman
is exalted
praise the mountain destroyer
praise Her who
    (together with An)
received the unchanging powers
praise my lady wrapped in beauty
PRAISE BE TO INANNA

Introduction to Sappho (c. 610–570 BC)

Even though Sappho was considered one of the more important poets during the clas-sical Greek and Hellenistic periods, we know little about her, and most of what we know comes from secondary sources that may not be accurate. She made her home in Mitylene, on the Isle of Lesbos, but whether she was born there is uncertain. A few accounts indicate that she was born somewhere in what is now Turkey. Her name in the Aeolic dialect of the region was Psappha, which is decidedly non-Greek and gives credence to reports that she was not a Greek but a Hittite. Sappho was a member of the aristocracy, which may explain her superior education; however, Lesbos was known in the ancient world for being progressive, especially with regard to women, so it is possible that her education was fairly typical. Her life changed dramatically around 610 BC, when the demagogue Pittacus led an army against the aristocracy, overthrew the leader Melanchrus, instituted a democracy, and exiled all the wealthy families. Sappho and her family fled to Syracuse, where they lived for at least a decade before they were able to return to Lesbos.

Sappho did not invent lyric poetry, but she advanced it to such a degree that her work became the quintessential model well into the Roman period and was included as standard reading in Greek, Roman, and even Byzantine academies. Over time, interest in her work declined, perhaps because she wrote in the Aeolic dialect of Greek, which fewer and fewer people used or understood. Like Enheduanna, Sappho wrote in the first person, which gives her work an undeniable appeal. In spite of her reputation throughout the ancient world as the greatest lyric poet, only one of her poems survived in its entirety. We know that the early Church leaders were intent on destroying pagan writing, and during the fourth and fifth centuries AD entire libraries were put to the torch throughout the Mediterranean. Concrete evidence is lacking, but it seems likely that Sappho may have received special attention in this regard owing to the homoerotic nature of some of her poems.

As W. Harris (2006) noted, translating Sappho is difficult for three reasons. First, and most obviously, only one complete poem exists, and translating fragments that lack contextualizing information is a challenge. Some translators have chosen to fill in missing words, phrases, and lines in an effort to provide a more detailed corpus, but as well-reasoned as their choices are, they remain merely guesses, and we cannot be certain that they reflect Sappho's original writing accurately. Second, the Aeolic dialect is sufficiently different from the more widely understood Attic Greek to prevent us from using Attic texts to tease out the exact meaning of words and phrases. And finally, Greek meter does not yield easily to an English equivalent. Because Sappho's poems were written to be sung to music, any translation is missing both pitch and melody. Much is lost, and the result is that even the most thoughtful translation into English leaves many readers left wondering what all the fuss is about.

Aphrodite was Sappho's personal god, and as in the works of Enheduanna, we find Sappho in the only complete poem asking the goddess to end her suffering. Her complaints are of the heart and involve longing for a loved one or loved ones. That Sappho was in close association with a group of young women seems evident, and it has led several scholars to propose that she ran a school for girls to prepare them for marriage (e.g., Fantham et al., 1994; Jaeger, 1976). Some readers may find the homoeroticism in Sappho's work unsettling, even though there is nothing in any of the surviving poems that could be characterized as titillating. It is important to understand that the ancient Greeks held views on sexuality that were different from our own. Homosexual relations between males are well known to us because they are mentioned so often in the literature of the period, nearly all of which was produced by men. The emphasis on keeping women separated from males was discussed in the general introduction, but we have no evidence that similar efforts were made to isolate women from other women. It seems, in fact, that women were relatively free to associate with one another. Given the easy acceptance of male homosexuality, it does not seem farfetched to propose that female homosexuality was not uncommon.[3]

Symonds (2002) suggested that, in all of Greece, Lesbos was particularly liberal and that many Lesbian women, not just Sappho, produced literature. They formed clubs in which they performed their poetry, much like the *symposia* that were so popular among Athenian men. If Sappho indeed ran a school to prepare girls for marriage, it probably included instruction in poetry and music, but her affiliation with Aphrodite suggests that it also may have provided instruction in sex and seduction, which given the age of the typical bride seems not only reasonable but perhaps necessary. Grooms commonly were in their late 20s or early 30s and therefore were more experienced than their teenage brides in all areas of life (Blundel, 1995; Duby and Perrot, 1992; Redfield, 1982). They were likely to have been introduced to sex in early adolescence through a homosexual relationship with an older male, and given the abundance of prostitutes in most cities, they also no doubt came to the marriage bed with years of heterosexual experience. Instruction in sex and seduction would have helped bridge the gap between bride and groom on the wedding night and afterwards. Exactly what Sappho's role was in this regard we cannot know, but in such circumstances, instruction, eroticism, and love can become blurred.

Readings 3–12

Sappho's Poetry

"With His Venom," "That Afternoon," "We Heard Them Chanting," "It's No Use," "Sleep, Darling," "I Have Had Not One Word," "Afraid," from *Sappho: A New Translation* edited and translated by M. Barnard. University of California Press, 1958. © 1958 by The Regents of the University of California, © renewed 1986 by Mary Barnard. Reprinted by permission of The University of California Press.

"He Seems to Me," "A Host of Horsemen," pp. 54–6 from *Greek Lyric: An Anthology in Translation*, edited and translated by Andrew M. Miller. Hackett Publishing, 1996. Reprinted by permission of Hackett Publishing Company, Inc. All rights reserved.

"To Aphrodite," from *Sappho: The Greek Poems*, edited and translated by William Harris. Retrieved October 21, 2008 from http://community.middlebury.edu/~harris/sappho.html.

3

With His Venom

With his venom

irresistible
and bittersweet

that loosener
of limbs, Love

reptile-like
strikes me down

---

[3] Given that the extant works make it clear that few men were exclusively homosexual (indeed, it was deemed an aberration), it would seem more accurate to use the term "bisexual" to characterize sexual orientations in this period.

4

That Afternoon

That afternoon

Girls ripe to marry
wove the flower-
heads into necklaces

5

We Heard Them Chanting

We heard them chanting:

FIRST
VOICE
Young Adonis is
dying! O Cytherea
What shall we do now?

SECOND
VOICE
Batter your breasts
with your fists, girls–
tatter your dresses!

6

It's No Use

It's no use

Mother dear, I
can't finish my
weaving
    You may
blame Aphrodite
soft as she is

she has almost
killed me with

love for that boy

7

Sleep, Darling

Sleep, darling

I have a small
daughter called
Cleis, who is

like a golden
flower
          I wouldn't
take all Croesus'
kingdom with love
thrown in, for her

8

I Have Had Not One Word

I have had not one word from her

Frankly I wish I were dead.
When she left, she wept

a great deal; she said to
me, "This parting must be
endured, Sappho. I go unwillingly."

I said, "Go, and be happy
but remember (you know
well) whom you leave shackled by love

"If you forget me, think
of our gifts to Aphrodite

and all the loveliness that we shared

"all the violet tiaras,
braided rosebuds, dill and
crocus twined around your young neck

"myrrh poured on your head
and on soft mats girls with
all that they most wished for beside them

"while no voices chanted
choruses without ours,
no woodlot bloomed in spring without
    song …"

9

Afraid

Afraid of losing you

I ran fluttering
like a little girl
after her mother

10

He Seems to Me

He seems to me equal to the gods,
that man who sits across from you
and listens close at hand to your sweet voice
and lovely laughter.
Truly it sets
my heart to pounding in my breast,
for the moment I glance at you, I can
no longer speak;
my tongue grows numb; at once a subtle
fire runs stealthily beneath my skin;
my eyes see nothing, my ears
ring and buzz,

the sweat pours down, a trembling seizes the whole of me, I turn paler
than grass, and I seem to myself
not far from dying.
But everything can be endured, because ...

11

A Host of Horsemen

Some say a host of horsemen is the most
    beautiful thing
on the black earth, some say a host of
    foot-soldiers,
some, a fleet of ships; but I say it is
whatever one loves.
Wholly easy it is to make this intelligible
to everyone, for she who by far surpassed
all humankind in beauty, Helen,
forsook her husband,
noblest of men, to sail away to Troy;
neither of child nor of beloved parents

did she take thought at all, being led
    astray by ...
[one line missing]
... for pliant ...
... lightly ...
... now has brought Anaktoria to my
    mind,
though she is absent:
I would rather see her lovely step
and the glancing brightness of her face
than Lydian chariots and foot soldiers
arrayed in armor.

12

To Aphrodite

Many colored throned immortal
Aphrodite,
daughter of Zeus, wile-weaver, I beg you
with reproaches and harms do not beat
    down
O Lady, my soul.

But come here, if ever at another time
My voice hearing, from afar
You have ear, and your father's home
    leaving
 – golden – you came

Yoking the chariot. And fair, swift
Doves brought you over the black earth
Dense wings whirring, from heaven down
through middle air.

Suddenly they arrived, and you, O Blessed
    One,

Smiling with your immortal countenance
Asked what hurt me, and for what
Now I cried out.

And what do I want to happen most
In my crazy heart. "Whom then
    Persuasion
..............to bring to you, dearest? Who,
Sappho, hurts you?

And if she flees, soon will she follow,
And if she does not take gifts, she will
    give,
If she does not love, she will love
Despite herself."

Come to me now, the harsh worry
Let loose, what my heart wants to be
Done, do it! And you yourself be
My battle-ally.

Study Questions

1   Prayer commonly involves efforts to flatter the divinity to whom it is addressed. What form does this flattery take in the first part of Poem 2? What purpose do you believe it serves? Given the powers attributed to Inanna, why would the god require praise?
2   Although Enheduanna was high priestess of the god Nanna, she seems to reject Nanna in Poem 3 to proclaim for the goddess Inanna. What do the autobiographical elements of the poem offer that might explain her decision?
3   From our modern perspective, the Greek attitude toward women seems repressive, and it is fairly common to find scholarly discussions of male suppression of women in ancient Greece. The Greeks of the period, however, probably viewed their social structures as a means of protecting females. What factors might have lent legitimacy to this view?
4   Although Sappho has long been labeled a writer of homoerotic poetry, this characterization may not do justice to the range of her themes. Reviewing the verses provided in the text, what are some additional themes, and what do they reveal about the poetess?
5   A popular view of the distant past is that people in the ancient world were significantly different from us. Do the selections from Enheduanna and Sappho tend to confirm or disconfirm this view?

Writing Topics

1   Women held important positions in religions until the rise of Christianity. Explore some of the factors that led to their disappearance from those roles.
2   Some of the selections from Enheduanna and Sappho illustrate women in distress asking for divine intervention. Examine a text produced by a man, such as Homer's *Iliad* or *Odyssey*, which also contains requests for divine intervention. Analyze and explain the differences and similarities.

Further Reading

Archilocus, selections.
Alcman, selections.
Fantham, E., Foley, H.P., Kampen, N.B., Pomeroy, S.B., and Shapiro, H.A. (1994). *Women in the classical world*. New York: Oxford.

3

The Sophists

Introduction to Protagoras (c. 490–420 BC)

Born at Abdera, Thrace, Protagoras is the earliest known Sophist. He reportedly worked as a porter of wood in his youth, but at some point he began studying philosophy and, calling himself a Sophist, began teaching poetry and public speaking for pay. His instruction was deemed so valuable that he supposedly charged up to 100 *minae* per pupil, but we must be cautious about this figure because it is remarkably high and because we have no information about the length of pupils' studies. In ancient Athens, the average daily wage was perhaps one *drachma*; 100 *minae* would be 10,000 times this amount.

Protagoras was a friend of Pericles, with whom he may have discussed politics and morality. In 445 BC, he was asked to help draft laws and/or a constitution for the Athenian colony of Thurii. He also was the author of various philosophical treatises, such as *On Truth* and *On the Gods*. All that remains of these works are fragments, included here. *On the Gods* offended many, and in 411 BC he was charged with impiety, found guilty, and banished from Athens. Legend has it that he lived to be about 70 and died when his ship sank in a storm as he was traveling to Sicily.

Throughout history, Protagoras has been held responsible for introducing the concepts of relativism, theological skepticism, and humanism. Relativism had a significant influence on rhetoric, as the general introduction noted, for it led to claims that Sophists aimed to make weak causes seem stronger, which had the potential to raise ethical questions related to language. In the hands of an unethical rhetorician, injustice could prevail owing to the power of speech. Both relativism and theological skepticism appear to have influenced Plato's philosophy of Ideal Forms, and given the history of the period, Plato may have believed that Protagoras' teaching was somehow related to the chaos of the Athenian civil war and the spread of democracy. Although we have no way of verifying any such relation, it is the case that Protagoras' assertion that "man is the measure of all things" can be understood as an endorsement of democratic ideals, for it does not differentiate by class or socioeconomic status. In a world in which charges of impiety could lead to confiscation of property, exile, or even death, this particular assertion directly challenged the cosmological alignment that puts mankind in thrall to deities.

Fragment 1: Man is the Measure

Because we lack a context for fragment 1, we do not know exactly what Protagoras was trying to communicate or why. However, Plato provided a detailed analysis in his dialogue *Theaetetus* that offers some insight into how it may have been understood at the time. Plato's analysis operates on two levels, the individual and the general. First, to claim that (a) man is the measure of all things raises inherent contradictions. One person may feel cold if the wind is blowing, whereas another may feel warm under the same conditions. Thus, for Plato, the claim leads to an unacceptable paradox inherent in subjective assessments of truth – the wind cannot be both cold and warm simultaneously.

Protagoras' claim is equally problematic at the general level, for it suggests that perception is knowledge. Perception, however, may differ from one person to the next. Plato argued that without an objective measure of knowledge (or truth) we cannot accept numerous incontrovertible conditions, such as the fact that some people "know" more than others, some are taller, and so on. Furthermore, we would have no means of differentiating justice from injustice, truth from falsehood, or good from evil. Justice would be simply what people perceive it to be, as would the good and other factors associated with morality and ethics. This is the path to social chaos and tyranny, of "might makes right." On this account, Plato rejected Protagoras' claim, as well as the logical implication that perception is knowledge.

Many scholars also contextualize Protagoras' statement in reference to Parmenides. Parmenides is known principally as the advocate of *Eleatic monism*, a philosophical position that maintains that change is an illusion and that reality is composed of and reducible to one substance (see Curd, 1997). Havelock (1986) argued that Parmenides was attempting to rein in preliterate ways of thinking and speaking, which described the world through poetic exaggeration (ironically through a mystical poem, *On Nature*). In such a world, Zeus can change into a swan and back again; the gods are called immortal and yet can be wounded, as they are in *The Iliad*, by a sharp blade; and men can become women, as in the case of the prophet Tiresias, and then can change back into a man. Stated another way, in this poetic preliterate world, a god is a god and also not a god; a man is a man and also not a man. This clearly creates a problem for any principled investigation of reality. As Parmenides (frag. 6) stated: People are "as much deaf as blind, an undiscerning horde, by whom to be and not to be are considered the same and not the same." Thus, the thrust of Havelock's argument is that Parmenides was attempting to shift language and thinking toward the sort of analytical modality that has often been associated with literacy and science (also see Goody, 1968, 1972, 1987; Goody and Watt, 1968; Ong, 1982). This argument should be viewed, however, in light of the way *On Nature* discounts the world of the senses as an illusion and celebrates rationalism as the Way of Truth: The real is only what can be conceived, not what can be seen.

In this context, Protagoras' statement appears to be a refutation of Parmenides. People have the ability to judge for themselves what is and what is not and are not entirely "undiscerning." This position is congruent with Sophistic rhetoric and the practice of *dissoi logoi,* which emphasized that a good speaker should be able to argue both sides of any issue. A more subtle reading of the fragment, however, leads to the suggestion that, contrary to monism, it is not *change* that is an illusion but rather the concept of an absolute reality, an absolute truth. A thermometer may indicate that the temperature is 75 degrees, but people will experience that absolute temperature differently, some finding it cool, others finding it warm. In this analysis, the statement that "man is the measure of all things" asserts the possibility that our *experiences* with the world can differ according to our sensibilities and sensitivities. This is a deep truth, indeed.

Reading 13

Fragment 1, *Man is the Measure*

Fragment 1, *Man Is the Measure*, p. 4 from *The Older Sophists*, edited by Rosamond Kent Sprague and translated by M. O'Brien (Hackett Publishing, 2001). Reprinted by permission of Hackett Publishing Company, Inc. All rights reserved.

"Of all things the measure is man, of things that are, that they are, and of things that are not, that they are not."

Fragment 2: On the Gods

The Greeks had a curious view of their gods. On the one hand, they recognized that the gods warranted the respect and veneration due to the divine, but on the other they imbued them with so many human frailties that often the only thing that separated god from man was supernatural power. The gods of Olympus were commonly portrayed as jealous, petty, licentious, and just plain mean.[1] As a result, it is easy for us today to suspect that the Greeks worshiped their gods largely out of fear, but the reality is that we will never know exactly how common people viewed them.

We do know, however, that by the fifth century BC, many educated people – not just philosophers – were questioning traditional depictions of the gods. Some conception of the divine has characterized all societies since prehistoric times, leading to speculation over the last few years that god and religion are part of our genetic makeup (see Hamner, 2004; Newberg, D'Aquili, and Rause, 2002). Nevertheless, after about 2500 BC, the old gods – and certainly the Greek gods as portrayed in Homer's epics, for example – were not important sources of moral guidelines; they offered personal protection and success to worshipers, albeit on a very haphazard basis. As intellectuals in the ancient world discovered more about the workings of nature, many came to view the gods as fanciful attempts to explain natural phenomena, which may explain why some, like Protagoras, were shifting to agnosticism. Plato's dialogues suggest that others were shifting to pagan monotheism, in which the unknown god referenced in *Timaeus* was conceived of as the ultimate manifestation of "the good" (see Athanassiadi and Frede, 2002).

Fragment 2 (Reading 14) is translated from Diogenes Laertius' (1964) *The Lives and Sayings of Eminent Philosophers*. It is more than an expression of agnosticism, however; it also is a statement on the limits of human understanding that came to characterize pagan monotheism. That is, even if the gods exist, their nature must be so different from our own that we are incapable of comprehending them.

Reading 14

Fragment 2, *On the Gods*

Fragment 2, *On the Gods*.

Περί μὲν θεῶν οὐκ ἔχω εἰδέναι οὔθ᾽ ὡς εἰσὶν οὔθ ὡς οὐκ εἰσὶν οὔθ᾽ ὁποῖοί τινες ἰδέαν. Πολλὰ γαρ τα κωλύοντα εἰδέναι ἤ τ᾽ ἀδηλότης καὶ βραχὺς ὢν ὁ βίοσ τοῦ ἀνθρώπου.

---

[1] Of course, these are characteristics of virtually all ancient deities.

About the gods, I am not able to know whether they exist or do not exist, nor what they are like in form; for the factors preventing knowledge are many: the obscurity of the subject, and the shortness of human life.

Fragment 3: Dissoi Logoi

This fragment is an expression of the *dissoi logoi*, or two arguments, orientation of Sophistic rhetoric. We do not know whether Protagoras originated this perspective or whether he merely made it popular. Moreover, we cannot be certain that Protagoras is the actual source of the fragment – only that it has been attributed to him throughout history. Various translations of the fragment exist because of the difficulty in determining the exact meaning of the words *logos* (λόγους) and *pragmata* (πράγματος). Efforts to locate the fragment in the framework of Sophistic rhetoric have resulted in translations of *logos* as "speeches" and "arguments" and of *pragmata* as "subject" or "question" (see Schiappa, 2003, for a detailed discussion). Some take the rhetorical orientation a step farther and insert the word "true" even though it does not exist in the original, yielding something along the lines of: "There are two arguments in every question, and both are true." But we have no evidence that Protagoras intended a rhetorical emphasis, and for this reason, my version below strives to approximate a literal translation.

The fragment seems related to, and perhaps an alternate expression of, Milesian dualism. Moreover, Protagoras' interests were not limited to rhetoric, so it seems possible that a statement of this kind, on the nature of things, would be inclusive rather than exclusive. All analyses are highly speculative in the end, of course, because we do not have the entire work from which the fragment came and therefore lack its proper context.

Reading 15

Fragment 3, *Dissoi Logoi*

Fragment 3, *Dissoi Logoi*.

Καὶ πρῶτος ἔφη δύο λόγους εἶναι περὶ παντὸς πράγματος ἀντικειμένουσ ἀλλήλοις

First it can be said that every object has two sides being certainly contrary to each other.

Fragment 4: Making the Worse Appear the Better

This fragment appears in *The Art of Rhetoric* (1402a) as Aristotle discusses the role of Sophistic probability in arguing cases. In a case involving assault, for example, a weak person could argue that it is improbable that he or she could be guilty owing to the very condition of being weak; a strong person, on the other hand, could also argue that it is improbable owing to the fact that his strength would make him a likely suspect and therefore he would not be so foolish as to commit the crime. The text then reads:

Reading 16

Fragment 4, *Making the Worse Appear the Better*

Fragment 4, *Making the Worse Appear the Better*, p. 335 reprinted by permission of the publishers and Trustees of the Loeb Classical Library from *Aristotle*, Volume XXII, Loeb Classical Library Volume 193, translated by John Henry Freese (Cambridge, MA: Harvard University Press, 1926). © 1926 by the President and Fellows of Harvard College. The Loeb Classical Library ® is a registered trademark of the President and Fellows of Harvard College.

For if a man is not likely to be guilty of what he is accused of, for instance if, being weak, he is accused of assault and battery, his defence will be that the crime is not probable; but if he is likely to be guilty, for instance, if he is strong, it may be argued again that the crime is not probable, for the very reason that it was bound to appear so. It is the same in all other cases; for a man must either be likely to have committed a crime or not. Here, both the alternatives appear equally probable, but the one is really so, the other not probable absolutely, but only in the conditions mentioned. And this is what "making the worse appear the better argument" means.

The idea that Sophists taught students how to make the worse appear the better argument is widespread in the existing literature. In Aristophanes' *The Clouds*, for example, the main character takes lessons from Socrates, characterized as the preeminent Sophist, so he can cheat his creditors by convincing them that he does not owe them money. Although some Sophists undoubtedly adopted this position – after all, it would have a tangible appeal in many cases – we cannot be certain that "making the worse appear the better argument" is what Protagoras wrote or meant.

It is important to consider that Protagoras' livelihood consisted of teaching rhetoric, which involved helping students speak successfully in the assembly and in court. Consequently, any reference to "argument" probably should be understood in this context. Schiappa's (2003) analysis of Fragment 4, noted in the general introduction, assumes increasing relevance on this account. Cole (1991) provided an equally cogent analysis, noting that the application of this approach "can only have involved … teaching a student to think, and make others think, about situations in ways that were better rather than worse for him" (p. 145).

Study Questions

1 How might a person today respond to Protragoras' assertion that he is unable to know whether or not the gods exist?
2 Why would the notion of making a weak case seem the stronger strike many ancient Greeks as being immoral? Does it seem immoral today?
3 Rhetoric in ancient Greece was oral and focused almost exclusively on government and law. What role, if any, does oral rhetoric play in society today?

Writing Topics

1 Examine the ways in which difficulties in translation can affect our understanding of Protagoras.

2   Suppose you are a teacher of rhetoric or communication. Would you urge
     students to adopt Fragment 4 as part of their repertoire of skills? Why or
     why not?
3   The idea that every object, including every argument, has two sides has been
     construed as an assertion of relativism and an attack on truth. We see *dissoi
     logoi* at work, for example, in the courtroom, where litigation is not about
     truth but rather the preponderance of evidence. On a more philosophical
     level, however, it has been suggested that *dissoi logoi* proposes that each
     side in an argument *believes* his or her position to be truth. Analyze how this
     could be possible given that the two sides are in opposition.

Further Reading

Plato, *Theaetetus*.
Parmenides, *On Nature*.

Introduction to Gorgias (c. 483–378 BC)

Gorgias was from Leontini, Sicily, where he had gained such a reputation as a speaker
that he was asked to serve as ambassador to Athens in 427 BC. His task was to persuade
the Athenian assembly to send military aid against the Syracusans. Although it is tempting to attribute his success in this endeavor to his skill as a rhetorician, we must recognize that the Athenians were eager to expand their empire and thus needed little
persuasion to attack Syracuse, a city of abundant wealth that, if conquered, would give
Athens a platform for the eventual control of all Sicily.

   Not long after his first visit, Gorgias returned to Athens, perhaps encouraged by his
success with the assembly, and began teaching rhetoric. He reportedly electrified audiences with his demonstration speeches, gained a large number of students, and became
a very wealthy man. Gorgias rejected the title "Sophist" in favor of "rhetorician," but he
nevertheless was, and is, classified as one of the Older Sophists.

   Unlike other Sophists, Gorgias did not claim to teach virtue, only the art of persuasion. In Plato's dialogue of the same name, he states that "persuasion is the chief end of
rhetoric" (453), to which Socrates replies, "Then rhetoric … is the artificer of a persuasion which creates belief about the just and unjust, but gives no instruction about
them?" (455). Gorgias obligingly responds with "True" (455). Whether Gorgias actually
advocated an ethics-free version of rhetoric is uncertain, but we do know, particularly
from *Encomium to Helen*, that he readily strove to approach a difficult subject from multiple directions. Helen, after all, was the femme fatale who "caused" the Trojan War,
which resulted not only in the deaths of countless men and women but also in the
destruction of Ilium. In producing his *Encomium*, Gorgias was flouting tradition, for
Helen had taken on all the characteristics of evil personified. She therefore provided an
excellent subject for a display speech, allowing Gorgias to demonstrate how his rhetorical teaching could succeed in even the most difficult circumstances. As a *technê*, the
Encomium also could serve as a tool for stimulating critical thinking among students,
illustrating how to generate several arguments in support of one's case.

   Gorgias traveled throughout Greece, giving demonstration speeches and teaching.
Although there are reports that he undertook this peregrinatory lifestyle to avoid paying
taxes in any city that could claim him as a permanent resident, the lack of evidence

makes such reports dubious. Apparently, he did not produce speeches for litigants in court but limited himself to teaching rhetoric. Gorgias died in Larissa, at the advanced age of 105.

Gorgias' rhetoric was famous for its stylistic features, particularly figures of speech. The most well known, sometimes referred to as "Gorgianic figures," are:

- *antithesis* – juxtaposing contrasting words or ideas (example: If our love is *wrong*, I don't want to be *right*.).
- *anadiplosis* – repetition of the last word (or phrase) from a previous line, clause, or sentence at the beginning of the next (example: (a) He knew the meaning of *love; love* was the source of all pleasure and all pain; (b) Raul knew *the man he wanted to be*; and *the man he wanted to be* would not lie.).
- *homoioteleuton* – ending a series of adjacent or parallel words in the same way (example: Macarena captured his imagination, for she spoke *softly,* danced *lightly,* and smiled *brightly.*).
- *isocolon* – a form of parallelism, a series of similarly structured elements having the same length (example: The gunman *turned, aimed, and fired.*).

Kairos

Gorgias made a significant contibution to rhetorical theory with his notion of *kairos,* or appropriate timing. As Sipiora (2002) noted, in Homer's epic poems *kairos* signified a point on an enemy's body that was vulnerable to attack. Over time, use of the word changed, and knowing exactly what Gorgias meant by *kairos* is problematic owing to the scarcity of sources. From the existing works, however, as well as from *Against the Sophists* by his student Alcidamas, Gorgias seems to have understood *kairos* as a nascent moment for speaking extemporaneously and appropriately to the occasion, and it is likely that he was influenced in this respect by the Pythagoreans, who viewed *kairos* as an elemental law of the universe and therefore fundamental to their philosophy and teaching (Untersteiner, 1971). We must be careful to differentiate *kairos* from *prepon,* or "fitness," although it is the case that the two terms became so intertwined that differentiating them is a challenge. For Gorgias, *kairos* was fluid, dynamic, associated with *pros kriseis,* those issues that required judicious analysis and pragmatic decision making – hence its link to extemporaneous speaking, at which he excelled. *Kairos,* from this perspective, was the starting point for deliberation and thus for examining issues of good and bad, right and wrong, just and unjust. Indeed, *kairos* is commonly linked to justice (*dikaion*). It appears to have been an important part of Gorgias' rhetorical teaching, although there is no evidence that he provided any insight into knowing how one could identify correctly an appropriate time for speaking. Nonetheless, his emphasis on *kairos* in rhetoric appears to have stimulated the thinking of both Plato and Aristotle on this topic (see Sipiora and Baumlin, 2002, for a detailed discussion of *kairos*).

Fragment 1

This fragment apparently was part of a larger work entitled *On the Nonexistent,* the substance of which was summarized in *Against the Schoolmasters,* a text written in the second century of the Christian Era by Sextus Empiricus (1972). Our initial response (which probably was shared by Gorgias' contemporaries) to this fragment may be to reject it as nonsense, for existence is evident everywhere, particularly in the substance of our own being. But there is more to it than this response allows. Generally, the statement has been understood as an expression of *nihilism*; as such it lends support to the assessment that Gorgias was more than a teacher of persuasive speech, that he was keenly attuned to the philosophical debates of the time.

The problem is this: Nihilism does not involve a denial of physical existence; it is a denial of meaning and truth. Nevertheless, Gorgias' fragment seems to deal specifically with the physical. This may be an unfortunate consequence of the lack of context, for we have no reason to believe that Gorgias doubted, for example, his own existence. Sextus' analysis of *On the Nonexistent* does not help us much here, for it gives the impression that the question is one of logic. That is, he reshaped the question along the lines of Milesian philosophy and created a logical contradiction, which does not help us understand Gorgias' statement. Consider this exerpt from *Against the Schoolmasters*:

More specifically, the nonexistent does not exist; for if the nonexistent exists, it will both exist and not exist at the same time, for insofar as it is understood as nonexistent, it will not exist, but insofar as it is nonexistent it will, on the other hand, exist. It would, however, be entirely absurd for something to exist and at the same time not to exist. The nonexistent, therefore does not exist. (67, p. 43)

If we locate Fragment 1 in its broader historical context, we note that many philosophers during the fifth and fourth centuries BC were pondering the nature of reality. Plato, for example, maintained that the world as we know it is merely a simulacrum of the Ideal Forms that exist beyond the range of our perception and that can be understood only through the study of philosophy. The influence of Parmenides seems evident here insofar as he espoused the Eleatic philosophy of monism, which maintains that reality is composed of and reducible to one substance and that change is an illusion. Although Paremenides admitted that, indeed, the world does appear to be made up of multiple elements and that change seems to occur everywhere, he argued that what we see is not how the world really operates and that we cannot trust our perceptions. Likewise, Protagoras advocated a form of relativism that emphasized the subjectivity of experience.

Questioning the nature of reality was new to the Greeks. The ideas of these philosophers challenged existing views and suggested not only that the world is unstable but also that everything around us is indifferent (*adiaphora*), unmeasurable (*astathmêta*), and indeterminate (*anepikrita*). Neither our senses nor our reason can help us discover truth, for just when we believe we have found it, we are forced to recognize that our neighbor, using senses and reason just as acute as our own, has discovered a truth that is exactly the opposite of ours. On this account, nihilism cannot be a denial of physical existence but rather a denial of meaning and belief. As a philosophical position, Gorgias' fragment offers a view of the world that is without meaning, purpose, or comprehension – it simply is.

But perhaps Gorgias was not attempting to stake out a philosophical position. As the passage from Sextus Empiricus suggests, *On the Nonexistent* may have been an exercise in logic. Moreover, some scholars have analyzed the fragment in the context of Gorgias' *Encomium to Helen,* a work that seems designed to shock contemporary audiences while simultaneously being playful, even joking. From this perspective, Gorgias was mocking Eleatic monism, particularly Zeno's *paradox of motion.* (Zeno was Paremenides' most famous student. He sought to prove the unchanging nature of reality by showing that motion is impossible, despite appearances to the contrary. To do so, he offered the story of the tortoise and Achilles, the swift-footed hero of *The Iliad.* If there is no motion, there can be no change, and thus monism is proved.)

As a sarcastic rebuttal to the argument that reality is unchanging (owing to the fact that motion is impossible), Gorgias' fragment claims that there is *no reality*, for, indeed, nothing exists; even if it did, we would not know it in any meaningful sense or be able to explain it, which makes a mockery of the Eleatics' attempts to describe the nature of reality. This analysis, however, presents a problem that may be difficult to overcome, for it reduces to a joke a fragment that strikes many as having a deep philosophical meaning that, as the fragment itself asserts, is difficult to describe.

Reading 17

Fragment 1, *On the Nonexistent*

Fragment 1, *On the Nonexistent*, p. 42 from *The Older Sophists*, edited by Rosamond Kent Sprague and translated by G. Kennedy (Hackett Publishing, 2001). Reprinted by permission of Hackett Publishing Company, Inc. All rights reserved.

First and foremost, ... nothing exists; second, ... even if it exists it is inapprehensible to man; third, ... even if it is apprehensible, still it is without a doubt incapable of being expressed or explained to the next man.

The Defense of Palamedes

Credited with inventing counting, coinage, weights and measures, military ranks, and the game of *pessoi* (a forerunner of chess) Palamedes symbolized for ancient Greeks the miscarriage of justice. He was one of the legendary heroes of the Trojan War. When King Agamemnon was gathering his forces for the expedition to Ilium, he sent Menelaus, Nestor, and Palamedes to Ithaca to recruit Odysseus, who, having been warned by an oracle that joining the war would keep him from his home and family for 20 years, feigned madness when the envoys arrived. Palamedes, however, was certain that Odysseus was pretending, and he threatened the life of Odysseus' infant son, Telemachus, as a way of proving the hero's sanity. Odysseus never forgot nor forgave Palamedes, and as the war was nearing its end, he arranged to make it appear that Palamedes had betrayed the Greeks to the Trojans. Although Palamedes declared his innocence, Agamemnon judged him guilty and sentenced him to death.

Gorgias' *Defense* illustrates a *technê*, or rhetorical exercise that students could study, and it is an excellent example of what Aristotle called *epideictic rhetoric*, which involves praise and blame and offers orators opportunities to demonstrate their abilities to argue difficult subjects. As a *technê*, *Defense* is not an example of applied rhetoric, but it does illustrate some of the theoretical as well as pragmatic principles of Sophistic rhetoric, such as argument from probability, which was the dominant method of argumentative proof prior to the beginning of the fourth century BC.

Reading 18

The Defense of Palamedes

The Defense of Palamedes, pp. 54–63 from *The Older Sophists*, edited by Rosamond Kent Sprague and translated by G. Kennedy (Hackett Publishing, 2001). Reprinted by permission of Hackett Publishing Company, Inc. All rights reserved.

IIa. (1) Prosecution and defense are not a means of judging about death; for Nature, with a vote which is clear, casts a vote of death against every mortal on the day on which he is born. The danger relates to dishonor and honor, whether I must die justly or whether I must die roughly with the greatest reproaches and most shameful accusation. (2) There are the two alternatives; you have the second within your power, I the first; justice is up to me, roughness is up to you. You will easily be able to kill me if you wish, for you have power over these matters, over which as it happens I have no power. (3) If then the accuser, Odysseus, made his accusation through good will toward Greece, either clearly knowing that I was betraying Greece to the barbarians or imagining somehow that this was the case, he would be best of men. For this would of course[2] be true of one who saves his homeland, his parents, and all Greece, and in addition punishes a wrongdoer. But if he has put together this allegation out of envy or conspiracy or knavery, just as in the former case he would be the finest of men, so in this he would be the worst of men. (4) Where shall I start to speak about these matters? What shall I say first? To what part of the defense shall I turn my attention? For an unsupported allegation creates evident perplexity, and because of the perplexity it follows that I am at a loss in my speech, unless I discover something out of the truth itself and out of the present necessity, having met with teachers more dangerous than inventive. (5) Now I clearly know that my accuser accuses me without <knowing> the matter clearly; for I know in my heart clearly that I have done no such thing; and I do not know how anyone could know what did not happen. But in case he made the accusation thinking it to be so, I shall show you in two ways that he is not speaking the truth. For I could not if I wished, nor would I if I could, put my hand, to such works as these.

(6) I come first to this argument, that I lack the capability of performing the action charged. There must have been some first beginning to the treason, and the beginning would have been speech, for before any future deeds it is necessary first for there to be discussions. But how could there be discussions unless there had been some meeting? And how could there have been a meeting unless the opponent sent to me or <some-one> went from me to him? For no message arrives in writing without a bearer. (7) But this can take place by speech. And suppose he is with me and I am with him – how does it take place? Who is with whom? Greek with barbarian. How do we listen and how talk to each other? By ourselves? But we do not know each other's language. With an interpreter then? A third person is added as a witness to things which need to be hidden. (8) But assume that this too has taken place, even though it has not. Next it was necessary to give and receive a pledge. What would the pledge be? An oath? Who was apt to trust me, the traitor? Perhaps there were hostages? Who? For instance, I might have given my brother (for I had no one else), and the barbarian might have given one of his sons; in this way the pledge would have been most secure to me from him and to him from me. But these things, if they happened, would have been clear to you all. (9) Someone will say that we made the contract for money, he giving it, I taking it. Was it for little? But it is not probable that a man would take a little money for a great service. For much money? Who was the go-between? How could one person bring it? Perhaps there were many? If many brought it, there would have been many witnesses of the plot, but if one brought it, what was brought would not have been anything much. (10) Did they bring it by day or by night? But the guards are many and closely placed and it is not possible to escape their notice. But by day? Certainly the light militates against such things. Well then. Did I go out and get it or did the opponent come bringing it? For both are impossible. If I had in fact taken it, how would I have hidden it both from those in the camp and from those outside it? Where would I have put it? How would I have protected it? If I made use of it, I would have been conspicuous; if I didn't, what advantage would I have gotten from it? (11) Still, assume that what did not happen has happened. We met, we talked, we reached an understanding, I took money from them, I was not detected after taking it, I hid it. It was then necessary to perform that for the sake of which these arrangements were made. Now this is still stranger than what has been discussed. For in doing it, I acted by myself or with others. But the action was not the work of one man. But was it with others? Who? Clearly my associates. Were

---

[2]   Without the emendation of Stephanus-Blass, the meaning would be "of course not."

they free men or slaves? My free associates are you. Who then among you was aware? Let him speak. How is it credible that I would use slaves? For they bring charges <both> in hopes of their freedom and out of necessity when hard pressed. (12) As for the action, how <would> it have taken place? Clearly enemy forces outnumbering you had to be brought in, which was impossible. How could I have brought them in? Through the gates? But it was not my job to shut or open them, but the commanders were in charge of these. But it was over the walls <by> a ladder? Wouldn't <I have been seen?> The whole place was full of guards. But it was through a hole made in the wall? It would then have been clear to all. Life under arms is carried on outdoors (for this is a camp!), in which <everybody> sees everything and everybody is seen by everybody. Altogether then and in every way it was impossible for me to do all these things.

(13) Consider among yourselves the following point as well. What reason was there to wish to do these things, assuming that I had a special capability? For no one wishes to run the greatest dangers without reward nor to be most wicked in the greatest wickedness. But what reason was there? (For again I revert to this point.) For the sake of rul<ing>? Over you or over the barbarians? But over you it would be impossible for me to rule, considering your numbers and nature and the fact that you have all manner of great resources: nobility of family, wealth of money, fame, strength of heart, the thrones of cities. (14) But over the <barbarians>? Who is going to betray them? By means of what power shall I, a Greek, take over the barbarians, when I am one and they are many? Persuading or constraining them? For they would not wish to be persuaded and I would not be able to constrain. But possibly there are those willing to betray them to a willing receiver by giving money in return for the surrender? But both to believe and accept this is very foolish. For who would choose slavery instead of sovereignty, the worst instead of the best? (15) Someone might say that I ventured on this out of a desire for wealth and money. But I have a moderate amount of money, and I have no need for much. Those who spend much money need

much, not those who are continent of the pleasures of nature, but those who are slaves to pleasures and seek to acquire honors from wealth and show. None of this applies to me. I shall offer my past life as sure evidence that I am speaking the truth, and you be witnesses to the witness, for you are my companions and thus know these things. (16) Nor, moreover, would a man even moderately prudent put his hand to such work even for honor. Honors come from goodness, not from badness. How would there be honor for a man who is the betrayer of Greece? And in addition, as it happens, I am not without honor. For I am honored for the most honorable reason by the most honorable men, that is, by you for wisdom. (17) Nor, moreover, would anyone do these things for the sake of security. For the traitor is the enemy of all: the law, justice, the gods, the bulk of mankind. For he contravenes the law, negates justice, destroys the masses, and dishonors what is holy, and a man does not have security whose life <is> of this sort among the greatest dangers. (18) But was I anxious to assist friends or harm enemies? For someone might commit injustice for these reasons. But in my case everything was the opposite. I was harming my friends and helping foes. The action therefore involved no acquisition of goods, and there is no one who does wrong out of desire to suffer loss. (19) The remaining possibility is that I did it to escape some fear or labor or danger. But no one could say that these motives applied to me in any way. All men do all things in pursuit of these two goals: either seeking some profit or escaping some punishment, and whatever knavery is done for reasons other than these <is apt to involve the doer in great evils. That I would most>[3] hurt myself in doing these things is not unclear. For in betraying Greece I was betraying myself, my parents, my friends, the dignity of my ancestors, the cults of my native land, the tombs of my family, and my great country of Greece. Those things which are all in all to all men, I would have entrusted to men who had been wronged.[4] (20) But consider the following as well. Would not my life have been unlivable if I had done these things? Where must I have turned for help? To Greece? Shall I make amends to those who have been wronged? Who

[3] The conjecture of Keil, which Diels approves in the *apparatus*.
[4] Perhaps "had done wrong"(?), Diels.

of those who suffered could keep his hands off me? Or must I remain among the barbarians? Abandoning everything important, deprived of the noblest honor, passing my life in shameful disgrace, throwing away the labors labored for virtue of my past life? And this of my own accord, although to fail through his own doing is most shameful for a man. (21) Moreover, not even among the barbarians would I be trusted. How could I be, if they knew that I had done something most untrustworthy, had betrayed my friends to my enemies? But life is not livable for a man who has lost the confidence of others. The man who loses his money <or> who falls from power or who is exiled from his country might get on his feet again, but he who throws away good faith would not any more acquire it. Therefore, that I would not <if I could, nor could if I would>, betray Greece has been demonstrated by what has been said.

(22) I wish next to address the accuser. What in the world do you trust when, being what you are, you accuse such a one as me? It is worth examining the kind of man you are who says the kind of things you do, like the worthless attacking the worthless. Do you accuse me, knowing accurately what you say, or imagining it? If it is with knowledge, you know either from seeing or participating or learning from someone <who was participating>. If then you saw, tell these judges <the manner>, the place, the time, when, where, how you saw. If you participated, you are liable to the same accusations. And if you heard from someone who participated, who is he? Let him come forward; let him appear; let him bear witness. For if it is witnessed in this way, the accusation will be more credible, since as it is, neither of us is furnishing a witness. (23) You will say perhaps that it is equitable for you not to furnish witnesses of what you allege to have happened, but that I should furnish witnesses of what has not happened. But this is not equitable. For it is quite impossible for what has not happened to be testified to by witnesses, but on the subject of what has happened, not only is it not impossible, but it is even easy, and not only is it easy, but <even necessary. But> for you it was not possible, <not> only to find witnesses, but even to find false witnesses, and for me it was possible to find neither of these. (24) Therefore, it is clear that you do not have knowledge of the things about which you make

accusation. It follows that since you do <not> have knowledge, you have an opinion. Do you then, O most daring of all men, trusting in opinion, a most untrustworthy thing, not knowing the truth, dare to bring a capital charge against a man? Why do you share knowledge that he has done such a deed? But surely it is open to all men to have opinions on all subjects, and in this you are no wiser than others. But it is not right to trust those with an opinion instead of those who know, nor to think opinion more trustworthy than truth, but rather truth than opinion.

(25) You accused me through spoken words of two directly opposed things, wisdom and madness, which the same man cannot have. Where you say that I am artful and clever and resourceful, you accuse me of wisdom, and where you say that I was betraying Greece, you accuse me of madness. For it is madness to undertake tasks which are impossible, inexpedient, and shameful, which will harm his friends, help his enemies, and make his own life disgraceful and perilous. Yet how can one trust a man of the sort who in a single speech says to the same man the most inconsistent things about the same subjects? (26) I would like to ask you whether you think wise men are witless or intelligent. If witless, your speech is novel, but not true; if intelligent, surely it is not right for intelligent men to make the worst mistakes and to prefer evils to present goods. If therefore I am wise, I have not erred; if I have erred, I am not wise. Thus in both cases you would be wrong.

(27) I do not want to introduce in reply the many enormities, both old and new, which you have committed, though I could. For <I wish> to escape this charge by means of my own virtues, not by means of your vices. So much, therefore, to you.

(28) To you, O judges, I wish to say something invidious, but true about myself, not appropriate to one who has <not> been accused, but fitting to one who has been accused. For I am now undergoing scrutiny and furnishing an account of my past life. I therefore beg of you, if I remind you of some of the fine things done by me, that no one be annoyed at what is said, but think it necessary for one who is dreadfully and falsely accused to say as well some true things among you who know them. This is the most pleasant for me. (29) First, then, and second and greatest, in every respect from beginning to end my past life has been blameless, free from all blame. No one could truthfully speak any imputation of evil to you

about me. For not even the accuser himself has provided any evidence of what he has said. Thus his speech has the impact of abuse lacking proof. (30) I might say, and saying it I would not lie nor would I be refuted, that I am not only blameless but also a great benefactor of you and the Greeks and all mankind, not only of those now alive but <also> of those to come. For who else would have made human life well provided instead of destitute and adorned instead of unadorned, by inventing military equipment of the greatest advantage and written laws, the guardians of justice, and letters, the tool of memory, and measures and weights, the convenient standards of commercial exchange, and number, the guardian of items, and very powerful beacons and very swift messengers, and draughts, the harmless game of leisure? Why do I remind you of these? (31) For the purpose of making it clear <on the one hand> that it is to this sort of thing that I apply myself, and on the other giving an indication of the fact that I abstain from shameful and wicked deeds. For it is impossible for one applying himself to the latter to apply himself to this sort of thing. And I think it right not to be harmed myself by you if I myself have done you no harm. (32) Nor am I, because of other activities, deserving of ill treatment at the hands of younger or older men. For I am inoffensive to the older, not unhelpful to the younger, not envious of the fortunate, but merciful to the unfortunate; not heedless of poverty nor valuing wealth ahead of virtue, but virtue ahead of wealth; neither useless in council nor lazy in war, doing what is assigned to me, obeying those in command. To be sure, it is not for me to praise myself, but the present occasion requires me to make my defense in every possible way since I have been accused of these things.

(33) For the rest, my speech is to you and about you; when I have said this I shall end my defense. Appeals to pity and entreaties and the intercession of friends are useful when a trial takes place before a mob, but among you, the first of the Greeks and men of repute, it is not right to persuade you with the help of friends or entreaties or appeals to pity, but it is right for me to escape this charge by means of the clearest justice, explaining the truth, not deceiving. (34) And it is necessary for you to avoid paying more attention to words than to actions, and not to prejudge the bases of the defense nor to think a short time affords wiser judgment than a long time nor to believe that slander is more reliable than firsthand knowledge. For in all matters good men must take great care against erring, and more so in matters irremediable than in those remediable. For these lie within the control of those who have exercised foresight, but are uncorrectable by those with hindsight. And it is a matter of this sort whenever men judge a man on a capital charge, which is now the case before you. (35) If then, by means of words, it were possible for the truth of actions to become free of doubt <and> clear to hearers, judgment would now be easy from what has been said. But since this is not the case, protect my body, wait for a longer while, and make your decision with truth. For your danger is great that by seeming unjust you lose one reputation and acquire another. To good men death is preferable to a shameful reputation. For one is the end of life, and the other is disease in life. (36) If you kill me unjustly, it will be evident to many, for I am <not> unknown, and your wickedness will be known and clear to all Greeks. And you, rather than the accuser, will have a responsibility for the injustice which will be clear to all. For the outcome of the trial rests with you. But greater error than this could not exist. If you give an unjust verdict, you will make a mistake, not only in regard to me and my parents, but by your action you will make yourselves responsible for a dreadful, godless, unjust, unlawful deed, having killed a man who is your fellow soldier, useful to you, a benefactor of Greece, Greeks killing Greek, though convicting him of no clear injustice nor credible fault.

(37) My side of the case is spoken and I rest. For to recapitulate briefly what has been spoken at length is logical before bad judges, but it is not appropriate to think that Greeks who are first of the first do not pay attention and do not remember what has been said.

The Encomium of Helen

The Encomium of Helen is another example of epideictic discourse, and like Gorgias' Defense, it is a techné designed to show how one can approach a difficult argument from multiple perspectives. It differs, however, in a couple of interesting ways. The structure is more organized than *Defense* insofar as it established, albeit still in a rudimentary fashion, an order that was to become characteristic of both epideictic and forensic rhetoric: a proem, or appealing statement; an introduction outlining the circumstances of the matter at hand; a narrative of facts; arguments and proofs; and a peroration or conclusion. In addition, the challenge here was significantly greater because of Helen's reputation. Helen was a daughter of Zeus, born from an egg after the god, in the shape of a swan, raped Leda, queen of Sparta. She grew into the most beautiful woman in the world and had many noble suitors. To avoid potential conflict, the suitors pledged to respect her choice of husband and to band together to punish anyone who attempted to break the matrimonial bond. This pledge was soon tested. Helen wed Menelaus, king of Sparta, and had been married for only a few years when Prince Paris of Troy arrived as an envoy from Ilium. Unlike Menelaus, Paris was handsome, sophisticated, and young, and he soon seduced Helen and convinced her to run away with him to Troy.

In some versions of the tale, Helen was a "gift" to Paris from Aphrodite. The goddesses Hera, Athena, and Aphrodite were arguing one day over which of them was the loveliest, and they decided to ask a mortal to judge their beauty. They chose Paris, and Aphrodite, unwilling to face the humiliation that would follow if she, the goddess of love and beauty, was not selected as the winner, offered Paris a bribe if he selected her over the other goddesses. The bribe was that he could have the most beautiful woman in the world. In this account, the gods were to blame for all the trouble that resulted from Helen's elopement with Paris. Be that as it may, as soon as he discovered his cuckoldry, Menelaus and his brother, King Agamemnon, called on all the former suitors to honor their pledge. The outcome was the Trojan War, which lasted for 10 years and which caused the death of thousands of Greeks, including its most illustrious heroes.

Over the centuries, Helen came to symbolize the antithesis of the feminine virtues of fidelity, motherhood, honesty, sensitivity, and compassion. She had broken her marriage vows, made a fool and a cuckold of her husband, abandoned her daughter, and caused a war. Her cultural status was significantly lower than that of a prostitute. Given this context, we can more readily imagine how disturbing audiences might find Gorgias' *Encomium*, which presents a comprehensive defense of Helen. Although finding an equivalent case as a basis of comparison is difficult, we might consider the reaction today to an enthusiastic defense of Adolf Hitler or James Earl Ray, the man who assassinated Martin Luther King, Jr.

Very logically and methodically, Gorgias identified four possible "causes" for Helen's actions: (1) It was the will of the gods; (2) Paris raped her and carried her away against her will; (3) it was the force of love; and (4) it was the power of speech. When viewed as a teaching tool, this approach also seems designed to stimulate critical thinking, showing students how a given action may have multiple causes. The last is particularly interesting because it offers a view of poetry and rhetoric that is very similar to Plato's: Both have the power to evoke strong emotional responses that influence actions.

Reading 19

The Encomium of Helen

The Encomium of Helen, pp. 50–4 from *The Older Sophists*, edited by Rosamond Kent Sprague and translated by G. Kennedy (Hackett Publishing, 2001). Reprinted by permission of Hackett Publishing Company, Inc. All rights reserved.

II. (1) What is becoming to a city is manpower, to a body beauty, to a soul wisdom, to an action virtue, to a speech truth, and the opposites of these are unbecoming. Man and woman and speech and deed and city and object should be honored with praise if praiseworthy and incur blame if unworthy, for it is an equal error and mistake to blame the praisable and to praise the blamable. (2) It is the duty of one and the same man both to speak the needful rightly and to refute <the unrightfully spoken. Thus it is right to refute>[5] those who rebuke Helen, a woman about whom the testimony of inspired poets has become univocal and unanimous as had the ill omen of her name, which has become a reminder of misfortunes. For my part, by introducing some reasoning into my speech, I wish to free the accused of blame and, having reproved her detractors as prevaricators and proved the truth, to free her from their ignorance.

(3) Now it is not unclear, not even to a few, that in nature and in blood the woman who is the subject of this speech is preeminent among preeminent men and women. For it is clear that her mother was Leda, and her father was in fact a god, Zeus, but allegedly a mortal, Tyndareus, of whom the former was shown to be her father because he was and the latter was disproved because he was said to be, and the one was the most powerful of men and the other the lord of all.

(4) Born from such stock, she had godlike beauty, which taking and not mistaking, she kept. In many did she work much desire for her love, and her one body was the cause of bringing together many bodies of men thinking great thoughts for great goals, of whom some had greatness of wealth, some the glory of ancient nobility, some the vigor of personal agility, some command of acquired knowledge. And all came because of a passion which loved to conquer and a love of honor which was unconquered. (5) Who it was and why and how he sailed away, taking Helen as his love, I shall not say. To tell the knowing what they know shows it is right but brings no delight. Having now gone beyond the time once set for my speech, I shall go on to the beginning of my future speech, and I shall set forth the causes through which it was likely that Helen's voyage to Troy should take place.

(6) For either by will of Fate and decision of the gods and vote of Necessity did she do what she did, or by force reduced or by words seduced <or by love possessed>. Now if through the first, it is right for the responsible one to be held responsible; for god's predetermination cannot be hindered by human premeditation. For it is the nature of things, not for the strong to be hindered by the weak, but for the weaker to be ruled and drawn by the stronger, and for the stronger to lead and the weaker to follow. God is a stronger force than man in might and in wit and in other ways. If then one must place blame on Fate and on a god, one must free Helen from disgrace.

(7) But if she was raped by violence and illegally assaulted and unjustly insulted, it is clear that the raper, as the insulter, did the wronging, and the raped, as the insulted, did the suffering. It is right then for the barbarian who undertook a barbaric undertaking in word and law and deed to meet with blame in word, exclusion in law, and punishment in deed. And surely it is proper for a woman raped and robbed of her country and deprived of her friends to be pitied rather than pilloried. He did the dread deeds; she suffered them. It is just therefore to pity her but to hate him.

(8) But if it was speech which persuaded her and deceived her heart, not even to this is it difficult to make an answer and to banish blame as follows. Speech is a powerful lord, which by means of the finest and most invisible body effects the divinest works: it can stop fear and banish grief and create joy and nurture pity. I shall show how this is the case, since (9) it is necessary to offer proof to the opinion of my hearers: I both deem and define all poetry as speech with meter. Fearful shuddering and tearful pity and grievous longing come upon its hearers, and at the actions and physical sufferings of others in good fortunes and in evil fortunes, through the agency of words, the soul is wont to experience a suffering of its own. But come, I shall turn from one argument to another. (10) Sacred incantations sung with words are bearers of pleasure and banishers of pain, for, merging with opinion in the soul, the power of the incantation is wont to beguile it and persuade it and alter it by witchcraft. There have been discovered two arts of witchcraft and magic: one consists of errors of soul and the other of deceptions of opinion. (11) All who have and do persuade people of things do so by molding a false argument. For if all men on all subjects had

---

[5] Accepting Diels's "sense" as given in the *apparatus criticus*.

<both> memory of things past and <awareness> of things present and foreknowledge of the future, speech would not be similarly similar, since as things are now it is not easy for them to recall the past nor to consider the present nor to predict the future. So that on most subjects most men take opinion as counselor to their soul, but since opinion is slippery and insecure it casts those employing it into slippery and insecure successes. (12) What cause then prevents the conclusion that Helen similarly, against her will, might have come under the influence of speech, just as if ravished by the force of the mighty? For it was possible to see how the force of persuasion prevails; persuasion has the form of necessity, but it does not have the same power.[6] For speech constrained the soul, persuading it which it persuaded, both to believe the things said and to approve the things done. The persuader, like a constrainer, does the wrong and the persuaded, like the constrained, in speech is wrongly charged. (13) To understand that persuasion, when added to speech, is wont also to impress the soul as it wishes, one must study: first, the words of astronomers who, substituting opinion for opinion, taking away one but creating another, make what is incredible and unclear seem true to the eyes of opinion; then, second, logically necessary debates in which a single speech, written with art but not spoken with truth, bends a great crowd and persuades; <and> third, the verbal disputes of philosophers in which the swiftness of thought is also shown making the belief in an opinion subject to easy change. (14) The effect of speech upon the condition of the soul is comparable to the power of drugs over the nature of bodies. For just as different drugs dispel different secretions from the body, and some bring an end to disease and others to life, so also in the case of speeches, some distress, others delight, some cause fear, others make the hearers bold, and some drug and bewitch the soul with a kind of evil persuasion.

(15) It has been explained that if she was persuaded by speech she did not do wrong but was unfortunate. I shall discuss the fourth cause in a fourth passage. For if it was love which did all these things, there will be no difficulty in escaping the charge of the sin which is alleged to have taken place. For the things we see do not have the nature which we wish them to have, but the nature which

belligerents in war buckle on their warlike accouterments of bronze and steel, some designed for defense, others for offense, if the sight sees this, immediately it is alarmed and it alarms the soul, so that often men flee, panic-stricken, from future danger <as though it were> present. For strong as is the habit of obedience to the law, it is ejected by fear resulting from sight, which coming to a man causes him to be indifferent both to what is judged honorable because of the law and to the advantage to be derived from victory. (17) It has happened that people, after having seen frightening sights, have also lost presence of mind for the present moment; in this way fear extinguishes and excludes thought. And many have fallen victim to useless labor and dread diseases and hardly curable madnesses. In this way the sight engraves upon the mind images of things which have been seen. And many frightening impressions linger, and what lingers is exactly analogous to <what is> spoken. (18) Moreover, whenever pictures perfectly create a single figure and form from many colors and figures, they delight the sight, while the creation of statues and the production of works of art furnish a pleasant sight to the eyes. Thus it is natural for the sight to grieve for some things and to long for others, and much love and desire for many objects and figures is engraved in many men. (19) If, therefore, the eye of Helen, pleased by the figure of Alexander, presented to her soul eager desire and contest of love, what wonder? If, <being> a god, <love has> the divine power of the gods, how could a lesser being reject and refuse it? But if it is a disease of human origin and a fault of the soul, it should not be blamed as a sin, but regarded as an affliction. For she came, as she did come, caught in the net of Fate, not by the plans of the mind, and by the constraints of love, not by the devices of art.

(20) How then can one regard blame of Helen as just, since she is utterly acquitted of all charge, whether she did what she did through falling in love or persuaded by speech or ravished by force or constrained by divine constraint?

(21) I have by means of speech removed disgrace from a woman; I have observed the procedure which I set up at the beginning of the speech; I have tried to end the injustice of blame and the ignorance of opinion, I wished to write a speech which would be a praise of Helen and a diversion to myself.

[6] Accepting Diels's "sense" as given in the *apparatus criticus*.

Study Questions

1 We can look at Zeno's paradox of motion and identify it as an argument that is logical but false. What does this mean, exactly? Can you provide other examples?
2 Of the four possible reasons for Helen's actions, Gorgias devoted the least amount of space to love. What might be some reasons for this?
3 In *Helen*, Gorgias indicated that poetry has the power to stir the emotions and that language has great power to influence others. Based on your experience, is this argument supportable? How easily are people persuaded by speech? He then created an analogy between poetry and speech by defining poetry as speech with meter. Is this a legitimate analogy?
4 How does Palamedes support his argument that he is innocent of the charges against him?

Writing Topics

1 Some scholars have suggested that postmodernism takes a "Gorgianic" stance. Analyze what this means, providing relevant examples.
2 Some scholars have viewed *Encomium of Helen* as an expression of feminism and as an indictment of patriarchy. Argue for or against this position.
3 Although Gorgias and Plato had similar views on the power of language to overcome reason by stimulating the emotions, neither addressed the fact that, with poetry, audiences are willing participants in the author's or performer's construction of a synthetic reality and that they also willingly – one might even say eagerly – surrender to the emotions that are stirred in the process. Analyze this issue with regard to rhetoric in general and *Encomium of Helen* in particular.

Further Reading

Isocrates, *Helen*.
Alcidamas, *Against the Sophists*.
Sextus Empiricus, *Against the Schoolmasters*.

Introduction to Antiphon (c. 479–411 BC)

Our understanding of Antiphon is complicated by the fact that "Antiphon" was a common name in ancient Athens and that three distinct Antiphons are mentioned in the relevant literature. There is the orator and politician, Antiphon of Rhamnus – a contemporary of Protagoras, Gorgias, and Socrates, born into an old aristocratic family, who led an oligarchic coup that overthrew the Athenian democracy in 411 BC. There is Antiphon the Sophist who debates Socrates in Xenophon's *Memorabilia* and who, as Aristotle noted in *Physics* (193a), proposed the method of mathematical exhaustion for squaring the circle. And there is Antiphon the tragic poet whom Aristotle mentioned in his *Rhetoric* (1385a) but who does not seem to be germane to rhetoric. Some scholars have concluded that the politician and the Sophist are one and the same, arguing for what is known as the "unitarian" position. Others insist that the two cannot be the same person and argue for what is known as the "separatist" position.

Gagarin (2002) and Gagarin and MacDowell (1998) noted that in recent years a growing number of scholars (themselves included) have tended to accept the unitarian position. Pendrick (2002), on the other hand, dismissed this argument and suggested that the move toward identifying Antiphon the politician with Antiphon the Sophist has been based, in part, on convenience. This approach, without question, makes the historiography easier, but the fact remains that we have two distinct sets of surviving works that do not fit together particularly well. The lack of fit can be, and has been, explained – Athiphon was writing for different audiences and/or at different times – but other problems remain. Any in-depth examination of these problems is beyond the scope of this text, but a brief summary seems warranted.

The significant extant works attributed to Antiphon consist of: (a) three court speeches delivered at separate homicide trials; (b) what is often identified as a political speech (*On the Revolution*) but which is the speech Antiphon gave in his own defense against a charge of treason; (c) three *technai* known as the *Tetralogies*; and (d) fragments of two philosophical works entitled *On Truth* and *On Concord,* respectively.[7]

The first problem emerges when we consider that Socrates names Rhamnus a teacher of rhetoric in *Menexenus* – albeit a very poor one – but this reference appears alongside Socrates' identification of Aspasia as the person who taught him rhetoric and cannot be taken seriously. Yet in *On the Revolution* (included here), Antiphon remarks that the prosecution identified him as one who takes money for writing speeches, not for teaching rhetoric. The *Tetralogies*, on the other hand, model legal cases that are clearly the sort of *technai* that students of rhetoric would use in their studies, which raises the question of why *On the Revolution* does not describe Antiphon as a Sophist and a *logographos*. The situation is further complicated by the fact that even in late antiquity scholars recognized that there were significant stylistic differences among the existing works. Hermogenes of Tarsus (c. second century AD), for example, commented on the stylistic differences between the legal speeches and the philosophical works and went on to state that, on the basis of these differences, he was convinced that they were produced by two writers rather than one – but that in deference to Plato he was at the same time *unconvinced*. Worthington (1993), among others, raised the possibility that legal speeches were joint efforts between clients and *logographoi*. Moreover, after a trial was over, the client owned the speech and could revise and publish it at will. If this were the case with regard to Antiphon, it might explain the differences in style. Collaboration of this sort appears logical from a modern perspective, but Worthington nevertheless argued that there is little evidence that it was widespread, if it occurred at all.

The historical record is of no help in differentiating between the Sophist and the politician because the only Antiphon for whom we have any credible background information is Rhamnus. What we know is this: Like many others during the Peloponnesian War, Antiphon of Rhamnus got caught up in the struggle between democracy and oligarchy, and his ancestry and inclination motivated him to resist the democratic movement. In 411 BC, he and a group of fellow aristocrats organized a coup, overthrew the democratic government, and replaced it with an oligarchy, calling themselves the Council of 400 in keeping with a tradition that, according to Plutarch (1959), went back at least to the time of Solon in which Athens was governed by a council made up of leading nobles whose lineage gave them the requisite *aretê*.

---

[7] Mann (2005) argued that Antiphon also was the author of the medical treatise known as *On the Art* (*Peri Technê*), but as of this writing, his appears to be a minority view.

The difficulties Antiphon's works presented to Hermogenes of Tarsus illustrate that the question of whether there was one person or two who produced them can be confusing. Moreover, the arguments presented by unitarian scholars such as Gagarin (2002) and separatist scholars such as Pendrick (2002) are equally compelling. It is possible – though unlikely – that new evidence will come to light that will give us a definitive answer to the question, but at this point it seems that the most prudent approach is to adopt a neutral stance.

In addition to his interest in law and politics, "Antiphon" is commonly recognized as the first Athenian rhetorician and *logographos*. He wrote numerous speeches for litigants and was quite successful doing so. Some 500 years after his death, approximately 60 works were attributed to him, but only three complete speeches survive today: *On Chreutes*, *On the Murder of Herodes*, and *Against the Stepmother for Poisoning*. The three *Tetralogies* illustrate model speeches in hypothetical homicide cases; each model contains a total of four speeches (hence the title), two for the prosecution and two for the defense. Various fragments attributed to Antiphon have survived; some are portions of legal and political speeches, whereas others treat such topics as politics, rhetoric, and the interpretation of dreams (see Sprague, 2001).

On Truth

The most well-known fragments are from two philosophical treatises: *On Truth* and *On Concord*. *On Truth*, included here, illustrates the association between rhetoric and politics. It is best known for its treatment of *nomos* and *physis*, which are in conflict in any society. The statements that man-made laws are based on "agreement" suggest that *nomoi* are central to the social contract. These statements, in conjunction with his observation that barbarian and Greek alike breathe air, laugh when happy, cry when sad, and walk on their feet, have led some scholars (e.g., Gagarin and MacDonald, 1998; Havelock, 1957; Luria, 1963; Wood, 1974) to argue that *On Truth* is an expression of egalitarianism, which seems incongruent with the man who led the oligarchic revolt against Athenian democracy in 411 BC. In addition, the key element of the first paragraph appears to be the statement that "we have become barbarians in our relations with one another," which may be understood as a criticism of the perpetual conflicts among the Greek city-states and thus an implicit expression of panhellenism. If even Greeks and barbarians are so much alike by virtue of "nature," Athenians, Spartans, and Thebeans must be even more alike.

Furthermore, close reading does not support the conclusion that nature compels equality but just the opposite. For we also find the following: "the majority of things sanctioned as just in terms of the law are enactments inimical (πολεμίως) to nature." So much of the whole work is missing that we cannot reasonably rely on the existing fragments to determine Antiphon's politics, but viewed on their face, these fragments seem to express, at the very least, some antipathy toward the rule of law in society as opposed to the rule of nature and, at the very most, support for a form of social Darwinism (see Moulton, 1972; Ostwald, 1990). Such antipathy is easier to understand when we consider that members of the *demos* regularly brought to trial on charges of financial malfeasance members of the aristocracy who had held public office. If found guilty, those charged were subject to severe penalties – and given the fact that a large percentage of jurors were from the lower classes, guilty verdicts were frequent. Antiphon's recitation of human commonalities, therefore, could very well have been an effort to emphasize the inherent unnaturalness of all societies (but especially democratic ones), where *nomos* rules over *physis*. On this account, it is possible to read *On Truth* as an expression of oligarchic, not democratic, sentiments. But considering that we have only about 400 lines of text remaining from what originally is thought to have been two complete books, all such interpretations are speculative.

Reading 20

On Truth

On Truth, from "Nomos and Phusis in Antiphon's Peri Alêtheias," pp. 293–6 from *Cabinet of the Muses: Rosenmeyer Festschrift*, translated by M. Ostwald (University of California Press, 1990)

The following translation, adapted from that by Jonathan Barnes, is based on the new text published in the first fascicle of the *Corpus dei papiri filosofici greci e latini* by F. Decleva Caizzi, who accepts, largely on the basis of papyrological arguments adduced by M. S. Funghi, an inversion of the sequence of fragments A and B as adopted by Diels. The translation of fragment C is based on Diels' text.

[Col. 2] ... (of more familiar societies) we understand and respect; those of distant societies

5   we neither understand nor respect. This means that we have become barbarians in our relations with one another,

10   for by nature we are all equally equipped in every respect to be barbarians and Greeks.

15   This is shown by examining those factors which are by nature necessary among all human beings and

20   are provided to all in terms of the same capacities; it is in these very factors that none of us is

25   differentiated as a [294] barbarian or a Greek. We all breathe into the

30   air with our mouths and with our nostrils, and we all laugh when there is joy in our [Col. 3] mind, or we weep when suffering pain; we receive sounds

5   through our hearing; we see when sunlight combines with our faculty of sight; we work with our hands

10   and we walk with our feet ... [gap] [Col. 4] ... each group of men came to an

5   agreement on terms of their liking and enacted the laws...

[Col. 1] ...

6   So justice consists in not transgressing the regulations (νόμιμα) of the city

10   of which one is a citizen. Thus a human being is likely to use justice to his own (15) best advantage, if he stresses the importance of the laws in the presence of witnesses,

20   but when he is alone and there are no witnesses (follows) the dictates of nature (τὰ τῆς φύσεως). For the dictates of the laws (τὰ τῶν νόμων) are

25   adventitious, whereas the dictates of nature are inescapable; dictates of the laws, based on agreement as they are, are not natural growths, whereas the dictates of nature (τὰ τῆς φύσεως), being natural growths, are not based on agreement.

[Col. 2] So he who transgresses the regulations (τὰ οὖν νόμιμα παραβαίνων)

5   is free from shame and penalty, if he remains undetected by those who are a party to the agreement; but this is not the case

10   if he is detected. However, if someone should try the impossible, namely to violate what is connate with nature, even if

15   he remains undetected by all men, the adverse effect will be no less, and if all see him,

20   it will be no greater. For he is not harmed through opinion but through truth.

The reason for our inquiry into

25   these matters is that the majority of things sanctioned as just in terms of the law are enactments inimical (πολεμίως)

30   to nature. For laws have been enacted for the eyes telling them what they must [Col. 3] see and what they must not; for the ears what they must hear and what

5   they must not; and for the tongue what it must say and what it must not; and for the hands

10   what they must do and what they must not; and for the feet where they must go and where

15   not; and for the mind what it must desire and what not. So the things from which the laws turn men away are in no way

20   less congenial and less close to nature than are the things they

25 turn us towards. For to live belongs to nature and also to die, and living results

30 from things advantageous for them, while dying comes from things that are not [Col. 4] [295] advantageous. The advantageous things that have been enacted by the sanction of the laws are fetters (δεσμοί) on nature, but those sanctioned by nature are free. Consequently, what brings discomfort does not,

10 by correct reasoning, profit nature more than what brings gladness; it follows that what brings pain could not be

15 advantageous to a greater degree than what brings pleasure. For things truly advantageous

20 must not bring harm but benefit. Those things, however, which are of advantage through nature … [short gap] …

31 and those who fight only to [Col. 5] defend themselves when attacked and do not themselves initiate action; and those who treat

5 their parents well despite the bad treatment they receive from them; and those who

10 put others on oath without themselves swearing an oath. One might find many of the things

15 I have enumerated inimical to nature (πολέμια τῆι φύσει); what characterizes them is the suffering of more discomfort, when it is possible to

20 suffer less, and the experience of less pleasure when it is possible to have more, and undergoing bad treatment when it is possible not to undergo it.

25 Now, if the laws would afford some protection (ἐπικούρησις) to those who let themselves be subjected to this kind of treatment

30 and would handicap those who do not let themselves be subjected to it but oppose it, [Col. 6] obedience that ties us to the laws would not be without benefit. But in fact it turns out that

5 for those who subject themselves to such treatment the justice that derives from law is inadequate to protect them; it allows

10 the victim to suffer in the first place and the perpetrator to act, and it did not attempt at the crucial moment

15 to prevent the victim from suffering nor the perpetrator from acting. And in administering

20 punishment it is no more partial to the victim than to the perpetrator,

25 for he must persuade those who will inflict the punishment that he has been a victim, or he must be able to obtain

30 justice by fraudulence. The same means are also at the disposal of the perpetrator, if he chooses [Col. 7] to deny … [short gap] … the

6 defendant has as much opportunity to make his defense as the plaintiff has to make his accusation;

10 persuasion available to victim balances persuasion available to perpetrator. For victory can also be attained

15 through verbiage and…

[Col. 1] when what is just is taken seriously, testifying truthfully for another

5 is conventionally thought to be [296] just and no less useful for men's pursuits.

10 Still the person who does this will not be just, if we accept the proposition that it is just not to wrong anyone, unless he is

15 wronging you; for when a person testifies – even if his testimony is truthful – he must necessarily wrong another person in some way

20 and at the same time be wronged later for the evidence he gave. This is inherent in the fact that the testimony given by him

25 leads to the conviction of the person he testified against and makes that person lose his property or his life because of someone whom he

30 is not wronging in any way. This means that he wrongs the person against whom he has testified in that he does wrong to a person who is not

35 wronging him; he is himself wronged by the person he testified against, because he incurs his hatred for having [Col. 2] given truthful testimony – and not only is he wronged by hatred, but also because for the rest

5 of his life he must be on guard against the man he testified against: he has a constant enemy

10 ready to say and do whatever evil he can do to him. Now, these wrongs turn out to be not inconsiderable,

15 neither those he suffers nor those he inflicts. For it is not possible that these acts are just and that at the same time

20 it is just neither to do wrong nor to be wronged oneself. On the contrary, it is necessarily true either that only one of them is just or that

25 they are both unjust. It is evident also that   30   may be. For what benefits some harms
sitting in judgment, passing verdicts, and acting   others. And this means that those who profit are
as an arbitrator are not just, whatever the   not wronged,
result   35   but those who are harmed are wronged....

On the Revolution

By 412 BC, the *demos* clearly had shown that it lacked the ability to execute the war against Sparta. Military blunders mounted, and so did the level of suffering in Athens. Even average citizens began to reflect nostalgically on the past, when the affairs of government were in the hands of a few rather than the many. Among the wealthy, those who had not been killed in the war or exiled by the supporters of democracy were being squeezed dry as the city taxed them to the edge of bankruptcy in the effort to keep troops in the field and ships on the seas.

Thucydides reported that in this moment of social and political tension, the notorious Alcibiades (see chapter 1, note 11) – who had fled to Persia after receiving a death sentence in Sparta for seducing King Agis' wife, Timaea – stirred the pot. Reciting his considerable credentials as a military leader, Alcibiades wrote to all the influential Athenians still alive and stated that he would secure the support of his current patron, Tissaphernes, satrap of Lydia and son-in-law of the Persian king Artaxerxes, if they overthrew the democracy, established an oligarchy, and installed him in a position of authority. This proposal was tempting for several reasons, but the most important was that the Persians had signed a treaty with the Spartans early in 412 BC and were rendering them significant support. If Alcibiades was true to his word, the treaty would be broken, and he would bring his unquestioned military genius to the aid of Athens. Even some diehard democrats were willing to entertain the prospect of changing the government if doing so led to victory.

But Alcibiades' word could not be trusted. Only months before his proposal, Alcibiades, in the service of the Spartans, wrested control of Miletus from Athens. Meanwhile, Tissaphernes learned of Alcibiades' double dealing and was not about to offer the Athenians any support. He decided to break the treaty with Sparta, let the two sides grind each other down to nothing, and then march into Greece at his leisure, making it his own. Although the leading oligarchs broke with Alcibiades when they discovered that he was trying to manipulate everyone concerned so as to further his own interests, the idea of overthrowing the democracy continued to burn in their breasts. Among them was Antiphon of Rahmnus, whom Thucydides identified in his *History of the Peloponnesian War* as the person who conceived the coup and brought it to pass. Likewise, Aristotle noted in *The Athenian Constitution* that Antiphon, Phrynichus, Peisander, and Theramenes were "the chief promoters of the revolution" (32). They mobilized a band of assassins to execute influential supporters of democracy and in so doing created a climate of fear that cowed the entire population. In this way, they were able to control the assembly and pass laws that ostensibly legitimized the forthcoming coup. As Thucydides noted, there was no opposition to their motions, for "If anyone should speak in opposition, he was immediately killed in some convenient way" (8.66.2). Having completed the work necessary to drape the new government in a cloak of legitimacy, the four leaders and their cohorts entered the council chamber, dismissed the elected leaders, and took control.

By all accounts, these were clever men, but it seems that they had not considered how they were to maintain power when the army and navy were composed almost entirely of average citizens who were staunch supporters of democracy. When in their first governmental act the oligarchs sought peace with Sparta, rebellion erupted among troops and sailors throughout the Aegean. The Spartans, for their part, saw the peace overtures as a sign of weakness and stepped up their attacks. In a characteristic twist, Alcibiades now came out in support of democracy, railed against the Council of 400 ruling Athens, and then persuaded the fleet stationed at Samos not only to grant him amnesty for his earlier sentence of death but also to elect him general.

Meanwhile, the oligarchs faced a dilemma. They could not get Sparta to agree to a peace treaty, and they could not pursue the war with the troops and sailors in revolt. They came to believe that the only way out of their predicament was simply to surrender Athens. Their envoys arranged for the Spartan commander Agesandridas to sail into the port at Piraeus. But when his ships were sighted, the few Athenian triremes defending the harbor sailed out to meet them, which Agesandridas apparently was not expecting. He refused to engage and went on to Euboea, wiping out the Athenian forces defending the island. This was a tremendous loss, for Athens depended on Euboea for grain. The Attic plain was occupied and unusable; with Euboea captured, the only other source of grain was the Bosporus, highly uncertain owing to the presence of Spartan forces.

In the wake of the Euboean disaster, the troops stationed at Piraeus marched on the council chambers and, weapons poised, brusquely notified the 400 that their government was finished. All but Antiphon fled. Peisander, for example, went over to the Spartans. Antiphon could have escaped with the others, and we have no idea why he chose to stay. He was charged with treason, found guilty, and executed. The fragment *On the Revolution* presented here comes from the speech he gave before the court in his defense and therefore is an example of applied rhetoric. Because he had worked as a *logographos* for years, he probably wrote the speech in advance of the trial; but it is possible that he revised it after the verdict as he was awaiting execution. Gagarin (1998, 2002) argued that the speech is similar to the one Socrates gave at his trial and that he used the occasion to defend his career as well as his life, but the fragments themselves do not seem to support this assessment fully, nor does the substance of the fragments differ significantly from other extant defense speeches.

Reading 21

On the Revolution

On the Revolution, pp. 203–4 from *The Older Sophists*, edited by Rosamond Kent Sprague and translated by J.S. Morrison (Hackett Publishing, 2001). Reprinted by permission of Hackett Publishing Company, Inc. All rights reserved.

Was this my motive for wanting a revolution, that, being elected to a public office, I had handled [large] sums of money and that there was an audit due which I had cause to fear, or that I had lost my citizen rights or that I had committed some crime or that I had a lawsuit hanging over me? No, this was not the reason, since none of these was the case with me. Was it, then, because you had confiscated my property? Or was it because [you had punished me] for some crime my ancestors had committed against you? [It is for reasons like this that men] begin to yearn for a different kind of political setup to the one they have, either to avoid paying the penalty of their crimes or so that they may take vengeance for some wrong done to them and suffer no compensating attack.

No, I had no such reason. The prosecution does [however] assert that I composed defenses for other people and that I made money out of it. Surely under an oligarchy I should not have had the chance to do this, while it is under a [demo]cra[cy] that I am the powerful man I have become; and whereas under oligarchy I was likely to be of no importance, under a democracy my importance is great. Answer then. What likelihood is there that I should want oligarchy? Am I too stupid to make this calculation? Am I the [only man] in Athens unable to appreciate his own advantage? Did the ... think? ... No, by the gods in heaven, if you are sensible, since Theramenes, who accused me in the Council. ...

Study Questions

1 The struggle between supporters of oligarchy and the supporters of democracy was intense, as this background information indicates. What may have been some factors that explain its intensity, and what do we learn from the struggle?
2 It is clear from the historical record that Antiphon could have fled Athens prior to his arrest for treason, but he did not. What might have been his reasons for staying when he knew that if found guilty he would be executed? What would you have done under those circumstances? Why?
3 The Greeks saw themselves as being different from – indeed, superior to – everyone else. Their view of the world could be characterized as an example of extreme diversity, divided into two groups: Greeks and everyone else. In *On Truth*, Antiphon rejected this view and focused on similarities, not differences. What benefits are there to emphasizing the similarities among people? Does this element of *On Truth* offer any wisdom for us today?
4 What features do *On the Revolution* and *Defense of Palamedes* have in common?

Writing Topics

1 Analyze Antiphon's *Tetralogies* so as to identify and explain the rhetorical strategies you see there.
2 Analyze one of Antiphon's legal speeches, such as *Against the Stepmother*, and explain whether (and if so how) the speech utilizes any of the rhetorical features illustrated in the *Tetralogies*.
3 Stylistic differences in the works attributed to Antiphon have figured significantly in the unitarian v. separatist debate on authorship. Stylistic studies today quantify style by examining such factors as average sentence length, average number of subordinate and relative clauses, average number of adverbials and adjectivals, sentence openings, and so forth. Examine your own style using this method to determine whether it has changed over a period of several years, using, for example, a paper you produced as a freshman or sophomore and one produced recently. What does your analysis reveal about style?

Further Reading

Lysias, *Against Agathos*.
Antiphon, *Against the Stepmother for Poisoning*.
Gagarin, M., and MacDowell, D. (1998). *Antiphon & Andocides*. University of Texas Press.

Introduction to Isocrates (c. 436–338 BC)

Like all Athenians, Isocrates was deeply affected by the Peloponnesian War. Born into a wealthy family, he received the best education available, studying rhetoric with Protagoras and Gorgias. His father's wealth, however, was consumed by the war, forcing Isocrates to fend for himself. He lacked any skills other than his training in rhetoric, so out of necessity he began a career as a *logographos*, at which he was quite successful. He grew more reflective as he aged (perhaps more self-confident as well) and came to deny ever having had a legal career, turning eventually to writing and distributing essays on education, politics, and philosophy.

Most, if not all, of Isocrates' works are extant, consisting of six forensic speeches, three orations, three encomia, three treatises on education, nine letters, and six political pamphlets. He may have produced a work entitled *The Art of Rhetoric*, but the authorship is uncertain, and in any event, it did not survive. Isocrates is included here among the Sophists, but unlike Protagoras, Gorgias, and Antiphon, he was not a public speaker; his early works were intended for others to use in litigation, whereas his later ones were intended to be read. Various scholars, such as Guthrie (1977), do not classify him as a Sophist but instead follow Isocrates' self-assessment in *Against the Sophists* and refer to him as an educator and/or a rhetorician. Usher (1999), on the other hand, identified him as a Sophist, but "of a peculiar kind": Isocrates' "discourses are derived not from live cases in the courts or from actual political debates in the Assembly or the Council, but from the lucubrations of a small academic circle dominated by a single mind ... [He] has no clearly identifiable predecessors among extant orators" (p. 297). In *Against the Sophists*, Isocrates was highly critical of Sophists and their teaching, yet its publication in 391 BC closely coincided with the opening of his school of rhetoric around 390 BC which should lead us to consider it, at least partially, as an effort to describe the ways in which his school was better than others rather than as a broadside motivated simply by his concern for the education of Athenians. His work and his teaching indeed differed from the Sophistic mainstream in important respects, but from this great distance the differences do not appear so radical that they necessitate putting him in a separate category.

Isocrates' school was in direct competition with Plato's Academy, founded about three years earlier, and later with Aristotle's Lyceum. Both Plato and Isocrates taught philosophy, but they approached the subject from different perspectives. Isocrates had little patience with Plato's metaphysics and generally deemed Plato's philosophy useless in the hurly-burly realpolitik of Athens. Isocrates' curriculum taught philosophy as a means of understanding the sociopolitical issues that men had to address daily, the issues *pros kriseis*. As such, this philosophy was more properly *phronesis*, or practical wisdom; it was not concerned with truth, for Isocrates did not believe that truth as Plato conceived it could ever be found.

Rather than rejecting rhetoric as a pernicious means of deception, Isocrates viewed it as a necessary tool in the deliberative processes that are at the heart of society's major institutions. Like the Sophists, Isocrates believed that *aretê* could be taught, but it seems that he developed a more substantive approach than they through the principled application of *phronesis* to questions of ethics and morality. Here, again, rhetoric played an important role, and the curriculum appears to have reflected the sentiments of Hesiod (1981), who in *Works and Days* wrote: "that man is altogether best who considers all things himself and marks what will be better afterwards and at the end; and he, again, is good who listens to a good adviser" (293). By combining rhetoric and ethics, Isocrates sought to provide an education that produced ethical leaders who could advise others to do what is "better afterwards and at the end." This approach became the cornerstone of Western education and was the basis, in the Roman period, of Cato the Elder's definition of rhetoric as *vir bonus dicendi peritus* – a good man speaking well – which was later embraced by both Cicero (106–43 BC) and Quintilian (35–95 AD). But in the fourth century BC, the concept was manifest, as Jaeger (1976) noted, in *kalos kagathos*, the good man of virtue. An important goal of Isocrates' educational program, therefore, was to use rhetoric and *phronesis* to develop students into virtuous men who could speak well (Johnson, 1959).[8]

Isocrates understood that *phronesis* was necessary if an orator was to "consider all things himself" in his own mind, but he also recognized that a successful rhetorician must know when to speak, when to present arguments and themes that resonated with a particular audience, and how to ensure that the arguments, style, and tone fit the occasion (see Sipiora, 2002; Sullivan, 1992). That is, both *kairos* and *prepon* were important factors in Isocratean education, and in his work *Against the Sophists* he criticized other teachers for neglecting them. Equally important, Isocrates' emphasis on *kairos* was based on his perception of rhetoric as a social action and the rhetor as a man of action working for the betterment of society. The *kalos kagathos* is not merely the good man speaking well but also the good man doing the right thing in his relationships with others. *Aretê*, therefore, is based on *conduct*, in clear distinction from the Platonic notion that it is based on philosophically enlightened *thoughts*.

In what appears to have been an innovative move, Isocrates extended this notion of *aretê* beyond the individual to government. The city-state had come to be viewed as a reflection of mankind's highest values, which made this extension feasible. In the fourth century, as in our own time, the general inclination was to judge the quality of government on the basis of its form. Thus, democracy was good, whereas plutocracy, oligarchy, and dictatorships were bad. Rejecting this simplistic assessment, Isocrates judged the quality of government on the basis of its actions: There can be bad democracies and good dictatorships, depending on how they serve the needs of citizens. As a teacher and a public intellectual, Isocrates believed that he had an obligation to educate not just individual students but the entire society, and he did so in his letters and treatises, such as *Panegyricus* and *Aeropagiticus*.

These works are not manuals for good government by any means. Instead, they are discourses designed to rally audiences to traditional values, perspectives, and behaviors. They are explicitly panhellenistic and without question mirror Isocrates' desire to prevent any further internal conflicts among the Greeks. He saw Philip of Macedonia as the leader with the wherewithal to unite Greece, bring an end to civil strife, and – perhaps more important – prepare to defend the homeland against what he understood was an inevitable renewal of the conflict between Greece and the people of the Middle East. These works also display a nostalgia for the past, for strong leaders like Solon, for a balance of political power between the *demos* and the aristocracy, and for the personal and civic virtue that Isocrates believed had been lost among Athenians. The failures of democracy inherent in the Peloponnesian War and the civil wars that followed left Isocrates with few illusions about the ability of the *demos* to govern responsibly, and he did not hesitate to criticize his fellow Athenians, as in the passage below from *Aeropagiticus*:

---

[8] Note that *vir bonum* translates into the English "good man" but that the translation lacks the full meaning of the Latin. A more accurate translation is "the *morally* good man," which makes the connection with Isocrates even stronger.

And yet how can we praise or tolerate a government which has in the past been the cause of so many evils and which is now year by year ever drifting on from bad to worse? And how can we escape the fear that if we continue to progress after this fashion we may finally run aground on rocks more perilous than those which at that time loomed before us? ... [Today, our] citizens ... [look] upon insolence as democracy, lawlessness as liberty, impudence of speech as equality, and license to do what they please as happiness. (Isocrates, 1929, 18–20, pp. 115–16)

Words like these, as well as the difficulty associated with interpreting Isocrates' concept of *aretê*, have led some scholars to conclude that he was an enemy of democracy who yearned for a return to oligarchy, or perhaps even monarchy (e.g., Leff, 2003; Mirhady and Too, 2000; Too, 1995). Other scholars, however, point out the commitment to democracy in his works and identify Isocrates as a democrat, even a liberal democrat (e.g., Depew and Poulakos, 2004; Freese, 1894; McGee, 2006; Ober, 1989, 2004). Jaeger (1965) went so far as to call Isocrates "the father of humanism" (p. 84). Such conflicting assessments seem rooted in the fact that Isocrates both affirmed and criticized democracy, exercising, as in the passage above, what he deemed to be a critical component of a viable democracy – *parrhesia*, or frank, critical speech – that had become impossible in Athens owing to what today we would call politically correct thinking among the *demos*, who eagerly shouted down or brought to trial on bogus charges anyone who dared to question ideologically based policies and decisions (Foucault, 1983).

We learn from *Antidosis* that writing was a central component of the curriculum at Isocrates' school, which indicates that literacy had expanded significantly in Greece over a relatively short time (see Lentz, 1989). In addition, the emphasis on writing illustrates a shift in rhetoric: From this point on, we begin to see less emphasis among the Greeks on display and practice speeches as a means of teaching rhetoric and more emphasis on what we may think of as training manuals, redefining the concept of *technê* in the process. After Isocrates, we continue to find rhetoricians who also are teachers of rhetoric, in the Sophistic tradition, but increasingly we find that teachers of rhetoric are not practicing rhetoricians – that is, not public speakers – the most notable example being Aristotle.

The question of Isocrates' significance is an interesting one, in part because he himself complained in *Antidosis* about being ignored by his contemporaries. Relegated to minor status for centuries, only recently has modern scholarship elevated his position. The problem in the past, and to a certain extent even today, was the perception that he did not contribute to rhetorical theory. In his introduction to Isocrates, for example, Freese (1894) stated that "it cannot be denied that there was little that was fresh or original in his ideas" (p. 3). This assessment is no doubt founded to a certain degree on the influence of Aristotle, who established the prominence of theory over practice in the intellectual realm, and also on the fact that virtually all rhetorical theories must inevitably be judged against the standard set by Aristotle in his *Art of Rhetoric* and just as inevitably come up short in the process. But the value of practice is better recognized today, and many scholars acknowledge that theory without practice is empty and, ultimately, meaningless. This point is amply illustrated by the fact that Aristotle taught rhetoric as a formal system based largely on theory and did not produce any significant rhetoricians; Isocrates, on the other hand, taught rhetoric as a practical endeavor and produced several. In addition, the influence Isocrates had on education in general and rhetorical education in particular is difficult to ignore. As part of the rehabilitation of Isocrates, Poulakos (1997) argued on the basis of works like *Aeropagiticus* that Isocrates made a lasting contribution to rhetoric because he gave it a "political orientation" (p. 4).

Yet we must note that rhetoric as practiced in the assembly was inherently political and predated Isocrates by many years. It therefore may be more accurate to acknowledge Isocrates as the progenitor of political philosophy (an enterprise that Aristotle quickly took over just a few years after Isocrates, applying significantly more depth and perspicacity in *Nicomachean Ethics* and *Politics*).[9]

The difficulty Isocrates faced during his lifetime and afterwards appears to lie in the nature of his work. Although his writing is typically categorized by form – speeches, letters, and so forth – when we look beneath the external appearance of his works we find a common genre, the encomium. In Aristotles' taxonomy, encomia fall under the more general heading of epideixis, which he deemed to be less substantial than deliberative and forensic rhetoric, suitable primarily for funeral orations and victory speeches. Isocrates, on the other hand, understood epideixis' inherent flexibility as an educational tool; it is fundamentally phatic. As Perelman and Olbrechts-Tyteca (1969, pp. 52–53) noted:

a moment's reflection enables one to see that … the speaker engaged in epideictic discourse is very close to being an educator. … The purpose of epideictic speech is to increase the intensity of adherence to values held in common by the audience and the speaker. The epideictic speech has an important part to play, for without such common values upon what foundation could deliberative and legal speeches rest?

On this basis, we may conclude that Isocrates was correct in seeing epideixis as an educational tool – and as an excellent vehicle for urging his fellow Athenians to recover the ideals that governed their city in the time of Solon, as well as for using the looming threat of the Persians and Arabs as an inducement for a unified Greece. The problem, however, is that the encomiast who would educate his audience must, again turning to Perelman and Olbrechts-Tyteca (1969), "nevertheless have a high reputation … [and] must have qualifications for speaking on his subject" (p. 52). Where these characteristics are lacking, the speaker can easily fall into the trap of producing an encomium to himself, which is exactly what we find in so much of Isocrates' work. Self-flattery often leads to disdain, not to a swelling of communal values.

Against the Sophists

Although Isocrates studied rhetoric with Protagoras and Gorgias, his contempt for Sophists in general is evident in his criticism of their claims and methods. Their reliance on *technai,* for example, did little to develop in students an understanding of rhetoric as a creative process. Nor did their instruction recognize that rhetoric is an "art." Isocrates' use of this term was important because it emphasized what had previously been a secondary meaning of *technê,* a meaning that, as Cole (1991) noted, came to dominate: a formal treatise.

After criticizing the Sophists, Isocrates begins to describe his own method, which focuses on teaching and practice while recognizing the need for natural talent.

---

[9] Plato is commonly deemed to be the originator of political philosophy on the basis of *The Republic,* dated between 360 and 350 BC and thus a few years prior to Isocrates' political works. Although *The Republic* addresses various political issues, the overall focus of the work, in my view, is education; politics and political systems are viewed as the outcome of education.

Unfortunately, the text ends abruptly at this point, and we are left wondering about the details of his curriculum. The reference to *eristic*, or adversarial, speeches offers a clue – supported in other works – that Isocrates did not limit instruction to eristic discourse, and the emphasis on epideixis in his own work suggests that this genre may have occupied a central place in his teaching.

Reading 22

Against the Sophists

Against the Sophists, pp. 163–77 (Greek on even-numbered pages omitted) reprinted by permission of the publishers and Trustees of the Loeb Classical Library from *Isocrates*, Volume II, Loeb Classical Library Volume 229, translated by George Norlin (Cambridge, MA: Harvard University Press, 1929). © 1929 by the President and Fellows of Harvard College. The Loeb Classical Library® is a registered trademark of the President and Fellows of Harvard College.

If all who are engaged in the profession of education were willing to state the facts instead of making greater promises than they can possibly fulfil, they would not be in such bad repute with the lay-public. As it is, however, the teachers who do not scruple to vaunt their powers with utter disregard of the truth have created the impression that those who choose a life of careless indolence are better advised than those who devote themselves to serious study.

Indeed, who can fail to abhor, yes to contemn, those teachers, in the first place, who devote themselves to disputation, since they pretend to search for truth, but straightway at the beginning of their professions attempt to deceive us with lies? For I think it is manifest to all that foreknowledge of future events is not vouchsafed to our human nature, but that we are so far removed from this prescience that Homer, who has been conceded the highest reputation for wisdom, has pictured even the gods as at times debating among themselves about the future – not that he knew their minds but that he desired to show us that for mankind this power lies in the realms of the impossible.

But these professors have gone so far in their lack of scruple that they attempt to persuade our young men that if they will only study under them they will know what to do in life and through this knowledge will become happy and prosperous. More than that, although they set themselves up as masters and dispensers of goods so precious, they are not ashamed of asking for them a price of three or four minae! Why, if they were to sell any other commodity for so trifling a fraction of its worth they would not deny their folly; nevertheless, although they set so insignificant a price on the whole stock of virtue and happiness, they pretend to wisdom and assume the right to instruct the rest of the world. Furthermore, although they say that they do not want money and speak contemptuously of wealth as "filthy lucre," they hold their hands out for a trifling gain and promise to make their disciples all but immortal! But what is most ridiculous of all is that they distrust those from whom they are to get this money – they distrust, that is to say, the very men to whom they are about to deliver the science of just dealing – and they require that the fees advanced by their students be entrusted for safe keeping to those who have never been under their instruction, being well advised as to their security, but doing the opposite of what they preach. For it is permissible to those who give any other instruction to be exacting in matters open to dispute, since nothing prevents those who have been made adept in other lines of training from being dishonourable in the matter of contracts. But men who inculcate virtue and sobriety – is it not absurd if they do not trust in their own students before all others? For it is not to be supposed that men who are honourable and just-dealing with others will be dishonest with the very preceptors who have made them what they are.

When, therefore, the layman puts all these things together and observes that the teachers of wisdom and dispensers of happiness are themselves in great want but exact only a small fee from their students, that they are on the watch for contradictions in words but are blind to inconsistencies in deeds, and that, furthermore, they pretend to have knowledge of the future but are incapable either of saying anything pertinent or of giving any counsel regarding the present, and when he observes that those who follow their judgements are more consistent and more successful than those who profess to have exact knowledge, then he has, I think, good reason to contemn such studies and regard them as stuff and nonsense, and not as a true discipline of the soul.

But it is not these sophists alone who are open to criticism, but also those who profess to teach political discourse. For the latter have no interest whatever in the truth, but consider that they are masters of an art if they can attract great numbers of students by the smallness of their charges and the magnitude of their professions and get something out of them. For they are themselves so stupid and conceive others to be so dull that, although the speeches which they compose are worse than those which some laymen improvise, nevertheless they promise to make their students such clever orators that they will not overlook any of the possibilities which a subject affords. More than that, they do not attribute any of this power either to the practical experience or to the native ability of the student, but undertake to transmit the science of discourse as simply as they would teach the letters of the alphabet, not having taken trouble to examine into the nature of each kind of knowledge, but thinking that because of the extravagance of their promises they themselves will command admiration and the teaching of discourse will be held in higher esteem – oblivious of the fact that the arts are made great, not by those who are without scruple in boasting about them, but by those who are able to discover all of the resources which each art affords.

For myself, I should have preferred above great riches that philosophy had as much power as these men claim; for, possibly, I should not have been the very last in the profession nor had the least share in its profits. But since it has no such power, I could wish that this prating might cease. For I note that the bad repute which results therefrom does not affect the offenders only, but that all the rest of us who are in the same profession share in the opprobium.

But I marvel when I observe these men setting themselves up as instructors of youth who cannot see that they are applying the analogy of an art with hard and fast rules to a creative process. For, excepting these teachers, who does not know that the art of using letters remains fixed and unchanged, so that we continually and invariably use the same letters for the same purposes, while exactly the reverse is true of the art of discourse? For what has been said by one speaker is not equally useful for the speaker who comes after him; on the contrary, he is accounted most skilled in this art who speaks in a manner worthy of his subject and yet is able to discover in it topics which are nowise the same as those used by others. But the greatest proof of the difference between these two arts is that oratory is good only if it has the qualities of fitness for the occasion, propriety of style, and originality of treatment, while in the case of letters there is no such need whatsoever. So that those who make use of such analogies ought more justly to pay out than to accept fees, since they attempt to teach others when they are themselves in great need of instruction.

However, if it is my duty not only to rebuke others, but also to set forth my own views, I think all intelligent people will agree with me that while many of those who have pursued philosophy have remained in private life, others, on the other hand, who have never taken lessons from any one of the sophists have become able orators and statesmen. For ability, whether in speech or in any other activity, is found in those who are well endowed by nature and have been schooled by practical experience. Formal training makes such men more skilful and more resourceful in discovering the possibilities of a subject; for it teaches them to take from a readier source the topics which they otherwise hit upon in haphazard fashion. But it cannot fully fashion men who are without natural aptitude into good debaters or writers, although it is capable of leading them on to self-improvement and to a greater degree of intelligence on many subjects.

But I desire, now that I have gone this far, to speak more clearly on these matters. For I hold that to obtain a knowledge of the elements out of which we make and compose all discourses is not so very difficult if anyone entrusts himself, not to those who make rash promises, but to those who have some knowledge of these things. But to choose from these elements those which should be employed for each subject, to join them together, to arrange them properly, and also, not to miss what the occasion demands but appropriately to adorn the whole speech with striking thoughts and to clothe it in flowing and melodious phrase – these things, I hold, require much study and are the task of a vigorous and imaginative mind: for this, the student must not only have the requisite aptitude but he must learn the different kinds of discourse and practise himself in their use; and the teacher, for his part, must so expound the principles of the art with the utmost possible exactness as to leave out nothing that can be taught, and, for the rest, he must in himself set such an example of oratory that the students who have taken form under his instruction and are able to pattern after him will, from the outset, show in their speaking a degree of grace and charm which is not found in others. When all of these requisites are found together, then the devotees of philosophy will achieve complete success; but according as any one of the things which I have mentioned is lacking, to this extent must their disciples of necessity fall below the mark.

Now as for the sophists who have lately sprung up and have very recently embraced these pretensions, even though they flourish at the moment, they will all, I am sure, come round to this position. But there remain to be considered those who lived before our time and did not scruple to write the so-called arts of oratory. These must not be dismissed without rebuke, since they professed to teach how to conduct law-suits, picking out the most discredited of terms, which the enemies, not the champions, of this discipline might have been expected to employ – and that too although this facility, in so far as it can be taught, is of no greater aid to forensic than to all other discourse. But they were much worse than those who dabble in disputation; for although the latter expounded such captious theories that were anyone to cleave to them in practice he would at once be in all manner of trouble, they did, at any rate, make professions of virtue and sobriety in their teaching, whereas the former, although exhorting others to study political discourse, neglected all the good things which this study affords, and became nothing more than professors of meddlesomeness and greed.

And yet those who desire to follow the true precepts of this discipline may, if they will, be helped more speedily towards honesty of character than towards facility in oratory. And let no one suppose that I claim that just living can be taught; for, in a word, I hold that there does not exist an art of the kind which can implant sobriety and justice in depraved natures. Nevertheless, I do think that the study of political discourse can help more than any other thing to stimulate and form such qualities of character.

But in order that I may not appear to be breaking down the pretensions of others while myself making greater claims than are within my powers, I believe that the very arguments by which I myself was convinced will make it clear to others also that these things are true.

Antidosis

As noted in the general introduction, wealthy citizens of Athens were required to support the city in various ways. One of the more costly expenses was the support of a warship (a trireme) for a year. A citizen who was selected to provide this support (a trierarch) could avoid what essentially was a tax on the rich by claiming that another person had more money and was thus better able to bear the costs involved. Few so named were willing to accept the claim, but if they resisted, the law allowed the claimant to demand an exchange of all property, which would then enable him to use the other's wealth to meet the burden of maintaining the warship. This procedure was called *antidosis*. The named person had the option of fighting the antidosis in court, and as far was we can determine, everyone so challenged exercised this option.

Perhaps because Isocrates had already served as a trierarch three times in the past – which would have bankrupted many fairly wealthy citizens – or perhaps because of some personal enmity, Megacleides,[10] when called upon to pay for a warship, named Isocrates as someone who could better afford the expense. Isocrates refused the honor,

[10] The name of the plaintiff in *Antidosis* is Lysimachus, which appears to be fictional.

so Megacleides filed an *antidosis* suit, requesting an exchange of property, and the matter went to trial. Apparently, Isocrates lost the case, for he comments in *Antidosis* that the trierarchy was imposed upon him. It seems that he bore the cost without great complaint, but what rankled was that his adversary in the case belittled him and his profession. Having lived a quiet but productive life and having contributed materially to the city, he had assumed that his fellow citizens held him in high esteem. The trial showed him that they did not. He therefore composed *Antidosis* some years after the trial as a response to the abuse he had received in court. He announces at the beginning of the piece that, after some deliberation, he determined that the best way to explain himself to the public was to "adopt the fiction of a trial," which would allow him to recite the calumnies of the prosecution and then refute them. Consequently, after this introduction, the beginning of the work has some of the characteristics of a legal speech. It deviates, however, when Isocrates launches into a description and defense of his career. *Antidosis* resembles Socrates' trial in several ways; for example, Isocrates indicates that, like Socrates, he was charged with corrupting the youth of Athens. Thus, *Antidosis* reflects an unusual combination of forensic rhetoric and encomium.

Reading 23

Antidosis

Antidosis (excerpt), pp. 185–93, 199–215, 285–313, 331–43, 365 (Greek on even-numbered pages omitted) reprinted by permission of the publishers and Trustees of the Loeb Classical Library from *Isocrates*, Volume II, Loeb Classical Library Volume 229, translated by George Norlin (Cambridge, MA: Harvard University Press, 1929). © 1929 by the President and Fellows of Harvard College. The Loeb Classical Library ® is a registered trademark of the President and Fellows of Harvard College.

If the discourse which is now about to be read had been like the speeches which are produced either for the law-courts or for oratorical display, I should not, I suppose, have prefaced it by any explanation. Since, however, it is novel and different in character, it is necessary to begin by setting forth the reasons why I chose to write a discourse so unlike any other; for if I neglected to make this clear, my speech would, no doubt, impress many as curious and strange.

The fact is that, although I have known that some of the sophists traduce my occupation, saying that it has to do with writing speeches for the courts, very much as one might have the effrontery to call Pheidias, who wrought our statue of Athena, a doll-maker, or say that Zeuxis and Parrhasius practised the same art as the sign-painters, nevertheless I have never deigned to defend myself against their attempts to belittle me, because I considered that their foolish babble had no influence whatever and that I had, myself, made it manifest to all that I had elected to speak and write, not on petty disputes, but on subjects so important and so elevated that no one would attempt them except those who had studied with me, and their would-be imitators.

Indeed, I had always thought, until well on in years, that, owing to this choice and to my retired life in general, I stood fairly well in the opinion of all the lay public. Then when my career was near its close, having been challenged to an exchange of property on the question of a trierarchy, and subjected to a trial on that issue, I came to realize that even outside of my profession there were those who were not disposed towards me as I had thought; nay, that some had been absolutely misled as to my pursuits and were inclined to listen to my detractors, while others, who were well aware of the nature of my work, were envious, feeling the same towards me as do the sophists, and rejoiced to see people hold false opinions of my character. They betrayed their sentiments at the trial; for, although my opponent made no argument whatever on the merits of the case, and did nothing but decry my "cleverness" of speech and indulge in extravagant nonsense about my wealth and the number of my pupils, they imposed the trierarchy upon me.

Now, I bore that expense in such a manner as is becoming to those who are neither too much upset by such things nor altogether reckless or even careless about money. But when my eyes were opened, as I have said, to the fact that a greater number than I supposed had mistaken ideas about me, I began to ponder how I could show to them and to posterity the truth about my character, my life, and the education to which I am devoted, and not suffer myself to be condemned on these issues without a trial nor to remain, as I had just been, at the mercy of my habitual calumniators. And as I kept thinking upon it, I came ever to the same conclusion, namely, that the only way in which I could accomplish this was to compose a discourse which would be, as it were, a true image of my thought and of my whole life; for I hoped that this would serve both as the best means of making known the truth about me and, at the same time, as a monument, after my death, more noble than statues of bronze.

I saw, however, that if I were to attempt a eulogy of myself, I should not be able to cover all the points which I proposed to discuss, nor should I succeed in treating them without arousing the displeasure or even the envy of my hearers. But it occurred to me that if I were to adopt the fiction of a trial and of a suit brought against me – if I were to suppose that a sycophant had brought an indictment and was threatening me with trouble and that he was using the calumnies which had been urged against me in the suit about the exchange of property, while I, for my part, cast my speech in the form of a defence in court – in this way it would be possible to discuss to the best advantage all the points which I wanted to make.

With these thoughts in mind I set myself to write this discourse – I who am no longer in the prime of youth but in my eighty-second year. Wherefore, you may well forgive me if my speech appears to be less vigorous than those which I have published in the past. For, I assure you, it has not been an easy nor a simple task, but one of great difficulty; for while some things in my discourse are appropriate to be spoken in a court-room, others are out of place amid such controversies, being frank discussions about philosophy and

expositions of its power. There is in it, also, matter which it would be well for young men to hear before they set out to gain knowledge and an education; and there is much, besides, of what I have written in the past, inserted in the present discussion, not without reason nor without fitness, but with due appropriateness to the subject in hand.

Now to view as a whole so great an extent of subject matter, to harmonize and bring together so many diverse varieties of discourse, to connect smoothly what follows with what goes before, and to make all parts consonant one with another, was by no means an easy undertaking. Yet I did not desist, in spite of my age, until I had accomplished it, such as it is. It is, at any rate, written with devotion to the truth; its other qualities I leave to the judgement of my hearers. But I urge all who intend to acquaint themselves with my speech, first, to make allowance, as they listen to it, for the fact that it is a mixed discourse, composed with an eye to all these subjects; next, to fix their attention even more on what is about to be said than on what has been said before; and, lastly, not to seek to run through the whole of it at the first sitting, but only so much of it as will not fatigue the audience. For if you comply with this advice, you will be better able to determine whether I speak in a manner worthy of my reputation.

These, then, are the things which it was necessary for me to say by way of introduction. I beg you now to listen to my defence, which purports to have been written for a trial, but whose real purpose is to show the truth about myself, to make those who are ignorant about me know the sort of man I am and those who are afflicted with envy suffer a still more painful attack of this malady; for a greater revenge upon them than this I could not hope to obtain.

[…]

Indeed no one may rely on the honesty of his life as a guarantee that he will be able to live securely in Athens; for the men who have chosen to neglect what is their own and to plot against what belongs to others do not keep their hands off citizens who live soberly and bring before you only those who do evil; on the contrary, they advertise their powers in their attacks upon men who are entirely innocent, and so get more money from those who are clearly guilty. This is exactly what Lysimachus had in mind when he subjected me to this trial; for he thought that this suit against me would bring him profit from other sources, and he expected that if he won in the debate with me, whom he calls the teacher of other men, everyone would regard his power as irresistible. He is confident that he will win easily; for he sees that you are over-ready to accept slanders and calumnies, while I, because of my age and my lack of experience in contests of this kind, shall not be able to reply to them in a manner worthy of my reputation; for I have so lived all my life till now that no man either under the oligarchy or under the democracy has ever charged me with any offence, whether of violence or injury, nor will any man be found to have sat either as arbitrator or as judge upon my actions. For I have schooled myself to avoid giving any offence to others, and, when I have been wronged by others, not to seek revenge in court but to adjust the matter in dispute by conferring with their friends. All this has availed me nothing; on the contrary, I who have lived to this advanced age without complaint from anyone could not be in greater jeopardy if I had wronged all the world.

Yet I am not utterly discouraged because I face so great a penalty; no, if you will only hear me with good will, I am very confident that those who have been misled as to my pursuits and have been won over by my would-be slanderers will promptly change their views, while those who think of me as I really am will be still more confirmed in their opinion.

But in order that I may not overtax your patience by speaking at undue length before coming to the subject, I shall leave off this discussion and attempt forthwith to inform you on the question which you are to vote upon.

[...]

Now, in fact, no citizen has ever been harmed either by my "cleverness" or by my writings, and I think the most convincing proof of this is furnished by this trial; for if any man had been wronged by me, even though he might have held his tongue up till now, he would not have neglected the present opportunity, but would have come forward to denounce me or bear witness against me. For when one who has never in his life heard a single disparaging word from me has put me in so great peril, depend upon it, had any suffered injury at my hands, they would now attempt to have their revenge. For surely it is neither probable nor possible both that I, on the one hand, have wronged many people and that those, on the other hand, who have been visited with

misfortune through me are silent and refrain from accusing me; nay, are kinder to me when my life is in peril than those who have suffered no injury, especially since all they have to do is to testify to the wrongs I have done them in order to obtain the fullest reparation. But neither in the past nor now will anyone be found to have made any such complaint.

If, therefore, I were to agree with my accuser and concede his claim that I am the "cleverest" of men and that I have never had an equal as a writer of the kind of speeches which are offensive to you, it would be much more just to give me credit for being an honest man than to punish me; for when a man has superior talents whether for speech or for action, one cannot fairly charge it to anything but fortune, but when a man makes good and temperate use of the power which nature has given him, as in my own case, all the world ought in justice to commend his character.

However, though I might advance this argument in my behalf, I shall never be found to have had anything to do with speeches for the courts. You can judge this from my habits of life, from which indeed, you can get at the truth much better than from the lips of my accusers ; for no one is, I think, blind to the fact that all people are wont to spend their time in the places where they elect to gain their livelihood. And you will observe that those who live upon your contracts and the litigation connected with them are all but domiciled in the courts of law, while no one has ever seen me either at the council-board, or at the preliminaries, or in the courts, or before the arbitrators; on the contrary, I have kept aloof from all these more than any of my fellow-citizens.

Moreover, you will find that these men are able to carry on a profitable business in Athens alone; if they were to sail to any other place they would starve to death; while my resources, which this fellow has exaggerated, have all come to me from abroad. Then again you will find associated with them either men who are themselves in evil case or who want to ruin others, while in my company are those who of all the Hellenes lead the most untroubled lives.

But you have heard also from my accuser that I have received many great presents from Nicocles, the king of the Salaminians. And yet, can any one of you be persuaded that Nicoles offered me these presents in order that he might learn how to plead cases in court – he who dispensed justice, like a master, to others in their disputes? So, from what my accuser has himself said, it is easy for you to conclude that I have nothing to do with litigation. Nay, everyone is aware of this also, that there is a superabundance of men who produce speeches for litigants in the courts. Nevertheless you will not find that any one of them, numerous as they are, has ever been thought worthy to have pupils, while I, as my accuser states, have had more than all the rest together who are occupied with philosophy. Yet how can anyone think that people who are so far apart in their ways of life are engaged in the same occupations?

But although I could point out many contrasts between my own career and that of the pleaders in the courts, I believe that the quickest way to disabuse your mind of this confusion would be to show that people do not study under me what my accuser says they do, and that I am not clever at the kind of oratory which has to do with private disputes. For I think, now that the charge under which I formerly laboured has been disproved, you are anxious to change your attitude and want to hear from me what sort of eloquence it is which has occupied me and given me so great a reputation.

Whether, indeed, it is going to profit me to speak the truth, I am not sure; for it is hard to conjecture what is in your thoughts. Yet, for all that, I am going to speak to you absolutely without reserve. For I should blush before my associates; if, after having told them again and again that I should be glad to have everyone of my fellow-citizens know the life I lead and the speeches which I compose, I did not now lay them open before you, but appeared rather to attempt to hide them away. Be assured, therefore, that you shall hear from me the whole truth, and in this spirit give me your attention.

First of all, then, you should know that there are no fewer branches of composition in prose than in verse. For some men have devoted their lives to researches in the genealogies of the demi-gods; others have made studies in the poets; others have elected to compose histories of wars; while still others have occupied themselves with dialogue, and are called dialecticians. It would, however, be no slight task to attempt to enumerate all the forms of prose, and I shall take up only that which is pertinent to me, and ignore the rest.

For there are men who, albeit they are not strangers to the branches which I have mentioned, have chosen rather to write discourses, not for private disputes, but which deal with the world of Hellas, with affairs of state, and are appropriate to be delivered at the Pan-Hellenic assemblies – discourses which, as everyone will agree, are more akin to works composed in rhythm and set to music than to the speeches which are made in court. For they set forth facts in a style more imaginative and more ornate; they employ thoughts which are more lofty and more original, and, besides, they use throughout figures of speech in greater number and of more striking character.

All men take as much pleasure in listening to this kind of prose as in listening to poetry, and many desire to take lessons in it, believing that those who excel in this field are wiser and better and of more use to the world than men who speak well in court. For they know that while the latter owe to a capacity for intrigue their expertness in forensic debate, the former have drawn from their pursuit of wisdom the eloquence which I have described; that while those who are thought to be adept in court procedure are tolerated only for the day when they are engaged in the trial, the devotees of philosophy are honoured and held in high esteem in every society and at all times; that, furthermore, while the former come to be despised and decried as soon as they are seen two or three times in court, the latter are admired more and more as they become better and more widely known; and, finally, that while clever pleaders are sadly unequal to the higher eloquence, the exponents of the latter could, if they so desired, easily master also the oratory of the courts. Reflecting on these facts, and considering it to be by far the better choice, they elect to have a part in that culture wherein, it would appear, neither have I myself been an alien but have, on the contrary, won a far more gracious reputation.

Now you have heard the whole truth about my power, my philosophy, my profession, or whatever you care to call it. However, I want to set up for myself a more difficult standard than for other people, and to make a proposition which may seem over-rash for my years. For I ask you not only to show me no mercy, if the oratory which I cultivate is harmful, but to inflict on me the extreme penalty if it is not superior to any other. But I should not have made so bold a proposal, if I were not about to show you what my eloquence is and to make it very easy for you to pass judgement upon it.

[...]

I suppose that you are not unaware of the fact that the government of the state is handed on by the older men to the youth of the coming generation; and that since the succession goes on without end, it follows of necessity that as is the education of our youth so from generation to generation will be the fortune of the state. Therefore, you must not let the sycophants have control of a thing so momentous, nor punish those who refuse to pay them money, while permitting those from whom they have received it to do whatever they please. But if philosophy has an influence which tends to corrupt our youth, you ought not merely to punish the occasional offender whom some sycophant hales into court but to banish all who are engaged in teaching it. If, however, it has the opposite effect and helps and improves and makes better men of its devotees, then you should call a halt on those who load this study with abuse; you should strip the sycophants of their rewards, and counsel our young men to occupy themselves with this pursuit above all others.

I would have given a good deal, assuming that I was doomed by fate to defend myself against this charge, if I could have faced this trial in the fullness of my vigour; for in that case I should have felt no misgiving but should have been better able both to protect myself from my accuser and to champion the cause of liberal education. Now, however, I am afraid that, although I have been enabled by this education to speak well enough on other themes, I may find that I have discoursed less ably upon this subject than upon matters which should have concerned me less. And yet I would rather lay down my life this day – for you shall have the truth even though the words be inept – after having spoken adequately upon this theme and persuaded you to look upon the study of eloquence in its true light, than live many times my allotted span and see it continue to fare among you as it now does.

My aspiration, then, is much greater than my power to do the subject justice; but yet I shall try as best I can to explain what is the nature of this education, what is its power, what of the other arts it is akin to, what benefit it is to its devotees, and what claims I make for it. For I think that when you know the truth about this you will be in a better position to deliberate and pronounce judgement upon it. But I beg of you, if I appear to carry on the discussion in a manner far removed from that which is customary here, not to be impatient but to bear with me, remembering that when a man is defending himself on a charge unlike any other, he must resort to a kind of pleading which is out of the ordinary. Be patient, therefore, with the manner of my discourse and with my frankness of speech; permit me to use up the time allotted to my defence; and then cast your ballots as each of you thinks is right and in accordance with the law.

In my treatment of the art of discourse, I desire, like the genealogists, to start at the beginning. It is acknowledged that the nature of man is compounded of two parts, the physical and the mental, and no one would deny that of these two the mind comes first and is of greater worth; for it is the function of the mind to decide both on personal and on public questions, and of the body to be servant to the judgements of the mind. Since this is so, certain of our ancestors, long before our time, seeing that many arts had been devised for other things, while none had been prescribed for the body and for the mind, invented and bequeathed to us two disciplines: physical training for the body, of which gymnastics is a part, and, for the mind, philosophy, which I am going to explain. These are twin arts – parallel and complementary – by which their masters prepare the mind to become more intelligent and the body to become more serviceable, not separating sharply the two kinds of education, but using similar methods of instruction, exercise, and other forms of discipline.

For when they take their pupils in hand, the physical trainers instruct their followers in the postures which have been devised for bodily contests, while the teachers of philosophy impart all the forms of discourse in which the mind expresses itself. Then, when they have made them familiar and thoroughly conversant with these lessons, they set them at exercises, habituate them to work, and require them to combine in practice the particular things which they have learned, in order that they may grasp them more firmly and bring their theories into closer touch with the occasions for applying them – I say "theories," for no system of knowledge can possibly cover these occasions, since in all cases they elude our science. Yet those who most apply their minds to them and are able to discern the consequences which for the most part grow out of them, will most often meet these occasions in the right way.

Watching over them and training them in this manner, both the teachers of gymnastic and the teachers of discourse are able to advance their pupils to a point where they are better men and where they are stronger in their thinking or in the use of their bodies. However, neither class of teachers is in possession of a science by which they can make capable athletes or capable orators out of whomsoever they please. They can contribute in some degree to these results, but these powers are never found in their perfection save in those who excel by virtue both of talent and of training.

I have given you now some impression of what philosophy is. But I think that you will get a still clearer idea of its powers if I tell you what professions I make to those who want to become my pupils. I say to them that if they are to excel in oratory or in managing affairs or in any line of work, they must, first of all, have a natural aptitude for that which they have elected to do; secondly, they must submit to training and master the knowledge of their particular subject, whatever it may be in each case; and, finally, they must become versed and practised in the use and application of their art; for only on these conditions can they become fully competent and pre-eminent in any line of endeavour. In this process, master and pupil each has his place; no one but the pupil can furnish the necessary capacity; no one but the master, the ability to impart knowledge; while both have a part in the exercises of practical application: for the master must painstakingly direct his pupil, and the latter must rigidly follow the master's instructions.

Now these observations apply to any and all the arts. If anyone, ignoring the other arts, were to ask me which of these factors has the greatest power in the education of an orator I should answer that natural ability is paramount and comes before all else. For given a man with a mind which is capable of finding out and learning the truth and of working hard and remembering what it learns, and also with a voice and a clarity of utterance which are able to captivate the audience, not only by what he says, but by the music of his words, and, finally, with an assurance which is not an expression of bravado, but which, tempered by sobriety, so fortifies the spirit that he is no less at ease in addressing all his fellow-citizens than in reflecting to himself – who does not know that such a man might, without the advantage of an elaborate education and with only a superficial and common training, be an orator such as has never, perhaps, been seen among the Hellenes? Again, we know that men

who are less generously endowed by nature but excel in experience and practice, not only improve upon themselves, but surpass others who, though highly gifted, have been too negligent of their talents. It follows, therefore, that either one of these factors may produce an able speaker or an able man of affairs, but both of them combined in the same person might produce a man incomparable among his fellows.

These, then, are my views as to the relative importance of native ability and practice. I cannot, however, make a like claim for education; its powers are not equal nor comparable to theirs. For if one should take lessons in all the principles of oratory and master them with the greatest thoroughness, he might, perhaps, become a more pleasing speaker than most, but let him stand up before the crowd and lack one thing only, namely, assurance, and he would not be able to utter a word.

But let no one of you think that before you I belittle my pretensions, while when I address those who desire to become my pupils I claim every power for my teaching; for it was to avoid just such a charge as this that, when I entered upon my profession, I wrote and published a discourse in which you will find that I attack those who make pretensions which are unwarranted, and set forth my own ideas. Now I am not going to quote from it my criticisms of others; for they are too long for the present occasion; but I shall attempt to repeat to you that part in which I express my own views. I begin at this point.

[...]

I do not, however, delude myself as to the people who are ill disposed towards my teaching: nothing of what I have said so far is enough to disabuse them of this feeling; and it will take many arguments of all sorts to convert them to a different opinion from that which they now hold. Accordingly I must not leave off expounding and speaking until I shall accomplish one of two things – until I have persuaded them to change their views or have proved that the slanders and charges which they repeat against me are false.

These charges are of two kinds. Some of them say that the profession of the sophist is nothing but sham and chicane, maintaining that no kind of education has ever been discovered which can improve a man's ability to speak or his capacity for handling affairs, and that those who excel in these respects owe their superiority to natural gifts; while others acknowledge that men who take this training are more able, but complain that they are corrupted and demoralized by it, alleging that when they gain the power to do so, they scheme to get other people's property.

Now there is not a sound or true word in either complaint, as I am very confident that I can prove to everyone. First of all I would have you note, in the case of those who assert that education is a sham, that they quite obviously talk rubbish themselves; for while they ridicule it as powerless to help us – nothing but humbug and chicane – at the same time they demand that my pupils show improvement from the moment they come to me; that when they have been with me a few days, they must be abler and wiser in speech than those who have the advantage over them both in years and in experience; and that when they have been with me no more than a year, they must all be good and finished orators; nor must the indolent be a whit less accomplished than the industrious, nor they who are lacking in ability than those who are blessed with vigorous minds. These are the requirements they set up, and yet they have never heard me make such promises, nor have they ever seen like results in the other arts and disciplines. On the contrary, all knowledge yields itself up to us only after great effort on our part, and we are by no means all equally capable of working out in practice what we learn. Nay, from all our schools only two or three students turn out to be real champions, the rest retiring from their studies into private life.

And yet how can we fail to deny intelligence to those who have the effrontery to demand powers which are not found in the recognized arts of this which they declare is not an art and who expect greater advantages to come from an art in which they do not believe than from arts which they regard as thoroughly perfected? Men of intelligence ought not to form contrary judgements about similar things nor refuse to recognize a discipline which accomplishes the same results as most of the arts. For who among you does not know that most of those who have sat under the sophists have not been duped nor affected as these men claim, but that some of them have been turned out competent champions and others able teachers; while those who have preferred to live in private have become more gracious in their social intercourse than before, and keener judges of discourses and more prudent counsellors than most? How then is it possible to scorn a discipline which is able to make of those who have taken advantage of it men of that kind?

Furthermore, this also will be agreed to by all men, namely, that in all the arts and crafts we regard those as the most skilled who turn out pupils who all work as far as possible in the same manner. Now it will be seen that this is the case with philosophy. For all who have been under a true and intelligent guide will be found to have a power of speech so similar that it is evident to everyone that they have shared the same training. And yet, had not a common habit and a common technique of training been instilled into them, it is inconceivable that they should have taken on this likeness.

Again, every one of you could name many of your schoolfellows who when they were boys seemed to be the dullest among their companions, but who, growing older, outstripped them farther in intelligence and in speech than they had lagged behind them when they were boys. From this fact you can best judge what training can do; for it is evident that when they were young they all possessed such mental powers as they were born with, but as they grew to be men, these outstripped the others and changed places with them in intelligence, because their companions lived dissolutely and softly, while they gave heed to their own opportunities and to their own welfare. But when people succeed in making progress through their own diligence alone, how can they fail to improve in a much greater degree both over themselves and over others if they put themselves under a master who is mature, of great experience, and learned not only in what has been handed down to him but in what he has discovered for himself?

But there remain still other reasons why everyone may well be astonished at the ignorance in men who venture so blindly to condemn philosophy. For, in the first place, they know that pains and industry give proficiency in all other activities and arts, yet deny that they have any such power in the training of the intellect; secondly, they admit that no physical weakness is so hopeless that it cannot be improved by exercise and effort, but they do not believe that our minds, which are naturally superior to our bodies, can be made more serviceable through education and suitable training; again, they observe that some people possess the art of training horses and dogs and most other animals by which they make them more spirited, gentle or intelligent, as the case may be, yet they do not think that any education has been discovered for training human nature, such as can improve men in any of those respects in which we improve the beasts. Nay, so great is the misfortune which they impute to us all, that while they would acknowledge that it is by our mental powers that every creature is improved and made more useful, yet they have the hardihood to claim that we ourselves, who are endowed with an intelligence through which we render all creatures of greater worth, cannot help each other to advance in excellence. But most absurd of all, they behold in the shows which are held year after year lions which are more gentle toward their trainers than some people are toward their benefactors, and bears which dance about and wrestle and imitate our skill, and yet they are not able to judge even from these instances the power which education and training have, nor can they see that human nature will respond more promptly than the animals to the benefits of education. In truth, I cannot make up my mind which should astonish us the more – the gentleness which is implanted in the fiercest of wild beasts or the brutishness which resides in the souls of such men.

One might say more upon this head, but if I say too much on questions about which most men are agreed, I fear you may suspect that I have little to say on questions which are in dispute. Therefore I shall leave this subject and turn my attention to a class of people who do not, to be sure, contemn philosophy but condemn it much more bitterly since they attribute the iniquities of those who profess to be sophists, but in practice are far different, to those whose ways have nothing in common with them. But I am speaking, not in behalf of all those who pretend to be able to educate the young, but in behalf of those only who have justly earned this reputation, and I think that I shall convince you that my accusers have shot very wide of the truth if only you are willing to hear me to the end.

In the first place, then, we must determine what are the objects which make people venture to do evil; for if we define these correctly, you will be better able to make up your minds whether the charges which have been made against us are true of false. Well then, I maintain that everyone does everything which he does for the sake of pleasure or gain or honour; for I observe that no desire springs up in men save for these objects. If this be so, it only remains to consider which of these objects we should attain by corrupting the young.

[…]

Perhaps, however, some might venture to reply that many men, because of their incontinence, are not amenable to reason, but neglect their true interests and rush on in the pursuit of pleasure. I grant you that many men in general and some who pretend to be sophists are of this nature. Nevertheless, no one even of their number is so incontinent as to desire his pupils also to show the same lack of control; for he would not be able to share in the pleasures which they might enjoy as the result of their incontinence, while he would bring down upon his own head most of the evil repute which would result from their depravity.

Again, whom would they corrupt and what manner of people would they get as pupils? For this is worth inquiring into. Would they get those who are already perverse and vicious? And who, pray, would make an effort to learn from another what his own nature teaches him? Would they, then, get those who are honest and ambitious to lead a useful life? But no such person would deign to speak with men who are evil in their words and in their deeds.

I should like to ask those who disapprove of me what they think about the students who cross the sea from Sicily, from the Pontus, and from other parts of the world in order to enjoy my instruction. Do they think that they voyage to Athens because of the dearth of evil-minded men at home? But anywhere on earth anyone can find no lack of men willing to aid him in depravity and crime. Do they think, then, that they come here in order to become intriguers and sycophants, at great expense to themselves? But, in the first place, people of this mind are much more inclined to lay hold of other people's property than to part with anything of their own; and, in the next place, who would pay out money to learn depravity, since it is easy to be depraved at no expense whatever, whenever one is so inclined? For there is no need of taking lessons in evil-doing; all that a man has to do is to set his hands to it.

No, it is evident that these students cross the sea and pay out money and go to all manner of trouble because they think that they themselves will be the better for it and that the teachers here are much more intelligent than those in their own countries. This ought to fill all Athenians with pride and make them appreciate at their worth those who have given to the city this reputation.

But, in fact, some of our people are extremely unreasonable. They know that neither the strangers who come here nor the men who preside over their education occupy themselves with anything harmful, but that they are, on the contrary, the most unofficious and the most peaceable of all who live in Athens, giving their minds to their own affairs and confining their intercourse to each other, and living, furthermore, day by day in the greatest simplicity and decorum, taking their pleasures in discourse – not the kind of discourse which is employed in petty litigation nor that which is offensive to anyone, but the kind which has the approbation of all men. Nevertheless, although they know all this about them, they do not refrain from traducing them and saying that they engage in this training in order that they may defeat the ends of justice in the courts and win their own advantage. And yet who that engages in the practice of injustice and of evil-doing would be willing to live more continently than the rest? Whom have these traducers ever seen reserving and treasuring up their depravities for future use instead of indulging from the first the evil instincts present in their nature?

But, apart from these considerations, if it be true that cleverness in speech results in plotting against other people's property, we should expect all able speakers to be intriguers and sycophants; for the same cause produces in every instance the same effect. In fact, however, you will find that among our public men who are living to-day or who have but lately passed away those who give most study to the art of words are the best of the statesmen who come before you on the rostrum, and, furthermore, that among the ancients it was the greatest and the most illustrious orators who brought to the city most of her blessings.

[...]

For I believe that the teachers who are skilled in disputation and those who are occupied with astronomy and geometry and studies of that sort do not injure but, on the contrary, benefit their pupils, not so much as they profess, but more than others give them credit for. Most men see in such studies nothing but empty talk and hair-splitting ; for none of these disciplines has any useful application either to private or to public affairs; nay, they are not even remembered for any length of time after they are learned because they do not attend us through life nor do they lend aid in what we do, but are wholly divorced from our necessities. But I am neither of this opinion nor am I far removed from it; rather it seems to me both that those who hold that this training is of no use in practical life are right and that those who speak in praise of it have truth on their side. If there is a contradiction in this statement, it is because these disciplines are different in their nature from the other studies which make up our education; for the other branches avail us only after we have gained a knowledge of them, whereas these studies can be of no benefit to us after we have mastered them unless we have elected to make our living from this source, and only help us while we are in the process of learning. For while we are occupied with the subtlety and exactness of astronomy and geometry and are forced to apply our minds to difficult problems, and are, in addition, being habituated to speak and apply ourselves to what is said and shown to us, and not to let our wits go wool-gathering, we gain the power, after being exercised and sharpened on these disciplines, of grasping and learning more easily and more quickly those subjects which are of more importance and of greater value. I do not, however, think it proper to apply the term "philosophy" to a training which is no help to us in the present either in our speech or in our actions, but rather I would call it a gymnastic of the mind and a preparation for philosophy. It is, to be sure, a study more advanced than that which boys in school pursue, but it is for the most part the same sort of thing; for they also when they have laboured through their lessons in grammar, music, and the other branches, are not a whit advanced in their ability to speak and deliberate on affairs, but they have increased their aptitude for mastering greater and more serious studies. I would, therefore, advise young men to spend some time on these disciplines, but not to allow their minds to be dried up by these barren subtleties, nor to be stranded on the speculations of the ancient sophists, who maintain, some of them, that the sum of things is made up of infinite elements; Empedocles that it is made up of four, with strife and love operating among them; Ion, of not more than three; Alcmaeon, of only two; Parmenides and Melissus, of one; and Gorgias, of none at all. For I think that such curiosities of thought are on a par with jugglers' tricks which, though they do not profit anyone, yet attract great crowds of the empty-minded, and I hold that men who want to do some good in the world must banish utterly from their interests all vain speculations and all activities which have no bearing on our lives.

Now I have spoken and advised you enough on these studies for the present. It remains to tell you about "wisdom" and "philosophy." It is true that if one were pleading a case on any other issue it would be out of place to discuss these words (for they are foreign to all litigation), but it is appropriate for me, since I am being tried on such an issue, and since I hold that what some people call philosophy is not entitled to that name, to define and explain to you what philosophy, properly conceived, really is. My view of this question is, as it happens, very simple. For since it is not in the nature of man to attain a science by the possession of which we can know positively what we should do or what we should say, in the next resort I hold that man to be wise who is able by his powers of conjecture to arrive generally at the best course, and I hold that man to be a philosopher who occupies himself with the studies from which he will most quickly gain that kind of insight.

What the studies are which have this power I can tell you, although I hesitate to do so; they are so contrary to popular belief and so very far removed from the opinions of the rest of the world, that I am afraid lest when you first hear them you will fill the whole court-room with your murmurs and your cries. Nevertheless, in spite of my misgivings, I shall attempt to tell you about them; for I blush at the thought that anyone might suspect me of betraying the truth to save my old age and the little of life remaining to me. But, I beg of you, do not, before you have heard me, judge that I could have been so mad as to choose deliberately, when my fate is in your hands, to express to you ideas which are repugnant to your opinions if I had not believed that these ideas follow logically on what I have previously said, and that I could support them with true and convincing proofs.

I consider that the kind of art which can implant honesty and justice in depraved natures has never existed and does not now exist, and that people who profess that power will grow weary and cease from their vain pretensions before such an education is ever found. But I do hold that people can become better and worthier if they conceive an ambition to speak well, if they become possessed of the desire to be able to persuade their hearers, and, finally, if they set their hearts on seizing their advantage – I do not mean "advantage" in the sense given to that word by the empty-minded, but advantage in the true meaning of that term; and that this is so I think I shall presently make clear.

For, in the first place, when anyone elects to speak or write discourses which are worthy of praise and honour, it is not conceivable that he will support causes which are unjust or petty or devoted to private quarrels, and not rather those which are great and honourable, devoted to the welfare of man and our common good; for if he fails to find causes of this character, he will accomplish nothing to the purpose. In the second place, he will select from all the actions of men which bear upon his subject those examples which are the most illustrious and the most edifying; and, habituating himself to contemplate and appraise such examples, he will feel their influence not only in the preparation of a given discourse but in all the actions of his life. It follows, then, that the power to speak well and think right will reward the man who approaches the art of discourse with love of wisdom and love of honour.

Furthermore, mark you, the man who wishes to persuade people will not be negligent as to the matter of character; no, on the contrary, he will apply himself above all to establish a most honourable name among his fellow-citizens; for who does not know that words carry greater conviction when spoken by men of good repute than when spoken by men who live under a cloud, and that the argument which is made by a man's life is of more weight than that which is furnished by words? Therefore, the stronger a man's desire to persuade his hearers, the more zealously will he strive to be honourable and to have the esteem of his fellow-citizens.

And let no one of you suppose that while all other people realize how much the scales of persuasion incline in favour of one who has the approval of his judges, the devotees of philosophy alone are blind to the power of good will. In fact, they appreciate this even more thoroughly than others, and they know, furthermore, that probabilities and proofs and all forms of persuasion support only the points in a case to which they are severally applied, whereas an honourable reputation not only lends greater persuasiveness to the words of the man who possesses it, but adds greater lustre to his deeds, and is, therefore, more zealously to be sought after by men of intelligence than anything else in the world.

I come now to the question of "advantage" – the most difficult of the points I have raised. If any one is under the impression that people who rob others or falsify accounts or do any evil thing get the advantage, he is wrong in his thinking; for none are at a greater disadvantage throughout their lives than such men; none are found in more difficult straits, none live in greater ignominy; and, in a word, none are more miserable than they. No, you ought to believe rather that those are better off now and will receive the advantage in the future at the hands of the gods who are the most righteous and the most faithful in their devotions, and that those receive the better portion at the hands of men who are the most conscientious in their dealings with their associates, whether in their homes or in public life, and are themselves esteemed as the noblest among their fellows.

This is verily the truth, and it is well for us to adopt this way of speaking on the subject, since, as things now are, Athens has in many respects been plunged into such a state of topsy-turvy and confusion that some of our people no longer use words in their proper meaning but wrest them from the most honourable associations and apply them to the basest pursuits.

[...]

I observe that when others who are placed in jeopardy here come to the end of their defence, they supplicate, they implore, they bring their children and their friends before the jury. I, however, consider that such expedients are unbecoming to one of my age; and, apart from this feeling, I should be ashamed to owe my life to any other plea than to the words which you have just heard. For I know that I have spoken with so just and clear a conscience both towards the city and our ancestors, and above all towards the gods, that if it be true that the gods concern themselves at all with human affairs I am sure that they are not indifferent to my present situation. Wherefore, I have no fear of what may come to me at your hands; nay, I am of good courage and have every confidence that when I close my life it will be when it is best for me; for I take it as a good sign that all my past life up to this day has been such as is the due of righteous and godfearing men.

Being assured, therefore, that I am of this mind, and that I believe that whatever you decide will be for my good and to my advantage, let each one cast his vote as he pleases and is inclined.

Study Questions

1 Throughout the Classical Period, the question of natural talent appeared repeatedly in discussions of teaching. We find it not only in Isocrates but also in Aristotle, Cicero, and Quintilian. Why do you think natural talent was such an important consideration during this period? Why do you think that today we find discussions of natural talent in sports but not education?

2 Isocrates raised several complaints in *Against the Sophists*. Which do you believe is the most significant?

3 In *Against the Sophists*, Isocrates argued that the knowledge that teachers of rhetoric conveyed could not be very valuable because they charged low fees. Is the argument legitimate? What might be some factors that influenced what Sophists charged? Teachers today receive very little monetary compensation. Does that mean that what they teach has little value?

4 *Antidosis* is often viewed as Isocrates' defense of his life and career, and he himself indicated that its aim was to rebut the calumnies uttered against him in court. But it also has been seen as an autobiographical encomium. Is the second characterization justified? Overall, how effective do you believe *Antidosis* is in repairing any damage to his reputation that Isocrates may have experienced?

5 How would you describe the curriculum at Isocrates' school?

Writing Topics

1 Isocrates stated in *Antidosis* that he had adopted the fiction of a trial so as to rebut statements made about him during litigation several years previously. Examine an actual trial speech, such as Lyias' *Against Ctesiphon* or Antiphon's *Against the Stepmother*, describe the key elements of such a speech, and then analyze *Antidosis* to determine whether it meets the standard.
2 Research Isocrates' approach to education and examine its influence throughout the Classical Period.
3 It has been argued that we live in a postmodern age that places little value on education or effective communication and no value at all on the concept of *kalos kagathos*, a virtuous person who speaks well. Examine the grounds for this view and argue for or against it.

Further Reading

Isocrates, *Aeropagiticus*.
Isocrates, *Panegyricus*.
Isocrates, *Against the Stepmother*.
Perelman, C., and Olbrechts-Tyteca, L. (1969). *The new rhetoric: A treatise on argumentation*. Notre Dame, IN: University of Notre Dame Press.

Introduction to Demosthenes (c. 384–322 BC)

Demosthenes has long been identified as one of the more influential orators in history (see Gibson, 2002). Until the modern era, only Cicero was more widely known and studied by students of oratory. He began his career, like Isocrates, as a *logographos* but eventually entered politics, writing a number of political speeches (rather than treatises) that took the practice of deliberative rhetoric in ancient Greece to its zenith. He is included in this chapter not because he was a Sophist but because he can be viewed as the finished product of the ideal Sophistic education (particularly as advocated by Isocrates) and because with him the time of the Sophists and the Classical Period of Greece essentially came to an end, giving way to the Hellenistic Period initiated by Alexander the Great. Understanding Demosthenes, as well as the end of the Classical Period, entails at least a nodding familiarity with the complex, tumultuous events that characterized his life and the course of history that he tried to shape.

He seemed destined for conflict from the beginning. The laws of Draco defined the family as a household (*oikos*) headed by a male and consisting of all persons living in the household, as well as its assets. Greek law did not recognize the autonomy of women, and it was not until Pericles' legal reforms that women were granted limited citizenship rights. Yet even with these rights, they remained under the legal authority of males. Until a woman married, for example, she was under the guardianship of her father. After marriage, she was under the protection (or control) of her husband. In the event of divorce (which was fairly easy to obtain in ancient Athens but nevertheless uncommon), the woman returned to her father's guardianship. In the event of the father's death, his property passed to the daughter, provided there were no male heirs, and she became an *epicleros,* or female property owner. This status was temporary, however, for the law required the father's closest male relative to marry the daughter and to assume control over the household.

A similar situation obtained when a wife became a widow. If she had a son who was of age, all the property passed to the son, not to the wife, and he became her guardian. If she did not have a son, or if the son had not reached his majority, the law required – as in the case of the *epicleros* – the deceased husband's closest male relative to marry the widow and become the head of the *oikos*.

The laws governing women and property had a significant effect on Demosthenes' life and career. He lost his father at age six or seven, and because he was a minor, both he and his mother were subject to the laws governing the *oikos*. The father's will specified Aphobus, a paternal nephew, as the closest male relative who was to marry Demosthenes' mother, but it also identified a maternal nephew, Demophon, and a friend from childhood, Therippides, as co-guardians. According to Demosthenes, this arrangement was designed to ensure the provident management of the inheritance.

After finishing grammar school, he began studying rhetoric, perhaps with deliberate intent, for by the time Demosthenes reached his majority, not only had Aphobus failed to marry his mother in keeping with the law and the father's will, but he and the other guardians had squandered the estate to such a degree that there was little left. Demosthenes studied under Isaeus, who specialized in forensic rhetoric, and he also may have studied with Isocrates. At age 18, according to Plutarch (1959), Demosthenes had the guardians arrested. He then took a courageous step: Drawing on his training in rhetoric, he sued them for reimbursement of his inheritance plus interest.[11] Having learned Isaeus' lessons in forensic rhetoric well, he won the suit, but the debtors refused to pay, and Demosthenes subsequently had to appear in court again before he collected any funds, which turned out to be only a small portion of the original inheritance.[12]

Demosthenes became quite well known after these trials, which enabled him to launch his career as a *logographos*. He wrote speeches for a number of high-profile cases, and according to Usher (1999), he was so successful that just four years after his victory over Aphobus he was able to support a trireme. With money and visibility, Demosthenes was well positioned to enter the political arena.

We have no records that shed light on his growing interest in politics, but it seems probable that current events and the quest for *aretê* were powerful stimulants. Within just a few decades of losing all of its territories at the end of the Peloponnesian War, Athens had reestablished its empire only to repeat the mistakes of greed, arrogance, and oppression that had preceded the conflict with Sparta and her allies. In 357 BC, Chios, Rhodes, and Cos revolted, plunging the region into what is known as the Social War. Athens was ill-prepared, for the city had not recovered from the losses suffered during the conflict with Sparta and lacked sufficient resources for extended military operations.

Philip, King of Macedonia, recognized Athens' weakness and used it to his advantage. He captured the former Athenian colony of Amphipolis in 357 BC, which gave him control of the gold and silver mines there, as well as control of the nearby forest. He then contacted Athens and offered to exchange Amphipolis for the Athenian port of Pydna. Desperate for gold to pay its soldiers and for timber to build its ships, Athens agreed, only to have Philip renege on the exchange at this sign of weakness and proceed to capture the cities of Potidaea and Crenides.

---

[11] According to legend, Demosthenes was not only frail and sickly but also suffered from a speech impediment. If true, his decision to sue the guardians could not have been made easily. According to the legend, he committed himself to rhetoric by exercising to build his strength; to improve his speaking ability, he isolated himself in a cave and practiced oratory with pebbles in his mouth. He thereby overcame the impediment and developed an unsurpassed clarity of speech.

[12] We have the related speeches from the trials in *Against Aphobus*, 1, 2, and 3.

Meanwhile, the Social War was going badly for Athens. A fleet led by General Chabrias was defeated off the coast of Chios, and he was killed. General Chares, in command of a second fleet, was defeated in the Battle of Embata and lost a significant number of ships. Needing money to pay his troops and to repair what ships remained in the fleet, Chares allied himself with the Persian satrap Atrabazus, who seems to have offered financial assistance only as a means of gaining intelligence on Athenian strength, for in 356 BC he demanded that Athens abandon Ionia and threatened war if the city did not comply. Faced with Philip to the north, Persians to the east, and military disasters throughout the Aegean, Athens had little choice but to withdraw from Asia Minor and to cobble together a hasty peace treaty with the rebelling cities that granted them independence in 355 BC. It was at this time that Isocrates wrote and distributed *On the Peace*, which argued against empire and imperialism and urged Athenians to lead by example rather than by force.

Demosthenes was about 30 years old during this turbulent period, and it is likely that he read *On the Peace*. Thus, when in the following year the Greek withdrawal from Ionia did not even reduce, much less end, the threats of war coming from Atrabazus, he may have been influenced by the tone of Isocrates' treatise. More foolhardy than wise, and unable to recognize the weakness of the city, many Athenians were clamoring for yet another war, this time against Persia. Demosthenes responded by delivering his first political speech, *On the Navy*, which echoes Isocrates' in its call for a united Greek front against a common enemy.[13] This speech also displays a sagacity and restraint that were not common in the assembly in those days, as when he stated:

> To your rash advisers, who are so eager to hurry you into war, I have this to say, that it is not difficult, when deliberation is needed, to gain a reputation for courage, nor when danger is at hand, to display skill in oratory; but there is something that is both difficult and essential – to display courage in the face of danger, and in deliberation to offer sounder advice than one's fellows. I believe, men of Athens, that the war with the King [of the Persian Empire] is a difficult undertaking for our city. ... [T]he first requisites for every war are necessarily ... fleets and money and strong positions, and I find that the King is more fully supplied with these than we are. (Demosthenes, 2004, p. 387)

This speech not only turned the tide against the hawks and avoided a war that would have been disastrous for Athens but also launched Demosthenes' political career and led eventually to his reputation as the most accomplished orator in Greek history.

It soon became apparent to Demosthenes, however, that the real threat to Greece was not the barbarians of Asia Minor but Philip of Macedonia. In a series of speeches called *The Philippics*, the first of which he delivered to the assembly in 351 BC, Demosthenes sought to rally Athens and the rest of Greece to stop Philip's growing power. He called for the formation of a "Hellenic League" that would have the strength to defeat the Macedonian forces. Even though by this time Demosthenes was recognized as the preeminent orator in Athens, not everyone agreed with his political assessment. Aeschines, another member of the assembly whose rhetorical skills were only slightly less than Demosthenes', argued that not even a unified Greece could withstand Philip, and he urged accommodation. Theirs became a bitter rivalry that resulted in two trials: Aeschines' *Against Ctesiphon* and Demosthenes' *On the Crown*, an excerpt of which is included here.

In retrospect, we can see that Aeschines was right and Demosthenes was wrong in thinking that Athens or Greece could resist Philip. With the exception of Sparta, whose

[13] How much – or even whether – Isocrates influenced Demosthenes is a matter of debate. Kennedy (1963), for example, stated with much conviction that the two had nothing in common. My assessment, however, is that Kennedy is correct with respect to rhetorical style but incorrect with respect to rhetorical purpose.

strength also had been seriously depleted by the Peloponnesian War, all Greek cities depended on citizen soldiers. Their successes in the past were legendary, but in Philip they faced innovations in weapons and tactics for which they were unprepared. Moreover, Philip had built a professional, rather than a citizen, army that was stronger, better equipped, and better trained than even the Spartan forces. He also had the distinct advantage of being a brilliant strategist and tactician. Athens had no chance of prevailing. Nevertheless, at the urging of Demosthenes, Athens sent its army to confront Philip at Chaeronea in 336 BC. The victory for Philip, thanks in part to the efforts of his son, Alexander, was decisive.[14]

When Philip was assassinated later that year, Demosthenes and other Athenians were jubilant, anticipating that they would no longer be threatened by the Macedonians. They had no way of knowing that whereas Philip had been a brilliant military commander, Alexander was a genius. Nor could they know that Alexander's ambitions exceeded his father's. Athens, Greece, and the entire Persian Empire were soon conquered and under Alexander's control. Alexander, however, contracted a fever while in Babylon and died in 323 BC, at age 32. Demosthenes immediately began urging his fellow Athenians and other Greeks to rise up against Antipater, who had served as the Greek viceroy during Alexander's campaign in Asia Minor. Ignoring the outcome of following Demosthenes' earlier advice, which had led to the disastrous defeat at Chaeronea, the Athenians rallied again. The result was the Lamian War (323–322 BC), which Antipater won decisively after initial setbacks. Utterly exhausted by nearly a hundred years of warfare (the Peloponnesian War began in 431 BC), its resources depleted beyond repair, Athens capitulated, bringing to a close Greek democracy and introducing a long period of military dictatorships. Never again would Athens enjoy the political, economic, or military influence it had wielded in the past.

After winning the Lamian War, Antipater demanded the arrest and execution of Demosthenes, but the orator fled Athens and sought safety on the island of Calauria. Soon discovered by Antipater's agents, Demosthenes committed suicide with poison rather than allow himself to be captured. A patriot to the end, he died in keeping with sentiments he had expressed years earlier, at his defense against Aeschines in *On the Crown*:

The man who deems himself born only to his parents will wait for his natural and destined end; the son of his country is willing to die rather than see her enslaved, and will look upon those outrages and indignities, which a commonwealth in subjection is compelled to endure, as more dreadful than death itself. (§210)

On the Treaty with Alexander

Demosthenes had made it abundantly clear to anyone who would listen that he believed Philip of Macedonia was a threat to Athens and all of Greece. He repeated this message so often that many Athenians soon grew weary of hearing him demonize Philip, who initially was dismissed as a rustic from the boondocks who did not pose a serious threat. Even when, in 349 BC, Philip moved against Olynthus, a city allied with Athens, the citizens failed to mobilize adequately. Demosthenes gave a quick set of three speeches called the *Olynthiacs* in which he urged Athenians to go to the aid of Olynthus, but the city sent troops to Euboea, instead, leaving Olynthus to stand alone. Philip destroyed

[14] According to Plutarch (1959), Demosthenes was determined to participate in the battle and donned the armor and weapons of a hoplite, or foot soldier. However, as soon as the battle started, he reportedly dropped his weapons, stripped off his armor, and fled the field.

the city. Seriously alarmed by the swiftness of this conquest, the Athenian assembly was eager to avoid a similar fate, so when King Philip communicated that he was willing to sign a treaty with Athens, the city leaders accepted. The orator Philocrates proposed that the assembly appoint a group of envoys to negotiate the treaty, and the members agreed, appointing Philocrates, Demosthenes, and Aeschines as the principals.

Demosthenes was perhaps a logical choice because his speaking ability and hostility toward Philip no doubt were viewed as being assets that would ensure favorable terms for Athens in the peace negotiations. Aeschines, Demosthenes' enemy, also a forceful rhetorician and a leader who had from the very beginning advocated accommodation in the hope of preserving Athenian independence, may have been chosen as a check on Demosthenes. Philocrates probably was selected simply because he had made the proposal. In any event, matters did not go well. According to Aeschines, Philip so intimidated Demosthenes that he could not speak and fell into a swoon, effectively squelching the prospect of negotiations even if Philip had been inclined to negotiate, which he was not. He understood the dynamics of power and clearly recognized that he could dictate terms. And the terms he put on the table were harsh, leaving Athens at a serious disadvantage. Athens' situation was made worse when Philocrates proved to be a quisling. Probably in response to a Macedonian bribe, he immediately accepted the terms, dismissing the objections of Demosthenes and Aeschines. As far as Philip was concerned, Philocrates' acceptance concluded the treaty, which became known as the Peace of Philocrates, and he left to initiate another campaign.

Not surprisingly, Demosthenes began distancing himself from the treaty almost at once. He was certain that Philip had no intention of adhering to its terms, and subsequent events proved him right. A provision of the treaty specified that it would pass to Philip's successor, and after the assassination, Alexander displayed even more willingness to violate its terms. Demosthenes soon realized that he had been entirely mistaken in thinking that Philip's assassination meant the end of the Macedonian threat. Alexander had taken up his father's crown and was pursuing the conquest of Greece more aggressively than anyone had imagined possible. In the oration *On the Treaty with Alexander*, Demosthenes recited for the audience the numerous infractions of the peace treaty they had already witnessed and reminded them of their honor and past glory. He then called for a declaration of war against Alexander. This speech is a prime example of deliberative rhetoric as practiced in the Athenian assembly.

Reading 24

On the Treaty with Alexander

On the Treaty with Alexander, pp. 465–83 (Greek omitted on even-numbered pages) reprinted by permission of the publishers and Trustees of the Loeb Classical Library from *Demosthenes*, Volume I, Loeb Classical Library Volume 238, translated by J.H. Vince (Cambridge, MA: Harvard University Press, 1930). © 1930 by the President and Fellows of Harvard College. The Loeb Classical Library® is a registered trademark of the President and Fellows of Harvard College.

Our hearty assent, men of Athens, is due to those who insist that we should abide by our oaths and covenants, provided that they do so from conviction; for I believe that nothing becomes a demo-cratic people more than zeal for equity and justice. Those, therefore, who are so emphatic in urging you to this course should not keep weary-ing you with speeches which are belied by their practice, but after submitting *now* to full inquiry, should either for the future be sure of your assent in these matters, or else make way for the counsels of those who show a truer conception of what is just, so that you may either voluntarily submit to wrong, making the wrongdoer a free gift of your submission, or having definitely resolved to put justice before all other claims, may pursue your own interests, clear from all reproach, without further hesitation. But from the very terms of the compact and from the oaths which ratified the general peace, you may at once see who are its transgressors; and that those transgressions are serious, I will prove to you concisely.

Now if you were asked, men of Athens, what form of compulsion would most rouse your indignation, I think that if the sons of Pisistratus had been alive at the present time and someone tried to compel you to restore them, you would snatch up your weapons and brave any danger rather than receive them back, or if you did consent, you would be slaves, as surely as if you had been bought for money; nay, more so, inasmuch as no one would intentionally kill his own servant, but the victims of tyranny may be seen executed without trial, as well as outraged in the persons of their wives and children. Therefore when Alexander, contrary to the oaths and the compacts as set forth in the general peace, restored those tyrants, the sons of Philiades, to Messene, had he any regard for justice? Did he not rather give play to his own tyrannical disposition, showing little regard for you and the joint agreement? It is surely wrong that you should be highly indignant when you are the victims of such coercion, but should neglect all safeguards if it is employed somewhere else, contrary to the sworn agreement with you, and that we here at Athens should be urged by certain speakers to abide by the oaths, while they grant this liberty of action to the men who have so notoriously made those oaths of no effect. But this can never happen, if you are willing to see justice done; for it is further stipulated in the compact that anyone who acts as Alexander has acted shall be the enemy of all the other parties to the compact, and his country shall be hostile territory, and all the parties shall unite in a campaign against him. So if we carry out the agreement, we shall treat the restorer of the tyrants as an enemy.

But these champions of tyranny might urge that the sons of Philiades were tyrants of Messene before the compact was made, and that that was why Alexander restored them. But it is a ridiculous principle to expel the Lesbian tyrants on the ground that their rule is an outrage – I mean the tyrants of Antissa and Eresus, who established themselves before the agreement – and yet to imagine that it is a matter of indifference at Messene, where the same harsh system prevails.

Again, the compact at the very beginning enjoins that the Greeks shall be free and independent. Is it not, then, the height of absurdity that the clause about freedom should stand first in the compact, and that one who has enslaved others should be supposed not to have acted contrary to the joint agreement? Therefore, men of Athens, if we are going to abide by our oaths and covenants and do what is just (for it is to this that these speakers, as I have said, are urging you), it is our bounden duty to seize our arms and take the field against the transgressors with all who will join us. Or do you think that opportunity sometimes so prevails that men pursue expediency even apart from justice – and yet now, when justice and opportunity and expediency all concur, will you actually wait for some other season to claim your liberties and the liberties of all the Greeks?

I come to another claim sanctioned by the compact. For the actual words are, "If any of the parties shall overthrow the constitution established in the several states at the date when they took the oaths to observe the peace, they shall be treated as enemies by all the parties to the peace." But just reflect, men of Athens, that the Achaeans in the Peloponnese enjoyed democratic government, and one of their democracies, that of Pellene, has now been overthrown by the Macedonian king, who has expelled the majority of the citizens, given their property to their slaves, and set up Chaeron, the wrestler, as their tyrant. But we ourselves are parties to the peace, which instructs us to treat as enemies those who are guilty of such acts. Now in view of this, are we to obey these joint instructions and treat them as enemies, or will anyone be blackguard enough to say no – one of the hirelings in the pay of the Macedonian king, one of those who have grown rich at your expense? For you may be sure they are not ignorant of these facts; but they have grown so insolent, with the tyrant's troops for their bodyguard, that they insist on your observing the already violated oaths, as if Alexander's absolute sovereignty extended over perjury also; and they compel you to rescind your own laws, releasing men who have been condemned in your courts and forcing you to sanction numberless other illegalities. And their conduct is natural; for men who have sold themselves to a policy antagonistic to the interests of their country cannot trouble themselves about laws and oaths; they are to them mere terms which they employ to lead astray the citizens who come to the Assembly for diversion and not for careful inquiry, and who forget that present inaction will some day result in wild confusion. My own advice, as I said at the start, is to believe them when they say that we ought to abide by the joint agreement, unless, when they insist on our abiding by the oaths, they interpret them as not forbidding any act of injustice, or imagine that no one will be sensible of the change from democracy to tyranny or of the overthrow of a free constitution.

Now for a still greater absurdity. For it is provided in the compact that it shall be the business of the delegates at the Congress and those responsible for public safety to see that in the states that are parties to the peace there shall be no executions and banishments contrary to the laws established in those states, no confiscation of property, no partition of lands, no cancelling of debts, and no emancipation of slaves for purposes of revolution. But these speakers are so far from seeking to prevent any of these evils, that they join in promoting them. And do they not then deserve death – the men who promote in the various states those terrible calamities which, because they are so serious, this important body has been commissioned to prevent?

I will point out a further breach of the compact. For it is laid down that it shall not be lawful for exiles to set out, bearing arms, from the states which are parties to the peace, with hostile intent against any of the states included in the peace; but if they do, then that city from which they set out shall be excluded from the terms of the treaty. Now the Macedonian king has been so unscrupulous about bearing arms that he has never yet laid them down, but even now goes about bearing arms, as far as is in his power, and more so indeed now than ever, inasmuch as he has reinstated the professional trainer at Sicyon by an edict, and other exiles elsewhere. Therefore if we are to keep this joint agreement, as these speakers say, the states that are guilty of these offences are excluded from our treaty. If, indeed, we ought to hush the matter up, we must never say that they are the Macedonian states; but if the men who are subservient to the Macedonian king against your interests never cease urging us to carry out the joint agreement, let us take them at their word, since their contention is just, and let us, as our oath demands, exclude the guilty parties from the treaty, and form a plan for dealing with men whose temper is so brutally dictatorial, and who are constantly either plotting or acting against us and mocking at the general peace. What, I ask you, can they urge against the correctness of this view? Will they claim that the agreement stands good as against our city, but demur to it where it protects our interests? Does it really seem fair that this should be so? And if there is anything in the treaty that favours our enemies against our city, will they always make the most of it, but if there is anything that tells the other way and is at once just and advantageous to us, will they think that unremitting opposition is their peculiar duty?

But to prove to you still more clearly that no Greeks will accuse you of transgressing any of the terms of the joint agreement, but will even be grateful to you for exposing the real transgressors, I will just touch upon a few of the many points that might be mentioned. For the compact, of course, provides that all the parties to the peace may sail the seas, and that none may hinder them or force a ship of any of them to come to harbour, and that anyone who violates this shall be treated as an enemy by all the parties to the peace. Now, men of Athens, you have most distinctly seen this done by the Macedonians; for they have grown so arrogant that they forced all our ships coming from the Black Sea to put in at Tenedos, and under one pretence or another refused to release them until you passed a decree to man and launch a hundred war-galleys instantly, and you put Menestheus in command. Is it not, then, absurd that others should be guilty of so many serious transgressions, but that their friends in Athens, instead of restraining the transgressors, should urge us to abide by the terms thus lightly regarded? As if there were a clause added, permitting some to violate them, but forbidding others even to defend their rights! But was not the conduct of the Macedonians as stupid as it was lawless, when they committed such a gross violation of their oaths as deservedly went near to cost them their right to command at sea? Even as it is, they have supplied us with this unquestionable claim against them, whenever we choose to press it. For surely their violation of the joint agreement is not lessened because they have now ceased to offend. But they are in luck, because they can make the most of your supineness, which prefers to take no advantage even of your due rights.

The greatest humiliation, however, that we have suffered is that all the other Greeks and barbarians dread your enmity, but these upstarts alone can make you despise yourselves, sometimes by persuasion, sometimes by force, as if Abdera or Maronea, and not Athens, were the scene of their political activities. Moreover, while they weaken your cause and strengthen that of your enemies, they at the same time admit unconsciously that our city is irresistible, because they bid her uphold justice by injustice, as though she could easily vanquish her enemies, if she preferred to consult her own interests. And they have taken up a reasonable attitude; for as long as we, singlehanded, can maintain an unchallenged supremacy at sea, we can devise other and stronger defences on land in addition to our existing forces, especially if by good fortune we can get rid of these politicians, who have for their bodyguard the hosts of tyranny, and if some of them are destroyed and others conclusively proved to be worthless.

Such then, in the matter of the ships, has been the violation of the compact by the Macedonian king, in addition to the other cases mentioned. But the most insolent and overbearing exploit of the Macedonians was that performed quite recently, when they dared to sail into the Piraeus, contrary to our mutual agreement. Moreover, men of Athens, because it was only a single wargalley, it must not be regarded as a slight matter, but as an experiment made to see whether we should overlook it, so that they could repeat it on a larger scale, and also as a proof that they cared as little for these terms of agreement as for those that have been already mentioned. For that it was an encroachment little by little and was meant to accustom us to suffering such intrusions into our harbours, is plain from the following considera-

tion. For the mere fact that the man who sailed the ship in, and whom you ought to have put out of existence at once, galley and all, asked permission to build small boats in our harbour – does it not make it perfectly plain that their scheme was not so much to enter the harbour as to be inside it from the first? And if we tolerate small craft, a little later it will be war-galleys as well; and if at first we sanction a few, there will soon be many. For they cannot allege as their excuse that there is plenty of timber for shipbuilding at Athens, where we import it with great trouble from distant parts, but that it is scarce in Macedonia, where there is a cheap supply for all who want it. No, they thought that they would build their ships here and also furnish them with crews in our harbour, though it is expressly stipulated in the joint agreement that nothing of the kind should be permitted; and they thought too that it would always be more and more in their power to do this. Thus on every hand they treat our city with contempt, thanks to their prompters here, who suggest to them everything they should do; and thus with their help they have discovered that there is an indescribable slackness and feebleness in our city, and that we take no thought for the morrow, and that it never occurs to us to consider how the tyrant is carrying out the joint agreement.

That agreement, men of Athens, I urge you to keep in the way that I have explained, and I would confidently assure you, with the authority that my age confers, that we shall at once be exercising our undoubted rights, and also making the safest use of those opportunities which impel us to secure our interests. For, indeed, there is this clause appended to the agreement, "if it is our wish to share in the common peace." But the words "if it is our wish" mean also the opposite – if it is ever our *duty* to abandon our disgraceful submission to the dictates of others, or even our forgetfulness of those high ideals, which from time immemorial we have cherished in greater measure than any other people. Therefore, if you approve, Athenians, I will now propose that, as the agreement directs, we declare war on the transgressors.

On the Crown

Demosthenes' efforts to rally Athens and other Greek cities against Philip and then Alexander resulted in one military defeat after another until, ironically, his vision of a unified Greece was realized, but with Macedonia in control rather than Athens. Nevertheless, Demosthenes was viewed by the majority of Athenians as a patriot who had worked tirelessly to preserve the city. As a way of recognizing its outstanding citizens, Athens had a long tradition of bestowing a golden crown upon the most worthy, and in 336 BC, a politician named Ctesiphon proposed to the assembly that Demosthenes be given this award for his service to Athens. The proposal stirred the enmity between Demosthenes and Aeschines, who immediately challenged the award on technical grounds as violating the constitution. By law, a person could be nominated for such an honor only when he was currently in office. Demosthenes held no office when Ctesiphon proposed that he be awarded the gold crown, hence the charge that the nomination was illegal. For reasons that are unclear, the case did not come to trial until 330 BC. When it did, Aeschines delivered a brilliant speech entitled *Against Ctesiphon* that was a sharp indictment of Demosthenes and his policies. Demosthenes responded with *On the Crown*, a lengthy defense of his record and a biting ad hominem attack on Aeschines. Considered by many to be the best example we have of forensic rhetoric from the period, *On the Crown* illustrates well the orator's use of persuasive discourse. The jury ruled against Aeschines, who was fined and exiled. He moved to Ionia, where he reportedly became a Sophist.

Reading 25

On the Crown

On the Crown (excerpt), edited by J.J. Murphy; translated by J.J. Keaney.

(1)[15] My first words, men of Athens, are a prayer to all our gods and goddesses that in this trial I may depend on as much good will from you as I have continually maintained toward our city and toward all of you; secondly – something which concerns your piety and your reputation to the highest degree – I pray the gods to implant in your minds the thought that you should not let my opponent advise you of the manner in which you should listen to me (for that would be harsh) (2) but that you be guided by the laws and your oath, which imposes the special obligation upon you to listen to both parties in the same manner. This means not only that you should make no prejudgment, nor even that you should give both parties an equal share of your good will; it means that you should allow each party in the trial to use the type of defense he has chosen and to arrange his defense as he wishes.

(3) In this trial, Aeschines has many advantages over me, but there are two important ones, men of Athens. The first is that the result of the trial cannot have the same meaning to both of us, for

it is not the same thing for me to fail to achieve your good will and for him to fail in his prosecution, while for me – I don't wish to say anything offensive at the beginning of my speech, but he accuses me from a superior position. Secondly, it is a natural characteristic of all men to enjoy listening to insults and accusations, but to be offended when they hear men praising themselves. (4) The pleasurable side is given to Aeschines, the part which irritates nearly everybody is left for me. If, to prevent this, I do not mention my achievements, I will seem to have no way of acquitting myself of the charges nor of pointing out the grounds for my claim that I deserve to be honored. But if I take up my actions and public policies, I will necessarily have to talk about myself frequently. I will attempt to do so as moderately as possible, but it is fair that Aeschines, who instituted this trial, bear the responsibility for whatever the situation itself compels me to say.

(5) I think all of you would agree that Ctesiphon and I are equally involved in this trial, and that it

---

[15] Numbers in parentheses refer to the traditional divisions of the text of the speech.

requires no less concern on my part. For it is a painful and cruel experience to be deprived of anything, especially if one's enemy is responsible; but it is particularly so to be deprived of your good will and affection, as to obtain these is the highest blessing. Since these are the issues in the trial, (6) I expect and ask to receive a fair hearing from all of you alike when I defend myself against the accusations, as indeed the laws require. It was Solon, a benevolent supporter of popular government, who was the original author of these laws, and he thought their validity should lie not only in the fact that they were enacted but also in that an oath was imposed on the jurors; his motive was not, it seems to me, mistrust of you, (7) but he saw that it was not possible for a defendant to avoid false and slanderous accusations – a strong advantage the prosecutor has since he addresses you first – unless each of you jurors, by preserving your piety toward the gods, would receive with good will the just arguments of the second speaker and would make your decision about the entire case on the basis of an equal and impartial hearing of both speakers.

(8) Since I am about to give an account of the whole of my personal life, it seems, today, as well as of my public policies, I wish again to invoke the gods and, in your presence, to pray, first, that in this trial I may depend on as much good will from you as I have continually maintained toward our city and toward all of you; secondly, that the gods may implant in you the ability to make a decision about this indictment which will prove to be conducive to the good reputation of all of you and the religious piety of each.

(9) If Aeschines had limited his accusations to the items contained in his indictment, I, too, would begin my defense with the Council's decree. But since he has spent at least as much of his time in discussing other matters, and mostly in lies about me, I think it at once necessary and fair that I speak briefly about these matters first, so that none of you be induced by arguments extraneous to the indictment to give an unfavorable hearing to the justice of my answer to it.

(10) See how simple and fair is my reply to the abusive slanders he has voiced at my personal life. If you know me to be the type of man he has accused me of being (for I have never lived anywhere but among you), do not tolerate the sound of my voice, not even if my statesmanship has been brilliantly successful, but stand up and condemn me now. But if you have always assumed and have personal knowledge that I (and my family) are far better, and better born, than he and inferior to none of our respectable citizens – to avoid an invidious term – do not trust what he says about other matters (clearly it is all woven from the same fabric) but grant me today also the same good will you have shown me in many previous trials.

(11) The duplicity of your character, Aeschines, has led you to the thoroughly simple notion that I would have to reply to your abuse and neglect to discuss my public actions and policies. I shall not do it; I am not so demented. I will review my policies, the subject of your abusive falsehoods, and will take up later your loose insults – language worthy of peasant women at a comic festival – if these jurors are willing to listen to them.

(12) I have been accused of many crimes, for some of which the laws provide grave and extreme penalties. But his purpose in this trial is not that: it is to allow an enemy to heap upon me spite, malice, abuse, dirt, and everything of the kind. The city cannot come close to exacting a penalty of the sort demanded by his charges and accusations, if they were, in fact, true. (13) To prevent me from appearing before the people and obtaining a hearing from them – and this because of his spite and his envy – is, by the gods, not right or constitutional or just, men of Athens. If he saw me committing crimes against our city which were as enormous as he has just described them in his theatrical style, he had an obligation to use the penalties which the laws provide when the crimes were being committed; if he saw that my actions deserved impeachment, by impeaching me and using this procedure for settling the matter in your courts; if I was proposing illegal measures, by indicting me on these grounds. For surely it cannot be that he is prosecuting Ctesiphon through me, but that he would not have indicted me, if he thought he could convict me. (14) Furthermore, if he saw me doing any of the other things with which he has now slandered me or any crime whatsoever against you, there are laws and punishments for all of them; there are processes and suits which carry grave and severe penalties, and all of these he could have used; if he had ever clearly done this and had taken advantage of such possible measures against me, his accusation now would be consistent with his behavior in the past. (15) As it is, he has stepped off the path of right

and justice and avoided investigating my actions at the time they were done; he is playing a stage part, piling up charges and jokes and abuse much after the events. In the second place, he accuses me, but brings Ctesiphon to trial; his enmity toward me is the pre-eminent feature of this whole trial but, never daring to meet me on that ground, he clearly seeks to deprive another man of his civic rights. (16) Yet, men of Athens, besides all the other arguments one could cite in support of Ctesiphon, it seems to me that one could say with much justice that it was fair for Aeschines and me to settle our personal feuds by ourselves, not to dismiss a personal confrontation and look for a third party to cause trouble to. This is the height of injustice.

(17) All of his accusations alike, one may see, are neither just nor based on the truth. I wish to examine them one by one, and especially the lies he has told about me in the matter of the Peace and the embassy, attributing to me what he himself did in conjunction with Philocrates. It is necessary, men of Athens, and fitting as well that I remind you of the chronology of the events so that you may observe each event in its temporal context.

[...]

(50) Although I still have much to say about the events surrounding the Peace, I think what I have said is more than enough. This man is to blame, who has spewed at me the garbage of his own villainy. I must defend myself to those of you who are too young to have witnessed the events; others of you were, perhaps, irritated at my remarks, I mean those of you who knew that he had been bribed, before I said anything about it. (51) And yet he calls this bribery an act of "friendship" and just now, somewhere in his speech, referred to him "who reproaches me with the friendship of Alexander." I reproach you with the friendship of Alexander? Where did you get it from? How did you deserve it? I would not call you – I am not insane – the guest of Philip or the friend of Alexander, unless one should also call farm hands or any other kind of hireling guests and friends of their employers. (52) Before, I called you the hireling of Philip and now, the hireling of Alexander, as do all of these here. If you don't believe me, ask them, or, rather, I will do it for you. Does Aeschines seem to you, men of Athens, to be the hireling or the friend of Alexander? You hear what they say.

(53) Finally, I wish to make my defense against the indictment itself, and to discuss my activities in detail so that Aeschines, although he already knows them, will hear my reasons for saying that I have a just claim on the rewards mentioned in the Council's resolution and much greater rewards than these. Please read the indictment.

Indictment (54–55)

(56) These are the details of Ctesiphon's decree, men of Athens, on which he bases his prosecution. In the first place, I think I will make clear to you, from these very details, that my whole defense will be fair. For I will use the same order of the items in the indictment as he; I will speak to each of these in order; and I will omit nothing willingly. (57) The words of Ctesiphon's proposal are that I "spoke and acted continually for the best interests of the people and was eager to do whatever good I was capable of and that I be praised for this." I believe that your judgment on the proposal should be based on my political actions. When these are examined, it will be found whether the items of Ctesiphon's proposal which concern me are true and deserved or whether they are in fact false. (58) As to the fact that Ctesiphon did not add the clause "when I pass the audit," and bade the Crown to be proclaimed in the theatre, I think that this too is connected with my political actions, that is, whether I deserve the Crown and the public proclamation or not. Further, I think that I should specify the legal basis of Ctesiphon's proposal. This is the simple and fair defense I have decided to make, and I will now proceed to my actions.

(59) But let no one think that my remarks are irrelevant to the indictment, if I happen to discuss foreign policy. For the prosecutor, who has called untrue that part of the proposal which states that my actions and speeches were for the best, is the same man who has made a discussion of all my policies relevant and necessary to the charge. Secondly, of the many areas of government which were open to me, I chose the one which deals with foreign policy, so that I can fairly begin my exposition in this sphere.

(60) I will pass over what Philip seized and held before I began to make speeches on public policy. None of this, I think, has anything to do with me.

I will mention and give a full account of what he was prevented from doing, beginning with the day on which I involved myself in this sphere, premising only this much. Philip had one large advantage, men of Athens. (61) For among the Greeks, not some but all alike, there grew a crop of traitors and hirelings and men hateful to the gods, the like of which no one can ever recall before. With these as his assistants and accomplices, he worsened the relations between the Greeks, which even before this were bad and faction-ridden. Some he deceived, others he bribed, others he thoroughly corrupted; he split the Greeks into many factions, although they all had a single interest, to prevent him from becoming powerful. (62) When all the Greeks were in this state and ignorant of the growing and gathering danger, you, men of Athens, should consider what was the proper course of action for our city to have chosen and expect an account of this from me. For I took my position in this area of government. (63) Should Athens, Aeschines, denying her pride and her dignity, have taken a position with the Thessalians and Dolopians, by this act obtaining the rule of Greece for Philip and nullifying the just and glorious deeds of our forefathers? That was not the proper course – it is truly unthinkable – but was it proper for Athens to allow acts to go on, which she knew long before would take place, if no one prevented them? (64) I would now like to ask the severest critic of our actions, on which side he would have wanted Athens to be: on that which shares the responsibility for the shameful and ugly results which befell Greece (here were the Thessalians and their followers) or on the side which overlooked what was going on in the hope of personal aggrandizement (here we would put the Arcadians, Messenians, and Argives). (65) But even many of these, rather all of them, fared worse than we. If Philip, after gaining control, had departed, kept peace afterward and harmed none of his own allies or the rest of the Greeks, there might be some grounds for accusing and blaming those who opposed his actions. But if he has taken away, from all alike, reputation, leadership, and freedom – and even the free governments of as many as he could – how could the decision you took at my urging fail to be most glorious?

[...]

(120) The next item is the proclamation of the Crown in the theatre. I pass over the innumerable times innumerable Crowns were so proclaimed, and that I myself was frequently crowned in this way before. But, for heaven's sake, Aeschines, are you so imperceptive and so stupid that you cannot grasp the fact that the gift of a Crown causes the same pride in its recipient wherever it is proclaimed? And that the proclamation in the theatre assists the purposes of the donors? All who hear the proclamation are encouraged to serve their city and they praise those who confer the favor more than its recipient. This is why the city has this law. Please read the law.

Law

(121) You hear, Aeschines, the clear statement of the law: "Except in cases which the people and Council approve: let the herald proclaim these." Why then, miserable man, do you make malicious accusations? Why do you fabricate arguments? Why don't you take hellebore to cure your madness? Do you feel no shame at bringing in a suit based on envy, not on any offense, at remaking laws and omitting parts of laws when it is only right that the whole law be read to jurors who have sworn to make their decision according to the laws? (122) You act like this, and then you list the qualities a public servant should have, just like one who contracts to have a statue made and then gets it back with the contract unfulfilled, or as if public servants were known by their words and not by their actions and policies. You scream every kind of filthy name at me, like a comic reveler from a wagon, names which suit you and your family, not me. There is also this to think of, men of Athens. (123) I believe that the difference between insult and accusation lies in this, that accusation is directed at crimes for which there are penalties in the laws, while insult involves slander, which naturally involves only the statements which personal enemies make about each other. It is my conviction that your forefathers built these courts, not so that we could collect you here to listen to men making libelous statements about each other for their own reasons, but so that we could convict anyone who has committed a crime against the city. (124) Aeschines knows this as well as I, but he has chosen to revel in slander rather than make accusations. It is not right that he should leave without getting as

much as he has given, I will now take up this point, asking him this small question. Should one say, Aeschines, that you are the city's enemy or mine? Mine, clearly. When it was possible for you to seek legal satisfaction from me, if I committed a crime, for the benefit of these Athenian citizens, in the audits, in civil suits, in the other trials, you neglected to do so. (125) Have you chosen to face me where I am immune in all respects: in respect to the laws, so the time that has passed, to the statute of limitations; immune because the facts of the case have been frequently argued in court, because I have never been convicted of any wrong against you citizens, because the city must have a larger or smaller share with me in the reputation she gained from her actions? Watch out that you don't prove to be the enemy of these citizens here, while you claim to be mine.

[...]

(129) I have no difficulty in finding things to say about you and your family; my difficulty is where to begin. Should I say that your father, Trembler, was a slave in the elementary school of Elpias near the Theseum, wearing leg-irons and a wooden collar? Or that your mother plied her trade of daylight marriages in the little shack near the statue of Kalamites, she who raised you, her pretty little doll, to be the paragon of third-rate actors? Everybody knows this and I don't have to mention it. But should I mention that the boatswain Phormio, the slave of Dion the Phrearrian, raised her out of this noble occupation? By all the gods in heaven, I hesitate to say what deserves to be said about you, lest I be thought to have chosen expressions unworthy of me. (130) I will let that be and begin from the kind of life Aeschines led. He was born of no ordinary parents; they were the type of parents solemnly cursed by the Athenian people. Late in his career – do I say late? It was yesterday or the day before that he became an Athenian citizen and an Athenian politician at the same time. By adding a syllable, he made his father Nontrembler instead of Trembler; his mother was endowed with the quite exalted name, Eyegleam, though everyone knows she was called Hobgoblin, a name derived from her occupation because she would do anything and submit to every request of her clients. How else did she get it? (131) You were elevated from slavery to freedom and from begging to riches thanks to these citizens, but you are such an ingrate and so deformed in your nature that you have no way to thank them except by

selling yourself and pursuing a policy detrimental to their interests. I will not mention his speeches; some might claim they were delivered in the city's interest. But I will remind you of his actions; their results have shown that they were clearly in our enemies' interest.

(132) Who among you does not know of the case of Antiphon? He was deprived of his citizenship, but returned to Athens after promising Philip that he would burn the dockyards. I found him hiding in Peiraios and, when I brought him before your Assembly, Aeschines, that malicious man, yelled and screamed that my action was outrageous in a democratic state, that I was insulting citizens who were down on their luck, that I had entered a home without a supporting order. He obtained Antiphon's release. (133) If the Council of the Areopagus, which learned of the case and saw that your ignorance of the facts was untimely, had not ordered a further investigation, arrested the man and brought him to you for trial, he would have been snatched from your grasp, avoided his penalty, and been sent on his way by this mouther of noble phrases. As it was, you tortured him and put him to death, the penalty which Aeschines should have received. (134) The Council of the Areopagus knew of his activities in that case; and when you elected him to argue your side in the dispute about the Delphic temple, out of the same ignorance of the facts which has caused you to sacrifice many of your interests, the Council, which the Assembly had made its associate and put in control of the matter, rejected him as a traitor and instructed Hypereides to take on the task. Their votes were solemnly placed on the altar, and no vote was cast for this morally polluted man. To prove that I speak the truth, call the witnesses.

[...]

(265) Compare the kind of lives each of us lived, calmly, Aeschines, not bitterly. Then ask these jurors whose luck each of them would choose. You taught school, I attended school. You initiated people, I was an initiate. You were a minor clerk, I was a member of the Assembly. You were a minor actor, I was a spectator. You were hissed off the stage, I joined in the hissing. Your policies supported our enemy, mine, our country. (266) I pass over the rest, but now, today, my qualifications to receive a Crown of honor are under examination, it is agreed that I have done no wrong; the reputation you have as a malicious accuser is set, you are

in constant danger, whether you must continue to behave like this or whether you will soon be stopped, by failing to receive a minimum of the votes. Good luck has marked your life – good, indeed! – and you accuse my luck.

(267) Bring here the evidence which deals with my voluntary services and let me read them to you. Alongside these, Aeschines, you read the verses you murdered, "I am come to the crypt of the dead and the gates of darkness" and "Be assured I have no wish to bring evil tidings" and "evil man, evilly" may you be destroyed, first by the gods and then by all of these jurors, bad citizen and bad actor alike.

Read the evidence.

[…]

(321) The well-meaning citizen (to speak about myself in this way cannot cause envy) must have two qualities, men of Athens: when he is in authority, he should persist in the policy which aims at the city's pre-eminence and honor, but at every time and in every action, he should be patriotic. For his nature controls this quality, other factors control his power and his strength. You will find that I have been constant in my patriotism. (322) Look at the facts. When Alexander demanded me, when they indicted me before the Amphictyonic Council, when they threatened me, when they made promises, when they set this whole damned group on me like wild animals, at no time did I betray my patriotism. From the very beginning of my political career, I chose the path of honesty and justice; I chose to foster, to increase, to associate myself with the honors, power, and reputation of our country. (323) I do not walk around the market place, with a smile on my face, exulting in the successes of our enemies, offering my hand and telling the good news to those I thought would report to Macedonia. I do not shudder and moan and hang my head when I hear of some good fortune of our city, like these impious men, who disparage our city, as if, by doing so, they are not disparaging themselves at the same time, who look abroad, who approve the success of another – a success gained at the expense of Greece – and say that we should ensure that his success last forever.

(324) I pray to all the gods that they refuse assent to this desire but rather implant in these men a better mind and a better spirit; if they are beyond cure, may they, and they alone, be quickly and utterly destroyed, wherever they might be, and may the rest of us be granted swift release and safe security from the terrors which hang over us.

Study Questions

1 *On the Treaty with Alexander* was designed to stir the emotions of Athenians. What are some of the ways the speech does this? Are the techniques Demosthenes used effective in all circumstances? Why or why not?

2 We find frequent use of ad hominem arguments and invective in *On the Crown*. Where do we most often find this approach today? Is it effective? Why or why not?

3 In *On the Crown*, Demosthenes spoke at length about his political career rather than addressing the legal issue involved. Why do you think he chose this approach? Was the verdict just? Why or why not?

Writing Topics

1 Demosthenes succeeded in marshaling Athenians to war against the forces of Philip and those of Alexander even when the city was no real match for the Macedonians, and Athens experienced defeat after defeat. Examine the various social and political factors of the time and offer a possible explanation for the Athenians' willingness to wage war against an obviously superior force. Was it merely due to the power of Demosthenes' oratory?

2   Although *On the Treaty with Alexander* and *On the Crown* were aimed at different audiences and had somewhat different aims, as examples of persuasive oratory they nevertheless have some features in common. Analyze the two works, identify their common features, and explain how they function as rhetorical devices.

Further Reading

Aeschines, *Against Ctesiphon*.
Demosthenes, *The Philippics*.

Plato on Philosophy and Rhetoric

Introduction to Plato (c. 427–347 bc)

The number of books, articles, and dissertations written on Plato and his works runs into the thousands for manifold reasons. Perhaps most obviously, Plato is one of the more influential people in history. And there is the so-called "Socratic problem." Socrates appears as the major figure in all of Plato's works except *Laws*: Do the words and ideas he expresses belong to the actual Socrates, or are they Plato's? Moreover, Plato's writing is difficult to understand, in part because it consists almost entirely of dialogues but also because the ideas contained therein are convoluted and hard to grasp fully. As a result of these and other factors, Plato's work lends itself to multiple interpretations, as different readers find different meanings and understanding in the corpus. Even scholars who have devoted their entire lives to studying Plato disagree on more issues than might seem reasonably possible (e.g., Clapp, 1950; Gagarin, 1969).

Certain basic facts about Plato and his writing are known and widely accepted, as indicated in the general introduction. But the multiple interpretations of his work create a significant obstacle for students who are in the early stages of their study of Plato, as well as a problem for this text: Providing a brief introduction that summarizes the various perspectives is not feasible. Quite simply, too many different views exist to allow it. What follows here, therefore, is but one way of approaching Plato.

Plato's philosophy

Reflecting on Plato, Candreva (2005) wrote: "Perhaps no other figure in Western political thought has been the object of so much disagreement" (p. 33). There are several reasons. Plato's philosophy is an early form of rationalism because it relies on reason rather than the senses to understand the world, and it is complex, dealing with abstractions such as truth, justice, virtue, and knowledge that he seldom defined concretely and that were subtly and implicitly embedded in the social and political issues of the time. Furthermore, Plato's position on these topics is inconsistent across the dialogues, and even within dialogues we find him abandoning a point and moving on to another at the very moment when we sense that clarity or resolution is forthcoming.

At the heart of his philosophy are the Ideal Forms. The Milesians, we recall, had emphasized dualities in their attempts to understand the world: hot/cold, wet/dry, and so on. Moreover, they attributed change to transitions of opposites: Something that is hot becomes something that is cold. Heraclitus of Ephesus, yet another Ionian, rejected this notion as absurd and proposed that what we perceive to be opposites are actually one and the same, which led to the conclusion that everything is in a perpetual state of flux. Plato apparently became convinced that Heraclitus was only half right. His philosophy of Ideal Forms is predicated on the idea that we may experience something as being simultaneously hot and cold or pleasant and painful, but in such instances our senses must be deceiving us, for if hot and cold can exist simultaneously, then being and not being must have the same status, which creates not only inconsistency but also a logical contradiction. The Ideal Forms solve the problem. In Plato's view, truth cannot be inconsistent, and given that our experiences with the world are rife with inconsistencies, they must be false. The uneducated may believe that these experiences are real and true, but this belief is merely opinion, not knowledge. The Ideal Forms represent the truth of things, an unchanging reality that exists apart from the (changeable and changing) things themselves.

We can perhaps best understand this concept by considering a circle. Geometry defines a circle as an unbroken curved line formed at an equal distance from a center point. If we try to draw such a line by hand, however, we usually find that the line is not consistently even, and the result may look more like an egg than a circle. To correct this problem we may use a compass or even graphing software, both of which provide a much better result, one that appears to meet our geometric definition. Yet if we were to examine these improved circles with a magnifying glass, we would find that the lines are uneven and that we still have not produced a figure that meets the definition. It is on this account that Plato proposed that the *concept* of "circle" exists outside of our *experiences* with circles; thus, a person can only know what a true circle is by studying geometry and thereby acquiring knowledge of its Ideal Form. And the same principle applies to everything in the world. The chairs we sit in are only imitations of their Ideal Forms; our pet dog is only an imitation, as are our shoes, our books, and so forth. Of special importance in this philosophy are not dogs, shoes, and books, but rather concepts, such as justice, truth, love, and virtue. What passes for justice and virtue in the world of experiences are simply imitations of the Ideal Forms that exist in the mind of God, imitations that delude us into believing that we are experiencing true justice and true virtue on the basis of their resemblance to the real things. The hard study of philosophy enables us not only to recognize that we live in a world of illusion but also to attain an understanding, or more properly a *recollection*, of the real. It can do so because our immortal souls contain within them a memory of the Ideal Forms from their existence prior to birth. We therefore say that Plato's Ideal Forms represent *a priori* truths – that is, truths that are knowable independent of experience on the basis of reflection alone by anyone who has acquired the relevant concepts and, equally important, the relevant techniques of reasoning.[1]

Plato and the Sophists

In the Platonic dialogue *Apology*, Socrates tells the court that he is "a sort of gadfly, given to the state by God" (30e). His mission in life was to walk about Athens questioning fellow citizens to show them that they knew nothing because they had not pursued philosophic inquiry. Understanding Plato and his work can be greatly enhanced by recognizing that he also seemed to view himself as something of a gadfly whose task was to challenge prevailing views on philosophy, education, poetry, and rhetoric.

---

[1] One of the more useful sources for understanding Plato's philosophy is Aristotle's *Metaphysics*, which provides far more details than what we find in Plato's dialogues or what can be summarized here.

Like the Sophists, Plato was heir to the proto-scientific legacy of Thales, Anaximander, and Anaximenes. However, he came of age in a fully literate society, which might lead us to expect him to have a superior set of logical tools that he could use to further scientism and thereby reduce the influence of *mythos*. Although the Sophists were, as Cole (1991) noted, part of a "rationalizing tradition ... [that] was concerned with rewriting history and mythology to meet the demands of logic, empirical observation, and Ionian 'science'" (p. 66), we must remember that they were transitional figures facilitating the shift from orality to literacy. Their rhetoric maintained certain features of oral poetry, and some of their speeches incorporated structural characteristics reminiscent of song. Even though they committed demonstration speeches to writing, their focus was on oration, which they used like rhapsodes to stir the emotions and move listeners rather than to discover truth. Their commitment to *dissoi logoi*, at least as it is described in the extant literature, demonstrated to many their lack of concern for truth, their subversive relativism. On this basis, it would be easy to propose that from Plato's more developed perspective the Sophists as a group had failed to live up to an important Milesian principle. Through their teaching, the Sophists were perpetuating *mythos* and ignorance just as surely as the rhapsodes and the epic poets – resulting in what might be considered a curious mixture of traditionalism and anti-traditionalism. From Plato's perspective, they could not possibly teach civic virtue because their poetic vision of the world was metaphorical, full of allegories that had little bearing on reality, and therefore fundamentally false. Like poetry, Sophistic rhetoric led people to base their actions on emotion and opinion rather than reason and knowledge.

There are clear indications that some of Plato's criticism of the Sophists was based on this assessment. For example, he held that there was a strong connection between Sophistic rhetoric and poetry, for both have the power to move an audience, to make people believe even in the absence of truth. The connection appears in works like *Gorgias*, where we find that "Tragedy has her face turned towards pleasure and the gratification of the audience" (502c), which is a kind of "flattery." And if "we strip all poetry of song and rhythm and metre" (502d), all that is left is speech:

SOCRATES: And this speech is addressed to a crowd of people?
CALLICLES: Yes.
SOCRATES: Then poetry is a sort of rhetoric?
CALLICLES: True.

SOCRATES: And do not the poets in the theatres seem to you to be rhetoricians?
CALLICLES: Yes ...
SOCRATES: Very good. (502e–503b)

Equating rhetoric with poetry was without question a clever rhetorical move, for it allowed Plato to draw on the cultural shift underway from *mythos* to logic and thereby persuade his audience more readily of Sophistic oratory's shortcomings. The resulting dichotomy was clear and easy to grasp: Poetry, rhetoric, and myth on the one hand; philosophy and truth on the other. And it had the added advantage of conforming to the dualisms that characterized Milesian philosophy and that were widely familiar. This dichotomy appears most memorably in Book X of *The Republic*, where Plato asserted that "there is an ancient quarrel between philosophy and poetry" (607b, 6–7). The "quarrel" is based on the fact that the poet does not intend "to please or affect the rational principle of the soul; but he will prefer the passionate and fitful temper" (605a, 2–3). And no one is immune:

The best of us, ... when we listen to a passage of Homer, or one of the tragedians, in which he represents some pitiful hero who is drawling out his sorrows in a long oration, or weeping, and smiting his breast – the best of us, you know, delight in giving way to sympathy, and are in raptures at the excellence of the poet who stirs our feelings most. (605c, 1–6)

Rhetoric and literature alike, in other words, stir the beast in us all and lead to chaos and moral disorder (see Havelock, 2005). It was rhetoric that appealed to the basest emotions of the *demos* and brought on the war with Sparta; it was rhetoric that forged those exiled by the Council of Thirty into an army that provoked the civil war and, ultimately, the execution of Socrates (see Kraut, 1997).

Plato's new paradigm

Although the above analysis has a certain appeal, it cannot be pushed too far. Doing so would entail reaching the unhappy and unbelievable conclusion that Plato was not particularly self-aware, given that he did not adhere to the proto-scientific principles of philosophy's founders, either. His work displays to a significant degree the mysticism of Pythagoras and Parmenides, particularly with regard to the concepts of truth and the immortal soul, and in many respects is far less concerned with purging traditional lore and poetic fabrications than anything the Sophists produced. He never embraced scientism, and although in his dialogues he demonstrated his ability to parse the meaning of an individual word down to its root, his use of classification and categorization was limited. He was not a naturalist and, unlike the Milesians, apparently had no interest whatsoever in the natural world or cosmology. Rejecting empirical observation, he focused on self-exploration that sought to know the individual's relation to universal concepts such as truth, love, justice, virtue, and wisdom – concepts that were quite marginal among the Milesians, when they were mentioned at all. If the words Socrates speaks in the dialogues reveal any of Plato's views, then *Phaedrus* conveys his sentiment concisely: "I am a lover of knowledge, and the men who dwell in the city are my teachers, and not the trees or the country" (230). Given these factors, Plato's criticism of the Sophists undoubtedly runs deeper than their failure to advance the social and intellectual move away from *mythos*.

Limiting the study of Plato to *Protagoras*, *Gorgias*, and *Phaedrus* can lead to the incorrect perception that Sophists and rhetoric were his central concerns. But when the Platonic dialogues are studied in their entirety, it becomes apparent that these three works fit into a kind of tapestry that examines, as well as indicts, Sophists, rhetoric, poetry, education, and human nature – the entire Sophistic enterprise associated with the social and cultural changes wrought by war, shifting economics, democracy, and literacy. Whether it was real or existed only in the imagination, the relatively stable world of the past, with its heroic absolutes of right and wrong, had given way to contingent morals after a century of nearly constant warfare that saw unprecedented levels of brutality, betrayal, and corruption. Plato took a stand in his dialogues against the new way of the world, constructing (as already noted) a philosophy predicated on the notion of *a priori* values. His dualisms were not linked to natural phenomena but rather to issues most relevant to his perception of a world undergoing a change for the worse. They were drawn directly from Parmenides: rhetoric/philosophy, injustice/justice, opinion/knowledge. In Parmenides' didactic poem, *On Nature*, the narrator describes an encounter with a goddess who explains to him the Way of Truth, which maintains that the only things that exist are those that the mind can conceive. Moreover, truth compels conviction. She then explains the Way of Belief, which identifies as illusion all things that are processed through the senses. Plato assimilated Parmenides' mystical rationalism, making it his own and giving birth to the Ideal Forms, until it reflected an unwavering and unrealistic faith in the power of reason to correct the human condition.[2] Infused with mysticism, Plato's dialogues seem to stand solidly in opposition to

[2] Commenting on Plato's rationalism, Nietzsche (1956) asserted that Plato was guilty of "the illusion that thought, guided by the thread of causation, might plumb the farthest abysses of being and even *correct* it" (pp. 93–94).

the proto-scientific approach to understanding the world initiated by the Milesians, which based reality, and consequently truth, on natural phenomena, with reason serving as an *interpretive* tool. Plato rejected this paradigm, discounted observation, and viewed reason as the sole means of *discovering* truth and understanding reality.

The implications of his new paradigm were significant and influence Western thought even today. Reason is a quality of Mind, and as such, was deemed by the Sophists to be subjective – a perspective that is inherent in Protagoras' assertion that "man is the measure of all things." Truth is both contingent and pragmatic, at least with respect to human behavior and perception. Plato's claim that reason is the sole means of discovering truth and reality constitutes a reversal in status, assigning to reason a veracious quality that elevates it from the subjective realm to the objective. Truth is theoretical, not pragmatic and certainly not contingent. From this perspective, observation, no matter how acute, is antithetical to discovering truth and reality not only because it is deemed subjective but also because the world and everything in it are merely simulacra that the senses cannot penetrate or fully understand. In fact, observation takes us away from truth because it seduces us into believing that the world of the senses is real.

Many scholars have noted, however, that Plato's paradigm is beset by problems. Oakeshott (1991) suggested, for example, that rationalism leads to debilitating political and intellectual isolation. It reduces epistemology to technique – in the case of Plato, to dialectic. Certainty and truth do not emerge through a process of observation, measurement, and testing but through strict adherence to the "correct" intellectual technique. Thus, in the dialogues, we find that Socrates' interlocutors generally do not adhere to the correct technique and are either reeducated or dismissed as intellectual hacks. Likewise, we find in *The Republic* that for his ideal state Plato advocated standardization over liberty, uniformity over variety, and rules over experience.

The notion that what we perceive is an illusion and that reality exists on a plane beyond our perception defies common sense. As a result, Plato's paradigm was not readily accepted among his contemporaries. It fared even less well among the Greeks of the Hellenistic Period and among the ever-practical Romans. Only toward the end of the Roman Period did Plato's vision gain wide popularity, especially when it was embraced by the early Christians – their world view being based almost entirely on faith in the existence of that which cannot be perceived – through the writings of neoplatonists such as Plotinus and Prophyry. After the fall of the Roman Empire, Plato's works disappeared in the West, and although scholars were teased by references and the occasional fragment in the texts of other authors, none of his writings was available in complete form until the fourteenth century AD, when Greek scholars started fleeing to the West as the Ottoman Turks began to threaten Constantinople. It then took two hundred years for Plato's ideas to be assimilated, at which point they became an enduring part of the British Enlightenment.

In addition, rhetoric as taught by the Sophists and as practiced in the assembly and the courts was concerned with *pros kriseis*, those things in the scope of human affairs that require an immediate decision. It was pragmatic by necessity, and observation was a central component involving close examination of the facts, witness testimony, relevant laws, and the best interests of the state. Dialectic and philosophy had little if any utility in such venues. Plato's assertion in *Phaedrus* that "Oratory is the art of enchanting the soul" (271) suggests that his conception of rhetoric had little in common with the realities of the courts and the assembly. He and the Sophists were operating with quite different premises. More critical to any examination of the history of rhetoric is the fact that his refusal to acknowledge oratory as a pragmatic endeavor – or what today we would call a "social action" – focused on decision making prevented him from formulating any substantive rhetorical theories of his own. Therefore, when he described the ideal rhetoric in *Phaedrus,* he concluded that he actually was describing philosophy, not oratory. Here, again, we see the influence of Parmenides insofar as the Platonic dialogues persistently ask the question "What is rhetoric?" even though the aim always is to expose what it is not.

For all his brilliance, Plato seemed unable to reconcile himself to the fact that most people's lives are governed by emotion, not reason. Consequently, his work can be seen as a rejection not only of rhetoric and the Sophistic curriculum but also of Athenian society. Nowhere is this more evident than in *The Republic,* a description of his ideal state, which bears a striking resemblance to Sparta (which in many respects was the antithesis of Athens), where philosopher kings regulate every facet of life, especially education. Rhetoric is banned, of course, but art, most forms of poetry, and even laughter are also proscribed.

Equally troubling to many readers is the fact that two persistent ironies – we might even say contradictions – are evident throughout the dialogues. They not only display Plato's own command of rhetoric but also frequently employ myth and allegory, the bread and butter of Greek poetry. Among the more famous is the Allegory of the Cave, which he used to great effect in describing the deception of the senses and the reality of the Ideal Forms. Grassi (2000) recognized the problem when he asked:

> If philosophy aims at being a theoretical mode of thought and speech, can it have a rhetorical character and be expressed in rhetorical terms? The answer seems obvious. Theoretical thinking, as a rational process, excludes every rhetorical element because pathetic influences – the influences of feeling – disturb the clarity of rational thought. (p. 1)

The presence of rhetorical elements in the dialogues suggests that Plato recognized as truth the words that he assigned to Socrates in *Phaedrus,* that "The art of disputation, then, is not confined to the courts and the assembly, but is one and the same in every use of language" (261). This idea is ignored immediately thereafter, like an unwelcome guest, but if we accept the dialogues as disputations with the Sophists and Athenian society, the strong rhetorical elements become inevitable, and we better understand, in keeping with Grassi's comment, why they fail to present a clearly delineated philosophy. In fact, one could argue that in many respects Plato's dialogues are more powerful rhetorically than they are philosophically: Among casual readers of Plato, it is common to find that the allegories – the Allegory of the Cave in *The Republic,* the Allegory of the Winged Horses in *Phaedrus,* and so on – are remembered long after everything else is forgotten.

Some readers will be tempted to suggest that Plato's use of rhetorical technique, if not his world view, remained anchored in the *mythos* of Greece's oral culture, perhaps even more so than did that of the Older Sophists. Certainly, one of his goals was quite conservative: to defend tradition against the changes that were transforming Greek society. This assessment is supported by his choice of genre – the dialogue. Cole (1991) argued that this choice was designed to recreate the poetic and persuasive force of oral discourse that the Sophists used so effectively, but twisted because Plato understood that "Poetry and oratory can do more than make lies sound like truth. They are also means for making truth sound like truth" (p. 140). This argument attains greater strength when we consider that until as late as the seventeenth century there was no such thing as "silent reading." Essentially all reading was done aloud. And when Plato's dialogues are read aloud, they resemble plays. If this analysis is correct, Plato was incapable of resolving the "ancient quarrel between philosophy and poetry" because he was unable to abandon poetic *mythos* completely, even though he would ban drama and most poetry from his ideal society. He was unalterably aligned with both.[3] It was left to his student Aristotle to resolve the quarrel.

Protagoras

Protagoras has been characterized as the dialogue most friendly (or less hostile) to the Sophists. Gagarin (1969), for example, stated that "*Protagoras* is essentially a positive statement about *aretê* and education, and not an attack on Protagoras and the sophists" (p. 134). This characterization is based, at least in part, on the fact that in the dialogue Socrates treats Protagoras with a measure of respect that we generally do not see in other dialogues involving Sophists, and he readily admits that Protagoras is everywhere held in high esteem. Such positive assessments of the dialogue, however, fail to recognize that in this work Plato's irony is more subtle than what we find in most of his other works, and they also fail to take proper account of the *dramatis personae* of the piece.

Wolfsdorf's (1998) analysis is particularly revealing in this regard because it focuses on the dialogue's historicity. The setting is the house of Callias, son of Hipponicus, who was infamous for squandering his inherited wealth and for his scandalous sexual affairs with young boys and married women. Inside the house we find Critias, Charmides, Eryximachus, Andron, Alcibiades, and others, all of whom "were notorious for their immorality" (p. 130). Wolfsdorf goes on to argue that "Plato's dramaturgical strategy of setting the dialogue at Callias' house and selecting certain notorious Athenians to be students of the Sophists there correlates Sophistic activity and the corruption of the Athenian people. ... [T]heir presence at Callias' house ... undermines Protagoras' claim to teach good counsel regarding domestic ... and political affairs" (p. 131).

In addition, *Protagoras* is rhetorically identical to other dialogues in the use of *aporia* and *elenchus*.[4] Socrates feigns ignorance and confusion on a variety of topics and encourages Protagoras to educate him. The Sophist readily complies, and the trap is set. Protagoras speaks of virtue in two different ways: Sometimes he considers it to be a whole quality, whereas at other times he describes it as consisting of separate elements, such as piety and temperance. Through cross-examination, Socrates demonstrates that Protagoras cannot possibly teach *aretê* because he does not know what it is: Virtue can be one, or it can be multiple parts, but it cannot be both. In the process, he develops a theory of virtue based on the concept of unity or identity in which all features of virtue – such as courage, temperance, fidelity, and so forth – are equated with knowledge (see, e.g., Brickhouse and Smith, 1997; Devereux, 1992; Ferejohn, 1982; Penner, 1973). On this basis, he rejects the simple notion that the good is what is pleasurable, for it leads to unacceptable hedonism. The good, like virtue, is knowledge, a position that allows Socrates to explore weakness of will (*akrasia*) and to conclude that evil actions are the result of ignorance, not evil intent. Morality, therefore, is predicated on knowledge of good and evil (see Watson, 1977).

---

[3] Grassi (2000) argued that this outcome was inevitable. In his view, philosophical discourse is apodictic, concerned with that which is demonstrably true on the basis of primary assertions. Because primary assertions are irreducible, they can be clarified and explained only on the basis of something else. Grassi asserted that they are necessarily imagistic and metaphorical. Imagery and metaphor, however, are inherently rhetorical, leading Grassi to conclude not only that rhetoric comes before philosophical speech but also that rational speech can have "only a rhetorical character. Thus the term 'rhetoric' assumes a fundamentally new significance; 'rhetoric' is not, nor can it be, the art, the technique, of an exterior persuasion; it is rather the speech which is the basis of the rational thought" (p. 2).

[4] *Aporia* is a figure of speech in which the speaker purports to be in doubt about a question or an interlocutor's statement. *Elenchus* literally means "to cross-examine," but in rhetoric and oratory it is a technique of examining and questioning statements and beliefs to test them for coherence and consistency.

Reading 26

Protagoras

Protagoras, translated by B. Jowett, 1892.

Persons of the Dialogue

SOCRATES, *who is the narrator of*   PROTAGORAS,
    the Dialogue to his Companion   HIPPIAS,   } *Sophists*
HIPPOCRATES   PRODICUS,
ALCIBIADES   CALLIAS, *a wealthy Athenian*
CRITIAS

Scene: The House of Callias

COM. WHERE do you come from, Socrates? And yet I need hardly ask the question, for I know that you have been in chase of the fair Alcibiades. I saw him the day before yesterday; and he had got a beard like a man, – and he is a man, as I may tell you in your ear. But I thought that he was still very charming.

SOC. What of his beard? Are you not of Homer's opinion, who says[5]

    'Youth is most charming when the beard first appears'?

And that is now the charm of Alcibiades.

COM. Well, and how do matters proceed? Have you been visiting him, and was he gracious to you?

SOC. Yes, I thought that he was very gracious; and especially today, for I have just come from him, and he has been helping me in an argument. But shall I tell you a strange thing? I paid no attention to him, and several times I quite forgot that he was present.

COM. What is the meaning of this? Has anything happened between you and him? For surely you cannot have discovered a fairer love than he is; certainly not in this city of Athens.

SOC. Yes, much fairer.

COM. What do you mean – a citizen or a foreigner?

SOC. A foreigner.

COM. Of what country?

SOC. Of Abdera.

COM. And is this stranger really in your opinion a fairer love than the son of Cleinias?

SOC. And is not the wiser always the fairer, sweet friend?

COM. But have you really met, Socrates, with some wise one?

SOC. Say rather, with the wisest of all living men, if you are willing to accord that title to Protagoras.

COM. What! Is Protagoras in Athens?

SOC. Yes; he has been here two days.

COM. And do you just come from an interview with him?

SOC. Yes; and I have heard and said many things.

COM. Then, if you have no engagement, suppose that you sit down and tell me what passed, and my attendant here shall give up his place to you.

SOC. To be sure; and I shall be grateful to you for listening.

COM. Thank you, too, for telling us.

SOC. That is thank you twice over. Listen then:

Last night, or rather very early this morning, Hippocrates, the son of Apollodorus and the brother of Phason, gave a tremendous thump with his staff at my door; some one opened to him, and he came rushing in and bawled out: Socrates, are you awake or asleep?

I knew his voice, and said: Hippocrates, is that you? and do you bring any news?

Good news, he said; nothing but good.

Delightful, I said; but what is the news? and why have you come hither at this unearthly hour?

He drew nearer to me and said: Protagoras is come.

Yes, I replied; he came two days ago: have you only just heard of his arrival?

---

[5] Il. xxiv. 348.

Yes, by the gods, he said; but not until yesterday evening.

At the same time he felt for the truckle-bed, and sat down at my feet, and then he said: Yesterday quite late in the evening, on my return from Oenoe whither I had gone in pursuit of my runaway slave Satyrus, as I meant to have told you, if some other matter had not come in the way; – on my return, when we had done supper and were about to retire to rest, my brother said to me: Protagoras is come. I was going to you at once, and then I thought that the night was far spent. But the moment sleep left me after my fatigue, I got up and came hither direct.

I, who knew the very courageous madness of the man, said: What is the matter? Has Protagoras robbed you of anything?

He replied, laughing: Yes, indeed he has, Socrates, of the wisdom which he keeps from me.

But, surely, I said, if you give him money, and make friends with him, he will make you as wise as he is himself.

Would to heaven, he replied, that this were the case! He might take all that I have, and all that my friends, have, if he pleased. But that is why I have come to you now, in order that you may speak to him on my behalf; for I am young, and also I have never seen nor heard him; (when he visited Athens before I was but a child;) and all men praise him, Socrates; he is reputed to be the most accomplished of speakers. There is no reason why we should not go to him at once, and then we shall find him at home. He lodges, as I hear, with Callias the son of Hipponicus: let us start.

I replied: Not yet, my good friend; the hour is too early. But let us rise and take a turn in the court and wait about there until day-break; when the day breaks, then we will go. For Protagoras is generally at home, and we shall be sure to find him; never fear.

Upon this we got up and walked about in the court, and I thought that I would make trial of the strength of his resolution. So I examined him and put questions to him. Tell me, Hippocrates, I said, as you are going to Protagoras, and will be paying your money to him, what is he to whom you are going? and what will he make of you? If, for example, you had thought of going to Hippocrates of Cos, the Asclepiad, and were about to give him your money, and some one had said to you: You are paying money to your name-sake Hippocrates, O Hippocrates; tell me, what

is he that you give him money? how would you have answered?

I should say, he replied, that I gave money to him as a physician.

And what will he make of you?

A physician, he said.

And if you were resolved to go to Polycleitus the Argive, or Pheidias the Athenian, and were intending to give them money, and some one had asked you: What are Polycleitus and Pheidias? and why do you give them this money? – how would you have answered?

I should have answered, that they were statuaries.

And what will they make of you?

A statuary, of course.

Well now, I said, you and I are going to Protagoras, and we are ready to pay him money on your behalf. If our own means are sufficient, and we can gain him with these, we shall be only too glad; but if not, then we are to spend the money of your friends as well. Now suppose, that while we are thus enthusiastically pursuing our object some one were to say to us: Tell me Socrates, and you Hippocrates what is Protagoras, and why are you going to pay him money – how should we answer? I know that Pheidias is a sculptor, and that Homer is a poet; but what appellation is given to Protagoras? how is he designated?

They call him a Sophist, Socrates, he replied.

Then we are going to pay our money to him in the character of a Sophist?

Certainly.

But suppose a person were to ask this further question: And how about yourself? What will Protagoras make of you, if you go to see him?

He answered, with a blush upon his face (for the day was just beginning to dawn, so that I could see him): Unless this differs in some way from the former instances, I suppose that he will make a Sophist of me.

By the gods, I said, and are you not ashamed at having to appear before the Hellenes in the character of a Sophist?

Indeed, Socrates, to confess the truth, I am.

But you should not assume, Hippocrates, that the instruction of Protagoras is of this nature: may you not learn of him in the same way that you learned the arts of the grammarian, or musician, or trainer, not with the view of making any of them a profession, but only as a part of education, and because a private gentleman and freeman ought to know them?

Just so, he said; and that, in my opinion, is a far truer account of the teaching of Protagoras.

I said: I wonder whether you know what you are doing?

And what am I doing?

You are going to commit your soul to the care of a man whom you call a Sophist. And yet I hardly think that you know what a Sophist is; and if not, then you do not even know to whom you are committing your soul and whether the thing to which you commit yourself be good or evil.

I certainly think that I do know, he replied.

Then tell me, what do you imagine that he is?

I take him to be one who knows wise things, he replied, as his name implies.

And might you not, I said, affirm this of the painter and of the carpenter also: Do not they, too, know wise things? But suppose a person were to ask us: In what are the painters wise? We should answer: In what relates to the making of likenesses, and similarly of other things. And if he were further to ask: What is the wisdom of the Sophist, and what is the manufacture over which he presides? – how should we answer him?

How should we answer him, Socrates? What other answer could there be but that he presides over the art which makes men eloquent?

Yes, I replied, that is very likely true, but not enough; for in the answer a further question is involved: Of what does the Sophist make a man talk eloquently? The player on the lyre may be supposed to make a man talk eloquently about that which he makes him understand, that is about playing the lyre. Is not that true?

Yes.

Then about what does the Sophist make him eloquent? Must not he make him eloquent in that which he understands?

Yes, that may be assumed.

And what is that which the Sophist knows and makes his disciple know?

Indeed, he said, I cannot tell.

Then I proceeded to say: Well, but are you aware of the danger which you are incurring? If you were going to commit your body to some one, who might do good or harm to it, would you not carefully consider and ask the opinion of your friends and kindred, and deliberate many days as to whether you should give him the care of your body? But when the soul is in question, which you hold to be of far more value than the body, and upon the good or evil of which depends the well-being of your all, – about this you never consulted either with your father or with your brother or with any one of us who are your companions. But no sooner does this foreigner appear, than you instantly commit your soul to his keeping. In the evening, as you say, you hear of him, and in the morning you go to him, never deliberating or taking the opinion of any one as to whether you ought to intrust yourself to him or not; – you have quite made up your mind that you will at all hazards be a pupil of Protagoras, and are prepared to expend all the property of yourself and of your friends in carrying out at any price this determination, although, as you admit, you do not know him, and have never spoken with him: and you call him a Sophist, but are manifestly ignorant of what a Sophist is; and yet you are going to commit yourself to his keeping.

When he heard me say this, he replied: No other inference, Socrates, can be drawn from your words.

I proceeded: Is not a Sophist, Hippocrates, one who deals wholesale or retail in the food of the soul? To me that appears to be his nature.

And what, Socrates, is the food of the soul?

Surely, I said, knowledge is the food of the soul; and we must take care, my friend, that the Sophist does not deceive us when he praises what he sells, like the dealers wholesale or retail who sell the food of the body; for they praise indiscriminately all their goods, without knowing what are really beneficial or hurtful: neither do their customers know, with the exception of any trainer or physician who may happen to buy of them. In like manner those who carry about the wares of knowledge, and make the round of the cities, and sell or retail them to any customer who is in want of them, praise them all alike; though I should not wonder, O my friend, if many of them were really ignorant of their effect upon the soul; and their customers equally ignorant, unless he who buys of them happens to be a physician of the soul. If, therefore, you have understanding of what is good and evil, you may safely buy knowledge of Protagoras or of any one; but if not, then, O my friend, pause, and do not hazard your dearest interests at a game of chance. For there is far greater peril in buying knowledge than in buying meat and drink: the one you purchase of the wholesale or retail dealer, and carry them away in other vessels, and before you receive them into the body as food, you may deposit them at home and call in any experienced friend who knows what is good to be eaten or drunken, and what not, and how much, and when; and then the danger of purchasing them is not so great. But you cannot buy the wares of knowledge and carry them away in another vessel; when you have paid for them you must receive them into the soul and go your way, either greatly harmed or greatly benefited; and therefore we should deliberate and take counsel with our elders; for we are still young – too young to determine such a matter. And now let us go, as we were intending, and hear Protagoras; and when we have heard what he has to say, we may take counsel of others; for not only is Protagoras at the house of Callias, but there is Hippias of Elis, and, if I am not mistaken, Prodicus of Ceos, and several other wise men.

To this we agreed, and proceeded on our way until we reached the vestibule of the house; and there we stopped in order to conclude a discussion which had arisen between us as we were going along; and we stood talking in the vestibule until we had finished and come to an understanding. And I think that the door-keeper, who was a eunuch, and who was probably annoyed at the great inroad of the Sophists, must have heard us talking. At any rate, when we knocked at the door, and he opened and saw us, he grumbled: They are Sophists – he is not at home; and instantly gave the door a hearty bang with both his hands. Again we knocked, and he answered without opening: Did you not hear me say that he is not at home, fellows? But, my friend, I said, you need not be alarmed; for we are not Sophists, and we are not come to see Callias, but we want to see Protagoras; and I must request you to announce us. At last, after a good deal of difficulty, the man was persuaded to open the door.

When we entered, we found Protagoras taking a walk in the cloister; and next to him, on one side, were walking Callias, the son of Hipponicus, and Paralus, the son of Pericles, who, by the mother's side, is his half-brother, and Charmides, the son of Glaucon. On the other side of him were Xanthippus, the other son of Pericles, Philippides, the son of Philomelus; also Antimoerus of Mende, who of all the disciples of Protagoras is the most famous, and intends to make sophistry his profession. A train of listeners followed him; the greater part of them appeared to be foreigners, whom Protagoras had brought with him out of the various cities visited by him in his journeys, he, like Orpheus, attracting them by his voice, and they following.[6] I should mention also that there were some Athenians in the company. Nothing delighted me more than the precision of their movements: they never got into his way at all; but when he and those who were with him turned back, then the band of listeners parted regularly on either side; he was always in front, and they wheeled round and took their places behind him in perfect order.

After him, as Homer says,[7] 'I lifted up my eyes and saw' Hippias the Elean sitting in the opposite cloister on a chair of state, and around him were seated on benches Eryximachus, the son of Acumenus, and Phaedrus the Myrrhinusian, and Andron the son of Androtion, and there were strangers whom he had brought with him from his native city of Elis, and some others: they were putting to Hippias certain physical and astronomical questions, and he, *ex cathedra*, was determining their several questions to them, and discoursing of them.

Also, 'my eyes beheld Tantalus;'[8] for Prodicus the Cean was at Athens: he had been lodged in a room which, in the days of Hipponicus, was a storehouse; but, as the house was full, Callias had cleared this out and made the room into a guest-chamber. Now Prodicus was still in bed, wrapped up in sheepskins and bedclothes, of which there seemed to be a great heap; and there was sitting by him on the couches near, Pausanias of the deme of Cerameis, and with Pausanias was a youth quite young, who is certainly remarkable for his good looks, and, if I am not mistaken, is also of a fair and gentle nature. I thought that I heard him called Agathon, and my suspicion is that he is the beloved of Pausanias. There was this youth, and also there were the two Adeimantuses, one the son of Cepis, and the other of Leucolophides, and some others. I was very anxious to hear what Prodicus was saying, for he seems to me to be an all-wise and inspired man; but I was not able to get into the inner circle, and

---

[6] Cp. Rep. x. 600 D.

[7] Od. xi. 601 foll.

[8] Od. xi. 582.

his fine deep voice made an echo in the room which rendered his words inaudible.

No sooner had we entered than there followed us Alcibiades the beautiful, as you say, and I believe you; and also Critias the son of Callaeschrus.

On entering we stopped a little, in order to look about us, and then walked up to Protagoras, and I said: Protagoras, my friend Hippocrates and I have come to see you.

Do you wish, he said, to speak with me alone, or in the presence of the company?

Whichever you please, I said; you shall determine when you have heard the purpose of our visit.

And what is your purpose? he said.

I must explain, I said, that my friend Hippocrates is a native Athenian; he is the son of Apollodorus, and of a great and prosperous house, and he is himself in natural ability quite a match for anybody of his own age. I believe that he aspires to political eminence; and this he thinks that conversation with you is most likely to procure for him. And now you can determine whether you would wish to speak to him of your teaching alone or in the presence of the company.

Thank you, Socrates, for your consideration of me. For certainly a stranger finding his way into great cities, and persuading the flower of the youth in them to leave the company of their kinsmen or any other acquaintances, old or young, and live with him, under the idea that they will be improved by his conversation, ought to be very cautious; great jealousies are aroused by his proceedings, and he is the subject of many enmities and conspiracies. Now the art of the Sophist is, as I believe, of great antiquity; but in ancient times those who practised it, fearing this odium, veiled and disguised themselves under various names, some under that of poets, as Homer, Hesiod, and Simonides, some, of hierophants and prophets, as Orpheus and Musaeus, and some as I observe, even under the name of gymnastic-masters, like Iccus of Tarentum, or the more recently celebrated Herodicus, now of Selymbria and formerly of Megara, who is a first-rate Sophist. Your own Agathocles pretended to be a musician, but was really an eminent Sophist; also Pythocleides the Cean; and there were many others; and all of them, as I was saying, adopted these arts as veils or disguises because they were afraid of the odium which they would incur. But that is not my way,

for I do not believe that they effected their purpose, which was to deceive the government, who were not blinded by them; and as to the people, they have no understanding, and only repeat what their rulers are pleased to tell them. Now to run away, and to be caught in running away, is the very height of folly, and also greatly increases the exasperation of mankind; for they regard him who runs away as a rogue, in addition to any other objections which they have to him; and therefore I take an entirely opposite course, and acknowledge myself to be a Sophist and instructor of mankind; such an open acknowledgment appears to me to be a better sort of caution than concealment. Nor do I neglect other precautions, and therefore I hope, as I may say, by the favour of heaven that no harm will come of the acknowledgment that I am a Sophist. And I have been now many years in the profession – for all my years when added up are many: there is no one here present of whom I might not be the father. Wherefore I should much prefer conversing with you, if you want to speak with me, in the presence of the company.

As I suspected that he would like to have a little display and glorification in the presence of Prodicus and Hippias, and would gladly show us to them in the light of his admirers, I said: But why should we not summon Prodicus and Hippias and their friends to hear us?

Very good, he said.

Suppose, said Callias, that we hold a council in which you may sit and discuss. – This was agreed upon, and great delight was felt at the prospect of hearing wise men talk; we ourselves took the chairs and benches, and arranged them by Hippias, where the other benches had been already placed. Meanwhile Callias and Alcibiades got Prodicus out of bed and brought in him and his companions.

When we were all seated, Protagoras said: Now that the company are assembled, Socrates, tell me about the young man of whom you were just now speaking.

I replied: I will begin again at the same point, Protagoras, and tell you once more the purport of my visit: this is my friend Hippocrates, who is desirous of making your acquaintance; he would like to know what will happen to him if he associates with you. I have no more to say.

Protagoras answered: Young man, if you associate with me, on the very first day you will return home a better man than you came, and better on the second day than on the first, and better every day than you were on the day before.

When I heard this, I said: Protagoras, I do not at all wonder at hearing you say this; even at your age and with all your wisdom, if any one were to teach you what you did not know before, you would become better no doubt: but please to answer in a different way – I will explain how by an example. Let me suppose that Hippocrates, instead of desiring your acquaintance, wished to become acquainted with the young man Zeuxippus of Heraclea, who has lately been in Athens, and he had come to him as he has come to you, and had heard him say, as he has heard you say, that every day he would grow and become better if he associated with him: and then suppose that he were to ask him, 'In what shall I become better, and in what shall I grow?' – Zeuxippus would answer, 'In painting.' And suppose that he went to Orthagoras the Theban and heard him say the same thing, and asked him, 'In what shall I become better day by day?' he would reply, 'In flute-playing.' Now I want you to make the same sort of answer to this young man and to me, who is asking questions on his account. When you say that on the first day on which he associates with you he will return home a better man, and on every day will grow in like manner, – in what, Protagoras, will he be better? and about what?

When Protagoras heard me say this, he replied: You ask questions fairly, and I like to answer a question which is fairly put. If Hippocrates comes to me he will not experience the sort of drudgery with which other Sophists are in the habit of insulting their pupils; who, when they have just escaped from the arts, are taken and driven back into them by these teachers, and made to learn calculation, and astronomy, and geometry, and music (he gave a look at Hippias as he said this); but if he comes to me, he will learn that which he comes to learn. And this is prudence in affairs private as well as public; he will learn to order his own house in the best manner, and he will be able to speak and act for the best in the affairs of the state.

Do I understand you, I said; and is your meaning that you teach the art of politics, and that you promise to make men good citizens?

That, Socrates, is exactly the profession which I make.

Then, I said, you do indeed possess a noble art, if there is no mistake about this; for I will freely confess to you, Protagoras, that I have a doubt whether this art is capable of being taught, and yet I know not how to disbelieve your assertion. And I ought to tell you why I am of opinion that this art cannot be taught or communicated by man to man. I say that the Athenians are an understanding people, and indeed they are esteemed to be such by the other Hellenes. Now I observe that when we are met together in the assembly, and the matter in hand relates to building, the builders are summoned as advisers; when the question is one of ship-building, then the ship-wrights; and the like of other arts which they think capable of being taught and learned. And if some person offers to give them advice who is not supposed by them to have any skill in the art, even though he be good-looking, and rich, and noble, they will not listen to him, but laugh and hoot at him, until either he is clamoured down and retires of himself; or if he persist, he is dragged away or put out by the constables at the command of the prytanes. This is their way of behaving about professors of the arts. But when the question is an affair of state, then everybody is free to have a say – carpenter, tinker, cobbler, sailor, passenger; rich and poor, high and low – any one who likes gets up, and no one reproaches him, as in the former case, with not having learned, and having no teacher, and yet giving advice; evidently because they are under the impression that this sort of knowledge cannot be taught. And not only is this true of the state, but of individuals; the best and wisest of our citizens are unable to impart their political wisdom to others: as for example, Pericles, the father of these young men, who gave them excellent instruction in all that could be learned from masters, in his own department of politics neither taught them, nor gave them teachers; but they were allowed to wander at their own free will in a sort of hope that they would light upon virtue of their own accord. Or take another example: there was Cleinias the younger brother of our friend Alcibiades, of whom this very same Pericles was the guardian; and he being in fact under the apprehension that Cleinias would be corrupted by Alcibiades, took him away, and placed him in the house of Ariphron to be educated; but before six months had elapsed, Ariphron sent him back, not knowing what to do with him. And I could mention numberless other instances of persons who were good themselves, and never yet made any one else good, whether friend or stranger.

Now I, Protagoras, having these examples before me, am inclined to think that virtue cannot be taught. But then again, when I listen to your words, I waver; and am disposed to think that there must be something in what you say, because I know that you have great experience, and learning, and invention. And I wish that you would, if possible, show me a little more clearly that virtue can be taught. Will you be so good?

That I will, Socrates, and gladly. But what would you like? Shall I, as an elder, speak to you as younger men in an apologue or myth, or shall I argue out the question?

To this several of the company answered that he should choose for himself.

Well, then, he said, I think that the myth will be more interesting.

Once upon a time there were gods only, and no mortal creatures. But when the time came that these also should be created, the gods fashioned them out of earth and fire and various mixtures of both elements in the interior of the earth; and when they were about to bring them into the light of day, they ordered Prometheus and Epimetheus to equip them, and to distribute to them severally their proper qualities. Epimetheus said to Prometheus: 'Let me distribute, and do you inspect.' This was agreed, and Epimetheus made the distribution. There were some to whom he gave strength without swiftness, while he equipped the weaker with swiftness; some he armed, and others he left unarmed; and devised for the latter some other means of preservation, making some large, and having their size as a protection, and others small, whose nature was to fly in the air or burrow in the ground; this was to be their way of escape. Thus did he compensate them with the view of preventing any race from becoming extinct. And when he had provided against their destruction by one another, he contrived also a means of protecting them against the seasons of heaven; clothing them with close hair and thick skins sufficient to defend them against the winter cold and able to resist the summer heat, so that they might have a natural bed of their own when they wanted to rest; also he furnished them with hoofs and hair and hard and callous skins under their feet. Then he gave them varieties of food, – herb of the soil to some, to others fruits of trees, and to others roots, and to some again he gave other animals as food. And some he made to have few young ones, while those who were their prey were very prolific; and in this manner the race was preserved. Thus did Epimetheus, who, not being very wise, forgot that he had distributed among the brute animals all the qualities which he had to give – and when he came to man, who was still unprovided, he was terribly perplexed. Now while he was in this perplexity, Prometheus came to inspect the distribution, and he found that the other animals were suitably furnished, but that man alone was naked and shoeless, and had neither bed nor arms of defence. The appointed hour was approaching when man in his turn was to go forth into the light of day; and Prometheus, not knowing how he could devise his salvation, stole the mechanical arts of Hephaestus and Athene, and fire with them (they could neither have been acquired nor used without fire), and gave them to man. Thus man had the wisdom necessary to the support of life, but political wisdom he had not; for that was in the keeping of Zeus, and the power of Prometheus did not extend to entering into the citadel of heaven, where Zeus dwelt, who moreover had terrible sentinels; but he did enter by stealth into the common workshop of Athene and Hephaestus, in which they used to practise their favourite arts, and carried off Hephaestus' art of working by fire, and also the art of Athene, and gave them to man. And in this way man was supplied with the means of life. But Prometheus is said to have been afterwards prosecuted for theft, owing to the blunder of Epimetheus.

Now man, having a share of the divine attributes, was at first the only one of the animals who had any gods, because he alone was of their kindred; and he would raise altars and images of them. He was not long in inventing articulate speech and names; and he also constructed houses and clothes and shoes and beds, and drew sustenance from the earth. Thus provided, mankind at first lived dispersed, and there were no cities. But the consequence was that they were destroyed by the wild beasts, for they were utterly weak in comparison of them, and their art was only sufficient to provide them with the means of life, and did not enable them to carry on war against the animals: food they had, but not as yet the art of government, of which the art of war is a part. After a while the desire of self-preservation gathered them into cities; but when they were gathered together, having no art of government, they evil intreated one another, and were again in process of dispersion and destruction. Zeus feared that the entire race would be exterminated, and so he sent Hermes to them, bearing reverence and justice to be the ordering principles of cities and the bonds of friendship and conciliation. Hermes asked Zeus how he should impart justice and reverence among men – Should he distribute them as the arts are distributed; that is to say, to a favoured few only, one skilled individual having enough of medicine or of any other art for many unskilled ones? 'Shall this be the manner in which I am to distribute justice and reverence among men, or shall I give them to all?' 'To all,' said Zeus; 'I should like them all to have a share; for cities cannot exist, if a few only share in the virtues, as in the arts. And further, make a law by my order, that he who has no part in reverence and justice shall be put to death, for he is a plague of the state.'

And this is the reason, Socrates, why the Athenians and mankind in general, when the question relates to carpentering or any other mechanical art, allow but a few to share in their deliberations; and when any one else interferes, then, as you say, they object, if he be not of the favoured few; which, as I reply, is very natural. But when they meet to deliberate about political virtue, which proceeds only by way of justice and wisdom, they are patient enough of any man who speaks of them, as is also natural, because they think that every man ought to share in this sort of virtue, and that states could not exist if this were otherwise. I have explained to you, Socrates, the reason of this phenomenon.

And that you may not suppose yourself to be deceived in thinking that all men regard every man as having a share of justice or honesty and of every other political virtue, let me give you a further proof, which is this. In other cases, as you are aware, if a man says that he is a good flute-player, or skilful in any other art in which he has no skill, people either laugh at him or are angry with him, and his relations think that he is mad and go and admonish him; but when honesty is in question, or some other political virtue, even if they know that he is dishonest, yet, if the man comes publicly forward and tells the truth about his dishonesty, then, what in the other case was held by them to be good sense, they now deem to be madness. They say that all men ought to profess honesty whether they are honest or not, and that a man is out of his mind who says anything else.

Their notion is, that a man must have some degree of honesty; and that if he has none at all he ought not to be in the world.

I have been showing that they are right in admitting every man as a counsellor about this sort of virtue, as they are of the opinion that every man is a partaker of it. And I will now endeavour to show further that they do not conceive this virtue to be given by nature, or to grow spontaneously, but to be a thing which may be taught; and which comes to a man by taking pains. No one would instruct, no one would rebuke, or be angry with those whose calamities they suppose to be due to nature or chance; they do not try to punish or to prevent them from being what they are; they do but pity them. Who is so foolish as to chastise or instruct the ugly, or the diminutive, or the feeble? And for this reason. Because he knows that good and evil of this kind is the work of nature and of chance; whereas if a man is wanting in those good qualities which are attained by study and exercise and teaching, and has only the contrary evil qualities, other men are angry with him, and punish and reprove him – of these evil qualities one is impiety, another injustice, and they may be described generally as the very opposite of political virtue. In such cases any man will be angry with another, and reprimand him, – clearly because he thinks that by study and learning, the virtue in which the other is deficient may be acquired. If you will think, Socrates, of the nature of punishment, you will see at once that in the opinion of mankind virtue may be acquired; no one punishes the evil-doer under the notion, or for the reason, that he has done wrong – only the unreasonable fury of a beast acts in that manner. But he who desires to inflict rational punishment does not retaliate for a past wrong which cannot be undone; he has regard to the future, and is desirous that the man who is punished, and he who sees him punished, may be deterred from doing wrong again. He punishes for the sake of prevention, thereby clearly implying that virtue is capable of being taught. This is the notion of all who retaliate upon others either privately or publicly. And the Athenians, too, your own citizens, like other men, punish and take vengeance on all whom they regard as evil doers; and hence, we may infer them to be of the number of those who think that virtue may be acquired and taught. Thus far, Socrates, I have shown you clearly enough, if I am not mistaken, that your countrymen are right in admitting the tinker and the cobbler to advise about politics, and also that they deem virtue to be capable of being taught and acquired.

There yet remains one difficulty which has been raised by you about the sons of good men. What is the reason why good men teach their sons the knowledge which is gained from teachers, and make them wise in that, but do nothing towards improving them in the virtues which distinguish themselves? And here, Socrates, I will leave the apologue and resume the argument. Please to consider: Is there or is there not some one quality of which all the citizens must be partakers, if there is to be a city at all? In the answer to this question is contained the only solution of your difficulty; there is no other. For if there be any such quality, and this quality or unity is not the art of the carpenter, or the smith, or the potter, but justice and temperance and holiness and, in a word, manly virtue – if this is the quality of which all men must be partakers, and which is the very condition of their learning or doing anything else, and if he who is wanting in this, whether he be a child only or a grown-up man or woman, must be taught and punished, until by punishment he becomes better, and he who rebels against instruction and punishment is either exiled or condemned to death under the idea that he is incurable – if what I am saying be true, good men have their sons taught other things and not this, do consider how extraordinary their conduct would appear to be. For we have shown that they think virtue capable of being taught and cultivated both in private and public; and, notwithstanding, they have their sons taught lesser matters, ignorance of which does not involve the punishment of death: but greater things, of which the ignorance may cause death and exile to those who have no training or knowledge of them – aye, and confiscation as well as death, and, in a word, may be the ruin of families – those things, I say, they are supposed not to teach them – not to take the utmost care that they should learn. How improbable is this, Socrates!

Education and admonition commence in the first years of childhood, and last to the very end of life. Mother and nurse and father and tutor are vying with one another about the improvement of the child as soon as ever he is able to understand what is being said to him: he cannot say or do anything without their setting forth to him that this is just and that is unjust; this is honourable, that is dishonourable; this is holy, that is unholy; do this and abstain from that. And if he obeys, well and good; if not, he is straightened by threats and blows, like a piece of bent or warped wood. At a later stage they send him to teachers, and enjoin them to see to his manners even more than to his reading and music; and the teachers do as they are desired. And when the boy has learned his letters and is beginning to understand what is written, as before he understood only what was spoken, they put into his hands the works of great poets, which he reads sitting on a bench at school; in these are contained many admonitions, and many tales, and praises, and encomia of ancient famous men, which he is required to learn by heart, in order that he may imitate or emulate them and desire to become like them. Then, again, the teachers of the lyre take similar care that their young disciple is temperate and gets into no mischief; and when they have taught him the use of the lyre, they introduce him to the poems of other excellent poets, who are the lyric poets; and these they set to music, and make their harmonies and rhythms quite familiar to the children's souls, in order that they may learn to be more gentle, and harmonious, and rhythmical, and so more fitted for speech and action; for the life of man in every part has need of harmony and rhythm. Then they send them to the master of gymnastic, in order that their bodies may better minister to the virtuous mind, and that they may not be compelled through bodily weakness to play the coward in war or on any other occasion. This is what is done by those who have the means, and those who have the means are the rich; their children begin to go to school soonest and leave off latest. When they have done with masters, the state again compels them to learn the laws, and live after the pattern which they furnish, and not after their own fancies; and just as in learning to write, the writing-master first draws lines with a style for the use of the young beginner, and gives him the tablet and makes him follow the lines, so the city draws the laws, which were the invention of good lawgivers living in the olden time; these are given to the young man, in order to guide him in his conduct whether he is commanding or obeying; and he who transgresses them is to be corrected, or, in other words, called to account, which is a term used not only in your country, but also in many others, seeing that justice calls men to account. Now when there is all this care about virtue private and public, why, Socrates, do you still wonder and doubt whether virtue can be taught? Cease to wonder, for the opposite would be far more surprising.

But why then do the sons of good fathers often turn out ill? There is nothing very wonderful in this; for, as I have been saying, the existence of a state implies that virtue is not any man's private possession. If so – and nothing can be truer – then I will further ask you to imagine, as an illustration, some other pursuit or branch of knowledge which may be assumed equally to be the condition of the existence of a state. Suppose that there could be no state unless we were all flute-players, as far as each had the capacity, and everybody was freely teaching everybody the art, both in private and public, and reproving the bad player as freely and openly as every man now teaches justice and the laws, not concealing them as he would conceal the other arts, but imparting them – for all of us have a mutual interest in the justice and virtue of one another, and this is the reason why every one is so ready to teach justice and the laws; – suppose, I say, that there were the same readiness and liberality among us in teaching one another flute-playing, do you imagine, Socrates, that the sons of good flute-players would be more likely to be good than the sons of bad ones? I think not. Would not their sons grow up to be distinguished or undistinguished according to their own natural capacities as flute-players, and the son of a good player would often turn out to be a bad one, and the son of a bad player to be a good one, and all flute-players would be good enough in comparison of those who were ignorant and unacquainted with the art of flute-playing? In like manner I would have you consider that he who appears to you to be the worst of those who have been brought up in laws and humanities, would appear to be a just man and a master of justice if he were to be compared with men who had no education, or courts of justice, or laws, or any restraints upon them which compelled them to practise virtue – with the savages, for example, whom the poet Pherecrates exhibited on the stage at the last year's Lenaean festival. If you were living among men such as the man-haters in his Chorus, you would be only too glad to meet with Eurybates and Phrynondas, and you

would sorrowfully long to revisit the rascality of this part of the world. And you, Socrates, are discontented, and why? Because all men are teachers of virtue, each one according to his ability; and you say, Where are the teachers? You might as well ask, Who teaches Greek? For of that too there will not be any teachers found. Or you might ask, Who is to teach the sons of our artisans this same art which they have learned of their fathers? He and his fellow-workmen have taught them to the best of their ability, – but who will carry them further in their arts? And you would certainly have a difficulty, Socrates, in finding a teacher of them; but there would be no difficulty in finding a teacher of those who are wholly ignorant. And this is true of virtue or of anything else; if a man is better able than we are to promote virtue ever so little we must be content with the result. A teacher of this sort I believe myself to be, and above all other men to have the knowledge which makes a man noble and good; and I give my pupils their money's-worth, and even more, as they themselves confess. And therefore I have introduced the following mode of payment: – When a man has been my pupil, if he likes he pays my price, but there is no compulsion; and if he does not like, he has only to go into a temple and take an oath of the value of the instructions, and he pays no more than he declares to be their value.

Such is my Apologue, Socrates, and such is the argument by which I endeavour to show that virtue may be taught, and that this is the opinion of the Athenians. And I have also attempted to show that you are not to wonder at good fathers having bad sons, or at good sons having bad fathers, of which the sons of Polycleitus afford an example, who are the companions of our friends here, Paralus and Xanthippus, but are nothing in comparison with their father; and this is true of the sons of many other artists. As yet I ought not to say the same of Paralus and Xanthippus themselves, for they are young and there is still hope of them.

Protagoras ended, and in my ear

'So charming left his voice, that I the while
Thought him still speaking; still stood fixed to hear.'[9]

At length, when the truth dawned upon me, that he had really finished, not without difficulty

[9] Borrowed by Milton, *Paradise Lost*, viii. 2–3.

I began to collect myself, and looking at Hippocrates, I said to him: O son of Apollodorus, how deeply grateful I am to you for having brought me hither; I would not have missed the speech of Protagoras for a great deal. For I used to imagine that no human care could make men good; but I know better now. Yet I have still one very small difficulty which I am sure that Protagoras will easily explain, as he has already explained so much. If a man were to go and consult Pericles or any of our great speakers about these matters, he might perhaps hear as fine a discourse; but then when one has a question to ask of any of them, like books, they can neither answer nor ask; and if any one challenges the least particular of their speech, they go ringing on in a long harangue, like brazen pots, which when they are struck continue to sound unless some one puts his hand upon them; whereas our friend Protagoras can not only make a good speech, as he has already shown, but when he is asked a question he can answer briefly; and when he asks he will wait and hear the answer; and this is a very rare gift. Now I, Protagoras, want to ask of you a little question, which if you will only answer, I shall be quite satisfied. You were saying that virtue can be taught – that I will take upon your authority, and there is no one to whom I am more ready to trust. But I marvel at one thing about which I should like to have my mind set at rest. You were speaking of Zeus sending justice and reverence to men; and several times while you were speaking, justice, and temperance, and holiness, and all these qualities, were described by you as if together they made up virtue. Now I want you to tell me truly whether virtue is one whole, of which justice and temperance and holiness are parts; or whether all these are only the names of one and the same thing: that is the doubt which still lingers in my mind.

There is no difficulty, Socrates, in answering that the qualities of which you are speaking are the parts of virtue which is one.

And are they parts, I said, in the same sense in which mouth, nose, and eyes, and ears, are the parts of a face; or are they like the parts of gold, which differ from the whole and from one another only in being larger or smaller?

I should say that they differed, Socrates, in the first way; they are related to one another as the parts of a face are related to the whole face.

And do men have some one part and some another part of virtue? Or if a man has one part, must he also have all the others?

By no means, he said; for many a man is brave and not just, or just and not wise.

You would not deny, then, that courage and wisdom are also parts of virtue?

Most undoubtedly they are, he answered; and wisdom is the noblest of the parts.

And they are all different from one another? I said.

Yes.

And has each of them a distinct function like the parts of the face – the eye, for example, is not like the ear, and has not the same functions; and the other parts are none of them like one another, either in their functions, or in any other way? I want to know whether the comparison holds concerning the parts of virtue. Do they also differ from one another in themselves and in their functions? For that is clearly what the simile would imply.

Yes, Socrates, you are right in supposing that they differ.

Then, I said, no other part of virtue is like knowledge, or like justice, or like courage, or like temperance, or like holiness?

No, he answered.

Well then, I said, suppose that you and I enquire into their natures. And first, you would agree with me that justice is of the nature of a thing, would you not? That is my opinion: would it not be yours also?

Mine also, he said.

And suppose that some one were to ask us, saying, 'O Protagoras, and you, Socrates, what about this thing which you were calling justice, is it just or unjust?' – and I were to answer, just: would you vote with me or against me?

With you, he said.

Thereupon I should answer to him who asked me, that justice is of the nature of the just: would not you?

Yes, he said.

And suppose that he went on to say: Well now, is there also such a thing as holiness?' – we should answer, 'Yes,' if I am not mistaken?

Yes, he said.

Which you would also acknowledge to be a thing – should we not say so?

He assented.

'And is this a sort of thing which is of the nature of the holy, or of the nature of the unholy?' I should be angry at his putting such a question, and should say, 'Peace, man nothing can be holy if holiness is not holy.' What would you say? Would you not answer in the same way?

Certainly, he said.

And then after this suppose that he came and asked us, 'What were you saying just now? Perhaps I may not have heard you rightly, but you seemed to me to be saying that the parts of virtue were not the same as one another.' I should reply, 'You certainly heard that said, but not, as you imagine, by me; for I only asked the question; Protagoras gave the answer.' And suppose that he turned to you and said, 'Is this true, Protagoras? and do you maintain that one part of virtue is unlike another, and is this your position?'—how would you answer him?

I could not help acknowledging the truth of what he said, Socrates.

Well then, Protagoras, we will assume this; and now supposing that he proceeded to say further, 'Then holiness is not of the nature of justice, nor justice of the nature of holiness, but of the nature of unholiness; and holiness is of the nature of the not just, and therefore of the unjust, and the unjust is the unholy:' how shall we answer him? I should certainly answer him on my own behalf that justice is holy, and that holiness is just; and I would say in like manner on your behalf also, if you would allow me, that justice is either the same with holiness, or very nearly the same; and above all I would assert that justice is like holiness and holiness is like justice; and I wish that you would tell me whether I may be permitted to give this answer on your behalf, and whether you would agree with me.

He replied, I cannot simply agree, Socrates, to the proposition that justice is holy and that holiness is just, for there appears to me to be a difference between them. But what matter? if you please I please; and let us assume, if you will, that justice is holy, and that holiness is just.

Pardon me, I replied; I do not want this 'if you wish' or 'if you will' sort of conclusion to be proven, but I want you and me to be proven: I mean to say that the conclusion will be best proven if there be no 'if.'

Well, he said, I admit that justice bears a resemblance to holiness, for there is always some point of view in which everything is like every other thing; white is in a certain way like black, and hard is like soft, and the most extreme opposites have some qualities in common; even the parts of the face which, as we were saying before, are distinct and have different functions, are still in a certain point of view similar, and one of them is like another of them. And you may prove that they are like one another on the same principle that all things are like one another; and yet things which are like in some particular ought not to be called alike, nor things which are unlike in some particular, however slight, unlike.

And do you think, I said in a tone of surprise, that justice and holiness have but a small degree of likeness?

Certainly not; any more than I agree with what I understand to be your view.

Well, I said, as you appear to have a difficulty about this, let us take another of the examples which you mentioned instead. Do you admit the existence of folly?

I do.

And is not wisdom the very opposite of folly?

That is true, he said.

And when men act rightly and advantageously they seem to you to be temperate?

Yes, he said.

And temperance makes them temperate?

Certainly.

And they who do not act rightly act foolishly, and in acting thus are not temperate?

I agree, he said.

Then to act foolishly is the opposite of acting temperately?

He assented.

And foolish actions are done by folly, and temperate actions by temperance?

He agreed.

And that is done strongly which is done by strength, and that which is weakly done, by weakness?

He assented.

And that which is done with swiftness is done swiftly, and that which is done with slowness, slowly?

He assented again.

And that which is done in the same manner, is done by the same; and that which is done in an opposite manner by the opposite?

He agreed.

Once more, I said, is there anything beautiful?

Yes.

To which the only opposite is the ugly?

There is no other.

And is there anything good?

There is.

To which the only opposite is the evil?

There is no other.

And there is the acute in sound?

True.

To which the only opposite is the grave?

There is no other, he said, but that.

Then every opposite has one opposite only and no more?

He assented.

Then now, I said, let us recapitulate our admissions. First of all we admitted that everything has one opposite and not more than one?

We did so.

And we admitted also that what was done in opposite ways was done by opposites?

Yes.

And that which was done foolishly, as we further admitted, was done in the opposite way to that which was done temperately?

Yes.

And that which was done temperately was done by temperance, and that which was done foolishly by folly?

He agreed.

And that which is done in opposite ways is done by opposites?

Yes.

And one thing is done by temperance, and quite another thing by folly?

Yes.

And in opposite ways?

Certainly.

And therefore by opposites – then folly is the opposite of temperance?

Clearly.

And do you remember that folly has already been acknowledged by us to be the opposite of wisdom?

He assented.

And we said that everything has only one opposite?

Yes.

Then, Protagoras, which of the two assertions shall we renounce? One says that everything has but one opposite; the other that wisdom is distinct from temperance, and that both of them are parts of virtue; and that they are not only distinct, but dissimilar, both in themselves and in their functions, like the parts of a face. Which of these two assertions shall we renounce? For both of them together are certainly not in harmony; they do not accord or agree: for how can they be said to agree if everything is assumed to have only one opposite and not more than one, and yet folly, which is one, has clearly the two opposites – wisdom and temperance? Is not that true, Protagoras? What else would you say?

He assented, but with great reluctance.

Then temperance and wisdom are the same, as before justice and holiness appeared to us to be nearly the same. And now, Protagoras, I said, we must finish the enquiry, and not faint. Do you think that an unjust man can be temperate in his injustice?

I should be ashamed, Socrates, he said, to acknowledge this, which nevertheless many may be found to assert.

And shall I argue with them or with you? I replied.

I would rather, he said, that you should argue with the many first, if you will.

Whichever you please, if you will only answer me and say whether you are of their opinion or not. My object is to test the validity of the argument; and yet the result may be that I who ask and you who answer may both be put on our trial.

Protagoras at first made a show of refusing, as he said that the argument was not encouraging; at length, he consented to answer.

Now then, I said, begin at the beginning and answer me. You think that some men are temperate, and yet unjust?

Yes, he said; let that be admitted.

And temperance is good sense?

Yes.

And good sense is good counsel in doing injustice?

Granted.

If they succeed, I said, or if they do not succeed?

If they succeed.

And you would admit the existence of goods?

Yes.

And is the good that which is expedient for man?

Yes, indeed, he said: and there are some things which may be inexpedient, and yet I call them good.

I thought that Protagoras was getting ruffled and excited; he seemed to be setting himself in an attitude of war. Seeing this, I minded my business, and gently said:

When you say, Protagoras, that things inexpedient are good, do you mean inexpedient for man only, or inexpedient altogether? and do you call the latter good?

Certainly not the last, he replied; for I know of many things, – meats, drinks, medicines, and ten thousand other things, which are inexpedient for man, and some which are expedient; and some which are neither expedient nor inexpedient for man, but only for horses; and some for oxen only, and some for dogs; and some for no animals, but only for trees; and some for the roots of trees and not for their branches, as for example, manure, which is a good thing when laid about the roots of a tree, but utterly destructive if thrown upon the shoots and young branches; or I may instance olive oil, which is mischievous to all plants, and generally most injurious to the hair of every animal with the exception of man, but beneficial to human hair and to the human body generally; and even in this application (so various and changeable is the nature of the benefit), that which is the greatest good to the outward parts of a man, is a very great evil to his inward parts: and for this reason physicians always forbid their patients the use of oil in their food, except in very small quantities, just enough to extinguish the disagreeable sensation of smell in meats and sauces.

When he had given this answer, the company cheered him. And I said: Protagoras, I have a wretched memory, and when any one makes a long speech to me I never remember what he is talking about. As then, if I had been deaf, and you were going to converse with me, you would have had to raise your voice; so now, having such a bad memory, I will ask you to cut your answers shorter, if you would take me with you.

What do you mean? he said: how am I to shorten my answers? shall I make them too short?

Certainly not, I said.

But short enough?

Yes, I said.

Shall I answer what appears to me to be short enough, or what appears to you to be short enough?

I have heard, I said, that you can speak and teach others to speak about the same things at such length that words never seemed to fail, or with such brevity that no one could use fewer of them. Please therefore, if you talk with me, to adopt the latter or more compendious method.

Socrates, he replied, many a battle of words have I fought, and if I had followed the method of disputation which my adversaries desired, as you want me to do, I should have been no better than another, and the name of Protagoras would have been nowhere.

I saw that he was not satisfied with his previous answers, and that he would not play the part of answerer any more if he could help; and I considered that there was no call upon me to continue the conversation; so I said: Protagoras, I do not wish to force the conversation upon you if you had rather not, but when you are willing to argue with me in such a way that I can follow you, then I will argue with you. Now you, as is said of you by others and as you say of yourself, are able to have discussions in shorter forms of speech as well as in longer, for you are a master of wisdom; but I cannot manage these long speeches: I only wish that I could. You, on the other hand, who are capable of either, ought to speak shorter as I beg you, and then we might converse. But I see that you are disinclined, and as I have an engagement which will prevent my staying to hear you at greater length (for I have to be in another place), I will depart; although I should have liked to have heard you.

Thus I spoke, and was rising from my seat, when Callias seized me by the right hand, and in his left hand caught hold of this old cloak of mine. He said: We cannot let you go, Socrates, for if you leave us there will be an end of our discussions: I must therefore beg you to remain, as there is nothing in the world that I should like better than to hear you and Protagoras discourse. Do not deny the company this pleasure.

Now I had got up, and was in the act of departure. Son of Hipponicus, I replied, I have always admired, and do now heartily applaud and love your philosophical spirit, and I would gladly comply with your request, if I could. But the truth is that I cannot. And what you ask is as great an impossibility to me, as if you bade me run a race with Crison of Himera, when in his prime, or with some one of the long or day course runners. To such a request I should reply that I would fain ask the same of my own legs; but they refuse to comply. And therefore if you want to see Crison and me in the same stadium, you must bid him slacken his speed to mine, for I cannot run quickly, and he can run slowly. And in like manner if you want to hear me and Protagoras discoursing, you must ask him to shorten his answers, and keep to the point, as he did at first; if not, how can there be any discussion? For discussion is one thing, and making an oration is quite another, in my humble opinion.

But you see, Socrates, said Callias, that Protagoras may fairly claim to speak in his own way, just as you claim to speak in yours.

Here Alcibiades interposed, and said: That, Callias, is not a true statement of the case. For our friend Socrates admits that he cannot make a speech – in this he yields the palm to Protagoras: but I should be greatly surprised if he yielded to any living man in the power of holding and apprehending an argument. Now if Protagoras will make a similar admission, and confess that he is inferior to Socrates in argumentative skill, that is enough for Socrates; but if he claims a superiority in argument as well, let him ask and answer – not, when a question is asked, slipping away from the point, and instead of answering, making a speech at such length that most of his hearers forget the question at issue (not that Socrates is likely to forget – I will be bound for that, although he may pretend in fun that he has a bad memory). And Socrates appears to me to be more in the right than Protagoras; that is my view, and every man ought to say what he thinks.

When Alcibiades had done speaking, some one – Critias, I believe – went on to say: O Prodicus and Hippias, Callias appears to me to be a partisan of Protagoras: and this led Alcibiades, who loves opposition, to take the other side. But we should not be partisans either of Socrates or of Protagoras; let us rather unite in entreating both of them not to break up the discussion.

Prodicus added: That, Critias, seems to me to be well said, for those who are present at such discussions ought to be impartial hearers of both the speakers; remembering, however, that impartiality is not the same as equality, for both sides should be impartially heard, and yet an equal meed should not be assigned to both of them; but to the wiser a higher meed should be given, and a lower to the less wise. And I as well as Critias would beg you, Protagoras and Socrates, to grant our request, which is, that you will argue with one another and not wrangle; for friends argue with friends out of good-will, but only adversaries and enemies wrangle. And then our meeting will be delightful; for in this way you, who are the speakers, will be most likely to win esteem, and not praise only, among us who are your audience; for esteem is a sincere conviction of the hearers' souls, but praise is often an insincere expression of men uttering falsehoods contrary to their conviction. And thus we who are the hearers will be gratified and not pleased; for gratification is of the mind when receiving wisdom and knowledge, but pleasure is of the body when eating or experiencing some other bodily delight. Thus spoke Prodicus, and many of the company applauded his words.

Hippias the sage spoke next. He said: All of you who are here present I reckon to be kinsmen and friends and fellow-citizens, by nature and not by law; for by nature like is akin to like, whereas law is the tyrant of mankind, and often compels us to do many things which are against nature. How great would be the disgrace then, if we, who know the nature of things, and are the wisest of the Hellenes, and as such are met together in this city, which is the metropolis of wisdom, and in the greatest and most glorious house of this city, should have nothing to show worthy of this height of dignity, but should only quarrel with one another like the meanest of mankind! I do pray and advise you, Protagoras, and you, Socrates, to agree upon a compromise. Let us be your peacemakers. And do not you, Socrates, aim at this precise and extreme brevity in discourse, if Protagoras objects, but loosen and let go the reins of speech, that your words may be grander and more becoming to you.[10] Neither do you, Protagoras, go forth on the gale with every sail set out of sight of land into an ocean of words, but let there be a mean observed by both of you. Do as I say. And let me also persuade you to choose an arbiter or overseer or president; he will keep watch over your words and will prescribe their proper length.

This proposal was received by the company with universal approval; Callias said that he would not let me off, and they begged me to choose an arbiter. But I said that to choose an umpire of discourse would be unseemly; for if the person chosen was inferior, then the inferior or worse ought not to preside over the better; or if he was equal, neither would that be well; for he who is our equal will do as we do, and what will be the use of choosing him? And if you say,

---

[10] Reading ὑμῖν.

'Let us have a better then,' – to that I answer that you cannot have any one who is wiser than Protagoras. And if you choose another who is not really better, and whom you only say is better, to put another over him as though he were an inferior person would be an unworthy reflection on him; not that, as far as I am concerned, any reflection is of much consequence to me. Let me tell you then what I will do in order that the conversation and discussion may go on as you desire. If Protagoras is not disposed to answer, let him ask and I will answer; and I will endeavour to show at the same time how, as I maintain, he ought to answer: and when I have answered as many questions as he likes to ask, let him in like manner answer me; and if he seems to be not very ready at answering the precise question asked of him, you and I will unite in entreating him, as you entreated me, not to spoil the discussion. And this will require no special arbiter – all of you shall be arbiters.

This was generally approved, and Protagoras, though very much against his will, was obliged to agree that he would ask questions; and when he had put a sufficient number of them, that he would answer in his turn those which he was asked in short replies. He began to put his questions as follows:

I am of opinion, Socrates, he said, that skill in poetry is the principal part of education; and this I conceive to be the power of knowing what compositions of the poets are correct, and what are not, and how they are to be distinguished, and of explaining when asked the reason of the difference. And I propose to transfer the question which you and I have been discussing to the domain of poetry; we will speak as before of virtue, but in reference to a passage of a poet. Now Simonides says to Scopas the son of Creon the Thessalian: –

'Hardly on the one hand can a man become truly good, built four-square in hands and feet and mind, a work without a flaw.'

Do you know the poem? or shall I repeat the whole?

There is no need, I said; for I am perfectly well acquainted with the ode, – I have made a careful study of it.

Very well, he said. And do you think that the ode is a good composition, and true?

Yes, I said, both good and true.

But if there is a contradiction, can the composition be good or true?

No, not in that case, I replied.

And is there not a contradiction? he asked. Reflect.

Well, my friend, I have reflected.

And does not the poet proceed to say, 'I do not agree with the word of Pittacus, albeit the utterance of a wise man: Hardly can a man be good?' Now you will observe that this is said by the same poet.

I know it.

And do you think, he said, that the two sayings are consistent?

Yes, I said, I think so (at the same time I could not help fearing that there might be something in what he said). And you think otherwise?

Why, he said, how can he be consistent in both? First of all, premising as his own thought, 'Hardly can a man become truly good;' and then a little further on in the poem, forgetting, and blaming Pittacus and refusing to agree with him, when he says, 'Hardly can a man be good,' which is the very same thing. And yet when he blames him who says the same with himself, he blames himself; so that he must be wrong either in his first or his second assertion.

Many of the audience cheered and applauded this. And I felt at first giddy and faint, as if I had received a blow from the hand of an expert boxer, when I heard his words and the sound of the cheering; and to confess the truth, I wanted to get time to think what the meaning of the poet really was. So I turned to Prodicus and called him. Prodicus, I said, Simonides is a countryman of yours, and you ought to come to his aid. I must appeal to you, like the river Scamander in Homer, who, when beleaguered by Achilles, summons the Simoïs to aid him, saying:

'Brother dear, let us both together stay the force of the hero.'[11]

And I summon you, for I am afraid that Protagoras will make an end of Simonides. Now is the time to rehabilitate Simonides, by the application of your philosophy of synonyms, which enables you to distinguish 'will' and 'wish,' and make other

[11] Il. xxi. 308.

charming distinctions like those which you drew just now. And I should like to know whether you would agree with me; for I am of opinion that there is no contradiction in the words of Simonides. And first of all I wish that you would say whether, in your opinion, Prodicus, 'being' is the same as 'becoming.'

Not the same, certainly, replied Prodicus.

Did not Simonides first set forth, as his own view, that 'Hardly can a man become truly good'?

Quite right, said Prodicus.

And then he blames Pittacus, not, as Protagoras imagines, for repeating that which he says himself, but for saying something different from himself. Pittacus does not say as Simonides says, that hardly can a man become good, but hardly can a man be good: and our friend Prodicus would maintain that being, Protagoras, is not the same as becoming; and if they are not the same, then Simonides is not inconsistent with himself. I dare say that Prodicus and many others would say, as Hesiod says,

> 'On the one hand, hardly can a man become good,
> For the gods have made virtue the reward of toil;
> But on the other hand, when you have climbed the height,
> Then, to retain virtue, however difficult the acquisition, is easy.'[12]

Prodicus heard and approved; but Protagoras said: Your correction, Socrates, involves a greater error than is contained in the sentence which you are correcting.

Alas! I said, Protagoras; then I am a sorry physician, and do but aggravate a disorder which I am seeking to cure.

Such is the fact, he said.

How so? I asked.

The poet, he replied, could never have made such a mistake as to say that virtue, which in the opinion of all men is the hardest of all things, can be easily retained.

Well, I said, and how fortunate are we in having Prodicus among us, at the right moment; for he has a wisdom, Protagoras, which, as I imagine, is more than humble and of very ancient date, and may be as old as Simonides or even older. Learned as you are in many things, you appear to know nothing of this; but I know, for I am a disciple of his. And now, if I am not mistaken, you do not understand the word 'hard' (χαλεπόν) in the sense which Simonides intended; and I must correct you, as Prodicus corrects me when I use the word 'awful' (δεινόν) as a term of praise. If I say that Protagoras or any one else is an 'awfully' wise man, he asks me if I am not ashamed of calling that which is good 'awful'; and then he explains to me that the term 'awful' is always taken in a bad sense, and that no one speaks of being 'awfully' healthy or wealthy, or 'awful' peace, but of 'awful' disease, 'awful' war, 'awful' poverty, meaning by the term 'awful,' evil. And I think that Simonides and his countrymen the Ceans, when they spoke of 'hard' meant 'evil,' or something which you do not understand. Let us ask Prodicus, for he ought to be able to answer questions about the dialect of Simonides. What did he mean, Prodicus, by the term 'hard'?

Evil, said Prodicus.

And therefore, I said, Prodicus, he blames Pittacus for saying, 'Hard is the good,' just as if that were equivalent to saying, Evil is the good.

Yes, he said, that was certainly his meaning; and he is twitting Pittacus with ignorance of the use of terms, which in a Lesbian, who has been accustomed to speak a barbarous language, is natural.

Do you hear, Protagoras, I asked, what our friend Prodicus is saying? And have you an answer for him?

You are entirely mistaken, Prodicus, said Protagoras; and I know very well that Simonides in using the word 'hard' meant what all of us mean, not evil, but that which is not easy – that which takes a great deal of trouble: of this I am positive.

I said: I also incline to believe, Protagoras, that this was the meaning of Simonides, of which our friend Prodicus was very well aware, but he thought that he would make fun, and try if you could maintain your thesis; for that Simonides could never have meant the other is clearly proved by the context, in which he says that God only has this gift. Now he cannot surely mean to say that to be good is evil, when he afterwards proceeds to say that God only has this gift, and that this is the attribute of him and of no other. For if this be his

---

[12] *Works and Days*, 264 foll.

meaning, Prodicus would impute to Simonides a character of recklessness which is very unlike his countrymen. And I should like to tell you, I said, what I imagine to be the real meaning of Simonides in this poem, if you will test what, in your way of speaking, would be called my skill in poetry; or if you would rather, I will be the listener.

To this proposal Protagoras replied: As you please; – and Hippias, Prodicus, and the others told me by all means to do as I proposed.

Then now, I said, I will endeavour to explain to you my opinion about this poem of Simonides. There is a very ancient philosophy which is more cultivated in Crete and Lacedaemon than in any other part of Hellas, and there are more philosophers in those countries than anywhere else in the world. This, however, is a secret which the Lacedaemonians deny; and they pretend to be ignorant, just because they do not wish to have it thought that they rule the world by wisdom, like the Sophists of whom Protagoras was speaking, and not by valour of arms; considering that if the reason of their superiority were disclosed, all men would be practising their wisdom. And this secret of theirs has never been discovered by the imitators of Lacedaemonian fashions in other cities, who go about with their ears bruised in imitation of them, and have the caestus bound on their arms, and are always in training, and wear short cloaks; for they imagine that these are the practices which have enabled the Lacedaemonians to conquer the other Hellenes. Now when the Lacedaemonians want to unbend and hold free conversation with their wise men, and are no longer satisfied with mere secret intercourse, they drive out all these laconizers, and any other foreigners who may happen to be in their country, and they hold a philosophical *séance* unknown to strangers; and they themselves forbid their young men to go out into other cities – in this they are like the Cretans – in order that they may not unlearn the lessons which they have taught them. And in Lacedaemon and Crete not only men but also women have a pride in their high cultivation. And hereby you may know that I am right in attributing to the Lacedaemonians this excellence in philosophy and speculation: If a man converses with the most ordinary Lacedaemonian, he will find him seldom good for much in general conversation, but at any point in the discourse he will be darting out some notable saying, terse and full

of meaning, with unerring aim; and the person with whom he is talking seems to be like a child in his hands. And many of our own age and of former ages have noted that the true Lacedaemonian type of character has the love of philosophy even stronger than the love of gymnastics; they are conscious that only a perfectly educated man is capable of uttering such expressions. Such were Thales of Miletus, and Pittacus of Mitylene, and Bias of Priene, and our own Solon, and Cleobulus the Lindian, and Myson the Chenian; and seventh in the catalogue of wise men was the Lacedaemonian Chilo. All these were lovers and emulators and disciples of the culture of the Lacedaemonians, and any one may perceive that their wisdom was of this character; consisting of short memorable sentences, which they severally uttered. And they met together and dedicated in the temple of Apollo at Delphi, as the first-fruits of their wisdom, the far-famed inscriptions, which are in all men's mouths, – 'Know thyself,' and 'Nothing too much.'

Why do I say all this? I am explaining that this Lacedaemonian brevity was the style of primitive philosophy. Now there was a saying of Pittacus which was privately circulated and received the approbation of the wise, 'Hard is it to be good.' And Simonides, who was ambitious of the fame of wisdom, was aware that if he could overthrow this saying, then, as if he had won a victory over some famous athlete, he would carry off the palm among his contemporaries. And if I am not mistaken, he composed the entire poem with the secret intention of damaging Pittacus and his saying.

Let us all unite in examining his words, and see whether I am speaking the truth. Simonides must have been a lunatic, if, in the very first words of the poem, wanting to say only that to become good is hard, he inserted μέν, 'on the one hand' ['on the one hand to become good is hard']; there would be no reason for the introduction of μέν, unless you suppose him to speak with a hostile reference to the words of Pittacus. Pittacus is saying 'Hard is it to be good,' and he, in refutation of this thesis, rejoins that the truly hard thing, Pittacus, is to become good, not joining 'truly' with 'good,' but with 'hard.' Not, that the hard thing is to be truly good, as though there were some truly good men, and there were others who were good but not truly good (this would be a very simple observation, and quite unworthy of Simonides); but you must suppose him to make a trajection of the word 'truly' (ἀλαθέως), construing the saying of Pittacus thus (and let us imagine Pittacus to be speaking and Simonides answering him): 'O my friends,' says Pittacus, 'hard is it to be good,' and Simonides answers, 'In that, Pittacus, you are mistaken; the difficulty is not to be good, but on the one hand, to become good, four-square in hands and feet and mind, without a flaw – that is hard truly.' This way of reading the passage accounts for the insertion of μέν, 'on the one hand,' and for the position at the end of the clause of the word 'truly,' and all that follows shows this to be the meaning. A great deal might be said in praise of the details of the poem, which is a charming piece of workmanship, and very finished, but such minutiae would be tedious. I should like, however, to point out the general intention of the poem, which is certainly designed in every part to be a refutation of the saying of Pittacus. For he speaks in what follows a little further on as if he meant to argue that although there is a difficulty in becoming good, yet this is possible for a time, and only for a time. But having become good, to remain in a good state and be good, as you, Pittacus, affirm, is not possible, and is not granted to man; God only has this blessing; 'but man cannot help being bad when the force of circumstances overpowers him.' Now whom does the force of circumstance overpower in the command of a vessel? – not the private individual, for he is always overpowered; and as one who is already prostrate cannot be overthrown, and only he who is standing upright but not he who is prostrate can be laid prostrate, so the force of circumstances can only overpower him who, at some time or other, has resources, and not him who is at all times helpless. The descent of a great storm may make the pilot helpless, or the severity of the season the husbandman or the physician, for the good may become bad, as another poet witnesses:

'The good are sometimes good and sometimes bad.'

But the bad does not become bad; he is always bad. So that when the force of circumstances overpowers the man of resources and skill and virtue, then he cannot help being bad. And

you, Pittacus, are saying, 'Hard is it to be good.' Now there is a difficulty in becoming good; and yet this is possible: but to be good is an impossibility:

'For he who does well is the good man, and he who does ill is the bad.'

But what sort of doing is good in letters? and what sort of doing makes a man good in letters? Clearly the knowing of them. And what sort of well-doing makes a man a good physician? Clearly the knowledge of the art of healing the sick. 'But he who does ill is the bad.' Now who becomes a bad physician? Clearly he who is in the first place a physician, and in the second place a good physician; for he may become a bad one also: but none of us unskilled individuals can by any amount of doing ill become physicians, any more than we can become carpenters or anything of that sort; and he who by doing ill cannot become a physician at all, clearly cannot become a bad physician. In like manner the good may become deteriorated by time, or toil, or disease, or other accident (the only real doing ill is to be deprived of knowledge), but the bad man will never become bad, for he is always bad; and if he were to become bad, he must previously have been good. Thus the words of the poem tend to show that on the one hand a man cannot be continuously good, but that he may become good and may also become bad; and again that

'They are the best for the longest time whom the gods love.'

All this relates to Pittacus, as is further proved by the sequel. For he adds:

'Therefore I will not throw away my span of life to no purpose in searching after the impossible, hoping in vain to find a perfectly faultless man among those who partake of the fruit of the broad-bosomed earth: if I find him, will send you word.'

(this is the vehement way in which he pursues his attack upon Pittacus throughout the whole poem).

'But him who does no evil, voluntarily I praise and love; – not even the gods war against necessity.'

All this has a similar drift, for Simonides was not so ignorant as to say that he praised those who did no evil voluntarily, as though there were some who did evil voluntarily. For no wise man, as I believe, will allow that any human being errs voluntarily, or voluntarily does evil and dishonourable actions; but they are very well aware that all who do evil and dishonourable things do them against their will. And Simonides never says that he praises him who does no evil voluntarily; the word 'voluntarily' applies to himself. For he was under the impression that a good man might often compel himself to love and praise another,[13] and to be the friend and approver of another; and that there might be an involuntary love, such as a man might feel to an unnatural father or mother, or country, or the like. Now bad men, when their parents or country have any defects, look on them with malignant joy, and find fault with them and expose and denounce them to others, under the idea that the rest of mankind will be less likely to take themselves to task and accuse them of neglect; and they blame their defects far more than they deserve, in order that the odium which is necessarily incurred by them may be increased: but the good man dissembles his feelings, and constrains himself to praise them; and if they have wronged him and he is angry, he pacifies his anger and is reconciled, and compels himself to love and praise his own flesh and blood. And Simonides, as is probable, considered that he himself had often had to praise and magnify a tyrant or the like, much against his will, and he also wishes to imply to Pittacus that he does not censure him because he is censorious.

'For I am satisfied,' he says, 'when a man is neither bad nor very stupid; and when he knows justice (which is the health of states), and is of sound mind, I will find no fault with him, for I am not given to finding fault, and there are innumerable fools'

(implying that if he delighted in censure he might have abundant opportunity of finding fault).

'All things are good with which evil is unmingled.'

In these latter words he does not mean to say that all things are good which have no evil in them, as you might say 'All things are white which have no black in them,' for that would be ridiculous; but he means to say that he accepts and finds no fault with the moderate or intermediate state.

['I do not hope,' he says, 'to find a perfectly blameless man among those who partake of the fruits of the broad-bosomed earth (if I find him, I will send you word); in this sense I praise no man. But he who is moderately good, and does no evil, is good enough for me, who love and approve every one']

(and here observe that he uses a Lesbian word, ἐπαίνημι (approve), because he is addressing Pittacus,

'Who love and *approve* every one *voluntarily*, who does no evil:'

and that the stop should be put after 'voluntarily'); 'but there are some whom I involuntarily praise and love. And you, Pittacus, I would never have blamed, if you had spoken what was moderately good and true; but I do blame you because, putting on the appearance of truth, you are speaking falsely about the highest matters.' – And this, I said, Prodicus and Protagoras, I take to be the meaning of Simonides in this poem.

Hippias said: I think, Socrates, that you have given a very good explanation of the poem; but I have also an excellent interpretation of my own which I will propound to you, if you will allow me.

Nay, Hippias, said Alcibiades; not now, but at some other time. At present we must abide by the compact which was made between Socrates and Protagoras, to the effect that as long as Protagoras is willing to ask, Socrates should answer; or that if he would rather answer, then that Socrates should ask.

I said: I wish Protagoras either to ask or answer as he is inclined; but I would rather have done with poems and odes, if he does not object, and come back to the question about which I was

[13] Reading φιλεν κα παινεν κα φλον τιν κ.τ.λ.

asking you at first, Protagoras, and by your help make an end of that. The talk about the poets seems to me like a commonplace entertainment to which a vulgar company have recourse; who, because they are not able to converse or amuse one another, while they are drinking, with the sound of their own voices and conversation, by reason of their stupidity, raise the price of flute-girls in the market, hiring for a great sum the voice of a flute instead of their own breath, to be the medium of intercourse among them: but where the company are real gentlemen and men of education, you will see no flute-girls, nor dancing-girls, nor harp-girls; and they have no nonsense or games, but are contented with one another's conversation, of which their own voices are the medium, and which they carry on by turns and in an orderly manner, even though they are very liberal in their potations. And a company like this of ours, and men such as we profess to be, do not require the help of another's voice, or of the poets whom you cannot interrogate about the meaning of what they are saying; people who cite them declaring, some that the poet has one meaning, and others that he has another, and the point which is in dispute can never be decided. This sort of entertainment they decline, and prefer to talk with one another, and put one another to the proof in conversation. And these are the models which I desire that you and I should imitate. Leaving the poets, and keeping to ourselves, let us try the mettle of one another and make proof of the truth in conversation. If you have a mind to ask, I am ready to answer; or if you would rather, do you answer, and give me the opportunity of resuming and completing our unfinished argument.

I made these and some similar observations; but Protagoras would not distinctly say which he would do. Thereupon Alcibiades turned to Callias, and said: Do you think, Callias, that Protagoras is fair in refusing to say whether he will or will not answer? for I certainly think that he is unfair; he ought either to proceed with the argument, or distinctly to refuse to proceed, that we may know his intention; and then Socrates will be able to discourse with some one else, and the rest of the company will be free to talk with one another.

I think that Protagoras was really made ashamed by these words of Alcibiades, and when the prayers of Callias and the company were superadded, he was at last induced to argue, and said that I might ask and he would answer.

So I said: Do not imagine, Protagoras, that I have any other interest in asking questions of you but that of clearing up my own difficulties. For I think that Homer was very right in saying that

'When two go together, one sees before the other,'[14]

for all men who have a companion are readier in deed, word, or thought; but if a man

'Sees a thing when he is alone,'

he goes about straightway seeking until he finds some one to whom he may show his discoveries, and who may confirm him in them. And I would rather hold discourse with you than with any one, because I think that no man has a better understanding of most things which a good man may be expected to understand, and in particular of virtue. For who is there, but you? – who not only claim to be a good man and a gentleman, for many are this, and yet have not the power of making others good – whereas you are not only good yourself, but also the cause of goodness in others. Moreover such confidence have you in yourself, that although other Sophists conceal their profession, you proclaim in the face of Hellas that you are a Sophist or teacher of virtue and education, and are the first who demanded pay in return. How then can I do otherwise than invite you to the examination of these subjects and ask questions and consult with you? I must, indeed. And I should like once more to have my memory refreshed by you about the questions which I was asking you at first, and also to have your help in considering them. If I am not mistaken the question was this. Are wisdom and temperance and courage and justice and holiness five names of the same thing? or has each of the names a separate underlying essence and corresponding thing having a peculiar function, no one of them being like any other of them? And you replied that the five names were not the names of the same thing, but that each of them had a separate object, and that all these objects

14 Il. x. 224.

were parts of virtue, not in the same way that the parts of gold are like each other and the whole of which they are parts, but as the parts of the face are unlike the whole of which they are parts and one another, and have each of them a distinct function. I should like to know whether this is still your opinion; or if not, I will ask you to define your meaning, and I shall not take you to task if you now make a different statement. For I dare say that you may have said what you did only in order to make trial of me.

I answer, Socrates, he said, that all these qualities are parts of virtue, and that four out of the five are to some extent similar, and that the fifth of them, which is courage, is very different from the other four, as I prove in this way: You may observe that many men are utterly unrighteous, unholy, intemperate, ignorant, who are nevertheless remarkable for their courage.

Stop, I said; I should like to think about that. When you speak of brave men, do you mean the confident, or another sort of nature?

Yes, he said; I mean the impetuous, ready to go at that which others are afraid to approach.

In the next place, you would affirm virtue to be a good thing, of which good thing you assert yourself to be a teacher.

Yes, he said; I should say the best of all things, if I am in my right mind.

And is it partly good and partly bad, I said, or wholly good?

Wholly good, and in the highest degree.

Tell me then; who are they who have confidence when diving into a well?

I should say, the divers.

And the reason of this is that they have knowledge?

Yes, that is the reason.

And who have confidence when fighting on horseback – the skilled horseman or the unskilled?

The skilled.

And who when fighting with light shields – the peltasts or the nonpeltasts?

The peltasts. And that is true of all other things, he said, if that is your point: those who have knowledge are more confident than those who have no knowledge, and they are more confident after they have learned than before.

And have you not seen persons utterly ignorant, I said, of these things, and yet confident about them?

Yes, he said, I have seen such persons far too confident.

And are not these confident persons also courageous?

In that case, he replied, courage would be a base thing, for the men of whom we are speaking are surely madmen.

Then who are the courageous? Are they not the confident?

Yes, he said; to that statement I adhere.

And those, I said, who are thus confident without knowledge are really not courageous, but mad; and in that case the wisest are also the most confident, and being the most confident are also the bravest, and upon that view again wisdom will be courage.

Nay, Socrates, he replied, you are mistaken in your remembrance of what was said by me. When you asked me, I certainly did say that the courageous are the confident; but I was never asked whether the confident are the courageous; if you had asked me, I should have answered 'Not all of them:' and what I did answer you have not proved to be false, although you proceeded to show that those who have knowledge are more courageous than they were before they had knowledge, and more courageous than others who have no knowledge, and were then led on to think that courage is the same as wisdom. But in this way of arguing you might come to imagine that strength is wisdom. You might begin by asking whether the strong are able, and I should say 'Yes;' and then whether those who know how to wrestle are not more able to wrestle than those who do not know how to wrestle, and more able after than before they had learned, and I should assent. And when I had admitted this, you might use my admissions in such a way as to prove that upon my view wisdom is strength; whereas in that case I should not have admitted, any more than in the other, that the able are strong, although I have admitted that the strong are able. For there is a difference between ability and strength; the former is given by knowledge as well as by madness or rage, but strength comes from nature and a healthy state of the body. And in like manner I say of confidence and courage, that they are not the same; and I argue that the courageous are confident but not all the confident courageous. For confidence may be given to men by art, and also, like ability, by madness and rage; but courage comes to them from nature and the healthy state of the soul.

I said: You would admit, Protagoras, that some men live well and others ill?

He assented.

And do you think that a man lives well who lives in pain and grief?

He does not.

But if he lives pleasantly to the end of his life, will he not in that case have lived well?

He will.

Then to live pleasantly is a good and to live unpleasantly an evil?

Yes, he said, if the pleasure be good and honourable.

And do you, Protagoras, like the rest of the world, call some pleasant things evil and some painful things good? – for I am rather disposed to say that things are good in as far as they are pleasant, if they have no consequences of another sort, and in as far as they are painful they are bad.

I do not know, Socrates, he said, whether I can venture to assert in that unqualified manner that the pleasant is the good and the painful the evil. Having regard not only to my present answer, but also to the whole of my life, I shall be safer, if I am not mistaken, in saying that there are some pleasant things which are not good, and that there are some painful things which are good, and some which are not good, and that there are some which are neither good nor evil.

And you would call pleasant, I said, the things which participate in pleasure or create pleasure?

Certainly, he said.

Then my meaning is, that in as far as they are pleasant they are good; and my question would imply that pleasure is a good in itself.

According to your favourite mode of speech, Socrates, 'let us reflect about this,' he said; and if the reflection is to the point, and the result proves that pleasure and good are really the same, then we will agree; but if not, then we will argue.

And would you wish to begin the enquiry? I said; or shall I begin?

You ought to take the lead, he said; for you are the author of the discussion.

May I employ an illustration? I said. Suppose some one who is enquiring into the health or some other bodily quality of another: – he looks at his face and at the tips of his fingers, and then he says, Uncover your chest and back to me that I may have a better view: – that is the sort of thing which I desire in this speculation. Having seen what your opinion is about good and pleasure, I am minded to say to you: Uncover your mind to me, Protagoras, and reveal your opinion about knowledge, that I may know whether you agree with the rest of the world. Now the rest of the world are of opinion that knowledge is a principle not of strength, or of rule, or of command: their notion is that a man may have knowledge, and yet that the knowledge which is in him may be overmastered by anger, or pleasure, or pain, or love, or perhaps by fear, – just as if knowledge were a slave, and might be dragged about anyhow. Now is that your view? or do you think that knowledge is a noble and commanding thing, which cannot be overcome, and will not allow a man, if he only knows the difference of good and evil, to do anything which is contrary to knowledge, but that wisdom will have strength to help him?

I agree with you, Socrates, said Protagoras; and not only so, but I, above all other men, am bound to say that wisdom and knowledge are the highest of human things.

Good, I said, and true. But are you aware that the majority of the world are of another mind; and that men are commonly supposed to know the things which are best, and not to do them when they might? And most persons whom I have asked the reason of this have said that when men act contrary to knowledge they are overcome by pain, or pleasure, or some of those affections which I was just now mentioning.

Yes, Socrates, he replied; and that is not the only point about which mankind are in error.

Suppose, then, that you and I endeavour to instruct and inform them what is the nature of this affection which they call 'being overcome by pleasure,' and which they affirm to be the reason why they do not always do what is best. When we say to them: Friends, you are mistaken, and are saying what is not true, they would probably reply: Socrates and Protagoras, if this affection of the soul is not to be called 'being overcome by pleasure,' pray, what is it, and by what name would you describe it?

But why, Socrates, should we trouble ourselves about the opinion of the many, who just say anything that happens to occur to them?

I believe, I said, that they may be of use in helping us to discover how courage is related to the other parts of virtue. If you are disposed to abide by our agreement, that I should show the way in which, as I think, our recent difficulty is most likely to be cleared up, do you follow; but if not, never mind.

You are quite right, he said; and I would have you proceed as you have begun.

Well then, I said, let me suppose that they repeat their question, What account do you give of that which, in our way of speaking, is termed being overcome by pleasure? I should answer thus: Listen, and Protagoras and I will endeavour to show you. When men are overcome by eating and drinking and other sensual desires which are pleasant, and they, knowing them to be evil, nevertheless indulge in them, would you not say that they were overcome by pleasure? They will not deny this. And suppose that you and I were to go on and ask them again: 'In what way do you say that they are evil, – in that they are pleasant and give pleasure at the moment, or because they cause disease and poverty and other like evils in the future? Would they still be evil, if they had no attendant evil consequences, simply because they give the consciousness of pleasure of whatever nature?' – Would they not answer that they are not evil on account of the pleasure which is immediately given by them, but on account of the after consequences – diseases and the like?

I believe, said Protagoras, that the world in general would answer as you do.

And in causing diseases do they not cause pain? and in causing poverty do they not cause pain; – they would agree to that also, if I am not mistaken?

Protagoras assented.

Then I should say to them, in my name and yours: Do you think them evil for any other reason, except because they end in pain and rob us of other pleasures: – there again they would agree?

We both of us thought that they would.

And then I should take the question from the opposite point of view, and say: 'Friends, when you speak of goods being painful, do you not mean remedial goods, such as gymnastic exercises, and military service, and the physician's use of burning, cutting, drugging, and starving? Are these the things which are good but painful?' – they would assent to me?

He agreed.

'And do you call them good because they occasion the greatest immediate suffering and pain; or because, afterwards, they bring health and improvement of the bodily condition and the sal-

vation of states and power over others and wealth?' – they would agree to the latter alternative, if I am not mistaken?

He assented.

'Are these things good for any other reason except that they end in pleasure, and get rid of and avert pain? Are you looking to any other standard but pleasure and pain when you call them good?' – they would acknowledge that they were not?

I think so, said Protagoras.

'And do you not pursue after pleasure as a good, and avoid pain as an evil?'

He assented.

'Then you think that pain is an evil and pleasure is a good: and even pleasure you deem an evil, when it robs you of greater pleasures than it gives, or causes pains greater than the pleasure. If, however, you call pleasure an evil in relation to some other end or standard, you will be able to show us that standard. But you have none to show.'

I do not think that they have, said Protagoras.

'And have you not a similar way of speaking about pain? You call pain a good when it takes away greater pains than those which it has, or gives pleasures greater than the pains: then if you have some standard other than pleasure and pain to which you refer when you call actual pain a good, you can show what that is. But you cannot.'

True, said Protagoras.

Suppose again, I said, that the world says to me: 'Why do you spend many words and speak in many ways on this subject?' Excuse me, friends, I should reply; but in the first place there is a difficulty in explaining the meaning of the expression 'overcome by pleasure;' and the whole argument turns upon this. And even now, if you see any possible way in which evil can be explained as other than pain, or good as other than pleasure, you may still retract. Are you satisfied, then, at having a life of pleasure which is without pain? If you are, and if you are unable to show any good or evil which does not end in pleasure and pain, hear the consequences: – If what you say is true, then the argument is absurd which affirms that a man often does evil knowingly, when he might abstain, because he is seduced and overpowered by pleasure; or again, when you say that a man knowingly refuses to do what is good because he is overcome at the moment by pleasure. And that this is ridiculous will be evident if only we give up the use of various names, such as pleasant and painful, and good and evil. As there are two things, let us call them by two names – first, good and evil, and then pleasant and painful. Assuming this, let us go on to say that a man does evil knowing that he does evil. But some one will ask, Why? Because he is overcome, is the first answer. And by what is he overcome? the enquirer will proceed to ask. And we shall not be able to reply 'By pleasure,' for the name of pleasure has been exchanged for that of good. In our answer, then, we shall only say that he is overcome. 'By what?' he will reiterate. By the good, we shall have to reply; indeed we shall? Nay, but our questioner will rejoin with a laugh, if he be one of the swaggering sort, 'That is too ridiculous, that a man should do what he knows to be evil when he ought not, because he is overcome by good. Is that, he will ask, because the good was worthy or not worthy of conquering the evil'? And in answer to that we shall clearly reply, Because it was not worthy; for if it had been worthy, then he who, as we say, was overcome by pleasure, would not have been wrong. 'But how,' he will reply, 'can the good be unworthy of the evil, or the evil of the good'? Is not the real explanation that they are out of proportion to one another, either as greater and smaller, or more and fewer? This we cannot deny. And when you speak of being overcome – 'what do you mean,' he will say, 'but that you choose the greater evil in exchange for the lesser good'? Admitted. And now substitute the names of pleasure and pain for good and evil, and say, not as before, that a man does what is evil knowingly, but that he does what is painful knowingly, and because he is overcome by pleasure, which is unworthy to overcome. What measure is there of the relations of pleasure to pain other than excess and defect, which means that they become greater and smaller, and more and fewer, and differ in degree? For if any one says: 'Yes, Socrates, but immediate pleasure differs widely from future pleasure and pain' – To that I should reply: And do they differ in anything but in pleasure and pain? There can be no other measure of them. And do you, like a skilful weigher, put into the balance the pleasures and the pains, and their nearness and distance, and weigh them, and then say which outweighs the other. If you weigh pleasures against pleasures, you of course take the more and greater; or if you weigh pains against pains, you take the fewer and

the less; or if pleasures against pains, then you choose that course of action in which the painful is exceeded by the pleasant, whether the distant by the near or the near by the distant; and you avoid that course of action in which the pleasant is exceeded by the painful. Would you not admit, my friends, that this is true? I am confident that they cannot deny this.

He agreed with me.

Well then, I shall say, if you agree so far, be so good as to answer me a question: Do not the same magnitudes appear larger to your sight when near, and smaller when at a distance? They will acknowledge that. And the same holds of thickness and number; also sounds, which are in themselves equal, are greater when near, and lesser when at a distance. They will grant that also. Now suppose happiness to consist in doing or choosing the greater, and in not doing or in avoiding the less, what would be the saving principle of human life? Would not the art of measuring be the saving principle; or would the power of appearance? Is not the latter that deceiving art which makes us wander up and down and take the things at one time of which we repent at another, both in our actions and in our choice of things great and small? But the art of measurement would do away with the effect of appearances, and, showing the truth, would fain teach the soul at last to find rest in the truth, and would thus save our life. Would not mankind generally acknowledge that the art which accomplishes this result is the art of measurement?

Yes, he said, the art of measurement.

Suppose, again, the salvation of human life to depend on the choice of odd and even, and on the knowledge of when a man ought to choose the greater or less, either in reference to themselves or to each other, and whether near or at a distance; what would be the saving principle of our lives? Would not knowledge? – a knowledge of measuring, when the question is one of excess and defect, and a knowledge of number, when the question is of odd and even? The world will assent, will they not?

Protagoras himself thought that they would.

Well then, my friends, I say to them; seeing that the salvation of human life has been found to consist in the right choice of pleasures and pains, – in the choice of the more and the fewer, and the greater and the less, and the nearer and remoter, must not this measuring be a consideration of their excess and defect and equality in relation to each other?

This is undeniably true.

And this, as possessing measure, must undeniably also be an art and science?

They will agree, he said.

The nature of that art or science will be a matter of future consideration; but the existence of such a science furnishes a demonstrative answer to the question which you asked of me and Protagoras. At the time when you asked the question, if you remember, both of us were agreeing that there was nothing mightier than knowledge, and that knowledge, in whatever existing, must have the advantage over pleasure and all other things; and then you said that pleasure often got the advantage even over a man who has knowledge; and we refused to allow this, and you rejoined: O Protagoras and Socrates, what is the meaning of being overcome by pleasure if not this? – tell us what you call such a state: – if we had immediately and at the time answered 'Ignorance,' you would have laughed at us. But now, in laughing at us, you will be laughing at yourselves: for you also admitted that men err in their choice of pleasures and pains; that is, in their choice of good and evil, from defect of knowledge; and you admitted further, that they err, not only from defect of knowledge in general, but of that particular knowledge which is called measuring. And you are also aware that the erring act which is done without knowledge is done in ingorance. This, therefore, is the meaning of being overcome by pleasure; – ignorance, and that the greatest. And our friends Protagoras and Prodicus and Hippias declare that they are the physicians of ignorance; but you, who are under the mistaken impression that ignorance is not the cause, and that the art of which I am speaking cannot be taught, neither go yourselves, nor send your children, to the Sophists, who are the teachers of these things – you take care of your money and give them none; and the result is, that you are the worse off both in public and private life – Let us suppose this to be our answer to the world in general: and now I should like to ask you, Hippias, and you, Prodicus, as well as Protagoras (for the argument is to be yours as well as ours) whether you think that I am speaking the truth or not?

They all thought that what I said was entirely true.

Then you agree, I said, that the pleasant is the good, and the painful evil. And here I would beg my friend Prodicus not to introduce his distinction of names, whether he is disposed to say pleasurable, delightful, joyful. However, by whatever name he prefers to call them, I will ask you, most excellent Prodicus, to answer in my sense of the words.

Prodicus laughed and assented, as did the others.

Then, my friends, what do you say to this? Are not all actions honourable and useful, of which the tendency is to make life painless and pleasant? The honourable work is also useful and good?

This was admitted.

Then, I said, if the pleasant is the good, nobody does anything under the idea or conviction that some other thing would be better and is also attainable, when he might do the better. And this inferiority of a man to himself is merely ignorance, as the superiority of a man to himself is wisdom.

They all assented.

And is not ignorance the having a false opinion and being deceived about important matters?

To this also they unanimously assented.

Then, I said, no man voluntarily pursues evil, or that which he thinks to be evil. To prefer evil to good is not in human nature; and when a man is compelled to choose one of two evils, no one will choose the greater when he may have the less.

All of us agreed to every word of this.

Well, I said, there is a certain thing called fear or terror; and here, Prodicus, I should particularly like to know whether you would agree with me in defining this fear or terror as expectation of evil.

Protagoras and Hippias agreed, but Prodicus said that this was fear and not terror.

Never mind, Prodicus, I said; but let me ask whether, if our former assertions are true, a man will pursue that which he fears when he is not compelled? Would not this be in flat contradiction to the admission which has been already made, that he thinks the things which he fears to be evil; and no one will pursue or voluntarily accept that which he thinks to be evil?

That also was universally admitted.

Then, I said, these, Hippias and Prodicus, are our premises; and I would beg Protagoras to explain to us how he can be right in what he said at first. I do not mean in what he said quite at first, for his first statement, as you may remember, was that whereas there were five parts of virtue none of them was like any other of them; each of them had a separate function. To this, however, I am not referring, but to the assertion which he afterwards made that of the five virtues four were nearly akin to each other, but that the fifth, which was courage, differed greatly from the others. And of this he gave me the following proof. He said: You will find, Socrates, that some of the most impious, and unrighteous, and intemperate, and ignorant of men are among the most courageous; which proves that courage is very different from the other parts of virtue. I was surprised at his saying this at the time, and I am still more surprised now that I have discussed the matter with you. So I asked him whether by the brave he meant the confident. Yes, he replied, and the impetuous or goers. (You may remember, Protagoras, that this was your answer.)

He assented.

Well then, I said, tell us against what are the courageous ready to go – against the same dangers as the cowards?

No, he answered.

Then against something different?

Yes, he said.

Then do cowards go where there is safety, and the courageous where there is danger?

Yes, Socrates, so men say.

Very true, I said. But I want to know against what do you say that the courageous are ready to go – against dangers, believing them to be dangers, or not against dangers?

No, said he; the former case has been proved by you in the previous argument to be impossible.

That, again, I replied, is quite true. And if this has been rightly proven, then no one goes to meet what he thinks to be dangers, since the want of self-control, which makes men rush into dangers, has been shown to be ignorance.

He assented.

And yet the courageous man and the coward alike go to meet that about which they are confident; so that, in this point of view, the cowardly and the courageous go to meet the same things.

And yet, Socrates, said Protagoras, that to which the coward goes is the opposite of that to which the courageous goes; the one, for example, is ready to go to battle, and the other is not ready.

And is going to battle honourable or disgraceful? I said.

Honourable, he replied.

And if honourable, then already admitted by us to be good; for all honourable actions we have admitted to be good.

That is true; and to that opinion I shall always adhere.

True, I said. But which of the two are they who, as you say, are unwilling to go to war, which is a good and honourable thing?

The cowards, he replied.

And what is good and honourable, I said, is also pleasant?

It has certainly been acknowledged to be so, he replied.

And do the cowards knowingly refuse to go to the nobler, and pleasanter, and better?

The admission of that, he replied, would belie our former admissions.

But does not the courageous man also go to meet the better, and pleasanter, and nobler?

That must be admitted.

And the courageous man has no base fear or base confidence?

True, he replied.

And if not base, then honourable?

He admitted this.

And if honourable, then good?

Yes.

But the fear and confidence of the coward or foolhardy or madman, on the contrary, are base?

He assented.

And these base fears and confidences originate in ignorance and uninstructedness?

True, he said.

Then as to the motive from which the cowards act, do you call it cowardice or courage?

I should say cowardice, he replied.

And have they not been shown to be cowards through their ignorance of dangers?

Assuredly, he said.

And because of that ignorance they are cowards?

He assented.

And the reason why they are cowards is admitted by you to be cowardice?

He again assented.

Then the ignorance of what is and is not dangerous is cowardice?

He nodded assent.

But surely courage, I said, is opposed to cowardice?

Yes.

Then the wisdom which knows what are and are not dangers is opposed to the ignorance of them?

To that again he nodded assent.

And the ignorance of them is cowardice?

To that he very reluctantly nodded assent.

And the knowledge of that which is and is not dangerous is courage, and is opposed to the ignorance of these things?

At this point he would no longer nod assent, but was silent.

And why, I said, do you neither assent nor dissent, Protagoras?

Finish the argument by yourself, he said.

I only want to ask one more question, I said. I want to know whether you still think that there are men who are most ignorant and yet most courageous?

You seem to have a great ambition to make me answer, Socrates, and therefore I will gratify you, and say, that this appears to me to be impossible consistently with the argument.

My only object, I said, in continuing the discussion, has been the desire to ascertain the nature and relations of virtue; for if this were clear, I am very sure that the other controversy which has been carried on at great length by both of us – you affirming and I denying that virtue can be taught – would also become clear. The result of our discussion appears to me to be singular. For if the argument had a human voice, that voice would be heard laughing at us and saying: 'Protagoras and Socrates, you are strange beings; there are you, Socrates, who were saying that virtue cannot be taught, contradicting yourself now by your attempt to prove that all things are knowledge, including justice, and temperance, and courage, – which tends to show that virtue can certainly be taught; for if virtue were other than knowledge, as Protagoras attempted to prove, then clearly virtue cannot be taught; but if virtue is entirely knowledge, as you are seeking to show, then I cannot but suppose that virtue is capable of being taught. Protagoras, on the other hand, who started by saying that it might be taught, is now eager to prove it to be anything rather than knowledge; and if this is true, it must be quite incapable of being taught.' Now I, Protagoras perceiving this terrible confusion of our ideas, have a great desire that they should be cleared up. And I should like to carry on the discussion until we ascertain what virtue is, and whether capable of being taught or not, lest haply Epimetheus should trip us up and deceive us in the argument, as he forgot us in the story; I prefer your Prometheus to your Epimetheus, for of him I make use, whenever I am busy about these questions, in Promethean care of my own life. And if you have no objection, as I said at first, I should like to have your help in the enquiry.

Protagoras replied: Socrates, I am not of a base nature, and I am the last man in the world to be envious. I cannot but applaud your energy and your conduct of an argument. As I have often said, I admire you above all men whom I know and far above all men of your age; and I believe that you will become very eminent in philosophy. Let us come back to the subject at some future time; at present we had better turn to something else.

By all means, I said, if that is your wish; for I too ought long since to have kept the engagement of which I spoke before, and only tarried because I could not refuse the request of the noble Callias. So the conversation ended, and we went our way.

Gorgias

It is a credit to the dramatic nature of Plato's dialogues that many readers forget that they are not transcriptions of debates between Socrates and his interlocutors. As a result, some become frustrated by the willingness of one character or another to let Socrates lead them into self-contradictions, or they may feel uncomfortable with the brusque tone Socrates uses with men of stature. These reactions can be particularly intense when reading Gorgias, arguably Plato's most bitter attack on rhetoric.

The dialogue has three main parts: The first consists of the interaction between Socrates and Gorgias, the second between Socrates and Polus, and the third between Socrates and Callicles. Socrates begins by asking about rhetoric, cautioning Gorgias that he will not tolerate lengthy answers to his interrogation. Gorgias states that he is a rhetorician and a teacher of rhetoric, which prompts Socrates to ask, "with what is rhetoric concerned?" After much circumlocution, the Sophist agrees to accept Socrates' definition of rhetoric as the "artificer of persuasion," which leads to questions about its substance. Gorgias' answer seems inconsistent with what we know about the real man and the Sophistic pedagogical enterprise (see McComiskey, 1992): "I answer Socrates, that rhetoric is the art of persuasion in courts and other assemblies, as I was just now saying, and about the just and the unjust." This simplistic response is quite different from Gorgias' characterization of rhetoric in his *Helen*, but it does allow Plato to lay the foundation for an exegesis of rhetoric and Sophistic teaching. If the substance of rhetoric includes "the just and the unjust," as a professed rhetorician and teacher of rhetoric, Gorgias' instruction must logically include consideration of the just and the unjust. But Socrates gets him to accept a number of propositions that lead to the following conclusion: "Then rhetoric, as would appear, is the artificer of a persuasion which creates belief about the just and unjust, but gives no instruction about them?" To which Gorgias responds: "True."

Additional contradictions force Gorgias to retire from the discussion, so it is taken up by his student Polus, who asks Socrates how he would describe rhetoric. The answer is that it is an "experience in producing a sort of delight or gratification." On this basis, Socrates develops his argument that rhetoric is merely *flattery*. Understanding what Plato meant by this term as applied to rhetoric requires that we consider briefly his concept of pleasure as presented in *Protagoras*. In that dialogue, Plato rejected the idea that the good is what is pleasurable and instead equated the good with knowledge. Among those who lack knowledge, pleasure creates the illusion of good. For example, the pursuit of pleasure may seem to be a pursuit of the good in the short term, but over the long term it may prove to be harmful, as in the case of someone overindulging in sweets. Over the short term, the pleasure is great and good, but over the long term, as the pounds pile up and the waistline expands, this pursuit of pleasure can lead to disease and pain.

Flattery, of course, tends also to provide short-term pleasure. It gratifies our sense of self, appeals to our vanity, and makes us feel recognized and appreciated. What too often is missed, however, is the insincerity of the person who flatters to gain some advantage, and this is the point emphasized in *Gorgias* that allows Plato to claim that rhetoric is flattery and a form of deception used to persuade. Even a moment's reflection allows us to construct from daily life mental scenarios of self-serving flattery (or rhetoric) in action: the employee seeking a promotion; the student trying to get into a closed class; the man or woman hoping to begin a romantic liaison.

Dismissing the claims of Gorgias and Polus that rhetoric is an art, Socrates asserts that "it is unable to explain or give a reason for the nature of its own applications," which he deems a defining characteristic of art. There is no question about whether rhetoric works; indeed, in Plato's view it works all too well. Thus, Socrates' denial of *technê* status is based on an underlying question that remains insufficiently examined in the dialogue: How or why does rhetoric work? In *Phaedrus* and *The Republic*, the answer is that rhetoric appeals to the emotional, as opposed to the rational, part of the soul, and it succeeds in those instances in which the audience lacks true knowledge. This idea appears again in *Gorgias*, with rhetoric providing belief without knowledge. A problem in each case is that Plato never provided a definition of "soul" or a substantive explanation of the difference between emotion and reason, which his emphasis on dialectic should lead us to expect.

The lack of definitions is especially troubling in *Gorgias*, in which Plato addressed *good*, *evil*, *power*, and *justice* – all important concepts central to his philosophy. He resorts to metaphor and parable, a technique that appears regularly whenever the process of definition is challenging. Power and happiness consist of self-control, of tempering ones desire to nothing (to which Callicles aptly remarks, "then stones and dead men would be the happiest of all!"). But when it comes to the definition of temperance, we get the parable of the vessels. Justice, then, is temperance in the use of power to create harmony or balance in the body politic. The terms are not defined but rather described in terms of something else that is based on a parable. And the circularity does not edify.

Without basic scaffolding, several of Socrates' main arguments founder. As both Polus and Callicles suggest, the arguments are logical but nevertheless false. The discussion of *will*, *good*, and *evil* offers one example. Proposing that "all things are either good or evil, or intermediate and indifferent," Socrates divides actions into good or evil, noting in the process that we sometimes do not find a direct connection between an action and our will. In his view, a person who must make a business trip does not "will" the trip but rather wills the money that is likely to result from the trip. Thus, a person can only "will" the ultimate good to be gained from his or her action; all intermediate actions are merely steps toward the ultimate good and are not willed but are incidental. Moreover, on the basis of this premise, we do not "will" evil, for evil is antithetical to our ultimate good.

One way of looking at this issue is to consider the phenomenological character of will. Will is related to commitment, but insofar as it involves an action, it is related to intention. Searle (1983) argued that the phenomenological content of an intention is an action, which, if correct, means that all actions are intentional. In addition, Searle suggested that intentions must meet a condition of satisfaction. That is, if a person intends to do something, he or she must actually do it. On this basis, the content of an intention also is causally self-referential. Along these lines, Bratman (1987) proposed that intentions involve a form of problem solving to the extent that if a person intends to do something he or she must form a mental plan of action to meet the specific conditions of satisfaction associated with the intention, and because plans typically involve selecting multiple steps from a variety of available options, what one intends is a subject of what one chooses (also see Cohen, Morgan, and Pollack, 1990). The question with regard to Plato's argument, therefore, is this: Can we perform an unintentional action, an action that is not willed? Clearly, we can. Hitting a baseball that inadvertently breaks someone's window is just one example. From the perspective of phenomenology, then, an action is performed only when one intends to do something and actually does it. If we apply this perspective to Plato's assertion regarding "will," the business trip he described is *necessarily intentional*: It is part of an intentional plan, and it is governed by "will" because it involves the person's commitment to meeting the conditions of satisfaction for the primary intention.

This analysis also suggests there may be a problem with the claim that we can only "will" actions that are "conducive to our good." If actions are intentional, the involvement of our will is determined by whether we meet the conditions of satisfaction of the intention, not by whether the action is good or evil. Furthermore, people do commit evil actions.[15] In some cases, they do so because they believe that their action is conducive to their good. Bank robbers, for example, rob banks because they want money, which they perceive as a personal good. In other cases, however, people commit evil actions not for any tangible object, such as money, but for the thrill of the act itself.

---

[15] Aristotle provided an important discussion of will and choice in *Nichomachean Ethics* that is congruent with the analysis here.

Although Plato excludes the irrational from his analysis, it is relatively easy to argue that bank robbers and the like are stupid, but it is quite difficult to argue that they are irrational. Finally, the argument is focused on the concept of individual good and does not consider actions in relation to society. Taking medicine, for example, is recognized as a good, even though it may be temporarily unpleasant, because it can restore the body to health. Failure to take medicine can lead to death in some instances, which may be the ultimate personal evil. Yet within societies men and women frequently perform altruistic actions that sacrifice their lives for the good of others. Again, whenever such actions are actually performed, they are intentional and willed. It is these sorts of issues that make *Gorgias* one of the more challenging of Plato's dialogues.

Reading 27

Gorgias

Gorgias, translated by B. Jowett, 1892.

Persons of the Dialogue

CALLICLES   SOCRATES   CHAEREPHON

GORGIAS   POLUS

Scene: The house of Callicles

CALLICLES. THE wise man, as the proverb says, is late for a fray, but not for a feast.

SOCRATES. And are we late for a feast?

CAL. Yes, and a delightful feast; for Gorgias has just been exhibiting to us many fine things.

SOC. It is not my fault, Callicles; our friend Chaerephon is to blame; for he would keep us loitering in the Agora.

CHAEREPHON. Never mind, Socrates; the misfortune of which I have been the cause I will also repair; for Gorgias is a friend of mine, and I will make him give the exhibition again either now, or, if you prefer, at some other time.

CAL. What is the matter, Chaerephon – does Socrates want to hear Gorgias?

CHAER. Yes, that was our intention in coming.

CAL. Come into my house, then; for Gorgias is staying with me, and he shall exhibit to you.

SOC. Very good, Callicles; but will he answer our questions? for I want to hear from him what is the nature of his art, and what it is which he professes and teaches; he may, as you [Chaerephon] suggest, defer the exhibition to some other time.

CAL. There is nothing like asking him, Socrates; and indeed to answer questions is a part of his exhibition, for he was saying only just now, that any one in my house might put any question to him, and that he would answer.

SOC. How fortunate! will you ask him, Chaerephon – ?

CHAER. What shall I ask him?

SOC. Ask him who he is.

CHAER. What do you mean?

SOC. I mean such a question as would elicit from him, if he had been a maker of shoes, the answer that he is a cobbler. Do you understand?

CHAER. I understand, and will ask him: Tell me, Gorgias, is our friend Callicles right in saying that you undertake to answer any questions which you are asked?

GORGIAS. Quite right, Chaerephon; I was saying as much only just now; and I may add, that many years have elapsed since any one has asked me a new one.

CHAER. Then you must be very ready, Gorgias.

GOR. Of that, Chaerephon, you can make trial.

POLUS. Yes, indeed, and if you like Chaerephon, you may make trial of me too, for I think that Gorgias, who has been talking a long time, is tired.

CHAER. And do you, Polus, think that you can answer better than Gorgias?

POL. What does that matter if I answer well enough for you?

CHAER. Not at all: – and you shall answer if you like.

POL. Ask: –

CHAER. My question is this: If Gorgias had the skill of his brother Herodicus, what ought we to call him? Ought he not to have the name which is given to his brother?

POL. Certainly.

CHAER. Then we should be right in calling him a physician?

POL. Yes.

CHAER. And if he had the skill of Aristophon the son of Aglaophon, or of his brother Polygnotus, what ought we to call him?

POL. Clearly, a painter.

CHAER. But now what shall we call him – what is the art in which he is skilled?

POL. O Chaerephon, there are many arts among mankind which are experimental, and have their origin in experience, for experience makes the days of men to proceed according to art, and inexperience according to chance, and different persons in different ways are proficient in different arts, and the best persons in the best arts. And our friend Gorgias is one of the best, and the art in which he is a proficient is the noblest.

SOC. Polus has been taught how to make a capital speech, Gorgias; but he is not fulfilling the promise which he made to Chaerephon.

GOR. What do you mean, Socrates?

SOC. I mean that he has not exactly answered the question which he was asked.

GOR. Then why not ask him yourself?

SOC. But I would much rather ask you, if you are disposed to answer: for I see, from the few words which Polus has uttered, that he has attended more to the art which is called rhetoric than to dialectic.

POL. What makes you say so, Socrates?

SOC. Because, Polus, when Chaerephon asked you what was the art which Gorgias knows, you praised it as if you were answering some one who found fault with it, but you never said what the art was.

POL. Why, did I not say that it was the noblest of arts?

SOC. Yes, indeed, but that was no answer to the question: nobody asked what was the quality, but what was the nature, of the art, and by what name we were to describe Gorgias. And I would still beg you briefly and clearly, as you answered Chaerephon when he asked you at first, to say what this art is, and what we ought to call Gorgias: Or rather, Gorgias, let me turn to you, and ask the same question, – what are we to call you, and what is the art which you profess?

GOR. Rhetoric, Socrates, is my art.

SOC. Then I am to call you a rhetorician?

GOR. Yes, Socrates, and a good one too, if you would call me that which, in Homeric language, 'I boast myself to be.'

SOC. I should wish to do so.

GOR. Then pray do.

SOC. And are we to say that you are able to make other men rhetoricians?

GOR. Yes, that is exactly what I profess to make them, not only at Athens, but in all places.

SOC. And will you continue to ask and answer questions, Gorgias, as we are at present doing, and reserve for another occasion the longer mode of speech which Polus was attempting? Will you keep your promise, and answer shortly the questions which are asked of you?

GOR. Some answers, Socrates, are of necessity longer; but I will do my best to make them as short as possible; for a part of my profession is that I can be as short as any one.

SOC. That is what is wanted, Gorgias; exhibit the shorter method now, and the longer one at some other time.

GOR. Well, I will; and you will certainly say, that you never heard a man use fewer words.

SOC. Very good then; as you profess to be a rhetorician, and a maker of rhetoricians, let me ask you, with what is rhetoric concerned: I might ask with what is weaving concerned, and you would reply (would you not?), with the making of garments?

GOR. Yes.

SOC. And music is concerned with the composition of melodies?

GOR. It is.

SOC. By Herè, Gorgias, I admire the surpassing brevity of your answers.

GOR. Yes, Socrates, I do think myself good at that.

SOC. I am glad to hear it; answer me in like manner about rhetoric: with what is rhetoric concerned?

GOR. With discourse.

SOC. What sort of discourse, Gorgias? – such discourse as would teach the sick under what treatment they might get well?

GOR. No.

SOC. Then rhetoric does not treat of all kinds of discourse?

GOR. Certainly not.

SOC. And yet rhetoric makes men able to speak?

GOR. Yes.

SOC. And to understand that about which they speak?

GOR. Of course.

SOC. But does not the art of medicine, which we were just now mentioning, also make men able to understand and speak about the sick?

GOR. Certainly.

SOC. Then medicine also treats of discourse?

GOR. Yes.

SOC. Of discourse concerning diseases?

GOR. Just so.

SOC. And does not gymnastic also treat of discourse concerning the good or evil condition of the body?

GOR. Very true.

SOC. And the same, Gorgias, is true of the other arts: – all of them treat of discourse concerning the subjects with which they severally have to do.

GOR. Clearly.

SOC. Then why, if you call rhetoric the art which treats of discourse, and all the other arts treat of discourse, do you not call them arts of rhetoric?

GOR. Because, Socrates, the knowledge of the other arts has only to do with some sort of external action as of the hand; but there is no such action of the hand in rhetoric which works and takes effect only through the medium of discourse. And therefore I am justified in saying that rhetoric treats of discourse.

SOC. I am not sure whether I entirely understand you, but I dare say I shall soon know better; please to answer me a question: – you would allow that there are arts?

GOR. Yes.

SOC. As to the arts generally, they are for the most part concerned with doing, and require little or no speaking; in painting, and statuary, and many other arts, the work may proceed in silence; and of such arts I suppose you would say that they do not come within the province of rhetoric.

GOR. You perfectly conceive my meaning, Socrates.

SOC. But there are other arts which work wholly through the medium of language, and require either no action or very little, as, for example, the arts of arithmetic, of calculation, of geometry, and of playing draughts; in some of these speech is pretty nearly coextensive with action, but in most of them the verbal element is greater – they depend wholly on words for their efficacy and power: and I take your meaning to be that rhetoric is an art of this latter sort?

GOR. Exactly.

SOC. And yet I do not believe that you really mean to call any of these arts rhetoric; although the precise expression which you used was, that rhetoric is an art which works and takes effect only through the medium of discourse; and an adversary who wished to be captious might say, 'And so, Gorgias, you call arithmetic rhetoric.' But I do not think that you really call arithmetic rhetoric any more than geometry would be so called by you.

GOR. You are quite right, Socrates, in your apprehension of my meaning.

SOC. Well, then, let me now have the rest of my answer: – seeing that rhetoric is one of those arts which works mainly by the use of words, and there are other arts which also use words, tell me what is that quality in words with which rhetoric is concerned: – Suppose that a person asks me about some of the arts which I was mentioning just now; he might say, 'Socrates, what is arithmetic?' and I should reply to him, as you replied to me, that arithmetic is one of those arts which take effect through words. And then he would proceed to ask: 'Words about what?' and I should reply, Words about odd and even numbers, and how many there are of each. And if he asked again: 'What is the art of calculation?' I should say, That also is one of the arts which is concerned wholly with words. And if he further said, 'Concerned with what?' I should say, like the clerks in the assembly, 'as aforesaid' of arithmetic, but with a difference, the difference being that the art of calculation considers not only the quantities of odd and even numbers, but also their numerical relations to themselves and to one another. And suppose, again, I were to say that astronomy is only words – he would ask, 'Words about what, Socrates?' and I should answer, that astronomy tells us about the motions of the stars and sun and moon, and their relative swiftness.

GOR. You would be quite right, Socrates.

SOC. And now let us have from you, Gorgias, the truth about rhetoric: which you would admit (would you not?) to be one of those arts which act always and fulfil all their ends through the medium of words?

GOR. True.

SOC. Words which do what? I should ask. To what class of things do the words which rhetoric uses relate?

GOR. To the greatest, Socrates, and the best of human things.

SOC. That again, Gorgias, is ambiguous; I am still in the dark: for which are the greatest and best of human things? I dare say that you have heard men singing at feasts the old drinking song, in which the singers enumerate the goods of life, first health, beauty next, thirdly, as the writer of the song says, wealth honestly obtained.

GOR. Yes, I know the song; but what is your drift?

SOC. I mean to say, that the producers of those things which the author of the song praises, that is to say, the physician, the trainer, the money-maker, will at once come to you, and first the physician will say: 'O Socrates, Gorgias is deceiving you, for my art is concerned with the greatest good of men and not his.' And when I ask, Who are you? he will reply, 'I am a physician.' What do you mean? I shall say. Do you mean that your art produces the greatest good? 'Certainly,' he will answer, 'for is not health the greatest good? What greater good can men have, Socrates?' And after him the trainer will come and say, 'I too, Socrates, shall be greatly surprised if Gorgias can show more good of his art than I can show of mine.' To him again I shall say, Who are you, honest friend, and what is your business? 'I am a trainer,' he will reply, 'and my business is to make men beautiful and strong in body.' When I have done with the trainer, there arrives the money-maker, and he, as I expect, will utterly despise them all. 'Consider, Socrates,' he will say, 'whether Gorgias or any one else can produce any greater good than wealth.' Well, you and I say to him, and are you a creator of wealth? 'Yes,' he replies. And who are you? 'A money-maker.' And do you consider wealth to be the greatest good of man? 'Of course,' will be his reply. And we shall rejoin: Yes; but our friend Gorgias contends that his art produces a greater good than yours. And then he will be sure to go on and ask, 'What good? Let Gorgias answer.' Now I want you, Gorgias, to imagine that this question is asked of you by them and by me; What is that which, as you say, is the greatest good of man, and of which you are the creator? Answer us.

GOR. That good, Socrates, which is truly the greatest, being that which gives to men freedom in their own persons, and to individuals the power of ruling over others in their several states.

SOC. And what would you consider this to be?

GOR. What is there greater than the word which persuades the judges in the courts, or the senators in the council, or the citizens in the assembly, or at any other political meeting? – if you have the power of uttering this word, you will have the physician your slave, and the trainer your slave, and the money-maker of whom you talk will be found to gather treasures, not for himself, but for you who are able to speak and to persuade the multitude.

SOC. Now I think, Gorgias, that you have very accurately explained what you conceive to be the art of rhetoric; and you mean to say, if I am not mistaken, that rhetoric is the artificer of persuasion, having this and no other business, and that this is her crown and end. Do you know any other effect of rhetoric over and above that of producing persuasion?

GOR. No: the definition seems to me very fair, Socrates; for persuasion is the chief end of rhetoric.

SOC. Then hear me, Gorgias, for I am quite sure that if there ever was a man who entered on the discussion of a matter from a pure love of knowing the truth, I am such a one, and I should say the same of you.

GOR. What is coming, Socrates?

SOC. I will tell you: I am very well aware that I do not know what, according to you, is the exact nature, or what are the topics of that persuasion of which you speak, and which is given by rhetoric; although I have a suspicion about both the one and the other. And I am going to ask – what is this power of persuasion which is given by rhetoric, and about what? But why, if I have a suspicion, do I ask instead of telling you? Not for your sake, but in order that the argument may proceed in such a manner as is most likely to set forth the truth. And I would have you observe, that I am right in asking this further question: If I asked, 'What sort of a painter is Zeuxis?' and you said, 'The painter of figures,' should I not be right in asking, 'What kind of figures, and where do you find them?'

GOR. Certainly.

soc. And the reason for asking this second question would be, that there are other painters besides, who paint many other figures?

gor. True.

soc. But if there had been no one but Zeuxis who painted them, then you would have answered very well?

gor. Quite so.

soc. Now I want to know about rhetoric in the same way; – is rhetoric the only art which brings persuasion, or do other arts have the same effect? I mean to say – Does he who teaches anything persuade men of that which he teaches or not?

gor. He persuades, Socrates, – there can be no mistake about that.

soc. Again, if we take the arts of which we were just now speaking: – do not arithmetic and the arithmeticians teach us the properties of number?

gor. Certainly.

soc. And therefore persuade us of them?

gor. Yes.

soc. Then arithmetic as well as rhetoric is an artificer of persuasion?

gor. Clearly.

soc. And if any one asks us what sort of persuasion, and about what,—we shall answer, persuasion which teaches the quantity of odd and even; and we shall be able to show that all the other arts of which we were just now speaking are artificers of persuasion, and of what sort, and about what.

gor. Very true.

soc. Then rhetoric is not the only artificer of persuasion?

gor. True.

soc. Seeing, then, that not only rhetoric works by persuasion, but that other arts do the same, as in the case of the painter, a question has arisen which is a very fair one: Of what persuasion is rhetoric the artificer, and about what? – is not that a fair way of putting the question?

gor. I think so.

soc. Then, if you approve the question, Gorgias, what is the answer?

gor. I answer, Socrates, that rhetoric is the art of persuasion in courts of law and other assemblies, as I was just now saying, and about the just and unjust.

soc. And that, Gorgias, was what I was suspecting to be your notion; yet I would not have you wonder if by-and-by I am found repeating a seemingly plain question; for I ask not in order to confute you, but as I was saying that the argument may proceed consecutively, and that we may not get the habit of anticipating and suspecting the meaning of one another's words; I would have you develop your own views in your own way, whatever may be your hypothesis.

gor. I think that you are quite right, Socrates.

soc. Then let me raise another question; there is such a thing as 'having learned'?

gor. Yes.

soc. And there is also 'having believed'?

gor. Yes.

soc. And is the 'having learned' the same as 'having believed,' and are learning and belief the same things?

gor. In my judgment, Socrates, they are not the same.

soc. And your judgment is right, as you may ascertain in this way: – If a person were to say to you, 'Is there, Gorgias, a false belief as well as a true?' – you would reply, if I am not mistaken, that there is.

gor. Yes.

soc. Well, but is there a false knowledge as well as a true?

gor. No.

soc. No, indeed; and this again proves that knowledge and belief differ.

gor. Very true.

soc. And yet those who have learned as well as those who have believed are persuaded?

gor. Just so.

soc. Shall we then assume two sorts of persuasion, – one which is the source of belief without knowledge, as the other is of knowledge?

gor. By all means.

soc. And which sort of persuasion does rhetoric create in courts of law and other assemblies about the just and unjust, the sort of persuasion which gives belief without knowledge, or that which gives knowledge?

gor. Clearly, Socrates, that which only gives belief.

soc. Then rhetoric, as would appear, is the artificer of a persuasion which creates belief about the just and unjust, but gives no instruction about them?

gor. True.

soc. And the rhetorician does not instruct the courts of law or other assemblies about things just and unjust, but he creates belief about them; for no one can be supposed to instruct such a vast multitude about such high matters in a short time?

GOR. Certainly not.

SOC. Come, then, and let us see what we really mean about rhetoric; for I do not know what my own meaning is as yet. When the assembly meets to elect a physician or a shipwright or any other craftsman, will the rhetorician be taken into counsel? Surely not. For at every election he ought to be chosen who is most skilled; and, again, when walls have to be built or harbours or docks to be constructed, not the rhetorician but the master workman will advise; or when generals have to be chosen and an order of battle arranged, or a proposition taken, then the military will advise and not the rhetoricians: what do you say Gorgias? Since you profess to be a rhetorician and a maker of rhetoricians, I cannot do better than learn the nature of your art from you. And here let me assure you that I have your interest in view as well as my own. For likely enough some one or other of the young men present might desire to become your pupil, and in fact I see some, and a good many too, who have this wish, but they would be too modest to question you. And therefore when you are interrogated by me, I would have you imagine that you are interrogated by them. 'What is the use of coming to you, Gorgias?' they will say – 'about what will you teach us to advise the state? – about the just and unjust only, or about those other things also which Socrates has just mentioned?' How will you answer them?

GOR. I like your way of leading us on, Socrates, and I will endeavour to reveal to you the whole nature of rhetoric. You must have heard, I think, that the docks and the walls of the Athenians and the plan of the harbour were devised in accordance with the counsels, partly of Themistocles, and partly of Pericles, and not at the suggestion of the builders.

SOC. Such is the tradition, Gorgias, about Themistocles; and I myself heard the speech of Pericles when he advised us about the middle wall.

GOR. And you will observe, Socrates, that when a decision has to be given in such matters the rhetoricians are the advisers; they are the men who win their point.

SOC. I had that in my admiring mind, Gorgias, when I asked what is the nature of rhetoric, which always appears to me, when I look at the matter in this way, to be a marvel of greatness.

GOR. A marvel, indeed, Socrates, if you only knew how rhetoric comprehends and holds under her sway all the inferior arts. Let me offer you a striking example of this. On several occasions I have been with my brother Herodicus or some other physician to see one of his patients, who would not allow the physician to give him medicine, or apply a knife or hot iron to him; and I have persuaded him to do for me what he would not do for the physician just by the use of rhetoric. And I say that if a rhetorician and a physician were to go to any city, and had there to argue in the Ecclesia or any other assembly as to which of them should be elected state-physician, the physician would have no chance; but he who could speak would be chosen if he wished; and in a contest with a man of any other profession the rhetorician more than any one would have the power of getting himself chosen, for he can speak more persuasively to the multitude than any of them, and on any subject. Such is the nature and power of the art of rhetoric! And yet, Socrates, rhetoric should be used like any other competitive art, not against everybody, – the rhetorician ought not to abuse his strength any more than a pugilist or pancratiast or other master of fence; – because he has powers which are more than a match either for friend or enemy, he ought not therefore to strike, stab, or slay his friends. Suppose a man to have been trained in the palestra and to be a skilful boxer, – he in the fulness of his strength goes and strikes his father or mother or one of his familiars or friends; but that is no reason why the trainers or fencing-masters should be held in detestation or banished from the city; – surely not. For they taught their art for a good purpose, to be used against enemies and evil-doers, in self-defence not in aggression, and others have perverted their instructions, and turned to a bad use their own strength and skill. But not on this account are the teachers bad, neither is the art in fault, or bad in itself; I should rather say that those who make a bad use of the art are to blame. And the same argument holds good of rhetoric; for the rhetorician can speak against all men and upon any subject, – in short, he can persuade the multitude better than any other man of anything which he pleases, but he should not therefore seek to defraud the physician or any other artist of his reputation merely because he has the power; he ought to use rhetoric fairly, as he would also use his athletic powers. And if after having become a rhetorician he makes a bad use of his strength and skill, his instructor surely ought not on that account to be held in detestation or banished. For he was intended by his teacher to make a good use of his instructions, but he abuses them. And therefore he is the person who ought to be held in detestation, banished, and put to death, and not his instructor.

soc. You, Gorgias, like myself, have had great experience of disputations, and you must have observed, I think, that they do not always terminate in mutual edification, or in the definition by either party of the subjects which they are discussing; but disagreements are apt to arise – somebody says that another has not spoken truly or clearly; and then they get into a passion and begin to quarrel, both parties conceiving that their opponents are arguing from personal feeling only and jealousy of themselves, not from any interest in the question at issue. And sometimes they will go on abusing one another until the company at last are quite vexed at themselves for ever listening to such fellows. Why do I say this? Why, because I cannot help feeling that you are now saying what is not quite consistent or accordant with what you were saying at first about rhetoric. And I am afraid to point this out to you, lest you should think that I have some animosity against you, and that I speak, not for the sake of discovering the truth, but from jealousy of you. Now if you are one of my sort, I should like to cross-examine you, but if not I will let you alone. And what is my sort? you will ask. I am one of those who are very willing to be refuted if I say anything which is not true, and very willing to refute any one else who says what is not true, and quite as ready to be refuted as to refute; for I hold that this is the greater gain of the two, just as the gain is greater of being cured of a very great evil than of curing another. For I imagine that there is no evil which a man can endure so great as an erroneous opinion about the matters of which we are speaking; and if you claim to be one of my sort, let us have the discussion out, but if you would rather have done, no matter; – let us make an end of it.

GOR. I should say, Socrates, that I am quite the man whom you indicate; but, perhaps, we ought to consider the audience, for, before you came, I had already given if long exhibition, and if we proceed the argument may run on to a great length. And therefore I think that we should consider whether we may not be detaining some part of the company when they are wanting to do something else.

CHAER. You hear the audience cheering, Gorgias and Socrates, which shows their desire to listen to you; and for myself, Heaven forbid that I should have any business on hand which would take me away from a discussion so interesting and so ably maintained.

CAL. By the gods, Chaerephon, although I have been present at many discussions, I doubt whether I was ever so much delighted before, and therefore if you go on discoursing all day I shall be the better pleased.

soc. I may truly say, Callicles, that I am willing, if Gorgias is.

GOR. After all this, Socrates, I should be disgraced if I refused, especially as I have promised to answer all comers; in accordance with the wishes of the company, then, do you begin, and ask of me any question which you like.

soc. Let me tell you then, Gorgias, what surprises me in your words; though I dare say that you may be right, and I may have misunderstood your meaning. You say that you can make any man, who will learn of you, a rhetorician?

GOR. Yes.

soc. Do you mean that you will teach him to gain the ears of the multitude on any subject, and this not by instruction but by persuasion?

GOR. Quite so.

soc. You were saying, in fact, that the rhetorician will have greater powers of persuasion than the physician even in a matter of health?

GOR. Yes, with the multitude, – that is.

soc. You mean to say, with the ignorant; for with those who know he cannot be supposed to have greater powers of persuasion.

GOR. Very true.

soc. But if he is to have more power of persuasion than the physician, he will have greater power than he who knows?

GOR. Certainly.

soc. Although he is not a physician: – is he?

GOR. No.

soc. And he who is not a physician must, obviously, be ignorant of what the physician knows.

GOR. Clearly.

soc. Then, when the rhetorician is more persuasive than the physician, the ignorant is more persuasive with the ignorant than he who has knowledge? – is not that the inference?

GOR. In the case supposed: – Yes.

SOC. And the same holds of the relation of rhetoric to all the other arts; the rhetorician need not know the truth about things; he has only to discover some way of persuading the ignorant that he has more knowledge than those who know?

GOR. Yes, Socrates, and is not this a great comfort? – not to have learned the other arts, but the art of rhetoric only, and yet to be in no way inferior to the professors of them?

SOC. Whether the rhetorician is or is not inferior on this account is a question which we will hereafter examine if the enquiry is likely to be of any service to us; but I would rather begin by asking, whether he is or is not as ignorant of the just and unjust, base and honourable, good and evil, as he is of medicine and the other arts; I mean to say, does he really know anything of what is good and evil, base or honourable, just or unjust in them; or has he only a way with the ignorant of persuading them that he not knowing is to be esteemed to know more about these things than some one else who knows? Or must the pupil know these things and come to you knowing them before he can acquire the art of rhetoric? If he is ignorant, you who are the teacher of rhetoric will not teach him – it is not your business; but you will make him seem to the multitude to know them, when he does not know them; and seem to be a good man, when he is not. Or will you be unable to teach him rhetoric at all, unless he knows the truth of these things first? What is to be said about all this? By heavens, Gorgias, I wish that you would reveal to me the power of rhetoric, as you were saying that you would.

GOR. Well, Socrates, I suppose that if the pupil does chance not to know them, he will have to learn of me these things as well.

SOC. Say no more, for there you are right; and so he whom you make a rhetorician must either know the nature of the just and unjust already, or he must be taught by you.

GOR. Certainly.

SOC. Well, and is not he who has learned carpentering a carpenter?

GOR. Yes.

SOC. And he who has learned music a musician?

GOR. Yes.

SOC. And he who has learned medicine is a physician, in like manner? He who has learned anything whatever is that which his knowledge makes him.

GOR. Certainly.

SOC. And in the same way, he who has learned what is just is just?

GOR. To be sure.

SOC. And he who is just may be supposed to do what is just?

GOR. Yes.

SOC. And must not[16] the just man always desire to do what is just?

GOR. That is clearly the inference.

SOC. Surely, then, the just man will never consent to do injustice?

GOR. Certainly not.

SOC. And according to the argument the rhetorician must be a just man?

GOR. Yes.

SOC. And will therefore never be willing to do injustice?

GOR. Clearly not.

SOC. But do you remember saying just now that the trainer is not to be accused or banished if the pugilist makes a wrong use of his pugilistic art; and in like manner, if the rhetorician makes a bad and unjust use of rhetoric, that is not to be laid to the charge of his teacher, who is not to be banished, but the wrong-doer himself who made a bad use of his rhetoric – he is to be banished – was not that said?

GOR. Yes, it was.

SOC. But now we are affirming that the aforesaid rhetorician will never have done injustice at all?

GOR. True.

SOC. And at the very outset, Gorgias, it was said that rhetoric treated of discourse, not [like arithmetic] about odd and even, but about just and unjust? Was not this said?

GOR. Yes.

SOC. I was thinking at the time, when I heard you saying so, that rhetoric, which is always discoursing about justice, could not possibly be an unjust thing. But when you added, shortly afterwards, that the

---

[16] Omitting the words τὸν ῥητορικὸν δίκαιον εἶναι and δέ in next clause.

rhetorician might make a bad use of rhetoric I noted with surprise the inconsistency into which you had fallen; and I said, that if you thought, as I did, that there was a gain in being refuted, there would be an advantage in going on with the question, but if not, I would leave off. And in the course of our investigations, as you will see yourself, the rhetorician has been acknowledged to be incapable of making an unjust use of rhetoric, or of willingness to do injustice. By the dog, Gorgias, there will be a great deal of discussion, before we get at the truth of all this.

POLUS. And do even you, Socrates, seriously believe what you are now saying about rhetoric? What! because Gorgias was ashamed to deny that the rhetorician knew the just and the honourable and the good, and admitted that to any one who came to him ignorant of them he could teach them, and then out of this admission there arose a contradiction – the thing which you so dearly love, and to which not he, but you, brought the argument by your captious questions – [do you seriously believe that there is any truth in all this?] For will any one ever acknowledge that he does not know, or cannot teach, the nature of justice? The truth is, that there is great want of manners in bringing the argument to such a pass.

SOC. Illustrious Polus, the reason why we provide ourselves with friends and children is, that when we get old and stumble, a younger generation may be at hand to set us on our legs again in our words and in our actions: and now, if I and Gorgias are stumbling, here are you who should raise us up; and I for my part engage to retract any error into which you may think that I have fallen – upon one condition:

POL. What condition?

SOC. That you contract, Polus, the prolixity of speech in which you indulged at first.

POL. What! do you mean that I may not use as many words as I please?

SOC. Only to think, my friend, that having come on a visit to Athens, which is the most free-spoken state in Hellas, you when you got there, and you alone, should be deprived of the power of speech – that would be hard indeed. But then consider my case: – shall not I be very hardly used, if when you are making a long oration, and refusing to answer what you are asked, I am compelled to stay and listen to you, and may not go away? I say rather, if you have a real interest in the argument, or, to repeat my former expression, have any desire to set it on its legs, take back any statement which you please; and in your turn ask and answer, like myself and Gorgias – refute and be refuted: for I suppose that you would claim to know what Gorgias knows – would you not?

POL. Yes.

SOC. And you, like him, invite any one to ask you about anything which he pleases, and you will know how to answer him?

POL. To be sure.

SOC. And now, which will you do, ask or answer?

POL. I will ask; and do you answer me, Socrates, the same question which Gorgias, as you suppose, is unable to answer: What is rhetoric?

SOC. Do you mean what sort of an art?

POL. Yes.

SOC. To say the truth, Polus, it is not an art at all, in my opinion.

POL. Then what, in your opinion, is rhetoric?

SOC. A thing which, as I was lately reading in a book of yours, you say that you have made an art.

POL. What thing?

SOC. I should say a sort of experience.

POL. Does rhetoric seem to you to be an experience?

SOC. That is my view, but you may be of another mind.

POL. An experience in what?

SOC. An experience in producing a sort of delight and gratification.

POL. And if able to gratify others, must not rhetoric be a fine thing?

SOC. What are you saying, Polus? Why do you ask me whether rhetoric is a fine thing or not, when I have not as yet told you what rhetoric is?

POL. Did I not hear you say that rhetoric was a sort of experience?

SOC. Will you, who are so desirous to gratify others, afford a slight gratification to me?

POL. I will.

SOC. Will you ask me, what sort of an art is cookery?

POL. What sort of an art is cookery?

SOC. Not an art at all, Polus.

POL. What then?

SOC. I should say an experience.

POL. In what? I wish that you would explain to me.

SOC. An experience in producing a sort of delight and gratification, Polus.

POL. Then are cookery and rhetoric the same?

SOC. No, they are only different parts of the same profession.

POL. Of what profession?

SOC. I am afraid that the truth may seem discourteous; and I hesitate to answer, lest Gorgias should imagine that I am making fun of his own profession. For whether or no this is that art of rhetoric which Gorgias practises I really cannot tell: – from what he was just now saying, nothing appeared of what he thought of his art, but the rhetoric which I mean is a part of a not very creditable whole.

GOR. A part of what, Socrates? Say what you mean, and never mind me.

SOC. In my opinion then, Gorgias, the whole of which rhetoric is a part is not an art at all, but the habit of a bold and ready wit, which knows how to manage mankind: this habit I sum up under the word 'flattery;' and it appears to me to have many other parts, one of which is cookery, which may seem to be an art, but, as I maintain, is only an experience or routine and not an art: – another part is rhetoric, and the art of attiring and sophistry are two others: thus there are four branches, and four different things answering to them. And Polus may ask, if he likes, for he has not as yet been informed, what part of flattery is rhetoric: he did not see that I had not yet answered him when he proceeded to ask a further question: Whether I do not think rhetoric a fine thing? But I shall not tell him whether rhetoric is a fine thing or not, until I have first answered, 'What is rhetoric?' For that would not be right, Polus; but I shall be happy to answer, if you will ask me, What part of flattery is rhetoric?

POL. I will ask, and do you answer? What part of flattery is rhetoric?

SOC. Will you understand my answer? Rhetoric, according to my view, is the ghost or counterfeit of a part of politics.

POL. And noble or ignoble?

SOC. Ignoble, I should say, if I am compelled to answer, for I call what is bad ignoble: – though I doubt whether you understand what I was saying before.

GOR. Indeed, Socrates, I cannot say that I understand myself.

SOC. I do not wonder, Gorgias; for I have not as yet explained myself, and our friend Polus, colt by name and colt by nature, is apt to run away.[17]

GOR. Never mind him, but explain to me what you mean by saying that rhetoric is the counterfeit of a part of politics.

SOC. I will try, then, to explain my notion of rhetoric, and if I am mistaken, my friend Polus shall refute me. We may assume the existence of bodies and of souls?

GOR. Of course.

SOC. You would further admit that there is a good condition of either of them?

GOR. Yes.

SOC. Which condition may not be really good, but good only in appearance? I mean to say, that there are many persons who appear to be in good health, and whom only a physician or trainer will discern at first sight not to be in good health.

GOR. True.

SOC. And this applies not only to the body, but also to the soul: in either there may be that which gives the appearance of health and not the reality?

GOR. Yes, certainly.

SOC. And now I will endeavour to explain to you more clearly what I mean: The soul and body being two, have two arts corresponding to them: there is the art of politics attending on the soul; and another art attending on the body, of which I know no single name, but which may be described as having two divisions, one of them gymnastic, and the other medicine. And in politics there is a legislative part, which answers to gymnastic, as justice does to medicine; and the two parts run into one another, justice having to do with the same subject as legislation, and medicine with the same subject as gymnastic, but with a difference. Now, seeing that there are these four arts, two attending on the body and two on the soul for their highest good; flattery knowing, or rather guessing their natures, has distributed herself into four shams or simulations of them; she puts on the likeness of some one or other of them, and pretends to be that which she simulates, and having no regard for men's highest interests, is ever making pleasure the bait of the unwary, and deceiving them into the belief that she is of the highest value to them. Cookery simulates the disguise of medicine, and pretends to know what food is the best for the body; and if the physician and the cook had to enter into a competition in which children were the judges, or men who had

---

[17] There is an untranslatable play on the name 'Polus,' which means 'a colt.'

no more sense than children, as to which of them best understands the goodness or badness of food, the physician would be starved to death. A flattery I deem this to be and of an ignoble sort, Polus, for to you I am now addressing myself, because it aims at pleasure without any thought of the best. An art I do not call it, but only an experience, because it is unable to explain or to give a reason of the nature of its own applications. And I do not call any irrational thing an art; but if you dispute my words, I am prepared to argue in defence of them.

Cookery, then, I maintain to be a flattery which takes the form of medicine; and tiring, in like manner, is a flattery which takes the form of gymnastic, and is knavish, false, ignoble, illiberal, working deceitfully by the help of lines, and colours, and enamels, and garments, and making men affect a spurious beauty to the neglect of the true beauty which is given by gymnastic.

I would rather not be tedious, and therefore I will only say, after the manner of the geometricians, (for I think that by this time you will be able to follow,)

as tiring : gymnastic : : cookery : medicine; or rather,

as tiring : gymnastic : : sophistry : legislation; and

as cookery : medicine : : rhetoric : justice.

And this, I say, is the natural difference between the rhetorician and the sophist, but by reason of their near connection, they are apt to be jumbled up together; neither do they know what to make of themselves, nor do other men know what to make of them. For if the body presided over itself, and were not under the guidance of the soul, and the soul did not discern and discriminate between cookery and medicine, but the body was made the judge of them, and the rule of judgment was the bodily delight which was given by them, then the word of Anaxagoras, that word with which you, friend Polus, are so well acquainted, would prevail far and wide: 'Chaos' would come again, and cookery, health, and medicine would mingle in an indiscriminate mass. And now I have told you my notion of rhetoric, which is, in relation to the soul, what cookery is to the body. I may have been inconsistent in making a long speech, when I would not allow you to discourse at length. But I think that I may be excused, because you did not understand me, and could make no use of my answer when I spoke shortly, and therefore I had to enter into an explanation. And if I show an equal inability to make use of yours, I hope that you will speak at equal length; but if I am able to understand you, let me have the benefit of your brevity, as is only fair: And now you may do what you please with my answer.

POL. What do you mean? do you think that rhetoric is flattery?

SOC. Nay, I said a part of flattery; if at your age, Polus, you cannot remember, what will you do by-and-by, when you get older?

POL. And are the good rhetoricians meanly regarded in states, under the idea that they are flatterers?

SOC. Is that a question or the beginning of a speech?

POL. I am asking a question.

SOC. Then my answer is, that they are not regarded at all.

POL. How not regarded? Have they not very great power in states?

SOC. Not if you mean to say that power is a good to the possessor.

POL. And that is what I do mean to say.

SOC. Then, if so, I think that they have the least power of all the citizens.

POL. What! are they not like tyrants? They kill and despoil and exile any one whom they please.

SOC. By the dog, Polus, I cannot make out at each deliverance of yours, whether you are giving an opinion of your own, or asking a question of me.

POL. I am asking a question of you.

SOC. Yes, my friend, but you ask two questions at once.

POL. How two questions?

SOC. Why, did you not say just now that the rhetoricians are like tyrants, and that they kill and despoil or exile any one whom they please?

POL. I did.

SOC. Well then, I say to you that here are two questions in one, and I will answer both of them. And I tell you, Polus, that rhetoricians and tyrants have the least possible power in states, as I was just now saying; for they do literally nothing which they will, but only what they think best.

POL. And is not that a great power?

SOC. Polus has already said the reverse.

SOC. No, by the great – what do you call him? – not you, for you say that power is a good to him who has the power.

POL. I do.

soc. And would you maintain that if a fool does what he thinks best, this is a good, and would you call this great power?

pol. I should not.

soc. Then you must prove that the rhetorician is not a fool, and that rhetoric is an art and not a flattery – and so you will have refuted me; but if you leave me unrefuted, why, the rhetoricians who do what they think best in states, and the tyrants, will have nothing upon which to congratulate themselves, if as you say, power be indeed a good, admitting at the same time that what is done without sense is an evil.

pol. Yes; I admit that.

soc. How then can the rhetoricians or the tyrants have great power in states, unless Polus can refute Socrates, and prove to him that they do as they will?

pol. This fellow –

soc. I say that they do not do as they will; – now refute me.

pol. Why, have you not already said that they do as they think best?

soc. And I say so still.

pol. Then surely they do as they will?

soc. I deny it.

pol. But they do what they think best?

soc. Aye.

pol. That, Socrates, is monstrous and absurd.

soc. Good words, good Polus, as I may say in your own peculiar style; but if you have any questions to ask of me, either prove that I am in error or give the answer yourself.

pol. Very well, I am willing to answer that I may know what you mean.

soc. Do men appear to you to will that which they do, or to will that further end for the sake of which they do a thing? when they take medicine, for example, at the bidding of a physician, do they will the drinking of the medicine which is painful, or the health for the sake of which they drink?

pol. Clearly, the health.

soc. And when men go on a voyage or engage in business, they do not will that which they are doing at the time; for who would desire to take the risk of a voyage or the trouble of business? – But they will, to have the wealth for the sake of which they go on a voyage.

pol. Certainly.

soc. And is not this universally true? If a man does something for the sake of something else, he wills not that which he does, but that for the sake of which he does.

pol. Yes.

soc. And are not all things either good or evil, or intermediate and indifferent?

pol. To be sure, Socrates.

soc. Wisdom and health and wealth and the like you would call goods, and their opposites evils?

pol. I should.

soc. And the things which are neither good nor evil, and which partake sometimes of the nature of good and at other times of evil, or of neither, are such as sitting, walking, running, sailing; or, again, wood, stones, and the like: – these are the things which you call neither good nor evil?

pol. Exactly so.

soc. Are these indifferent things done for the sake of the good, or the good for the sake of the indifferent?

pol. Clearly, the indifferent for the sake of the good.

soc. When we walk we walk for the sake of the good, and under the idea that it is better to walk, and when we stand we stand equally for the sake of the good?

pol. Yes.

soc. And when we kill a man we kill him or exile him or despoil him of his goods, because, as we think it will conduce to our good?

pol. Certainly.

soc. Men who do any of these things do them for the sake of the good?

pol. Yes.

soc. And did we not admit that in doing something for the sake of something else, we do not will those things which we do, but that other thing for the sake of which we do them?

pol. Most true.

soc. Then we do not will simply to kill a man or to exile him or to despoil him of his goods, but we will to do that which conduces to our good, and if the act is not conducive to our good we do not will it; for we will, as you say, that which is our good, but that which is neither good nor evil, or simply evil, we do not will. Why are you silent, Polus? Am I not right?

pol. You are right.

soc. Hence we may infer, that if any one, whether he be a tyrant or a rhetorician, kills another or exiles another or deprives him of his property, under the idea that the act is for his own

GORGIAS

157

interests when really not for his own interests, he may be said to do what seems best to him?

POL. Yes.

SOC. But does he do what he wills if he does what is evil? Why do you not answer?

POL. Well, I suppose not.

SOC. Then if great power is a good as you allow, will such a one have great power in a state?

POL. He will not.

SOC. Then I was right in saying that a man may do what seems good to him in a state, and not have great power, and not do what he wills?

POL. As though you, Socrates, would not like to have the power of doing what seemed good to you in the state, rather than not; you would not be jealous when you saw any one killing or despoiling or imprisoning whom he pleased, Oh, no!

SOC. Justly or unjustly, do you mean?

POL. In either case is he not equally to be envied?

SOC. Forbear, Polus!

POL. Why 'forbear'?

SOC. Because you ought not to envy wretches who are not to be envied, but only to pity them.

POL. And are those of whom I spoke wretches?

SOC. Yes, certainly they are.

POL. And so you think that he who slays any one whom he pleases, and justly slays him, is pitiable and wretched?

SOC. No, I do not say that of him: but neither do I think that he is to be envied.

POL. Were you not saying just now that he is wretched?

SOC. Yes, my friend, if he killed another unjustly, in which case he is also to be pitied; and he is not to be envied if he killed him justly.

POL. At any rate you will allow that he who is unjustly put to death is wretched, and to be pitied?

SOC. Not so much, Polus, as he who kills him, and not so much as he who is justly killed.

POL. How can that be, Socrates?

SOC. That may very well be, inasmuch as doing injustice is the greatest of evils.

POL. But is it the greatest? Is not suffering injustice a greater evil?

SOC. Certainly not.

POL. Then would you rather suffer than do injustice?

SOC. I should not like either, but if I must choose between them, I would rather suffer than do.

POL. Then you would not wish to be a tyrant?

SOC. Not if you mean by tyranny what I mean.

POL. I mean, as I said before, the power of doing whatever seems good to you in a state, killing, banishing, doing in all things as you like.

SOC. Well then, illustrious friend, when I have said my say, do you reply to me. Suppose that I go into a crowded Agora, and take a dagger under my arm. Polus, I say to you, I have just acquired rare power, and become a tyrant; for if I think that any of these men whom you see ought to be put to death, the man whom I have a mind to kill is as good as dead; and if I am disposed to break his head or tear his garment, he will have his head broken or his garment torn in an instant. Such is my great power in this city. And if you do not believe me, and I show you the dagger, you would probably reply: Socrates, in that sort of way any one may have great power – he may burn any house which he pleases, and the docks and triremes of the Athenians, and all their other vessels, whether public or private – but can you believe that this mere doing as you think best is great power?

POL. Certainly not such doing as this.

SOC. But can you tell me why you disapprove of such a power?

POL. I can.

SOC. Why then?

POL. Why, because he who did as you say would be certain to be punished.

SOC. And punishment is an evil?

POL. Certainly.

SOC. And you would admit once more, my good sir, that great power is a benefit to a man if his actions turn out to his advantage, and that this is the meaning of great power; and if not, then his power is an evil and is no power. But let us look at the matter in another way: – do we not acknowledge that the things of which we were speaking, the infliction of death, and exile, and the deprivation of property are sometimes a good and sometimes not a good?

POL. Certainly.

SOC. About that you and I may be supposed to agree?

POL. Yes.

SOC. Tell me, then, when do you say that they are good and when that they are evil – what principle do you lay down?

POL. I would rather, Socrates, that you should answer as well as ask that question.

SOC. Well, Polus, since you would rather have the answer from me, I say that they are good when they are just, and evil when they are unjust.

POL. You are hard of refutation, Socrates, but might not a child refute that statement?

SOC. Then I shall be very grateful to the child, and equally grateful to you if you will refute me and deliver me from my foolishness. And I hope that refute me you will, and not weary of doing good to a friend.

POL. Yes, Socrates, and I need not go far or appeal to antiquity; events which happened only a few days ago are enough to refute you, and to prove that many men who do wrong are happy.

SOC. What events?

POL. You see, I presume, that Archelaus the son of Perdiccas is now the ruler of Macedonia?

SOC. At any rate I hear that he is.

POL. And do you think that he is happy or miserable?

SOC. I cannot say, Polus, for I have never had any acquaintance with him.

POL. And cannot you tell at once, and without having an acquaintance with him, whether a man is happy?

SOC. Most certainly not.

POL. Then clearly, Socrates, you would say that you did not even know whether the great king was a happy man?

SOC. And I should speak the truth; for I do not know how he stands in the matter of education and justice.

POL. What! and does all happiness consist in this?

SOC. Yes, indeed, Polus, that is my doctrine; the men and women who are gentle and good are also happy, as I maintain, and the unjust and evil are miserable.

POL. Then, according to your doctrine, the said Archelaus is miserable?

SOC. Yes, my friend, if he is wicked.

POL. That he is wicked I cannot deny; for he had no title at all to the throne which he now occupies, he being only the son of a woman who was the slave of Alcetas the brother of Perdiccas; he himself therefore in strict right was the slave of Alcetas; and if he had meant to do rightly he would have remained his slave, and then, according to your doctrine, he would have been happy. But now he is unspeakably miserable, for he has been guilty of the greatest crimes: in the first place he invited his uncle and master, Alcetas, to come to him, under the pretence that he would restore to him the throne which Perdicoas has usurped, and after entertaining

him and his son Alexander, who was his own cousin, and nearly of an age with him, and making them drunk, he threw them into a waggon and carried them off by night, and slew them, and got both of them out of the way; and when he had done all this wickedness he never discovered that he was the most miserable of all men, and was very far from repenting: shall I tell you how he showed his remorse? He had a younger brother, a child of seven years old, who was the legitimate son of Perdiccas, and to him of right the kingdom belonged; Archelaus, however, had no mind to bring him up as he ought and restore the kingdom to him; that was not his notion of happiness; but not long afterwards he threw him into a well and drowned him, and declared to his mother Cleopatra that he had fallen in while running after a goose, and had been killed. And now as he is the greatest criminal of all the Macedonians, he may be supposed to be the most miserable and not the happiest of them, and I dare say that there are many Athenians, and you would be at the head of them, who would rather be any other Macedonian than Archelaus!

SOC. I praised you at first, Polus, for being a rhetorician rather than a reasoner. And this, as I suppose, is the sort of argument with which you fancy that a child might refute me, and by which I stand refuted when I say that the unjust man is not happy. But, my good friend, where is the refutation? I cannot admit a word which you have been saying.

POL. That is because you will not for you surely must think as I do.

SOC. Not so, my simple friend, but because you will refute me after the manner which rhetoricians practise in courts of law. For there the one party think that they refute the other when they bring forward a number of witnesses of good repute in proof of their allegations, and their adversary has only a single one or none at all. But this kind of proof is of no value where truth is the aim; a man may often be sworn down by a multitude of false witnesses who have a great air of respectability. And in this argument nearly every one, Athenian and stranger alike, would be on your side, if you should bring witnesses in disproof of my statement; – you may, if you will, summon Nicias the son of Niceratus, and let his brothers, who gave the row of tripods which stand in the precincts of Dionysus, come with him; or you may summon Aristocrates, the son of Scellius, who is the giver of that famous offering which is at Delphi; summon, if you will, the whole house of Pericles, or any other great Athenian family whom you choose; – they will all agree with you: I only am left alone and cannot agree, for you do not convince me; although you produce many false witnesses against me, in the hope of depriving me of my inheritance, which is the truth. But I consider that nothing worth speaking of will have been effected by me unless I make you the one witness of my words; nor by you, unless you make me the one witness of yours; no matter about the rest of the world. For there are two ways of refutation, one which is yours and that of the world in general; but mine is of another sort – let us compare them, and see in what they differ. For, indeed, we are at issue about matters which to know is honourable and not to know disgraceful; to know or not to know happiness and misery – that is the chief of them. And what knowledge can be nobler? or what ignorance more disgraceful than this? And therefore I will begin by asking you whether you do not think that a man who is unjust and doing injustice can be happy, seeing that you think Archelaus unjust, and yet happy? May I assume this to be your opinion?

POL. Certainly.

SOC. But I say that this is an impossibility – here is one point about which we are at issue: – very good. And do you mean to say also that if he meets with retribution and punishment he will still be happy?

POL. Certainly not; in that case he will be most miserable.

SOC. On the other hand, if the unjust be not punished, then, according to you, he will be happy?

POL. Yes.

SOC. But in my opinion, Polus, the unjust or doer of unjust actions is miserable in any case, – more miserable, however, if he be not punished and does not meet with retribution, and less miserable if he be punished and meets with retribution at the hands of gods and men.

POL. You are maintaining a strange doctrine, Socrates.

SOC. I shall try to make you agree with me, O my friend, for as a friend I regard you. Then these are the points at issue between us – are they not? I was saying that to do is worse than to suffer injustice?

POL. Exactly so.

SOC. And you said the opposite?

POL. Yes.

SOC. I said also that the wicked are miserable, and you refuted me?

POL. By Zeus, I did.

SOC. In your own opinion, Polus.

POL. Yes, and I rather suspect that I was in the right.

SOC. You further said that the wrong-doer is happy if he be unpunished?

POL. Certainly.

SOC. And I affirm that he is most miserable, and that those who are punished are less miserable – are you going to refute this proposition also?

POL. A proposition which is harder of refutation than the other, Socrates.

SOC. Say rather, Polus, impossible for who can refute the truth?

POL. What do you mean? If a man is detected in an unjust attempt to make himself a tyrant, and when detected is racked, mutilated, has his eyes burned out, and after having had all sorts of great injuries inflicted on him, and having seen his wife and children suffer the like, is at last impaled or tarred and burned alive, will he be happier than if he escape and become a tyrant, and continue all through life doing what he likes and holding the reins of government, the envy and admiration both of citizens and strangers? Is that the paradox which, as you say, cannot be refuted?

SOC. There again, noble Polus, you are raising hobgoblins instead of refuting me; just now you were calling witnesses against me. But please to refresh my memory a little; did you say – 'in an unjust attempt to make himself a tyrant'?

POL. Yes, I did.

SOC. Then I say that neither of them will be happier than the other,—neither he who unjustly acquires a tyranny, nor he who suffers in the attempt, for of two miserables one cannot be the happier, but that he who escapes and becomes a tyrant is the more miserable of the two. Do you laugh, Polus? Well, this is a new kind of refutation, – when any one says anything, instead of refuting him to laugh at him.

POL. But do you not think, Socrates, that you have been sufficiently refuted, when you say that which no human being will allow? Ask the company.

SOC. O Polus, I am not a public man and only last year, when my tribe were serving as Prytanes, and it became my duty as their president to take the votes, there was a laugh at me, because I was unable to take them. And as I failed then, you must not ask me to count the suffrages of the company now; but if, as I was saying, you have no better argument than numbers, let me have a turn, and do you make trial of the sort of proof which, as I think, is required; for I shall produce one witness only of the truth of my words, and he is the person with whom I am arguing; his suffrage I know how to take; but with the many I have nothing to do, and do not even address myself to them. May I ask then whether you will answer in turn and have your words put to the proof? For I certainly think that I and you and every man do really believe, that to do is a greater evil than to suffer injustice: and not to be punished than to be punished.

POL. And I should say neither I, nor any man: would you yourself, for example, suffer rather than do injustice?

SOC. Yes, and you, too; I or any man would.

POL. Quite the reverse; neither you, nor I, nor any man.

SOC. But will you answer?

POL. To be sure, I will; for I am curious to hear what you can have to say.

SOC. Tell me, then, and you will know, and let us suppose that I am beginning at the beginning: which of the two, Polus, in your opinion, is the worst? – to do injustice or to suffer?

POL. I should say that suffering was worst.

SOC. And which is the greater disgrace? – Answer.

POL. To do.

SOC. And the greater disgrace is the greater evil?

POL. Certainly not.

SOC. I understand you to say, if I am not mistaken, that the honourable is not the same as the good, or the disgraceful as the evil?

POL. Certainly not.

SOC. Let me ask a question of you: When you speak of beautiful things, such as bodies, colours, figures, sounds, institutions, do you not call them beautiful in reference to some standard: bodies, for example, are beautiful in proportion as they are useful, or as the sight of them gives pleasure to the spectators; can you give any other account of personal beauty?

POL. I cannot.

SOC. And you would say of figures or colours generally that they were beautiful, either by reason of the pleasure which they give, or of their use, or of both?

POL. Yes, I should.

SOC. And you would call sounds and music beautiful for the same reason?

POL. I should.

SOC. Laws and institutions also have no beauty in them except in so far as they are useful or pleasant or both?

POL. I think not.

SOC. And may not the same be said of the beauty of knowledge?

POL. To be sure, Socrates; and I very much approve of your measuring beauty by the standard of pleasure and utility.

SOC. And deformity or disgrace may be equally measured by the opposite standard of pain and evil?

POL. Certainly.

SOC. Then when of two beautiful things one exceeds in beauty, the measure of the excess is to be taken in one or both of these; that is to say, in pleasure or utility or both?

POL. Very true.

SOC. And of two deformed things, that which exceeds in deformity or disgrace, exceeds either in pain or evil – must it not be so?

POL. Yes.

SOC. But then again, what was the observation which you just now made, about doing and suffering wrong? Did you not say, that suffering wrong was more evil, and doing wrong more disgraceful?

POL. I did.

SOC. Then, if doing wrong is more disgraceful than suffering, the more disgraceful must be more painful and must exceed in pain or in evil or both: does not that also follow?

POL. Of course.

SOC. First, then, let us consider whether the doing of injustice exceeds the suffering in the consequent pain: Do the injurers suffer more than the injured?

POL. No, Socrates; certainly not.

SOC. Then they do not exceed in pain?

POL. No.

SOC. But if not in pain, then not in both?

POL. Certainly not.

SOC. Then they can only exceed in the other?

POL. Yes.

SOC. That is to say, in evil?

POL. True.

soc. Then doing injustice will have an excess of evil, and will therefore be a greater evil than suffering injustice?

pol. Clearly.

soc. But have not you and the world already agreed that to do injustice is more disgraceful than to suffer?

pol. Yes.

soc. And that is now discovered to be more evil?

pol. True.

soc. And would you prefer a greater evil or a greater dishonour to a less one? Answer, Polus, and fear not; for you will come to no harm if you nobly resign yourself into the healing hand of the argument as to a physician without shrinking, and either say 'Yes' or 'No' to me.

pol. I should say 'No.'

soc. Would any other man prefer a greater to a less evil?

pol. No, not according to this way of putting the case, Socrates.

soc. Then I said truly, Polus, that neither you, nor I, nor any man, would rather, do than suffer injustice; for to do injustice is the greater evil of the two.

pol. That is the conclusion.

soc. You see, Polus, when you compare the two kinds of refutations, how unlike they are. All men, with the exception of myself, are of your way of thinking; but your single assent and witness are enough for me, – I have no need of any other, I take your suffrage, and am regardless of the rest. Enough of this, and now let us proceed to the next question; which is, Whether the greatest of evils to a guilty man is to suffer punishment, as you supposed, or whether to escape punishment is not a greater evil, as I supposed. Consider: – You would say that to suffer punishment is another name for being justly corrected when you do wrong?

pol. I should.

soc. And would you not allow that all just things are honourable in so far as they are just? Please to reflect, and tell me your opinion.

pol. Yes, Socrates, I think that they are.

soc. Consider again: – Where there is an agent, must there not also be a patient?

pol. I should say so.

soc. And will not the patient suffer that which the agent does, and will not the suffering have the quality of the action? I mean, for example, that if a man strikes, there must be something which is stricken?

pol. Yes.

soc. And if the striker strikes violently or quickly, that which is struck will be struck violently or quickly?

pol. True.

soc. And the suffering to him who is stricken is of the same nature as the act of him who strikes?

pol. Yes.

soc. And if a man burns, there is something which is burned?

pol. Certainly.

soc. And if he burns in excess or so as to cause pain, the thing burned will be burned in the same way?

pol. Truly.

soc. And if he cuts, the same argument holds – there will be something cut?

pol. Yes.

soc. And if the cutting be great or deep or such as will cause pain, the cut will be of the same nature?

pol. That is evident.

soc. Then you would agree generally to the universal proposition which I was just now asserting: that the affection of the patient answers to the act of the agent?

pol. I agree.

soc. Then, as this is admitted, let me ask whether being punished is suffering or acting?

pol. Suffering, Socrates; there can be no doubt of that.

soc. And suffering implies an agent?

pol. Certainly, Socrates; and he is the punisher.

soc. And he who punishes rightly, punishes justly?

pol. Yes.

soc. And therefore he acts justly?

pol. Justly.

soc. Then he who is punished and suffers retribution, suffers justly?

pol. That is evident.

soc. And that which is just has been admitted to be honourable?

pol. Certainly.

soc. Then the punisher does what is honourable, and the punished suffers what is honourable?

pol. True.

soc. And if what is honourable, then what is good, for the honourable is either pleasant or useful?

pol. Certainly.

SOC. Then he who is punished suffers what is good?

POL. That is true.

SOC. Then he is benefited?

POL. Yes.

SOC. Do I understand you to mean what I mean by the term 'benefited'? I mean, that if he be justly punished his soul is improved.

POL. Surely.

SOC. Then he who is punished is delivered from the evil of his soul?

POL. Yes.

SOC. And is he not then delivered from the greatest evil? Look at the matter in this way: – In respect of a man's estate, do you see any greater evil than poverty?

POL. There is no greater evil.

SOC. Again, in a man's bodily frame, you would say that the evil is weakness and disease and deformity?

POL. I should.

SOC. And do you not imagine that the soul likewise has some evil of her own?

POL. Of course.

SOC. And this you would call injustice and ignorance and cowardice, and the like?

POL. Certainly.

SOC. So then, in mind, body, and estate, which are three, you have pointed out three corresponding evils – injustice, disease, poverty?

POL. True.

SOC. And which of the evils is the most disgraceful? – Is not the most disgraceful of them injustice, and in general the evil of the soul?

POL. By far the most.

SOC. And if the most disgraceful, then also the worst?

POL. What do you mean, Socrates?

SOC. I mean to say, that what is most disgraceful has been already admitted to be most painful or hurtful, or both.

POL. Certainly.

SOC. And now injustice and all evil in the soul has been admitted by us to be most disgraceful?

POL. It has been admitted.

SOC. And most disgraceful either because most painful and causing excessive pain, or most hurtful, or both?

POL. Certainly.

SOC. And therefore to be unjust and intemperate, and cowardly and ignorant, is more painful than to be poor and sick?

POL. Nay, Socrates; the painfulness does not appear to me to follow from your premises.

SOC. Then, if, as you would argue, not more painful, the evil of the soul is of all evils the most disgraceful; and the excess of disgrace must be caused by some preternatural greatness, or extraordinary hurtfulness of the evil.

POL. Clearly.

SOC. And that which exceeds most in hurtfulness will be the greatest of evils?

POL. Yes.

SOC. Then injustice and intemperance, and in general the depravity of the soul, are the greatest of evils!

POL. That is evident.

SOC. Now, what art is there which delivers us from poverty? Does not the art of making money?

POL. Yes.

SOC. And what art frees us from disease? Does not the art of medicine?

POL. Very true.

SOC. And what from vice and injustice? If you are not able to answer at once, ask yourself whither we go with the sick, and to whom we take them.

POL. To the physicians, Socrates.

SOC. And to whom do we go with the unjust and intemperate?

POL. To the judges, you mean.

SOC. – Who are to punish them?

POL. Yes.

SOC. And do not those who rightly punish others, punish them in accordance with a certain rule of justice?

POL. Clearly.

SOC. Then the art of money-making frees a man from poverty; medicine from disease; and justice from intemperance and injustice?

POL. That is evident.

SOC. Which, then, is the best of these three?

POL. Will you enumerate them?

SOC. Money-making, medicine, and justice.

POL. Justice, Socrates, far excels the two others.

SOC. And justice, if the best, gives the greatest pleasure or advantage or both?

POL. Yes.

SOC. But is the being healed a pleasant thing, and are those who are being healed pleased?

POL. I think not.

SOC. A useful thing, then?

POL. Yes.

SOC. Yes, because the patient is delivered from a great evil; and this is the advantage of enduring the pain – that you get well?

POL. Certainly.

SOC. And would he be the happier man in his bodily condition, who is healed, or who never was out of health?

POL. Clearly he who was never out of health.

SOC. Yes; for happiness surely does not consist in being delivered from evils, but in never having had them.

POL. True.

SOC. And suppose the case of two persons who have some evil in their bodies, and that one of them is healed and delivered from evil, and another is not healed, but retains the evil – which of them is the most miserable?

POL. Clearly he who is not healed.

SOC. And was not punishment said by us to be a deliverance from the greatest of evils, which is vice?

POL. True.

SOC. And justice punishes us, and makes us more just, and is the medicine of our vice?

POL. True.

SOC. He, then, has the first place in the scale of happiness who has never had vice in his soul; for this has been shown to be the greatest of evils.

POL. Clearly.

SOC. And he has the second place, who is delivered from vice?

POL. True.

SOC. That is to say, he who receives admonition and rebuke and punishment?

POL. Yes.

SOC. Then he lives worst, who, having been unjust, has no deliverance from injustice?

POL. Certainly.

SOC. That is, he lives worst who commits the greatest crimes, and who, being the most unjust of men, succeeds in escaping rebuke or correction or punishment; and this, as you say, has been accomplished by Archelaus and other tyrants and rhetoricians and potentates?[18]

POL. True.

SOC. May not their way of proceeding, my friend, be compared to the conduct of a person who is afflicted with the worst of diseases and yet contrives not to pay the penalty to the physician for his sins against his constitution, and will not be cured, because, like a child, he is afraid of the pain of being burned or cut: – Is not that a parallel case?

POL. Yes, truly.

SOC. He would seem as if he did not know the nature of health and bodily vigour; and if we are right, Polus, in our previous conclusions, they are in a like case who strive to evade justice, which they see to be painful, but are blind to the advantage which ensues from it, not knowing how far more miserable a companion a diseased soul is than a diseased body, a soul, I say, which is corrupt and unrighteous and unholy. And hence they do all that they can to avoid punishment and to avoid being released from the greatest of evils; they provide themselves with money and friends, and cultivate to the utmost their powers of persuasion. But if we, Polus, are right, do you see what follows, or shall we draw out the consequences in form?

POL. If you please.

SOC. Is it not a fact that injustice and the doing of injustice, is the greatest of evils?

POL. That is quite clear.

SOC. And further, that to suffer punishment is the way to be released from this evil?

POL. True.

SOC. And not to suffer, is to perpetuate the evil?

POL. Yes.

SOC. To do wrong, then, is second only in the scale of evils; but to do wrong and not to be punished, is first and greatest of all?

POL. That is true.

SOC. Well, and was not this the point in dispute, my friend? You deemed Archelaus happy, because he was a very great criminal and unpunished: I, on the other hand, maintained that he or any other who like him has done wrong and has not been punished, is, and ought to be, the most miserable of all men; and that the doer of injustice is more miserable than the sufferer; and he who escapes punishment, more miserable than he who suffers. – Was not that what I said?

POL. Yes.

SOC. And it has been proved to be true?

POL. Certainly.

---

18 Cp. Rep. ix. 579, 580.

soc. Well, Polus, but if this is true, where is the great use of rhetoric? If we admit what has been just now said, every man ought in every way to guard himself against doing wrong, for he will thereby suffer great evil?

POL. True.

soc. And if he, or any one about whom he cares, does wrong, he ought of his own accord to go where he will be immediately punished; he will run to the judge, as he would to the physician, in order that the disease of injustice may not be rendered chronic and become the incurable cancer of the soul; must we not allow this consequence, Polus, if our former admissions are to stand: – is any other inference consistent with them?

POL. To that, Socrates, there can be but one answer.

soc. Then rhetoric is of no use to us, Polus, in helping a man to excuse his own injustice, or that of his parents or friends, or children or country; but may be of use to any one who holds that instead of excusing he ought to accuse – himself above all, and in the next degree his family or any of his friends who may be doing wrong; he should bring to light the iniquity and not conceal it, that so the wrong-doer may suffer and be made whole; and he should even force himself and others not to shrink, but with closed eyes like brave men to let the physician operate with knife or searing iron, not regarding the pain, in the hope of attaining the good and the honourable; let him who has done things worthy of stripes, allow himself to be scourged, if of bonds, to be bound, if of a fine, to be fined, if of exile, to be exiled, if of death, to die, himself being the first to accuse himself and his own relations, and using rhetoric to this end, that his and their unjust actions may be made manifest, and that they themselves may be delivered from injustice, which is the greatest evil. Then, Polus, rhetoric would indeed be useful. Do you say 'Yes' or 'No' to that?

POL. To me, Socrates, what you are saying appears very strange, though probably in agreement with your premises.

soc. Is not this the conclusion, if the premises are not disproven?

POL. Yes; it certainly is.

soc. And from the opposite point of view, if indeed it be our duty to harm another, whether an enemy or not – I except the case of self-defence – then I have to be upon my guard – but if my enemy injures a third person, then in every sort of way, by word as well as deed, I should try to prevent his being punished, or appearing before the judge; and if he appears, I should contrive that he should escape, and not suffer punishment: if he has stolen a sum of money, let him keep what he has stolen and spend it on him and his, regardless of religion and justice; and if he have done things worthy of death, let him not die, but rather be immortal in his wickedness; or, if this is not possible, let him at any rate be allowed to live as long as he can. For such purposes, Polus, rhetoric may be useful, but is of small if of any use to him who is not intending to commit injustice; at least, there was no such use discovered by us in the previous discussion.

CAL. Tell me, Chaerephon, is Socrates in earnest, or is he joking?

CHAER. I should say, Callicles, that he is in most profound earnest; but you may as well ask him.

CAL. By the gods, and I will. Tell me, Socrates, are you in earnest, or only in jest? For if you are in earnest, and what you say is true, is not the whole of human life turned upside down; and are we not doing, as would appear, in everything the opposite of what we ought to be doing?

soc. O Callicles, if there were not some community of feelings among mankind, however varying in different persons – I mean to say, if every man's feelings were peculiar to himself and were not shared by the rest of his species – I do not see how we could ever communicate our impressions to one another. I make this remark because I perceive that you and I have a common feeling. For we are lovers both, and both of us have two loves apiece: – I am the lover of Alcibiades, the son of Cleinias, and of philosophy; and you of the Athenian Demus, and of Demus the son of Pyrilampes. Now, I observe that you, with all your cleverness, do not venture to contradict your favourite in any word or opinion of his; but as he changes you change, backwards and forwards. When the Athenian Demus denies anything that you are saying in the assembly, you go over to his opinion; and you do the same with Demus, the fair young son of Pyrilampes. For you have not the power to resist the words and ideas of your loves; and if a person were to express surprise at the strangeness of what you say from time to time when under their influence, you would probably reply to him, if you were honest, that you cannot help saying what your loves say unless they are prevented; and that you can only be silent when they are. Now you must understand that my words are an echo too, and therefore you need not wonder at me; but if you want to silence me, silence philosophy, who is my love, for she is always telling me what I am now telling you, my friend; neither is she capricious like my other love, for the son of Cleinias says one thing to-day and another thing to-morrow, but philosophy is always true. She is the teacher at whose words you are now wondering, and you have heard her yourself. Her you must refute, and either show, as I was saying, that to do injustice and to escape punishment is not the worst of all evils; or, if you leave her word unrefuted, by the dog the god of Egypt, I declare, O Callicles, that Callicles will never be at one with himself, but that his whole life will be a discord. And yet, my friend, I would rather that my lyre should be inharmonious, and that there should be no music in the chorus which I provided; aye, or that the whole world should be at odds with me, and oppose me, rather than that I myself should be at odds with myself, and contradict myself.

CAL. O Socrates, you are a regular declaimer, and seem to be running riot in the argument. And now you are declaiming in this way because Polus has fallen into the same error himself of which he accused Gorgias: – for he said that when Gorgias was asked by you, whether, if some one came to him who wanted to learn rhetoric, and did not know justice, he would teach him justice, Gorgias in his modesty replied that he would, because he thought that mankind in general would be displeased if he answered 'No;' and then in consequence of this admission, Gorgias was compelled to contradict himself, that being just the sort of thing in which you delight. Whereupon Polus laughed at you deservedly, as I think; but now he has himself fallen into the same trap. I cannot say very much for his wit when he conceded to you that to do is more dishonourable than to suffer injustice, for this was the admission which led to his being entangled by you; and because he was too modest to say what he thought, he had his mouth stopped. For the truth is, Socrates, that you, who pretend to be engaged in the pursuit of truth, are appealing now to the popular and vulgar notions of right, which are not natural, but only conventional. Convention and nature are generally at variance with one another: and hence, if a person is too modest to say what he thinks, he is compelled to contradict himself; and you, in your ingenuity perceiving the advantage to be thereby gained, slyly ask of him who is arguing conventionally a question which is to be determined by the rule of nature; and if he is talking of the rule of nature, you slip away to custom: as, for instance, you did in this very discussion about doing and suffering injustice. When Polus was speaking of the conventionally dishonourable, you assailed him from the point of view of nature; for by the rule of nature, to suffer injustice is the greater disgrace because the greater evil; but conventionally, to do evil is the more disgraceful. For the suffering of injustice is not the part of a man, but of a slave, who indeed had better die than live; since when he is wronged and trampled upon, he is unable to help himself, or any other about whom he cares. The reason, as I conceive, is that the makers of laws are the majority who are weak; and they make laws and distribute praises and censures with a view to themselves and to their own interests; and they terrify the stronger sort of men, and those who are able to get the better of them, in order that they may not get the better of them; and they say, that dishonesty is shameful and unjust; meaning, by the word injustice, the desire of a man to have more than his neighbours; for knowing their own inferiority, I suspect that they are too glad of equality. And therefore the endeavour to have more than the many, is conventionally said to be shameful and unjust, and is called injustice,[19] whereas nature herself intimates that it is just for the better to have more than the worse, the more powerful than the weaker; and in many ways she shows, among men as well as among animals, and indeed among whole cities and races, that justice consists in the superior ruling over and having more than the inferior. For on what principle of justice did Xerxes invade Hellas, or his father the Scythians? (not to speak of numberless other examples). Nay, but these are the men who act according to nature; yes, by Heaven, and according to the law of nature: not perhaps, according to that artificial law, which we invent and impose upon our fellows, of whom we take the best and strongest from their youth upwards, and tame them like young lions, – charming them

[19] Cp. Rep. ii. 358.

with the sound of the voice, and saying to them, that with equality they must be content, and that the equal is the honourable and the just. But if there were a man who had sufficient force, he would shake off and break through, and escape from all this; he would trample under foot all our formulas and spells and charms, and all our laws which are against nature: the slave would rise in rebellion and be lord over us, and the light of natural justice would shine forth. And this I take to be the sentiment of Pindar, when he says in his poem, that

'Law is the king of all, of mortals as well as of immortals;'

this, as he says,

'Makes might to be right, doing violence with highest hand; as I infer from the deeds of Heracles, for without buying them—'[20]

– I do not remember the exact words, but the meaning is, that without buying them, and without their being given to him, he carried off the oxen of Geryon, according to the law of natural right, and that the oxen and other possessions of the weaker and inferior properly belong to the stronger and superior. And this is true, as you may ascertain, if you will leave philosophy and go on to higher things: for philosophy, Socrates, if pursued in moderation and at the proper age, is an elegant accomplishment, but too much philosophy is the ruin of human life. Even if a man has good parts, still, if he carries philosophy into later life, he is necessarily ignorant of all those things which a gentleman and a person of honour ought to know; he is inexperienced in the laws of the State, and in the language which ought to be used in the dealings of man with man, whether private or public, and utterly ignorant of the pleasures and desires of mankind and of human character in general. And people of this sort, when they betake themselves to politics or business, are as ridiculous as I imagine the politicians to be, when they make their appearance in the arena of philosophy. For, as Euripides says,

'Every man shines in that and pursues that, and devotes the greatest portion of the day to that in which he most excels,'[21]

but anything in which he is inferior, he avoids and depreciates, and praises the opposite from partiality to himself, and because he thinks that he will thus praise himself. The true principle is to unite them. Philosophy, as a part of education, is an excellent thing, and there is no disgrace to a man while he is young in pursuing such a study; but when he is more advanced in years, the thing becomes ridiculous, and I feel towards philosophers as I do towards those who lisp and imitate children. For I love to see a little child, who is not of an age to speak plainly, lisping at his play; there is an appearance of grace and freedom in his utterance, which is natural to his childish years. But when I hear some small creature carefully articulating its words, I am offended; the sound is disagreeable, and has to my ears the twang of slavery. So when I hear a man lisping, or see him playing like a child, his behaviour appears to me ridiculous and unmanly and worthy of stripes. And I have the same feeling about students of philosophy; when I see a youth thus engaged, – the study appears to me to be in character, and becoming a man of liberal education, and him who neglects philosophy I regard as an inferior man, who will never aspire to anything great or noble. But if I see him continuing the study in later life, and not leaving off, I should like to beat him, Socrates; for, as I was saying, such a one, even though he have good natural parts, becomes effeminate. He flies from the busy centre and the marketplace, in which, as the poet says, men become distinguished; he creeps into a corner for the rest of his life, and talks in a whisper with three or four admiring youths, but never speaks out like a freeman in a satisfactory manner. Now I, Socrates, am very well inclined towards you, and my feeling may be compared with that of Zethus towards Amphion, in the play of Euripides, whom I was mentioning just now: for I am disposed to say to you much what Zethus said to his brother, that you, Socrates, are careless about the things of which you ought to be careful; and that you

---

20 Fragm. Incert. 151 (Böckh).
21 Antiope, fragm. 20 (Dindorf).

'Who have a soul so noble, are remarkable for
  a puerile exterior;
Neither in a court of justice could you state a
  case, or give any reason or proof,
Or offer valiant counsel on another's behalf.'

And you must not be offended, my dear Socrates,
for I am speaking out of good-will towards you, if
I ask whether you are not ashamed of being thus
defenceless; which I affirm to be the condition
not of you only but of all those who will carry the
study of philosophy too far. For suppose that
some one were to take you, or any one of your
sort, off to prison, declaring that you had done
wrong when you had done no wrong, you must
allow that you would not know what to do: –
there you would stand giddy and gaping, and not
having a word to say; and when you went up
before the Court, even if the accuser were a poor
creature and not good for much, you would die if
he were disposed to claim the penalty of death.
And yet, Socrates, what is the value of

'An art which converts a man of sense into a
  fool,'

who is helpless, and has no power to save either
himself or others, when he is in the greatest
danger and is going to be despoiled by his enemies of all his goods, and has to live, simply
deprived of his rights of citizenship? – he being a
man who, if I may use the expression, may be
boxed on the ears with impunity. Then, my good
friend, take my advice, and refute no more:

'Learn the philosophy of business, and acquire
  the reputation of wisdom. But leave to others
  these niceties,'

whether they are to be described as follies or
absurdities:

'For they will only

Give you poverty for the inmate of your dwelling.'
Cease, then, emulating these paltry splitters of
words, and emulate only the man of substance
and honour, who is well to do.

soc. If my soul, Callicles, were made of gold,
should I not rejoice to discover one of those
stones with which they test gold, and the very
best possible one to which I might bring my soul;
and if the stone and I agreed in approving of her
training, then I should know that I was in a satisfactory state, and that no other test was needed
by me.

cal. What is your meaning, Socrates?

soc. I will tell you; I think that I have found in
you the desired touchstone.

cal. Why?

soc. Because I am sure that if you agree with
me in any of the opinions which my soul forms, I
have at last found the truth indeed. For I consider
that if a man is to make a complete trial of the
good or evil of the soul, he ought to have three
qualities – knowledge, good-will, outspokenness,
which are all possessed by you. Many whom I
meet are unable to make trial of me, because they
are not wise as you are; others are wise, but they
will not tell me the truth, because they have not
the same interest in me which you have; and these
two strangers, Gorgias and Polus, are undoubtedly wise men and my very good friends, but they
are not outspoken enough, and they are too
modest. Why, their modesty is so great that they
are driven to contradict themselves, first one and
then the other of them, in the face of a large company, on matters of the highest moment. But you
have all the qualities in which these others are
deficient, having received an excellent education;
to this many Athenians can testify. And you are
my friend. Shall I tell you why I think so? I know
that you, Callicles, and Tisander of Aphidnae,
and Andron the son of Androtion, and Nausicydes
of the deme of Cholarges, studied together: there
were four of you, and I once heard you advising
with one another as to the extent to which the
pursuit of philosophy should be carried, and, as I
know, you came to the conclusion that the study
should not be pushed too much into detail. You
were cautioning one another not to be overwise;
you were afraid that too much wisdom might
unconsciously to yourselves be the ruin of you.
And now when I hear you giving the same advice
to me which you then gave to your most intimate
friends, I have a sufficient evidence of your real
good-will to me. And of the frankness of your
nature and freedom from modesty I am assured
by yourself, and the assurance is confirmed by
your last speech. Well then, the inference in the
present case clearly is, that if you agree with me
in an argument about any point, that point will
have been sufficiently tested by us, and will not

require to be submitted to any further test. For you could not have agreed with me, either from lack of knowledge or from superfluity of modesty, nor yet from a desire to deceive me, for you are my friend, as you tell me yourself. And therefore when you and I are agreed, the result will be the attainment of perfect truth. Now there is no nobler enquiry, Callicles, than that which you censure me for making, – What ought the character of a man to be, and what his pursuits, and how far is he to go, both in maturer years and in youth? For be assured that if I err in my own conduct I do not err intentionally, but from ignorance. Do not then desist from advising me, now that you have begun, until I have learned clearly what this is which I am to practise, and how I may acquire it. And if you find me assenting to your words, and hereafter not doing that to which I assented, call me 'dolt,' and deem me unworthy of receiving further instruction. Once more, then, tell me what you and Pindar mean by natural justice: Do you not mean that the superior should take the property of the inferior by force; that the better should rule the worse, the noble have more than the mean? Am I not right in my recollection?

CAL. Yes; that is what I was saying, and so I still aver.

SOC. And do you mean by the better the same as the superior? for I could not make out what you were saying at the time – whether you meant by the superior the stronger, and that the weaker must obey the stronger, as you seemed to imply when you said that great cities attack small ones in accordance with natural right, because they are superior and stronger, as though the superior and stronger and better were the same; or whether the better may be also the inferior and weaker, and the superior the worse, or whether better is to be defined in the same way as superior: this is the point which I want to have cleared up. Are the superior and better and stronger the same or different?

CAL. I say unequivocally that they are the same.

SOC. Then the many are by nature superior to the one, against whom, as you were saying, they make the laws?

CAL. Certainly.

SOC. Then the laws of the many are the laws of the superior?

CAL. Very true.

SOC. Then they are the laws of the better; for the superior class are far better, as you were saying?

CAL. Yes.

SOC. And since they are superior, the laws which are made by them are by nature good?

CAL. Yes.

SOC. And are not the many of opinion, as you were lately saying, that justice is equality, and that to do is more disgraceful than to suffer injustice? – is that so or not? Answer, Callicles, and let no modesty be found to come in the way;[22] do the many think, or do they not think thus? – I must beg of you to answer, in order that if you agree with me I may fortify myself by the assent of so competent an authority.

CAL. Yes; the opinion of the many is what you say.

SOC. Then not only custom but nature also affirms that to do is more disgraceful than to suffer injustice, and that justice is equality; so that you seem to have been wrong in your former assertion, when accusing me you said that nature and custom are opposed, and that I, knowing this, was dishonestly playing between them, appealing to custom when the argument is about nature, and to nature when the argument is about custom?

CAL. This man will never cease talking nonsense. At your age, Socrates, are you not ashamed to be catching at words and chuckling over some verbal slip? do you not see – have I not told you already, that by superior I mean better: do you imagine me to say, that if a rabble of slaves and nondescripts, who are of no use except perhaps for their physical strength, get together, their *ipsissima verba* are laws?

SOC. Ho! my philosopher, is that your line?

CAL. Certainly.

SOC. I was thinking, Callicles, that something of the kind must have been in your mind, and that is why I repeated the question, – What is the superior? I wanted to know clearly what you meant; for you surely do not think that two men are better than one, or that your slaves are better than you because they are stronger? Then please to begin again, and tell me who the better are, if they are not the stronger; and I will ask you, great Sir, to be a little milder in your instructions, or I shall have to run away from you.

[22] Cp. what is said of Gorgias by Callicles at p. 165.

CAL. You are ironical.

SOC. No, by the hero Zethus, Callicles, by whose aid you were just now saying many ironical things against me, I am not: – tell me, then, whom you mean by the better?

CAL. I mean the more excellent.

SOC. Do you not see that you are yourself using words which have no meaning and that you are explaining nothing? – will you tell me whether you mean by the better and superior the wiser, or if not, whom?

CAL. Most assuredly, I do mean the wiser.

SOC. Then according to you, one wise man may often be superior to ten thousand fools, and he ought to rule them, and they ought to be his subjects, and he ought to have more than they should. This is what I believe that you mean (and you must not suppose that I am word-catching), if you allow that the one is superior to the ten thousand?

CAL. Yes; that is what I mean, and that is what I conceive to be natural justice – that the better and wiser should rule and have more than the inferior.

SOC. Stop there, and let me ask you what you would say in this case: Let us suppose that we are all together as we are now; there are several of us, and we have a large common store of meats and drinks, and there are all sorts of persons in our company having various degrees of strength and weakness, and one of us, being physician, is wiser in the matter of food than all the rest, and he is probably stronger than some and not so strong as others of us – will he not, being wiser, be also better than we are, and our superior in this matter of food?

CAL. Certainly.

SOC. Either, then, he will have a larger share of the meats and drinks, because he is better, or he will have the distribution of all of them by reason of his authority but he will not expend or make use of a larger share of them on his own person, or if he does, he will be punished; – his share will exceed that of some, and be less than that of others, and if he be the weakest of all, he being the best of all will have the smallest share of all, Callicles: – am I not right, my friend?

CAL. You talk about meats and drinks and physicians and other nonsense; I am not speaking of them.

SOC. Well, but do you admit that the wiser is the better? Answer 'Yes' or 'No.'

CAL. Yes.

SOC. And ought not the better to have a larger share?

CAL. Not of meats and drinks.

SOC. I understand: then, perhaps, of coats – the skilfullest weaver ought to have the largest coat, and the greatest number of them, and go about clothed in the best and finest of them?

CAL. Fudge about coats!

SOC. Then the skilfullest and best in making shoes ought to have the advantage in shoes; the shoemaker, clearly, should walk about in the largest shoes, and have the greatest number of them?

CAL. Fudge about shoes! What nonsense are you talking?

SOC. Or, if this is not your meaning, perhaps you would say that the wise and good and true husbandman should actually have a larger share of seeds, and have as much seed as possible for his own land?

CAL. How you go on, always talking in the same way, Socrates!

SOC. Yes, Callicles, and also about the same things.

CAL. Yes, by the Gods, you are literally always talking of cobblers and fullers and cooks and doctors, as if this had to do with our argument.

SOC. But why will you not tell me in what a man must be superior and wiser in order to claim a larger share; will you neither accept a suggestion, nor offer one?

CAL. I have already told you. In the first place, I mean by superiors not cobblers or cooks, but wise politicians who understand the administration of a state, and who are not only wise, but also valiant and able to carry out their designs, and not the men to faint from want of soul.

SOC. See now, most excellent Callicles, how different my charge against you is from that which you bring against me, for you reproach me with always saying the same; but I reproach you with never saying the same about the same things, for at one time you were defining the better and the superior to be the stronger, then again as the wiser, and now you bring forward a new notion; the superior and the better are now declared by you to be the more courageous: I wish, my good friend, that you would tell me, once for all, whom you affirm to be the better and superior, and in what they are better?

CAL. I have already told you that I mean those who are wise and courageous in the administration of a state – they ought to be the rulers of their states, and justice consists in their having more than their subjects.

SOC. But whether rulers or subjects will they or will they not have more than themselves, my friend?

CAL. What do you mean?

SOC. I mean that every man is his own ruler; but perhaps you think that there is no necessity for him to rule himself; he is only required to rule others?

CAL. What do you mean by his 'ruling over himself'?

SOC. A simple thing enough; just what is commonly said, that a man should be temperate and master of himself, and ruler of his own pleasures and passions.

CAL. What innocence! you mean those fools, – the temperate?

SOC. Certainly: – any one may know that to be my meaning.

CAL. Quite so, Socrates; and they are really fools, for how can a man be happy who is the servant of anything? On the contrary, I plainly assert, that he who would truly live ought to allow his desires to wax to the uttermost, and not to chastise them; but when they have grown to their greatest he should have courage and intelligence to minister to them and to satisfy all his longings. And this I affirm to be natural justice and nobility. To this however the many cannot attain; and they blame the strong man because they are ashamed of their own weakness, which they desire to conceal, and hence they say that intemperance is base. As I have remarked already, they enslave the nobler natures, and being unable to satisfy their pleasures, they praise temperance and justice out of their own cowardice. For if a man had been originally the son of a king, or had a nature capable of acquiring an empire or a tyranny or sovereignty, what could be more truly base or evil than temperance – to a man like him, I say, who might freely be enjoying every good, and has no one to stand in his way, and yet has admitted custom and reason and the opinion of other men to be lords over him? – must not he be in a miserable plight whom the reputation of justice and temperance hinders from giving more to his friends

than to his enemies, even though he be a ruler in his city? Nay, Socrates, for you profess to be a votary of the truth, and the truth is this: – that luxury and intemperance and licence, if they be provided with means, are virtue and happiness – all the rest is a mere bauble, agreements contrary to nature, foolish talk of men, nothing worth.[23]

SOC. There is a noble freedom, Callicles, in your way of approaching the argument; for what you say is what the rest of the world think, but do not like to say. And I must beg of you to persevere, that the true rule of human life may become manifest. Tell me, then: – you say, do you not, that in the rightly-developed man the passions ought not to be controlled, but that we should let them grow to the utmost and somehow or other satisfy them, and that this is virtue?

CAL. Yes; I do.

SOC. Then those who want nothing are not truly said to be happy?

CAL. No indeed, for then stones and dead men would be the happiest of all.

SOC. But surely life according to your view is an awful thing; and indeed I think that Euripides may have been right in saying,

'Who knows if life be not death and death life;'

and that we are very likely dead; I have heard a philosopher say that at this moment we are actually dead, and that the body ($\sigma\tilde{\omega}\mu\alpha$) is our tomb ($\sigma\tilde{\eta}\mu\alpha$[24]), and that the part of the soul which is the seat of the desires is liable to be tossed about by words and blown up and down; and some ingenious person, probably a Sicilian or an Italian, playing with the word, invented a tale in which he called the soul – because of its believing and make-believe nature – a vessel,[25] and the ignorant he called the uninitiated or leaky, and the place in the souls of the uninitiated in which the desires are seated, being the intemperate and incontinent part, he compared to a vessel full of holes, because it can never be satisfied. He is not of your way of thinking, Callicles, for he declares, that of all the souls in Hades, meaning the invisible world ($\dot{\alpha}\epsilon\iota\delta\grave{\epsilon}\varsigma$), these uninitiated or leaky persons are

[23] Cp. Rep. i. 348.

[24] Cp. Phaedr. 250 C.

[25] An untranslateable pun, – διὰ τὸ πιθανόν τε καὶ πιστικὸν ὠνόμασε πίθον.

the most miserable, and that they pour water into a vessel which is full of holes out of a colander which is similarly perforated. The colander, as my informer assures me, is the soul, and the soul which he compares to a colander is the soul of the ignorant, which is likewise full of holes, and therefore incontinent, owing to a bad memory and want of faith. These notions are strange enough, but they show the principle which, if I can, I would fain prove to you; that you should change your mind, and, instead of the intemperate and insatiate life, choose that which is orderly and sufficient and has a due provision for daily needs. Do I make any impression on you, and are you coming over to the opinion that the orderly are happier than the intemperate? Or do I fail to persuade you, and, however many tales I rehearse to you, do you continue of the same opinion still?

CAL. The latter, Socrates, is more like the truth.

SOC. Well, I will tell you another image, which comes out of the same school: – Let me request you to consider how far you would accept this as an account of the two lives of the temperate and intemperate in a figure: – There are two men, both of whom have a number of casks; the one man has his casks sound and full, one of wine, another of honey, and a third of milk, besides others filled with other liquids, and the streams which fill them are few and scanty, and he can only obtain them with a great deal of toil and difficulty; but when his casks are once filled he has no need to feed them any more, and has no further trouble with them or care about them. The other, in like manner, can procure streams, though not without difficulty; but his vessels are leaky and unsound, and night and day he is compelled to be filling them, and if he pauses for a moment, he is in an agony of pain. Such are their respective lives: – And now would you say that the life of the intemperate is happier than that of the temperate? Do I not convince you that the opposite is the truth?

CAL. You do not convince me, Socrates, for the one who has filled himself has no longer any pleasure left; and this, as I was just now saying, is the life of a stone: he has neither joy nor sorrow after he is once filled; but the pleasure depends on the superabundance of the influx.

SOC. But the more you pour in, the greater the waste; and the holes must be large for the liquid to escape.

CAL. Certainly.

SOC. The life which you are now depicting is not that of a dead man, or of a stone, but of a cormorant; you mean that he is to be hungering and eating?

CAL. Yes.

SOC. And he is to be thirsting and drinking?

CAL. Yes, that is what I mean; he is to have all his desires about him, and to be able to live happily in the gratification of them.

SOC. Capital, excellent; go on as you have begun, and have no shame; I, too, must disencumber myself of shame: and first, will you tell me whether you include itching and scratching, provided you have enough of them and pass your life in scratching, in your notion of happiness?

CAL. What a strange being you are, Socrates! a regular mob-orator.

SOC. That was the reason, Callicles, why I scared Polus and Gorgias, until they were too modest to say what they thought; but you will not be too modest and will not be scared, for you are a brave man. And now, answer my question.

CAL. I answer, that even the scratcher would live pleasantly.

SOC. And if pleasantly, then also happily?

CAL. To be sure.

SOC. But what if the itching is not confined to the head? Shall I pursue the question? And here, Callicles, I would have you consider how you would reply if consequences are pressed upon you, especially if in the last resort you are asked, whether the life of a catamite is not terrible, foul, miserable? Or would you venture to say, that they too are happy, if they only get enough of what they want?

CAL. Are you not ashamed, Socrates, of introducing such topics into the argument?

SOC. Well, my fine friend, but am I the introducer of these topics, or he who says without any qualification that all who feel pleasure in whatever manner are happy, and who admits of no distinction between good and bad pleasures? And I would still ask, whether you say that pleasure and good are the same, or whether there is some pleasure which is not a good?

CAL. Well, then, for the sake of consistency, I will say that they are the same.

SOC. You are breaking the original agreement, Callicles, and will no longer be a satisfactory companion in the search after truth, if you say what is contrary to your real opinion.

CAL. Why, that is what you are doing too, Socrates.

SOC. Then we are both doing wrong. Still, my dear friend, I would ask you to consider whether pleasure, from whatever source derived, is the good; for, if this be true, then the disagreeable consequences which have been darkly intimated must follow, and many others.

CAL. That, Socrates, is only your opinion.

SOC. And do you, Callicles, seriously maintain what you are saying?

CAL. Indeed I do.

SOC. Then, as you are in earnest, shall we proceed with the argument?

CAL. By all means.[26]

SOC. Well, if you are willing to proceed, determine this question for me: – There is something, I presume, which you would call knowledge?

CAL. There is.

SOC. And were you not saying just now, that some courage implied knowledge?

CAL. I was.

SOC. And you were speaking of courage and knowledge as two things different from one another?

CAL. Certainly I was.

SOC. And would you say that pleasure and knowledge are the same, or not the same?

CAL. Not the same, O man of wisdom.

SOC. And would you say that courage differed from pleasure?

CAL. Certainly.

SOC. Well, then, let us remember that Callicles, the Acharnian, says that pleasure and good are the same; but that knowledge and courage are not the same, either with one another, or with the good.

CAL. And what does our friend Socrates, of Foxton, say – does he assent to this, or not?

SOC. He does not assent; neither will Callicles, when he sees himself truly. You will admit, I suppose, that good and evil fortune are opposed to each other?

CAL. Yes.

SOC. And if they are opposed to each other, then, like health and disease, they exclude one another; a man cannot have them both, or be without them both, at the same time?

CAL. What do you mean?

SOC. Take the case of any bodily affection: – a man may have the complaint in his eyes which is called ophthalmia?

CAL. To be sure.

SOC. But he surely cannot have the same eyes well and sound at the same time?

CAL. Certainly not.

SOC. And when he has got rid of his ophthalmia, has he got rid of the health of his eyes too? Is the final result, that he gets rid of them both together?

CAL. Certainly not.

SOC. That would surely be marvellous and absurd?

CAL. Very.

SOC. I suppose that he is affected by them, and gets rid of them in turns?

CAL. Yes.

SOC. And he may have strength and weakness in the same way, by fits?

CAL. Yes.

SOC. Or swiftness and slowness?

CAL. Certainly.

SOC. And does he have and not have good and happiness, and their opposites, evil and misery, in a similar alternation?[27]

CAL. Certainly he has.

SOC. If then there be anything which a man has and has not at the same time, clearly that cannot be good and evil – do we agree? Please not to answer without consideration.

CAL. I entirely agree.

SOC. Go back now to our former admissions. – Did you say that to hunger, I mean the mere state of hunger, was pleasant or painful?

CAL. I said painful, but that to eat when you are hungry is pleasant.

SOC. I know; but still the actual hunger is painful: am I not right?

CAL. Yes.

SOC. And thirst, too, is painful?

CAL. Yes, very.

SOC. Need I adduce any more instances, or would you agree that all wants or desires are painful?

CAL. I agree, and therefore you need not adduce any more instances.

---

[26] Or, 'I am in profound earnest.'
[27] Cp. Rep. iv. 436.

soc. Very good. And you would admit that to drink, when you are thirsty, is pleasant?

CAL. Yes.

soc. And in the sentence which you have just uttered, the word 'thirsty' implies pain?

CAL. Yes.

soc. And the word 'drinking' is expressive of pleasure, and of the satisfaction of the want?

CAL. Yes.

soc. There is pleasure in drinking?

CAL. Certainly.

soc. When you are thirsty?

CAL. Yes.

soc. And in pain?

CAL. Yes.

soc. Do you see the inference: – that pleasure and pain are simultaneous, when you say that being thirsty, you drink? For are they not simultaneous, and do they not affect at the same time the same part, whether of the soul or the body? – which of them is affected cannot be supposed to be of any consequence: Is not this true?

CAL. It is.

soc. You said also, that no man could have good and evil fortune at the same time?

CAL. Yes, I did.

soc. But you admitted, that when in pain a man might also have pleasure?

CAL. Clearly.

soc. Then pleasure is not the same as good fortune, or pain the same as evil fortune, and therefore the good is not the same as the pleasant?

CAL. I wish I knew, Socrates, what your quibbling means.

soc. You know, Callicles, but you affect not to know.

CAL. Well, get on, and don't keep fooling: then you will know what a wiseacre you are in your admonition of me.

soc. Does not a man cease from his thirst and from his pleasure in drinking at the same time?

CAL. I do not understand what you are saying.

GOR. Nay, Callicles, answer, if only for our sakes; – we should like to hear the argument out.

CAL. Yes, Gorgias, but I must complain of the habitual trifling of Socrates; he is always arguing about little and unworthy questions.

GOR. What matter? Your reputation, Callicles, is not at stake. Let Socrates argue in his own fashion.

CAL. Well, then, Socrates, you shall ask these little peddling questions, since Gorgias wishes to have them.

soc. I envy you, Callicles, for having been initiated into the great mysteries before you were initiated into the lesser. I thought that this was not allowable. But to return to our argument: – Does not a man cease from thirsting and from the pleasure of drinking at the same moment?

CAL. True.

soc. And if he is hungry, or has any other desire, does he not cease from the desire and the pleasure at the same moment?

CAL. Very true.

soc. Then he ceases from pain and pleasure at the same moment?

CAL. Yes.

soc. But he does not cease from good and evil at the same moment, as you have admitted: do you still adhere to what you said?

CAL. Yes, I do; but what is the inference?

soc. Why, my friend, the inference is that the good is not the same as the pleasant, or the evil the same as the painful; there is a cessation of pleasure and pain at the same moment; but not of good and evil, for they are different. How then can pleasure be the same as good, or pain as evil? And I would have you look at the matter in another light, which could hardly, I think, have been considered by you when you identified them: Are not the good good because they have good present with them, as the beautiful are those who have beauty present with them?

CAL. Yes.

soc. And do you call the fools and cowards good men? For you were saying just now that the courageous and the wise are the good – would you not say so?

CAL. Certainly.

soc. And did you never see a foolish child rejoicing?

CAL. Yes, I have.

soc. And a foolish man too?

CAL. Yes, certainly; but what is your drift?

soc. Nothing particular, if you will only answer.

CAL. Yes, I have.

soc. And did you ever see a sensible man rejoicing or sorrowing?

CAL. Yes.

soc. Which rejoice and sorrow most – the wise or the foolish?

CAL. They are much upon a par, I think, in that respect.

SOC. Enough: And did you ever see a coward in battle?

CAL. To be sure.

SOC. And which rejoiced most at the departure of the enemy, the coward or the brave?

CAL. I should say 'most' of both; or at any rate, they rejoiced about equally.

SOC. No matter; then the cowards, and not only the brave, rejoice?

CAL. Greatly.

SOC. And the foolish; so it would seem?

CAL. Yes.

SOC. And are only the cowards pained at the approach of their enemies, or are the brave also pained?

CAL. Both are pained.

SOC. And are they equally pained?

CAL. I should imagine that the cowards are more pained.

SOC. And are they not better pleased at the enemy's departure?

CAL. I dare say.

SOC. Then are the foolish and the wise and the cowards and the brave all pleased and pained, as you were saying, in nearly equal degree; but are the cowards more pleased and pained than the brave?

CAL. Yes.

SOC. But surely the wise and brave are the good, and the foolish and the cowardly are the bad?

CAL. Yes.

SOC. Then the good and the bad are pleased and pained in a nearly equal degree?

CAL. Yes.

SOC. Then are the good and bad good and bad in a nearly equal degree, or have the bad the advantage both in good and evil? [i. e. in having more pleasure and more pain.]

CAL. I really do not know what you mean.

SOC. Why, do you not remember saying that the good were good because good was present with them, and the evil because evil; and that pleasures were goods and pains evils?

CAL. Yes, I remember.

SOC. And are not these pleasures or goods present to those who rejoice – if they do rejoice?

CAL. Certainly.

SOC. Then those who rejoice are good when goods are present with them?

CAL. Yes.

SOC. And those who are in pain have evil or sorrow present with them?

CAL. Yes.

SOC. And would you still say that the evil are evil by reason of the presence of evil?

CAL. I should.

SOC. Then those who rejoice are good, and those who are in pain evil?

CAL. Yes.

SOC. The degrees of good and evil vary with the degrees of pleasure and of pain?

CAL. Yes.

SOC. Have the wise man and the fool, the brave and the coward, joy and pain in nearly equal degrees? or would you say that the coward has more?

CAL. I should say that he has.

SOC. Help me then to draw out the conclusion which follows from our admissions; for it is good to repeat and review what is good twice and thrice over, as they say. Both the wise man and the brave man we allow to be good?

CAL. Yes.

SOC. And the foolish man and the coward to be evil?

CAL. Certainly.

SOC. And he who has joy is good?

CAL. Yes.

SOC. And he who is in pain is evil?

CAL. Certainly.

SOC. The good and evil both have joy and pain, but, perhaps, the evil has more of them?

CAL. Yes.

SOC. Then must we not infer, that the bad man is as good and bad as the good, or, perhaps, even better – is not this a further inference which follows equally with the preceding from the assertion that the good and the pleasant are the same: – can this be denied, Callicles?

CAL. I have been listening and making admissions to you, Socrates; and I remark that if a person grants you anything in play, you, like a child, want to keep hold and will not give it back. But do you really suppose that I or any other human being denies that some pleasures are good and others bad?

SOC. Alas, Callicles, how unfair you are! you certainly treat me as if I were a child, sometimes saying one thing, and then another, as if you were meaning to deceive me. And yet I thought at first that you were my friend, and would not have deceived me if you could have helped. But I see that I was mistaken; and now I suppose that I must make the best of a bad business, as they said of old, and take what I can get out of you. – Well, then, as I understand you to say, I may assume that some pleasures are good and others evil?

CAL. Yes.

SOC. The beneficial are good, and the hurtful are evil?

CAL. To be sure.

SOC. And the beneficial are those which do some good, and the hurtful are those which do some evil?

CAL. Yes.

SOC. Take, for example, the bodily pleasures of eating and drinking, which we were just now mentioning – you mean to say that those which promote health, or any other bodily excellence, are good, and their opposites evil?

CAL. Certainly.

SOC. And in the same way there are good pains and there are evil pains?

CAL. To be sure.

SOC. And ought we not to choose and use the good pleasures and pains?

CAL. Certainly.

SOC. But not the evil?

CAL. Clearly.

SOC. Because, if you remember, Polus and I have agreed that all our actions are to be done for the sake of the good; – and will you agree with us in saying, that the good is the end of all our actions, and that all our actions are to be done for the sake of the good, and not the good for the sake of them? – will you add a third vote to our two?

CAL. I will.

SOC. Then pleasure, like everything else, is to be sought for the sake of that which is good, and not that which is good for the sake of pleasure?

CAL. To be sure.

SOC. But can every man choose what pleasures are good and what are evil, or must he have art or knowledge of them in detail?

CAL. He must have art.

SOC. Let me now remind you of what I was saying to Gorgias and Polus; I was saying, as you will not have forgotten, that there were some processes which aim only at pleasure, and know nothing of a better and worse, and there are other processes which know good and evil. And I considered that cookery, which I do not call an art, but only an experience, was of the former class, which is concerned with pleasure, and that the art of medicine was of the class which is concerned with the good. And now, by the god of friendship, I must beg you, Callicles, not to

jest, or to imagine that I am jesting with you; do not answer at random and contrary to your real opinion; – for you will observe that we are arguing about the way of human life; and to a man who has any sense at all, what question can be more serious than this? – whether he should follow after that way of life to which you exhort me, and act what you call the manly part of speaking in the assembly, and cultivating rhetoric, and engaging in public affairs, according to the principles now in vogue; or whether he should pursue the life of philosophy; – and in what the latter way differs from the former. But perhaps we had better first try to distinguish them, as I did before, and when we have come to an agreement that they are distinct, we may proceed to consider in what they differ from one another, and which of them we should choose. Perhaps, however, you do not even now understand what I mean?

CAL. No, I do not.

SOC. Then I will explain myself more clearly: seeing that you and I have agreed that there is such a thing as good, and that there is such a thing as pleasure, and that pleasure is not the same as good, and that the pursuit and process of acquisition of the one, that is pleasure, is different from the pursuit and process of acquisition of the other, which is good – I wish that you would tell me whether you agree with me thus far or not – do you agree?

CAL. I do.

SOC. Then I will proceed, and ask whether you also agree with me, and whether you think that I spoke the truth when I further said to Gorgias and Polus that cookery in my opinion is only an experience, and not an art at all; and that whereas medicine is an art, and attends to the nature and constitution of the patient, and has principles of action and reason in each case, cookery in attending upon pleasure never regards either the nature or reason of that pleasure to which she devotes herself, but goes straight to her end, nor ever considers or calculates anything, but works by experience and routine, and just preserves the recollection of what she has usually done when producing pleasure. And first, I would have you consider whether I have proved what I was saying, and then whether there are not other similar processes which have to do with the soul – some of them processes of art, making a provision for the soul's highest interest – others despising the interest, and, as in the previous case, considering only the pleasure of the soul, and how this may be acquired, but not considering what pleasures are good or bad, and having no other aim but to afford gratification, whether good or bad. In my opinion, Callicles, there are such processes, and this is the sort of thing which I term flattery, whether concerned with the body or the soul, or whenever employed with a view to pleasure and without any consideration of good and evil. And now I wish that you would tell me whether you agree with us in this notion, or whether you differ.

CAL. I do not differ; on the contrary, I agree; for in that way I shall soonest bring the argument to an end, and shall oblige my friend Gorgias.

SOC. And is this notion true of one soul, or of two or more?

CAL. Equally true of two or more.

SOC. Then a man may delight a whole assembly, and yet have no regard for their true interests?

CAL. Yes.

SOC. Can you tell me the pursuits which delight mankind – or rather, if you would prefer, let me ask, and do you answer, which of them belong to the pleasurable class, and which of them not? In the first place, what say you of flute-playing? Does not that appear to be an art which seeks only pleasure, Callicles, and thinks of nothing else?

CAL. I assent.

SOC. And is not the same true of all similar arts, as, for example, the art of playing the lyre at festivals?

CAL. Yes.

SOC. And what do you say of the choral art and of dithyrambic poetry? – are not they of the same nature? Do you imagine that Cinesias the son of Meles cares about what will tend to the moral improvement of his hearers, or about what will give pleasure to the multitude?

CAL. There can be no mistake about Cinesias, Socrates.

SOC. And what do you say of his father, Meles the harp-player? Did he perform with any view to the good of his hearers? Could he be said to regard even their pleasure? For his singing was an infliction to his audience. And of harp-playing and dithyrambic poetry in general, what would you say? Have they not been invented wholly for the sake of pleasure?

CAL. That is my notion of them.

SOC. And as for the Muse of Tragedy, that solemn and august personage – what are her aspirations? Is all her aim and desire only to give pleasure to the spectators, or does she fight against them and refuse to speak of their pleasant vices, and willingly proclaim in word and song truths welcome and unwelcome? – which in your judgment is her character?

CAL. There can be no doubt, Socrates, that Tragedy has her face turned towards pleasure and the gratification of the audience.

SOC. And is not that the sort of thing, Callicles, which we were just now describing as flattery?

CAL. Quite true.

SOC. Well now, suppose that we strip all poetry of song and rhythm and metre, there will remain speech?[28]

CAL. To be sure.

SOC. And this speech is addressed to a crowd of people?

CAL. Yes.

SOC. Then poetry is a sort of rhetoric?

CAL. True.

SOC. And do not the poets in the theatres seem to you to be rhetoricians?

CAL. Yes.

SOC. Then now we have discovered a sort of rhetoric which is addressed to a crowd of men, women, and children, freemen and slaves. And this is not much to our taste, for we have described it as having the nature of flattery.

CAL. Quite true.

SOC. Very good. And what do you say of that other rhetoric which addresses the Athenian assembly and the assemblies of freemen in other states? Do the rhetoricians appear to you always to aim at what is best, and do they seek to improve the citizens by their speeches, or are they too, like the rest of mankind, bent upon giving them pleasure, forgetting the public good in the thought of their own interest, playing with the people as with children, and trying to amuse them, but never considering whether they are better or worse for this?

CAL. I must distinguish. There are some who have a real care of the public in what they say, while others are such as you describe.

SOC. I am contented with the admission that rhetoric is of two sorts; one, which is mere flattery and disgraceful declamation; the other, which is

---

[28] Cp. Rep. iii. 392 foll.

noble and aims at the training and improvement of the souls of the citizens, and strives to say what is best, whether welcome or unwelcome, to the audience; but have you ever known such a rhetoric; or if you have, and can point out any rhetorician who is of this stamp, who is he?

CAL. But, indeed, I am afraid that I cannot tell you of any such among the orators who are at present living.

SOC. Well, then, can you mention any one of a former generation, who may be said to have improved the Athenians, who found them worse and made them better, from the day that he began to make speeches? for, indeed, I do not know of such a man.

CAL. What! did you never hear that Themistocles was a good man, and Cimon and Miltiades and Pericles, who is just lately dead, and whom you heard yourself?

SOC. Yes, Callicles, they were good men, if, as you said at first, true virtue consists only in the satisfaction of our own desires and those of others; but if not, and if, as we were afterwards compelled to acknowledge, the satisfaction of some desires makes us better, and of others, worse, and we ought to gratify the one and not the other, and there is an art in distinguishing them, – can you tell me of any of these statesmen who did distinguish them?

CAL. No, indeed, I cannot.

SOC. Yet, surely, Callicles, if you look you will find such a one. Suppose that we just calmly consider whether any of these was such as I have described. Will not the good man, who says whatever he says with a view to the best, speak with a reference to some standard and not at random; just as all other artists, whether the painter, the builder, the shipwright, or any other look all of them to their own work, and do not select and apply at random what they apply, but strive to give a definite form to it? The artist disposes all things in order, and compels the one part to harmonize and accord with the other part, until he has constructed a regular and systematic whole; and this is true of all artists, and in the same way the trainers and physicians, of whom we spoke before, give order and regularity to the body: do you deny this?

CAL. No; I am ready to admit it.

SOC. Then the house in which order and regularity prevail is good; that in which there is disorder, evil?

CAL. Yes.

SOC. And the same is true of a ship?

CAL. Yes.

SOC. And the same may be said of the human body?

CAL. Yes.

SOC. And what would you say of the soul? Will the good soul be that in which disorder is prevalent, or that in which there is harmony and order?

CAL. The latter follows from our previous admissions.

SOC. What is the name which is given to the effect of harmony and order in the body?

CAL. I suppose that you mean health and strength?

SOC. Yes, I do; and what is the name which you would give to the effect of harmony and order in the soul? Try and discover a name for this as well as for the other.

CAL. Why not give the name yourself, Socrates?

SOC. Well, if you had rather that I should, I will; and you shall say whether you agree with me, and if not, you shall refute and answer me. 'Healthy,' as I conceive, is the name which is given to the regular order of the body, whence comes health and every other bodily excellence: is that true or not?

CAL. True.

SOC. And 'lawful' and 'law' are the names which are given to the regular order and action of the soul, and these make men lawful and orderly: – and so we have temperance and justice: have we not?

CAL. Granted.

SOC. And will not the true rhetorician who is honest and understands his art have his eye fixed upon these, in all the words which he addresses to the souls of men, and in all his actions, both in what he gives and in what he takes away? Will not his aim be to implant justice in the souls of his citizens and take away injustice, to implant temperance and take away intemperance, to implant every virtue and take away every vice? Do you not agree?

CAL. I agree.

SOC. For what use is there, Callicles, in giving to the body of a sick man who is in a bad state of health a quantity of the most delightful food or drink or any other pleasant thing, which may be really as bad for him as if you gave him nothing, or even worse if rightly estimated. Is not that true?

CAL. I will not say No to it.

SOC. For in my opinion there is no profit in a man's life if his body is in an evil plight – in that case his life also is evil: am I not right?

CAL. Yes.

SOC. When a man is in health the physicians will generally allow him to eat when he is hungry and drink when he is thirsty, and to satisfy his desires as he likes, but when he is sick they hardly suffer him to satisfy his desires at all: even you will admit that?

CAL. Yes.

SOC. And does not the same argument hold of the soul, my good sir? While she is in a bad state and is senseless and intemperate and unjust and unholy, her desires ought to be controlled, and she ought to be prevented from doing anything which does not tend to her own improvement.

CAL. Yes.

SOC. Such treatment will be better for the soul herself?

CAL. To be sure.

SOC. And to restrain her from her appetites is to chastise her?

CAL. Yes.

SOC. Then restraint or chastisement is better for the soul than intemperance or the absence of control, which you were just now preferring?

CAL. I do not understand you, Socrates, and I wish that you would ask some one who does.

SOC. Here is a gentleman who cannot endure to be improved or to subject himself to that very chastisement of which the argument speaks!

CAL. I do not heed a word of what you are saying, and have only answered hitherto out of civility to Gorgias.

SOC. What are we to do, then? Shall we break off in the middle?

CAL. You shall judge for yourself.

SOC. Well, but people say that 'a tale should have a head and not break off in the middle,' and I should not like to have the argument going about without a head;[29] please then to go on a little longer, and put the head on.

CAL. How tyrannical you are, Socrates! I wish that you and your argument would rest, or that you would get some one else to argue with you.

SOC. But who else is willing? – I want to finish the argument.

CAL. Cannot you finish without my help, either talking straight on, or questioning and answering yourself?

SOC. Must I then say with Epicharmus, 'Two men spoke before, but now one shall be enough'? I suppose that there is absolutely no help. And if I am to carry on the enquiry by myself, I will first of all remark that not only I but all of us should have an ambition to know what is true and what is false in this matter, for the discovery of the truth is a common good. And now I will proceed to argue according to my own notion. But if any of you think that I arrive at conclusions which are untrue you must interpose and refute me, for I do not speak from any knowledge of what I am saying; I am an enquirer like yourselves, and therefore, if my opponent says anything which is of force, I shall be the first to agree with him. I am speaking on the supposition that the argument ought to be completed; but if you think otherwise let us leave off and go our ways.

GOR. I think, Socrates, that we should not go our ways until you have completed the argument; and this appears to me to be the wish of the rest of the company; I myself should very much like to hear what more you have to say.

SOC. I too, Gorgias, should have liked to continue the argument with Callicles, and then I might have given him an 'Amphion' in return for his 'Zethus';[30] but since you, Callicles, are unwilling to continue, I hope that you will listen, and interrupt me if I seem to you to be in error. And if you refute me, I shall not be angry with you as you are with me, but I shall inscribe you as the greatest of benefactors on the tablets of my soul.

CAL. My good fellow, never mind me, but get on.

SOC. Listen to me, then, while I recapitulate the argument: – Is the pleasant the same as the good? Not the same. Callicles and I are agreed about that. And is the pleasant to be pursued for the sake of the good? or the good for the sake of the pleasant? The pleasant is to be pursued for the sake of the good. And that is pleasant at the presence of which we are pleased, and that is good at the presence of which we are good? To be sure. And we are good, and all good things whatever

[29] Cp. Laws vi. 752 A.
[30] p. 166.

are good when some virtue is present in us or them? That, Callicles, is my conviction. But the virtue of each thing, whether body or soul, instrument or creature, when given to them in the best way comes to them not by chance but as the result of the order and truth and art which are imparted to them: Am I not right? I maintain that I am. And is not the virtue of each thing dependent on order or arrangement? Yes, I say. And that which makes a thing good is the proper order inhering in each thing? Such is my view. And is not the soul which has an order of her own better than that which has no order? Certainly. And the soul which has order is orderly? Of course. And that which is orderly is temperate? Assuredly. And the temperate soul is good? No other answer can I give, Callicles dear; have you any?

CAL. Go on, my good fellow.

SOC. Then I shall proceed to add, that if the temperate soul is the good soul, the soul which is in the opposite condition, that is, the foolish and intemperate, is the bad soul. Very true.

And will not the temperate man do what is proper, both in relation to the gods and to men; – for he would not be temperate if he did not? Certainly he will do what is proper. In his relation to other men he will do what is just; and in his relation to the gods he will do what is holy; and he who does what is just and holy must be just and holy? Very true. And must he not be courageous? for the duty of a temperate man is not to follow or to avoid what he ought not, but what he ought, whether things or men or pleasures or pains, and patiently to endure when he ought; and therefore, Callicles, the temperate man, being, as we have described, also just and courageous and holy, cannot be other than a perfectly good man, nor can the good man do otherwise than well and perfectly whatever he does; and he who does well must of necessity be happy and blessed, and the evil man who does evil, miserable: now this latter is he whom you were applauding – the intemperate who is the opposite of the temperate. Such is my position, and these things I affirm to be true. And if they are true, then I further affirm that he who desires to be happy must pursue and practise temperance and run away from intemperance as fast as his legs will carry him: he had better order his life so as not to need punishment; but if either he or any of his friends, whether private individual or city, are in need of punishment, then justice must be done and he must suffer punishment, if

he would be happy. This appears to me to be the aim which a man ought to have, and towards which he ought to direct all the energies both of himself and of the state, acting so that he may have temperance and justice present with him and be happy, not suffering his lusts to be unrestrained, and in the never-ending desire to satisfy them leading a robber's life. Such a one is the friend neither of God nor man, for he is incapable of communion, and he who is incapable of communion is also incapable of friendship. And philosophers tell us, Callicles, that communion and friendship and orderliness and temperance and justice bind together heaven and earth and gods and men, and that this universe is therefore called Cosmos or order, not disorder or misrule, my friend. But although you are a philosopher you seem to me never to have observed that geometrical equality is mighty, both among gods and men; you think that you ought to cultivate inequality or excess, and do not care about geometry. – Well, then, either the principle that the happy are made happy by the possession of justice and temperance, and the miserable miserable by the possession of vice, must be refuted, or, if it is granted, what will be the consequences? All the consequences which I drew before, Callicles, and about which you asked me whether I was in earnest when I said that a man ought to accuse himself and his son and his friend if he did anything wrong, and that to this end he should use his rhetoric – all those consequences are true. And that which you thought that Polus was led to admit out of modesty is true, viz. that, to do injustice, if more disgraceful than to suffer, is in that degree worse; and the other position, which, according to Polus, Gorgias admitted out of modesty, that he who would truly be a rhetorician ought to be just and have a knowledge of justice, has also turned out to be true.

And now, these things being as we have said, let us proceed in the next place to consider whether you are right in throwing in my teeth that I am unable to help myself or any of my friends or kinsmen, or to save them in the extremity of danger, and that I am in the power of another like an outlaw to whom any one may do what he likes, – he may box my ears, which was a brave saying of yours; or take away my goods or banish me, or even do his worst and kill me; a condition which, as you say, is the height of disgrace. My answer to you is one which has been already often repeated, but may as well be repeated once more. I tell you, Callicles, that to be boxed on the ears wrongfully is not the worst evil which can befall a man, nor to have my purse or my body cut open, but that to smite and slay me and mine wrongfully is far more disgraceful and more evil; aye, and to despoil and enslave and pillage, or in any way at all to wrong me and mine, is far more disgraceful and evil to the doer of the wrong than to me who am the sufferer. These truths, which have been already set forth as I state them in the previous discussion, would seem now to have been fixed and riveted by us, if I may use an expression which is certainly bold, in words which are like bonds of iron and adamant; and unless you or some other still more enterprising hero shall break them, there is no possibility of denying what I say. For my position has always been, that I myself am ignorant how these things are, but that I have never met any one who could say otherwise, any more than you can, and not appear ridiculous. This is my position still, and if what I am saying is true, and injustice is the greatest of evils to the doer of, injustice, and yet there is if possible a greater than this greatest of evils,[31] in an unjust man not suffering retribution, what is that defence of which the want will make a man truly ridiculous? Must not the defence be one which will avert the greatest of human evils? And will not the worst of all defences be that with which a man is unable to defend himself or his family or his friends? – and next will come that which is unable to avert the next greatest evil; thirdly that which is unable to avert the third greatest evil; and so of other evils. As is the greatness of evil so is the honour of being able to avert them in their several degrees, and the disgrace of not being able to avert them. Am I not right, Callicles?

CAL. Yes, quite right.

SOC. Seeing then that there are these two evils, the doing injustice and the suffering injustice – and we affirm that to do injustice is a greater, and to suffer injustice a lesser evil – by what devices can a man succeed in obtaining the two advantages, the one of not doing and the other of not suffering injustice? must he have the power, or only the will to obtain them? I mean to ask whether a man will escape injustice if he has only the will to escape, or must he have provided himself with the power?

CAL. He must have provided himself with the power; that is clear.

SOC. And what do you say of doing injustice? Is the will only sufficient, and will that prevent him from doing injustice, or must he have provided himself with power and art; and if he have not studied and practised, will he be unjust still? Surely you might say, Callicles, whether you think that Polus and I were right in admitting the conclusion that no one does wrong voluntarily, but that all do wrong against their will?

CAL. Granted, Socrates, if you will only have done.

SOC. Then, as would appear, power and art have to be provided in order that we may do no injustice?

CAL. Certainly.

SOC. And what art will protect us from suffering injustice, if not wholly, yet as far as possible? I want to know whether you agree with me; for I think that such an art is the art of one who is either a ruler or even tyrant himself, or the equal and companion of the ruling power.

CAL. Well said, Socrates; and please to observe how ready I am to praise you when you talk sense.

SOC. Think and tell me whether you would approve of another view of mine: To me every man appears to be most the friend of him who is most like to him – like to like, as ancient sages say: Would you not agree to this?

CAL. I should.

SOC. But when the tyrant is rude and uneducated, he may be expected to fear any one who is his superior in virtue, and will never be able to be perfectly friendly with him.

CAL. That is true.

SOC. Neither will he be the friend of any one who is greatly his inferior, for the tyrant will despise him, and will never seriously regard him as a friend.

CAL. That again is true.

SOC. Then the only friend worth mentioning, whom the tyrant can have, will be one who is of the same character, and has the same likes and dislikes, and is at the same time willing to be subject and subservient to him; he is the man who

---

[31] Cp. Republic, 9. 578 ff.

will have power in the state, and no one will injure him with impunity: – is not that so?

CAL. Yes.

SOC. And if a young man begins to ask how he may become great and formidable, this would seem to be the way – he will accustom himself, from his youth upward, to feel sorrow and joy on the same occasions as his master, and will contrive to be as like him as possible?

CAL. Yes.

SOC. And in this way he will have accomplished, as you and your friends would say, the end of becoming a great man and not suffering injury?

CAL. Very true.

SOC. But will he also escape from doing injury? Must not the very opposite be true, if he is to be like the tyrant in his injustice, and to have influence with him? Will he not rather contrive to do as much wrong as possible, and not be punished?

CAL. True.

SOC. And by the imitation of his master and by the power which he thus acquires will not his soul become bad and corrupted, and will not this be the greatest evil to him?

CAL. You always contrive somehow or other, Socrates, to invert everything: do you not know that he who imitates the tyrant will, if he has a mind, kill him who does not imitate him and take away his goods?

SOC. Excellent Callicles, I am not deaf, and I have heard that a great many times from you and from Polus and from nearly every man in the city, but I wish that you would hear me too. I dare say that he will kill him if he has in mind – the bad man will kill the good and true.

CAL. And is not that just the provoking thing?

SOC. Nay, not to a man of sense, as the argument shows: do you think that all our cares should be directed to prolonging life to the uttermost, and to the study of those arts which secure us from danger always; like that art of rhetoric which saves men in courts of law, and which you advise me to cultivate?

CAL. Yes, truly, and very good advice too.

SOC. Well, my friend, but what do you think of swimming; is that an art of any great pretensions?

CAL. No, indeed.

SOC. And yet surely swimming saves a man from death, and there are occasions on which he must know how to swim. And if you despise the swimmers, I will tell you of another and greater art, the art of the pilot, who not only saves the souls of men, but also their bodies and properties from the extremity of danger, just like rhetoric. Yet his art is modest and unpresuming: it has no airs or pretences of doing anything extraordinary, and, in return for the same salvation which is given by the pleader, demands only two obols, if he brings us from Aegina to Athens, or for the longer voyage from Pontus or Egypt, at the utmost two drachmae, when he has saved, as I was just now saying, the passenger and his wife and children and goods, and safely disembarked them at the Piraeus, – this is the payment which he asks in return for so great a boon; and he who is the master of the art, and has done all this, gets out and walks about on the sea-shore by his ship in an unassuming way. For he is able to reflect and is aware that he cannot tell which of his fellow-passengers he has benefited, and which of them he has injured in not allowing them to be drowned. He knows that they are just the same when he has disembarked them as when they embarked, and not a whit better either in their bodies or in their souls; and he considers that if a man who is afflicted by great and incurable bodily diseases is only to be pitied for having escaped, and is in no way benefited by him in having been saved from drowning, much less he who has great and incurable diseases, not of the body, but of the soul, which is the more valuable part of him; neither is life worth having nor of any profit to the bad man, whether he be delivered from the sea, or the law-courts, or any other devourer; – and so he reflects that such a one had better not live, for he cannot live well.[32]

And this is the reason why the pilot, although he is our saviour, is not usually conceited, any more than the engineer, who is not at all behind either the general, or the pilot, or any one else, in his saving power, for he sometimes saves whole cities. Is there any comparison between him and the pleader? And if he were to talk, Callicles, in your grandiose style, he would bury you under a mountain of words, declaring and insisting that we ought all of us to be engine-makers, and that no other profession is worth thinking about; he would have plenty to say. Nevertheless you despise him and his art, and sneeringly call him an engine-maker, and you will not allow your daughters to

[32] Cp. Rep. iii. 407 E.

marry his son, or marry your son to his daughters. And yet, on your principle, what justice or reason is there in your refusal? What right have you to despise the engine-maker, and the others whom I was just now mentioning? I know that you will say, 'I am better, and better born.' But if the better is not what I say, and virtue consists only in a man saving himself and his, whatever may be his character, then your censure of the engine-maker, and of the physician, and of the other arts of salvation, is ridiculous. O my friend! I want you to see that the noble and the good may possibly be something different from saving and being saved: – May not he who is truly a man cease to care about living a certain time? – he knows, as women say, that no man can escape fate, and therefore he is not fond of life; he leaves all that with God, and considers in what way he can best spend his appointed term; – whether by assimilating himself to the constitution under which he lives, as you at this moment have to consider how you may become as like as possible to the Athenian people, if you mean to be in their good graces, and to have power in the state; whereas I want you to think and see whether this is for the interest of either of us; – I would not have us risk that which is dearest on the acquisition of this power, like the Thessalian enchantresses, who, as they say, bring down the moon from heaven at the risk of their own perdition. But if you suppose that any man will show you the art of becoming great in the city, and yet not conforming yourself to the ways of the city, whether for better or worse, then I can only say that you are mistaken, Callicles; for he who would deserve to be the true natural friend of the Athenian Demus, aye, or of Pyrilampes' darling who is called after them, must be by nature like them, and not an imitator only. He, then, who will make you most like them, will make you as you desire, a statesman and orator: for every man is pleased when he is spoken to in his own language and spirit, and dislikes any other. But perhaps you, sweet Callicles, may be of another mind. What do you say?

CAL. Somehow or other your words, Socrates, always appear to me to be good words; and yet, like the rest of the world, I am not quite convinced by them.[33]

SOC. The reason is, Callicles, that the love of Demus which abides in your soul is an adversary to me; but I dare say that if we recur to these same matters, and consider them more thoroughly, you may be convinced for all that. Please, then, to remember that there are two processes of training all things, including body and soul; in the one, as we said, we treat them with a view to pleasure, and in the other with a view to the highest good, and then we do not indulge but resist them: was not that the distinction which we drew?

CAL. Very true.

SOC. And the one which had pleasure in view was just a vulgar flattery: – was not that another of our conclusions?

CAL. Be it so, if you will have it.

SOC. And the other had in view the greatest improvement of that which was ministered to, whether body or soul?

CAL. Quite true.

SOC. And must we not have the same end in view in the treatment of our city and citizens? Must we not try and make them as good as possible? For we have already discovered that there is no use in imparting to them any other good, unless the mind of those who are to have the good, whether money, or office, or any other sort of power, be gentle and good. Shall we say that?

CAL. Yes, certainly, if you like.

SOC. Well, then, if you and I, Callicles, were intending[34] to set about some public business, and were advising one another to undertake buildings, such as walls, docks or temples of the largest size, ought we not to examine ourselves, first, as to whether we know or do not know the art of building, and who taught us? – would not that be necessary, Callicles?

CAL. True.

SOC. In the second place, we should have to consider whether we had ever constructed any private house, either of our own or for our friends, and whether this building of ours was a success or not; and if upon consideration we found that we had had good and eminent masters, and had been successful in constructing many fine buildings, not only with their assistance, but without them, by our own unaided skill – in that case prudence would not dissuade us from

[33] Cp. Symp. 216: 1 Alcib. 135.
[34] Reading with the majority of MSS. πράξοντες.

proceeding to the construction of public works. But if we had no master to show, and only a number of worthless buildings or none at all, then, surely, it would be ridiculous in us to attempt public works, or to advise one another to undertake them. Is not this true?

CAL. Certainly.

SOC. And does not the same hold in all other cases? If you and I were physicians, and were advising one another that we were competent to practise as state-physicians, should I not ask about you, and would you not ask about me, Well, but how about Socrates himself, has he good health? and was any one else ever known to be cured by him, whether slave or freeman? And I should make the same enquiries about you. And if we arrived at the conclusion that no one, whether citizen or stranger, man or woman, had ever been any the better for the medical skill of either of us, then, by Heaven, Callicles, what an absurdity to think that we or any human being should be so silly as to set up as state-physicians and advise others like ourselves to do the same, without having first practised in private, whether successfully or not, and acquired experience of the art! Is not this, as they say, to begin with the big jar when you are learning the potter's art; which is a foolish thing?

CAL. True.

SOC. And now, my friend, as you are already beginning to be a public character, and are admonishing and reproaching me for not being one, suppose that we ask a few questions of one another. Tell me, then, Callicles, how about making any of the citizens better? Was there ever a man who was once vicious, or unjust, or intemperate, or foolish, and became by the help of Callicles good and noble? Was there ever such a man, whether citizen or stranger, slave or freeman? Tell me, Callicles, if a person were to ask these questions of you, what would you answer? Whom would you say that you had improved by your conversation? There may have been good deeds of this sort which were done by you as a private person, before you came forward in public. Why will you not answer?

CAL. You are contentious, Socrates.

SOC. Nay, I ask you, not from a love of contention, but because I really want to know in what way you think that affairs should be administered among us – whether, when you come to the administration of them, you have any other aim but the improvement of the citizens? Have we not already admitted many times over that such is the duty of a public man? Nay, we have surely said so; for if you will not answer for yourself I must answer for you. But if this is what the good man ought to effect for the benefit of his own state, allow me to recall to you the names of those whom you were just now mentioning, Pericles, and Cimon, and Miltiades, and Themistocles, and ask whether you still think that they were good citizens.

CAL. I do.

SOC. But if they were good, then clearly each of them must have made the citizens better instead of worse?

CAL. Yes.

SOC. And, therefore, when Pericles first began to speak in the assembly, the Athenians were not so good as when he spoke last?

CAL. Very likely.

SOC. Nay, my friend, 'likely' is not the word; for if he was a good citizen, the inference is certain.

CAL. And what difference does that make?

SOC. None; only I should like further to know whether the Athenians are supposed to have been made better by Pericles, or, on the contrary, to have been corrupted by him; for I hear that he was the first who gave the people pay, and made them idle and cowardly, and encouraged them in the love of talk and of money.

CAL. You heard that, Socrates, from the laconising set who bruise their ears.

SOC. But what I am going to tell you now is not mere hearsay, but well known both to you and me: that at first, Pericles was glorious and his character unimpeached by any verdict of the Athenians – this was during the time when they were not so good – yet afterwards, when they had been made good and gentle by him, at the very end of his life they convicted him of theft, and almost put him to death, clearly under the notion that he was a malefactor.

CAL. Well, but how does that prove Pericles' badness?

SOC. Why, surely you would say that he was a bad manager of asses or horses or oxen, who had received them originally neither kicking nor butting nor biting him, and implanted in them all these savage tricks? Would he not be a bad manager of any animals who received them gentle, and made them fiercer than they were when he received them? What do you say?

CAL. I will do you the favour of saying 'yes.'

SOC. And will you also do me the favour of saying whether man is an animal?

CAL. Certainly he is.

SOC. And was not Pericles a shepherd of men?

CAL. Yes.

SOC. And if he was a good political shepherd, ought not the animals who were his subjects, as we were just now acknowledging, to have become more just, and not more unjust?

CAL. Quite true.

SOC. And are not just men gentle, as Homer says? – or are you of another mind?

CAL. I agree.

SOC. And yet he really did make them more savage than he received them, and their savageness was shown towards himself; which he must have been very far from desiring.

CAL. Do you want me to agree with you?

SOC. Yes, if I seem to you to speak the truth.

CAL. Granted then.

SOC. And if they were more savage, must they not have been more unjust and inferior?

CAL. Granted again.

SOC. Then upon this view, Pericles was not a good statesman?

CAL. That is, upon your view.

SOC. Nay, the view is yours, after what you have admitted. Take the case of Cimon again. Did not the very persons whom he was serving ostracize him, in order that they might not hear his voice for ten years? and they did just the same to Themistocles, adding the penalty of exile; and they voted that Miltiades, the hero of Marathon, should be thrown into the pit of death, and he was only saved by the Prytanis. And yet, if they had been really good men, as you say, these things would never have happened to them. For the good charioteers are not those who at first keep their place, and then, when they have broken-in their horses, and themselves become better charioteers, are thrown out – that is not the way either in charioteering or in any profession. – What do you think?

CAL. I should think not.

SOC. Well, but if so, the truth is as I have said already, that in the Athenian State no one has ever shown himself to be a good statesman – you admitted that this was true of our present statesmen, but not true of former ones, and you preferred them to the others; yet they have turned out to be no better than our present ones; and

therefore, if they were rhetoricians, they did not use the true art of rhetoric or of flattery, or they would not have fallen out of favour.

CAL. But surely, Socrates, no living man ever came near any one of them in his performances.

SOC. O, my dear friend, I say nothing against them regarded as the serving-men of the State; and I do think that they were certainly more serviceable than those who are living now, and better able to gratify the wishes of the State; but as to transforming those desires and not allowing them to have their way, and using the powers which they had, whether of persuasion or of force, in the improvement of their fellow-citizens, which is the prime object of the truly good citizen, I do not see that in these respects they were a whit superior to our present statesmen, although I do admit that they were more clever at providing ships and walls and docks, and all that. You and I have a ridiculous way, for during the whole time that we are arguing, we are always going round and round to the same point, and constantly misunderstanding one another. If I am not mistaken, you have admitted and acknowledged more than once, that there are two kinds of operations which have to do with the body, and two which have to do with the soul: one of the two is ministerial, and if our bodies are hungry provides food for them, and if they are thirsty gives them drink, or if they are cold supplies them with garments, blankets, shoes, and all that they crave. I use the same images as before intentionally, in order that you may understand me the better. The purveyor of the articles may provide them either wholesale or retail, or he may be the maker of any of them, – the baker, or the cook, or the weaver, or the shoemaker, or the currier; and in so doing, being such as he is, he is naturally supposed by himself and every one to minister to the body. For none of them know that there is another art – an art of gymnastic and medicine which is the true minister of the body, and ought to be the mistress of all the rest, and to use their results according to the knowledge which she has and they have not, of the real good or bad effects of meats and drinks on the body. All other arts which have to do with the body are servile and menial and illiberal; and gymnastic and medicine are, as they ought to be, their mistresses. Now, when I say that all this is equally true of the soul, you seem at first to know and understand and assent to my words, and then a little while afterwards you come repeating, Has not the State had good and noble citizens? and when I ask you who they are, you reply, seemingly quite in earnest, as if I had asked, Who are or have been good trainers? – and you had replied, Thearion, the baker, Mithoecus, who wrote the Sicilian cookery-book, Sarambus, the vintner: these are ministers of the body, first-rate in their art; for the first makes admirable loaves, the second excellent dishes, and the third capital wine; – to me these appear to be the exact parallel of the statesmen whom you mention. Now you would not be altogether pleased if I said to you, My friend, you know nothing of gymnastics; those of whom you are speaking to me are only the ministers and purveyors of luxury, who have no good or noble notions of their art, and may very likely be filling and fattening men's bodies and gaining their approval, although the result is that they lose their original flesh in the long run, and become thinner than they were before; and yet they, in their simplicity, will not attribute their diseases and loss of flesh to their entertainers; but when in after years the unhealthy surfeit brings the attendant penalty of disease, he who happens to be near them at the time, and offers them advice, is accused and blamed by them, and if they could they would do him some harm; while they proceed to eulogize the men who have been the real authors of the mischief. And that, Callicles, is just what you are now doing. You praise the men who feasted the citizens and satisfied their desires, and people say that they have made the city great, not seeing that the swollen and ulcerated condition of the State is to be attributed to these elder statesmen; for they have filled the city full of harbours and docks and walls and revenues and all that, and have left no room for justice and temperance. And when the crisis of the disorder comes, the people will blame the advisers of the hour, and applaud Themistocles and Cimon and Pericles, who are the real authors of their calamities; and if you are not careful they may assail you and my friend Alcibiades, when they are losing not only their new acquisitions, but also their original possessions; not that you are the authors of these misfortunes of theirs, although you may perhaps be accessories to them. A great piece of work is always being made, as I see and am told, now as of old, about our statesmen. When the State treats any of them as malefactors, I observe that there is a great uproar and indignation at the supposed wrong which is done to them; 'after all their many services to the State,

that they should unjustly perish,' – so the tale runs. But the cry is all a lie; for no statesman ever could be unjustly put to death by the city of which he is the head. The case of the professed statesman is, I believe very much like that of the professed sophist; for the sophists, although they are wise men, are nevertheless guilty of a strange piece of folly; professing to be teachers of virtue, they will often accuse their disciples of wronging them, and defrauding them of their pay, and showing no gratitude for their services. Yet what can be more absurd than that men who have become just and good, and whose injustice has been taken away from them, and who have had justice implanted in them by their teachers, should act unjustly by reason of the injustice which is not in them? Can anything be more irrational, my friends, than this? You, Callicles, compel me to be a mob-orator, because you will not answer.

CAL. And you are the man who cannot speak unless there is some one to answer?

SOC. I suppose that I can; just now, at any rate, the speeches which I am making are long enough because you refuse to answer me. But I adjure you by the god of friendship, my good sir, do tell me whether there does not appear to you to be a great inconsistency in saying that you have made a man good, and then blaming him for being bad?

CAL. Yes, it appears so to me.

SOC. Do you never hear our professors of education speaking in this inconsistent manner?

CAL. Yes, but why talk of men who are good for nothing?

SOC. I would rather say, why talk of men who profess to be rulers, and declare that they are devoted to the improvement of the city, and nevertheless upon occasion declaim against the utter vileness of the city: – do you think that there is any difference between one and the other? My good friend, the sophist and the rhetorician, as I was saying to Polus, are the same, or nearly the same; but you ignorantly fancy that rhetoric is a perfect thing, and sophistry a thing to be despised; whereas the truth is, that sophistry is as much superior to rhetoric as legislation is to the practice of law, or gymnastic to medicine. The orators and sophists, as I am inclined to think, are the only class who cannot complain of the mischief ensuing to themselves from that which they teach others, without in the same breath accusing themselves of having done no good to those whom they profess to benefit. Is not this a fact?

CAL. Certainly it is.

SOC. If they were right in saying that they make men better, then they are the only class who can afford to leave their remuneration to those who have been benefited by them. Whereas if a man has been benefited in any other way, if, for example, he has been taught to run by a trainer, he might possibly defraud him of his pay, if the trainer left the matter to him, and made no agreement with him that he should receive money as soon as he had given him the utmost speed; for not because of any deficiency of speed do men act unjustly, but by reason of injustice.

CAL. Very true.

SOC. And he who removes injustice can be in no danger of being treated unjustly: he alone can safely leave the honorarium to his pupils, if he be really able to make them good – am I not right?[35]

CAL. Yes.

SOC. Then we have found the reason why there is no dishonour in a man receiving pay who is called in to advise about building or any other art?

CAL. Yes, we have found the reason.

SOC. But when the point is, how a man may become best himself, and best govern his family and state, then to say that you will give no advice gratis is held to be dishonourable?

CAL. True.

SOC. And why? Because only such benefits call forth a desire to requite them, and there is evidence that a benefit has been conferred when the benefactor receives a return; otherwise not. Is this true?

CAL. It is.

SOC. Then to which service of the State do you invite me? determine for me. Am I to be the physician of the State who will strive and struggle to make the Athenians as good as possible; or am I to be the servant and flatterer of the State? Speak out, my good friend, freely and fairly as you did at first and ought to do again, and tell me your entire mind.

CAL. I say then that you should be the servant of the State.

SOC. The flatterer? well, sir, that is a noble invitation.

CAL. The Mysian, Socrates, or what you please. For if you refuse, the consequences will be –

SOC. Do not repeat the old story – that he who likes will kill me and get my money; for then I shall have to repeat the old answer, that he will be a bad man and will kill the good, and that the money will be of no use to him, but that he will wrongly use that which he wrongly took, and if wrongly, basely, and if basely, hurtfully.

CAL. How confident you are, Socrates, that you will never come to harm! you seem to think that you are living in another country, and can never be brought into a court of justice, as you very likely may be brought by some miserable and mean person.

SOC. Then I must indeed be a fool, Callicles, if I do not know that in the Athenian State any man may suffer anything. And if I am brought to trial and incur the dangers of which you speak, he will be a villain who brings me to trial – of that I am very sure, for no good man would accuse the innocent. Nor shall I be surprised if I am put to death. Shall I tell you why I anticipate this?

CAL. By all means.

SOC. I think that I am the only or almost the only Athenian living who practises the true art of politics; I am the only politician of my time. Now, seeing that when I speak my words are not uttered with any view of gaining favour, and that I look to what is best and not to what is most pleasant, having no mind to use those arts and graces which you recommend, I shall have nothing to say in the justice court. And you might argue with me, as I was arguing with Polus: – I shall be tried just as a physician would be tried in a court of little boys at the indictment of the cook. What would he reply under such circumstances, if some one were to accuse him, saying, 'O my boys, many evil things has this man done to you: he is the death of you, especially of the younger ones among you, cutting and burning and starving and suffocating you, until you know not what to do; he gives you the bitterest options, and compels you to hunger and thirst. How unlike the variety of meats and sweets on which I feasted you!' What do you suppose that the physician would be able to reply when he found himself in such a predicament? If he told the truth he could only say, 'All these evil things, my boys,

---

[35] Cp. Protag. 328.

I did for your health,' and then would there not just be a clamour among a jury like that? How they would cry out!

CAL. I dare say.

SOC. Would he not be utterly at a loss for a reply?

CAL. He certainly would.

SOC. And I too shall be treated in the same way, as I well know, if I am brought before the court. For I shall not be able to rehearse to the people the pleasures which I have procured for them, and which, although I am not disposed to envy either the procurers or enjoyers of them, are deemed by them to be benefits and advantages. And if any one says that I corrupt young men, and perplex their minds, or that I speak evil of old men, and use bitter words towards them, whether in private or public, it is useless for me to reply, as I truly might: – 'All this I do for the sake of justice, and with a view to your interest, my judges, and to nothing else.' And therefore there is no saying what may happen to me.

CAL. And do you think, Socrates, that a man who is thus defenceless is in a good position?

SOC. Yes, Callicles, if he have that defence, which as you have often acknowledged he should have – if he be his own defence, and have never said or done anything wrong, either in respect of gods or men; and this has been repeatedly acknowledged by us to be the best sort of defence. And if any one could convict me of inability to defend myself or others after this sort, I should blush for shame, whether I was convicted before many, or before a few, or by myself alone; and if I died from want of ability to do so, that would indeed grieve me. But if I died because I have no powers of flattery or rhetoric, I am very sure that you would not find me repining at death. For no man who is not an utter fool and coward is afraid of death itself, but he is afraid of doing wrong. For to go to the world below having one's soul full of injustice is the last and worst of all evils. And in proof of what I say, if you have no objection, I should like to tell you a story.

CAL. Very well, proceed; and then we shall have done.

SOC. Listen, then, as story-tellers say, to a very pretty tale, which I dare say that you may be disposed to regard as a fable only, but which, as I believe, is a true tale, for I mean to speak the truth. Homer tells us,[36] how Zeus and Poseidon and Pluto divided the empire which they inherited from their father. Now in the days of Cronos there existed a law respecting the destiny of man, which has always been, and still continues to be in Heaven, – that he who has lived all his life in justice and holiness shall go, when he is dead, to the Islands of the Blessed, and dwell there in perfect happiness out of the reach of evil; but that he who has lived unjustly and impiously shall go to the house of vengeance and punishment, which is called Tartarus. And in the time of Cronos, and even quite lately in the reign of Zeus, the judgment was given on the very day on which the men were to die; the judges were alive, and the men were alive; and the consequence was that the judgments were not well given. Then Pluto and the authorities from the Islands of the Blessed came to Zeus, and said that the souls found their way to the wrong places. Zeus said: 'I shall put a stop to this; the judgments are not well given, because the persons who are judged have their clothes on, for they are alive; and there are many who, having evil souls, are apparelled in fair bodies, or encased in wealth or rank, and when the day of judgment arrives: numerous witnesses come forward and testify on their behalf that they have lived righteously. The judges are awed by them, and they themselves too have their clothes on when judging; their eyes and ears and their whole bodies are interposed as a veil before their own souls. All this is a hindrance to them; there are the clothes of the judges and the clothes of the judged. – What is to be done? I will tell you: – In the first place, I will deprive men of the fore knowledge of death, which they possess at present: this power which they have Prometheus has already received my orders to take from them: in the second place, they shall be entirely stripped before they are judged, for they shall be judged when they are dead; and the judge too shall be naked, that is to say, dead – he with his naked soul shall pierce into the other naked souls; and they shall die suddenly and be deprived of all their kindred, and leave their brave attire strewn upon the earth – conducted in this manner, the judgment will be just. I knew all about the matter before any of you, and therefore I have made my sons judges; two from Asia, Minos and Rhadamanthus, and one

---

[36] Il. xv. 187. foll.

from Europe, Aeacus. And these, when they are dead, shall give judgment in the meadow at the parting of the ways, whence the two roads lead, one to the Islands of the Blessed, and the other to Tartarus. Rhadamanthus shall judge those who come from Asia, and Aeacus those who come from Europe. And to Minos I shall give the primacy, and he shall hold a court of appeal, in case either of the two others are in any doubt: – then the judgment respecting the last journey of men will be as just as possible.'

From this tale, Callicles, which I have heard and believe, I draw the following inferences: – Death, if I am right, is in the first place the separation from one another of two things, soul and body; nothing else. And after they are separated they retain their several natures, as in life; the body keeps the same habit, and the results of treatment or accident are distinctly visible in it: for example, he who by nature or training or both, was a tall man while he was alive, will remain as he was, after he is dead; and the fat man will remain fat; and so on; and the dead man, who in life had a fancy to have flowing hair, will have flowing hair. And if he was marked with the whip and had the prints of the scourge, or of wounds in him when he was alive, you might see the same in the dead body; and if his limbs were broken or misshapen when he was alive, the same appearance would be visible in the dead. And in a word, whatever was the habit of the body during life would be distinguishable after death, either perfectly, or in a great measure and for a certain time. And I should imagine that this is equally true of the soul, Callicles; when a man is stripped of the body, all the natural or acquired affections of the soul are laid open to view. – And when they come to the judge, as those from Asia come to Rhadamanthus, he places them near him and inspects them quite impartially, not knowing whose the soul is: perhaps he may lay hands on the soul of the great king, or of some other king or potentate, who has no soundness in him, but his soul is marked with the whip, and is full of the prints and scars of perjuries and crimes with which each action has stained him, and he is all crooked with falsehood and imposture, and has no straightness, because he has lived without truth. Him Rhadamanthus beholds, full of all deformity and disproportion, which is caused by

licence and luxury and insolence and incontinence, and despatches him ignominiously to his prison, and there he undergoes the punishment which he deserves.

Now the proper office of punishment is twofold: he who is rightly punished ought either to become better and profit by it, or he ought to be made an example to his fellows, that they may see what he suffers, and fear and become better. Those who are improved when they are punished by gods and men, are those whose sins are curable; and they are improved, as in this world so also in another, by pain and suffering; for there is no other way in which they can be delivered from their evil. But they who have been guilty of the worst crimes, and are incurable by reason of their crimes, are made examples; for, as they are incurable, the time has passed at which they can receive any benefit. They get no good themselves, but others get good when they behold them enduring for ever the most terrible and painful and fearful sufferings as the penalty of their sins – there they are, hanging up as examples, in the prison-house of the world below, a spectacle and a warning to all unrighteous men who come thither. And among them, as I confidently affirm, will be found Archelaus, if Polus truly reports of him, and any other tyrant who is like him. Of these fearful examples, most, as I believe, are taken from the class of tyrants and kings and potentates and public men, for they are the authors of the greatest and most impious crimes, because they have the power. And Homer witnesses to the truth of this; for they are always kings and potentates whom he has described as suffering everlasting punishment in the world below: such were Tantalus and Sisyphus and Tityus. But no one ever described Thersites, or any private person who was a villain, as suffering everlasting punishment, or as incurable. For to commit the worst crimes, as I am inclined to think, was not in his power, and he was happier than those who had the power. No, Callicles, the very bad men come from the class of those who have power.[37] And yet in that very class there may arise good men, and worthy of all admiration they are, for where there is great power to do wrong, to live and to die justly is a hard thing, and greatly to be praised, and few there are who attain to this. Such good and true men, however, there have been, and will

[37] Cp. Rep. x. 615 E.

be again, at Athens and in other states, who have fulfilled their trust righteously; and there is one who is quite famous all over Hellas, Aristeides, the son of Lysimachus. But, in general, great men are also bad, my friend.

As I was saying, Rhadamanthus, when he gets a soul of the bad kind, knows nothing about him, neither who he is, nor who his parents are; he knows only that he has get hold of a villain; and seeing this, he stamps him as curable or incurable, and sends him away to Tartarus, whither he goes and receives his proper recompense. Or, again, he looks with admiration of the soul of some just one who has lived in holiness and truth; he may have been a private man or not; and I should say, Callicles, that he is most likely to have been a philosopher who has done his own work, and not troubled himself with the doings of other men in his lifetime; him Rhadamanthus sends to the Islands of the Blessed. Aeacus does the same; and they both have sceptres, and judge; but Minos alone has a golden sceptre and is seated looking on, as Odysseus in Homer[38] declares that he saw him:

'Holding a sceptre of gold, and giving laws to the dead.'

Now I, Callicles, am persuaded of the truth of these things, and I consider how I shall present my soul whole and undefiled before the judge in that day. Renouncing the honours at which the world aims, I desire only to know the truth, and to live as well as I can, and, when I die, to die as well as I can. And, to the utmost of my power, I exhort all other men to do the same. And, in return for your exhortation of me, I exhort you also to take part in the great combat, which is the combat of life, and greater than every other earthly conflict. And I retort your reproach of me, and say, that you will not be able to help yourself when the day of trial and judgment, of which I was speaking, comes upon you; you will go before the judge, the son of Aegina, and, when he has got you in his grip and is carrying you off, you will gape and your head will swim round, just as mine would in the courts of this world, and very likely some one will shamefully box you on the ears, and put upon you any sort of insult.

Perhaps this may appear to you to be only an old wife's tale, which you will contemn. And there might be reason in your contemning such tales, if by searching we could find out anything better or truer: but now you see that you and Polus and Gorgias, who are the three wisest of the Greeks of our day, are not able to show that we ought to live any life which does not profit in another world as well as in this. And of all that has been said, nothing remains unshaken but the saying, that to do injustice is more to be avoided than to suffer injustice, and that the reality and not the appearance of virtue is to be followed above all things, as well in public as in private life; and that when any one has been wrong in anything, he is to be chastised, and that the next best thing to a man being just is that he should become just, and be chastised and punished; also that he should avoid all flattery of himself as well as of others, of the few or of the many: and rhetoric and any other art should be used by him, and all his actions should be done always, with a view to justice.

Follow me then, and I will lead you where you will be happy in life and after death, as the argument shows. And never mind if some one despises you as a fool, and insults you, if he has a mind; let him strike you, by Zeus, and do you be of good cheer, and do not mind the insulting blow, for you will never come to any harm in the practice of virtue, if you are a really good and true man. When we have practised virtue together, we will apply ourselves to politics, if that seems desirable, or we will advise about whatever else may seem good to us, for we shall be better able to judge then. In our present condition we ought not to give ourselves airs, for even on the most important subjects we are always changing our minds; so utterly stupid are we! Let us, then, take the argument as our guide, which has revealed to us that the best way of life is to practise justice and every virtue in life and death. This way let us go; and in this exhort all men to follow, not in the way to which you trust and in which you exhort me to follow you; for that way, Callicles, is nothing worth.

---

[38] Odyss. xi. 569.

Phaedrus

Phaedrus is complex in both structure and content, and it very well may be the most frequently studied of Plato's works among those who are interested in rhetoric and oratory. Many scholars believe that Plato wrote the dialogue as a further exploration of some of the ideas he raised in *Gorgias*.

Phaedrus begins with three speeches on love (*eros*), and throughout much of the dialogue, but especially in the first half, the sexual innuendoes are frequent, imbuing the work with the heavy scent of pederastic seduction. Some translators, such as Jowett, the translator here, as well as various interpreters of Plato's work, such as Rutherford (1995), strove to attenuate the sexual aspects of the work. Rutherford, for example, suggested that Socrates was merely trying to "woo" Phaedrus to philosophy. Weaver (1953) argued that the discussion of love is a rhetorical figure that embodies "three types of discourse" (p. 6). But given the undeniable interweaving of *eros* with the soul (*psyche*), persuasion, rhetoric, and philosophy, efforts to mask or recast the sexuality in the dialogue would seem to reduce its overall force.

The first speech, read by Phaedrus, was supposedly written by Lysias, the prominent Sophist who played such a crucial role in the Athenian civil war. Its argument is that a young boy should choose the non-lover over the lover as his intimate. Socrates responds with a speech in which he describes the various disadvantages to the boy if he chooses the lover, but he breaks off without completing it and refuses to continue. Together, these two speeches can be viewed as a competition, one that Socrates won, based on Phaedrus' assessment, even though his speech was incomplete. This outcome may represent Plato's effort to demonstrate that rhetoricians did not possess any special skill and that even when the philosopher meets the rhetorician on his home court, so to speak, using rhetoric rather than dialectic, the philosopher's discourse is superior.

After breaking off his speech, Socrates states that he is guilty of impiety, for he has slandered Eros, the god of love; to make amends, he offers yet another speech on love very different from the previous ones. In it he provides two dissertations that on the surface do not seem to be closely related: one on love as divine madness, the other on the immortality of the soul. Both dissertations, however, prove to be important to the later discussion of rhetoric.

Socrates concludes his second speech with a prayer that Phaedrus will "dedicate himself wholly to love and to philosophy," which sets in motion what can only be characterized as an awkward transition to a discussion of rhetoric. Socrates indicates that he will examine "the rules of writing and speech" and gives every indication that he will offer a fully developed theory of rhetoric. Yunis (2005) interpreted Socrates' proposal as Plato's response to the uncomfortable reality that rhetoric had become institutionalized in Athenian society, and therefore *Phaedrus* was an effort to "confront the entire rhetorical establishment on its own terms" (p. 108), using rhetoric as a persuasive tool enhanced by dialectic to demonstrate the inadequacy of the one and the superiority of the other. And the "rules" that Socrates enunciates are consistent with Plato's philosophical paradigm: "[H]e who would be a master of the art must understand the real nature of everything." Plato then mentions structure, organization, division, and classification as important elements of oratory. Weaver (1953) also saw in *Phaedrus* an effort to join rhetoric and dialectic, arguing that we find in the dialogue a depiction of "the true rhetorician ... who works though dialectic and through poetic or analogical association" (p. 18), for there is "no true rhetoric without dialectic" (p. 17).

If this was Plato's aim in *Phaedrus*, he was less than successful, for the resulting dialectical rhetoric has inherent flaws. Plato's paradigm focuses on appealing to the souls of auditors – hence the lengthy discussion of the soul in *Phaedrus* – which is congruent with his definition of rhetoric as *paideia*. Whereas Sophistic rhetoric aims only at influencing opinion, Plato's dialectical rhetoric aims at conviction and belief, involving the exercise of judgment regarding truth. And as Socrates tells Phaedrus, its "whole effort is directed to the soul."[39] The difference between the Sophists and Plato is therefore clear: The Sophists structured their pedagogical curriculum around the concept of rhetoric as a tool to help the student become a better citizen, a better leader, and a successful pleader in the courts. Plato's pedagogy is based on making the student a better person, just as the lover strives to become a better person through adoration of the beloved.

In *Phaedrus* (and other dialogues), Plato's definition of terms and syllogistic reasoning create the appearance that his dialectical method is a discovery procedure that leads his interlocutors to correct judgments of truth and falsehood through the application of logic. Unlike Sophistic rhetoric, the emphasis is on discovery, not persuasion. But as Theodorakakou (2005) pointed out, judgment must follow discovery, and it always must have certitude. Thus, the purpose of dialectical rhetoric is to shepherd the interlocutor's soul through discovery to the certain judgment of philosophical truth. Dialectical syllogisms, however, have certainty of form, but they do not have certainty of matter: False premises can yield legitimate conclusions owing to the logical structure of the syllogism. Aristotle explained this difficulty in *Topics* and *Posterior Analytics* and noted that dialectical syllogisms are commonly constructed using premises based on widely held opinions that may be probable but not necessarily true. In his analysis, dialectical rhetoric cannot serve as a means of discovering truth but only as a means of confirming the opinions manifested in its premises. Plato's dialectical syllogisms, accordingly, do not represent the application of reason to support the argument but instead serve to enhance the credibility of Socrates' character by giving his rhetoric the appearance of rationality. If, however, dialectical rhetoric fails as a discovery procedure because it merely confirms opinions already held, it cannot lead to certitude in judgment of truth. Only the demonstrative syllogism of the sort used, for example, in geometry can do so.[40] But Plato eschewed demonstrative syllogisms and scientism.

Plato's use of dialectic is further complicated by the fact that even as he advocated the accurate, concrete definition of terms, he did not consistently meet his own criteria. As in the previous dialogues, we see an emphasis on knowing the nature of justice and injustice, good and evil, and again "the good" is equated with knowledge of *a priori* truths. Exactly what these truths are, however, is difficult to determine. Plato did not attempt to define what he means by the "soul," and he never considered justice and injustice in terms of law. Many readers are likely to sense that Plato used terms like "justice," "good," "truth," and so forth as semantic primitives – that is, as terms that have a single meaning in all languages and all contexts, such as "sky," "I," "you," "plants," and "hair" – when clearly they are not. The problem this presents is evident, for example, when Socrates states that it is important to define "the nature and power of love," but then in his long disquisition on the topic he merely describes the *effects* of *eros* without attempting a definition. Brownstein (1965) argued that even if Plato had been able

---

[39] Note that Kennedy (1980) and others have referred to dialectical rhetoric as "philosophical rhetoric."

[40] A demonstrative syllogism must have a middle term that is explanatory and correctly positioned between the first premise and the conclusion. For example:

Only animals that produce milk are mammals.
Snakes do not produce milk.
Therefore, snakes are not mammals.

to develop a dialectic that included formal, concrete definitions of abstract terms, he would not have been any closer to a knowledge-based discourse because such definitions cannot possibly lead to an understanding of ethics or ethical behavior. As various scholars have noted (e.g., Fisher, 1985; Hikins, 1981; Scott, 1967), Plato assumed that definitions and the dialectic of which they are a part are fundamentally objective, whereas rhetoric is not, and that the mere act of definition and classification produces truths. What we find, however, is that these truths ultimately cannot be defined with objective exactitude and that the dialogues reveal the intersubjectivity of discourse, particularly, as is so often the case, when the contributions of the secondary characters become empty formalities and Socrates engages in a conversation with himself. Even more problematic, we find Plato asserting in *Phaedrus* that "Thrasymachus [the Sophist] or any one else who teaches rhetoric in earnest will give an exact description of the nature of the soul," and it seems reasonable to expect that anyone engaged in philosophy would face an even stronger imperative. Yet as Socrates introduces this topic, he admits that the true nature of the soul is beyond "mortal discourse," and he is reduced to relying on a poetic allegory.

Some readers may conclude that Plato's mysticism, as well as his own deep immersion in a society that had institutionalized rhetorical figures, prevented him from stepping outside conventional ways of thinking with regard to rhetoric.[41] Doing so required the perspectives of an outsider. Aristotle, a *metic* with an inclination toward empiricism and science, brought the necessary tools to the task.[42]

---

[41] Arguably this was not the case with regard to *The Republic*, which strikes some readers as being more Laconian than Athenian in perspectives on government and society.

[42] Aristotle explored the nature of the soul (*psyche*) in several works, the most significant, perhaps, being *De Anima*. His approach was different from Plato's in several ways: For example, he viewed the study of *psyche* as being partially in the realm of the natural sciences, partially in the realm of philosophy. As a result, his investigation of *psyche* is commonly viewed as work in psychology, not metaphysics (see Ackrill, 1972; Frede, 1992; Scaltsas, 1996). The natural science aspect of *psyche* is evident in *The Art of Rhetoric*, which devotes an entire book to an exploration of audience psychology

Reading 28

Phaedrus

Phaedrus, translated by B. Jowett, 1892.

Persons of the Dialogue

SOCRATES   PHAEDRUS

Scene: Under a plane-tree, by the banks of the Ilissus.

SOCRATES. My dear Phaedrus, whence come you, and whither are you going?

PHAEDRUS. I come from Lysias the son of Cephalus, and I am going to take a walk outside the wall, for I have been sitting with him the whole morning; and our common friend Acumenus tells me that it is much more refreshing to walk in the open air than to be shut up in a cloister.

SOC. There he is right. Lysias then, I suppose, was in the town?

PHAEDR. Yes, he was staying with Epicrates, here at the house of Morychus; that house which is near the temple of Olympian Zeus.

SOC. And how did he entertain you? Can I be wrong in supposing that Lysias gave you a feast of discourse?

PHAEDR. You shall hear, if you can spare time to accompany me.

SOC. And should I not deem the conversation of you and Lysias 'a thing of higher import,' as I may say in the words of Pindar, 'than any business'?

PHAEDR. Will you go on?

SOC. And will you go on with the narration?

PHAEDR. My tale, Socrates, is one of your sort, for love was the theme which occupied us – love after a fashion: Lysias has been writing about a fair youth who was being tempted, but not by a lover; and this was the point: he ingeniously proved that the non-lover should be accepted rather than the lover.

SOC. O that is noble of him! I wish that he would say the poor man rather than the rich, and the old man rather than the young one; – then he would meet the case of me and of many a man; his words would be quite refreshing, and he would be a public benefactor. For my part, I do so long to hear his speech, that if you walk all the way to Megara, and when you have reached the wall come back, as Herodicus recommends, without going in, I will keep you company.

PHAEDR. What do you mean, my good Socrates? How can you imagine that my unpractised memory can do justice to an elaborate work, which the greatest rhetorician of the age spent a long time in composing. Indeed, I cannot; I would give a great deal if I could.

SOC. I believe that I know Phaedrus about as well as I know myself, and I am very sure that the speech of Lysias was repeated to him, not once only, but again and again; – he insisted on hearing it many times over and Lysias was very willing to gratify him; at last, when nothing else would do, he got hold of the book, and looked at what he most wanted to see, – this occupied him during the whole morning; – and then when he was tired with sitting, he went out to take a walk, not until, by the dog, as I believe, he had simply learned by heart the entire discourse, unless it was unusually long, and he went to a place outside the wall that he might practise his lesson.

There he saw a certain lover of discourse who had a similar weakness; – he saw and rejoiced; now thought he, 'I shall have a partner in my revels.' And he invited him to come and walk with him. But when the lover of discourse begged that he would repeat the tale, he gave himself airs and said, 'No I cannot,' as if he were indisposed; although, if the hearer had refused, he would sooner or later have been compelled by him to listen whether he would or no. Therefore, Phaedrus, bid him do at once what he will soon do whether bidden or not.

PHAEDR. I see that you will not let me off until I speak in some fashion or other; verily therefore my best plan is to speak as I best can.

SOC. A very true remark, that of yours.

PHAEDR. I will do as I say; but believe me, Socrates, I did not learn the very words – O no; nevertheless I have a general notion of what he said, and will give you a summary of the points in which the lover differed from the non-lover. Let me begin at the beginning.

SOC. Yes, my sweet one; but you must first of all show what you have in your left hand under your cloak, for that roll, as I suspect, is the actual discourse. Now, much as I love you, I would not have you suppose that I am going to have your memory exercised at my expense, if you have Lysias himself here.

PHAEDR. Enough; I see that I have no hope of practising my art upon you. But if I am to read, where would you please to sit?

SOC. Let us turn aside and go by the Ilissus; we will sit down at some quiet spot.

PHAEDR. I am fortunate in not having my sandals, and as you never have any, I think that we may go along the brook and cool our feet in the water; this will be the easiest way, and at midday and in the summer is far from being unpleasant.

SOC. Lead on, and look out for a place in which we can sit down.

PHAEDR. Do you see the tallest plane-tree in the distance?

SOC. Yes.

PHAEDR. There are shade and gentle breezes, and grass on which we may either sit or lie down.

SOC. Move forward.

PHAEDR. I should like to know, Socrates, whether the place is not somewhere here at which Boreas is said to have carried off Orithyia from the banks of the Ilissus?

SOC. Such is the tradition.

PHAEDR. And is this the exact spot? The little stream is delightfully clear and bright; I can fancy that there might be maidens playing near.

SOC. I believe that the spot is not exactly here, but about a quarter of a mile lower down, where you cross to the temple of Artemis, and there is, I think, some sort of an altar of Boreas at the place.

PHAEDR. I have never noticed it; but I beseech you to tell me, Socrates, do you believe this tale?

SOC. The wise are doubtful, and I should not be singular if, like them, I too doubted. I might have a rational explanation that Orithyia was playing with Pharmacia, when a northern gust carried her over the neighbouring rocks; and this being the manner of her death, she was said to have been carried away by Boreas. There is a discrepancy, however, about the locality; according to another version of the story she was taken from Areopagus, and not from this place. Now I quite acknowledge that these allegories are very nice, but he is not to be envied who has to invent them; much labour and ingenuity will be required of him; and when he has once begun, he must go on and rehabilitate Hippocentaurs and chimeras dire. Gorgons and winged steeds flow in apace, and numberless other inconceivable and portentous natures. And if he is sceptical about them, and would fain reduce them one after another to the rules of probability, this sort of crude philosophy will take up a great deal of time. Now I have no leisure for such enquiries; shall I tell you why? I must first know myself, as the Delphian inscription says; to be curious about that which is not my concern, while I am still in ignorance of my own self, would be ridiculous. And therefore I bid farewell to all this; the common opinion is enough for me. For, as I was saying, I want to know not about this, but about myself: am I a monster more complicated and swollen with passion than the serpent Typho, or a creature of a gentler and simpler sort, to whom Nature has given a diviner and lowlier destiny? But let me ask you, friend: have we not reached the plane-tree to which you were conducting us?

PHAEDR. Yes, this is the tree.

SOC. By Herè, a fair resting-place, full of summer sounds and scents. Here is this lofty and spreading plane-tree, and the agnus castus high and clustering, in the fullest blossom and the greatest fragrance; and the stream which flows beneath the plane-tree is deliciously cold to the feet. Judging from the ornaments and images, this must be a spot sacred to Achelous and the Nymphs. How delightful is the breeze: – so very sweet; and there is a sound in the air shrill and summerlike which makes answer to the chorus of the cicadae. But the greatest charm of all is the grass, like a pillow gently sloping to the head. My dear Phaedrus, you have been an admirable guide.

PHAEDR. What an incomprehensible being you are, Socrates: when you are in the country, as you say, you really are like some stranger who is led about by a guide. Do you ever cross the border? I rather think that you never venture even outside the gates.

SOC. Very true, my good friend; and I hope that you will excuse me when you hear the reason, which is, that I am a lover of knowledge, and the men who dwell in the city are my teachers, and not the trees or the country. Though I do indeed believe that you have found a spell with which to draw me out of the city into the country, like a hungry cow before whom a bough or a bunch of fruit is waved. For only hold up before me in like manner a book, and you may lead me all round Attica, and over the wide world. And now having arrived, I intend to lie down, and do you choose any posture in which you can read best. Begin.

PHAEDR. Listen. You know how matters stand with me; and how, as I conceive, this affair may be arranged for the advantage of both of us. And I maintain that I ought not to fail in my suit, because I am not your lover: for lovers repent of the kindnesses which they have shown when their passion ceases, but to the non-lovers who are free and not under any compulsion, no time of repentance ever comes; for they confer their benefits according to the measure of their ability, in the way which is most conducive to their own interest. Then again, lovers consider how by reason of their love they have neglected their own concerns and rendered service to others: and when to these benefits conferred they add on the troubles which they have endured, they think that they have long ago made to the beloved a very ample return. But the non-lover has no such tormenting recollections; he has never neglected his affairs or quarrelled with his relations; he has no troubles to add up or excuse to invent; and being well rid of all these evils, why should he not freely do what will gratify the beloved? If you say that the lover is more to be esteemed, because his love is thought to be greater; for he is willing to say and do what is hateful to other men, in order to please his beloved; – that, if true, is only a proof that he will prefer any future love to his present, and will injure his old love at the pleasure of the new. And how, in a matter of such infinite importance, can a man be right in trusting himself to one who is afflicted with a malady which no experienced person would attempt to cure, for the patient himself admits that he is not in his right mind, and acknowledges that he is wrong in his mind, but says that he is unable to control himself? And if he came to his right mind, would he ever imagine that the desires were good which he conceived when in his wrong mind? Once more, there are many more non-lovers than lovers; and if you choose the best of the lovers, you will not have many to choose from; but if from the non-lovers, the choice will be larger, and you will be far more likely to find among them a person who is worthy of your friendship. If public opinion be your dread, and you would avoid reproach, in all probability the lover, who is always thinking that other men are as emulous of him as he is of them, will boast to some one[43] of his successes, and make a show of them openly in the pride of his heart; – he wants others to know that his labour has not been lost; but the non-lover is more his own master, and is desirous of solid good, and not of the opinion of mankind. Again, the lover may be generally noted or seen following the beloved (this is his regular occupation), and whenever they are observed to exchange two words they are supposed to meet about some affair of love either past or in contemplation; but when non-lovers meet, no one asks the reason why, because people know that talking to another is natural, whether friendship or mere pleasure be the motive. Once more, if you fear the fickleness of friendship, consider that in any other case a quarrel might be a mutual calamity; but now, when you have given up what is most precious to you, you will be the greater loser, and therefore, you will have more reason in being afraid of the lover, for his vexations are many, and he is always fancying that every one is leagued against him. Wherefore also he debars his beloved from society; he will not have you intimate with the wealthy, lest they should exceed him in wealth, or with men of education, lest they

should be his superiors in understanding; and he is equally afraid of anybody's influence who has any other advantage over himself. If he can persuade you to break with them, you are left without a friend in the world; or if, out of a regard to your own interest, you have more sense than to comply with his desire, you will have to quarrel with him. But those who are non-lovers, and whose success in love is the reward of their merit, will not be jealous of the companions of their beloved, and will rather hate those who refuse to be his associates, thinking that their favourite is slighted by the latter and benefited by the former; for more love than hatred may be expected to come to him out of his friendship with others. Many lovers too have loved the person of a youth before they knew his character or his belongings; so that when their passion has passed away, there is no knowing whether they will continue to be his friends; whereas, in the case of non-lovers who were always friends, the friendship is not lessened by the favours granted; but the recollection of these remains with them, and is an earnest of good things to come. Further, I say that you are likely to be improved by me, whereas the lover will spoil you. For they praise your words and actions in a wrong way; partly, because they are afraid of offending you, and also, their judgment is weakened by passion. Such are the feats which love exhibits; he makes things painful to the disappointed which give no pain to others; he compels the successful lover to praise what ought not to give him pleasure, and therefore the beloved is to be pitied rather than envied. But if you listen to me, in the first place, I, in my intercourse with you, shall not merely regard present enjoyment, but also future advantage, being not mastered by love, but my own master; nor for small causes taking violent dislikes, but even when the cause is great, slowly laying up little wrath – unintentional offences I shall forgive, and intentional ones I shall try to prevent; and these are the marks of a friendship which will last. Do you think that a lover only can be a firm friend? reflect: – if this were true, we should set small value on sons, or fathers, or mothers; nor should we ever have loyal friends, for our love of them arises not from passion, but from other associations. Further, if we ought to shower favours on those who are the most eager suitors, – on that principle, we ought always to do

---

[43] Reading τῷ λέγειν; cf. infra, τῷ διαλέγεσθαι.

good, not to the most virtuous, but to the most needy; for they are the persons who will be most relieved, and will therefore be the most grateful; and when you make a feast you should invite not your friend, but the beggar and the empty soul; for they will love you, and attend you, and come about your doors, and will be the best pleased, and the most grateful, and will invoke many a blessing on your head. Yet surely you ought not to be granting favours to those who besiege you with prayer, but to those who are best able to reward you; nor to the lover only, but to those who are worthy of love; nor to those who will enjoy the bloom of your youth, but to those who will share their possessions with you in age; nor to those who, having succeeded, will glory in their success to others, but to those who will be modest and tell no tales; nor to those who care about you for a moment only, but to those who will continue your friends through life; nor to those who, when their passion is over, will pick a quarrel with you, but rather to those who, when the charm of youth has left you, will show their own virtue. Remember what I have said; and consider yet this further point: friends admonish the lover under the idea that his way of life is bad, but no one of his kin-dred ever yet censured the non-lover, or thought that he was ill-advised about his own interests.

'Perhaps you will ask me whether I propose that you should indulge every non-lover. To which I reply that not even the lover would advise you to indulge all lovers, for the indiscriminate favour is less esteemed by the rational recipient, and less easily hidden by him who would escape the cen-sure of the world. Now love ought to be for the advantage of both parties, and for the injury of neither.

'I believe that I have said enough; but if there is anything more which you desire or which in your opinion needs to be supplied, ask and I will answer.'

Now, Socrates, what do you think? Is not the discourse excellent, more especially in the matter of the language?

SOC. Yes, quite admirable; the effect on me was ravishing. And this I owe to you, Phaedrus, for I observed you while reading to be in an ecstasy, and thinking that you are more experienced in these matters than I am, I followed your example,

and, like you, my divine darling, I became inspired with a phrenzy.

PHAEDR. Indeed, you are pleased to be merry.

SOC. Do you mean that I am not in earnest?

PHAEDR. Now don't talk in that way, Socrates, but let me have your real opinion; I adjure you, by Zeus, the god of friendship, to tell me whether you think that any Hellene could have said more or spoken better on the same subject.

SOC. Well, but are you and I expected to praise the sentiments of the author, or only the clear-ness, and roundness, and finish, and tournure of the language? As to the first I willingly submit to your better judgment, for I am not worthy to form an opinion, having only attended to the rhe-torical manner; and I was doubting whether this could have been defended even by Lysias himself; I thought, though I speak under correction, that he repeated himself two or three times, either from want of words or from want of pains; and also, he appeared to me ostentatiously to exult in showing how well he could say the same thing[44] in two or three ways.

PHAEDR. Nonsense, Socrates; what you call rep-etition was the especial merit of the speech; for he omitted no topic of which the subject rightly allowed, and I do not think that any one could have spoken better or more exhaustively.

SOC. There I cannot go along with you. Ancient sages, men and women, who have spoken and writ-ten of these things, would rise up in judgment against me, if out of complaisance I assented to you.

PHAEDR. Who are they, and where did you hear anything better than this?

SOC. I am sure that I must have heard; but at this moment I do not remember from whom; perhaps from Sappho the fair, or Anacreon the wise; or, possibly, from a prose writer. Why do I say so? Why, because I perceive that my bosom is full, and that I could make another speech as good as that of Lysias, and different. Now I am certain that this is not an invention of my own, who am well aware that I know nothing, and therefore I can only infer that I have been filled through the ears, like a pitcher, from the waters of another, though I have actually forgotten in my stupidity who was my informant.

---

[44] Reading ταὐτά.

PHAEDR. That is grand: – but never mind where you heard the discourse or from whom; let that be a mystery not to be divulged even at my earnest desire. Only, as you say, promise[45] to make another and better oration, equal in length and entirely new, on the same subject; and I, like the nine Archons, will promise to set up a golden image at Delphi, not only of myself, but of you, and as large as life.

SOC. You are a dear golden ass if you suppose me to mean that Lysias has altogether missed the mark, and that I can make a speech from which all his arguments are to be excluded. The worst of authors will say something which is to the point. Who, for example, could speak on this thesis of yours without praising the discretion of the non-lover and blaming the indiscretion of the lover? These are the commonplaces of the subject which must come in (for what else is there to be said?) and must be allowed and excused; the only merit is in the arrangement of them, for there can be none in the invention; but when you leave the commonplaces, then there may be some originality.

PHAEDR. I admit that there is reason in what you say, and I too will be reasonable, and will allow you to start with the premiss that the lover is more disordered in his wits than the non-lover; if in what remains you make a longer and better speech than Lysias, and use other arguments, then I say again, that a statue you shall have of beaten gold, and take your place by the colossal offerings of the Cypselids at Olympia.

SOC. How profoundly in earnest is the lover, because to tease him I lay a finger upon his love! And so, Phaedrus, you really imagine that I am going to improve upon the ingenuity of Lysias?

PHAEDR. There I have you as you had me, and you must just speak 'as you best can.' Do not let us exchange 'tu quoque' as in a farce, or compel me to say to you as you said to me, 'I know Socrates as well as I know myself, and he was wanting to speak, but he gave himself airs.' Rather I would have you consider that from this place we stir not until you have unbosomed yourself of the speech; for here are we all alone, and I am stronger, remember, and younger than you: – Wherefore perpend, and do not compel me to use violence.

SOC. But, my sweet Phaedrus, how ridiculous it would be of me to compete with Lysias in an extempore speech! He is a master in his art and I am an untaught man.

PHAEDR. You see how matters stand; and therefore let there be no more pretences; for, indeed, I know the word that is irresistible.

SOC. Then don't say it.

PHAEDR. Yes, but I will; and my word shall be an oath. 'I say, or rather swear' – but what god will be witness of my oath? – 'By this plane-tree I swear, that unless you repeat the discourse here in the face of this very plane-tree, I will never tell you another; never let you have word of another!'

SOC. Villain! I am conquered; the poor lover of discourse has no more to say.

PHAEDR. Then why are you still at your tricks?

SOC. I am not going to play tricks now that you have taken the oath, for I cannot allow myself to be starved.

PHAEDR. Proceed.

SOC. Shall I tell you what I will do?

PHAEDR. What?

SOC. I will veil my face and gallop through the discourse as fast as I can, for if I see you I shall feel ashamed and not know what to say.

PHAEDR. Only go on and you may do anything else which you please.

SOC. Come, O ye Muses, melodious, as ye are called, whether you have received this name from the character of your strains, or because the Melians[46] are a musical race, help, O help me in the tale which my good friend here desires me to rehearse, in order that his friend whom he always deemed wise may seem to him to be wiser than ever.

Once upon a time there was a fair boy, or, more properly speaking, a youth; he was very fair and had a great many lovers; and there was one special cunning one, who had persuaded the youth that he did not love him, but he really loved him all the same; and one day when he was paying his addresses to him, he used this very argument – that he ought to accept the non-lover rather than the lover; his words were as follows:

'All good counsel begins in the same way; a man should know what he is advising about, or his counsel will all come to nought. But people

---

[45] Reading ὑπόσχες εἰπεῖν.
[46] In the original, λίγειαι, Λίγυες.

imagine that they know about the nature of things, when they don't know about them, and, not having come to an understanding at first because they think that they know, they end, as might be expected, in contradicting one another and themselves. Now you and I must not be guilty of this fundamental error which we condemn in others; but as our question is whether the lover or non-lover is to be preferred, let us first of all agree in defining the nature and power of love, and then, keeping our eyes upon the definition and to this appealing, let us further enquire whether love brings advantage or disadvantage.

'Every one sees that love is a desire, and we know also that non-lovers desire the beautiful and good. Now in what way is the lover to be distinguished from the non-lover? Let us note that in every one of us there are two guiding and ruling principles which lead us whither they will; one is the natural desire of pleasure, the other is an acquired opinion which aspires after the best; and these two are sometimes in harmony and then again at war, and sometimes the one, sometimes the other conquers. When opinion by the help of reason leads us to the best, the conquering principle is called temperance; but when desire, which is devoid of reason, rules in us and drags us to pleasure, that power of misrule is called excess. Now excess has many names, and many members, and many forms, and any of these forms when very marked gives a name, neither honourable nor creditable, to the bearer of the name. The desire of eating, for example, which gets the better of the higher reason and the other desires, is called gluttony, and he who is possessed by it is called a glutton; the tyrannical desire of drink, which inclines the possessor of the desire to drink, has a name which is only too obvious, and there can be as little doubt by what name any other appetite of the same family would be called; – it will be the name of that which happens to be dominant. And now I think that you will perceive the drift of my discourse; but as every spoken word is in a manner plainer than the unspoken, I had better say further that the irrational desire which overcomes the tendency of opinion towards right, and is led away to the enjoyment of beauty, and especially of personal beauty, by the desires which are her own kindred – that supreme

desire, I say, which by leading[47] conquers and by the force of passion is reinforced, from this very force, receiving a name, is called love (ἐρρωμέ-νως ἔρως).'

And now, dear Phaedrus, I shall pause for an instant to ask whether you do not think me, as I appear to myself, inspired?

PHAEDR. Yes, Socrates, you seem to have a very unusual flow of words.

SOC. Listen to me, then, in silence; for surely the place is holy; so that you must not wonder, if, as I proceed, I appear to be in a divine fury, for already I am getting into dithyrambics.

PHAEDR. Nothing can be truer.

SOC. The responsibility rests with you. But hear what follows, and perhaps the fit may be averted; all is in their hands above. I will go on talking to my youth. Listen:

Thus, my friend, we have declared and defined the nature of the subject. Keeping the definition in view, let us now enquire what advantage or disadvantage is likely to ensue from the lover or the non-lover to him who accepts their advances.

He who is the victim of his passions and the slave of pleasure will of course desire to make his beloved as agreeable to himself as possible. Now to him who has a mind diseased anything is agreeable which is not opposed to him, but that which is equal or superior is hateful to him, and therefore the lover will not brook any superiority or equality on the part of his beloved; he is always employed in reducing him to inferiority. And the ignorant is the inferior of the wise, the coward of the brave, the slow of speech of the speaker, the dull of the clever. These, and not these only, are the mental defects of the beloved; – defects which, when implanted by nature, are necessarily a delight to the lover, and when not implanted, he must contrive to implant them in him, if he would not be deprived of his fleeting joy. And therefore he cannot help being jealous, and will debar his beloved from the advantages of society which would make a man of him, and especially from that society which would have given him wisdom, and thereby he cannot fail to do him great harm. That is to say, in his excessive fear lest he should come to be despised in his eyes he will be compelled to banish from him divine philosophy; and there is no greater injury which he can inflict

---

[47] Reading ἀγωγῇ

upon him than this. He will contrive that his beloved shall be wholly ignorant, and in everything shall look to him; he is to be the delight of the lover's heart, and a curse to himself. Verily, a lover is a profitable guardian and associate for him in all that relates to his mind.

Let us next see how his master, whose law of life is pleasure and not good, will keep and train the body of his servant. Will he not choose a beloved who is delicate rather than sturdy and strong? One brought up in shady bowers and not in the bright sun, a stranger to manly exercises and the sweat of toil, accustomed only to a soft and luxurious diet, instead of the hues of health having the colours of paint and ornament, and the rest of a piece? – such a life as any one can imagine and which I need not detail at length. But I may sum up all that I have to say in a word, and pass on. Such a person in war, or in any of the great crises of life, will be the anxiety of his friends and also of his lover, and certainly not the terror of his enemies; which nobody can deny.

And now let us tell what advantage or disadvantage the beloved will receive from the guardianship and society of his lover in the matter of his property; this is the next point to be considered. The lover will be the first to see what, indeed, will be sufficiently evident to all men, that he desires above all things to deprive his beloved of his dearest and best and holiest possessions, father, mother, kindred, friends, of all whom he thinks may be hinderers or reprovers of their most sweet converse; he will even cast a jealous eye upon his gold and silver or other property, because these make him a less easy prey, and when caught less manageable; hence he is of necessity displeased of his possession of them and rejoices at their loss; and he would like him to be wifeless, childless, homeless, as well; and the longer the better, for the longer he is all this, the longer he will enjoy him.

There are some sort of animals, such as flatterers, who are dangerous and mischievous enough, and yet nature has mingled a temporary pleasure and grace in their composition. You may say that a courtesan is hurtful, and disapprove of such creatures and their practices, and yet for the time they are very pleasant. But the lover is not only hurtful to his love; he is also an extremely disagreeable

companion. The old proverb says that 'birds of a feather flock together'; I suppose that equality of years inclines them to the same pleasures, and similarity begets friendship; yet you may have more than enough even of this; and verily constraint is always said to be grievous. Now the lover is not only unlike his beloved, but he forces himself upon him. For he is old and his love is young, and neither day nor night will he leave him if he can help; necessity and the sting of desire drive him on, and allure him with the pleasure which he receives from seeing, hearing, touching, perceiving him in every way. And therefore he is delighted to fasten upon him and to minister to him. But what pleasure or consolation can the beloved be receiving all this time? Must he not feel the extremity of disgust when he looks at an old shrivelled face and the remainder to match, which even in a description is disagreeable, and quite detestable when he is forced into daily contact with his lover; moreover he is jealously watched and guarded against everything and everybody, and has to hear misplaced and exaggerated praises of himself, and censures equally inappropriate, which are intolerable when the man is sober, and, besides being intolerable, are published all over the world in all their indelicacy and wearisomeness when he is drunk.

And not only while his love continues is he mischievous and unpleasant, but when his love ceases he becomes a perfidious enemy of him on whom he showered his oaths and prayers and promises, and yet could hardly prevail upon him to tolerate the tedium of his company even from motives of interest. The hour of payment arrives, and now he is the servant of another master; instead of love and infatuation, wisdom and temperance are his bosom's lords; but the beloved has not discovered the change which has taken place in him, when he asks for a return and recalls to his recollection former sayings and doings; he believes himself to be speaking to the same person, and the other, not having the courage to confess the truth, and not knowing how to fulfil the oaths and promises which he made when under the dominion of folly, and having now grown wise and temperate, does not want to do as he did or to be as he was before. And so he runs away and is constrained to be a defaulter; the oyster-shell[48] has fallen with the other side uppermost – he changes pursuit into

---

[48] In allusion to a game in which two parties fled or pursued according as an oyster-shell which was thrown into the air fell with the dark or light side uppermost.

flight, while the other is compelled to follow him with passion and imprecation not knowing that he ought never from the first to have accepted a demented lover instead of a sensible non-lover; and that in making such a choice he was giving himself up to a faithless, morose, envious, disagreeable being, hurtful to his estate, hurtful to his bodily health, and still more hurtful to the cultivation of his mind, than which there neither is nor ever will be anything more honoured in the eyes both of gods and men. Consider this, fair youth, and know that in the friendship of the lover there is no real kindness; he has an appetite and wants to feed upon you:

'As wolves love lambs so lovers love their loves.'

But I told you so, I am speaking in verse, and therefore I had better make an end; enough.

PHAEDR. I thought that you were only half-way and were going to make a similar speech about all the advantages of accepting the non-lover. Why do you not proceed?

SOC. Does not your simplicity observe that I have got out of dithyrambics into heroics, when only uttering a censure on the lover? And if I am to add the praises of the non-lover, what will become of me? Do you not perceive that I am already overtaken by the Nymphs to whom you have mischievously exposed me? And therefore I will only add that the non-lover has all the advantages in which the lover is accused of being deficient. And now I will say no more; there has been enough of both of them. Leaving the tale to its fate, I will cross the river and make the best of my way home, lest a worse thing be inflicted upon me by you.

PHAEDR. Not yet, Socrates; not until the heat of the day has passed; do you not see that the hour is almost noon? there is the midday sun standing still, as people say, in the meridian. Let us rather stay and talk over what has been said, and then return in the cool.

SOC. Your love of discourse, Phaedrus, is superhuman, simply marvellous, and I do not believe that there is any one of your contemporaries who has either made or in one way or another has compelled others to make an equal number of speeches. I would except Simmias the Theban, but all the rest are far behind you. And now I do verily believe that you have been the cause of another.

PHAEDR. That is good news. But what do you mean?

SOC. I mean to say that as I was about to cross the stream the usual sign was given to me, – that sign which always forbids, but never bids, me to do anything which I am going to do; and I thought that I heard a voice saying in my ear that I had been guilty of impiety, and that I must not go away until I had made an atonement. Now I am a diviner, though not a very good one, but I have enough religion for my own use, as you might say of a bad writer – his writing is good enough for him; and I am beginning to see that I was in error. O my friend, how prophetic is the human soul! At the time I had a sort of misgiving, and, like Ibycus, 'I was troubled; I feared that I might be buying honour from men at the price of sinning against the gods.' Now I recognize my error.

PHAEDR. What error?

SOC. That was a dreadful speech which you brought with you, and you made me utter one as bad.

PHAEDR. How so?

SOC. It was foolish, I say, – to a certain extent, impious; can anything be more dreadful?

PHAEDR. Nothing, if the speech was really such as you describe.

SOC. Well, and is not Eros the son of Aphrodite, and a god?

PHAEDR. So men say.

SOC. But that was not acknowledged by Lysias in his speech, nor by you in that other speech which you by a charm drew from my lips. For if love be, as he surely is, a divinity, he cannot be evil. Yet this was the error of both the speeches. There was also a simplicity about them which was refreshing; having no truth or honesty in them, nevertheless they pretended to be something, hoping to succeed in deceiving the manikins of earth and gain celebrity among them. Wherefore I must have a purgation. And I bethink me of an ancient purgation of mythological error which was devised, not by Homer, for he never had the wit to discover why he was blind, but by Stesichorus, who was a philosopher and knew the reason why; and therefore, when he lost his eyes, for that was the penalty which was inflicted upon him for reviling the lovely Helen, he at once purged himself. And the purgation was a recantation, which began thus,

'False is that word of mine – the truth is that thou didst not embark in ships, nor ever go to the walls of Troy;'

and when he had completed his poem, which is called 'the recantation,' immediately his sight returned to him. Now I will be wiser than either Stesichorus or Homer, in that I am going to make my recantation for reviling love before I suffer; and this I will attempt, not as before, veiled and ashamed, but with forehead bold and bare.

PHAEDR. Nothing could be more agreeable to me than to hear you say so.

SOC. Only think, my good Phaedrus, what an utter want of delicacy was shown in the two discourses; I mean, in my own and in that which you recited out of the book. Would not any one who was himself of a noble and gentle nature, and who loved or ever had loved a nature like his own, when we tell of the petty causes of lovers' jealousies, and of their exceeding animosities, and of the injuries which they do to their beloved, have imagined that our ideas of love were taken from some haunt of sailors to which good manners were unknown – he would certainly never have admitted the justice of our censure?

PHAEDR. I dare say not, Socrates.

SOC. Therefore, because I blush at the thought of this person, and also because I am afraid of Love himself, I desire to wash the brine out of my ears with water from the spring; and I would counsel Lysias not to delay, but to write another discourse, which shall prove that 'ceteris paribus' the lover ought to be accepted rather than the non-lover.

PHAEDR. Be assured that he shall. You shall speak the praises of the lover, and Lysias shall be compelled by me to write another discourse on the same theme.

SOC. You will be true to your nature in that, and therefore I believe you.

PHAEDR. Speak, and fear not.

SOC. But where is the fair youth whom I was addressing before, and who ought to listen now; lest, if he hear me not, he should accept a non-lover before he knows what he is doing?

PHAEDR. He is close at hand, and always at your service.

SOC. Know then, fair youth, that the former discourse was the word of Phaedrus, the son of Vain Man, who dwells in the city of Myrrhina

(Myrrhinusius). And this which I am about to utter is the recantation of Stesichorus the son of Godly Man (Euphemus), who comes from the town of Desire (Himera), and is to the following effect: 'I told a lie when I said' that the beloved ought to accept the non-lover when he might have the lover, because the one is sane, and the other mad. It might be so if madness were simply an evil; but there is also a madness which is a divine gift, and the source of the chiefest blessings granted to men. For prophecy is a madness, and the prophetess at Delphi and the priestesses at Dodona when out of their senses have conferred great benefits on Hellas, both in public and private life, but when in their senses few or none. And I might also tell you how the Sibyl and other inspired persons have given to many an one many an intimation of the future which has saved them from falling. But it would be tedious to speak of what every one knows.

There will be more reason in appealing to the ancient inventors of names,[49] who would never have connected prophecy (μαντικὴ), which foretells the future and is the noblest of arts, with madness (μανικὴ), or called them both by the same name, if they had deemed madness to be a disgrace or dishonour; – they must have thought that there was an inspired madness which was a noble thing; for the two words, μαντικὴ and μανικὴ, are really the same, and the letter τ is only a modern and tasteless insertion. And this is confirmed by the name which was given by them to the rational investigation of futurity, whether made by the help of birds or of other signs – this, for as much as it is an art which supplies from the reasoning faculty mind (νοῦς) and information (ἱστορία) to human thought (οἴησις), they originally termed οἰονοιστικὴ, but the word has been lately altered and made sonorous by the modern introduction of the letter Omega (οἰονοιστικὴ and οἰωνιστικὴ), and in proportion as prophecy (μαντικὴ) is more perfect and august than augury, both in name and fact, in the same proportion, as the ancients testify, is madness superior to a sane mind (σωφροσύνη), for the one is only of human, but the other of divine origin. Again, where plagues and mightiest woes have bred in certain families, owing to some ancient blood-guiltiness, there madness has entered with holy prayers and rites, and by inspired utterances found a way of

---

[49] Cp. Cratylus 388 foll.

deliverance for those who are in need; and he who has part in this gift, and is truly possessed and duly out of his mind, is by the use of purifications and mysteries made whole and exempt from evil, future as well as present, and has a release from the calamity which was afflicting him. The third kind is the madness of those who are possessed by the Muses; which taking hold of a delicate and virgin soul, and there inspiring frenzy, awakens lyrical and all other numbers; with these adorning the myriad actions of ancient heroes for the instruction of posterity. But he who, having no touch of the Muses' madness in his soul, comes to the door and thinks that he will get into the temple by the help of art – he, I say, and his poetry are not admitted; the sane man disappears and is nowhere when he enters into rivalry with the madman.

I might tell of many other noble deeds which have sprung from inspired madness. And therefore, let no one frighten or flutter us by saying that the temperate friend is to be chosen rather than the inspired, but let him further show that love is not sent by the gods for any good to lover or beloved; if he can do so we will allow him to carry off the palm. And we, on our part, will prove in answer to him that the madness of love is the greatest of heaven's blessings, and the proof shall be one which the wise will receive, and the witling disbelieve. But first of all, let us view the affections and actions of the soul divine and human, and try to ascertain the truth about them. The beginning of our proof is as follows:

[50]The soul through all her being is immortal, for that which is ever in motion is immortal; but that which moves another and is moved by another, in ceasing to move ceases also to live. Only the self-moving, never leaving self, never ceases to move, and is the fountain and beginning of motion to all that moves besides. Now, the beginning is unbegotten, for that which is begotten has a beginning; but the beginning is begotten of nothing, for if it were begotten of something, then the begotten would not come from a beginning. But if unbegotten, it must also be indestructible; for if beginning were destroyed, there could be no beginning out of anything, nor anything out of a beginning; and all things must have a beginning. And therefore the self-moving is the beginning of motion; and this can neither be destroyed nor begotten, else the whole heavens and all creation would collapse and stand still, and never again have motion or birth. But if the self-moving is proved to be immortal, he who affirms that self-motion is the very idea and essence of the soul will not be put to confusion. For the body which is moved from without is soulless; but that which is moved from within has a soul, for such is the nature of the soul. But if this be true, must not the soul be the self-moving, and therefore of necessity unbegotten and immortal? Enough of the soul's immortality.

Of the nature of the soul, though her true form be ever a theme of large and more than mortal discourse, let me speak briefly, and in a figure. And let the figure be composite – a pair of winged horses and a charioteer. Now the winged horses and the charioteers of the gods are all of them noble and of noble descent, but those of other races are mixed; the human charioteer drives his in a pair; and one of them is noble and of noble breed, and the other is ignoble and of ignoble breed; and the driving of them of necessity gives a great deal of trouble to him. I will endeavour to explain to you in what way the mortal differs from the immortal creature. The soul in her totality has the care of inanimate being everywhere, and traverses the whole heaven in divers forms appearing: – when perfect and fully winged she soars upward, and orders the whole world; whereas the imperfect soul, losing her wings and drooping in her flight at last settles on the solid ground – there, finding a home, she receives an earthly frame which appears to be self-moved, but is really moved by her power; and this composition of soul and body is called a living and mortal creature. For immortal no such union can be reasonably believed to be; although fancy, not having seen nor surely known the nature of God, may imagine an immortal creature having both a body and also a soul which are united throughout all time. Let that, however, be as God wills, and be spoken of acceptably to him. And now let us ask the reason why the soul loses her wings!

The wing is the corporeal element which is most akin to the divine, and which by nature tends to soar aloft and carry that which gravitates downwards into the upper region, which is the habitation of the gods. The divine is beauty, wisdom, goodness, and the like; and by these the

---

[50] Translated by Cic. Tus. Quaest. s. 24.

wing of the soul is nourished, and grows apace; but when fed upon evil and foulness and the opposite of good, wastes and falls away. Zeus, the mighty lord, holding the reins of a winged chariot, leads the way in heaven, ordering all and taking care of all; and there follows him the array of gods and demi-gods, marshalled in eleven bands; Hestia alone abides at home in the house of heaven; of the rest they who are reckoned among the princely twelve march in their appointed order. They see many blessed sights in the inner heaven, and there are many ways to and fro, along which the blessed gods are passing, every one doing his own work; he may follow who will and can, for jealousy has no place in the celestial choir. But when they go to banquet and festival, then they move up the steep to the top of the vault of heaven. The chariots of the gods in even poise, obeying the rein, glide rapidly; but the others labour, for the vicious steed goes heavily, weighing down the charioteer to the earth when his steed has not been thoroughly trained: – and this is the hour of agony and extremest conflict for the soul. For the immortals, when they are at the end of their course, go forth and stand upon the outside of heaven, and the revolution of the spheres carries them round, and they behold the things beyond. But of the heaven which is above the heavens, what earthly poet ever did or ever will sing worthily? It is such as I will describe; for I must dare to speak the truth, when truth is my theme. There abides the very being with which true knowledge is concerned; the colourless, formless, intangible essence, visible only to mind, the pilot of the soul. The divine intelligence, being nurtured upon mind and pure knowledge, and the intelligence of every soul which is capable of receiving the food proper to it, rejoices at beholding reality, and once more gazing upon truth, is replenished and made glad, until the revolution of the worlds brings her round again to the same place. In the revolution she beholds justice, and temperance, and knowledge absolute, not in the form of generation or of relation, which men call existence, but knowledge absolute in existence absolute; and beholding the other true existences in like manner, and feasting upon them, she passes down into the interior of the heavens and returns home; and there the charioteer, putting up his horses at the stall, gives them ambrosia to eat and nectar to drink.

Such is the life of the gods; but of other souls, that which follows God best and is likest to him lifts the head of the charioteer into the outer world, and is carried round in the revolution, troubled indeed by the steeds, and with difficulty beholding true being; while another only rises and falls and sees, and again fails to see by reason of the unruliness of the steeds. The rest of the souls are also longing after the upper world and they all follow, but not being strong enough they are carried round below the surface, plunging, treading on one another, each striving to be first; and there is confusion and perspiration and the extremity of effort; and many of them are lamed or have their wings broken through the ill-driving of the charioteers; and all of them after a fruitless toil, not having attained to the mysteries of true being, go away, and feed upon opinion. The reason why the souls exhibit this exceeding eagerness to behold the plain of truth is that pasturage is found there, which is suited to the highest part of the soul; and the wing on which the soul soars is nourished with this. And there is a law of Destiny, that the soul which attains any vision of truth in company with a god is preserved from harm until the next period, and if attaining always is always unharmed. But when she is unable to follow, and fails to behold the truth, and through some ill-hap sinks beneath the double load of forgetfulness and vice, and her wings fall from her and she drops to the ground, then the law ordains that this soul shall at her first birth pass, not into any other animal, but only into man; and the soul which has seen most of truth shall come to the birth as a philosopher, or artist, or some musical and loving nature; that which has seen truth in the second degree shall be some righteous king or warrior chief; the soul which is of the third class shall be a politician, or economist, or trader; the fourth shall be a lover of gymnastic toils, or a physician; the fifth shall lead the life of a prophet or hierophant; to the sixth the character of a poet or some other imitative artist will be assigned; to the seventh the life of an artisan or husbandman; to the eighth that of a sophist or demagogue; to the ninth that of a tyrant; – all these are states of probation, in which he who does righteously improves, and he who does unrighteously, deteriorates his lot.

Ten thousand years must elapse before the soul of each one can return to the place from whence she came, for she cannot grow her wings in less;

only the soul of a philosopher, guileless and true, or the soul of a lover, who is not devoid of philosophy, may acquire wings in the third of the recurring periods of a thousand years; he is distinguished from the ordinary good man who gains wings in three thousand years: – and they who choose this life three times in succession have wings given them, and go away at the end of three thousand years. But the others[51] receive judgment when they have completed their first life, and after the judgment they go, some of them to the houses of correction which are under the earth, and are punished; others to some place in heaven whither they are lightly borne by justice, and there they live in a manner worthy of the life which they led here when in the form of men. And at the end of the first thousand years the good souls and also the evil souls both come to draw lots and choose their second life, and they may take any which they please. The soul of a man may pass into the life of a beast, or from the beast return again into the man. But the soul which has never seen the truth will not pass into the human form. For a man must have intelligence of universals, and be able to proceed from the many particulars of sense to one conception of reason; – this is the recollection of those things which our soul once saw while following God – when regardless of that which we now call being she raised her head up towards the true being. And therefore the mind of the philosopher alone has wings; and this is just, for he is always, according to the measure of his abilities, clinging in recollection to those things in which God abides, and in beholding which He is what He is. And he who employs aright these memories is ever being initiated into perfect mysteries and alone becomes truly perfect. But, as he forgets earthly interests and is rapt in the divine, the vulgar deem him mad, and rebuke him; they do not see that he is inspired.

Thus far I have been speaking of the fourth and last kind of madness, which is imputed to him who, when he sees the beauty of earth, is transported with the recollection of the true beauty; he would like to fly away, but he cannot; he is like a bird fluttering and looking upward and careless of the world below; and he is therefore thought to be mad. And I have shown this of all inspirations to be the noblest and highest and the offspring of the highest to him who has or shares in it, and that he who loves the beautiful is called a lover because he partakes of it. For, as has been already said, every soul of man has in the way of nature beheld true being; this was the condition of her passing into the form of man. But all souls do not easily recall the things of the other world; they may have seen them for a short time only or they may have been unfortunate in their earthly lot, and, having had their hearts turned to unrighteousness through some corrupting influence, they may have lost the memory of the holy things which once they saw. Few only retain an adequate remembrance of them; and they, when they behold here any image of that other world, are rapt in amazement; but they are ignorant of what this rapture means, because they do not clearly perceive. For there is no light of justice or temperance or any of the higher ideas which are precious to souls in the earthly copies of them: they are seen through a glass dimly; and there are few who, going to the images, behold in them the realities, and these only with difficulty. There was a time when with the rest of the happy band they saw beauty shining in brightness, – we philosophers following in the train of Zeus, others in company with other gods; and then we beheld the beatific vision and were initiated into a mystery which may be truly called most blessed, celebrated by us in our state of innocence, before we had any experience of evils to come, when we were admitted to the sight of apparitions innocent and simple and calm and happy, which we beheld shining in pure light, pure ourselves and not yet enshrined in that living tomb which we carry about, now that we are imprisoned in the body, like an oyster in his shell. Let me linger over the memory of scenes which have passed away.

But of beauty, I repeat again that we saw her there shining in company with the celestial forms; and coming to earth we find her here too, shining in clearness through the clearest aperture of sense. For sight is the most piercing of our bodily senses; though not by that is wisdom seen; her loveliness would have been transporting if there had been a visible image of her, and the other ideas, if they had visible counterparts, would be equally lovely. But this is the privilege of beauty,

---

[51] The philosopher alone is not subject to judgment (κρίσις), for he has never lost the vision of truth.

that being the loveliest she is also the most palpable to sight. Now he who is not newly initiated or who has become corrupted, does not easily rise out of this world to the sight of true beauty in the other; he looks only at her earthly namesake, and instead of being awed at the sight of her, he is given over to pleasure, and like a brutish beast he rushes on to enjoy and beget; he consorts with wantonness, and is not afraid or ashamed of pursuing pleasure in violation of nature. But he whose initiation is recent, and who has been the spectator of many glories in the other world, is amazed when he sees any one having a god-like face or form, which is the expression of divine beauty; and at first a shudder runs through him, and again the old awe steals over him; then looking upon the face of his beloved as of a god he reverences him, and if he were not afraid of being thought a downright madman, he would sacrifice to his beloved as to the image of a god; then while he gazes on him there is a sort of reaction, and the shudder passes into an unusual heat and perspiration; for, as he receives the effluence of beauty through the eyes, the wing moistens and he warms. And as he warms, the parts out of which the wing grew, and which had been hitherto closed and rigid, and had prevented the wing from shooting forth, are melted, and as nourishment streams upon him, the lower end of the wings begins to swell and grow from the root upwards; and the growth extends under the whole soul – for once the whole was winged. During this process the whole soul is all in a state of ebullition and effervescence, – which may be compared to the irritation and uneasiness in the gums at the time of cutting teeth, – bubbles up, and has a feeling of uneasiness and tickling; but when in like manner the soul is beginning to grow wings, the beauty of the beloved meets her eye and she receives the sensible warm motion of particles which flow towards her, therefore called emotion (ἵμερος), and is refreshed and warmed by them, and then she ceases from her pain with joy. But when she is parted from her beloved and her moisture fails, then the orifices of the passage out of which the wing shoots dry up and close, and intercept the germ of the wing; which, being shut up with the emotion, throbbing as with the pulsations of an artery, pricks the aperture which is nearest, until at length the entire soul is pierced

and maddened and pained, and at the recollection of beauty is again delighted. And from both of them together the soul is oppressed at the strangeness of her condition, and is in a great strait and excitement, and in her madness can neither sleep by night nor abide in her place by day. And wherever she thinks that she will behold the beautiful one, thither in her desire she runs. And when she has seen him, and bathed herself in the waters of beauty, her constraint is loosened, and she is refreshed, and has no more pangs and pains; and this is the sweetest of all pleasures at the time, and is the reason why the soul of the lover will never forsake his beautiful one, whom he esteems above all; he has forgotten mother and brethren and companions, and he thinks nothing of the neglect and loss of his property; the rules and proprieties of life, on which he formerly prided himself, he now despises, and is ready to sleep like a servant, wherever he is allowed, as near as he can to his desired one, who is the object of his worship, and the physician who can alone assuage the greatness of his pain. And this state, my dear imaginary youth to whom I am talking, is by men called love, and among the gods has a name at which you, in your simplicity, may be inclined to mock; there are two lines in the apocryphal writings of Homer in which the name occurs. One of them is rather outrageous, and not altogether metrical. They are as follows:

'Mortals call him fluttering love,
But the immortals call him winged one,
Because the growing of wings[52] is a necessity
to him.'

You may believe this, but not unless you like. At any rate the loves of lovers and their causes are such as I have described.

Now the lover who is taken to be the attendant of Zeus is better able to bear the winged god, and can ensure a heavier burden; but the attendants and companions of Ares, when under the influence of love, if they fancy that they have been at all wronged, are ready to kill and put an end to themselves and their beloved. And he who follows in the train of any other god while he is unspoiled and the impression lasts, honours and imitates him, as far as he is able; and after the manner of his god he behaves in his intercourse with his beloved and with the rest of the world during the first period of his earthly exist-

[52] Or, reading πτερόφοιτον, 'the movement of wings.'

ence. Every one chooses his love from the ranks
of beauty according to his character, and this he
makes his god, and fashions and adorns as a sort
of image which he is to fall down and worship.
The followers of Zeus desire that their beloved
should have a soul like him; and therefore they
seek out some one of a philosophical and imperial nature, and when they have found him and
loved him, they do all they can to confirm such a
nature in him, and if they have no experience of
such a disposition hitherto, they learn of any one
who can teach them, and themselves follow in
the same way. And they have the less difficulty in
finding the nature of their own god in themselves, because they have been compelled to gaze
intensely on him; their recollection clings to
him, and they become possessed of him, and
receive from him their character and disposition,
so far as man can participate in God. The qualities of their god they attribute to the beloved,
wherefore they love him all the more, and if, like
the Bacchic Nymphs, they draw inspiration from
Zeus, they pour out their own fountain upon
him, wanting to make him as like as possible to
their own god. But those who are the followers
of Herè seek a royal love, and when they have
found him they do just the same with him; and
in like manner the followers of Apollo, and of
every other god walking in the ways of their
god, seek a love who is to be made like him
whom they serve, and when they have found
him, they themselves imitate their god, and persuade their love to do the same, and educate him
into the manner and nature of the god as far as
they each can; for no feelings of envy or jealousy
are entertained by them towards their beloved,
but they do their utmost to create in him the
greatest likeness of themselves and of the god
whom they honour. Thus fair and blissful to the
beloved is the desire of the inspired lover, and
the initiation of which I speak into the mysteries
of true love, if he be captured by the lover and
their purpose is effected. Now the beloved is
taken captive in the following manner:

As I said at the beginning of this tale, I divided
each soul into three – two horses and a charioteer;
and one of the horses was good and the other bad:
the division may remain, but I have not yet
explained in what the goodness or badness of
either consists, and to that I will proceed. The

right-hand horse is upright and cleanly made; he
has a lofty neck and an aquiline nose; his colour is
white, and his eyes dark; he is a lover of honour
and modesty and temperance, and the follower
of true glory; he needs no touch of the whip, but
is guided by word and admonition only. The other
is a crooked lumbering animal, put together
anyhow; he has a short thick neck; he is flat-faced
and of a dark colour, with grey eyes and blood-
red complexion;[53] the mate of insolence and
pride, shag-eared and deaf, hardly yielding to whip
and spur. Now when the charioteer beholds the
vision of love, and has his whole soul warmed
through sense, and is full of the prickings and
ticklings of desire, the obedient steed, then as
always under the government of shame, refrains
from leaping on the beloved; but the other, heedless of the pricks and of the blows of the whip,
plunges and runs away, giving all manner of trouble to his companion and the charioteer, whom
he forces to approach the beloved and to remember the joys of love. They at first indignantly
oppose him and will not be urged on to do terrible and unlawful deeds; but at last, when he per-
sists in plaguing them, they yield and agree to do
as he bids them. And now they are at the spot and
behold the flashing beauty of the beloved; which
when the charioteer sees, his memory is carried
to the true beauty, whom he beholds in company
with Modesty like an image placed upon a holy
pedestal. He sees her, but he is afraid and falls
backwards in adoration, and by his fall is compelled to pull back the reins with such violence as
to bring both the steeds on their haunches, the
one willing and unresisting, the unruly one very
unwilling; and when they have gone back a little,
the one is overcome with shame and wonder, and
his whole soul is bathed in perspiration; the other,
when the pain is over which the bridle and the fall
had given him, having with difficulty taken
breath, is full of wrath and reproaches, which he
heaps upon the charioteer and his fellow-steed,
for want of courage and manhood, declaring that
they have been false to their agreement and guilty
of desertion. Again they refuse, and again he
urges them on, and will scarce yield to their
prayer that he would wait until another time.
When the appointed hour comes, they make as if
they had forgotten, and he reminds them, fighting and neighing and dragging them on, until at

[53] Or with grey and blood-shot eyes.

length he, on the same thoughts intent, forces them to draw near again. And when they are near he stoops his head and puts up his tail, and takes the bit in his teeth and pulls shamelessly. Then the charioteer is worse off than ever; he falls back like a racer at the barrier, and with a still more violent wrench drags the bit out of the teeth of the wild steed and covers his abusive tongue and jaws with blood, and forces his legs and haunches to the ground and punishes him sorely. And when this has happened several times and the villain has ceased from his wanton way, he is tamed and humbled and follows the will of the charioteer, and when he sees the beautiful one he is ready to die of fear. And from that time forward the soul of the lover follows the beloved in modesty and holy fear.

And so the beloved who, like a god, has received every true and loyal service from his lover, not in pretence but in reality, being also himself of a nature friendly to his admirer,[54] if in former days he has blushed to own his passion and turned away his lover, because his youthful companions or others slanderously told him that he would be disgraced, now as years advance, at the appointed age and time, is led to receive him into communion. For fate which has ordained that there shall be no friendship among the evil has also ordained that there shall ever be friendship among the good. And the beloved when he has received him into communion and intimacy, is quite amazed at the good-will of the lover; he recognises that the inspired friend is worth all other friends or kinsmen; they have nothing of friendship in them worthy to be compared with his. And when his feeling continues and he is nearer to him and embraces him, in gymnastic exercises and at other times of meeting, then the fountain of that stream, which Zeus when he was in love with Ganymede named Desire, overflows upon the lover, and some enters into his soul, and some when he is filled flows out again; and as a breeze or an echo rebounds from the smooth rocks and returns whence it came, so does the stream of beauty, passing through the eyes which are the windows of the soul, come back to the beautiful one; there arriving and quickening the passages of the wings, watering them and inclining them to grow, and filling the soul of the beloved also with love. And

thus he loves, but he knows not what; he does not understand and cannot explain his own state; he appears to have caught the infection of blindness from another; the lover is his mirror in whom he is beholding himself, but he is not aware of this. When he is with the lover, both cease from their pain, but when he is away then he longs as he is longed for, and has love's image, love for love (Anteros) lodging in his breast, which he calls and believes to be not love but friendship only, and his desire is as the desire of the other, but weaker; he wants to see him, touch him, kiss, embrace him, and probably not long afterwards his desire is accomplished. When they meet, the wanton steed of the lover has a word to say to the charioteer; he would like to have a little pleasure in return for many pains, but the wanton steed of the beloved says not a word, for he is bursting with passion which he understands not; – he throws his arms round the lover and embraces him as his dearest friend; and, when they are side by side, he is not in a state in which he can refuse the lover anything, if he ask him; although his fellow-steed and the charioteer oppose him with the arguments of shame and reason. After this their happiness depends upon their self-control; if the better elements of the mind which lead to order and philosophy prevail, then they pass their life here in happiness and harmony – masters of themselves and orderly – enslaving the vicious and emancipating the virtuous elements of the soul; and when the end comes, they are light and winged for flight, having conquered in one of the three heavenly or truly Olympian victories; nor can human discipline or divine inspiration confer any greater blessing on man than this. If, on the other hand, they leave philosophy and lead the lower life of ambition, then probably, after wine or in some other careless hour, the two wanton animals take the two souls when off their guard and bring them together, and they accomplish that desire of their hearts which to the many is bliss; and this having once enjoyed they continue to enjoy, yet rarely because they have not the approval of the whole soul. They too are dear, but not so dear to one another as the others, either at the time of their love or afterwards. They consider that they have given and taken from each other the most sacred pledges, and they may not break them and fall into enmity.

---

[54] Omitting εἰς ταὐτὸν ἄγει τὴν φιλίαν.

At last they pass out of the body, unwinged, but eager to soar, and thus obtain no mean reward of love and madness. For those who have once begun the heavenward pilgrimage may not go down again to darkness and the journey beneath the earth, but they live in light always; happy companions in their pilgrimage, and when the time comes at which they receive their wings they have the same plumage because of their love.

Thus great are the heavenly blessings which the friendship of a lover will confer upon you, my youth. Whereas the attachment of the non-lover, which is alloyed with a worldly prudence and has worldly and niggardly ways of doling out benefits, will breed in your soul those vulgar qualities which the populace applaud, will send you bowling round the earth during a period of nine thousand years, and leave you a fool in the world below.

And thus, dear Eros, I have made and paid my recantation, as well and as fairly as I could; more especially in the matter of the poetical figures which I was compelled to use, because Phaedrus would have them.[55] And now forgive the past and accept the present, and be gracious and merciful to me, and do not in thine anger deprive me of sight, or take from me the art of love which thou hast given me, but grant that I may be yet more esteemed in the eyes of the fair. And if Phaedrus or I myself said anything rude in our first speeches, blame Lysias, who is the father of the brat, and let us have no more of his progeny; bid him study philosophy, like his brother Polemarchus; and then his lover Phaedrus will no longer halt between two opinions, but will dedicate himself wholly to love and to philosophical discourses.

PHAEDR. I join in the prayer, Socrates, and say with you, if this be for my good, may your words come to pass. But why did you make your second oration so much finer than the first? I wonder why. And I begin to be afraid that I shall lose conceit of Lysias, and that he will appear tame in comparison, even if he be willing to put another as fine and as long as yours into the field, which I doubt. For quite lately one of your politicians was abusing him on this very account; and called him a 'speech-writer' again and again. So that a feeling

of pride may probably induce him to give up writing speeches.

SOC. What a very amusing notion! But I think, my young man, that you are much mistaken in your friend if you imagine that he is frightened at a little noise; and possibly, you think that his assailant was in earnest?

PHAEDR. I thought, Socrates, that he was. And you are aware that the greatest and most influential statesmen are ashamed of writing speeches and leaving them in a written form, lest they should be called Sophists by posterity.

SOC. You seem to be unconscious, Phaedrus, that the 'sweet elbow'[56] of the proverb is really the long arm of the Nile. And you appear to be equally unaware of the fact that this sweet elbow of theirs is also a long arm. For there is nothing of which our great politicians are so fond as of writing speeches and bequeathing them to posterity. And they add their admirers' names at the top of the writing, out of gratitude to them.

PHAEDR. What do you mean? I do not understand.

SOC. Why, do you not know that when a politician writes, he begins with the names of his approvers?

PHAEDR. How so?

SOC. Why, he begins in this manner: 'Be it enacted by the senate, the people, or both, on the motion of a certain person,' who is our author; and so putting on a serious face, he proceeds to display his own wisdom to his admirers in what is often a long and tedious composition. Now what is that sort of thing but a regular piece of authorship?

PHAEDR. True.

SOC. And if the law is finally approved, then the author leaves the theatre in high delight; but if the law is rejected and he is done out of his speech-making, and not thought good enough to write, then he and his party are in mourning.

PHAEDR. Very true.

SOC. So far are they from despising, or rather so highly do they value the practice of writing.

PHAEDR. No doubt.

SOC. And when the king or orator has the power, as Lycurgus or Solon or Darius had, of attaining an immortality or authorship in a state,

---

[55] See p. 196

[56] A proverb, like 'the grapes are sour,' applied to pleasures which cannot be had, meaning sweet things which, like the elbow, are out of the reach of the mouth. The promised pleasure turns out to be a long and tedious affair.

is he not thought by posterity when they see his compositions, and does he not think himself, while he is yet alive, to be a god?

PHAEDR. Very true.

SOC. Then do you think that any one of this class, however ill-disposed, would reproach Lysias with being an author?

PHAEDR. Not upon your view; for according to you he would be casting a slur upon his own favourite pursuit.

SOC. Any one may see that there is no disgrace in the mere fact of writing.

PHAEDR. Certainly not.

SOC. The disgrace begins when a man writes not well, but badly.

PHAEDR. Clearly.

SOC. And what is well and what is badly – need we ask Lysias, or any other poet or orator, who ever wrote or will write either a political or any other work, in metre or out of metre, poet or prose writer, to teach us this?

PHAEDR. Need we? For what should a man live if not for the pleasures of discourse? Surely not for the sake of bodily pleasures, which almost always have previous pain as a condition of them, and therefore are rightly called slavish.

SOC. There is time enough. And I believe that the grasshoppers chirruping after their manner in the heat of the sun over our heads are talking to one another and looking down at us. What would they say if they saw that we, like the many, are not conversing, but slumbering at mid-day, lulled by their voices, too indolent to think? Would they not have a right to laugh at us? They might imagine that we were slaves, who, coming to rest at a place of resort of theirs, like sheep lie asleep at noon around the well. But if they see us discoursing, and like Odysseus sailing past them, deaf to their siren voices, they may perhaps, out of respect, give us of the gifts which they receive from the gods that they may impart them to men.

PHAEDR. What gifts do you mean? I never heard of any.

SOC. A lover of music like yourself ought surely to have heard the story of the grasshoppers, who are said to have been human beings in an age before the Muses. And when the Muses came and song appeared they were ravished with delight; and singing always, never thought of eating and drinking, until at last in their forgetfulness they died. And now they live again in the grasshop-pers; and this is the return which the Muses make to them – they neither hunger, nor thirst, but from the hour of their birth are always singing, and never eating or drinking; and when they die they go and inform the Muses in heaven who honours them on earth. They win the love of Terpsichore for the dancers by their report of them; of Erato for the lovers, and of the other Muses for those who do them honour, according to the several ways of honouring them; – of Calliope the eldest Muse and of Urania who is next to her, for the philosophers, of whose music the grasshoppers make report to them; for these are the Muses who are chiefly concerned with heaven and thought, divine as well as human, and they have the sweetest utterance. For many reasons, then, we ought always to talk and not to sleep at mid-day.

PHAEDR. Let us talk.

SOC. Shall we discuss the rules of writing and speech as we were proposing?

PHAEDR. Very good.

SOC. In good speaking should not the mind of the speaker know the truth of the matter about which he is going to speak?

PHAEDR. And yet, Socrates, I have heard that he who would be an orator has nothing to do with true justice, but only with that which is likely to be approved by the many who sit in judgment; nor with the truly good or honourable, but only with opinion about them, and that from opinion comes persuasion, and not from the truth.

SOC. The words of the wise are not to be set aside; for there is probably something in them; and therefore the meaning of this saying is not hastily to be dismissed.

PHAEDR. Very true.

SOC. Let us put the matter thus: – Suppose that I persuaded you to buy a horse and go to the wars. Neither of us knew what a horse was like, but I knew that you believed a horse to be of tame animals the one which has the longest ears.

PHAEDR. That would be ridiculous.

SOC. There is something more ridiculous coming: – Suppose, further, that in sober earnest I, having persuaded you of this, went and composed a speech in honour of an ass, whom I entitled a horse beginning: 'A noble animal and a most useful possession, especially in war, and you may get on his back and fight, and he will carry baggage or anything.'

PHAEDR. How ridiculous!

SOC. Ridiculous! Yes; but is not even a ridiculous friend better that a cunning enemy?

PHAEDR. Certainly.

SOC. And when the orator instead of putting an ass in the place of a horse puts good for evil being himself as ignorant of their true nature as the city on which he imposes is ignorant; and having studied the notions of the multitude, falsely persuades them not about 'the shadow of an ass,' which he confounds with a horse, but about good which he confounds with evil, – what will be the harvest which rhetoric will be likely to gather after the sowing of that seed?

PHAEDR. The reverse of good.

SOC. But perhaps rhetoric has been getting too roughly handled by us, and she might answer: What amazing nonsense you are talking! As if I forced any man to learn to speak in ignorance of the truth! Whatever my advice may be worth, I should have told him to arrive at the truth first, and then come to me. At the same time I boldly assert that mere knowledge of the truth will not give you the art of persuasion.

PHAEDR. There is reason in the lady's defence of herself.

SOC. Quite true; if only the other arguments which remain to be brought up bear her witness that she is an art at all. But I seem to hear them arraying themselves on the opposite side, declaring that she speaks falsely, and that rhetoric is a mere routine and trick, not an art. Lo! a Spartan appears, and says that there never is nor ever will be a real art of speaking which is divorced from the truth.

PHAEDR. And what are these arguments, Socrates? Bring them out that we may examine them.

SOC. Come out, fair children, and convince Phaedrus, who is the father of similar beauties, that he will never be able to speak about anything as he ought to speak unless he have a knowledge of philosophy. And let Phaedrus answer you.

PHAEDR. Put the question.

SOC. Is not rhetoric, taken generally, a universal art of enchanting the mind by arguments; which is practised not only in courts and public assemblies, but in private houses also, having to do with all matters, great as well as small, good and bad alike, and is in all equally right, and equally to be esteemed – that is what you have heard?

PHAEDR. Nay, not exactly that; I should say rather that I have heard the art confined to speaking and writing in lawsuits, and to speaking in public assemblies – not extended farther.

SOC. Then I suppose that you have only heard of the rhetoric of Nestor and Odysseus, which they composed in their leisure hours when at Troy, and never of the rhetoric of Palamedes?

PHAEDR. No more than of Nestor and Odysseus, unless Gorgias is your Nestor, and Thrasymachus or Theodorus your Odysseus.

SOC. Perhaps that is my meaning. But let us leave them. And do you tell me, instead, what are plaintiff and defendant doing in a law-court – are they not contending?

PHAEDR. Exactly so.

SOC. About the just and unjust – that is the matter in dispute?

PHAEDR. Yes.

SOC. And a professor of the art will make the same thing appear to the same persons to be at one time just, at another time, if he is so inclined, to be unjust?

PHAEDR. Exactly.

SOC. And when he speaks in the assembly, he will make the same things seem good to the city at one time, and at another time the reverse of good?

PHAEDR. That is true.

SOC. Have we not heard of the Eleatic Palamedes (Zeno), who has an art of speaking by which he makes the same things appear to his hearers like and unlike, one and many, at rest and in motion?

PHAEDR. Very true.

SOC. The art of disputation, then, is not confined to the courts and the assembly, but is one and the same in every use of language; this is the art, if there be such an art, which is able to find a likeness of everything to which a likeness can be found, and draws into the light of day the likenesses and disguises which are used by others?

PHAEDR. How do you mean?

SOC. Let me put the matter thus: When will there be more chance of deception – when the difference is large or small?

PHAEDR. When the difference is small.

SOC. And you will be less likely to be discovered in passing by degrees into the other extreme than when you go all at once?

PHAEDR. Of course.

SOC. He, then, who would deceive others, and not be deceived, must exactly know the real likenesses and differences of things?

PHAEDR. He must.

SOC. And if he is ignorant of the true nature of any subject, how can he detect the greater or less degree of likeness in other things to that of which by the hypothesis he is ignorant?

PHAEDR. He cannot.

SOC. And when men are deceived and their notions are at variance with realities, it is clear that the error slips in through resemblances?

PHAEDR. Yes, that is the way.

SOC. Then he who would be a master of the art must understand the real nature of everything; or he will never know either how to make the gradual departure from truth into the opposite of truth which is effected by the help of resemblances, or how to avoid it?

PHAEDR. He will not.

SOC. He then, who being ignorant of the truth aims at appearances, will only attain an art of rhetoric which is ridiculous and is not an art at all?

PHAEDR. That may be expected.

SOC. Shall I propose that we look for examples of art and want of art, according to our notion of them, in the speech of Lysias which you have in your hand, and in my own speech?

PHAEDR. Nothing could be better; and indeed I think that our previous argument has been too abstract and wanting in illustrations.

SOC. Yes; and the two speeches happen to afford a very good example of the way in which the speaker who knows the truth may, without any serious purpose, steal away the hearts of his hearers. This piece of good-fortune I attribute to the local deities; and perhaps, the prophets of the Muses who are singing over our heads may have imparted their inspiration to me. For I do not imagine that I have any rhetorical art of my own.

PHAEDR. Granted; if you will only please to get on.

SOC. Suppose that you read me the first words of Lysias' speech.

PHAEDR. 'You know how matters stand with me, and how, as I conceive, they might be arranged for our common interest; and I maintain that I ought not to fail in my suit, because I am not your lover. For lovers repent –'

SOC. Enough: – Now, shall I point out the rhetorical error of those words?

PHAEDR. Yes.

SOC. Every one is aware that about some things we are agreed, whereas about other things we differ.

PHAEDR. I think that I understand you; but will you explain yourself?

SOC. When any one speaks of iron and silver, is not the same thing present in the minds of all?

PHAEDR. Certainly.

SOC. But when any one speaks of justice and goodness we part company and are at odds with one another and with ourselves?

PHAEDR. Precisely.

SOC. Then in some things we agree, but not in others?

PHAEDR. That is true.

SOC. In which are we more likely to be deceived, and in which has rhetoric the greater power?

PHAEDR. Clearly, in the uncertain class.

SOC. Then the rhetorician ought to make a regular division, and acquire a distinct notion of both classes, as well of that in which the many err, as of that in which they do not err?

PHAEDR. He who made such a distinction would have an excellent principle.

SOC. Yes; and in the next place he must have a keen eye for the observation of particulars in speaking, and not make a mistake about the class to which they are to be referred.

PHAEDR. Certainly.

SOC. Now to which class does love belong – to the debatable or to the undisputed class?

PHAEDR. To the debatable, clearly; for if not, do you think that love would have allowed you to say as you did, that he is an evil both to the lover and the beloved, and also the greatest possible good?

SOC. Capital. But will you tell me whether I defined love at the beginning of my speech? for, having been in an ecstasy, I cannot well remember.

PHAEDR. Yes, indeed; that you did, and no mistake.

SOC. Then I perceive that the Nymphs of Achelous and Pan the son of Hermes, who inspired me, were far better rhetoricians than Lysias the son of Cephalus. Alas! how inferior to them he is! But perhaps I am mistaken; and Lysias at the commencement of his lover's speech did insist on our supposing love to be something or other which he fancied him to be, and according to this model he fashioned and framed the remainder of his discourse. Suppose we read his beginning over again:

PHAEDR. If you please; but you will not find what you want.

SOC. Read, that I may have his exact words.

PHAEDR. 'You know how matters stand with me, and how, as I conceive, they might be arranged for our common interest; and I maintain I ought not to fail in my suit because I am not your lover, for lovers repent of the kindnesses which they have shown, when their love is over.'

SOC. Here he appears to have done just the reverse of what he ought; for he has begun at the end, and is swimming on his back through the flood to the place of starting. His address to the fair youth begins where the lover would have ended. Am I not right, sweet Phaedrus?

PHAEDR. Yes, indeed, Socrates; he does begin at the end.

SOC. Then as to the other topics – are they not thrown down anyhow? Is there any principle in them. Why should the next topic follow next in order, or any other topic. I cannot help fancying in my ignorance that he wrote off boldly just what came into his head, but I dare say that you would recognize a rhetorical necessity in the succession of the several parts of the composition?

PHAEDR. You have too good an opinion of me if you think that I have any such insight into his principles of composition.

SOC. At any rate, you will allow that every discourse ought to be a living creature, having a body of its own and a head and feet; there should be a middle, beginning, and end, adapted to one another and to the whole?

PHAEDR. Certainly.

SOC. Can this be said of the discourse of Lysias? See whether you can find any more connexion in his words than in the epitaph which is said by some to have been inscribed on the grave of Midas the Phrygian.

PHAEDR. What is there remarkable in the epitaph?

SOC. It is as follows:

'I am a maiden of bronze and lie on the
    tomb of Midas;
So long as water flows and tall trees grow,
So long here on this spot by his sad tomb
    abiding,
I shall declare to passers-by that Midas sleeps
    below.'

Now in this rhyme whether a line comes first or comes last, as you will perceive, makes no difference.

PHAEDR. You are making fun of that oration of ours.

SOC. Well, I will say no more about your friend's speech lest I should give offence to you; although I think that it might furnish many other examples of what a man ought rather to avoid. But I will proceed to the other speech, which, as I think, is also suggestive to students of rhetoric.

PHAEDR. In what way?

SOC. The two speeches, as you may remember, were unlike; the one argued that the lover and the other that the non-lover ought to be accepted.

PHAEDR. And right manfully.

SOC. You should rather say 'madly;' and madness was the argument of them, for, as I said, 'love is a madness.'

PHAEDR. Yes.

SOC. And of madness there were two kinds; one produced by human infirmity, the other was a divine release of the soul from the yoke of custom and convention.

PHAEDR. True.

SOC. The divine madness was subdivided into four kinds, prophetic, initiatory, poetic, erotic, having four gods presiding over them; the first was the inspiration of Apollo, the second that of Dionysus, the third that of the Muses, the fourth that of Aphrodite and Eros. In the description of the last kind of madness, which was also said to be the best, we spoke of the affection of love in a figure, into which we introduced a tolerably credible and possibly true though partly erring myth, which was also a hymn in honour of Love, who is your lord and also mine, Phaedrus, and the guardian of fair children, and to him we sung the hymn in measured and solemn strain.

PHAEDR. I know that I had great pleasure in listening to you.

SOC. Let us take this instance and note how the transition was made from blame to praise.

PHAEDR. What do you mean?

SOC. I mean to say that the composition was mostly playful. Yet in these chance fancies of the hour were involved two principles of which we should be too glad to have a clearer description if art could give us one.

PHAEDR. What are they?

SOC. First, the comprehension of scattered particulars in one idea; as in our definition of love, which whether true or false certainly gave clearness and consistency to the discourse, the speaker should define his several notions and so make his meaning clear.

PHAEDR. What is the other principle, Socrates?

SOC. The second principle is that of division into species according to the natural formation, where the joint is, not breaking any part as a bad carver might. Just as our two discourses, alike assumed, first of all, a single form of unreason; and then, as the body which from being one becomes double and may be divided into a left side and right side, each having parts right and left of the same name – after this manner the speaker proceeded to divide the parts of the left side and did not desist until he found in them an evil or left-handed love which he justly reviled; and the other discourse leading us to the madness which lay on the right side, found another love, also having the same name, but divine, which the speaker held up before us and applauded and affirmed to be the author of the greatest benefits.

PHAEDR. Most true.

SOC. I am myself a great lover of these processes of division and generalization; they help me to speak and to think. And if I find any man who is able to see 'a One and Many' in nature, him I follow, and 'walk in his footsteps as if he were a god.' And those who have this art, I have hitherto been in the habit of calling dialecticians; but God knows whether the name is right or not. And I should like to know what name you would give to your or to Lysias' disciples, and whether this may not be that famous art of rhetoric which Thrasymachus and others teach and practise? Skilful speakers they are, and impart their skill to any who is willing to make kings of them and to bring gifts to them.

PHAEDR. Yes, they are royal men; but their art is not the same with the art of those whom you call, and rightly, in my opinion, dialecticians: – Still we are in the dark about rhetoric.

SOC. What do you mean? The remains of it, if there be anything remaining which can be brought under rules of art, must be a fine thing; and, at any rate, is not to be despised by you and me. But how much is left?

PHAEDR. There is a great deal surely to be found in books of rhetoric?

SOC. Yes; thank you for reminding me. – There is the exordium, showing how the speech should begin, if I remember rightly; that is what you mean – the niceties of the art?

PHAEDR. Yes.

SOC. Then follows the statement of facts, and upon that witnesses; thirdly, proofs; fourthly, probabilities are to come; the great Byzantine word-maker also speaks, if I am not mistaken, of confirmation and further confirmation.

PHAEDR. You mean the excellent Theodorus.

SOC. Yes; and he tells how refutation or further refutation is to be managed, whether in accusation or defence. I ought also to mention the illustrious Parian, Evenus, who first invented insinuations and indirect praises; and also indirect censures, which according to some he put into verse to help the memory. But shall I 'to dumb forgetfulness consign' Tisias and Gorgias, who are not ignorant that probability is superior to truth, and who by force of argument make the little appear great and the great little, disguise the new in old fashions and the old in new fashions, and have discovered forms for everything, either short or going on to infinity. I remember Prodicus laughing when I told him of this; he said that he had himself discovered the true rule of art, which was to be neither long nor short, but of a convenient length.

PHAEDR. Well done, Prodicus!

SOC. Then there is Hippias the Elean stranger, who probably agrees with him.

PHAEDR. Yes.

SOC. And there is also Polus, who has treasuries of diplasiology, and gnomology, and eikonology, and who teaches in them the names of which Licymnius made him a present; they were to give a polish.

PHAEDR. Had not Protagoras something of the same sort?

SOC. Yes, rules of correct diction and many other fine precepts; for the 'sorrows of a poor old man,' or any other pathetic case, no one is better than the Chalcedonian giant; he can put a whole company of people into a passion and out of one again by his mighty magic, and is first-rate at inventing or disposing of any sort of calumny on any grounds or none. All of them agree in asserting that a speech should end in a recapitulation, though they do not all agree to use the same word.

PHAEDR. You mean that there should be a summing up of the arguments in order to remind the hearers of them.

SOC. I have now said all that I have to say of the art of rhetoric: have you anything to add?

PHAEDR. Not much; nothing very important.

SOC. Leave the unimportant and let us bring the really important question into the light of day, which is: What power has this art of rhetoric, and when?

PHAEDR. A very great power in public meetings.

SOC. It has. But I should like to know whether you have the same feeling as I have about the rhetoricians? To me there seem to be a great many holes in their web.

PHAEDR. Give an example.

SOC. I will. Suppose a person to come to your friend Eryximachus, or to his father Acumenus, and to say to him: 'I know how to apply drugs which shall have either a heating or a cooling effect, and I can give a vomit and also a purge, and all that sort of thing; and knowing all this, as I do, I claim to be a physician and to make physicians by imparting this knowledge to others,' – what do you suppose that they would say?

PHAEDR. They would be sure to ask him whether he knew 'to whom' he would give his medicines, and 'when,' and 'how much.'

SOC. And suppose that he were to reply: 'No; I know nothing of all that; I expect the patient who consults me to be able to do these things for himself'?

PHAEDR. They would say in reply that he is a madman or a pedant who fancies that he is a physician because he has read something in a book, or has stumbled on a prescription or two, although he has no real understanding of the art of medicine.

SOC. And suppose a person were to come to Sophocles or Euripides and say that he knows how to make a very long speech about a small matter, and a short speech about a great matter, and also a sorrowful speech, or a terrible, or threatening speech, or any other kind of speech, and in teaching this fancies that he is teaching the art of tragedy – ?

PHAEDR. They too would surely laugh at him if he fancies that tragedy is anything but the arranging of these elements in a manner which will be suitable to one another and to the whole.

SOC. But I do not suppose that they would be rude or abusive to him: Would they not treat him as a musician would a man who thinks that he is a harmonist because he knows how to pitch the highest and lowest note; happening to meet such an one he would not say to him savagely, 'Fool, you are mad!' But like a musician, in a gentle and harmonious tone of voice, he would answer: 'My good friend, he who would be a harmonist must certainly know this, and yet he may understand nothing of harmony if he has not got beyond your stage of knowledge, for you only know the preliminaries of harmony and not harmony itself.'

PHAEDR. Very true.

SOC. And will not Sophocles say to the display of the would-be tragedian, that this is not tragedy but the preliminaries of tragedy? and will not Acumenus say the same of medicine to the would-be physician?

PHAEDR. Quite true.

SOC. And if Adrastus the mellifluous, or Pericles heard of these wonderful arts, brachylogies and eikonologies and all the hard names which we have been endeavouring to draw into the light of day, what would they say? Instead of losing temper and applying uncomplimentary epithets, as you and I have been doing, to the authors of such an imaginary art, their superior wisdom would rather censure us, as well as them. 'Have a little patience, Phaedrus and Socrates, they would say; you should not be in such a passion with those who from some want of dialectical skill are unable to define the nature of rhetoric, and consequently suppose that they have found the art in the preliminary conditions of it, and when these have been taught by them to others, fancy that the whole art of rhetoric has been taught by them; but as to using the several instruments of the art effectively, or making the composition a whole, – an application of it such as this is they regard as an easy thing which their disciples may make for themselves.'

PHAEDR. I quite admit, Socrates, that the art of rhetoric which these men teach and of which they write is such as you describe – there I agree with you. But I still want to know where and how the true art of rhetoric and persuasion is to be acquired.

SOC. The perfection which is required of the finished orator is, or rather must be, like the perfection of anything else, partly given by nature, but may also be assisted by art. If you have the natural power and add to it knowledge and practice, you will be a distinguished speaker; if you fall short in either of these, you will be to that extent defective. But the art, as far as there is an art, of rhetoric does not lie in the direction of Lysias or Thrasymachus.

PHAEDR. In what direction then?

SOC. I conceive Pericles to have been the most accomplished of rhetoricians.

PHAEDR. What of that?

SOC. All the great arts require discussion and high speculation about the truths of nature; hence come loftiness of thought and completeness of execution. And this, as I conceive, was the quality which, in addition to his natural gifts, Pericles acquired from his intercourse with Anaxagoras whom he happened to know. He was thus imbued with the higher philosophy, and attained the knowledge of Mind and the negative of Mind, which were favourite themes of Anaxagoras, and applied what suited his purpose to the art of speaking.

PHAEDR. Explain.

SOC. Rhetoric is like medicine.

PHAEDR. How so?

SOC. Why, because medicine has to define the nature of the body and rhetoric of the soul – if we would proceed, not empirically but scientifically, in the one case to impart health and strength by giving medicine and food, in the other to implant the conviction or virtue which you desire, by the right application of words and training.

PHAEDR. There, Socrates, I suspect that you are right.

SOC. And do you think that you can know the nature of the soul intelligently without knowing the nature of the whole?

PHAEDR. Hippocrates the Asclepiad says that the nature even of the body can only be understood as a whole.[57]

SOC. Yes, friend, and he was right: – still, we ought not to be content with the name of Hippocrates, but to examine and see whether his argument agrees with his conception of nature.

PHAEDR. I agree.

SOC. Then consider what truth as well as Hippocrates says about this or about any other nature. Ought we not to consider first whether that which we wish to learn and to teach is a simple or multiform thing, and if simple, then to enquire what power it has of acting or being acted upon in relation to other things, and if multiform, then to number the forms; and see first in the case of one of them, and then in the case of all of them, what is that power of acting or being acted upon which makes each and all of them to be what they are?

PHAEDR. You may very likely be right, Socrates.

SOC. The method which proceeds without analysis is like the groping of a blind man. Yet, surely, he who is an artist ought not to admit of a comparison with the blind, or deaf. The rhetorician, who teaches his pupil to speak scientifically, will particularly set forth the nature of that being to which he addresses his speeches; and this, I conceive, to be the soul.

PHAEDR. Certainly.

SOC. His whole effort is directed to the soul; for in that he seeks to produce conviction.

PHAEDR. Yes.

SOC. Then clearly, Thrasymachus or any one else who teaches rhetoric in earnest will give an exact description of the nature of the soul; which will enable us to see whether she be single and same, or, like the body, multiform. That is what we should call showing the nature of the soul.

PHAEDR. Exactly.

SOC. He will explain, secondly, the mode in which she acts or is acted upon.

PHAEDR. True.

SOC. Thirdly, having classified men and speeches, and their kinds and affections, and adapted them to one another, he will tell the reasons of his arrangement, and show why one soul is persuaded by a particular form of argument, and another not.

PHAEDR. You have hit upon a very good way.

SOC. Yes, that is the true and only way in which any subject can be set forth or treated by rules of art, whether in speaking or writing. But the writers of the present day, at whose feet you have sat, craftily conceal the nature of the soul which they know quite well. Nor, until they adopt our method of reading and writing, can we admit that they write by rules of art?

PHAEDR. What is our method?

SOC. I cannot give you the exact details; but I should like to tell you generally, as far as is in my power, how a man ought to proceed according to rules of art.

PHAEDR. Let me hear.

[57] Cp. Charmides, 156 C.

soc. Oratory is the art of enchanting the soul, and therefore he who would be an orator has to learn the differences of human souls – they are so many and of such a nature, and from them come the differences between man and man. Having proceeded thus far in his analysis, he will next divide speeches into their different classes: – 'Such and such persons,' he will say, 'are affected by this or that kind of speech in this or that way,' and he will tell you why. The pupil must have a good theoretical notion of them first, and then he must have experience of them in actual life, and be able to follow them with all his senses about him, or he will never get beyond the precepts of his masters. But when he understands what persons are persuaded by what arguments, and sees the person about whom he was speaking in the abstract actually before him, and knows that it is he, and can say to himself, 'This is the man or this is the character who ought to have a certain argument applied to him in order to convince him of a certain opinion;' – he who knows all this, and knows also when he should speak and when he should refrain, and when he should use pithy sayings, pathetic appeals, sensational effects, and all the other modes of speech which he has learned; – when, I say, he knows the times and seasons of all these things, then, and not till then, he is a perfect master of his art; but if he fail in any of these points, whether in speaking or teaching or writing them, and yet declares that he speaks by rules of art, he who says 'I don't believe you' has the better of him. Well, the teacher will say, is this, Phaedrus and Socrates, your account of the so-called art of rhetoric, or am I to look for another?

PHAEDR. He must take this, Socrates, for there is no possibility of another, and yet the creation of such an art is not easy.

soc. Very true; and therefore let us consider this matter in every light, and see whether we cannot find a shorter and easier road; there is no use in taking a long rough round-about way if there be a shorter and easier one. And I wish that you would try and remember whether you have heard from Lysias or any one else anything which might be of service to us.

PHAEDR. If trying would avail, then I might; but at the moment I can think of nothing.

soc. Suppose I tell you something which somebody who knows told me.

PHAEDR. Certainly.

soc. May not 'the wolf,' as the proverb says, 'claim a hearing'?

PHAEDR. Do you say what can be said for him.

soc. He will argue that there is no use in putting a solemn face on these matters, or in going round and round, until you arrive at first principles; for, as I said at first when the question is of justice and good, or is a question in which men are concerned who are just and good, either by nature or habit, he who would be a skilful rhetorician has no need of truth – for that in courts of law men literally care nothing about truth, but only about conviction: and this is based on probability, to which he who would be a skilful orator should therefore give his whole attention. And they say also that there are cases in which the actual facts, if they are improbable, ought to be withheld, and only the probabilities should be told either in accusation or defence, and that always in speaking, the orator should keep probability in view, and say good-bye to the truth. And the observance of this principle throughout a speech furnishes the whole art.

PHAEDR. That is what the professors of rhetoric do actually say, Socrates. I have not forgotten that we have quite briefly touched upon this matter[58] already; with them the point is all-important.

soc. I dare say that you are familiar with Tisias. Does he not define probability to be that which the many think?

PHAEDR. Certainly, he does.

soc. I believe that he has a clever and ingenious case of this sort: – He supposes a feeble and valiant man to have assaulted a strong and cowardly one, and to have robbed him of his coat or of something or other; he is brought into court, and then Tisias says that both parties should tell lies: the coward should say that he was assaulted by more men than one; the other should prove that they were alone, and should argue thus: 'How could a weak man like me have assaulted a strong man like him?' The complainant will not like to confess his own cowardice, and will therefore invent some other lie which his adversary will thus gain an opportunity of refuting. And there are other devices of the same kind which have a place in the system. Am I not right, Phaedrus?

---

[58] Cp. p. 210.

PHAEDR. Certainly.

SOC. Bless me, what a wonderfully mysterious art is this which Tisias or some other gentleman, in whatever name or country he rejoices, has discovered. Shall we say a word to him or not?

PHAEDR. What shall we say to him?

SOC. Let us tell him that, before he appeared, you and I were saying that the probability of which he speaks was engendered in the minds of the many by the likeness of the truth, and we had just been affirming that he who knew the truth would always know best how to discover the resemblances of the truth. If he has anything else to say about the art of speaking we should like to hear him; but if not, we are satisfied with our own view, that unless a man estimates the various characters of his hearers and is able to divide all things into classes and to comprehend them under single ideas, he will never be a skilful rhetorician even within the limits of human power. And this skill he will not attain without a great deal of trouble, which a good man ought to undergo, not for the sake of speaking and acting before men, but in order that he may be able to say what is acceptable to God and always to act acceptably to Him as far as in him lies; for there is a saying of wiser men than ourselves, that a man of sense should not try to please his fellow-servants (at least this should not be his first object) but his good and noble masters; and therefore if the way is long and circuitous, marvel not at this, for, where the end is great, there we may take the longer road, but not for lesser ends such as yours. Truly, the argument may say, Tisias, that if you do not mind going so far, rhetoric has a fair beginning here.

PHAEDR. I think, Socrates, that this is admirable, if only practicable.

SOC. But even to fail in an honourable object is honourable.

PHAEDR. True.

SOC. Enough appears to have been said by us of a true and false art of speaking.

PHAEDR. Certainly.

SOC. But there is something yet to be said of propriety and impropriety of writing.

PHAEDR. Yes.

SOC. Do you know how you can speak or act about rhetoric in a manner which will be acceptable to God?

PHAEDR. No, indeed. Do you?

SOC. I have heard a tradition of the ancients, whether true or not they only know; although if we had found the truth ourselves, do you think that we should care much about the opinions of men?

PHAEDR. Your question needs no answer; but I wish that you would tell me what you say that you have heard.

SOC. At the Egyptian city of Naucratis, there was a famous old god, whose name was Theuth; the bird which is called the Ibis is sacred to him, and he was the inventor of many arts, such as arithmetic and calculation and geometry and astronomy and draughts and dice, but his great discovery was the use of letters. Now in those days the god Thamus was the king of the whole country of Egypt; and he dwelt in that great city of Upper Egypt which the Hellenes call Egyptian Thebes, and the god himself is called by them Ammon. To him came Theuth and showed his inventions, desiring that the other Egyptians might be allowed to have the benefit of them; he enumerated them, and Thamus enquired about their several uses, and praised some of them and censured others, as he approved or disapproved of them. It would take a long time to repeat all that Thamus said to Theuth in praise or blame of the various arts. But when they came to letters, This, said Theuth, will make the Egyptians wiser and give them better memories; it is a specific both for the memory and for the wit. Thamus replied: O most ingenious Theuth, the parent or inventor of an art is not always the best judge of the utility or inutility of his own inventions to the users of them. And in this instance, you who are the father of letters, from a paternal love of your own children have been led to attribute to them a quality which they cannot have; for this discovery of yours will create forgetfulness in the learners' souls, because they will not use their memories; they will trust to the external written characters and not remember of themselves. The specific which you have discovered is an aid not to memory, but to reminiscence, and you give your disciples not truth, but only the semblance of truth; they will be hearers of many things and will have learned nothing; they will appear to be omniscient and will generally know nothing; they will be tiresome company, having the show of wisdom without the reality.

PHAEDR. Yes, Socrates, you can easily invent tales of Egypt, or of any other country.

SOC. There was a tradition in the temple of Dodona that oaks first gave prophetic utterances.

The men of old, unlike in their simplicity to young philosophy, deemed that if they heard the truth even from 'oak or rock,' it was enough for them; whereas you seem to consider not whether a thing is or is not true, but who the speaker is and from what country the tale comes.

PHAEDR. I acknowledge the justice of your rebuke; and I think that the Theban is right in his view about letters.

SOC. He would be a very simple person, and quite a stranger to the oracles of Thamus or Ammon, who should leave in writing or receive in writing any art under the idea that the written word would be intelligible or certain; or who deemed that writing was at all better than knowledge and recollection of the same matters?

PHAEDR. That is most true.

SOC. I cannot help feeling, Phaedrus, that writing is unfortunately like painting; for the creations of the painter have the attitude of life, and yet if you ask them a question they preserve a solemn silence. And the same may be said of speeches. You would imagine that they had intelligence, but if you want to know anything and put a question to one of them, the speaker always gives one unvarying answer. And when they have been once written down they are tumbled about anywhere among those who may or may not understand them, and know not to whom they should reply, to whom not: and, if they are maltreated or abused, they have no parent to protect them; and they cannot protect or defend themselves.

PHAEDR. That again is most true.

SOC. Is there not another kind of word or speech far better than this, and having far greater power – a son of the same family, but lawfully begotten?

PHAEDR. Whom do you mean, and what is his origin?

SOC. I mean an intelligent word graven in the soul of the learner, which can defend itself, and knows when to speak and when to be silent.

PHAEDR. You mean the living word of knowledge which has a soul, and of which the written word is properly no more than an image?

SOC. Yes, of course that is what I mean. And now may I be allowed to ask you a question: Would a husbandman, who is a man of sense, take the seeds, which he values and which he wishes to bear fruit, and in sober seriousness plant them during the heat of summer, in some garden of Adonis, that he may rejoice when he sees them in eight days appearing in beauty? at least he would do so, if at all, only for the sake of amusement and pastime. But when he is in earnest he sows in fitting soil, and practises husbandry, and is satisfied if in eight months the seeds which he has sown arrive at perfection?

PHAEDR. Yes, Socrates, that will be his way when he is in earnest; he will do the other, as you say, only in play.

SOC. And can we suppose that he who knows the just and good and honourable has less understanding, than the husbandman, about his own seeds?

PHAEDR. Certainly not.

SOC. Then he will not seriously incline to 'write' his thoughts 'in water' with pen and ink, sowing words which can neither speak for themselves nor teach the truth adequately to others?

PHAEDR. No, that is not likely.

SOC. No, that is not likely – in the garden of letters he will sow and plant, but only for the sake of recreation and amusement; he will write them down as memorials to be treasured against the forgetfulness of old age, by himself, or by any other old man who is treading the same path. He will rejoice in beholding their tender growth; and while others are refreshing their souls with banqueting and the like, this will be the pastime in which his days are spent.

PHAEDR. A pastime, Socrates, as noble as the other is ignoble, the pastime of a man who can be amused by serious talk, and can discourse merrily about justice and the like.

SOC. True, Phaedrus. But nobler far is the serious pursuit of the dialectician, who, finding a congenial soul, by the help of science sows and plants therein words which are able to help themselves and him who planted them, and are not unfruitful, but have in them a seed which others brought up in different soils render immortal, making the possessors of it happy to the utmost extent of human happiness.

PHAEDR. Far nobler, certainly.

SOC. And now, Phaedrus, having agreed upon the premises we decide about the conclusion.

PHAEDR. About what conclusion?

SOC. About Lysias, whom we censured, and his art of writing, and his discourses, and the rhetorical skill or want of skill which was shown in them – these are the questions which we sought to determine, and they brought us to this point. And I think that we are now pretty well informed about the nature of art and its opposite.

PHAEDR. Yes, I think with you; but I wish that you would repeat what was said.

SOC. Until a man knows the truth of the several particulars of which he is writing or speaking, and is able to define them as they are, and having defined them again to divide them until they can be no longer divided, and until in like manner he is able to discern the nature of the soul, and discover the different modes of discourse which are adapted to different natures, and to arrange and dispose them in such a way that the simple form of speech may be addressed to the simpler nature, and the complex and composite to the more complex nature – until he has accomplished all this, he will be unable to handle arguments according to rules of art, as far as their nature allows them to be subjected to art, either for the purpose of teaching or persuading; – such is the view which is implied in the whole preceding argument.

PHAEDR. Yes, that was our view, certainly.

SOC. Secondly, as to the censure which was passed on the speaking or writing of discourses, and how they might be rightly or wrongly censured – did not our previous argument show – ?

PHAEDR. Show what?

SOC. That whether Lysias or any other writer that ever was or will be, whether private man or statesman, proposes laws and so becomes the author of a political treatise, fancying that there is any great certainty and clearness in his performance, the fact of his so writing is only a disgrace to him, whatever men may say. For not to know the nature of justice and injustice, and good and evil, and not to be able to distinguish the dream from the reality, cannot in truth be otherwise than disgraceful to him, even though he have the applause of the whole world.

PHAEDR. Certainly.

SOC. But he who thinks that in the written word there is necessarily much which is not serious, and that neither poetry nor prose, spoken or written, is of any great value, if, like the compositions of the rhapsodes, they are only recited in order to be believed, and not with any view to criticism or instruction; and who thinks that even the best of writings are but a reminiscence of what we know, and that only in principles of justice and goodness and nobility taught and communicated orally for the sake of instruction and graven in the soul,

which is the true way of writing, is there clearness and perfection and seriousness, and that such principles are a man's own and his legitimate offspring; – being, in the first place, the word which he finds in his own bosom; secondly, the brethren and descendants and relations of his others; – and who cares for them and no others – this is the right sort of man; and you and I, Phaedrus, would pray that we may become like him.

PHAEDR. That is most assuredly my desire and prayer.

SOC. And now the play is played out; and of rhetoric enough. Go and tell Lysias that to the fountain and school of the Nymphs we went down, and were bidden by them to convey a message to him and to other composers of speeches – to Homer and other writers of poems, whether set to music or not; and to Solon and others who have composed writings in the form of political discourses which they would term laws – to all of them we are to say that if their compositions are based on knowledge of the truth, and they can defend or prove them, when they are put to the test, by spoken arguments, which leave their writings poor in comparison of them, then they are to be called, not only poets, orators, legislators, but are worthy of a higher name, befitting the serious pursuit of their life.

PHAEDR. What name would you assign to them?

SOC. Wise, I may not call them; for that is a great name which belongs to God alone, – lovers of wisdom or philosophers is their modest and befitting title.

PHAEDR. Very suitable.

SOC. And he who cannot rise above his own compilations and compositions, which he has been long patching and piecing, adding some and taking away some, may be justly called poet or speech-maker or law-maker.

PHAEDR. Certainly.

SOC. Now go and tell this to your companion.

PHAEDR. But there is also a friend of yours who ought not to be forgotten.

SOC. Who is he?

PHAEDR. Isocrates the fair: – What message will you send to him, and how shall we describe him?

SOC. Isocrates is still young, Phaedrus; but I am willing to hazard a prophecy concerning him.

PHAEDR. What would you prophesy?

SOC. I think that he has a genius which soars above the orations of Lysias, and that his character is cast in a finer mould. My impression of him is that he will marvellously improve as he grows older, and that all former rhetoricians will be as children in comparison of him. And I believe that he will not be satisfied with rhetoric, but that there is in him a divine inspiration which will lead him to things higher still. For he has an element of philosophy in his nature. This is the message of the gods dwelling in this place, and which I will myself deliver to Isocrates, who is my delight; and do you give the other to Lysias, who is yours.

PHAEDR. I will; and now as the heat is abated let us depart.

SOC. Should we not offer up a prayer first of all to the local deities?

PHAEDR. By all means.

SOC. Beloved Pan, and all ye other gods who haunt this place, give me beauty in the inward soul; and may the outward and inward man be at one. May I reckon the wise to be the wealthy, and may I have such a quantity of gold as a temperate man and he only can bear and carry. – Anything more? The prayer, I think, is enough for me.

PHAEDR. Ask the same for me, for friends should have all things in common.

SOC. Let us go.

Study Questions

1 Sophistic rhetoric was pragmatic and focused on dealing with the everyday issues of law and government. With the possible exception of *The Republic,* Plato was not concerned with such issues but rather with philosophy and how it could improve the individual soul. How might Plato respond to the claim that his focus ignored the practical needs of society?

2 In *Protagoras,* Socrates questions his young friend on the basis of an assumption: that training in rhetoric affects the soul. What is the soul, and what is the basis for Socrates' assumption?

3 In attempting to prove that wisdom is holy, Socrates in *Protagoras* applies a bit of mathematical logic: if a = b and b = c, then a = c. The procedure is based on the assertion that every thing has only one opposite, but it leads to the conclusion that "folly" has two opposites, "wisdom" and "temperance." What is the error in reasoning here?

4 In *Gorgias,* Plato suggested that desires should be strictly controlled, if not eliminated completely, if a person is to be happy. This sentiment is similar to the Buddha's assertion that "desire is pain." Callicles responds: "then stones and dead men would be the happiest of all!" At issue here are two different perspectives on *being* and *becoming*. Given your knowledge of human nature, which is more important to happiness and fulfillment?

5 Socrates claims in *Gorgias* that it is better to suffer than commit an injustice. Do you agree? If not, why not? If so, how does your belief influence how you live your life?

6 The allegory of the souls in *Phaedrus* attempts to explain a basic conflict in human nature. What is that nature, and is Plato's description accurate, even though couched in metaphor?

7 In *Phaedrus,* Socrates declares that "rhetoric is like medicine." What does this mean? If this assertion is correct, what are the implications for communication?

8 Form a cast of characters from members of your class and have them read aloud a portion of one of the dialogues as though performing a play. Was this performance more or less effective than reading the dialogue silently to yourself? Why or why not?

Writing Topics

1 Select a modern speech and analyze it from a Platonic perspective.
2 Compare and contrast Isocrates' and Plato's views of rhetoric.
3 "Plato's views on rhetoric, education, and the soul are relevant to our lives today." Argue for or against this claim.

Further Reading

Plato, *The Republic.*
Plato, *Apology.*
Plato, *Symposium.*

Aristotle and the Systemization of Rhetoric

Introduction to Aristotle (c. 384–322 BC)

As the previous chapters suggested, the development of rhetoric in Greece was a complex enterprise. The Sophists created and applied pedagogical approaches to language in response to a number of social, political, educational, and intellectual changes that affected the Mediterranean region in general and Athens in particular. Plato, in turn, responded to the Sophists and the cultural changes of which they were a part. It is understandable, then, that Aristotle's *Rhetoric* and *Poetics* should be viewed as responses to Plato, with whom he studied and worked for nearly 20 years. Limiting ourselves to this view, however, leads to the incorrect assessment that *Rhetoric* and *Poetics* are merely detailed manuals on oratory and poetry, respectively, which makes it difficult to recognize that they are part of Aristotle's comprehensive philosophy of ethics and politics.

There is no question that we find certain correspondences between Plato and Aristotle with regard to rhetoric and philosophy. Both placed significant value, for example, on the notion of *kairos* in rhetoric. Kinneavy and Eskin (2000) noted that the term appears only 16 times in Aristotle's *Rhetoric* but that the concept nevertheless permeates the work, as in the definition of rhetoric as the faculty of observing or discovering in each case the available means of persuasion (also see Kinneavy, 2002; Smith, 2002). Kinneavy and Eskin concluded that, "As in Plato, Aristotle's art [of rhetoric] is to be applied to a particular kairos" (p. 434). Overall, however, there are more differences between the two than similarities. One of the more obvious is the far greater breadth of Aristotle's interests. His known works – dealing with logic, natural science, zoology, psychology, ethics, politics, rhetoric, and poetry – are indicative of a mind capable of truly encyclopedic knowledge. Although Aristotle saw these different areas as being discrete with regard to topics, he did not see them as being discrete with regard to investigative principles. His theory of argumentation, for example, is embedded in his more general theory of syllogisms, which supports his concepts of dialectic and logic. His general inclination was to approach topics from a scientific perspective, and his genius enabled him to understand that seemingly very different topics are all interrelated within the framework of human nature and experience. On this basis, poetry, for example, is related to ethics and psychology; rhetoric is related to politics, psychology, and poetry; and everything is related to the goal (*telos*) of existence.

Aristotle's philosophy

The popular understanding of philosophy today seems to focus on a personal philosophy of "how to" – how to live a rewarding life, how to be a whole person, how to accomplish specific goals, and so forth. Missing from this popular view is the broader, historical conceptualization of philosophy as a theory of human nature that includes not only individual but also social and political behaviors and outcomes. Reflecting on this broader conceptualization, Sowell (2002) argued that, historically, philosophy has been dominated by two competing visions, or theories, of human nature, with conflicting notions of reason, justice, equality, and power. The "constrained" vision, Sowell maintained, holds that human nature is flawed and very difficult, if not impossible, to change, whereas the "unconstrained" vision holds that human nature can be changed, given the right circumstances, and is, in fact, perfectible. We can see these two competing theories in the work of Plato and Aristotle.

To understand how Aristotle's *Rhetoric* and *Poetics* are part of his exploration of human nature, we need to know something about his philosophy, which is tangled in unexpected ways and thus difficult to summarize without oversimplification and which is developed in a number of treatises, not just these two works. Nevertheless, we can begin to understand at least some part of it by considering *being* and *change*, topics that received a great deal of attention during the Classical Period. Change presents an obvious problem for being. If something is, how can it remain consistently the same if it is subject to change? Plato attempted to answer this question through his unchanging Ideal Forms and the argument that our experiences of change are tied to a world of illusions. Aristotle, however, viewed this approach as being illogical. Moreover, it was unacceptable as theory because it lacked a basic requirement: the empirical evidence necessary for validation.

Aristotle believed that change was a basic component of all things. He saw unity in being and change, which gave him an understanding of reality quite different from Plato's. The issue of the perfect circle was discussed in the previous chapter, and we saw that when viewed under a magnifying glass, even a line drawn with computer software is uneven and therefore is not a perfect circle. From Aristotle's perspective, whether we draw a circle by hand or with computer software does not detract from the *essence* of the circle itself, even though one may be better formed than the other, because both conform to the general characteristics of "circle." We know this because we have the evidence of our experience with numerous circles – some drawn by hand, some produced with software; some large, some small – because we understand from this experience that circles may differ in various ways, and because we have constructed a mental model of "circle" that contains certain universal characteristics that define type but that also has sufficient flexibility to allow for a wide range of tokens. Therefore, the form of something cannot be separate from the thing itself; indeed, form is an inherent part of a thing's being.

This conclusion only makes sense, however, if we recognize that change also is inherent in a thing's being, a fundamental part of its nature. A "circle" can change in various ways – big, small, regular, irregular – and still be a circle. More important for Aristotle was the idea that change is necessary for existence. We can understand this if we consider, say, an acorn. An acorn is not a tree, but it has within itself the *potential* to become a tree. In fact, this potential is inextricable from the thing itself and from its goal (*telos*) in the universe. Aristotle argued on this account that what a thing is must be part of what it has the potential to become. As he stated in *Rhetoric*: "Change … is pleasant, since change is in the order of nature" (1371).

The idea of change allows us to see that, at the most basic level, Aristotle's philosophy is predicated on the concept of ethical action and the conscious choices one makes to live a good life (Sherman, 1989). An important consequence of this concept is a view of education quite different from Plato's. For Plato, education consisted of applying a specific technique, dialectic, to help students recollect memories of the real submerged in the recesses of the soul. For Aristotle, it consisted of a *process* – an action – that constructed the morphology of reality through close observation and classification to determine the unique nature (*ousia*) of a thing on the basis of quantity; quality; relationship to other things (similar and dissimilar); its location, or habitat; its structure; its activity; and how it is affected by other forces. When applied, this ecological process provides an understanding of a thing's being, its essence, and when applied consistently to experience, it provides an understanding of reality.[1] Aristotle's scientific research reflected his quest to understand physical reality, but his investigations of ethics, politics, rhetoric, and poetry reflected a quest to understand the reality of human nature. He applied his ecological process to both, which explains why *The Art of Rhetoric* and *The Art of Poetry* display the same sort of close observation and classification, discussion of structure, activity, and so forth, that characterizes his other works. The aim was not specifically to provide *technoi* on rhetoric and poetry but rather to determine the unique nature, or essence, of what to Aristotle were important elements of human nature.

Like Plato, Aristotle recognized that humans are imperfect beings, but his teleology led to a new assessment of life's goal. Plato held that the goal was the acquisition of knowledge through rigorous philosophical inquiry. Recall that "the good" in Plato's dialogues equates to knowledge. For Aristotle, however, the goal of life was happiness, a point that he expressed in detail in both *The Art of Rhetoric* and *Nicomachean Ethics*. Happiness is achieved when one lives in accordance with his nature as a human being. This nature compels people to learn, so the person who applies his mind to acquiring knowledge will be happier than the person who does not. Likewise, people are by nature social, so the person who develops close friendships will be happier than the person who does not. People are "political animals," and thus friendships produce the social capital that not only binds people together into a political unit but also makes government possible. And participation in government, making decisions about the right functioning of the polity and engaging in actions that benefit others, is congruent with the right functioning of the individual and brings out the best in both. Aristotle therefore rejected Plato's ideal of philosopher kings who control every facet of political existence in favor of a participatory government in which virtuous citizens engaged in meaningful deliberation on the affairs of state with the aim of furthering the attainment of every person's human potential toward happiness. If we were to use Sowell's (2002) analysis, we would say on this basis that Aristotle's view of human nature is "unconstrained." People not only can change, but they must because change is inherent in their nature. In addition, people have the *potential* of perfectibility – and not just philosophers, either, but everyone who strives for excellence and applies practical reason (*phronesis*) in making life choices that are congruent with human nature.

This is not to suggest that Aristotle's view of human nature was in any way naïve. He fully recognized that our potential is seldom realized. In *Rhetoric*, for example, he reminded us in his pithy, understated way that "most men are rather bad than good," that "as a rule men do wrong whenever they can" (1382), and that "most human things

---

[1] Although Aristotle necessarily understood the value of definitions, in this concept of education, definition is not central to understanding the essence of things.

turn out badly" (1389). Excellence and virtue, though implicit in our nature, do not come naturally to anyone but a select few. Unlike the acorn, whose nature is sufficiently simple to allow it to achieve its potential through relatively uncomplicated means, human nature is highly complicated, one might even say storm tossed, owing to selfishness, desires, and passions that too frequently conflict with right reason (*orthos logos*). In light of this fairly obvious handicap, our pursuit of excellence must be aided if we are to achieve our potential. Reason is our primary aid, for it is our distinguishing characteristic. It gives us the means – through discipline, deliberate effort, and close observation and study of virtuous behavior – to overcome our inclination to be bad. Reaching our potential as political creatures is especially challenging because we live in societies governed by written laws, unwritten conventions, and social reciprocity. As Aristotle recognized in *Nicomachean Ethics*, within every society the truths of human experience and political life are ambiguous, unlike the precise truths of science. Grasping these truths requires a knowledge of human nature itself – not of the soul, but of the desires and emotions that influence our decisions and actions, what today we think of as psychology. With this knowledge, a person may better understand not only the social dynamics that characterize the *polis* but also him- or herself. We see, therefore, that for Aristotle governance of the city and governance of the self were interrelated, with the goal of both being to move toward fulfilling their potential. Achieving this goal, however, involves deliberative democracy and thus requires a knowledge of how to speak in ways that not only, as Nichols (1987) stated, "convey the ambiguous truths of political life" (p. 657) but that also persuade or move others to right action, that helps them contest their own inclination to "do wrong whenever they can." The art (*technê*) that provides the necessary tools for political life, of course, is rhetoric.[2]

Rhetoric and society

Aristotle brought to rhetoric the same qualities of mind that enabled him to conduct seminal work in science: close observation, detailed classification and categorization, and rigorous logic. The result was the first fully developed study of rhetoric that includes both technical and theoretical components. As such, his *Rhetoric* represents a *technê* in the complete sense of formal handbook and of "art" as it was understood at the time. The work consists of three books that address matter, audience psychology, and style, respectively. The organizational structure, therefore, is roughly divided into matter, style, and arrangement, in keeping with Aristotle's statement at the beginning of Book III: "[F]or it is not sufficient to know what one ought to say, but one must also know how to say it" (1403b).

The Art of Rhetoric rises above the level of a mere handbook, however, for a number of reasons. For example, it addresses Plato's criticisms of rhetoric, especially those found in *Gorgias* and *Phaedrus*, but it goes far beyond them. The previous chapter noted that Plato's ideal rhetoric in *Phaedrus* turns out to be dialectic, which consists of private conversations with individuals and the application of dialectical syllogisms to discover truth. Hackforth (1972) concluded in this regard that Plato viewed the dialectical syllogism as a "counterpart of the real world of Forms" (p. 21). Because each soul is different, the dialectician must tailor his or her discourse to meet the unique needs of each individual for the discovery to occur. But Aristotle noted that dialectic serves primarily as a means of refutation, and, as such, it does not lead to discovery of truth; instead, it merely reveals the absence of truth and knowledge. Rhetoricians, moreover,

---

[2] Modern explorations of rhetoric and deliberative democracy are readily available in the works of political theorists such as Jay Bregman, Jürgen Habermas, and John Rawls.

deliver their speeches to groups of people, which means that there is no chance of fitting a given speech to the different individual souls that comprise the audience.

In Plato's view, no truth can be found in such an endeavor, only the appearance of truth designed to deceive auditors into believing that they have been brought closer to knowledge. Aristotle effectively dismissed this concern by shifting the ground of the discussion and thus the matters at issue. He did so by rejecting Plato's definition of rhetoric as the artificer of persuasion. It is, rather:

1   a counterpart (*antistrophos*) of dialectic, for both deal with common matters rather than a special science.

2   an art, because it can be reduced to a system.

3   the faculty of discovering the possible means of persuasion in each particular case.

4   an offshoot of dialectic and the science of ethics, or politics.

Not one of these statements is simple, for each is intricately connected to Aristotle's investigative principles and to his views on ethics and politics, making any detailed discussion impossible in the limited space here. But statements 3 and 4 are so important that they warrant some exploration, with the caveat that we again must engage in some oversimplification.

The third statement suggests that Plato (and others) misunderstood the goal of rhetoric, which is not persuasion at all but rather discovering the means of persuasion. This reorientation has significant consequences. It immediately counters Plato's claim that rhetoric was merely "a knack" and aligns oratory with science via implied discovery procedures, methods of analysis and application, pedagogical principles, and, particularly important, validation through empirical evidence. Although Aristotle noted that rhetoric could never achieve the status of a science because it deals with general rather than specific topics, his definition nevertheless established a theoretical and applied framework similar to that which characterizes fields such as psychology, linguistics, physics, and medicine, thereby raising its status well above a mere "knack."

The fourth statement, identifying rhetoric as a branch of ethics and politics, may be even more important because of the temptation to consider *The Art of Rhetoric* as merely a treatise on communication without regard to Aristotle's view that rhetoric functions as a tool to further political and ethical development. It does more than offer a response to Plato's complaints about rhetoric and the Sophists' teaching of *aretê*. In keeping with his emphasis on dialectic, which entails dialogue, Plato's discussion of civic virtue focused on the individual, leading him to develop what essentially is a simple equation: knowledge = the good = justice. In *The Republic*, he expanded his idea of virtue to include entire classes of people – the philosopher kings had the virtue of wisdom, whereas the common people had the virtue of moderation – but because the common people were incapable of benefiting from the special education the rulers received, their concept of justice was, at best, less than fully formed. His ideal society would be just because it was governed by a group of guardians who, owing to their philosophical education, had knowledge of the good, not because the common people who made up that society shared that knowledge or engaged in virtuous behavior in accordance with just laws. Rhetoric in the hands of such people had the clear potential of being put to bad use. Thus, by limiting civic virtue to individual virtue, Socrates could dismiss Gorgias' claim that rhetoric is ethically neutral.

Aristotle's view was radically different: As Tessitore (1996) noted, for Aristotle "the aim of ethical study is not knowledge (*gnosis*) but action (*praxis*)" (p. 15).[3] From this

---

[3] In *Nicomachean Ethics*, Aristotle differentiated intellectual virtue from moral, or ethical, virtue. The discussion here is limited to ethical virtue.

perspective, debates about whether virtue is one thing or many (as in *Gorgias*) fail to be productive. Ethical virtue (*êthikê aretê*) in the individual must be developed through practice, like any other action. With sufficient practice, virtuous behavior becomes ingrained, a matter of habit as doing right comes to feel more natural than doing wrong. Furthermore, this practice can only be exercised by functioning members of society, in keeping with a person's human nature and the goal of reaching his or her full potential as a social and political animal. This position can be viewed as an answer to the question Plato raised in *Gorgias* and *The Republic*: If what we are morally required to do can be contrary to what we would *choose* to do for our personal pleasure and gain, why should we behave morally? Aristotle's answer was perspicacious: Because it is in our nature. Plato's focus on the ethics of the individual fails here because, as Oakeshott (1991) recognized, it is isolating, exclusive, and ultimately antisocial. It elevates philosophers, the only ones capable of knowing the highest virtue (justice), to an elite class. In addition, it does not lead to civic participation but rather to confrontation and conflict with society, as the case of Socrates well illustrates.

Aristotle recognized that the practice of ethical virtue must have some guidance beyond our capacity to reason because this capacity varies greatly from person to person, and he emphasized the role of society in helping citizens achieve this part of their potential. By and large, society has a concrete, if somewhat imprecise, standard of good behavior that is established by decent people who apply right reason to distinguish justice from injustice. This standard is expressed in different ways, but the most germane in Aristotle's view is in laws. Aristotle believed that the laws themselves motivate (and educate) citizens to pursue ethical virtue and justice by establishing standards of behavior and by codifying altruistic punishments for violations of those standards. Stated another way, ethical virtue is a consequence of right actions at the individual as well as the social level. Aristotle argued that it is in the best interests of the state to be concerned with ethics, and for this reason he asserted in *Nicomachean Ethics* that the education and pursuits of the young should be prescribed by law. To reduce the likelihood that bad people will use rhetoric for bad purposes, Aristotle would improve the laws so that society can exert more influence over both ethical and unethical behavior. Clearly written, strict laws, in his view, were necessary to ensure that ethical virtue became a matter of habit; fear of punishment, especially among the common people, is a powerful motivator. Laws also provide opportunities for deliberation, whether in regard to making and rescinding statutes or in regard to questions in the courts concerning justice and injustice, equality and equity, as they apply to the commonweal. Such deliberations require rhetoric, and it is probably for this reason that Aristotle viewed deliberative rhetoric as being more important than the other two categories he identified: forensic and epideictic.

The enthymeme and rhetorical proofs

A hallmark of Aristotle's rhetoric is the enthymeme, which is described in different ways: a truncated syllogism because in some instances a premise is missing; a rhetorical counterpart to the dialectical syllogism associated with refutation; and a manifestation of the fuzzy logic associated with argument from probability, as opposed to the precise syllogism used in logical demonstration (see McBurney, 1936; Simonson, 1945). Although accurate, none of these descriptions gets at the fundamental difference between the enthymeme and the syllogism, which is that the former is based on generally accepted opinions (*endoxa*), whereas the latter is based on what is known to be true. The examples below illustrate the difference:

Syllogism
- All men are mortal.
- Socrates is a man.

- Therefore, Socrates is mortal.

Enthymeme
- Anyone who lies cannot be trusted.
- Socrates has lied in the past.

- Therefore, Socrates cannot be trusted.

The enthymeme is interesting for a variety of reasons, which no doubt accounts for the numerous books and scholarly articles that examine it in detail. For our purposes here, we need only consider a few points. Aristotle connected enthymemes to *topoi*, or "topics," stating in Book II (1403b) of *The Art of Rhetoric* that a *topos*, or topic, "is a head under which several enthymemes are included." Although the meaning is not particularly clear in *Rhetoric* (as well as in *Topics*, his major work on the syllogism), Aristotle appears to be suggesting that a *topos* is a general category or source from which a specific argument can be constructed. He identified two types of *topoi*, common and special – the former consisting of such categories as laws, contracts, and comparisons; the latter consisting of such categories as justice and injustice, good and evil, and truth and falsehood.

Another factor that makes enthymemes interesting is that, in the example above, the first premise is not a fact but rather a widely accepted opinion, one that we use on a regular basis to make judgments about people. Thus, in order for speakers to develop arguments using enthymemes, they must know something about prevailing opinions. The second premise may or may not be a fact; it stands merely as an allegation and therefore is the weakest part of the argument. The conclusion will only be accepted if auditors believe the allegation.

Aristotle recognized these difficulties, which explains why Book II of *The Art of Rhetoric* examines psychology, the first serious treatment of the subject in history. He not only defined a wide range of mental and emotional states but considered their causes, giving the student of rhetoric the means to choose enthymemic first premises more judiciously. In his view, an understanding of human emotions was central to knowing one's audience, which in turn was necessary if a speaker was to discover all available means of persuasion. He addressed the issue of the second premise with a thorough consideration of rhetorical proofs (*pisteis*), of which there are two types: inartificial and artificial. The inartificial proofs consist of concrete evidence and are not of great importance to Aristotle's discussion. The artificial proofs, however, "make a man a master of rhetorical argument" (1354b). They are *ethos* (character), *logos* (reason or the speech itself), and *pathos* (emotion).

Some types of oratory may rely more heavily on one type of proof than another. Today, for example, we note that a great deal of advertising uses *ethos* extensively through celebrity endorsements, but it might not use *pathos*. It is clear from Aristotle's discussion in *Rhetoric*, however, that, overall, the three proofs work in conjunction to persuade (see Grimaldi, 1972). Moreover, it is equally clear that ethical character is the lynch pin that holds everything together. As Aristotle stated, "moral character ... constitutes the most effective means of proof" (1356a). An audience is just not likely to respond positively to a speaker of bad character: His or her statement of premises will be met with skepticism; he or she will find it difficult to rouse the emotions appropriate to the situation; and the quality of the speech itself will be viewed negatively.

The enthymeme and its proofs return us to the question of ethical virtue and prompt us to reflect on the fact that *ethos* and *êthikê* have the same root, literally and metaphorically. We see here that even the more technical features of Aristotle's rhetoric are bound to broader issues of philosophy. The moral character necessary to utilize *ethos* in a speech derives from living within the well-ordered community, from which one can learn justice and proper conduct, and from performing ethical actions as part of that community. These actions, as we learn from *Nicomachean Ethics* and *Politics*, have the greatest effect when they are undertaken for the benefit of others rather than for selfish motives, which is the essence of statecraft and the *kalos kagathos*. Education in the art of rhetoric, therefore, is not a simple matter. Rather it demands the comprehensive study of several fields, perhaps the most important being psychology, ethics, and statecraft. This approach, of course, was not entirely new: It bears a striking similarity to the education advocated by Isocrates.[4]

---

[4] This point is reinforced by the fact that Aristotle cites Isocrates more times in *Rhetoric* than he does any other person.

Reading 29

The Art of Rhetoric

The Art of Rhetoric (excerpt), pp. 3–51, 169–207, 345–77 reprinted by permission of the publishers and Trustees of the Loeb Classical Library from *Aristotle*, Volume XXII, Loeb Classical Library Volume 193, translated by J.H. Freese (Cambridge, MA: Harvard University Press, 1926). © 1926 by the President and Fellows of Harvard College. The Loeb Classical Library ® is a registered trademark of the President and Fellows of Harvard College.

Book I

1. Rhetoric is a counterpart[5] of Dialectic: for both have to do with matters that are in a manner within the cognizance of all men and not confined[6] to any special science. Hence all men in a manner have a share of both; for all, up to a certain point, endeavour to criticize or uphold an argument, to defend themselves or to accuse. Now, the majority of people do this either at random or with a familiarity arising from habit. But since both these ways are possible, it is clear that matters can be reduced to a system, for it is possible to examine the reason why some attain their end by familiarity and others by chance; and such an examination all would at once admit to be the function of an art.[7]

Now, previous compilers of "Arts"[8] of Rhetoric have provided us with only a small portion of this art, for proofs are the only things in it that come within the province of art; everything else is merely an accessory. And yet they say nothing about enthymemes which are the body of proof, but chiefly devote their attention to matters outside the subject; for the arousing of prejudice, compassion, anger, and similar emotions has no connexion with the matter in hand, but is directed only to the dicast.[9] The result would be that, if all

---

[5] Not an exact copy, but making a kind of pair with it, and corresponding to it as the antistrophe to the strophe in a choral ode.

[6] Or "and they (Rhetoric and Dialectic) are not confined."

[7] The special characteristic of an art is the discovery of a system or method, as distinguished from mere knack (ἐμπειρία).

[8] Manuals or handbooks treating of the rules of any art or science.

[9] His functions were a combination of those of the modern judge and juryman.

trials were now carried on as they are in some States, especially those that are well administered, there would be nothing left for the rhetorician to say. For all men either think that all the laws ought so to prescribe,[10] or in fact carry out the principle and forbid speaking outside the subject, as in the court of Areopagus, and in this they are right. For it is wrong to warp the dicast's feelings, to arouse him to anger, jealousy, or compassion, which would be like making the rule crooked which one intended to use. Further, it is evident that the only business of the litigant is to prove that the fact in question is or is not so, that it has happened or not; whether it is important or unimportant, just or unjust, in all cases in which the legislator has not laid down a ruling, is a matter for the dicast himself to decide; it is not the business of the litigants to instruct him.

First of all, therefore, it is proper that laws, properly enacted, should themselves define the issue of all cases as far as possible, and leave as little as possible to the discretion of the judges; in the first place, because it is easier to find one or a few men of good sense, capable of framing laws and pronouncing judgements than a large number; secondly, legislation is the result of long consideration, whereas judgements are delivered on the spur of the moment, so that it is difficult for the judges properly to decide questions of justice or expediency. But what is most important of all is that the judgement of the legislator does not apply to a particular case, but is universal and applies to the future, whereas the member of the public assembly and the dicast have to decide present and definite issues, and in their case love, hate, or personal interest is often involved, so that they are no longer capable of discerning the truth adequately, their judgement being obscured by their own pleasure or pain.

All other cases, as we have just said, should be left to the authority of the judge as seldom as possible, except where it is a question of a thing having happened or not of its going to happen or not, of being or not being so; this must be left to the discretion of the judges, for it is impossible for the legislator to foresee such questions. If this is so, it is obvious that all those who definitely lay down, for instance, what should be the contents of the exordium or the narrative, or of the other parts of the discourse, are bringing under the rules of art what is outside the subject; for the only thing to which their attention is devoted is how to put the judge into a certain frame of mind. They give no account of the artificial proofs,[11] which make a man a master of rhetorical argument.

Hence, although the method of deliberative and forensic Rhetoric is the same, and although the pursuit of the former is nobler and more worthy of a statesman than that of the latter, which is limited to transactions between private citizens, they say nothing about the former, but without exception endeavour to bring forensic speaking under the rules of art. The reason of this is that in public speaking it is less worth while to talk of what is outside the subject, and that deliberative oratory lends itself to trickery less than forensic, because it is of more general interest.[12] For in the assembly the judges decide upon their own affairs, so that the only thing necessary is to prove the truth of the statement of one who recommends a measure, but in the law courts this is not sufficient; there it is useful to win over the hearers, for the decision concerns other interests than those of the judges, who, having only themselves to consider and listening merely for their own pleasure, surrender to the pleaders but do not give a real decision.[13] That is why, as I have said before, in many places the law prohibits speaking outside the subject in the law courts, whereas in the assembly the judges themselves take adequate precautions against this.

It is obvious, therefore, that a system arranged according to the rules of art is only concerned

---

[10] That is, forbid speaking of matters that have nothing to do with the case.

[11] Systematic logical proofs (enthymeme, example), including testimony as to character and appeals to the emotions (2. 3), which the rhetorician has to invent (εὑρεῖν, *inventio*) for use in particular cases. They are contrasted with "inartificial" proofs, which have nothing to do with the rules of the art, but are already in existence, and only need to be made use of.

[12] κοινότερον: or, "more intelligible to the ordinary man."

[13] The case as a rule being a matter of personal indifference, the judges are likely to be led away by the arguments which seem most plausible.

with proofs; that proof is a sort of demonstration,[14] since we are most strongly convinced when we suppose anything to have been demonstrated; that rhetorical demonstration is an enthymeme, which, generally speaking, is the strongest of rhetorical proofs; and lastly, that the enthymeme is a kind of syllogism. Now, as it is the function of Dialectic as a whole, or of one of its parts,[15] to consider every kind of syllogism in a similar manner, it is clear that he who is most capable of examining the matter and forms of a syllogism will be in the highest degree a master of rhetorical argument, if to this he adds a knowledge of the subjects with which enthymemes deal and the differences between them and logical syllogisms. For, in fact, the true and that which resembles it come under the purview of the same faculty, and at the same time men have a sufficient natural capacity for the truth and indeed in most cases attain to it; wherefore one who divines well in regard to the truth will also be able to divine well in regard to probabilities.[16]

It is clear, then, that all other rhetoricians bring under the rules of art what is outside the subject, and[17] have rather inclined to the forensic branch of oratory. Nevertheless, Rhetoric is useful, because the true and the just are naturally superior to their opposites, so that, if decisions are improperly made, they must owe their defeat to their own advocates; which is reprehensible. Further, in dealing with certain persons, even if we possessed the most accurate scientific knowledge, we should not find it easy to persuade them by the employment of such knowledge. For scientific discourse is concerned with instruction,[18] but in the case of such persons instruction is impossible, our proofs and arguments must rest on generally accepted principles, as we said in the *Topics*,[19] when speaking of converse with the multitude. Further, the orator should be able to prove opposites, as in logical arguments; not that we

should do both (for one ought not to persuade people to do what is wrong), but that the real state of the case may not escape us, and that we ourselves may be able to counteract false arguments, if another makes an unfair use of them. Rhetoric and Dialectic alone of all the arts prove opposites; for both are equally concerned with them. However, it is not the same with the subject matter, but, generally speaking, that which is true and better is naturally always easier to prove and more likely to persuade. Besides, it would be absurd if it were considered disgraceful not to be able to defend oneself with the help of the body, but not disgraceful as far as speech is concerned, whose use is more characteristic of man than that of the body. If it is argued that one who makes an unfair use of such faculty of speech may do a great deal of harm, this objection applies equally to all good things except virtue, and above all to those things which are most useful, such as strength, health, wealth, generalship; for as these, rightly used, may be of the greatest benefit, so, wrongly used, they may do an equal amount of harm.

It is thus evident that Rhetoric does not deal with any one definite class of subjects, but, like Dialectic, [is of general application]; also, that it is useful; and further, that its function is not so much to persuade, as to find out in each case the existing means of persuasion.[20] The same holds good in respect to all the other arts. For instance, it is not the function of medicine to restore a patient to health, but only to promote this end as far as possible; for even those whose recovery is impossible may be properly treated. It is further evident that it belongs to Rhetoric to discover the real and apparent means of persuasion, just as it belongs to Dialectic to discover the real and apparent syllogism. For what makes the sophist is not the faculty but the moral purpose. But there is a difference: in Rhetoric, one who acts in accordance with sound argument, and one who

---

[14] Exact scientific proof (ἀπόδειξις), which probable proof (πίστις) only to a certain extent resembles.

[15] Dialectic here apparently includes logic generally, the "part" being either the *Analytica Priora*, which deals with the syllogism, or the *Sophistici Elenchi*, on Fallacies.

[16] ἔνδοξα, "resting on opinion"; defined in the *Topics* (i. 1) as "things generally admitted by all, or by most men, or by the wise, and by all or most of these, or by the most notable and esteemed."

[17] διότι either = ὅτι, "that"; or, (it is clear) "why."

[18] Almost equivalent to demonstration or strictly logical proof.

[19] i. 2. The *Topics* is a treatise in eight books on Dialectic and drawing conclusions from probabilities.

[20] The early sophistical definition was "the art of persuasion."

acts in accordance with moral purpose, are both called rhetoricians; but in Dialectic it is the moral purpose that makes the sophist, the dialectician being one whose arguments rest, not on moral purpose but on the faculty.[21]

Let us now endeavour to treat of the method itself, to see how and by what means we shall be able to attain our objects. And so let us as it were start again, and having defined Rhetoric anew, pass on to the remainder of the subject.

2. Rhetoric then may be defined as the faculty of discovering the possible means of persuasion in reference to any subject whatever. This is the function of no other of the arts, each of which is able to instruct and persuade in its own special subject; thus, medicine deals with health and sickness, geometry with the properties of magnitudes, arithmetic with number, and similarly with all the other arts and sciences. But Rhetoric, so to say, appears to be able to discover the means of persuasion in reference to any given subject. That is why we say that as an art its rules are not applied to any particular definite class of things.

As for proofs, some are inartificial, others artificial. By the former I understand all those which have not been furnished by ourselves but were already in existence, such as witnesses, tortures, contracts, and the like; by the latter, all that can be constructed by system and by our own efforts. Thus we have only to make use of the former, whereas we must invent the latter.

Now the proofs furnished by the speech are of three kinds. The first depends upon the moral character of the speaker, the second upon putting the hearer into a certain frame of mind, the third upon the speech itself, in so far as it proves or seems to prove.

The orator persuades by moral character when his speech is delivered in such a manner as to render him worthy of confidence; for we feel confidence in a greater degree and more readily in persons of worth in regard to everything in general, but where there is no certainty and there is room for doubt, our confidence is absolute. But this confidence must be due to the speech itself, not to any preconceived idea of the speaker's character; for it is not the case, as some writers of rhetorical treatises lay down in their "Art," that the worth of the orator in no way contributes to his powers of persuasion; on the contrary, moral character, so to say, constitutes the most effective means of proof. The orator persuades by means of his hearers, when they are roused to emotion by his speech; for the judgements we deliver are not the same when we are influenced by joy or sorrow, love or hate; and it is to this alone that, as we have said, the present-day writers of treatises endeavour to devote their attention. (We will discuss these matters in detail when we come to speak of the emotions.) Lastly, persuasion is produced by the speech itself, when we establish the true or apparently true from the means of persuasion applicable to each individual subject.

Now, since proofs are effected by these means, it is evident that, to be able to grasp them, a man must be capable of logical reasoning, of studying characters and the virtues, and thirdly the emotions – the nature and character of each, its origin, and the manner in which it is produced. Thus it appears that Rhetoric is as it were an offshoot of Dialectic and of the science of Ethics, which may be reasonably called Politics.[22] That is why Rhetoric assumes[23] the character of Politics, and those who claim to possess it, partly from ignorance, partly from boastfulness, and partly from other human weaknesses, do the same. For, as we said at the outset, Rhetoric is a sort of division or likeness of Dialectic, since neither of them is a science that deals with the nature of any

---

[21] The essence of sophistry consists in the moral purpose, the deliberate use of fallacious arguments. In Dialectic, the dialectician has the power or faculty of making use of them when he pleases; when he does so deliberately, he is called a sophist. In Rhetoric, this distinction does not exist; he who uses sound arguments as well as he who uses false ones, are both known as rhetoricians.

[22] Rhetoric, as dealing with human actions, characters, virtues, and emotions, is closely connected with Politics, which includes Ethics. The two latter treat of the same subject from a different point of view. Both deal with happiness and virtue, but the object of Politics is, by comparison of the different forms of States to find the one in which man will be most virtuous. Lastly, Rhetoric, as an important factor in the training and education of the individual citizen and of the members of the State as a whole, may be described as an offshoot of Politics, with which the sophistical rhetoricians *identifies* it.

[23] Or, "slips into the garb of" (Jebb). Probably a stage metaphor.

definite subject, but they are merely faculties of furnishing arguments. We have now said nearly enough about the faculties of these arts and their mutual relations.

But for purposes of demonstration, real or apparent, just as Dialectic possesses two modes of argument, induction and the syllogism, real or apparent, the same is the case in Rhetoric; for the example is induction, and the enthymeme a syllogism, and the apparent enthymeme an apparent syllogism. Accordingly I call an enthymeme a rhetorical syllogism, and an example rhetorical induction. Now all orators produce belief by employing as proofs either examples or enthymemes and nothing else; so that if, generally speaking, it is necessary to prove any fact whatever either by syllogism or by induction – and that this is so is clear from the *Analytics*[24] – each of the two former must be identical with each of the two latter.[25] The difference between example and enthymeme is evident from the *Topics*,[26] where, in discussing syllogism and induction, it has previously been said that the proof from a number of particular cases that such is the rule, is called in Dialectic induction, in Rhetoric example; but when, certain things being posited, something different results by reason of them alongside of them, from their being true, either universally or in most cases, such a conclusion in Dialectic is called a syllogism, in Rhetoric an enthymeme.

It is evident that Rhetoric enjoys both these advantages[27] – for what has been said in the *Methodica*[28] holds good also in this case – for rhetorical speeches are sometimes characterized by examples and sometimes by enthymemes, and orators themselves may be similarly distinguished by their fondness for one or the other. Now arguments that depend on examples are not less calculated to persuade, but those which depend upon enthymemes meet with greater approval. The origin and the way in which each should be used will be discussed later;[29] for the moment let us define more clearly these proofs themselves.

Now, that which is persuasive is persuasive in reference to some one, and is persuasive and convincing either at once and in and by itself, or because it appears to be proved by propositions that are convincing[30]; further, no art has the particular in view, medicine for instance what is good for Socrates or Callias, but what is good for this or that class of persons (for this is a matter that comes within the province of an art, whereas the particular is infinite and cannot be the subject of a true science); similarly, therefore, Rhetoric will not consider what seems probable in each individual case, for instance to Socrates or Hippias, but that which seems probable to this or that class of persons. It is the same with Dialectic, which does not draw conclusions from any random premises – for even madmen have some fancies – but it takes its material from subjects which demand reasoned discussion, as Rhetoric does from those which are common subjects of deliberation.

The function of Rhetoric, then, is to deal with things about which we deliberate, but for which we have no systematic rules; and in the presence of such hearers as are unable to take a general view of many stages, or to follow a lengthy chain of argument. But we only deliberate about things which seem to admit of issuing in two ways; as for those things which cannot in the past, present, or future be otherwise, no one deliberates about them if he supposes that they are such; for nothing would be gained by it. Now, it is possible to draw conclusions and inferences partly from what has been previously demonstrated syllogistically, partly from what has not, which however needs demonstration, because it is not probable.[31] The

---

[24] *Anal. Priora*, ii. 23; *Anal. Posteriora*, i. 1.

[25] That is, enthymeme and example must be the same as syllogism and induction.

[26] From the definitions of syllogism (i. 1) and induction (i. 12). No particular passage, however, explains the difference here mentioned.

[27] The employment of syllogism and induction, τὸ εἶδος τῆς ῥητορικῆς being taken as simply = ἡ ῥητορική. Another rendering is: "that each kind of Rhetoric (that which depends upon example or upon enthymeme) enjoys some special advantage.

[28] A lost treatise, mentioned by Diogenes Laërtius in his *Life of Aristotle*, xxiv., and by Dionysius of Halicarnassus in the first letter to Ammaeus, vi. It is supposed to have dealt with some branch of Logic.

[29] ii. 20–24.

[30] Or, "by persons who are so" (Jebb).

[31] Certain propositions, which seem paradoxical and improbable to a popular audience, must be proved before it is able to understand them.

first of these methods is necessarily difficult to follow owing to its length, for the judge is supposed to be a simple person; the second will obtain little credence, because it does not depend upon what is either admitted or probable. The necessary result then is that the enthymeme and the example are concerned with things which may, generally speaking, be other than they are, the example being a kind of induction and the enthymeme a kind of syllogism, and deduced from few premises, often from fewer than the regular[32] syllogism; for if any one of these is well known, there is no need to mention it, for the hearer can add it himself. For instance, to prove that Dorieus[33] was the victor in a contest at which the prize was a crown, it is enough to say that he won a victory at the Olympic games; there is no need to add that the prize at the Olympic games is a crown, for everybody knows it.

But since few of the propositions of the rhetorical syllogism are necessary, for most of the things which we judge and examine can be other than they are, human actions, which are the subject of our deliberation and examination, being all of such a character and, generally speaking, none of them necessary; since, further, facts which only generally happen or are merely possible can only be demonstrated by other facts of the same kind, and necessary facts by necessary propositions (and that this is so is clear from the *Analytics*),[34] it is evident that the materials from which enthymemes are derived will be sometimes necessary, but for the most part only generally true; and these materials being probabilities and signs, it follows that these two elements must correspond to these two kinds of propositions, each to each.[35] For that which is probable is that which generally happens, not however unreservedly, as some define it but that which is concerned with things that may be other than they are, being so

related to that in regard to which it is probable as the universal to the particular. As to signs, some are related as the particular to the universal, others as the universal to the particular. Necessary signs are called *tekmēria*; those which are not necessary have no distinguishing name. I call those necessary signs from which a logical syllogism can be constructed, wherefore such a sign is called *tekmērion*; for when people think that their arguments are irrefutable, they think that they are bringing forward a *tekmērion*, something as it were proved and concluded; for in the old language *tekmar* and *peras* have the same meaning (limit, conclusion).

Among signs, some are related as the particular to the universal; for instance, if one were to say that all wise men are just, because Socrates was both wise and just. Now this is a sign, but even though the particular statement is true, it can be refuted, because it cannot be reduced to syllogistic form. But if one were to say that it is a sign that a man is ill, because he has a fever, or that a woman has had a child because she has milk, this is a necessary sign. This alone among signs is a *tekmērion*; for only in this case if the fact is true, is the argument irrefutable. Other signs are related as the universal to the particular, for instance, if one were to say that it is a sign that this man has a fever, because he breathes hard; but even if the fact be true, this argument also can be refuted, for it is possible for a man to breathe hard without having a fever. We have now explained the meaning of probable, sign, and necessary sign, and the difference between them; in the *Analytics*[36] we have defined them more clearly and stated why some of them can be converted into logical syllogisms, while others cannot.

We have said that example is a kind of induction and with what kind of material it deals by way of induction. It is neither the relation of part

<hr>

[32] πρῶτος: the primary, typical syllogism of the first figure.

[33] Son of Diagoras of Rhodes, and like his father celebrated for his victories in the Greek athletic contests. He played a considerable part in political and naval affairs in support of the Spartans (412–407 BC), whom he afterwards offended, and by whom he is said to have been put to death.

[34] *Anal. Priora*, i. 8, 13–14.

[35] That is, probabilities and signs correspond to general and necessary propositions. This is not strictly correct; only the τεκμήρια correspond to the necessary propositions, the other signs and the probabilities to the general or contingent propositions.

[36] *Anal. Priora*, ii. 27.

to whole, nor of whole to part, nor of one whole to another whole, but of part to part, of like to like, when both come under the same genus, but one of them is better known than the other. For example, to prove that Dionysius is aiming at a tyranny, because he asks for a bodyguard, one might say that Pisistratus before him and Theagenes of Megara did the same, and when they obtained what they asked for made themselves tyrants. All the other tyrants known may serve as an example of Dionysius, whose reason, however, for asking for a bodyguard we do not yet know. All these examples are contained under the same universal proposition, that one who is aiming at a tyranny asks for a bodyguard.

We have now stated the materials of proofs which are thought to be demonstrative. But a very great difference between enthymemes has escaped the notice of nearly every one, although it also exists in the dialectical method of syllogisms. For some of them belong to Rhetoric, some syllogisms only to Dialectic, and others to other arts and faculties, some already existing and others not yet established. Hence it is that this escapes the notice of the speakers, and the more they specialize in a subject, the more they transgress the limits of Rhetoric and Dialectic. But this will be clearer if stated at greater length.

I mean by dialectical and rhetorical syllogisms those which are concerned with what we call "topics," which may be applied alike to Law, Physics, Politics, and many other sciences that differ in kind, such as the topic of the more or less, which will furnish syllogisms and enthymemes equally well for Law, Physics, or any other science whatever, although these subjects differ in kind. Specific topics on the other hand are derived from propositions which are peculiar to each species or genus of things; there are, for example,

propositions about Physics which can furnish neither enthymemes nor syllogisms about Ethics, and there are propositions concerned with Ethics which will be useless for furnishing conclusions about Physics; and the same holds good in all cases. The first kind of topics will not make a man practically wise about any particular class of things, because they do not deal with any particular subject matter; but as to the specific topics, the happier a man is in his choice of propositions, the more he will unconsciously produce a science quite different from Dialectic and Rhetoric. For if once he hits upon first principles, it will no longer be Dialectic or Rhetoric, but that science whose principles he has arrived at.[37] Most enthymemes are constructed from these specific topics, which are called particular and special, fewer from those that are common or universal. As then we have done in the *Topics*,[38] so here we must distinguish the specific and universal topics, from which enthymemes may be constructed. By specific topics I mean the propositions peculiar to each class of things, by universal those common to all alike. Let us then first speak of the specific topics, but before doing so let us ascertain the different kinds of Rhetoric, so that, having determined their number, we may separately ascertain their elements and propositions.[39]

3. The kinds of Rhetoric are three in number, corresponding to the three kinds of hearers. For every speech is composed of three parts: the speaker, the subject of which he treats, and the person to whom it is addressed, I mean the hearer, to whom the end or object of the speech refers. Now the hearer must necessarily be either a mere spectator or a judge, and a judge either of things past or of things to come[40] For instance, a member of the general assembly is a judge of things to come; the dicast, of things past; the mere spectator,

[37] The common topics do not deal with particular subject matter, as the specific topics do. In making use of the latter, the "better" (that is, in regard to a special science) the propositions chosen by a man, the more he will without knowing it quit the domain of Rhetoric and Dialectic, and become a professor of that special science whose first principles he has hit upon.

[38] *Sophistici Elenchi (Fallacies)*, 9. This treatise is really the ninth and concluding part of the *Topics*.

[39] Propositions (or premises), the name given to the two first statements in a syllogism from which the conclusion is drawn: All men are mortal (major premise); Socrates is a man (minor premise); therefore Socrates is mortal.

[40] All three kinds of hearers are regarded as judges (the mere spectator as a "critic"), although strictly κριτής should be limited to the law courts.

of the ability of the speaker. Therefore there are necessarily three kinds of rhetorical speeches, deliberative, *forensic*, and epideictic.

The deliberative kind is either hortatory or dissuasive; for both those who give advice in private and those who speak in the assembly invariably either exhort or dissuade. The forensic kind is either accusatory or defensive; for litigants must necessarily either accuse or defend. The epideictic kind has for its subject praise or blame.

Further, to each of these a special time is appropriate: to the deliberative the future,[41] for the speaker, whether he exhorts or dissuades, always advises about things to come; to the forensic the past, for it is always in reference to things done that one party accuses and the other defends; to the epideictic most appropriately the present, for it is the existing condition of things that all those who praise or blame have in view. It is not uncommon, however, for epideictic speakers to avail themselves of other times, of the past by way of recalling it, or of the future by way of anticipating it.

Each of the three kinds has a different special end, and as there are three kinds of Rhetoric, so there are three special ends. The end of the deliberative speaker is the expedient or harmful; for he who exhorts recommends a course of action as better, and he who dissuades advises against it as worse; all other considerations, such as justice and injustice, honour and disgrace, are included as accessory in reference to this. The end of the forensic speaker is the just or the unjust; in this case also all other considerations are included as accessory. The end of those who praise or blame is the honourable and disgraceful; and they also refer all other considerations to these. A sign that what I have stated is the end which each has in view is the fact that sometimes the speakers will

not dispute about the other points. For example, a man on trial does not always deny that an act has been committed or damage inflicted by him, but he will never admit that the act is unjust; for otherwise a trial would be unnecessary. Similarly, the deliberative orator, although he often sacrifices everything else, will never admit that he is recommending what is inexpedient or is dissuading from what is useful; but often he is quite indifferent about showing that the enslavement of neighbouring peoples, even if they have done no harm, is not an act of injustice.[42] Similarly, those who praise or blame do not consider whether a man has done what is expedient or harmful, but frequently make it a matter for praise that, disregarding his own interest, he performed some deed of honour. For example, they praise Achilles because he went to the aid of his comrade Patroclus,[43] knowing that he was fated to die, although he might have lived. To him such a death was more honourable, although life was more expedient.

From what has been said it is evident that the orator must first have in readiness the propositions on these three subjects.[44] Now, necessary signs, probabilities, and signs are the propositions of the rhetorician; for the syllogism universally[45] consists of propositions, and the enthymeme is a syllogism composed of the propositions above mentioned. Again, since what is impossible can neither have been done nor will be done, but only what is possible, and since what has not taken place nor will take place can neither have been done nor will be done, it is necessary for each of the three kinds of orators to have in readiness propositions dealing with the possible and the impossible, and as to whether anything has taken place or will take place, or not. Further, since all, whether they praise or blame, exhort or dissuade,

[41] In i. 6. 1 and 8.7 the present is also mentioned as a time appropriate to deliberative Rhetoric.

[42] The omission of οὐκ before ἄδικον has been suggested. The sense would then be: "As to the injustice of enslaving … he is quite indifferent." There is no doubt a reference to the cruel treatment by Athens of the inhabitants of the island of Melos (416 BC) for its loyalty to the Spartans during the Peloponnesian war (Thuc. v. 84–116). The Athenian envoys declined to discuss the question of right or wrong, which they said was only possible between equal powers, and asserted that *expediency* was the only thing that had to be considered. The question of justice or injustice (in the Melian case entirely disregarded), even when taken into account, was merely accessory and intended to serve as a specious justification for the policy of might.

[43] To protect his body and avenge his death (*Iliad*, xviii.).

[44] The expedient, the just, the honourable, and their contraries.

[45] ὅλως: or, reading ὅλος, "the syllogism as a whole."

accuse or defend, not only endeavour to prove what we have stated, but also that the same things, whether good or bad, honourable or disgraceful, just or unjust, are great or small, either in themselves or when compared with each other, it is clear that it will be necessary for the orator to be ready with propositions dealing with greatness and smallness and the greater and the less, both universally and in particular; for instance, which is the greater or less good, or act of injustice or justice; and similarly with regard to all other subjects. We have now stated the topics concerning which the orator must provide himself with propositions; after this, we must distinguish between each of them individually, that is, what the three kinds of Rhetoric, deliberative, epideictic, and forensic, are concerned with.

4. We must first ascertain about what kind of good or bad things the deliberative orator advises, since he cannot do so about everything, but only about things which may possibly happen or not. Everything which of necessity either is or will be, or which cannot possibly be or come to pass, is outside the scope of deliberation. Indeed, even in the case of things that are possible advice is not universally appropriate; for they include certain advantages, natural and accidental, about which it is not worth while to offer advice. But it is clear that advice is limited to those subjects about which we take counsel; and such are all those which can naturally be referred to ourselves and the first cause of whose origination is in our own power; for our examination is limited to finding out whether such things are possible or impossible for us to perform.

However, there is no need at present to endeavour to enumerate with scrupulous exactness or to classify those subjects which men are wont to discuss, or to define them as far as possible with strict accuracy, since this is not the function of the rhetorical art but of one that is more intelligent and exact, and further, more than its legitimate subjects of inquiry have already been assigned to it. For what we have said before is true[46]: that Rhetoric is composed of analytical science and of that branch of political science which is concerned with Ethics, and that it resembles partly Dialectic and partly sophistical arguments. But in proportion as anyone endeavours to make of Dialectic or Rhetoric, not what they are, faculties, but sciences, to that extent he will, without knowing it, destroy their real nature, in thus altering their character, by crossing over into the domain of sciences,[47] whose subjects are certain definite things, not merely words. Nevertheless, even at present we may mention such matters as it is worth while to analyse, while still leaving much for political science to investigate.

Now, we may say that the most important subjects about which all men deliberate and deliberative orators harangue, and five in number, to wit: ways and means, war and peace, the defence of the country, imports and exports, legislation.

Accordingly, the orator who is going to give advice on ways and means should be acquainted with the nature and extent of the State resources, so that if any is omitted it may be added, and if any is insufficient, it may be increased. Further, he should know all the expense of the State, that if any is superfluous, it may be removed, or, if too great, may be curtailed. For men become wealthier, not only by adding to what they already possess, but also by cutting down expenses. Of these things it is not only possible to acquire a general view from individual experience, but in view of advising concerning them it is further necessary to be well informed about what has been discovered among others.

In regard to war and peace, the orator should be acquainted with the power of the State, how great it is already and how great it may possibly become; of what kind it is already and what additions may possibly be made to it; further, what wars it has waged and its conduct of them. These things he should be acquainted with, not only as far as his own State is concerned, but also in reference to neighbouring States and particularly those with whom there is a likelihood of war, so that towards the stronger a pacific attitude may be maintained, and in regard to the weaker, the deci-

---

[46] The analytical science is Dialectic, incorrectly regarded as a branch of Analytics, which properly implies scientific demonstration.

[47] Taking εἰς ἐπιστήμας with μεταβαίνειν. If taken with ἐπισκευάζων, the sense will be: "by changing his ground (μεταβαίνειν being used absolutely) while altering their characters from faculties to sciences."

sion as to making war on them may be left to his own State. Again, he should know whether their forces are like or unlike his own, for herein also advantage or disadvantage may lie. With reference to these matters he must also have examined the results, not only of the wars carried on by his own State, but also of those carried on by others; for similar results naturally arise from similar causes.

Again, in regard to the defence of the country, he should not be ignorant how it is carried on; he should know both the strength of the guard, its character, and the positions of the guard-houses (which is impossible for one who is unacquainted with the country) so that if any guard is insufficient it may be increased, or if any is superfluous it may be disbanded, and greater attention devoted to suitable positions.

Again, in regard to food, he should know what amount of expenditure is sufficient to support the State; what kind of food is produced at home or can be imported; and what exports and imports are necessary, in order that contracts and agreements may be made with those[48] who can furnish them; for it is necessary to keep the citizens free from reproach in their relations with two classes of people – those who are stronger and those who are useful for commercial purposes.

With a view to the safety of the State, it is necessary that the orator should be able to judge of all these questions but an understanding of legislation is of special importance, for it is on the laws that the safety of the State is based. Wherefore he must know how many forms of government there are; what is expedient for each; and the natural causes of its downfall, whether they are peculiar to the particular form of government or opposed to it. By being ruined by causes peculiar to itself, I mean that, with the exception of the perfect form of government, all the rest are ruined by being relaxed or strained to excess. Thus democracy, not only when relaxed, but also when strained to excess, becomes weaker and will end in an oligarchy; similarly, not only does an aquiline or snub nose reach the mean, when one of

these defects is relaxed, but when it becomes aquiline or snub to excess, it is altered to such in extent that even the likeness of a nose is lost. Moreover, with reference to acts of legislation, it is useful not only to understand what form of government is expedient by judging in the light of the past, but also to become acquainted with those in existence in other nations, and to learn what kinds of government are suitable to what kinds of people. It is clear, therefore, that for legislation books of travel are useful, since they help us to understand the laws of other nations, and for political debates historical works.[49] All these things, however, belong to Politics and not to Rhetoric.

Such, then, are the most important questions upon which the would-be deliberative orator must be well informed. Now let us again state the sources whence we must derive our arguments for exhortation or discussion on these and other questions.

5. Men, individually and in common, nearly all have some aim, in the attainment of which they choose or avoid certain things. This aim, briefly stated, is happiness and its component parts. Therefore, for the sake of illustration, let us ascertain what happiness, generally speaking, is, and what its parts consist in; for all who exhort or dissuade discuss happiness and the things which conduce or are detrimental to it. For one should do the things which procure happiness or one of its parts, or increase instead of diminishing it, and avoid doing those things which destroy or hinder it or bring about what is contrary to it.

Let us then define happiness as well-being combined with virtue, or independence of life, or the life that is most agreeable combined with security, or abundance of possessions and slaves,[50] combined with power to protect and make use of them[51]; for nearly all men admit that one or more of these things constitutes happiness. If, then, such is the nature of happiness, its component parts must necessarily be: noble birth, numerous friends, good friends, wealth, good children, numerous children, a good old

---

[48] τούτους: those who will receive exports and send imports.

[49] This rendering, although convenient, hardly represents the Greek, which, literally translated, is "the *investigations of those who write about human actions*" (*cf.* ἱστορικός, § 8).

[50] This is the usual rendering, although it is hardly satisfactory. Jebb translates "a flourishing state … of body."

[51] Or, "bring about," "effect them."

age; further, bodily excellences, such as health, beauty, strength, stature, fitness for athletic contests, a good reputation, honour, good luck, virtue. For a man would be entirely independent, provided he possessed all internal and external goods; for there are no others. Internal goods are those of mind and body; external goods are noble birth, friends, wealth, honour. To these we think should be added certain capacities[52] and good luck; for on these conditions life will be perfectly secure. Let us now in the same way define each of these in detail.

Noble birth, in the case of a nation or State, means that its members or inhabitants are sprung from the soil,[53] or of long standing; that its first members were famous as leaders, and that many of their descendants have been famous for qualities that are highly esteemed. In the case of private individuals, noble birth is derived from either the father's or the mother's side, and on both sides there must be legitimacy and, as in the case of a State, it means that its founders were distinguished for virtue, or wealth, or any other of the things that men honour, and that a number of famous persons, both men and women, young and old, belong to the family.

The blessing of good children and numerous children needs little explanation. For the commonwealth it consists in a large number of good young men, good in bodily excellences, such as stature, beauty, strength, fitness for athletic contests; the moral excellences of a young man are self-control and courage. For the individual it consists in a number of good children of his own, both male and female, and such as we have described. Female bodily excellences are beauty and stature, their moral excellences self-control and industrious habits, free from servility.[54] The object of both the individual and of the community should be to secure the existence of each of these qualities in both men and women; for all those States in which the character of women is unsatisfactory, as in Lacedaemon,[55] may be considered only half-happy.

Wealth consists in abundance of money, ownership of land and properties, and further of movables, cattle, and slaves, remarkable for number, size, and beauty, if they are all secure, liberal, and useful. Property that is productive is more useful, but that which has enjoyment for its object is more liberal. By productive I mean that which is a source of income, by enjoyable that which offers no advantage beyond the use of it – at least, none worth mentioning.

[. . .]

Book II

1. Such then are the materials which we must employ in exhorting and dissuading, praising and blaming, accusing and defending, and such are the opinions and propositions that are useful to produce conviction in these circumstances; for they are the subject and source of enthymemes, which are specially suitable to each class (so to say) of speeches.[56] But since the object of Rhetoric is judgement – for judgements are pronounced in deliberative rhetoric and judicial proceedings are a judgement – it is not only necessary to consider how to make the speech itself demonstrative and convincing, but also that the speaker should show himself to be of a certain character and should know how to put the judge into a certain frame of mind. For it makes a great difference with regard to producing conviction – especially in demonstrative, and, next to this, in forensic oratory – that the speaker should show himself to be possessed of certain qualities and that his hearers should think that he is disposed in a certain way

---

[52] *i.e.* of mind and body; or δυνάμεις may mean "positions of authority and influence."

[53] This was a favourite boast of the Athenians.

[54] ἀνελευθερία: literally, qualities unbecoming to a free man or woman, ungentlemanly, unladylike; hence, mean, servile, sordid.

[55] A similar charge against the Spartan women is made in the *Politics* (ii. 9. 5): "Further, the looseness (ἄνεσις) of the Spartan women is injurious both to the purpose of the constitution and the well-being of the State … their life is one of absolute luxury and intemperance" (compare Euripides, *Andromache*, 595–6 "even if she wished it, a Spartan girl could not be chaste") The opinion of Xenophon and Plutarch is much more favourable.

[56] This is Cope's interpretation. Jebb renders: "If we take each branch of Rhetoric by itself." The classes are of course the deliberative, forensic, and epideictic.

towards them; and further, that they themselves should be disposed in a certain way towards him.[57] In deliberative oratory, it is more useful that the orator should appear to be of a certain character, in forensic, that the hearer should be disposed in a certain way; for opinions vary, according as men love or hate, are wrathful or mild, and things appear either altogether different, or different in degree; for when a man is favourably disposed towards one on whom he is passing judgement, he either thinks that the accused has committed no wrong at all or that his offence is trifling; but if he hates him, the reverse is the case. And if a man desires anything and has good hopes of getting it, if what is to come is pleasant, he thinks that it is sure to come to pass and will be good; but if a man is unemotional or not hopeful[58] it is quite the reverse.

For the orator to produce conviction three qualities are necessary; for, independently of demonstrations, the things which induce belief are three in number. These qualities are good sense, virtue, and goodwill; for speakers are wrong both in what they say and in the advice they give because they lack either all three or one of them. For either through want of sense they form incorrect opinions, or, if their opinions are correct, through viciousness they do not say what they think, or, if they are sensible and good,[59] they lack goodwill; wherefore it may happen that they do not give the best advice, although they know what it is. These qualities are all that are necessary, so that the speaker who appears to possess all three will necessarily convince his hearers. The means whereby he may appear sensible and good must be inferred from the classification of the virtues;[60] for to make himself appear such he would employ the same means as he would in the case of others. We must

now speak of goodwill and friendship in our discussion of the emotions.

The emotions are all those affections which cause men to change their opinion in regard to their judgements, and are accompanied by pleasure and pain; such are anger pity, fear, and all similar emotions and their contraries. And each of them must be divided under three heads; for instance, in regard to anger, the disposition of mind which makes men angry, the persons with whom they are usually angry, and the occasions which give rise to anger. For if we knew one or even two of these heads, but not all three, it would be impossible to arouse that emotion. The same applies to the rest. Just as, then, we have given a list of propositions[61] in what we have previously said, we will do the same here and divide the emotions in the same manner.

2. Let us then define anger as a longing, accompanied by pain, for a real or apparent revenge for a real or apparent slight,[62] affecting a man himself or one of his friends, when such a slight is undeserved. If this definition is correct, the angry man must always be angry with a particular individual (for instance, with Cleon, but not with men generally), and because this individual has done, or was on the point of doing, something against him or one of his friends; and lastly, anger is always accompanied by a certain pleasure, due to the hope of revenge to come. For it is pleasant to think that one will obtain what one aims at; now, no one aims at what is obviously impossible of attainment by him, and the angry man aims at what is possible for himself. Wherefore it has been well said of anger, that

Far sweeter than dripping honey down the throat it spreads in men's hearts.[63]

---

[57] The instructions given for enthymematic or logical proof should suffice; but since the function of Rhetoric is to find the available means of persuasion and its end is a judgement; and since an appeal to the speaker's own character and to the passions of those who are to give the judgement is bound to carry great weight, the speaker must be provided with rules for ethical and "pathetic" (emotional) proofs. In i. 5 Aristotle mentions appeals to the emotions with disapproval, but this does not apply to all such appeals, but only to those which are likely to bias the judges unfairly (*e.g.* stirring up envy, hatred, a desire for revenge).

[58] Opposed to εὐέλπιδι. Others render "in a bad humour."

[59] ἐπιεικής and σπουδαῖος both = ἀγαθός. In a restricted sense ἐπιεικής is "respectable," σπουδαῖος is "serious."

[60] i. 9.

[61] In i. generally (cp. i. 2. 22).

[62] Gomperz translates φαινομένης "real or apparent"; Jebb omits φαινομένης and translates φαινομένην "apparent"; Cope confines both to the meaning "manifest."

[63] *Iliad*, xviii. 109 (cp. i. 11. 9).

for it is accompanied by a certain pleasure, for this reason first,[64] and also because men dwell upon the thought of revenge, and the vision that rises before us produces the same pleasure as one seen in dreams.

Slighting is an actualization of opinion in regard to something which appears valueless; for things which are really bad or good, or tend to become so, we consider worthy of attention, but those which are of no importance or trifling[65] we ignore. Now there are three kinds of slight: disdain, spitefulness, and insult. For he who disdains, slights, since men disdain those things which they consider valueless and slight what is of no account. And the spiteful man appears to show disdain; for spitefulness consists in placing obstacles in the way of another's wishes, not in order that any advantage may accrue to him who spites, but to prevent any accruing to the other. Since then he does not act in this manner from self-interest, it is a slight; for it is evident that he has no idea that the other is likely to hurt him, for in that case he would be afraid of him instead of slighting him; nor that he will be of any use to him worth speaking of, for in that case his thought would be how to become his friend.[66]

Similarly, he who insults another also slights him; for insult[67] consists in causing injury or annoyance whereby the sufferer is disgraced, not to obtain any other advantage for oneself besides the performance of the act, but for one's own pleasure; for retaliation is not insult, but punishment. The cause of the pleasure felt by those who insult is the idea that, in ill-treating others, they are more fully showing superiority. That is why the young and the wealthy are given to insults; for they think that, in committing them, they are showing their superiority. Dishonour is characteristic of insult; and one who dishonours another slights him; for that which is worthless has no value, either as good or evil. Hence Achilles in his wrath exclaims:

> He has dishonoured me, since he keeps the prize he has taken for himself,[68]

and

> [has treated me] like a dishonoured vagrant,[69]

as if being wrath for these reasons. Now men think that they have a right to be highly esteemed by those who are inferior to them in birth, power, and virtue, and generally, in whatever similar respect[70] a man is far superior to another; for example, the rich man to the poor man in the matter of money, the eloquent to the incompetent speaker in the matter of oratory, the governor to the governed, and the man who thinks himself worthy to rule to one who is only fit to be ruled. Wherefore it has been said:

> Great is the wrath of kings cherished by Zeus,[71]

and

> Yet it may be that even afterwards he cherishes his resentment,[72]

for kings are resentful in consideration of their superior rank. Further, men are angry at slights from those by whom they think they have a right to expect to be well treated; such are those on whom

---

[64] The thought of revenge in the future, as distinguished from dwelling upon it in the present.

[65] Or, "those in which this tendency does not exist, or is trifling."

[66] Or, "how to make him his friend," φιλος being for φίλον by attraction.

[67] In Attic law ὕβρις (insulting, degrading treatment) was a more serious offence than αἰκία (bodily ill-treatment). It was the subject of a State criminal prosecution (γραφή), αἰκία of a private action (δίκη) for damages. The penalty was assessed in court, and might even be death. It had to be proved that the defendant struck the first blow (ii. 24. 9). One of the best known instances is the action brought by Demosthenes against Midas for a personal outrage on himself, when *choregus* of his tribe and responsible for the equipment of a chorus for musical competitions at public festivals.

[68] *Iliad*, i. 356.

[69] *Iliad*, ix. 648. μετανάστης, lit. "one who changes his home," used as a term of reproach.

[70] ταὐτῷ. Other readings are ταὐτα, or τις.

[71] *Iliad*, ii. 196.

[72] *Iliad*, i. 82. The words are those of the soothsayer Calchas to Achilles, and the reference is to Agamemnon.

they have conferred or are conferring benefits, either themselves, or some one else for them, or one of their friends; and all those whom they desire, or did desire, to benefit.

It is now evident from these considerations what is the disposition of those who are angry, with whom they are angry, and for what reasons. Men are angry when they are pained, because one who is pained aims at something; if then anyone directly opposes him in anything, as, for instance, prevents him from drinking when thirsty, or not directly, but seems to be doing just the same; and if anyone goes against him or refuses to assist him, or troubles him in any other way when he is in this frame of mind, he is angry with all such persons. Wherefore the sick, the necessitous, [those at war], the love-sick, the thirsty, in a word, all who desire something and cannot obtain it, are prone to anger and easily excited, especially against those who make light of their present condition; for instance, the sick man is easily provoked in regard to his illness,[73] the necessitous in regard to his poverty, the warrior in regard to warlike affairs, the lover in regard to love-affairs, and so with all the rest; for the passion[74] present in his mind in each case paves the way for his anger. Again, men are angry when the event is contrary to their expectation, for the more unexpected a thing is, the more it pains; just as they are overjoyed if, contrary to expectation, what they desire comes to pass. From this it is obvious what are the seasons, times, states of mind, and conditions of age in which we are easily moved[75] to anger; and what are the various times, places, and reasons, which make us more prone to anger in proportion as we are subject to their influence.

Such then are the dispositions of those who are easily roused to anger. As to the objects of their anger, men are angry with those who ridicule, mock, and scoff at them, for this is an insult. And with those who injure them in ways that are indications of insult. But these acts must be of such a kind that they are neither retaliatory nor advantageous to those who commit them; for if

they are, they then appear due to gratuitous insult. And men are angry with those who speak ill of or despise things which they themselves consider of the greatest importance; for instance, if a man speaks contemptuously of philosophy or of personal beauty in the presence of those who pride themselves upon them; and so in all others cases. But they are far more angry if they suspect that they do not possess these qualities, either not at all, or not to any great extent, or when others do not think they possess them. For when they feel strongly that they do possess those qualities which are the subject of mockery, they pay no heed to it. And they are more angry with those who are their friends than with those who are not, for they think that they have a right to be treated well by them rather than ill. And they are angry with those who have been in the habit of honouring and treating them with respect, if they no longer behave so towards them; for they think that they are being treated with contempt by them, otherwise they would treat them as before. And with those who do not return their kindnesses nor requite them in full; and with those who oppose them, if they are inferiors; for all such appear to treat them with contempt, the latter as if they regarded them as inferiors, the former as if they had received kindnesses from inferiors.

And they are more angry with those who are of no account, if they slight them; for anger at a slight was assumed to be felt at those who ought not to behave in such a manner; for inferiors ought not to slight their superiors. And they are angry with friends, if they neither speak well of nor treat them well, and in an even greater degree, if they do the opposite. And if they fail to perceive that they want something from them, as Plexippus[76] in Antiphon's tragedy reproached Meleager; for failure to perceive this is a sign of slight; since, when we care for people, these things are noticed.[77] And they are angry with those who rejoice, or in a general way are cheerful when they are unfortunate;

---

[73] τοῖς πρὸς τὴν νόσον: lit. "the sick man [is angry with those who slight him] in regard to his illness," that is, by making light of it.

[74] Or, "his suffering at the moment."

[75] εὐκίνητοι refers grammatically to διαθέσεις and ἡλικίαι.

[76] Plexippus was the uncle of Meleager. The allusion is obscure. It may refer to Meleager giving the skin of the Calydonian boar to Atalanta, which his uncle wanted. One of Antiphon's tragedies was named *Meleager* (T.G.F. p. 792).

[77] Literally, "for the things which (= the persons whom) one respects, do not escape notice."

for this is an indication of enmity or slight. And with those who do not care if they pain them; whence they are angry with those who bring bad news. And with those who listen to the tale of their faults, or look on them with indifference, for they resemble slighters or enemies; for friends sympathize and all men are pained to see their own faults exposed.[78] And further, with those who slight them before five classes of persons: namely, their rivals, those whom they admire, those by whom they would like to be admired, those whom they respect, or those who respect them; when anyone slights them before these, their anger is greater. They are also angry with those who slight such persons as it would be disgraceful for them not to defend, for instance, parents, children, wives, and dependents.[79] And with those who are ungrateful,[80] for the slight is contrary to all sense of obligation. And with those who employ irony, when they themselves are in earnest; for irony shows contempt. And with those who do good to others, but not to them; for not to think them worthy of what they bestow upon all others also shows contempt. Forgetfulness also is a cause of anger, such as forgetting names, although it is a mere trifle, since even forgetfulness seems a sign of slight; for it is caused by indifference, and indifference is a slight. We have thus stated at one and the same time the frame of mind and the reasons which make men angry, and the objects of their anger. It is evident then that it will be necessary for the speaker, by his eloquence, to put the hearers into the frame of mind of those who are inclined to anger, and to show that his opponents are responsible for things which rouse men to anger and are people of the kind with whom men are angry.

3. And since becoming angry is the opposite of becoming mild, and anger of mildness, we must determine the state of mind which makes men mild, towards whom they become mild, and the reasons which make them so. Let us then define making mild as the quieting and appeasing of anger. If then men are angry with those who slight them, and slight is voluntary, it is evident that they are mild towards those who do none of these things, or do them involuntarily, or at least appear to be such; and towards those who intended the opposite of what they have done, and all who behave in the same way to themselves, for no one is likely to slight himself. And towards those who admit and are sorry for a slight; for finding as it were satisfaction in the pain the offenders feel at what they have done, men cease to be angry. Evidence of this may be seen in the punishment of slaves; for we punish more severely those who contradict us and deny their offence, but cease to be angry with those who admit that they are justly punished. The reason is that to deny what is evident is disrespect, and disrespect is slight and contempt; anyhow, we show no respect for those for whom we entertain a profound contempt. Men also are mild towards those who humble themselves before them and do not contradict them, for they seem to recognize that they are inferior; now, those who are inferior are afraid, and no one who is afraid slights another. Even the behaviour of dogs proves that anger ceases towards those who humble themselves, for they do not bite those who sit down.[81] And men are mild towards those who are serious with them when they are serious, for they think they are being treated seriously, not with contempt. And towards those who have rendered them greater services.[82] And towards those who want something and deprecate their anger, for they are humbler. And towards those who refrain from insulting, mocking, or slighting anyone, or any virtuous man, or those who resemble themselves. And generally speaking, one can determine the reasons that make for mildness by their opposites. Thus, men

---

[78] The real friend, therefore, would feel as much pain as the other whose faults are exposed.

[79] Cope translates "rulers and governors"; but can ἄρχεσθαι be used in a middle sense?

[80] To avoid the apparent tautology (§ 17), Roemer (*Rhein. Mus.* xxxix. p. 503) boldly conjectures χαίρειν: "not to return another's greeting."

[81] ἐξαπίνης δ' Ὀδυσῆα ἴδον κύνες ὑλακόμωροι | οἱ μὲν κεκλήγοντες ἐπέδραμον· αὐτὰρ Ὀδυσσεὺς | ἕζετο κερδοσύνη (*Odyssey*, xiv. 29–31).

[82] That is, greater than their present disservices.

are mild towards those whom they fear or respect, as long as they feel so towards them, for it is impossible to be afraid and angry at the same time. And against those who have acted in anger they either feel no anger or in a less degree, for they do not seem to have acted from a desire to slight. For no one slights another when angry, since slight is free from pain, but anger is accompanied by it. And men are not angry with those who usually show respect for them.[83]

It is also evident that those are mild whose condition is contrary to that which excites anger, as when laughing, in sport, at a feast, in prosperity, in success, in abundance,[84] And, in general, in freedom from pain, in pleasure which does not imply insult, or in virtuous hope. Further, those whose anger is of long standing and not in its full flush, for time appeases anger. Again vengeance previously taken upon one person appeases anger against another, even though it be greater. Wherefore Philocrates,[85] when someone asked him why he did not justify himself when the people were angry with him, made the judicious reply, "Not yet." "When then?" "When I see someone accused of the same offence"; for men grow mild when they have exhausted their anger upon another, as happened in the case of Ergophilus.[86] For although the Athenians were more indignant with him than with Callisthenes, they acquitted him, because they had condemned Callicrates to death on the previous day. Men also grow mild towards those whom they pity[87]; and if an offender has suffered greater evil than those who

are angry would have inflicted, for they have an idea that they have as if were obtained reparation. And if they think that they themselves are wrong and deserve what they suffer, for anger is not aroused against what is just; they no longer think that they are being treated otherwise than they should be, which, as we have said, is the essence of anger. Wherefore we should inflict a preliminary verbal chastisement, for even slaves are less indignant at punishment of this kind. And men are milder if they think that those punished will never know that the punishment comes from *them* in requital for their own wrongs; for anger has to do with the individual, as is clear from our definition.[88] Wherefore it is justly said by the poet:

Tell him that it is Odyssesus, sacker of cities,[89]

as if Polyphemus would not have been punished,[90] had he remained ignorant who had blinded him and for what. So that men are not angry either with any others who cannot know who punishes them,[91] or with the dead, since they have paid the last penalty and can feel neither pain nor anything else, which is the aim of those who are angry.[92] So then, in regard to Hector, Homer, when desirous of restraining the anger of Achilles against a dead man, well says:

For it is senseless clay that he outrages in his wrath.[93]

It is evident, then, that men must have recourse to these topics when they desire to appease their

[83] They regard the disrespectful treatment as merely a temporary lapse.

[84] πλήρωσις: lit. "filling up." The reference may be to the "fulfilment" of one's desires, or to "repletion" in the matter of food (L. and S.), which seems less likely; "in fulness of content" (Jebb).

[85] Opponent of Demosthenes, and one of the pro-Macedonian party. Impeached for his share in the disastrous "Peace of Philocrates," he went into exile and was condemned to death during his absence.

[86] Ergophilus failed in an attack on Cotys, king of Thrace, while Callisthenes concluded a premature peace with Perdiccas, king of Macedonia.

[87] Another reading is ἐὰν ἕλωσι "if they have convicted him." This is adopted by Roemer, who refers to Plato, *Republic*, 558 A, where, in speaking of the freedom allowed to all who live under a democracy, it is remarked that, even if a man is convicted by a court of justice, he takes no heed of the sentence, which is very often not enforced.

[88] Therefore, if you think that a man will never learn *who* took vengeance on him, you will be less cruel; for anger is personal, and so Odysseus, because he was angry, inflicted a savage punishment, and wished Polyphemus to know it.

[89] *Odyssey*, ix. 504.

[90] Or, "as if Odysseus would not have considered himself avenged, had P. remained ignorant ..."

[91] Or, "with any who can no longer feel their anger." Cope translates: "with all the rest (besides those actually within reach) who are out of sight."

[92] To make the offender *feel* pain as part of the punishment.

[93] *Iliad*. xxiv. 54.

audience, putting them into the frame of mind required and representing those with whom they are angry as either formidable or deserving of respect, or as having rendered them great services, or acted involuntarily, or as exceedingly grieved at what they have done.

4. Let us now state who are the persons that men love[94] or hate, and why, after we have defined love and loving. Let loving, then, be defined as wishing for anyone the things which we believe to be good, for his sake but not for our own, and procuring them for him as far as lies in our power. A friend is one who loves and is loved in return, and those who think their relationship is of this character consider themselves friends. This being granted, it necessarily follows that he is a friend who shares our joy in good fortune and our sorrow in affliction, for our own sake and not for any other reason. For all men rejoice when what they desire comes to pass and are pained when the contrary happens, so that pain and pleasure are indications of their wish. And those are friends who have the same ideas of good and bad, and love and hate the same persons, since they necessarily wish the same things; wherefore one who wishes for another what he wishes for himself seems to be the other's friend.

We also like those who have done good either to us or to those whom we hold dear, if the services are important, or are cordially rendered, or under certain circumstances and for our sake only; and all those whom we think desirous of doing us good. And those who are friends of our friends and who like those whom we like and those who are liked by those who are liked by us; and those whose enemies are ours, those who hate those whom we ourselves hate, and those who are hated by those who are hated by us; for all such persons have the same idea as ourselves of what is good, so that they wish what is good for us, which, as the said, is the characteristic of a friend. Further, *we like those* who are ready to help others in the matter of money or personal safety; wherefore men honour those who are liberal and courageous and just. And such we consider those who do not live upon others; the sort of men who live by their exertions, and among them agriculturists, and, beyond all others, those who work with their own hands.[95] And the self-controlled, because they are not likely to commit injustice; and those who are not busybodies, for the same reason. And those with whom we wish to be friends, if they also seem to wish it; such are those who excel in virtue and enjoy a good reputation, either generally, or amongst the best, or amongst those who are admired by us or by whom we are admired.[96] Further, those who are agreeable to live or spend the time with; such are those who are good-tempered and not given to carping at our errors, neither quarrelsome nor contentious, for all such persons are pugnacious, and the wishes of the pugnacious appear to be opposed to ours.

And those are liked who are clever at making or taking a joke, for each has the same end in view as his neighbour, being able to take a joke and return it in good taste. And those who praise our good qualities, especially those which we ourselves are afraid we do not possess; those who are neat in their personal appearance and dress, and clean-living; those who do not make our errors or the benefits they have conferred a matter of reproach, for both these are inclined to be censorious; those who bear no malice and do not cherish the memory of their wrongs, but are easily appeased; for we think that they will be to ourselves such as we suppose them to be to others; and those who are neither given to slander, or eager to know the faults of their neigh-

---

[94] φιλεῖν may be translated "to love" or "to like"; φιλία by "love," "liking," or "friendship" ; for φίλος "friend" alone is suitable. For the two meanings cp. the use of *aimer* in French, and *lieben* in German.

[95] Aristotle's opinion of husbandry, in which tillage and planting, keeping of bees, fish, and fowl were included, was not nearly so favourable as that of Xenophon in his *Oeconomicus*. In two lists of the elements of a State given in the *Politics*, it comes first at the head of the lower occupations. In its favour it is said that it forms the best material of a rural democracy, furnishes good sailors, a healthy body of men, not money-grabbers like merchants and tradesmen, and does not make men unfit to bear arms. On the other hand, it claims so much of a man's time that he is unable to devote proper attention to political duties, and should be excluded from holding office. He further says that husbandmen, if possible, should be slaves (neither of the same race nor hot-tempered, for they will work better and are less likely to revolt) or, as the next best alternative, barbarians or serfs. The favourable view taken by Aristotle here and in the *Oeconomics* (probably not his) does not agree with that put forward in the *Politics*.

[96] Spengel reads ἢ ἐν οἷς θαυμάζουσιν αὐτοί and brackets [ἢ ἐν τοῖς θαυμαζομένοις ὑφ᾽ αὐτῶν]. ἅπασιν, βελτίστοις, and οἷς will then be neuter.

bours nor our own, but only the good qualities; for this is the way in which the good man acts. And those who do not oppose us when we are angry or occupied, for such persons are pugnacious; and those who show any good feeling towards us; for instance, if they admire us, think us good men, and take pleasure in our company, especially those who are so disposed towards us in regard to things for which we particularly desire to be either admired or to be thought worthy or agreeable. And we like those who resemble us and have the same tastes, provided their interests do not clash with ours and that they do not gain their living in the same way; for then it becomes a case of

Potter [being jealous] of potter.[97]

And those who desire the same things, provided it is possible for us to share them; otherwise the same thing would happen again. And those with whom we are on such terms that we do not blush before them for faults merely condemned by public opinion, provided that this is not due to contempt; and those before whom we do blush for faults that are really bad. And those whose rivals we are,[98] or by whom we wish to be emulated, but not envied, – these we either like or wish to be friends with them. And those whom we are ready to assist in obtaining what is good, provided greater evil does not result for ourselves. And those who show equal fondness for friends, whether absent or present; wherefore all men like those who show such feeling for the dead.

In a word, men like those who are strongly attached to their friends and do not leave them in the lurch; for among good men they chiefly like those who are good friends. And those who do not dissemble with them; such are those who do not fear to mention even their faults. (For, as we have said, before friends we do not blush for faults merely condemned by public opinion; if then he who blushes for such faults is not a friend, he who does not is not likely to be one).[99] And men like those who are not formidable, and in whom they have confidence; for no one likes one whom he fears.

Companionship, intimacy, kinship, and similar relations are species of friendship. Things that create friendship are doing a favour, and doing it unasked, and not making it public after doing it; for then it seems to have been rendered for the sake of the friend, and not for any other reason.

As for enmity and hatred, it is evident that they must be examined in the light of their contraries. The causes which produce enmity are anger, spitefulness, slander. Anger arises from acts committed against us, enmity even from those that are not; for if we imagine a man to be of such and such a character, we hate him. Anger has always an individual as its object, for instance Callias or Socrates, whereas hatred applies to classes; for instance, every one hates a thief or informer. Anger is curable by time, hatred not; the aim of anger is pain, of hatred evil; for the angry man wishes to see what happens;[100] to one who hates it does not matter. Now, the things which cause pain are all perceptible, while things which are especially bad, such as injustice or folly, are least perceptible; for the presence of vice causes no pain. Anger is accompanied by pain, but hatred not; for he who is angry suffers pain, but he who hates does not. One who is angry might feel compassion in many cases, but one who hates, never; for the former wishes that the object of his anger should suffer in his turn, the latter, that he should perish. It is evident, then, from what we have just said, that it is possible to prove that men are enemies or friends, or to make them such if they are not; to refute those who pretend that they are, and when they oppose us through anger or enmity, to bring them over to whichever side may be preferred. The things and persons that men fear and in what frame of mind, will be evident from the following considerations.

5. Let fear be defined as a painful or troubled feeling caused by the impression of an imminent evil that causes destruction or pain; for men do not fear all evils, for instance, becoming unjust or slow-witted, but only such as involve great pain or destruction, and only if they appear to be not

---

[97] Two of a trade never agree (Hesiod, *Works and Days*, 25).

[98] Those with whom we are ambitious of entering into competition "in the race for distinction" (Cope). There is no unfriendliness, whereas envy produces it.

[99] A parenthetical remark. Aristotle explains that he is not thinking of merely conventional faults; if, then, one who *is* ashamed of these is no friend, then one who is *not* …

[100] He wishes to see and know the result of the measures taken against those with whom he is angry. Or, it may mean that he wishes the object of his anger to feel his wrath, and to know by whom, and for what, he is punished.

far off but near at hand and threatening, for men do not fear things that are very remote; all know that they have to die, but as death is not near at hand, they are indifferent. If then this is fear, all things must be fearful that appear to have great power of destroying or inflicting injuries that tend to produce great pain. That is why even the signs of such misfortunes are fearful for the fearful thing itself appears to be near at hand, and danger is the approach of anything fearful. Such signs are the enmity and anger of those able to injure us in any way; for it is evident that they have the wish,[101] so that they are not far from doing so. And injustice possessed of power is fearful, for the unjust man is unjust through deliberate inclination.[102] And outraged virtue when it has power, for it is evident that it always desires satisfaction, whenever it is outraged, and now it has the power. And fear felt by those able to injure us in any way, for such as these also must be ready to act. And since most men are rather bad than good and the slaves of gain and cowardly in time of danger, being at the mercy of another is generally fearful, so that one who has committed a crime has reason to fear his accomplices as likely to denounce or leave him in the lurch. And those who are able to ill-treat others are to be feared by those who can be so treated; for as a rule men do wrong whenever they can. Those who have been, or think they are being, wronged, are also to be feared, for they are ever on the look out for an opportunity. And those who have committed some wrong, when they have the power, since they are afraid of retaliation, which was assumed to be something to be feared. And those who are our rivals for the same things, whenever it is impossible to share them, for men are always contending with such persons. And those who are feared by those who are stronger than we are, for they would be better able to injure us, if they could injure those stronger than ourselves; and those whom those who are stronger than ourselves are afraid of, for the same reason. And those who have overthrown those who are stronger than us and those who attack those who are weaker, for they are either already to be feared, or will be, when they have grown stronger.

And among those whom we have wronged, or are our enemies or rivals, we should fear not the hot-tempered or outspoken, but those who are mild, dissemblers, and thorough rascals; for it is uncertain whether they are on the point of acting, so that one never knows whether they are far from it.[103] All things that are to be feared are more so when, after an error has once been committed, it is impossible to repair it, either because it is absolutely impossible, or no longer in our power, but in that of our opponents; also when there is no possibility of help or it is not easy to obtain. In a word, all things are to be feared which, when they happen, or are on the point of happening, to others, excite compassion. These are, so to say, nearly all the most important things which are to be feared and which men fear. Let us now state the frame of mind which leads men to fear.

If then fear is accompanied by the expectation that we are going to suffer some fatal misfortune, it is evident that none of those who think that they will suffer nothing at all is afraid either of those things which he does not think will happen to him, or of those from whom he does not expect them, or at a time when he does not think them likely to happen. It therefore needs be that those who think they are likely to suffer anything should be afraid, either of the persons at whose hands they expect it, or of certain things, and at certain times. Those who either are, or seem to be, highly prosperous do not think they are likely to suffer anything; wherefore they are insolent, contemptuous, and rash, and what makes them such is wealth, strength, a number of friends, power. It is the same with those who think that they have already suffered all possible ills and are coldly indifferent to the future, like those who are being beaten to death; for it is a necessary incentive to fear that there should remain some hope of being saved from the cause of their distress. A sign of this is that fear makes men deliberate, whereas no one deliberates about things that are hopeless. So that whenever it is preferable that the audience should feel afraid it is necessary to make them think they are likely to suffer, by reminding them that others greater than they have suffered, and showing that their equals are

---

[101] By the definitions of anger and hatred.
[102] And therefore, having the inclination to be unjust, if he has the power, he will be so.
[103] Or simply, "near … far from us."

suffering or have suffered, and that at the hands of those from whom they did not expect it, in such a manner and at times when they did not think it likely.

Now, since we have made clear what fear and fearful things are, and the frame of mind in each case which makes men fear, one can see from this what confidence is, what are the things that give it, and the frame of mind of those who possess it; for confidence is the contrary of fear and that which gives confidence of that which causes fear, so that the hope of what is salutary is accompanied by an impression that it is quite near at hand, while the things to be feared are either non-existent or far off.

[…]

Book III

1. There are three things which require special attention in regard to speech: first, the sources of proofs; secondly, style; and thirdly, the arrangement of the parts of the speech. We have already spoken of proofs and stated that they are three in number, what is their nature, and why there are only three; for in all cases persuasion is the result either of the judges themselves being affected in a certain manner, or because they consider the speakers to be of a certain character, or because something has been demonstrated. We have also stated the sources from which enthymemes should be derived – some of them being special, the others general commonplaces.

We have therefore next to speak of style; for it is not sufficient to know what one ought to say, but one must also know how to say it, and this largely contributes to making the speech appear of a certain character. In the first place, following the natural order, we investigated that which first presented itself – what gives things themselves their persuasiveness; in the second place, their arrangement by style; and in the third place, delivery, which is of the greatest importance, but has not yet been treated of by any one. In fact, it only made its appearance late in tragedy and rhapsody, for at first the poets themselves acted their tragedies.[104] It is clear, therefore, that there is something of the sort in rhetoric as well as in poetry, and it has been dealt with by Glaucon of Teos among others. Now delivery is a matter of voice, as to the mode in which it should be used for each particular emotion; when it should be loud, when low, when intermediate; and how the tones, that is, shrill, deep, and intermediate, should be used; and what rhythms are adapted to each subject. For there are three qualities that are considered, – volume, harmony, rhythm. Those who use these properly nearly always carry off the prizes in dramatic contests, and as at the present day actors have greater influence on the stage than the poets, it is the same in political[105] contests, owing to the corruptness of our forms of government. But no treatise has yet been composed on delivery, since the matter of style itself only lately came into notice; and rightly considered it is thought vulgar.[106] But since the whole business of Rhetoric is to influence opinion,[107] we must pay attention to it, not as being right, but necessary; for, as a matter of right, one should aim at nothing more in a speech than how to avoid exciting pain or pleasure. For justice should consist in fighting the case with the facts alone, so that everything else that is beside demonstration is superfluous; nevertheless, as we have just said, it is of great importance owing to the corruption of the hearer. However, in every system of instruction there is some slight necessity to pay attention to style; for it does make a difference, for the purpose of making a thing clear, to speak in this or that manner still, the difference is not so very great, but all these things[108] are mere outward show for pleasing the hearer; wherefore no one teaches geometry in this way.

---

[104] Since the authors of tragedies acted their own plays, there was no need for professional actors, nor for instruction in the art of delivery or acting. This explains why no attempt had been made to deal with the question. Similarly, the rhapsodists (reciters of epic poems) were at first as a rule the composers of the poems themselves.

[105] In the law courts and public assembly.

[106] Cope prefers: "is thought vulgar, and rightly so considered."

[107] Or, "is concerned with appearance."

[108] *i.e.* style, delivery, and acting, which are of no use to serious students.

Now, when delivery comes into fashion, it will have the same effect as acting. Some writers have attempted to say a few words about it, as Thrasymachus, in his *Eleoi*[109]; and in fact, a gift for acting is a natural talent and depends less upon art, but in regard to style it is artificial. Wherefore people who excel in this in their turn obtain prizes, just as orators who excel in delivery; for written speeches owe their effect not so much to the sense as to the style.

The poets, as was natural, were the first to give an impulse to style; for words are imitations, and the voice also, which of all our parts is best adapted for imitation, was ready to hand; thus the arts of the rhapsodists, actors, and others, were fashioned. And as the poets, although their utterances were devoid of sense, appeared to have gained their reputation through their style, it was a poetical style that first came into being, as that of Gorgias.[110] Even now the majority of the uneducated think that such persons express themselves most beautifully, whereas this is not the case, for the style of prose is not the same as that of poetry. And the result proves it; for even the writers of tragedies do not employ it in the same manner but as they have changed from the tetrametric to the iambic metre, because the latter, of all other metres, most nearly resembles prose, they have in like manner discarded all such words as differ from those of ordinary conversation, with which the early poets used to adorn their writings, and which even now are employed by the writers of hexameters. It is therefore ridiculous to imitate those who no longer employ that manner of writing. Consequently, it is evident that we need not enter too precisely into all questions of style, but only those which concern such a style as we are discussing. As for the other kind of style,[111] it has already been treated in the *Poetics*.

2. Let this suffice for the consideration of these points. In regard to style, one of its chief merits may be defined as perspicuity. This is shown by the fact that the speech, if it does not make the meaning clear, will not perform its proper function; neither must it be mean, nor above the dignity of the subject, but appropriate to it; for the poetic style may be is not mean, but it is not appropriate to prose. Of nouns and verbs it is the proper ones that make style perspicuous[112]; all the others which have been spoken of in the *Poetics*[113] elevate and make it ornate; for departure from the ordinary makes it appear more dignified. In this respect men feel the same in regard to style as in regard to foreigners and fellow citizens. Wherefore we should give our language a "foreign[114] air"; for men admire what is remote, and that which excites admiration is pleasant. In poetry many things conduce to this and there it is appropriate; for the subjects and persons spoken of are more out of the common. But in prose such methods are appropriate in much fewer instances, for the subject is less elevated; and even in poetry, if fine language were used by a slave or a very young man, or about quite unimportant matters, it would be hardly becoming; for even here due proportion consists in contraction and amplification as the subject requires. Wherefore those who practise this artifice must conceal it and avoid the appearance of speaking artificially instead of naturally; for that which is natural persuades, but the artificial does not. For men become suspicious of one whom they think to be laying a trap for them, as they are of mixed wines. Such was the case with the voice of Theodorus as contrasted with that of the rest of the actors; for his seemed to be the voice of the speaker, that of the others the voice of some one else. Art is cleverly concealed when the speaker chooses his words from ordinary language[115] and

---

[109] A treatise on Pathos.

[110] Of Leontini in Sicily, Greek sophist and rhetorician.

[111] *i.e.* the poetic style. See *Poetics*, 22, where the choice of words and the extent to which out-of-the-way words and phrases may be used in poetry is discussed.

[112] "Nouns and verbs" is a conventional expression for all the parts of speech. Cp. Horace, *Ars Poetica*, 240, "non ego inornata et dominantia nomina solum | verbaque," where *dominantia* is a literal adaptation of κύρια, the usual Latin equivalent for which is *propria*.

[113] Ch. 21.

[114] It is impossible to find a satisfactory English equivalent for the terms ξένος, ξενικός τὸ ξενίζον, as applied to style. "Foreign" does not really convey the idea, which is rather that of something opposed to "home-like," – out-of-the-way, as if from "abroad." Jebb suggests "distinctive."

[115] Cp. Horace, *Ars Poetica*, 46, where it is said that the choice and use of words requires subtlety and care, skill in making an old word new by clever combination (*callida iunctura*) being especially praised.

puts them together like Euripides, who was the first to show the way.

Nouns and verbs being the components of speech, and nouns being of the different kinds which have been considered in the *Poetics*, of these we should use strange, compound, or coined words only rarely and in few places. We will state later[116] in what places they should be used; the reason for this has already been mentioned, namely, that it involves too great a departure from suitable language. Proper and appropriate words and metaphors are alone to be employed in the style of prose; this is shown by the fact that no one employs anything but these. For all use metaphors in conversation, as well as proper and appropriate words; wherefore it is clear that, if a speaker manages well, there will be something "foreign" about his speech, while possibly the art may not be detected, and his meaning will be clear. And this, as we have said, is the chief merit of rhetorical language. (In regard to nouns, homonyms are most useful to the sophist, for it is by their aid that he employs captious arguments, and synonyms to the poet. Instances of words that are both proper and synonymous are "going" and "walking": for these two words are proper and have the same meaning.)[117]

It has already been stated, as we have said, in the *Poetics*,[118] what each of these things[119] is, how many kinds of metaphor there are, and that it is most important both in poetry and in prose. But the orator must devote the greater attention to them in prose, since the latter has fewer resources than verse. It is metaphor above all that gives perspicuity, pleasure and a foreign air, and it cannot be learnt from anyone else;[120] but we must make use of metaphors and epithets that are appropriate. This will be secured by observing due proportion; otherwise there will be a lack of propriety, because it is when placed in juxtaposition that contraries are most evident. We must consider, as a red cloak suits a young man, what suits an old one; for the same garment is not suitable for both. And if we wish to ornament our subject, we must derive our metaphor from the better species under the same genus; if to depreciate it, from the worse. Thus, to say (for you have two opposites belonging to the same genus) that the man who begs prays, or that the man who prays begs (for both are forms of asking)[121] is an instance of doing this; as, when Iphicrates[122] called Callias[123] a mendicant priest instead of a torch-bearer, Callias replied that Iphicrates himself could not be initiated, otherwise he would not have called him mendicant priest but torch-bearer[124]; both titles indeed have to do with a divinity, but the one is honourable, the other dishonourable. And some call actors flatterers of Dionysus, whereas they call themselves "artists." Both these names are metaphors, but the one is a term of abuse, the other the contrary. Similarly, pirates now call themselves purveyors;[125] and so it is allowable to say that the man who has committed a crime has "made a mistake," that the man who has "made a mistake" is "guilty of crime," and that one who has committed a theft has either "taken" or "ravaged." The saying in the *Telephus* of Euripides,

Ruling over the oar and having landed in Mysia,

is inappropriate, because the word "ruling" exceeds the dignity of the subject, and so the

---

[116] Chs. 3 and 7.

[117] This is a parenthetical note.

[118] Chs. 21, 22.

[119] The different kinds of words.

[120] *Poetics*, 22. 9: "for this alone cannot be borrowed from another."

[121] Begging (as a beggar does) and praying (as a priest might) are both forms of asking, and by substituting one for the other, you can amplify or depreciate.

[122] See i. 7. 32.

[123] Head of a distinguished Athenian family which held the office of torch-bearer at the Eleusinian mysteries. A man of notoriously dissipated character, he took some part in politics.

[124] The δᾳδοῦχος or hereditary torch-bearer ranked next to the hierophant or chief priest. In addition to holding the torch during the sacrifices, he took part in the recitation of the ritual and certain purificatory ceremonies. The μητραγύρται or mendicant priests collected alms on behalf of various deities, especially the great Mother Cybele (whence their name). They included both men and women of profligate character, addicted to every kind of lewdness.

[125] *Cf.* "'convey' the wise it call" (*Merry Wives*, I. iii.). Either the euphemistic or unfavourable application of the term may be adopted.

artifice can be seen. Forms of words also are faulty, if they do not express an agreeable sound; for instance, Dionysius the Brazen[126] in his elegiacs speaks of poetry as

the scream of Calliope;

both are sounds, but the metaphor is bad, because the sounds have no meaning.[127]

Further, metaphors must not be far-fetched, but we must give names to things that have none by deriving the metaphor from what is akin and of the same kind, so that, as soon as it is uttered, it is clearly seen to be akin, as in the famous enigma,

I saw a man who glued bronze with fire upon another.

There was no name for what took place, but as in both cases there is a kind of application, he called the application of the cupping-glass "gluing."[128] And, generally speaking, clever enigmas furnish good metaphors; for metaphor is a kind of enigma, so that it is clear that the transference is clever. Metaphors should also be derived from things that are beautiful, the beauty of a word consisting, as Licymnius says, in its sound or sense, and its ugliness in the same. There is a third condition, which refutes the sophistical argument; for it is not the case, as Bryson[129] said, that no one ever uses foul language, if the meaning is the same whether this or that word is used; this is false; for one word is more proper than another, more of a likeness, and better suited to putting the matter before the eyes. Further, this word or that does not signify a thing under the same conditions; thus for this reason also it must be admitted that one word is fairer or fouler than the other. Both, indeed, signify what is fair or foul, but not *qua* fair or foul; or if they do, it is in a greater or less degree. Metaphors therefore should be

derived from what is beautiful either in sound, or in signification, or to sight, or to some other sense. For it does make a difference, for instance, whether one says "rosy-fingered morn" rather than "purple-fingered," or, what is still worse "red-fingered."

As for epithets, they may be applied from what is vile or disgraceful, for instance, "the matricide," or from what is more honourable, for instance, "the avenger of his father."[130] When the winner in a mule-race offered Simonides a small sum, he refused to write an ode, as if he thought it beneath him to write on half-asses; but when he gave him a sufficient amount, he wrote.

Hail, daughters of storm-footed steeds![131]

and yet they were also the daughters of asses. Further, the use of diminutives amounts to the same. It is the diminutive which makes the good and the bad appear less, as Aristophanes in the *Babylonians* jestingly uses "goldlet cloaklet, affrontlet, diseaselet" instead of "gold, cloak, affront, disease." But one must be careful to observe the due mean in their use as well as in that of epithets.

3. Frigidity of style arises from four causes: first, the use of compound words, as when Lycophron[132] speaks of "the many-faced sky of the mighty-topped earth," "narrow-passaged shore"; and Gorgias of "a begging-poet flatterer," "those who commit perjury and those who swear right solemnly."[133] And as Alcidamas says, "the soul full of anger and the face fire-coloured," "he thought that their zeal would be end-accomplishing," "he made persuasive words end-accomplishing," and "the azure-coloured floor of the sea," for all these appear poetical because they are compound.

This is one cause of frigidity; another is the use of strange words; as Lycophron calls Xerxes "a

---

[126] According to Athenaeus, xv. p. 669, he was a poet and rhetorician who recommended the Athenians to use bronze money.

[127] A scream is neither articulate nor agreeable, like the sound of poetry, although both are voices or sound, and to that extent the metaphor is correct.

[128] Athenaeus, p. 452.

[129] Rhetorician and sophist of Heraclea in Pontus.

[130] Euripides, *Orestes*, 1588. In the preceding line Menelaus accuses Orestes as a matricide and ready to heap murder on murder, to which Orestes replies, you should rather call me the avenger of my father Agamemnon, who had been murdered by his wife Clytaemnestra, the mother of Orestes. "Matricide" and "avenger of his father" show the good and bad sides of the deed of Orestes.

[131] Frag. 7 (*P.L.G.* iii. p. 390). The winner of the mule-race was Anaxilaus of Rhegium.

[132] A sophist, not the poet (author of the obscure *Alexander* or *Cassandra*), who was later than Aristotle.

[133] Lobeck conjectured κατεπιορκήσαντας, "who commit out-and-out perjury."

monster of a man." Sciron "a human scourge"[134]; and Alcidamas says "plaything in poetry," "the audaciousness of nature," "whetted with unmitigated wrath of thought."

A third cause is the use of epithets that are either long or unseasonable or too crowded; thus, in poetry it is appropriate to speak of white milk, but in prose it is less so; and if epithets are employed to excess, they reveal the art and make it evident that it is poetry. And yet such may be used to a certain extent, since it removes the style from the ordinary and gives a "foreign" air. But one must aim at the mean, for neglect to do so does more harm than speaking at random; for a random style lacks merit, but excess is vicious. That is why the style of Alcidamas appears frigid; for he uses epithets not as a seasoning but as a regular dish, so crowded, so long, and so glaring are they. For instance, he does not say "sweat" but "damp sweat"; not "to the Isthmian games" but "to the solemn assembly of the Isthmian games"; not "laws," but "the laws, the rulers of states"; not "running," but "with a race-like impulse of the soul"; not "museum," but "having taken up the museum of nature";[135] and "the scowling anxiety of the soul"; "creator," not "of favour," but of "all-popular favour"; and "dispenser of the pleasure of the hearers"; "he hid," not "with branches" but "with the branches of the forest"; "he covered," not "his body," but "the nakedness of his body." He also calls desire "counter-initiative of the soul" – an expression which is at once compound and an epithet, so that it becomes poetry – and "the excess of his depravity so beyond all bounds." Hence those who employ poetic language by their lack of taste make the style ridiculous and frigid, and such idle chatter produces obscurity; for when words are piled upon one who already knows, it destroys perspicuity by a cloud of verbiage. People use compound words, when a thing has no name and the word is easy to combine, as χρονοτριβεῖν, to pass time; but if the practice is abused, the style becomes entirely poetical. This is why compound words are especially employed by dithyrambic poets, who are full of noise; strange words by epic poets, for they imply dignity and self-assertion; metaphor to writers of iambics, who now employ them, as we have stated.

The fourth cause of frigidity of style is to be found in metaphors; for metaphors also are inappropriate, some because they are ridiculous – for the comic poets also employ them – others because they are too dignified and somewhat tragic; and if they are far-fetched, they are obscure, as when Gorgias says: "Affairs pale and bloodless";[136] "you have sown shame and reaped misfortune"; for this is too much like poetry. And as Alcidamas calls philosophy "a bulwark of the laws."[137] and the *Odyssey* "a beautiful mirror of human life," and "introducing no such plaything in poetry." All these expressions fail to produce persuasion, for the reasons stated. As for what Gorgias said to the swallow which, flying over his head, let fall her droppings upon him, it was in the best tragic style. He exclaimed, "Fie, for shame, Philomela!"; for there would have been nothing in this act disgraceful for a bird, whereas it would have been for a young lady. The reproach therefore was appropriate, addressing her as she was, not as she is.

---

[134] Sciron and Sinnis were both robbers slain by Theseus, but Lycophron turns Sinnis into a γλῶττα, using it adjectivally = "destructive"; *cf.* σῖνος, "harm"; σίντης = σίννις.

[135] The meaning of παραλαβών is quite obscure: various renderings are "having taken to himself," "received," "grasped," "inherited." The word μουσεῖον, originally a haunt of the Muses, came to mean a school of art or literature. The fault appears to consist in the addition of τῆς φύσεως, but it is difficult to see why. Cope confesses his inability to understand the passage. Jebb translates: "he does not say, 'having taken to himself a school of the Muses,' but 'to *Nature's* school of the Muses.'"

[136] On this passage Thompson (*Gorgias*, p. 179) says: "The metaphor of reaping and sowing is a mere commonplace … but 'pallid and bloodless affairs' is a phrase which would need apology even from a modern." On the other hand, it is difficult to see what objection there is to calling the *Odyssey* "a beautiful mirror of human life." Another reading is ἔναιμα, which Cope translates "events fresh with the blood in them." If the two extracts are taken together, it is suggested (apparently by the editor of Cope's notes) that the sense may be: "things green and unripe (flushed with sap), and this was the crop which you ...," the adjectives referring to green and unripe stalks of corn.

[137] Or, "a barrier against the laws." This is the general meaning of ἐπιτείχισμα, a border fortress commanding an enemy's country.

4. The simile also is a metaphor; for there is very little difference. When the poet says of Achilles,[138]

he rushed on like a lion,

it is a simile; if he says, "a lion, he rushed on," it is a metaphor; for because both are courageous, he transfers the sense and calls Achilles a lion. The simile is also useful in prose, but should be less frequently used, for there is something poetical about it. Similes must be used like metaphors, which only differ in the manner stated. The following are examples of similes. Androtion[139] said of Idrieus that he was like curs just unchained; for as they attack and bite, so he when loosed from his bonds was dangerous. Again, Theodamas likened Archidamus to a Euxenus ignorant of geometry, by proportion;[140] for Euxenus "will be Archidamus acquainted with geometry." Again, Plato in the *Republic*[141] compares those who strip the dead to curs, which bite stones, but do not touch those who throw them; he also says that the people is like a ship's captain who is vigorous, but rather deaf;[142] that poets' verses resemble those who are in the bloom of youth but lack beauty;[143] for neither the one after they have lost their bloom, nor the others after they have been broken up,[144] appear the same as before. Pericles said that the Samians were like children who cry while they accept the scraps.[145] He also compared the Boeotians to holm-oaks; for just as these are beaten down by knocking against each other,[146] so are the Boeotians by their civil strife. Demosthenes compared the people to passengers who are seasick.[147] Democrates said that orators resembled nurses who gulp down the morsel and rub the babies' lips with the spittle. Antisthenes likened the skinny Cephisodotus to incense, for he also gives pleasure by wasting away. All such expressions may be used as similes or metaphors, so that all that are approved as metaphors will obviously also serve as similes which are metaphors without the details. But in all cases the metaphor from proportion should be reciprocal and applicable to either of the two things of the same genus;[148] for instance, if the goblet is the shield of Dionysus, then the shield may properly be called the goblet of Ares.[149]

5. Such then are the elements of speech. But purity, which is the foundation of style, depends upon five rules. First, connecting particles should be introduced in their natural order, before or after, as they require; thus, μέν and ἐγὼ μέν require to be followed by δέ and ὁ δέ. Further, they should be made to correspond whilst the hearer still recollects; they should not be put too far apart, nor should a clause be introduced before the necessary

---

[138] Compare *Iliad*, xxii. 164 ἐνάντιον ὦρτο λεὼν ὥς.

[139] Pupil of Isocrates and historical writer. Idrieus was a prince of Caria, who had been imprisoned.

[140] Meaning that there was no difference between Euxenus without a knowledge of geometry and Archidamus with a knowledge of geometry. The proportion of geometrical knowledge will remain the same, so that Archidamus can be called an ungeometrical Euxenus, and Euxenus a geometrical Archidamus (see note 149 for "by proportion").

[141] 469 D.

[142] 488 A.

[143] 601 B.

[144] If metrical restrictions have been removed and they are read as prose.

[145] Meaning that they did not appreciate the benefits received from the Athenians, who conquered the islands (440 B.C.).

[146] Or, "are cut down by axes, the handles of which are made of their own wood."

[147] It is disputed whether Demosthenes is the orator or the Athenian general in the Peloponnesian War. The point of the comparison is that in a democracy the general instability of political conditions makes the people sick of the existing state of things and eager for a change.

[148] Aristophanes, *Knights*, 715–718.

[149] As the shield is to Ares, so is the goblet to Dionysus. Proportion is defined (*Ethics*, v. 3. 8) as "an equality of ratios, implying four terms at the least," and the proportional metaphor is one in which the second term is to the first as the fourth is to the third; for then one can by metaphor substitute the fourth for the second, or the second for the fourth. Let A be Dionysus, B a goblet, C Ares, D a shield. Then by the definition, the goblet is to Dionysus as the shield is to Ares. The metaphor consists in transferring to the goblet the name belonging to its analogue the shield. Sometimes an addition is made by way of explanation of the word in its new sense, and the goblet may be described as the shield of Dionysus and the shield as the goblet of Ares. The shield and the goblet both come under the same genus, being characteristics of a deity, and can therefore be reciprocally transferred (*Poetics*, 21. 4).

connexion;[150] for this is rarely appropriate. For instance, "As for me, I, after he had told me – for Cleon came begging and praying – set out, taking them with me." For in this phrase several connecting words have been foisted in before the one which is to furnish the apodosis; and if the interval between "I" and "set out" is too great, the result is obscurity. The first rule therefore is to make a proper use of connecting particles; the second, to employ special, not generic terms. The third consists in avoiding ambiguous terms, unless you deliberately intend the opposite, like those who, having nothing to say, yet pretend to say something; such people accomplish this by the use of verse, after the manner of Empedocles.[151] For the long circumlocution takes in the hearers, who find themselves affected like the majority of those who listen to the soothsayers. For when the latter utter their ambiguities, they also assent; for example,

> Croesus, by crossing the Halys, shall ruin a mighty dominion.[152]

And as there is less chance of making a mistake when speaking generally, diviners express themselves in general terms on the question of fact; for, in playing odd or even, one is more likely to be right if he says "even" or "odd" than if he gives a definite number, and similarly one who says "it will be" than if he states "when." This is why sooth-sayers do not further define the exact time. All such ambiguities are alike, wherefore they should be avoided, except for some such reason.[153] The fourth rule consists in keeping the genders distinct – masculine, feminine, and neuter,[154] as laid down by Protagoras; these also must be properly introduced: "She, having come (*fem.*) and having conversed (*fem.*) with me, went away." The fifth rule consists in observing number, according as many, few, or one are referred to: "They, having come (*pl.*), began to beat (*pl.*) me."

Generally speaking, that which is written should be easy to read or easy to utter, which is the same thing. Now, this is not the case when there is a number of connecting particles, or when the punctuation is hard, as in the writings of Heraclitus.[155] For it is hard, since it is uncertain to which word another belongs, whether to that which follows or that which precedes; for instance, at the beginning of his composition he says: "Of this reason which exists[156] always men are ignorant," where it is uncertain whether "always" should go with "which exists" or with "are ignorant." Further, a solecism results from not appropriately connecting or joining two words with a word which is equally suitable to both. For instance, in speaking of "sound" and "colour," the word "seeing" should not be used, for it is not suitable to both, whereas "perceiving" is. It also causes obscurity, if you do not say at the outset what you mean, when you intend to insert a number of details in the middle; for instance, if you say: "I intended after having spoken to him thus and thus and in this way to set out" instead of "I intended to set out after having spoken to him," and then this or that happened, in this or that manner.

6. The following rules contribute to loftiness of style. Use of the description instead of the name of a thing; for instance, do not say "circle," but "a plane figure, all the points of which are equidistant

---

[150] The apodosis. ἀποδιδόναι is used in the sense of introducing a clause answering to the πρότασις, and ἀπόδοσις for this answering clause.

[151] Of Agrigentum (*c.* 490–430), poet, philosopher, and physician. Among other legends connected with him, he is said to have thrown himself into the crater of Etna, so that by suddenly disappearing he might be thought to be a god. His chief work was a poem called Nature, praised by Lucretius. The principles of things are the four elements, fire, air, water, and earth, which are unalterable and indestructible. Love and hate, alternately prevailing, regulate the periods of the formation of the world. The existing fragments corroborate Aristotle's statement.

[152] Herodotus, i. 53, 91. Croesus consulted the Delphian oracle whether he should attack Cyrus the Persian or not. Encouraged by the ambiguous oracle, he did so, but was utterly defeated.

[153] The deliberate intention to mislead.

[154] σκεύη, "inanimate things," the classification probably being male, female and inanimate, not the grammatical one of masculine, feminine, and neuter.

[155] Heraclitus of Ephesus (*c.* 535–475). His chief work was on Nature. From the harshness of his language and the carelessness of his style he was called ὁ σκοτεινός (the obscure). According to him, fire was the origin of all things; all things become fire, and then fire becomes all other things. All things are in a constant state of flux; all is the same and yet not the same. Knowledge is founded upon sensual perception, but only the gods possess knowledge in perfection.

[156] Or, "although this reason exists for ever men are born ... without understanding" (Welldon).

from the centre." But for the purpose of conciseness the reverse – use the name instead of the description. You should do the same to express anything foul or indecent; if the foulness is in the description, use the name; if in the name, the description. Use metaphors and epithets by way of illustration, taking care, however, to avoid what is too poetical. Use the plural for the singular, after the manner of the poets, who, although there is only one harbour, say

to Achaean harbours,

and,

Here are the many-leaved folds of the tablet.[157]

You should avoid linking up, but each word should have its own article: τῆς γυναικὸς τῆς ἡμετέρας. But for conciseness, the reverse: τῆς ἡμετέρας γυναικός. Employ a connecting particle or for conciseness omit it, but avoid destroying the connexion; for instance "having gone and having conversed with him," or, "having gone, I conversed with him." Also the practice of Antimachus is useful, that of describing a thing by the qualities it

does not possess; thus, in speaking of the hill Teumessus,[158] he says,

There is a little swind-swept hill;

for in this way amplification may be carried on *ad infinitum*. This method may be applied to things good and bad, in whichever way it may be useful. Poets also make use of this in inventing words, as a melody "without strings" or "without the lyre"; for they employ epithets from negations, a course which is approved in proportional metaphors, as for instance, to say that the sound of the trumpet is a melody without the lyre.

7. Propriety of style will be obtained by the expression of emotion and character, and by proportion to the subject matter. Style is proportionate to the subject matter when neither weighty matters are treated offhand nor trifling matters with dignity, and no embellishment is attached to an ordinary word; otherwise there is an appearance of comedy, as in the poetry of Cleophon,[159] who used certain expressions that reminded one of saying 'madam fig.'"

[...]

---

[157] Euripides, *Iphig. Taur.* 727.

[158] In Boeotia. The quotation is from the *Thebaid* of Antimachus of Claros (*c.* 450 BC). The Alexandrians placed him next to Homer among the epic poets. In his eulogy of the little hill, he went on to attribute to it all the good qualities it did *not* possess, a process which could obviously be carried on *ad infinitum*.

[159] By some identified with the tragic poet spoken of in the *Poetics*, 2. His manner of expression, due to the wish to use fine language, was ridiculous owing to its being out of harmony with the subject. Others consider that he was not a poet at all but an orator. πότνια [which Freese translated strangely as "madam fig" but which is more properly translated as "queen" or "mistress"] was a title of respect, applied to females, whether they were goddesses or ordinary women.

Poetics (*The Art of Poetry*)

In the previous chapter, we saw that Plato would proscribe most types of poetry as well as rhetoric from his ideal society. His rationale for banning poetry was twofold: First, it disrupts the soul by stimulating the emotions; and second, it is an imitation (*mimêsis*) of life, which already is an imitation of the Ideal Forms, and thus is twice removed from reality. Given that in many of his works Aristotle refuted the views of his teacher, it is understandable that *Poetics* has often been characterized as a rebuttal to Plato's position. Although there is little question that *it* serves as a counterstatement to Plato in this regard, an unmitigated focus on this aspect can lead to an incomplete appreciation of the work, as we find when it is classified simply as a treatise on literary theory. Such an approach might be justified if we could find Aristotle displaying any literary inclination in his other works, but this is not the case. With the exception of his scientific treatises, his extant work concentrates on exploring human nature. Viewing *Poetics* as being outside the context of Aristotle's philosophy therefore would seem to ignore his comprehensive vision.

The importance Aristotle placed on poetry as an element of our nature is evident in Chapter IV, where Aristotle noted that "the desire to imitate or represent is instinctive in man from childhood; in fact one of man's distinguishing marks is that he is the most mimetic of all animals, and it is through his mimetic activity that he first begins to learn." From the earlier discussion of education, we see that learning and *mimêsis* are related in two ways. The first involves imitative behavior of the cognitive kind, as when we learn to dance, tie a shoe lace, write a check, and so forth. The second, on the other hand, involves behavior of the ethical kind, as when we follow the examples of decent people and when we adhere to regulatory laws. We also must take into account that *Poetics* deals primarily with tragedy, even though the time of the great Greek tragedies had passed before Aristotle was born.[160] We can only speculate on the reasons for this focus, but it seems reasonable to suggest that Aristotle may have been motivated by the fact that Greek tragedy, rooted as it was in religion and morality,[161] is an action that offers insight into virtuous behavior in a concentrated and moving form.

This assessment is congruent with poetry's long-standing role in ancient Greek society as a source of ethical instruction. We saw in the general introduction that poetry occupied a central place in moral education and that the Sophists had been teaching virtue through the study of poetry for years before they incorporated their pedagogical methods into their teaching of rhetoric. Given this context, it seems unlikely that Aristotle intended *Poetics* to be a handbook for would-be playwrights, even though it generally follows the tripartite division of *The Art of Rhetoric*: matter, arrangement, and style.[162] Evidence for this perspective also comes from the work itself. In Chapter II, for example, we find that the objects of *mimêsis* that "the poet as mimetic artist represents are human beings in action. Such agents must be either good or bad, for the diversities of human character are nearly always secondary to the primary distinction between virtue and vice." Also telling is the fact that the agents, or characters, of drama in Aristotle's view are not particularly important – but the action or plot is because it deals with *universal issues* related to human nature and ethical virtue. Thus, the work has many of the characteristics of philosophy and few of the characteristics of a handbook.

Close reading of the text shows more fully how *Poetics* fits into the broad scope of Aristotle's philosophy and how it is related to rhetoric.[163] Chapter VI discusses the crucial elements of tragedy, and we find that it emphasizes action and character so as to reveal "moral purpose." The language of tragedy "belongs to the provinces of statecraft (*politikê*) and oratory (*rhêtorikê*)." In Chapter IX we find that tragedy "is a representation of an action that is not only complete but that consists of events inspiring fear and pity." Golden (1962) noted that Aristotle saw drama as a form of learning but incorrectly concluded, perhaps owing to his conviction that *The Art of Poetry* must be interpreted on its own merits without considering how the work fits into the context of Aristotle's philosophy, that it somehow "involves learning about pity and fear" (p. 55). Yet in *Politics* Aristotle indicated that fear and pity are universal emotional experiences, not intellectual ones, and in *The Nicomachean Ethics* (1982) he clearly connected fear and pity to virtue:

---

[160] We must keep in mind that Greek tragedy was written and performed in verse.

[161] Tragedies were performed as part of the Athenian religious festival called the City Dionysia.

[162] Aristotle's treatment of style in *The Art of Poetry* is quite limited, however.

[163] For a detailed discussion of the relation between rhetoric and poetry, see Walker (2000).

The capacities are the faculties in virtue of which we can be said to be liable to the emotions, for example, capable of feeling anger or pain or pity … [O]ne can be frightened or bold, feel desire or anger or pity, and experience pleasure and pain in general, either too much or too little, and in both cases wrongly; whereas to feel these feelings at the right time, on the right occasion, towards the right people, for the right purpose and in the right manner, is to feel the best amount of them, which is the mean amount – and the best amount is of course the mark of virtue. (1105b–1106b)

Part of the difficulty is that fear and pity cannot be characterized as pleasant emotions, but Aristotle nevertheless stated that our experience of them when viewing a tragedy is pleasant. In Chapter XIV, we find that the proper aim, or goal, of tragedy is "to produce through *mimêsis* the kind of pleasure that comes from responding with pity and fear," provided that, as indicated in Chapter VI, the incidents arousing pity and fear are presented "in such a way as to accomplish a purgation (*katharsis*) of such emotions." Exactly what Aristotle meant by *katharsis* is unclear. Although he promised in *Politics* to provide a thorough treatment of the term in *Poetics,* by the time he actually got around to producing this treatise it seems he forgot to do so![164]

Katharsis is derived from *kathairein,* meaning "to purify" or "to purge." The adjectival form, *katharos,* means "clean," "pure," or "free from offense." In *Politics,* Aristotle used the word to signify a purgation in the medical sense. Illness in ancient Greece was considered to be an imbalance of bodily elements (fire, water, earth, and air) or of bodily humors. Treatment focused on "purgation" of the element or humor causing the imbalance and restoring physical harmony. *Katharsis* when used in regard to spiritual or moral matters indicated purification. A person who had defiled a sacred ritual, for example, would go to a temple for cathartic cleansing of the soul. In *The Nicomachean Ethics,* Aristotle used the term with respect to moral purification.

The tendency among many scholars has been to interpret *katharsis* as signifying medical purgation. Golden (1962, 1992), however, argued that both the purgation and purification interpretations are incorrect and that *katharsis* in *Poetics* is used in a pedagogical sense to indicate "intellectual clarification" (also see Nehamas, 1992; Nussbaum, 2001). Although not everyone accepts this cognitive view of *katharsis* (see Halliwell, 1998), it is widely influential. An unresolved problem, however, is that the intellectual clarification argument requires us to read *Poetics* not only outside the context of poetry's role as a source of ethical instruction but also outside the context of Aristotle's other works and his effort to develop a comprehensive philosophy of human nature. Golden suggested that the intellectual clarification of *katharsis* is simply the pleasure one has when viewing the representation of the incidents that aroused the emotions, but for Aristotle pleasure and virtue were linked, not through education, for education itself does not develop virtue, but through law and the imitation of virtuous people. From this perspective, the discussion of fear and pity in *Poetics* is analogous to the discussion of emotions in *The Art of Rhetoric*: Both are associated with awareness of the psyche and human nature. As Cole (1991) suggested, the ability of drama to arouse the emotions leads to a "determination of the best thing to do in any given situation" (p. 142). Tragedy, then, is moral drama, showing what happens to those who step outside the boundaries of ethical behavior and giving the audience insight into how to walk the right path.

---

[164] It may be that what we have was not written by Aristotle but rather consists of student notes on his lectures. This question remains unresolved, but in the end it may not be particularly relevant.

Its goal is to raise the emotions of pity and fear vicariously. *Katharsis*, in this case, would signify the moment of resolution when the audience is released from the grip of those vicariously generated emotions and left in a state of elevated being similar to the relief one feels after hurrying back to a restaurant and finding that the pocketbook he or she left behind is still there. As Aristotle declared in *The Nicomachean Ethics*, every art, like every practical undertaking, aims to achieve some good. The good of tragedy is that, like the law, it serves as a guide for ethical behavior.

Reading 30

The Art of Poetry

The Art of Poetry (excerpt), from *Aristotle*, translated by P. Wheelwright (The Odyssey Press, 1935).

i. Mimêsis: Its Means

In studying the 'art of poetry' (*poiêtikê*) our task will be to treat of: (1) the intrinsic nature of poetry, (2) its various kinds, (3) the essential 'function and potentiality' (*dynamis*) of each, (4) the kind of plot (*mythos*)-construction requisite to a good poem (*poiêsis*), (5) the number and nature of a poem's constituent parts, and anything else that falls within the scope of the inquiry. Let us follow the natural order, starting with what is most basic.

Epic poetry and tragedy, as well as comedy and dithyrambic poetry, and most flute and lyre playing, all share the general characteristic of being 'modes of mimetic representation' (*mimêsis*). But at the same time they differ from one another in three respects: in the medium which they employ, in the objects represented, and in the manner of representing.

Just as there are persons who – whether by conscious art or by a skill based on habit – represent various objects by making likenesses of them through the medium of color and form or by the voice; so in the arts above mentioned the representing is done through the medium of rhythm, language, and melodic intervals, whether simply or in certain combinations. Flute and lyre playing employ a combination of rhythm and melodic intervals; and this is the case with any other arts that function similarly, like that of the shepherd's pipe. Rhythm alone, without melody, is the dancer's means of representation; for the dancer too represents human characters, feelings, and actions, by the use of rhythmical gestures.

There is also an art which represents by language alone – either in prose or verse, and if in verse either in one meter or in several. This kind of representation has not yet received a name. For there is no common term we could apply to the mimes[165] of Sophron or Xenarchus and to the Socratic discourses; nor would the difficulty be removed if both of these contrasting types of imitative art were couched in, say, [iambic] trimeter or elegiac meter or the like. It is common practice, of course, to attach to the word 'poet' (*poiêtes*) the name of the meter that he makes (*poiein*) and in speaking of elegiac poets and epic poets, to bestow the title not by reason of the principle of mimetic representation embodied in their work but indiscriminately because of the meter they write in. Even when a treatise on medicine or natural science is published in verse the same practice prevails. It would be better, however, when we compare say Homer and Empedocles, who have nothing in common except meter, to distinguish the one as a poet, the other not as a poet but as a natural scientist. ... Such then are the ways in which arts may be distinguished with respect to *medium*.

ii. The Objects of Mimêsis

The *objects* which the poet as mimetic artist represents are human beings in action. Such agents

---

[165] The Greek *mimos* was a sort of burlesqued drama written in rhythmic but colloquial prose.

must be either good or bad, for the diversities of human character are nearly always secondary to the primary distinction between virtue and vice. Accordingly they must be represented as either better than our everyday selves or as worse or as similar. It is the same with painters: Polygnotus was wont to portray men as better than in real life, Pauson as worse, and Dionysius as they actually are. It is clear that each of the modes of representation that we have mentioned will admit of these differences in the character of the object, and that each will become a distinct species of art by representing objects that are thus distinct. ... It is this kind of difference that distinguishes tragedy from comedy: the one aims to represent men as superior, the other as inferior to their actual condition.

iii. The Manner of Mimêsis

A third difference among the arts under consideration is found in the *manner* in which any of the foregoing types of objects may be represented. Given a certain medium and a certain type of objects to be represented, the poet may represent them [in one of three ways]: he may alternate between narrative and the speeches of individuals as Homer does, or he may speak from the standpoint of a single individual throughout, or he may represent his character as living and acting before our eyes.

So, as we declared at the outset, artistic representation is distinguishable in three ways – in respect of medium, objects, and manner. Accordingly, Sophocles' mimetic art is akin to Homer's in one respect, namely that both portray characters of a worthier sort, and to Aristophanes' in another, namely that both set their characters before us as living and acting. ...

iv. Origin and Early Development of Poetry

Broadly considered, the origin of poetry may be traced to two causes (*aitia*), each of them inherent in man's nature. On the one hand the desire to 'imitate or represent' is instinctive in man from childhood; in fact one of man's distinguishing marks is that he is the most mimetic of all animals, and it is through his mimetic activity that he first begins to learn. Moreover, such imitating and representing is always a source of delight, as experience plainly shows: for even where the objects themselves are disagreeable to behold – repulsive animals, for instance, or dead bodies – we take delight in artistically exact reproductions of them. The reason for this is that learning gives the keenest pleasure – not only to philosophers but even to the rest of mankind despite the scant attention they bestow on it. Hence the reason why men enjoy seeing a picture is that in contemplating it they are incidentally learning and inferring in their recognition of particulars, as when they exclaim, "Ah, that is so-and-so!" For if they happen not to have seen the original, any pleasure that they get will be due not to the picture in its representational role but to the execution or coloring or some other such cause.

Now since mimetic representation is natural to us on the one hand, and harmonic intervals and rhythms on the other (meters being obviously only special kinds of rhythm), it was through these natural human aptitudes that men originally made rude improvisations, which, as practice gradually improved them, developed into poetry.

Poetry split into two kinds, corresponding to a difference of character in the poets. The more serious poets would represent noble actions performed by noble men, the more trivial ones the actions of the ignoble. Hence the one class of poets took to composing hymns and panegyrics, the other lampoons. ... Iambic came into use as the meter best suited to the latter style: which explains why even today iambic connotes the meter in which people lampoon or 'iambize' one another.

Homer, who stands supreme among serious poets by reason not only of the literary but of the dramatic qualities of his representations, also established the outlines of comedy by dramatizing the ludicrous instead of merely lampooning. Thus his *Margites* stands in the same relation to later comedies as the *Iliad* and *Odyssey* stand to later tragedies. With the emergence of tragedy and comedy the two types of poet continued to follow their natural bent: instead of lampoons the one type took to the writing of comedy, and instead of epics the other type began to compose tragedies, since these new art forms had wider possibilities and were more highly esteemed than the old.[166]

---

[166] "Whether present-day tragedy has fully realized its formative possibilities is a matter for separate inquiry, and would have to be judged not only on the intrinsic merits of the case but with reference to essential theatrical requirements as well." (Aristotle's gloss.)

Tragedy arose, as did comedy, from improvisation – as practiced respectively by choral leaders of the dithyramb and of phallic songs such as are still in vogue in many of our cities. Thence tragedy developed little by little as its possibilities were gradually brought to light, and only after a long succession of changes did it reach the end of its development by finding its natural form. Thus, Aeschylus first increased the number of actors from one to two, curtailed the chanting of the chorus, and gave dialogue the leading role. The third actor and the use of painted scenery were introduced by Sophocles. Meanwhile tragedy had been developing beyond the short plots and grotesque diction of the early satyr-plays and attaining to greater magnitude and dignity, while the meter changed from [trochaic] tetrameter to iambic [double trimeter]. Tetrameter was employed in early times as being better suited to the kind of poetry then in vogue, namely the satyr-play, which involved more dancing than plays do now; but as soon as dialogue was introduced, nature herself discovered the proper meter. For iambic is the most conversational of all meters, as evidenced by the fact that it is the one we most readily fall into when talking with one another, whereas meters such as the [dactyllic] hexameter are used rarely and only when we depart from a conversational tone. As for other changes in the development of tragedy – the division into episodes, and the introduction of various embellishments [like masks, costumes, and stage properties] – all this had better be taken as told, for a detailed account would doubtless be a very long task.

v.   Comedy, Epic

Comedy, as we have said, is a representation of men who are morally inferior – not in the sense of being thoroughly evil, but only in the sense of being ludicrous. For the ludicrous is a subdivision of the morally ugly, consisting in some defect or ugliness which does not produce actual harm and hence causes no pain to the beholder: as a comic mask is ugly and distorted without causing pain. ...

Epic poetry is similar to tragedy in being a representation of serious subjects in stately verse, but differs in being limited to a single meter and by reason of its narrative form. It differs also in respect of length: for whereas tragedy tries to confine itself to a single revolution of the sun or not much more than that, the action of an epic has no fixed time limit. This is a point of difference between them, although originally tragedies had the same freedom as epics in this respect. Finally, they differ in constituent parts, some of which are common to both forms while others are peculiar to tragedy. Therefore, since all the elements of the epic are to be found in tragedy but not all those of tragedy in the epic, it follows that whoever can judge of good and bad in tragedy can do so in the epic also.

vi.   Definition of Tragedy; Its Six Formative Elements

Let us postpone discussion of epic poetry and of comedy till later,[167] and proceed now with a discussion of tragedy, deriving from what has been said a definition of what it essentially is. Tragedy, then, is a representation (*mimêsis*) of an action (*praxis*) that is serious, complete, and of a certain magnitude; in language pleasurably and variously embellished suitably to the different parts of the play; in the form of actions directly presented, not narrated; with incidents arousing pity and fear in such a way as to accomplish a purgation (*katharsis*) of such emotions. By 'language pleasurably embellished' I refer to the use of rhythm, 'harmonic modes' (*harmonia*), and song (*melos*). By 'variously for the different parts' I mean that some parts of the play produce their effects through verse alone, others through song.

Since tragic representation consists of showing people in action, it follows that staging (*opsis*) will

---

[167]   Epic poetry is discussed in Chaps. xxiii–xxvi [not included in this excerpt]. The purposed discussion of comedy was not written.

be one of the necessary aspects of tragedy. Next come song (*melos*) and diction (*lexis*), these being the immediate instruments of representation. By diction I mean simply the metrical arrangement of words; song has its customary signification. Next, since the subject represented is an action, and since actions are performed by agents, each of whom is distinguished by certain traits of character and thought – for it is from such traits that a man's actions and hence his eventual success or failure springs, whether in drama or in real life – it follows that the representation of action in the play will have the form of a 'story or plot' *(mythos)* [and will include character (*êthos*) and thought (*dianoia*) as necessary elements]. By story or plot I mean the way in which the incidents are constructed into a whole; by character, that by which we ascribe certain qualities to the agents or persons of the drama; by thought, that which is expressed when they argue a point or even merely enunciate a general truth.

Every tragedy, therefore, must have six aspects, which make it what it is: story, characters, diction, thought, staging, and song. Two of these elements [diction and song] may be regarded as the media of representation, one of them [the staging] as the manner of representation, and three of them [story, characters, and thought] as the objects of representation. The list is exhaustive. All six of these 'formative elements' (*eidos*) are generally taken account of in writing a tragedy, for all tragedies involve just these elements of staging, character, story, diction, song, and thought.

The most important of the six is the structure of incidents [which form the story]. Tragedy is a representation essentially not of men but of 'human action' (*praxis*): i.e., of human life, its happiness and its misery; for on the stage these must find expression in action, and the proper end [of dramatic representation] therefore is a mode of action, not some sort of quality. [The persons of a drama] will be of one sort or another according to their several characters, but [they must be shown to] achieve happiness or misery according to their actions. What they do, then, is not simply a way of representing their characters; rather, their characters are developed as subsidiary and instrumental to the action. Hence the incidents and the story or plot [which they constitute] are the real end of the tragedy; and the real end is of course our principal concern.

[That plot is more essential than character] is further indicated by the fact that while there cannot be a tragedy without action, there may be one without character. The tragedies of most modern dramatists are lacking in character portrayal – a lack which is to be found among modern poets generally, and which has its counterpart in the paintings of Zeuxis as compared with those of Polygnotus; for whereas Polygnotus is a good character painter, the paintings of Zeuxis offer nothing in the way of character. Moreover, even though a writer string together a number of speeches expressing character in polished style as regards both diction and thought, he may utterly fail to produce the proper tragic effect; whereas he will succeed much better with a tragedy which, however deficient in those respects, yet has a plot consisting of well-arranged incidents. Again, it is in the plot that we find those elements whereby tragedy achieves its most powerful emotional effect, namely 'reversals of the situation' (*peripeteia*) and recognition scenes. Still another indication is found in the fact that novices in the tragic art achieve competence in language and character-portrayal before they are able to construct a good pattern of incidents: as is the case with nearly all the early poets.

The story or plot, then, is the "initiating principle" (*archê*) and, so to speak, the soul of tragedy; character being in second place. Tragedy is the representation of an action; and it is principally in carrying out this function that it represents agents likewise.

Third [in importance] comes thought; i.e., the faculty of saying what is possible and appropriate [in a given situation]. This element, which is found in the dialogue and speeches of a tragedy [not in the choral parts], belongs to the provinces of statecraft (*politikê*) and oratory (*rhêtorikê*), for the older poets made their personages talk like statesmen, the modern like orators. Character, as distinguished from thought, reveals 'moral purpose' (*proairesis*) – that is, what a dramatic personage will choose or shun in situations where the ground of choice is obscure. Speeches that do not manifest any concern with choice or avoidance are not expressive of character. Thought, on the other hand, finds expression whenever anyone argues for or against some point or enunciates some generalization.

Fourth among the literary[168] elements of tragedy comes diction: by which I mean, as already explained, the interpretive use of language, this being the essential function of diction whether in verse or in prose.

Of the two remaining elements we may say that musical composition holds chief place among the embellishments of tragedy. The 'visual aspect of the staging' (*opsis*), despite its emotional appeal, is the least artistic of all the elements and has least to do with the art of poetry. For the 'essential power' (*dynamis*) of tragedy is independent of a 'stage presentation' (*agôn*) and of actors, and moreover the production of scenic effects lies more in the province of the 'costumer and stage-manager' (*skeuopoios*) than of the poet.

vii. Plot Requirements: Proper Magnitude

Having thus distinguished the formative elements, let us now discuss the proper arrangement of incidents [into a story or plot], since this is the first and most important aspect of tragedy. According to our definition, tragedy is a representation of an action that is whole, complete, and of a certain magnitude – for a thing might be completely whole and yet lack magnitude. Now a whole involves having a beginning, a middle, and an end. A beginning is that which does not follow as a necessary consequent upon something else, but which is followed by something else existing or occurring as its own natural result; an end, on the contrary, is that which follows as a natural result, either inevitably or usually, from something else, but has nothing following it in turn; while a middle both follows and is followed by something else. That is to say, a well-constructed plot must neither begin nor end at random, but must observe these distinctions.

Furthermore, any beautiful object, whether a living creature or anything else made up of parts, must not only have its parts well arranged but must also be of an appropriate size, for beauty depends on size and order. Thus, a very minute creature cannot be beautiful to us, for our perception of it is instantaneous without any clear discrimination of its parts; nor, on the other hand, could a monstrously large creature, miles and miles in length, be beautiful to us, for our inability to see it all at once would leave us without any sense of its unity and wholeness. Now just as there is a proper size for living creatures and other physical bodies – a size, namely, which the eye can take in; so there is a proper size for stories and plots – a size, namely, that can be taken in by the memory. ... The limit must be set by the nature of the case, but in general the greater the length the more beautiful the story will be in this respect, provided it can still be grasped as a whole. In general, a sufficient length will mean one which allows of a development, by steps whose connection [appears] inevitable or at any rate plausible, from misfortune to happiness or from happiness to misfortune.

viii. Plot Requirements: Unity

A plot does not have unity, as some believe, merely because it deals with a single hero. The incidents that befall even a single man are numberless, and not all of them will fit into a unified conception of what happens to him; likewise his actions are numerous and cannot all be combined into one action. Whence the mistake of all those poets who have composed a *Heracleid*, a *Theseid*, or the like: they suppose that because Heracles was one individual the story about him must correspondingly be one. Homer, on the other hand, whether by conscious art or instinctive genius, seems to have been well aware of this principle – another evidence of his superiority to other poets. In composing the *Odyssey* he did not introduce all that ever befell his hero. There was the incident of Odysseus' being wounded on Mount Parnassus, for example, and there was the incident of his feigning madness when the army was being mustered,[169] but the two incidents had no necessary or even plausible

---

[168] The first four elements of tragedy – story, character, thought, and diction – belong to it as a work of literature and are shared by the epic; the fifth and sixth elements – music and staging – are accessories, which attach to tragedy only when it is enacted on the stage.

[169] The first of these incidents, as a matter of fact, is briefly narrated in Book XIX, lines 560 ff., but it plays no part in the real action of the *Odyssey*. The second incident occurred at the outset of the Trojan War. To avoid conscription Odysseus feigned madness by ploughing his field with an ox and a horse; but when Palamedes laid the infant Telemachus in the way of the plough, Odysseus stopped, thereby revealing his sanity.

relation with each other, and Homer was building the *Odyssey*, as he had built the *Iliad*, around a unity of action in the sense here defined. In short, just as in the other mimetic arts the *mimêsis* or representation is one when the object mimed or represented is one, so the plot, being a representation of an action, should represent an action that is single and whole – that is to say, an action whose component parts hang together in such a way that to displace or remove any one of them would disturb and even destroy the whole. For a part that can be present or absent indifferently is no real part of the whole.

ix. Poetry Compared With History

The poet's function, then, as appears from the foregoing discussion, is to describe not what has actually happened but the kind of thing that might well happen – i.e., what is [dramatically] possible in the sense of being either plausible or inevitable. The difference between a historian and a poet is not that the one writes in prose and the other in verse. Herodotus' writings, for example, even though they were versified would still be a kind of history, the meter notwithstanding. No, the real difference consists in this, that the one speaks of what has occurred, the other of what might occur. Hence poetry is something more philosophical and more highly serious than history, for poetry tends to express universals, history particulars. By universal is meant what a man of a certain sort will say or do, either probably or inevitably; and this is what poetry aims at, despite the particular names it employs. By particular is meant [some such thing as] what Alcibiades did or had done to him.

The distinction has lately become obvious in the field of comedy; for modern comedy writers – as distinguished from the ancient iambic poets who wrote about particular persons – first construct their plots out of plausible incidents, then affix proper names at random. Writers of tragedy, on the contrary, still adhere to the use of real names. Their reason for doing so is that only the possible has credibility, and we are apt to be unsure of the possibility of what has never actually occurred, whereas when something *has* occurred its very occurrence proves that it must be possible. Nevertheless there are some tragedies that employ only one or two familiar names, the rest being fictitious; and there are some, like Agathon's *The Blossoming*, without even a single familiar name, the names being as fictitious as the incidents, although the play is no whit less effective on that account. It is by no means absolutely essential, then, that a poet confine himself to the traditional stories. Such a restriction would be inconsistent in any case, because the familiar stories are familiar only to a few, yet they give delight to all.

From all this it is manifest that the poet [which is to say, the maker] must be primarily a maker of plots rather than of verses, for he is a poet by virtue of the representing (*mimêsis*) that he does, and the object that he represents is actions. Even though he should happen to take a subject from history, he is none the less a poet on that account; for there is nothing to prevent certain historical events from being plausible and [dramatically] possible, and it is in relation to this aspect of them that he is their proper maker, or poet.

The worst kind of plot and dramatic action is the episodic; by which I mean a plot in which the episodes follow one another in a way that is neither plausible nor inevitable. Bad poets commit this fault through want of skill, while good ones do so through adapting the action to the actors, for in meeting the requirements of a theatrical contest they stretch the plot beyond its natural capacity and thereby, frequently, have to sacrifice dramatic continuity.

Tragedy, however, is a representation of an action that is not only complete but that consists of events inspiring fear and pity; and this effect is best produced when the events are at once unexpected and causally related. For thereby they stir our wonder more than if they happened by themselves or by mere chance. Even coincidences appear most remarkable when they have some appearance of design: when, for instance, the statue of Mitys at Argos toppled over on Mitys' very murderer at a festival, the occurrence did not seem entirely accidental. Accordingly, plots which have this [double aspect of unexpectedness and apparent causal relation] are the best.

x. Simple and Complex Plots

Some plots are simple, others are complex; for the actions they represent are similarly distinguishable.

I call dramatic action simple when (granted that it has the unity and continuity prescribed) the 'change in the hero's fortune' (*metabasis*) is produced without employing either reversal or discovery in the technical sense; complex, when the catastrophe is attended by reversal or discovery or both. These devices should arise out of the very structure of the plot, so that what follows comes to be the result, plausible or inevitable, of what has preceded. There is a great difference between happening *because of* something and merely happening *after* it.

xi. Reversal and Discovery

A reversal (*peripeteia*) is a change of the situation into its opposite [from good fortune to bad or from bad to good], as has been said, and in a way that is either plausible or inevitable, as has also been said.[170] In the *Oedipus*, for example, the messenger who comes to gladden Oedipus and release him from his fears about his mother, actually produces just the opposite effect through revealing the secret of his birth. …

A discovery (*ana-gnôrisis*), as the word itself indicates, is a change from ignorance to knowledge, and thereby to either friendship or enmity, according as the characters involved are marked for good or evil fortune. The best kind of discovery is one combined with reversals, like the reversal in the *Oedipus*. There are no doubt other kinds. It is possible to 'discover,' within our meaning of the word, whether a person has done something or not, and there may even be discoveries about trivial inanimate things. But the kind of discovery most intimately connected with the plot and the dramatic action is such as we have been describing. This kind of discovery, combined with reversal, will arouse either pity or fear; and according to our theory, it is actions productive of

such effects that are properly represented in tragedy. Moreover, it is upon situations such as these that good or bad fortune will depend. Confining the term 'discovery,' then, to relations between persons, we may distinguish between cases where one person's identity is already known and cases where each must discover the identity of the other. Thus Iphigeneia became known to Orestes through sending the letter, but a separate act of discovery was required to make him known to Iphigeneia.[171]

So much, then, for these two elements of the plot, reversal and discovery, which involve the kind of incident here described. A third element is the 'scene of pathos' (*pathos*), which may be defined as 'dramatic action' (*praxis*) involving destruction or pain, such as deaths on the stage, agonies, woundings, and the like.

xii. The Technical Divisions of Tragedy

The formative elements of tragedy having been discussed, we may now examine the quantitatively distinct parts which it comprises: prologue, episode, and exode on the one hand, and chorus on the other; which last is divided into parode and stasimon, both of which are found in all tragedies, whereas songs by an individual actor and *kommoi* are found in some tragedies and not in others. The prologue is all that portion of a tragedy which precedes the parode [or entrance chant] of the chorus; the episode is all that portion which comes between whole choric songs; the exode is all that part which has no choric song following it. Of the choric portion, the parode is the entire first utterance of the chorus; the stasimon is [any later] choric song;[172] the kommos, a lamentation carried on between the chorus and an actor.

---

[170] The reference here is presumably to the last sentence of Chap. vii, although reversal was not there mentioned. How technical reversal differs from simple change of fortune is well stated by Bywater: "Every tragedy, according to Aristotle, describes a transition from happiness to misery or vice versa; but in the 'complex story' the change, however gradual it may be, seems to the hero to come upon him all at once, by a sudden reversal of the state of things; he thinks himself a happy man (let us say) at the beginning of an [episode], and a miserable man at the end of it." (*Aristotle on the Art of Poetry*, p. 199.)

[171] Euripides, *Iphigeneia in Tauris*, I. 11.

[172] What Aristotle actually says is, "a choric song without anapests or trochees," but this does not apply to the surviving Greek tragedies. The more usual definition of a stasimon is a 'stationary song' (W. Rhys Roberts), sung after the chorus has taken up its station in the orchestra.

xiii. Aim and Proper Effect of Tragedy

The next points to consider, after the matters just mentioned, are: what should be aimed at and what avoided in the construction of plots; and by what means the 'proper effect' (*ergon*) of tragedy is to be achieved.

Tragedy at its best, as we have seen, will have not a simple but a complex type of construction, and also it will represent actions arousing pity and fear. Since this latter operation is the distinctive function of tragic *mimêsis*, it evidently follows that there are three types of plot to be avoided. First a [thoroughly] good man should not be shown passing from prosperity to misfortune, for such a situation does not arouse either pity or fear, but merely offends us by its brutality. Nor, on the other hand, should a bad man be shown passing from adversity to prosperity – a situation entirely alien to tragedy, meeting none of its requirements, for it excites neither our pity and fear nor our moral sympathies. Finally, it must not be an utterly wicked man who is shown passing from prosperity to adversity. Such a situation may excite our moral sympathies but it will not arouse our pity nor our fear: pity is aroused by undeserved misfortune, and fear by the misfortune of someone like ourselves, so that an event of the sort described is neither piteous nor fear-inspiring. The remaining case is that of the man who is a mean between these extremes: who, though not outstandingly virtuous and just, yet falls into misfortune not through vice or depravity but through some 'tragic flaw' (*hamartia*); and moreover he should be drawn from the ranks of men who have enjoyed great reputation and prosperity, like Oedipus, Thyestes, and men of equally illustrious families.

Ideally, then, tragedy is at its best when constructed in the way described, and those critics are wrong who censure Euripides for constructing many of his plays on that principle and so giving them unhappy endings. In this respect he was right, as we have said; the best proof of which is that when well produced and performed upon the stage such plays are the most pronouncedly tragic, and Euripides himself, although he sometimes handles his subjects badly, is still the most tragic of poets.

Of second rank, although there are some who put it first, is the double dramatic construction like that of the *Odyssey*, in which there are opposite outcomes for the good characters and the bad. That it passes for the best is owing to the sentimentality of theatre audiences, to whose cravings the dramatist has accommodated his writing. But the pleasure which such dramas produce is not essentially tragic; it belongs rather to comedy, where those whom the story presents as bitter enemies, like Orestes and Aegisthus, quit the stage as good friends, with no slaying or being slain.

xiv. Kinds of Action Arousing Pity and Fear

Fear and pity may be aroused by spectacular staging, or they may be aroused by the dramatic construction. The latter method is the one which better poets employ. For the plot ought to be constructed in such a way that anyone, by merely hearing an account of the incidents and without seeing them, will be filled with horror and pity at what occurs. That is how anyone hearing the story of Oedipus would be affected. To rely on spectacular staging is less artistic and makes the production more dependent upon 'financial backing' (*chorêgia*).[173] Those who stage the play in such a way as to produce an effect which is not terrible but merely showy are not really writers of tragedy at all. For what we should expect of tragedy is not any random pleasure, but only such pleasure as is proper to it. And since the dramatist's task is to produce through *mimêsis* the kind of pleasure that comes from responding with pity and fear, it is clear that this effect should be drawn from the incidents themselves.

Let us examine, then, what kinds of incident strike us as terrible and as pitiable. Logically, the persons involved must be either friends or enemies or indifferent to each other. If an enemy performs a

---

[173] The *chorêgos* was a man of wealth who voluntarily assumed responsibility for "assembling and hiring a body of *choreutae*, engaging a trainer to drill them, purchasing or renting costumes for the chorus, employing mute characters, providing showy extras of various kinds, etc. ... There was no surer method of displaying one's wealth and of currying favor with the populace than by voluntary and lavish assumption of the choregia." (Roy C. Flickinger, *The Greek Theatre and its Drama*.)

deed against an enemy, there is nothing to arouse our pity in either the deed or the intention; our pity is confined to the suffering which results. The same will be true when the participants are neither friends nor enemies. But when the 'tragic occurrence' (*pathos*) takes place between friends – when, for instance, some such crime as murder is done or planned by brother against brother, or by son against father, or by son against mother or mother against son – here is the kind of situation that the dramatist should look for. Traditional stories, then, like Orestes' slaying of Clytemnestra and Alcmaeon's of Eriphyle, should not be radically altered; it is left for the poet to show his inventiveness by his skillful handling of the traditional material. What I mean by skillful handling I will next explain.

A dreadful deed may be done in full consciousness of what it involves, as in the older poets and in the scene where Euripides has Medea slay her children. Or it may be done in ignorance of its dreadful nature, which becomes revealed only later when some intimate relationship is discovered, as in Sophocles' *Oedipus*. In that case, to be sure, the deed lies outside the play, but there are other examples where the deed lies within the play itself. Thirdly, a character may be about to do some irreparable deed through ignorance and make the discovery in time to desist. [And lastly, one may be about to act in full knowledge of what is involved and then change his mind.] These exhaust the possibilities, for the deed must either be done or not be done, and either knowingly or unwittingly.

The worst of these situations is where one is about to act in full knowledge and then changes his mind. Such a situation is not tragic but merely revolting, for no tragic feeling is involved. Hence it is rarely employed, the scene between Haemon and Creon in the *Antigone* being one of the few exceptions. Next [in ascending order of merit] comes the doing of the deed [in full knowledge]. Still better is the acting in ignorance and subsequent discovery, for there is nothing revolting about it and the discovery is [effectively] startling. Best of all is the remaining type of situation. In the *Cresphorites* [of Euripides], for example, Merope intends to kill her son but discovers who he is and so spares his life; there is a

similar situation in Euripides' *Iphigeneia in Tauris* between sister and brother; and in the *Helle*[174] a son discovers the identity of his mother just as he is about to surrender her.

Thus we see the reason why tragedies, as we said just now, deal with the fortunes of a few [illustrious] families. For it is not technical proficiency but the happy chance [of having discovered suitable situations in the traditional tales about those families] that enabled the tragic poets to embody such incidents in their plots. Accordingly they still feel bound to have recourse to the families in which such tragic occurrences took place.

Enough now has been said about the proper arrangement of incidents and the character of plots.

xv. Requirements of Tragic Characters

Respecting the characters (*êthos*) in tragedy, there are four things to be aimed at. First and foremost they must be good. The play will have an 'element of character, or ethical element' (*êthos*) if, as has already been remarked, some kind of 'moral purpose' (*proairesis*) is expressed, either in the 'speeches and dialogue' (*logos*) or in the action; and the character will be good if the moral purpose is good. The rule holds for all classes of people – even of women and slaves, although it is doubtless true that the one is an inferior type of person and the other without any personal worth whatever. Secondly, the characters should be appropriate; manly valor, for instance, has its proper place, but manly valor and domination are hardly appropriate in a woman. Thirdly, the characters should resemble [their models], which is something quite distinct from making them good or, in the sense here defined, appropriate. Fourthly, they should be consistent: for even where an inconsistent person is to be represented, he should be consistently represented as inconsistent. Menelaos in the *Orestes* [of Euripides] is an example (*paradeigma*) of unnecessary badness of character; Melanippe's speech[175]

---

[174] Nothing is known of this play.

[175] In *Melanippe the Wise*, a lost play of Euripides, of which only certain fragments have been preserved. Melanippe, seduced by Neptune, bore him twins and concealed them in her father's stable. Her father, taking them for monstrous offspring of his cows, ordered them burned. Melanippe, in order to save them without exposing her indiscretion, had recourse to a 'masculine' type of argument, based upon the principles of Anaxagoras, to prove that monstrous births are 'natural.' Of the *Scylla* nothing is known.

exemplifies character that is incongruous; Odysseus' lament in the *Scylla*, character that does not resemble its model; and Iphigeneia in Aulis [in Euripides' play of that name], character that is inconsistent – for Iphigeneia as suppliant is quite unlike her later self. In short, the rule in character drawing, just as in plot construction, is that one should always seek what is [dramatically] inevitable or [at least] dramatically plausible, so that it becomes inevitable or [at least] plausible that a given person should speak or act in a certain way, and inevitable or [at least] plausible that one incident should follow another.

[To digress for a moment.] It is clear from this last point that the 'denouement or resolution' (*lysis*) of a plot should arise out of the plot itself and not be produced by a mechanical device as in the *Medea* [of Euripides] and in the account of the [supernaturally prevented] return of the Greek army in the *Iliad*. The mechanical device[176] should only be employed for what lies outside the drama; that is, in the explaining or foretelling of unfamiliar events that precede or follow the drama itself. [In such cases it is permissible to introduce a god by mechanical device,] for the gods are credited with omniscience. In short, there should be no supernatural elements within the drama proper, but only, if at all, peripheral to it, as in Sophocles' *Oedipus*.

[Returning to the subject of character portrayal] we may remark that since tragedy is a representation of men better than ordinary, the example of good portrait painters should be followed. Their method is to produce a likeness of a man's distinctive features and beautify him at the same time. Analogously the poet, when representing a man who is irascible or lazy or otherwise morally defective, should set him forth with these very traits while at the same time ennobling him. This is how both Agathon and Homer have represented Achilles.[177]

Such are the rules to be observed in the writing of tragedy. There is also, of course, the question of theatrical effects to be considered, for there are many ways in which a play can go wrong when it is being presented on the stage; but this subject has been sufficiently treated in our published writings.

xvi. Kinds of "Discovery"

The general nature of 'discovery' has already been explained; let us now distinguish its species.

The first and least artistic kind of discovery, usually a mark of incompetence, is discovery by means of visible signs: whether they be congenital, such as birthmarks, or acquired, such as bodily scars on the one hand and external tokens like necklaces on the other. The treatment of such signs admits of varying degrees of skill: compare, for instance, the way in which he was recognized by his nurse with the way in which he was recognized by the swineherds.[178] A discovery in which the signs are deliberately shown as a means of proof, or any other such labored contrivance, is artistically inferior to one in which (as in the incident just cited, of Odysseus being bathed by the old nurse) they occur as a spontaneous reversal of the situation.

Secondly, there are discoveries arbitrarily invented by the poet: e.g., where Orestes, in the *Iphigeneia* [*in Tauris*], reveals his identity. Whereas Iphigeneia becomes known to Orestes by means of the letter, he becomes known to her by speaking what the poet and not what the plot requires. This second fault, then, comes close to the one already mentioned, for [when Orestes describes things at home in order to prove his identity] it is virtually as if he had brought some tokens to show. Another example is offered by the 'voice of the shuttle' device in Sophocles' *Tereus*.[179]

---

[176] This epithet appears to have a double and perhaps shifting meaning in the present paragraph: (1) the *deus ex machina*, a mechanical contraption, standard in the Greek theatre, for lowering a god on to the stage; (2) hence, the kind of artificial resolution of plot which the use of the contraption ordinarily involved.

[177] Professor Jaeger quotes the rhetor Dio of Prusa to similar effect: "Homer praised almost everything – animals and plants, water and earth, weapons and horses. He passed over nothing without somehow honoring and glorifying it. Even the one man whom he abused, Thersites, he called a clear-voiced speaker." (Werner Jaeger, *Paideia*, Vol. I, p. 42; Oxford University Press.)

[178] The old nurse Eurycleia sees Odysseus' scar by a natural accident (*Odyssey*, xix, 386 ff.) whereas Odysseus deliberately shows it to the herdsmen in order to convince them of his identity (*Odyssey*, xxi, 205 ff.). The former of these constitutes a 'dramatic reversal.'

[179] A lost play. After Tereus had raped Philomela and cut out her tongue, the wronged girl succeeded in telling her sister Procne what had happened by weaving the story into the embroidery. The shuttle with which she wove thereby had a 'voice.' Aristotle regards such disclosure as too deliberate to be artistically effective.

Thirdly, there is discovery through memory, whereby the sight of something stirs an emotional recollection. Thus when Odysseus heard the minstrel Alcinoüs play the lyre he remembered the past and burst into tears, thereby being recognized.[180]

The fourth kind of discovery comes about through rational inference. An example is [Electra's] reasoning in [Aeschylus'] *Choëphori*: "Someone like myself has come here, no one resembles me but Orestes, therefore Orestes has come." ...

But of all discoveries the best is that which arises from the action itself, where the shock of surprise is the outcome of a plausible succession of events. Such is the discovery in Sophocles' *Oedipus*. Another example is found in the *Iphigeneia* [*in Tauris*], for it is plausible enough that Iphigeneia should want to send a letter home.

The last type of discovery, being the only one entirely free from artificial contrivances, is best. Second in excellence is the type that depends on inference.

xvii.   Practical Advice for the Tragic Poet

In constructing his plots and elaborating them in language (*lexis*) the poet should keep the scene before his eyes as far as possible. Thereby, seeing everything as vividly as if he were an actual spectator, he will discover what is appropriate and will detect incongruities.

Moreover, he should work out the action even down to gestures. To be entirely convincing he must be able to enter into the emotions of his characters through sharing in their nature. One enacts agitation or anger most convincingly when he is actually feeling them. That is why poetry requires either a natural talent or an enthusiasm that verges on madness: by the one a man is adaptable, by the other ecstatically inspired.

As for the story – whether the poet takes it ready-made or invents it himself – he should first sketch its general outline, then write the episodes

and otherwise amplify it. ... He should take care that the episodes are appropriate: as illustrated by the madness of Orestes, which led to his capture, and the ritual purification which saved him.[181]

The episodes in a drama should be short, whereas in an epic they are used for lengthening out the action. ...

xviii.   On Plot Construction

Every tragedy falls into two parts – the complication or 'tying up' and the resolution or 'unraveling.' The complication usually contains not only elements within the drama proper but incidents referred to as occurring outside it; the rest is dramatic resolution. In other words, the complication is everything from the beginning of the story up to that crucial point which is followed by a change from prosperity to adversity; the resolution is all that extends from this turning-point to the end of the play. The soundest basis on which to compare or contrast one tragedy with another is plot – specifically, by comparing them with respect to complication and resolution. Many poets are good at tying the knot but poor at untying it. Both arts should be mastered.

There are four species of tragedy, corresponding to the four elements which have just been discussed:[182] (1) complex tragedy, depending entirely on reversal and discovery, (2) tragedy 'of suffering' (*pathêtikos*), like the various *Ajaxes* and *Ixions*, (3) tragedy 'of character' (*êthikos*), like *The Phthiotides* and *Peleus*, and finally, (4) tragedy depending upon spectacle, exemplified by *The Phorcides*, *Prometheus*, and all those plays whose scene is laid in Hades. A poet should aim to combine all four elements if possible, or at any rate as many of them in as significant a way as he can – especially in these days when there is so much ill-considered criticism of poets. Just because there have been poets who were adept at writing one or another particular species of tragedy, critics now expect a poet to show his superiority by combining all the different excellences of his predecessors into one.

[180]   *Odyssey*, viii, 521 ff.
[181]   This situation, in Euripides' *Iphigeneia in Tauris*, takes place after Orestes has murdered his mother. Although the ritual purification is merely a stratagem by Iphigeneia to 'save' them from their captors, the madness is ethically appropriate in view of Orestes' crime, and the purification and 'saving' (the Greek word *sôtêria* here connotes both escape from captivity and religious salvation) is appropriate symbolically.
[182]   The reference is apparently to Chaps. xi ff. In the traditional arrangement this paragraph is introduced three sentences earlier.

Again, the poet should remember what has been repeatedly said, and not construct a tragedy in the manner of an epic (which comprises a number of stories) by trying to dramatize, for instance, the entire *Iliad*. An epic is long enough to allow of the parts being as long as they need to be, but a drama so constructed will fail of its intended effect. A proof of this is that poets who have dramatized the entire story of Troy's fall, instead of presenting it part by part like Euripides, or the entire story of Niobe instead of selecting a portion of it like Aeschylus, either fail utterly or at any rate come out badly in the competition. ...

The Chorus should be considered as one of the persons in the drama; it should be an integral part of the whole and have a share in the action – following the practice of Sophocles, not Euripides. The rest [of the moderns] use songs that have no more to do with the plot of the tragedy that contains them than with any other. Hence they come to be sung as mere interludes – a practice which Agathon first began. And yet how is the singing of interludes any better than transferring a speech or an entire scene from one play to another?

xix.   Diction and Thought

The other aspects of tragedy having been discussed, it remains to speak of the diction and the thought. As for thought, we may refer to what has been said about it in our *Rhetoric*, for it is to that field of study that the subject more properly belongs. The 'thought' of a tragedy includes whatever effects are produced by the speeches and dialogues: wherever anyone is engaged in proving or disproving, arousing some emotion (such as pity, fear, anger, and the like), or exaggerating or belittling. Dramatic incidents, to be sure, can have essentially the same effect as speeches, arousing pity or horror or suggesting that something is important or probable. The only difference is that dramatic incident must make its impression without explanation, whereas in the speeches the effect is produced by the speaker, in consequence of what he *says* – the speech being necessary where the thought is not adequately conveyed by incident alone.
[...]

Study Questions

1   How would you account for the tendency to view *The Art of Rhetoric* and *Poetics* as handbooks rather than as elements of Aristotle's ethical philosophy?

2   Samuel Coolridge said that every person is either a Platonist or an Aristotelian. What does this mean? How would you characterize yourself?

3   We find examples of Aristotle's artificial proofs not only in speeches but also in advertising. Select three pieces of advertising (without regard to medium) and explain how each uses *ethos*, *pathos*, and *logos*.

4   Aristotle's three classes of rhetoric – deliberative, forensic, and epidiectic – are associated with persuasion. Yet there are other types of discourse that lie outside these classes. Academic writing, for example, seems to be a different genre – argument rather than persuasion. What is the difference between argument and persuasion?

5   How does Aristotle differentiate rhetoric from dialectic?

6   Explain the difference between an enthymeme and a syllogism. Which do we use more frequently on our lives?

7   In Book III of the *Rhetoric*, are style and delivery differentiated? If so, how?

8   *The Art of Poetry* indicates that tragedy should involve noble people engaged in serious actions that inspire fear and pity in the audience. Today, however, we seem to have very few dramas on the stage, on TV, or in cinema that meet these criteria. Why do you think that is? Do they qualify as tragedy? What *is* tragedy?

9   Aristotle conceived of protagonists as noble characters with a fatal flaw, usually hubris, or pride. They were larger than life, heroes, whose human tendency to err brought them down. How do today's protagonists differ?

Writing Topics

1   Analyze a set of 3 to 5 print or video ads in terms of their use of artificial proofs. How does the use of proof differ among the ads? Are their any generalizable patterns? Which seems to be the most effective proof?

2   In Book I of *The Art of Rhetoric*, Aristotle asserted that truth does not always persuade. Analyze what he meant by this claim, placing it in the context of rhetoric and everyday life, and then argue for or against the claim.

3   Book III of *The Art of Rhetoric* addresses style, which Aristotle indicated is one of the more important features of discourse. Studies of style in composition received a great deal of attention during the late 1960s and early 1970s but since the mid-1980s have been largely ignored. Summarize the history of stylistic studies and explain the lack of attention over the last 20 years.

4   Some communication theorists maintain that, at a fundamental level, the purpose of communication is to transmit information. Examine *The Art of Rhetoric* from this perspective and explain whether Aristotle's theory of rhetoric is also a theory of communication.

Further Reading

Aristotle, *Politics*.

Aristotle, *Nicomachean Ethics*.

Aristotle, *Topics*.

Belfiore, E. (1992). *Tragic pleasures: Aristotle on plot and emotion*. Princeton: Princeton University Press.

Rorty, A. (Ed.). (1992). *Essays on Aristotle's* Poetics. Princeton: Princeton University Press.

Part II

Classical Roman Rhetoric

6

Introduction to Roman Rhetoric and Oratory

Rome's history is vast and complex. Summarizing it here so as to develop a context for Roman rhetoric that has even a semblance of detail is unrealistic. To address this problem, what follows punctuates summary with what may be thought of as "snapshots" – selected details designed to give some texture to a greatly abbreviated account of the various social and cultural factors that influenced rhetoric and oratory during the Roman Period. Matters are made more difficult by the fact that in many instances scholars have interpreted the available evidence in different, often conflicting, ways. As a result, the summary presented here should be viewed as one interpretation among several.

As the title of this chapter suggests, Romans differentiated the instruction that they observed in the Greek schools of rhetoric from the more virile public speaking practiced in Rome. They therefore used, with some exceptions, the term "rhetoric" to refer to instruction and the term "oratory" to refer to public speaking. This distinction will be used throughout Part II.

Rome was founded in 750 BC by the Etruscans, a group of people who appeared in central Italy in the tenth or eleventh century. Their origins are uncertain, although for years many scholars speculated, on the basis of the Etruscan's highly advanced culture, that they came from Asia Minor, a view supported by a recent mitrochondrial DNA study showing that they were closely related to population groups in western Anatolia (Vernesi, et al., 2004). The Etruscan's superior culture and fierceness in war allowed them to conquer the Latins and several other tribes and to consolidate tribal villages into fortified hilltop towns. Rome was one such town. They ruled Rome for at least two hundred years, until Roman nobles overthrew King Tarquin in 509 BC. The nature of the coup d'état made it unfeasible to continue with a monarchy, so the nobles established a "republic" that enabled them to share power among themselves through a governing senate, and for the next 450 years the very idea of being ruled by a king was anathema in Rome.

The Republic collapsed after years of civil war driven by personal ambition, profligate corruption, and class conflict, only to emerge as an empire under Octavian (c. 63 BC –14 AD). The western portion of the empire fell to Germanic invaders in 476 AD, whereas the eastern portion, with its capital in Constantinople, was conquered by Turks in 1456 AD. Thus, classical Rome's history spanned either one or two thousand years, depending on one's perspective.

Class Structure and Government

Etruscan culture was rigidly hierarchical, and under Etruscan rule Roman society was organized into two classes: a small group of wealthy landowners, known as *patricians*, and a large group of farmers and craftsmen, known as *plebeians*. The patricians became Rome's hereditary nobility and solidified their status by claiming to be descended from the gods. They ruled as a group but selected from their ranks two chief administrators, or *consuls*, who were then ratified by the citizens in a plebiscite. The consular appointment was limited to one year, and the most significant duty (owing to the frequency of warfare) was to serve as commander-in-chief of the military.

Almost from the beginning of the Republic, Rome experienced often bitter conflict between patricians and plebeians. This conflict had a direct influence on every facet of Rome's existence, including rhetoric and oratory, and given the connection between democracy and rhetoric, it raises the important question of whether the Republic was a democracy or an oligarchy. As we saw in Part I, rhetoric thrived in Greece before the Hellenistic Period (4th century BC–1st century AD) for a number of reasons. The value Greeks placed on language was historical, reaching back beyond the time of Homer to the heroic age of the Mycenaeans. After reforms implemented by Solon (c. 638–558 BC) and Pisistratus (c. 600–527 BC), Athens (and other cities) practiced direct democracy; all citizens could participate in the assembly, where debates on government decisions made skill in public speaking important and where citizens voted on those decisions, thereby guiding the ship of state. The requirement that litigants present their own cases also served as a powerful motivator for rhetorical skill.

Rome was different. The division of society into legal classes – initially patricians and plebeians, but later including *equites*, or knights – was a source of continual social tension that the Romans, unlike the Greeks, seemed incapable of addressing effectively. Republics are representative, with greater or lesser degrees of citizen participation, and do not allow for direct democracy. In fact, republics typically are antagonistic toward direct democracy, for many of the same reasons Athenian aristocrats opposed this system of government – claiming that it is the rule of the mob, that common people lack sufficient education and intelligence to reason soundly when considering complex issues, and that they lack virtue and honor.

Few people or groups have ever been able to give up power willingly, and certainly such was the case in Rome. The patricians who formed the Roman Republic resisted power sharing to the very end. Only when warfare expanded the size of the Republic and made many plebeians rich in the process, owing to the patrician disdain for engaging in any moneymaking activity other than agriculture, did the Senate allow members of this "lower" class to join its august ranks, provided they were wealthy. These "new men" (*homines novi*), however, were for the most part as committed to aristocratic values as their patrician counterparts and usually aligned themselves with patricians against the common people. Only toward the end of the Republic did they begin pursuing populist agendas, but even then their efforts generally were more about increasing their own power than about true social reform. Cicero (c. 103–43 BC) is among the most well-known *homines novi* – a plebeian who became wealthy through oratory and who throughout his career managed to convince the *populus* that he was their man, even though in his senatorial speeches and private correspondence his contempt and disdain for the common people was bitter and deep.

Growing social unrest left patricians with little choice but to implement reforms, albeit grudgingly. To placate the people, the Senate created the position of *tribune*, from which patricians were barred, and invested the office with the power to veto laws passed by the Senate. In 471 BC, the Senate created the *comitia plebus*, or people's assembly, and the *comitia tributa*, the assembly of tribes. The former was initially authorized to meet periodically to express the plebeians' views to their tribunes, who would then pass them on to the Senate, and any decisions it reached were binding only on plebeians. The *comitia tributa*, on the other hand, was a voting assembly of all Romans in their respective tribes, and its decisions were binding on everyone, provided they were not blocked by tribune veto or annulled by the Senate on the ground that they were contrary to the constitution. In 287 BC, a law was passed (*Lex Hortensia*) that expanded the power of the *comitia plebus* so that its decisions were binding on all classes, thus making it the chief legislative body in the Republic. The influence of the *comitia tributa* began to decline thereafter, and fewer and fewer citizens attended its meetings.

These and other reforms designed to allow the common people greater participation in government suggest that the Roman Republic managed to control the inherent conflict between rich and poor by infusing government with vigorous democratic components that balanced the ambitions of the aristocrats with the needs of the people. But the democratic nature of Roman government during the Republic is far from clear, and there is an ongoing debate among scholars about whether the Republic was an oligarchy or a true republic with elected representatives.

Gelzer (1969) and Syme (1939), among others, argued that the bulk of the evidence indicates that Rome remained a harsh oligarchy and that the Senate's democratic reforms were merely a sham. According to Syme, *res publica populi Romani* was nothing more than a name, and "Roman history, Republican or Imperial, is the history of the governing class" (pp. 11–12). There is substantial evidence to support this view. Certainly during the early years of the Republic, power and government were in the hands of the Senate. Membership in this body was long based solely on the amount of real property one owned; only under pressure from wealthy plebeians did the Senate modify the laws to allow membership to those without vast real property holdings, but it remained the province of the rich elite. Grant (1992) noted that over a three hundred year period, only 14 men from outside the nobility – *homines novi* such as the very wealthy Cicero – were admitted to the Senate and rose to be consul. Moreover, most of the important offices in the various branches of government were staffed by nobles. None of these positions provided any compensation, which may have been an institutionalized method of ensuring that only men of wealth could afford to serve in the higher administrative posts. Although by law tribunes were to come from the *equites* or plebeian classes, the Senate had no qualms about declaring a patrician to be a plebeian (e.g., Clodius Pulcher (c. 92–52 BC)), thereby allowing one of their own to stand for election when it was politically expedient.[1] But those who had enough wealth to stand for tribune understandably had more in common with patricians than with the masses, and rampant bribery and widespread corruption could always buy enough votes (and frequently did) to ensure that election results were congruent with patrician interests.[2]

The argument that Rome was an often brutal oligarchy – not a true republic and certainly not a democracy – also takes into account the fact that money was so important in Rome that class distinctions were a matter of law. The failure of a plebeian to show deference to a patrician was a criminal offense. Marriage between plebeians and patricians was illegal until 442 BC on the grounds that class miscegenation would contaminate the pure blood of the patricians. The majority of the population during the early Republic – perhaps as much as 90 percent – were peasants who either worked their

[1] Intially, tribunes had to be members of the plebeian class; toward the latter part of the Republic, however, the position was opened to members of the *equites*.
[2] Plutarch (1958) reported, for example, that Julius Caesar's distributions of cash to the people enabled Marc Antony's election to tribune. In this case, however, it is important to point out that Caesar (and therefore Antony) had aligned himself with the people against the oligarchs in the Senate. Even so, Antony's election illustrates how bribery influenced outcomes. Note that Marc Antony, although from a wealthy family and related to Caesar through his mother, Julia, was not a patrician. Class status was passed on from the father, not the mother. Julia was patrician, but Antony's father, Marcus Antonius Cretius, was not.

own small farms or hired themselves out as laborers. As has often been the case throughout history, poverty was seen as a moral failure, and the poor were believed to deserve their fate owing to their moral deficiency. Not even members of the nobility were exempt. Cicero, for example, in his second oration against Lucius Catilina (c. 108–62 BC) near the end of the Republic, alleged that Catiline and his cohorts were impoverished and linked their poverty to moral vices that threatened the *res publica*.

Patronage

All male plebeians were eligible to attend the *comitia plebus*, but there is some question as to how much political power this body actually possessed, in part because of the influence exerted by Rome's system of patronage. In the most simple terms, patronage can be viewed as a form of welfare inherent in the tribalism that dominated sociopolitical relations among the Latin people even before the founding of the Republic. Wealthy citizens provided for the needs of those of lesser means – "clients" – in return for their support and allegiance. Poor clients called on their patrons to pay homage and to receive food and a few coins in return. Sometimes they would be given odd jobs. Powerful patrons capable of providing a wide range of benefits to their clients were visited every morning, and they were accompanied by an entourage of clients whenever they left their homes (Veyne, 1987). Common people did not have access to the courts, so if they had a cause of legal action, they were required to ask their patron to serve as advocate. Clients of higher standing may not have called on their patrons daily, but they were expected to do so on a fairly regular basis. Rather than food or a job, they sought recommendations for government positions, or they might ask their patron to stand as surety for a loan.

The benefits of patronage for clients are obvious, but the benefits for patrons are less so unless seen through the lens of tribalism. At its heart is unbridled competition with other tribes for resources, power, and honor. Even as the Republic grew to control all of Italy and then the Mediterranean, it retained various features of tribal culture, such as relentless competition and preferential treatment based on kinship. Among aristocratic Romans, competition became an obsession that eventually led to civil war and the collapse of the Republic. The wealth of the ruling class was so great and so easily maintained that there was little in the way of material goods that they lacked. Consequently, they focused their individual energies on competing for and increasing personal power.

Clients served as one means of doing so and therefore can be analyzed as a form of altruistic giving designed to advertise the patron's power and superiority, what in anthropology is referred to as the Potlatch Effect. As Veyne (1987) indicated, honor and dignity were viewed as commodities in Rome. Clients therefore served as a kind of currency for obtaining greater levels of both; they provided an entourage and inflated the wealthy man's sense of power owing to their dependency on him for favors. The currency of a broad client base was valuable in the political arena because, according to Gelzer (1969) and Syme (1939), it gave the wealthy significant influence over plebeian voting in the various people's assemblies. Plebeians could be expected to vote in keeping with the best interests of their patrons.

The argument for democracy

Over the past several decades, various scholars have challenged the view that the Republic was an oligarchy (e.g., Brunt, 1974; Gruen, 1995; Millar, 1984, 1989, 1998).

Plate 1   View of the Acropolis, Athens, showing the Parthenon. Photo © Guy Vanderelst / Getty Images.

Plate 2   Socrates, marble bust, Hellenistic. Museo Archeologico Nazionale, Naples. Photo © Alinari / Bridgeman Art Library.

Plate 3   Plato, marble bust. Vatican, Museo Pio-Clementino. © 1990, photo Scala, Florence.

Plate 4   Aristotle, marble bust, Roman copy of a Greek original by Lysippos, fl.370–310 BC. Musée du Louvre, Paris. Photo © Giraudon / Bridgeman Art Library.

Plate 5 Demosthenes, portrait bust, Roman copy after Greek bronze statue by Polyclitus, 280 BC. Marble, height 44 cm. Musée du Louvre, Paris. Photo © Erich Lessing / akg-images.

Plate 6 Cicero, marble bust. Musei Capitolini, Rome. Photo bpk / Alfredo Dagli Orti.

Plate 7 Portrait of a young woman, "The Poetess of Pompeii" (Sappho?), Roman fresco. Museo Archeologico Nazionale, Naples. © 2003, photo Scala, Florence / Fotografica Foglia, courtesy of the Ministero Beni e Att. Culturali.

Plate 8 Livia (58BC–29AD), wife of Caesar Augustus. Basalt head, 1st century AD. Musée du Louvre, Paris. Photo © Erich Lessing / akg-images.

Plate 9 Hypothetical reconstruction of the Roman Forum in Imperial Times, Southern Part, watercolor, 1892. Soprintendenza alle Antichita, Rome. © 1990, photo Scala, Florence / courtesy of the Minstero Beni et Att. Culturali.

Plate 10 Antonello da Messina, painting of St. Augustine. Palermo, Galleria Nazionale della Sicilia, inv. 50. © 1990, photo Scala, Florence.

Millar (1989), perhaps the most vigorous challenger, noted that oratory played a significant part in Roman politics and that it could only do so if democratic mechanisms were
in place. Relying significantly on the writing of the historian Polybius (c. 203–120 BC),
Millar (1984) also cited the frequency with which treaties were ratified in the public
assemblies as evidence of democratic elements at work. In *The Crowd in the Late Roman
Republic*, Millar (1998) argued that democracy must vest the power to legislate in the
votes of citizens and that these votes must count equally. He also examined more closely
the role of oratory as a suasive tool in the political dynamics and decision making of the
Republic. He concluded from his analyses that the Republic was a "direct democracy"
because "the most fundamental of all rights of the people was … that they, and they
alone, could legislate" (p. 209). The power to legislate was vested in the popular assemblies, which raises the question of how much influence Rome's elite exercised through
the patronage system. Although this influence was no doubt significant, it would seem
unlikely that the system could have included all the poor in the city.

As well-supported as these analyses are, it is important to recognize that during the
latter half of the Republic control of legislation and the courts shifted back and forth
between the aristocrats and the common people. Only toward the end of the Republic,
when gangs from both groups used violence and intimidation to exert control, did the
plebeians have absolute control to legislate, and it was fleeting. The public assemblies
could pass only those bills introduced by a tribune, and because the tribunes were from the
wealthy elite, even though technically they were plebeians, no tribune introduced a bill
seriously at odds with Senate goals until 133 BC. In addition, Mouritsen (2001) and Wade
(2002) argued that the popular assemblies may have been structured as manifestations of
democratic political apparatuses in keeping with the ideology of *libertas*, or freedom, but
that the very nature of Roman politics prevented them from having much substance.
Wade noted, for example, that voting in the Republic never rose above 2 percent of eligible
citizens. Certainly, determining just how many voters that percentage represented is a
challenge because of the difficulty in knowing the exact size of the Rome's population (see
Beloch, 1886; Cascio, 1994; Oates, 1934; Parkin, 1992). Cascio (1994) indicated that the last
Republican census, conducted in 70 BC, gave a figure of 900,000. The population during the
middle Republic most certainly was much smaller, perhaps 300,000. Even so, after analyzing the sizes of available meeting places in the city, Mouritsen concluded that the popular
assemblies could not have involved more than 5,000 people because there was no area
large enough to contain more. If this figure is accurate, the potential influence of patronage must be viewed in a different light, for the elite quite easily could control groups of this
size, particularly given the widespread practice of buying votes.

Also worth considering is Mouritsen's (2001) proposal that the actual number was
much smaller than 5,000 owing to the time-consuming nature of political life. *Contiones*
were nonvoting meetings that were usually held a day or more before voting occurred
in the *comitia*. In a *contio*, the crowd listened to the speech of the magistrate proposing
legislation and expressed its sentiments for or against a proposal through group accla-
mation or dissent. As for the *comitia*, according to Pernot (2005), the "Roman citizen
was summoned around twenty times at least during the year, for sessions that could last
several days" (p. 88) owing to the amount of time required for voting. Mouritsen pointed
out that involvement at such a level was impossible for the majority of Roman plebeians, who had to work for a living as shopkeepers, craftsmen, and laborers. Even at the
height of the public dole around the end of the Republic, most Romans worked for
their daily bread. Thus, Mouritsen concluded that the popular assemblies did not reflect
political participation of the masses but rather were limited to the indigent rabble and
to those whose personal wealth allowed them the leisure required to attend frequent

meetings that lasted for days: "[W]orking-class citizens *de facto* would have been excluded from the political scene by the lack of public remuneration, which in effect left the *comitia* in the hands of the propertied classes for whom political activity did not entail any material sacrifices" (p. 37).

Moreover, voting was conducted on the basis of tribes, not individual citizens. The concept of one man, one vote, simply did not exist. By law, the number of urban tribes was fixed at four, whereas the number of rural tribes was set at 17, only to be increased to 31 in 241 BC. Each tribe had one vote regardless of the number of members, which meant that those in the country always had more voting power than those in the cities. The majority of rural citizens were farmers and laborers who either worked directly on the estates of the wealthy elite or were beholden to them in one way or another through the client system. Consequently, even after the countryside was depopulated during the wars against Carthage[3] and subsequent urbanization swelled the number of people living in city, the rural tribal votes outweighed the urban by a factor of eight to one.

What seems clear is that as the Republic matured, it enacted various reforms aimed at increasing democratic structures to provide more balance between the wealthy elite and the common people. But these reforms nearly always were a response to demands in the form of riots and protests; they were not undertaken freely. Several reforms led to the development of a professional class of jurists for whom rhetoric was a necessity, but whether they significantly increased the level of social and legal equity between rich and poor is highly questionable. After reviewing the central factors in the democracy v. oligarchy debate, North (1990) argued that the influence of tribes may not have been as powerful as numerous scholars have claimed, but he nevertheless concluded that "If there was such a thing as Roman democracy, it was nonparticipatory to an extreme degree and therefore in many ways the opposite pole to the Athenian democracy. ... The popular will of the Roman people found expression in the context, and only in the context, of divisions within the oligarchy" (pp. 284–285).

A careful review of the plethora of laws enacted between 241 and 49 BC, such as the one Botsford (2005) conducted, shows that the popular will was regularly manipulated by patricians and *equites* as these two groups alternately aligned and fought for political supremacy. The *comitia tributa* and *comitia plebus* could convene only if summoned by a magistrate and could not consider any subject other than what was proposed to them. If the popular assembly passed a law, it could be annulled by the *comitia centuriata*, which was always controlled by patricians, as occurred in the case of Cicero, who was exiled by the *comitia plebus* but then recalled by the *comitia centuriata*. Furthermore, there was no open discussion or deliberation in the popular assemblies, which meant that deliberative oratory as practiced in Greece was restricted to the Senate, which was closed to the public. In the *comitia*, the people listened to the rogation and could respond only if granted permission to do so on an individual basis. Botsford concluded that "Notwithstanding the theory of popular sovereignty, these conditions prevented the rise of real democracy" (p. 346).

If this conclusion is correct, then rhetoric and oratory – at least as they were applied in the political arena and perhaps even in the courts, which often served as stages for the subplots of political intrigue – must be viewed as a tool operating within oligarchic divisions and competition for power. Kennedy's (1972) assessment, therefore, warrants special consideration: "Persuasion in Rome before the second century BC was relatively nonverbal and nonargumentative and rested on family prestige, personal authority, and resources of power or money" (p. 7).

---

[3] The Punic Wars began in 264 BC and ended in 146 BC.

Revolution and Rhetoric

The end of the Second Punic War in 201 BC and the defeat of Hannibal (c. 247–183 BC) marked a turning point in Roman history. Romans began to shed their provincialism. Their victory over Carthage caused them to look for the first time at the world beyond the borders of the Italian peninsula. What they saw were limitless opportunities for conquest and riches aplenty. With such wealth came a guilty pleasure in luxuries that was to trouble Romans for centuries – reflected not only in the magisterial position of censor, who had the authority to punish those whose actions deviated from what was deemed morally proper for a Roman citizen, but also in the various sumptuary laws that the Senate passed in an effort to control how much people (particularly women) spent on food, clothing, and jewelry. In addition, the nature of war had changed. Increasingly, it was put in the hands of professionals, leaving politicians free to pursue less strenuous activities, and conquest led to a slave-based economy that provided the wealthy with more leisure time. Greek culture became more influential and alluring, at least among the upper class and to some degree the middle class as well. The Macedonian Wars (215–148 BC) increased Roman exposure to things Greek and turned allure into lust. Rome's conquering generals raided schools, estates, and temples, sending shiploads of art, literature, and artifacts back home (Holland, 2003). Captured philosophers became especially prized slaves in the households of the rich and famous. Romans adopted so many features of Greek culture that their civilization is often referred to as *Greco-Roman*.

Few Romans became philosophers themselves, however. It was simply too unmanly. But rhetoric was a different matter. Rhetoric could be used to enhance one's oratory, sharpening it into a tool, or weapon, that improved chances of success in the rough-and-tumble politics of Rome. In the past, the ambitious who sought political power had to meet three requirements: extravagant wealth, patrician lineage, and military success. Ideally, a man met all three. The changes in Roman society, however, made this ideal combination increasingly less common. Many young patricians squandered their family wealth, turning themselves into penniless blue-bloods. *Equites* had wealth but the wrong ancestors. The professionalization of the military meant that success in war was not as certain for amateurs as it once was. In this changing environment, with the plebeians becoming a force to be reckoned with – and manipulated – the study of rhetoric emerged as a new avenue to power.

The Punic Wars also altered the military. Consuls continued to command armies as needed during their tenure, but afterwards they were eligible to serve as *proconsuls*, or governors, of outlying provinces, which increasingly were where Rome had the greatest need for seasoned generals. The Senate began awarding the most dangerous assignments (and therefore also the most lucrative in terms of potential honor and plunder) to proven commanders for multi-year terms so that effective leaders were no longer replaced after one year. Serving for years under the same commander produced strong bonds of loyalty between troops and their generals that apparently had not existed previously. The generals quickly recognized that these bonds gave them unprecedented power as well as independence from the Senate. Moreover, the Senate was losing the support of plebeians at home. As Hannibal destroyed farms and burned villages, the small farmers and laborers who survived had no alternative but to flee to the city, depopulating the countryside and causing the deterioration of Rome's already inadequate infrastructure. Plebeians in the city initially welcomed their country cousins, until the stream of internal refugees turned into a flood that not only made living conditions unbearable but also reduced workers' wages as the competition for jobs became brutal. In desperation, the displaced farmers had no alternative but to sell their land to Rome's wealthy elite, who, of course, were predominantly members of the Senate and their cronies. The situation was exacerbated when legions were demobilized.[4] Thousands of soldiers found that although through sheer luck the farms they had left in the care of wives and children had been spared Hannibal's depredations, economic hardship had forced their families to sell (Rosenstein, 2004). Men who for years had fought for Rome learned at war's end that they had no homes. By the end of the Second Punic War, Roman agriculture was dominated by large estates owned by wealthy, absentee landowners, and the era of the small farmer who owned his land was at an end.

The plight of the plebeians could have been ameliorated were it not for the fact that the Punic Wars, as well as those that soon followed in Macedonia and the eastern Mediterranean, provided Rome with so many slaves that the number is difficult to calculate. Holland (2003) suggested that it may well have been in the millions, and Bradley (1994) speculated that approximately 30 percent of the people in Italy were slaves by the first century AD. The economics of slavery were so lucrative for the wealthy that the Senate resisted all efforts at land reform. When the wars ended, plebeians who had taken refuge in the city had nowhere to go. They had sold their land at fire-sale prices, and they could not even return to the country as laborers, for essentially all agricultural work was being performed by slaves (Grant, 1992). Rome, like Athens, shifted to a slave economy fairly early, and it experienced similar difficulties, but unlike Athens, Rome proved incapable of instituting the reforms necessary for an equitable distribution of power. Food riots were frequent, and the threat of revolt by slaves and citizens alike was a continuing concern that minor reforms, such as the creation of public assemblies, could not eliminate.

The Gracchi: Revolution begins

Rome's class tensions escalated as successful military campaigns and increasing corruption among the patricians and *equites* made the rich richer and the poor poorer. Without a police force to control the angry crowds, Rome became a dangerous place. *Equites* and patricians escalated their struggle for control of the state, and both sides sought to use the *populus* to further their aims (Enos, 1995). In this hot environment, two ideologies emerged that often are equated with political parties but are not, for there was no clear membership, just an orientation, a perspective, that defined goals and objectives. The *optimates* were those whose values were aligned with the aristocrats and whose goals were fundamentally conservative and aimed to preserve traditional class structures and privileges. The *populares*, on the other hand, were those who were aligned with the welfare and interests of the common people. But the unruliness of the *populus* grew so violent that the ideology of the *optimates* could seldom be expressed in public assemblies. Speakers therefore strove to outdo one another in speeches that pandered to the crowds, and reform oratory was the order of the day – in public, at least. In the confines of the Senate chamber, the wealthy elite kept up a

---

[4] Rosenstein (2004) argued that military service did not have a significant effect on Roman agricultural manpower. In his view, only young men were recruited, leaving older men behind to work the farms and sire more offspring. He concluded that the result was overpopulation: With the young men gone, the older men left behind took advantage of the lopsided male-to-female ratio. We should note, however, that, as Cowan (2003) pointed out, all male citizens between the ages of 17 and 46 were liable for military duty and that in times of severe emergency, such as the Punic Wars, the legions essentially took every male who owned a sword.

steady stream of invective against the unwashed mob. Apprehensive about the power of speech to stir the *populus*, the Senate banned the teaching of rhetoric and closed all the schools in 161 BC.

Tiberius (c. 163–133 BC) and Gaius (c. 154–121 BC) Gracchus – well-educated, wealthy brothers who were members of the *equites* – sought to use the existing class tensions. Whether they were true reformers or merely demagogues seeking power is uncertain, but they aligned themselves with the *populares* and spoke forcefully against existing inequities. Elected as tribune, Tiberius proposed a bill that limited land ownership to five hundred *iugera* (about 312 acres); any holdings over this amount would be seized and distributed among the poor. Senators, many of whom owned thousands of acres, were appalled, while the masses were thrilled. The bill was immediately passed by the popular assembly but vetoed by another tribune, Octavius, the Senate's man. Tiberius submitted the bill again and again; each time, it was approved by the people, and each time it was vetoed by Octavius.

When his term as tribune expired, Tiberius proclaimed to the crowds that the goal of social justice warranted illegal acts, and he stood again for election to tribune, which was specifically prohibited by the constitution. The Senate, meanwhile, began to make subtle, and sometimes not so subtle, threats against him. Tiberius used these threats to further incite the crowds, and at a gathering that was so large that the majority of the people could not hear his words, he tried to communicate his message using hand gestures that his enemies interpreted as signaling that he wanted to be crowned king. Alarmed, Senators agreed that it was time to bring Tiberius down. A group left the chamber and headed toward the assembly, collecting a gang of supporters, as well as clubs, along the way. Tiberius tried to flee when he saw them approaching, but the great number of people surrounding the Rostra made movement difficult. He tripped and fell. Then the thugs were upon him, beating him to death with their clubs in the name of the Roman constitution.

Sentiments smoldered for a decade. Then, in 123, Gaius Gracchus, brother of the slain Tiberius, was elected tribune. He took up the land reform issue of his dead brother, which had been annulled by the Senate, so as to appeal to those living in the rural areas. In an effort to detach the city's poor from their patrons and thus gain more control over voting, he proposed a commodities law that fixed the retail price of grain well below the market rate (eventually, grain was distributed free of charge to urban Romans). This law endeared him further to the poor, who depended on their patrons for food distributions, especially in times of scarcity, but it also wrought economic chaos. In violation of the law, Gaius ran for tribune a second time and won. When he ran a third time, the *optimates* put forward their own candidate, Marcus Livius Drusus (c. 124–91 BC), whose speeches to the plebeians were even more radically liberal than those of Gaius. Gaius lost the election, which allowed the Senate to repeal all the laws he had passed. In response, Gaius and a large group of *populares* marched on the Senate to protest. The Senate promptly declared him an enemy of the people and dispatched the militia to deal with the protesters, many of whom were carrying weapons. In the melee that followed, Gaius and about 3,000 of his supporters died.

With the advantage of historical perspective, we can see that the conflict between the *optimates* and *populares* reached a critical point with the death of Gaius and his supporters. The willingness of Rome's poor to use violence in support of their demagogues may have been driven by desperation, or it may have been motivated simply by the need to feel that their voices mattered. But the result was unequivocal: It eliminated the checks and balances that had restrained the personal ambitions of Rome's wealthy men. The Senate was powerless in the face of an angry crowd, and the Gracchi showed how easy it was for educated men to use rhetoric and oratory to further their ambitions. Both sides began using gangs more frequently as a tool of intimidation to influence legislation. Many Romans must have given thanks to the gods that neither the Gracchi nor the Senate had been in command of a loyal army during their contest over the status quo.

Gaius Marius and Cornelius Sulla

It was inevitable that a time came when just such a situation arose. The conflict between the *populares* and *optimates* was sporadic over three decades and then exploded when two extremely powerful and popular generals, Gaius Marius (c. 156–86 BC) and Lucius Cornelius Sulla (c. 138–48 BC), began competing with each other for the consulship and command of the army that was to wage war against Mithridates, a king in Anatolia. They were bitter enemies, even though – or perhaps because – Sulla had served under Marius. Plutarch (1958) reported that Marius was born to poor, indigent parents who supported themselves by their daily labor, but it seems more likely that they were members of the *equites*, which enabled Marius to use connections with the Roman nobility to secure a military commission.

Sulla was of the patrician class, but his family had fallen on hard times when his father died, and as a youth Sulla had, as Holland (2003) stated, "sunk into a world of seedy lodgings and even seedier companions" (p. 61). Even so, he received an excellent education, for he was fluent in Greek and evidently received solid training in rhetoric. His fortunes changed when he received two large inheritances at age 30 that allowed him to embark on the Roman *cursus honorum*, the ladder of successive political offices that culminated in the consulship. His fondness for Greek culture in general and Aristotle in particular no doubt influenced his decision in 84 BC, upon his return from Greece, to bring with him Aristotle's entire library. Conservative as well as brilliant and ambitious, Sulla aligned himself with the *optimates*.

Marius and Sulla both stood for the consulship the same year. During the political campaign, Sulla freely used the rhetoric of military crisis to excite the fear of the populus and to proclaim that only a young, vigorous commander could deal with the new threat from the East. His speech making and politicking were successful, perhaps enhanced by his familiarity with the demimonde, which allowed him to adopt easily the salty language of the poor; he was elected consul and also received command of the armies that would march on Mithridates. But Sulla underestimated Marius, and he also overestimated his own position. Enter Tribune Publius Sulpicius Rufus, a strong advocate for granting full citizenship to Rome's Italian allies. Sulpicius prepared a bill that he wanted to present to the public assemblies, but he understood that his rogation would fail without consular support. He therefore conferred privately with Sulla and Pompeius Rufus, the second consul. No doubt some *quid pro quo* was involved, but in any event, the consuls told Sulpicius that they would endorse the bill. Yet when the bill came before the people, both consuls opposed it (probably after conferring with other members of the Senate, which historically opposed extending citizenship), and without their support, the bill was defeated.

Sulla then left Rome to rejoin his legions stationed outside the town of Nola, several days travel to the south. Meanwhile, Marius had stayed in Rome to monitor the political scene. Seeing an opportunity, he approached Sulpicius and made an agreement that would serve both their interests. With Sulla away, Sulpicius presented his bill to the people again, this time with Marius at his side urging the people to accept it. Very likely, Marius had instructed his aides to pack the assembly with *populares*, a move that by this time was fairly common, and money was probably distributed to ensure the proper level of enthusiasm. Sulpicius' oration, no doubt given in a lower-class accent that was the hallmark of a *popularis* aristocrat, whipped the crowd into a frenzy, and after passing the bill the mob took to the streets and began rioting. When Sulla learned of the situation, he returned to Rome as quickly as possible, only to be attacked by the mob and nearly killed. He had to suffer the indignity of slipping out of the city in the dead of night. He therefore was conveniently out of the way when Sulpicius, again with Marius as sponsor, presented a bill to the people that ordered the dismissal of Sulla's co-consul, Pompeius Rufus, and that stripped Sulla of the Asian command.

For Sulla, the events in Rome must have resembled a nightmare. After a lifetime of struggle, he had finally achieved Rome's highest honor only to have everything blow up in his face. Then, to be dismissed from the Asian command as though he were merely a hired hand was more than his honor could bear. While Marius was gloating over his triumph, he apparently never expected that Sulla might apply to Rome's internal politics one of the more effective political tools that had been used repeatedly to subdue external enemies – war. Yet when we consider how leaders (including Marius) had been using gangs and street violence for decades to attain their political ends, bringing the army into the fray seems like a logical next step. Standing before his legions at Nola, Sulla described his humiliation to his troops, whose loyalty to him was unquestioned, and asked if they would march with him against his enemies. They shouted their support and urged him to descend on Rome immediately.

What followed was a protracted civil war between the forces of Marius and Sulla that can be viewed as a contest between the ideologies of *populares* and *optimates*. Marius had his subordinates draw up lists of enemies – proscription lists – who were summarily executed, their properties confiscated. Sulla was victorious and was named *dictator rei publicae constituendae* – dictator for reorganizing the government. Sulla and his forces had their own list of victims, and the bloodletting continued long after he became Rome's first dictator. Claiming that he was restoring Rome to her ancient traditions and saving the Republic, Sulla tossed out a majority of the legislation that had been passed over the preceding decades and implemented his own laws. He barred tribunes, for example, from standing for consul and from presenting bills to the public assemblies. Their right to address the people in *contiones* was severely limited. The effect was to dismantle the democratic reforms of the previous centuries and to return power to the Senate, although as dictator his was the real power.

Julius Caesar

With command of loyal legions, Sulla used sheer brutality and fear to suppress the hostility between *optimates* and *populares*, but he could not eliminate it. Further violence needed only a small spark to set off another civil war. The spark involved, once again, competition for honor between two mighty generals – Pompeius Magnus (c. 106–48 BC) and Gaius Julius Caesar (c. 100–44 BC). The story of Julius Caesar is one of the more intriguing in history, but it cannot be explored here (see Goldsworthy, 2006, for a detailed biography). Suffice it to say that he was brilliant, driven by ambition, a master politician, one of the world's great generals, and complex beyond full understanding. He was cold-hearted and brutal, dispatching enemies without a second thought, and also charitable and merciful, frequently granting clemency (*clementia*) to those who had betrayed him. Although his assassination in 44 BC precludes any definitive conclusions about his political goals, the evidence of his life suggests that he was a true reformer, perhaps the only politician during the last decades of the Republic genuinely devoted to improving the lot of the common people and to modernizing Rome's government. For his efforts, he received the implacable enmity of the Senate.

Pompeius Magnus, or Pompey, was a military hero who had literally doubled the size of the Republic and in the process became the second richest man in Rome. When Pompey returned from his victories in Asia, many feared that, like Sulla before him, he would use his legions to set himself up as dictator. Instead, he released his troops and set about indulging himself in extravagant luxuries that only someone with his limitless wealth could afford. He had the misfortune, however, of living at the same time as Marcus Porcius Cato (c. 95–46 BC) (also known as Cato the Younger to differentiate him from his father, referred to as Cato the Elder), who saw himself as the defender of the Republic as it had existed two or three hundred years in the past. A Stoic, a pedant, and an abrasive moralist who despised the masses, he insisted on maintaining a poor man's diet, wearing simple woolen clothes and often going barefoot.[5] As a very rich man, he could easily play at being poor. He abhorred even the idea of progress and believed that his purpose in life was to stamp out frivolity and immorality in the Republic so as to return Romans to the rectitude that supposedly characterized them before the great expansion made possible by the victory over Carthage. Infatuated with his own sense of morality, he wore it like a badge to display his presumed superiority and was always eager to denounce anyone whom he suspected of even the most trivial venality. He objected to everything that was Pompey: the boyish coiffure, the expensive clothes, the obvious quest for connections and status. But most of all, he loathed Pompey's spend-thrift ways.

Even before Pompey returned from his victories in Asia, Cato began strategizing to bring down the *homo novus* hero and put him in his place. He began by blocking all tokens of respect, such as a triumphal entrance into Rome, that were regularly awarded to returning heroes. He ridiculed Pompey's successes in the East by remarking that the general had been fighting against women. He then refused to allow the Senate to recognize treaties Pompey had secured for the governing of Asia and successfully urged the Senate to deny the distribution of any land or benefits to Pompey's demobilized legionaries. Dazed and confused by these rebuffs, Pompey gradually came to realize that he was out of his depth politically and needed an adroit ally if he wanted the recognition he felt he deserved. He found one in Julius Caesar.

The Catiline Conspiracy

In 63 BC, Cicero competed against Lucius Catilina, or Catiline, for the consulship. Both men distributed a fortune in bribes to buy votes, and when Cicero won, Catiline – now bankrupt – did not take the loss lightly. He conspired to assassinate Cicero and take over the government by force with the help of several ambitious, but reckless, senators. The plot was discovered, and Cicero denounced Catiline on the floor of the Senate. The alleged conspirators were arrested, and Cicero proposed that they should be executed without trial. Caesar, who was serving at that time as a *praetor*, or judge, stood to speak. We know from both Plutarch and the historian Sallust that Caesar used his exceptional oratorical skills to argue for adherence to the law, for due process, an investigation and a trial, and for exile rather than death. His speech was so persuasive that many senators changed their minds even though only moments before they had agreed to execution without trial. Cato immediately rose to oppose Caesar's motion. After slyly suggesting

---

[5] Stoicism arguably was the world's most popular philosophy, especially among the ruling elite. In Rome, it provided a means of reconciling personal wealth and government service, for it maintained that the order of the world (and thus society) was based on natural law, giving Stoics a rational basis for advocating plutocracy and monarchy.

that Caesar urged clemency because he was a fellow conspirator, Cato reminded the senators of Rome's early days – before the *populus* had forced enactment of bothersome laws governing trials and sentences – when criminals met justice without the annoyance of a hearing. Cicero then responded, reinforcing Cato's oration with a speech describing the death and destruction that Catiline's treason would have brought. Stirred by this speech, and perhaps fearing the outcome of an investigation, the Senate voted overwhelmingly in favor of immediate execution, and Cicero ordered the prisoners removed to a prison cellar in the dead of night and garroted.[6] Meanwhile, Cato was incensed by Caesar's opposition speech, which he viewed as sheer impertinence. From this point forward, he was Caesar's mortal enemy. He hated Caesar easily, perhaps because Caesar had recently taken Cato's sister, Servilia, as his mistress, perhaps because the two men were polar opposites. Caesar was handsome, charming, generous to a fault, vigorous, a risk taker, and wildly popular with the people. Cato was not.

For the rest of his life, Cicero took every opportunity to describe himself as the savior of Rome. Many people, however, had a different view. At the end of his tenure as consul, Cicero, as was the custom, prepared an elaborate speech giving an account of his service with special emphasis on the Catiline conspiracy. The people's tribune, Metellus, refused him permission to speak. The common people were disturbed by the executions, and street gangs were making threats against senators, most of whom were afraid to appear in public. To restore calm, Metellus drafted a proposal authorizing Pompey to use his troops to restore order. Before he could present it to the people, Cato, outraged by the thought of Pompey receiving yet another honor, jumped onto the Rosta and ordered Metellus to be silent, ripping the written proposal from the tribune's hands. Surrounded by a gang of *optimate* henchmen, Cato informed Metellus and Caesar that they were dismissed from their magistracies by authority of the Senate. Riots ensued and raged for days until the Senate was forced to rescind its decision in order to restore calm.

Matters went from bad to worse for Cicero in 58 BC. One of the men he had executed was Publius Cornelius Lentelus Sura, stepfather of Marc Antony (c. 83–30 BC), who by that time, as Caesar's lieutenant, had accumulated enough power to make Cicero apprehensive. Nevertheless, he did not hesitate to make yet another enemy – Clodius Pulcher, a strong supporter of Caesar who had been caught violating the sacred rites of Bona Dea, goddess of fertility. Because these rites excluded males, Clodius had dressed as a woman to gain entrance, perhaps for a tryst with one of the ladies. Tried for sacrilege and facing a possible death sentence, Clodius offered witnesses who claimed that he had been away from the city during the religious rites, but he was undone when Cicero came forward and testified that, contrary to what the witnesses declared, Clodius was indeed in Rome that day. Clodius escaped a guilty verdict only by bribing the jury, and he never forgave Cicero. Four years later, he abandoned his patrician status so that he could stand for tribune, and he promptly proposed a law to the *comitia plebus*, to be applied retroactively, that the execution of an accused Roman citizen without trial was a crime punishable by exile. Everyone knew that the law targeted Cicero, and it was approved overwhelmingly by the people. Rather than face a trial, Cicero fled the city, was found guilty in absentia, declared an outlaw, and forced into exile. His property was confiscated, and his Roman mansion was burned to the ground. A year and a half later, however, the Senate succeeded in getting the *comitia centuriata* to overturn the *plebus* decision, and it then recalled Cicero.

---

[6] Cicero's actions were particularly disturbing because the Republic did not impose the death penalty for crimes except in the most extreme circumstances.

Crossing the Rubicon: *Vae Victus*

These actions of the Senate confirmed what many Romans had believed for a long time, that the government was broken and that the rule of law was no longer in effect. If more evidence was needed, it came during Caesar's consulship in 59 BC. Displaying an unsurpassed political ability, Caesar had managed the year before to forge an alliance that had the potential to curtail the Senate's corruption, reduce the conflict between *optimates* and *populares*, and restore functional government. Crassus, an *equites* who was the richest man in Rome and its supreme business leader, set aside his hostility toward Pompey and joined Caesar in what became known as the First Triumvirate. Thus, the interests of the *populus*, the army, and the wealthy middle class were finally represented in a union of powerful leaders. Caesar invited Cicero to join the alliance so that the conservatives would also be represented, but the orator refused the invitation when it became obvious to him that he would not be the group's leader.

The conservatives – led by Cato and Marcus Claudius Marcellus – then did everything possible to block Caesar's election to consul when he stood in 59 BC. Despite their efforts, Caesar was elected in a landslide. He at once began implementing a policy of reconciliation so that he could involve the Senate in badly needed legislation that would return functionality to the government, but the Senate, again with Cato in the lead, blocked him at every turn. Frustrated when the Senate refused to pass his comprehensive land-reform bill, Caesar abandoned his conciliatory efforts and took the proposal to the *populus*. The Senate sent several tribunes, as well as the second consul, Marcus Bibulus (Cato's son-in-law), to block the plebiscite. When the tribunes exercised their legal authority and vetoed the law, Caesar ignored them. When Bibulus stepped to the Rosta and exercised his consular veto, Caesar's supporters threw dung over his head and chased him from the Forum. The law was passed, and from that point on, Caesar ignored the Senate and took his bills directly to the *contiones* and *comitia*. In addition to the land-reform measure, the most important legislation during Caesar's consulship was the *Leges Juliae*, a comprehensive body of laws governing acts of violence, fraud, and corruption. Among the latter – and arguably the most threatening to Senate interests – was *Lex de Repetundis*, which aimed to prevent peculation among magistrates.

The ruling elite had enriched themselves at the expense of the Republic for generations, and they understood that Caesar's reform efforts were a serious challenge to their way of life. Those who opposed Caesar claimed publicly and privately that he was destroying the Republic and that their opposition was based on their patriotism, but it is clear that their real concern was preserving their status and privileges. The more timid among them retired for a time. Traumatized by this experience on the Rosta, Bibulus closed himself in his house and did not leave it for the entire year of Caesar's consulship. Cicero, stewing over the erosion of aristocratic privileges and pouting because not even his gift for self-promotion could enable him to step outside Caesar's extensive shadow, left the city for his country estate, where he spent his time writing letters to friends that bemoaned Caesar's "tyranny."

The less timid, however, were resolute in their ambition to destroy Caesar. Because consuls and proconsuls were immune from prosecution, these members of the Senate determined to indict Caesar as soon as he became a private citizen. They would charge him with treason for ignoring the tribunal vetoes. To humiliate Caesar and to ensure that he did not have access to a significant number of troops, the Senate appointed him at the end of his consular year to the governorship of woods and forests in northern Italy. But fate intervened when the governor of Gaul fell ill and died. The public assembly quickly ordered that Caesar be assigned to Gaul and extended his proconsulship to five years (later extended to ten).

Caesar's adventures in Gaul are legendary. But while he was away from Rome, political intrigue continued, led by Cato and Marcus Claudius Marcellus. As for Cicero, his relationship with Caesar was complex: At times he expressed praise and admiration for him, but he also worked quietly in the background to oppose him. Pompey, meanwhile, fell victim to his own ego and his overweening desire to be accepted by patricians like Cato, who succeeded in persuading him to break with Caesar and abandon the cause of the *populares*. With his term as proconsul drawing to a close, Caesar met with members of the Senate in the town of Lucca and proposed that he be allowed to stand for consul a second time while absent from Rome, which would ensure that he was immune from the prosecution that his enemies had readied. The proposal was not particularly unusual and was accepted by the Senate and ratified by the people.

The Senators, however, were caught in a dilemma and had accepted the proposal under duress. On the one hand, they were afraid that if they did not grant this request Caesar might use his legions to become another Sulla, dictator with unlimited power. On the other hand, they knew with absolute certainty that a second consulship would result in more Julian laws to curtail their corruption and undermine their privileges. Caesar was so popular with the citizens that no amount of money would be sufficient to rig the election. They therefore conspired to find a third option that would free them from these dangers. Now the Senate's creature and convinced that Caesar was trying to eclipse him as the hero of Rome, Pompey proposed a law forbidding any candidate from standing for the consulship who was not physically present in the city – that is, a law in direct conflict with the legally binding agreement for Caesar that he had recently supported. Informing Caesar that trouble was brewing again in Asia, the Senate ordered him to send two of his legions to Rome for duty in the East, but when they arrived, Pompey made them part of the army he was mobilizing to confront Caesar. The Senate then passed a resolution informing Caesar that he was incorrect in thinking that his proconsulship ended just prior to the upcoming election; instead, it ended six months earlier. The man who only a few years later gave the world a more accurate calendar (which was not modified until 1582) had the date wrong, they asserted. He was ordered to dismiss his army and return to Rome as a private citizen. If he complied, his enemies would have ample time to prosecute him for treason or find a less troublesome means of eliminating him. If he failed to comply, he would be declared an enemy of the state, hunted down as a criminal, and executed.

Everyone knew very well that the Senate lacked any authority for these measures and that they were blatantly illegal. And it appears that the Senate knew that Caesar would not – indeed, as an eminent Roman general could not – accept such a humiliating dismissal. Putting its faith in Pompey's heretofore unequaled military ability, the Senate declared a state of emergency and ordered him to prepare for war.

Caesar reviewed the Senate's orders and then assembled his troops. He shared with them the edicts of the Senate and asked whether they would support him in his effort to right the wrongs done against him and to thwart the Senate's attack on the constitution. The legionaries responded by declaring that they would follow him anywhere and would even serve without pay. His officers and regular troops offered to contribute their own funds to cover the expenses of the war. Caesar ordered the men to strike camp, and on January 10 or 11, 49 BC, he crossed a narrow river called the Rubicon. Thus began the final series of conflicts in a protracted civil war that had started with the Gracchi 84 years earlier. The conflict did not end when Caesar was assassinated by colleagues in the Senate on the Ides of March, 44 BC, but continued as his nephew and adopted heir, Octavian, allied with longtime lieutenant Marc Antony, pursued and finally destroyed the assassins – and resumed after a brief pause until Octavian defeated Antony in the Battle of Actium in 31 BC. Octavian took the name Augustus and replaced the Republic, which had long outlived its effectiveness, with empire.

Some Characteristics of Republican Rhetoric and Oratory

The cultural history of Rome was inextricably linked to Greece. This was especially true with regard to rhetoric and oratory, which were influenced significantly by Aristotle, the last of the great figures in the history of Greek rhetoric. During the Hellenistic Period that followed Alexander's death, formal rhetoric was widely studied and practiced throughout the Greek-controlled Mediterranean (Kennedy, 1994), but it predominantly followed the course set by Aristotle, not Plato or the Sophists. When we examine theory and practice in this period, we find certain advances (see Higgins, 2005). Aristotle's student Theophrastus, for example, elaborated on his teacher's discussion of style, developing the idea of stylistic genres – the grand style, the middle style, and the simple style – that became central to Roman rhetoric in the *Rhetorica ad Herennium* and the work of Cicero. Hermagoras of Temnos also drew on Aristotle to develop the concept to *stasis*, which had been discussed only briefly in *The Art of Rhetoric*.

In Aristotle, *stasis* was a discovery procedure that involved asking a series of questions to determine the point at issue. The questions involved fact, definition, quality, and jurisdiction, as illustrated below:

- *Fact*: Did the defendant commit the act?
- *Definition*: What did the defendant do?
- *Quality*: Was the defendant's action justified or unjustified?
- *Jurisdiction*: What is the proper forum for determining the issue?

Throughout the Hellenistic Period, philosophers and rhetoricians alike studied *stasis* and how it operated in the various fields of rhetoric, and in time it emerged as a theory of rhetorical classification that shed light on the underlying structure of arguments. During the Republic, stasis theory as developed by Hermagoras became central to rhetorical instruction, and it also was an important (and often the dominant) feature of forensic oratory.

In addition to explorations of *stasis*, two other developments in the Hellenistic Period warrant attention. Schools of rhetoric followed the Isocratean emphasis on writing, and before students could engage in oratorical practice they were subjected to a regimen of written exercises called *progymnasmata*. Teachers would assign a rhetorical genre, and students would produce a composition that followed a strict outline. In the case of encomia, for example, the outline included: (1) reference to family background; (2) description of upbringing and education; (3) narration of worthy deeds attributed to the person's excellent qualities; (4) a comparison to some other worthy person or legendary hero; and (5) an epilogue that encouraged the audience to emulate the person being praised. After students had mastered the structure of the various rhetorical genres in writing, they went on to produce practice speeches, or declamations (*meletê* in Greek, *declamatio* in Latin).[7]

Declamations were of two types: *suasoriae* (persuasive) and *controversiae* (adversarial). *Suasoriae* initially had some connection to the real world and tended to be based on historical figures and deliberative decisions. A student might be asked, for example, to advise the Athenian assembly on whether the city should accept the Spartan's peace offer

---

[7] See Russell (1983) for an informative and detailed discussion of declamations.

of 410 BC. During the Roman Period, however, the topics for *suasoriae* became increasingly unrelated to reality, probably because opportunities for deliberative rhetoric, which were never great to begin with, declined precipitously after the collapse of the Republic. *Controversiae* were intended to provide students with practice in forensic rhetoric and required them to produce an oration that followed the structure expected in a court of law. For reasons that are unclear, many of the *controversiae* topics dealt with crimes of violence. Seneca (1974) provided one of the more complete discussions of these topics in his *Controversiae* and offered the following example, first stating the law – "a girl who has been raped may choose either marriage to her ravisher without a dowry or his death" – and then the matter at issue – "On a single night a man raped two girls. One demands his death, the other marriage" (I.5).

Whether these developments represented major advances is debatable, and their heavy reliance on Aristotle's work suggests that rhetoricians during the Hellenistic Period did not break much new ground. There are several possible, interrelated explanations. Perhaps the most obvious is that *The Art of Rhetoric* so thoroughly covered the central issues that there was little left for scholars who followed Aristotle to do but refine and clarify his ideas. The socio-historical context of the period no doubt further hindered originality. After Plato's death, the Academy fell on hard times, sinking deeper and deeper into the quagmire of mysticism until, as Green (1990) noted, Platonism "ended as just one more syncretic mishmash" (p. 609). The Lyceum fared better, but Aristotle's successors stripped their intellectual agenda of the polymath's excursions into morality and ethics and decried as ridiculous his notion that the universe was directed by a divine "Unmoved Mover." Eventually, they focused their efforts, instead, on expanding and refining what they saw as the real value of Aristotle's legacy: pure scientific investigation of the natural world, which had no bearing whatsoever on rhetoric.

We also need to remember that classical Greek rhetoric flourished in the context of deliberative democracy, where citizens met regularly to discuss, debate, and decide matters important to the city-state. When Alexander unified Greece and established himself as king, deliberative democracy as practiced in Athens disappeared, and the city-state that made it practicable was no longer a viable political entity. The situation became worse after his untimely death in 323 BC. In the absence of an adult heir to the empire, Alexander's generals tossed aside their many years of friendship and camaraderie and began fighting among themselves for control. By 322 BC, the empire was split into three parts, with Ptolemy controlling Egypt, Antigenes controlling Macedonia and Greece, and Seleucus Asia. Nearly 200 years of warfare followed: When these dynasties were not fighting against warrior tribes seeking to topple them, they were fighting among themselves.

War and the threat of war took a toll on the Greek ideal of the *kalos kagathos* engaged in bettering himself through service to the community. Government was in the hands of kings, tyrants, and warlords, which rendered the concept of communal, civic virtue quaint, if not obsolete. Aristotle's declaration that happiness was the goal of human existence became even more provocative in these uncertain times, but it took on a new meaning as philosophers and the educated public reinterpreted it as a manifesto for increased individuality. Epicureanism, Cynicism, and Stoicism gained adherents from one end of the Mediterranean to the other. Despite their several differences, these philosophical systems shared a common goal, which as Green (1990) noted was "the achievement of *apatheia* or *ataraxia*, freedom from worry or suffering, the Hellenistic age's characteristically negative ideal" (p. 603). In this unsettled environment, the anonymous *Rhetorica ad Alexandrum* became paradigmatic, decoupling oratory from democracy and advocating normative argumentation to maintain the status quo of rigid class structures in the hope of finding some measure of security there.

Interest in rhetoric nevertheless grew, not because it continued to be a tool for political engagement but because it became a status symbol. Hellenistic culture spread among rulers and the wealthy elite (usually indistinguishable) even as it was rejected by the common people. Greeks had always considered non-Greeks to be barbarians, and Hellenism encouraged a haughty disdain for everything indigenous, as evidenced by the fact that after three hundred years of Greek domination, Cleopatra (c. 69–30 BC) was the only ruler among Alexander's Hellenistic dynasties to learn the native language.[8] But for young men of means, studying rhetoric was the thing to do, and new schools of rhetoric were founded in various places throughout the Mediterranean to accommodate them. Rhetoricians continued to produce handbooks, for students needed texts, but few displayed originality, and most were poorly written. The quality of *technai* did not begin to change until toward the end of the Roman Republic, a gap of nearly 250 years between Aristotle and the first significant Roman text, *Rhetorica ad Herrenium*. However, *ad Herrenium*, as well as Cicero's works on rhetoric, was based on Greek models, particularly *The Art of Rhetoric*. As Russell (1967) stated, "It could easily be argued that all later rhetoric is a commentary on Aristotle" (p. 133). Cicero, for example, could describe his *De Oratore* as being written *Aristotelio more*, "in the manner of Aristotle," in a letter to Publius Cornelius Lentulus Spinther. But we should note that Cicero also recognized the importance of Isocrates. Kirby (1997) pointed out that it was Cicero's regard for Aristotle *and* Isocrates that motivated him to summarize in *De Oratore* their venerable work (*omnem antiquarum et Aristoteliam et Iscoratiam rationem oratoriam complectuntur*).

The passage of so much time between *The Art of Rhetoric* and *Rhetorica ad Herrenium* should not be interpreted to mean that Romans in the early Republic did not engage in oratory. They obviously did. Morstein-Marx (2004) showed that public assemblies were a vital part of Roman society. In these assemblies, magistrates gave speeches on important issues, and individuals had opportunities to ask questions and offer comments, provided the magistrate conducting the meeting invited a person to do so. There is little question that these speeches were inherently rhetorical (although not necessarily deliberative) and that non-deliberative *contiones* existed long before orators like Cicero and Caesar enjoyed the benefit of formal rhetorical training.

The absence of formal training becomes understandable when we consider Rome's history and character. Greek cities dotted Southern Italy; they had excellent schools with a long history of teaching rhetoric. But the early Republic was so primitive and isolated that she was of little interest to either the Greek cities in Italy or the fragmented sections of Alexander's empire. Her contact with the Greek cities to the south appears to have been sporadic, and the finer elements of Greek culture that the Etruscans could transmit may not have been welcome. Consequently, the early Republic adopted certain pragmatic elements of Greek culture and ignored the rest. The situation changed, however, when the Punic Wars gave Rome control of Southern Italy and Sicily.

What Romans found in the Greek cities that dotted the region did not please them much: people who pursued luxury without shame and who talked endlessly, speculating and disputing about philosophy, government, and the nature of reality. To the Romans, these were not manly virtues. They quickly developed an ambivalent attitude toward rhetoric and everything Greek. They tended to see themselves as warriors – men and women of action – and to view anything Greek as weak and effeminate. Kennedy's

[8] Although Kennedy (1994, p. 81) asserted that Greek was used by "a significant segment of the population" during the Hellenistic Period, Green (1990) argued that it was limited to Greeks, the educated ruling class, middle-class property owners, and merchants who depended on it for trade. The non-Greek populations and the poor throughout the fragments of Alexander's empire continued to use their own languages and were so hostile to arrogant Greek rule that they resisted inculturation.

(1972) assessment in this regard was accurate: "the ideal Roman ... was austere and laconic, a man of action rather than words" (p. 5), which meant that public speaking was probably quite simple in the early Republic.

The Latinization of rhetoric

Roman rhetoric and oratory came of age during the tumultuous period between the reforms of the Gracchi and Caesar's crossing the Rubicon. As already noted, the impetus for its development was the expansion of the Republic that resulted in close encounters with Greek culture and more opportunities for those who excelled in public speaking. The Romans modified what they learned from the Greeks, but most of these modifications were minor.

The first step was to shift instruction from Greek to Latin, which seems like a logical move but which nevertheless raised objections in 92 BC among the censors, who claimed that the Latin schools provided only a superficial education and that they should be closed. Clarke (1968) suggested that the teachers in these schools were endeavoring to make rhetoric more Roman by eliminating some of the subtleties and complexities of Greek theory, thereby aligning it with Roman pragmatism. This effort would make sense in light of the widespread attitude among Romans that Greeks and their culture were feminine, an attitude so strong that well-educated people, such as Cato the Elder and Cicero, often concealed their extensive knowledge of things Greek. In any event, the censorial assessment appears to have had no effect on the schools, as evidenced by Cicero's report in *Brutus* that as a youth he had the opportunity to attend a Latin school but chose a Greek one, instead, and by the fact that he wrote his *De Inventione* in Latin sometime between 88 and 81 BC. The *Rhetorica ad Herennium*, written at about the same time, was also in Latin.

Following Aristotle and the author of *Rhetorica ad Alexandrum*, these early texts divided the study of rhetoric into five parts or "offices": invention (*inventio*), arrangement (*dispositio*), style and presentation (*elocutio*), memory (*memoria*), and delivery (*actio*). The discussion of invention relied on Aristotle and Hermagoras, particularly the latter's description of *stasis*. Their treatment of style drew on the work of Theophrastus and his classification of plain, middle, and grand, but Romans were influenced to a great degree by the style of Greek oratory that developed in the Eastern Mediterranean, especially at Rhodes. Known as *Asianism*, this style was very ornate and, to a certain degree, artificial. Discussing Asianism in *Brutus*, Cicero stated that:

[O]rationis Asiaticum adulescentiae magis concessum quam senectuti. Genera autem Asiaticae dictionis duo sunt, unum sententiosum et argutum, sententiis non tam gravibus et severis quam concinnis et venustis. ... Aliud autem genus est non tam sententiis frequentatum quam verbis volucre atque incitatium, quale est nunc Asia tota, nec flumine solum orationis, sed etiam exornator et faceto genere verborum. ...

[The Asiatic style] is more suited to youth than to old age. It consists of two types. One is pithy and deliberate, characterized not so much by depth of thought as by its elegance and charm. ... The other sort is not so remarkable for the richness of its sententious[9] phrasing as for its rapidity [*volucre*] and speed [*incitatum*] of expression,[10] which at present is the ruling taste in Asia; but, besides its uncommon fluency, it also is generally characterized by a choice of words that are delicate and embellished. (XCV, 325)

---

[9] *Sententia* – moral or philosophical maxims – became popular in forensic oratory toward the end of the Republic and increased in popularity during the Empire. Orators infused their speeches with these maxims so as to project the image of a sage. The *Rhetorica ad Herennium*, however, advised caution so as to avoid seeming too moralistic: "Maxims should be inserted discreetly, so that the speaker is seen as a judicial advocate, not a teacher of morals" (*Sententias interponi raro convenit, ut rei actores, non vivendi praeceptores videamur esse*) (4.25).

[10] Although *volucre* and *incitatum* seem very similar in English, they are not in Latin. *Volucre* is related to *volucer*, or bird. Thus, the connotation here is that the Asiatic style is as swift as a bird.

According to the historian Strabo (c. 64 BC–24 AD), Hegesias of Magnesia was the originator of Asianism, which was contrasted with a more direct and natural style of speaking, known as *Atticism*. Isocrates and Demosthenes were deemed to represent the ideal form of Atticism, which in addition to its directness was characterized by a full periodic structure that gave it texture and depth; Hegesias reportedly broke the periodic sentences into short, rhythmic clauses to produce a staccato effect that made speeches resemble songs.

Asianism was popular in Rome when Cicero was young, and it influenced his work, as evidenced in several of his orations, particularly the early ones. He tried, however, to attain a more balanced style later in his career – although he was not entirely successful – and criticized Hortensius, his contemporary and rival, for having a florid Asiatic style full of gestures and bodily motions that drew applause from youthful audiences but scorn from older ones. This scorn is understandable when we consider that, as Richlin (1997) pointed out, one of the dangers of Asianism for Roman orators was the risk of seeming unmanly, not only because Romans viewed Asians as being womanish but also because the Asiatic style emphasized an exaggerated delivery (*actio*). Richlin's assessment is insightful here: "The problem was that [Asiatic] orators used their bodies in performance in ways that resembled what actors did on stage. ... [A]nd it is startling to realize that a Roman orator must have looked more like a hula dancer than like a television anchorman" (p. 100). Ironically, during the Empire, Asianism flourished among rhetoricians and orators, in large part because orations no longer had much social purpose but became more aligned with literature, influenced by the notion of *ars gratia artis*, "art for art's sake." In this environment, *kairos* became less important, for rhetoric was shifting from persuasive oratory to artful expression. In written texts, *kairos* had little place at all, at least in its traditional sense of correct or appropriate timing, replaced by *prepon*, or fitness, which increasingly was understood as appropriate style.[11]

The growing emphasis on style in rhetoric and oratory was fueled by Stoics and by several young orators, such as Brutus and Gaius Licinius Calvus, who, calling themselves "Attici," argued for less reliance on extravagant and florid language. Calvus complained, for example, that Cicero's style was overblown and self-indulgent.[12] Always hypersensitive when it came to his reputation, Cicero responded with *Orator*, which purports to be a description of the ideal orator but which is primarily Cicero's defense of his career against the Attici. Stoics, however, offered the only organized opposition to Asianism, and they based their oratorical style on the concept of *scientia recte decendi*, or knowledge of correct speaking. What this consisted of, exactly, is unclear, although in *Brutus*, Cicero indicated that their style was poorly suited to public speeches because it was not sufficiently "eloquent," leading to speculation that it reduced reliance on *ethos* and *pathos*, stressing *logos*, instead. The little we know of Stoic rhetorical theory suggests that it eschewed ornamentation and exaggerated delivery of the sort that made those using the Asiatic style look like hula dancers and that it emphasized brevity and conciseness. On this basis, Atherton (1988) concluded that "What distinguishes Stoic orators and rhetoricians is their skill and shrewdness in argument and the importance they attached to proof" (p. 400).

---

[11] Horace's *Ars Poetica*, for example, treats appropriateness at length and illustrates the interconnectivity between rhetoric and poetry that began with the Sophists.

[12] In his *Dialogus*, Tacitus (18.5) reported that Cicero was often criticized for his style, which was characterized as *fractum atque elumbem*. The literal translation of this epithet is "weak and without hips," which at the time and in the context of Asianism's perceived effeminacy probably meant "weak and without balls."

Deliberative rhetoric

Of some significance were the differences between Greek and Roman rhetoric with regard to genres and artificial proofs. Aristotle identified three genres – deliberative, forensic, and epideictic – and as we saw in Part I, each was practiced extensively in Athens and other democratic city-states. During the Republic, however, epideictic oratory existed almost exclusively as funeral speeches and received little theoretical attention. Examining the other two genres in turn, we find that Rome had three venues where deliberative oratory might occur: the Senate, the *comitia*, and the *contiones*. Even though the Senate is often considered to have been the principal place for deliberative oratory (e.g., Cruttwell, 2005; Kennedy, 1994), we cannot be certain to what extent the orations of the senators were truly deliberative, given that so many Senate decisions were worked out in private, not in the Senate chamber.

The speeches regarding Catiline, as well as others that were preserved (e.g., see Appian's (1996) *The Civil Wars, Book III*, for an interesting pair of speeches supposedly given by Cicero and Piso), indicate that senators sometimes engaged in deliberations, but whether these are typical or representative cannot be readily determined; moreover, they suggest that many senatorial speeches involved declamation rather than deliberation. Given the nature of politics among the senators, its seems likely that deliberative oratory in the Senate did not, as a rule, address broad issues of government unless they involved class struggles but rather focused on more narrow issues related to the infighting associated with personal ambitions and conflicts. Thus, in the speeches by Cicero and Piso mentioned above, we find Cicero charging Marc Antony with very serious crimes on the basis, as Piso points out, of his utter hatred of the man, not on the basis of facts. In many respects, senatorial speeches frequently appear to have been similar to those we find in the US Senate. That is, they functioned as displays rather than as persuasive discourse. Cicero seemed acutely aware of the problem. As Fantham (1996) observed, his Brutus "reflects the feeling that political oratory, like the orator and the free republic, has been silenced" (p. 45).

Contesting the notion that the Senate was in general a venue for true deliberative oratory, the above analysis raises two questions: Why was Cicero esteemed among fellow senators for his speaking ability, and why was he recognized as one of the leaders of the conservatives? In the context of a deliberative body, it is reasonable to assume that leadership and esteem are bestowed owing to one's ability to influence decision making. In the absence of deliberation, some other factors must be involved. One such factor with regard to Cicero probably was his rhetorical inventiveness. His speeches illustrate a level of creativeness unmatched by other orators of the period. In the first oration against Catiline, for example, Cicero abandoned convention and opened with a series of emotion-charged questions rather than with a calm exordium: *Quo usque tandem abutere, Catilina, patientia nostra? Quam diu etiam furor iste tuus nos eludet?* – "How long, Catiline, will you abuse our patience? How long will that madness of yours continue to mock us?" (I.1). In addition, he, more so than any of his contemporaries, was a master not only of narrative and *stasis* but also of *ethos*, which he used effectively in two ways – to portray his clients in the most favorable terms and to demolish the characters of his adversaries.[13]

---

[13] *Pro Murena* illustrates what may be one of Cicero's more skillful uses of *ethos*. His adversaries are Sulpicius and Cato, well known for their morality and ethical behavior and whose characters were above reproach. Cicero faced the challenge of recognizing their rectitude while simultaneously convincing the jury that their code of ethics had little applicability to the real world.

Another factor may well have been his ability to present himself to the people as a supporter of *populares* values while simultaneously working to maintain the status and privileges of the *optimates*.[14] This ability would have had tangible benefits for the aristocracy. Two speeches – one to the Senate and one to the people – that Cicero gave upon his installation as consul in 63 BC are illustrative. In both he argued against the proposed agrarian law of tribune Publius Rullus. His oration to the Senate repeatedly noted that the law would remove control of state revenues from the ruling class and put it in the hands of ten commissioners, and he asserted that as consul he would do everything in his power to defeat the proposed law, which he compared to "the corrupting liberality of the Gracchi" (*First Oration*, VII). In the second speech, after stressing his humble origins and status of *homo novus*, he ensured popular antipathy toward the law by drawing on Roman hostility toward kingship, referring to the commissioners as "ten kings of the treasury" (*Second Oration*, VI). But especially interesting is that he again mentioned the Gracchi, but from a quite different perspective:

Nam vere dicam, quirites, genus ipsum legis agrariae vituperare non possum. Venit enim mihi in mentem duos clarissimos, ingeniosissimos, amantissimos plebei Romanae viros Tiberius et Gaius Gracchos, plebem in agris publicis constituisse, qui agri a privatis antea possidebantur. Non sum autem ego ..., ut plerique, nefas esse arbitrer Gracchos laudare, quorum consiliis, sapientia, legibus multas esse video rei publicae partis constitutas.

My fellow Romans, to tell you the truth, I cannot find any fault with the general principle of an agrarian law, and this particular proposal prompts me to remember that two most illustrious men, two most able men, two men most thoroughly dedicated to serving the Roman people, Tiberius and Gaius Gracchus, succeeded in relocating citizens on public lands that had until then been controlled by private individuals. And unlike many here in Rome, I am not the sort of man who maintains that it is wrong ... to praise the Gracchi, for I fully recognize that their counsel, their wisdom, and the laws they championed made our Republic stronger. (*Second Oration*, V)

If we assume that the *comitia* provided venues for deliberative rhetoric, we face similar problems. It was fairly common for the magistrate who called the assembly together to identify one or more speakers prior to voting, and it was the case that these invited orators sometimes spoke against the pending rogation, which gives the appearance of deliberation and debate. But this appearance seems belied by reality, for by packing a *comitatus* with supporters, the magistrate could ensure that those speaking in opposition to the proposed legislation would be shouted down so as to suggest overwhelming support for his bill.[15] No debate was involved, and the only decision for those attending the assembly was whether to vote for or against the bill, but in nearly every instance, this decision had already been made in the *contiones*. Arguing for just such an analysis, Mouritsen (2001) found that during the Republic there were very few instances in which the *comitia* voted against a rogation, which we would not expect in a deliberative environment. Because measures were "vetted" in the *contiones* prior to voting, only those laws that could lay claim to having the support of the *populus*, whether real or manufactured, ever went to the *comitia*.

---

[14] Cicero had little or no sympathy for the plebeian efforts to gain some measure of political power through democratic reform. In Book I of *De Re Publica*, for example, he wrote: *Cum omnia per populum geruntur quamvis iustum atque moderatum, tamen ipsa aequabilitas est iniqua, cum habet nullos gradus dignitatis* – "When all political action is controlled by the people, however just and moderate they may be, this very equality is unjust and unequal in having no recognition of degrees of merit" (I.43)

[15] This reality may explain why Publicus Rullus and his supporters declined Cicero's invitation to debate with him the agrarian reform bill in a public forum.

Kennedy (1994) proposed that deliberative oratory was common in the *contiones*, perhaps on the basis of the connection between these meetings and the voting assemblies that followed them. But the nature of these meetings appears to have precluded deliberation as it is normally understood: A magistrate called the *contio*, made his speech, and then, only if he chose, invited individuals to speak in turn. The magistrate was under no obligation to allow someone to speak in opposition to his rogation or even to entertain minor amendments to the proposed law. The crowd itself was involved only insofar as it shouted approval or disapproval, and in the last decades of the Republic bribes and patronage ensured that there was more of the former than the latter. As Olmsted (2006) observed, "Roman orators were more likely to lead the people than to deliberate with them about contested values and conflicting interests" (p. 26).

Because any magistrate could call a *contio*, there frequently were competing meetings, which allowed both sides to claim that their positions represented the will of the people. There is no compelling evidence, however, to indicate that any deliberation or debate took place. The absence of deliberative oratory in these meetings is evident in the *contio* Caesar called during his first consulship to present his agrarian-reform measure to the people. When he asked Bibulus whether he had any objections, he was not inviting debate. Rather, as Morstein-Marx (2004) stated, the invitation to speak:

> was instead a form of political theater designed to stampede opposition to popular measures by forcing opponents to confront the ostensibly manifest Will of the Roman People, or at minimum to elicit an outrageous response from the audience that could then be represented as a *significatio* of the people's "judgment and will." (p. 167)

Given these limitations, we can better understand why deliberative rhetoric and oratory as practiced in the schools had little connection with what could be observed in the political realm.

Forensic rhetoric

The Roman legal system was complex. Over the centuries Romans had enacted numerous laws that were often conflicting and frequently unclear. Courts were divided into two types: *judicia privata*, which handled civil cases, such as property disputes, probate, adultery, and so forth; and *judicia publica*, which handled criminal cases, including homicides and political crimes, such as electoral fraud (*de ambitu*), extortion (*de rebus repentundis*), and public violence (*de vi*). In 103 BC, the *Lex Appuleia* established yet another court to handle exclusively cases involving magistrates accused of "diminishing the greatness of the Roman people" (*maiestatem populi Romani minuere*). Patricians and *equites* struggled to control the jury system during the Republic, and depending on which group was dominant, juries at times were composed solely of one or the other, which had especially significant consequences for political trials.[16] Matters were further complicated by bribery and the ways in which family and political connections frequently determined the outcome of trials, not guilt or innocence.

Rampant bribery and prejudice notwithstanding, Cicero observed in *Brutus* that the multiplicity of courts and the complexity of the laws made skill in forensic rhetoric invaluable. To illustrate this point, he described a case involving a contested will that pitted the two premier jurists of the day, Lucinius Crassus and Mucius Scaevola. Scaevola was a very good orator but a master of the law, whereas Crassus was a master orator who knew the law reasonably well. Arguing his side of the case, Scaevola showed that

---

[16] During the Empire, Augustus and Caligula revised the jury system to allow common citizens to serve.

the law clearly supported his client; Crassus, on the other hand, said little about the law but instead focused on gaining the favor of the jury through his skill in oratory (see Fantham, 2004). Eloquence, not legal knowledge, triumphed. Of course, as Cruttwell (2005) pointed out, "With more eloquence they had less justice" (p. 75).

Both deliberative and forensic oratory faced tangible pressures that did not allow them to play the same role in Rome that they had played in Athens. Aristotle could observe that deliberative rhetoric was the superior genre, but in Rome skill in forensic oratory appears to have been more highly valued, especially in the late Republic. Certainly, Cicero's successes in the courts gave him the public attention he needed, as well as the funds, for a political career. Although by law patrons who spoke on behalf of their clients could not receive a fee, they were free to accept gifts, and Cicero's clients were generous, bestowing upon him houses and land. Caesar also began his political career as a jurist, prosecuting Cornelius Dolabella for extortion (*de rebus repentundis*) in 77 BC.

Rhetorical proofs

The majority of what we know about rhetoric and oratory in the Republic is based on the Ciceronian canon, and when we examine his speeches to gain insight into oratorical practice, we need to remember that he revised them, perhaps substantially, before they were published. They are simulations that no doubt vary from the actual speeches in a number of ways. Even so, it seems safe to assume that in most cases their global features – organization and use of proofs, for example – did not change much as Cicero wrote them out in revised form.[17]

Of particular interest is the light these orations shed on the use of rhetorical proofs. Whether analyzing a political speech or a judicial one, we find that Aristotle's artificial proofs – *ethos, logos, and pathos* – tended to be interpreted in keeping with Cicero's view that the aim of forensic oratory was *probare, delectare*, and *flectere* – to prove, to delight, and to persuade. Moreover, Aristotle's proofs were applied in the context of Roman society, with its emphasis on *dignitas* and *auctoritas*, or dignity and authority. In trials, especially, the patron used his character as a member of the aristocracy to color the proceedings, linking (and in some cases identifying) his *ethos* with that of his client. This blurring of characters had the advantage of enabling the patron to assume the role of his client and thereby provide prejudiced testimony that otherwise would not be allowed. According to Quintilian (c. 35–95 AD) in *Institutio Oratoria*, Cicero approached the jury *nec advocati studium, sed testis aut judicis ... fidem* – "not with the enthusiasm of an advocate but rather with the convincing testimony of a witness" (X.1.111). At the same time, *ethos* was used against the opposition, resulting in virulent attacks on character, or ad hominem arguments. What this meant in practical terms was that *ethos* and *pathos* regularly dominated *logos*, which often was limited to the questions associated with *stasis* theory. The successful orator would commonly conceal his lack of evidence (*logos*) by using *ethos* and *pathos* to stir up the jurors, putting them into an emotional frenzy that short circuited reason. Increasingly, eloquence came to be understood as passion – the passionate orator who was able to inflame the passions of the audience.

Pro Milone, which is frequently identified as Cicero's most eloquent forensic oration, illustrates his extensive use of *ethos* and *pathos* to make (not necessarily support) his

---

[17] In all likelihood, Cicero did not write any of his orations; instead, he probably dictated them to a slave who did the writing.

argument.[18] Milo – Cicero's friend, a wealthy young aristocrat, and a leader among the *optimates* – had organized a gang that included several former gladiators, and he and his thugs made a pastime out of roaming about the city assaulting *populares*. Enter Clodius Pulcher once again, advocate of the *populares*. He had a gang of his own, and the two groups squared off in several street fights, each one more intense and violent than the last. In 52 BC, they had a chance encounter outside the city. In the melee that followed, Clodius and a number of his men were wounded, then run down and killed as they tried to escape. Cicero volunteered to defend his friend when Milo was brought to trial for murder, and the Senate thought it prudent to post armed guards throughout the Forum to discourage partisan violence. Cicero began his speech by feigning fear of the armed guards, no doubt with the aim of making himself, and thus his client, seem more sympathetic to the jury.

Cicero also emphasized *ethos* and *pathos* in his political speeches. In his first oration against Catiline there is much *ethos* and *pathos*, but very little *logos* (although we need to keep in mind that he already had informed the Senate of Catiline's acts). The excerpt below illustrates how Cicero combined the two in a single passage to cast himself as a stern but loving father while simultaneously playing on the audiences' fears:

Cupio, patres conscripti, me esse clementem, cupio in tantis rei publicae periculis me non dissolutum videri, sed iam me ipse inertiae nequitiaeque condemno. Castra sunt in Italia contra populum Romanum in Etruriae faucibus conlocata, crescit in dies singulos hostium numerus; eorum autem castrorum imperatorem ducemque hostium intra moenia atque adeo in senatu videmus intestinam aliquam cotidie perniciem rei publicae molientem.

I wish, my fellow senators, to be merciful. At the same time, I do not wish to appear negligent, given the present danger to the state. But I now must nevertheless accuse myself of being both negligent and guilty of inactivity. An armed camp is pitched in Italy, at the entrance of Etruria, and it is hostile to the Republic. The number of our enemies there grows every day, while the general of that camp, the very leader of those enemies, we see within the walls of Rome – yes, even here in the Senate – planning every day to harm the Republic. (1.4–5)

Roman Women

Women in Rome, like their Greek counterparts, married as young as 12 or 13 and were under the guardianship of either father or husband, but they had far more freedom than women in Greece. They were able to divorce their husbands, travel, and inherit and own property. We know very little about women of the lower classes, unfortunately, but those in the country must have been hardy as well as independent: The men in their lives were often away at war for years at a time, leaving them to work the farms, raise their children, and supervise slaves. Those in the city were equally industrious and commonly worked alongside their husbands in small family businesses in leather, ceramics, meat and produce, clothing, and so forth.[19] Most were probably poorly educated, and literacy may have been the exception rather than the rule (see Harris, 1991). Women of the middle and upper classes, on the other hand, tended to be well educated. A common

---

[18] The actual speech was unsuccessful – Milo was found guilty and exiled from Rome. The historian Asconius wrote an account of the fight in which Clodius was murdered, providing numerous details that cannot be presented here.

[19] Most people in the lower classes could not afford to purchase new clothes, so Rome had a thriving used clothing market that employed many women.

motif in Roman frescos was the image of a young woman writing. They were not allowed to attend schools of rhetoric, but they were regular attendees of public lectures on history, philosophy, literature, mathematics, and other subjects. Many immersed themselves in literature and philosophy and were avid readers. Advances in binding led to a decline in the use of scrolls and to a rapid increase in bound books, or codices: Educated women were able to pursue their intellectual interests in the many bookstores that sprang up throughout the city, and they could visit Rome's public libraries, the first of which opened during the second century BC. The educational and autodidactic activities of women increased in the Empire: For example, Julia Domna (c. 170–217 AD), wife of Emperor Septimus Severus, was devoted to philosophy and formed a circle of mathematicians and philosophers who met regularly in her salon for intellectual discussions.[20]

Political involvement during the Republic was limited, but beginning in the middle of the second century BC women were allowed to attend political meetings. Toward the end of that century, restrictions had relaxed to such a degree that they occasionally were allowed to speak in public assemblies (Bauman, 1992; Fantham et al., 1994). Tradition required a woman to be represented in court by her husband or a male patron, but extant records show that during the latter part of the Republic this tradition was often ignored.[21] Valerius Maximus, writing in the first century BC, identified two such women: Amaesia Sentia and Gaia Arania. According to Valerius, Gaia Arania was the wife of a senator, had a litigious nature, and was a frequent complainant, which suggests that she may have found some pleasure in forensic oratory.

In Appian's (1996) history of the civil wars we find reference to Hortensia, daughter of Quintus Hortensius, a successful orator and jurist. In 42 BC, the triumvirs – Octavian, Marc Antony, and Lepidus – needed to raise funds to continue the war against Caesar's assassins and proposed a tax that targeted wealthy women whose husbands or fathers had been proscribed for crimes against the state. Hortensia, like many of the women whom the tax would affect, was a young woman in her twenties without a male protector, having lost both her father and her husband. Dismayed by the prospect of being assigned a special tax, she organized women to oppose it, and they marched on the Forum, where the triumvirs were meeting. Her speech against taxation without representation was successful, and the triumvirs agreed to forgo the tax:

Why should we pay taxes when we hold no public office and have no part in the honors or the commands of government – the very things you fight one another for with such harmful results? "Because this is a time of war," you say? But when has there not been war? When have taxes ever been imposed on women, who are exempted by virtue of their sex? ... We will never submit to paying taxes for civil wars, and we will not help you fight against one another! We did not pay taxes to Caesar or to Pompey. Neither Marius nor Cinna asked us to pay taxes. Nor did Sulla, even though he was a tyrant with absolute power over the country. (4.33)

Although in many respects Romans were highly civilized – as their libraries, theaters, and public baths attest – in other respects they were backward, in part owing to a general lack of intellectual curiosity. They bathed regularly, sometimes twice a day (see

---

[20] Nevertheless, educated women seem to have been a source of some anxiety. Fragments of an essay Plutarch (1958) wrote on the education of women suggest that he believed that they should be instructed only in household management. The Stoic Musonius Rufus took a slightly more liberal approach insofar as he allowed that men and women alike are blessed with reason and can benefit from the study of philosophy, but he also argued that education should conform to the nature of the student. In the case of women, his view was that their nature necessarily should confine their education to, once again, household management.

[21] The poor, male and female alike, had little or no access to the court system, however.

Fagan, 1999), but they never invented soap. Health care and sanitation were abysmal, and as a result both men and women had short life spans. Women frequently died in childbirth, and men who were not killed outright in battle usually died if wounded. Nevertheless, a relatively large number of women in the propertied class accumulated great wealth through inheritance combined with sharp business sense.

Most marriages among the upper classes were based entirely on politics, as families tried to consolidate wealth and power, but historical records and epitaphs indicate that a great many of these unions involved deep love and respect. Aristocratic women appear to have recognized their political value and to have used it to effect. Caesar's mistress Servilia was deeply involved not only in his political career but also in that of her son, Brutus. During the Empire, many aristocratic women – such as Octavian's wife, Livia (c. 58 BC–29 AD), Marc Antony's wife Fulvia (c. 77 BC–40 BC), the above mentioned Julia Domna, and Nero's mother Agrippina – were very influential politically. Fulvia – whose first husband was Clodius Pulcher and whose political actions she may have inspired – appears to have acted as de facto consul while Antony was campaigning, raised troops against Octavian, and issued orders like a commander. Cassius Dio Cocceianus (1917) reported that she not only exhorted these soldiers with her oratory but also wore a sword.

The Empire

The fall of the Roman Empire has been the subject of research and speculation for centuries. What caused the richest, most powerful and enlightened society in the world to collapse? Edward Gibbon (1993), whose *Decline and Fall of the Roman Empire* became an instant classic when published in the late eighteenth century, argued for two principle causes. First, Rome shifted to using foreign mercenaries, whose loyalties were not to the state but rather to whomever was paying their wages. The result was twofold: Mercenaries did not fight as hard as Roman citizens, so they could not hold back the encroachments of hostile northern tribes; in addition, with little regard for government or tradition, the armies usurped the political process and soon were declaring one general or another to be emperor, leading to political instability. In 69 AD, for example, Rome had four different emperors (see MacMullen, 1988; Morgan, 2006). Second, Gibbon argued that Christianity was a profoundly debilitating influence. It emasculated Roman society and turned attention away from the day-to-day concerns necessary to build social capital and to maintain a vast empire, leading large segments of the population to abandon their earthly responsibilities and to focus on a dreamy afterlife. The spread of Christianity figures significantly in all considerations of the Empire, but it is important to acknowledge its broader effect: Christianity dismantled most of the religious, philosophical, social, and intellectual foundations that had supported Western culture for a thousand years or more. What it could not dismantle, it assimilated.

The appeal of philosophy

Hollywood depictions would have us believe that the iron boot of the legions or the crushing avarice of the *publicani* (hired tax collectors) made life in the Empire pure hell. Certainly there were incidents of abuse, and we must always keep in mind that a large percentage of the population was held in slavery, but overall Roman rule was characterized by noninterference until the reign of Constantine (c. 272–327 AD), provided everyone obeyed Roman law. Failure to do so typically resulted in an overwhelming response designed to provide a lesson to the whole Empire. Thus, rebellions were the exception rather than the rule, and for countless millions, life in the Empire was good. The early period of the Empire (27 BC to 180 AD) was in fact so tranquil that it came to be known as the period of the *Pax Romana*, or Roman peace. Moreover, Rome brought material improvements to the entire Mediterranean: paved roads, irrigation, plumbing, temples, and so on. It also stabilized trade, which raised the standard of living throughout the region, and in 212 AD extended citizenship to everyone except slaves. The primary motivation for the franchise may have been to implement uniform taxation, but it had the considerable benefit of engendering a sense of *communitas*, or community, to large numbers of the subject peoples.

Peace and economic prosperity especially affected the Eastern Mediterranean, reviving elements of a culture that had essentially been comatose since coming under Roman domination. Intellectual activity increased and set a tone for the rest of the Empire; leaders ceased being embarrassed by their knowledge of and fascination with things Greek, and a new concept of *paideia* emerged, no longer meaning simply edification but now meaning *culture* or *cultured*. Moreover, "cultured" was understood in the very narrow sense of being thoroughly versed in Greek literature and philosophy, even though as Momigliano (1986) pointed out, "There was no work in the Greek world from 100 BC to AD 300 that could compare with the literature in Latin of the Caesarean and Augustan period [sic]: the imperial Greeks never had their Cicero or Virgil" (p. 285).

In spite of the tangible benefits of empire, it appears that by the second century AD a growing number of people felt that something was missing in their lives. A malaise had gripped the Empire that peace and prosperity could not mollify, and as the century progressed, intangible social forces motivated segments of the population to disengage from society. Foucault (1990) argued that the people of the Empire experienced a great turn inward that made them more reflective and less inclined to base their identity on civic involvement. The cause may well have been the Empire's rigid social structure, as well as the aforementioned peace and prosperity. The quest for honor that had driven men in the Greek city-states and the Roman Republic had largely disappeared owing to lack of opportunities. And in the vastness of the Empire, where corruption was rampant, the Greek ideal of *aretê*, civic virtue, had become quaint. Among the more visible examples of disengagement were the emperors themselves, who were becoming increasingly isolated from their subjects. Arguably, their detachment did not serve the goal of *communitas* very well. Brown (1992) attributed this detachment to the size of the Empire (it could take more than a month to travel from Rome to Byzantium) and the inability of the Romans to develop a more effective system of government, with serious political consequences: Although the emperor held absolute power, government itself was weak and getting weaker owing to the inability to improve communication with and oversight of provincial governors.

The problem of imperial detachment was not limited to government or the creation of social capital and civic virtue. Several years after his assassination, Caesar had been declared a god. Augustus was declared a living god. Then each successive emperor made minor adjustments to the bureaucracy to strengthen his own divine status. To us this may seem strange, but in the ancient world (with the notable exception of the Jews) the idea that a man could become a god was not farfetched. In pagan cosmology, gods and men were not terribly far removed, which enabled a man to become godlike on the basis of his clear superiority to mere mortals. But the divine emperor's detachment was something new, something different. The concept of divinity that was being modeled had nothing in common with traditional religious views. Quite simply, the emperors were no longer part of this world. Yet one of the distinguishing characteristics of the pagan gods for 2,000 years had been that they were immersed in this world, not removed from it.[22]

We saw in Part I that around the time of Enheduanna's priesthood the concept of the divine had shifted: The distance between gods and people decreased considerably. They became personal patrons who might bring succor to those in trouble. In Rome, individuals made private appeals to the gods, and every home had a small shrine for worship of the *dii familiaris*, or family god, but the practice of religion overall was a significantly public affair that celebrated the state as well as the gods. In the Empire, however, increasing numbers of people were growing dissatisfied with the old ways, and they began exploring alternatives to established religious practices. The old religions were not being replaced, but they were being questioned with an intensity that the Mediterranean had not seen since the days of the Milesian *hoi physikoi*. Sophisticated Romans increasingly viewed the traditional accounts of the gods as nothing more than fairy tales and strove to find the godhead in Plato's Ideal Forms or Aristotle's Unmoved Mover. Contact with Judaism influenced sophisticated and unsophisticated alike, and monotheistic paganism, evident as early as the fourth century BC in Plato's works, spread as growing numbers embraced the idea that there was one god and that the other gods were merely different manifestations of the supreme being.

In this environment, the old philosophies of Greece were resuscitated seemingly overnight. Epicureanism and Stoicism were among the more popular, and they held out the prospect of attaining the sort of calm detachment associated with Aristotle's Unmoved Mover. Epicurus (c. 341–270 BC) sought to help his disciples achieve the sort of inner peace (*ataraxia*) known only to the gods through the application of doctrines that aimed to rid them of ignorance and superstition. The focus was on abstention and acquisition of knowledge. Food and wine were to be consumed in moderation, nothing to excess. Sex was not banned, but it was deemed to be a biological necessity, like eating, that should be indulged in limited portions. A principal goal was to find pleasure in a simple life, with friendship serving as the cornerstone of inner peace.

Detachment from civic life was antithetical to Roman traditions, and it was alien to Greek as well, evident in Aristotle's description of man as a political animal defined by his existence and participation in the city-state. In other words, detachment was a new occurrence in the world, which may explain why Cicero railed against the Epicureans in senatorial orations and letters. More problematic during these times of inward reflection was that Epicureanism denied the existence of an afterlife. Epicurus had scoffed at the idea as being the worst sort of superstition, and he urged his followers to abandon their fear of death, which he described as merely the absence of all thought and sensation. Only the most strong-willed could follow this path, and as the sense of personal emptiness grew among citizens of the Empire, the longing for hope made Epicureanism less attractive. In addition, the indefinable malaise of the times had produced a prudish morality, and the emphasis on finding pleasure in a simple life was too often interpreted as hedonism by those who were not members of the Epicurean community: Epicureans treated men and women equally, which only fed prurient imaginations that their meetings were nothing more than hedonistic orgies. In a society that had come to view sex as something that must be limited to married couples, and even then only with the aim of producing children, the mental images were too much to bear.

---

[22] The biblical evidence that Jesus claimed to be divine is sparse, unclear, and incongruent with first-century Judaism. As Paul traveled from Tarsus into Ionia and Greece, the ease with which Greeks accepted apotheosis may have been inspirational.

Stoicism was an attractive alternative to Epicureanism in part because it demanded less sacrifice, and people throughout the Mediterranean region embraced it, especially members of the upper classes. Unlike Epicureanism, which focused on finding pleasure in life, Stoicism sought to apply reason (*logos*) to the world of experience. It maintained that there was a natural order in the world and that life was governed by natural laws. Thus, Stoicism advocated the supremacy of *physis* over *nomos* and the view that the world is as it is for a reason. One obvious consequence of this philosophy was that it supported the status quo, with imperial and aristocratic rule accepted as part of the natural order. Perhaps the principal difficulty for Stoicism (also true of most philosophies as well as religions) was the existence of evil, which always seems to defy reason. Like Christianity, Stoicism tended to fall back on the claim that some forms of evil, such as natural disasters that wipe out entire towns, are beyond the capacity of our reason to understand but that they nevertheless fit into a larger order or purpose that would make sense if it could be known.

The primary focus of Stoicism, however, was not on cosmology or theology but rather on applying reason to our experiences so as to enhance personal well-being. Stoics recognized that the source of most human suffering is human desire – for wealth, fame, power, love, immortality, freedom, and so forth. The goal of the Stoic, therefore, was to eliminate desire by understanding the nature of the world and his or her own place in it. Accomplishing this goal would produce inner peace through *apatheia*, or detachment. This perspective is perhaps best expressed in *The Enchiridion*, attributed to Epictetus (c. 55–135 AD) (1948) but actually written by his student Flavius Arrian in about 138 AD:

There are things which are within our power, and there are things which are beyond our power. ... [A]ltogether restrain desire; for if you desire any of the things not within our own power, you must necessarily be disappointed ... With regard to whatever objects either delight the mind or contribute to use or are tenderly beloved, remind yourself of what nature they are, beginning with the merest trifles: if you have a favorite cup, that it is but a cup of which you are fond – for thus, if it is broken, you can bear it; if you embrace your child or your wife, that you embrace a mortal – and thus, if either of them dies, you can bear it. (I–III)

The popularity of Epicureanism and Stoicism over many centuries is a greater testament to the human yearning for peace in a troubled world than it is to the viability of their doctrines. In their focus on abstention and elimination of desire, both philosophies were antithetical to human nature. The irrefutable logic of philosophical materialism does nothing to attenuate the need to believe, contrary to everything we know about life, that we continue to exist beyond this mortal plane. Moreover, the detachment they advocated – for Epicureans, manifested in communities striving to live apart from their fellow men; for the Stoics, manifested in emotional dissociation – was incomplete. Epicureans continued to interact with the larger community because they had no other way to support themselves; Stoics tended to be civic leaders and members of the upper class who usually failed – as evidenced in the *Meditations* of perhaps the most famous Stoic, Emperor Marcus Aurelius (c. 121–180 AD) – to attain the proper level of *apatheia* in the face of life's vicissitudes. But perhaps the most significant shortcoming of these philosophies was that they could not provide followers with a sense that life has a greater purpose, some meaning beyond our basic biological functions and existence as social creatures in an indifferent universe. Rooted in intellectualism, they ultimately were impersonal.

Detachment and dissociation may bring some measure of inner calm, but they may not bring much fulfillment. Aristotle understood this, hence his recognition that man is a political, and therefore a social, creature and that virtue develops through civic action, civic engagement. Opportunities for civic action were limited in the stratified and controlled Empire, and as Gibbon (1993) noted, the result was a decline in civic virtue, with all the predictable negative consequences. Civic virtue and individual virtue, or more simply individual *character,* are linked; a decline in one involves a decline in the other, leading to an increase in criminals and freeloaders. In an environment where civic virtue is in decline, detachment and anonymity act *against* ethical behavior (see Fukuyama, 1999; Putnam, 2002). Moreover, despite the intense investigation of *ethos* by Plato, Aristotle, and other Greek thinkers, their discussions were largely inaccessible to the majority of Roman citizens, and perhaps even irrelevant. They lack the personal immediacy necessary for application in the quotidian world of everyday people wrestling with issues of good and bad, people who in the Empire generally had few avenues for redressing wrongs committed against them. What people wanted was a different type of ethics that promised rewards to those who were good and punishments to those who were not – that is, a deontological ethics that would offer a more effective guide to behavior because they were god-given. And religion certainly can be an effective means of policing society.

Philo of Alexandria (c. 20 BC–50 AD) was among the first to try formulating a set of deontological ethics. His aim was to reconcile Platonism and Judaism by equating Plato's concept of "the good," or highest Ideal Form, with God, asserting that spirituality consisted of intellectual contemplation. Thus, what Philo meant by "virtue" was significantly different from the ancient concept of *aretê,* for he viewed religion – not education, literature, philosophy, or the city-state – as the foundation for ethical behavior. He drew on the Old Testament for his deontological system and identified four virtues – wisdom, self-control, courage, and justice – that are present in everyone at a rudimentary level, implanted by God. Good deeds can enhance one's virtue, but influenced by Stoicism, he suggested that *ataraxia* and moderation also are useful paths. True or complete virtue, however, is attainable only by combining the wisdom of philosophy with the love of God. He conceptualized God as perfect reason, pure *logos.* The surest path to virtue was to dedicate one's life to reason, thereby emulating God and ultimately attaining union with Him. Like the Stoics, Philo argued that a person also must reject all earthly concerns that were not necessary for living a simple life so as to rid oneself of superfluities.

In addition to the resurgent interest in philosophy, the early Empire saw a growing fascination with exotic religions, and mystery cults from Egypt and the Middle East found new initiates throughout the Mediterranean. We know little about the ancient cults of Dionysus, Demeter, and Eleusis, but what we do know suggests that their rituals were intended to give initiates contact with the divine. Burkert (1987) concluded that the cults provided initiates a personal religious experience but not necessarily a spiritual one. Mithraism, which originated in Persia or India, became especially popular among legionaries, perhaps because its emphasis on hierarchy resembled the hierarchical structure of legions themselves. According to Cumont (1956), initiation involved a ritual baptism of blood (*taurobolium*) and a sacrament of bread and wine. Doctrine declared the existence of immortal souls, which God places into our bodies at birth, and God's judgment at the end of life. The souls of the good return to heaven, whereas those of the bad are sent to hell, to be tormented by demons throughout eternity. The path to a good life involves abstinence, celibacy, and self-control.

Christianity

In this context, Christianity emerged as yet one more Eastern cult, but even though in many ways it resembled others – Epicureanism in its focus on establishing distinct communities detached from the mainstream, Mithraism in its eschatology, sacraments, and emphasis on celibacy – it had some important differences that appealed to the personal needs of the time. Greek philosophy taught that death was a part of life and should be accepted as such, neither feared nor overly mourned. Greek paganism was largely indifferent to the question of an afterlife. When the issue emerged, the afterlife was described as unpleasant (even for great heroes like Achilles), but not torturous – the ghostly shades merely were adrift, dreaming of their previous existence, yearning hopelessly for the faintest sensation of life.[23]

For reasons that are obscure, people throughout the Empire during the first and second centuries became deeply worried, one might even say obsessed, with their own mortality. Stroumsa (2005) argued that Christianity's perspective on this issue was embedded in a socio-psychological shift involving a radical concern for self. Rather than accepting death, as had been the norm in the past, Christians sought to overcome it. This desire was reflected in the cardinal importance they placed on the afterlife and in the vigorous way in which they asserted the resurrection of Jesus. To add strength to the assertion, they claimed the authority of direct testimony. In First Corinthians 1:15, Paul assured his audience that he *saw* Jesus after the resurrection and that many others did also. His task was to proclaim the Good News that all who believed the message he brought to them of Christ's resurrection were saved from death. Like Jesus, they, too, would be resurrected, in Paradise. Death would be conquered.[24] Moreover, owing to God's compassion, access to heaven was (initially, at least) open to all who believed in Jesus and who tried to live a spiritual life. Once there, they would live in bliss as immortals, praising God.

Under the influence of leaders such as Jerome and especially Augustine, the message changed: God became more judgmental. Compassion gave way to vindictiveness and a desire to punish sinners, and hell became a more frequent topic. Only God's chosen few would get to heaven, and the overwhelming majority of people, whether Christian or not, would burn for eternity. This was deontological ethics with a vengeance. Predestinationism guaranteed immortal bliss for a few and immortal torment for the majority, and the ethical system remained in force because one could never know whether he or she was among the chosen. Thus, as Christianity spread, it produced a fundamental social shift. Until this time, ethics and morality in the classical world were primarily the province of education and philosophy. Christianity concentrated them in religion, using the threat of eternal punishment as a motivator for good behavior as doctrinally defined by the Church.

The early Christian leaders were wise in the ways of leadership. They understood that one of the surest methods of creating strong social bonds was to cast the group in the role of persecuted outsider at odds with misguided traditions and the status quo. They preached that the emperor and the Empire were the enemy, and as evidence they pointed to the many temples and shrines erected by emperors over the years and the

---

[23] In *The Republic*, Plato took a different view in the Myth of Er, but even the few outside the Academy who knew *The Republic* probably classified the story as a poetic fairy tale with an unconvincing account of resurrection into the afterlife.

[24] This portion of First Corinthians, especially 15–19, is rhetorically and logically challenging. After emphasizing that he has worked harder than any of Christ's 12 apostles, Paul asks: "Now if Christ is proclaimed as raised from the dead, how can some of you say there is no resurrection of the dead? If there is no resurrection of the dead, then Christ has not been raised; and if Christ has not been raised, then our proclamation has been in vain and your faith has been in vain." These tautologies are repeated for several lines without ever addressing the veracity of the central issue. Few Greeks would have accepted the absence of rhetorical finesse evident here.

state support of the pagan priesthood. The early leaders did not deny the existence of the pagan gods – quite the contrary. They argued that these gods were all too real, but that they were demons whose aim was to torment men and women and to prevent them from finding salvation.

With this idea planted, Christian communities could not view their goal of detachment from the mainstream as some sort of intellectual exercise; they had to accept it as a matter of survival. Anyone who crossed the boundaries and interacted willingly in any way with pagans risked damnation. Resistance to the non-Christian world was considered an act of faith. This perception reinforced the need to forge a distinct Christian identity, and it gave rise to a completely new phenomenon – religious martyrdom. Burkert (1987) explored how the early Christian leaders created an alternative, self-sustaining society in which followers relied on fear and economic cooperation to gain a degree of independent detachment that the Epicureans never achieved. Brown (1987) argued that Christian leaders used chastity effectively to further set the new religion apart, a radical position indeed considering that Roman society already embraced a strict morality that only condoned sex between man and wife when it was for procreation: "Lacking the clear ritual boundaries provided in Judaism by circumcision and dietary laws, Christians tended to make their exceptional sexual discipline bear the full burden of expressing the difference between themselves and the pagan world" (p. 263) (see Gaca, 2003, for an alternative view). By the end of the third century, significant numbers of upper-class married couples were vowing upon conversion to live in chaste unions, which the clergy encouraged because the lack of offspring made it more certain that these couples would will their estates to the Church. But nothing more clearly defined Christians, and nothing more clearly set them apart from non-Christians, than their eager willingness to sacrifice their lives for their religion. When the first persecutions began in the latter part of the first century, martyrdom became a popular expression of faith.

Contrary to popular belief, the initial converts were not the poor and downtrodden but rather members of the middle and upper classes who lived in the Empire's major cities: Alexandria, Antioch, Byzantium, and Corinth. The first Christian communities were in the Greek-speaking East, not in Rome, and all of the sacred texts, including Paul's letters to these communities, were in Greek. Ironically, Paul himself was not particularly well educated in the sense of *paideia*, even though he was fluent in Greek, and he had little understanding of the Greek intellectual tradition. He also had a strong hostility toward learning, and it seems that his visit to Athens may have increased this sentiment.[25] In Romans 1:22, for example, he observed of pagans that, "Professing themselves to be wise, they became fools." Then, in First Corinthians, Paul declared: "For it is written, I will destroy the wisdom of the wise"; for "The foolishness of God is wiser than men" (1:19, 1:25). On this basis, Freeman (2002) concluded:

> As Paul's writings came to be seen as authoritative, it became a mark of the committed Christian to be able to reject rational thought, and even the evidence of empirical experience. Christians would often pride themselves on their lack of education, associating independent philosophical thinking with the sin of pride. (p. 120)

The state religion

Monotheistic religions like Christianity are based on the concept of revealed truth that, like the monotheistic god himself, is one and universal. Their hostility toward education

---

[25] In Acts 17–32, Luke reported that when Paul spoke to a group of Athenian philosophers, they "scoffed" at his talk of resurrection.

and philosophy is based on the belief that neither is revealed and therefore is the product of men and women – sinners tempted by the devil – who are incapable of discovering the one universal truth on their own. For early Christians, the only legitimate object of study was the Bible, as indicated in Augustine's *Confessions,* in which he dismissed not only education but curiosity:

[T]here is yet another form of temptation still more complex in its peril ..., a certain vain and curious longing in the soul, ... cloaked under the name of knowledge and learning. ... This malady of curiosity is the reason for all those strange sights exhibited in the theater. It is also the reason why we proceed to search out the secret powers of nature – those which have nothing to do with our destiny – which do not profit us to know about, and concerning which men desire to know only for the sake of knowing. And it is with this same motive of perverted curiosity for knowledge that we consult the magical arts. (X.54–55)

In *De Doctrina Christiana,* Augustine stated that "We were ensnared by the wisdom of the serpent: We are set free by the foolishness of God. Moreover, just as the former was called wisdom, but was in reality the folly of those who despised God, so the latter is called foolishness, but is true wisdom in those who overcome the devil" (I.14.13).

The concept of revealed truth also establishes the fundamental doctrine among monotheistic religions that all other religions are false and therefore must be eradicated. As a consequence of this doctrine, those who follow these false religions must be either converted or eliminated.[26] As Stark (2003) indicated, the chief duty of those who embrace monotheism is "to spread knowledge of the One True God: the duty to missionize is inherent in dualistic monotheism" (p. 35). This doctrine and its related duty help us understand why Christians were determined to destroy paganism, and they also offer insight into Christianity's rapid growth throughout the Empire.

The early Church leaders, however, quickly found that the revealed truth of the Bible frequently made little sense unless it was interpreted allegorically. They recognized that even on the most basic level, the New Testament and the Old Testament were incompatible. But the act of interpretation is an open process, not a closed one. As a result, by the end of the second century, Christians did not have one universal revealed truth – they had many. Each leader preached his own interpretation of the Bible and claimed that it was revealed truth, often provided via direct communication with God, and each leader attracted parishioners who not only accepted his version of the truth but also sought actively to impose it on others.

By the fourth century, the number of competing groups identifying themselves as Christians, even though they espoused different doctrines, had grown substantially. The situation became worse when Emperor Constantine ordered toleration of Christianity (the Edict of Milan) after winning a battle in 312 AD, a victory he attributed to God's intervention when he ordered his troops to paint a cross on their shields. Afterwards, Constantine issued several edicts that benefited the Christian churches, such as granting them tax-exempt status, and that clearly favored Christianity over the traditional religions. The Edict of Milan freed the Christian groups from fear of persecution, and it also appears to have exacerbated their doctrinal conflicts. Three major controversies emerged that so embroiled the faithful in argument and riots (in the East, at any rate) that they threatened the stability of an empire already under considerable stress from

---

[26] This generalization does not include the sort of pagan monotheism found in Plato and others (see Frede, 2002). Jaffee (2001) argued that monotheism's innate hostility toward other religions is not due to the failure of monotheistic ethics but rather to the fundamental incompatibility of their symbolic systems, which always include identification of an exclusive and select group of "chosen ones."

unrelenting barbarian raids: Donatism, Arianism, and Plegianism (see Bowder, 1978; Kousoulas, 1997). Each of these controversies is interesting in its own right, but Arianism had the more lasting influence on Western culture. Christians could not decide on the exact nature of Jesus. Was Jesus God? Divine but not God? Or a human filled with God's Spirit? Arius, a Christian leader in Alexandria, asserted option two.

Probably for the sake of domestic stability in the face of growing external pressures, Constantine determined to put an end to the arguing and ordered a select group of bishops to convene in council at Nicea, in Anatolia. The bishops duly traveled to Nicea in May of 325 and began debating doctrine. After many days of discussion the bishops could not reach an agreement. Constantine therefore intervened and settled the matter by using his considerable influence to persuade the bishops to accept the notion that Jesus, God, and the Holy Spirit are both separate and one – what came to be known as the Nicene Creed of the Holy Trinity (see Drake, 2002; Eusebius, 1999; Freeman, 2002; Shenk, 2002). He then took the provocative step of ordering the excommunication of Arius and other leaders who refused to sign the statement of trinitarianism.

After Nicea, the growth of Christianity was nurtured and even accelerated by government support. Constantine continued to intervene in doctrine and policy, transforming Christianity until it was as much a political movement as a religious one. This confluence of faith and politics was to affect the Western world from that point forward. Under Emperor Theodosius (c. 347–395 AD), all other religions were outlawed, and Christianity became the official religion of the state; anyone caught practicing the old religions was subject to execution as Christianity and the imperial government formed a symbiotic relationship (see Bowersock, 1986). Emperors, for example, found that the notion of one supreme god was a useful metaphor to reflect their own status: God ruled the heavens, while the emperor ruled the earth (Hall, 1992).

Increasingly after Constantine, we find emperors declaring themselves to be God's chosen vicars as they sought to stabilize the Empire. But the Church leaders exacted a price, most evident in 390 AD, when Bishop Ambrose of Milan (c. 340–397) forced Emperor Theodosius to humiliate himself publicly for a military incursion into Thessalonica. Yet the hope of stability began to unravel as external pressures mounted. Christian emperors called upon their Christian subjects to defend the borders against the barbarians, only to have them routinely refuse on the grounds that it was against their religion. For its part, the growing Church needed an administrative hierarchy, and it found an efficient model in the imperial government. Thus, Christians who initially had opposed the Empire and Rome as the new Babylon, the capital of sin, essentially became the Empire. They were ill-suited to preserving it. Their focus was on the spiritual realm, not the temporal, and their radical concern for self could not be aligned with the classical concept of civic virtue. Regularly during the fourth and fifth centuries, Rome used bribes to keep the barbarians at bay, until the Germanic leader Odoacer dethroned Romulus Augustus in 476 and thereby ended the Western Roman Empire.[27]

Rhetoric and Oratory in the Empire

In the early part of the Empire, rhetoric was essentially indistinguishable from what had existed in the Republic. The elevation of Octavian to Augustus brought to an end the free-for-all competition for individual honor and power that had characterized the

---

[27] See Burns (2003) for an in-depth discussion of the complex relations between barbarians and the Empire.

Republic, and it also brought to an end the politically infused oratory of the Senate and the popular assemblies. This change had a negative effect on oratory. Only a hundred years or so after his death, Cicero already had achieved "classic" status, motivating Quintilian (c. 35–95 AD) to argue that the perfect orator would model himself after the savior of the Republic, declaring that "Cicero is not the name of a man, but of eloquence" (X.1.112).

Other changes were inevitable. This was an age of cities: Rome, Byzantium, Alexandria, Corinth, Athens, Antioch. The emperor, intellectuals, and the wealthy elite traveled regularly from city to city, diminishing the status of Rome as a political and cultural center.[28] With power in the hands of the emperor, whatever opportunities for deliberative oratory that previously had existed in the Senate all but disappeared. Both Seneca (in Book I of *Controversiae*) and Tacitus (in *Annals* and *Dialogus de Oratoribus*) described Roman rhetoric and oratory in decline. Seneca attributed the decline primarily to moral weakness. Tacitus' keener perception found the cause in the Empire itself: The government's rigid control of society constrained oratory in numerous ways, preventing the art from rising above the standard set by Cicero. Probing Tacitus' assessment, Rudich (1997) argued that the reigns of Clodius (c. 10 BC–54 AD) and Nero (c. 37–68 AD) deteriorated social conditions significantly, requiring the elite to engage in *dissimulatio*, the concealment of true feelings beneath a show of false sentiment, leading to "a sort of socio-political schizophrenia" (p. 4) in which the distinction between truth and fiction, content and style, became blurred, and life itself became rhetoricized.

In this environment, epideixis emerged after centuries of neglect from the obscurity of funeral orations, as evidenced by Menander Rhetor's (c. 4th century) publication of *On Epideictic Oratory*. Speakers sought to outdo one another in their praise of the emperor and those whom he favored – and may have trembled in fear that their words might be misinterpreted. To honor themselves, provincial governors commissioned municipal Sophists to write panegyrics and deliver them to the crowds.

Peace, an improved standard of living, and more leisure time created among city dwellers such a demand for entertainment that the gladiatorial contests, theaters, and feasts could not meet the people's needs. The craving for entertainment moved declamation out of the schools, where it had become ever more artificial, and into the public arena, with orators often contesting to win the acclaim of audiences. In addition, many people turned to the law courts, which had offered some measure of entertainment during the Republic but which during the Empire became more exciting than ever as *delatores*, professional informers, alleged that, one after another, some of the Empire's more important men and women were engaged in conspiracies, adultery, and/or witchcraft. Beginning with Augustus, high-profile political trials were heard either by the emperor or by the Senate, but those without significant political import allowed audiences to witness the eloquence of the greatest jurists and experience the high emotions of the wealthy and powerful as they struggled to retain their property and their lives against charges of unlawful fornication or of using black magic. Fantham's (1997) examination of legal rhetoric in the late Republic suggested that forensic orators shaped their speeches to appeal to the spectators as much as to the juries, recognizing that their hostility or sympathy could influence the outcome of a case. There is no reason to assume that this facet of forensic oratory changed significantly during the Empire.

---

[28] The Eastern portion of the Empire steadily grew more important, until Constantine moved the capital to Byzantium, renamed Constantinople, in 330 AD (see Mitchell, 2006).

Declamation and epideixis

Even the emperors became enamored of rhetoric and oratory. Vespasian (c. 9–79 AD) established state-supported chairs of Greek and Latin rhetoric and appointed Quintilian as the first holder of the Latin chair (see Anderson, 1993). By the beginning of the second century, most major cities, as well as some of middling stature, had their own chairs supported by local funds. In nearly all instances, those who held these positions were teachers of rhetoric, and their frequent public declamations became high-stakes contests for status. If a chaired orator performed poorly against his opponent, he could be turned out. Students committed themselves to their teacher's particular style of ora- tory, and the schools competed against one another in public displays of declamation. Rivalries were vicious, and students from competing schools engaged in frequent street fights that left them bloodied and bruised.

Declamations were usually held in public buildings: temples, libraries, theaters, and in some cities, lecture halls designed specifically for these events. The accounts that have come down to us, even if somewhat exaggerated, indicate that declamations were among the more important social events in the cities.[29] People were moved to laughter and tears by these speeches, looked forward to them with great anticipation, and discussed and analyzed them a length afterwards, often memorizing certain parts when the oration was published. It is difficult for us today to understand this enthusiasm for public speak- ing. Ours is a different age, one in which the effective use of language is neglected, and the concept of someone being treated as a celebrity simply owing to his or her speaking ability is hard to grasp. Only indirectly, through the accounts that have come down to us, can we get a sense of how popular declamations were. The orator Libanius (c. 314–394 AD), for example, recounted in his autobiography that people camped out overnight at the entrance to the building where he was to speak so as to be first in line. In *Orations* (1997) the second-century orator Aristides (c. 129–180 AD) related a similar scene:

> Before I even entered the city, people were coming to meet me because they had heard about me. … Despite the fact that my appearance was impromptu, and most people knew nothing about it, the Council Chamber was so full that you could see nothing but human faces – and you couldn't have thrust your hand between those in the crowd because the chamber was so fully packed. Even so, the noise and the good will, or rather (to tell the truth) the enthusiasm, were so universal that there was no one to be seen sitting down either during my preliminary speech or when I stood up and declaimed. (51. 29–34)

Declamations continued to involve *suasoriae* and *controversiae*, with orations character- istically embedded in a largely mythologized history, leading Russell (1983) to conclude that "the concentration on the past must have been escapism" (p. 109). Perhaps, but this focus appears to have served other purposes: sheer entertainment, as well as a celebra- tion of the city and its people through a form of historical revisionism that reinforced a cultural identity that many citizens of the Empire desired to forge for themselves. In any event, we find that imperial rhetoric was largely lacking in philosophical elements; even the sort of secondhand philosophical musing found in Cicero disappeared.

As for epideixis, its popularity grew until it occupied an important place in display speeches. In classical Greek oratory, epideixis focused on encomia, speeches that praised

---

[29] It is important to understand that ancient societies operated at a different pace than ours. People typically rose at dawn and worked until about 2 pm, unless they were slaves. They therefore had significantly more time available for family, friends, entertainment, and cultural events than we do today.

someone who was worthy owing to accomplishments or contributions to the city-state. Thus, traditional epideixis was phatic in that its performative force served to build community. But this role changed somewhat in the Empire. As already noted, *logos* in Roman oratory was subordinated to *ethos* and *pathos*, which accelerated a trend already evident in Greek rhetoric, especially the forensic speeches of Demosthenes – the use of invective to ridicule an opponent. By the second century AD, we find that Roman epideixis was clearly divided into the contrastive subgenres of encomia and invective.

Kennedy (1994) described clearly how encomia were further divided into additional subgenres: *panegyric*, used to celebrate the gods during religious festivals; *gamelion*, used during wedding celebrations, *genethliac*, used to celebrate a birthday; *epithalamion*, used to celebrate a newly wedded couple when they arrive at their home after the wedding ceremony; *prosphonetic*, used to praise a ruler; *epitaphios*, used to praise the departed at a funeral; and *protreptic*, used to praise an athlete. Overall, however, encomia had lost much of their community-building performative force by this time. They had become set pieces that emphasized *sententiae* and exaggerated eloquence, moving toward litera-ture and away from phatic oratory, expressing little more than greeting-card platitudes. As Holloway (1998) noted, "The skillful use of *sententiae* became one of the hallmarks of Roman *urbanitas*" (pp. 34–35).

Invective, on the other hand, grew into an effective political tool that the ruling elite used in their struggles for power and control within their ranks. Craig (2004) listed "sev-enteen conventional *loci* of invective established in Greek and Roman practice by Cicero's time" (p. 190) and concluded that in the courts humiliation was more impor-tant rhetorically than truth, whereas in judicial speeches invective was expected to "flow within the narrower banks of plausibility" (p. 197). We see the power of invective at the end of the fourth century, when the Roman poet Claudian unleashed an invective against Eutropius (*In Eutropium*), consul of the Eastern portion of the Empire, that seems to have contributed to the consul's deposition and assassination (Long, 1996).

The Second Sophistic

The cultural shift toward reflection and contemplation was accompanied by increased interest in literature, philosophy, and declamation as the Empire matured. Romans' long-standing ambivalence toward everything Greek tempered significantly. Many rhet-oricians, such as Aristides and Lucian, began viewing the ascendancy of Asianism as a perversion of the art's original goals, for the practitioners of this artificial style had increased the scope of their gyrations to such a degree that their oratory was as much about posturing as it was about speech. The focus was on sheer performance with little substance (Anderson, 1993). The study of theory and practice from Athens' Golden Age expanded as these rhetoricians sought to develop a more authentic, purer style and to season their work with philosophy. They found a ready model in the Greek Sophists, and widespread imitation of the Attic style followed, with Demosthenes frequently identified as the premier model. In an effort to locate the roots of Atticism, Philostratus (c. 170–247 AD) recounted the lives of various orators, beginning with Gorgias, who were successful in merging philosophy and rhetoric and concluded that history was witnessing a new wave of sophistry, which he dubbed in his *Lives of the Sophists* as a "Second Sophistic."

There is no question that rhetoric and oratory were undergoing a change, particu-larly in the Eastern Mediterranean, but scholars are divided over the exact nature of the Second Sophistic. Even identifying the inclusive dates of the Second Sophistic with cer-tainty is problematic, some asserting that it ended around 250 AD, whereas others extend it to the close of the fourth century and the death of Libanius (see Pernot, 1993). Bowersock (1969) and Swain (1996) affirmed that an explicit goal of the new Sophists was the purification of language and a reduction of Asiatic extremes, but they also recognized that it entailed a revival of philosophical rhetoric. Equally important, they linked the Second Sophistic to a renaissance of Greek culture, which the emperors may have encouraged so as to promote a common cultural history. Anderson (1993), on the other hand, argued that there was no real break in the sophistic tradition from Gorgias onward but that the Second Sophistic, largely limited to the Greek-speaking East, was a nostalgic response to Roman domination. Through their declamations, sophistic orators gave audiences the opportunity to relive the glory days of Athens. Brunt (1994) insisted that the idea of a Greek renaissance lacks foundation and that the term "Sophist" was just as pejorative during the first three centuries of the Empire as it had been in the days of Plato and Isocrates.[30] On this account, he suggested that the Second Sophistic, at least if it is conceptualized as a revival of the rhetorical and intellectual climate of classical Greece, was largely a creation of Philostratus' imagination. What is clear is that the Older Sophists existed in a democratic environment that was absent in the Empire, and over time, the Empire became more rigidly authoritarian, not less. On this basis alone, the term "Second Sophistic" is misleading in that it contains a false connotation. Whether the Second Sophistic was real or imaginary, however, may not be as important as how attempting to recapture the past – or revisioning their present – led intellectuals to perceive themselves and their place in society.

Rhetoric and oratory were inextricably linked to the Greek intellectual tradition, and the Second Sophistic emphasized this connection by stressing its location in the context of *paideia*, which as Brown (1992) suggested, was as much about politics as education: "Only a young man who had 'installed Demosthenes in his soul' at an early age could be trusted to behave correctly when governing a province"; "*paideia* united potentially conflicting segments of the governing class. It joined imperial administrators and provincial notables in a shared sense of common excellence" (pp. 38–39). From this perspective, immersion in and dedication to Greek literature and philosophy served to enhance already existing social distinctions. In addition, their education gave these notables a shared language and set of values that facilitated government. If a provincial governor needed a new aqueduct for his capital, for example, he could appeal to Rome using the commonplaces of *aretê*, civic virtue.

A knowledge of literature, therefore, was deemed a fundamental requirement among the elite. Rhetoricians played an important role in providing the "shared sense of common excellence," and literature was a significant part of the curriculum in schools of rhetoric. Public orations were delivered to large audiences from all classes, so orators nurtured a shared culture in entire communities, not just among the elite. Whitmarsh (2001) went a step further and proposed that the Second Sophistic involved creating a social identity through "the politics of imitation":

> *Paideia*, then, was not simply a form of social practice ... at a more abstract level, it was also a means of constructing and reifying idealized identities for Greek and Roman, a privileged space of complex cultural interaction ... between Roman ideology and Greek identity, a foundation upon which both peoples constructed their own sense of their place in the world. (p. 16)

---

[30] Winter (1997) showed that Philo of Alexandria (c. 20 BC–50 AD) did not use the term "Sophist" pejoratively. Although some popular orators, such as Aristides (c. 117–181 AD), seem to have taken care to call themselves rhetors, not Sophists, this was not universal. Libanius, for example, regularly used "Sophist" nonpejoratively to mean both "teacher" and "orator."

Orators during the Second Sophistic imitated historical speeches so convincingly that many declamations were indistinguishable from real speeches, leading Russell (1983) to conclude that the Pseudo-Herodes' *Peri Politeias* was, contrary to most scholarly opinion, written in the third or fourth century AD, not the fifth century BC. The difficulty in distinguishing between the real speeches of the ancient Greeks and the contemporary imitations seems to support Whitmarsh's (2001) perspective, and the conclusion that declamation may have served the purpose of historical revisionism is tempting. We know from the extant works that rhetoricians and orators celebrated long-extinct political virtues and linked them to the existing authoritarian government, creating the illusion of freedom, political participation, and truly deliberative oratory. Their encomia – commonly produced as commissions – regularly compared emperors, provincial governors, and even city prefects to the great leaders of ancient Athens – men like Solon, Pericles, and Demosthenes – who floated like ghosts in the cultural memory and lent themselves easily to the creation of an artificial identity, an artificial reality. These comparisons were expressed with particular enthusiasm (although often with little sincerity) in the East, no doubt with the objective of locating Roman rulers in the narrative of Greek history and traditions so as to relieve the burden of political domination.

By the middle of the third century AD, however, both politics and education were undergoing irreversible changes. The western portion of the Empire was becoming more Latinized, a process that accelerated in the fourth century. It had developed its own literary canon during the Silver Age (the first two centuries of the Empire), significantly reducing the historical dependence on Greek culture even as the Greek-dominated East seemed to undergo fossilization, caught in a resigned focus on past literary and cultural glories that were widely accepted as unmatchable. Displaying a haughty disdain for Latin texts, the schools of rhetoric in the East, with few exceptions, did not include Latin literature in the curriculum. The formal split of the Empire into eastern and western domains exacerbated the situation, encouraging political as well as cultural autonomy. Thus, by the end of the fourth century, the bilingualism that had characterized Roman intellectuals during Cicero's lifetime was a rarity, and so few people spoke Latin in the East that Latin schools popped up in all major cities, their success forcing schools of rhetoric to compete fiercely for students (Cribiore, 2007; Herrin, 1987).

The sociopolitical nature of the Second Sophistic made its decline and ultimate demise inevitable in the face of the Christian revolution. Christianity created a new culture that, unlike *paideia*, did not require any familiarity with literature, philosophy, or history. Faith was what mattered, not education. The surviving works of early Christian leaders (such as Gregory of Nazianzus [c. 325–389] and Augustine) – most of whom were trained in rhetoric – frequently reveal the mental conflicts they experienced in trying to reconcile their love of *paideia* with their religious conversion, but they all realized that they could not serve two masters. Starting in 389 AD, the powerful application of faith to politics led Emperor Theodosius to issue a series of edicts against paganism that concluded in 391 with a law making pagan worship illegal. In celebration, Christian mobs took to the streets, assaulting non-Christians, robbing and destroying temples, and burning libraries to eradicate the texts of the devil worshipers. Over the next several decades, followers of the old gods were presented with a choice – convert or face execution. The Christian ranks subsequently swelled remarkably.

During the Golden Age of Athens, politics and manmade laws guided human conduct, and the city state was viewed as a manifestation of the highest human values, giving rise to political philosophy. Christianity effected a reversal that changed the course of Western society. It focused on the individual and his relationship to God, and it advocated a mythico-poetic world view that required a new cultural identity and a new educational curriculum. Establishing a new curriculum divorced from *paideia* required dismantling the old. To this end, Emperor Justinian (c. 483–565 AD) cut off all state funding to chairs of rhetoric, essentially bringing the classical tradition to a close.

Letteraturizzazione *and Christian rhetoric*

Kennedy (1980) used the term *"letteraturizzazione"* to describe what he saw as a transition during the Empire to "literary rhetoric." In his analysis, *letteraturizzazione* involved a shift from the *primary* use of rhetoric – persuasive speech in a public venue – to a *secondary* use: written texts intended to be read that were principally either literary or about literature. While asserting that the work of Isocrates can be characterized as literary because it meets the necessary criteria, Kennedy indicated that *letteraturizzazione* began in earnest during the Silver Age of Rome with writers such as Ovid, Seneca, and Juvenal producing "the first truly rhetorical literature" (p. 113). Several factors, according to Kennedy, contributed to *letteraturizzazione,* but perhaps the most significant was that Greek literature was oral and therefore "made much use of the forms of oratory" (p. 110), which facilitated the transition.

Kennedy's (1980) identification of the shift from primary to secondary rhetoric is extremely valuable. His analysis did not reference, however, the early connection of literature and rhetoric evident in Plato's assertion that rhetoric was merely poetry without rhyme or meter, nor did it consider Aristotle's *Art of Poetry* as a companion piece to *The Art of Rhetoric.* Recognizing that the association between rhetoric and literature – specifically, poetics – extends far into the past is necessary to understanding fully the historical influences underlying *letteraturizzazione,* particularly in light of the evidence suggesting that formal rhetoric emerged out of the Older Sophists' study of poetry and that its earliest instances made much use of poetic devices, not vice versa.

These issues aside, the emergence of writing as the primary medium for the application of rhetoric is an important factor in the field. Unfortunately, identifying the stimuli for *letteraturizzazione* is difficult and necessarily forces a measure of speculation, although some factors seem more likely than others. A large number of highly educated Greeks lived in Rome toward the end of the Republic, and as teachers, writers, and readers with a long tradition of attention to linguistic correctness, they would have exerted significant influence on Roman letters (Rawson, 1985). This influence may have been especially strong during the Republic's last years, when Roman intellectuals were assessing language in its totality as they debated the relative merits of Latin and Greek as the proper language for writing. Marcus Terentius Varro's (c. 116–27 BC) massive treatise *On the Latin Language* perhaps best represents the intellectual climate of the times. Education also probably played a significant role. We know from Quintilian's *Institutio Oratoria* that the *schola grammatici* had significantly expanded the instruction they provided young boys, moving beyond grammar and literature to include rhetoric. It seems likely that a course of study that combined literature and rhetoric would lead to a fusion of the two, making literary expression more rhetorical and oratory more literary. Quintilian hinted at this conflation when he noted that the *grammatici* had laid claim not only to "the principles of correct speech … but [also to] the knowledge of almost all the major arts" (II.1.5).[31] Nevertheless, he indicated that the ideal student of oratory would read poetry to gain inspiration "as regards the matter, sublimity of language, and the power to excite every kind of emotion" (X.1.27–28). Horace's *Ars Poetica* – which well

---

[31] Increased patronage may also have encouraged *letteraturizzazione,* for it freed poets from economic concerns and enable them to be more productive than they would have been even 50 years earlier.

exemplifies the fusion of literature and rhetoric – may, therefore, be characterized as the inevitable outcome of the *grammatici*'s importation of rhetoric into their traditional literary instruction.

By the fourth century, the lines between rhetoric and literature were blurred. The *grammatici* continued to give students the foundation in literature (and often in rhetoric) that was necessary for more advanced study in one of the many schools of rhetoric. *Paideia* required significant knowledge of classical works. Consequently, when Libanius traveled to Athens for rhetorical training, his study of literature and philosophy was rigorous. As his letters and autobiography show, he insisted that his own students not only master literature as part of their training but that they continuing reading the great works as a lifelong endeavor after leaving school and taking their place in the world.

Efforts to spread, legitimize, and standardize Christianity also constituted a major force in the transition to secondary rhetoric. The early Church leaders found that the Empire's poor and poorly educated were receptive to Christianity's messages, but the messages had to be communicated using literary devices that were easy to understand. Many of the educated, on the other hand, after that first blush, struggled with Christianity. Large numbers of rhetoricians, perhaps a majority, were pagans, not Christians, well into the fifth century. They had been trained in a tradition that stretched back nearly a thousand years to the Milesians. Moreover, the logical flaws, inept style, and immorality they perceived in the Bible made it difficult for many to believe that this was a divinely inspired work.

The need to repudiate this assessment drove early Christians with a grim purpose. Christian rhetoricians like Origen (c. 184–254 AD), Jerome (c. 340–420 AD), and Augustine applied their training and intellects to homilies and hermeneutics in an effort to reshape the perception of the Bible, creating the core of Christian rhetoric in the process. Origen explained the Bible's problems by claiming that it was written on different levels: the literal, the moral, and the spiritual. The deepest level, the spiritual, is nearly impenetrable and therefore requires interpretation because God did not want his secret messages to be understood easily, which would lead people to take them for granted. He argued that only the exercise of allegorical interpretation can unlock these secrets, hence the need for exegesis.

Augustine, with his solid rhetorical training and fertile imagination, was the true master of exegesis. His allegorical interpretations of the Gospel necessarily required an allegorical interpretation of the world and human experience, and he – perhaps more than anyone else – completed the transition from primary to secondary rhetoric. His written work encompassed massive treatises, such as *De Doctrina Christiana* and *De Civitae Dei*, but it also included numerous argumentative pamphlets and letters that he produced in his persecution of those Christians whom he perceived to be heretics – especially the Pelegians, the Donatists, and the Arians. Polemical yet also literary in its use of metaphor and allegory, the sheer force of his writing is evidenced by his success in persuading Emperor Honorius to outlaw the Donatists and to declare that they would be executed if they met in worship. This sort of persuasive power had an influence that extended far beyond contemporary doctrinal disputes – it silenced inquiry and shut down independent thought. Natural laws were rejected and replaced by *mythos*. Physics disappeared, and the supernatural permeated every facet of life once again. In other words, society had come full circle, returning the Mediterranean to its pre-Milesian state.

Understandably, Augustine and other leaders recognized the value of rhetoric, but as already noted, their relation with it was an ambivalent one. Gregory of Nazianzus, for example, attested to the value of encomia, but he asserted that they should be used only to celebrate the lives of religious figures. He saw the utility in recognizing rhetorical genres, but bound them to sanctioned topics; thus, encomia, moral edification, and exposition of Christian dogma were to characterize Christian rhetoric. Because he worked in both poetry and prose, his writing appears to reflect the rhetorical instability of the time, for his poetry is highly rhetorical, whereas his prose is highly poetic. Augustine had very little Greek and did not seem to know Aristotle except for a few badly translated works; his knowledge of Plato was limited to Cicero's references and to Plotinus' revisionism and therefore was highly distorted. His rhetorical training was based almost entirely on Cicero, whose influence is most evident in Book Four of *De Doctrina Christiana*. As a result of this influence, Augustine placed great emphasis on style, but like Origen, his principal focus was on discovering and interpreting the Bible's hidden truths. At times he struggled: The principles of Greek rhetoric did not always lend themselves comfortably to scriptural hermeneutics. Nevertheless, Augustine's own work demonstrated beyond doubt the persuasive power of rhetorically based writing to transcend time and space.

Biblical exegesis and rhetorical proofs

The traditional proofs of *ethos*, *pathos*, and *logos* were transformed in Christian rhetoric. Kennedy's (1980) work is perhaps the most insightful here: Even though *logos* had never figured significantly in Roman rhetoric, under Christian influence it lost any vestigial denotation of argument based on reason or evidence and came to be understood as God's divine message; *ethos* and *pathos* underwent similar changes. *Ethos* was recast as the authority of the priest to interpret and communicate the Word of God. This authority, however, was not based on his standing in the Church or on his qualities as a man but rather on his piety and thus on his relationship with God, which determined whether he was able to serve effectively as a vessel through which God communicated his Truths to an audience. The concept of *vir bonus dicendi peritus* vanished as Augustine argued successfully that God could communicate his divine truths even through the broken instrument of a sin-corrupted priest, provided it was God's will. *Pathos* was recast as *grace*, the ability to open the hearts of an audience to receive the Spirit and the Word of the Lord. More often than not, this ability was understood to be passion, leading priests to strive to make their sermons as passionate as possible so as to stir the emotions and raise the spirits of audiences.

Augustine's life may well reflect the tensions and struggles the early Church leaders faced in transforming their training and practice to meet the needs of a Christian rhetoric that would affirm the faith of those who believed in Scripture. None was as successful in this transformation as Augustine. His writing was so influential that it became the model not just for Biblical exegesis but for the interpretation of all forms of literature. He also laid the groundwork for the rhetoric that dominated the Middle Ages: *ars predicandi* (art of preaching). With his death, the period of classical rhetoric came to an end.

7

Cicero and the Latinization of Greek Rhetoric

Introduction to Cicero (c. 106–43 BC)

Marcus Tullius Cicero was born in Arpinum, a village located in the hills about 65 miles from Rome. His *equites* parents were not wealthy, but they had sufficient means to provide him with an excellent education, including training in rhetoric. Everitt (2001) suggested that Cicero attended one of Rome's public schools (*ludus litterarius*) in his youth, but as Clarke (1968) noted, this seems highly unlikely. Young boys and girls of the propertied class typically were tutored at home, studying reading, writing, and arithmetic until age 10 or 12, at which point they began their secondary studies in a school conducted by a *grammaticus*. The secondary curriculum included Greek language and literature (which were taught before students moved on to Latin), as well as music, geometry, and the fundamentals of rhetoric. At age 14, Cicero already was well along in his rhetorical studies and wanted to work with a Latin rhetor but was persuaded to pursue advanced studies with a Greek teacher, instead. Following the custom of the time, Cicero's father sought to apprentice him to a worthy mentor after he reached his majority at age 16. The family apparently had important patronage connections, for Rome's leading orator, Lucius Linius Crassus agreed to take the boy on.

While living with Crassus, Cicero would have observed his mentor preparing and delivering orations, and he also would have been able to observe the philosophical and political discussions that constituted common dinner entertainment among the elite. The association with Crassus had another great advantage, for Crassus was related to Rome's premier jurist, Quintus Mucius Scaevola. Crassus arranged for Cicero to study law under Scaevola's tutelage, which gave him the training and knowledge he needed to pursue a career as a jurist. His studies were interrupted by the Social War, which erupted in 91 BC, but lacking any military inclination, he returned to them as soon as he was able.

According to Plutarch (1958), Cicero kept a low profile during the civil war between Marius and Sulla, immersing himself in reading philosophy and the law. He was aided greatly in his study of philosophy when Philo of Larissa, the head to Plato's Academy, fled Athens for Rome in the wake of King Mithridates' efforts to throw off Roman rule. A skeptic much influenced by Stoicism, Philo incorporated *dissoi logoi* into his teaching as a way of helping students evaluate philosophical and ethical arguments. In so doing, he essentially advocated the application to philosophy of techniques associated with rhetoric. Cicero began studying with Philo, whose influence was considerable, as seen in the discussions of philosophy in both *De Oratore* and *Academia* (see Brittain, 2001, 2006; Reinhardt, 2006).

Even though Cicero was well connected, it is unlikely that he was able to plead any significant cases when he began to practice as a jurist. In addition, he also may have been hindered by nerves. None of the available evidence suggests that Cicero was a courageous man, and if the historian Cassius Dio Cocceianus (1917) can be believed, he found speaking in court difficult, as indicated in the excerpt below from a speech against Cicero by Quintus Rufius Calenus:

> Why, you always come to the courts trembling, as if you were going to fight as a gladiator, and after uttering a few words in a meek and half-dead voice you take your departure, without having remembered a word of the speech you thought out at home before you came, and without having found anything to say on the spur of the moment. In making assertions and promises you surpass all mankind in audacity, but in the trials themselves, apart from reviling and abusing people, you are most weak and cowardly. Or do you think anyone is ignorant of the fact that you never delivered one of those wonderful speeches of yours that you have published, but wrote them all out afterwards, like persons who fashion generals and cavalry leaders out of clay? (XLVI.7)

If Cicero truly was nervous before the court, it did not prevent him from recognizing an opportunity to advance his career when one appeared (nor could it have been a serious obstacle to his career, for his successes in court are beyond dispute). In 80 BC, Sextus Roscius was accused of murdering his wealthy father. Even by Roman standards, the politics of the case were complicated. News of the murder reached Chrysogonus, a former slave who had become rich and powerful as a favorite of Sulla. Chrysogonus put the dead man's name on Sulla's proscription list, even though the list had been closed, which enabled him to seize the man's property, leaving Sextus penniless and without a home. Influential friends sought justice, only to be put off with promises while Chrysogonus tried to assassinate Sextus. When these attempts failed, Chrysogonus had his cronies accuse Sextus of patricide. Accepting the case meant challenging Chrysogonus, characterizing him as a villain who abused his power to gain financial advantage. Given Sulla's history of killing anyone whom he found even slightly irritating, Cicero was putting himself directly in harm's way, for the abuses of Chrysogonus were symptomatic of Sulla's dictatorship. We have no way of knowing the details of the actual trial, but Cicero's published version of his speech is brilliant in its use of *pathos* and *ethos* to cultivate sympathy for the accused and then to destroy the characters of the accusers. A turning point in the trail came when Cicero shifted his focus to motive, asking *Cui bono?* – Who stood to gain? In the process, he managed to avoid offending Sulla by declaring that the dictator was not involved and, indeed, was too busy guiding the Republic to take notice of the individual actions of his many subordinates. The result was a total success: Sextus Roscius was acquitted, Sulla did not kill Cicero, and the orator was instantly famous. He solidified his social position about this time by marrying Terentia, the daughter of a wealthy nobleman.

His legal practice flourished, and he became rich. But only a year after his defense of Sextus, Cicero decided to take time off to travel to Athens for further training in rhetoric. When he returned to Rome two years later, he ran for public office, and with friends in high places willing to help him buy votes and with his skill as a speaker, he easily won election to *quaestor*, or magistrate, and was assigned to assist the governor of Sicily, Gaius Verres. Cicero had successfully entered the *cursus honorum*. He concentrated on cultivating his alliances, and one of the more important was with Pompey, who had become the most powerful man in Rome. Jimenez (2000), for example, noted that "[Cicero] had just been elected a praetor [in 66 BC], and he knew that when he stood for the Consulship in two years, the support of Pompey would be crucial" (pp. 36–37).

As already discussed in the general introduction, Cicero then went on to defeat Lucius Catilina for the consulship in 63 at age 46, making him among the youngest men ever to hold this office during the Republic. As consul, he discovered Catiline's plot to take over the government and had the conspirators executed.

Cicero was convinced that his leadership during the Catiline conspiracy had saved the Republic, but his hasty actions earned him lifelong enemies whose power and influence were significantly greater than his own. Clodius Pulcher forced him into exile and confiscated his property, but even more problematic was that one of those whom Cicero had executed was the stepfather of Marc Antony, Caesar's most trusted lieutenant. When he returned from exile, Cicero began playing a dangerous game, juggling his allegiance between Pompey and Caesar, ultimately throwing in with Pompey as civil war seemed inevitable. He urged Pompey to march his troops north as soon as possible, and he wrote numerous letters to those in positions of authority urging them to take up arms against Caesar. Pompey, however, chose to abandon Italy rather than engage Caesar, sailing for Greece with his troops and several senators, including Cato and Brutus. After weeks of indecisiveness, Cicero finally left Italy to join Pompey. This proved to be a bad move, for not long afterwards Caesar soundly defeated Pompey at Pharsalus. Cicero had no other option than to return to Italy and hope that he could count on Caesar's famous willingness to pardon those who had opposed him.

The fact that Cicero survived the turmoil and chaos of the war is testimony to his rhetorical and political skills, but what seems clear is that he was unaware of the extent to which he had been under Caesar's protection throughout the conflict. Caesar's assassination brought this protection to an end, and Cicero made matters worse for himself by expressing his delight in the murder. A month after the assassination, Cicero (1978) wrote to his friend Atticus that "Nothing so far gives me pleasure except the Ides of March" (14.6.1). Meanwhile, Marc Antony took control of Rome. For years he had been forced to suppress his anger and bitterness over Cicero's execution of his stepfather; these feelings were intensified by the knowledge that the orator had witnessed the assassination of Caesar and had done nothing to help the man who had treated him with kindness and generosity. He also learned that immediately after the murder, Brutus had raised his bloody dagger in salute to Cicero, signifying implicit, if not explicit, culpability made even more damning when Cicero pressed hard for granting general amnesty to the assassins.[1]

By the summer of 43 BC, Antony and Octavian had joined forces with the aim of stabilizing the Republic and bringing to justice all those involved in killing Caesar. A proscription list was drawn up, and Antony insisted that Cicero be included. Terrified, Cicero hoped to flee to Athens, but he dithered, finally taking to the roads only when it was too late. The executioners found him being carried in a litter, and as Plutarch (1958) reported: "He was all covered with dust; his hair was long and disordered, and his face was pinched and wasted with his anxieties – so that most of those who stood by covered their faces while Herennius was killing him. His throat was cut as he stretched his neck out from the litter" (p. 48).

Although he was a complex and conflicted person, most readers today limit their consideration of Cicero either to rhetoric and oratory or to Roman history, often ignoring his role in shaping Western thinking and politics through his influence on such

---

[1] The hostility between Antony and Cicero was intense. Appian reported that Cicero also tried to have Antony executed without trial (*The Civil Wars*, 3.50–70). Even if all the other offenses were erased, this attempt would have sealed Cicero's fate. Given the personal politics of Rome, Cicero's action signaled a struggle to the death.

figures as Machiavelli, Grotius, Hobbes, and Locke. Wood (1988) provided one of the more insightful analyses of Cicero's political thoughts and concluded that the orator's views were generally humane, in spite of his intractable adherence to aristocratic values. The problem for modern readers is twofold. As Wood noted:

> Cicero, the sworn enemy of popular rule, the implacable foe of social amelioration and economic reform, a leader of the Roman landed oligarchy who decried any drift toward arithmetical equality or social parity, could hardly have attracted the intellectual spokesmen of the ... [modern era's] impetus for fundamental change. (p. 6)

The social and political ideals expressed in Cicero's works are inconsistent with modern sentiments, which focus on human rights, social equity, and social justice. Consequently, his status has declined significantly over the last 250 years.

In addition, today we live in a world of emotive images and signs where words are often deemed intrusive, making Cicero's speeches seem overblown and tedious in their verbosity. Given our modern sensibilities, it is important to remember that Cicero, following the Aristotelian tradition, shaped his speeches to match his audiences, for whom less was rarely accepted as more. And recovering the full effect of Cicero's speeches from their textual form borders on the impossible. Gotoff (1993) pointedly reminded us that courtroom drama was Cicero's trademark and that the texts of his speeches resist efforts to recreate that aspect of his craft. Certainly, part of the difficulty modern readers face when studying Cicero is the tendency to apply Plato's perspective more than Aristotle's. Doing so makes Cicero seem to be the very personification of the rhetorical pandering and deceit that Plato ridiculed, and as such a representative of the worst sort of rhetoric and oratory. A more seasoned perspective, however, locates Cicero and his work in the context of his time, and it recognizes that his many weaknesses and inconsistencies were all too human.

De Inventione

Cicero wrote *De Inventione* in his youth, although the exact date of composition is uncertain, with most scholars suggesting that it was produced sometime between 88 and 81 BC The date is important because Cicero refers to the views of Aristotle in Book I (identifying rhetoric as a part of politics, for example) and asserts in the preface to Book II that he has extracted the best ideas from all the most significant rhetoricians of the past. Various scholars, such as Kennedy (1994), have expressed doubt that the young Cicero had much access to what at the time would have been ancient works, especially Aristotle's *Art of Rhetoric*, and the speculation is that he drew on some unknown secondary work or on the lectures of his Greek teachers. We should remember, however, that Sulla returned from Greece with Aristotle's entire library in 84 BC. Given Cicero's connections, he certainly could have had access to this collection, provided that he actually completed the work after Sulla's return. A very feasible date, therefore, would be 83 BC.

In *De Oratore*, Cicero dismissed *De Inventione* as "sketchy and immature," and in comparison to the major expositions he produced later – *De Oratore*, *Brutus*, and *Orator* – it is. Nevertheless, the overall quality of the work gives us a fairly good sense of his intelligence and learning at an early age. We also need to consider that *De Inventione* was among the first (if not the first) major rhetorical treatises in Latin. Considering the censors' objection to using Latin in schools of rhetoric, Cicero's decision to write in his native language rather than in Greek seems to reflect either the bold confidence of youth or a perspicacity beyond his years.

The original plan appears to have been to produce a complete *technê* in four or five books, but we have only the first two. It is uncertain whether he completed the plan and the last books were lost or whether he was unable to finish the task. Book I examines the nature of eloquence and the materials, scope, and parts of rhetoric. It then offers a discussion of exordia and how to win the support of an audience; narration and how to make it both clear and plausible; arrangement; confirmation, including a consideration of syllogisms; refutations; and conclusions. Book II offers an extended discussion of forensic rhetoric and *stasis,* examining *stasis* of fact, definition, procedure, and quality. This discussion is followed by sections on written documents, deliberation, and epideixis.

As the above outline suggests, *De Inventione* owes much to Greek rhetoric, particularly the work of Aristotle, Isocrates, and Hermagoras (see Solmsen, 1938, 1941). Cicero's definition of "invention," for example, as the "discovery of valid or seemingly valid arguments to render one's cause probable" (I.vii) bears a striking resemblance to Aristotle's definition of rhetoric as a tool for discovering "in each case the existing means of persuasion" with the aim of securing a judgment. Cicero explored the notion of eloquence in all of his rhetorical works, and in *De Inventione* he distinguished it from argumentative skill by limiting it to diction and delivery. But we also see the influence of Attic philosophy, especially in Book I, which begins with a reflective introduction on the nature of societies and rhetoric, concluding with what became a famous statement on eloquence:

Ac me quidem diu cogitantem ratio ipsa in hanc potissimum sententiam ducit, ut existimem sapientiam sine eloquentia parum prodesse civitatibus, eloquentiam vero sine sapientia nimium obesse plerumque, prodesse numquam.	After long consideration, reason itself leads me to think that wisdom without eloquence has been of little benefit to states, but eloquence without wisdom has for the most part been a great hindrance and never an advantage. (I.1)

The work cannot be characterized as a slavish duplication of the Aristotelian framework, however. Cicero deviated from Aristotle in several respects, probably owing to the influence of Hellenistic rhetoricians such as Hermagoras. Leff (1996) pointed out, for example, that Cicero's presentation of topoi in *De Inventione* differs significantly from Aristotle's. Whereas in *Rhetoric* topoi are associated with enthymemes and lead to conclusions, in *De Inventione* they "operate as a process of discovery, ... invented and completed before dealing with the case at hand" (p. 448).

De Inventione was superseded by Cicero's later works on rhetoric, but for about 1,500 years it was the most popular of his treatises, shaping rhetoric and oratory well into the Renaissance. The explanation lies in the nature of the work and the ways in which it differs from those that followed. As a handbook, it generally offers a straightforward, easily accessible outline that provides useful information to students of the art. *De Oratore, Brutus,* and *Orator,* on the other hand, are dialogues in the Platonic tradition and have frequent digressions that make them impossible to use as a ready resource or guide. In addition, they are significantly more philosophical; and while Cicero's musings are interesting, particularly from a historical perspective, they are not entirely relevant to students preparing to plead cases in the courts. The irony here is significant, considering that Cicero insisted that the study of philosophy was central to the education of the ideal orator.

The excerpt presented here comes from Book I of *De Inventione* and introduces several of the fundamental technical issues associated with rhetoric and oratory.

Reading 31

De Inventione (On Invention)

De Inventione (On Invention) (excerpt), pp. 13, 15, 17, 19, 21, 23, 25, 27, 29, 31, 33 reprinted by permission of the publishers and Trustees of the Loeb Classical Library from *Cicero*, Volume II, Loeb Classical Library Volume 386, translated by H.M. Hubbell (Cambridge, MA: Harvard University Press, 1949). © 1949 by the President and Fellows of Harvard College. The Loeb Classical Library ® is a registered trademark of the President and Fellows of Harvard College

But before I speak of the rules of oratory I think I should say something about the nature of the art itself, about its function, its end, its materials, and its divisions. For if these are understood the mind of each reader will be able more easily and readily to grasp the outline and method of the subject.

6   V. There is a scientific system of politics which includes many important departments. One of these departments – a large and important one – is eloquence based on the rules of art, which they call rhetoric. For I do not agree with those who think that political science has no need of eloquence, and I violently disagree with those who think that it is wholly comprehended in the power and skill of the rhetorician. Therefore we will classify oratorical ability as a part of political science. The function of eloquence seems to be to speak in a manner suited to persuade an audience, the end is to persuade by speech. There is this difference between function and end : in the case of the function we consider what should be done, in the case of the end what result should be produced. For example, we say that the function of the physician is to treat the patient in a manner suited to heal him, the end is to heal by treatment. So in the case of the orator we may understand what is meant by function and end when we call what he ought to do the function, and the purpose for which he ought to do it, the end.

7   By the material of the art I mean that with which the art as a whole and the power produced by the art are concerned. For example, we say the material of medicine is diseases and wounds because medicine is wholly concerned with these; in the same way we call the material of the art of rhetoric those subjects with which the art and power of oratory are concerned. However, some have thought that there are more and some less of these subjects. To cite one example, Gorgias of Leontini, almost the earliest teacher of oratory, held that the orator could speak better than anyone else on all subjects. Apparently he assigned to the profession a vast – and in fact infinite – material. Aristotle, on the other hand, who did much to improve and adorn this art, thought that the function of the orator was concerned with three classes of subjects, the epideictic, the deliberative, and the judicial. The epideictic is devoted to the praise or censure of a particular individual; the deliberative is at home in a political debate and involves the expression of an opinion; the judicial is at home in a court of law and involves accusation and defence or a claim and counter-plea. According to my opinion, at least, the art and faculty of the orator must be thought of as concerned with this threefold material.

VI. For Hermagoras indeed does not seem to 8 notice what he says or understand what he promises when he divides the material of the orator into "special cases" and "general questions," and defines "special cases" as a matter involving a controversy conducted by a speech with the introduction of definite individuals (this we too say is assigned to the orator, for we give him the three parts which we have already mentioned: judicial, deliberative, epideictic).

"General question" he defines as a matter involving a controversy conducted by a speech without the introduction of definite individuals, as for example, "Is there any good except honour?" "Can the senses be trusted?" "What is the shape of the world?" "How large is the sun?" I think that everyone understands perfectly that these questions are far removed from the business of an orator. It seems the height of folly to assign to an orator as if they were trifles these subjects in which we know that the sublime genius of philosophers has spent so much labour.

But if Hermagoras had possessed great skill in dealing with these subjects – a skill acquired by study and training – he would seem to have laid down a false principle about the profession of the orator through confidence in his own knowledge, and to have described not what the art, but what he himself could accomplish. But as a matter of fact the man's ability is such that one will more readily deny him the power of rhetoric than grant him acquaintance with philosophy. Not that I think the text-book which he published is very faulty, for he seems to have done well enough at arranging topics which he had chosen with ingenuity and care from earlier authors, and to have added something new himself; but for an orator it is a very slight thing to talk about his art, as he has done; by far the most important thing is to speak in accordance with the principles of his art, which we all see he was wholly incapable of doing.

9   VII. Therefore the material of the art of rhetoric seems to me to be that which we said Aristotle approved. The parts of it, as most authorities have stated, are Invention, Arrangement, Expression, Memory, Delivery. Invention is the discovery of valid or seemingly valid arguments to render one's cause plausible. Arrangement is the distribution of arguments thus discovered in the proper order. Expression is the fitting of the proper language to the invented matter. Memory is the firm mental grasp of matter and words. Delivery is the control of voice and body in a manner suitable to the dignity of the subject matter and the style.

Now that these terms have been defined briefly we shall postpone to another time the discussion in which we could explain the nature, the end and the function of this art; for they require lengthy treatment and are not so intimately connected with the description of the art and the transmission of rules. But we think that one who is to write a text-book of rhetoric ought to write about the other two subjects, the material of the art and its divisions. And I think I should treat material and divisions together. Therefore let us consider what the character of invention should be; this is the most important of all the divisions, and above all is used in every kind of pleading.

10   VIII. Every subject which contains in itself a controversy to be resolved by speech and debate involves a question about a fact, or about a definition, or about the nature of an act, or about legal processes. This question, then, from which the whole case arises, is called *constitutio* or the "issue." The "issue" is the first conflict of pleas which arises from the defence or answer to our accusation, in this way: "You did it"; "I did not do it," or "I was justified in doing it." When the dispute is about a fact, the issue is said to be conjectural (*coniecturalis*), because the plea is supported by conjectures or inferences. When the issue is about a definition, it is called the definitional issue, because the force of the term must be defined in words. When, however, the nature of the act is examined, the issue is said to be qualitative, because the controversy concerns the value of the act and its class or quality. But when the case depends on the circumstance that it appears that the right person does not bring the suit, or that he brings it against the wrong person, or before the wrong tribunal, or at a wrong time, under the wrong statute, or the wrong charge, or with a wrong penalty, the issue is called translative because the action seems to require a transfer to another court or alteration in the form of pleading. There will always be one of these issues applicable to every kind of case; for where none applies, there can be no controversy. Therefore it is not fitting to regard it as a case at all.

As to the dispute about a fact, this can be   11 assigned to any time. For the question can be "What has been done?" *e.g.* "Did Ulysses kill Ajax?" and "What is being done?," *e.g.* "Are the Fregellans friendly to the Roman people?," and what is going to occur, *e.g.* "If we leave Carthage untouched, will any harm come to the Roman state?"

The controversy about a definition arises when there is agreement as to the fact and the question is by what word that which has been done is to be described. In this case there must be a dispute about the definition, because there is no agreement about the essential point, not because the fact is not certain, but because the deed appears differently to different people, and for that reason different people describe it in different terms. Therefore, in cases of this kind the matter must be defined in words and briefly described. For example, if a sacred article is purloined from a private house, is the act to be adjudged theft or sacrilege? For when this question is asked, it will be necessary to define both theft and sacrilege, and to show by one's own description that the act in dispute should be called by a different name from that used by the opponents.

IX. There is a controversy about the nature or   12 character of an act when there is both agreement as to what has been done and certainty as to how the act should be defined, but there is a question nevertheless about how important it is or of what kind, or in general about its quality, *e.g.* was it just or unjust, profitable or unprofitable? It includes all such cases in which there is a question about the quality of an act without any controversy about definition. Hermagoras divided this genus into four species: deliberative, epideictic, equitable, and legal. I think I ought to criticize this error of his – no inconsiderable error as I think – but briefly lest if we pass it by in silence we be thought to have failed to follow him without good reason, or if we linger on the point too long, we seem to have hindered and delayed the presentation of the rules to be laid down in the rest of the book.

If deliberative and epideictic are genera of argument they cannot rightly be thought to be species of any one genus of argument. For the same thing can be genus in relation to one thing and species in relation to another, but cannot be both genus and species in relation to the same thing. Moreover the deliberative and epideictic are genera of arguments. For either there is no classification of arguments or there are only forensic arguments, or there are three genera, forensic, epideictic, and deliberative. To say that there is no classification of arguments when he says that there are many and gives rules for them, is madness. How can there be only one genus – the forensic – when deliberative and epideictic are not similar to each other and are far different from the forensic kind and each has its own end to which it may be referred? It follows, therefore, that there are, in all, three genera of arguments. Deliberative and epideictic cannot rightly be regarded as species of any kind of argument. He was wrong then, in saying that they are species of the qualitative issue.

13   X. Wherefore if they cannot rightly be regarded as species of a genus of argument, there will be much less justification for regarding them as sub-heads of a species of argument. But the "issue" is nothing but a sub-head of argument. For the argument is not subsumed under the issue but the issue is subsumed under the argument. But epideictic and deliberative cannot rightly be regarded as species of a genus of argument, because they are themselves the genera of argument; there will be much less justification for regarding them as sub-heads of this species which is here described. In the second place, if the issue, either entire or any part of it, is an answer to an accusation, then that which is not an answer to an accusation cannot be either an issue or a sub-head of an issue. But if what is not an answer to an accusation is neither an issue or [sic] a sub-head of an issue,

deliberative and epideictic speeches are not an issue or a sub-head of an issue. If, then, the issue, either entire or any part of it, is the answer to an accusation, deliberative and epideictic speeches cannot be either an issue or a sub-head of an issue. But he himself is of the opinion that the issue is the answer to an accusation. He ought, therefore, to be of the opinion that epideictic and deliberative speeches are not the issue or a sub-head of the issue. And he will be pressed by the same argument whether he defines issue as the first assertion of his cause by the accuser or the first plea of the defendant. For all the same difficulties will attend him.

Furthermore a conjectural argument cannot at 14 one and the same time and from the same point of view and under the same system of classification be both conjectural and definitive, nor can a definitive argument be at one and the same time and from the same point of view and under the same system of classification both definitive and translative. And, to put it generally, no issue or sub-head of an issue can have its own scope and also include the scope of another issue, because each one is studied directly by itself and in its own nature, and if another is added, the number of issues is doubled but the scope of any one issue is not increased. But a deliberative argument generally includes at one and the same time and from the same point of view and under the same system of classification an issue, or *constitutio*, the conjectural, qualitative, definitional, or translative, either any one of these or at times more than one. Therefore it is not itself an issue or a sub-head of an issue. The same thing is wont to occur in the demonstrative (or epideictic) speech. These, then, as we said before, are to be regarded as the genera of oratory and not as sub-heads under any issue.

XI. Therefore this issue, which we call the qualitative issue, seems to us to have two subdivisions, equitable and legal. The equitable is that in which there is a question about the nature of justice and right or the reasonableness of reward or punishment. The legal is that in which we examine what the law is according to the custom of the community and according to justice: at Rome the jurisconsults are thought to be in charge of the study of this subject. The equitable is itself divided into 15 two parts, the absolute and the assumptive. The absolute is that which contains in itself the question of right and wrong done. The assumptive is that which of itself provides no basis for a counter plea, but seeks some defence from extraneous circumstances. It has four divisions, *concessio* (confession and avoidance), *remotio criminis* (shifting the charge), *relatio criminis* (retort of the accusation), and *comparatio* (comparison). Confession and avoidance is used when the accused does not defend the deed but asks for pardon. This is divided into two parts: *purgatio* and *deprecatio*. It is *purgatio* when the deed is acknowledged but *intent* is denied; it has three parts, ignorance, accident, necessity. *Deprecatio* is used when the defendant acknowledges that he has given offence and has done so intentionally, and still asks to be forgiven; this can very rarely occur. It is shifting of the charge when the defendant tries to shift to another the charge brought against himself by transferring to another either the act or the intent or the power to perform the act. This can be done in two ways: either the cause or the act itself is attributed to another. The cause is attributed when the deed is said to have been done because of the power and authority of another; the deed is transferred when it is alleged that another should have done it or could have done it. The retort of the charge is used when the defendant claims that the deed was done lawfully because some one had first illegally provoked him. Comparison is used when it is argued that some other action was lawful and advantageous, and then it is pleaded that the misdemeanour which is charged was committed in order to make possible this advantageous act.

In the fourth issue which we call the translative 16 there is a controversy when the question arises as to who ought to bring the action or against whom, or in what manner or before what court or under what law or at what time, and in general when there is some argument about changing or invalidating the form of procedure. Hermagoras is thought to be the inventor of this issue, not that orators did not use it before his day – many did use it frequently – but because earlier writers of text-books did not notice it nor include it with the issues. Since his invention of the term many have found fault with it, not misled by ignorance, I think, for the case is perfectly plain, so much as they have been kept from adopting it by a spirit of envy and desire to disparage a rival.

De Oratore

Cicero completed *De Oratore* in 55 BC, when he was middle-aged and had the benefit of his decades as an orator in the Senate, the courts, and the assemblies. Experience had taught him that memorization of rules, taxonomies, and *topoi*, and mastery of *stasis* theory's intricacies provided only limited preparation for the realities an orator faced in the Forum. In this respect, *De Oratore* is in the Isocratean tradition, for it criticizes the contemporary system of rhetorical instruction and offers a more personal and pragmatic approach, one that combines speaking and writing and that advocates a broad education in numerous subjects, especially philosophy. Cicero had succumbed to the allure of philosophy as a teenager under the tutelage of Philo of Larissa, and its appeal had grown stronger as he aged. The infusion of philosophy in a work on rhetoric thus conformed to his personal inclination, but it was something of a novelty at the time. Romans generally were averse to philosophy, considering it Greek and effeminate, and the schools of rhetoric during this period gave the subject little attention. We may suspect, in addition, that the discussions of philosophy in *De Oratore* were motivated by Cicero's desire to display his knowledge and by his desire to pay homage to a tradition that he greatly admired. The decision to set the work as a Platonic dialogue tends to support the latter perspective.

De Oratore ostensibly is addressed to Cicero's brother, Quintus, in order to offer a description of those precepts of rhetoric and oratory that are not available in the schools but that can be found only in "the authority of those who have been granted the highest praise for their oratorical qualities" (I.23). It relates a fictional gathering, much like a Greek *symposium*, at Lucius Crassus' villa in Tusculum.[2] Crassus is joined by Marcus Antonius, Quintus Mucius Scaevola, Gaius Aurelius Cotta, Publius Sulpicius Rufus, Quintus Lutatius Catulus, and Gaius Julius Caesar Strabo Vopiscus. The dialogue is set in 91 BC, just before the outbreak of the Social War between Rome and her Italian allies. The primary speakers in the dialogue are Crassus and Antonius, whom Cicero generally uses to express his views.

Of all Cicero's theoretical works, *De Oratore* is generally deemed to be his master-piece – not so much for its elaboration of the techniques and theories of oratory, how-ever, as for its humane and elevated treatment of the art. Antonius, for example, states that:

> there is nothing more magnificent than the perfect orator. ... [T]here is nothing that can give a more pleasant impression either to the human ear or to the human mind. What song can be found that is sweeter than a well-measured speech? ... [T]here is no subject ... that does not belong to the orator. (II. 34)

This characteristic of the work has pleased some and upset others: Whately (1963), for example, complained that the work was unsystematic and insufficiently focused on the technical features of rhetoric and that Cicero "is perpetually drawn off from the rigid philosophical analysis of its principles into discursive declamations, always eloquent indeed, and often highly interesting, but adverse to regularity of system and frequently as unsatisfactory to the practical student as to the philosopher" (p. 7). In other words, *De Oratore* is neither fish nor fowl. This criticism should strike us as overly harsh and as failing to consider adequately the context of the work. Cicero already had dealt with technical features in *De Inventione*; moreover, there was no shortage of contemporary schools where students could study technical rhetoric. But more to the point, by middle age, Cicero had concluded that such studies were insufficient for the education of the ideal orator. Whately, it seems, wanted *De Oratore* to be a *technê*, which Cicero pur-posely chose not to produce.

The question of *De Oratore*'s theoretical substance, however, is more problematic. Cicero took up the traditional quarrel between rhetoric and philosophy, but rather than explore it in depth and consider the various issues raised by Plato, he sought to dismiss it by arguing that the quarrel is superficial. The comment by Crassus is relevant here. He notes, for example, that in *Gorgias* Plato, "while making fun of orators, ... appeared to be a supreme orator himself. It is, after all, really a fight over a mere word that has been tormenting those petty Greeks for such a long time, fonder as they are of an argu-ment than of the truth" (1.47). Cicero strove to conflate rhetoric and philosophy, claim-ing that the perfect orator is a philosopher and that the philosopher must be an orator to convey his truths.

Cicero could incorporate the philosopher's historical focus on ethics by defining ora-tory as *vir bonus dicendi peritus* – the good man speaking well – but the reality of oratory during the late Republic demanded regular ethical compromises that were contrary to this ideal. Through the character of Scaevola, Cicero raised the problem in *De Oratore*

---

[2] The Roman equivalent of the Greek *symposium* was the *convivium*, but it differed in several ways. The *sym-posium* emphasized the equality of the participants, for example, which encouraged not only more lively singing but also a freer exchange of ideas. Like Roman society, however, the *convivium* emphasized hierarchy and social distinctions, with those of higher status receiving the best food and drink and an individual couch upon which to recline, whereas those of lower status received food of poorer quality and had to recline several to a couch (D'Arms, 1990).

of making the worse appear the better argument but failed to examine it in either theoretical or practical terms. Perhaps he had not read *Gorgias* thoroughly, or perhaps the
conventional reality of the late Republic made it impossible for him to recognize that
the ethical use of rhetoric was a central philosophical issue in Plato's criticism. In any
event, his forensic speeches, such as *Pro Milone*, included here, demonstrate his willingness to fabricate and obfuscate so as to make the worse case seem the better in defense
of someone who was clearly guilty of murder. Plato without doubt would have condemned this willingness and argued that it illustrates the inherent problem of rhetoric –
a pervasive lack of ethical concern for truth and justice. The disconnect between
Cicero's theory and practice and his failure to examine it in any depth is a shortcoming
that has lead many readers to applaud the elevated rhetorical sentiments in *De Oratore*
even as they criticize the work for being both theoretically and philosophically weak.

The excerpt provided here samples each of *De Oratore*'s three books. The length of
the treatise, however, means that even a fairly substantial sampling cannot provide a
clear view of the whole work. To ameliorate this problem, May and Wisse's (2001) outline of the entire dialogue precedes the excerpt.

Reading 32

Outline of *De Oratore* (*On the Ideal Orator*)

Outline of *De Oratore* (*On the Ideal Orator*) (excerpt), translated by J.M. May and J. Wisse.

Horizontal lines indicate incisions that are signalled by Cicero either by an explicit transition to a new
subject (see, e.g., the beginning of Antonius' treatment of arrangement in 2.307) or by the insertion of
a brief conversation between some of the interlocutors (e.g., at 1.96–113a; Catulus' brief intervention
in 2.74–76 fulfills a similar function).

References such as "113a" and "113b" indicate the first and second half of the section in question.

Book 1

1.1–23	Prologue	
	1–5	Cicero's personal situation and reasons for writing *De oratore*
	6–20	The difficulty of oratory, and the exacting requirements for the ideal orator
	21–23	The work; Cicero will rely on the authority of the greatest of Roman orators
1.24–29	Setting of the dialogue, with introduction of the interlocutors of the first day (Crassus, Antonius, Scaevola, Cotta, and Sulpicius)	
1.30–34	Crassus extols eloquence: its powers, and its role in politics and the courts, in conversation, and in the development of human culture	
1.35–44	Scaevola's objections	
	35–40	In politics and in the development of culture, the role of eloquence has been restricted or even harmful
	41–44	The orator has no competence to express himself in discussions of all sorts; the requisite knowledge belongs to the philosophers

Book 2

2.41–73		Antonius on the orator's subject matter, explaining why he will concentrate on judicial and deliberative oratory (with interventions by Catulus and Caesar)
	41–43a	Divisions of oratory
	43b–50	Judicial and deliberative oratory the two essential and most difficult genres; other genres need no rules but can be dealt with on the principle of analogy; some examples
	51–64a	The same is true for historiography
	64b–73	And also for general, philosophical questions (*theses*)
2.74–76		Interlude: Catulus on practice vs. (Greek) theory
2.77–84		Antonius on art: the standard rhetorical rules
2.85–87		Antonius on natural abilities
2.88–98		Antonius on imitation and training
	88–92a	General rules for imitation
	92b–95	History shows the importance of imitation
	96–98	Imitation and training
2.99–306		INVENTION (mainly Antonius)
2.99–113		Getting to know the case (status theory)
2.114–128a		Introduction to main discussion of invention
	114–120a	General remarks on the three means of persuasion (arguments, ethos, pathos)
	120b–128a	The division of labor between Antonius and Crassus (Antonius, Crassus, Catulus)
2.128b–177		Arguments
	128b–151	Preliminaries: (128b–131) introduction; (132–138a) determining the nature of the case; (138b–145a) the technical rules here are oversystematic; (145b–151) the right approach; diligence
	152–161	The philosophical background: Aristotle (Antonius, Catulus)
	162–177	The system of abstract commonplaces
2.178–216a		The other two means for persuasion: ethos and pathos
	178–181	Introduction
	182–184	Ethos
	185–211a	Pathos: (185–188) introduction; (189–196) feeling the emotions yourself; (197–204a) an example from Antonius' practice: the Norbanus case; (204b–211a) the individual emotions
	211b–216a	Handling of ethos and pathos
2.216b–290		Excursus on wit (mainly Caesar)
	216b–234	General discussion; Caesar is persuaded to treat the subject
	235–236	Five questions; brief treatment of the first three
	237–247	The fourth question: to what extent must the humorous be employed?

3.213–227	DELIVERY (mainly Crassus)
	213–216a Introduction
	216b–219 The voice
	220 Gesture
	221–223a The face, especially the eyes
	223b–227 The universal nature of delivery; preserving and using the voice
3.228–230	Coda

Reading 33

De Oratore (On the Ideal Orator)

De Oratore (On the Ideal Orator) (excerpt), translated by J.M. May and J. Wisse.

Book 1

1–5 Prologue I: Cicero's personal situation and reasons for writing De oratore

1 Whenever my reflections and reminiscences take me back to times gone by, my dear brother Quintus, it always seems to me that the men of that era were tremendously fortunate.[3] Living in the best days of our State, and prospering in the enjoyment of high honors and the glory of their accomplishments, they could maintain a course of life that offered them the opportunity for political activity without peril, as well as the possibility for leisure with dignity. There was, in fact, a time when I believed that, once an end had come to my ceaseless work in the forum and to my concern with political campaigning, after holding all important public offices and having reached a turning point in my life,[4] I too would have almost everyone's approval for entering on a period of well-deserved rest, in which I could redirect my attention to the splendid intellectual pursuits we both love. But these hopes that I cher- 2 ished in my thoughts and plans have been foiled by the disastrous events in our community as well as by personal misfortunes of all kinds. Just when the circumstances promised, so it seemed, to be utterly peaceful and undisturbed, an enormous mass of troubles and incredibly turbulent storms arose. So, for all my hopes and prayers, I have not been granted the benefit of leisure that would allow me to pursue and revive, together with you, the arts to which we have been dedicated from boyhood. For it so happened that in my early years I witnessed the 3 very disruption of traditional order and morals; then during my consulship, I had to confront a critical conflict of universal proportion; and all my time since that consulship I have spent in trying to break the waves that, while prevented by my intervention from wreaking general destruction, have recoiled upon me personally.[5]

[3] Cicero looks back nostalgically to times of greater stability in the State, to which he contrasts the turbulent events in his own lifetime.

[4] Cicero's consulship (in 63 BC) was the capstone of his political career.

[5] Cicero refers, first, to the period of 91 to 79 BC, with the Social War, the bloody civil wars between Marius and Sulla, and the proscriptions under the latter's regime; then to the Catilinarian conspiracy of 63; and finally to the difficult political circumstances after his consulship, marked especially by his exile in 58. This exile was brought about by Cicero's enemies in the aftermath of the conspiracy of 63, partly as a reaction to the role he as consul had played in its suppression.

Nevertheless, despite this difficult situation and these constraints upon my time, I will heed the call of our studies and will devote, especially to writing, as much leisure time as I am afforded by the intrigue of my enemies, the cause of my friends, and my duty to the State. You, Quintus, urge me to do this, and I shall not fail you, for no one's authority or wish could carry more weight with me than yours. To this end, it is appropriate for me to recall something that happened long ago. Though the story is not remembered in every detail, it is, I think, particularly suited to your request, and you will learn from it the ideas of the most eloquent and illustrious men about all the principles of oratory. For as you have often told me, you would like me to publish something more polished and mature on this subject, since the sketchy and unsophisticated work that found its way out of my notebooks when I was a boy (or rather a youth)[6] is hardly worthy of my present age and of the experience I have acquired from pleading so many momentous cases. Moreover, when our discussions on occasion turn to this topic, you generally disagree with me.[7] I maintain that eloquence is founded upon the intellectual accomplishments of the most learned; you, on the other hand, believe that it has nothing to do with the refinements of education, but is, rather, one of the things that depend on natural ability and practice.[8]

6–20   Prologue II: The difficulty of oratory; the ideal orator

For my part, whenever I reflect upon the greatest and most gifted men, it always seems that the following question requires an answer: why have more people come forward to distinguish themselves in every other art than in oratory? Turn your thoughts and attention where you will, and you see a great many who excel in each kind of endeavor – not merely in the minor arts, but in those we might call the most important.[9] For instance, should anyone choose to evaluate the knowledge of illustrious men in terms of the usefulness or importance of their accomplishments, would he not grant precedence to the general over the orator? Yet there is no doubt that, even from our State alone, we could produce an almost endless list of absolutely outstanding leaders in war, but could name barely a few who have excelled in oratory. Furthermore, many have emerged who had the ability to guide and steer the State by counsel and thought – many in our own memory, more in our fathers', and even more in our ancestors' – whereas for quite a long time there were no good speakers at all, and entire generations scarcely produced even a tolerable one.

But some perhaps think that this art of oratory[10] should be compared with other pursuits, namely those involved with abstruse branches of study and with varied and extensive reading, rather than with the qualities of the general or the wisdom of the good senator. If so, let them indeed turn their attention to these kinds of arts and examine who and how many have distinguished themselves in each. In this way, they will quite easily infer how very small the number of orators is and always has been. For instance, as you of course know, the most learned consider philosophy, as the Greeks call it, to be the creator and mother of all the valuable arts; so to speak.[11] Yet even here in philosophy it is difficult to reckon how many people there have been (so notable for their abundant knowledge and for the variety and vast range of their studies!) who have not only worked as specialists in one single

---

[6] This work is Cicero's *On Invention*, written probably ca. 89 BC, when he was about seventeen.

[7] "… on occasion … generally …": the Latin is differently phrased, but this is clearly the implication.

[8] Although the well-known triad, theory, natural ability, and practice, stands in the background, Cicero here modifies it, for he replaces rhetorical theory ("art") with "the intellectual accomplishments of the most learned," and contrasts this with the other two. This modification reflects the central theme of the work.

[9] In what follows, it appears that "the most important arts" with which Cicero first compares oratory are those of war and politics. The minor arts are not mentioned again (these are probably the arts of song and swordsmanship, mentioned in 3.86–87, and others like these). Instead, oratory is also compared, in 1.8–11, with the "esoteric" arts of philosophy, mathematics, music, and grammar.

[10] The Latin phrase translated here as "this art of oratory" (*hanc dicendi rationem*) means more properly something like "practical oratory based on the understanding of its principles"; "art" in the sense of theory is certainly not meant.

[11] This was at least Posidonius' view (cf. Seneca, *Epistle* 90); but see also Cicero's own remarks in 1.186–190 on the role of dialectic in the development of an art.

area, but have embraced all that exists in their thorough investigations or their dialectical rea-
10 sonings. We all know how obscure the subjects handled by the so-called mathematicians are, and how abstruse, complex, and exact is the art with which they deal. Yet even in this area, so many geniuses have emerged that almost no one who has devoted his energies to mastering it appears to have been unsuccessful. As to the theory of music, and the study of language and literature so popular nowadays (the profession of the so-called grammarians)[12] – has anyone really dedicated himself to them without managing to acquire enough knowledge to cover the
11 complete, almost infinite range and material of those arts? I think I am justified in saying that, of all those who have been involved in the pursuit and study of the truly noble arts, the smallest contingent to emerge has been that of outstanding poets and speakers. Yet again, if you look at this group, where excellence is so very rare, and are willing to make a careful selection both from our number and from that of the Greeks, you will find that there have been far fewer good orators than good poets.
12   This fact is all the more amazing when we realize that the study of the other arts draws as a rule upon abstruse and hidden sources, whereas all the procedures of oratory lie within everyone's reach, and are concerned with everyday experience and with human nature and speech. This means that in the other arts the highest achievement is precisely that which is most remote from what the uninitiated can understand and perceive, whereas in oratory it is the worst possible fault to deviate from the ordinary mode of speaking and the gen-
13 erally accepted way of looking at things. One cannot even truly maintain that more people dedicate themselves to the other arts, or that those who do are motivated to master them because these offer more pleasure or richer hopes or greater rewards. And in this respect, I need not mention Greece, which has always aspired to the leading position in eloquence, or the famous city

of Athens, the inventor of all learning, where oratory in its highest form was both discovered and perfected, for surely even in this community of ours, no study has ever enjoyed more vigorous popularity than the study of eloquence. Once we 14 had established our authority over all nations and a stable peace had provided us with leisure,[13] almost every ambitious young man thought he should devote himself to oratory with all the energy he had. At first, it is true, they accomplished only as much as their own natural ability and reflection allowed, for they were unaware of any theory, and assumed there was no definite method of practicing or any rule of art whatsoever. But once they had heard Greek orators, had come to know Greek writings on the subject, and had called in teachers, our people were fired with a really incredible zeal for learning all these things. They were urged on by the scope, vari- 15 ety, and frequency of cases of every type, so that the theoretical knowledge that each had acquired by his own study was supplemented by constant practice, which was more effective than the precepts of all teachers. In addition, there were laid before them, just as there are now, the greatest rewards for this pursuit, in terms of influence, power, and prestige. Moreover, there are many indications that the natural ability of our people was far superior to that of all others, from every other nation.
        Considering all this, who would not rightly be 16 amazed that, in the entire history of generations, of ages, and of communities, such a slight number of orators is to be found? The truth of the matter is, however, that this faculty is something greater, and is a combination of more arts and pursuits, than is generally supposed. For, in view of the enormous number of apprentices, the rich supply of available teachers, the exceptional talents engaged, the infinite variety of cases, and the utterly magnificent rewards held out for eloquence, the only conceivable explanation of this scarcity is surely the incredible scope and difficulty of oratory. To begin with[14], one 17

---

[12] The (originally Greek) term *grammaticus* was used to describe "scientific" grammarians as well as elementary teachers of literature. The treatment of poetry was central to the activity of both groups.
[13] Beginning in 201 BC, the Romans won a series of victories in the Mediterranean and the East, defeating Carthage in the war with Hannibal (201 BC), King Philip V of Macedonia (197), Antiochus the Great, King of the Seleucid Empire in the East (the peace of 188), and Perseus (at the Battle of Pydna in 168 BC).
[14] In these two sections (17–18) Cicero sketches in bold strokes his "ideal orator"; the rest of the work will develop this picture.

must acquire knowledge of a very great number of things, for without this a ready flow of words is empty and ridiculous; the language itself has to be shaped, not only by the choice of words but by their arrangement as well; also required is a thorough acquaintance with all the emotions with which nature has endowed the human race, because in soothing or in exciting the feelings of the audience the full force of oratory and all its available means must be brought into play. In addition, it is essential to possess a certain esprit and humor, the culture that befits a gentleman,[15] and an ability to be quick and concise in rebuttal as well as attack, combined with refinement, 18 grace, and urbanity. Moreover, one must know the whole past with its storehouse of examples and precedents, nor should one fail to master statutes and the civil law. Surely I don't need to add anything about delivery? This must be regulated by the movement of the body, by gesture, by facial expression, and by inflecting and varying the voice.[16] Just how much effort this requires, even by itself, is indicated by the trivial art of actors on the stage. For although every one of them strives to regulate his facial expression, voice, and movement, we all know how really few actors there are, and have been, whom we can watch without irritation. What shall I say about that universal treasure-house, the memory? It is clear that unless this faculty is applied as a guard over the ideas and words that we have devised and thought out for our speech, all the qualities of the orator, however brilliant, will go to waste.

19   Let us stop wondering, then, why there are so few eloquent speakers, seeing that eloquence depends on the combination of all these accomplishments, any one of which alone would be a tremendous task to perfect. Let us rather encourage our children, and all others whose fame and reputation are dear to us, to appreciate fully its enormous scope. They should not rely on the precepts or the teachers or the methods of practice in general use, but be confident that they can achieve their goals by means that are of a quite different order. It is at least my opinion that it will 20 be impossible for anyone to be an orator endowed with all praiseworthy qualities, unless he has gained a knowledge of all the important subjects and arts. For it is certainly from knowledge that a speech should blossom and acquire fullness: unless the orator has firmly grasped the underlying subject matter, his speech will remain an utterly empty, yes, almost childish verbal exercise.[17]

21–23 *Prologue III: The present work*

Nevertheless, it is not my intention to lay upon 21 orators – least of all upon ours who are so intensely occupied with life at Rome – this enormous burden of having to know everything, even though the essence of the notion "orator," and the very claim of being able to speak well seem to imply a definite promise to speak distinctively and abundantly[18] about whatever subject has been put for- 22 ward. I have no doubt, however, that this would seem to most people an immense and infinite task. Moreover, I see that even the Greeks (who are amply endowed with natural ability and learning, and also with leisure time and enthusiasm for study) have already made a certain division of the arts, and have not, in their individual efforts, attempted to cover the entire field. Rather, they have set aside from the other forms of speaking that part of oratory which is involved with disputes before the courts and in deliberative assemblies, leaving only speeches of that sort for the orator. In this work, therefore, I shall not include anything more than what the highest authorities, after inquiry and much debate, have almost unanimously assigned to that form of speaking.[19] And 23

[15] Literally, "free man."

[16] All the traditional aspects of delivery.

[17] Substance, i.e., subject matter (*res*), and therefore knowledge, must be the foundation of words (*verba*); this was already indicated in 1.17 and will remain an important theme throughout the work.

[18] I.e., *ornate* and *copiose*.

[19] Cicero here, by way of concession, says that he will not focus on the (ideal) orator's ability to speak "about whatever subject has been put forward," but will restrict his scope to the two types of oratory that traditionally received most attention (viz., the judicial and deliberative genres). This concession, however, will be seen to be temporary, not so much because Antonius in Book 2 adds a brief discussion of the third genre (that of praise and blame: 2.341–349), but because the ideal of universal eloquence will receive much stress. It will be discussed in Book 1, and be emphasized again in Book 3.

in doing so, I shall not draw upon the elementary schooling that we received long ago as boys, and present some string of precepts. Instead, I will write about the things that, as I was once told, were the subject of a discussion between our most eloquent speakers, men of the highest possible reputation. Not that I despise what the Greek experts and teachers of oratory have left behind, but those things are evident and readily accessible to all, and could not, by any exposition of mine, either be set out with more distinction or be described more clearly. I suppose you will forgive me, my dear brother,[20] if I do not rely on the Greeks, but rather on the authority of those who have been granted the highest praise for their oratorical qualities by our own countrymen.

24–29 *Setting of the dialogue*

24   Well then, I remember being told that, when the consul Philippus was ever more fiercely attacking the policy of our leading statesmen, and when the power of Drusus in his tribunate, an office he had undertaken to support the Senate's authority, already seemed weakened to the point of collapse, Lucius Crassus retired during the Roman Games to his villa at Tusculum as if to reinvigorate himself.[21] Quintus Mucius Scaevola, the father of his late wife,[22] joined him there, along with Marcus Antonius, who was an ally of Crassus in his political objectives and united to him in closest friendship. Crassus had
25 also brought with him from Rome two young men, both very good friends of Drusus, in whom their elders then placed high hopes for the preservation of their political standing: Gaius Cotta, who was at that time a candidate for the tribuneship of the plebs, and Publius Sulpicius, who was

thought likely to stand for the same office in the 26 following year. On the first day they talked for a long time, until sunset, about the present crisis and the political situation in general – the actual reason they had assembled. And in this conversation, Cotta used to tell me, these three former consuls[23] discussed developments they found deplorable in such inspired fashion, that no evil subsequently fell upon our community that they had not seen hanging over it, even at that time. Once this whole conversation had been brought 27 to an end, however, Crassus displayed such geniality that, after they had taken their bath and reclined for dinner, all the gloom of the previous day's discussion was driven away; his pleasantness and conversational charm were such, that while their day together had been spent in the atmosphere of the Senate House, their dinner seemed to be quite appropriate for a Tusculan villa. On the next day, Cotta reported, when the older 28 members of the party had taken enough rest, they all gathered in the garden-walk. Then, after they had completed two or three turns, Scaevola said: "Say, Crassus, why don't we follow the example of Socrates as he appears in Plato's *Phaedrus*? For your plane tree here suggests this to me, by spreading its broad boughs to shade this place exactly like that other plane tree whose shade Socrates sought – which seems to me to have grown not so much because of that little stream described there as owing to Plato's own words.[24] But what Socrates did, despite his extremely tough feet, can more justifiably be conceded to mine: he threw himself on the grass and there uttered the famous words that the philosophers say were spoken in inspired fashion."[25]

"But certainly we can make things even more 29 comfortable," Crassus replied. He called for

---

[20] Cicero speaks tongue in cheek; we already know from 1.5 that Quintus prefers practice to theory. Cf. also 2.10, where Marcus reveals his brother's dislike for systematic rhetorical handbooks.

[21] Place and dramatic date of the dialogue are thus established: Philippus was consul in 91 BC and the *Ludi Romani*, the "Roman Games," were given annually, and in this period from the 4th or 5th until the 18th of September. The crisis alluded to was especially connected with the demands for Roman citizenship by Rome's Italian Allies [sic], and was soon to erupt into the War [sic] with the Allies [sic]. The group around Crassus consisted of (probably moderate) conservatives, who believed in the supremacy of the Senate as a political body, and who were trying to solve the crisis by peaceful means. The prologue to Book 3 (3.2–5) provides a dramatic description of the immediate sequel, the clash between Philippus and Crassus in the Senate.

[22] Crassus had been married to Scaevola's daughter, who apparently had since died.

[23] I.e., Crassus, Antonius, and Scaevola.

[24] Cicero alludes to the literary and fictional nature of Plato's plane tree, as he does at the beginning of *On the Laws*. The scene, including the plane tree and the grass, is described by Plato, *Phaedrus* 229 A–230 C.

[25] Socrates always went barefoot (see, e.g., *Phaedrus* 229 A). "The philosophers" possibly refers to Plato alone.

cushions and they all sat down on the benches that were under the plane tree. Then, as Cotta used to tell me, to relieve the minds of all from the tension of the conversation on the day before, Crassus initiated a discussion about the pursuit of oratory.

30–34   *Crassus extols eloquence*

30   He began by saying that there seemed to be no need for him to encourage Sulpicius and Cotta, but rather to praise both of them for having already developed such oratorical skill that they were not only considered the best of their own generation, but were even challenging comparison with their seniors.[26] "Actually," he continued, "I think nothing is more admirable than being able, through speech, to have a hold on human minds, to win over their inclinations, to drive them at will in one direction, and to draw them at will from another. It is this ability, more than anything else, that has ever flourished, ever reigned supreme in every free nation and especially in

31   quiet and peaceful communities. What could be so wonderful as when out of an infinite crowd one human being emerges who – alone or with very few others – is able to use with effect the faculty that is a natural gift to all? Or what is so pleasing to the mind and to the ear as speech distinguished and refined by wise thoughts and impressive words? Or what so powerful and so splendid as when a single man's speech reverses popular upheavals, the scruples of jurors, or the

32   authority of the Senate? Again, what is so regal, so generous, so magnanimous, as lending aid to those in distress,[27] raising up the afflicted, offering people safety, freeing them from dangers, saving them from exile? At the same time, what is so vital as always having the weapons available with which you can shield yourself and challenge the wicked or take revenge when provoked? But really, let us not always be preoccupied with the forum, with the court-benches, the *rostra*,[28] and the Senate House: if we consider our leisure time, what can be more pleasant or more properly human than to be able to engage in elegant conversation and show oneself a stranger to no subject? For the one thing that most especially sets us above animals is that we converse with one another, and that we can express our thoughts through speech. Who, then, would not rightly 33 admire this ability, and would not think that he should take the greatest pains in order to surpass other human beings in the very thing which especially makes humans themselves superior to beasts? But let us now turn to what is surely the most important point of all: what other force could have gathered the scattered members of the human race into one place, or could have led them away from a savage existence in the wilderness to this truly human, communal way of life, or, once communities had been founded, could have established laws, judicial procedures, and legal arrangements?[29] And to avoid enumerating 34 still more points (they are actually almost numberless), let me summarize everything in a few words: I assert that the leadership and wisdom of the perfect orator provide the chief basis, not only for his own dignity, but also for the safety of countless individuals and of the State at large. Therefore, young men, continue your present efforts and devote all your energies to the pursuit you are following, so that you can bring honor to yourselves, service to your friends, and benefit to the State."

---

[26] The contemporaries of Sulpicius and Cotta included Quintus Varius, Gnaeus Pomponius, Gaius Curio, Lucius Fufius, Marcus Drusus, and Publius Antistius; after Sulpicius and Cotta, Cicero ranked Pomponius a distant third, although some preferred Curio (see *Brutus* 201 ff.). Their seniors would include, in addition to Antonius and Crassus, Lucius Philippus, Lucius Gellius, Decimus Brutus, Julius Caesar Strabo, Gnaeus Octavius (cf. *Brutus* 173 ff.).

[27] The Latin word (*supplices*) is a general word for "suppliants," "people in distress"; among others, it is used to refer to people who are on trial.

[28] The platform in the Roman Forum from which speakers addressed the people, adorned with the beaks or rams of ships (*rostra*) captured during the battle of Antium in 338 BC.

[29] The establishment of human civilization was a so-called topos, i.e., a subject that could be used in many different ways, according to the inclinations and ideas of an author (see, e.g., *On Invention* 1.1–5). Cicero's contemporary readers will have recognized that Crassus, by claiming eloquence as the force behind the civilizing process, emphatically opposes the view of the philosophers, who claimed that role for philosophy. Note, however, that Crassus claims the role for eloquence, and not for the theoretical discipline of rhetoric. Thus, Cicero's characteristic middle position in the struggle between philosophers and rhetoricians is immediately made clear.

35–40   Scaevola objects: the role of eloquence

35   Then Scaevola, in his usual gracious manner, said, "I agree with Crassus on almost all points, for I don't want to depreciate either the skill or the glory of my father-in-law, Gaius Laelius, or of my son-in-law here. But Crassus, I'm afraid you mentioned two points that I cannot grant you: first, that communities were initially founded and also often preserved by orators; and secondly, that leaving aside the forum with its public meetings, courts, and Senate, the orator is perfectly
36 accomplished in every kind of refined conversation which is so characteristic of human culture. Who would grant you that in the beginning the human race, scattered throughout mountains and forests, went to live in the protection of city walls because it was soothed by the words of skilled speakers, not because it was driven by the counsels of wise men? Or that the other useful institutions involved in the foundation or preservation of communities were indeed established by the distinguished words of skilled speakers rather than the wisdom of men of resolute
37 action? Do you really believe that when Romulus gathered his shepherds and refugees, or established the right to intermarry with the Sabines, or checked the violence of his neighbors, he did this by means of eloquence and not by the singular wisdom of his counsels? What about Numa Pompilius, or Servius Tullius, or the rest of the kings, who made many outstanding contributions to the organization of the State – do you find even a trace of eloquence in them? And after the kings had been expelled (and it is clear that even this expulsion was effected by the mind of

Lucius Brutus, not by his tongue),[30] don't we see that all subsequent accomplishments were the result of an abundance of counsel accompanied by a complete absence of words? Indeed, if I wanted, I could actually give you examples 38 from our own community as well as from others to show that men of supreme eloquence have more often damaged their states than they have supported them. But let me pass over the rest, and only mention Tiberius and Gaius Gracchus. I think that of all the men I have heard, excepting you and Antonius, they were the most eloquent. Their father, who possessed wisdom and authority, but was by no means eloquent, proved to be the salvation of the State on many occasions, and particularly when he was censor. It was not by any carefully prepared flow of words, but by a nod and a single word, that he restricted registration of the freedmen into the urban tribes[31]; had he not done this, the State, which we are now barely managing to preserve, would have ceased to exist long ago. His sons, on the other hand, were accomplished speakers and equipped for speaking with all the instruments that talent and instruction can offer. But while the community they took over was in a most flourishing condition thanks to their father's counsel and their grandfather's arms,[32] they shattered the State by what you maintain is a splendid guide of commu- 39 nities, by eloquence.[33] What about our ancient laws and ancestral tradition? What about the auspices over which both of us, Crassus, preside to the great benefit of the State?[34] What about our religious customs and ceremonies? And what about the civil law, in which our family has already been engaged for a long time without any reputation for eloquence? Were these things

---

[30] According to tradition, Rome was governed by kings from its foundation by Romulus in 753 BC. The last king, Tarquin the Proud, ruled like a tyrant and was expelled by Lucius Junius Brutus in 509. At his expulsion, the magistracy of the consulship was created, and the highest authority in the State was given to the two annually elected consuls.

[31] Tiberius Sempronius Gracchus was censor in 169–168 BC; in 168 he instituted a measure that (with some exceptions) restricted the registration of freedmen (i.e., of slaves set free by their masters) as citizens to the four urban tribes. The details are obscure, but it seems that from then on, this rule was followed, though several attempts were made to alter the arrangement. Since there were 35 tribes, and voting was conducted tribe by tribe, the measure served to limit the political influence of these ex-slaves (many of whom were of non-Roman origin).

[32] Their mother Cornelia was the daughter of Scipio Africanus Maior, who defeated Hannibal in 202 BC.

[33] During their tribunates in 133 and 123–122 BC respectively, Tiberius and Gaius Gracchus initiated many measures that most of their fellow aristocrats regarded as subversive, such as "agrarian laws" that proposed redistribution of land.

[34] Scaevola and Crassus were both members of the College of Augurs, and as such took the "auspices," signs of the will of the gods interpreted from the flight of birds, thunder and lightning, etc.

invented or mastered or even handled at all by
40 your crowd of orators? I well remember that
Servius Galba, a brilliant speaker, and Marcus
Aemilius Porcina, and Gaius Carbo, the man
whom you struck down when you were young,
were all ignorant of our statutes, at a loss about
our ancestral customs, and knew nothing of the
civil law. And as for your own generation, you are
an exception, Crassus (and you have learned civil
law from us owing to your own dedication, rather
than because it is one of the tasks required of an
accomplished speaker); but your contemporaries
are so ignorant of the civil law that it sometimes
makes me blush.

41–44   Scaevola continues: the orator compared with the philosophers

41 "And as to the territory you appropriated at the
end of your statement,[35] as if by right, declaring
that the orator has the ability to express himself
with all fullness in every discussion, whatever
the subject of the conversation might be – were
we not here in your own domain, I would not
have put up with that. I would have dictated the
legal formula to many who would contend with
you in court for an injunction from the praetor,
or who would summon you from court to
engage in a struggle for ownership, because you
42 had encroached so recklessly upon the possessions of others.[36] To begin with, all the
Pythagoreans would call you into court, and the
followers of Democritus and the rest of the
natural philosophers would legitimately seek
reparation, men who are all distinguished and
impressive speakers and with whom you could
not contend successfully. The troupes of the
other philosophers besides, starting right with

the ultimate source of them all, Socrates, would
press you hard. They would prove that you have
learned nothing about the good in life, about
the evil, about the emotions, about human
character, about the conduct of life; that you
have examined nothing about these things, that
you know nothing about them at all. And after
this collective attack, the individual schools 43
would bring suit against you. The Academy
would assail you, and would force you, whatever you had asserted, to deny it again.[37]
Certainly our Stoics would hold you ensnared in
the nets of their debating and questioning. And
the Peripatetic philosophers would succeed in
proving that even these things you assume to be
the exclusive property of orators, the tools and
ornaments of speaking, should actually be
obtained from them; and they would demonstrate that Aristotle and Theophrastus have
written not only better, but even much more on
such topics than all the teachers of rhetoric put 44
together. And I won't even mention the mathematicians, the grammarians, and the music
theorists: with their fields, that oratorical faculty of yours hasn't even the slightest thing in
common. So I don't think, Crassus, you should
make so many extravagant claims. The accomplishment you can guarantee[38] is great enough:
that in court, the case you are pleading, whatever it is, will appear the stronger and more
plausible; that in public meetings and when
declaring your opinion in the Senate, your
speech will have the most power to persuade;
finally, that you appear to intelligent listeners to
speak skillfully, to ignorant ones truthfully as
well. If you are able to do any more than this, I
will reckon that you have this capability not as
an orator, but as Crassus, and that you owe it to
your own special faculty, not to that common to
all orators."

[35] Actually Crassus made this point in 1.32, *before* the argument that Scaevola addresses in 1.36–40.

[36] In these sections, Scaevola treats Crassus' description of an orator's abilities as an unlawful encroachment upon other people's territory, and employs the vocabulary of the law. As jurisconsult he threatens to instruct a mob of clients on the legal formula necessary for either of the two procedures mentioned. In the first, they would try to obtain a praetor's injunction (*interdictum*) against Crassus, an order that secured possession of the disputed property. The second procedure, *conserere manum*, translated here as "struggle for ownership," was the formal challenge over the ownership of an object. Originally the parties engaged in a conventional struggle before the praetor, bringing the actual object or a piece of it into court, and ceremonially laying their hands on it. Even after the procedure of a "struggle" was discontinued, the formal challenge was maintained.

[37] The Academy, the philosophical school founded by Plato, had adopted a sceptical position in the third century BC, and was therefore given to contradiction.

[38] Scaevola again employs legal terminology.

45–47 Crassus begins his reply: his visit to Athens[39]

45 To this, Crassus made the following reply: "I am not unaware, Scaevola, that the Greeks commonly raise such arguments in their discussions. For I heard the most eminent among them when I, as quaestor, had come to Athens from Macedonia.[40] At that time, the Academy, led by Charmadas, Clitomachus, and Aeschines, was said to be flourishing. Metrodorus was there, too; together with these three, he had been an attentive pupil of Carneades himself, reportedly the most sharp-witted and copious speaker of all. Two others who were influential were Mnesarchus and Diodorus, the first a pupil of 46 your friend, Panaetius, the other of Critolaus the Peripatetic.[41] There were also many other quite illustrious philosophers, and I saw that all these people, almost in chorus, drove the orator from the helm of State, and excluded him from all learning and from knowledge of the more important subjects, pushing him aside and confining him only to the courts and petty public meetings, 47 like a slave put to a treadmill. But I agreed neither with them nor with the unsurpassed master of impressive eloquence, Plato, who invented this line of argument. During this stay in Athens, I read his *Gorgias* with some care, together with Charmadas. In this work I particularly admired Plato for the way in which, while making fun of orators, he appeared to be a supreme orator himself. It is, after all, really a fight over a mere word that has been tormenting those petty Greeks for such a long time, fonder as they are of an argument than of the truth.

48–57 Crassus: the orator needs much knowledge, no matter which of the two interpretations of his task is preferred

48 "For if someone wants to define the orator as one who can speak with fullness only before a prae-

tor[42] or a jury or before the people or in the Senate, then he must still concede that this same orator should be granted many qualities. After all, to be engaged with sufficient resourcefulness and expertise even in these fields alone is impossible without having thoroughly examined public affairs of all sorts, without knowledge of statutes, tradition, and law, and without an understanding of human character and behavior. But if someone has actually learned all this (and without it no one can handle even the smallest elements of a case adequately), can he be said to lack in any way knowledge of the most important matters?

"If, however, you want to restrict the task of the orator to speaking in a well-ordered, distinguished, and abundant fashion, how could he achieve even this without the knowledge that you and all those others refuse to grant him? For excellence in speaking cannot exist unless the speaker has grasped the subject he will speak 49 about. If, therefore, Democritus, the renowned natural philosopher, spoke with distinction (as I think is rightly said about him), the material he spoke about belonged to the province of the natural philosopher, but the actual distinction of his language must be considered the property of the orator. If Plato spoke on subjects far removed from judicial and political controversy with the voice of a god (as I concede), and if, likewise, Aristotle and Theophrastus and Carneades were eloquent in the matters that they discussed, and spoke with charm and distinction, then let it be admitted that the subjects of their discussions are at home in certain other pursuits, but surely their speech itself is the special and exclusive property of this art of oratory that we are examining. 50 Indeed, we see that the discussions of these same subjects by certain others are barren and dry, such as those by Chrysippus, a man, so they say, of extremely keen intellect; yet the fact that they had no ability in this art of speaking (which, after all, belongs to others), did not mean that they failed to satisfy the demands of philosophy. What, then, is the difference, and how do you distinguish the

---

[39] For a more detailed analysis of this difficult passage (45–73), see [Reading 32].

[40] Crassus had been quaestor in Asia in 111 BC, and afterward apparently returned to Rome via Macedonia and Athens.

[41] Panaetius had been head of the Stoic school, and Mnesarchus was therefore a Stoic (and possibly Panaetius' successor as head of the school). Thus, Crassus mentions representatives from each of the three philosophical schools most involved in the quarrel (Academy, Stoa, and Peripatos)

[42] "Before a praetor" refers to the first stage of a civil procedure.

richness and fullness of those mentioned earlier from the dryness of those who do not employ this refinement and variety of speech? Surely it is one particular quality that marks good speakers: speech that is well ordered, distinguished, and characterized by a particular kind of artistry and polish. And unless the orator has fully grasped the underlying subject matter, such speech is utterly 51 impossible – or at best everyone will make fun of it. For what can be more insane than the hollow sound of even the best and most distinguished words, if they are not based upon thought and knowledge? Thus, whatever the theme may be, from whatever art or from whatever area, when the orator has learned about it just as he learns about a case from his client, he will address the subject better and with greater distinction than even the expert who invented it can.

"I realize someone may say that only certain 52 pronouncements[43] and cases, and only knowledge that is restricted by the barriers of the forum, are the special property of orators, and I certainly admit that our oratorical activities are in general more often involved with these. All the same, even here there is much that these so-called rhetoricians do not teach, or even understand. For every- 53 one knows that the power of an orator is most manifest in dealing with people's feelings, when he is stirring them to anger or to hatred and resentment, or is calling them back from these same emotions to mildness and compassion. And this will only be accomplished by someone who has gained a thorough understanding of human character and the whole range of human nature, and of the causes by which feelings are stirred or calmed 54 – otherwise, his speech will not achieve its purpose. All the same, this whole subject is generally

considered the property of the philosophers, and I will never support an orator who challenges their claim. But, although he will leave the investigation of such things to the philosophers (because they have chosen to concentrate on this alone), the treatment of them in speech, which is totally impossible without this kind of knowledge, he will still claim for himself. For this, as I have already repeatedly said, is the orator's own province: impressive and distinguished speech that is adapted to the way most people think and feel. I 55 acknowledge that Aristotle and Theophrastus have written about all this; but I'm afraid, Scaevola, that this point is wholly in my favor. For what the orator and they share, I need not borrow from them, whereas they do admit that what they have to say about such matters belongs to the orators; it is for this reason that they call their other books by the name of the subject involved, but entitle these books *On Rhetoric*, and refer to them as 56 such.[44] Indeed, when it happens, as it often does when we are speaking, that we have to take up general subjects, and talk about the immortal gods and dutifulness, harmony and friendship, laws concerning the citizens, concerning human beings in general, and the law valid for all nations, equity, self-control, greatness of spirit, and every kind of virtue, then, I suppose, all the gymnasia and all the schools of the philosophers[45] will cry out that all these topics belong to them and are not the orator's business. Well, I give them leave to discuss such matters in their secluded corners,[46] 57 just to pass their leisure time. Yet I will definitely grant the orator this role: to take the same themes about which they debate in plain and meager language, and develop them with all the attractiveness and dignity he can muster.

---

[43] "Pronouncements" translates *sententiae*, which indicates pronouncements made in the Senate or in a public meeting.

[44] Crassus' argument is as follows: the orators and the philosophers share the subject of human nature and the emotions, as well as many general subjects that the orator treats in his speech; these are thus proven not to be alien to the orators. But the actual treatment of such material in speech belongs exclusively to the orators. The latter point is then confirmed by reference to the titles of Aristotle's and Theophrastus' books: generally, these were not about disciplines with specific practitioners but about (philosophical) subjects (e.g., *On Justice*), but their books on speaking were called "rhetorical <books>," i.e., books on "the art of the *rhetor* = speaker." This shows that the material on speaking belongs to the orators and not to the philosophers.

[45] Both these expressions refer to protests from the philosophers, since philosophers often gathered and taught in gymnasia.

[46] This proverbial taunt of the impractical and secluded life of the philosopher goes back to Plato, *Gorgias* 485 D, where Callicles contemptuously describes the philosopher as "spending the rest of his life whispering in a corner with three or four lads." Since Callicles is there portrayed as being in the wrong, our passage is most probably an ironical rejoinder to Plato.

"All this I personally discussed with the philosophers themselves while I was in Athens, for our friend Marcus Marcellus urged me to do so. He is now serving as curule aedile, and if he were not putting on the games at this moment, he would surely be taking part in our conversation.[47] At that time he was a young man, but already remarkably dedicated to these pursuits.

58–73   Crassus restates his position from several perspectives

58 "But now, on the subjects of legislation, war, peace, allies, those paying taxes, and the description of the rights of citizens according to property and age classifications, the Greeks, if they wish, are welcome to assert that Lycurgus and Solon (who I still believe should certainly be ranked among the eloquent) had better knowledge than even Hyperides or Demosthenes, both consummately polished speakers. Or let our countrymen, in this field, rank the Board of Ten, the drafters of the Twelve Tables and surely wise men, above both Servius Galba and your father-in-law Gaius Laelius, who, as everyone 59 agrees, earned outstanding glory as speakers. I shall never deny that there are particular pursuits that belong to those who have invested all of their energy in examining them and dealing with them; but I do maintain that the complete and perfect orator is he who can speak about all subjects with fullness and variety. In fact, even in those cases that everyone admits to be the domain of the orators, there is often some element that cannot be derived from experience in the forum (the only province that you grant them), but must be taken from outside, from some more obscure branch of know- 60 ledge. For let me ask you, is it really possible to support or oppose the military command of a general without experience in military affairs, or actually, in many cases, without geographical knowledge of lands and seas?[48] Can one speak before the people on ratifying or rejecting laws, or address the Senate on all dimensions of public affairs, without the deepest knowledge and understanding of political matters? Can speech be applied to kindle the

emotions or to quench them again – precisely the thing most essential for an orator – without having investigated with the utmost care all the theories that the philosophers have developed about human character and behavior? You will, I'm afraid, be 61 even less easily persuaded of another point; still I will not hesitate to give you my opinion. Physics, which you mentioned, and the subjects that you posited just now as the special property of mathematics and of the other arts, do belong to the expertise of those who make them their profession; yet if anyone wishes these same arts to be elucidated in speech, he must resort to the skill of the orator. For instance, if it is true that Philo, the architect who designed the arsenal for the Athenians, expressed himself quite fluently when he gave an account of his plans before the people, we must not attribute this fluency to the craft of the architect rather than to that of the orator. And if Marcus Antonius here had been called upon to speak on behalf of Hermodorus about his work on the dockyards, he then, after learning about the circumstances from him, would not have failed to speak with distinction and fullness about another man's craft. Again, Asclepiades whom I knew as a doctor and as a friend, at the time he surpassed the other doctors in eloquence, did not employ his skill in medicine when speaking with such distinction, but rather his faculty for eloquence. In fact, what Socrates used to say, that all people are sufficiently 63 eloquent about what they know, is quite plausible, but nevertheless untrue. It is nearer the truth to say that no one can express himself well without knowing his subject; nor will anyone, if he knows a subject intimately but is ignorant about how to fashion and polish his speech, be able to express himself well about the very subject he knows. Accordingly, 64 then, if we want to capture the true meaning of the word 'orator' in a complete definition, it is my opinion that an orator worthy of this grand title is he who will speak on any subject that occurs and requires verbal exposition in a thoughtful, well-disposed, and distinguished manner, having accurately memorized his speech, while also displaying a certain dignity of delivery.[49]

---

[47] Marcellus here functions as a link between the debate in Athens and the present discussion in Tusculum, while at the same time reminding the reader of the dialogue's historical setting during the Roman Games (*Ludi Romani*).

[48] Cicero's readers would perhaps recall that in 66 BC, he (along with Caesar) had spoken on behalf of the Lex Manilia, which conferred on Pompey the command in the East against Mithradates and Tigranes, and granted him *imperium* over all the provinces of Asia Minor.

[49] Crassus here refers to the five traditional "activities" of the orator.

65 "If anyone thinks that my claim about speaking 'on any subject' is too unrestricted, he may trim and prune away from it as much as he sees fit. Yet I shall hold on to one thing: suppose the orator knows only about what occurs in the practice of judicial and political disputes, but is ignorant of the subject matter of the other pursuits and arts; even then, if he should be required to speak about these very subjects, the orator, once he has been instructed about the contents of each field by those who do know it, will speak far better than the experts in those arts themselves. For example, 66 if Sulpicius here will be required to speak about military affairs, he will ask my relative Gaius Marius[50] about it, and once he has been instructed, he will express himself in such a way that even Marius will have the impression that Sulpicius knows these things almost better than he does. If the topic is civil law, he will consult with you, and despite your exceptional understanding and experience, he will, through his oratorical skill, surpass 67 you in the very matters he has learned from you. And should an occasion arise in which he must speak about human nature and its vices, about desires, moderation, self-control, pain, or death, he will, if he sees fit – but the orator should certainly have knowledge of all this, – consult with Sextus Pompeius, who is quite knowledgeable about philosophy. One thing he will certainly accomplish: whomever he consults, and whatever the subject may be, he will speak about it with much more distinction than the very person who 68 has instructed him. But perhaps he will listen to my advice: seeing that philosophy is divided into three parts, the mysteries of nature, the subtleties of dialectic, and the study of human life and conduct, we may give up the first two as a concession to our laziness – but if we don't hold on to the third part (which has always belonged to the orators), we will leave the orator nothing in which 69 he can be truly great. For this reason, this entire topic of human life and conduct must be thoroughly mastered by the orator. As to other subjects, even if he has not learned about them, he will, whenever the need arises, be able to give

them distinction by his speech, if only the material has been handed over to him. Indeed, if scholars agree that a man who knew no astronomy, Aratus, spoke about the heavens and the stars in very fine and distinguished verses, or that Nicander of Colophon, a complete stranger to country life, wrote splendid lines on farming by virtue of the skill of a poet, not that of a farmer, I don't see why an orator couldn't speak eloquently about what he has learned for a particular case or occasion. The 70 poet, after all, closely resembles the orator. While the former is slightly more restricted as to rhythm, and enjoys greater license in his choice of words, they have an almost equal share in many of the devices of style. And however that may be, the poet is certainly almost identical to the orator in this respect: he does not restrict or confine his right of possession by any boundaries that will prevent him from wandering – employing this same ability to express himself copiously – wherever he wishes to go.

"As for your declaration, Scaevola, that if you 71 were not in my own domain, you would not have put up with my statement that the orator should be perfectly accomplished in every kind of conversation and in all aspects of human culture[51]: I would surely never say this if I thought myself to be the man I am here portraying. But I agree with 72 what Gaius Lucilius often used to say – he had some hard feelings toward you, and for that reason was not as close to me as he wished, but he was still a learned and very cultured man.[52] He said that no one should be ranked an orator who is not thoroughly accomplished in all arts that befit a gentleman.[53] Even if we do not employ these arts when speaking, still it is quite apparent whether we are ignorant of them or have actually learned 73 about them. Those who play ball do not in the game itself use the skills peculiar to the palaestra,[54] but by their very movements betray whether or not they have learned the exercise of the palaestra; those who are sculpting something cannot hide whether or not they know how to paint, even though they are not in any way using the art of painting at that time; and it is just the same for

[50] Marius was related to Crassus because his son Gaius Marius (consul in 82 BC) had married Crassus' daughter, Licinia, in or soon after 95 BC.

[51] See 1.35 and 41.

[52] The poet Lucilius, in the second book of his *Satires*, had ridiculed Scaevola in connection with an extortion trial in 119/118 BC.

[53] As in 1.17, literally "free man."

[54] In the palaestra, one exercised in running, wrestling, boxing, jumping, javelin throwing, etc.

what we are now talking about, the speeches before the courts, public meetings, and the Senate: although the other arts are not employed directly, it is nevertheless readily evident whether the one who is speaking has merely been jostled about while training his voice in one of the common rhetorical workshops, or has applied himself to speaking only after he has been fitted out with all the noble arts."

74–79   Conclusion of the debate between Crassus and Scaevola

74 Scaevola laughed, and said: "I am not going to wrestle with you any longer, Crassus. In fashioning this whole reply of yours you have resorted to some sort of trick: you did agree with me about the things that I refused to allow as part of the orator's province, but then you managed somehow to wrench these same things away from me again, and hand them over to the orator as his own prop-
75 erty. When I was praetor and was visiting Rhodes,[55] I discussed the arguments I had heard from Panaetius[56] with Apollonius, that distinguished teacher of your rhetorical discipline. What he did was to mock philosophy and to scorn it, as he used to, and many of his remarks, rather than being serious, were made in a spirit of jest. Your argument, however, was of a different sort, for you scorned no art or branch of learning, but claimed
76 them all as the companions and attendants of the orator. Surely, if a single individual should master all of these, and should also join to them this faculty for distinguished speech, he would be an exceptional and admirable human being – I will not deny that. But such a man – if there were, or ever had been, or ever could be such a man – would surely be you alone. For in my judgment as well as everyone else's, you have left the other orators – with all due respect to those present –
77 scarcely any possibility for winning glory. But if even you yourself, though you have a complete knowledge of political, judicial, and civil affairs, have not embraced all the knowledge that you assign to the orator, let's be careful not to attribute to him more than reality and truth itself allow."

To this Crassus replied, "You must remember 78 that I have not been talking about my own ability, but about the ability of the true orator. For what did I learn, or what did I have any chance of knowing? I entered an active life of pleading cases before I had begun acquiring knowledge, and my actual practice in the forum, in campaigning for office, in affairs of State, and in my obligations to friends, exhausted my energies before I could even begin to have an inkling about such lofty 79 subjects. So, as you think, I may not have been totally devoid of talent, but I certainly lacked instruction, leisure time, and – oh yes – that passionate enthusiasm for learning. If you still find so much merit in me, don't you see what a truly great sort of orator we will have if someone perhaps more talented than I should in addition master these things, which I have not even touched?

[...]

113b–121   Natural ability: its importance

"Well, then," said Crassus, "in my opinion it is, in the first place, natural ability and talent that make a very important contribution to oratory. And in fact, in the writers of rhetorical handbooks, whom Antonius mentioned a little while ago,[57] it was not knowledge of the principles and methods of speaking that was lacking, but rather native ability. For a certain quickness of the mind and intellect is required, which displays itself in the keenness of its thoughts, in the richness with which it unfolds and elaborates them, and in the strength and retentiveness of its memory.[58] And 114 if there is anyone who thinks that these powers can be conferred by art (which is false: we ought to be well satisfied if art can kindle and stimulate them, but they surely cannot be implanted or bestowed by art, for they are all gifts of nature), then what about the qualities that no one doubts are innate: I mean flexibility of the tongue, the sound of the voice, powerful lungs, physical vigor, and a certain build and shape of the face and body as a whole. By this I do not mean to say

---

[55]   120 BC.

[56]   Obviously antirhetorical arguments like those of his pupil Mnesarchus (1.45–46).

[57]   In 1.91

[58]   These requirements correspond roughly to four of the regular oratorical "activities": invention, arrangement, style, memory; sections 114b–115 cover the fifth, delivery.

115 that some people cannot be refined by art – for I am well aware that what is good can be made better by teaching, and that what is not very good can still somehow be honed and corrected. But there are certain people whose tongues are so faltering, whose voices are so harsh, or whose facial expression and bodily movements are so uncouth and rude that they can never enter the ranks of the orators, even if they are intellectually gifted and have a firm command of the art. On the other hand, some are so well suited in these same respects and so richly endowed with the gifts of nature that they seem not to have been born of human stock, but to have been fashioned by some divinity.

116 "It is a huge burden and a huge responsibility you undertake, when you claim that, before a vast assembly of people where all others stand silent, you alone are to be heard on affairs of the highest importance. For there is hardly anyone in such a crowd who will not notice the speaker's faults with a sharper and more discriminating eye than he does his merits; thus, whatever mistake 117 he makes smothers even his points of excellence. By these arguments I'm not implying that I want to deter young men from the pursuit of oratory altogether, should they happen to lack a particular natural endowment. For anyone can see that my contemporary, Gaius Coelius, a new man,[59] won highest renown precisely because of whatever modest speaking skills he has managed to achieve for himself; and everyone understands that your contemporary, Quintus Varius, an uncouth and ugly fellow, has attained considerable influence in 118 our society precisely through whatever speaking ability he possesses. But because we are considering the orator as such,[60] we must fashion, in our discussion, a picture of an orator free from all possible faults and endowed with all praiseworthy qualities. For even if the great number of trials, the variety of cases, and the disorder and crudeness that rule the forum nowadays offer room to even the most fault-ridden orators, that will be no reason for us to lose sight of our objective. By the same token, when we are dealing with the arts that do not aim at fulfilling practical needs but at a certain disinterested pleasure of the mind, how scrupulously and almost fastidiously we pass judgment on them! For in the theater there are no legal quarrels or disputes that force us to sit through a performance of bad actors, as there are in the forum, where we are compelled to put up with mediocre 119 speakers. The orator, therefore, must scrupulously see to it not so much that he satisfies those whom he must, as that he wins the admiration of those who are free to make a disinterested judgment.

"And if you really want to know, I'll speak plainly and – being among very close friends – disclose an opinion that up till now I have always kept to myself, and thought it right to keep to myself. Unless they are nervous when they set out to speak and are upset while uttering their first words, I think that even the best orators, those who can speak with the utmost ease and distinction, are little less than shameless. Yet this cannot really happen, seeing that the better a man 120 speaks, the more frightened he feels about the difficulty of speaking, the unpredictable outcome of a speech, and the expectations of the audience. A speaker, on the other hand, who can produce not a single utterance that is worthy of his case, worthy of the title of orator, worthy of his audience's ears, I think such a man is shameless, however agitated he may be during his speech. For it is not by feeling ashamed, but by not doing what is inappropriate that we must escape the label of shamelessness. A speaker, however, who has no 121 sense of shame – as I see is the case with a great many orators – in my opinion deserves not only to be blamed, but even to be punished.[61] For my own part, I very frequently experience what I always observe happening to you also: during the beginning of my speech I find myself turning deathly pale, and I tremble with my whole heart and in every limb. In fact, as a very young man, I was once so beside myself when opening the case for the prosecution that Quintus Maximus

---

[59] In the *Brutus* (165), Cicero says that Coelius possessed extraordinary industry and personal qualities, and that his oratorical skills were just good enough to help his friends and sustain his senatorial position.

[60] The text here alludes to the title of our treatise, *"De oratore,"* "On the Orator," which implies "On the Ideal Orator," that is, "On the Orator as Such."

[61] Crassus, then, mentions three types of orators: (1) excellent speakers who do not become agitated when beginning their speeches; if such existed, he would consider them shameless; (2) those who are not good speakers, but are nervous when speaking; these, too, are shameless; (3) speakers who have no sense of shame and, according to Crassus, are actually deserving of punishment.

couldn't have done me a greater favor than when he adjourned the proceedings the moment he saw that I was incapacitated and unnerved by fear."[62]

122–133   Natural ability continued: the demands on the orator

118 At this point, all the others began to express their agreement, exchanging nods, looks, and comments. For there was an amazing kind of modesty[63] in Crassus, which, far from hindering his oratory, actually benefitted it by recommending his decency.

"I have often noticed, as you say, Crassus," Antonius said, "that both you and the other first-rate orators (though no one, in my opinion, has ever been your equal) are agitated at the beginning of a speech. And when I tried to think of a reason for this phenomenon, why it was that the greater the ability of an orator, the more frightened he felt, I found the follow- 123 ing two explanations: first, because those who have learned the lessons of nature and experience realize that the outcome of a speech is sometimes not entirely satisfactory to the orator, even if he is first-rate; accordingly, they fear with good reason, whenever they speak, 124 that what can happen at some time will, in fact, happen then. The second reason is this – it is something I often complain about. If, on some occasion, something in the performance of recognized and esteemed practitioners of the other arts does not meet their usual standards, they are thought to have failed in what they basically knew how to do because they didn't feel like it, or because they were prevented by ill health. People say, for example, 'Roscius didn't feel like acting today, or per-

haps his stomach was upset.'[64] But if some mistake is noticed in the performance of an orator people think this is due to stupidity. And for stupidity, there is no excuse, since people surely never suppose that someone was stupid because his stomach was upset or because he 125 felt like it. On this account, the judgment to which we are subjected when speaking is actually more severe.[65] For we are judged every time we speak: if an actor makes just one mistake in gesture, people do not immediately conclude that he does not know how to make gestures; but if some fault is found with a speaker, he will earn a reputation for slow-wittedness that will last forever, or at least for a very long time.

"Now you also said[66] that there are quite a 126 number of things that an orator must possess by nature, or else he cannot be helped much by a teacher – and really, I couldn't agree more. On this score, I had the greatest respect for the well-known and distinguished teacher, Apollonius of Alabanda. Though he taught for pay, he still did not allow those whom he judged incapable of becoming orators to waste their efforts with him, but sent them away, and he would urgently encourage them to take up that art for which he thought each was best suited. For in order to 127 acquire the other arts, it is enough merely to resemble a human being, and to be able to grasp with the mind and guard with the memory what is being taught, or even hammered in if someone is a little slow-witted: there is no need for flexibility of the tongue, for a quick flow of words, or finally, for any of the things we cannot fashion for ourselves, namely a particular stature, face, and tone of voice. In an orator, however, we 128 have to demand the acumen of a dialectician,[67] the thoughts of a philosopher, the words, I'd almost

---

[62] This was the prosecution of C. Papirius Carbo in 119 BC. Crassus was 21 years old at the time. Quintus Fabius Maximus, as praetor, presided over the court. Cf. 1.40. Crassus' nervousness at the beginning of a speech, be it historical or not, reflects Cicero's own emotional state when beginning an oration (see e.g., *Divinatio against Caecilius* 41–42, *In defense of Cluentius* 51, *In defense of King Deiotarus* 1).

[63] "Modesty" here renders the Latin *pudor*, the opposite of *impudentia*, which was translated by "shamelessness" in 1.120–121.

[64] Roscius was one of the great actors of Cicero's time.

[65] With "actually more severe" (*etiam gravius*), Antenius seems to refer to what Crassus has said in 1.118, that bad orators are tolerated more easily than bad actors. Antonius is now talking, not about orators in general as Crassus was, but about great orators; and where such absolute standards are concerned, the judgment passed on orators is "actually more severe" than that passed on actors.

[66] See 1.114–115.

[67] Dialectic was the art of reasoning, close, but not identical to our logic.

say, of a poet, the memory of a jurisconsult,[68] the voice of a tragic performer, and gestures close to those of a consummate actor. This is why nothing in the human race is more rarely to be found than a perfect orator. For practitioners of these individual arts are respected if they have mastered their subjects to a moderate degree, but the orator cannot win respect unless he exhibits all of them at the highest level."[69]

129 "Yes," said Crassus at that point, "but look how those involved in an extremely insubstantial and trivial art devote much more careful attention to what they do than those involved in our pursuit, which everyone agrees is of greatest importance. Time and again I hear Roscius say that he has, as yet, been unable to find a pupil of whom he could truly approve, not because there weren't some who were acceptable, but because he personally found it intolerable if there was any fault in them at all. For nothing is so conspicuous or so indelibly imprinted 130 on the memory as something that annoys you in any way. So let us take the example of this actor as a standard for oratorical merit: don't you see how he does nothing without perfection, nothing without consummate charm, and only in a manner that is appropriate and that moves and delights all? In this way he has, already long ago, won the distinction that anyone who excels in any art is called a 'Roscius' in his own field. Now it is shameless of me to demand this absolute perfection in an orator, while I am personally far removed from it: I want to be pardoned myself, but I do not pardon others. For I believe that someone who does not have the ability, who gets it all wrong, who, in short, is not fit for the task, should, as Apollonius directed, be demoted to the job that he can handle."

131 "Would you then," said Sulpicius, "direct me or Cotta here to learn civil law or the military art? For who can attain the height of universal perfection that you demand?"

"No," replied Crassus, "I have said all this precisely because I have observed an extraordinary and exceptional talent for oratory in you two; my remarks were tailored less to deterring those who do not have the ability than to rousing you who do. And though I have discerned in both of you a very high level of natural ability and devotion, those qualities that are connected with one's physical appearance (about which I have perhaps said more than the Greeks generally do)[70] are present in you beyond human measure, Sulpicius. For indeed, I don't believe that I have heard another 132 speaker whose bodily movements, bearing, and appearance were more suitable, or whose voice was richer or more pleasant. Those who have been less well endowed by nature with such gifts can still succeed in making tempered and sensible use of what they have, in a way that avoids being inappropriate.[71] For avoiding that is especially necessary, and at the same time it is especially difficult to give instructions on this topic – not only for me who am talking about these things like a head of a household would,[72] but even for Roscius himself. I have often heard him say that the essence of an art is to see to it that what you do is appropriate, though on the other hand, this is the one thing that cannot be taught by art. But if you don't 133 mind, let's change the subject, and at last talk the way we usually do, instead of like rhetoricians."

"Certainly not," said Cotta, "for now that you are retaining us in this pursuit and are not sending us away to some other art, we are obliged to beg you to explain your own oratorical power, whatever you make it out to be (nor are we too greedy: what you call your average eloquence[73] is enough for us). And since you say that we are not exceedingly deficient in the qualities that must be obtained from nature, we only ask you (in order to avoid achieving more than the little bit that you have achieved in oratory), what you think we must acquire in addition?"

[...]

[68] The memory of Roman jurists had to be highly developed since their *responsa* ("replies," approximately "legal opinion, advice") had to take all precedents into account.

[69] Note here the echo of the theme of the difficulty of oratory and the arguments found in the prologue, 1.16–20.

[70] The rhetoricians, who were still mainly Greeks at that time, emphasized their theoretical system, and obviously said very little about such natural endowments. Crassus' remarks were made in 1.114–115 (and 116) above.

[71] This remark is particularly apt in Cotta's presence. Cicero's description of him in *Brutus* 202 begins as follows: "Cotta possessed keenness in invention, purity and fluency in diction. Because his lungs were not strong, he had quite sensibly abandoned all vehemence, and accommodated his manner of speaking to his physical weakness."

[72] For the interpretation of *unus pater familias* (not "any ordinary head of a household"), see Pinkster 1988: 109–115.

[73] "Average eloquence" (*mediocri eloquentia*) is, in fact, an oxymoron, since "eloquence" in *De oratore* indicates an absolutely high level. The remark refers to 1.130, where Crassus (again) rated his own "eloquence" so low.

147–159 *Crassus on training*

147 "Also, you must make it your concern to practice in some way or other – though you, of course, have already been in full career for sometime. But for those who are just entering this pursuit, it is really necessary. Already at this stage, by practicing in mock exercise, they can learn in advance

148 the things that must be done in the front line of the forum, so to speak." "This," said Sulpicius, "is exactly what we want to know about. Still, we are eager to hear more on what you treated so cursorily when you were talking about the art, even though we, too, have heard such things before. But we can talk of that soon enough; now, we are asking you what you actually think about this matter of practice."

149 "For my part," said Crassus, "I approve of your habit of taking as a starting point some case very similar to those brought into the forum, and of speaking on it in a manner that is as true to life as possible. Most people, however, when doing this, merely exercise their voices (and not very knowledgeably at that), build their strength, quicken the speed of their tongues, and revel in the flood of their words. They have heard the saying that

150 the way to become a speaker is to speak, and this misleads them. For there is another saying that is equally true: the easiest way to become a wretched speaker is to speak wretchedly. For this reason, although it is also useful, in these practice sessions of yours, to speak extemporaneously on a regular basis, it is still more useful to take some time for reflection, in order to speak better prepared and with greater care.

"What is most fundamental, however, is something that, to be honest, we do least of all (for it involves a great deal of effort, which most of us try to avoid) – I mean writing as much as possible. It is the pen, the pen, that is the best and most eminent teacher and creator of speaking. And I am saying this with very good reason: if extemporaneous and random speech is easily surpassed by preparation and reflection, the latter, in turn, will certainly be outdone by con-

151 stant and diligent writing. For as we investigate the matter and consider it with all of our powers of discernment, all commonplaces (at least as far as they are inherent in the subject on which we are writing), those provided by the art as well as those provided, in a way, by natural ability and intelligence, occur to us, revealing themselves to our minds. All the thoughts and all the words that are most appropriate to each type of subject, and that are most clear and brilliant, cannot help but pass under the point of our pen one after the other. In addition, writing perfects the ability of actually arranging and combining words, not in a poetic, but in a kind of oratorical

152 measure and rhythm. These are the things that win a good orator shouts of approval and admiration, and no one will master them unless he has written long and written much even if he has trained himself ever so vigorously in those extemporaneous speeches. Also, whoever comes to oratory after much practice in writing brings this ability along: even when he is improvising, what he says will still turn out to resemble a written text. And what is more, should he take a piece of text with him when he is going to speak, once he has stopped following this, the remain-

153 der of his speech will continue to resemble it. A ship at full speed, when once the rowers rest upon their oars,[74] still maintains its own momentum and course, even though the thrust of the oar strokes has been interrupted. The same thing happens in the case of a speech: when the written text leaves off, the remainder of the speech still maintains a like course, sped on by the similarity to what was written and by its impulse.

154 "What I used to do as a very young man in my daily practice sessions was to apply myself especially to the same exercise that I knew Gaius Carbo, my old enemy, had always employed.[75] I would set up as a model some verses, as impressive as possible, or I would read a speech, as much of it as I could manage to memorize, and then I would express exactly what I had read, choosing different words as much as I could.[76] But after a while, I noticed this method had a defect: the words that were most fitting in each case, and

[74] "Rest upon their oars" (i.e., stop rowing) reflects what Cicero intends to say, not the actual meaning of the Latin nautical term he uses (*inhibere*), which is "backwater" (i.e., rowing backward). Ten years later, Cicero realized that he had always misunderstood the term (cf. *Letters to Atticus* 13.21.3).

[75] Carbo was known for his habit of practicing intensely; cf. *Brutus* 105; Quintilian 10.7.27.

[76] Later, paraphrasing a text became a common form of exercise in grammatical and rhetorical education (cf. Suetonius, *On Grammarians and Rhetoricians* 4.5; Quintilian 10.5.4–11).

that were the finest and most distinguished, had already been appropriated by Ennius (if I was practicing with his verses) or by Gracchus, if I happened to use a speech of his as my model.[77] If, therefore, I chose the same words, I gained nothing, and if I chose others, I was actually doing myself harm, because I was getting used to employing words that were less appropriate. 155 Afterward, it seemed a good idea – and this was the practice I adopted when I was a bit older – to take speeches of the great orators from Greece and reformulate them. The advantage of choosing these was not only that, when rendering in Latin what I had read in Greek, I could use the finest words that were nevertheless common, but also that, by imitating Greek words, I could coin certain others that were new to our language – provided they were appropriate.

156   "Now as to the voice, the breath, and the movement of the entire body and of the tongue itself, the exercise of these requires hard work rather than art.[78] Here we must carefully consider who are to be our models, and whom we want to resemble. We must observe actors as well as orators to make sure that we do not, through bad practice, develop any tasteless or ugly habits. We 157 must also exercise our memory, by learning by heart as many passages as possible, from our own writings as well as from those of others. And when you are practicing this, I don't think there is any objection against also applying, if that is what you are used to doing, the traditional system of places and images that the rhetorical handbooks teach.[79] But next, our speech-making must be led out from the sheltered training ground of our home right into the fray, into the dust and the din, into the camp and the front line of the forum. We must confront the gaze of the whole world. The powers of our native ability must be put to the test, and our secluded preparation must be brought out into the light of reality.

158   "Also, we must read poetry, acquire a knowledge of history, and select teachers and writers of all the noble arts, read them attentively, and, for the sake of practice, praise, expound, correct,

criticize, and refute them. We must argue every question on both sides, and on every topic we must elicit as well as express every plausible argu- 159 ment. We must thoroughly learn the civil law, acquire knowledge of the statutes, and get to know the whole of the past.[80] We must acquire knowledge of the conventions of the Senate, the organization of the State, the legal standing of our allies, treaties, pacts, and effective foreign policy. And from all types of urbanity we must take bits of witticism and humor that we can sprinkle, like a little salt, throughout all of our speech. Well, I've poured out all my views for you. But you would probably have received the same answers to your questions, if you had gone to any social gathering and accosted some head of a household."

[...]

178–181 Antonius introduces the other two means of persuasion (ethos and pathos)

"I am running through these things in a hurry, 178 being a half-educated man among the learned, so that we might at last arrive at those other, more important matters. For nothing in oratory, Catulus, is more important than for the orator to be favorably regarded by the audience, and for the audience itself to be moved in such a way as to be ruled by some strong emotional impulse rather than by reasoned judgment. For people make many more judgments under the influence of hate or affection or partiality or anger or grief or joy or hope or fear or delusion or some other emotion, than on the basis of the truth or an objective rule, whether some legal standard or a formula for a trial or the laws. So, 179 with your permission, let's move on to these subjects."

"There is one small thing, Antonius," said Catulus, "that still seems to be missing from your account, and you must discuss that before setting out in the direction that you say you are going to take." "What is it?" asked Antonius. "What do

---

[77] Of the two brothers mentioned at 1.38, Gaius is obviously meant here: Cicero considered him the greatest orator of his generation (cf. *Brutus* 125).

[78] The exercises described in 1.151–155 concern invention and style. Crassus now adds remarks on practicing delivery (1.156) and developing the memory (1.157).

[79] This system is known to us especially from the extensive account in *Rhetoric for Herennius* 3.28–40; it is discussed by Antonius in the second book (2.350–360).

[80] Unlike "history" in 1.158, this refers to the past as a "storehouse of examples and precedents" (cf. 1.18).

you think is the best order of the arguments," Catulus answered, "and the best way to arrange them? It always seems to me that, in this area, you have the abilities of a god."[81]

180   "Look at how much of a god I am at that sort of thing, Catulus," said Antonius. "I swear, if it hadn't been for your reminder, the thought wouldn't have crossed my mind – which might show you that the successes that I sometimes seem to attain are merely due to my oratorical experience, or rather to chance, and that I always just happen upon them. In fact, this subject that you mention, but that I didn't know about and thus passed by just as I would some stranger, is so powerful in oratory that nothing contributes more to winning a case. For all that, I think you

181 were too quick in asking me for an account of order and of the arrangement of the material. If I had made the force of an orator entirely dependent on arguments and on proving the case in and of itself, then certainly it would now be time to say something about the order of the arguments and their arrangement. But since I have claimed that there are three factors that come into play, and only one of them has been dealt with, the question of arranging the whole of a speech should be posed only after I have also dealt with the other two.

182–184 Ethos

182 "Well then, the character, the customs, the deeds, and the life, both of those who do the pleading and of those on whose behalf they plead, make a very important contribution to winning a case. These should be approved of, and the corresponding elements in the opponents should meet with disapproval, and the minds of the audience should, as much as possible, be won over to feel goodwill toward the orator as well as toward his client. Now people's minds are won over by a man's prestige, his accomplishments, and the reputation he has acquired by his way of life. Such things are easier to embellish if present than to fabricate if

totally lacking, but at any rate, their effect is enhanced by a gentle tone of voice on the part of the orator, an expression on his face intimating restraint, and kindliness in the use of his words; and if you press some point rather vigorously, by seeming to act against your inclination, because you are forced to do so. Indications of flexibility, on the part of the orator and the client, are also quite useful,[82] as well as signs of generosity, mildness, dutifulness, gratitude, and of not being desirous or greedy. Actually all qualities typical of people who are decent and unassuming, not severe, not obstinate, not litigious, not harsh, really win goodwill, and alienate the audience from those who do not possess them. And these same considerations must likewise be employed to ascribe the opposite qualities to the opponents. But this entire mode of speaking is most effective 183 in cases where there is not much opportunity to use some form of sharp and violent emotional arousal to set the juror's heart aflame. For we don't always have to employ vigorous oratory, but often we should rather speak in a quiet, low-keyed, and gentle manner. This is particularly effective in recommending parties [rei] to the audience. (By 'parties' [rei] I mean not only those who are accused, but all those whose interests [res] are at stake – for this is how the word was used in the old days).[83] Portraying their characters in your speech, 184 then, as being just, upright, conscientious toward the gods, subject to fear, and patient of injustice, is enormously influential. And if this is handled agreeably and with taste, it is actually so powerful – whether done in the prologue or when narrating the facts or when bringing the speech to its conclusion – that it often has more influence than the case itself. Moreover, so much is accomplished by speaking thoughtfully and with a certain taste, that the speech may be said to mold an image of the character of the orator. Employing thoughts of a certain kind and words of a certain kind, and adopting besides a delivery that is gentle and shows signs of flexibility, makes speakers appear as decent, as good in character – yes, as good men.

[81] Catulus, like Cicero's contemporary readers, expects that now that the arguments have been discussed, the whole of invention has been treated. He therefore anticipates a discussion of the next "activity" of the orator, arrangement. That is, he has not yet understood that, for Antonius, invention must also include ethos and pathos, something that Antonius will now again emphasize.

[82] "Orator and client": not in the Latin, but implied by the context.

[83] The Latin word *reus* (plural *rei*) regularly indicates the defendant in a court case. Here and frequently elsewhere in *De oratore* (cf. 2.78, "litigants"; 2.321) Cicero prefers an older usage (etymologically linking the word with *res*, "interests"), which includes both plaintiff and defendant; this usage is witnessed in ancient law.

185–196   Introduction to pathos; the orator's own emotions

185 "Related to this, though of a different order, is the other mode of speaking I mentioned, which stirs the hearts of the jurors quite differently, impelling them to hate or to love, to envy someone or to want his safety, to fear or to hope, to feel favor or aversion, to feel joy or grief, to pity or to want punishment, or to be led to whatever feelings are near and akin to these and other such 186 emotions. Of course, the most desirable situation for the orator is when the jurors themselves come to the case in an emotional state of mind suited to what his own interests demand. For, as the saying goes, it is easier to spur on a willing horse than to rouse a sluggish one. But if this is not the case, or if the situation is rather unclear, then my method is that of a diligent doctor: before attempting to apply treatment to a patient, he must find out, not only about the disease of the person he wants to cure, but also about his routine when healthy and his physical constitution. I do likewise myself: when I set out to work upon the emotions of the jurors in a difficult and uncertain case, I carefully concentrate all of my thoughts on considering, on scenting out as keenly as I can, what their feelings, their opinions, their hopes, and their wishes are, and in what direction my speech may most easily lead 187 them. If they put themselves into my hands and, as I just said, are inclined, of their own accord, to lean in the direction I am pushing them, I accept what is offered and spread my sails to catch any breeze that happens to be blowing. If, however, the jurors are unbiased and unemotional, more effort is required; for then, the given situation offers no help, and all feelings must be stirred by my speech alone. But such enormous power is wielded by what one of our good poets rightly describes as 'soul-bending, the queen of all the world – speech,'[84] that it cannot only straighten up someone who is bending over and bend over someone who is standing, but also, like a good and brave general take prisoner someone who is offering resistance and is fighting back.

"Such are the things Crassus was pressing me for 188 just now, making fun of me and saying that I always handle them with brilliance, and praising my supposedly outstanding treatment of them in the cases of Manius Aquillius, Gaius Norbanus, and some others.[85] But I swear, Crassus, that on my part, I always shudder when you handle these matters in your cases: such mental vigor, such energy, such passion always show from your eyes, your face, your gestures, and even from your finger[86]; so overwhelming is the flow of the best and most impressive words; and so sincere are your thoughts, so true, so novel, and so devoid of immature frills, that it seems to me that you are not just setting the jurors on fire, but are ablaze yourself.

"In fact, it is impossible for the hearer to grieve, 189 to hate, to envy, to become frightened at anything, to be driven to tears and pity, unless the self-same emotions the orator wants to apply to the juror seem to be imprinted and branded onto the orator himself.[87] Now if, for instance, the grief that we must assume would somehow be unreal and pretended, and if this mode of speaking would involve nothing but deception and imitation and feigning, then we would probably require some quite powerful art. Well, I'm not sure what happens to you, Crassus, or to others; but since I am in the company of great experts who are at the same time my closest friends, I have no reason to lie about myself. I swear to you that every time I have ever wanted to arouse grief or pity or envy or hate in the hearts of jurors through my oratory, I was invariably, while working to stir the jurors, thoroughly stirred myself by the same feelings to which I was trying to lead 190 them. It isn't easy to make a juror get angry at the person you choose, if you are seen to take the matter calmly yourself; or to make him hate the person that you want him to, unless he has first seen you burning with hate; or to bring him into a state of pity, unless you have shown him signs of your own grief by your words, thoughts, voice, face, and even by bursting into tears. For no material is so easy to kindle, that it can catch fire unless fire is actually applied to it; likewise, no mind is so susceptible to an orator's power, that it can be set

---

[84] From the *Hermione* of Pacuvius (line 187 *ROL*), who imitates Euripides, *Hecuba* 816.

[85] Antonius refers to Crassus' remarks in 1.124–125 and 127.

[86] The index finger, which was employed in all sorts of gestures; Crassus obviously used it to great effect. Cf. Quint. 11.3.94.

[87] The question about the sincerity of an orator's emotions was probably a matter of debate.

on fire unless the orator who approaches it is
191 burning and all ablaze himself. But you shouldn't
think this is somehow a difficult and surprising
thing, that someone, especially over other people's affairs, should so often get angry, so often
feel grief, so often be moved by every possible
emotion: the power of the thoughts that you treat
and of the commonplaces that you handle when
you are speaking is great enough to preclude any
need for pretence and deception. For oratory that
aims at stirring the hearts of others, will, by its
very nature, stir the orator himself even more
192 strongly than it will any member of his audience.
And we shouldn't be surprised that this might
happen to us when pleading, when appearing in
trials, when assisting prosecuted friends in their
danger, before a crowd, in the public eye, in the
forum, when not only our reputation as gifted
speakers is at stake – for that would be less important, though if you have claimed to be able to do
what only a few others can, even that is no small
thing.[88] But other things are much more important: our loyalty, moral duty, and diligence. If we
are led by these, we cannot, even if we are defending total strangers, keep on regarding them as
strangers, if we want to be considered good men
193 ourselves. But as I said, you shouldn't think this
surprising when it happens to us orators, for what
can be so unreal as poetry, the stage, the theater?
Yet, in such performances, I have often seen
myself how the eyes of an actor seemed to blaze
forth from his mask, when he was speaking these
lines at another's prompting:[89]

> Did you dare to let him be parted from you, or
> without him enter Salamis?

Did you not, then, fear your father's mien?

Never did he say the word 'mien' without making
me see Telamon infuriated and raging with grief
for his son. Just as when this same man, his voice
lowered to a pitiful tone, seemed to mourn and to
be in tears when he spoke the next words:

> When at the end of my years, bereft
> Of children – so you tore me to shreds, left me
> desolate, killed me, with
> no thought for your slaughtered
> Brother, nor for his little son, who was
> entrusted to you in guardianship.

Now if this actor, although he went on stage every
day, could not perform these lines rightly without
feeling grief, do you really think Pacuvius was in a
calm and relaxed state of mind when he wrote
them? That is surely out of the question. For I
have often heard (people say that Democritus and 194
Plato have left this statement on record) that no
one can become a good poet without emotional
fire and without a kind of inspired frenzy.[90]

"So, do not imagine that I (who have no desire
to use my speeches for imitating and sketching
out the ancient misfortunes and unreal, fictional
griefs of heroes – I am not an actor of another's
character, but the author of my own) – do not
imagine that I didn't feel enormous grief in doing
what I did when concluding my speech for Manius
Aquillius, when I had to preserve his status as a 195
citizen.[91] For I remembered him to have been
consul, to have been *imperator*, that he had been
honored by the Senate, and had climbed the
Capitol in celebration of his *ovatio*.[92] So, when

---

[88] This sentence is grammatically irregular (a so-called anacoluthon). Antonius is carried away himself here!
[89] Viz., at the prompting of the poet (whether this is what Cicero actually wrote is, however, uncertain, since the text
is corrupt). The following two quotations, which fit together (1½ plus 2½ lines), are from the *Teucer* of Pacuvius.
Teucer was Ajax' half-brother and comrade in the Trojan War, but was not there when Ajax committed suicide.
Telamon, their father and king of Salamis, is here addressing Teucer on his return from Troy, reproaching him for
not bringing back Ajax; he will eventually banish him.
[90] This idea was well known in Cicero's time (cf. *In defense of Archias* 18), and is likewise coupled with Democritus
and Plato in Cicero's *On Divination* 1.80. For Democritus, see also Horace, *The Art of Poetry* 295–298; for Plato, see
especially *Ion* 533 E–534 E; *Phaedrus* 245 A; and Murray 1995: 6–12, 235–238.
[91] The case was already mentioned in 2.124 by Crassus, and in 2.188 by Antonius himself. Loss of citizen status
would entail going into exile.
[92] Aquillius, consul in 101 BC together with Marius, from 101–99 held a command in Sicily to put down a slave revolt.
In 100, his troops acclaimed him *imperator* (an honorary title thus conferred at a victory). In 99, he finished the paci-
fication of Sicily, and was "honored by the Senate" with an *ovatio*. The latter was a victory celebration on a scale less
grand than a *triumphus* (e.g., because, as in this case, the enemies had been slaves). E.g., in the procession, the general
ascended the Capitol on foot or horse back (not in a chariot as in a *triumphus*).

I saw him crushed, weakened, mourning, brought to the brink of disaster, I did not attempt to arouse pity in others before having been overwhelmed with pity myself. I clearly sensed that the jurors were especially moved at the point when I called forward the grieving old man, dressed in mourning clothes,[93] and when I was prompted not by rhetorical theory (I wouldn't know what to say about that), but by deep grief and passion, to do 196 what you, Crassus, were praising – I ripped open his tunic and exposed his scars. Gaius Marius, who was present at the trial among his supporters, strongly heightened the sorrow of my speech with his tears, and I, repeatedly addressing him, commended his colleague to his protection, and appealed to him to support the defense of the common fortune of generals. When I uttered these lamentations, and also invoked all gods and men, all citizens and allies, it was not without shedding tears and feeling enormous grief myself. If there had been no grief in all of the words that I delivered on that occasion, my speech, so far from stirring pity, would actually have been ridiculous. For this reason, Sulpicius, I am teaching you two this (being, of course, such a good and learned teacher): to be able to get angry when you are speaking, and to grieve, and to weep.

[...]

19–212 STYLE

19–24 Words and content

19 "Because of your authority and your friendship," Crassus began, "and because Antonius has been so obliging, I am deprived of the possibility of refusing, even though my case for doing so is very strong.[94] Nevertheless, in assigning the parts for our discussion, when he took it upon himself to deal with the things an orator must say, while leaving it to me to discuss how they must be given a distinguished style, he divided two things that cannot exist separately.[95] For since all discourse is made up of content and words, the words cannot have any basis if you withdraw the content, and the content will remain in the dark if you remove the 20 words. For my part, I have the impression that those great men of the past, having grasped in their minds something of a higher order, have thereby seen much more than our mind's eye, today, is able to contemplate[96]: they said that all the universe above and below us is a unity and is bound together by a single, natural force and harmony. For there is nothing in the world, of whatever sort, that can either exist on its own if it is severed from all other things, or that can be dispensed with by the other things if they are to preserve their own force and eternal existence. But if 21 this conception seems too vast for mortal senses or thought to comprehend, there is also this true saying of Plato's, which is certainly familiar to you, Catulus: that all the teachings of our noble and humane arts are held together by one common bond.[97] Since, once it is perceived how forceful the method is on which the knowledge of causes and outcomes is based, there emerges, so to speak, an agreement and harmony between all disciplines that is quite extraordinary.[98] But if 22 this also seems too lofty for us to be able to raise our eyes to it – in our lowly position upon the ground –, we should at least know and understand

---

[93] Defendants regularly wore mourning clothes (which were black and often dirty).

[94] See the end of Book 2 (2.361–367).

[95] For this "division of labor," see 2.123 and 350; for Crassus' protest, already 2.366.

[96] "Those great men of the past," to whom Crassus refers are the Eleatic philosophers (6th–5th century BC), who proclaimed that the universe is One (see e.g., Cicero, *Lucullus* 118 on Xenophanes). The idea to which he alludes in what follows, however, is more specifically the (contemporary) Stoic concept of "cosmic sympathy" (Greek συμπάθεια; see especially Cicero, *On Divination* 2.33–34); it is probable that the Stoics claimed the Eleatics as their forerunners in this idea.

[97] "Our noble and humane arts" refers to what are commonly called the *artes liberales*, i.e., the "arts" that it befitted a free man to learn (especially grammar, rhetoric, dialectic, music, and mathematics). The saying was originally found in the pseudo-Platonic *Epinomis*, 991 E5–992 A1; there, however, the bond (δεσμός, in Greek) is between the mathematical arts only. By Cicero's time, the saying was obviously known in isolation from its original context, and had been reinterpreted to refer to the *artes liberales* (cf. also, Cicero, *In defense of Archias*, 2). See also next note.

[98] I.e., the disciplines are united through the causal principles underlying the world. This is also a radical reinterpretation of the original "saying," since in the *Epinomis* not only are the arts the mathematical ones, but the bond is probably also of a mathematical nature.

that which we have embraced, the profession we lay claim to, the task we have taken upon ourselves. For, as I said yesterday, and as Antonius 23 indicated at several points in this morning's conversation,[99] eloquence forms a unity, into whatever realms or areas of discourse it travels: whether it is speaking about the nature of the heavens or of the earth, or about divine or human nature, whether in trials, in the Senate, or from the *rostra*,[100] whether its purpose is to urge people on or to teach them or to deter them, or to stir them or to curb them, or to kindle their emotions or to calm them, whether its audience be few or many, or strangers or one's friends or oneself: speech is like a river, branching out into little streams, yet issuing from the same source; and in whatever direction it goes, it is attended by the same equipment and adornment.[101] But we are 24 now laboring under the opinions not only of the crowd, but also of half-educated people. They find it easier to deal with things they cannot grasp in their entirety, if they split them apart and almost tear them to pieces, and they separate words from thoughts just like a body from its soul – which in both cases can only wreak destruction.[102] In my discussion, therefore, I will undertake no more than is assigned to me.[103] I would only indicate briefly that discovering[104] words for a distinguished style is impossible without having produced and shaped the thoughts, and that no thought can shine clearly without the enlightening power of words.

25–37a Preliminaries to style: the variety of eloquence

25 "But before attempting to touch upon the ways of lending distinction to a speech and giving it

brilliance and clarity, I will first briefly formulate my views about oratory as a whole. It seems to me that every category of natural phenomena includes many things that are different from one another but are nevertheless equally highly valued. For instance, all of the many delightful sounds caught by our ears consist of tones, but they are often so varied that what you have heard last seems most pleasant. The number of pleasing sensations gathered by our eyes is almost infinite, but the manner in which they captivate us is such that they delight this one sense in different ways. Each of the other senses is also charmed by dissimilar pleasures, so that it is always difficult to 26 judge which experience is most agreeable. This feature of natural phenomena can be observed in the arts as well. There is one art of sculpture; among its most outstanding practitioners were Myron, Polyclitus, and Lysippus, all of whom were different from one another, but still in such a way that you could not wish any one of them to be different from what he was. There is one systematic art of painting, yet Zeuxis, Aglaophon, and Apelles are entirely different from one another; but there is not one among them whose art seems deficient in any respect. And if this is surprising but still true in the case of these so-called silent arts, it is certainly much more surprising in the case of speech, that is, language. Although this is invariably concerned with words and thoughts, it admits of the most striking differences – not in the sense that some deserve praise and others criticism, but in the sense that the people who are generally agreed to deserve praise are, nonetheless, praised as representatives of dissimilar types.[105] In the first place, in the case of 27 the poets (who are closely akin to the orators), we can observe how different Ennius, Pacuvius, and

---

[99] Yesterday, i.e., in Book 1 (see especially 1.49–73 and 158–159); "in this morning's conversation," i.e., in Book 2 (see especially 2.34–38, 41–73, 337).

[100] Literally, the Latin says, "whether from a lower, equal, or higher place," which is more general than our translation suggests. The chief reference, however, does seem to be to the main three physical spheres of activity for an orator: speaking from below the jurors, who were seated on a raised platform, to senators on an equal level in the Senate, and to the people from the elevated level of the speaker's platform (the *rostra*).

[101] The metaphor in "equipment and adornment" (*instructu ornatuque*) suggests richness of both content and form.

[102] Crassus here alludes to the rhetoricians: in standard rhetoric, content (invention and arrangement) and words (style) were treated separately.

[103] This concession mirrors the concession made by Cicero in his own person in 1.22; it is likewise a temporary one.

[104] Crassus deliberately chooses the word usually employed for the "discovery" of content, i.e., for "invention" (*invenire, inventio*).

[105] "Type" (Latin, *genus*), here and in what follows, is not to be taken as a technical term; nor, with respect to oratory, does it denote only style, for it covers all aspects of an orator's performance. The usual assumption that *genus* refers

Accius are from one another, and among the Greeks, Aeschylus, Sophocles, and Euripides. Yet in their different types of writing, they are all accorded almost equal merit.[106]

28 "Now turn your eyes to the people whose skill we are examining, to the orators, and look at how different their aims and abilities are: Isocrates had charm, Lysias refined precision, Hyperides pointedness, Aeschines sonority, Demosthenes force. Surely each of them was outstanding, while at the same time resembling no one but himself. Scipio had weight, Laelius gentleness, Galba fierceness, Carbo a sort of fluency and melodiousness. Surely each of these men was an eminent speaker in
29 those days. At the same time, each was eminent in his own type. But why should I actually search for old examples when I have the opportunity to use living ones who are here with us? Our ears have certainly never been struck by anything more pleasant than the language of Cotulus here. It is so very pure that he seems almost the only one who speaks Latin. It is impressive, but its unique dignity is still combined with all possible humanity and charm. What more should I say? Whenever I listen to this man, my personal judgment about the way he speaks is always that even the smallest addition or alteration or subtraction
30 would diminish its perfection and make it worse. What about our friend Caesar here? Hasn't he come up with a new approach to oratory, and introduced an almost unique type of speaking? Did anyone except him ever treat tragic subjects almost in the manner of comedy, gloomy subjects lightly, serious ones cheerfully, and the business of the forum with a charm almost like that of the stage? Nevertheless, the importance of these subjects does not preclude his humor, while his jokes do not diminish his seriousness.[107] And look, we
31 have two close contemporaries present here, Sulpicius and Cotta. Where could we find a greater difference? And where could we find

people who are more outstanding in their own types of oratory? The one is polished and precise, setting out his case in proper and fitting words.[108] He always sticks to the issue, and when his sharp eyes have seen what he must prove to the jurors, he leaves aside all other arguments, focusing his attention and his speech on that point.[109] Sulpicius, on the other hand, has enormous mental vigor and a very rich and strong voice; his body is full of energy, his movements dignified, and his language is also so impressive and copious that his natural abilities seem to make him better equipped for oratory than anyone else.

32 "I now return to us, since it has always been our fate that when people talk about us, we are, so to speak, brought before a court, as if there were some legal conflict between us. There can surely be no greater difference than between Antonius' oratory and mine, since he is an orator of such stature that no one could be more outstanding, and I – well, although I am really dissatisfied with myself, I am still especially linked and compared with him. You know what Antonius' type of oratory is like. It is vigorous, vehement, excited in delivery, fortified and protected on every side of the case, intense, precise, to the point, lingering on each and every aspect, giving ground without dishonor, pursuing vigorously, intimidating, begging, displaying the greatest possible variety of expression, without ever
33 satiating our ears. When you look at me, on the other hand, whatever my speaking abilities are (I know you think I am of some account), there is certainly a great difference between his type of oratory and mine. What mine is like is not for me to say because everyone is least known to himself and can form an opinion about his own qualities only with great difficulty. Nevertheless, you can understand the nature of the difference when you consider that my abilities in movement are only average, that I almost always conclude my speech

in a technical way to style is untenable, for this as well as many other passages; the word is as general and vague as are "sort, kind, type, class" in English.

[106] All six are tragedians , which makes their variety all the more remarkable (Ennius is here obviously mentioned as such, although he wrote many other works).

[107] Part of Crassus' phrasing in this section recalls Caesar's activity as a writer of drama (tragedies). Normally, the world of the stage was considered too lowly for a Roman orator; Caesar's ability to use an approach that recalled the stage without losing his dignity was therefore one of the paradoxical features of his oratory.

[108] "Proper words" are such as are used in their proper meaning, i.e., nonmetaphorical, usual words. That words should be "fitting" was a generally accepted requirement of style (cf. 1.144; 3.37).

[109] That is, Cotta always strictly concentrated on the "point of decision" (iudicatio, κρινόμενον; see 2.132, excluding other rational arguments, as well as ethos and pathos.

along the same lines that I followed in the beginning, and that I am considerably more tormented and anxious in choosing words than in choosing thoughts, for fear that my speech, if it is a little too trite, may seem not to have deserved the high expectations and silent attention of the audience.[110] Between all of us here, then, there are great differences, and each of us has clear and specific traits. And amid this variety, the better is generally distinguished from the worse more by ability than by the type to which each belongs, and everything that is perfect in its own type is praised. So don't you think that if we chose to include all orators who are or have ever been active anywhere, we would have to say something like, 'so many orators, so many types of speaking'?

"Perhaps my argument will give rise to a further notion: if there is indeed an almost countless number of, let us say, forms and kinds of speaking, different in appearance but praiseworthy in their own types, then these mutually different things cannot be molded by the same rules and by one method of instruction. But this is not true. It is the responsibility of those who provide instruction and education to observe very carefully where each pupil's natural abilities seem to lead him. In fact, when we look at the schools run by expert teachers who were superior in their own different types, we see that each one produced pupils who were different from one another and still praiseworthy, since every teacher adapted his instruction to the natural abilities of each individual pupil. The most striking example of this (to leave aside the other arts) is probably that the incomparable teacher Isocrates said that he always used the spurs on Ephorus, but the bridle on Theopompus. He checked the latter, who was unrestrained in his bold use of words, while he urged on the former, who was hesitant and modest, so to speak. Yet he did not make them alike; he added to the one and filed away from the other only as much as was necessary to reinforce in each what his natural abilities allowed.

"I had to make these preliminary remarks for a specific reason: my suggestions may not all fit the aims of each of you and the type of oratory that each of you favors, so I wanted you to realize that I am describing the type that I myself favor most.

37b–38   Introduction of the four qualities of style

"Well then, the orator must deliver the material discussed by Antonius, as well as express it in a certain way. And tell me, is there a better way of expression – for I will see to delivery later[111] – than to speak correct Latin, clearly, with distinction, and in a manner that is suitable and appropriate to the particular matter at issue?[112] Now I don't think that I am expected to give an account of the two elements that I mentioned first, pure and lucid language. For we do not attempt to teach someone to speak who doesn't know how to talk, and we cannot hope, if someone cannot speak correct Latin, that he is going to speak with distinction – or, for that matter, if someone cannot say something that we might understand, that he will be able to say something that we might admire. So let us leave these two elements aside. Learning them is easy, using them is indispensable. For the first is taught when we are learning our ABCs in our elementary lessons, and the reason for applying the second is to ensure that everybody will make himself understood – which is indeed indispensable, but nevertheless only a minimum prerequisite.

39–51   The first two qualities of style: correct Latin (especially pronunciation) and clarity

"Still, every aspect of refined diction, though it can be polished by a knowledge of grammar, can nonetheless be developed by reading the orators and the poets.[113] For almost all of the ancients, though they were not yet able to impart distinction to what they said, expressed themselves very well, and people who have become accustomed to their language cannot fail to speak anything but correct Latin, even if they should try. This is not to say that we should employ the words that are not employed in normal usage anymore, except

---

[110] Cicero thus again makes it clear that Crassus is the right person to discuss style.

[111] In 3.213–227.

[112] Crassus here refers to the four qualities around which his discussion of style will be built, and which he already mentioned in 1.144.

[113] Grammar was largely based on literature, and usually included some examination of poetry. Crassus, however, proceeds to recommend more thorough reading.

sparingly, for the sake of imparting distinction to what we say, as I will point out later.[114] But in the employment of words in common use you will be able to use the choicest among them if you have thoroughly and devotedly immersed yourself in the writings of the ancients.

40 "But in order to speak correct Latin we must not only be careful to utter words that no one might justifiably criticize, and to use them in the proper case, tense, class, and number, so that there is no confusion, want of agreement, or incorrect order[115]; but we must also control our

41 tongue, our breath, and the actual sound of our voice. I don't like letters to be overarticulated with too much affectation, and I don't like them to be obscured by being pronounced too carelessly; I don't like words to sound thin by being pronounced with too little breath, and I don't like them to be puffed up and uttered, as it were, with too full and heavy a breath. As to the voice, I am not yet speaking about the points that fall under the category of delivery, but about what, as it seems to me, is somehow connected with the normal use of language. There are, of course, certain faults that everyone wants to avoid: a voice that is soft or effeminate, or unmusically

42 harsh, so to speak, and discordant. But there is also a fault that is cultivated intentionally by some people. There are those who delight in a countrified and coarse pronunciation because they think that if their language sounds this way, it will seem to preserve more of the past. For example, Lucius Cotta, who is a close friend of yours, Catulus, seems to me to take great delight in a heavy pronunciation and a coarse-sounding voice, and he imagines that what he says will seem truly old if it comes straight from the country. I myself take pleasure in the sound of your voice, Catulus, and

in your refinement. I won't mention the refinement in choice of words, fundamental though it is; this is provided by theory, taught by grammar, and strengthened by daily practice in both reading and speaking. What I mean here is a pleasant sound produced by the mouth itself. In the Latin language this belongs especially to the city of Rome, just as in Greece it belongs to the inhabitants of Attica.[116] In Athens, learning among the 43 Athenians themselves has long since perished, and the city has remained merely the seat of several branches of study. The citizens themselves are not involved in them at all, but foreigners[117] avail themselves of them, somehow captivated by the name and prestige of the city. Nevertheless, any unschooled Athenian will easily outdo the most erudite people from Asia, not in their choice of words, but in the sound of their voice, and not so much in the correctness as in the pleasantness of their language. People in our city are less devoted to literary pursuits than are the people from Latium. Nevertheless, among those in the city whom you know and who have very little familiarity with literature, there is no one who, in terms of the smoothness of his voice or the sound of his distinct pronunciation, is not easily superior to the most literate man of all those who wear the toga,[118] Quintus Valerius from Sora.[119] 44 Thus, there is a particular kind of accent characteristic of the Romans who are from the city itself, in which there is nothing that can give offense, nothing unpleasant, nothing to provoke criticism, and nothing to sound or smell of foreignness. So let us cultivate this accent, and learn to avoid not only countrified roughness, but also peculiar foreign pronunciation.

"I must say that when I hear my mother-in-law, 45 Laelia, speaking – for the old pronunciation is

---

[114] See 3.153.

[115] As elements of correct Latin, Crassus first mentions the two categories of school rhetoric, word choice and correct "syntax." (The ancients had no complicated notion of syntax in our sense; the relevant concepts here are morphological regularity and grammatical agreement between the elements of a sentence.) The description of the latter is brief and untechnical, partly because some of the terms are applicable to both the verb and the noun.

[116] Attica was the territory around, and including, Athens. The dialect spoken in Athens is therefore known as "Attic" Greek.

[117] The foreigners in Athens were, as the sequel shows, primarily Greeks from Asia (i.e., Asia Minor). Romans, of course, also visited the city for their education, but that became more common only in Cicero's own generation, having been less normal in the time of Crassus and Antonius.

[118] I.e., the inhabitants of Rome and its surroundings, including Latium (the area south-east of Rome). The toga was apparently the traditional dress of all these people, though it was sometimes, as in 1.111, considered typical of Roman citizens (not all the people from Latium had citizenship in 91 BC, the dramatic date of the dialogue).

[119] Sora was a town in (Greater) Latium, about 60 miles east of Rome, and near Cicero's home town Arpinum.

more easily preserved intact by women; they are not exposed to the language of a lot of people, so they always hold on to what they originally learned – anyway, when I hear her speaking, I seem to be hearing Plautus or Naevius. The actual sound of her voice is so straight-forward and unaffected that there is obviously nothing ostentatious or inauthentic to it. From this I conclude that this was the way her father used to speak, as well as her ancestors – not roughly, like the man I mentioned,[120] nor in a harsh or countrified or disjointed way, but distinctly and steadily 46 and smoothly. For this reason, it seems to me, Sulpicius, that this friend of ours, Lucius Cotta, whose broad sounds you sometimes imitate when you drop the letter I and pronounce a very full E instead,[121] is imitating farmhands rather than the orators of the past."

Sulpicius himself laughed at this, and Crassus said, "This is the way I'll deal with you: since you wanted me to talk, I'll be telling you a bit about your own faults." "If only you would!" Sulpicius replied. "For that is precisely what we want, and if you do so, we will probably lay aside many of our 47 faults here today." "But surely," said Crassus, "I cannot criticize you, Sulpicius, without risk to myself because Antonius said that he thinks that you very much resemble me."[122] "He did so," said the other, "when he advised us to imitate the strongest points in each of our models.[123] Accordingly I fear that I have imitated nothing from you but the stamping of your foot, a few expressions, and perhaps some movements." "Then I will not criticize the points you've gotten from me," said Crassus, "in order not to make fun of myself – though they are much more numerous as well as more important than you say. But the qualities that are either clearly your own or that you have formed by imitating someone else, of these I will remind you, if there happens to be an occasion that prompts me to do so.

48   "Let us, then, pass over the rules for speaking correct Latin, which are taught in our elementary lessons, fostered by a more precise, systematic knowledge of grammar, or by the practice

of daily conversation at home, and strengthened by books and the reading of the ancient orators and poets. And really, let us not spend more time on the second point, on discussing in what ways 49 we can see to it that what we say will be understood – obviously by speaking correct Latin, by employing words in common use that properly designate the things we want to be signified and indicated, by avoiding ambiguous words or language, excessively long periodic sentences, and spun-out metaphors, by not breaking up the train of thought, confusing the chronology, mixing up people, or muddling the order. Why say more? The whole thing is so easy that I am often absolutely astonished that it is so difficult to understand what a pleader is trying to say – more difficult than it would be if the person who actually enlists the pleader were speaking about his case himself. The instruction we get from the 50 people who entrust their cases to us is usually so satisfactory that you couldn't ask for a clearer statement. But as soon as Fufius or your contemporary Pomponius[124] begins to treat the same material, I don't understand them as clearly, unless I pay really close attention – so confused and muddled are their speeches that nothing comes first, nothing second, and there is such a jumble of strange words, that the speech, which ought to shed light on the content, actually obscures and darkens it, and they somehow seem to drown themselves out when they are 51 speaking.[125] But I expect that, at least to you, the older ones here, these subjects are pretty tiresome and pedantic. So if you don't mind, let's move on to the other points, which are a little more troublesome."

"Actually," said Antonius, "I'm sure you see how little attention we are paying, how grudgingly we are listening to you. No (I can guess this when I look at myself), we can be made to abandon everything else to become your followers and listen to you. You discuss what is crude with such brilliance, what is barren with such fullness, and what is common with such originality!"

---

[120] Lucius Cotta, see 3.42.

[121] E.g., in the country the word *villa* was probably pronounced *vella* (Varro, *On Agriculture* 1.2.14).

[122] See 2.89.

[123] See 2.90–92.

[124] Crassus is still addressing Cotta and Sulpicius, for Pomponius was their (near-)contemporary.

[125] Both these orators often shouted when speaking (for Fufius, cf. 2.91; for Pomponius, *Brutus* 221).

52–55 True eloquence and the remaining two qualities of style (distinction and appropriateness)

52 "That, Antonius," Crassus replied, "is because the two parts that I just ran through, or rather, virtually passed over, are so very easy – speaking correct Latin and speaking clearly. The parts that remain are important, intricate, varied, and difficult, and on them alone depend the admiration for our talents and the praise of our eloquence. Nobody has ever admired an orator for speaking correct Latin; if he doesn't, they actually make fun of him, and not only consider him no orator, but not even a human being. Nor has anyone ever extolled a man for having spoken in such a way that those present understood what he was saying; on the contrary, everyone has always despised 53 people who proved incapable of doing so. Who is it, then, who sends shivers down your spine? At whom do people stare in stunned amazement when he speaks? For whom do they cheer? Whom do they consider, if I may use the expression, a god among men? Certainly those whose speech is well shaped, is unfolded with clarity and abundance, and is brilliant, both in its content and in its words, and who, where the actual form of the speech is concerned, produce something resembling rhythm and verse[126] – that is, those who practice what I call speaking with d istinction. Those who also regulate their speech in the way required by the relative importance of the subject matter and the people concerned, deserve praise for the quality that I call suitability and appropriateness.[127] 54 Antonius denied that he had ever yet seen such

speakers, and said that to them alone the title of eloquence should be awarded.[128] For this reason you have my blessing when you deride and scorn all those people who imagine they have embraced the entire power of oratory by using the precepts of the rhetoricians, as they are nowadays called, but who have never yet been able to understand what role they are assuming or what claim they are making. For the true orator ought to have examined and heard and read and discussed and thoroughly treated all aspects of human life, since it is with them that the orator is engaged, and it is 55 this that constitutes his material. Eloquence, after all, has its own place among the supreme virtues. Of course, all the virtues are equal and equivalent, but still, one is more beautiful and splendid in appearance than another.[129] This is the case with the power that I am talking about: having acquired all-embracing knowledge, it unfolds the thoughts and counsels of the mind in words, in such a way that it can drive the audience in whatever direction it has applied its weight. And the greater this power is, the more necessary it is to join it to integrity and the highest measure of good sense. For if we put the full resources of speech at the disposal of those who lack these virtues, we will certainly not make orators of them, but will put weapons into the hands of madmen.[130]

56–62 The original unity of speech and knowledge and its destruction

"I contend that this method of thought and 56 expression, this power of speaking is what the Greeks of old called wisdom. This is what

---

[126] By mentioning "something resembling rhythm and verse," Crassus anticipates his account of prose rhythm, much later in the book (3.173–198). "Verse," as he indicates, is not to be taken literally; elsewhere, he indeed emphasizes the difference with the poets in this respect (cf. 1.70, 3.175, 182, and 184).

[127] Crassus here refers to the two remaining (of the four) qualities of style announced in 3.37. His grandiose description of especially the first (speaking with distinction), however, is unlike the technical ones found in the handbooks, and this prepares the way for the broadened scope of what follows.

[128] Crassus here refers to Antonius' "little book" (libellus), first mentioned by Antonius himself in 1.94.

[129] Crassus here refers half-ironically to Stoic ideas (defended in almost the same words by Mnesarchus in 1.83). He starts by accepting their estimation of eloquence as a virtue, but in doing so talks of "supreme virtues," which is markedly un-Stoic, because to them, all virtues are equal. He proceeds, therefore, to "apologize," conceding that all virtues are indeed equal – only to qualify this again by saying that some are more beautiful than others. Eloquence, of course, is one of the more beautiful ones!

[130] This section is the only one in which Cicero places a moral demand on the (ideal) orator; perhaps surprisingly, this plays no further part in the work. Note that Crassus (Cicero) does not say that supreme eloquence, which is based on knowledge, will automatically be morally upright; on the contrary, it is "necessary" to join such powerful eloquence to moral qualities. The comparison with giving weapons to a madman goes back to Plato's Gorgias (456 C–457 C, and especially 469 C–470 C), but had probably become widespread.

produced people like Lycurgus, Pittacus, and Solon,[131] and from something analogous to it came Romans like Coruncanius, Fabricius, Cato, and Scipio (although the latter were perhaps not as learned, they were driven by a similar mentality and disposition). Others, who had the same intelligence but a different attitude toward the goals of life, chose an existence of peace and leisure, such as Pythagoras, Democritus, and Anaxagoras. They transferred their attention entirely from the government of communities to the study of the universe. Because of the tranquillity this brought with it and because of the attractiveness of pure knowledge, which is more pleasant for a human being than anything else, 57 more people took delight in this style of life than was beneficial for the states in which they lived. It was precisely the most gifted people who devoted themselves to this pursuit. Thus, on account of their unlimited supply of unoccupied, free time, these very learned people, richly gifted as they were with too much leisure and extremely fertile intellects, came to think that many more things were worthy of their care and their devoted investigations than was really necessary. For the old form of learning seems to have taught both right actions and good speech. Nor were the teachers separated from each other, but the same people gave instructions for living and for speaking, such as Phoenix in Homer, who says that Achilles' father Peleus had assigned him to the young Achilles to accompany him to the war, in order to make him 'a speaker of words and a doer of deeds.[132]' But 58 when people who are used to uninterrupted,

daily labor are prevented from work because of the weather, they often turn to ball games and dicing,[133] or even think up some new game for themselves during their leisure time. Something similar happened to the people I mentioned. Being either shut out from the affairs of state, just as from work, by the stormy circumstances of the time,[134] or having taken time off from these of their own accord, they transferred their attention entirely, some to the poets, some to mathematics, some to music; and others, such as the dialecticians,[135] even produced a new game for themselves to pursue. And in these arts, which were devised to educate children's minds in humane culture and virtue, they spent all of their time – yes, their whole lives.

"As I said, however, there were people (and not a 59 few of them) who either prospered in the state because of this twofold wisdom in action and speech, which cannot exist when split apart (for instance Themistocles, Pericles, and Theramenes),[136] or who were not themselves involved in the state, but were still teachers of this same wisdom (for instance Gorgias, Thrasymachus, and Isocrates). But in reaction to this, others appeared who on their part were amply endowed with learning and natural ability, but shirked politics and its responsibilities on deliberate principle; they criticized and scorned this practice of speaking. The most impor- 60 tant among them was Socrates. According to the unanimous testimony of the learned and the verdict of the whole of Greece, he easily ranked above all others, wherever he directed his attention – not only because of his intelligence, acumen, charm, and refinement, but also because of his eloquence,

---

[131] Pittacus and Solon were two of the Seven Wise Men, and Lycurgus was an early lawgiver of Sparta. All are here seen as statesmen, which was not unusual. In the quarrel between rhetoricians and philosophers, these figures were claimed by both camps: the rhetoricians said that they were orators, and used this as an argument for the value of rhetorical rules; the philosophers claimed that they were thinkers, and used this as an argument for the value of philosophy. Crassus takes an emphatic middle position: these people were thinkers as well as orators (but the latter here implies the value of oratory, not of rhetorical rules).

[132] Crassus here paraphrases *Iliad* 9.438–443, ending with a translation of 443. The line, and the position of eloquence in the Homeric epics in general, was probably a bone of contention in the quarrel between the rhetoricians and philosophers. The exact positions of the two camps are somewhat obscure, but Cicero clearly takes an idiosyncratic stand.

[133] In the Latin, Crassus actually mentions two forms of dicing, one with four-sided knucklebones (*tali*), and one with six-sided dice (*tesserae*).

[134] Cicero is here probably thinking about his own exile in 58–57 BC and his political isolation in the 50s.

[135] The study of the poets was part of the ancient art of "grammar."

[136] Athenian statesmen of the 5th century BC. Through Crassus' mention of Themistocles and Pericles, Cicero distances himself from Plato, who, in a famous passage of his *Gorgias* (515 B–517 A), attacked these two (together with Cimon and Miltiades) for misusing their eloquence.

variety, and fullness.[137] The people who discussed, practiced, and taught the subjects and activities we are now examining bore one and the same name (because knowledge of the most important things as well as practical involvement in them was, as a whole, called 'philosophy'),[138] but he robbed them of this shared title. And in his discussions he split apart the knowledge of forming wise opinions and of speaking with distinction, two things that are, in fact, tightly linked. (His genius and his varied conversations were rendered immortal by Plato in his writings, since Socrates himself had left not a single written syllable.) This 61 was the source of the rupture, so to speak, between the tongue and the brain,[139] which is quite absurd, harmful, and reprehensible, and which has resulted in our having different teachers for thinking and for speaking.[140] For many people virtually took their origin from Socrates, since different followers seized upon different aspects of his discussions, which had been varied and diverse and had branched out in all directions. Thus, mutually disagreeing families, so to speak, were bred, which were very much distinct and dissimilar,

though all philosophers still wanted to be called followers of Socrates, and indeed believed that 62 they were.[141] In the first place, from Plato himself came Aristotle and Xenocrates, whose schools were respectively called Peripatos and Academy.[142] Next, from Antisthenes, who, in Socrates' conversations, had been captivated particularly by the ideas about endurance and hardness, came first the Cynics, and then the Stoics. From Aristippus, finally, who had been more delighted by Socrates' discussions about pleasure, came Cyrenaic philosophy, which he and his descendants used to defend candidly and without qualification – whereas those who today measure everything by the standard of pleasure,[143] while doing so with greater modesty, neither satisfy the claims of the honorable, which they do not reject, nor manage to defend pleasure, which they want to embrace. There were also other families of philosophers, almost all of whom claimed to be followers of Socrates: the Eretrians, the Erillians, the Megarians, and the Pyrrhonians. These, however, were crushed and wiped out long ago by the forceful arguments of the schools now still in existence.[144]

[137] Note that Crassus stresses the paradoxical nature of Socrates' attitude by saying that he was himself truly eloquent.

[138] This claim is generally correct: in early Greek, the word *philosophia* (φιλοσοφία) had a much broader meaning than after, say, 300 BC: it included knowledge of a practical kind, especially about politics. It is doubtful, however, whether the actual *practice* of politics was also included in its meaning, as is here claimed; Cicero may be wrong, or may be deliberately exaggerating.

[139] Literally, "between the tongue and the heart"; the heart was considered the seat of the intellect.

[140] In the preface to his early *De inventione* (1.1–5), Cicero posited a similar rupture, but there he put it in a vague, distant past; there are also other, essential differences.

[141] This reasoning ("For many people …"), of which the following sections are partly a development (3.62–68), explains why the activity of Socrates has been decisive for bringing about the rupture just mentioned: for all their great differences, all later philosophers were his followers, and thus "inherited" his hostility to eloquence.

[142] In this section, Cicero (through Crassus) presents a "family tree" that comprises all existing philosophical schools. Such "family trees" were known as "Successions of the Philosophers," since they were built around the lines of succession in the philosophical schools, where each head on his death or resignation was succeeded by the next. These "Successions" were a common way of organizing the history of these schools, even though they involved a number of unhistorical and forced links; the approach is best known from Diogenes Laertius' compendium on the lives and doctrines of the ancient philosophers (written probably shortly after 200 AD). Cicero's version differs from all other variants that have come down to us in two ways, both of which are meant to make the schema as comprehensive as possible and thus to tie all the philosophers clearly to Socrates (see previous note): (1) he adds the Epicureans (see next note); (2) at the end of this section, he adds a list of the schools that are no longer extant; such lists were normally found in a different context (see, note 145).

[143] That is, the Epicureans, whose name is avoided also in the more extensive treatment in 3.63–64. The same criticism of inconsistency is found elsewhere (*On the Highest Good and the Highest Evil* 1.23, 26; 2.114). In line with what is said at the end of 3.61, Cicero here suggests (but is careful not to say) that the Epicureans were also followers of Socrates; this was not true, but in this way, Cicero can also force them into his explanation of the philosophers' hostility to eloquence (see the two previous notes).

[144] All of these "schools" (some of which were probably not formally organized) had apparently disappeared well before 200 BC. Lists such as these were normally found in the context of the so-called "division of Carneades" (cf., e.g., *On the Highest Good and the Highest Evil* 5.16–23).

63–68   *The present philosophical schools and the orator*

63 "Of the remaining schools, the philosophy that has taken up the patronage of pleasure, even if some may think it is true, still has nothing to do with the man whom we are looking for and whom we want to be an author of public policy, a guide in governing the community, and a leader who employs his eloquence in formulating his thoughts in the Senate, before the people, and in public court cases. All the same, this philosophy will suffer no wrong from us, for it will not be excluded from an area where it desires to go. Rather, it will be reposing in its delicate gardens,[145] where it wants to be. From there, while reclining in softness and effeminacy, it even tries to beckon us from the *rostra*,[146] from the courts, 64 and from the Senate House – perhaps wisely so, especially in the present political situation. But the question I am asking now is not which philosophy is the truest, but which has the most affinity with the orator. So let us dismiss these people, but without insulting them, for they are good folk and, since they think so themselves, they are blissful as well. Let us merely remind them to keep their opinion to themselves, and guard it as a holy secret, even if it should be quite true – I mean their claim that it is not the part of a wise man to be involved in politics. If they convince us as well as all the best people of the truth of this, then they themselves will not be able to do what they desire most – that is, to live in undisturbed peace.

65 "The Stoics, of whom I by no means disapprove, I still dismiss, without fearing their anger, seeing that they don't know how to get angry at all.[147] I am actually grateful to them, because they are the only ones among all the philosophers who have said that eloquence is a virtue and a form of wisdom.[148] But whatever the truth of that, something in their views is quite at odds with the orator that we are trying to equip. For instance, they say that all those who are not wise are slaves, bandits, enemies, and mentally deranged, and just the same, that no one is wise.[149] It would be rather absurd to entrust a public meeting, a Senate meeting, or any gathering of people to someone who thinks that none of those present is sane, none a citizen, none a free man. An additional problem is the way that 66 they speak. It is perhaps refined and certainly precise, but, from the point of view of an orator, it is meager, strange, foreign to the ears of the crowd, obscure, empty, and barren. Apart from this, it's the sort that one could never use before a crowd; good and bad do not mean to Stoics what they mean to the rest of the citizens, or rather, to the rest of the nations on earth, and they also have different conceptions of honor and disgrace, and of reward and punishment. Whether these are true or not is irrelevant for our present purpose, but if we follow their ideas, we would never be able to make anything understood through speech.

"That leaves the Peripatetics and Academics, 67 though the latter are really two schools of thought under one name. On the one hand Speusippus, Plato's nephew, and Xenocrates, Plato's pupil, as well as Xenocrates' pupils Polemo and Crantor, differed on no point to any great extent from Aristotle, who had heard Plato's lectures in their company – although they were perhaps not his equals in richness and variety of speaking. Polemo's pupil Arcesilaus was then the first to adopt, from the varied books of Plato and from Socrates' dialogues, especially the idea that there is no certainty that can be grasped either by the senses or by the mind. In this complete rejection of the mind and senses as instruments of judgment, he is said to have employed an exceptionally charming manner of speaking, and also to have been the first to establish the practice – although this was very characteristic of Socrates – of not revealing his own view, but of always arguing against any view that anyone else would

---

[145] The Epicureans were constantly associated with gardens: the school was originally located in the gardens belonging to Epicurus and was therefore known as the "Garden."

[146] *rostra*, the speaker's platform

[147] An important point of the philosophy of the Stoics was their ideal of being without emotions (ἀπαθεία).

[148] See 1.83 and 3.55.

[149] These are the so-called Stoic paradoxes (i.e., doctrines contrary to expectation), which follow from the absolute and uncompromising ethical doctrines of Stoic philosophy. Later, in 46 BC, Cicero wrote an (unserious) defense of these paradoxes, the *Paradoxa Stoicorum*.

68 assert.[150] This was the source of the more recent Academy of our own day, in which Carneades came forward as a man of superhuman quickness of mind and richness of speaking. I did meet many of his pupils personally when I was in Athens,[151] but I can cite two people as my most reliable authorities. In his youth, my father-in-law, Scaevola, heard him lecture in Rome,[152] and my friend Quintus Metellus, the son of Lucius, a man of great distinction, used to say that when he was a young man, he had heard Carneades lecture in Athens over the course of several days, when he was already quite old.

69–73 Restatement

69 "So, just as the rivers part at the watershed of the Apennines the disciplines parted when flowing down from the common ridge of wisdom. The philosophers flowed into the Ionian Sea on the East, as it were, which is Greek and well provided with harbors, while the orators came down into our barbarian Tyrrhenian Sea on the West, which is full of reefs and dangers, and where even Odysseus himself had lost his way.[153]

70 "Accordingly, if we are content with the present sort of eloquence and the present kind of orator, who knows that you must[154] either deny the charge brought against you, or if you cannot do that, then demonstrate that what the defendant has done was either done justly, or because of another's fault or another's wrongdoing, or in accordance with the law, or not against the law, or out of ignorance or necessity, or that it should not be designated by the name under which he is accused, or that the procedure is not as it ought to be and is allowed to be; and if you think it enough to learn what those handbook-writers teach, which was, for that matter, expounded by Antonius with much more distinction than by those people themselves, and with more fullness too[155] – I say, if you are content with all of this, and even with the things that you wanted me to tell you, then you are driving the orator away from a vast and immense field and forcing him into a pretty narrow circle. If, however, you want 71 to follow the famous Pericles of old, or if you want to follow Demosthenes, who is more familiar to us because of his numerous writings, and if you have come to love the splendid and outstanding appearance and the beauty of the perfect orator, then you must master the power of 72 Carneades or that of Aristotle. For, as I said before, those great men of the past, all the way down to Socrates, used to link the principles of oratory with the entire study and knowledge of everything that was relevant to human conduct, to human life, to virtue, and to the state. Then subsequently, as I have described, the learned were separated from the skillful speakers, first by Socrates himself, and after that likewise by all of Socrates' followers. The philosophers despised eloquence, and the orators wisdom, and each side did not so much as touch what belonged to the others, except for what each borrowed one from the other – whereas they would be drawing jointly from their common source had they preferred to remain in their former partnership.[156] 73

[150] That is, Arcesilaus (head of the Academy from ca. 270 BC) introduced a sceptical orientation into the school. The statement that this was already Socratic and Platonic reflects the claims of Arcesilaus himself and his successors to be real "Socratics." On the other hand, in this section the history of the Peripatos and Academy (a contested issue in Cicero's time) is not presented from a one-sided "sceptical" point of view. In a characteristically Ciceronian, balanced way, the rival view of the antisceptical Academic "rebel" Antiochus of Ascalon (ca. 130–69 BC) is also given its due; especially the claim that the early Academy and Aristotle resembled one another was typical of Antiochus.

[151] See 1.45.

[152] This is obviously supposed to have happened during the famous embassy in 156/155 BC (see 2.155). Cicero, however, most probably made a chronological mistake here, for Scaevola was born between 168 (or even 165) and 160 BC.

[153] In antiquity, Odysseus' wanderings were generally considered to have taken place in this area. The fact that "even he," astute as he was, lost his way, indicates the greatness of the dangers.

[154] In what follows, Crassus gives a deliberately monotonous summary of one of standard rhetoric's standard doctrines, viz., status theory.

[155] Crassus refers to Antonius' discussion in Book 2 (2.99 ff.). Antonius himself had repeatedly emphasized the differences from standard rhetoric, but his discussion did remain essentially technical, while Crassus' aim here goes beyond that.

[156] "Borrowing" implies only irregular and infrequent use of what belongs to another party, instead of the shared possession that Crassus insists upon. Cf. his language in 1.55, "I need not borrow from them."

But it is just as with the priests of the past. Because of the great number of sacrifices, they wanted there to be a Committee of Three Banquet Supervisors, even though they had themselves been appointed by Numa to conduct the sacrificial banquet at the games as well.[157] In the same way, the followers of Socrates dissociated the pleaders of cases from themselves and from the shared title of philosophy, though the ancients had intended there to be an amazing sort of communion between speaking and understanding.

[157] According to the (unhistorical) tradition, Numa was the second king of Rome, known for his wisdom, and responsible for many of Rome's religious practices, including the institution of the college of priests (*pontifices*). The institution of the committee of "Banquet Supervisors" (*epulones*) can be dated to 196 BC. This passage alludes to the political situation surrounding the dialogue, since one of the (two) banquets for which these *epulones* were responsible was (almost certainly) the "Banquet for Jupiter," held on September 13. That is, such a banquet was to be held on the day of the dramatic Senate meeting described in 3.2–6.

Pro Milone

The context for *Pro Milone* was discussed in the general introduction to Part II, so only a brief review is necessary here. In the last years of the Republic, law and order had largely disintegrated in Rome, and both the *populares* and the *optimates* were using gang warfare to influence politics. The two most notorious gang leaders were Clodius Pulcher, aligned with the *populares*, and Titus Annius Milo, aligned with the *optimates*. On January 18, 52 BC, Clodius and his entourage were traveling along the Appian Way several miles from the city when they had a chance encounter with Milo and his gang. A battle ensued, and Clodius and most of his men were slain, whereas only two of Milo's men lost their lives. Milo was indicted and brought to trial for murder.

Cicero was determined to defend Milo as a matter of principle: He and Clodius had hated each other for years. Clodius was responsible for sending Cicero into exile, and the enmity this engendered was exacerbated by Pulcher's support of the *populares*.[158] No doubt Cicero also was motivated by the knowledge that the case would give him one last opportunity to attack the character of his bitter enemy. Yet Cicero's task at trial was difficult, and it seems that he was so unnerved by the presence of Clodius' supporters and the very real threat they presented to his own welfare after the trial that he offered a weak, perhaps even incompetent, defense. The speech that has come down to us represents what Cicero wanted to say at the trial but did not.

The factors that alarmed Cicero were clear. The Senate was determined to try to rein in the gang warfare that had been plaguing the city for years and therefore had ordered a special court to handle the case, even though Milo was one of their own. The Senate also may have been sensitive to the fact that plebeians throughout Rome were attached to Clodius, not only because he supported their interests but also because he was a liberal spender when it came to providing bribes and festivals. When the common people first learned of the murder, riots broke out across the city, with plebeians eager to take matters into their own hands. The Senate bestowed special powers on Pompey so that he could restore some semblance of order. Tempers cooled somewhat after Clodius' closest supporters made the mistake of cremating their leader on the floor of the Senate house. They succeeded in burning down the entire building – and seriously damaged their public support in the process, for Romans of all classes were outraged by the stupidity of this excess. Nevertheless, the Senate needed at least to make a show of

[158] Cicero actually may have been operating behind the scenes, encouraging Milo to use his gang of slaves and gladiators to attack Clodius.

securing justice, for the plebeians were a fickle lot, and the situation could easily turn ugly if a trial did not take place.

Another complication for Cicero was that Milo and his thugs had not managed to kill all the members of Clodius' gang, and the survivors were ready to stand as witnesses for the prosecution. The situation was made even worse by the fact that the wounded Clodius and some of his men had taken refuge in an inn along the Appian Way, and when Milo and his crew arrived they killed the innkeeper as they dragged Clodius outside to finish him off. The several guests at the inn were also ready to testify against Milo. Thus, Cicero could not deny that his client had killed Clodius and was forced to find an alternative defense. In the heavily revised speech that Cicero produced after the trial, we find that the core argument to the court is the claim that Milo had acted in self-defense, but an important secondary claim is that the murder was justified because Clodius' death benefited the Republic.

Both claims required the skillful application of stasis theory and argument from probability, and the speech therefore provides an excellent opportunity to see intersections with Cicero's rhetorical treatises (*De Inventione* and *De Oratore*). Because the fact of the murder was indisputable, Cicero had to accept the prosecution's initial claim of *kataphasis* – Milo committed the act – and he was forced to apply the stasis of quality to offer the counterclaim that the killing was justified. This, then, was the issue that the jury had to decide. Cicero therefore ignored the most likely scenario – that the encounter was accidental – and argued that Clodius had previously threatened to kill Milo, that the violence of January 18 was premeditated, and that Clodius had obtained information regarding Milo's travel and had staged an ambush.[159] Self-defense, of course, is an affirmative defense in a murder case. But the number of witnesses against Milo presented such a serious problem that Cicero had no alternative but to concentrate on the secondary claim. Even if Clodius was not killed in self-defense, his murder was justified on the grounds that he was a terrible person despised by all.

Supporting this argument required significant reliance on *ethos* and *pathos*, and we find Cicero using both with abundance throughout the speech. He portrays Milo and Clodius as polar opposites, characterizing one as a saint and the other as a monster. He goes so far as to claim that Milo's entourage of gladiators and street ruffians consisted primarily of female servants and a boys' choir, "Whereas Clodius, who was habitually escorted by whores and homosexuals and streetwalkers, was not escorted on this occasion by any companions at all – except some individuals who were all of the same tough type" (XXI.55). In this respect, *Pro Milone* offers a useful model not only of applied oratory but also of forensic rhetoric as performance. Gotoff's (1993) analysis is insightful here: "The orator creates dramatic characters for himself and the prosecutor as well as for his client. Cicero provides everybody with a mask or masks; no one wears more than he does himself" (p. 292). Thus, typical of court speeches during this period, Cicero also devotes considerable time to discussing his own troubled relationship with Clodius, particularly the matter of his exile, to lend his authority as one of Rome's leading figures in support of his client. This *ethokoi* device is likely to strike modern readers as distracting because it frequently seems excessively vain, but in the context of Roman culture it was effective. As Paterson (2004) argued, self-reference and self-flattery in forensic speeches were congruent with the advocate's role as patron.

Cicero's failure at trial to use his oratorical skills fully no doubt contributed to Milo's conviction, but the preponderance of evidence against his client was so great that it is

---

[159] As a good advocate, he omitted to mention that Milo had made similar threats against Clodius, but it is very likely that the judges and jurors in the case were well aware of them.

very likely that the verdict would have been guilty even if Cicero had presented his revised speech. In exile, Milo took up residence in Massilia (today the city of Marseilles) and lived there for four years. Being removed from the hurly-burly politics of Rome and unable to practice his brand of political agitation became too much to bear, however. He knew full well that as an exile he was subject to immediate execution if he returned to Italy, but he nevertheless left Massilia in 48 BC. He was captured almost as soon as he arrived in Italy and was executed in the town of Cosa.

Reading 34

Pro Milone (For Milo)

Pro Milone (For Milo) (excerpt), pp. 217–36 and 277–8 from *Selected Political Speeches of Cicero*, translated by Michael Grant (Penguin, 1969).

For a speaker, who is beginning the defence of an extremely courageous man, to exhibit fear is a disgraceful thing, I must admit. And the fact, judges, that my client Titus Annius himself shows more concern for our country's salvation than for his own makes it particularly unbecoming that I am unable to muster the same intrepid spirit when I speak on his behalf. However, the unfamiliar aspect of this unfamiliar tribunal exercises an alarming effect on me. Wherever my eyes turn, they look in vain for the customary sights of the Forum and the traditional procedure of the courts. The usual circle of listeners is missing; the habitual crowds are nowhere to be seen. Instead you can see military guards, stationed in front of all the temples. They are posted there, it is true, in order to protect us from violence, but all the same they cannot fail to have an inhibiting effect on oratory. This ring of guards is, I repeat, both protective and necessary, and yet the very freedom from fear which they are there to guarantee has something frightening about it.

If I believed these precautions to be aimed against Milo, gentlemen, I should bow to necessity and conclude that amid all this weapon-power there was no place for an advocate at all. But on this point the wisdom of the sage and fair-minded Cnaeus Pompeius has relieved and reassured me. For once he has committed a man to a court to be tried, he would certainly not regard it as compatible with his sense of justice to place that same man at the mercy of troops bristling with arms. And it would also, surely, be inconsistent with his sound judgement to add official incitement to the violence of a wild and excited mob. In other words, what all these weapons and centurions and cohorts surely promise is not danger but a safeguard. They are meant to encourage us to be not only calm but determined as well; as I speak in defence of Milo they assure me physical security, but they also guarantee an uninterrupted hearing.

All the other Roman citizens in this audience are sympathetic. From any and every point overlooking the Forum you can see crowds gazing this way, and there is not a single soul among them who does not applaud the sterling qualities of Milo. And every one of these persons feels the same conviction: that not only Milo's future but his own, and the future of his children and his entire country, everything he possesses in the whole world, is at stake in this court today.

The people who are against us, on the other hand, the people who bear us ill-will, are those whom the hysteria of Publius Clodius has fed with loot and incendiarism and every sort of national calamity. They are the same crowd who at yesterday's mass-gathering were whipped up to dictate to you the verdict you are supposed to give today. And if their racket reaches your ears, it should, I hope, warn you of the necessity of cherishing as a fellow-citizen the man who has always spurned individuals of that type, however loud they shout, because his one preoccupation is with the safety of you all.

So give me your attention, gentlemen. If you feel any nervousness, dismiss it from your minds. For here is the greatest opportunity you have ever had to declare your attitude towards a fine and gallant gentleman, a citizen of proven loyalty. You who are members of our country's most distinguished Orders have often expressed your appreciation of goodness and bravery by looks and words, but this is your unequalled chance to clothe those sentiments in actual votes and deeds. For here and now a vital decision is yours and yours alone to give. We, for our part, have never failed in devotion to your authority, and now it is for you to decide whether we must continue to pine away in miserable hardship or whether instead, by your staunch, courageous and wise support, our prolonged persecution by these ruffians can at long last come to an end, so that we may begin to live again.

For the situation in which my client and myself find ourselves is in the highest degree painful and anxious and distressing. When he and I originally took up politics, we nourished the ambition that honourable rewards might come our way. But what has happened? Instead we suffer from incessant, tormenting fears of terrible penalties. I always realized Milo would be buffeted by storms and tempests of every other kind, that is to say of the kind encountered on the troubled waters of popular meetings. There was very good reason for this, since he has invariably backed the patriotic cause against disloyalty in all its forms. But in a trial, conducted in a court of law, where the most eminent members of all the Orders in the state pronounce their judgements, I never imagined for a moment that the enemies of Milo could entertain the smallest hope that such men might lend themselves to damaging his splendid reputation – much less that they would actually be willing to ruin him utterly.

And yet I do not propose to defend Titus Annius, gentlemen, by exploiting the success that he made of his tribuneship, or by dwelling on all the noble actions he performed at that time in the interests of our country. Far be it from me, I repeat, to ask that you should condone anything he may now have done on the grounds of his many outstanding services to the state. On the contrary, what I propose to do instead is to make you see, with your own eyes, that it was Clodius who subjected Milo to a treacherous attack. And if, again the death of Publius Clodius has in fact proved your salvation, it is by no means my purpose to allow you to ascribe this to Milo's valour – when the credit should rather go to the good fortune of Rome itself. However, if I can make it as clear as day (as I shall) that it was Clodius who laid this plot, then, gentlemen, and then only, I shall have one favour to ask of you most earnestly. It is this. Even if all else be taken from us, do not, I beg and beseech you, deprive us of this inalienable right: the right to defend our own lives when they are threatened by the brutal weapons of our foes.

But before I start dealing explicitly with the events you have come here to investigate, I feel it incumbent upon me to refute certain persistent allegations which have been spread by hostile individuals speaking in the Senate, as well as by scoundrels holding forth at public meetings – and just now they have been repeated by the prosecuting counsel as well. When I have dealt with this point, you will be in a position to examine, without any further risk of misapprehension, the issue which is before you. What these people are maintaining is that a person who has killed someone and confesses to the deed has by that very act lost all right to look upon the light of day and live. But the people who say this are evidently not very intelligent, if you consider the place in which they have chosen to develop this argument. For that place is actually the self-same city where the very first defendant in any capital trial was the valiant Marcus Horatius. And he was the man who, even in those days before the state was liberated from despotism, won his own liberation at the hands of the Assembly of the Roman people which absolved him from the charge of murder – in spite of his own voluntary admission that he had killed his sister with his own hands.[160]

Surely everyone must realize that any investigation into a murder offers two alternatives: either the deed is categorically denied, or it is admitted with the defence that it was justified and right. When a seditious tribune of the people, Gaius Carbo, asked Publius Africanus at an open meeting what he thought about the death of Tiberius Gracchus,[161] you will not, I am sure, accuse the

[160] According to the legend Marcus Horatius, after his two brothers had fallen in the fight in which they killed the three Curiatii of Alba, slew his sister Horatia because she displayed grief at the death of one of the Albans, who was her betrothed.

[161] The reference is to an inquiry made of P. Cornelius Scipio Aemilianus by C. Papirius Carbo after the murder of Ti. Sempronius Gracchus (133).

great man of mental aberration for his reply that, in his opinion, the killing was deserved. And if, again, it was automatically wrong to put Roman citizens guilty of criminal acts to death, then the famous Servilius Ahala, and Publius Nasica, and Lucius Opimius, and Gaius Marius,[162] and the Senate during my own consulship, would all have to be regarded as having acted sinfully. But the true conclusion, gentlemen, is that of the myth, handed down to us by the most eminent of writers, which tells of the man who slew his mother to avenge his father.[163] The votes of the human judges were divided; yet he was absolved by a verdict pronounced by the voice of divinity itself, speaking through the wisest among all the goddesses. Besides, the Twelve Tables themselves ordained that a thief by night may be killed under any circumstances – and that he may be killed also by day if he attempts to defend himself with a weapon. That being so, it is impossible to argue that every act of homicide must necessarily deserve punishment, since in certain circumstances the laws themselves place a sword in our hands to inflict death upon our fellow-men.

There are, in fact, many occasions on which homicide is justifiable. In particular, when violence is needed in order to repel violence, such an act is not merely justified but unavoidable. Once upon a time a soldier in the army of Gaius Marius was indecently assaulted by a military tribune who was a relative of the general. But the victim of the assault slew his seducer because he was an honourable young man who believed that resistance, whatever the perils involved, was preferable to shameful compliance; and the great commander acquitted him and let him go free. And so, equally, to end the life of a man who is a bandit and a brigand can never be a sin. For what, if it were, would be the point of the bodyguards we take around with us, the swords we carry? We should obviously not be allowed to have them if they were never intended for use.

And indeed, gentlemen, there exists a law, not written down anywhere but inborn in our hearts; a law which comes to us not by training or custom or reading but by derivation and absorption and adoption from nature itself; a law which has come to us not from theory but from practice, not by instruction but by natural intuition. I refer to the law which lays it down that, if our lives are endangered by plots or violence or armed robbers or enemies, any and every method of protecting ourselves is morally right. When weapons reduce them to silence, the laws no longer expect one to await their pronouncements. For people who decide to wait for these will have to wait for justice, too – and meanwhile they must suffer injustice first. Indeed, even the wisdom of the law itself, by a sort of tacit implication, permits self-defence, because it does not actually forbid men to kill; what it does, instead, is to forbid the bearing of a weapon with the intention to kill. When, therefore, an inquiry passes beyond the mere question of the weapon and starts to consider the motive, a man who has used arms in self-defence is not regarded as having carried them with a homicidal aim. So, for the purpose of the present trial, let us regard that principle as established. For if you bear in mind that the slaying of a man who waylays another may on occasion be justifiable – and you can scarcely do otherwise – I am certain I shall be able to convince you that my case for the defence should prevail.

The next point is one which Milo's enemies repeatedly stress. The fatal skirmish which resulted in the death of Publius Clodius, they emphasize, has been defined by the Senate as an act contrary to the interests of the state. And yet the Senate really approved of the deed. It showed that it did so, both by votes it had registered on earlier occasions, and by other clear manifestations of sympathy as well. Think of all the times I have pleaded this very same cause in the Senate and received its approbation in unanimous, unconcealed, outspoken terms. Even at its most crowded meetings there have never been more than four or at most five members who failed to support Milo's policy. This was openly admitted by that tribune[164] (half-roasted by the conflagration in the Senate House) whose dead–alive harangues, day after day, malignantly attacked what he called my

---

[162] C. Servilius Ahala killed Sp. Maelius (439), P. Cornelius Nasica Serapio led the attack on Tio Sempronius Gracchus (133), and L. Opimius on C. Sempronius Gracchus (121); C. Marius was regarded as responsible for the deaths of L. Appuleius Saturninus and C. Servilius Glaucia (100).

[163] Aeschylus and Latin tragedians told of the slaying of Clytaemnestra by her son Orestes to avenge his father Agamemnon.

[164] T. Munatius Plancus Bursa is described, perhaps accurately, as having sustained burns in the fire in the Senate House caused by the supporters of the dead Clodius who cremated him there (19 January). He was one of the extremely few men ever prosecuted by Cicero (for violence).

'supremacy', declaring that the Senate's resolutions did not reflect its own opinions at all, but merely echoed mine. Supremacy, as a matter of fact, is not the right word for what is really just a modest influence for the good, based on a considerable record of public service – or it could be described as a measure of popularity among right-minded people because of all the efforts I have made to help them in the courts. However, call it supremacy if you will, provided you concede that I use it to save loyal citizens from the frenzied attacks of scum.

I am not saying there is anything unfair about the court conducting this trial. All the same, the Senate has never on any previous occasion regarded the establishment of such a commission as a necessity. For laws and courts covering murder and violence already existed – and the grief and lamentation aroused in the Senate by the news of Clodius death were not so overwhelmingly large as to necessitate the institution of an altogether novel tribunal. Since the Senate had not been allowed to appoint the judges who tried Clodius for immorality and sacrilege,[165] it seems very strange that this same body should have thought it imperative to set up a brand-new investigating commission to report on the circumstances of his death. For, if that needed to be done, why was the Senate itself perfectly prepared, on its own account and without any such special machinery, to pronounce that the burning of the Senate House, and the attack on the house of Marcus Aemilius Lepidus,[166] and the bloodshed which is the subject of the present case, were all acts that contravened the interests of the nation? And they were quite right to do so, because in a free country any and every violence used by one citizen against another cannot fail to be contrary to the welfare of our country. Even self-defence against violence, which I was upholding just now, is very far from being actually desirable. Nevertheless, sometimes it is necessary. Take, for example, those occasions on which Tiberius Gracchus and Gaius Gracchus were killed, and the armed action of Saturninus was put down. Their repression could not fail to

convulse the Republic; though it was to safeguard the Republic that it had to be carried out.

That is why, bearing in mind that a death was the outcome of that skirmish on the Appian Way, I refrained from voting in favour of the proposition that the man who had caused it in self-defence acted against the interests of the state. Instead, conscious that violence and treacherous attack were involved, I voted my disapproval of the whole affair, leaving, however, the question of guilt to be decided by a court of law. And if that demented tribune had allowed the Senate to do as it had wished, we should never have been obliged to have this freshly created court. For what the Senate had wanted was that the action, while accorded a special degree of priority, should be tried by existing laws. But the motion was brought forward in two parts, on someone or other's proposal[167] (there is no need for me to expose the deplorable errors of each and every individual!). The first part denounced the deed, and the proposal to which I have just referred became the second part; but it failed to come to anything because bribery managed to get it stopped by a veto.

You may, perhaps, suggest that Cnaeus Pompeius' bill made it clear what opinion he himself held regarding not only the facts of the case but the distribution of blame as well, since the terms of his measure referred explicitly to the fight on the Appian Way 'in which Publius Clodius was killed'. But the point of his measure, in fact, was that there must be an investigation. Now the inquiry had no need to consider whether the act had been committed or not, because there is no disagreement about this. By whom was it committed? That too is obvious. In other words, Cnaeus Pompeius fully appreciated that avowal of the deed by no means excludes the possibility of justification. Had he not realized that a man who confessed to such action might reasonably be acquitted, he would never, once he had heard the confession, have ordered an inquiry to be held at all, and would not, therefore, have given you the choice of recording upon your tablets, instead of C for condemn,[168] the welcome A for absolve.

---

[165] Clodius was accused of bursting into the rites of the Bona Dea in woman's clothes in order to prosecute his affair with Caesar's wife Pompeia (December 62). The religious violation could be classified as *incestum*. Much to Cicero's disappointment he was acquitted.

[166] After Clodius' death his gangs attacked the house of M. Aemilius Lepidus the Interrex (appointed to conduct the elections), the future triumvir.

[167] Q. Fufius Calenus. Any Senator could demand the division of a composite motion. The 'demented tribune' was T. Munatius Plancus Bursa.

[168] A (*absolvo*) and C (*condemno*) were marked on either side of the voting tablets of the judges, who erased one of the letters.

As I see it, Cnaeus Pompeius has definitely refrained from making any sort of pronouncement in Milo's disfavour. What he has done instead is to point out what you yourselves ought to look for when you come to your decision. For by ensuring that the result of the confession should not be a penalty but a chance to plead justification, he has indicated his conviction that it is not the actual fact of the death that needs investigating at all; the subject of the examination must instead be the circumstances in which that death occurred. And as to his reasons for this step, which he took entirely upon his own initiative – whether he meant it as a tribute to the virtues of Publius Clodius or a concession to a critical situation – he himself will no doubt shortly be explaining to us what his intentions were.

The noble Marcus Drusus,[169] who was tribune of the people, champion and in those difficult times virtually patron of the Senate – and he was also the uncle of the valiant Marcus Cato who is sitting on our bench today – succumbed to murder in his own house. And yet no motion of any kind bearing upon his death was proposed before the Assembly of the people; no special inquiry was decreed by the Senate. Our fathers have also told us of the great grief into which the city was plunged when Publius Africanus the younger,[170] resting quietly at his home, was fatally struck down during the night. There was universal sorrow and burning indignation that the man whom everyone wanted to become immortal, if such a thing be possible, should not even have been permitted to last out the natural term of his mortal life. Well, was there any special commission to look into the death of Africanus? There was not. And why? Because there is no distinction, as a crime, between the murder of the great and the murder of the humblest citizen in the land. In life, it is true, the positions of the highest and lowest are very different. But as to their death, when this is feloniously brought about, the same penalties and laws have to apply universally. A man who kills his father is just as much a parricide

when the victim is a nonentity as when he has held office as a consul.

And, that being so, the death of Publius Clodius does not assume any the graver significance because he was killed among the monuments of his ancestors. For that is what the other side keep on repeating. They seem to imagine that the famous Appius Claudius Caecus had built his Appian Way[171] not for public use at all, but as a place where his descendants might prey on their fellows with impunity. That, I can only suppose, must be why Publius Clodius was able to murder a very distinguished knight, Marcus Papirius,[172] without the crime apparently calling for any punishment whatever. For the murderer was an aristocrat, surrounded by his own family memorials; and the man he was disposing of was merely a Roman knight. And now, on this occasion, what sagas are being woven round the name of this same Appian Way, with its Claudian origins! When its stones were drenched in the blood of an innocent, honourable man, this aspect was not even mentioned. But now that the blood is of a robber and a traitor, the talk about it never stops.

Nor need we restrict ourselves to instances from the past. For this very Publius Clodius himself posted a slave in the temple of Castor to assassinate Cnaeus Pompeius. The slave was caught, and the dagger was wrenched from his hand, and he confessed. From then onwards Pompeius kept away from the Forum and the Senate and the public gaze altogether. Evidently, he did not consider his rights under the laws and courts to be sufficient protection: the shelter of his own door and walls seemed preferable. Yet on that occasion, again, no new law was proposed, no novel court of inquiry set in motion. But surely no previous occasion, or personage, or emergency, had ever pointed so imperatively to the need for such a step! The conspirator was stationed right inside the Forum; he was actually within the forecourt of the Senate House itself. Moreover, the proposed victim of his ambush was the personage on whose life the whole future of the country depended – and the criminal design was entered

[169] M. Livius Drusus was killed after proposing a law to extend the franchise to Italians (91).

[170] It was suspected that P. Cornelius Scipio Aemilianus was the victim of assassination owing to his resistance to the Gracchan land commission (129).

[171] The Appian Way was built by Ap. Claudius Caecus (censor 312) and lined with tombs of the Claudii.

[172] M. Papirius and others were trying to prevent the escape (from Pompeius' custody) of Tigranes I, whom Clodius was hoping to restore to the kingdom of Armenia (58).

upon at such a grave hour of national crisis that if Pompeius had fallen, and even if he had been the one and only man to fall, this country of ours and all the nations of the world would have collapsed in ruin. For you will not, I imagine, wish to suggest that the failure of the plot exonerates it from punishment. Such a proposition would signify that the laws take no cognizance of intentions, and are only interested in results. The fact that the assassination did not come off gave us less cause to grieve, it is true, but surely did not diminish in any way the need to punish the attempt.

And many is the time that I too, gentlemen, have narrowly managed to escape from Publius Clodius' weapons and gory hands. If, by my own good fortune and that of Rome itself, I had not succeeded in dodging them, I am perfectly sure that no one would have proposed a special investigation into my death!

But how ridiculous of me to presume to compare Drusus, Africanus, Pompeius and myself with Publius Clodius. The actions against them were, I suppose, not beyond our endurance; but obviously no one could be expected to bear with equanimity the death of a man of Clodius' calibre! See how the Senate grieves for him! The knights have broken hearts, the whole country is in a state of collapse, deepest mourning shrouds every town, the colonial settlements are plunged in abject misery. For how could the entire population be anything but inconsolable at the loss of this citizen who was so noteworthy for his kindly and benevolent and gentle personality?

No, members of the bench: that was certainly *not* why Pompeius decided upon the establishment of a special commission. The fact of the matter rather was that his lofty wisdom, a wisdom which is not as other men's, appreciated a number of considerations. That Clodius had been his enemy, that Milo was his friend, he was perfectly well aware. Yet, if he associated himself with the universal rejoicing at Clodius' death, he was afraid that the authenticity of his recent reconciliation with Clodius might take on a dubious appearance. And, among the many other factors that he bore in mind, one predominated over all the rest: he was absolutely certain that, however severe the terms of his own proposal, your decision would still be impartial.

With this in view, the judges he selected were the brightest luminaries of the most excellent Orders in the state. The allegation that his choice was specially directed to exclude my own friends is quite untrue. For one thing, he was much too fair-minded a person ever to have considered such an idea at all. And besides, even if he had, the adoption of such a course would have been incompatible with his determination to choose good men. My most intimate associates, I admit, are not perhaps very numerous, because, after all, one can only have close and constant relationships with a limited number of people; but my adherents are by no means restricted to them. On the contrary, any influence I may possess is derived from the fact that public life has brought me into touch with a wide range of good men. And so Pompeius, bent on selecting for this case the best judges he could find, and well aware that his own reputation was deeply involved in the choice, could not have failed to nominate people who felt warmly towards myself.

Moreover, Pompeius' strong desire that you, Lucius Domitius,[173] should preside over the court demonstrates his single-minded intention to go for justice, authority, humaneness and integrity. As a preliminary he had enacted that the chairman must be of consular rank – evidently believing that it is the special function of our national leaders to stand up against the emotionalism of the crowd and the importunity of agitators. And out of all the consulars it was you upon whom his choice fell: for from your earliest years you have given ample proof of the disgust with which you view the excesses of agitators.

And now, gentlemen, we must come to the charge which is the reason for this trial. I have shown that confession of such a deed is not wholly without precedent. I have suggested that the only pronouncements the Senate has offered about our case were in complete conformity with what we ourselves should have wished. I have pointed out that the proposer of the law himself, even though there is no argument about the facts, desired the investigation to go further and look into the rights of the matter. And I have stressed that the judges and president chosen to conduct the action are personages whose deliberations will be both just and wise. It only remains then, gentlemen, for you

---

[173] L. Domitius Ahenobarbus, of the extreme right wing, was actually appointed president of the court by the Assembly – no doubt on the initiative of Pompeius.

to decide which of the two men involved laid the plot against the other. So as to help you to obtain a clearer view of the true circumstances, I will now give a brief account of what happened; and I ask for your close attention.

Publius Clodius was determined to use the post of praetor[174] to convulse the government by every sort of evil-doing. But the elections of the previous year had dragged on so protractedly that he saw his own praetorship would be restricted to a period of no longer than a few months. Advancement in rank, which appeals to other men, was not his object at all. One of the purposes that carried more weight in his mind was a strong desire to avoid having an excellent man like Lucius Paullus as his colleague. But Clodius' main ambition was to have an entire year to devote to the disruption of our state. And so he suddenly abandoned the idea of being praetor in the earliest year to which he was entitled, and transferred his candidature to the following year instead. His motive in so doing was very far from involving the religious scruples which sometimes cause people to take such a step. On the contrary – as he himself admitted – what he wanted was to have a full and continuous year for the exercise of his praetorship: that is to say, for the subversion of the Republic.

All the same, in regard to the latter year as well, a worrying thought continued to nag him. This was the consideration that if Milo was elected to the consulate for that year his own praetorship would once again be hampered and paralysed. Indeed, as Clodius clearly appreciated, there was every likelihood of Milo becoming consul, and by the unanimous vote of the Roman people at that. In this situation he attached himself to Milo's competitors, and did so in such a way that he himself should have complete control of their electoral campaigns – whether they liked it or not. That is to say, as he himself frequently expressed it, his intention was to carry the entire election upon his own shoulders. And so he proceeded to marshal the tribes, acting as a go-between in every negotiation and mobilizing disreputable toughs who virtually amounted to a new Colline tribe[175] in themselves.

And yet the more flagrantly Clodius' disturbances raged, the stronger waxed Milo's position

every day, until finally it became evident to Clodius, through the unmistakable voice of public opinion expressing itself in a series of popular votes, that this courageous man, his inveterate enemy, was certain to become consul. And so Clodius, who was ready to stop at nothing, now began to operate openly: and he declared straight out that Milo must be killed.

Clodius had a gang of rustic and barbarous slaves whom he had recruited to ravage the national forests and harass the Etrurian countryside. These he now brought down from the Apennines – and you have seen the creatures yourselves. There was not the slightest concealment, for he himself asserted repeatedly and publicly that even if the consulate could not be taken away from Milo, the same could not be said about his life. Clodius frequently gave indications to this effect in the Senate, and he said it at mass meetings too. Moreover, when the gallant Marcus Favonius asked him what purpose all this violence could possibly serve while Milo was alive to resist it, Clodius replied that within three or, at most, four days Milo would be dead. And Favonius promptly reported this remark to Marcus Cato here.

Meanwhile Clodius became aware (and it was an easy enough fact to discover) that on 18 January Milo was under an obligation, prescribed by ritual and law, to proceed to Lanuvium. He held the local office of dictator[176] and it was his duty to make a nomination to the priesthood of the town. Equipped with this knowledge, Clodius left Rome without notice on the previous day. As subsequent events demonstrated, his plan was to take up a position in front of his own country manor, and set an ambush for Milo on that spot. Clodius' departure from Rome meant that he had to absent himself from a turbulent public gathering on that same day. His usual violent contributions were greatly missed at the meeting, and he would certainly never have failed to play his part had he not formed the deliberate intention to be punctually in the locality set for the ambush at the appropriate time.

Meanwhile Milo, on the other hand, attended the Senate on that day, until the meeting was

---

[174] Clodius had been aedile in 56 and according to the *Lex Villia* could have been elected praetor in 54.
[175] The Colline tribe was composed of the lowest class of citizens.
[176] 'Dictator' was an ancient title of office at Milo's home town Lanuvium, going back to its independent days and now limited to religious duties.

concluded. Then he proceeded to his home, changed his shoes and his clothes, waited for the usual period while his wife got ready, and then started off at just about the time when Clodius could have got back to Rome if it had been his intention to return at all on the day in question. But instead he encountered Clodius in the country. The man was lightly equipped, not seated in a coach but riding on horseback, unimpeded by any baggage, with none of his usual Greek companions, and even without his wife who nearly always travelled with him. Milo, on the other hand, was sitting in a coach with his wife, wearing a heavy travelling cloak and accompanied by a substantial, heavily laden, feminine, unwarlike retinue of maids and pages.[177] And this was our so-called waylayer, the man who had allegedly planned the expedition with the explicit purpose of committing a murder!

And so at about five in the afternoon, or thereabouts, he found himself confronted by Clodius before the gates of the latter's house. Milo was instantly set upon by a crowd of armed men who charged down from higher ground; while, simultaneously, others rushed up from in front and killed the driver of the coach. Milo flung back his cloak, leapt out of the vehicle, and defended himself with energy. But meanwhile the people with Clodius were brandishing their drawn swords, and while some of them ran towards the coach in order to fall upon Milo from the rear, others believed he was already slain and began to attack his slaves who had been following behind him. A number of these slaves of Milo's lost their lives defending their master with loyal determination. Others, however, who could see the fight round the coach but were unable to get to their master's help, heard from Clodius' own lips that Milo was slain, and believed the report. And so these slaves, without the orders or knowledge or presence of their master – and I am going to speak quite frankly, not with any aim of denying the charge but just exactly as the situation developed – did what every man would have wished his own slaves to do in similar circumstances.

The incident, gentlemen, took place precisely as I have described it. The attacker was defeated. Force was frustrated by force; or, to put the matter more accurately, evil was overcome by good. Of the gain to our country and yourselves and all loyal citizens, I say nothing. It is not my intention to urge that the deed be counted in favour of Milo – the man whose self-preservation was destined to mean the preservation of the Republic and yourselves. No, my defence is that he was justified in acting to save his life. Civilized people are taught this by logic, barbarians by necessity, communities by tradition; and the lesson is inculcated even in wild beasts by nature itself. They learn that they have to defend their own bodies and persons and lives from violence of any and every kind by all the means within their power. That being so, if you come to the conclusion that this particular action was criminal, you are in the same breath deciding that every other man in the history of the world who has ever fought back against a robber deserves nothing better than death – and that if the robber's weapons did not manage to produce this result, then you yourself would be quite prepared to bring it about! If Milo had been of the same mind, he would have done better to offer his throat to Clodius, who had already attacked him repeatedly, than to refuse the death-blow from Clodius merely so that it could be death him subsequently by yourselves.

If, then, you are all agreed that self-defence is not necessarily wrong, you need not trouble about the question *whether* Clodius was killed. For we fully admit that he was. What you have to consider instead is that issue which has so frequently been raised in a variety of different cases – namely, whether the act was justifiable or not. That a plot existed is generally agreed, and indeed the plot is what the Senate has denounced as having been contrary to the national interests. But the point that needs to be settled is which of the two men was the conspirator, and this is the problem you were appointed to investigate. What the Senate censured was the deed itself, and not any particular individual; and the inquiry set up by Pompeius was intended to determine not the facts, but the question of justification. So quite clearly the only matter before the court is this: which man plotted against the other? If Milo plotted against Clodius, let him be punished; if Clodius plotted against Milo, then the only proper verdict is Milo's acquittal.

How, then, can it be proved that it was Clodius who laid the plot against Milo? When we are dealing with such an audacious and despicable monster as Clodius, it will surely carry conviction if we can prove that there was a strong incentive for him to

---

[177] Asconius says Milo was accompanied by a large number of slaves including gladiators.

kill Milo; and that he had high hopes and the prospect of great benefits from his death. We must consequently apply to the two men's characters that famous maxim of Cassius, *Who stood to gain?*[178] And to that it is only necessary to add that personal advantage will never drive a good man to crime, while a bad man will succumb even if the advantage is trivial. Now, if Milo had been killed, Clodius would have gained in two ways. First, he would not have been compelled to serve as praetor under a consul who would have made it impossible for him to indulge in mischievous behaviour. Secondly, the consuls who would have held office in Milo's place might have been expected by Clodius, if not actually to collaborate with him, at the very least to connive in allowing him a free hand to carry out his appalling designs. For no doubt he reasoned that, even if it were within their power to hamper his efforts, they would not be keen to do so since they were under such heavy obligations towards him. Besides, even if their intentions were obstructive, they might in any case scarcely possess the power to crush this loathsome creature's programme – so well established as it was, following a long list of previous outrages.

[...]

If only heaven had arranged – forgive me, Rome, for what I am now about to say, for the wish I am expressing in Milo's interests may, I fear, be criminally harmful to your own. But I am obliged to pronounce the wish that Publius Clodius had lived after all! And had not only lived but become praetor and consul and even dictator

– anything rather than that I should have survived to see what I am seeing today. For Milo, heaven knows, is a truly valiant man: a man whom you will do well to preserve. He himself, it is true, speaks in different terms. Of Clodius he says it is good that he received the punishment he merited. 'But as for myself,' he goes on, 'let me, if I must, be punished as well – though I have done nothing whatever to deserve it.'

Milo was born to serve his country. Surely, then, it cannot be right that he should be forbidden to die within its bounds – or at least while continuing to fight on its behalf. The reminders of his heroism will always be with you – and yet do you really propose to allow him no corner of Italian soil for the burial of his body? If Milo went into exile, he would be welcomed by every other city in the world. How, then, could anyone venture to vote for the banishment of such a man as that? Blessed is the land which shall give sanctuary to this hero! Ungrateful Rome, if it shall cast him out! Unhappy Rome, if it shall be bereft of him!

But enough. Tears choke my voice; and my client does not want a tearful defence. What I am asking you, gentlemen, and asking you urgently, is that when you come to cast your votes, you should be brave enough to act as you really think is right. If you do, believe me, your fearlessness, impartiality and integrity will meet with sincere approval from the person who, in picking the judges, has permitted his choice to fall upon men who are conspicuous for their loyalty and their wisdom and their courage.

---

[178] *Cui bono* was the maxim of L. Cassius Longinus, tribune of the people in 137.

Study Questions

1   Although in the beginning of *De Inventione* Cicero follows Aristotle in linking rhetoric with political science, he quickly shifts the discussion from deliberative to forensic oratory and does not examine in depth the role of rhetoric in politics. How would you relate this shift to the socio-historical context of the time?

2   In *De Oratore*, Cicero stated that only someone who has "gained a knowledge of all the important subjects and arts" could be an outstanding orator. How might this position expose Cicero to Plato's criticism?

3   What does Crassus mean in *De Oratore* when he states that the "petty Greeks" are "fonder ... of an argument than of the truth"?

4   Cicero wrote that the aim of oratory was to prove, delight, and persuade. What features of *De Oratore* seem intended to delight Cicero's readers?

5   *Pro Milone* illustrates the use of encomium and invective to praise Milo and condemn Clodius Pulcher, even though a majority of the jurors in this case probably knew something about these men and their characters. What are some of the rhetorical challenges an orator faces under this condition?

6   Where in *Pro Milone* do we find *stasis* and argument from probability? How do they function to support Cicero's defense of Milo?

Writing Topics

1   Evaluate *De Oratore* as a work designed to prove, delight, and persuade. Does one feature tend to dominate? If so, why?

2   Analyze *Pro Milone* to determine the extent to which Cicero's applied rhetoric follows the precepts provided in *De Inventione* and *De Oratore*.

3   The formal principles of oratory emerged in the context of court cases but immediately became entangled with issues associated with philosophy. Describe a rhetoric totally disentangled from philosophy.

4   Using concrete examples to illustrate your argument, examine to what extent, if any, *probare, delectare*, and *flectere* influence modern communications.

Further Reading

Cicero, *Academica*.

Cicero, *Brutus*.

Cicero, *Orator*.

Morstein-Marx, R. (2004). *Mass oratory and political power in the late Roman republic*. Cambridge: Cambridge University Press.

8

Horace and the Revival of Poetry

Introduction to Horace (65–8 BC)

Quintus Horatius Flaccus, or Horace, was born in Venusia, located in the southeastern region of Italy. His father, a former slave who succeeded in freeing himself before the birth of his son, served as a *coactor argentarius* (auction broker) and *publicanus* (tax collector), earning enough money to purchase a small estate and to provide Horace with an excellent education. As a boy, Horace studied grammar, literature, and rhetoric in Rome, and even at this early age his interest in poetry motivated him to compose verses in Greek. After finishing his studies in Rome, he traveled to Athens for more advanced work in literature, philosophy, and rhetoric.

This tranquil life of ease and luxury ended abruptly with the assassination of Julius Caesar. Brutus and Cassius, the principal conspirators in the assassination, had misjudged the sentiments of the Roman people and were forced to flee to Greece after the murder. There they took control of the Eastern portion of the Empire and began assembling two large armies to face the inevitable assault of Octavian and Marc Antony, who were determined to punish them. Horace was studying with a group of wealthy young Romans, and this association no doubt led to an introduction to Brutus, who was using Athens as his headquarters while preparing his forces. Even though a plebeian of limited means compared to the young aristocrats flocking to Brutus' army, Horace sided with the *optimates* and volunteered for duty. For reasons that are unclear, Brutus made him a military tribune despite the fact that he had no experience.

As Brutus and Cassius marched their troops to Philippi, in Thrace, Horace may have had some misgivings, owing to his total lack of military training. Nevertheless, he was with Brutus in October of 42 BC when the assassins' armies engaged the forces of Antony and Octavian. The fighting was hard on both sides, for the legionaries were seasoned veterans who knew the taste of war. In two major battles, Brutus and Cassius lost approximately three-quarters of their men, with only about 24,000 surviving out of an estimated 100,000 troops and cavalry. Stunned by their defeat, both Brutus and Cassius committed suicide rather than face capture.

Horace was among the lucky few who lived. He made his way back to Italy, only to discovered that his father was dead, perhaps owing to a proscription, and that his property had been confiscated. How he supported himself over the next few years is uncertain, but when Augustus issued a general amnesty, in 39 BC, Horace was able to obtain a position as a public clerk. He had ample time for writing, and somehow he became acquainted with Gaius Maecenas (c. 70–8 BC), an extremely wealthy aristocrat, close advisor to Augustus, and patron of the arts. Maecenas encouraged Horace's literary ambitions, and with his patronage Horace was able to devote more time to writing. His first significant work was a book of satires, which may have been published around 35 BC. The satires mocked the rich for their obsessive pursuit of wealth and status while carefully flattering Maecenas, who in gratitude may have gifted Horace two years later with a farm, which Horace celebrated in much of his poetry as a pastoral ideal (see Meuke, 2007).

The patronage relationship between Horace and Maecenas evolved into a close friendship and gave the poet access to the most elite level of society. The emperor was an admirer and granted him a commission. Horace, however, never lost sight of his heritage, and in many of his poems he reflected on the good fortune that had made Maecenas his patron. He was not ashamed of the fact that he was the son of a freedman and extolled the virtues of a simple life. Nor did he allow his head to be turned by the many solicitations for favors that resulted from his connections to the imperial court. Horace captured the essence of his modest sentiments in his second book of satires. *Satire vi* relates the story of a simple country mouse whose city-slicker cousin persuades him to leave the country to enjoy a life of luxury and high society. Just as the two are settled onto velvet cushions, ready to feast, they are tumbled to the ground by the entry of barking, ferocious dogs. The country mouse exclaims, "I don't need any of this, and so good-bye to it. I long for my safe woods, simple hole, and a small meal of grain" (vi, 114–117).

The satires were followed by the *Epodes*, written, perhaps, around 29 BC. These poems reflect a variety of themes: for example, celebrating Maecenas, rejoicing in the virtues of a simple life in the country, ridiculing the posturing of a young "upstart," and warning of the repellent smell of garlic on the breath. There is the sense throughout that Horace was a man conflicted by his heritage and his destiny: born to relatively modest circumstances on the one hand and elevated to imperial-court poet on the other (see L. Watson, 2007). Approximately six years later, he produced three books of lyric poems entitled *Odes*, which Hardison and Golden (1995) described as "among the loveliest and most finished lyrics in the Latin language" (p. 24). All of these works have a playful quality that encourages good humor despite life's difficulties (see Barchiesi, 2007). The *Odes*, for example, celebrate life in the face of inevitable death. It was in the first of these books that Horace gave us the immortal phrase *"carpe diem"*:

Dum loquimur, fugerit invida   Even while we speak, jealous time has passed:
Aetas: carpe diem, quam minimum credula postero. seize the day, putting as little trust as possible in
(I, xi)   tomorrow.

Around 20 BC, Horace produced his first book of *Epistles*, or "letters" in verse. The *Epistles* are generally reflective, tinged with philosophical elements, the most prominent being Epicureanism, which also was an important factor in his earlier work. Horace shaped a dramatic monologue to project the persona of a retired poet commenting on life from his country farm and offering advice to friends (see Ferri, 2007; Kilpatrick, 1986). *Epistle II* is less substantial, but it also has a philosophical tone and provides an interesting comparative analysis of ancient and modern Roman poets; thus, it represents a venture into literary criticism.

The modern response to the *Epistles* is mixed, with many scholars deeming them to be inferior to Horace's other work. Fantham (1996), for example, noted that Horace was unable or unwilling to abandon satire, the genre that had launched his career, and that the presence in the *Epistles* of satire and philosophy is an unfortunate pairing. The same could be said, of course, about any attempt to philosophize in verse, for poetry's metaphors and allegories do not lend themselves to the depth and precision of thought that philosophy demands. Kiernan (1999) took a stronger stand and asserted that if Horace "had seriously hoped to become an established philosopher and guide, he must be said to have failed" (p. 137). There is little evidence, however, that Horace sought to become a philosopher, so Kiernan's assessment may assume too much. Like all well-educated Romans, Horace had studied philosophy, and it was a matter of social convention among the well educated to display their learning in keeping with *paideia*. The most obvious comparison is with Cicero, whose demonstrations of knowledge regarding Greek rhetoric and philosophy at times seems gratuitous. The presence of philosophical references in Horace's work, therefore, should not be construed as an attempt to wear the mantle of philosopher but rather as conformity with convention. Moreover, as Mayer (1986) pointed out, "Philosophy in Horace's lifetime ... was a profession" (p. 55), and it is clear that Horace never saw himself as anything other than a poet. Again, the comparison to Cicero is relevant: Both he and Horace expressed philosophical sentiments in their writing, but their aim was protreptic, designed to persuade audiences of the benefits to be found in philosophy. If, as seems likely, the playful qualities of his poetry reflect something of Horace's personality, he probably was not temperamentally suited to producing serious philosophy.

Ars Poetica

Horace's *Ars Poetica* has long been accepted as the most significant statement of literary criticism in Latin, with its influence being particularly strong during the Renaissance (Hardison and Golden, 1995). In the sixteenth century, however, scholars raised a number of questions about the work and its many puzzles, and this process continues today. The central issue is this: Does *Ars Poetica* represent a serious discussion of literary principles along the lines of Aristotle's *Poetics*, or is it something else?

Dating Ars Poetica

Four hundred years of investigation and debate have yet to provide any definitive answers to this question, in part because any assessment of the poem is colored by what readers expect the work to be, in part because we know so little about it. We cannot, for example, accurately date the poem. Elmore (1935) indicated that it was produced between 28 and 27 BC, whereas other scholars, such as A. Campbell (1924), Villeneuve (1934), and Pontani (1953), argued that it was produced between 23 and 20 BC. Brink's (1963) influential analysis suggested that the poem was written between 13 and 8 BC, near the end of Horace's life, a view that has become widely accepted (see Laird, 2007). Rudd (1989) took a further step, concluding that "the Ars Poetica was Horace's last work" (p. 21). On the basis of stylistic features, Duckworth (1965) argued that *Ars Poetica* was written around 18 BC. Frischer (1991), after reexamining Duckworth's approach, proposed that the poem was most likely written between 24 and 20 BC, that is, around the middle of Horace's career. Unfortunately, this sort of stylistic analysis is suspect because it is based on three premises that are difficult to substantiate: a writer's style is consistent irrespective of genre, audience, and aim; a writer's style changes measurably over time; and such changes follow a consistent pattern.

The Pisones

Critics have generally assumed that Horace wrote *Ars Poetica* in response to a request from Piso père, yet even after centuries of research the identity of the Pisones is uncertain. The Piso family was influential for generations in both the Republic and the Empire. Lucius Calpurnius Piso Caesoninus served as consul in 58 BC and became Julius Caesar's father-in-law when Caesar married Calpurnia. A patron of the arts and a successful politician, he maintained what may have been Rome's largest private library at his vast estate at Herculaneum, which was a regular gathering place for intellectuals. His son (or sons) followed in his footsteps, continuing the tradition of patronage and political involvement. Gnaeus Calpurnius Piso served as consul in 23 BC, and Lucius Calpurnius Piso Pontifex served in 15 BC. In his commentary on *Ars Poetica*, Pomponius Porphyrio, a Latin *grammaticus* of the second or third century, identified Pontifex as the addressee,[1] but not all scholars have accepted his assessment. Some have argued that *Ars Poetica* was addressed to Caesoninus, even though he would have been quite old by the time the poem was written regardless of the proposed dates (e.g., Fraenkel, 1957; Frischer, 1991). Others have argued it was addressed to Gnaeus (see Brink, 1963, 1981).

Porphyrio's identification of Pontifex is appealing because this Piso was close to Augustus and seems never to have lost the emperor's favor; moreover, he was something of a poet and a generous supporter of literature. Frischer (1991) argued on the basis of internal evidence that Porphyrio was wrong, noting that lines 386–390 identify Piso père as a critic and concluding that Caesoninus must be the addressee. Cicero characterized Caesoninus as an incompetent critic in his *In Pisonem,* which renders these lines highly ironic, if this Piso was the addressee. It is important to point out, however, that in lines 24–25 we find the statement: "Most of us poets, father and youths worthy of such a father, can be mislead by what appears to be right" (*Maxima pars vatum pater et juvenes patre digni decipimur specie recti*). The Latin *maxima pars vatum* is ambiguous, for it could include the father among the poets. The possibility that Piso Pontifex engaged in both poetry and criticism does not seem farfetched, rendering Frischer's argument somewhat less than compelling.

If Porphyrio was correct, the poem would have to be dated toward the end of Horace's life, certainly after 13 BC, because Piso Pontifex was born in 48 BC. We also must consider that Horace referred to the elder offspring as *major juvenum*. This phrase translates as "oldest son" but must be understood in the context of Roman society, where a *juvenus* could be between the ages of 20 and 45, depending on whether he had the means to support himself, even though he reached legal emancipation at age 25. The average age of male first marriages is another factor that may help in determining which Piso was the addressee. Saller (1987) and Scheidel (2006) proposed that it was 25 for members of the Senatorial class (30 for plebeians), whereas Lelis, Percy, and Verstraete (2003) proposed that is was 20. If we accept the latter age, the "oldest son" of the poem would could not have been born before 29 BC, giving us a date of 9 BC for the poem's creation. Equally significant are census records that show that the "median age of paternity appears to have been around 37–38 years" (Scheidel, p. 8). Dating *Ars Poetica* to 20 BC therefore makes it impossible for Pontifex to have a son of the right age; the same can be said of 13 BC, when Pontifex would have been 35, for it is extremely unlikely that Pontifex married and had a child at age 15. Even if we assign 9 BC as the earliest possible date for the poem, using Lelis et al., for the average date of marriage, the data regarding the siring of offspring cast some doubt on the conclusion. Pontifex would have been an exception, marrying young, at age 19, and having a son immediately. But there is no evidence that this was the case. Indeed, we cannot conclusively determine from the existing records whether Pontifex had any children (see Syme, 1960).

---

[1] Hunc librum, qui inscribitur de arte poetica, ad Lucium Pisonem, qui postea urbis custos fuit, eiusque liberos misit; nam et ipse Piso poeta fuit, et studiorum liberalium antistes (I.1).

There is no doubt that proposing Caesoninus as the addressee is delectable because doing so adds to the ironic tone of the poem, for the "boys" to whom Horace offers guidance would have been well-educated, mature men who would have little need for the level of instruction *Ars Poetica* offers. Whether Caesoninus lived to the age of 80 is unknown, although we do know that Piso Pontifex did so and that longevity often is genetic. Horace's vagueness on this point may have been deliberate, a possibility supported by the fact that he named the Pisones only twice in the entire poem, at lines 6 and 235. Toohey (1996) viewed this lack of significant attention to the Pisones as part of a purposeful focus on a general audience, which allowed Horace to work in the familiar form of the epistle while nevertheless evoking "an addressee who is, for want of a better description, us" (p. 152). Another possibility, however, is that Horace drew on the centuries-old Hellenistic tradition of the fictional letter (see Costa, 2002; Rosenmeyer, 2006), in which case the Pisones are merely faux addressees.

Epistle or treatise?

As Toohey made clear, the fact that *Ars Poetica* appears to be a verse letter to the Pisones greatly confounds our understanding of the work. It is playful and often ironic, as we might expect in a letter to a friend, and in this respect it seems to follow the *Epistles*. If we are to view *Ars Poetica* as a letter, however, how are we to account for the title, with *ars* seeming to signify a formal treatise? The question is complicated by the lack of evidence regarding what the work was originally called. In his discussion of style, Quintilian identified the poem as *Ars Poetica*,[2] but for centuries the work has also been called *Epistula ad Pisones – Letter to the Pisones*. This alternative title is commonly justified on the ground that, after all, the work is in the form of a verse letter. Yet if Horace titled the poem *Epistula ad Pisones*, why would Quintilian, writing about a hundred years later, refer to the work as *Ars Poetica*, with no suggestion whatever that Horace called it an epistle? This question is salient because, on its face, the work does not have many of the characteristics of a treatise on poetic composition. As Russell (1973) pointed out, "The poem before us does not … look at all like a versified treatise" (p. 114). It offers very little in the way of specific instruction and even less in the way of literary or compositional theory. Instead, the poem presents numerous general observations that all but the dullest student would find commonsensical – such as the dictum that poetry and drama should "delight and guide" the audience (99–100) and that the writer should be consistent, even while *Ars Poetica* itself seems to violate the basic premises of consistency.

The question of organization

Equally problematic is the issue of organization, which many view as chaotic at best, nonexistent at worst. Surely Horace was not so incompetent as to produce a treatise on poetics that is structurally deficient. Porphyrio offered a tantalizing hint regarding a

---

[2] Note that Quintilian's reference to Horace consists of nothing more than a casual example, which makes the assumption that he renamed *Ars Poetica* less credible. He provided no analysis or commentary, as the relevant lines show: "To these stylistic blemishes may be added faulty arrangement, or ανοικονομητον, the faulty use of figures, or ασχηματιστον, and the faulty collocation of words, or κακοσυμθετον. Having already discussed matters associated with arrangement, I will confine myself here to the consideration of figures and structure. There is also a stylistic fault known as Σαρδισμος, which consists of the indiscriminate use of several dialects, such as would result from mixing Doric, Ionic, and even Aeolic words with Attic. A similar fault exists in Latin, as when we find the indiscriminate mixture of grand words with common ones, old words with new ones, and poetic language with colloquial. The result is a monstrous hodgepodge like that Horace described in the opening portion of his *Ars Poetica*: 'If a painter choose / To place a man's head on a horse's neck' (Quintilian, VIII.iii.59–60).

possible organizational principle. He remarked that "In this book [*Ars Poetica*, Horace] brought together Neoptolemus' precepts on the art of poetry, not indeed all of them, but the most prominent. The first precept is about consistency" – *In quem librum congessit praecepta Neoptolemi* του Παριανου *de arte poetica, non quidem omina sed eminentissima. Primum praeceptum est* περι της ακολουθας.

On the basis of this comment, scholars have diligently sought an organizational schema. Some proposed rearranging the verses on the premise that they had been scrambled by poor copyists; others declared that there was no reason to expect organization and "spoke of the 'art of artlessness' and the 'form of formlessness'" (Greenberg, 1961, p. 264). Many others, however, asserted that such measures were unnecessary because the poem was well organized, but according to unknown Neoptolemeic principles. Norden (1905) believed that he discovered these principles when he observed that *Ars Poetica* could be roughly divided into two parts at line 294: the first dealing with *ars*, the second with *artifex*, or the artist.

We know very little about Neoptolemus of Parium. What we do know comes from fragments of a work titled *On Poems* written by Philodemus – a philosopher and poet, contemporary of Cicero and friend to Lucius Calpurnius Piso Caesoninus – that were excavated from the ruins of Caesoninus' estate at Herculaneum (see Jensen, 1923; Mangoni, 1993). In Book V of *On Poems*, Philodemus critiqued various earlier writers, including Neoptolemus, noting that he placed the poet (*poiêtês*) alongside the poem (*poiêma*) and craftsmanship (*poiêsis*). Jensen (1923) and Dahlmann (1953) argued that Norden's (1905) bipartite schema was incorrect. Jensen stated that *poiêtês, poiêma*, and *poiêsis* would necessitate a tripartite organizational schema.

Poiêtês, poiêma, and *poiêsis* have a long history. Already by the fifth century BC we find Herodotus using the terms as though they were well established. Plato and Aristotle used them as well. In *The Art of Rhetoric*, for example, Aristotle stated that prose must be rhythmical but not metrical, or it will be a *poiêma*—διο ρυθμον δει εχειν τον λογον, μετρον δε μη ποιημα γαρ εσται (1408b3). In *The Art of Poetry*, Aristotle stated (1447b8) that *poiêsis* must have a *mythos* (μυθοσ) – a narrative, story, or plot that provides a representation (or mimesis) of life – to be successful. Horace's treatment of *poiêtês* and *poiêma* are clear enough, but this is not the case with *poiêsis*. Dahlmann therefore rejected the entire notion that *Ars Poetica* employs a Neoptolemeic organization, proposing that Neoptolemus did not use these terms to describe a structural schema but rather defined them as part of an introduction to poetics (see Greenberg, 1961; Janko, 2003; Rudd, 1989).

Ars Poetica and rhetoric

Given the sister relationship between poetic and rhetoric, it is understandable that various scholars have sought to ground *Ars Poetica* in classical rhetoric, giving credence thereby to its status as a serious treatise. Grant and Fiske (1924), for example, sought to concretize the rhetorical nature of Horace's *Ars Poetica* by identifying parallels between it and Cicero's *De Inventione, Orator*, and *De Oratore* (also see Brink, 1971; Herrick, 1946; Kilpatrick, 1990; Oliensis, 1998; Schneider, 1995; Walker, 2000). Finding that in both Horace and Cicero "the poet and the orator ... seek to make an emotional appeal to their audience" (p. 15), they stressed the similar emphasis placed on *prepon* in *Ars Poetica* and *Orator*, with the clear suggestion that Horace drew on the sister relationship to construct a treatise similar to Aristotle's *Poetics*. Likewise, Rudd (1989) noted that, following Aristotle, Horace viewed poetry as mimesis and insisted that the fundamental criterion of literary quality is unity. White (1977) argued that Horace's discussion of *communia* and *proprie* – the universal and the particular – is based on Aristotle's *Poetics*.[3] Horace followed Cicero – and, it should be added,

Aristotle in both *Rhetoric* and *Poetics* – when he stressed (220–250) the importance of appropriateness (*prepon/decorum*). In this regard, Brink (1963) argued that *Ars Poetica* has more in common with Aristotle's *Rhetoric* than his *Poetics*, pointing to the similar treatments of word choice, meter, and rhyme. Horace differed from Aristotle, however, in that he balanced mimesis with appropriateness: Not all natural acts are appropriate for poetic consideration, so mimesis must be constrained.

The existence of Aristotelian and Ciceronian rhetorical precepts in *Ars Poetica* do little to establish the work as a viable treatise: By the early Empire they were commonplaces taught by *grammatici* at the elementary level. Horace's inclusion of these precepts illustrates that he was familiar with them, exactly what we would expect given his education in Rome and Athens. It seems impossible that a work purporting to be an *ars*, whether formal or informal, could ignore them. But Horace made no discernible effort to move beyond the commonplaces and delve more deeply into rhetorical principles or theory, rendering them as little more than adornments that provide little aid to the student. Consequently, one could never hope to become even a mediocre poet, much less an accomplished one, with *Ars Poetica* as his or her textbook. It not only lacks sufficient pedagogical devices but also offers the student scant encouragement. Toohey (1996) therefore suggested that the work should not be taken seriously, for to do so is to ignore the sense of play that is palpable throughout the poem, a sense of play that ultimately requires us to recognize *Ars Poetica* as "a piece of sophisticated leisure entertainment" (p. 156). If Toohey (1996) is correct, it is a mistake to view *Ars Poetica* as a serious treatise or even an example of didactic verse.

The problems inherent in classifying *Ars Poetica* as a treatise on poetics can be ameliorated by emphasizing the epistolary nature of the work. If the poem actually is a letter written to the Piso boys at the request of their father, with Horace giving sage advice based on his success as a poet, we should not expect it to have the characteristics of a well-organized and highly cogent treatise with the depth and scope of Aristotle's *Poetics*. Consequently, Quintilian's title, *Ars Poetica*, may be explained by proposing that in the hundred years following its composition, the poem had become widely used by *grammatici* as an elementary textbook, its epistolary status notwithstanding. Hence, the work became an *ars* by default. The problem with this notion, however, is the complexity of the work itself. The Latin is challenging, with numerous plays on language, as are the various literary allusions; and the excursions into moral philosophy would most likely be beyond the ability of children.

On the other hand, if we accept the general designation of *major juvenum* to signify a young man of at least 20, we face the problem of explaining how the son could have reached this age without having already undergone extensive training in literature, philosophy, and rhetoric far beyond the elementary level presented in *Ars Poetica*. A viable solution would be to suggest that Horace used the phrase *major juvenum* as an honorific to flatter a young boy of age 8 or 9. The appeal of this proposal is that it allows Pontifex to marry in 23 BC, at 25, which would be congruent with Saller's (1987) and Scheidel's (2006) analyses of male's average age of first marriage. He then would have his first child four or five years later, which would put fatherhood closer to the median age reported by Scheidel.

Any emphasis on the epistolary nature of *Ars Poetica*, however, must address the fact that the work has only a marginal resemblance to Horace's other letters. Using his

---

[3] Consider, however, that Aristotle insisted that poetry deals with universals, whereas history deals with particulars. Horace proposed a more difficult task for the poet, making the universal particular – difficile est proprie communia dicere, tuque rectius Iliacum carmen deducis in actus quam si proferres ignota indictaque primus (128–30).

Epistles as a benchmark, we note immediately that the opening lines are significantly different from the beginnings of these earlier works. *Epistle 2.1*, for example, begins with a discussion of poetic taste, which among the Romans, Horace complains, is too conservative, and then goes on to compare Greek and Roman poetry. *Epistle 2.2*, begins with exaggerated flattery of his young friend Florus (bono claroque fidelis amici Neroni – Nero's good, faithful friend) and then releases an avalanche of clever reasoning to explain why he has stopped writing. *Ars Poetica*, on the other hand, offers in its first lines the bizarre image of a human head on a horse's neck and compares poetry to painting. *Ars Poetica* offers no advice on lyric, Horace's forte, and instead focuses on epic and drama – two genres that he never even dabbled in – clearly at odds with Horace's expertise. We know, admittedly, that Piso Pontifex was patron to the poet Antipater, who not only celebrated the consul in about one hundred epigrams but who also may have produced an epic poem celebrating Pontifex's victory in the Thracian War (Syme, 1989). The inclusion of epic, therefore, could be viewed as following the pattern of flattery that we find in several of Horace's works.

Even so, it is clear that some statements in *Ars Poetica* about poetry and poets frequently contradict the views we find in his other poems, raising the question of why a man who had achieved significant success through his poetry would, near the end of life, produce a work on poetics disconnected from his poetic practice. We can be certain, for example, that Horace did not leave a poem in a drawer for 9 years before publishing it, as he advises in *Ars Poetica*, which raises the question of why Horace would flatter the father and then give poor (or at best imprecise and misleading) advice to the son. Furthermore, the argument for epistolary status is based on a significant and unsubstantiated assumption – that Quintilian renamed the work. Quintilian certainly knew the difference between a letter and a handbook, which makes his choice of *Ars Poetica* seem incomprehensible unless we credit him with using, if not Horace's title, the title by which the work was widely known.

Setting aside such concerns, Rudd (1989) chose to call the poem *Epistula ad Pisones* and by way of support pointed out that Charisius, writing in the fourth century, used the phrase "Horatius in Epistularum" when referencing a line from the poem. Various scholars have found Charisius not only suggestive but compelling (e.g., Armstrong, 1989; Kilpatrick, 1990; Norden, 1905). However, he is by no means dispositive. Whether "Horatius in Epistularum" refers to *Ars Poetica* is uncertain owing to his questionable reliability: Sometimes he cited authors by name and title of the work, other times by name alone, and some of the names are not quite correct, the result either of an error on his part or corruption of the text during copying. Moreover, there seems to be no record in the extant ancient texts of the poem being called anything other than *Ars Poetica*. As Frischer (1991) noted, "no one seems to have called the *Ars Poetica* the *Epistula ad Pisones* before Jason De Nores, the professor of Moral Philosophy in Padua from 1577 to his death in 1590, who in 1553 wrote a commentary on the poem in which he passed on the ideas of his friend and teacher, Padua professor Trifone Gabriele" (pp. 8–9).

The lack of significant epistolary and treatise-like qualities suggests that *Ars Poetica* lies outside the parameters of Horace's *oeuvre*, that it may have been an experiment. Brink (1971) argued that the work is a hybrid and that efforts to classify the work as either a poetic epistle or a treatise may be misguided. The poem includes some of the elements of Horace's earlier *Epistles* – such as the avuncular tone of epistolography's sage advice – and the mocking tone of his *Satires*, but it is distinct from both genres. And although the work resembles Aristotle's *Art of Poetry* in some ways, Horace's venture cannot readily be characterized as a poetic treatise because "It lacks Aristotle's clarity of concept and coherence of argument" (Brink, p. 81; also see

Laird, 2007). Thus, Brink's assessment was that as a hybrid, *Ars Poetica* is a com-plicated, often incoherent, didactic poem (a conclusion also reached by A. Campbell, 1924). Toohey (1996) concurred: The scant attention to the Pisones and the focus on a general audience, noted earlier, confirmed for him that the *Ars Poetica* "possess all the characteristics of didactic poetry" (p. 150).

Viewing the work as a didactic poem has not reduced the tendency to classify *Ars Poetica* as a serious effort at literary criticism. Few scholars have entertained the possibil-ity that the voice in the poem is a poetic persona, not Horace responding honestly to a friend's request to provide advice on poetics. Applying just this perspective, Frischer (1991) offered one of the more interesting examinations of the poem and concluded that *Ars Poetica* is a "parody" of the sort of advice provided by incompetent *grammatici* and would-be critics like Lucius Calpurnius Piso Caesoninus: "[R]ight from the start, Horace portrays the speaker of the poem as a pedant and an ignoramus. This charac-terization, like the attack on his authority, is consistent with a parodic reading of the work" (p. 52). The motivation for producing such a parody, according to Frischer, is found in the date of composition in the middle period of Horace's career, when the *grammatici* were highly critical of his poetry and he had yet to find a wide audience. The poetic voice of *Ars Poetica*, on this account, is not Horace at all but rather the persona of the pedant *grammaticus* spouting nonsense that mixes advice about poetry with dis-cussions about drama and satyr plays, the latter of which seem not even to have existed in Rome.[4]

Ars and technê

Both Brink's (1971) and Frischer's (1991) perspectives offer valuable insight into the work, but questions remain. Classifying *Ars Poetica* as a hybrid sheds little light on the issues of internal contradictions, the uncertain organization, or Horace's purpose in writing the poem unless one is willing to propose that the poet nodded off at his scrib-ing table in his dotage. And most scholars have resisted calling *Ars Poetica* a parody owing to an unwillingness to entertain the notion that Horace was capable of such a monumental joke.

Previous endeavors to analyze its rhetorical features appear to come closest to pro-viding a comprehensive understanding of the poem, but they are not entirely satisfy-ing. Efforts to identify the influences of Aristotle, Neoptolemus, and Cicero have tended to generate as much heat as light, and they have not yet led to a reconciliation of the various inconsistencies. A more valuable approach may be to locate Horace in the broader Hellenistic tradition that includes Greco-Roman display oratory and fictional letters. Doing so suggests that Horace was an important precursor of the Second Sophistic.

The title remains a significant obstacle, creating problems for readers over the centu-ries because it necessarily engenders the expectation of a treatise along the lines of Aristotle's *Technê Rhêtorikê*. At the heart of this issue is the word *"ars."* The Indo-European root of *ars*, "ar," means to join closely, to fit; it connotes not only purposeful motion or a goal orientation but also skill in joining things together. The Greek equiva-lent is *arti* (αρτι), meaning "just" or "exactly," and *artios* (αρτιος), meaning "suitable," "complete," or "exactly fitted." How these words were used in early Greek is uncertain, but we find Homer using *artios* in both the *Iliad* and the *Odyssey* to signify speaking to a specific purpose (*Iliad*, 14.92; *Odyssey*, 8.240). In early Latin, *ars* was used in the context of building, and it came to signify skill in a craft.

---

[4] See Wiseman (1988) for an examination of the indirect evidence for the existence of Roman satyr plays.

The Indo-European root of *technê*, "tek/x," means to form, to generate and to do so skillfully. (The Latin word *texo* – to weave, to fit together, or to construct – is a derivative.) The earliest uses of *technê* are found in Homer and Pindarus, who used the word to signify skill in a craft; in this respect, the early uses of *technê* and *ars* were nearly identical. Pindarus also used *technê* in the sense of "agency," which seems indicative of language change at work: We know that by the fifth century Herodotus, Euripides, and Aristophanes were using *technê* to indicate a cunning kind of skill associated with any action that did not involve a craft. The creation of mimetic forms – poetry, painting, and sculpture – was deemed to represent just such an action. Indeed, the negative connotations of the term were so strong that Greek required a syntactic adjustment, and we find writers using *technê* in conjunction with *epistêmê*, or craftsman-like knowledge, to create a positive semantic frame. Thus, *technê* begins to signify "art" during this period, but not in a positive way: The aesthetic, imitative nature of "art" was viewed as a form of trickery or deception embedded in the semantics of the term (see Ford, 2002).

The emergence of formal rhetoric in the fifth century led to another shift in meaning. The peregrinatory lifestyle of the Sophists necessitated that they appear in the agora soon upon arriving in a new city and that they offer a *display speech* to the crowd so as to demonstrate their skills and attract students. These speeches, designed to illustrate the Sophist's skill and eloquence, did not represent a craft, though they were skillfully constructed, and they did not represent art, though they contained numerous poetic elements. In many respects, they resembled *artios* in that they were speech with a specific purpose. As the popularity of rhetoric grew, many display speeches – such as Gorgias' *Helen* and *Palamedes* – were put into writing to provide students with models of the sort Plato criticized in *Phaedrus*. The epidictic nature of such works underlie Cole's (1991) observation that *technê* "can be used to apply to both the systematic, theoretical treatise … and the practical demonstration text" (p. 81). The evidence is indirect but nevertheless pertinent. In *Phaedrus*, Socrates remarks that, with his paradoxes, Zeno "has an art of speaking [λέγοντα οὐκ ἰσ̇μεν τέχνη] by which he makes the same things appear to his hearers like and unlike, one and many, at rest and in motion" (261). In *Sophist* (224a), Socrates sets out to define the Sophist, likening him to a merchant who travels from city to city hawking wares for the soul, one of which is the "art of the display" (ἐπιδεικτικη δικαιότατα). The Sophist, then, is a τεχνοπωλικόν, an "art seller."

As Sophists turned their display speeches into written texts, the distinction between display piece and instructional handbook became blurred. In *Against the Sophists*, Isocrates criticized such handbooks based on display speeches, stating: But there remain to be considered those who lived before our time and did not scruple to write the so-called arts of oratory (295). Referring to "previous compilers" of *technai* (1354a), Aristotle also seems to be commenting on Sophists who converted display speeches into written texts that purported to serve as models (albeit deficient) for students of rhetoric. The monumental status of his *Rhetoric, however,* quickly gave preference to the meaning of *technê* as "formal treatise" (see Cole, 1991; Papillion, 1995; Schiappa, 2003). Experiencing a different linguistic history, the Romans conflated the semantics of *artios* and *technê* into *ars*.

Ars Poetica as a display piece

A characteristic of Sophistic display speeches is that they fail to offer a balance between the generalities associated with theory and the details necessary for application. Their *topoi*, for example, are usually specific and are the equivalent of case studies or exercises that offered students several possible solutions to real-life problems. Lacking significant development of general principles, a given *technê* might illustrate half a dozen different argumentative approaches, but it would fail as a pedagogical tool the moment the orator was faced with the need for a seventh. Such *technai* may give the appearance of effective models but ultimately have little if any paradigmatic usefulness, as in the case of Gorgias' *Helen*, *Defense of Palamedes*, and perhaps most strikingly, *On the Nonexistent*.

Nevertheless, spoken and written *technai* were popular. Rhetoric had become a pop-culture phenomenon owing to social, political, and educational changes associated with the shift from an oral to a literate society (Havelock, 1963, 1986), and display speeches and handbooks found eager audiences. Although Plato, Aristotle, and Isocrates dismissed Sophistic handbooks, the display speeches were not entirely devoid of worth, frequently reflecting a moral didacticism with a phatic quality that was valuable in a world concerned with *aretê*. *Palamedes* illustrates this characteristic as well as a tendency in *technai* to use imaginary speeches presented by contemporary and historical figures as a source of entertainment.

The decline of the First Sophistic during the Hellenistic Period did not lead to the demise of the display speech. Its obvious pedagogical value motivated both *grammatici* and Sophists to incorporate epideixis into their *progymnasmata*. In the process, the display speech became a "practice speech" intended initially as a vocal exercise (*anaphônêsis*) for students that became a school tradition. When the practice speech became an established part of the Greek curriculum, it was no longer termed *anaphônêsis* but simply *meletê*, or "exercise." As Russell (1983) noted, the Romans appear to have translated *anaphônêsis* as *declamatio*, or "declamation," which denoted "an exercise in delivery rather than composition" but that owing to semantic shift came to be "used for the speech composed to be delivered in training, not the delivery of it" (p. 9).

The display speech was not limited to students enrolled in schools of rhetoric; it survived in the work of professional rhetoricians, predominantly in the Greek East. A hallmark of the display speech was that it offered an opportunity for the rhetorician to showcase his eloquence and creativity, and competition among professionals during their demonstrations was fierce. We find, however, that these rhetoricians did not generally refer to their display speeches as either epeideiktkiê, technê, or *meletê* but rather as either "oration" (*logon*) or "declamation" (*rhetoria*), with *logon* being used most frequently (e.g., Libanius' *Autobiography*).

Ars Poetica manifests many of the characteristics of a display speech. Like the epeideiktkoi of the Older Sophists, it is abstract and general so as to highlight Horace's eloquence, versatility, and imaginative approach to a difficult subject. In addition, *Ars Poetica* has little paradigmatic usefulness but is appealing because it nevertheless displays mastery of technique and blends philosophy with poetic and rhetorical devices. To grasp the importance of eloquence in understanding the poem, we need first to consider that until as late as the seventeenth century there was no such thing a "silent reading." Essentially all reading was done aloud, even when one was alone, and reading aloud served to showcase eloquence. The proem of *Ars Poetica* is what we would expect of a display speech, designed to grab the attention of the audience rather than offer a technical discourse on unity. Gorgias' *Helen* is the closest Greek equivalent, with a proem that has little to do with the substance of the speech itself. We also must consider Philodemus once more. Book I of *On Poems* summarizes and then refutes a series of Hellenistic critics who maintained that the quality of verse does not reside in its meaning but solely in whether it is pleasing to the ear. As Janko (2003) indicated, this was the dominant literary theory during the period between Aristotle and Horace. The exact influence Philodemus had on Horace is unclear but is unlikely to have been absolute, leaving open the possibility that Horace produced *Ars Poetica* in keeping with the long-standing Hellenistic tradition.

If indeed the most likely date of the poem is near the end of Horace's life, such a display would serve as a fitting epilogue to a successful career, demonstrating that his powers were still intact. But if Horace's goal was to produce a final display of his poetic skill, why put it in the form of a verse letter? The success of his earlier *Epistles* is an obvious answer, but it is worth noting that Sophistic *technai* typically took the form of an imaginary speech that, as Cole (1991) noted, were structured so as to appear occasional and thus "come from the mouth [or in Horace's case the pen] of the person most qualified to present it" (p. 101). In addition, the tradition of the fictional letter may have motivated Horace to experiment, to demonstrate that age had not diminished his creativity. As a fictional epistle to a quasi-fictional father who had requested advice on poetry for his sons, *Ars Poetica* matches these characteristics quite well. Unlike Greek *technai*, however, *Ars Poetica* does not serve a true pedagogical function; it does not consist of a master's demonstration of how poetry or drama should be done, for the general principles are never actualized into concrete example. As Laird (2007) noted, "The *Ars Poetica* is far more of a guide to inform the judgment of readers and audiences than the manual for practicing writers it pretends to be" (p. 142) Even so, there is no question that the poem was successful pedagogically insofar as it influenced generations of would-be poets to study its general principles.

Questions clearly remain. Papillion (1995) pointed out that Cicero's study of Greek rhetoric failed to recognize that *technê* signified both a handbook and display speeches, and we have no way of knowing what factors in Horace's rhetorical education may have provided this knowledge. Nevertheless, *Ars Poetica* indicates that his training in Rome and Athens gave him the requisite grounding not only in rhetorical theory and practice but also in history. His knowledge of rhetorical history would answer the obvious question: Why did Horace choose the word *ars* rather than *declamatio* for the title if he intended to produce a display piece? *Declamatio* is inappropriate because *Ars Poetica* is neither an *anaphônêsis* nor a *meletê*. *Ars* was the best available choice owing to its similarity to *technê*. And no doubt the most significant question is how can we know with certainty what Horace intended to produce. Clearly, we cannot. Yet *Ars Poetica* contains many of the characteristics of Greek *technai*, and although ultimately speculative, this analysis does resolve some of the more troubling facets of the work.

Reading 35

Ars Poetica (*The Art of Poetry*)

Ars Poetica (The Art of Poetry) (excerpt), pp. 451–9, 465–7, 475–81 (Latin on even-numbered pages omitted) reprinted by permission of the publishers and Trustees of the Loeb Classical Library from *Horace*, Volume II, Loeb Classical Library Volume 194, translated by H.R. Fairclough (Cambridge, MA: Harvard University Press, 1926). © 1926 by the President and Fellows of Harvard College. The Loeb Classical Library® is a registered trademark of the President and Fellows of Harvard College.

If a painter chose to join a human head to the neck of a horse, and to spread feathers of many a hue over limbs picked up now here now there, so that what at the top is a lovely woman ends below in a black and ugly fish, could you, my friends, if favoured with a private view, refrain from laughing? Believe me, dear Pisos, quite like such pictures would be a book, whose idle fancies shall be shaped like a sick man's dreams, so that neither head nor foot can be assigned to a single shape. "Painters and poets," you say, "have always had an equal right in hazarding anything." We know it: this licence we poets claim and in our turn we grant the like; but not so far that savage should mate with tame, or serpents couple with birds, lambs with tigers.

14. Works with noble beginnings and grand promises often have one or two purple patches so stitched on as to glitter far and wide, when Diana's grove and altar, and

The winding stream a-speeding 'mid fair fields

or the river Rhine, or the rainbow is being described. For such things there is a place, but not just now. Perhaps, too, you can draw a cypress. But what of that, if you are paid to paint a sailor swimming from his wrecked vessel in despair? That was a wine jar, when the moulding began: why, as the wheel runs round, does it turn out a pitcher? In short be the work what you will, let it at least be simple and uniform.

24. Most of us poets, O father and ye sons worthy of the father, deceive ourselves by the semblance of truth. Striving to be brief, I become obscure. Aiming at smoothness, I fail in force and fire. One promising grandeur, is bombastic; another, over-cautious and fearful of the gale, creeps along the ground. The man who tries to vary a single subject in monstrous fashion, is like a painter adding a dolphin to the woods, a boar to the waves. Shunning a fault may lead to error, if there be lack of art.

32. Near the Aemilian School, at the bottom of the row, there is a craftsman who in bronze will mould nails and imitate waving locks, but is unhappy in the total result, because he cannot represent a whole figure. Now if I wanted to write something, I should no more wish to be like him, than to live with my nose turned askew, though admired for my black eyes and black hair.

38. Take a subject, ye writers, equal to your strength; and ponder long what your shoulders refuse, and what they are able to bear. Whoever shall choose a theme within his range, neither speech will fail him, nor clearness of order. Of order, this if I mistake not, will be the excellence and charm that the author of the long-promised poem shall say at the moment what at that moment should be said, reserving and omitting much for the present, loving this point and scorning that.

46. Moreover, with a nice taste and care in weaving words together, you will express yourself most happily, if a skilful setting makes a familiar word new. If haply one must betoken abstruse things by novel terms, you will have a chance to fashion words never heard of by the kilted Cethegi, and licence will be granted, if used with modesty ; while words, though new and of recent make, will win acceptance, if they spring from a Greek fount and are drawn therefrom but sparingly. Why indeed shall Romans grant this licence to Caecilius and Plautus, and refuse it to Virgil and Varius? And why should I be grudged the

right of adding, if I can, my little fund, when the tongue of Cato and of Ennius has enriched our mother-speech and brought to light new terms for things? It has ever been, and ever will be, permitted to issue words stamped with the mint-mark of the day. As forests change their leaves with each year's decline, and the earliest drop off: so with words, the old race dies and, like the young of human kind, the new-born bloom and thrive. We are doomed to death – we and all things ours ; whether Neptune, welcomed within the land, protects our fleets from northern gales – a truly royal work – or a marsh, long a waste where oars were plied, feeds neighbouring towns and feels the weight of the plough; or a river has changed the course which brought ruin to corn-fields and has learnt a better path: all mortal things shall perish, much less shall the glory and glamour of speech endure and live. Many terms that have fallen out of use shall be born again, and those shall fall that are now in repute, if Usage so will it, in whose hands lies the judgement, the right and the rule of speech.

[…]

99. Not enough is it for poems to have beauty; they must have charm, and lead the hearer's soul where they will: As men's faces smile on those who smile, so they respond to those who weep. If you would have me weep, you must first feel grief yourself: then, O Telephus or Peleus, will your misfortunes hurt me: if the words you utter are ill suited, I shall laugh or fall asleep. Sad tones befit the face of sorrow; blustering accents that of anger; jests become the merry, solemn words the grave. For Nature first shapes us within to meet every change of fortune: she brings joy or impels to anger, or bows us to the ground and tortures us under a load of grief; then, with the tongue for interpreter, she proclaims the emotions of the soul. If the speaker's words sound discordant with his fortunes, the Romans, in boxes and pit alike, will raise a loud guffaw. Vast difference will it make, whether a god be speaking or a hero, a ripe old man or one still in the flower and fervour of youth, a dame of rank or a bustling nurse, a roaming trader or the tiller of a verdant field, a Colchian or an Assyrian, one bred at Thebes or Argos.

[…]

179. Either an event is acted on the stage, or the action is narrated. Less vividly is the mind stirred by what finds entrance through the ears than by

what is brought before the trusty eyes, and what the spectator can see for himself. Yet you will not bring upon the stage what should be performed behind the scenes, and you will keep much from our eyes, which an actor's ready tongue will narrate anon in our presence; so that Medea is not to butcher her boys before the people, nor impious Atreus cook human flesh upon the stage, nor Procne be turned into a bird, Cadmus into a snake. Whatever you thus show me, I discredit and abhor.

189. Let no play be either shorter or longer than five acts, if when once seen it hopes to be called for and brought back to the stage. And let no god intervene, unless a knot come worthy of such a deliverer, nor let a fourth actor essay to speak.

193. Let the Chorus sustain the part and strenuous duty of an actor, and sing nothing between acts which does not advance and fitly blend into the plot. It should side with the good and give friendly counsel; sway the angry and cherish the righteous. It should praise the fare of a modest board, praise wholesome justice, law, and peace with her open gates; should keep secrets, and pray and beseech the gods that fortune may return to the unhappy, and depart from the proud.

[...]

285. Our own poets have left no style untried, nor has least honour been earned when they have dared to leave the footsteps of the Greeks and sing of deeds at home, whether they have put native tragedies or native comedies upon the stage. Nor would Latium be more supreme in valour and glory of arms than in letters, were it not that her poets, one and all, cannot brook the toil and tedium of the file. Do you, O sons of Pompilius, condemn a poem which many a day and many a blot has not restrained and refined ten times over to the test of the close-cut nail.

295. Because Democritus believes that native talent is a greater boon than wretched art, and shuts out from Helicon poets in their sober senses, a goodly number take no pains to pare their nails or to shave their beards; they haunt lonely places and shun the baths – for surely one will win the esteem and name of poet if he never entrusts to the barber Licinus a head that three Anticyras cannot cure. Ah, fool that I am, who purge me of my bile as the season of spring comes on! Not another man would compose better poems. Yet it's not worth while. So I'll play a whetstone's part, which makes steel sharp, but of itself cannot cut.

Though I write naught myself, I will teach the poet's office and duty; whence he draws his stores; what nurtures and fashions him; what befits him and what not; whither the right course leads and whither the wrong.

309. Of good writing the source and fount is wisdom. Your matter the Socratic pages can set forth, and when matter is in hand words will not be loath to follow. He who has learned what he owes his country and his friends, what love is due a parent, a brother, and a guest, what is imposed on senator and judge, what is the function of a general sent to war, he surely knows how to give each character his fitting part. I would advise one who has learned the imitative art to look to life and manners for a model, and draw from thence living words. At times a play marked by attractive passages and characters fitly sketched, though lacking in charm, though without force and art, gives the people more delight and holds them better than verses void of thought, and sonorous trifles.

323. To the Greeks the Muse gave native wit, to the Greeks she gave speech in well-rounded phrase; they craved naught but glory. Our Romans, by many a long sum, learn in childhood to divide the *as* into a hundred parts. "Let the son of Albinus answer. If from five-twelfths one ounce be taken, what remains? You might have told me by now." "A third." "Good! you will be able to look after your means. An ounce is added; what's the result?" "A half." When once this canker, this lust of petty gain has stained the soul, can we hope for poems to be fashioned, worthy to be smeared with cedar-oil, and kept in polished cypress?

333. Poets aim either to benefit, or to amuse, or to utter words at once both pleasing and helpful to life. Whenever you instruct, be brief, so that what is quickly said the mind may readily grasp and faithfully hold: every word in excess flows away from the full mind. Fictions meant to please should be close to the real, so that your play must not ask for belief in anything it chooses, nor from the Ogress's belly, after dinner, draw forth a living child. The centuries of the elders chase from the stage what is profitless; the proud Ramnes disdain poems devoid of charms. He has won every vote who has blended profit and pleasure, at once delighting and instructing the reader. That is the book to make money for the Sosii; this the one to cross the sea and extend to a distant day its author's fame.

347. Yet faults there are which we can gladly pardon; for the string does not always yield the sound which hand and heart intend, but when you call for a flat often returns you a sharp; nor will the bow always hit whatever mark it threatens. But when the beauties in a poem are more in number, I shall not take offence at a few blots which a careless hand has let drop, or human frailty has failed to avert. What, then, is the truth? As a copying clerk is without excuse if, however much warned he always makes the same mistake, and a harper is laughed at who always blunders on the same string: so the poet who often defaults, becomes, methinks, another Choerilus, whose one or two good lines cause laughter and surprise; and yet I also feel aggrieved, whenever good Homer "nods," but when a work is long, a drowsy mood may well creep over it.

361. A poem is like a picture: one strikes your fancy more, the nearer you stand; another, the farther away. This courts the shade, that will wish to be seen in the light, and dreads not the critic insight of the judge. This pleased but once; that though ten times called for, will always please.

Study Questions

1 Aristotle's *Art of* Poetry is imbedded in his philosophy of ethics and society. Horace, on the other hand, twice advised poets to follow "nature." What does he mean by this, and how might following "nature" lead to a theory of poetics different from Aristotle's?

2 In *De Oratore*, Cicero noted the importance of matching one's style to the audience. How does Horace translate this observation to poetry?

3 In lines 103–104, Horace asserted: "If you want to move me to tears/You must first grieve yourself." What does this imply for the student of poetry/drama?

4 The classical world placed far less emphasis on novel plots than we do today. What was Horace's advice in this regard? What does his advice tell us about audiences at the beginning of the Empire?

5 Horace's discussion of character has been linked directly to Aristotle's *Art of Rhetoric*. What is the basis of this linkage and how does it reflect the concurrence of rhetoric and poetry?

6 Jonathan Swift reduced Horace's views on appropriateness, or decorum, to a dictum: "proper words in proper places." Consider drama today. Does it reflect Horace's notion of decorum? Why or why not?

Writing Topics

1 Framing a work as a letter or extended missive offering advice to a friend or relative was a common literary device. *De Oratore*, for example, was supposedly composed as a guide for Cicero's brother, Quintus. Examine how Horace's *Ars Poetica* reflects the conventions of this device.

2 Horace devoted considerable attention to the notion of appropriateness in drama. Examine the factors that influenced appropriateness when Horace was writing and that influence appropriateness today, considering commonalities, differences, and how writers determine what is appropriate and what is not.

3 Aristotle's *Art of Poetry* is often deemed to have been a significant influence on Horace's *Ars Poetica*. Examine the two works and argue for or against this supposed influence.

Further Reading

Horace, vol. 1: Odes and Epodes. (2004). (N. Rudd, trans.). Harvard University Press.

Horace, vol. 2: Satires, Epistles, Ars Poetica. (1926). (H.R. Fairclough, trans.) Harvard University Press.

Horace and Greek Lyric Poetry. (2002). (M. Paschalis, ed). University of Crete Press.

9

Quintilian the Educator

Introduction to Quintilian (c. 35–95 AD)

We know relatively little about Quintilian's life, and only a few details can be established with any certainty. He was born in Spain, in the town of Calagurris, and both his father and grandfather may have been rhetoricians. Clarke (1967) suggested that his family were not Roman colonists but rather were native to Spain, but there is no concrete evidence to verify this. Quintilian probably received his elementary education at home, but as a young adolescent he traveled to Rome for his rhetorical training, studying with Domitius Afer, an outstanding rhetorician of dubious character whose activities as a *delator*, or professional informer, seem to have led to his downfall.[1] We also know that sometime in the early 70s Emperor Vespasian selected Quintilian to hold the first chair of rhetoric in Rome, providing him with generous compensation. This appointment probably was related to Vespasian's efforts to rebuild Rome after the neglect of the previous emperors and the depredations of the civil wars that preceded his reign. Quintilian indicated in *Institutio Oratoria* that he held this position for two decades.[2] He did not marry until his forties, wedding a young girl of 12 or 13 with whom he had two children, both boys. The youngest died at age 5, and his mother followed soon after. The oldest boy died several years later, at age 10.[3]

Quintilian's appointment to the Latin chair of rhetoric established a patronage relationship with Vespasian and his family, so when the emperor died in 79, the accession of his son Titus to the throne had no effect on Quintilian's position. Indeed, when Vespasian's second son, Domitian, became emperor after his brother's untimely death in 81, the orator's ties to the imperial court appear to have grown stronger. In the early 90s, while working on *Institutio Oratoria*, he was asked to tutor the emperor's appointed heirs (his sister's grandsons), a great honor that reflected the esteem with which Quintilian was held by the imperial family. *Institutio Oratoria* is Quintilian's only extant

---

[1] *Delatores* had to be accomplished orators because they prosecuted the people they informed on when the cases went to trial. When successful, they received substantial fees, often a percentage of the convicted person's confiscated property. If unsuccessful, however, the *delator* was subject to severe penalties.

[2] Some of his comments suggest that he may have continued to handle legal cases during this period, but there is insufficient evidence to determine whether he actually did.

[3] Quintilian wrote about the death of his wife and children in the preface to Book VI. Their deaths struck him hard. Of his wife he stated: "*Ego vel hoc uno malo sic eram adflictus ut me iam nulla fortuna posset efficere felicem. Nam cum, omni virtute quae in feminas cadit functa, insanabilem attulit marito dolorem, tum aetate tam puellari, praesertim meae comparata, potest et ipsa numerari inter vulnera orbitatis*" – "Her death was such an awful blow that thereafter no amount of good fortune could bring me happiness. She possessed every virtue that a woman could possess, and my grief upon her death left me inconsolable."

work, and the consensus is that he began writing it in the late 80s or more likely the early 90s, completing it a year or two before his death in 95.

We know that Quintilian lived in turbulent times. Even a brief summary can provide insight into just how troubled the Empire was during his lifetime. Emperors Caligula (c. 12–41 AD) and Claudius (c. 10 BC–54 AD) had steadily eroded the already minuscule authority of the Senate and were infamous for their extravagance and cruelty. The historian Suetonius (1997) labeled Caligula a depraved "monster"; and to emphasize the utter disdain the emperor had for the Senate, he reported the rumor that Caligula gave serious consideration to appointing his favorite horse to that august body.[4] Troubled by his tyrannical behavior, the praetorian guard assassinated Caligula after only four years of rule. The guard then declared Claudius emperor, even though, according to Suetonius he stuttered, drooled, and walked with a limp, defects that most Romans ridiculed. As for the new emperor, Suetonius described him as "cruel and bloodthirsty" owing to the eagerness with which he dispatched anyone (commonly without trial) who displeased him, regardless of rank. He characterized Claudius' third wife, Valeria Messalina, as a teenage nymphomaniac who organized wild orgies for years until Claudius grew tired of her antics and ordered her executed for adultery. The emperor then married his niece Agrippina (Caligula's sister), who brought to the union her young son by a previous marriage, Lucius Domitius Ahenobarbus, better known to the world as Nero. Agrippina is generally thought to have poisoned Claudius so that Nero would be named emperor. Because he was still a teenager, Agrippina acted as her son's regent and ran the Empire herself, but according to Tacitus, Nero quickly came to resent his mother's power and ordered her exile in 55 and her execution in 59.

By 68, Nero had murdered his mother and two wives and had ordered his tutor and guardian, Seneca, to commit suicide. Sunk so deep in depravity that he was either deranged or appeared to be so, he had lost the regard of most people in Rome.[5] Government was in a shambles, and a food shortage in the city was looming. In this cloudy environment, Gaius Julius Vindex (c. 37–69), governor of Gallia Lugdunensis (the northern portion of modern-day France), appears to have seen an opportunity – he decided that Nero should be deposed and communicated with various governors in an effort to induce them to join him in rebellion. Among them was Servius Sulpicius Galba (c. 3 BC–69 AD): governor of northern and eastern Spain (Tarraconensis), 70 or 71 years old, from an ancient family that had been active in Roman politics since the earliest days of the Republic, a disciplinarian who even in his forties could run 20 miles, and so prudent that he had managed to survive the reign of five emperors. Suetonius reported that Galba did not even bother to respond to Vindex's call to rebellion until he was informed that Nero had decided to have him executed, at which point he began mobilizing. He was aided significantly by the governor of western Spain (Lusitania), Marcus Salvius Otho (c. 32–69).

---

[4] Much of what we know about this period comes from Suetonius, Tacitus, Plutarch, and Cassius Dio. It is important to note here that Roman historians were significantly influenced by the rhetorical view that the writing of history was a form of literature on a par with epic poetry. As a result, the work of these four historians often includes speculative reconstruction unsupported by evidence. Suetonius' work, for example, includes numerous anecdotes and rumors that are interesting but that cannot be accepted as true with any certainty.

[5] Nero wanted more than anything to be an artist, but he was unable to perceive that he had no talent. He required Senators and members of the wealthy elite to attend his displays of poetry and singing, which were so bad that, according to Suetonius (1997), many in the audience feigned sudden death so that they could be carried away and escape the horror of Nero's fractured voice.

Ironically, mobilization alone was enough to depose Nero. The assassination of Caligula and subsequent elevation of Claudius had already demonstrated the imperial guard's power in affairs of state. For reasons that are not entirely clear, the prefect of the praetorians, Nymphidius Sabinius, chose to support Galba as Nero's most suitable replacement. He promised the guards a huge bribe if they supported Galba as emperor, and once an agreement was reached, he communicated to the Senate that Nero had lost the support of the praetorians. Seeing which way the political winds were blowing, the Senate promptly declared Nero an enemy of the state, even though he continued to have support among several of its members (Morgan, 2006). Nero fled the city in panic, retreating to a country estate where he committed suicide, which allowed Galba to enter Rome and assume the position of emperor without even having to unsheathe his sword.[6]

Galba's reign did not last long, however. Otho became enraged when, despite the considerable support he had provided, the new but aged emperor did not name him heir to the throne. He organized the praetorians and had them assassinate Galba on January 15, 69, using strength of arms to force the Senate to name him emperor. His rule ended four months later, brought to an end when Aulus Vitellius (c. 15–69), governor of Germania Inferior (southern and western Netherlands, Belgium and Luxembourg, parts of northeastern France, and western Germany), refused to recognize Otho, was proclaimed emperor by his troops, and began moving his legions toward Rome. After losing the Battle of Bedriacum in April 69, Otho committed suicide. But Vitellius' reign was only slightly longer than Otho's. Hearing reports relating Vitellius' profligate waste of the imperial treasury, the legions under Titus Flavius Vespasianus (c. 9–79), governor of Africa, proclaimed him emperor. In the ensuing civil war, Vitellius was captured and executed on or about December 20, 69.

Amid such turmoil, Quintilian finished his formal education in or about the year 53. It was fairly common for young men to begin their professional careers at an early age, so he probably started pleading cases in the courts at age 18 or 19. Much about Quintilian's life in the years immediately afterwards has been liberally reconstructed on the basis of two brief entries in St Jerome's (c. 340–420) *Chronicle*. The first states that Quintilian returned to Italy with Galba during the "211th Olympiad." From this entry it has been concluded that he traveled back to Spain after practicing law in Rome for several years, perhaps in 63, and that he there came to the attention of Galba. The second entry indicates that Quintilian's appointment to the Roman chair of rhetoric occurred during the "216th Olympiad."

Although Jerome's account has been widely accepted (e.g., Clarke, 1953, 1967; Kennedy, 1969; 1994; Tellegen-Couperus, 2003) and used to rationalize the reconstructed history, there are several reasons why it seems suspect. We must consider not only that the *Chronicle* was written about 300 years after Quintilian's death but also that it is a translation into Latin of a work in Greek by Eusebius (c. 275–339), the original of which no longer exists, raising the question of the accuracy of his translation. In addition, the lack of a uniform calendar for either the Greek or early Roman periods was problematic. Eusebius was forced to use the Olympiads as a dating system because the four-year cycle of the games at least offered some consistency, and Jerome adopted this system. Each Olympiad covers four years, which means that when an event was recorded as occurring in, say, the 210th Olympiad, there is no way to determine whether the year was 61, 62, 63, or 64. Thus, the precise identification of dates is rendered difficult, requiring

---

[6] Galba did not engage in any battles on his march to Rome, but he certainly ordered a large number of executions among civilians as well as soldiers.

cross-referencing with other sources. Eusebius' preface discusses the problem of accurate dating at length, and in spite of his projection of confidence, it is clear that he was simply guessing in many instances, such as the time of Moses and the Trojan War.

Even more problematic is the fact that the *Chronicle* contains various reporting errors. It notes, for example, that Nero canceled the games of the 211th Olympiad (which would have corresponded to the years 65, 66, 67, and 68) but then states that Nero won several competitions in the games of 65. This confusion was probably the result of the fact that Nero did not cancel the games but merely postponed them two years, which means that he participated in 67, not 65. Likewise, Jerome reported that Nero killed his second wife, Octavia, in 67, yet Tacitus (c. 56–117), who lived during Nero's reign and by this token alone may be a more reliable source, reported in his *Annals* that Octavia was murdered in 62 or 63.

Complicating matters is the dearth of autobiographical information in Quintilian's *Institutio Oratoria*,[7] as well as the fact that no other historical sources provide any biographical details. According to Suetonius (1997), Galba assembled a group of senior dignitaries as political advisors during the mobilization in Spain, and it is possible that Quintilian was part of this group, although he would have been only in his early thirties at the time, which would not readily put him in the category of "senior,"[8] and if in Spain he had continued his work as a jurist, it is unlikely (although not impossible) that he merited the status of "dignitary." Furthermore, even those scholars who accept Jerome's entries as veridical acknowledge that the date of 85 (or 87 if we adjust for Nero's postponement of the Olympic games) that Jerome gave for Quintilian's appointment to the chair of rhetoric is difficult to reconcile with Quintilian's comment in *Institutio Oratoria* that he had taught for 20 years.[9]

Quintilian's return to Calagurris certainly is a possibility and would seem quite reasonable given the dangers he would have faced in Rome with Nero dispatching anyone whom he found annoying. The motivation to leave the city no doubt would have been greater by the early 60s, when Nero's dissolution and erratic behavior were becoming more apparent. But even if Quintilian did return to live in Calagurris at some point before 68, the idea that Galba would ask an orator to join the rebel army he was marching to overthrow the emperor seems farfetched, as does the idea that Quintilian would want to do so. Galba did not make friends easily, and his concern with pedigrees was so intense that the likelihood of him socializing with someone of Quintilian's modest background approaches zero. Also, for at least a century, Roman armies had been made up of professional soldiers, so it is unlikely that an orator aged 30 or so with no military training or experience would have been invited (or drafted) to take up sword and shield in support of the rebellion. A more likely scenario, assuming that Quintilian had returned to Spain in the early 60s, would have him relocating to Rome on his own after learning that Nero was dead. He would have had every reason to assume that the new emperor would restore order and sanity to Rome, for Galba had been, by most accounts, an excellent (although harsh) governor in Spain. Quintilian's return in 68, the same year that Galba entered Rome, would in this case be mere coincidence.

---

[7] The only other work that Quintilian seems to have written was *De Causis Corruptae Eloquentiae* – or *On the Causes of Corrupt Eloquence*. We have no reason to assume that this work survived to Jerome's day or that it contained any autobiographical information.

[8] Latin has two words for young man, *adulescens* (from which came the English "adolescent") and *juvenis* (from which came the English "juvenile"). Both could be applied to a man well into his thirties if he had not yet made his mark in the world.

[9] Note that Clarke (1967) and Kennedy (1994) use the date 88 rather than 85 or 87.

Another possibility, however, is that Quintilian never went back to Spain at all but stayed in Rome. With the city in a rising state of anxiety over political events between 64, the year of the Great Fire that destroyed much of the city, and 67, when several aristocrats began conspiring to depose Nero, Quintilian may have found his legal practice suffering and decided to begin offering classes as a way to supplement his income.[10] This scenario has some significant advantages. It does not rely on Jerome's dubious entries concerning the orator, and it does not require speculation regarding a supposed relationship with Galba for which there is no evidence. In addition, it would give Quintilian several years of teaching experience, which seems necessary if we are to understand why in 71 Emperor Vespasian would single him out from among the numerous orators and rhetoricians in Rome to hold a lucrative chair in rhetoric. Also worth considering is that Vespasian seems to have had a significant reason for restricting rather than advancing the career of a Galba protégé: Suetonius (1997) indicated that Galba tried to have him assassinated, which led Vespasian, after he became emperor, to veto a Senate decree for a Galba memorial. Given these factors, using Jerome to date events related to Quintilian may be unwarranted at best, inaccurate at worst.

When Titus died in 81 after only 26 months as emperor, Domitian assumed the throne. The historical portrait of Domitian is in many ways contradictory: Suetonius (1997) described him as an able administrator who at the same time evidenced a frightening inclination toward cruelty that degenerated during the last years of his rule into a reign of terror. Some modern scholars (e.g., Jones, 1993; Morgan, 2006) have argued that ancient historians' views should not be taken at face value in this instance and that the reported brutality was greatly exaggerated. On this account, we would need to consider that Tacitus, for example, became a Senator under Domitian and saw many of his colleagues executed during the so-called reign of terror in 93–96; the experience left him bitter and angry, as his references to the emperor attest. This issue, although perhaps impossible to settle satisfactorily, is important owing to Quintilian's positive attitude toward Domitian in *Institutio Oratoria* on the one hand and his emphasis on the ideal orator's ethics and morality on the other.

Institutio Oratoria (The Orator's Education)

Institutio Oratoria is a massive work of 12 books – arguably the most comprehensive treatment on how to educate an orator ever produced. In many respects, Quintilian followed the educational model Cicero described in *Brutus*, *De Oratore*, and *Orator*, so there are necessarily a number of similarities. Both asserted, for example, that education could only enhance what a student already possessed by nature and that the ideal orator had to be a good man. The scope of Quintilian's vision, however, is somewhat broader than Cicero's, as the brief outline below suggests. Included in this chapter are excerpts from Books I and II:

---

[10] Suetonius (1997) reported in his biography of Vespasian that the courts had been unable to process complaints owing to the civil wars, but the interruption of legal proceedings probably started earlier. Suetonius also reported that Caligula often intervened in court cases and abused the legal process by hearing cases himself *in camera*, or closed sessions.

Quintilian's rhetorical theory

Institutio Oratoria is primarily a guide to education, and as a result it lacks some of the characteristics of a traditional *technê* such as Aristotle's *Art of Rhetoric* or Cicero's *De Inventione*. Even so, the amount of information related to rhetoric is considerable, especially in Books III through IX, which often are viewed as comprising the core of Quintilian's rhetorical theory. A broader perspective, however, recognizes that his theory is woven into the entire work. Essentially Aristotelian, the influences of Isocrates and Cicero are nevertheless strong, but Quintilian was not reluctant to "correct" the ideas of these lofty figures. He misquoted Aristotle's definition of rhetoric seemingly to dismiss Cicero's view that rhetoric is simply the power of persuasion, noting in this regard that "money also persuades, as do influence, the speaker's authority and dignity, and even the mere look of a man" (II.15.6).

Quintilian followed Aristotle and Cicero regarding rhetoric's five offices: invention (*inventio*), arrangement (*dispositio*), style and presentation (*elocutio*), memory (*memoria*), and delivery (*actio*). He accepted Aristotle's division of rhetoric into three types – forensic, deliberative, and epideictic – which allowed him to view the subject matter of rhetoric as being essentially limitless, "for there is nothing that does not come under these heads" (II, 21.24). Because opportunities for deliberative rhetoric in the Empire were essentially nil, Quintilian's comments on deliberative oratory may seem out of touch with contemporary realities, but his predominant focus on forensic oratory offsets this perspective. Moreover, he was writing about the education of the ideal orator, and perhaps we should assume that were it possible for such a person to exist, he or she would live in an equally ideal world that allowed and even encouraged these three types of speech. Quintilian also strove to ameliorate the problem by suggesting in Book III that the traditional view of deliberative rhetoric was too narrow, connected historically as it was to politics, and that anyone who gives advice (such as a friend) may be understood to be practicing deliberative oratory.

The argument on this point is weak, however, for the rhetorical nature of a friend's advice is similar to political deliberations only at the most superficial level. The two speech acts are fundamentally different with regard to rhetorical stances and aims, performative and illocutionary force, and adherence to linguistic pragmatics.[11] Advice to a friend, for example, may be neutral rather than persuasive, and unlike deliberative oratory in a governing assembly, it typically does not have consequences for the body politic, nor does it commonly involve issues *pros kriseis*. Quintilian rejected the idea that deliberative oratory must involve such issues, embracing instead Cicero's claim (ironic

---

[11] Advice to a friend, for example, would be governed by Grice's (1975) Cooperative Principle, which describes how people behave linguistically in conversations. Deliberative oratory, like debate, is not necessarily governed by all of Grice's maxims.

in light of Cicero's actions) that the primary focus of this type of speech should be with what is honorable (Book III). Aristotle might have accepted the idea that deliberation should be honorable, but he was too much of a realist to argue this point with much force. Aristotle also might have suggested that advice to a friend is akin to dialectic because, like dialectic, this use of language is isolated and detached from the *polis*.

Throughout *Institutio Oratoria*, we find Quintilian following the pattern suggested above – identifying a traditional element in rhetoric as part of his rhetorical theory and then adjusting it in one way or another to differentiate his views from those of previous masters. Book III and its discussion of stasis theory offer another example. Cicero and most orators who followed him limited stasis to questions of law; but Quintilian expanded the traditional application to include questions of reason, thereby allowing him to conclude that stasis can be applied to all three divisions of rhetoric, not solely to forensic. In doing so, he was very close to Aristotle's position on stasis, which included both forensic and deliberative oratory. The questions applicable to the law – Did it happen? Was it wrong? Was it injurious? and so forth – are transformed in deliberation by simply changing the verb to "will" and the adjective "injurious" to "expedient." The application of stasis theory to epideixis, on the other hand, seems problematic, as evidenced by the difficulty Quintilian had in explaining what this would entail.

The cornerstone of Quintilian's rhetorical theory, however, does not lie in such specific issues but rather in the notion that rhetoric must be combined with ethics and that the education of the orator therefore must emphasize the ethical practice of the art. From the very beginning of *Institutio*, he stressed that the orator must be a good man, Cato's and Cicero's *vir bonus dicendi peritus*. But good in what sense? Quintilian's definition of rhetoric as *bene dicendi scientiam* – the science of speaking well – is drawn directly from Stoic rhetoric and its focus on *scientia recte decendi* – knowledge of correct speaking. We therefore might be tempted to conclude that Quintilian's "good man" is a philosopher similar to the Stoic's "wise man" who has attained true knowledge (*katalepseis*). But this conclusion would not be entirely accurate.

Quintilian valued philosophy and identified it as an important element in the education of the ideal orator, even though he did not have much regard for contemporary philosophers. His strong argument in Books I, II, and XII that students should read extensively to gain knowledge seems congruent with the Stoic view that rhetoric and wisdom are interrelated. He stated in Book XII, for example, that:

Atqui ego illum quem instituo Romanum quendam velim esse sapientem, qui non secretis disputationibus sed rerum experimentis atque operibus vere civilem virum exhibeat.

And yet the person whose character I would mold should be a wise man in the Roman

sense, that is, not displaying his skills in private disputations and debates but in the real experience and practice of civic life. (XII.2.7)

The emphasis here on civic life is congruent with Roman patriotic sensibilities, but it also reminds us of Aristotle and Isocrates, both of whom saw rhetoric as a crucial factor in the concept of *aretê* as civic virtue.[12] The parallels appear early: In Book I he declared that his ideal orator is the man "who can really play his part as a citizen, who is fit for the management of public and private business, and who can guide cities by his counsel,

---

[12] We also see this influence in the stress Quintilian placed on having students write regularly as part of their training. Furthermore, Quintilian followed both Aristotle and Isocrates in his understanding that rhetorical training must focus on *poema, poetis, and poesis* – the work, the orator, and making meaning.

give them a firm basis by his laws, and put them right by his judgements" (I.10). In other words, Quintilian's *vir bonus* closely aligns oratory and rhetorical education with civic ethics and morality, not simply wisdom or knowledge. This alignment was evident in Cicero, but for Quintilian it was fundamental.

From the modern perspective, the emphasis Quintilian placed on ethics and morality creates several difficulties. One of the more obvious is the suggestion that morality is absolute; like Plato, Quintilian does not allow for any gradations – people are either good or bad, and the ideal orator must be good. Although speculative, the similarity here to Plato may be related to the fact that both men lived in turbulent times characterized by civil war and social disruptions. The desire to find moral absolutes in a chaotic, immoral world is understandable. Moral dilemmas, however, are an inevitable consequence of absolutism, and Plato's efforts to resolve them frequently led to paradoxical assertions, such as his arguments in *Gorgias* that it is better to suffer injustice than to commit an unjust act.

Quintilian was not a philosopher, and the *Institutio* gives us no reason to believe that he was Plato's intellectual equal. Whereas readers admire the subtleties of Plato's response to moral dilemmas, Quintilian's treatment in Book XII strikes some as unsatisfactory. Will the perfect orator lie? What should he do when asked to represent in court someone who is guilty? Quintilian's Roman pragmatism forced him to equivocate with regard to lies, and he acknowledged that even the perfect orator cannot always tell the truth because there are different types of lies. Some are actually beneficial, as when a parent praises a child's artwork even when a picture shows little evidence of ability. Likewise, in a case that requires the orator to defend a guilty person, Quintilian advised that one should approach the task with the firm belief that if his skill leads to an acquittal the client may mend his ways and become a model citizen. It is highly unlikely that he actually witnessed such a reformation, of course, and we see in this instance a conflict between Quintilian's ideals and the hard realities of legal practice, which entail having to defend the guilty as well as the innocent.

More problematic is the apparent disconnect between Quintilian's stance on ethics and morality and his praise of Emperor Domitian, leading Walzer (2006), for one, to characterize Quintilian as a moral quisling. Given Domitian's brutality, so the argument goes, Quintilian's flattery of the emperor in Books IV and X contradicts his emphasis on morality at best and makes him indirectly complicit at worst. After noting that Domitian exiled some of Rome's street philosophers and executed some others, Walzer asked: "[I]s it merely coincidental that the view toward philosophy and philosophers that Quintilian advances in the *Institutes* is consonant with that of the Flavian rulers?" (p. 266). The clear implication is that it was not.

Such criticisms may be overwrought. Quite small is the number of rhetoricians in the history of classical rhetoric who in their published works showed overt concern for political conditions. The question of whether Plato's treatment of contemporary political conditions was overt or covert, for example, is the source of interesting discussions, but the fact that there is disagreement on this point is revealing. Aristotle's *The Art of Rhetoric* and *The Art of Poetry* seem devoid of politics per se. Cicero set *De Oratore* almost 40 years in the past, perhaps as a way of justifying his lack of reference to the tumultuous political events that began with the outbreak of the Social War in 91 BC.

Analyzing *Institutio Oratoria* in its historical context requires us to recognize that Quintilian owed his success to the Flavians, who became his patrons the moment that Vespasian took over as emperor, and this relationship was solidified when Quintilian received the appointment as city rhetorician. The patron/client relationship was not just between individuals but between families; thus, even if Vespasian's sons had not succeeded to the throne, their patronage of Quintilian would have remained intact as a legacy. Moreover, any readily visible criticism of Domitian would have been a violation of the traditional bonds between patron and client, contrary to a cornerstone of Roman culture.[13] On a more pragmatic level, all emperors from Caligula to Domitian had shown intolerance for anyone who was annoying or who criticized their administrations, sending an unknown number of men and women to their deaths. Quintilian would have been foolhardy to express overtly any complaints about political or social conditions, which leaves open, however, the question of covert criticism.

Another factor to consider is that Quintilian's praise of Domitian does not lie outside literary convention. We need only consider that Horace flattered Emperor Augustus in his epistles and odes, even though the poet had fought against him at Pharsalus. *Odes IV*, a work of 15 lyric poems that celebrate Emperor Augustus and his family, can be hastily dismissed as purchased propaganda, but these lyrics are far more subtle than this characterization allows. Johnson (2005), for example, identified in the lyrics a wide range of richly textured ambiguities in which words of praise change to words of criticism when readers shift their perspective slightly. The result, according to Johnson, is "sympotic" insofar as the ambiguities require reflection on the very nature of identities: the identity of the Emperor; the identity of the individual reader; the identity of Rome as a community; and the identities of the culture and ideologies that drove and sustained Roman society. Given Cicero's palpable hostility toward Julius Caesar and the abuse he heaped on him in his letters, it seems inconceivable that he would celebrate the man whom he saw as an enemy of the Republic, yet in *Brutus* we find fulsome praise. Caesar is called Cicero's "counterpart" in oratory, a "genius." Brutus comments:

Itaque et lectis utitur verbis et frequentibus [or senten-tiis] et spendore vocis degnitate motus fit speciosum et illustre quod dicitur, omniaque sic suppletunt, ut ei nullam deesse virtutem oratoris putem.	His fine voice and dignified actions give his speeches an undeniable charm and brilliance. His command of oratory is so skillful that I am certain that he lacks no quality that an orator should have. (LXXI.250)

Brutus probably was written in 46 BC, at which time Caesar had been in power for about 3 years, and so it seems certain that multiple motives led Cicero to offer this assessment, motives that from this distance we cannot truly uncover. But it is the case that he could have written less.

Likewise, Quintilian no doubt had multiple motives for praising Domitian, and most are unknowable. A socio-rhetorical analysis, however, suggests that one such motive may be located in the literary and social framework that ineluctably influenced his writing. Declamation had grown increasingly artificial, dealing with topics that were removed from reality. Although Quintilian criticized the practice of declamation, it would have been difficult for him to escape its influence, for all around him Roman orators and rhetoricians were engaged in what Whitmarsh (2001) called the "politics of imitation," which constructed "idealized identities for Greek and Roman" alike (p. 16).

---

[13] We do not have to look far for cases in which these bonds were violated in the past, of course. Perhaps the most graphic example was the assassination of Julius Caesar, who as dictator was essentially the patron of all Romans. But as the events following the assassination show, Romans did not take such violations lightly.

If Whitmarsh's analysis is correct, panegyrics for men like Julius Caesar, Augustus, and Domitian can be understood as celebrating an ideal that extends back to Homer's "speaker of words and a doer of deeds" – the warrior king who also excels in oratory. This ideal had little basis in reality: Augustus reportedly was a poor speaker; Nero and Otho were incompetent commanders. But what mattered was that the celebration of the ideal created a sense of community through share values, not that anyone lived up to the ideal in a world of faded authenticity. *Institutio Oratoria* seems congruent with this analysis, for Quintilian repeatedly acknowledged that the overwhelming obstacles that stood in the way of educating the ideal orator must not detract from the ideal itself. Another possibility, to be found in a careful reading of the text, is that the praise of Domitian was designed, at least in part, to deflect attention from the subtle criticism of the imperial regime that is inherent in Quintilian's rhetorical theory and in his call for the reform of rhetoric and oratory.

Book I

One of the more distinctive features of *Institutio Oratoria* is Quintilian's attention to elementary education, which is the focus of Book I. Education must begin in the nursery, and parents must ensure that the "the nurses speak properly" (I.1.4). Molding the ideal orator requires that the child have certain natural advantages to begin with – specifically the great advantage of highly educated parents. To his credit, Quintilian noted that mothers must be included in this assessment, and by way of example he recalled the mother of the Gracchi brothers, who owed much of their eloquence to the influence she exerted on them owing to her superior education.

Quintilian's recommendation that education should begin in infancy appears to be related to his goal of combining rhetoric and morals. In his view, "language is based on Reason, Antiquity, Authority, and Usage" (I.6.1). The initial suggestion is that authority is derived from correct usage, following the models of history and master orators, but it becomes clear as the *Institutio* progresses that reliance on such authority is superficial, for true authority comes from the orator's *ethos*, his moral character (see Fernández-Lopez, 2003; Winterbottom, 1998). That is, the moral education of the orator begins in infancy: First comes habit, then nature (I.2.8). If the child is not raised in a moral home, there can be no hope of shaping the good man who speaks well, leading Quintilian to complain, "If only we did not ourselves damage our children's characters!" (I. 2.6). Book I therefore can be said to lay the foundation for Book XII, which examines moral issues with regard to the ideal orator. It also advances the Ciceronian agenda of creating a philosophical rhetoric, and there are clear parallels with sophistic notions of *aretê*. But Quintilian's approach differed from the Sophists' and from Cicero's. His view was that rhetoric preceded philosophy and that the art should retake what it had lost to presumptuous "students of wisdom." To support this view, Quintilian pointed out that philosophers do not own the topics and discourses of nature and justice. Even country folk ask questions about natural phenomena and matters of right and wrong: "Who – if not an utter villain – does not speak about justice and equity and goodness?" (I. prf.).

Book I had a significant influence on elementary education in the West. The range of subjects that Quintilian recommended in Book I for a child's education became institutionalized, and with some variations over the centuries formed the basis for the elementary curriculum: reading, writing, grammar, language, mathematics and geometry, music, and art. Ironically, Quintilian's treatise may, therefore, be said to have had a greater influence on education than on rhetoric and oratory.

Reading 36

Book I

Book I (excerpt), pp. 53–85 (Latin on even-numbered pages omitted) reprinted by permission of the publishers and Trustees of the Loeb Classical Library from *Quintilian*, Volume I, Loeb Classical Library Volume 124N, translated by D.A. Russell (Cambridge, MA: Harvard University Press, 1949). © 1949 by the President and Fellows of Harvard College. The Loeb Classical Library ® is a registered trademark of the President and Fellows of Harvard College.

Prooemium

When at last I won leisure for my studies, which for twenty years I had devoted to the training of the young, some friends asked me to write something on the theory of oratory. I resisted for a long time, because I knew that some very famous authors, in both Greek and Latin, had left to posterity many very carefully composed works relevant to this subject. But the reason that made me think I should have an easier excuse for saying no served only to inflame their enthusiasm. They urged that there was a difficulty in choosing between the different and in some instances contradictory opinions of my predecessors. They seemed therefore to be justified in imposing upon me the task of passing judgement on old ideas, if not of discovering new ones. I was moved to comply not so much because I felt confident that I could meet their requirements, but because I was ashamed to refuse. However, as the subject opened up more widely, I voluntarily undertook a heavier load than was being imposed upon me, partly to oblige my loving friends by fuller compliance, and partly to avoid going along the beaten track and finding myself merely treading in others' footsteps. For almost all others who have committed their teaching on the art of oratory to writing have started with the assumption that their pupils were perfect in every other branch of learning, and that they simply had to add the finishing touch; this was either because they despised the earlier stages of education as trivial, or because they thought they were not their concern (the roles of the professions being distinct), or, most probably, because they had no hope of winning favour for their talents by dealing with subjects which, however necessary, are very far from being showy – just as, in buildings, the rooftops are seen, but the foundations are hidden. For my part, however – holding as I do that nothing is foreign to the art of oratory which must be admitted to be essential for the making of an orator, and that one cannot reach the top in any subject without going through the elementary stages – I shall certainly not refuse to stoop to those matters which, though minor, cannot be neglected without blocking the way to greater things. I shall proceed exactly as if a child were put into my hands to be educated as an orator, and shall plan his studies from his infancy.

I dedicate this work to you, Marcus Vitorius. You are a very good friend of mine, and you have a burning enthusiasm for literature; but these are not the only reasons (strong as they are) why I regard you as particularly worthy of this pledge of our mutual affection. It is also because I think that these books will be useful for the education of your son Geta, whose early years already show such clear promise of talent. To carry the work through from the very cradle of eloquence, as it were, through all the skills that may be of some service to the future orator, right to the conclusion of the whole matter, shall be my urgent task – all the more urgent because two books on the Art of Rhetoric are already circulating in my name, though they were never published by me nor prepared for this purpose. One is a two days' lecture course which was taken down by the slaves to whom the responsibility was given. The other lecture course, which spread over several days, was taken down by shorthand (as best they could) by some excellent young men who were nevertheless too fond of me, and therefore rashly honoured it with publication and wide circulation. In the present work, therefore, there will be some things the same, many things changed, and very many things added, and the whole will be better written and worked up to the best of my ability.

I am proposing to educate the perfect orator, who cannot exist except in the person of a good man. We therefore demand of him not only exceptional powers of speech, but all the virtues of character as well. I cannot agree that the principles of upright and honourable living should, as some have held, be left to the philosophers. The man who can really play his part as a citizen, who is fit for the management of public and private business, and who can guide cities by his counsel, give them a firm basis by his laws, and put them right by his judgements, is surely no other than our orator. And so, although I admit that I shall use some ideas found in philosophical books, I would contend that these truly and rightfully belong to our work, and are strictly relevant to the art of oratory. We are often obliged to speak of justice, courage, temperance, and the like – indeed, scarcely a Cause can be found in which some question relating to these is not involved – and all these topics have to be developed by Invention and Elocution: how then can there be any doubt that wherever intellectual power and fullness of diction are required, the orator has the leading role? These two disciplines, as Cicero very clearly argues, were once so closely joined by nature and united in function, that philosophers and orators were taken to be the same. The subject then split into two, and it came about, through failure of art, that there were thought to be more arts than one. For as soon as the tongue began to offer a way of making a living, and the practice developed of making a bad use of the good gifts of eloquence, those who were counted able speakers abandoned moral concerns, and these, left to themselves, became, as it were, the prey of weaker minds. At this point, some, disdaining the effort of speaking well, returned to the business of forming character and establishing rules of life, and kept for themselves what would be, if the division were possible, the more important part; they laid claim, however, to a very presumptuous name, wishing to be regarded as the only "students of wisdom" – a distinction which neither the greatest generals nor the most famous statesmen and administrators have ever dared claim for themselves, because they have always preferred to do right rather than to profess it. I am very ready to admit that many of the old philosophers taught honourable principles and lived in accordance with their teaching; but in our day, very great vices have been concealed under this name in many persons. They did not try by virtue or learning to be regarded as philosophers; instead, they put on a gloomy face and an eccentric form of dress as a cover for their immorality. In fact, we all regularly handle the themes which philosophy claims for its own. Who – if not an utter villain – does not speak about justice and equity and goodness? Who – even among

country folk – does not ask some questions about the causes of natural phenomena? As for verbal precision and distinctions, this should be a study common to all who care for language. But it is the orator who will both know these things best and best express them in words; and if the perfect orator had existed at some epoch, there would be no need to apply to the schools of the philosophers for the precepts of virtue. As things are, we must return to those authors who, as I said, took possession of the better part of rhetoric when it was unoccupied, and demand its return, as ours by right – not appropriate their discoveries but show them that they have appropriated what was not theirs. So let our orator be the sort of man who can truly be called "wise," not only perfect in morals (for in my view that is not enough, though some people think otherwise) but also in knowledge and in his general capacity for speaking. Such a person has perhaps never yet existed; but that is no reason for relaxing our efforts to attain the ideal. Many of the ancients indeed acted on this principle, and handed down precepts of wisdom, despite their belief that no "wise" man had yet been found. Consummate eloquence is surely a real thing, and the nature of human abilities does not debar us from attaining it. But even if we fail, those who make an effort to get to the top will climb higher than those who from the start despair of emerging where they want to be, and stop right at the foot of the hill.

This will be a further reason for forgiving me if I do not pass over even minor details, which are nevertheless essential to the work. Book One will deal with what comes before the rhetor begins his duties. In Book II, I shall handle the first elements taught by the rhetor, and problems connected with the nature of rhetoric itself. The next five books will be given over to Invention (Disposition forms an appendix to this), and the following four to Elocution, with which are associated Memory and Delivery. There will be one further book, in which the orator himself is to be portrayed: I shall there discuss (as well as my poor powers allow) his character, the principles of undertaking, preparing, and pleading cases, his style, the end of his active career, and the studies he may undertake thereafter. With all these discussions, I shall combine, as appropriate at each point, a method of teaching which is not only intended to instruct students in the topics to which some teachers confine the name of "the art," and thus, as it were, interpret the law of rhetoric, but which can also nourish their powers of speech and develop their eloquence. The familiar dry textbooks, with their striving for excessive subtlety, merely weaken and cripple any generous stylistic tendencies there may be, drain off all the juice of the mind, and expose the bones – which must of course be there, and be bound together by the proper sinews, but which also need to be covered by the flesh. This is why I have not (like most writers) confined myself to this small part of the subject, but have gathered together in these twelve books everything that I think useful for the orator's education. I shall set it all out briefly, for if I were to go into everything that can be said on each subject, the work would have no end.

There is one point which I must emphasize at the start: without the help of nature, precepts and techniques are powerless. This work, therefore, must not be thought of as written for persons without talent, any more than treatises on agriculture are meant for barren soils. And there are other aids also, with which individuals have to be born: voice, strong lungs, good health, stamina, good looks. A modest supply of these can be further developed by methodical training; but sometimes they are so completely lacking as to destroy any advantages of talent and study, just as these themselves are of no profit without a skilled teacher, persistence in study, and much continuous practice in writing, reading, and speaking.

Chapter 1

Elementary education

As soon as his son is born, the father should form the highest expectations of him. He will then be more careful about him from the start. There is no foundation for the complaint that only a small minority of human beings have been given the power to understand what is taught them, the majority being so slow-witted that they waste time and labour. On the contrary, you will find the greater number quick to reason and prompt to learn. This is natural to man: as birds are born for flying, horses for speed, beasts of prey for ferocity, so are we for mental activity and resourcefulness. This is why the soul is believed to have its origin in heaven. Dull and unteachable persons are no more normal products of human nature

than prodigious and monstrous births [but these have been very few]. The proof of this is that the promise of many accomplishments appears in children, and when it fades with age, this is plainly due to the failure not of nature but of care. "But some have more talent than others." I agree: then some will achieve more and some less, but we never find one who has not achieved something by his efforts. A parent who grasps this must devote the keenest possible care, from the moment he becomes a parent, to fostering the promise of the orator to be.

First of all, make sure the nurses speak properly. Chrysippus wished them, had it been possible, to be philosophers; failing that, he would have us choose the best that our circumstances allowed. No doubt the more important point is their character; but they should also speak correctly. These are the first people the child will hear, theirs are the words he will try to copy and pronounce. We naturally retain most tenaciously what we learned when our minds were fresh: a flavour lasts a long time when the jar that absorbs it is new, and the dyes that change wool's pristine whiteness cannot be washed out. Indeed, the worse these impressions are, the more persistent they are. Good is easily changed to worse: can you ever hope to change bad to good? So do not let the child become accustomed, even in infancy, to a type of speech which he will have to unlearn.

As to the parents, I should wish them to be as highly educated as possible. (I do not mean only the fathers. We are told that the eloquence of the Gracchi owed much to their mother Cornelia, whose highly cultivated style is known also to posterity from her letters; Laelia, Gaius Laelius' daughter, is said to have echoed her father's elegance in her own conversation; and the speech delivered before the triumvirs by Hortensia, the daughter of Quintus Hortensius, is still read – and not just because it is by a woman.) However, those who have not been lucky enough to learn themselves should not for that reason take less trouble about their sons' teaching; on the contrary, it should make them all the more careful in other matters.

As to the slave boys with whom the child born to such high hopes is to be brought up, I would repeat what I said about the nurses. Regarding his *paedagogi*, I would add that they should either be thoroughly educated (this is the first priority) or know themselves to be uneducated. Nothing can be worse than those who, having got just beyond the alphabet, delude themselves that they have acquired some knowledge. They both scorn to give up the role of instructor and, conceiving that they have a certain title to authority (a frequent source of vanity in this class of persons), become imperious and sometimes even brutal teachers of their own foolishness. Their failings have an equally bad moral effect: Alexander's *paedogogus*, Leonides, according to Diogenes of Babylon, infected him with some faults which clung to him as a result of his childhood education even when he was a grown man and had become a mighty king.

If anyone thinks I am asking too much, let him reflect that we are educating an orator, which is a hard enough business even if there is nothing lacking for his education, and that more and greater difficulties are still to come. He needs continuous application, first-class teachers, and many different branches of study. We must therefore recommend the optimum procedure: if anyone finds this too hard, the fault will lie with the individual, not with the principle. But if it is not possible to secure the sort of nurses, young companions, and *paedagogi* that I should most prefer, let there be anyway one person always at hand who knows the right ways of speaking, and who can correct on the spot any faulty expression used by the others in the pupil's presence, and so stop it becoming a habit. But it must be understood that this is only a remedy: what I said above is the ideal course.

I prefer a boy to begin by speaking Greek, because he will imbibe Latin, which more people speak, whether we will or no; and also because he will need to be taught Greek learning first, it being the source of ours too. However, I do not want a fetish to be made of this, so that he spends a long time speaking and learning nothing but Greek, as is commonly done. This gives rise to many faults both of pronunciation (owing to the distortion of the mouth produced by forming foreign sounds) and of language, because the Greek idioms stick in the mind through continual usage and persist obstinately even in speaking the other tongue. So Latin ought to follow not far behind, and soon proceed side by side with Greek. The result will be that, once we begin to pay equal attention to both languages, neither will get in the way of the other.

Some have held that children should not be taught to read under the age of seven, on the ground that this is the earliest age which can grasp the subjects taught and sustain the effort. This view is attributed to Hesiod by most writers who lived before Aristophanes the grammarian, who was the first to deny that the *Hypothecae*, in which this can be found, was by that poet. Other authorities also, including Eratosthenes, have given the same advice. But one finds better advice in those who believe that no age should be without some interest, like Chrysippus, who gives the nurses the first three years, but holds that they too should already have a part in forming the mind on the best possible principles. But why should an age already capable of moral instruction not be capable of learning its letters? I know of course that in all this period one can hardly get the results that a single year later on can achieve; still, those who have taken this line seem to me to have spared the teachers rather than the pupils. What better thing can they be doing anyway, from the moment they are able to speak? Something at least they must be doing! Or why should we despise the gains to be made before the age of seven, however small they are? For though the knowledge contributed by the early years may be small, still the boy will be learning some more important things in the year in which he would otherwise have been learning more elementary matters. Carried forward year by year, this all adds up, and the time saved in childhood is a gain for the period of adolescence. The same advice may be taken to apply to the subsequent years: let the child not begin too late to learn what he has to learn. Let us therefore not waste the earliest years, especially as the elements of reading and writing are entirely a matter of memory, which not only already exists in little children, but is then at its most retentive.

I am not so careless of age differences as to think that the very young should be forced on prematurely, and that set tasks should be demanded of them. For one of the first things to take care of is that the child, who is not yet able to love study, should not come to hate it and retain his fear of the bitter taste he has experienced even beyond his first years. Let it be a game; let him be questioned and praised and always feel glad that he has done something; sometimes, when he refuses a lesson, it should be given to another child, of whom he can be jealous; sometimes he should compete, and more often than not think he is the winner; and finally, he should be encouraged by rewards suitable to his age.

These are trivial recommendations for one who claims to be educating an orator; but study also has its infancy, and, as the rearing of what will one day be the strongest bodies begins with breast feeding and the cradle, so the great speaker of the future once cried as a baby, tried to speak with an uncertain voice, and was puzzled by the shapes of letters. If learning something is not sufficient in itself, it does not follow that it is not necessary. If no one blames a father for thinking these things should not be neglected in his son, why should a person be criticized for bringing into public view what he would rightly do in his own home? All the more so, because little children grasp little things more easily, and, just as the body can only be trained to flex the limbs in certain ways when it is young and tender, so the acquisition of strength itself makes the mind also more resistant to many kinds of learning. Would King Philip of Macedon have chosen that his son Alexander be taught his letters by Aristotle, the greatest philosopher of the age, or would Aristotle have accepted the commission, if they had not believed that elementary instruction is best given by the most accomplished teacher and that it is important for the ultimate outcome? So let us imagine that an Alexander is entrusted to our care, that the child placed in our lap deserves as much attention (though of course every father thinks this of his son): ought I to be ashamed to point out a short way of teaching even for the first elements?

At any rate, I do not like the procedure (which I see is very common) by which children learn the names and sequence of the letters before their shapes. This is an obstacle to the recognition of the letters, since they do not when the time comes pay attention to the actual outlines, because they follow the promptings of their memory, which runs ahead of their observation. This is why teachers, even when they think they have sufficiently fixed the letters in a child's mind in the order in which they are commonly first written, next reverse this, or muddle it up in various ways, until the pupils come to recognize the letters by their shape and not by the order in which they come. It will be best therefore for them to be taught the appearance and the name side by side: it is like recognizing people.

But what is an obstacle in learning letters will do no harm when we come to syllables. Nor do I rule out the well-known practice of giving ivory letter-shapes to play with, so as to stimulate little children to learn – or indeed anything else one can think of to give them more pleasure, and which they enjoy handling, looking at, or naming.

Once the child has begun to trace the outlines, it will be useful to have these inscribed as neatly as possible on a tablet, so that the stilus is guided by the grooves. In this way, the child will not make mistakes as on wax (for he will be constrained by the edges on both sides, and will not be able to stray beyond the marks), and, by following these well-defined traces so quickly and often, he will strengthen his fingers, and not need the help of a guiding hand placed over his own. Practice in writing well and quickly, which people of standing tend to neglect, is not an irrelevance. Writing in one's own hand is important in our studies, and is the only way of ensuring real, deep-rooted progress; slow writing delays thought, ill-formed or confused writing is unintelligible, and this produces a second laborious stage of dictating what needs to be copied out. So, at all times and in all places, and especially in confidential and familiar letters, one will find pleasure in not having neglected this skill either.

With syllables, there is no short cut. They must all be learned; there is no point in the common practice of postponing the most difficult questions relating to them, to be discovered only when we come to write words. We must beware also of trusting the first memory too readily: it is better to have repeated syllable-drill over a long period, and not be in a hurry to achieve continuity or speed in reading either, unless the sequences of letters are produced without hesitation or doubt, and anyway without the child having to stop and think. Only then let him begin to construct words with the syllables themselves and form connected sentences with the words. It is unbelievable how much further delay in reading is produced by haste. The result is hesitation, interruption, and repetition, because they are venturing beyond their powers, and then, when they make mistakes, losing confidence also in what they already know. Reading must therefore first be sure, then connected, and for a long time quite slow, until practice enables correctness to be combined with speed. For to look forward to the right (as is universally taught), and so foresee what is coming, is a matter not only of theory but of practice, since we have to keep our eyes on what follows while reading out what precedes, and (most difficult of all) divide the attention of the mind, the voice doing one thing and the eyes another.

One will never regret making sure that, when the child (according to the usual practice) begins to write names, he does not waste his time on common words that occur all the time. Right from the start, he can, incidentally, learn the explanations of obscure words (what the Greeks call "glosses"), and so, at this elementary stage, acquire knowledge which would need time for itself later on. And, as we are still dealing with minor matters, I should like to suggest that the lines set for copying should not be meaningless sentences, but should convey some moral lesson. The memory of such things stays with us till we are old, and the impression thus made on the unformed mind will be good for the character also. The child may also be allowed to learn, as a game, the sayings of famous men and especially selected passages from the poets (which children particularly like to know). Memory (as I shall show in due time) is very necessary to the orator; there is nothing like practice for nourishing and strengthening it, and, since the age-group of which we are now speaking cannot as yet produce anything on its own, it is almost the only faculty which the teacher's attention can help to develop.

It would be a good idea, at this age, in order to develop the vocal organs and make the speech more distinct, to get the child to rattle off, as fast as he can, words and verses designed to be difficult, formed of strings of syllables which clash with one another, and are really rocky, as it were: the Greeks call them *chalinoi* (tongue twisters). This sounds no great matter; but its omission leads to many faults of pronunciation which, unless removed in early years, persist through life as an incurable bad habit.

Chapter 2

Home or school?

But now our boy is to grow up little by little, leave the nursery, and begin his education seriously. This is therefore the best place to discuss the question whether it is better to keep him studying at home, within one's own walls, or hand him over to the general society of the schools and teachers who, as it were, are available to the public. I know this has been the favoured course of those who have established the customs of the most famous cities, and of other very eminent authorities besides. But we must not conceal the fact that there are some who disagree with this publicly approved custom because of private convictions of their own. They seem to have two main reasons. First, they are making (they think) better provision for morality by avoiding the crowd of persons of an age which is particularly liable to vice; and I only wish that the view that this has often been a cause of shameful behaviour were false! Secondly, the future teacher, whoever he is, seems likely to give a single pupil more of his time than if he had to divide it among several.

The first point is certainly serious. If it were agreed that schools were good for study, but bad for morals, I should put a higher value on respectability of life than on any excellence as a speaker. In my view, however, the two are inseparably connected. I hold that no one can be an orator unless he is a good man; and even if it *is* possible, I do not want it to happen. So I take this question first.

People think that morals are corrupted in schools. Sometimes indeed they are, but so they are at home, and there are numerous instances of this, and also of course of the most scrupulous preservation of good repute in both situations. The whole difference lies in the nature of the individual and the attention he receives. Given a natural bent towards evil, and some carelessness in developing and guarding modesty in early years, privacy will give just as much opportunity for sin. The teacher employed at home may be of bad character, and the company of bad slaves is no safer than that of immodest companions of good birth. On the other hand, if the boy's natural bent is good, and the parents are not sunk in blind indifference, it is possible to choose a teacher of unexceptionable character (this is the wise parent's prime concern) and the strictest system of education conceivable, and at the same time to attach some respectable man or loyal freedman to one's son as a friend, whose regular companionship may even improve those who gave rise to our fears.

Book II

Having examined the role of elementary education in developing the ideal orator, Quintilian in Book II turned to the more specific issue of rhetorical instruction. His discussion of preliminary exercises, or *progymnasmata*, follows the approach that by his time had become standard, with students beginning with the practice of simple narratives and then moving on to more complicated matters: refutation and confirmation, encomia and invectives, commonplaces, and so on. What stands out in the early chapters is not how Quintilian would organize instruction but rather his humane approach to education. In II.4.5, for example, he urges teachers to "take trouble to nourish the tender minds gently, like nurses"; in II.4.10, he cautions against harsh correction of students' errors, noting how easily young students can be hurt by criticism.

After expressing his concern for the gentle treatment of young students, Quintilian begins weaving the second major theme of *Institutio Oratoria* – the reformation of rhetoric. Then, after a cursory discussion of commonplaces and themes, he introduces in Chapter 4 his view that a principle factor in effective oratory is the law. His discussion is somewhat anachronistic, more appropriate to the Republic than to the Empire, when members of the Senate were free to question whether a given law was "right and ... expedient." Nevertheless, it provides the foundation for further examination of rhetoric and the law in Chapter 10.

The problem with contemporary rhetoricians, Quintilian argues, is that their teaching was detached from reality. They focused almost exclusively on training their students in declamation, which dealt with "magicians ... plagues ... oracles ... stepmothers more cruel than any in tragedy ... and ... other still more fabulous elements" (II.10.5). Rhetoricians had lost sight of the purpose of declamation, which was to prepare students for forensic oratory; they "completely fail[ed] to see the reason why this exercise was invented. If it is not a preparation for the courts, it is like nothing so much as a stage performance or the cries of a lunatic" (II.10.8). Indeed, the training students received in Rome's schools of rhetoric – no matter how effective in other respects – was useless for any practical purpose, leaving orators "novices in court" (II.10.9). Only a reformed rhetoric, Quintilian argued, would prepare students for the practice of law. At this point, his comments in Chapter 4, mentioned above, regarding the questioning of whether a law was right and expedient become clear: The orator in court must be able to attack the law that his client allegedly violated. The focus should be on the question of right, which Quintilian expanded to include justice, piety, and religion. Is the law just?, pious?, conforming to religious beliefs?

Another area of reform was the practice of insisting that orations follow what amounted to a recipe, with proemium, narrative, proposition, and so forth. Quintilian notes that "Rhetoric would be a very easy and trivial affair if it could be comprised in a single short set of precepts" (II.13.1), and then he dismisses this approach as being incongruent with the realities of courtroom practice. He compared legal proceedings to a battle, for both are in a continual state of flux that borders on chaos. Thus, the orator must be able to respond quickly and versatilely to the fluid conditions of the trial. Training that takes a recipe approach is too rigid and fails to prepare students for the challenges of forensic oratory. The criticism of contemporary rhetoric continues in Chapter 15, where Quintilian considers earlier definitions of rhetoric and found fault in them all.

It is at this point that Quintilian offers an interpretation of Plato's *Gorgias* that leads him to assert that rhetoric and oratory as practiced by the ideal orator are not concerned solely with justice in the courts but are also a crucial component of *ars civilitatis* – the art of government. Querzoli (2003) recognized this expansion of rhetoric and oratory as being a significant feature of Quintilian's reform effort: "In Quintilian's theory, the orator was not only just, but also engaged in propagating *iustita* [justice], which he practised in leading the *res publica*" (p. 47). The ideal orator therefore renders philosophers, who claimed province of both justice and political theory, irrelevant. A more significant consequence of the agenda for reforming education and rhetoric is also quite subtle, helping us to understand better his repeated emphasis on characterizing the ideal orator as *vir bonus*, a good man. Quintilian's assertion that the province of the ideal orator includes justice as well as government appears to be a criticism of both as they existed. Possessing personal as well as civic virtue, the ideal orator *propagates* – to use Querzoli's term – justice in society, which is necessary where justice does not prevail – or where it does not exist. From this perspective, *Institutio Oratoria* cannot so easily be criticized for its flattery of Emperor Domitian, which ultimately seems trivial given Quintilian's skillful criticism of society in general, and the legal system and government in particular.

Reading 37

Book II

Book II (excerpt), pp. 263–91 (Latin on even-numbered pages omitted) reprinted by permission of the publishers and Trustees of the Loeb Classical Library from *Quintilian*, Volume I, Loeb Classical Library Volume 124N, translated by D.A. Russell (Cambridge, MA: Harvard University Press, 1949). © 1949 by the President and Fellows of Harvard College. The Loeb Classical Library ® is a registered trademark of the President and Fellows of Harvard College.

Chapter 1

When should the study of rhetoric be begun?

The custom has come to prevail, and grows stronger every day, of sending pupils to the teachers of rhetoric later than reason demands – invariably as regards Latin rhetors, but sometimes also as regards Greek. There are two reasons for this: the rhetors, and certainly our own, have abandoned their own sphere, and the *grammatici* have taken over what belongs to others. The rhetors think that their only function is to declaim and teach the theory and practice of declamation, restricted moreover to deliberative and judicial themes (because they regard everything else as beneath the dignity of their profession). The *grammatici* do not think it is enough to pick up what was left for them (and we should

indeed be grateful to them for this), but make inroads as far as *prosopopoeiae* and *suasoriae*, in which the burden of speaking is very great. Hence subjects which once formed the first stages of one discipline have come to form the final stages of another, and an age-group which ought to go on to higher studies is kept back in a lower school, and practises rhetoric under the *grammatici*. So (ridiculous as it is) a boy is not thought fit to go to the declamation master until he knows how to declaim.

Grammaticus and rhetor: the place of progymnasmata in the curriculum

We must however give the two professions their proper spheres. *Grammaticē* (it has been translated *litteratura* in Latin) must learn to know its own limits, especially as it has advanced so far beyond the modest bounds which its name implies, within which its earlier professors confined themselves. At its source a tiny trickle, it has gathered strength [from historians and critics] and now flows in full flood, having come to comprise not only the principles of correct speech (in itself no inconsiderable matter) but the knowledge of almost all the major arts. Rhetoric for its part, named as it is from the power of speaking, must not shirk its proper duties or rejoice to see burdens which belong to it taken up by others; indeed, by surrendering some of the work, it has almost been driven out of its rightful possessions. I shall not deny, of course, that some individual among those who profess *grammaticē* may progress to a stage of knowledge which makes him fully capable of teaching these things too; but when he does so, he will be performing the rhetor's function, not his own.

We next ask when a boy may be thought mature enough to grasp the precepts of rhetoric. For this purpose, we must think not of the actual age of the person, but of what progress he has already made in his studies. To save longer discussion of the question "When should he be sent on to the rhetor?" the best answer, I think, is "When he is fit."

But this itself depends on the previous question. For if the duties of the *grammaticus* are extended to include *suasoriae*, the rhetor will not be needed till later. But if the rhetor does not shirk the first duties of his task, he is needed as soon as the pupil gets to Narratives and short Encomia and Vituperations. Have we forgotten that the ancients developed their eloquence by the exercises of Thesis and Commonplace, and others which do not have a particular context of circumstances and persons, such as form the substance of real and imaginary *controversiae*? It is surely plain now that it is a scandal that rhetorical teaching has abandoned its original, and for a long time its only, sphere. And what is there in the exercises of which I have just spoken which does not fall within the general functions of the rhetor, and indeed also within the forensic genre? Do we not have to give Narratives in court? I suspect it may be the most important thing we do there. Are not Encomium and Vituperation frequently introduced in our contests? Do not Commonplaces belong at the very heart of lawsuits, whether they are like those which we read that Cicero composed, against vices, or are general discussions of questions, like those published also by Quintus Hortensius –

"should small arguments carry weight?" "for witnesses," and "against witnesses?" These are, in a sense, weapons always to be kept ready, to be used as the occasion demands. Anyone who denies that these things are not relevant to oratory might as well believe that a statue is not begun when the limbs are being cast!

No one should criticize this haste of mine (as some will think it) as though I were recommending that the pupil who has been handed over to the rhetor should forthwith be taken away from the *grammatici*. They will have their place in the timetable at this stage also, and there is no reason to fear that a boy will be overloaded by having two masters, for the work that was formerly all done under one will not increase, but simply be divided, and each teacher will be more serviceable in his own department. The Greeks still maintain this system, the Latins have given it up – excusably, we may think, because others have taken over this work from the *grammatici*.

Chapter 2

The duties and personal qualifications of the rhetor

So as soon as the boy has progressed in his studies to the point when he can follow what I have called the first stage of instruction in rhetoric, he should be handed over to the teachers of that art.

The first necessity will be to inquire into their good character. The reason which leads me to tackle this issue particularly in the present context is not that I do not think that the most careful inquiries possible are necessary in regard to other teachers also (as I showed in the previous book) but because the age of the pupils makes it more essential to discuss it now. Boys are approaching adulthood when they are passed on to the rhetor, and they remain with him even as young men; that is why we must take particular care at this stage that the impeccable character of the teacher should preserve the younger pupils from injury, and his authority deter the more aggressive from licentious behaviour. It is not sufficient that he should himself set an example of perfect self-control unless he also restrains the behaviour of those who attend his classes by the severity of his discipline.

First of all, then, let him adopt a paternal attitude towards his pupils, and regard himself as taking the place of those whose children are entrusted to him. Let him be free of vice himself and intolerant of it in others. Let him be strict but not grim, and friendly but not too relaxed, so as to incur neither hatred nor contempt. He should talk a great deal about what is good and honourable; the more often he has admonished his pupils, the more rarely will he need to punish them. He must not be given to anger, but he must not turn a blind eye to things that need correction; he must be straightforward in his teaching, willing to work, persistent but not obsessive. He must answer questions readily, and put questions himself to those who do not ask any. In praising his pupils' performances he must be neither grudging nor fulsome: the one produces dislike of the work, the other complacency. In correcting faults, he must not be biting, and certainly not abusive. Many have been driven away from learning because some teachers rebuke pupils as though they hate them. He should himself deliver at least one speech, preferably several, a day, for his class to take away with them. For even if he provides them with plenty of examples for imitation from their reading, better nourishment comes, as they say, from the "living voice," and especially from a teacher whom, if they are properly taught, the pupils love and respect. It is difficult to overestimate how much readier we are to imitate those whom we like.

We should definitely not allow boys (as happens in many teachers' classrooms) to stand up or jump out of their seats to applaud. Even young adults, when they are listening to a speech, should be restrained in their approval. In this way, the pupil will come to depend on the teacher's judgement, and think that he has spoken well when *he* approves. The extremely undesirable "humanity," as it is now called, which consists of mutual praise without any regard to quality, is unseemly, reeks of the theatre, and is quite alien to properly disciplined schools; it is also a very dangerous enemy of study, because, if there is praise on hand for every effusion, care and effort appear superfluous. The audience, therefore, as well as the pupil who is speaking, should keep their eyes on the teacher's face; they will thereby learn to distinguish what deserves approval from what does not, and will thus acquire judgement by listening as well as facility by writing. Nowadays however, leaning

forward, all ready to go, they not only stand up at the end of every sentence, but rush forward with shouts of unseemly enthusiasm. It is a mutual service; this is what makes the declamation a success. The result is a swollen head and a very false idea of themselves, carried to the point where, intoxicated by their fellow-students' uproar, they come to have bad feelings about their teacher if he fails to praise them warmly enough.

But teachers too should expect to be heard attentively and quietly. The master does not have to speak to suit the pupils' judgement, the pupil has to speak to suit his. If possible, too, he should watch to see what each boy praises and how, and should be pleased if the good things in his speech are appreciated, not so much for his own sake as for that of the pupils who judge it correctly.

I do not approve of boys and young men sitting all together. Even if a teacher who is the right type to be in charge of studies and morals may be able to keep the young men also under control, the weaker should all the same be kept apart from the stronger, and one must avoid not only charges of immorality but the bare suspicion. I thought a brief note was needed on this; there is surely no need even to specify that both teacher and school must be free from the grosser vices. And should there be any father who fails to avoid obvious vices in choosing his son's teacher, let him have no doubt that, if this is neglected, everything else that we are trying to put together for the use of young people is pointless.

Chapter 3

Should the best teacher be employed from the start?

I must not pass over in silence the view of those who, even when they have judged boys fit for the rhetor, still do not think they ought to be put straight into the charge of the most eminent teacher, but keep them for a time with lesser men, as though a mediocre teacher were better suited to the early stages of the art, both because he is easier to understand and to imitate and because he will not be too proud to take on the troublesome business of elementary teaching. On this, I do not think there is any need to emphasize how much better it is to absorb the best models, and how hard it is at a later stage to eradicate faults which have once become ingrained, because this puts a double burden on the teachers who take over, namely that of unteaching, which is a heavier task than teaching, and has to be given priority. It is for this reason that the famous piper Timotheus is said to have charged those who had had another teacher double the fee he asked of complete beginners.

The mistake here, however, is twofold. (1) For the time being, they think the lesser men perfectly adequate, and are indeed comfortable and content with them. This complacency is certainly in itself blameworthy, but it would still be tolerable, if it was only the quantity, and not the quality, of such persons' teaching that was inferior. (2) Secondly – an even commoner error – they think that those who have acquired superior gifts of eloquence will not condescend to lesser matters, and that the reason for this is sometimes that they disdain to take trouble over what is beneath them, and sometimes that they just cannot do it. Personally, I do not count anyone who is unwilling to do this as a teacher at all; and, as for capacity, my view is that the best man, if he chooses, will do it best, because (1) it is reasonable to believe that a man who surpasses others in eloquence has thoroughly understood the steps by which eloquence is attained; (2) the reasoning faculty, which is most highly developed in the most learned, is of crucial importance in teaching; and (3) no one excels in big things who fails in small things. Or are we to think that, though Phidias' Zeus is a masterpiece, the decorative additions to that work would have been better done by someone else? Or that an orator will not know how to conduct an ordinary conversation? Or that a great doctor will not be able to treat minor illnesses?

What then? Is there not a type of eloquence too great to be understood by immature boys? I admit that there is. But our eloquent teacher will also need to be sensible and knowledgeable about teaching, and prepared to come down to his pupil's level, just as a very fast walker, if he were walking with a child, would give him his hand, shorten his own stride, and never go beyond what his companion could manage. Again, it commonly happens that what the most learned teachers say is also easier to understand and much clearer. For clarity is the first virtue of eloquence, and the less talented a speaker is, the harder he will strive after elevation and expansion, just as

little men walk on tiptoe and weak men use more threats. As for the turgid, the perverse, the jingling, and any who suffer from any other species of affectation, I am persuaded that they do so not out of strength but out of weakness, just as bodies swell not with strength but with illness, and people who are tired of the direct road often turn aside from it. So the worse a teacher is, the more obscure he will be also.

I have not forgotten that I said in the previous book, when I was arguing that school education was preferable to home education, that the beginnings and the early progress of the young are stimulated more by imitating fellow pupils, because this is easier. Some may interpret this as implying that the position I am now defending is contrary to my earlier one. But that is far from my intention; perhaps the strongest reason why the boy should be entrusted to the best possible teacher is that the pupils are better taught in his school and will themselves either speak in a way worth imitating or be corrected at once if they make mistakes, whereas the unlearned teacher may well approve faulty work and force his pupils to like it because of his own judgement.

So the teacher who (like Phoenix in Homer) teaches his pupils "to speak and to do" must be as distinguished for his eloquence as for his character.

Chapter 4

Preliminary exercises (Progymnasmata)

I shall now proceed to indicate what I take to be the first areas to be covered by the rhetor, postponing for the moment what is commonly regarded as the sole field of the "art of rhetoric." The handiest approach seems to me to be by way of something which is closely related to what the child has learned with the *grammatici*.

Narrative

We are told that there are three species of Narrative, apart from the one used in actual Causes. One is Fable, found in tragedies and poems, and remote not only from truth but from the appearance of truth. The second is Plot, which is the false but probable fiction of comedy. The third is History, which contains the narration of actual events. We have given poetical Narratives to the *grammatici*; the rhetor should begin with historical ones, which are more grown-up because they are more real.

I shall discuss what I think to be the best principles of Narrative later, when I come to speak of forensic oratory. Meanwhile, it is sufficient to note that it should be neither quite dry and jejune (for why spend so much labour on our studies if it was thought satisfactory to set things out baldly and without embellishment?) nor, on the other hand, tortuous and revelling in those irrelevant Descriptions to which many are tempted by their wish to imitate the licence of poets. Both are faults, but the one which comes from deficiency is worse than the one which comes from abundance. In boys, a perfect style is neither to be demanded nor expected; but there is a better prospect in a fertile mind, ambitious effort, and a spirit that sometimes has too many bold ideas. I should never feel troubled by a certain amount of excess in a pupil of this age. Indeed, I should like the teachers themselves to take trouble to nourish the tender minds gently, like nurses, and let them have their fill of the milk, as it were, of pleasanter learning. That will put flesh on them for a time, but growing up will in due course slim them down. This is where one sees hope of future strength. The baby whose limbs are all distinctly visible from the start threatens to be skinny and weak later on. The young should be more daring and inventive, and take pleasure in their inventions, even if for the time being these are not sober and correct enough. Exuberance is easily remedied; no effort can overcome barrenness. The quality in a boy which, to my mind, gives least promise is the premature growth of judgement at the expense of creative talent. I like the raw material at the start to be over-abundant, poured out more generously even than it ought to be. The passing years will reduce it greatly, method will file it down, use will rub some of it away, so long as there is something there to be cut out and chiselled; and that will be so, if we do not draw the plate too thin to begin with, so that it breaks if the engraving goes too deep. That I think in this way about the young will be less surprising to anyone who has read Cicero's words: "I like fecundity to run riot in a young man."

It is therefore especially important, particularly with little boys, to avoid a dry teacher, just as we avoid a dry soil without moisture for young plants. For with this sort of teaching, they instantly become stunted, and look down at the ground, as it were, because they dare not rise above the level of daily speech. They think leanness means health and weakness good judgement, and while they think it is enough to be without fault they fall into the fault of being without virtues. I would not want even maturity to come too soon, or the must to become tart straight away in the vat; in this way it will bear its years better and improve with age.

It is worth noting too that boys' minds sometimes cannot stand up to undue severity in correction. They despair, they feel hurt, they come ultimately to hate the work, and (most damaging of all) they make no effort because they are frightened of everything. Farmers know this: they do not believe in applying the pruning hook to the tender leaves, because these seem to be afraid of the knife and not yet able to bear a scar. So at this stage the teacher should be particularly kind, so that the remedies, which are otherwise harsh by nature, can be made easier by a gentle touch. He must praise some things, tolerate others, suggest changes (always also giving reasons for them), and brighten up passages by putting in something of his own. He will sometimes also find it useful to dictate whole themes himself for the boy to imitate and sometimes love as if they were his own. If, however, the written work is so careless that it cannot be corrected, I have found that it helped if I treated the same theme again myself and made my pupil write it out afresh, telling him he could do even better; for nothing makes for happy work as much as hope. But different ages need different methods of correction, and the original assignment and the correction have both to be proportionate to the pupil's strength. I used to say to boys who ventured on some rather free or exuberant expression that I approved of it now, but the time would come when I should not let it pass. So they were happy with their creativity, and not deceived in their judgement.

But to return to the point from which I digressed. I want written Narratives to be as carefully composed as possible. When children are first being taught to talk, it is useful for them to repeat what they have heard, so as to improve their facility of speech, and they may quite properly be made to tell the story orally in reverse, and to start in the middle and go either backwards or forwards, but only privately with the teacher, and only so long as they cannot do more, but are merely beginning to put things and words together; this helps to strengthen the memory from the start. Similarly, when they are beginning to understand the nature of correct and accurate speech, extempore chatter, not waiting to think and hardly hesitating before getting up, suggests simply the self-advertisement of a street-seller's patter. Ignorant parents get a foolish pleasure from this, but the boys themselves come to despise their work, lose all shame, acquire very bad habits of speaking, practise their faults, and develop an arrogant conceit of themselves – a development which has often put a stop to impressive progress. There will be a proper time for acquiring facility, and I shall not neglect that topic. Meanwhile, it is enough if a boy, by taking pains and working as hard as his age permits, writes something that one can approve. Let him get used to this, and make it second nature. It is only the pupil who learns to speak correctly before he learns to speak quickly who will be able to achieve our ideal, or the nearest thing to it.

Refutation and confirmation

To Narrative is usefully added the exercise of refuting and confirming, which is called *anaskeuē* and *kataskeuē*. This too can be applied not only to mythical and poetic traditions, but also to the records of history. For example, there is a great deal to be said on both sides if we ask whether it is credible that a raven should have settled on Valerius' head as he was fighting, and struck the face and eyes of his Gallic opponent with its beak and wings; or we can take the serpent by which Scipio is supposed to have been begotten, or Romulus' she-wolf, or Numa's Egeria. (Greek

historical narratives often display an almost poetic licence.) The time and place of a supposed occurrence, and sometimes also the person involved, is often questioned. Thus Livy very frequently expresses doubt, and historians very frequently disagree with one another.

Encomia and invectives

The pupil will then gradually begin to attempt more ambitious themes: Encomia of famous men and Invective against the wicked. This is useful in more ways than one: the mind is exercised by the variety and multiplicity of the material; the character is moulded by the contemplation of right and wrong; a wide knowledge of facts is acquired, and this provides the speaker with a ready-made store of examples – a very powerful resource in all sorts of cases – which he will use when occasion demands. From this follows the exercise of Comparison: which of the two men is the better and which is the worse? This rests on a similar principle, but doubles the material and handles not only the nature of virtues and vices but their degree. The method of Encomium and its opposite (which form the third part of rhetoric) I shall prescribe when its time comes.

Commonplaces

Commonplaces (I mean those in which we orate against vices in themselves – the adulterer, the gambler, the profligate – without naming individuals) are at the heart of judicial cases: if you add the defendant's name, they become accusations. But the usual treatment of Commonplaces is to modify the generality by bringing it down to some more specific case: a *blind* adulterer, a *poor* gambler, an *old* profligate. They sometimes contribute to a defence, for we speak "in defence of luxury" or "in defence of love," and a pimp or a parasite may occasionally be defended, so as to plead the cause not of the individual but of the crime itself.

Study Questions

1   What is the basis for Quintilian's argument that orators should take over the "principles of upright and honorable living" from philosophers?
2   In Book I, Quintilian asked, "Who – if not an utter villain – does not speak about justice and equity and goodness?" What does this question imply about Romans, and does it have any basis in fact?
3   Societies today recognize that education is a sorting mechanism for children, and curricula are designed with the understanding that some students will fail. The elementary education that Quintilian advocated is challenging, yet *Institution Oratoria* does not acknowledge that not all students could complete his curriculum successfully. What does this tell us about Roman society at the time?
4   Like the Sophists, Quintilian was deeply concerned that teachers dedicate themselves to the moral education of their students. What is the status of moral education in schools today?
5   Quintilian complained in Book II that *grammatici* were expanding their curricula, adding rhetoric to the standard instruction in literature. What may have been some consequences of this expansion?
6   Quintilian expressed displeasure with what he called "humanity," which consisted of "mutual praise without regard to quality." Why would he object to this practice, given that it would make education appear more egalitarian?

Writing Topics

1   Compare Quintilian's educational program to Isocrates', as outlined in *Antidosis*, giving particular attention to explaining differences between the two.
2   Quintilian's *vir bonus decendi* is not only a moral man but one displaying significant civic virtue. Examine the socio-historical factors that may have led to this emphasis on morality and civic virtue.
3   Stressing the importance of imitation in learning, Quintilian recommended that teachers deliver at least one speech a day to students. What role does imitation play in education today?
4   Quintilian recommended that *progymnasmata* begin with narratives. Examine modern research on cognition, learning, and communication to determine whether there is a basis for supporting or rebutting this recommendation.

Further Reading

Brink, C.O. (1989). Quintilian's *De Causis Corruptae Eloquentiae* and Tacitus' *Diologus de Oratoribus*. *Classical Quarterly, 39*, 472–503.

Clarke, M.L. (1967). Quintilian: A biographical sketch. *Greece & Rome, 14, 1*, 24–37.

Kennedy, G. (1962). An estimate of Quintilian. *American Journal of Philology, 83*, 130–46.

Kennedy, G. (1969). *Quintilian*. New York: Twayne.

The End of the Classical Period: Libanius and Augustine

This chapter explores the state of rhetoric at the end of the Classical Period through the work of two representative figures – Libanius and Augustine. Libanius (c. 314–394 AD) was one of the more successful rhetoricians in the Eastern Empire, a pagan who strove to preserve the old traditions that he loved. Augustine (c. 354–430 AD) was trained in those traditions and became a successful rhetorician, first in Carthage and then in Rome, only to convert to Christianity, dedicate his life and his considerable skills to disparaging *paideia*, and transforming rhetoric into an apparatus for biblical herme- neutics. Similar in many ways and yet so different, their lives overlapped chronologi- cally. Together, Libanius and Augustine offer important perspectives on the state of rhetoric and oratory in the latter days of the Classical Period.

The events and social conditions of the fourth and fifth centuries were so complex and volatile that a brief chapter cannot possibly begin to provide significant insights. What follows, therefore, is a greatly simplified and abbreviated summary of a few key factors.

The Fourth Century

By the early fourth century, political power had shifted from Italy to Constantinople.[1] Christianity had spread significantly, but the Empire nevertheless stood divided not just physically into the eastern and western regions but also socially and ideologically. A majority of the people living in the great cities were now adherents to the new religion, whereas those in the countryside remained predominantly pagan. Emperor Constantine and his half brothers and sisters – Julius Constantius I, Flavius Dalmatius, Hannibalianus, Constantia, and Anastasia – had converted, and they raised their chil- dren to be Christians. Perhaps recognizing the direction of social change, a growing number of intellectuals also were converting.

But the new religion did little to improve social or political conditions. Inflation was out of control, and food shortages were frequent, undermining the middle class and leaving the poor in dire straights. Grinding taxation was ruinous for Christian and pagan alike. Imposed initially to provide the outrageous bribes that barbarian leaders demanded in return for limiting their incursions along the frontiers, high taxes were raised even higher in order to meet the costs of Constantine's ever more extravagant lifestyle.

---

[1] Emperor Diocletian was the first to divide the Empire into the Eastern and Western portions in 286. Julian united the two parts, but with the death of Emperor Theodosius in 395, the Empire was permanently divided.

Pagans were increasingly uneasy, and with good reason. Although it is not entirely clear whether Constantine or Constantius II was responsible for banning blood sacrifices (see Barnes, 2001; Bradbury, 1994), the central component of pagan worship, they nevertheless were prohibited. Pagans fully recognized that their religion as well as their culture was threatened, but they inexplicably responded with what appears to have been nothing more than passive resignation.

Constantine no doubt added to the social tensions when he ordered the execution of his second wife, Fausta, and his son Crispus. In addition, doctrinal disputes within the Church led to frequent riots, prompting Constantine, as already noted, to seek sectarian peace at the Council of Nicea. He brought an official end to Arianism by forcing the congregating bishops to sign a declaration affirming the Trinitarian Creed; he then excommunicated Arius and sent him into exile. His efforts were not effective over the short term, however: Bishops like Eusebius of Nicomedia continued to advocate, albeit less vocally, the doctrine of one God and a created Son, and parishioners loyal to Arianism rioted after the Creed was announced. Moreover, Arius' supporters – including Constantia, the emperor's sister – lobbied on his behalf, and Constantine was persuaded to recall Arius from exile in 328; he was then quickly reinstated in the Church.

In this uncertain environment, Constantine's surviving children – Constantine II, Constantius II, and Constans – began jostling for power. When the emperor died in 337, Constantius II embarked on a violent purge, murdering all his royal uncles and their children, with the notable exception of Julian (c. 332–363) and his half-brother Gallus.[2] Meanwhile, Arianism still commanded a wide level of support. Even before Constantine's death, several bishops who had led the opposition to Arius' views were dismissed, replaced by Arians, most notably Eusebius of Nicomedia. Constantius II was an Arian, and after consolidating his power he collaborated with Eusebius in an effort to overturn the Nicene Creed.[3] Moreover, a majority of the recently converted Germanic people in the western portion of the Empire were Arians.

As for Gallus and Julian, Gallus was exiled, and Julian was placed under house arrest. Julian is interesting for many reasons. Caught between paganism on the one hand and Christianity on the other, his life serves as a metaphor for the Empire as the struggle between the old ways and the new was played out in many venues. While a youth, Julian underwent the traditional education of a young aristocrat, studying ancient literature and philosophy. His studies instilled in him a deep devotion to classical culture and religion that was not diminished when the emperor exiled him to a fortress outside Cappadocia, where he spent approximately 6 years receiving a Christian education. In 348, he began studying rhetoric, first in Constantinople and then in Nicomedia, where he became acquainted with Libanius, one of the more celebrated teachers in the Eastern Empire. A few years later, he intensified his study of philosophy with Maximus of Ephesus, a neo-Platonist who introduced him to Mithraism. In 355, he received permission to travel to Athens, where he continued his studies of literature and philosophy.

Julian's Christian education did not take. When Constantius II died in 361, Julian became emperor, and he immediately sought to subvert Christianity and return the Empire to the old gods. But although he barred Christians from teaching, he proved incapable (perhaps owing to youthful naïveté) of using widespread persecution, proscription, or exile to dismantle the Christian infrastructure, and his untimely death just 2 years later ensured that his efforts to reestablish paganism became little more than a historical footnote.

[2] DiMaio and Arnold (1992) suggested that Constantius II may have taken advantage of the religious rioting between Arians and non-Arians to launch the purge.

[3] Emperor Valens (c. 328–358), who succeeded to the throne shortly after the death of Julian, also was an Arian.

The struggle between paganism and Christianity spilled over into rhetoric. As the Empire neared its end, a majority of rhetoricians were pagans firmly committed to the classical tradition, and they faced increasingly difficult social, political, and professional challenges in a changing world. They could not display their religious views openly without risk; their theurgic rituals were decried as magic, punishable by death; and accusations of magical practice became a popular way of attacking enemies and rivals.

Christian rhetoricians faced challenges of a different sort. Many were torn between their love of *paideia* and the Church's doctrinaire hostility toward the classical tradition. Rhetoric was so thoroughly embedded in pagan literature and philosophy that mental conflict was inevitable: Rhetoric could not be separated from *paideia*, and *paideia* could not be separated from paganism. Gregory of Nazianzus (c. 329–374), a leading Christian as well as a rhetorician, illustrates the dilemma. He disparaged rhetoric and *paideia* in several of his epistles (e.g., *Epistles 176, 178, 191, 233*), and in *Epistle 110* he identified oratory with vanity and argued for the value of silence. Yet it seems that after studying in Athens for about 10 years, he taught rhetoric in Cappadocia, and he often made reference to Greek literature in his writing (Cribiore, 2007). He wrote literally thousands of poems, and although they focus on the power of faith, their language and imagery draws considerably on ancient themes and traditions, such as Homer (see Azkoul, 1995).

The Fifth Century

As difficult as life was during the fourth century, it became even more difficult in the fifth. For generations, Rome had been using bribes to appease the barbarian tribes on the frontiers. Some tribal leaders were beginning to reconsider this arrangement. Rome had grown weak, ripe for the picking, and tribal leaders wondered why they should continue to accept yearly tribute when an easy invasion would allow them to plunder the riches of the Empire (see Gibbon, 1993; Heather, 2006). The Huns, a nomadic warrior people, may have initiated the final collapse. Near the end of the fourth century, they rode westward out of the Steppes, cutting a swath of devastation across Eastern Europe, driving Germanic tribes, such as the Suevi, Visigoths, and Vandals before them. Rome's efforts to halt the advance of these tribes proved futile, so Emperor Valens negotiated a treaty with the Visigoths in 376 that allowed them to settle on lands along the River Danube. Trouble began immediately, for the Romans did everything possible to exploit the Visigoths and to show them that they were unwelcome. Resentment soon reached a boiling point, and in 378 the Visigoths rebelled. Emperor Valens rushed approximately 40,000 troops to crush the barbarians, only to lead his army to a humiliating defeat at Adrianople and get himself killed in the process. A treaty was thereafter concluded that granted the Visigoths considerable compensation, but Rome's frontier defenses were greatly weakened, leaving the entire western frontier vulnerable. The Vandals, harried by the Huns, and seeing the opportunity provided by the Roman conflict with the Visigoths, crossed the Rhine into Roman territory and destroyed the legions guarding the border. They gained control of a significant part of Gaul, which they occupied for nearly 3 years before moving on into Spain. There they routed the Roman forces and settled throughout central and southern Iberia.

Rome achieved détente with the Visigoths under Emperor Theodosius, who tried to ameliorate conditions by integrating Visigoths into the military (Heather, 2006). He appointed the Visigoth noble Alaric, for example, to serve as a general in the Roman army. But when Theodosius died in 395, relations deteriorated, and Roman prejudice against the barbarians escalated. Again feeling maltreated, the Visigoths declared Alaric their king; he then led his warriors against Rome, first attacking Greece and ravaging several of its cities before returning to the Balkans. In 401, he marched his troops into Italy and attacked Rome. The attack was thwarted by the Roman general Stilicho, but Alaric soon returned, ultimately sacking and occupying Rome in 410. After installing a puppet government, Alaric marched into southern Italy, conquering cities en route, with the aim of taking his forces to Africa. He died, however, before he could implement this plan, and his successor, Athaulf, reversed course, moving the Visigoths back into Gaul.

The Visigoths left Gaul a few years later to attack the Vandals in Spain. Hard pressed, the Vandals built a fleet and sailed to North Africa, established bases there, and began rapacious pirate activity throughout the western Mediterranean. Recognizing that even greater plunder was to be had in the affluent North African cities, the Vandal king, Gaiseric, mobilized an army of almost a hundred thousand. Nearly all the Vandals were Christians by this time, but Gaiseric and his forces nevertheless proceeded to conquer city after city, slaughtering fellow Christians indiscriminately as they made their way toward Carthage. Roman governor Boniface tried to stop the Vandals at Hippo, where Augustine was bishop, but was driven inside the city's walls. Gaiseric immediately laid siege and over the next 14 months starved the city into submission, despite the fervent prayers that Augustine and his priests sent up daily asking for relief from the barbarian invaders. Augustine died on August 28, 430, while the city was still under siege, so he did not live to see Boniface surrender Hippo to the Vandals, who made it their capital.

Introduction to Libanius (314–394 AD)

Of all the imperial rhetors, Libanius arguably comes closest to matching Quintilian's ideal orator. He immersed himself in the political and social affairs of the state, striving to make it better. He does not appear to have ventured into rhetorical theory, devoting himself, instead, to the application of rhetoric in both his teaching and practice. He never produced a *technê*, but he was a prolific writer. Dozens of his orations and declamations have survived, as well as an autobiography.[4] He maintained steady correspondence with civic leaders, politicians, former classmates, fellow rhetoricians, former students, and the parents of current students. More than 1,500 of his letters are extant. This wealth of material, a great deal of which has not yet been translated into English, offers unequaled insight into Libanius' life and the times in which he lived, leading Russell (1996) to conclude that we know more about Libanius than any other classical orator. The sheer quantity of material also presents a serious obstacle to any definitive study and is especially problematic here owing to space restrictions.

The middle of three sons, he was born in Antioch, one of the leading cities of the Eastern Empire, known for its beauty, culture, and affluence. His family was among the wealthy elite, but when his paternal grandfather and uncle were executed owing to a proscription in 303, his father and surviving family members were left in difficult straights that became even more strained after his father's untimely death. At age 14, Libanius made the decision to put away his boyhood and begin studying rhetoric, but when his teacher died and he could find no suitable replacement, he attached himself to

---

[4] Note that Libanius' autobiography is commonly referred to in the literature as *Oration I*. I refer to it here simply as "autobiography" to more clearly differentiate it from his many orations.

a *grammaticus* who instructed him in literature and rhetoric. He never married, but he found a lifelong companion in a woman of lower station to whom he was deeply devoted and with whom he had a son.

In his autobiography, Libanius reported that after he had "committed to memory the works of those who were most renowned for their stylistic abilities, the urge for ... [the Sophist's] way of life came over me" (*Autobiography*, 11). Even though his education had departed from the typical path, making him quite a bit older than students beginning their advanced training in the art, his desire to travel to Athens, the center of the intellectual world, was irrepressible. His mother objected, as did his elder uncle, who had assumed the role of family provider. But their resistance was tempered somewhat by the fact that Libanius was a model young man who, according to his own assessment, "acted as ... the rescuer of others ..., putting an end to the harmful pranks to which many youngsters who neglected their studies betook themselves" (*Autobiography*, 11). Finally obtaining his mother's permission, he set off on a long, difficult journey, every mile seeming to make him more uncomfortable and ill, until he finally "crossed the Bosporus little better than a corpse" (*Autobiography*, 14).

His experience in Athens was not entirely pleasant. Gangs of students roamed the streets just as frequently as they had a century earlier, and they created as much mischief. New students were hazed as a matter of course, and it was common practice for advanced students to kidnap new arrivals fresh off the boat and drag them to their schools, forcing them to vow fidelity regardless of where the students had originally hoped to study. So it was that such a group of students captured Libanius when he entered the city, and they locked him in a closet "about as big as a barrel" (*Autobiography*, 16), releasing him only after he pledged allegiance to the school and swore to accept his condition. He was not overly impressed with the quality of instruction once he began attending lectures and demonstrations, which suggests that the training he had received from his *grammaticus* was more than rudimentary. Nevertheless, he continued his studies for 4 years, winning significant recognition for his abilities, and he wanted to stay on yet another 4 to ensure that he had a firm grasp of the material, but as he wrote in his autobiography, Fortune intervened.

His good friend Crispinus finished his studies and was called home to Heraclea. In ancient Athens, during the time of Plato and Aristotle, young boys coming of age were not granted citizenship simply as a matter of birth but had to demonstrate their qualifications. To gauge their capacity to assume the rights of citizenship, they were subjected to a public examination, or *dokimasia*, by the city leaders. The Eastern Empire had preserved this tradition over the centuries insofar as the young men who left their homes to study rhetoric were expected to return for a rhetorical *dokimasia*. They had to demonstrate how much they had learned by providing a panegyric to the home city that displayed their oratorical skill.

These examinations were not trivial affairs: A young man's career and reputation were a stake. Many of those who attended the oration – the father, government officials, and city notables – were all well trained in oratory, characterized in Libanius' autobiography as "clever and highly cultured people" (*Autobiography*, 27). The audience also included those of lesser means, people who lacked formal training but who had attended so many declamations and orations that they were well able to differentiate gold from dross.[5] The assessment was sharp and informed, making no allowance for a poor performance. Consequently, many students chose to extend their studies as long

[5] In Libanius' *Oration 25*, we get a sense of who these people were: merchants, artisans, and soldiers.

as possible as a way of postponing the *dokimasia*, and when the inevitable moment came, the stress was considerable (Cribiore, 2007). Crispinus asked his friend to accompany him to lend moral support during the examination, and Libanius agreed. Their journey, however, became an oratorical tour. At every town along the way to Heraclea, they declaimed, showing their skills while simultaneously honing them. Their reception was so positive that any anxiety Libanius may have felt about his own *dokimasia* appears to have vanished, and he gave up his plan to continue his studies in Athens. When invited to open a school in Constantinople, he accepted.[6]

Libanius the rhetorician

Libanius attracted students to his school in Constantinople by participating in the public competitions in oratory. He reported in his autobiography that he was so successful that in a matter of days he had 80 pupils and that the emperor issued an edict preventing him from leaving the city. Moreover, "People who had been all of a flutter about the chariot races or the theatrical performances had changed to a sudden interest in rhetoric" (*Autobiography*, 37). Success, however, was fraught with dangers owing to the high stakes of oratorical competition and the volatile climate of the times. Bemarchius, the city's official Sophist, was immediately jealous of Libanius and sought to belittle him through a set of public speeches. When this effort failed (and even backfired), Bemarchius, though a pagan himself, accused Libanius of practicing magic – that is, of engaging in proscribed theurgic rituals that had enlisted the aid of the old gods to raise the level of his oratory. Because Christians considered pagan religious rituals to be a form of black magic, Libanius, known to be a pagan, was an easy target. He was arrested, and Libanius stated that the Christian governor "prayed Fortune that his tenure would last at least long enough for him to be able to kill me" (*Autobiography*, 46).

Libanius' enemies, however, had assumed that they could extract testimony from his assistant, and they were wrong. No amount of torture could force him to commit perjury against his employer, and Libanius was released, although he judiciously left the city, traveling first to Nicea and then to Nicomedia, where he reestablished himself and where he came into contact with the future emperor, Julian. As he reflected on his life in his later years, he identified the time he spent in Nicomedia as the happiest. But this does not mean it was entirely tranquil. His success in attracting students led yet another rival to accuse him of magical practice, and to ensure a conviction he added murder to the charge. Libanius again escaped a trial, yet he could not escape the censure of his pagan friends, who may have concluded that his repeated ability to avoid prosecution was the result of his generally cordial relations with Christian rulers. Although Libanius was adamantly opposed to Christianity and grieved over Christian suppression of the old religion, he was pragmatic and understood that he could not survive as an orator or rhetorician if he did not curry favor with the Christian elite. More problematic and stressful was that his growing reputation prompted the emperor to order his return to Constantinople to serve as the city's official Sophist. Unable to refuse, in 349 Libanius returned to the city he loathed and renewed his work there – teaching and giving regular orations and declamations. All the while, he searched for a way to relocate.

[6] It appears, however, that he did not undergo his own examination until many years later, in 353, when he finally returned to Antioch for the first time since leaving as a young man to study in Athens. The success of his *dokimasia* led eventually to his installation as Antioch's municipal rhetorician. The panegyric to Antioch that Libanius gave in 353 should not be confused with the panegyric he gave in 360 to celebrate the city's hosting of the Olympic games. The two orations probably had much in common, but the speech of 360 is the only one extant.

In 353, on the grounds that he needed to return home to Antioch to attend to family business, Libanius received permission from the emperor to leave the city. His return to his hometown was a cause for celebration, and he began concocting a plan that would allow him to settle there permanently. He tarried, even when the emperor ordered him to return to Constantinople, claiming that ill health prevented him from traveling. After a year of negotiation, Libanius was granted leave to remain in Antioch, where he was appointed to the position of city Sophist.

No doubt one of the high points of his life was the year that Julian became emperor. He "laughed and danced, joyfully composed and delivered ... orations, for the alters received their blood offerings, smoke carried the savour of burnt sacrifice up to heaven" (*Autobiography*, 119). This joy was short-lived, however, for the "enemy to the unbelievers" died in a campaign against the Persians in 363. Julian's successor, Flavius Julius Valens (c. 328–378), was an Arian with little tolerance for pagans, and for the next two decades Libanius was the object of accusation and investigation: for magical practice, conspiracy, and association with unsavory characters.

His official position in Constantinople had provided an income that was reliable and probably generous, and it may have been at this time that Libanius began giving instruction to some students free of charge. His letters and orations indicate that he continued and actually expanded this practice in Antioch. His decision to waive tuition has been discussed at some length (e.g., Cribiore, 2007; Martin, 1996; Petit, 1955), and the consensus is that it was based not only on his generous nature and desire to help those in need but also on necessity. Oppressive taxation and the requirement that curial families bear the additional burden of paying for certain government expenses out of their own pockets had impoverished many old families of means. It was these families, however, that provided the principal source of students for teachers like Libanius. Not everyone was granted a tuition waiver, but classes full of students from prominent (even if impoverished) families served as a recruiting device for those who could pay. In *Institutio Oratoria*, Quintilian advised that a teacher should "adopt a paternal attitude towards his pupils, and regard himself as taking the place of those whose children are entrusted to him" (II.2). Although Libanius' lack of Latin makes it doubtful that he knew Quintilian, his gentle nature inclined him to adopt just such an attitude. In his letters, Libanius often referred to students as his "children" and to himself as their "second father" (e.g., *Epistle 833*). Because rhetorical training provided opportunities for socioeconomic advancement, Libanius could expect that students from good families would go on to lucrative careers (and many did) and that their quasi-familial bond would result in generous gifts from alumni (e.g., *Epistle 911*). Thus, the fee arrangement was not a simple one. It allowed significant flexibility to ensure that classes were full and that those students without the resources to pay their tuition felt an obligation of honor that motivated them to provide payment afterwards.[7]

Another factor that influenced Libanius' decision to offer free instruction in some cases was the fierce competition for students. By the fourth century, there were signs that the popularity of rhetoric was waning. There were few opportunities to practice oratory outside the stylized conventions of declamation and oration, and the number of teaching positions like Libanius' was limited. Most young men went into government service after completing their studies, not teaching. And while advanced training in rhetoric continued to have benefits in this regard, they were not as great as they had

---

[7] Nevertheless, Libanius' letters contain frequent complaints about the failure of students to provide tuition and the inadequate gifts of alumni (e.g., *Epistle 24*).

been in the past. One reason was that the *grammatici* were having an adverse effect on the schools of rhetoric. Quintilian's complaint (II.1.5) that they were overreaching their traditional roles did nothing to reverse a trend, and as Libanius' own education illustrates, *grammatici* in the fourth century were not only teaching rhetoric but were also doing a reasonably good job of it at a lower cost. Furthermore, the Christianization of the governing class was eroding the traditional expectation that a young man have solid training in literature and oratory, which resulted in a lowering of standards: Increasingly, those with some training rather than advanced training were able to secure important positions in the government through their family and Church connections alone. Therefore, offering a free education to some students increased Libanius' ability to compete. Human nature being what it is, however, the immediate benefits of Libanius' fee waivers were offset by negative consequences over the long term, for families began to conclude that anything offered for free could not have much inherent value.

Libanius also had to contend with the rising popularity of two other types of schools, which were siphoning the available pool of students. Centuries earlier, Cicero had noted that training in rhetoric as well as training in law provided paths to success. He argued emphatically, however, that the former was superior. But conditions had changed over time. Roman law had grown quite complex, requiring specialized training. The demand for competent jurists who could represent clients in court does not appear to have been particularly high, but it was for administrators who knew and could apply the law with some degree of accuracy. As a result, many students were choosing to study law rather than rhetoric. Because all the Empire's law books were in Latin, and because knowledge of that language was of great utility in the East, where Latin speakers were scarce, Latin schools became another source of competition. "[W]ell aware how critical the situation was" (*Autobiography*, 214), Libanius (who did not read or speak the language) responded by adding Latin to his curriculum, but doing so does not appear to have had the desired effect, probably because the focus at his school remained on rhetoric and because the instruction therein was so demanding that students had insufficient time or energy for the additional burden of studying Latin.

Declamations and orations

Devoted to the goals and orators of the Second Sophistic, Libanius immersed his students in classical literature to lay the foundation for the *paideia* that created a fraternity among the educated elite. He also trained them in the Attic style of speaking, emphasizing eloquence in measured speech rather than the singsong rhythms of the Asian style. Students engaged in a variety of rhetorical exercises, many of which are extant, that gave them practice in what had been a standard curriculum for centuries: narratives, anecdotes, commonplaces, encomia and invectives, refutations and confirmations. The study of Demosthenes occupied a central place in the curriculum. Libanius wrote an introduction to Demosthenes that summarized his speeches and provided a reconstruction of the historical context for each. Called *Hypotheses to the Orations of Demosthenes*, this student handbook served not only to introduce pupils to the orator's work but also to provide instruction in rhetorical and stylistic criticism, including stasis theory and stylistic classifications.

From his autobiography and letters, we know that students wrote out their speeches and that Libanius and his assistants checked and corrected them each day. Advanced students also served as teaching assistants, providing instruction to those who were just beginning their studies. In a world without any means of amplifying sound, training included exercises to strengthen the voice so that it would carry to audiences that could

number up to 1,000. Rhetoric schools were therefore noisy places, with students practicing their delivery at the top of their lungs.

Fifty-four of Libanius' declamations are extant and, following Foerster (1903–1913),
are usually grouped according to subject matter: Socrates; Greek mythology; Athenian
history; Demosthenes; non-Athenian history; and stock themes involving conflicts
between rich and poor, parents and children, husbands and wives. These declamations
exemplify traditional structure and themes. That is, they generally begin with a
proemium, or introduction, that sets the scene for the speech, followed by a *prokatastasis*,
or preliminary narrative, then the *katastasis*, or main narrative, one or more *antitheses*,
and finally the *epilogue*. Russell (1996) noted that declamations were dramatic mono-
logues and involved some measure of acting not only to convey more clearly the underlying conflict but also to entertain.

Of the 64 orations that are extant, just a fraction have been translated into English.
Although it can be argued that some of the panegyric orations, such as the encomium
to Antioch, were designed to entertain, they differ significantly from Libanius' declamations in terms of their overall seriousness.[8] His epideictic orations deal with such topics
as greed (*Oration 6*), poverty (*Oration 8*), and slavery (*Oration 25*). *Oration 30* calls upon
Emperor Theodosius to take action to end the destruction of pagan temples, and
Oration 50 protests the local administrator's forced-labor policy. *Orations 48* and *49* offer
advice on good government.

What emerges from these works is a portrait of Libanius as a social and political
spokesman for decency and fairness who sought to use his position and reputation
for the welfare of others. As might be expected, his outspoken support of the poor
and oppressed was met with hostility among certain groups, and this hostility
appears to have escalated when, after the accession of Theodosius, Libanius gave
orations that were implicitly critical of Constantine (e.g., *Orations 48* and *49*). The
situation became so stressful that he fell ill and could not teach for weeks, and after
finding a dead and rather suspicious chameleon in a classroom, Libanius was convinced that his enemies were using sympathetic magic to destroy him (see
Autobiography, 248–250).

Having the courage to speak publicly on social issues no doubt was an important
factor in Libanius' reputation – for good as well as bad – but as Norman (1976) noted, it
was his style "upon which his fame among the Byzantines was based" (p. 23). Any
attempt to analyze that style based on translations is essentially futile, but a few characteristics are observable, such as his nuanced blend of eloquence and straightforward
expression. The overall seriousness of the orations does not allow for much humor, yet
the first part of the *Autobiography* is laced with it, and this work suggests that Libanius
displayed substantial wit when teaching and conversing.

Letter writing

Epistolography, or letter writing, was an integral part of late Roman society. The
Empire was vast, and travel was difficult even for those with sufficient wealth to travel
first-class. Letters and communiqués served as a vital means of fostering and nurturing
the social, personal, financial, and governmental networks necessary for the functioning of the Empire. Although Christianity was creating a new cultural milieu, *paideia*

---

[8] Unlike the Antiochene panegyric, the encomium for Contantius and Constans (*Oration 59*) is difficult to
characterize as entertaining; its long introduction is a recitation of what appears to be the official history of
Constantine, serving as mere flattery with little regard for historical accuracy.

continued to project a shared heritage that connected the various parts of the Empire in important ways. The schools in intellectual centers such as Alexandria, Antioch, Constantinople, and Athens played a central role in maintaining both *paideia* and the fragile illusion of a shared cultural history for East and West and the various far-flung hinterlands in between. Graduates of those schools used letters to preserve bonds formed in school, to recommend a student or friend for a position, and to expand their network of associations. We learn from Libanius' letters that it was common practice for the recipient to read his letter aloud in the public square, sharing whatever news it contained. In a time when newspapers did not exist, such accounts suggest that letters were a valuable means of disseminating information from one part of the Empire to another. Given these factors, letters may be said to have functioned as a kind of social adhesive.

The Empire had no public mail system, which meant that regular communication was difficult and somewhat haphazard. To get a letter from Antioch to Alexandria, for example, the writer had to find someone who was traveling to Egypt and who was willing to convey not just the written text but also a great deal of oral information. Letters were not always complete in themselves but often were rather limited or terse, in many cases containing a fairly vague or imprecise message. It was the responsibility of the letter carrier to fill in the details, and it also was his responsibility to convey any confidential information.

The semipublic nature of letters motivated writers to exercise care in their composition. The basic principles of epistolography had been formalized in the first century by Demetrius, in his work *On Style* (see Roberts, 1902), but it was Libanius who raised letter writing to an art form. He did so not through any true innovation but rather by skillfully adhering in his letters to the same Attic principles of rhetoric that he applied to oratory. These included not only clarity and grace but also what Norman (1992) referred to as "harmony of subject and diction, with avoidance of exaggeration" (p. 19). Libanius was keenly aware that letters could be as public as declamations and orations (although he sometimes complained when his letters were indiscriminately publicized), and he recognized that his reputation demanded that his correspondence display the same level of skill and artistry. Moreover, he accepted the traditional view that a letter was a gift, and he could not bring himself to bestow a shoddy gift upon a friend, acquaintance, or politician. By the same token, he was offended when he received letters that were poorly written, and he sometimes chided his former students when their epistles fell short of the standard he set for them. Even though they were no longer enrolled in classes, he remained their teacher and expected them to perform admirably.

Declamations

Libanius' *The Silence of Socrates* is a companion piece to his *Defence of Socrates*. In the latter work, Libanius recreated Socrates' trial, but he chose not to represent the philosopher speaking on his own behalf; instead, he proposed that Socrates was represented by a *synêgoros*, or professional advocate. In *The Silence of Socrates*, Libanius explored the possibility of a second punishment – the imposition of silence on a man whose life was devoted to talking in an effort to discover if not truth at least ignorance. As Russell noted in his introduction to this declamation, some scholars have read the work as a criticism of Christian legislation that had banned – or silenced – pagan rituals. Although *The Silence of Socrates* is not quite as sensational as many declamations of the period, it well illustrates the rhetorical features of the genre.

Reading 38

The Silence of Socrates

The Silence of Socrates, pp. 59–66 from *Libanius: Imaginary Speeches: A Selection of Declamations*, translated by D.A. Russell (Duckworth, 1996). Reprinted by permission of Gerald Duckworth & Co. Ltd.

[1] It is difficult to advance even the most justified of arguments on Socrates' behalf before you who have already condemned him, and believed the first slanders that were directed against him. However, since the malicious prosecutors have now gone too far and are doing wrong not only to Socrates but to the common rights of all the unfortunate, it is incumbent upon me to say this much to you: many have been condemned in your court, and some have died justly, some unjustly, but none has ever died in silence. [2] You ordered Socrates to die. He obeys, uncomplaining. But they are imposing a second penalty upon him: to be silent and not to talk to anyone, until he dies. This is to kill him before the hemlock comes. It is of course easy for Socrates – he is as capable of silence as he is of speech – but you need to take care for yourselves, lest gods and men should charge you with taking away from Socrates the common right of all who live, and robbing him not only of his life but, even before that, of his voice. [3] Now I am one of those who visit Socrates and listen to him; it is a marvellous thing, the man teaching philosophy in prison, and dying with cheerfulness. I have therefore risen to oppose this cruel proposition, because I think it will be damaging not to Socrates but to us, if we are not to have some small benefit from Socrates' remaining days.

[4] Socrates is to die as a result of a malicious accusation which transgresses all the rules of justice, and of false charges which are totally unworthy of his philosophy. Of all men, he has been most pious and the most helpful to the young, always obeying the city's laws, as citizen and as soldier, opposing tyrants and oligarchies, and, uniquely, making no demand for money or a fee from pupils for his lessons; he has mastered two evil natures as well as he could, and turned many others into good citizens; he has made our city famous and admired throughout Greece, through the foreigners who come to gather round him and the discussions that are disseminated throughout the world.

[5] That such is the Socrates who has been the victim of this malicious prosecution, and that the judges cast their vote with more haste than was proper, will, I believe, be proved by time and by the gods. I pray only that this may come to pass without anger and without any public damage to the city! I know very well that the jury would have changed its mind, had it been given a second opportunity to judge the matter – just as you once changed your minds over Mitylene. [6] But when the day was won by those who bore a grudge against Socrates because of the way he had refuted them in argument, you heard him talking as a philosopher even in court. He neither wept nor begged for mercy nor contrived any rescue that might be shameful or unworthy of philosophy. He obeyed the god who led him to this end; he went happily with the Eleven, and proceeded to prison as cheerfully as to the Lyceum or the Academy or the Ilissus or any of the places where he used to pass his time; and he intended to talk and converse there also. Of course he did – he was a human being, and still alive. Indeed he discusses philosophy energetically with his friends. Even in chains, he is still Socrates. His physical discomfort has not overcome him. He expounds arguments so divine and beautiful that if you had all heard them you would surely have let him go free.

[7] The right thing then is to think of Socrates as fortunate, because he is happy in the presence of death and talks and discusses philosophy, not grudging it to those who listen to him and are capable of benefiting thereby for their whole life. But Anytus and Meletus, it seems, are more cruel than the prison governor. *He* lets visitors see Socrates; *they* both render his life useless to us and devise a new sort of fetter to bind him with – so that not only are his feet and hands tied before he is allowed to die, but his tongue too. [8] What envy, what brutality, what uncivilized wickedness! Is Socrates, o lord Apollo, not to talk, while he is yet alive, while he has a voice? Does our Solon propose a decree like this relating to an individual, when the laws explicitly and plainly forbid

the proposal of any law or decree relating to an individual which does not apply generally to all Athenians? [9] 'He is a criminal, and condemned.' Let us assume he is a criminal. Let us assume there is nothing unbelievable in the accusation or in the denunciations of Anytus and Meletus. I know that the time will come when you will be proud of Socrates, as the Ephesians are of Heraclitus, the Samians of Pythagoras, the Lacedaemonians of Chilon, the Milesians of Thales, the Lesbians of Pittacus, the Corinthians of Periander – and you yourselves once of Solon! All these wise men were opposed by the envy of their neighbours while they were alive; now they are dead, their wisdom is judged without prejudice, with a sensibility that feels no pain.

[10] Let the decision stand as it has been taken. What was resolved in court should not now be an issue. It was resolved that Socrates should drink hemlock, like other condemned men before him. Socrates does not reject this; he would never seek to escape your judgment, nor to flee the country, even if some of his friends want to snatch him away to Boeotia or to the Peloponnese or to Thessaly, and every city in Greece invites him: no, he would tolerate no furtive escape, he is more eager than you are yourselves for his death; he is thirsty for hemlock. [11] But it is surely scandalous and illegal to seek to add by a vote something which the court never decided, and which is not enjoined by the laws governing the treatment of convicted prisoners? It is wrong for any of us to add to judgments any measure of clemency over and above that which is obligatory under the law; it is equally wrong to show more bitterness than is regular. Both of these courses – both adding some mitigation in favour of the condemned, and depriving those who are in this condition of their due – are contrary to the law. The court herald did not announce that the Eleven were taking charge of Socrates and ordering that he should be silent till his death and not talk, but only that he should die. [12] Even you who accused Socrates and once asked for the death penalty, did not ask for an additional penalty of silence. That would have meant two assessments of penalty. Thus you are now inventing something over and above the original decision – something that you did not venture to add at the time, when the jurors were most angry, and most grievously misled. [13] If Socrates is guilty

of some further novel offence, and you are adding some charges, after the jury has voted, outside the terms of the previous indictment, tell us what it is, give us the facts. If his offence is to open his mouth and talk, who was ever punished for that? What condemned man has ever been ordered to be silent? Who has ever been brought before the people for talking? When did a criminal condemned to death at Athens last have his tongue cut out? You are making us Thracians, not Athenians; barbarians, not Greeks. [14] Miltiades was once in chains here; he was not silent in his chains. You once condemned the nine generals all together, though Socrates was unwilling and would have no part in the illegality. He thought the law a stronger consideration than your anger; you condemned the men all the same, but you did not order them to be silent. [15] Murderers, temple-robbers, traitors, perpetrators of every dreadful crime, are condemned, but never told to keep silent and not converse with others: some give their last instructions to their dearest, some talk to their relations, friends and connections, some invoke the gods, some lament their fate. It is dreadful to think that, when all this happens, this one man alone, since time began, is to be ordered, when near his death, not to talk, when he is the man who most deserves to talk!

[16] It was only Critias, the tyrant, who laid on Socrates the command that he should not hold his discussions – Critias, the bad pupil who condemned his teacher. So the democracy has come to imitate the tyrants; the Athenians, by a free vote, make a decision equivalent to the tyrants' commands. [17] But Critias merely forbade Socrates to hold discussions with the young, not to stop talking altogether, only to refrain from those similes about shepherds and herdsmen; Critias was annoyed by the moral of Socrates' imagery, that it is a bad shepherd who diminishes the flock; for it was against the tyrants that Socrates used this argument. You, on the other hand, demand that Socrates shall not discuss anything with anybody – not even with the warder or Xanthippe or the children; if Lamprocles or Sophroniscus asks his father a question, Socrates is not to answer, but to wait for the hemlock, gagged as it were and deprived of the common privilege of all mankind, even the unfortunate and the criminal. [18] Man is by nature a talking

animal, and the Athenians as a people love words and are full of them; when death is near, this love of talk takes hold of one, one wants to hear much and speak much, because one is shortly to be deprived of the power. No one grudges a man saying all he chooses when he is shortly to keep a long silence.

[19] 'Let him wait for the hemlock', says the prosecution, 'Theramenes died in silence.' But Theramenes had made a long speech before at the Council's hearth. Under the oligarchy some 1,500 persons drank the hemlock; not one of them died because of Socrates, who refused to obey when he was sent to arrest Leon of Salamis, and would not bring him to the tyrants to die – and it is Socrates who is to die now! And of all those who were killed in these days, not one is said to have drunk the poison in silence. Neither Dracontides nor Peison nor Charicles, nor any of those people, gave orders that anyone should keep his mouth shut or not bear witness before he died. [20] You are laying upon Socrates a much worse burden than those who had power under that savage tyranny. When people are under the knife, they are bound to groan; prisoners cry out; shall a man who is about to lose his life die without a word about anything, a dumb corpse even before the end comes? You are inflicting many deaths on Socrates.

[21] Philosophers tell us that ghosts have a voice, and that this remains even with shadows. Homer seems to offer proof of this. When he writes of the ghost of Patroclus, he says it came in all respects 'like him', in body *and in voice*. And you are cutting out Socrates' voice while he is yet alive! Again: most men talk more when they are unhappy, and the dumb son of Croesus of Lydia is said to have found his voice at the moment of his father's disaster. And is Socrates alone not to lament or invoke the gods in his present misfortune? [22] This is not indeed a Socratic thing to do; but it is a universal right which he too should be guaranteed. Everyone else in the prison talks and chatters, however uneducated or unskilled, being near the end, and philosophizes about death itself; shall Socrates not be allowed to let his philosophy have the same term as his life?

[23] 'His words were unsuitable and unjust', they say. That is what he is to die for, is it not? If you have no further charge to bring, beyond that on which he has been convicted, do not ask for any penalty greater than that which has already been assessed. 'He corrupts.' What boy has come to see him in

prison? Apollodorus, Crito, Phaedo, Simmias and Cebes, Hermogenes, Epigenes, Antisthenes, Aeschines – these are grown men or old men, Socrates' associates. If Socrates utters any damaging or wicked words, they have been corrupted long since; and if what he says is good and useful, they do not deserve to be deprived of it even at this late hour. [24] So let things be and do not do anything more. Is it not a scandal that Gorgias and Protagoras should speak, and Polus and that pretentious humbug Prodicus, and Hippias, sophists all, traffickers in words, and that the Greeks, individually and publicly, should pay to listen to them – to men of Elis and Ceos and Abdera and Leontini – while the Athenian Socrates is not to speak even in the prospect of death?

[25] You will have your fill, malicious as you are, of Socrates' silence. The Lyceum will be dumb, the Academy dumb, the wrestling-schools silent. All the haunts of beauty will be taken over by barbarism and silence. Socrates will not be talking in the gymnasia, in the porticoes – the King Archon's or the Painted Portico – at the bankers', in the courts, in Agathon's house or Callias's or Damon's – no Socrates in the city, nor in Piraeus, nor above Ilissus under that beautiful plane tree – only the cicadas will be singing there; no Socrates at Potidaea, nor at Delium; no discussions with Thrasymachus on justice, with Charmides on temperance, with Laches on courage, with Chaerephon on brotherly love, with Meno on virtue, with Hippias on beauty, with Gorgias on rhetoric, with Protagoras on the practice of virtue, with Euthyphro on piety, or with Xenophon on not kissing the beautiful young man. You will indeed have your fill of the absence of Socrates. He will have so many silences.

[26] So now, while he is with us, allow him to talk for this day or two. Now is the supreme test of Socrates' wisdom – if he feels no pain even in his chains, if he utters no lament when he is about to die, if he still practises philosophy as the end comes upon him. Let him speak, even in his chains. I commend Xenophon, because when he was a prisoner at Thebes he did not neglect Prodicus' teaching, but found a surety and attended the lecture. Do you expect the pupil to be more of a philosopher than the teacher? Are you compelling Socrates to be silent when he will soon cease altogether? Why do you make him like a man in pain? Let him speak above all now, just before death, when he is nearer truth.

[27] Let Socrates philosophize now; let him also prophesy, I beg you. Swans sing before they die, and release their soul in song; the death of a musical bird is a musical death. Let the Attic nightingale and the swan sing. Socrates is their fellow-slave, he too is consecrated to Apollo. The god of Pytho once proclaimed 'Socrates is the wisest of all men.' And now the wisest of all men is under order to die without wisdom!

[28] There have been unjust judgments before now. It was decided once that Palamedes, the wisest of the Greeks of those days, should die unjustly. At Ilium too there were men like Anytus and Meletus. But even Palamedes was not ordered to be silent before he died; he was allowed to speak and write. He wrote the story of his misfortune on the oar and sent his father Nauplius the letter telling of death. [29] Socrates never writes a malicious or bitter word, he bears the court no grudge, but dies happily and is convinced he is going to join the gods. He devotes himself even now to discussion, as he did in life. Do not be surprised. Such is the nature of the wise. Their wisdom does not fail even in hard times. [30] Music did not desert Orpheus even after death. The women of Thrace rent him to pieces, as these wrongful accusers have done to Socrates, but he kept on singing, though his body was torn apart. Orpheus' head floated down the River Strymon, recalling its own songs. Marsyas, the Phrygian piper who was punished, wants to return gift for gift; he cannot do so, but he hears someone else play, and the song brings him to life. Such is Socrates' case also.

[31] So do not be grudging, do not distrust philosophy. What are you afraid of? That he is going to pray to the gods against you all, if he is allowed to talk? When he spoke, he said nothing of that kind; and one could make such a prayer without speaking. Are you afraid to give him the hemlock when he is talking? If he is silent, he is not Socrates. Let him talk, as though he were at a party. Let him respond to the loving-cup which the divine power gives him.

[32] I thought that the strongest refutation of Socrates' false accusers was produced just now, when he was seen cheerful and happy in the midst of misfortune, and when he expounded arguments like those which he is expressing now. For what arguments do you order him to be silent? What does he say that is against the constitution or the laws or the authorities or the ways of our fathers? He gives us in fact a most pious philosophical defence of the laws, and says he will never run away from these his masters, nor take up residence as an alien in Megara or Boeotia or be a foreign guest of Peloponnesians or Thessalians, but will stay here and obey the Athenians' decision.

[33] Socrates – most lawful of men, most patriotic of any Athenian I have ever known – even now you do not want to leave Athens! He is practising and composing poetry, writing hymns to the gods in his prison, making poems to Apollo. In his last hours Socrates has become a poet too. And yet you are telling Socrates to be silent even in prose! [34] Your orders are contrary to the god's. You, Apollo, are deliberately holding back the Delian festival as a hostage for Socrates, you are not sending the Athenians the sacred ship, because you want to prolong your servant's days of life; you have commanded the winds not to bear her to Athens, so that Socrates can be a philosopher longer. Yet these men make your favour useless!

[35] 'Let him not speak', says the prosecution, 'not even if there is an audience there, not even if Socrates chooses.' Is he not to speak when he puts up his leg or rests because of the pain of his fetters? Is he not to theorize about the kinship of pleasure and pain? Simmias and Cebes ask him a question about the soul: is he not to speak about that? Are Athenians to practise philosophy, and one individual Athenian stay silent? He is cheerful in the prospect of death. His friends marvel at that. He is not to talk? Why? Not even if a man believes the soul is immortal? If he owes a god a sacrifice, may he not even tell one of his friends to pay it? If he is to drink the hemlock, may he not pour a libation or say his customary prayer? [36] What is he saying that is pointless or out of season? Some people, when they die, give instructions about property or children, the disposal of their body or the grave; Socrates sits there saying that one should not weep or groan or think that the present is to be our only life, but rather that another life follows, longer than that which we share with the body; when we are freed from bones and flesh and this whole prison, be it body or tomb, we shall all go to our rightful destiny; while we live, therefore, we must practise philosophy and make our lives a rehearsal for death, seeking to recall much of the ancient learning in which we seem to persist in this life; then, when our destined lot comes, we shall be carried hence, lightly borne aloft, towards gods who are our masters and spirits who will judge our souls. To those who

have lived purely and justly and have endured their earthly life with true philosophy, they assign the company of gods, the voyage above heaven, the vision of real justice, beauty, immortality, and blessed souls; whereas for those who have lived lawlessly and unjustly and whose souls are burdened with many wickednesses, there await Tartarus and Cocytus and Pyriphlegethon, ghastly chastisements and enduring punishments, where they are driven unceasingly along in fire and darkness and strange streams. [37] This is what Socrates says, this is his instruction to us, this is his testament. Who shall grudge us Socratic immortality? Let us hear him again and have confirmation of these hopes of blessedness. It is no harm to Socrates if he does not speak: a long life awaits him, many discussions, gods to listen to him; he will speak to them, he will practise philosophy when he is freed, he will tell them everything. It is for us, who will be left behind as Socrates' orphans, that it is so dreadful that he is never again to answer our doubts, and none of us is again to enjoy his presence here.

[38] Hold back the ship a little longer, Apollo; let the sacred delegation be delayed again at Delos. I have a question to ask Socrates about words and silence and salvation. False accusers, let us have benefit from Socrates while he is alive. Alas, maybe the ship will arrive today. Socrates dreamed that it would. Do not grudge us this one day. Indeed, while I am busy here, Socrates is talking to his companions. I shall be able to hear about it from those companions who have heard his words; but there is nothing to compare with hearing Socrates himself.

[39] My request to you, Socrates, is the opposite of these men's commands: it is to go on talking not only in your lifetime nor only with your own lips, but to talk even after the hemlock, not to stop even when you die. Every soul is immortal – I believe you – and yours more than any other. If any wise spirit visits the souls of his friends, do not keep silent, Socrates, but speak to us in dreams, as the gods do now.

Orations

Augustine is commonly considered to be the father of autobiography, but as Misch (2003) illustrated, the genre is significantly older than late antiquity. Misch traced the classical tradition to fourth-century Athens and works such as Plato's *Letter VII*, Isocrates' *Antidosis*, and Demosthenes' *On the Crown*. Libanius' *Autobiography* displays many of the characteristics of some of these earlier works, such as *Antidosis*, but it also represents a significant step forward for the genre with regard to the amount of personal information and detail that it presents. We should note, however, that none of these writers actually called their work "autobiographies," and it is important to avoid confusing the modern concept of the genre with its classical version. The actual title of Libanius' work, for example, is Βιοσ Η Περι Τησ Εαυτου Τυχησ – *Life, Or About Fortune*.

By his own account, Libanius started writing this work in 374. Like Isocrates, Libanius wanted to set the record straight concerning his life and stated as much in the introduction. Several themes resonant throughout the work: Libanius' standing as a rhetorician, his love of oratory and his students, his relations with government officials, and, significantly, the somewhat fickle nature of Fortune. The text is widely considered to consist of two parts, and Norman (1992) identified §155 as the division point. The first part of the *Autobiography*, despite Libanius' frequent encounters with adverse Fortune, is generally upbeat. It portrays a man at the height of his power, confident in his abilities, and able to laugh at his own mishaps. Indeed, Libanius' humor, as well as his humanity, in the first part is both charming and revealing of character.

The second part of the text, however, has a distinctly different tone – frequently rambling, seldom humorous, often rancorous, with touches of braggadocio. Unlike the first part of the work, it resembles a personal diary, lacking the polished cohesion of something intended for the public, and it creates the impression that Libanius had been beaten down by life. His relations with local governors had usually been cordial during much of his career, but as he aged, they became contentious, and the narrative and its language reflect this change, as well as a strikingly dyspeptic outlook that is absent from the first portion of the work. In §221, for example, he "prayed that Proclus [local governor at the time] should lose his office he had turned into a tyranny, and my prayers were not in vain." In §262, he noted in regard to a later administrator that "The rule of our pot-bellied governor was a harsh one, for his wrath had been kindled by a piece of deceit."

The loss of cordial relations with politicians was accompanied by problems with his school: difficulties with recruitment, lack of commitment among students, a dawning recognition that the glory days of oratory were passing. Enemies seem to emerge from every corner. In §257, we find that even one of his ex-pupils turned against him and tried to bring suit against him as well as his son. Through it all, Libanius asserts that he consistently managed to parry the attacks of a legion of enemies and that, indeed, his reputation emerged even brighter in the end – but the accounts of these glorious victories are likely to strike many readers as hollow, the words of a man who has grown bitter with age.

The excerpt presented here covers the period of Libanius' life from childhood to his mid-20s, when he left Athens with his friend Crispinus.

Reading 39

Autobiography

Autobiography (excerpt), pp. 53–87 (Latin on even-numbered pages omitted) reprinted by permission of the publishers and Trustees of the Loeb Classical Library from *Libanius: Autobiography and Selected Letters*, Volume I, Loeb Classical Library Volume 478, translated by A.F. Norman (Cambridge, MA: Harvard University Press, 1992). © 1992 by the President and Fellows of Harvard College. The Loeb Classical Library ® is a registered trademark of the President and Fellows of Harvard College.

1. Some people labour under a misapprehension in the opinions they entertain about my career. There are some who, as a result of this applause which greets my oratory, assert that I am the happiest of men: there are, on the other hand, those who, considering my incessant perils and pains, would have it that I am the wretchedest man alive. Now each of these verdicts is far removed from the truth, and I must endeavour to correct them by a narration of my past and present circumstances, so that all may know that heaven has granted me a mixture of fortune, and that I am neither the happiest nor the unhappiest of men. And I pray that the bolt of Nemesis may not light upon me.

2. First then, if it is conducive to good fortune to be a citizen of a great and famous city, let us consider the size and character of the city of Antioch, the extent of its territory, the streams which water it, and the breezes in which it basks. Even without seeing it, one can have full knowledge of it from hearsay, for there is no corner of land or sea to which the fame of the city has not spread. My family was one of the greatest in a great city – in education, wealth, the provision of shows and games, and in the oratory which opposes itself to the excesses of governors. 3. There is a notion current that my great-grandfather came from Italy – a mistaken idea arising from a speech which he composed in Latin. The fact is that, although he was versed in Latin, he originated from nowhere else but here. Acquaintance with Latin was not his only endowment: he had the power of divination, and it was through this that he foresaw that his own sons would perish by the sword, noble, great, and eloquent though they were. Their execution drained our household of great wealth, so that my father

in his compassion maintained his sisters after they had reached an age for marriage. Moreover my maternal grandfather, who was especially preeminent as a speaker, barely escaped a like fate. He died of an illness and left the leadership of the city council to his two sons, of whom one died after holding a governmental office, the other after declining it. So in this, part of my fortune was good, part bad.

4. My father took his bride from such a family and had three sons, of whom I am the middle one. He died before his prime when he had recovered a little of these great losses, and he was followed almost immediately by my maternal grandfather. My mother was a prudent woman and feared the dishonesty of guardians and the litigation which would inevitably arise with them, and so she herself set out to be all in all to us. In general, she succeeded very well by dint of her exertions, but though she paid out fees to schoolmasters for us, she did not have the heart to get annoyed with her sleepyhead of a son, for she thought it was a loving mother's part never never to upset her child. Thus it came about that we spent the greater part of the year in the countryside rather than in the study. 5. Four years passed by in this way, but when I was nearly fifteen my interest was kindled and an earnest love of study began to possess me. Hence the charms of the countryside were put aside: I sold my pigeons, pets which are apt to get a strong hold on a boy; the chariot races and everything to do with the stage were discarded, and I remained aloof, far from the sight of those gladiatorial combats where men, whom you would swear to be the pupils of the three hundred at Thermopylae, used to conquer or die. My attitude in this caused the greatest amazement both to young and old. The person responsible for the presentation of these shows was my maternal uncle, and though he invited me to the spectacle, I still stayed wedded to my books. The story goes that he, all that time ago, foretold for me the position of sophist that has actually come to pass. 6. In which category, then, shall I put my orphan's state? Gladly would I have beheld my father in his old age, but of one thing I am certain – that if my father had come to a ripe old age, I would now be engaged upon a very different way of life. If you compare the present with the might-have-been – a career in local politics, for instance, or law, or even in the imperial administration – you would have no dif-

ficulty in discovering which would be the correct estimate of my fortune. 7. Moreover, not even the most self-indulgent of men would dare deny that we children were fortunate in our mother's goodness, which drove countless admirers from our doors – once it is granted that it is a fine thing to be able to express oneself naturally, and that this is ensured not only by one's own conduct in life but by that of one's parents too. Many people, in fact, who have shown themselves to be personally beyond reproach, have been reduced to silence by the ill-repute of their forebears.

8. Again, I was lucky as a pupil in that I attended the lectures of a teacher with a fine flow of oratory; my bad luck was that my attendance was not as regular as it should have been but occurred only in a most perfunctory fashion, and then, when my desire did spur me on to study, I found none to instruct me, for death had stopped his flow. So, though I longed for my dead teacher, I began to frequent the living, mere shadows of teachers, as men eat loaves of barley bread for want of anything better. However, when I found that I was making no progress but was running the risk of falling into the bottomless pit of ignorance through following blind guides, I had done with them. I restrained my mind from composing, my tongue from speaking, and my hand from writing, and I concentrated upon one thing only – the memorization of the works of classical authors – and studied under a man of prodigious memory who was capable of instilling into his pupils an appreciation of the excellence of the classics. I attached myself to him so wholeheartedly that I would not leave him even after class had been dismissed, but would trail after him, book in hand, even through the city square, and he had to give me some instruction, whether he liked it or not. At the time he was obviously annoyed at this importunity, but in later days he was full of praise for it. 9. For these five years my life was entirely devoted to these pursuits, and heaven helped me by placing no hindrance of illness in my course, and then the incident of the thunderbolt occurred. This was as follows: I was standing by my teacher's chair engrossed in the *Acharnians* of Aristophanes, when the sun was hidden by such a pall of cloud that you could hardly tell the difference then between day and night. The heavens resounded with a mighty crash and a thunderbolt hurtled down, blinding my eyes with its flash and stunning my head with

its roar. My first thought was that I had suffered no permanent ill-effect and that the shock would soon settle. However, after I had reached home and was at the lunch table, I seemed again to sense that crash and the thunderbolt hurtling past the house. I broke out into a sweat of fear, and leapt up from the table to the refuge of my bed. I decided that I ought to say nothing of the matter and to keep it secret and not suffer the inconvenience of telling it to the doctors and being dragged from my usual routine to take medicine or undergo professional treatment. 10. This caused the malady which, as the saying goes, could have been removed with no trouble at all in its early stages, to take a deeper root. Hence my affliction was my constant companion abroad, growing great with increase, and it has returned home with me. There have been some fluctuations, of course, but it never stops worrying me, for even when it seems to abate, it never ceases completely. However, as I have said, except for this, I was untroubled by illness all this time, and even this did not prevent me from enjoying my pleasures to the full.

11. Now when I had committed to memory the works of those who were most renowned for their stylistic abilities, the urge for this way of life came over me. I had as a fellow student a Cappadocian, Iasion by name, and he, though late come to learning, had an infinite capacity for taking pains. This Iasion, almost every day, would tell me the tales he had heard from his elders about Athens and the goings-on there. Names like Callinicus and Tlepolemus were always on his tongue, and he would tell the tale of the rhetorical prowess of many another sophist too and of the orations by which they won or lost their disputations, and as a result of all this a longing for Athens began to possess my soul. 12. Later on I intended to let the news out that I had to go there; in the meantime there spread through the town the report of the labours upon which I was engaged and also of my youthful discretion. I make mention of this discretion with confidence, for I have witnesses still alive to rise and testify to it, should you so desire; many of them, indeed, I see seated here. I was incorruptible, not through the vigilance or the deterrents of any attendant, for them the orphan state of their charges tends to make unreliable, but through the providence of Fortune whereby I acted as my own protector and as the rescuer of others besides, putting an

end to the harmful pranks to which many youngsters who neglected their studies betook themselves. Well then, when the whole town buzzed with the account of both these virtues of mine, those fathers who had daughters on their hands approached me through my two uncles – one outbidding another in the size of the dowry he offered, 'but never for a moment did they win my heart.' I think that I would have followed Odysseus' example and spurned even marriage with a goddess for a glimpse of the smoke of Athens. 13. My mother was in tears and could not bear even the mention of the matter. Of my uncles, the elder thought that he should support her and he bade me give up this wild-goose chase, for, however much I hankered after it, he would not give his consent. However, after the younger of the two had presented the Olympic festival in honour of Zeus and I had yielded to necessity, Fate afflicted the city, or rather the whole world, with the death of Panolbius – as the elder of my uncles was called. My mother could not now prevail so well upon the other by her laments, for Phasganius was not the man to give way before idle tears. He persuaded her to bear her grief, for it would not be of long duration and it gave promise of great returns, and so he opened the door for me.

14. In this account the good luck and the bad are perfectly clear. However, once I had set out, I began to realize at last how terribly hard it is to leave behind one's kith and kin. So I went on my way with weeping and wailing, often turning round in longing for the sight of the city walls. As far as Tyana, I was in tears all the way: from there onwards, I was in a fever as well. I was torn between two desires, but the fear of the shame I would incur was added to the one and weighted the balance in its favour, and so I continued on my way perforce, ill though I was. My illness grew worse with the journey, and I crossed the Bosporus little better than a corpse, with my mules in much the same shape. There the man on whom I relied to send me on to Athens by the Imperial Post had fallen from his previous position of influence. He was most zealous in the other duties of hospitality, but this was the one thing which he said he could not provide. 15. I transferred my attention to the sea, but it was now closed to seafarers because of the season. However, I lit upon a well-known sea captain, won him over easily enough by the mention of a

fare, embarked, found Poseidon favourable and went on my way rejoicing. I sailed past Perinthus, and from the deck I gazed upon Rhoeteum, Sigeum and the ill-fated city of Priam. I crossed the Aegean and enjoyed a wind no worse than Nestor did, and so my host's inability turned out to my advantage. 16. So I made landfall at Geraestus, and then at one of the harbours of Attica, where I got a bed for the night. Next night I was in Athens – in the hands of people I wanted none of; and the day after, I was in the hands of yet other people, and these I wanted none of, either. I was unable even to catch a glimpse of the teacher from whom I had come to learn, for I was cooped up in a cell about as big as a barrel – such is the reception they give students on their arrival. My teacher had lost me and I him, so we began to set up a hullabaloo from our separate stations. My captors, however, took no account of our outcries, but I was kept under lock and key until I took the oath, like any Aristodemus, Syrian though I was. After I had sworn the oath to put up with my present condition, the door was opened and I began to attend the lectures of Diophantus as his regular pupil straightaway and those of the other two according to the normal practice of public declamation. 17. Though the applause that arose was enough to deceive those who experienced it then for the first time, I began to realize that I was present at nothing out of the ordinary, for the guidance of students had been monopolized by people who were little better than students themselves. So my attitude was held to be derogatory towards Athens and I was held guilty of not respecting my professors. It was with difficulty, therefore, that I allayed their anger, telling them that I was listening in respectful silence, for vocal demonstrations had been made impossible because of my illness. Finally, I produced some exercises of my own from my notebooks and the like, and made it appear that my attitude was satisfactory, despite my lack of enthusiasm.

18. From this narrative you can get a good idea of my fortune. Thus, my ailments and the fact that, like a merchant venturer, I found my ports of call to fall below expectation – highly spoken of but far different in experience – all this can be placed on the debit side. Yet that my winter sailing weather was no worse than that of summer, and that what occurred was not what I intended but resulted from duress – these are the favours of Fortune. You would probably agree with me on the matter of my voyage and accept my account as consistent with my theme, but for me to assert, with regard to my teachers, that I was lucky in experiencing such compulsion would perhaps seem to you a very queer argument. I must then resolve the riddle, and to this topic I will now proceed.

19. From my boyhood, gentlemen, I had heard tales of the fighting between the schools which took place in the heart of Athens: I had heard of the cudgels, the knives and stones they used and of the wounds they inflicted, of the resultant court actions, the pleas of the defence and the verdicts upon the guilty, and of all those deeds of derring-do which students perform to raise the prestige of their teachers. I used to think them noble in their hardihood and no less justified than those who took up arms for their country: I used to pray heaven that it should be my lot too to distinguish myself so, to go hot-foot to the Peiraeus or Sunium or other ports to kidnap students at their landing, and then go off hot-foot once more to Corinth to stand trial for the kidnapping, give a string of parties, run through all that I had, and then look to someone to make me a loan. 20. Well, Fortune knew that I would be heading for ruin in this specious trap with its high sounding title of head of the school, and so, in her usual wisdom, she withdrew me from the teacher whom I used to regard as the proper recipient of such services on my part, and took me off to be the pupil of someone else, under whom I would become acquainted only with the labours connected with rhetoric. This, in fact, is precisely what happened. I felt myself outraged by the compulsion of the oath and refused to perform any of the services I have mentioned, and no one else would order me to do them because of my unwilling bondage, and there was also the fear that, in my resentment of the imposition, I might take some fresh line with regard to the oath, basing my case upon the compulsion to which I was subjected. 21. Thus I took no part in the sallies, skirmishes, martial affrays, and pitched battles. In fact, even on the occasion of the great riot, when everyone was involved, even those excused by their age, I alone stayed in my seat far away from it all, hearing of the harm which befell each one and remaining aloof from the blows they dealt each other in their anger, giving none and receiving none, and with no intention of so doing, either. Why, a Cretan coming out from his bath

once met me, as I was going in for mine with a companion on either side of me. Without any provocation at all, he brutally clouted one of them on both cheeks, and never even glanced at me; for all that, I felt myself the victim of such an outrage committed before my very eyes. 22. Thus when I was present, everyone made a point of getting all to behave decently, for I never so much as touched a ball all the time I was in Athens, and I kept myself well away from the carousals and the company of those who raided the houses in the meaner quarters at night, and I made it quite clear too that the singing girls – Scylla's heads, or neighbours perhaps more dangerous than Sirens – who have wrecked the career of many a man, sang to me in vain.

23. But to return to my point – from all those disasters I was preserved by Fortune, and so I saw Corinth neither as defendant nor as plaintiff, but only once when I passed through on my way to attend the festival of the Whippings at Sparta, and again when I went to Argos to be initiated in the local mysteries. So much for that. Moreover, with regard to my studies, if I had become an imitator of the man I had set out to attend, for affection would have ensured this happening, I would have followed in the steps of individuals I would prefer not to mention – you know well enough whom I mean. So imagine what I would now be like, if I reminded you of some wretched starveling hack instead of those classic writers who are now the models for my oratory.

24. This, then, was one of the excellent dispositions of Fate. There was the added fact that, as I followed my proper guides, I needed no doctor for my bodily ailments. So I applied myself to study day in and day out, save those reserved for official holidays, and they were not many. Since it was agreed that the peak of a man's career was to be deemed worthy of holding a professorial chair at Athens, Fortune devised this and granted me it in the following manner. 25. An Italian was governor, a martinet who demanded that the students there should not misconduct themselves at all. As a result of rioting by the students, he dismissed their teachers as being no good shepherds, and he began to look around for three others to take their places as professors. So an Egyptian and a fellow citizen of my own, both resident in Athens, were recommended. My professional success matched theirs, though I was but twenty-five years old and the Egyptian was ten years older

and the other older still. So I was bound to accept the invitation. However, the governor's temper was soothed in the course of time, and the professors retained their posts, but I had been marked for distinction by this choice. After this, the atmosphere was charged with suspicion: there was no rest either for them or for me, for their intrigues caused them sleepless nights, while the expectation of having to undergo some unpleasant experience had the same effect on me. Yet here too Fortune had not abandoned me to the misconduct of the students; rather did she restrain their heightened tempers and vindictiveness.

26. Now let me mention yet another signal proof that I was under the protection of Fortune. My father's estate was going to be sold, and the goddess, naturally, had foreknowledge of this. My intention was to spend another four years additional to those I had already completed and then to leave Athens, since I felt that my intellect needed to be improved still further: however sufficient my ability might seem to other people, it did not seem so to me, and I was harassed by the dread that the pundits, who were everywhere about me, would wish to trip me up by exhaustive examination, and so I must still continue to research and increase my knowledge. 27. If the news of the sale had reached me in Athens, I would certainly be there now, making no use at all of my acquired learning, a fate that has befallen many students who, unable to get one of the professorial chairs there, reach old age with no chance of showing their eloquence. However, Fortune devised the following remedy. I had a close friend in Crispinus from Heraclea, a lad in my own year there who possessed a natural gift of eloquence. He, though of my own age, looked upon me as a father, and in all things great and small he followed my precepts, doing nothing to sully the virtues of his house, for modesty was his guide in his every word. He was summoned home by his revered uncle – revered indeed, for he consorted more with gods than with men on earth: despite the law which banned it and the death penalty inflicted on any who dared do so, he yet went his way through life in the company of the gods, and he laughed to scorn that evil law and its sacrilegious enactor. As I have said, Crispinus was called home and could no longer stay, and, as Homer puts it, 'his heart was sore afraid within him' – more so even than if he were going out to do battle against the foe, for that skill

in declamation which he had acquired in Athens he was going to demonstrate among his fellow citizens, clever and highly cultured people, and so, being a prudent lad and without experience of such an ordeal, he was not unnaturally alarmed. 28. He needed an ally and friend to stand by him and to be near to encourage him, and such a one was not far to seek when I was there. He told me of his predicament and of his need, and naturally I, considering the length of the journey, hesitated, but friendship overcame my hesitation. I also had the notion that, if my performance before such an assemblage proved at all inadequate, I would excuse myself from any second journey for this purpose. 29. This was the consideration which set me on my way, and by the grace of Hermes and the Muses, from Plataea onwards we began to make the most of our accomplishments, and, in every town through which we passed, we had praises and blessings showered upon us and were entitled benefactors of Athens. Nor yet did the Macedonian, whose habit it was to set upon travellers passing through Macedonia to their discomfiture, cause any discomfort to us. He engaged with us, indeed, but went off, himself for once discomfitted.

Oration 18: Funeral Oration over Julian

Although Julian was killed in 363, Libanius did not finish the funeral oration until toward the end of 365 (Norman, 1969). The delay was caused, in part, by his need to collect information that he did not have at hand about the emperor's life and death. In addition, a combination of grief and serious illness hampered his work. His grief was caused not only by the death of someone whom he considered a friend and the potential savior of paganism but also by the persecutions against nonbelievers that the Christians initiated immediately upon learning of the emperor's passing. The oration obviously was not presented at Julian's funeral, and given the dangerous conditions following the emperor's death, it is unlikely that he ever performed it in a public venue. Doing so would have put him at far too great a risk of retribution for praising a leader whom the Christians hated. At the very best, he invited a small group of trustworthy friends (probably no more than half a dozen) to a private presentation. The sheer length of the oration, however, may have made even this limited performance problematic, in which case he would have distributed the text of the oration to that same small group, perhaps with the understanding that they would not widely circulate it.

The oration follows the established tradition, beginning with a panegyric to the emperor's family and then moving on to consider his many accomplishments. The excerpt offered here concludes at the point where Julian's military victories in Gaul were elevating his reputation among soldiers and civilians alike, a circumstance that alarmed Constantius II and would have led to armed conflict had he not died before battle could be joined. Libanius' adherence to the traditional funeral oration extends beyond structure, however. The work recalls the panegyrics for Julius Caesar, and by reciting Julian's accomplishments as a scholar, an orator, a military leader, and as a moral, just man, Libanius was celebrating the Greek ideal that first found expression in Homer's description of Achilles – the "speaker of words and a doer of deeds," the warrior king who also excelled in oratory.

Reading 40

Oration 18: Funeral Oration over Julian

Oration 18: Funeral Oration over Julian (excerpt), pp. 279–311 (Latin on even-numbered pages omitted) reprinted by permission of the publishers and Trustees of the Loeb Classical Library from *Libanius: Selected Orations*, Volume I, Loeb Classical Library Volume 451, translated by A.F. Norman (Cambridge, MA: Harvard University Press, 1969). © 1969 by the President and Fellows of Harvard College. The Loeb Classical Library ® is a registered trademark of the President and Fellows of Harvard College.

1. GENTLEMEN here present, what I and all men hoped for should have come to pass: the Persian empire should now lie in ruins, and Roman governors instead of satraps should now be administering their territory under our laws: our temples here should be adorned with booty got from them, while the victor in this contest should be seated on his imperial throne, receiving the orations composed in honour of his exploits. Such, I am sure, would be right and proper, a fitting reward for all the many sacrifices he offered. 2. Yet since the spirit of envy has prevailed over our reasonable expectations, and his dead body has been brought back from the borders of Babylon, when he was so near the objective at which he aimed; since tears, as you would expect, have flowed from every eye and still could not prevent his death, let us perform the one thing left for us and most acceptable to him, and tell something of what he did, but before a different audience, for he has been prevented from hearing the praises of the deeds he wrought. 3. For first of all, it would be unjust that, though he ventured all to ensure his praises be sung, we should yet rob him of his reward. Moreover, it would be utterly disgraceful not to grant him in death the honours we gave him in life. For besides the fact that it would be the grossest kind of flattery to fawn upon the living and forget the dead, one may oblige the living in many other ways, even without an oration. Yet with regard to the dead, there is but one recourse for us – the praise and narration that transmit their glorious achievements to all posterity.

4. Now, in all my attempts to speak in his praise, I have ever found my words insufficient for the greatness of his deeds, and, to be sure, I did not take umbrage that my beloved emperor's genius should outstrip the powers of the teacher that loved him. I considered it advantageous to all the states of the empire alike that he who had ascended the throne for the salvation of the whole world should make it impossible for words to match his deeds. Since I cannot deal adequately merely with the high qualities he demonstrated in the West, how would I go on to-day, now that I am put to it, to entrust to a single oration both that topic and his expedition against Persia? 5. Indeed, I believe that, if he secured of the gods below permission to return on condition of assisting me in this task and if, unawares to everyone else, he shared such a labour of love with me, not even so would there be a true measure of his deeds. It would be better expressed than now, but even then as an entirety it would not be treated as it should be. What then must I consider my position to be if I choose so great a task without such assistance? 6. Had I not before now observed your awareness of the fact that victory belongs to the world of action, while you yet derive pleasure from oratory, it would be best for me to stay silent. However, since on those occasions you were prompt to praise and remained in enjoyment of my orations, I feel that there is no just cause for silence, and so I will attempt to do justice to my emperor and my friend.

7. Now there have been many emperors who, though not deficient in character, were not of distinguished ancestry, and who, though knowledgeable in preserving the empire, were ashamed to mention their parentage, with the result that those who made speeches in their praise had some difficulty in salving this sore. However, in his case there is nothing that does not redound to his credit. 8. In the first place, as regards his parentage, his grandfather was an emperor who held wealth in especial contempt and won the especial affection of his subjects. His father was an emperor's son and an emperor's brother and, though more fitted to rule than the actual ruler, he yet held his peace and congratulated him on his accession and continued as a loyal and affectionate member of the family. 9. He married the daughter of a wise and virtuous prefect, whom the

victorious enemy respected, advising his own subordinates to take him as the pattern for their administration, and he became the father of this excellent prince and honoured his father-in-law by giving his son the same name. 10. When Constantine fell ill and died, murder stalked through practically all the family, fathers and sons alike. Our prince and his elder brother escaped this massacre, Gallus saved by an illness which was thought quite enough to be the death of him anyway, Julian by his tender years, for he was but newly weaned. 11. Now while Gallus preferred to devote himself to other pursuits than eloquence, believing that he would thereby encounter less unpopularity, Julian's guardian angel urged him on to the love of learning, and therein he spent his time in the greatest city of the empire next to Rome. He went to school, an emperor's grandson, an emperor's nephew and an emperor's cousin, with no swagger, causing no trouble, and claiming no attention by a host of attendants and the hubbub that they create. An excellent eunuch was the guardian of his virtue and another attendant who was not without his share of learning. Julian's dress was nothing out of the ordinary: his demeanour was no more proud than that of others: he spoke to people before he was spoken to, and he did not repulse the poor: he would enter a room when invited, and until invited he would wait: he would stand where the rest usually did, listen to exactly the same as the rest, would leave with the rest, and would never claim any extra attention. So, if you had come from abroad and viewed the class without knowing who they were and who their parents, you would never have discovered from his outward appearance anything to mark the superiority of his station.

12. However, he was not on a level with them in every particular, for in his understanding and appreciation of his lessons, in his grasp and retention of them, and in his perseverance in his labours, he opened up a great gap between himself and the rest. I saw that and regretted that it was not I that had the cultivation of such genius. A good-for-nothing teacher had the lad as a reward for his abuse of the gods, and the boy was actually being brought up with such notions of religion and was enduring this incompetence in rhetoric because of the war waged against the altars by his teacher. 13. He was now on the threshold of manhood, and the princeliness of his

nature was attested by many notable signs. This allowed Constantius no rest, and so, fearful that his capital, which was so influential in the formulation of public opinion and in matters of government the peer of Rome, should be attracted to the young man's excellence, with some untoward consequences for himself, he had him packed off to Nicomedeia, since that city would cause him not nearly so much alarm, and there he provided facilities for his education. Julian did not attend my lectures, though I had established myself there and had chosen the peaceful calm of that city in preference to the teeming dangers of the capital. Still, he bought copies of my speeches and so maintained an association with me. 14. The reason for the fact that he found pleasure in my oratory and yet avoided its author was that marvellous teacher of his. He had bound him with many fearsome oaths never to be or to be called my pupil and never to be enrolled on the list of my students. 15. Though resenting his teacher's imposition of such an oath, he did not break it, but since he was so desirous of me, he discovered a method whereby he could share in my oratory without perjuring himself. He got someone, at considerable expense, to convey to him my lectures each day. And here he proved the power of his genius in the highest degree, for with no personal association with me, he imitated my style better than any of my regular pupils. By this more obscure path he surpassed the brilliance of their approach in the fruitfulness of his labours, and this is surely the reason why, in the orations he afterwards composed, there is some affinity with my own and he was thought to have been one of my students.

16. While he interested himself in this, his brother came to share the throne in a junior capacity. Constantius had two wars on his hands, first against Persia, and then against the usurper Magnentius. He certainly required a colleague, and so he sent Gallus from Italy to safeguard his Eastern empire. In times past his father's position had been that of an emperor's brother: so was Julian's now. 17. Now, when Gallus passed through Bithynia with his retinue, the two brothers had an interview, but his rise to fortune did not affect Julian's outlook, nor did he make it an excuse for idleness that his brother was a ruling emperor. Instead he increased his passion for learning still further, and increased the efforts that he applied to its pursuit, for he felt that, if he remained in a

private station, he would possess in place of majesty an attribute more divine – wisdom, while if he were called to the throne, he would adorn his majesty with wisdom. 18. Thus for his studies he made use of sunlight, and when evening fell, of lamplight. His aim was not to make his possessions any greater, easy though that was to do, but to improve his intellect. Finally, he met with people who were steeped with the learning of Plato, and he learned of gods and spirits and the real creators and saviours of this whole universe: he gained knowledge of the nature of the soul, its origin and its destination, the causes of its glory and elevation, and of its ruin and debasement: he discovered its bondage and its freedom, and the means to avoid the one and attain the other, and he washed a sour story clean with sweet discourse, casting out all that earlier nonsense and in its place introducing into his soul the beauty of truth, no less than if he had brought into some mighty temple statues of gods that had been in times past befouled and besmirched. 19. Despite the change in his beliefs, he kept the same appearance as before, since to reveal them was out of the question. Aesop here would have composed a fable not of an ass in a lion's skin but of a lion in an ass's hide: though he really knew what was right to know, he pretended a knowledge of what was safer. 20. His fame spread on all sides, and devotees of the Muses, and of the other gods too, travelled by land and sea, eager to look on him, to make his acquaintance, to address him themselves and to hear him address them. Once they came, it was not easy for them to go away again. Siren-like he detained them, not just by his eloquence, but by his natural attractiveness. By his gift for deep affection he instilled the capacity for it into others also, so that being so nobly compounded together they were separated not without difficulty.

21. He gathered together wisdom of every kind and displayed it – poetry, oratory, the various schools of philosophy, much use of Greek and not a little of Latin, for he interested himself in both. On the lips of every man of sense was the prayer that the lad should become the ruler of the empire, that an end be put to the ruin of civilization, and that there be put in charge of the troubled world one who knew how to cure such ills. 22. I would not go so far as to say that he disapproved of such prayers. I shall make no such boast about him. I feel that this was his desire too, but that it arose from a longing not for luxury, power

or the imperial purple, but for the restoration by his own efforts of the worship of the gods in particular to the empire whence it had been expelled. 23. It was this that shook him to the core, as he saw their temples in ruins, their ritual banned, their altars overturned, their sacrifices suppressed, their priests sent packing and their property divided up between a crew of rascals. If one of the gods promised him a cure for these ills at another's doing, I am sure that he would have insisted on refusing the throne. His anxiety, therefore, was not for power but for the well-being of the cities.

24. As this desire was growing in the hearts of men of learning, that the world might be cured by his will, a false accusation was brought against Gallus and a letter containing highly treasonable material was discovered. Those responsible for it were punished, for after being the victim of such calumny he was not likely to reward them with garlands of greeting, but, by inflicting this punishment, he was held to be guilty of the crime he had punished, and he was condemned to death unheard, for his execution took place before he could make any plea. 25. Julian was arrested immediately, and he was surrounded by armed guards, grim of face and harsh of tongue, whose behaviour was such that imprisonment seemed a mere trifle in comparison. Besides that, he was unable to remain in any single place: he was shifted from one locality to another to his discomfort. All this he endured without a single charge, great or small, being brought against him. How could there be, when he lived a distance of three hundred days' journey away from his brother and corresponded – and not very often, at that – by letters that were confined merely to greetings? So, though there was none to level accusation however false against him, he was victimized as I have said for no other reason than that the pair of them had a single father. 26. Here again there is reason to admire him: he made no denunciation of his dead brother to flatter his murderer, nor did he make any pronouncement on his behalf and so inflame the living against himself. He honoured his brother with concealed grief and allowed Constantius no excuse to kill him, though he was greatly desirous of it. He kept a good tight rein on his tongue, though hardly prompted to do so by all the discomforts that beset him, so that, by his patience, he stopped the mouths of the wickedest blackguards. 27. Yet

not even this served to protect him, nor did it assuage the wrath of Constantius in his stupid ill-temper, but as he was lying tempest-tossed, an Ino Cadmus' daughter, the wife of Constantius, saw him, took pity on him, and soothed her husband. With many a plea she set free this lover of Greece and especially of Athens, the most precious part of Greece, to send him to the land he loved. 28. Now this must surely be a token of a spirit sent from heaven, that in choosing a residence he showed no desire for gardens, villas, woodlands, seaside estates or the luxury of the many other possessions that were all his in Ionia, but regarded all this seeming good fortune as of little account compared with Athens, the home of Plato, Demosthenes and the various other branches of learning. 29. So he went there with all speed, to add to his store of knowledge and to consort with teachers who could offer something beyond what he already had. Upon associating with them and giving proof of his qualities and gaining proof of theirs, he astonished them more than they him. He alone of the youngsters who came to Athens left after giving instruction rather than receiving it. At any rate, there could always be seen about him swarms of men, young and old, of philosophers and rhetors. And the gods also fixed their eyes on him, well aware that he was the one who would restore them their age-old privileges. 30. He was equally remarkable for his eloquence and his shyness, for none of his utterances was made without a blush. Everyone enjoyed the kindness of his disposition, but it was only the best among them who enjoyed his confidence, and foremost among them was our fellow-citizen, the one person without reproach and by his excellence rising superior to idle gossip.

31. Now, the lad's intention was to live and die in Athens, and that he thought to be the most perfect bliss. However, the situation demanded a second emperor, for the cities near the Rhine were in ruins and the commanders sent to that theatre of war aspired to something higher than their lawful station. So the student of philosophy at Athens was summoned to the throne, and in consequence of his very philosophy he inspired confidence in the man who had wronged him most. Though he had been the murderer of his father and his brothers, some long before, the last but recently, he still had hopes that his assurances would be loyally kept and that his disposition would be stronger than the complaints he could

level against him. 32. So, in summoning him, he was not far wrong in his hopes, but Julian had no grounds for believing that this advancement would not turn out to be a snare, for the blood already shed gave him reason to come to this conclusion. However, there was no way of avoiding it, and he tearfully invoked the goddess and prayed her to help him, and so took his departure. On becoming a partner on the throne, he was immediately detailed for a task that required the hands of Heracles to deal with it, for the position in Gaul, the most distant province by the ocean's edge, was as follows.

33. When Constantius was at war with Magnentius who had usurped the empire of another and was governing it himself with regard for law and order, he felt that he must have recourse to every means to secure his downfall, and sending letters to the barbarians he actually opened up Roman territory to them, for he told them that he permitted them to occupy as much as they could. 34. They were given a clear field and the terms of their treaties were rescinded by these despatches, and they swept in with absolutely none to stop them, for Magnentius had his forces in Italy. They ravaged the prosperous cities to their hearts' content: villages were laid waste, walls were battered down: goods, women and children were carried off. The menfolk, as slaves, followed them, the poor devils carrying their own possessions on their backs. If they could not endure slavery and the sight of wives and daughters assaulted, they were murdered in the midst of their laments: the pick of what we possessed was transferred to the barbarians, and the victors farmed with their own hands the land that belonged to us and by those of their captives that which was their own. 35. Those cities that escaped the sack by the strength of their walls had no land save for a very small area: their folk were ravaged by famine and had recourse to anything that could serve for food, until the inhabitants were so reduced in number that the cities themselves formed both city and farmland and the uninhabited spaces inside the defences provided land enough for farming. Yes, oxen were yoked, furrows drawn, the seed set, and the corn grew, was reaped and threshed, all inside the city gates, so that the captives could not have been said to be any worse off than they who remained at home.

36. Constantius, after buying his victory at such cost, at first rejoiced and was glad, but after

the final defeat of his foe, his treason stood revealed and Rome practically cried out aloud that she had been foully mutilated. He had not the courage to eject the intruders at the risk of his own skin, so he called on this student, whom he had just now fetched from college to a career of arms, to undertake the expedition. But the oddest thing was his prayer that this same person should at the same time overcome and be overcome by the enemy, such emotions being due to his desire to recover his territory and to his envy. 37. He gave immediate proof that he was sending him out to death no less than to victory, for, though he had an army that in times past was big enough to keep three empires in order, with masses of infantry and cavalry so invulnerably equipped as to lend them a terrible aspect, he detailed three hundred of his most unreliable infantry to act as his escort: he would, he said, find his army in those already stationed there, that is, in men who had long been schooled in defeat and whose job had long been to stand siege. 38. Yet none of this worried Julian or caused him alarm. Though this was his first taste of action and campaigning, and though he was going to put into the field unsteady troops against the all-conquering foe, he wore his gear as if he had from the start been used to handling a shield instead of books, and he advanced with such confidence as if he were commander of a host of heroes. 39. There were two good reasons for such behaviour. First, there was his philosophy and his knowledge that strategy was more effective than brute strength. Secondly, he had confidence that the gods fought on his side. He knew that Heracles too had escaped the Styx because Athena tipped the scale in his favour.

40. Right from the start there was a clear indication of the goodwill of the gods towards him. He left Italy in mid-winter, a season when anyone not protected under cover was liable to die from the snowstorms and frost, but his march was accompanied by such brilliant sunshine that, as they advanced, they called it the season of spring, and the cold was conquered even before his enemies were. 41. Moreover, here was another indication of his better fortune: as he was passing through the first township of the province allotted to him, one of the garlands of greenery – our parishes hang them in large numbers suspended on strings in mid-air between the pillars and the house walls and we decorate our towns with them – lost its fastenings, dropped on the emper-

or's head and fitted exactly. A cheer rose up on all sides: for by this crown, obviously, his future triumphs were foretold, and the fact that he came to conquer.

42. Now, if the emperor that sent him had allowed him to go into action straightaway and to use his own initiative, the situation there would have been improved immediately, but in fact he had authority for nothing save to wear the uniform. Executive powers were vested in his military officers, for it had been Constantius' decision that they should command and he be subordinate to them. He, mindful of Odysseus and his companions, put up with the position, but the generals, it seemed, preferred to stay fast asleep, and it encouraged the enemy that, after the arrival of an emperor, they should have all they had had before. 43. But for all that, even if action were denied him and his tours of his provinces were only for inspection – and that was all he was allowed to do – the influence of his title and presence was such that one of those who had long been cooped up like fish in a barrel sallied out and captured a barbarian tilling the land close to the wall, and one or two more people did the same. Finally a night attack made by a large force of young warriors was repulsed by a few old men who had been released from military service because of their age. The assailants, with ladders, attacked alongside an unguarded gate – their favourite method of capturing a city – but the inhabitants, as soon as the alarm was raised, used everything in sight as a weapon and charged with aging step, shouting the emperor's name as the battle cry. And the old fellows won, just like those of Myronides, killing some of the assailants themselves, while others of the attackers threw themselves to their death from the wall. 44. From the other side the young men made a sally against the barbarians, something quite contrary to their custom hitherto. They revelled in the killing, and the enemy turned and fled. They did not actually see the emperor but had been inspired by his nearness, while others, who were on the point of settling elsewhere, cast away their fears and stayed. 45. And when the barbarians launched an attack from the depths of the forest upon the rear of the column of march, the change in the situation was such that they who had expected to throw him into disorder were annihilated. Their killers brought in their dead foes' heads as proof, for there was a price set on every head, and much

eagerness for head-hunting. With great clever-ness he used their desire for gain to purge their souls of cowardice, and acquisitiveness inspired courage. Some of the enemy sought refuge on the islands formed by the Rhine and fell prey to those of our people who crossed by swimming or in boats; and the cities feasted on their cattle. 46. In fact, of the two most important cities, he found that one had been harried by countless inroads and the other was lying desolate and in ruins as a result of a single recent attack. He lent a helping hand for the rebuilding of this last, and placed a garrison in it. The other, that had become com-pletely destitute, so that it had been reduced to using the most outlandish things for food, he con-soled with hopes of better things. 47. On seeing this, the chieftain of a not inconsiderable native tribe came to him with his excuses: he pleaded

that he had done no great harm, and asked for peace and offered to become an ally. Since there seemed to be something in what he said, Julian made a truce with him for a short period, render-ing him better disposed through fear of what might follow.

48. So, in his tours of inspection of the prov-ince, such and more was the influence he exerted, though he had not yet reached a position where he could put all his schemes into practice. That commander who showed cowardice in face of the enemy and reserved his violence for his own people was withdrawn, and as his successor there came a first-rate man with an expert acquaint-ance with warfare. Hence most of the obstacles were removed, and now at last the time had come for the emperor to prove himself beyond all doubt.

Oration 30: To Emperor Theodosius, for the Temples

Christians resented and were angered by Emperor Julian's efforts to return the Empire to the old gods. His untimely death motivated many to engage in violent reprisals against pagans. Tensions between Christians and non-Christians escalated, especially in the eastern portion of the Empire, where Christianity was strongest. The ban on blood sacrifices was designed to end paganism through slow strangulation of its rituals, but those who followed the old gods were innovative in finding alternative ways to honor them, such as substituting bread and fruit or the aroma of incense for the sacrificial animal. Seeing these substitutions as a form of defiance, church leaders became agita-tors, particularly against those who were less able to defend themselves – the farmers and peasants in the predominantly pagan countryside. Local priests, bishops, and monks began a campaign of persecution and desecration that continued well into the sixth century, resulting in the near total destruction of shrines, temples, and artwork across the Empire (Sardi-Mendelovici, 1990).

Oration 30 illustrates the role Libanius held as a public intellectual engaged in argu-ing for justice and ethics. Protesting the ongoing destruction of temples and art, as well as the loss of life, which was being facilitated by the local governor, Cynegius, Libanius pleads with Emperor Theodosius to intervene. The thrust of his argument is twofold. First, he points out that the victims of this violence are innocent of wrongdo-ing and that the perpetrators are committing unlawful acts that the emperor is duty-bound to punish. Second, he locates the emperor in the socio-historical context of the Greco-Roman tradition, arguing that the pagan temples and art are nothing less than the legacies of that tradition. An attack on them is the equivalent to an attack on the Empire itself, and the emperor therefore is obligated to enforce the law and protect these treasures.

Libanius' appeal never had any real chance of succeeding: His arguments were based on a classical foundation that had little support in a Christian context. Given the climate of the times, producing such an oration took great intrepidity. Libanius was facing social, political, and cultural changes that dwarfed him, and he could have been eliminated with a single word. Moreover, whether he knew it or not, his oration brought him indirectly into conflict with Ambrose, Bishop of Milan, whose influence over Theodosius was considerable and who effectively argued that the emperor, as a Christian, was neither part of nor the defender of the Greco-Roman tradition. Rather he was the defender of Christianity and therefore was obligated to use his authority and power to further the aims of Christian militants. Sizgorich (2007) noted that Ambrose successfully located Theodosius in the Christian narrative as Defender of the Faith. The extent of Ambrose's success can be measured by the Theodosian Decrees, which not only strengthened the existing ban on blood sacrifices but made it illegal for anyone even to set foot inside a temple (see Williams and Friell, 1994). Delivering the sermon at Thedosius' funeral in 395, Ambrose no doubt gloated in his description of the emperor as a "smasher of idols and a scourge of heretics" (pp. 97–98).

Reading 41

Oration 30: To Emperor Theodosius, for the Temples

Oration 30: To Emperor Theodosius, for the Temples, pp. 101–21 (Latin on even-numbered pages omitted) reprinted by permission of the publishers and Trustees of the Loeb Classical Library from *Libanius: Selected Orations*, Volume II, Loeb Classical Library Volume 452, translated by A.F. Norman (Cambridge, MA: Harvard University Press, 1977). © 1977 by the President and Fellows of Harvard College. The Loeb Classical Library ® is a registered trademark of the President and Fellows of Harvard College.

1. On many previous occasions, Sire, when I have tendered advice, you have felt that I have reached a proper conclusion, and I have prevailed over those whose words and wishes were opposed to mine because of the superior merits of my counsel. Now too I come on the same errand, inspired with the same hope, and now too especially lend me your ears. If, however, I fail to convince you, do not consider the speaker to be hostile to your administration. Apart from anything else, reflect upon the great distinction you have bestowed upon me and consider that the beneficiary cannot but reasonably feel the strongest affection for his benefactor. Simply for this reason I feel that I must advise on matters where I believe I have something worth while to say. In no other way could I show my gratitude to my sovereign, only perhaps by my oratory and what follows from it.

2. To many people it will appear that I am courting much danger by embarking upon an address to you about the temples and the need for them not to be abused as they are now, but in my view such people, in entertaining these fears, are very much mistaken in their assessment of you.

To my mind, it is the choleric, ill-tempered man who proceeds immediately to condemn the expression of opinions, when anything is said that is displeasing to him: the kindly, humane gentle character – your own qualities, Sire – merely refuses the counsel of which he does not approve. For where it lies with the hearer of a discourse whether to be convinced by it or not, it is unjustified for him to refuse a hearing, since no harm can come of it, or to become angry and resort to punishment if he disagrees with any remarks when anyone has the courage to say what he conceives to be right. 3. I beg you then, Sire, to turn your gaze on me as I speak, and not to let your eyes light upon those who will wish by various means to delude both you and me, for often enough the influence of a nod has more effect than the force of truth. I submit that they too should allow me to develop my argument quietly and without abuse and afterwards attempt by argument themselves to refute what I have said.

4. The first men who appeared on earth, Sire, occupied the high places and protected themselves in caves and huts, and soon gained a notion

of gods and realized how much their good will means to mankind. They raised the kind of temples to be expected of primitive man and made idols for themselves. As their culture advanced towards urbanization and building techniques became adequate for it, many cities made their appearance at the mountain's foot or on the plains, and in each and every one of them the first buildings to be erected after the wall were shrines and temples, for they believed that from such governance they would have the utmost protection also. 5. And if you travel the whole length of the Roman world, you will find this everywhere the case. Even in our second capital some temples still exist, robbed of all honour, admittedly, but though they be but few out of very many, still they have not vanished from it completely. And it was with these gods to aid them that the Romans used to march against the foe, engage them in battle, conquer them and, as conquerors, grant the vanquished a condition of life better than that which they had before their defeat, removing their fears and allowing them a share in their own civic life.

6. While I was still a boy, the ruler who held a reign of terror in Rome was brought down by the leader of an army of Gauls – Gauls who, originally worshippers of the gods, turned against them and attacked them. He, after overcoming the person who had infused new life into the cities, thought it to his own advantage to recognize some other as a god, and he employed the sacred treasures on the building of the city upon which his heart was set. For all that, he made absolutely no alteration in the traditional forms of worship, but, though poverty reigned in the temples, one could see that all the rest of the ritual was fulfilled. 7. To his son passed the government, or rather the shadow of it, for the reins of power were held by others who, through their control of his earliest upbringing, had gained a supremacy absolutely equal to his own. He, then, ruling under orders from them, was induced to adopt several misguided policies, in particular, the banning of sacrifices. His cousin, a paragon of all virtue, restored them. Of his actions and intentions I make no mention here, but after his death in Persia, the performance of sacrifice lasted for some little time until, after some untoward incidents, it was banned by the two imperial brothers, an exception, however, being made in the case of offerings of incense. This particular exception has

also been confirmed by a law of your own, so that we do not so much lament what we have lost as show gratitude for the concession we have obtained. 8. You then have neither ordered the closure of temples nor banned entrance to them. From the temples and altars you have banished neither fire nor incense nor the offerings of other perfumes. But this black-robed tribe, who eat more than elephants and, by the quantities of drink they consume, weary those that accompany their drinking with the singing of hymns, who hide these excesses under an artificially contrived pallor – these people, Sire, while the law yet remains in force, hasten to attack the temples with sticks and stones and bars of iron, and in some cases, disdaining these, with hands and feet. Then utter desolation follows, with the stripping of roofs, demolition of walls, the tearing down of statues and the overthrow of altars, and the priests must either keep quiet or die. After demolishing one, they scurry to another, and to a third, and trophy is piled on trophy, in contravention of the law. 9. Such outrages occur even in the cities, but they are most common in the countryside. Many are the foes who perpetrate the separate attacks, but after their countless crimes this scattered rabble congregates and calls for a tally of their activities, and they are in disgrace unless they have committed the foulest outrage. So they sweep across the countryside like rivers in spate, and by ravaging the temples, they ravage the estates, for wherever they tear out a temple from an estate, that estate is blinded and lies murdered. Temples, Sire, are the soul of the countryside: they mark the beginning of its settlement, and have been passed down through many generations to the men of today. 10. In them the farming communities rest their hopes for husbands, wives, children, for their oxen and the soil they sow and plant. An estate that has suffered so has lost the inspiration of the peasantry together with their hopes, for they believe that their labour will be in vain once they are robbed of the gods who direct their labours to their due end. And if the land no longer enjoys the same care, neither can the yield match what it was before, and, if this be the case, the peasant is the poorer, and the revenue jeopardized, for whatever a man's willingness, surely his inability frustrates him.

11. So the outrages committed by these hooligans against the estates bear upon vital matters of state. They claim to be attacking the temples, but

these attacks are a source of income, for, though some assail the shrines, others plunder the wretched peasantry of what they have, both the produce stored from the land and their stock; and the invaders depart with the loot from the places they have stormed. Others are not satisfied with this, but they appropriate the land too, claiming that what belongs to this or that body is temple property, and many a man has been robbed of his family acres on this false title. Others, again, claim to worship their god with fasting, and yet grow fat on the misfortunes of other folk. And if the victims of this looting come to the "pastor" in town – for that is the title they give to a fellow who is not all that he should be –, if they come and tearfully recount their wrongs, this pastor commends the looters and sends the victims packing with the assurance that they are lucky to have got off so lightly. 12. Yet, Sire, these victims are your subjects too, and as workers are more useful than idlers, so are they more useful than their oppressors. These are as the bees, those the drones. And if they hear that an estate has something worth looting, it is straightaway involved in sacrifices and is committing all manner of crimes: an armed visitation is called for, and up come the justices, which is the term they use to describe these – for want of a better word – footpads, for footpads at least try not to be found out and they deny their misdeeds. Call one of them a footpad and you insult him. But this crew flaunt their excesses, boast of them, advertise them to those who are unaware of them, and claim that they should be rewarded. 13. But it is nothing else than war in peace time waged against the peasantry. Ill-usage at the hands of their fellows is no alleviation for their misfortunes, except for the fact that it is even worse that those allies they might normally have had in times of trouble are responsible for their experiencing the above-mentioned outrages in time of peace.

14. Then what is your purpose, Sire, in maintaining your forces, equipping your armies and conferring with commanders? Why send them to where they are needed, post despatches to them on matters of urgency, despatch replies to their queries? What is the point of these fresh fortifications, these labours of midsummer? What is the object of all this? What is it that allows both town and country to live in security, to sleep soundly and not to quake with expectations of war, save the universal conviction that any invader will retire after suffering more damage than he has caused? So, while you keep external foes at arm's length, if one group of your subjects attacks another and prevents them sharing in the general prosperity, they inevitably do harm to your precautions, your policies and your task, Sire, and by their activities they rebel against your will also.

15. The assertion is, of course, that they were punishing those who offer sacrifice and so contravene the law that bans it. This assertion, Sire, is always a lie. None of these ignorant rustics is so impudent as to claim to be above the law, and when I say the law, I mean its formulator. Do you really believe that those who cringe even at the tax-collector's uniform would despise the emperor's majesty? Yet this was the argument so often put to Flavianus, but it was never proved – nor is it now. 16. Now look! I challenge the guardians of this law. Who has seen anyone out of all the persons you have dispossessed who has sacrificed on the altars in the manner forbidden by the law, whether you be young or old, man or woman, a fellow-villager who disagrees with sacrifices to the gods, or any native of the neighbourhood? Spite and envy could provide reason enough for neighbours to start proceedings against them, but for all that neither from them nor from anywhere else has anyone come forward, nor will he, if he has any qualms about perjury – not to mention the flogging for it. So what basis is there for the charge, save the mere assertion that they have performed an illegal sacrifice? But this will not do for the emperor.

17. "They did not sacrifice, then?" will be the comment. Of course they did, but for a banquet, a dinner, a feast, and the oxen were slaughtered elsewhere: no altar received the blood offering, no single part of the victim was burned, no offering of meal began the ceremony, nor did libations follow it. If people assemble in some beauty spot, slaughter a calf or a sheep, or both, and boil or roast it, and then lie down on the ground and eat it, I do not see that they have broken the laws at all. 18. You, Sire, have put no legal ban on these acts. By banning the performance of one specific action you automatically permit everything else. So even if they were in the habit of drinking together amid the scent of every kind of incense, they broke no law, nor yet if in their toasts they sang hymns and invoked the gods, unless indeed you intend to use a man's private life as grounds for accusation. 19. It used

to be the custom for country folk to assemble in large numbers at the homes of the village notables at holiday time, to make a sacrifice and then hold a feast. This they did while ever it was permitted to do so, and thereafter all the rest, with the exception of sacrifice, remained permissible. So, summoned on the usual day, they dutifully honoured it and the shrine in a manner that involved no risk. That they also thought fit to offer sacrifice no single person has ever said or heard, alleged convincingly or believed. Nor yet could any of their enemies assert that he either had personally witnessed a sacrifice or could produce an informant about one. But if he had these proofs, or even one of them, who would have put up with arrests, a hue and cry, and charges made by these people, not in Flavianus' court but in a real court of law? For they might expect more success in doing away with sacrifices if they did away with some individuals who had performed them. 20. But it is not their way, they will say, to hand a man over to execution, even though he be guilty of the most heinous crime. I forebear to mention the numbers they have murdered in their riotings in utter disregard of the name they share, in case such incidents be described as due to over-hasty action: but your expulsion of people who by their personal care provided relief for poverty among old men and women and fatherless children, the majority of them suffering from severe physical handicaps – is not this murder? Isn't it execution? Isn't this sentencing them to death, and to a death worse than ever, by starvation? For when their means of support have gone, this is surely the fate in store for them. Then in massacring their protectors, you have been massacring these innocents, but you wouldn't dream of doing so if they had broken the law! This by-passing of the courts of law is proof that their victims did not offer sacrifice. This killing without trial is a confession that there are no good grounds to try them.

21. And if they prate to me of the teachings of the scriptures that they profess to obey, I will counter them with the despicable acts they have committed.

Letters

A hallmark of Libanius' letters is their *charis*, or grace. That is, he strove to find just the right words and phrases for the recipient and the occasion. In *Letter 6, To Aristaenetus*, Libanius is writing to a close friend. He begins by expressing his grief upon learning that Aristaenetus' wife had died from an undisclosed illness. After acknowledging that there is nothing he can do to console his friend, Libanius goes on to share events of the last few months, perhaps hoping in this way to ease Aristaenetus' grief. *Letter 6* is followed by *Letter 8*, which was written after Libanius learned that the passage of time had not solved the pain of Aristaenetus' loss. He gently chides his friend for mourning excessively and urges him to seek consolation.

The recipient of *Letter 3*, Hierocles, was another friend who had suffered a loss, the death of his nephew. This letter well illustrates how Libanius applied his rhetorical training to epistolography, for the body is essentially a short funeral oration similar in many respects to the much longer *Funeral Oration over Julian*.

Reading 42

Letters 6, 8, & 3

Letters 6, 8, & 3, pp. 363–71, 373–5, 343–51 (Greek on even-numbered pages omitted) reprinted by permission of the publishers and Trustees of the Loeb Classical Library from *Libanius: Autobiography and Selected Letters*, Volume I, Loeb Classical Library Volume 478, translated by A.F. Norman (Cambridge, MA: Harvard University Press, 1992). © 1992 by the President and Fellows of Harvard College. The Loeb Classical Library ® is a registered trademark of the President and Fellows of Harvard College.

6. To Aristaenetus

1. When I heard of your wife's sickness, I sympathized as I reflected how you were sure to feel about her illness, and on learning of her death I groaned aloud for I grieved that Aristaenetus, for whom festivals are more fitting, should be in mourning. 2. I set out to console you with an oration, but then I stopped myself, for I was afraid that, though seeming to know you through and through, I should then be found not to know you at all. For the words with which I intended to console you, those quotations from Pindar and Simonides and all the passages from the tragedians which we normally adduce as a cure for grief, all these, it seemed to me, you knew long ago and would repeat them to other people. 3. I reflected, then, that if these were the means to assuage your grief, you would be your own physician, and if not, then for someone else to utter them would be labour in vain. Hence, I put this aside, and give you a report of the events which have occurred during the winter. 4. I began my teaching with a prologue and a competitive passage against a bit of Demosthenes. The first was a plea to Fortune for my stay here to be confirmed, while the competitive piece contained many variations. When I set up in practice, seventeen students attended me. "Plato, I believe, was ill" – the good Zenobius, that is. 5. Then I settled down to teaching, and they came in droves, citizens and strangers and those who wanted to know what I was like at this job too, for it had been agreed that I was a composer of no bad orations, but now this other aspect was under examination. 6. Some people thought that in this I was no worse, others that I was better even, and in consequence in a few days my class numbered fifty. I had no time for lunch, but had to work on until evening, and it was a source of surprise, besides everything else, that I controlled my belly. 7. Strategius arrived, and I welcomed him with a short speech – normal procedure, to my mind, in an address of welcome – but it gained his approval when delivered, and that of others too. My rival – I give him the description which he gives himself – threatened to deliver a speech, but his discourse went no further than his promise. 8. Then, seeing that the pedagogues ruled the roost from the sale of their students and that discipline in the schools had been ruined, I counselled my fellow citizens not to turn a blind eye to this, but to resent and stop it; and no little anger was directed against the culprits. My rival threatened to speak in their support. Here too his discourse went no further than his promise. 9. Zenobius died, and after his funeral I composed a monody; and a little later I produced a eulogy of my teacher in a longer speech, and it was felt that he had won no little reward. My rival promised to deliver a speech if his father died – but he is alive still. At this, those who had firmly made up their minds to be stubborn as mules – there were three who behaved so in return for his lavish hospitality – finally gave in. 10. Although I began to be in need of a rest, my uncle would have none of it, it seemed; Quirinus too was one of those who kept me up to scratch. His son is a pupil of mine, and he is like you in his attitude towards me, and like me towards you. 11. I took part in a declamation on one of those contrived topics, and they began to dance for joy, since that is what they had been brought up in, and when I reached the middle of the oration they began to ask me to write its rebuttal too with the same technique. I did so, and produced it as soon as I could. The oration was twin to the previous one, and my enemies were shaken to the core. 12. In fear that he would be stripped of everything, he entered the lists with the idea of checking the flow of desertions, but he actually caused some that would never have happened, had he kept quiet. For in his introduction he begged permission to relate his conclusion, but Quirinus refused, so he gave himself permission to jump this gap. And from that day, he has sat there alone, and the oaths, and all the constraints and bonds and everything else he relied upon to retain his students, have been trampled upon and melted away. 13. After that, a despatch from the emperor arrived, summoning me to return, to which I replied that, owing to migraine and kidney trouble, I could not. Having so settled this, I delivered an oration "On Genius," a kind of diatribe, the sort of thing you adore. It needed a second day for its delivery, and Clematius participated in that. 14. It is not my place to speak of his emotion at it. But *this* I *could* say and it was widely reported, that Aristaenetus had been my tutor in this, and indeed of all else that merited praise.

8. To Aristaenetus

1. I am told that your grief has got the better of you and that you spend all your time at her grave. If you were not in mourning I would reprove you; similarly, now that you mourn so excessively, I do not approve. That would have been out of keeping with your character; this is out of keeping with your upbringing. 2. So if you need some consolation from someone else besides, Olympius will provide it. He is good at freeing both souls and bodies from their ills.

3. To Hierocles

1. If laziness consists of a wilful refusal to do as much as one can, I am far from being blamed for it, for although my letter was briefer than the occasion warranted, I could not write more because of illness. 2. Yet be assured that the ill-feeling you have come to entertain for this man is a great blow to me. For to see people who should be in complete harmony at odds with one another, and to be pained at the occurrence without being able to stop it is obviously to be accounted a disaster by myself, your brothers, and all who entertain goodwill towards you. 3. But even worse than this is the death of Chromatius, by Zeus and the gods – I repeat, of Chromatius. He was a credit to Palestine, by reason of his birth there, and to Athens, by reason of his ready acceptance of its learning. 4. He was a glory to his family, a haven of refuge to his friends. Of all the men I know he gained most admiration and least envy. He startled with his eloquence, and attracted with his character, for in himself he was both an able orator and a good man. 5. What should I first call to mind? what should be the first reason for me to lament his passing? Our sojourn under the same roof at Athens? the way that we shared a single table, the same enjoyments, the same deliberations? or how we acted as whetstone to each other by our mutual criticism? 6. But at the time of my first homecoming, he excelled everyone in the applause and other marks of appreciation which are thought to be of service to the professorial station. Moreover, he urged me to return home again, and upon my arrival was worth many a supporter. 7. And this he did, though he knew that, through his devotion to me, he would annoy a certain person; but for all that, it did not distract him

from his courageous support of me that some reproach from someone or other would surely follow, but he generously acted as he thought was just, and those persons who expected him to oblige them by acting unjustly he shook off as being of not very sound disposition. 8. During such efforts on my behalf he fell ill, and though oppressed by such affliction, he endured it in silence. Then he rose from his bed and set out to Cilicia – and to his death. And the place to which he had removed, and which previously seemed so pleasant, now, as you can imagine, I felt to be utterly unfriendly. 9. When I first heard the news, I was struck dumb for a very long time, and when I could utter a word, the first words I uttered were that the noblest being on earth had passed away, a man more prudent than Peleus, no less dear to god than Sophocles, able in speech, better in judgement, a true friend, in no way inferior to those Syracusans who gave testimony to their fidelity in the tyranny of Dionysius. 10. Such was the story I told, Hierocles, amid my tears. Then in consequence of the very cause of my tears, I somehow came to consider that there was, after all, no need for tears, for to have lived a life of such nobility is consolation for his death. His fate is common to all men, but the objects for which he is praised are not. 11. Indeed you should rather rejoice at having had such a nephew and son-in-law than be shocked at his death. Reflect that everything happens by will of the gods, and that gods would never harm a man of such virtue, for they are just and would never punish one whom they ought to honour. 12. He died, surely, not in order to suffer some dire fate, but for better things. It seems to me that they regarded him as too good for a life on earth and as fitted for their own company, and so translated him from here to heaven. That is the way you must think of it too, and persuade your daughter to do the same, and you must believe that your ability to endure this is fitting tribute to his high qualities. 13. I could say more too upon the death of my companion, but there is no need, for it would be a tale told to one who knows already. As regards the disturbance here, my care is to have it allayed, and your part is no small one. Such occurrences require sound sense, and you, if anyone is, are renowned for sense. 14. Then, just as I would call upon you, if you were a helmsman, to show your skill in time of storm, so, since you hold the palm for your tact, reconcile one who is angered.

Introduction to Augustine (354–430 AD)

Augustine is difficult for readers today because his works seem very modern in the way they focus on the individual and at the same time somewhat alien in the way they relate all experiences to God. Adding to the difficulty is the complexity of Augustine's thinking and writing, which is so remarkable that it has produced centuries of commentary and analysis. His most important works are widely considered to be:

- *Confessions* (Confessiones), an extended prayer that recounts his life to the time of his conversion and assumption of ecclesiastical duties.
- *On Christian Doctrine* (De Doctrina Christiana), a treatise on how to teach and interpret the Scriptures.
- *On the Trinity (De Trinitae)*, a treatise explaining the Nicene Creed and the nature of the Holy Trinity.

- *City of God (De Civitae Dei)*, a treatise conceived as a defense against charges that the Christian suppression of pagan religions was responsible for the sack of Rome in 410, it developed into an interpretation of history and Scripture designed to show their congruence and how historical events led ineluctably to the founding of the Church and that will lead ultimately to the establishment of God's divine city.

Modern readers often fail to appreciate fully the influence of Augustine's writing because a large number of his ideas have become embedded in the Western world's cultural framework. But many of these ideas were controversial during his lifetime and continue to be so today. His call for the rejection of reason in favor of faith and ecclesiastical authority may be perceived as marking the end of the Classical Period and the beginning of the Middle Ages. As a principal source for Catholic doctrine, he was largely responsible for the concept of Original Sin and for the view that human nature is inherently and inescapably sinful.[9] He also developed perhaps the most comprehensive argument for the contested notion of predestination, basing it on his assessment that God exists in a timeless present in which there is neither past nor future and that He therefore had knowledge of Adam's sin before the sin occurred and also knew the fixed number of fallen men who would be saved at the end of the world and human time. Even more controversial was his concept of free will, which for Adam and Eve consisted of the ability to choose between good and evil but which was lost forever after the Fall, leaving man with only the ability to choose between one sin or another.

If anyone warrants the characterization of a "God-intoxicated man," it is Augustine. After his conversion, he viewed everything through the lens of his faith. In *De Civitae Dei*, he applied a quasi-political framework to his interpretation of the Scriptures that related history to the founding of the Church and the establishment of God's divine city, in which the saved would live eternally in peace and happiness (see von Heyking, 2001). In *De Doctrina Christiana*, he argued that all secular learning had to be subordinated to Scriptures and that it had no validity unless it furthered understanding of the Bible. In *Confessions*, he took the additional step of claiming that all life experiences should be seen as a means of moving closer to the divine.

---

[9] Kirwan (1989) argued that Augustine's doctrine of Original Sin was based, ironically, on a faulty translation of St. Paul's writings. Scriptural support for the concept of Original Sin is sparse, existing in only five texts.

Deane (1963) argued that, despite Augustine's voluminous oeuvre, he never produced a systematic treatment of his views on law, justice, obedience, or even theology. The reason is that, according to Deane, Augustine's writing is highly polemical, produced almost entirely in response to circumstances, often designed to suppress what he saw as heresy or an attack on Catholicism. Augustine's concept of predestination, for example, emerged in his attack on the Donatists, a Christian sect that claimed to have established a church of the saved and the pure, which clearly implied that Catholics had not. In Deane's assessment: "[S]ystem building and architectonic skill were not his forte; he is the master of the phrase or the sentence that embodies a penetrating insight ...; he is the rhetorician, the epigrammist, the polemicist, but not the patient, logical, systematic philosopher" (p. viii). Whether or not one accepts Deane's assessment, it is the case that Augustine's views on issues of law and justice – even his theology – are not always easily extracted from his writing, and efforts to do so leave much to interpretation, making the achievement of clarity difficult and tempting readers to impose a system where one may not exist. Rejecting rational processes, Augustine grounded his method in faith and love. Yet theory demands ratiocination. Some might argue that these powerful pathetic influences, evident in all his writing, served as a significant obstacle to developing systematic theory.

The frenetic pace at which Augustine had to work and his ceaseless self-questioning and reflection on complex issues added to the problem. His thought evolved over time, and he was unable (or did not choose) to make revisions to earlier work, which resulted in certain inconsistencies that can be confusing. This evolution is perhaps most clear in *De Civitae Dei*. Working on the text over some 13 years, Augustine praised Greek philosophy, especially Platonism, in the first 10 books for having many similarities to Christianity, yet after Book X the praise turns to criticism and then hostility, and Augustine ultimately condemns pagan philosophers to eternal punishment at world's end, along with demons and the ungodly. *De Civitae Dei*, following the Gospels, recognizes the legitimacy as well as the utility of the earthly city. Augustine noted that members of the Church will "obey the laws of the earthly city, whereby the things necessary for the maintenance of this mortal life are administered" (XIX.17).[10] Subjecting all life experiences to biblical authority, however, leads to an inherent conflict that is not easily resolved. As von Heyking (2001) pointed out, how can one "articulate transpolitical or transhistorical principles where those very principles seem to be suspended or changed by God's will? For example, how can one's laws prohibit killing when Abraham himself was specifically commanded by God to kill his son?" (p. 3). Augustine also emphasized that God is perfectly at rest, unchanging, existing in the eternal present, without past or future, free from the desires and cares of the mortal plain – but did not clearly explain why an entity so conceived would demand mankind's love. Equally problematic is that in *De Trinitae* Augustine argued that as long as a person acknowledges his dependence on God, recognizes God as the creator of all things, and obeys His commands, he will be happy, yet Augustine's conversion to Christianity did not bring him inner peace or happiness. For all his prayers and devotion, the character of Augustine that emerges from his writing is that of a truly tortured man obsessed with the perception of his own sinfulness.

---

[10]   Deane (1963) argued that Christianity's use of state authority to suppress and eventually eliminate paganism resulted in a change in the perceived role of government. The classical concept of the state as the expression of man's highest values was replaced by the view that the principle role of the state was to punish the wicked. Thus, for Augustine, Plato's vision of the perfect earthly society in *The Republic* was impossible; such perfection could only be found in the *civitas Dei*, the city of God. The significance of this new perception cannot be overestimated: It marked a shift in the West from an emphasis on individuals as members of a sociopolitical entity to an emphasis on individuals as members of a religious entity.

Augustine's early life

As in the case of Libanius, a great deal of what we know about Augustine comes from his autobiography, *Confessiones*, usually translated as *Confessions*.[11] He was born in the town of Thagaste, in modern-day Algeria, to parents of modest circumstances, with a brother and possibly a sister (Chadwick, 1986). Augustine's mother, Monica, was a devout Catholic, whereas his father, Patricius, if he had any religious inclinations at all, was a pagan who seems to have become a catechumen late in life to appease his wife. Although in *Confessions* Augustine discussed his mother in detail, the silence surrounding his father is palpable, and consequently we know little about him (we know nothing at all about the brother other than that he appeared at his mother's deathbed).

The few comments in *Confessions* suggest that Augustine was never close to his father but was instead a "momma's boy." In Book II, he described his father as *municipis Thagastensis admodum tenuis*, "a quite insignificant citizen of Thagaste."[12] In light of the fact that the family owned income-generating property, van Oort (1991) interpreted this statement to mean that Patricius was a member of the town council, but this is uncertain. What is certain is that Patricius' circumstances were strained. Consequently, he received the praise of friends and associates for spending well beyond his means "so that his son could be equipped with what was necessary" (*Confessions*, II.3) for the long journey to Carthage, where Augustine would begin advanced studies.[13] Rather than feeling appreciation for what must have been significant sacrifices, Augustine complained that his father was "not at all interested in how I was growing up in ... [God's] sight or whether I was chaste or not" (II.3) – which seems an unusual criticism to level against a pagan who had become a reluctant convert only near the end of his life. Also revealing is that Patricius died when Augustine was 17 or 18, but there is no expression of grief in *Confessions* at his father's passing.

It appears that Patricius recognized his son's exceptional intelligence, was proud of him, and did everything possible to provide him with a good education. At Carthage, Augustine studied oratory and law, with the aim of becoming a jurist. Education in the Western Empire at this time was thoroughly Latin, focusing on Cicero and Roman poets such as Terence and Virgil. Untranslated Greek works (few and far between) probably were not part of the reading: The bilingualism that had characterized Rome during the time of Cicero had eroded so significantly that there were relatively few in the West who were proficient in Greek (Herrin, 1987), which may explain Augustine's hatred of his instruction in the language as a boy (*Confessions*, I.13) and why he seems never to have mastered it (Brown, 1967; Marrou, 1938). His

[11] Whether this work truly is an autobiography is the subject of debate (e.g., Brown, 1967; Condon, 2001; Olney, 1998). Also, Wills (1999) translated the title as *The Testimony*, arguing that *Confessions* is a transliteration, or modern homology, of *Confessiones* that fails to capture the full meaning of the original Latin. Missing from the translation into *Confessions* is the connotation of "acknowledgment" in the original, but "testimony" is *testimonium* in Latin, which suggests that Wills' choice is not quite right, either. In the Pine-Coffin translation selected for this text, "confession" appears repeatedly where the word "acknowledge" provides a slightly better fit.

[12] Note that Pine-Coffin rendered *tenuis* as "modest," whereas I translated it here as "insignificant," which I believe is more in keeping with Augustine's attitude toward his father and thus a better choice. Worth considering in this regard is Condon's (2001) argument that Patricius is among the "unnamed and defaced" figures in *Confessions*.

[13] We learn from another work, *Contra Academicos*, that when Patricius' resources proved inadequate, his patron, Romanianus, contributed significantly to funding Augustine's education.

knowledge of the Greek canon therefore was limited, and there is no indication that he had a grasp of *paideia*, which indicates that his education was significantly different from what students received in the school of Libanius or from the rhetoricians in Athens and Constantinople. When he mentioned Greek works – for example, Aristotle's *Categories* in *Confessions* IV.16 – he most likely was referring to Latin translations, and his failure to locate this particular work in the context of Aristotle's broader investigation into the nature of being in *Metaphysics* suggests that they may not have been particularly good translations. He knew the basics of arithmetic and geometry, but his "science" consisted merely of a passing fascination with supposed *mirabilia* – "miracles."

The quality of Augustine's education in rhetoric and oratory is a matter of some debate. Completely missing is the broad education advocated by Quintilian. With Cicero the focus of the curriculum, Brown (1967), Marrou (1938), and O'Meara (1990), for example, argued that, essentially cut off from the Greek intellectual tradition, instruction focused on close reading of a limited number of Latin texts, with an emphasis on memorization. Students would repeatedly study a text word by word, dissecting it to analyze the relations between structure and meaning. The entire process must have been tedious in the extreme, which no doubt explains Augustine's harsh criticism of rhetorical education.

Experiencing the hormonal rush of adolescence, Augustine wanted to marry, but his parents objected on the grounds that he must finish his education and probably also that he was too young. But freed from the surveillance and restrictions of home when he arrived in Carthage, Augustine met a young woman, fell in love, and began cohabiting with her. They called the child that was soon born of their union Adeodatus.[14] Even though Augustine and the mother of his son were together for about 15 years, they never married, perhaps owing to his mother's resistance to seeing him wed a woman lacking social standing.[15]

In the course of his studies, his life's path was altered when he read a work of Cicero's called *Hortensius*, now lost except for a few fragments. These fragments suggest that *Hortensius* was a treatise on philosophy that reflected Stoic influences insofar as it advocated that the only meaningful purpose in life was the pursuit of happiness through emotional detachment and the pursuit of wisdom through reason. Augustine's encounter with *Hortensius* – and no doubt the constant exhortations of his mother – moved him to begin studying the Bible in earnest. During his boyhood, Augustine was a catechumen (I.11), but it seems that this religious instruction did not penetrate deeply. His study of the Bible was a disappointing experience. The biblical writing was inferior to the Latin classics, and he noted that it "seemed to me unworthy of comparison with the grand style of Cicero" (*Confessions*, III.5).

After completing his education, Augustine became a teacher of rhetoric and oratory, first in Thagaste, then in Carthage, achieving some success. Contrasting his

[14] Willis (1999) speculated that this liaison began in Thagaste, not Carthage. Where they met, however, seems less significant than the fact that Augustine was able to continue and complete his studies uninterrupted by the birth of his son. Even assuming that he had minimal involvement in child rearing, the financial strain must have been considerable, raising the question of whether (and why) his patron Romanianus agreed to foot the bill.

[15] The similar circumstances of Libanius and Augustine with regard to their relationships is worth noting. Libanius decided to forgo marriage because he felt that he was wedded to rhetoric. There is no evidence that he had any other woman in his life after the mother of his son died. Augustine's situation was more complex. He abandoned the mother of his son and found a replacement whom he dismissed in turn as soon as he was baptized, at which point he took a vow of chastity and essentially was wedded to the Church.

teaching career with Libanius is unavoidable. In a perpetual state of emotional and intellectual turmoil, Augustine must have found it difficult to concentrate on teaching, and he seems to have disliked most of his students. Nevertheless, he sensed that the world was opening to him, and it stimulated his ambition. He decided to move to Rome, where the fees for teaching oratory were much higher than they were in Carthage, where he could advance his reputation, and where the students were not as rowdy. To do so, however, he had to devise a way to escape from his mother, whom he recognized clung to him in an unnatural way. Only by deceiving her, in the dead of night, could he and his family board the boat that would take them to Rome.

Ambrose and Neoplatonism

Augustine's investigations into spirituality and his quest for what he identified as true happiness led him to Manichaeism, a dualistic religion from Persia that had attracted a large number of followers and that had embraced many of Christianity's fundamental beliefs. One of the doctrinal difficulties that Christianity faced was reconciling the existence of evil in a world created by a being that is all good as well as all powerful. Proposing that evil emerged out of goodness creates an ontological contradiction, and clearly an all powerful God has the ability to eliminate evil with merely a thought. The fact that evil exists in the world therefore suggests that evil did not emerge out of goodness but rather existed from the beginning; and the fact that evil continues to exists suggests that God lacks the power to end it. Manichaeism proposed a solution: There were two co-equal forces – or gods – in the universe, one good, the other evil, one a force of light, the other a force of darkness. These gods are in perpetual battle, which explains why good and evil coexist in the world.

Augustine was a follower of this religion for nearly a decade, and it seemed to appeal to his early, logical view of the universe. When he arrived in Rome, he was able to trade on his affiliation with Manichaeism to gain the attention of Symmachus, Prefect of Rome. Symmachus, a pagan, was caught up in a losing contest to preserve the old gods, and he used his position to lobby (unsuccessfully) a succession of Christian emperors to honor tradition (see Sogno, 2006). At every turn, he was opposed by Bishop Ambrose, whose remarkable influence over the emperors was enhanced by the fact that the seat of imperial government was no longer in Rome but in Milan, giving him easy access to the emperor and his court. Symmachus was eager to find some way to counter Ambrose's influence, and when the chair of rhetoric for the city of Milan became vacant, he saw an opportunity in Augustine. As holder of the chair, Augustine the Manichaean would have regular contact with the imperial court and thus opportunities to use his oratorical abilities to sway the Emperor into preserving some measure of pre-Christian religious tolerance. By serving as Augustine's patron in the matter of securing the chair, Symmachus would have counted on his client's willingness to cooperate.

Symmachus could never have anticipated, however, that Ambrose would quickly sweep Augustine up and make him his own. Augustine had grown skeptical of Manichaeism, finding certain flaws in its doctrines and a lack of intellect in its leaders. He also may have come to doubt Manichaeism's dualism, which suggested that evil is a material force in the world. Arriving in Milan to take up his position, he attended some of Ambrose's services. Like many other well-educated Christians, Ambrose was drawn to Neoplatonism, which grew out of attempts to merge Plato's philosophical system with religion.[16] Ambrose's sermons, such as *On Isaac and the Soul* and *On the Goodness of Death*, illustrate that he was well acquainted with Neoplatonism, and the effect on Augustine was immediate (see Starnes, 1990). Caught inextricably in the Christian revolution now, he underwent what Foucault (1990) characterized as a great turn inward, and his upbringing made him especially sensitive to the complex mysticism of this philosophy. He delved into the intricacies of Neoplatonism and promptly began experiencing a spiritual crisis exacerbated by the arrival of his dogged mother.

Conversion and baptism

In Milan, Catholicism became more attractive to Augustine daily, and he began establishing a network of friends and associates who were connected to the Church and the imperial court. Growing more aware of his position and the opportunities it afforded him, he realized that in due time he might well use his influential friends to obtain the governorship of a province and that he could then "marry a wife with money so that she would not increase my expenses" (*Confessions*, VI.11).

His mother encouraged these ambitions (*Confessions*, VI.13), and Augustine probably drew on his connections to identify a suitable marriage partner, a young girl aged 10 from an affluent family. Because the girl was too young to marry, the betrothal was scheduled to last 2 years, at the end of which she would be of legal age and the wedding could proceed.[17] Augustine's mother apparently insisted that he break with the woman who had been at his side since his student days and who was the mother of his child. Failure to do so was an impediment to his marriage. Augustine never named her, but he did relate that his companion returned to North Africa and spent the rest of her life in a convent. Though he grieved for her, Augustine, characterizing himself as "a slave to lust," soon found another woman to take her place. Adeodatus, intellectually gifted and now about 15, stayed in Milan with his father, only to die of unknown causes a year or so later.

Even as Augustine was laying the foundation for a new life, his spiritual crisis deepened. During a break in the school year, he and a small group of friends traveled to the countryside to meditate and reflect on their lives. Augustine was by now fairly certain that he wanted to be baptized into the Catholic Church and that he wanted to be a priest, but his fondness for the things of the nonspiritual world, especially sexual pleasure, held him back. In the courtyard of his retreat, he threw himself on the ground, weeping and chastising himself for his weakness. He thought he heard a child's voice in a nearby house saying *"tolle lege, tolle lege"* – "take it and read it, take it and read it"

---

[16] Origen of Alexandria (c. 185–232) was among the first to attempt this merger. He applied his thorough knowledge of classical Greek philosophy to a number of Christianity's central tenets. In his is most influential work, *On First Principles*, he drew on Middle Platonic triadic emanation schemata to develop the doctrine of the Trinity, replacing the Platonic terms of *monad*, *dyad*, and *world-soul* with "Father," "Christ," and "Holy Spirit." He viewed the Father, however, as an incorporeal mind existing in perfect unity that applied itself through *logos*, which he identified as Christ the Son. The Holy Spirit "proceeds from the Son" and is subordinate to him. The problem for Origen was that this view of the Trinity was in conflict with the Nicene Creed, and he eventually was denounced as a heretic for denying the coequal status of God, Jesus, and the Holy Spirit. Also worth noting is that Origen believed in the preexistence of souls and their eventual restoration or return to God (*apokatastasis*), a view that Augustine came to reject vigorously.

[17] Hopkins (1965) noted that "As late as A.D. 530 and at least as far back as the reign of Augustus, the legal minimum age of marriage for girls was 12" (p. 313). His review of the epigraphic evidence from 325 female funeral stones showed that more than a third of the Christian and non-Christian girls had married before the age of 13 and that 3 percent of the Christian girls, apparently in violation of the law, had married before the age of 12.

(*Confessions*, VIII.12). He picked up his copy of the New Testament, opened it at random, and his eyes came upon Romans 13.13–14, in which Paul urged the abandonment of earthly pleasures for Jesus Christ. This experience signaled his conversion. Shortly thereafter, he broke off his betrothal, resigned his position as city rhetorician, was baptized, made a priest, and sent to Hippo to shepherd the small Catholic community there. Four years later, he was named bishop of Hippo, one of several hundred bishops in North Africa.

Hippo was a backwater farming community, so isolated that most of the common people working the farms outside the town did not speak Latin (Brown, 1967). Beyond the farms were the nomads and herders who had never been absorbed into the Empire and who were largely untouched by the Christian revolution. Augustine did not venture into their territory. This isolation may have been an important factor in his professional life. The usual distractions of a vibrant city were absent (although he traveled to Carthage at least once a year), and he was able to focus his considerable energies on producing a voluminous body of work, of which more than 100 major texts, 200 letters, and nearly 500 sermons are extant. To expedite production, he dictated to a team of shorthand transcribers, who took down his words and then turned them over to copyists. The total output is remarkable, especially considering that he had other responsibilities. He gave sermons daily and managed a range of ecclesiastical duties. Moreover, in 407, Emperor Honorius gave bishops judicial authority to enforce the laws against Jews, pagans, and heretics, which meant that Augustine frequently spent entire days hearing court cases. The obvious disadvantage of being isolated, however, was that it deprived Augustine of the vibrant intellectual give-and-take that provides scholars with the stimulation they need if the are to sharpen and refine their ideas. He had to make do with correspondence, which the lack of an organized postal service rendered haphazard.

Although Augustine identified himself as a Christian, his writing is not clearly Christocentric. Given the importance Augustine gave to the Pauline texts, his corpus could easily be characterized as Paulocentric (see Martin, 2000), but doing so may mask the tension that necessarily underlies attempts to reconcile the Old and New Testaments and their different portrayals of God. Like Libanius, as Augustine aged his thinking became more rigid, his view of life and human nature more negative. Mirroring the New Testament, *Confessions* expresses the hopeful optimism that love and devotion to God offer a path to happiness and salvation. As he wrote *De Civitae Dei* toward the end of his life, optimism gave way to harsh predestinationism and what may be considered an Old Testament perspective. His glorification of God's love and mercy not withstanding, Augustine argued in *De Civitae Dei* that there is nothing a person can do to ensure salvation. Christian and non-Christian alike are condemned as *massa damnata* – the damned masses – who will suffer God's just and eternal punishment at the end of the world. Decades of battling those who disagreed with Catholic doctrine had taken a toll, and with the barbarians savaging Rome, the Old Testament God was ascendant.

Augustine and allegoresis

Augustine did not pursue the philosophical path to fulfillment, but Neoplatonism nevertheless shaped his thinking for the rest of his life, particularly with respect to allegory. Although Neoplatonism purported to be a representation of Plato's philosophy, it actually was a distorted, and in many respects original, reconstruction by Plotinus (c. 204–270) and his student Prophyry (c. 233–304). Their writing was convoluted, difficult, but it gave Augustine a new perspective on the problem of evil, which the Neoplatonists maintained was merely a departure from innate goodness, not a material force. He gained from this perspective the hope that he could rid himself of what he viewed obsessively as his own inclination toward evil and thus find the inner goodness that connected him to the divine.[18] This hope began to fade, however, when further reading of Plotinus' *Enneads* emphasized that a lifetime of disciplined intellectual toil was required to guide the soul to its true state in what was called the "Intelligible Realm," where the soul could contemplate "the One," the supreme principle that defies description and definition. Freeman (2002) concluded that Augustine's enthusiasm for Neoplatonism was thus irreparably damaged because he "yearned for a more immediate means of bridging the gap between the human soul and the incorporeal God" (p. 281).

Drawing on Porphyry, Ambrose had embraced allegoresis, the use of allegory as an interpretive tool, to comprehend the Bible. Allegoresis first emerged in Greece as a way of defending poetry and myth against the new proto-scientific thinking that tended to dismiss both as nonsensical (and often immoral) stories (see Clarke, 1996). Something was lost, it was thought, when texts describing Zeus hurling his thunderbolts came to be understood as an allegorical representation of a natural phenomenon, not as the god's anger. Ford (2002) traced allegoresis in the third century to Porphyry's commentary on Homer: "When the Iliad recounts how the Olympians descended to the Trojan plain to fight one another…, Porphyry observes that Homer's 'unsuitable' stories about the gods could be defended by appealing to his 'mode of expression (*lexis*), holding that everything is spoken by way of allegory (*allêgoria*)'" (p. 68).

No doubt following this lead, Ambrose argued that the Scriptures must be understood as allegories requiring interpretation to make them comprehensible, which assuaged Augustine's discomfort regarding what he saw as the Bible's stylistic irregularities, logical flaws, and frequent lapses in morals. His rhetorical training had schooled him well in hermeneutics, so interpretation was not new to him. But Ambrose's approach relied on sheer imagination, freeing interpretation from the text.

It swept through Augustine's mind like a cleansing wind.[19] As a student of rhetoric, he no doubt had learned that allegory was related to structure, a figure of speech like metaphor and synecdoche. Donatus, writing in the fourth century, included allegory as a trope in his widely influential *Ars Grammatica* (Kennedy, 1980), classifying it as an

---

[18] Augustine thought of himself as being among the worst of sinners, and *Confessions* too often has been used to characterize him as a libertine. An objective reading of the text, however, shows that he was not. Even though he made much of this theft of some pears as a boy, this act would have been deemed petty by most of his contemporaries. Despite his obvious interest in sex, he was clearly not licentious. He began living with the mother of this son and was faithful to her for 15 years. When she returned to Africa, he began a new relationship, but it was short-lived. Thus the sum total of his sexual experience appears to have been limited to two women.

[19] Neoplatonism also influenced Augustine's approach to the Trinity. Ambrose was a hard-line supporter of the Nicene Creed, which 60 years after the Council of Nicea continued to be a topic of great controversy owing to the fact that the concept of the Trinity had little if any scriptural support, as critics eagerly pointed out. (Ambrose produced a defense of the Creed, *De Fide*, around 380, using his hermeneutic approach to argue that Jesus and God were of the same substance and thus coequal.) Indeed, Arianism seemed in many respects stronger than ever, having been embraced not only by many leading intellectuals but also by the northern barbarians, the Vandals and the Goths. The fact that Christian leaders – generally men of good faith – struggled with the Creed is evidence that the concept is not easy to grasp. Plotinus had wrestled with a similar problem and provided both Ambrose and Augustine a useful model. He argued that the supreme principle – the One – emanates into multiple manifestations; it is simultaneously one and many, "begetting" itself into "intelligence," which is the source of "Being" and "Soul." To make sense of this problematic ontology, Plotinus relied on mysticism to claim that the One was not accessible through reason but had to be approached through intuition and prayer. This rejection of reason and reliance on intuition, or faith, was entirely compatible with Christian doctrine, particularly the teaching of Paul, with whom Augustine felt a special bond.

element of style. Ambrose's use of allegory, however, whether he was aware of it or not, went beyond allegoresis; it drew on an older approach – *hyponoia*, the ability to find deeper levels of meaning hidden below the surface meaning. (In *Symposium*, for example, Socrates belittled rhapsodes because they merely sang a poem without knowing the *hyponoiai* of the work.) Tracing the transition of allegory into rhetoric as a figure that was more complex than a simple substitution of one meaning for another, Cole (1991) stated: "When the rhetorically transmitted meaning is not a simple extension of the meaning [that] a text would have if it were put forward in a perfectly straightforward, nonrhetorical way, it can easily be supplied from textual context or referential situation. If it cannot, this is a sign that the text has failed as rhetoric" (p. 57). *Hyponoia* did not meet this criterion, nor did Ambrose's or Augustine's allegorical interpretations of Scripture. Their free interpretation was simply incongruent with rhetorical allegory. It signaled a reversal to the realm of *mythos* in which all things – but especially the Bible – are imbued with mystical hidden meanings that have little relation to the textual context or referential situation. Moreover, this approach treated the Bible as a work of literature insofar as it became an object for the application of hermeneutical critical tools. Ford's (2002) comment on the Greek literary tradition seems relevant here: "hermeneutics arises in heavily literate cultures that need to understand texts whose author is absent" (p. 81). The contention that the Bible contained eternal, albeit hidden, truths had lasting implications for all literature and for the entire hermeneutic enterprise.

We find a cursory treatment of allegoresis in *Confessions* XII.18, where Augustine wrote:

> Provided, therefore, that each of us tries as best he can to understand in the Holy Scriptures what the writer meant by them, what harm is there if a reader believes what you, the Light of all truthful minds, show him to be the true meaning? It may not even be the meaning which the writer had in mind, and yet he too saw in them a true meaning, different though it may have been from this.

His formal treatment, however, appears in *De Doctrina Christiana*, where Augustine noted that words are "signs," of which there are two classes, "natural" and "conventional." Signs can be approached on two levels, "what they are in themselves" and "what they signify" (II.1). Words are conventional signs, and the words of the Scriptures are obscure because they were "divinely arranged for the purpose of subduing pride by toil" (II.6). Augustine wrote that fear of God, piety, and knowledge of the Holy canon are key factors in biblical interpretation, but the central guiding principle is that interpretation must be congruent with "the judgment of the greater number of Catholic Churches" (II.8) – that is, all interpretation is free as long as it supports Church doctrine.

De Doctrina Christiana expressed Augustine's view that the process of free interpretation was a discovery procedure that led to truth, however multifaceted it might be. With respect to Scriptures, two governing factors made this view conceivable: (1) the conviction that the Scriptures were absolutely true, thus making it impossible for a person of faith and goodwill to produce falsehood in any interpretation; and (2) the proposition that interpretations should be shared only with Christians, who were predisposed to receive the truth. On this basis, Patton (1977) and Troup (1999) argued that Augustine viewed interpretation as rhetorical invention that aimed to provide an adaptation of the biblical text to match the beliefs of the audience while simultaneously making the obscure language of the Bible comprehensible. But the depth of Augustine's religious convictions enabled him to transcend conventional notions of allegoresis and thereby see the act of interpretation as a discovery procedure unbound by the dimensions of text. Thus, we find that in *Confessions* he extended the application of free interpretation beyond Scripture to his life, and in *De Civitae Dei* he extended it further to the totality of human history. The result was a rejection of any knowledge that was incongruent with Scripture, as when, arguing against those who suggested that the earth was ancient, he claimed that the earth was less than 6,000 years old (*De Civitae Dei*, XII.10–11). In so doing, Augustine reversed the tradition that had begun with the Melisians, which maintained that the only reality that exists is what can be perceived and that it exists independently of the observer. Stated another way, reality is independent of mind. Augustine, however, saw reality as a subjective invention.

De Doctrina Christiana offers numerous examples that embody this reversal, but only one can be examined here. In Book II, Augustine illustrated how allegory reveals the connection between the Church and Scripture by interpreting a line from the *Song of Solomon* (4.2): "Thy teeth are like a flock of sheep that are shorn, which came up from the washing, whereof every one bears twins, and none is barren among them." The "teeth" are:

"holy men ... of the Church, tearing men away from their errors, and bringing them into the Church's body, with all their harshness softened down, just as if they had been torn off and masticated by the teeth. It is with the greatest pleasure, too, that I recognize them under the figure of sheep that have been shorn, lying down the burdens of the world like fleeces, and coming up from the washing, i.e., from baptism, and all bearing twins, i.e., the twin commandments of love, and none among them barren in that holy fruit" (II.6).

Considering the line from the *Song of Solomon* in its broader context offers some insight into the degree of freedom Augustine's allegoresis entailed:

1 Behold, thou art fair, my love; behold, thou art fair; thou hast doves' eyes within thy locks: Thy hair is as a flock of goats, that appear from Mount Gilead.

2 Thy teeth are like a flock of sheep that are shorn, which came up from the washing; whereof every one bears twins, and none is barren among them.

3 Thy lips are like a thread of scarlet, and thy speech is comely; they temples are like a piece of pomegranate within thy locks.

4 Thy neck is like the tower of David builded for an armoury, whereon there hang a thousand bucklers, all shields of mighty men.

5 Thy two breasts are like two young roes that are twins, which feed among the lilies.

6 Until the day break, and the shadows flee away, I will get me to the mountain of myrrh, and to the hill of frankincense.

7 Thou art all fair, my love; there is no spot in thee.

Rejecting the eroticism inherent in the text, clearly evident in lines 5 and 6, both Jews and Christians viewed the *Song of Solomon* as purely religious allegory. The Jews saw it as an allegorical expression of God's love for his chosen people. The Christians, on the other hand, saw it as an expression of the love relationship between Jesus and the Catholic Church. This issue aside, Augustine's interpretation seems like a far stretch. Perhaps only a herding people can eagerly accept with a warm heart the effort to describe the beauty of a woman's hair by comparing it to a flock of goats coming down from Mount Gilead or imaging the whiteness of her teeth by comparing them to shorn and washed sheep. But after a moment's hesitation, required to adjust one's perspective, the images work easily enough, almost as easily as Shakespeare's comparison of his lover to a summer's day, even though she is more lovely and more temperate. It is a testimony to Augustine's influence that modern readers are likely to applaud his interpretive approach here as a sign of creativity, without considering that it signaled a significant break with classical tradition and conventional reality.

Augustine and rhetoric

Augustine's relation to rhetoric was ambivalent. In *Confessions*, he rejected rhetoric as a manifestation of pride that encouraged men to seek fame and fortune. It sustained the illusion that the material world had value and thus was based on a perpetual lie. The perceived rejection of rhetoric led Troup (1999) to argue that "Augustine effectively dismantled the entire rhetorical system of the Late Roman Empire" (p. 11). But this assessment is difficult to support: In *De Doctrina Christiana*, Augustine stated that it is both wise and "lawful" for the Christian preacher to use rhetoric (IV.2) because it enables him to teach the Gospel and move parishioners to greater belief in God. Nearly everything he knew about rhetoric came from Cicero, but rather than dismantling Cicero Augustine adapted him to match his own needs. In *De Doctrina Christiana*, he embraced Cicero's three styles of oratory, for example, but accepted Quintilian's modification of *probare, delectare,* and *flectere* (to prove, delight, and persuade) to *docere, delectare, movere* (to teach, delight, and move). Cicero's rhetoric was largely forensic, whereas Augustine's was not, so there was need for neither proving nor persuading. His goal was to transform the art so as to create a Christian rhetoric that focused on interpreting the Bible, using allegoresis to teach parishioners and enlisting eloquence to move them to a higher level of receptivity that would allow their hearts to open to God's Word. Thus, what Augustine objected to in *Confessions* was not rhetoric per se but rather its pagan tradition and *paideia*, to which it was linked.

The passion with which Augustine rejected rhetoric of the perpetual lie has a resonance leading some to label his rhetoric as Platonic. Mazzeo (1962), for example, stated that "St. Augustine's analysis of rhetoric reveals an authentic platonism which he recreated out of the contemporary materials furnished by neoplatonists and Academics" (p. 175). Hagendahl (1967) perceived in Augustine a "deep-seated hostility" toward rhetoric that echoed Plato's sentiments (p. 715), and Hartelius (2006) found that Plato and Augustine had much in common with regard to language as a vehicle for learning. Although Neoplatonism's influence certainly gave many of Augustine's views a Platonic flavor, identifying his rhetoric as Platonic is a somewhat exaggerated characterization. Plato would have had little patience with Augustine's assertion that allegoresis, a central feature of Christian rhetoric, leads to knowledge and truth; rhetoric leads to belief but not to truth. Plato no doubt would have advised that if Augustine hoped to discover truth he should employ the dialectical syllogism, not allegoresis. He also would have complained that Christian rhetoric appeals to the emotional, rather than the rational, part of the soul and that it therefore functions to overcome reason. It succeeds because it deals with topics concerning which neither the preacher nor the audience has true knowledge. Augustine's claim that allegoresis provides this knowledge does not stand up to dialectical analysis, nor does it lead to certitude of judgment.[20] On some level, Augustine must have understood this. His claim that the Bible is absolutely true can be seen not only as an affirmation of belief but also as a means of avoiding the problems of uncertainty and relativity inherent in *doxa*. He reduced challenges to the initial premise by preaching to Christians rather than to heathens or

---

[20] An Aristotelian perspective is equally uncharitable: Allegoresis may have certainty of form, but it cannot have certainty of matter. Consequently, Augustine's interpretive technique does not discover truth but serves only as a means of confirming beliefs manifested in its premises, beliefs already held by parishioners.

heretics. For the latter, he accepted the use of force. As Kennedy (1980) noted in this regard, "The function of Christian eloquence in Augustine's system is to convert belief into works, to impel the faithful to the Christian life" (p. 157). That is, preaching did not convert individuals.

But an open heart was necessary if the individual was to receive God's grace. An effective preacher needed to know the Bible, and Augustine viewed rhetoric as a means of gaining wisdom owing to its function as a discovery procedure through interpretation. Biblical knowledge then had to be transferred to parishioners, and Augustine argued that this was accomplished by delighting the audience through eloquence, or style, which therefore assumed a significant role in his reconfiguration of rhetoric. For centuries, rhetorical education had involved the extensive study of rhetorical rules, and students had modeled their style on the classical canon. Libanius, for example, had required his students to study Demosthenes closely. Augustine dismissed the study of rules as being a waste of time and proposed that Scripture, particularly the writings of Paul, offered better stylistic models. Perhaps the most striking feature of Augustine's Christian rhetoric, however, was his abandonment of the concept of *vir bonus*, which had been at the core of rhetorical theory since its beginning in ancient Greece. The ideal preacher was, of course, a good man who lived according to the truth of the Gospels, but for Augustine God's truth transcended the individual orator. Using Paul as an example of a man who initially was bad owing to his persecution of Christians but who, against his will, had been called to spread the Good News, Augustine held that even a bad man could be an excellent preacher, provided God spoke through him.

The significance of Augustine's position on this point is easy to overlook. As shown in the general introductions, the concepts of *aretê* and *kalos kagathos* were central to rhetoric as a sociopolitical tool in Greece, and they were translated into the ideal of *vir bonus* in Rome. The *ethoi* of speaker and speech – the good man speaking well – were wedded in this ideal so as to ensure (in theory, at least) that rhetoric and oratory served the common good of civic virtue. The truth of the speech was measured against the perceived character of the speaker. Augustine's reconfiguration of rhetoric and oratory severed the connection. In Christian rhetoric, the preacher is essentially a conduit of God's eternal truths, and although it is highly desirous that he be a good man in the sense that he is a good Christian, ultimately his character is irrelevant if God chooses to speak through him.

Confessions

Augustine's *Confessions* is commonly accepted as an autobiography, but this assessment fails to do justice to the work. Even a cursory comparison with Libanius' autobiography shows that *Confessions* is something entirely different. Libanius' autobiography is in the classical tradition; it reflects his engagement in the politics and life of the city. *Confessions*, on the other hand, illustrates the Christian turn inward. The focus is on Augustine's internal life, on his inner struggles, and the external world is only minimally present. These characteristics have led some scholars to conclude that *Confessions* does not readily fit into the genre of autobiography. In his introduction to the translation offered here, Pine-Coffin described the work as a long prayer. Brown (1967) also identified it as "a prayer to God that was common to a long tradition in religious philosophy" (p. 159).

Written when Augustine had entered middle age, *Confessions* consists of two parts, only the first of which, books I–IX, contains any autobiographical information. In these books, Augustine looked back on his youth and acknowledged his own sinful nature and unworthiness by recounting events in his life that were a source of shame. When considered in tandem with other works, such as *De Civitae Dei*, Augustine's acknowledgment can be seen as an important component in his views on human nature, rhetoric, theology, and predestination.

One of the more memorable parts of the work is his narration of the theft of pears from an orchard. What makes it memorable is the pettiness of the crime itself contrasted with the extreme remorse and self-recrimination that Augustine expressed as a result of the act, and the power of the narrative easily obscures the message: Evil is inherent in our natures, even in infants, as a result of Adam's Original Sin, perpetuated from generation to generation through sex. Augustine's confession involved opening his heart to receive God's grace, which is a central factor in his rhetorical theory. From this perspective, *Confessions* can be understood as an act of reflexive preaching.

In *De Civitae Dei*, Augustine noted that many Christian converts – indeed, many within the Catholic Church – had not given up their sinful ways and would not be saved. Outwardly, they posed as good Christians, while inwardly they remained prideful and self-centered, attributes that in Augustine's theology lie in the very heart of sin. *Confessions* therefore served also as a teaching instrument to show other members of the Church how to humble themselves before God and their fellow men and how to seek forgiveness. Moreover, the autobiographical portions of the text indicate fairly clearly that the magnitude of one's personal sins is irrelevant, overwhelmed as they are by the weight of Original Sin that condemns all mankind. We can see that the prayerful confession of sin is not unidirectional: In opening his heart and acknowledging his unworthiness, Augustine seemed to be hoping that God *would acknowledge him*.

The last four books of *Confessions* are significantly different from the first nine. If books I–IX can be characterized as a prayer of and for acknowledgment, books X–XIII are a prayer for wisdom. Augustine identified curiosity as a sin of pride, but these books show that his restless mind could not stop seeking answers. Book X is a detailed investigation of memory, whereas Book XI is an exploration of time. Books XII and XIII, on the other hand, are an exegesis of the first chapters of Genesis, presaging Augustine's fuller treatise on allegoresis in *De Doctrina Christiana*.

Books X and XI illustrate Augustine's mind at work as it attempts to use reason alone to unravel two very challenging topics. As Tell (2006) and Teske (2001) noted, the central question of *Confessions* is "How, then, do I look for you, O Lord?" (X.20), and the principal focus of this search is memory, conducted through *verbum mentis*, or the "mental word." The Platonic influence here seems strong, for Plato maintained that our immortal souls contain within them a memory of the Ideal Forms. On this basis, Tell concluded that "if in the *Confessions* Augustine finds God in Memory, *De Trinitae* suggests that it is more accurate to say that Augustine finds God in the inner word that reveals memories-from-within" (p. 244). But *Confessions* seems to stand as testimony that the *verbum mentis* cannot exist as thought alone but must be expressed, must be a performative act in the same sense that the *logos* or Word of God was a performative act.

The power of remembrance is first described in Book IV, where Augustine recounts the death of his best friend and his subsequent grief. In IV.6, he states that "I felt that our two souls had been as one, living in two bodies, and life to me was fearful because I did not want to live with only half a soul. Perhaps this, too, is why I shrank from death, for fear that one whom I had loved so well might be wholly dead." Condon (2001) argued that this passage reveals how Augustine:

equates memory with the soul and the soul with one's real, if not always *true*, self. Augustine tells us that who we are, at least how we know that we exist, is by our memory. How, then, are we able to understand, rather, *discover*, our true selves? It is to be discovered in those images that are retrieved from memory. (p. 51)

Augustine's initial reflection on memory leads to a deeper philosophical analysis in Book X.28 linking memory and time. Here Augustine asks, "But how can the future be diminished or absorbed when it does not yet exist? And how can the past increase when it no longer exists? It can only be that the mind, which regulates this process, performs three functions, those of expectation, attention, and memory." Because the present "has no duration," a recited psalm, for example, can exist as a whole only in the memory; it emerges from memory through expectation and attention only to pass "into the province of memory" when the recitation is finished. In a striking move, Augustine then takes an additional step: The province of memory is the locus "of any longer action in which I may be engaged and of which the recitation of the psalm may only be a small part. It is true of man's whole life, of which all his actions are parts. It is true of the whole of human history of mankind, of which each man's life is a part." But if the province of God is man, as Augustine argued, then the whole of human history and each man's life exists as a whole only in God's memory. On this basis, Condon (2001) noted that "Soul death ... may be avoided so long as one is predestined for redemption and the remembrance of God" (p. 53). If this analysis is correct, it provides an important insight into the nature of *Confessions* as both a prayer and religious philosophy. The prayerful effort to seek God's acknowledgment would be a performative act of great urgency, for immortality consists of being remembered by God.

Reading 43

Confessiones (Confessions)

Confessiones (Confessions) (excerpt), from *Confessions* by St. Augustine, translated by R.S. Pine-Coffin (Penguin, 1961). © R.S. Pine-Coffin, 1961. Reproduced by permission.

Book I

1

Can any praise be worthy of the Lord's majesty?[21] *How magnificent his strength! How inscrutable his wisdom!*[22] Man is one of your creatures, Lord, and his instinct is to praise you. He bears about him the mark of death, the sign of his own sin, to remind him that you *thwart the proud.*[23] But still, since he is a part of your creation, he wishes to praise you. The thought of you stirs him so deeply that he cannot be content unless he praises you, because you made us for yourself and our hearts find no peace until they rest in you.

Grant me, Lord, to know and understand whether a man is first to pray to you for help or to praise you, and whether he must know you before he can call you to his aid. If he does not know you, how can he pray to you? For he may call for some other help, mistaking it for yours.

Or are men to pray to you and learn to know you through their prayers? *Only, how are they to call upon the Lord until they have learned to believe in him? And how are they to believe in him without a preacher to listen to?*[24]

---

[21] Ps. 144.3 (145.3). In references to the Psalms the number according to the Vulgate is given first. This is followed by the Authorized Version number in brackets.
[22] Ps. 146.5 (147.5).
[23] I Pet., v. 5.
[24] Rom. 10.14.

Those who look for the Lord will cry out in praise of him,[25] because all who look for him shall find him, and when they find him they will praise him. I shall look for you, Lord, by praying to you and as I pray I shall believe in you, because we have had preachers to tell us about you. It is my faith that calls to you, Lord, the faith which you gave me and made to live in me through the merits of your Son, who became man, and through the ministry of your preacher.

2

How shall I call upon my God for aid, when the call I make is for my Lord and my God to come into myself? What place is there in me to which my God can come, what place that can receive the God who made heaven and earth? Does this then mean, O Lord my God, that there is in me something fit to contain you? Can even heaven and earth, which you made and in which you made me, contain you? Or, since nothing that exists could exist without you, does this mean that whatever exists does, in this sense, contain you? If this is so, since I too exist, why do I ask you to come into me? For I should not be there at all unless, in this way, you were already present within me. I am not in hell, and yet you are there too, for *if I sink down to the world beneath, you are present still.*[26] So, then, I should be null and void and could not exist at all, if you, my God, were not in me.

Or is it rather that I should not exist, unless I existed in you? For *all things find in you their origin, their impulse, the centre of their being.*[27] This, Lord, is the true answer to my question. But if I exist in you, how can I call upon you to come to me? And where would you come from? For you, my God, have said that you *fill heaven and earth,*[28] but I cannot go beyond the bounds of heaven and earth so that you may leave them to come to me.

[...]

4

What, then, is the God I worship? He can be none but the Lord God himself, for *who but the Lord is*

God? *What other refuge can there be, except our God?*[29] You, my God, are supreme, utmost in goodness, mightiest and all-powerful, most merciful and most just. You are the most hidden from us and yet the most present amongst us, the most beautiful and yet the most strong, ever enduring and yet we cannot comprehend you. You are unchangeable and yet you change all things. You are never new, never old, and yet all things have new life from you. You are the unseen power that brings decline upon the proud. You are ever active, yet always at rest. You gather all things to yourself, though you suffer no need. You support, you fill, and you protect all things. You create them, nourish them, and bring them to perfection. You seek to make them your own, though you lack for nothing. You love your creatures, but with a gentle love. You treasure them, but without apprehension. You grieve for wrong, but suffer no pain. You can be angry and yet serene. Your works are varied, but your purpose is one and the same. You welcome all who come to you, though you never lost them. You are never in need yet are glad to gain, never covetous yet you exact a return for your gifts. We give abundantly to you so that we may deserve a reward; yet which of us has anything that does not come from you? You repay us what we deserve, and yet you owe nothing to any. You release us from our debts, but you lose nothing thereby. You are my God, my Life, my holy Delight, but is this enough to say of you? Can any man say enough when he speaks of you? Yet woe betide those who are silent about you! For even those who are most gifted with speech cannot find words to describe you.

[...]

6

[...]

This much is hidden from me. But, although I do not remember it all myself, I know that when I came into the world all the comforts which your mercy provides were there ready for me. This I was told by my parents, the father who begat me and the mother who conceived me, the two from

---

[25] Ps. 21.27 (22.26).
[26] Ps. 138.8 (139.8).
[27] Rom. 11.36.
[28] Jer. 23.24.
[29] Ps. 17.32 (18.31).

whose bodies you formed me in the limits of time. So it was that I was given the comfort of woman's milk.

But neither my mother nor my nurses filled their breasts of their own accord, for it was you who used them, as your law prescribes, to give me infant's food and a share of the riches which you distribute even among the very humblest of all created things. It was also by your gift that I did not wish for more than you gave, and that my nurses gladly passed on to me what you gave to them. They did this because they loved me in the way that you had ordained, and their love made them anxious to give to me what they had received in plenty from you. For it was to their own good that what was good for me should come to me from them; though, of course, it did not come to me from them but, through them, from you, because you, my God, are the source of all good and *everywhere you preserve me.*[30] All this I have learned since then, because all the gifts you have given to me, both spiritual and material, proclaim the truth of it. But in those days all I knew was how to suck, and how to lie still when my body sensed comfort or cry when it felt pain.

Later on I began to smile as well first in my sleep, and then when I was awake. Others told me this about myself, and I believe what they said, because we see other babies do the same. But I cannot remember it myself. Little by little I began to realize where I was and to want to make my wishes known to others, who might satisfy them. But this I could not do, because my wishes were inside me, while other people were outside, and they had no faculty which could penetrate my mind. So I would toss my arms and legs about and make noises, hoping that such few signs as I could make would show my meaning, though they were quite unlike what they were meant to mime. And if my wishes were not carried out, either because they had not been understood or because what I wanted would have harmed me, I would get cross with elders, who were not at my beck and call, and with people who were not my servants, simply because they did not attend to my wishes; and I would take my revenge by bursting into tears. By watching babies I have learnt that this is how they behave, and they, quite unconsciously, have done more than those who brought me up and knew all about it to con-vince me that I behaved in just the same way myself.

[...]

I do acknowledge you, Lord of heaven and earth, and I praise you for my first beginnings, although I cannot remember them. But you have allowed men to discover these things about them-selves by watching other babies, and also to learn much from what women have to tell. I know that I was a living person even at that age, and as I came towards the end of infancy I tried to find signs to convey my feelings to others. Where could such a living creature come from if not from you, O Lord? Can it be that any man has skill to fabricate himself? Or can there be some channel by which we derive our life and our very existence from some other source than you? Surely we can only derive them from our Maker, from you, Lord, to whom living and being are not different things, since infinite life and infinite being are one and the same. For you are infinite and never change. In you "today" never comes to an end: and yet our "today" does come to an end in you, because time, as well as everything else, exists in you. If it did not, it would have no means of passing. And since your years never come to an end, for you they are simply "today." The count-less days of our lives and of our forefathers' lives have passed by within your "today." From it they have received their due measure of duration and their very existence. And so it will be with all the other days which are still to come. But you your-self are eternally the same. In your "today" you will make all that is to exist tomorrow and there-after, and in your "today" you have made all that existed yesterday and for ever before.

Need it concern me if some people cannot understand this? Let them ask what it means, and be glad to ask: but they may content themselves with the question alone. For it is better for them to find you and leave the question unanswered than to find the answer without finding you.

7

Hear me, O God! How wicked are the sins of men! Men say this and you pity them, because you made man, but you did not make sin in him.

Who can recall to me the sins I committed as a baby? For in your sight no man is free from sin,

---

[30] II Kings (2 Sam.) 23.5.

not even a child who has lived only one day on earth. Who can show me what my sins were? Some small baby in whom I can see all that I do not remember about myself? What sins, then, did I commit when I was a baby myself? Was it a sin to cry when I wanted to feed at the breast? I am too old now to feed on mother's milk, but if I were to cry for the kind of food suited to my age, others would rightly laugh me to scorn and remonstrate with me. So then too I deserved a scolding for what I did; but since I could not have understood the scolding, it would have been unreasonable, and most unusual, to rebuke me. We root out these faults and discard them as we grow up, and this is proof enough that they are faults, because I have never seen a man purposely throw out the good when he clears away the bad. It can hardly be right for a child, even at that age, to cry for everything, including things which would harm him; to work himself into a tantrum against people older than himself and not required to obey him; and to try his best to strike and hurt others who know better than he does, including his own parents, when they do not give in to him and refuse to pander to whims which would only do him harm. This shows that, if babies are innocent, it is not for lack of will to do harm, but for lack of strength.

I have myself seen jealousy in a baby and know what it means. He was not old enough to talk, but whenever he saw his foster-brother at the breast, he would grow pale with envy. This much is common knowledge. Mothers and nurses say that they can work such things out of the system by one means or another, but surely it cannot be called innocence, when the milk flows in such abundance from its source, to object to a rival desperately in need and depending for his life on this one form of nourishment? Such faults are not small or unimportant, but we are tender-hearted and bear with them because we know that the child will grow out of them. It is clear that they are not mere peccadilloes, because the same faults are intolerable in older persons.

You, O Lord my God, gave me my life and my body when I was born. You gave my body its five senses; you furnished it with limbs and gave it its proper proportions; and you implanted in it all the instincts necessary for the welfare and safety of a living creature. For these gifts you command me to acknowledge you and *praise you and sing in honour of your name*,[31] because you are Almighty God, because you are good, and because I owe you praise for these things, even if you had done nothing else. No one but you can do these things, because you are the one and only mould in which all things are cast and the perfect form which shapes all things, and everything takes its place according to your law.

I do not remember that early part of my life, O Lord, but I believe what other people have told me about it and from watching other babies I can conclude that I also lived as they do. But true though my conclusions may be, I do not like to think of that period as part of the same life I now lead, because it is dim and forgotten and, in this sense, it is no different from the time I spent in my mother's womb. But if *I was born in sin and guilt was with me already when my mother conceived me*,[32] where, I ask you, Lord, where or when was I, your servant, ever innocent? But I will say no more about that time, for since no trace of it remains in my memory, it need no longer concern me.

8

The next stage in my life, as I grew up, was boyhood. Or would it be truer to say that boyhood overtook me and followed upon my infancy – not that my infancy left me, for, if it did, where did it go? All the same, it was no longer there, because I ceased to be a baby unable to talk, and was now a boy with the power of speech. I can remember that time, and later on I realized how I had learnt to speak. It was not my elders who showed me the words by some set system of instruction, in the way that they taught me to read not long afterwards; but, instead, I taught myself by using the intelligence which you, my God, gave to me. For when I tried to express my meaning by crying out and making various sounds and movements, so that my wishes should be obeyed, I found that I could not convey all that I meant or make myself understood by everyone whom I wished to understand me. So my memory prompted me. I noticed that people would name some object and then turn towards whatever it was that they had named. I watched them and understood that the sound they made

[31] Ps. 91.2 (91.1).
[32] Ps. 50.7 (51.5).

when they wanted to indicate that particular thing was the name which they gave to it, and their actions clearly showed what they meant, for there is a kind of universal language, consisting of expressions of the face and eyes, gestures and tones of voice, which can show whether a person means to ask for something and get it, or refuse it and have nothing to do with it. So, by hearing words arranged in various phrases and constantly repeated, I gradually pieced together what they stood for, and when my tongue had mastered the pronunciation, I began to express my wishes by means of them. In this way I made my wants known to my family and they made theirs known to me, and I took a further step into the stormy life of human society, although I was still subject to the authority of my parents and the will of my elders.

9

But, O God my God, I now went through a period of suffering and humiliation. I was told that is was right and proper for me as a boy to pay attention to my teachers, so that I should do well at my study of grammar and get on in the world. This was the way to gain the respect of others and win for myself what passes for wealth in this world. So I was sent to school to learn to read. I was too small to understand what purpose it might serve and yet, if I was idle at my studies, I was beaten for it, because beating was favoured by tradition. Countless boys long since forgotten had built up this stony path for us to tread and we were made to pass along it, adding to the toil and sorrow of the sons of Adam.

But we found that some men prayed to you, Lord, and we learned from them to do the same, thinking of you in the only way that we could understand, as some great person who could listen to us and help us, even though we could not see you or hear you or touch you. I was still a boy when I first began to pray to you, my Help and Refuge. I used to prattle away to you, and though I was small, my devotion was great when I begged you not to let me be beaten at school. Sometimes, for my own good, you did not grant my prayer, and then my elders and even my parents, who certainly wished me no harm, would laugh at the beating I got – and in those days beatings were my one great bugbear.

[...]

10

And yet I sinned, O Lord my God, creator and arbiter of all natural things, but arbiter only, not creator, of sin. I sinned, O Lord, by disobeying my parents and the masters of whom I have spoken. For, whatever purpose they had in mind, later on I might have put to good use all the things which they wanted me to learn. I was disobedient, not because I chose something better than they proposed to me, but simply from the love of games. For I liked to score a fine win at sport or to have my ears tickled by the make-believe of the stage, which only made them itch the more. As time went on my eyes shone more and more with the same eager curiosity, because I wanted to see the shows and sports which grown-ups enjoyed. The patrons who pay for the production of these shows are held in esteem such as most parents would wish for their children. Yet the same parents willingly allow their children to be flogged if they are distracted by these displays from the studies which are supposed to fit them to grow rich and give the same sort of shows themselves. Look on these things with pity, O Lord, and free us who now call upon you from such delusions. Set free also those who have not yet called upon you, so that they may pray to you and you may free them from this folly.

11

While still a boy I had been told of the eternal life promised to us by Our Lord, who humbled himself and came down amongst us proud sinners. As a catechumen, I was blessed regularly from birth with the sign of the Cross and was seasoned with God's salt, for, O Lord, my mother placed great hope in you. Once as a child I was taken suddenly ill with a disorder of the stomach and was on the point of death. You, my God, were my guardian even then, and you saw the fervour and strength of my faith as I appealed to the piety of my own mother and to the mother of us all, your Church, to give me the baptism of Christ your Son, who is my God and my Master. My earthly mother was deeply anxious, because in the pure faith of her heart, she was in greater labour to ensure my eternal salvation than she had been at my birth. Had I not quickly recovered, she would have hastened to see that I was admitted to the sacraments of salvation and washed clean by acknowledging you, Lord Jesus, for the pardon of my sins. So my washing in the waters of baptism was postponed, in the surmise that, if I continued to live, I should defile myself again with sin and, after baptism, the guilt of pollution would be greater and more dangerous. Even at that age I already believed in you, and so did my mother and the whole household except for my father. But, in my heart, he did not gain the better of my mother's piety and prevent me from believing in Christ just because he still disbelieved himself. For she did all that she could to see that you, my God, should be a Father to me rather than he. In this you helped her to turn the scales against her husband, whom she always obeyed because by obeying him she obeyed your law, thereby showing greater virtue than he did.

I ask you, my God – for, if it is your will, I long to know – for what purpose was my baptism postponed at that time? Was it for my good that the reins which held me from sin were slackened? Or is it untrue that they were slackened? If not, why do we continually hear people say, even nowadays, "Leave him alone and let him do it. He is not yet baptized"? Yet when the health of the body is at stake, no one says "Let him get worse. He is not yet cured." It would then, have been much better if I had been healed at once and if all that I and my family could do had been done to make sure that once my soul had received its salvation, its safety should be left in your keeping, since its salvation had come from you. […]

12

These temptations were thought to be less of a danger in boyhood than in adolescence. But even as a boy I did not care for lessons and I disliked being forced to study. All the same I was compelled to learn and good came to me as a result, although it was not of my own making. For I would not have studied at all if I had not been obliged to do so, and what a person does against his will is not to his own credit, even if what he does is good in itself. Nor was the good which came of it due to those who compelled me to study, but to you, my God. For they had not the insight to see that I might put the lessons which

they forced me to learn to any other purpose than the satisfaction of man's insatiable desire for the poverty he calls wealth and the infamy he knows as fame. But you, who *take every hair of our heads into your reckoning,*[33] used for my benefit the mistaken ideas of all those who insisted on making me study; and you used the mistake I made myself, in not wishing to study, as a punishment which I deserved to pay, for I was a great sinner for so small a boy. In this way you turned their faults to my advantage and justly punished me for my own. For this is what you have ordained and so it is with us, that every soul that sins brings its own punishment upon itself.

13

Even now I cannot fully understand why the Greek language, which I learned as a child, was so distasteful to me. I loved Latin, not the elementary lessons but those which I studied later under teachers of literature. The first lessons in Latin were reading, writing, and counting, and they were as much of an irksome imposition as any studies in Greek. But this, too, was due to the sinfulness and vanity of life, since I was *flesh and blood, no better than a breath of wind that passes by and never returns.*[34] For these elementary lessons were far more valuable than those which followed, because the subjects were practical. They gave me the power, which I still have, of reading whatever is set before me and writing whatever I wish to write. But in the later lessons I was obliged to memorize the wanderings of a hero named Aeneas, while in the meantime I failed to remember my own erratic ways. I learned to lament the death of Dido, who killed herself for love, while all the time, in the midst of these things, I was dying, separated from you, my God and my Life, and I shed no tears for my own plight.

What can be more pitiful than an unhappy wretch unaware of his own sorry state, bewailing the fate of Dido, who died for love of Aeneas, yet shedding no tears for himself as he dies for want of loving you? O God, you are the Light of my heart, the Bread of my inmost soul, and the Power that weds my mind and the thoughts of my heart. But I did not love you. *I broke my troth with you*[35]

---

[33] Matt. 10.30.
[34] Ps. 77.39 (78.39).
[35] Ps. 72.27 (73.27).

and embraced another while applause echoed about me. For to love this world is to break troth with you,[36] yet men applaud and are ashamed to be otherwise. I did not weep over this, but instead I wept for Dido, who surrendered her life to the sword, while I forsook you and surrendered myself to the lowest of your created things. And if I were forbidden to read these books, I was sad not to be able to read the very things that made me sad. Such folly is held to be a higher and more fruitful form of study than learning to read and write.

But now, my God, let your voice ring in my soul and let your truth proclaim to me that it is wrong to think this. Tell me that reading and writing are by far the better study. This must be true, for I would rather forget the wanderings of Aeneas and all that goes with them, than how to read and write. It is true that curtains are hung over the entrances to the schools where literature is taught, but they are not so much symbols in honour of mystery as veils concealing error. The schoolmasters need not exclaim at my words, for I no longer go in fear of them now that I confess my soul's desires to you, my God, and gladly blame myself for my evil ways so that I may enjoy the good ways you have shown me. Neither those who traffic in literature nor those who buy their wares need exclaim against me. For if I put to them the question whether it is true, as the poet says, that Aeneas once came to Carthage, the less learned will plead ignorance and the better informed will admit that it is not true. But if I ask how the name of Aeneas is spelt, anyone who has learnt to read will give me the right answer, based on the agreed convention which fixes the alphabet for all of us. If I next ask them whether a man would lose more by forgetting how to read and write or by forgetting the fancies dreamed up by the poets, surely everyone who is not out of his wits can see the answer they would give. So it was wrong of me as a boy to prefer empty romances to more valuable studies. In fact it would be truer to say that I loved the one and hated the other. But in those days "one and one are two, two and two are four" was a loathsome jingle, while the wooden horse and its crew of soldiers, the burning of Troy and even the ghost of Creusa made a most enchanting dream, futile though it was.

14

If this was so, why did I dislike Greek literature, which tells these tales, as much as the Greek language itself? Homer, as well as Virgil, was a skilful spinner of yarns and he is most delightfully imaginative. Nevertheless, as a boy, I found him little to my taste. I suppose that Greek boys think the same about Virgil when they are forced to study him as I was forced to study Homer. There was of course the difficulty which is found in learning any foreign language, and this soured the sweetness of the Greek romances. For I understood not a single word and I was constantly subjected to violent threats and cruel punishments to make me learn. As a baby, of course, I knew no Latin either, but I learned it without fear and fret, simply by keeping my ears open while my nurses fondled me and everyone laughed and played happily with me. I learned it without being forced by threats of punishment, because it was my own wish to be able to give expression to my thoughts. I could never have done this if I had not learnt a few words, not from schoolmasters but from people who spoke to me and listened when I delivered to their ears whatever thoughts I had conceived. This clearly shows that we learn better in a free spirit of curiosity than under fear and compulsion. But your law, O God, permits the free flow of curiosity to be stemmed by force. From the schoolmaster's cane to the ordeals of martyrdom, your law prescribes bitter medicine to retrieve us from the noxious pleasures which cause us to desert you.

[…]

16

[…]

This traditional education taught me that Jupiter punishes the wicked with his thunderbolts and yet commits adultery himself. The two roles are quite incompatible. All the same he is represented in this way, and the result is that those who follow his example in adultery can put a bold face on it by making false pretences of thunder. But can any schoolmaster in his gown listen unperturbed to a man who challenges him on his own ground and says "Homer invented these stories and attributed human sins to the gods. He would have done better to provide men with example of divine goodness"?[37]

[36] See James, 4.4.

[37] Cicero, *Tusculanae disputationes* I, 26.

It would be nearer the truth to say that Homer certainly invented the tales but peopled them with wicked human characters in the guise of gods. In this way their wickedness would not be reckoned a crime, and all who did as they did could be shown to follow the example of the heavenly gods, not that of sinful mortals.

And yet human children are pitched into this hellish torrent, together with the fees which are paid to have them taught lessons like these. Much business is at stake, too, when these matters are publicly debated, because the law decrees that teachers should be paid a salary in addition to the fees paid by their pupils. And the roar of the torrent beating upon its boulders seems to say "This is the school where men are made masters of words. This is where they learn the art of persuasion, so necessary in business and debate" – as much as to say that, but for a certain passage in Terence, we should never have heard of words like "shower," "golden," "lap," "deception," "sky," and the other words which occur in the same scene. Terence brings on to the stage a dissolute youth who excuses his own fornication by pointing to the example of Jupiter. He looks at a picture painted on the wall, which "shows how Jupiter is said to have deceived the girl Danae by raining a golden shower into her lap." These are the words with which he incites himself to lechery, as though he had heavenly authority for it: "What a god he is! His mighty thunder rocks the sky from end to end. You may say that I am only a man, and thundering is beyond my power. But I played the rest of the part well enough, and willingly too!"[38]

[...]

17

Let me tell you, my God, how I squandered the brains you gave me on foolish delusions. I was set a task which troubled me greatly, for if I were successful, I might win some praise: if not, I was afraid of disgrace or a beating. I had to recite the speech of Juno,[39] who was pained and angry because she could not prevent Aeneas from sailing to Italy. I had been told that Juno had never really spoken the words, but we were compelled to make

believe and follow the flight of the poet's fancy by repeating in prose what he had said in verse. The contest was to be won by the boy who found the best words to suit the meaning and best expressed feelings of sorrow and anger appropriate to the majesty of the character he impersonated.

What did all this matter to me, my God, my true Life? Why did my recitation win more praise than those of the many other boys in my class? Surely it was all so much smoke without fire? Was there no other subject on which I might have sharpened my wits and my tongue? I might have used them, O Lord, to praise you in the words of your Scriptures, which could have been a prop to support my heart, as if it were a young vine, so that it would not have produced this crop of worthless fruit, fit only for the birds to peck at. For offerings can be made to those birds of prey, the fallen angels, in more ways than one.

[...]

19

It was at the threshold of a world such as this that I stood in peril as a boy. I was already being prepared for its tournaments by a training which taught me to have a horror of faulty grammar instead of teaching me, when I committed these faults, not to envy others who avoided them. All this, my God, I admit and confess to you. By these means I won praise from the people whose favour I sought, for I thought that the right way to live was to do as they wished. I was blind to the whirlpool of debasement in which I had been plunged away from the sight of your eyes. For in your eyes nothing could be more debased than I was then, since I was even troublesome to the people whom I set out to please. Many and many a time I lied to my tutor, my masters, and my parents, and deceived them because I wanted to play games or watch some futile show or was impatient to imitate what I saw on the stage. I even stole from my parents' larder and from their table, either from greed or to get something to give to other boys in exchange for their favourite toys, which they were willing to barter with me. And in the games I played with them I often cheated in order to come off the better, simply because a vain desire to win

---

[38] Terence, *Eunuchus* III, 5.

[39] Virgil, *Aeneid* I, 37–49.

had got the better of me. And yet there was nothing I could less easily endure, nothing that made me quarrel more bitterly, than to find others cheating me as I cheated them. All the same, if they found me out and blamed me for it, I would lose my temper rather than give in.

[...]

Book II

1

I must now carry my thoughts back to the abominable things I did in those days, the sins of the flesh which defiled my soul. I do this, my God, not because I love those sins, but so that I may love you. For love of your love I shall retrace my wicked ways. The memory is bitter, but it will help me to savour your sweetness, the sweetness that does not deceive but brings real joy and never fails. For love of your love I shall retrieve myself from the havoc of disruption which tore me to pieces when I turned away from you, whom alone I should have sought, and lost myself instead on many a different quest. For as I grew to manhood I was inflamed with desire for a surfeit of hell's pleasures. Foolhardy as I was, I ran wild with lust that was manifold and rank. In your eyes my beauty vanished and I was foul to the core, yet I was pleased with my own condition and anxious to be pleasing in the eyes of men.

2

I cared for nothing but to love and be loved. But my love went beyond the affection of one mind for another, beyond the arc of the bright beam of friendship. Bodily desire, like a morass, and adolescent sex welling up within me exuded mists which clouded over and obscured my heart, so that I could not distinguish the clear light of true love from the murk of dust. Love and lust together seethed within me. In my tender youth they swept me away over the precipice of my body's appetites and plunged me in the whirlpool of sin. More and more I angered you, unawares. For I had been deafened

by the clank of my chains, the fetters of the death which was my due to punish the pride in my soul. I strayed still farther from you and you did not restrain me. I was tossed and spilled, floundering in the broiling sea of my fornication, and you said no word. How long it was before I learned that you were my true joy! You were silent then, and I went on my way, farther and farther from you, proud in my distress and restless in fatigue, sowing more and more seeds whose only crop was grief.

Was there no one to lull my distress, to turn the fleeting beauty of these new-found attractions to good purpose and set up a goal for their charms, so that the high tide of my youth might have rolled in upon the shore of marriage? The surge might have been calmed and contented by the procreation of children. Which is the purpose of marriage, as your law prescribes, O Lord. By this means you form the offspring of our fallen nature, and with a gentle hand you prune back the thorns that have no place in your paradise. For your almighty power is not far from us, even when we are far from you. Or, again, I might have listened more attentively to your voice from the clouds, saying of those who marry that they will *meet with outward distress, but I leave you your freedom;*[40] that *a man does well to abstain from all commerce with women,*[41] and that *he who is unmarried is concerned with God's claim, asking how he is to please God; whereas the married man is concerned with the world's claim, asking how he is to please his wife.*[42] These were the words to which I should have listened with more care, and if I had made myself a *eunuch for love of the kingdom of heaven,*[43] I should have awaited your embrace with all the greater joy.

But, instead, I was in a ferment of wickedness. I deserted you and allowed myself to be carried away by the sweep of the tide. I broke all your lawful bounds and did not escape your lash. For what man can escape it? You were always present, angry and merciful at once, strewing the pangs of bitterness over all my lawless pleasures to lead me on to look for others unallied with pain. You meant me to find them nowhere but in yourself, O Lord, for you teach us by inflicting pain,[44] you smite so that you may heal,[45] and you kill us so

---

[40] I Cor. 7.28.
[41] I Cor. 7.1.
[42] I Cor. 7.32, 33.
[43] Matt. 19.12.
[44] See Ps. 93.20 (94.20).
[45] See Deut. 32.39.

that we may not die away from you. Where was I then and how far was I banished from the bliss of your house in that sixteenth year of my life? This was the age at which the frenzy gripped me and I surrendered myself entirely to lust, which your law forbids but human hearts are not ashamed to sanction. My family made no effort to save me from my fall by marriage. Their only concern was that I should learn how to make a good speech and how to persuade others by my words.

3

In the same year my studies were interrupted. I had already begun to go to the near-by town of Madaura to study literature and the art of public speaking, but I was brought back home while my father, a modest citizen of Thagaste whose determination was greater than his means, saved up the money to send me farther afield to Carthage. I need not tell all this to you, my God, but in your presence I tell it to my own kind, to those other men, however few, who may perhaps pick up this book. And I tell it so that I and all who read my words may realize the depths from which we are to cry to you. Your ears will surely listen to the cry of a penitent heart which lives the life of faith.

No one had anything but praise for my father who, despite his slender resources, was ready to provide his son with all that was needed to enable him to travel so far for the purpose of study. Many of our townsmen, far richer than my father, went to no such trouble for their children's sake. Yet this same father of mine took no trouble at all to see how I was growing in your sight or whether I was chaste or not. He cared only that I should have a fertile tongue, leaving my heart to bear none of your fruits, my God, though you are the only Master, true and good, of its husbandry.

In the meanwhile, during my sixteenth year, the narrow means of my family obliged me to leave school and live idly at home with my parents. The brambles of lust grew high above my head and there was no one to root them out, certainly not my father. One day at the public baths he saw the signs of active virility coming to life in me and this was enough to make him relish the thought of having grandchildren. He was happy to tell my mother about it, for his happiness was due to the intoxication which causes the world to forget you, its Creator, and to love the things you have created instead of loving you, because the world is drunk with the invisible wine of its own perverted, earth-bound will. But in my mother's heart you had already begun to build your temple and laid the foundations of your holy dwelling, while my father was still a catechumen and a new one at that. So, in her piety, she became alarmed and apprehensive, and although I had not yet been baptized, she began to dread that I might follow in the crooked path of those who do not keep their eyes on you but turn their backs instead.

How presumptuous it was of me to say that you were silent, my God, when I drifted farther and farther away from you! Can it be true that you said nothing to me at that time? Surely the words which rang in my ears, spoken by your faithful servant, my mother, could have come from none but you? Yet none of them sank into my heart to make me do as you said. I well remember what her wishes were and how she most earnestly warned me not to commit fornication and above all not to seduce any man's wife. It all seemed womanish advice to me and I should have blushed to accept it. Yet the words were yours, though I did not know it. I thought that you were silent and that she was speaking, but all the while you were speaking to me through her, and when I disregarded her, your handmaid, I was disregarding you, though I was both her son and your servant. But I did this unawares and continued headlong on my way. I was so blind to the truth that among my companions I was ashamed to be less dissolute than they were. For I heard them bragging of their depravity, and the greater the sin the more they gloried in it, so that I took pleasure in the same vices not only for the enjoyment of what I did, but also for the applause I won.

Nothing deserves to be despised more than vice; yet I gave in more and more to vice simply in order not to be despised. If I had not sinned enough to rival other sinners, I used to pretend that I had done things I had not done at all, because I was afraid that innocence would be taken for cowardice and chastity for weakness. These were the companions with whom I walked the streets of Babylon. I wallowed in its mire as if it were made of spices and precious ointments, and to fix me all the faster in the very depths of sin the unseen enemy trod me underfoot and enticed me to himself, because I was an easy prey for his seductions. For even my mother, who by now had escaped from the centre of Babylon, though she still loitered in its outskirts, did not act upon what she had heard about me from her husband with the same earnestness as she had advised me about chastity. She saw that I was already infected with a disease that would become dangerous later on, but if the growth of my passions could not be cut back to the quick, she did not think it right to restrict them to the bounds of married love. This was because she was afraid that the bonds of marriage might be a hindrance to my hopes for the future – not of course the hope of the life to come, which she reposed in you, but my hopes of success at my studies. Both my parents were unduly eager for me to learn, my father because he gave next to no thought to you and only shallow thought to me, and my mother because she thought that the usual course of study would certainly not hinder me, but would even help me, in my approach to you. To the best of my memory this is how I construe the characters of my parents. Furthermore, I was given a free rein to amuse myself beyond the strict limits of discipline, so that I lost myself in many kinds of evil ways, in all of which a pall of darkness hung between me and the bright light of your truth, my God. What malice proceeded from my pampered heart![46]

4

It is certain, O Lord, that theft is punished by your law, the law that is written in men's hearts and cannot be erased however sinful they are. For no thief can bear that another thief should steal from him, even if he is rich and the other is driven to it by want. Yet I was willing to steal, and steal I did, although I was not compelled by any lack, unless it were the lack of a sense of justice or a distaste for what was right and a greedy love of doing wrong. For of what I stole I already had plenty, and much better at that, and I had no wish to enjoy the things I coveted by stealing, but only to enjoy the theft itself and the sin. There was a pear-tree near our vineyard, loaded with fruit that was attractive neither to look at nor to taste. Late one night a band of ruffians, myself included, went off to shake down the fruit and carry it away, for we had continued our games out of doors until well after dark, as was our pernicious habit. We took away an enormous quantity of pears, not to eat them ourselves, but simply to throw them to the pigs. Perhaps we ate some of them, but our real pleasure consisted in doing something that was forbidden.

[...]

6

If the crime of theft which I committed that night as a boy of sixteen were a living thing, I could speak to it and ask what it was that, to my shame, I loved in it. It had no beauty because it was a robbery. It is true that the pears which we stole had beauty, because they were created by you, the good God, who are the most beautiful of all beings and the Creator of all things, the supreme Good and my own true Good. But it was not the pears that my unhappy soul desired. I had plenty of my own, better than those, and I only picked them so that I might steal. For no sooner had I picked them than I threw them away, and tasted nothing in them but my own sin, which I relished and enjoyed. If any part of one of those pears passed my lips, it was the sin that gave it flavour.

And now, O Lord my God, now that I ask what pleasure I had in that theft, I find that it had no beauty to attract me. I do not mean beauty of the sort that justice and prudence possess, nor the beauty that is in man's mind and in his memory and in the life that animates him, nor the beauty of the stars in their allotted places or of the earth and sea, teeming with new life born to replace the old as it passes away. It did not even have the shadowy, deceptive beauty which makes vice attractive – pride, for instance, which is a pretence of superiority, imitating yours, for you alone are God, supreme over all; or ambition, which is only a craving for honour and glory, when you alone are to be honoured before all and you alone are glorious for ever. Cruelty is the weapon of the powerful, used to make others fear them: yet no one is to be feared but God alone, from whose power nothing can be snatched away or stolen by any man at any time or place or by any means. The lustful use caresses to win the love they crave for, yet no caress is sweeter than your charity and no love is more rewarding than the love of your truth, which shines in beauty above all else. Inquisitiveness has all the appearance of a thirst for knowledge, yet you have supreme knowledge of all things. Ignorance, too, and stupidity choose

---

[46] See Ps. 72.7 (73.7).

to go under the mask of simplicity and innocence, because you are simplicity itself and no innocence is greater than yours. You are innocent even of the harm which overtakes the wicked, for it is the result of their own actions. Sloth poses as the love of peace: yet what certain peace is there besides the Lord? Extravagance masquerades as fullness and abundance: but you are the full, unfailing store of never-dying sweetness. The spendthrift makes a pretence of liberality: but you are the most generous dispenser of all good. The covetous want many possessions for themselves: you possess all. The envious struggle for preferment: but what is to be preferred before you? Anger demands revenge: but what vengeance is as just as yours? Fear shrinks from my sudden, unwonted danger which threatens the things that it loves, for its only care is safety: but to you nothing is strange, nothing unforeseen. No one can part you from the things that you love, and safety is assured nowhere but in you. Grief eats away its heart for the loss of things which it took pleasure in desiring, because it wants to be like you, from whom nothing can be taken away.

So the soul defiles itself with unchaste love when it turns away from you and looks elsewhere for things which it cannot find pure and unsullied except by returning to you. All who desert you and set themselves up against you merely copy you in a perverse way; but by this very act of imitation they only show that you are the Creator of all nature and, consequently, that there is no place whatever where man may hide away from you.

What was it, then, that pleased me in the act of theft? Which of my Lord's powers did I imitate in a perverse and wicked way? Since I had no real power to break his law, was it that I enjoyed at least the pretence of doing so, like a prisoner who creates for himself the illusion of liberty by doing something wrong, when he has no fear of punishment, under a feeble halucination of power? Here was the slave who ran away from his master and chased a shadow instead! What an abomination! What a parody of life! What abysmal death! Could I enjoy doing wrong for no other reason than that it was wrong?

[...]

8

It brought me no happiness, for *what harvest did I reap from acts which now make me blush*,[47] particularly from that act of theft? I loved nothing in it except the thieving, though I cannot truly speak of that as a "thing" that I could love, and I was only the more miserable because of it. And yet, as I recall my feelings at the time, I am quite sure that I would not have done it on my own. Was it then that I also enjoyed the company of those with whom I committed the crime? If this is so, there was something else I loved besides the act of theft; but I cannot call it "something else," because companionship, like theft, is not a thing at all.

[...]

9

How can I explain my mood? It was certainly a very vile frame of mind and one for which I suffered; but how can I account for it? *Who knows his own frailties?*[48]

We were tickled to laughter by the prank we had played, because no one suspected us of it although the owners were furious. Why was it, then, that I thought it fun not to have been the only culprit? Perhaps it was because we do not easily laugh when we are alone. True enough: but even when a man is all by himself and quite alone, sometimes he cannot help laughing if he thinks or hears or sees something especially funny. All the same, I am quite sure that I would never have done this thing on my own.

My God, I lay all this before you, for it is still alive in my memory. By myself I would not have committed that robbery. It was not the takings that attracted me but the raid itself, and yet to do it by myself would have been no fun and I should not have done it. This was friendship of a most unfriendly sort, bewitching my mind in an inexplicable way. For the sake of a laugh, a little sport, I was glad to do harm and anxious to damage another; and that without thought of profit for myself or retaliation for injuries received! And all because we are ashamed to hold back when others say "Come on! Let's do it!"

[...]

[47] Rom. 6.21.
[48] Ps. 18.13 (19.12).

Book III

1

I went to Carthage, where I found myself in the midst of a hissing cauldron of lust. I had not yet fallen in love, but I was in love with the idea of it, and this feeling that something was missing made me despise myself for not being more anxious to satisfy the need. I began to look around for some object for my love, since I badly wanted to love something. I had no liking for the safe path without pitfalls, for although my real need was for you, my God, who are the food of the soul, I was not aware of this hunger. I felt no need for the food that does not perish, not because I had had my fill of it, but because the more I was starved of it the less palatable it seemed. Because of this my soul fell sick. It broke out in ulcers and looked about desperately for some material, worldly means of relieving the itch which they caused. But material things, which have no soul, could not be true objects for my love. To love and to have my love returned was my heart's desire, and it would be all the sweeter if I could also enjoy the body of the one who loved me.

So I muddied the stream of friendship with the filth of lewdness and clouded its clear waters with hell's black river of lust. And yet, in spite of this rank depravity, I was vain enough to have ambitions of cutting a fine figure in the world. I also fell in love, which was a snare of my own choosing. My God, my God of mercy, how good you were to me, for you mixed much bitterness in that cup of pleasure! My love was returned and finally shackled me in the bonds of its consummation. In the midst of my joy I was caught up in the coils of trouble, for I was lashed with the cruel, fiery rods of jealousy and suspicion, fear, anger, and quarrels.

2

I was much attracted by the theatre, because the plays reflected my own unhappy plight and were tinder to my fire. Why is it that men enjoy feeling sad at the sight of tragedy and suffering on the stage, although they would be most unhappy if they had to endure the same fate themselves? Yet they watch the plays because they hope to be made to feel sad, and the feeling of sorrow is what they enjoy. What miserable delirium this is! The more a man is subject to such suffering himself, the more easily he is moved by it in the theatre. Yet when he suffers himself, we call it misery: when he suffers out of sympathy with others, we call it pity. But what sort of pity can we really feel for an imaginary scene on the stage? The audience is not called upon to offer help but only to feel sorrow, and the more they are pained the more they applaud the author. Whether this human agony is based on fact or is simply imaginary, if it is acted so badly the audience is not moved to sorrow, they leave the theatre in a disgruntled and critical mood; whereas, if they are made to feel pain, they stay to the end watching happily.

This shows that sorrow and tears can be enjoyable. Of course, everyone wants to be happy; but even if no one likes being sad, is there just the one exception that, because we enjoy pitying others, we welcome their misfortunes, without which we could not pity them? If so, it is because friendly feelings well up in us like the waters of a spring. But what course do these waters follow? Where do they flow? Why do they trickle away to join that stream of boiling pitch, the hideous flood of lust? For by their own choice they lose themselves and become absorbed in it. They are diverted from their true course and deprived of their original heavenly calm.

Of course this does not mean that we must arm ourselves against compassion. There are times when we must welcome sorrow on behalf of others. But for the sake of our souls we must beware of uncleanness. My God must be the Keeper of my soul, the God of our fathers, who is to be exalted and extolled for ever more. My soul must guard against uncleanness.

I am not nowadays insensible to pity. But in those days I used to share the joy of stage lovers and their sinful pleasure in each other even though it was all done in make-believe for the sake of entertainment; and when they were parted, pity of a sort led me to share their grief. I enjoyed both these emotions equally. But now I feel more pity for a man who is happy in his sins than for one who has to endure the ordeal of forgoing some harmful pleasure or being deprived of some enjoyment which was really an affliction. Of the two, this sort of pity is certainly the more genuine, but the sorrow which it causes is not a source of pleasure. For although a man who is sorry for the sufferings of others deserves praise for his charity, nevertheless, if his pity is genuine, he would prefer that there should be no cause for his sorrow. If the impossible could happen and kindness were unkind, a man whose sense of pity was true and sincere might want others to suffer so that he could pity them. Sorrow may therefore be commendable but never desirable. For it is powerless to stab you, Lord God, and this is why the love you bear for our souls and the compassion you show for them are pure and unalloyed, far purer than the love and pity which we feel ourselves. But *who can prove himself worthy of such a calling?*[49]

However, in those unhappy days I enjoyed the pangs of sorrow. I always looked for things to wring my heart and the more tears an actor caused me to shed by his performance on the stage, even though he was portraying the imaginary distress of others, the more delightful and attractive I found it. Was it any wonder that I, the unhappy sheep who strayed from your flock, impatient of your shepherding, became infected with a loathsome mange? Hence my love of things which made me sad. I did not seek the kind of sorrow which would wound me deeply, for I had no wish to endure the sufferings which I saw on the stage; but I enjoyed fables and fictions, which could only graze the skin. But where the fingers scratch, the skin becomes inflamed. It swells and festers with hideous pus. And the same happened to me. Could the life I led be called true life, my God?

3

Yet all the while, far above, your mercy hovered faithfully about me. I exhausted myself in depravity, in the pursuit of an unholy curiosity. I deserted you and sank to the bottom-most depths of scepticism and the mockery of devil-worship. My sins were a sacrifice to the devil, and for all of them you chastised me. I defied you even so far as to relish the thought of lust, and gratify it too, within the walls of your church during the celebration of your mysteries. For such a deed I deserved to pluck the fruit of death, and you punished me for it with a heavy lash. But, compared with my guilt, the penalty was nothing. How infinite is your mercy, my God! You are my Refuge from the terrible dangers amongst which I wandered, head on high, intent upon withdrawing still further from you. I loved my own way, not yours, but it was a truant's freedom that I loved.

Besides these pursuits I was also studying for the law. Such ambition was held to be honourable and I determined to succeed in it. The more unscrupulous I was, the greater my reputation was likely to be, for men are so blind that they even take pride in their blindness. By now I was at the top of the school of rhetoric. I was pleased with my superior status and swollen with conceit. All the same, as you well know, Lord, I behaved far more quietly than the "Wreckers," a title of ferocious devilry which the fashionable set chose for themselves. I had nothing whatever to do with their outbursts of violence, but I lived amongst them, feeling a perverse sense of shame because I was not like them. I kept company with them and there were times when I found their friendship a pleasure, but I always had a horror of what they did when they lived up to their name. Without provocation they would set upon some timid newcomer, gratuitously affronting his sense of decency for their own amusement and using it as fodder for their spiteful jests. This was the devil's own behavior or not far different. "Wreckers" was a fit name for them, for they were already adrift and total wrecks themselves. The mockery and trickery which they loved to practise on others was a secret snare of the devil, by which they were mocked and tricked themselves.

4

These were the companions with whom I studied the art of eloquence at that impressionable age. It was my ambition to be a good speaker, for the unhallowed and inane purpose of gratifying human vanity. The prescribed course of study brought me to a work by an author named Cicero, whose writing nearly everyone admires, if not the spirit of it. The title of the book is *Hortensius* and it recommends the reader to study philosophy. It altered my outlook on life. It changed my prayers to you, O Lord, and provided me with new hopes and aspirations. All my empty dreams suddenly lost their charm and my heart began to throb with a bewildering passion for the wisdom of eternal truth. I began to climb out of the depths to which I had sunk, in order to return to you. For I did not use the book as a whetstone to sharpen my tongue. It was not the style of it but the contents which won me over, and yet the allowance which my

[49] II Cor. 2.16.

mother paid me was supposed to be spent on putting an edge on my tongue. I was now in my nineteenth year and she supported me, because my father had died two years before.

My God, how I burned with longing to have wings to carry me back to you, away from all earthly things, although I had no idea what you would do with me! For *yours is the wisdom.*[50] In Greek the word "philosophy" means "love of wisdom," and it was with this love that the *Hortensius* inflamed me. There are people for whom philosophy is a means of misleading others, for they misuse its great name, its attractions, and its integrity to give colour and gloss to their own errors. Most of these so-called philosophers who lived in Cicero's time and before are noted in the book. He shows them up in their true colours and makes quite clear how wholesome is the admonition which the Holy Spirit gives in the words of your good and true servant, Paul: *Take care not to let anyone cheat you with his philosophizings, with empty fantasies drawn from human tradition, from worldly principles; they were never Christ's teaching. In Christ the whole plenitude of Deity is embodied and dwells in him.*[51]

But, O Light of my heart, you know that at that time, although Paul's words were not known to me, the only thing that pleased me in Cicero's book was his advice not simply to admire one or another of the schools of philosophy, but to love wisdom itself, whatever it might be, and to search for it, pursue it, hold it, and embrace it firmly. These were the words which excited me and set me burning with fire, and the only check to this blaze of enthusiasm was that they made no mention of the name of Christ. For by your mercy, Lord, from the time when my mother fed me at the breast my infant heart had been suckled dutifully on his name, the name of your Son, my Saviour. Deep inside my heart his name remained, and nothing could entirely captivate me, however learned, however neatly expressed, however true it might be, unless his name were in it.

5

So I made up my mind to examine the holy Scriptures and see what kind of books they were.

I discovered something that was at once beyond the understanding of the proud and hidden from the eyes of children. Its gait was humble, but the heights it reached were sublime. It was enfolded in mysteries, and I was not the kind of man to enter into it or bow my head to follow where it led. But these were not the feelings I had when I first read the Scriptures. To me they seemed quite unworthy of comparison with the stately prose of Cicero, because I had too much conceit to accept their simplicity and not enough insight to penetrate their depths. It is surely true that as the child grows these books grow with him. But I was too proud to call myself a child. I was inflated with self-esteem, which made me think myself a great man.

[...]

8

Surely it is never wrong at any time or in any place for a man to *love God with his whole heart and his whole soul and his whole mind* and to *love his neighbour as himself?*[52] Sins against nature, therefore, like the sin of Sodom, are abominable and deserve punishment wherever and whenever they are committed. If all nations committed them, all alike would be held guilty of the same charge in God's law, for our Maker did not prescribe that we should use each other in this way. In fact the relationship which we ought to have with God is itself violated when our nature, of which he is the Author, is desecrated by perverted lust.

On the other hand, offences against human codes of conduct vary according to differences of custom, so that no one, whether he is a native or a foreigner, may, to suit his own pleasure, violate the conventions established by the customary usage or the law of the community or the state. For any part that is out of keeping with the whole is at fault. But if God commands a nation to do something contrary to its customs or constitutions, it must be done even if it has never been done in that country before. If it is a practice which has been discontinued, it must be resumed, and if it was not a law before, it must be enacted. In his own kingdom a king has the right to make orders which neither he nor any other has ever made before.

---

[50] Job, 12.13.
[51] Col. 2.8, 9.
[52] Matt. 22.37, 39.

Obedience to his orders is not against the common interest of the community; in fact, if they were disobeyed, the common interest would suffer, because it is the general agreement in human communities that the ruler is obeyed. How much more right, then, has God to give commands, since he is the Ruler of all creation and all his creatures must obey his commandments without demur! For all must yield to God just as, in the government of human society, the lesser authority must yield to the greater.

With sins of violence the case is the same as with sins against nature. Here the impulse is to injure others, either by word or by deed, but by whichever means it is done, there are various reasons for doing it. A man may injure his enemy for the sake of revenge; a robber may assault a traveller to secure for himself something that is not his own; or a man may attack someone whom he fears in order to avoid danger to himself. Or the injury may be done from envy, which will cause an unhappy man to harm another more fortunate than himself or a rich man to harm someone whose rivalry he fears for the future or already resents. Again, it may be done for the sheer joy of seeing others suffer, as is the case with those who watch gladiators or make fun of other people and jeer at them.

These are the main categories of sin. They are hatched from the lust for power, from gratification of the eye, and from gratification of corrupt nature – from one or two of these or from all three together. Because of them, O God most high, most sweet, our lives offend against your *ten-stringed harp*,[53] your commandments, the three which proclaim our duty to you and the seven which proclaim our duty to men.

But how can sins of vice be against you, since you cannot be marred by perversion? How can sins of violence be against you, since nothing can injure you? Your punishments are for the sins which men commit against themselves, because although they sin against you, they do wrong to their own souls and their malice is self-betrayed.[54] They corrupt and pervert their own nature, which you made and for which you shaped the rules, either by making wrong use of the things which you allow, or by becoming inflamed with passion to make unnatural use of things which you do not allow. Or else their guilt consists in raving against you in their hearts and with their tongues and *kicking against the goad*,[55] or in playing havoc with the restrictions of human society and brazenly exulting in private feuds and factions, each according to his fancies or his fads.

[...]

Book IV

1

During the space of those nine years, from the nineteenth to the twenty-eighth year of my life, I was led astray myself and led others astray in my turn. We were alike deceivers and deceived in all our different aims and ambitions, both publicly when we expounded our so-called liberal ideas, and in private through our service to what we called religion. In public we were cocksure, in private superstitious, and everywhere void and empty. On the one hand we would hunt for worthless popular distinctions, the applause of an audience, prizes for poetry, or quickly fading wreaths won in competition. We loved the idle pastimes of the stage and in self-indulgence we were unrestrained. On the other hand we aspired to be purged of these lowly pleasures by taking food to the holy elect, as they were called, so that in their paunches it might pass through the process of being made into angels and gods who would set us free. These were the objects I pursued and the tasks I performed together with friends who, like myself and through my fault, were under the same delusion.

Let the proud deride me, O God, and all whom you have not yet laid low and humiliated for the salvation of their souls; but let me still confess my sins to you for your honour and glory. Allow me, I beseech you, to trace again in memory my past deviations and to offer you a sacrifice of joy. Without you I am my own guide to the brink of perdition. And even when all is well with me, what am I but a creature suckled on your milk and feeding on yourself, the food that never perishes? And what is any man, if he is only man? Let

---

[53] Ps. 143.9 (144.9).
[54] See Ps. 26.12 (27.12).
[55] Acts, 9.5.

the strong and mighty laugh at men like me: let us, the weak and the poor, confess our sins to you.

2

During those years I was a teacher of the art of public speaking. Love of money had gained the better of me and for it I sold to others the means of coming off the better in debate. But you know, Lord, that I preferred to have honest pupils, in so far as honesty has any meaning nowadays, and I had no evil intent when I taught the tricks of pleading, for I never meant them to be used to get the innocent condemned but, if the occasion arose, to save the lives of the guilty. From a distance, my God, you saw me losing my foothold on this treacherous ground, but through clouds of smoke you also saw a spark of good faith in me; for though, as I schooled my pupils, I was merely abetting their futile designs and their schemes of duplicity, nevertheless I did my best to teach them honestly.

In those days I lived with a woman, not my lawful wedded wife but a mistress whom I had chosen for no special reason but that my restless passions had alighted on her. But she was the only one and I was faithful to her. Living with her I found out by my own experience the difference between the restraint of the marriage alliance, contracted for the purpose of having children, and a bargain struck for lust, in which the birth of children is begrudged, though, if they come, we cannot help but love them.

I remember too that once, when I had decided to enter a competition for reciting dramatic verse, a sorcerer sent to ask me how much I would pay him to make certain that I won. I loathed and detested these foul rites and told him that even if the prize were a crown of gold that would last for ever, I would not let even a fly be killed to win it. For he would have slaughtered living animals in his ritual, and by means of these offerings he would have pretended to invoke the aid of his demons in my favour. But, O God of my heart, it was not from a pure love of you that I rejected this wickedness. I had not learnt how to love you, for when I thought of you I imagined you as some

splendid being, but entirely physical. Does not the soul which pines for such fantasies *break its troth with you?*[56] Does it not trust in false hopes and *play shepherd to the wind?*[57] But while I would not let this man offer sacrifice for me to his devils, all the time I was offering myself as a sacrifice to them because of my false beliefs. For if we play shepherd to the wind, we find pasture for the devils, because by straying from the truth we give them food for laughter and fill their cup of pleasure.

3

The same reasoning did not prevent me from consulting those impostors, the astrologers, because I argued that they offered no sacrifices and said no prayers to any spirit to aid their divination. Nevertheless, true Christian piety rightly rejects and condemns what they do.

[…]

4

During those years, when I first began to teach in Thagaste, my native town, I had found a very dear friend. We were both the same age, both together in the heyday of youth, and both absorbed in the same interests. We had grown up together as boys, gone to school together, and played together. Yet ours was not the friendship which should be between true friends, either when we were boys or at this later time. For though they cling together, no friends are true friends unless you, my God, bind them fast to one another through that love which is sown in our hearts by the Holy Ghost, who is given to us. Yet there was sweetness in our friendship, mellowed by the interests we shared. As a boy he had never held firmly or deeply to the true faith and I had drawn him away from it to believe in the same superstitious, soul-destroying fallacies which brought my mother to tears over me. Now, as a man, he was my companion in error and I was utterly lost without him. Yet in a moment, before we had reached the end of the first year of a friendship that was sweeter to me than all the joys of life as I lived it then, you took him from this world. For you are the God of vengeance[58] as well

---

[56] Ps. 72.27 (73.27).

[57] Osee (Hosea), 12.1.

[58] See Ps. 93.1 (94.1).

as the fountain of mercy. You follow close behind the fugitive and recall us to yourself in ways we cannot understand.

No man can count your praises, even though he is but one man and reckons only the blessings he has received in his own life. How can I understand what you did at that time, my God? How can I plumb the unfathomable depth of your judgement? My friend fell gravely ill of a fever. His senses were numbed as he lingered in the sweat of death, and when all hope of saving him was lost, he was baptized as he lay unconscious. I cared nothing for this, because I chose to believe that his soul would retain what it had learnt from me, no matter what was done to his body when it was deprived of sense. But no such thing happened. New life came into him and he recovered. And as soon as I could talk to him – which was as soon as he could talk to me, for I never left his side since we were so dependent on each other – I tried to chaff him about his baptism, thinking that he too would make fun of it, since he had received it when he was quite incapable of thought or feeling. But by this time he had been told of it. He looked at me in horror as though I were an enemy, and in a strange, new-found attitude of self-reliance he warned me that if I wished to be his friend, I must never speak to him like that again. I was astonished and confused, but I did not tell him what I felt, hoping that when he was better and had recovered his strength, he would be in a condition to listen to what I had to say. But he was rescued from my folly and taken into your safe keeping, for my later consolation. For a few days after this, while I was away from him, the fever returned and he died.

My heart grew sombre with grief, and wherever I looked I saw only death. My own country became a torment and my own home a grotesque abode of misery. All that we had done together was now a grim ordeal without him. My eyes searched everywhere for him, but he was not there to be seen. I hated all the places we had known together, because he was not in them and they could no longer whisper to me "Here he comes!" as they would have done had he been alive but absent for a while. I had become a puzzle to myself, asking my soul again and again "Why are you downcast? Why do you distress me?"[59]

But my soul had no answer to give. If I said "Wait for God's help," she did not obey. And in this she was right because, to her, the well-loved man whom she had lost was better and more real than the shadowy being in whom I would have her trust. Tears alone were sweet to me, for in my heart's desire they had taken the place of my friend.

[...]

6

But why do I talk of these things? It is time to confess, not to question. I lived in misery, like every man whose soul is tethered by the love of things that cannot last and then is agonized to lose them. Only then does he realize the sorry state he is in, and was in even before his loss. In such a state was I at that time, as I wept bitter tears and found my only consolation in their very bitterness. This was the misery in which I lived, and yet my own wretched life was dearer to me than the friend I had lost. Gladly though I would have changed it, I was more loth to lose my life than I had been to lose my friend. True or not, the story goes that Orestes and Pylades were ready to die together for each other's sake, because each would rather die than live without the other. But I doubt whether I should have been willing, as they were, to give my life for my friend. I was obsessed by a strange feeling, quite the opposite of theirs, for I was sick and tired of living and yet afraid to die. I suppose that the great love which I had for my friend made me hate and fear death all the more, as though it were the most terrible of enemies, because it had snatched him away from me. I thought that, just as it had seized him, it would seize all others too without warning. I still remember how these thoughts filled my mind.

My heart lies before you, O my God. Look deep within. See these memories of mine, for you are my hope. You cleanse me when unclean humours such as these possess me, by drawing my eyes to yourself and *saving my feet from the snare*.[60]

I wondered that other men should live when he was dead, for I had loved him as though he would never die. Still more I wondered that he should die and I remain alive, for I was his second self. How well the poet put it when he called his friend the

---

[59] See Ps. 41.12 (42.5).
[60] Ps. 24.15 (25.15).

half of his soul![61] I felt that our two souls had been as one, living in two bodies, and life to me was fearful because I did not want to live with only half a soul. Perhaps this, too, is why I shrank from death, for fear that one whom I had loved so well might then be wholly dead.

7

What madness, to love a man as something more than human! What folly to grumble at the lot man has to bear! I lived in a fever, convulsed with tears and sighs that allowed me neither rest nor peace of mind. My soul was a burden, bruised and bleeding. It was tired of the man who carried it, but I found no place to set it down to rest. Neither the charm of the countryside nor the sweet scents of a garden could soothe it. It found no peace in song or laughter, none in the company of friends at table or in the pleasures of love, none even in books or poetry. Everything that was not what my friend had been was dull and distasteful. I had heart only for sighs and tears, for in them alone I found some shred of consolation. But if I tried to stem my tears, a heavy load of misery weighed me down. I knew, Lord, that I ought to offer it up to you, for you would heal it. But this I would not do, nor could I, especially as I did not think of you as anything real and substantial. It was not you that I believed in, but some empty figment. The god I worshipped was my own delusion, and if I tried to find in it a place to rest my burden, there was nothing there to uphold it. It only fell and weighed me down once more, so that I was still my own unhappy prisoner, unable to live in such a state yet powerless to escape from it. Where could my heart find refuge from itself? Where could I go, yet leave myself behind? Was there any place where I should not be a prey to myself? None. But I left my native town. For my eyes were less tempted to look for my friend in a place where they had not grown used to seeing him. So from Thagaste I went to Carthage.

8

Time never stands still, nor does it idly pass without effect upon our feelings or fail to work its wonders on the mind. It came and went, day after day, and as it passed it filled me with fresh hope and new thoughts to remember. Little by little it pieced me together again by means of the old pleasures which I had once enjoyed. My sorrow gave way to them. But it was replaced, if not by sorrow of another kind, by things which held the germ of sorrow still to come. For the grief I felt for the loss of my friend had struck so easily into my inmost heart simply because I had poured out my soul upon him, like water upon sand, loving a man who was mortal as though he were never to die. My greatest comfort and relief was in the solace of other friends who shared my love of the huge fable which I loved instead of you, my God, the long-drawn lie which our minds were always *itching to hear*,[62] only to be defiled by its adulterous caress.

But if one of my friends died, the fable did not die with him. And friendship had other charms to captivate my heart. We could talk and laugh together and exchange small acts of kindness. We could join in the pleasure that books can give. We could be grave or gay together. If we sometimes disagreed, it was without spite, as a man might differ with himself, and the rare occasions of dispute were the very spice to season our usual accord. Each of us had something to learn from the others and something to teach in return. If any were away, we missed them with regret and gladly welcomed them when they came home. Such things as these are heartfelt tokens of affection between friends. They are signs to be read on the face and in the eyes, spoken by the tongue and displayed in countless acts of kindness. They can kindle a blaze to melt our hearts and weld them into one.

9

This is what we cherish in friendship, and we cherish it so dearly that in conscience we feel guilty if we do not return love for love, asking no more of our friends than these expressions of goodwill. This is why we mourn their death, which shrouds us in sorrow and turns joy into bitterness, so that the heart is drenched in tears and life becomes a living death because a friend is lost. Blessed are those who love you, O God, and love

[61] Horace, *Odes* I, 3.8.
[62] II Tim. 4.3.

their friends in you and their enemies for your sake. They alone will never lose those who are dear to them, for they love them in one who is never lost, in God, our God who made heaven and earth and fills them with his presence, because by filling them he made them. No one can lose you, my God, unless he forsakes you. And if he forsakes you, where is he to go? If he abandons your love, his only refuge is your wrath. Wherever he turns, he will find your law to punish him, for your law is the truth and the truth is yourself.

[...]

16

When I was only about twenty years of age Aristotle's book on the "Ten Categories" came into my hands. Whenever my teacher at Carthage and others who were reputed to be scholars mentioned this book, their cheeks would swell with self-importance, so that the title alone was enough to make me stand agape, as though I were poised over some wonderful divine mystery. I managed to read it and understand it without help, though I now ask myself what advantage I gained from doing so. Other people told me that they had understood it only with difficulty, after the most learned masters had not only explained it to them but also illustrated it with a wealth of diagrams. But when I discussed it with them, I found that they could tell me no more about it than I had already discovered by reading it on my own.

The meaning of the book seemed clear enough to me. It defined *substance*, such as man, and its attributes. For instance, a man has a certain shape; this is *quality*. He has height, measured in feet, which is *quantity*. He has *relation* to other men; for example, he is another man's brother. You may say *where* he is and *when* he was born, or describe his *position* as standing or sitting. You may name his *possessions* by saying that he has shoes or carries arms. You may define *what he does* and *what is done to him*. I have mentioned these examples, but there are countless others, all falling into these nine categories or the main category of substance.

What profit did this study bring me? None. In fact it made difficulties for me, because I thought that everything that existed could be reduced to these ten categories, and I therefore attempted to understand you, my God, in all your wonderful immutable simplicity, in these same terms, as though you too were substance, and greatness and beauty were your attributes in the same way that a body has attributes by which it is defined. But your greatness and beauty are your own self: whereas a body is not great or beautiful simply because it is a body. It would still be a body, even if it were less great or less beautiful. My conception of you was quite untrue, a mere falsehood. It was a fiction based on my own wretched state, not the firm foundation of your bliss. It was your command that *the ground should yield me thorns and this-tles*[63] and that I should *earn my bread with the sweat of my brow.*[64] And your word was accomplished in me.

I read and understood by myself all the books that I could find on the so-called liberal arts, for in those days I was a good-for-nothing and a slave to sordid ambitions. But what advantage did I gain from them? I read them with pleasure, but I did not know the real source of such true and certain facts as they contained. I had my back to the light and my face was turned towards the things which it illumined, so that my eyes, by which I saw the things which stood in the light, were themselves in darkness. Without great difficulty and without need of a teacher I understood all that I read on the arts of rhetoric and logic, on geometry, music, and mathematics. You know this, O Lord my God, because if a man is quick to understand and his perception is keen, he has these gifts from you. But since I made no offering of them to you, it did me more harm than good to struggle to keep in my own power so large a part of what you had given to me and, instead of preserving my strength for you,[65] to leave you and *go to a far country*[66] to squander your gifts on loves that sold themselves for money. For what good to me was my ability, if I did not use it well? And ability I had, for until I tried to instruct others I did not realize that these subjects are very difficult to master, even for pupils who are studious and intelligent, and a student who could follow my instruction without faltering was reckoned a very fine scholar.

---

[63] Gen. 3.18.

[64] Gen. 3.19.

[65] See Ps. 58.10 (59.9).

[66] Luke, 15.13.

But what value did I gain from my reading as long as I thought that you, Lord God who are the Truth, were a bright, unbounded body and I a small piece broken from it? What utter distortion of the truth! Yet this was my belief; and I do not now blush to acknowledge, my God, the mercies you have shown to me, nor to call you to my aid, just as in those days I did not blush to declare my blasphemies aloud and snarl at you like a dog. What, then, was the value to me of my intelligence, which could take these subjects in its stride, and all those books, with their tangled problems, which I unravelled without the help of any human tutor, when in the doctrine of your love I was lost in the most hideous error and the vilest sacrilege? And was it so great a drawback to your faithful children that they were slower than I to understand such things? For they did not forsake you, but grew like fledglings in the safe nest of your Church, nourishing the wings of charity on the food of the faith that would save them.

[...]

Book V

1

Accept my confessions, O Lord. They are a sacrifice offered by my tongue, for yours was the hand that fashioned it and yours the spirit that moved it to acknowledge you. Heal all my bones and let them say *Lord, there is none like you.*[67]

If a man confesses to you, he does not reveal his inmost thoughts to you as though you did not know them. For the heart may shut itself away, but it cannot hide from your sight. Man's heart may be hard, but it cannot resist the touch of your hand. Whenever you will, your mercy or your punishment can make it relent, and just as none can hide away from the sun, *none can escape your burning heat.*[68]

Let my soul praise you, so that it may show its love; and let it make avowal of your mercies, so that for these it may praise you. No part of your creation ever ceases to resound in praise of you. Man turns his lips to you in prayer and his spirit praises you. Animals too and lifeless things as well praise you through the lips of all who give them

thought. For our souls lean for support upon the things which you have created, so that we may be lifted up to you from our weakness and use them to help us on our way to you who made them all so wonderfully. And in you we are remade and find true strength.

2

Let the wicked go upon their way and fly from you, for they know no rest. But your eye can pierce the darkness; you can see them. All the world about them teems with beauty and they alone defile it. What harm have they been able to inflict on you? Have they been able to bring disgrace upon your rule, which reaches in its indivisible justice from the heights of heaven to the meanest things of earth? Where did they find refuge when they turned from your face and fled? What hiding place can they find where you cannot seek them out? They have fled and hidden their eyes from you, knowing that yours are on them. They are blind and do not see the God they have offended; but you are there, because you abandon no part of your creation. They have offended against your justice and for this they have justly suffered, because they have stolen away from your gentle mercy and sinned against your law, and so they have fallen down upon your anger.

Clearly the wicked do not know that you are everywhere. But you are not bound within the limits of any place. You alone are always present, even to those who set themselves apart from you. Let them then turn back and look for you. They will find that you have not deserted your creatures as they have deserted their Creator. Let them turn back, and they will find you in their hearts, in the hearts of all who confess to you and throw themselves upon your mercy, in the hearts of all who have left the hard path and come to weep upon your breast. Gently you wipe away their tears. They weep the more, but now their tears are tears of joy, because it is not some man of flesh and blood but you, O Lord, their Maker, who remakes them and consoles them.

But where was I when I looked for you? You were there before my eyes, but I had deserted even my own self. I could not find myself, much less find you.

[67] Ps. 34.10 (35.10).
[68] Ps. 18.7 (19.6).

3

In the sight of my God I will describe the twenty-ninth year of my age.

A Manichean bishop named Faustus had recently arrived at Carthage. He was a great decoy of the devil and many people were trapped by his charming manner of speech. This I certainly admired, but I was beginning to distinguish between mere eloquence and the real truth, which I was so eager to learn. The Manichees talked so much about this man Faustus that I wanted to see what scholarly fare he would lay before me, and I did not care what words he used to garnish the dish. I had already heard that he was very well versed in all the higher forms of learning and particularly in the liberal sciences.

I had read a great many scientific books which were still alive in my memory. When I compared them with the tedious tales of the Manichees, it seemed to me that, of the two, the theories of the scientists were the more likely to be true. For *their thoughts could reach far enough to form a judgement about the world around them*, though *they found no trace of him who is Master of it*.[69] You, Lord, *who are so high above us; yet look with favour on the humble, look on the proud too, but from far off*.[70] You come close only to men who are humble at heart.[71] The proud cannot find you, even though by dint of study they have skill to number stars and grains of sand, to measure the tracts of constellations and trace the paths of planets.

The reason and understanding by which they investigate these things are gifts they have from you. By means of them they have discovered much and foretold eclipses of the sun and moon many years before they happened. They calculated the day and the hour of the eclipse, and whether it would be total or partial, and their reckonings were found correct because it all happened as they had predicted. They wrote down the principles which they had discovered, and their books are still read and used to forecast the year, the month, the day, and the hour of eclipses of the sun and moon, and the degree of their totality. And these eclipses will take place just as they foretell.

These powers are a source of wonder and astonishment to men who do not know the secrets. But the astronomers are flattered and claim the credit for themselves.

[...]

All the same I remembered many of the true things that they had said about the created world, and I saw that their calculations were borne out by mathematics, the regular succession of the seasons and the visible evidence of the stars. I compared it all with the teaching of Manes, who had written a great deal on these subjects, all of it extremely incoherent. But in his writings I could find no reasonable explanation of the solstices and the equinoxes or of eclipses and similar phenomena such as I had read about in books written by secular scientists. Yet I was expected to believe what he had written, although it was entirely at variance and out of keeping with the principles of mathematics and the evidence of my own eyes.

[...]

6

For almost the whole of those nine years during which my mind was unsettled and I was an aspirant of the Manichees, I awaited the coming of this man Faustus with the keenest expectation. Other members of the sect whom I happened to meet were unable to answer the questions I raised upon these subjects, but they assured me that once Faustus had arrived I had only to discuss them with him and he would have no difficulty in giving me a clear explanation of my queries and any other more difficult problems which I might put forward.

At last he arrived. I found him a man of agreeable personality, with a pleasant manner of speech, who pattered off the usual Manichean arguments with a great deal more than the usual charm. But my thirst was not to be satisfied in this way, however precious the cup and however exquisite the man who served it. My ears were already ringing with these tales and they seemed to me none the better for being better expressed, nor true simply because they were eloquently told. Neither did I think that a pleasant face and a gifted tongue were proof of a wise mind. Those who had given me such assurances about him must have been poor

---

[69] Wisd. 13.9.

[70] Ps. 137.6 (138.6).

[71] See Ps. 33.19 (34.18).

judges. They thought him wise and thoughtful simply because they were charmed by his manner of speech.

I have known men of another sort, who look on truth with suspicion and are unwilling to accept it if it is presented in fine, rounded phrases. But in your wonderful, secret way, my God, you had already taught me that a statement is not necessarily true because it is wrapped in fine language or false because it is awkwardly expressed. I believe that it was you who taught me this, because it is the truth and there is no other teacher of the truth besides yourself, no matter how or where it comes to light. You had already taught me this lesson and the converse truth, that an assertion is not necessarily true because it is badly expressed or false because it is finely spoken. I had learnt that wisdom and folly are like different kinds of food. Some are wholesome and others are not, but both can be served equally well on the finest china dish or the meanest earthenware. In just the same way, wisdom and folly can be clothed alike in plain words or the finest flowers of speech.

My long and eager expectation of Faustus's arrival was amply rewarded by the way in which he set about the task of disputation and the goodwill that he showed. The ease with which he found the right words to clothe his thoughts delighted me, and I was not the only one to applaud it, though perhaps I did so more than most. But I found it tiresome, when so many people assembled to hear him, not to be allowed to approach him with my difficulties and lay them before him in the friendly give-and-take of conversation. As soon as the opportunity arose I and some of my friends claimed his attention at a time when a private discussion would not be inappropriate. I mentioned some of my doubts, but soon discovered that except for a rudimentary knowledge of literature he had no claims to scholarship. He had read some of Cicero's speeches, one or two books of Seneca, some poetry, and such books as had been written in good Latin by members of his sect. Besides his daily practice as a speaker, this reading was the basis of his eloquence, which derived extra charm and plausibility from his attractive personality and his ability to make good use of his mental powers.

O Lord my God, is this not the truth as I remember it? You are the Judge of my conscience, and my heart and my memory lie open before you. The secret hand of your providence guided me then, and you set my abject errors before my eyes so that I might see them and detest them.

7

As soon as it became clear to me that Faustus was quite uninformed about the subjects in which I had expected him to be an expert, I began to lose hope that he could lift the veil and resolve the problems which perplexed me. Of course, despite his ignorance of these matters he might still have been a truly pious man, provided he were not a Manichee. The Manichean books are full of the most tedious fictions about the sky and the stars, the sun and the moon. I badly wanted Faustus to compare these with the mathematical calculations which I had studied in other books, so that I might judge whether the Manichean theories were more likely to be true or, at least, equally probable, but I now began to realize that he could not give me a detailed explanation. When I suggested that we should consider these problems and discuss them together, he was certainly modest enough not to undertake the task. He knew that he did not know the answers to my questions and was not ashamed to admit it, for unlike many other talkative people whom I have had to endure, he would not try to teach me a lesson when he had nothing to say. He had a heart, and though his approach to you was mistaken, he was not without discretion. He was not entirely unaware of his limitations and did not want to enter rashly into an argument which might force him into a position which he could not possibly maintain and from which he could not easily withdraw. I liked him all the better for this, because modesty and candour are finer equipment for the mind than scientific knowledge of the kind that I wished to possess. I found that his attitude towards all the more difficult and abstruse questions was the same.

The keen interest which I had had in Manichean doctrines was checked by this experience, and my confidence in the other teachers of the sect was further diminished when I saw that Faustus, of whom they spoke so much, was obviously unable to settle the numerous problems which troubled me. His enthusiasm for literature, which I was then teaching to students at Carthage, often brought us together, and I set out to read with him either the books which he knew by repute and was eager to study or such works as I thought suitable for a man of his intelligence. But once I had come to know him well all my endeavours to make progress in the sect, as I had intended, were abandoned. I did not cut myself off entirely from the Manichees, but as I could find nothing better than the beliefs which I had stumbled upon more or less by chance, I decided to be content with them for the time being, unless something preferable clearly presented itself to me.

[...]

8

It was, then, by your guidance that I was persuaded to go to Rome and teach there the subjects which I taught at Carthage. I will not omit to confess to you how I was persuaded to do this, because even in matters like these we need to reflect upon your sublime secrets and the mercy which you are always ready to show to us.

It was not because I could earn higher fees and greater honours that I wanted to go to Rome, though these were the rewards promised me by my friends, who urged me to go. Naturally these considerations influenced me, but the most important reason, and almost the only one, was that I had heard that the behaviour of young students at Rome was quieter. Discipline was stricter and they were not permitted to rush insolently and just as they pleased into the lecture-rooms of teachers who were not their own masters. In fact they were not admitted at all without the master's permission. At Carthage, on the other hand, the students are beyond control and their behaviour is disgraceful. They come blustering into the lecture-rooms like a troop of maniacs and upset the orderly arrangements which the master has made in the interest of his pupils. Their recklessness is unbelievable and they often commit outrages which ought to be punished by law, were it not that custom protects them. Nevertheless, it is a custom which only proves their plight the more grievous, because it supposedly sanctions behaviour which your eternal law will never allow. They think that they do these things with impunity, but the very blindness with which they do them is punishment in itself and they suffer far more harm than they inflict.

As a student I had refused to take part in this behaviour, but as a teacher I was obliged to endure it in others. This was why I was glad to go to a place where, by all accounts, such disturbances did not occur. But it was to save my soul that you obliged me to go and live elsewhere, you who are *my only Refuge, all that is left me in this world of living men.*[72] You applied the spur that would drive me away from Carthage and offered me enticements that would draw me to Rome, and for your purpose you made use of men whose hearts were set upon this life of death, some acting like madmen, others promising me vain rewards. In secret you were using my own perversity and theirs to set my feet upon the right course. For those who upset my leisure were blind in their shameless violence, and those who tempted me to go elsewhere knew only the taste of worldly things. As for myself, life at Carthage was a real misery and I loathed it: but the happiness I hoped to find at Rome was not real happiness.

You knew, O God, why it was that I left one city and went to the other. But you did not make the reason clear either to me or to my mother. She wept bitterly to see me go and followed me to the water's edge, clinging to me with all her strength in the hope that I would either come home or take her with me. I deceived her with the excuse that I had a friend whom I did not want to leave until the wind rose and his ship could sail. It was a lie, told to my own mother – and to such a mother, too! But you did not punish me for it, because you forgave me this sin also when in your mercy you kept me safe from the waters of the sea, laden though I was with detestable impurities, and preserved me to receive the water of your grace. This was the water that would wash me clean and halt the flood of tears with which my mother daily watered the ground as she bowed her head, praying to you for me.

But she would not go home without me and it was all I could do to persuade her to stay that night in a shrine dedicated to Saint Cyprian, not far from the ship. During the night, secretly, I sailed away, leaving her alone to her tears and her prayers. And what did she beg of you, my God, with all those tears, if not that you would prevent me from sailing? But you did not do as she asked you then. Instead, in the depth of your wisdom, you granted the wish that was closest to her heart. You did with me what she had always asked you to do. The wind blew and filled our sails, and the shore

---

[72] Ps. 114.6 (142.5).

disappeared from sight. The next morning she was wild with grief, pouring her sighs and sorrows in your ear, because she thought you had not listened to her prayer. But you were letting my own desires carry me away on a journey that was to put an end to those same desires, and you used her too jealous love for her son as a scourge of sorrow for her just punishment. For as mothers do, and far more than most, she loved to have me with her, and she did not know what joys you had in store for her because of my departure. It was because she did not know this that she wept and wailed, and the torments which she suffered were proof that she had inherited the legacy of Eve, seeking in sorrow what with sorrow she had brought into the world. But at last she ceased upbraiding me for my deceit and my cruelty and turned again to you to offer her prayers for me. She went back to her house, and I went on to Rome.

[...]

10

[...]

I began to think that the philosophers known as Academics were wiser than the rest, because they held that everything was a matter of doubt and asserted that man can know nothing for certain. This is the common belief about their teaching and it seemed evident to me that it was what they thought, but I did not yet understand what they really meant. At the same time I did not scruple to discourage my host from placing too much confidence, as I saw that he did, in the tales which fill the pages of the Manichean books. Nevertheless I remained on more familiar terms with the Manichees than with others who did not share their heresy. I no longer advocated their cause with my old enthusiasm, but many of them were to be found in Rome, living unobtrusively, and their friendship made me slow to seek another, especially since I had lost hope of being able to find the truth in your Church, O Lord of heaven and earth, Creator of all things visible and invisible. The Manichees had turned me away from it: at the same time I thought it outrageous to believe that you had the shape of a human body and were limited within the dimensions of limbs like our own. When I tried to think of my God, I could think of him only as a bodily substance, because I could not conceive of the existence of anything else. This was the principal and almost the only cause of the error from which I could not escape.

For the same reason I believed that evil, too, was some similar kind of substance, a shapeless, hideous mass, which might be solid, in which case the Manichees called it earth, or fine and rarefied like air. This they imagine as a kind of evil mind filtering through the substance they call earth. And because such little piety as I had compelled me to believe that God, who is good, could not have created an evil nature, I imagined that there were two antagonistic masses, both of which were infinite, yet the evil in a lesser and the good in a greater degree.

All my other sacrilegious beliefs were the outcome of this first fatal mistake. For when I tried to fall back upon the Catholic faith, my mind recoiled because the Catholic faith was not what I supposed it to be. My theories forced me to admit that you were finite in one point only, in so far as the mass of evil was able to oppose you; but, O my God, whose mercies I now aver, if I believed that you were infinite in all other ways, I thought that this was a more pious belief than to suppose that you were limited, in each and every way, by the outlines of a human body. And it seemed to me better to believe that you had created no evil than to suppose that evil, such as I imagined it to be, had its origin in you. For, ignorant as I was, I thought of evil not simply as some vague substance but as an actual bodily substance, and this was because I could not conceive of mind except as a rarefied body somehow diffused in space. I also thought of our Saviour, your only Son, as somehow extended or projected for our salvation from the mass of your transplendent body, and I was so convinced of this that I could believe nothing about him except such futile dreams as I could picture to myself. I did not believe that a nature such as his could have taken birth from the Virgin Mary unless it were mingled with her flesh; and, if it were such as I imagined it to be, I could not see how it could be mingled with her flesh without being defiled. So I dared not believe in his incarnation, for fear that I should be compelled to believe that the flesh had defiled him.

Those who have the gifts of your Holy Spirit will laugh at me, in all kindness and charity, if they read of this confusion in my mind. But this was the man that I was.

[...]

12

I began actively to set about the business of teaching literature and public speaking, which was the purpose for which I had come to Rome. At first I taught in my house, where I collected a number of pupils who had heard of me, and through them my reputation began to grow. But I now realized that there were difficulties in Rome with which I had not had to contend in Africa. True enough, I found that there was no rioting by young hooligans, but I was told that at any moment a number of students would plot together to avoid paying their master his fees and would transfer in a body to another. They were quite unscrupulous, and justice meant nothing to them compared with the love of money.

[...]

13

So, when the Prefect of Rome received a request from Milan to find a teacher of literature and elocution for the city, with a promise that travelling expenses would be charged to public funds, I applied for the appointment, armed with recommendations from my friends who were so fuddled with the Manichean rigmarole. This journey was to mean the end of my association with them, though none of us knew it at the time. Eventually Symmachus, who was then Prefect, set me a test to satisfy himself of my abilities and sent me to Milan.

In Milan I found your devoted servant the bishop Ambrose, who was known throughout the world as a man whom there were few to equal in goodness. At that time his gifted tongue never tired of dispensing the richness of your corn, the joy of your oil, and the sober intoxication of your wine.[73] Unknown to me, it was you who led me to him, so that I might knowingly be led by him to you. This man of God received me like a father and, as bishop, told me how glad he was that I had come. My heart warmed to him, not at first as a teacher of the truth, which I had quite despaired of finding in your Church, but simply as a man who showed me kindness. I listened attentively when he preached to the people, though not with the proper intention; for my purpose was to judge for myself whether the reports of his powers as a speaker were accurate, or whether eloquence flowed from him more, or less, readily than I had been told. So while I paid the closest attention to the words he used, I was quite uninterested in the subject-matter and was even contemptuous of it. I was delighted with his charming delivery, but although he was a more learned speaker than Faustus, he had not the same soothing and gratifying manner. I am speaking only of his style for, as to content, there could be no comparison between the two. Faustus had lost his way among the fallacies of Manicheism, while Ambrose most surely taught the doctrine of salvation. But *your mercy is unknown to sinners*[74] such as I was then, though step by step, unwittingly, I was coming closer to it.

14

For although I did not trouble to take what Ambrose said to heart, but only to listen to the manner in which he said it – this being the only paltry interest that remained to me now that I had lost hope that man could find the path that led to you – nevertheless his meaning, which I tried to ignore, found its way into my mind together with his words, which I admired so much. I could not keep the two apart, and while I was all ears to seize upon his eloquence, I also began to sense the truth of what he said, though only gradually. First of all it struck me that it was, after all, possible to vindicate his arguments. I began to believe that the Catholic faith, which I had thought impossible to defend against the objections of the Manichees, might fairly be maintained, especially since I had heard one passage after another in the Old Testament figuratively explained. These passages had been death[75] to me when I took them literally, but once I had heard them explained in their spiritual meaning I began to blame myself for my despair, at least in so far as it had led me to suppose that it was quite impossible to counter people who hated and derided the law and the prophets.

[...]

---

[73] These phrases are modifications of verses from the Psalms. Cf. Ps. 4.8 (4.7), 44.8 (45.7), and 80.17 (81.16). The words "sober intoxication" are borrowed from Saint Ambrose's hymn "Splendor paternae gloriae."

[74] Ps. 118.155 (119.155).

[75] See II Cor. 3.6.

Book VI

[...]

4

[...]

Anxiety about what I could believe as certain gnawed at my heart all the more sharply as I grew more and more ashamed that I had been misled and deluded by promises of certainty for so long, and had talked wildly, like an ignorant child, about so many unconfirmed theories as though they were beyond question. It was only later that I realized that they were false. But by now I was sure at least that there was no certainty in them, though I had taken them for true when I blindly attacked your Catholic Church. Though I had not yet discovered that what the Church taught was the truth, at least I had learnt that she did not teach the doctrines which I so sternly denounced. This bewildered me, but I was on the road to conversion and I was glad, my God, that the one Church, the Body of your only Son, in which the name of Christ had been put upon me as a child, had no liking for childish absurdities and there was nothing in the sound doctrine which she taught to show that you, the Creator of all things, were confined within a measure of space which, however high, however wide it might be, was yet strictly determined by the form of a human body.

I was glad too that at last I had been shown how to interpret the ancient Scriptures of the law and the prophets in a different light from that which had previously made them seem absurd, when I used to criticize your saints for holding beliefs which they had never really held at all. I was pleased to hear that in his sermons to the people Ambrose often repeated the text: *The written law inflicts death, whereas the spiritual law brings life,*[76] as though this were a rule upon which he wished to insist most carefully. And when he lifted the veil of mystery and disclosed the spiritual meaning of texts which, taken literally, appeared to contain the most unlikely doctrines, I was not aggrieved by what he said, although I did not yet know whether it was true.

[...]

5

From now on I began to prefer the Catholic teaching. The Church demanded that certain things should be believed even though they could not be proved, for if they could be proved, not all men could understand the proof, and some could not be proved at all. I thought that the Church was entirely honest in this and far less pretentious than the Manichees, who laughed at people who took things on faith, made rash promises of scientific knowledge, and then put forward a whole system of preposterous inventions which they expected their followers to believe on trust because they could not be proved. Then, O Lord, you laid your most gentle, most merciful finger on my heart and set my thoughts in order, for I began to realize that I believed countless things which I had never seen or which had taken place when I was not there to see – so many events in the history of the world, so many facts about places and towns which I had never seen, and so much that I believed on the word of friends or doctors or various other people. Unless we took these things on trust, we should accomplish absolutely nothing in this life. Most of all it came home to me how firm and unshakeable was the faith which told me who my parents were, because I could never have known this unless I believed what I was told. In this way you made me understand that I ought not to find fault with those who believed your Bible, which you have established with such great authority amongst almost all the nations of the earth, but with those who did not believe it; and that I ought to pay no attention to people who asked me how I could be sure that the Scriptures were delivered to mankind by the Spirit of the one true God who can tell no lie. It was precisely this that I most needed to believe, because in all the conflicting books of philosophy which I had read no misleading proposition, however contentious, had been able, even for one moment, to wrest from me my belief in your existence and in your right to govern human affairs; and this despite the fact that I had no knowledge of what you are.

[...]

[76] II Cor. 3.6.

11

I found much to bewilder me in my memories of the long time which had passed since I was nineteen, the age at which I had first begun to search in earnest for truth and wisdom and had promised myself that, once I had found them, I would give up all the vain hopes and mad delusions which sustained my futile ambitions. I realized that I was now thirty years old and was still floundering in the same quagmire, because I was greedy to enjoy what the world had to offer, though it only eluded me and wasted my strength. And all the time I had been telling myself one tale after another.

"Tomorrow I shall discover the truth. I shall see it quite plainly, and it will be mine to keep. ...

"Faustus will come and explain everything. ...

"The Academics! What wonderful men they are! Is it true that we can never know for certain how we ought to manage our lives? ...

"No, not that! we must search all the more carefully and never despair. I can see now that the passages in Scripture which I used to think absurd are not absurd at all. They can be understood in another sense, quite fairly. I shall fix my foot firmly on the step where my parents set me as a boy, until I find the manifest truth. But where and when am I to look for it? Ambrose has no time to spare and I have no time for reading. Where am I to look for the books I need? Where and when can I buy them or get someone to lend them to me? I must plan my time and arrange my day for the good of my soul. ...

"Great hope is born in me, because I have found that the doctrines of the Catholic faith are not what I thought them to be, and my accusations were unfounded. The learned men of the Church hold it wrong to believe that God is limited by the shape of a human body. Why, then, do I hesitate to knock, so that the door may be opened to reveal what is still hidden from me? ...

"My pupils keep me busy all the morning, but how do I use the rest of my day? Why should I not spend it knocking at God's door? Yet if I did, when could I visit my influential friends, whose patronage I need? When could I prepare the lessons for which I am paid by my students? When could I refresh my own mind by giving it a rest from the troubles which absorb it? ...

"All this must go by the board. I must dismiss all these futile trifles from my mind and devote myself entirely to the search for truth. Life is a misery and I do not know when death may come. If it steals upon me, shall I be in a fit state to leave this world? Where could I then learn all that I have neglected to learn in this life? Is it not more probable that I should have to pay a heavy penalty for my negligence? ...

"Suppose death puts an end to all care. Suppose that it cuts it off together with the senses of the body. This is another problem to be solved ...

"But it is unthinkable that this could be true. It is not for nothing, not mere chance, that the towering authority of the Christian faith has spread throughout the world. God would never have done so much, such wonderful things for us if the life of the soul came to an end with the death of the body. Why then do I delay? Why do I not abandon my worldly hopes and give myself up entirely to the search for God and the life of true happiness? ...

"But not so fast! This life too is sweet. It has its own charms. They are not of small account and a man must not lightly undertake to detach his mind from them, because to return to them later would be a disgrace. ...

"It would need little effort to win myself a position of some standing in the world, and what more could a man ask? I have many influential friends, and if I press for nothing more, I may at least obtain a governor's post. I could marry a wife who would bring me a small dowry, so that the expense would be no burden, and this would be the limit of my ambitions. There have been many great men who have dedicated themselves to the pursuit of wisdom even though they were married, and I might do well to follow their example."

As I reasoned with myself in this way, my heart was buffeted hither and thither by winds blowing from opposite quarters. Time was passing and I kept delaying my conversion to you, my God. Day after day I postponed living in you, but I never put off the death which I died each day in myself. I longed for a life of happiness but I was frightened to approach it in its own domain; and yet, while I fled from it, I still searched for it. I thought it would be too much for me to bear if I were to be deprived of woman's love. In your mercy you have given us a remedy to cure this weakness, but I gave it no thought because I had never tried it for myself. I believed that continence was to be achieved by man's own power, which I knew that I did not possess. Fool that I was, I did not know that no man *can be master of himself, except of God's bounty*,[77] as your Bible tells us. And you would have given me this strength, if I had allowed the cries of my soul to beat upon your ears and had had faith firm enough to shed my troubles on to you.

12

It was Alypius who prevented me from marrying, because he insisted that if I did so, we could not possibly live together in uninterrupted leisure, devoted to the pursuit of wisdom, as we had long desired to do. As for himself, even as a grown man he was quite remarkably self-controlled in matters of sex. In early adolescence he had had the experience of sexual intercourse, but it had not become habitual. In fact he had been ashamed of it and thought it degrading and, ever since, he had lived a life of the utmost chastity. For my part I answered his arguments by pointing to the example of married men who had been lovers of wisdom, had served God well, and had retained the affection of their friends, whom they had loyally loved in return. But I was far from being the equal of these noble spirits. I was bound down by this disease of the flesh. Its deadly pleasures were a chain that I dragged along with me, yet I was afraid to be freed from it; and I refused to accept the good advice of Alypius, repelling the hand that meant to loose my bonds, as though it only rubbed my sores.

Moreover, the serpent used me as a mouth-piece to speak to Alypius himself. Satan twisted my words into snares that were meant to entice, and strewed them in the path to trap the feet of his victim, who walked in all innocence with no burden to bear.

Alypius could not understand how it was that I, of whom he thought so highly, could be so firmly caught in the toils of sexual pleasure as to assert, whenever we discussed the subject, that I could not possibly endure the life of a celibate. When I saw that he was puzzled by my words, I used to defend them by saying that there was a great difference between his own hasty, furtive experience and my enjoyment of a settled way of life. In his case, since he could scarcely remember the occasion, he might easily disparage it: but in mine, it

required only the respectable name of marriage and he need no longer wonder why I found it impossible to turn my back upon it. [...]

13

I was being urged incessantly to marry, and had already made my proposal and been accepted. My mother had done all she could to help, for it was her hope that, once I was married, I should be washed clean of my sins by the saving waters of baptism. She was delighted that, day by day, I was becoming more fitted for baptism, and in my acceptance of the faith she saw the answer to her prayers and the fulfilment of your promises. At my request and by her own desire she daily beseeched you with heartfelt prayers to send her some revelation in a vision about my future marriage, but this you would not do. She had some vague and fanciful dreams, which were the result of her preoccupation with these thoughts, and when she told me about them, she treated them as of no importance and did not speak with the assurance that she always had when you sent her visions. She always said that by some sense, which she could not describe in words, she was able to distinguish between your revelations and her own natural dreams. All the same, the plans for my marriage were pushed ahead and the girl's parents asked for their consent. She was nearly two years too young for marriage, but I liked her well enough and was content to wait.

[...]

15

Meanwhile I was sinning more and more. The woman with whom I had been living was torn from my side as an obstacle to my marriage and this was a blow which crushed my heart to bleeding, because I loved her dearly. She went back to Africa, vowing never to give herself to any other man, and left with me the son whom she had borne me. But I was too unhappy and too weak to imitate this example set me by a woman. I was impatient at the delay of two years which had to pass before the girl whom I had asked to marry became my wife, and because I was more a slave

---

[77] Wisd. 8.21.

of lust than a true lover of marriage, I took another mistress, without the sanction of wedlock. This meant that the disease of my soul would continue unabated, in fact it would be aggravated, and under the watch and ward of uninterrupted habit it would persist into the state of marriage. Furthermore the wound that I had received when my first mistress was wrenched away showed no signs of healing. At first the pain was sharp and searing, but then the wound began to fester, and though the pain was duller there was all the less hope of a cure.

[...]

Book VIII

1

My God, let me be thankful as I remember and acknowledge all your mercies. Let my whole self be steeped in love of you and all my being cry *Lord, there is none like you!*[78] *You have broken the chains that bound me; I will sacrifice in your honour.*[79] I shall tell how it was that you broke them and, when they hear what I have to tell, all who adore you will exclaim, "Blessed be the Lord in heaven and on earth. Great and wonderful is his name."

[...]

7

[...]

Many years of my life had passed – twelve, unless I am wrong – since I had read Cicero's *Hortensius* at the age of nineteen and it had inspired me to study philosophy. But I still postponed my renunciation of this world's joys, which would have left me free to look for that other happiness, the very search for which, let alone its discovery, I ought to have prized above the discovery of all human treasures and kingdoms or the ability to enjoy all the pleasures of the body at a mere nod of the head. As a youth I had been woefully at fault, particularly in early adolescence. I had prayed to you for chastity and said "Give me chastity and continence, but not yet." For I was afraid that you would answer my prayer at once and cure me too soon of the disease of lust, which I wanted satisfied, not quelled. I had wandered on along the road of vice in the sacrilegious superstition of the Manichees, not because I thought that it was right, but because I preferred it to the Christian belief, which I did not explore as I ought but opposed out of malice.

I had pretended to myself that the reason why, day after day, I staved off the decision to renounce worldly ambition and follow you alone was that I could see no certain goal towards which I might steer my course. But the time had now come when I stood naked before my own eyes, while my conscience upbraided me. "Am I to be silent? Did you not always say that you would not discard your load of vanity for the sake of a truth that was not proved? Now you know that the truth is proved, but the load is still on your shoulders. Yet here are others who have exchanged their load for wings, although they did not wear themselves out in the search for truth or spend ten years or more in making up their minds."

[...]

8

My inner self was a house divided against itself. In the heat of the fierce conflict which I had stirred up against my soul in our common abode, my heart, I turned upon Alypius. My looks betrayed the commotion in my mind as I exclaimed, "What is the matter with us? What is the meaning of this story? These men have not had our schooling, yet they stand up and storm the gates of heaven while we, for all our learning, lie here grovelling in this world of flesh and blood! Is it because they have led the way that we are ashamed to follow? Is it not worse to hold back?"

I cannot remember the words I used. I said something to this effect and then my feeling proved too strong for me. I broke off and turned away, leaving him to gaze at me speechless and astonished. For my voice sounded strange and the expression of my face and eyes, my flushed cheeks, and the pitch of my voice told him more of the state of my mind than the actual words that I spoke.

There was a small garden attached to the house where we lodged. We were free to make use of it as well as the rest of the house because our host, the owner of the house, did not live there. I now

[78] Ps. 34.10 (35.10).
[79] Ps. 115.7 (116.7).

found myself driven by the tumult in my breast to take refuge in this garden, where no one could interrupt that fierce struggle, in which I was my own contestant, until it came to its conclusion. What the conclusion was to be you knew, O Lord, but I did not. Meanwhile I was beside myself with madness that would bring me sanity. I was dying a death that would bring me life. I knew the evil that was in me, but the good that was soon to be born in me I did not know. So I went out into the garden and Alypius followed at my heels. His presence was no intrusion on my solitude, and how could he leave me in that state? We sat down as far as possible from the house. I was frantic, overcome by violent anger with myself for not accepting your will and entering into your covenant. Yet in my bones I knew that this was what I ought to do. In my heart of hearts I praised it to the skies. And to reach this goal I needed no chariot or ship. I need not even walk as far as I had come from the house to the place where we sat, for to make the journey, and to arrive safely, no more was required than an act of will. But it must be a resolute and whole-hearted act of the will, not some lame wish which I kept turning over and over in my mind, so that it had to wrestle with itself, part of it trying to rise, part falling to the ground.

During this agony of indecision I performed many bodily actions, things which a man cannot always do, even if he wills to do them. If he has lost his limbs, or is bound hand and foot, or if his body is weakened by illness or under some other handicap, there are things which he cannot do. I tore my hair and hammered my forehead with my fists; I locked my fingers and hugged my knees; and I did all this because I made an act of will to do it. But I might have had the will to do it and yet not have done it, if my limbs had been unable to move in compliance with my will. I performed all these actions, in which the will and the power to act are not the same. Yet I did not do that one thing which I should have been far, far better pleased to do than all the rest and could have done at once, as soon as I had the will to do it, because as soon as I had the will to do so, I should have willed it wholeheartedly. For in this case the power to act was the same as the will. To

will it was to do it. Yet I did not do it. My body responded to the slightest wish of my mind by moving its limbs at the least hint from me, and it did so more readily than my mind obeyed itself by assenting to its own great desire, which could be accomplished simply by an act of will.

[...]

12

I probed the hidden depths of my soul and wrung its pitiful secrets from it, and when I mustered them all before the eyes of my heart, a great storm broke within me, bringing with it a great deluge of tears. I stood up and left Alypius so that I might weep and cry to my heart's content, for it occurred to me that tears were best shed in solitude. I moved away far enough to avoid being embarrassed even by his presence. He must have realized what my feelings were, for I suppose I had said some thing and he had known from the sound of my voice that I was ready to burst into tears. So I stood up and left him where we had been sitting, utterly bewildered. Somehow I flung myself down beneath a fig tree and gave way to the tears which now streamed from my eyes, the sacrifice that is acceptable to you.[80] I had much to say to you, my God, not in these very words but in this strain: *Lord, will you never be content?*[81] *Must we always taste your vengeance? Forget the long record of our sins.*[82] For I felt that I was still the captive of my sins, and in my misery I kept crying "How long shall I go on saying 'tomorrow, tomorrow'? Why not now? Why not make an end of my ugly sins at this moment?"

I was asking myself these questions, weeping all the while with the most bitter sorrow in my heart, when all at once I heard the singsong voice of a child in a nearby house. Whether it was the voice of a boy or a girl I cannot say, but again and again it repeated the refrain "Take it and read, take it and read." At this I looked up, thinking hard whether there was any kind of game in which children used to chant words like these, but I could not remember ever hearing them before. I stemmed my flood of tears and stood up, telling myself that this could only be a divine command to open my book of Scripture and read

---

[80] See Ps. 50.19 (51.17).

[81] Ps. 6.4 (6.3).

[82] Ps. 78.5, 8 (79.5, 8).

the first passage on which my eyes should fall. For I had heard the story of Antony, and I remembered how he had happened to go into a church while the Gospel was being read and had taken it as a counsel addressed to himself when he heard the words *Go home and sell all that belongs to you. Give it to the poor, and so the treasure you have shall be in heaven; then come back and follow me.*[83] By this divine pronouncement he had at once been converted to you.

So I hurried back to the place where Alypius was sitting, for when I stood up to move away I had put down the book containing Paul's Epistles. I seized it and opened it, and in silence I read the first passage on which my eyes fell: *Not in revelling and drunkenness, not in lust and wantonness, not in quarrels and rivalries. Rather, arm yourselves with the Lord Jesus Christ; spend no more thought on nature and nature's appetites.*[84] I had no wish to read more and no need to do so. For in an instant, as I came to the end of the sentence, it was as though the light of confidence flooded into my heart and all the darkness of doubt was dispelled.

I marked the place with my finger or by some other sign and closed the book. My looks now were quite calm as I told Alypius what had happened to me. He too told me what he had been feeling, which of course I did not know. He asked to see what I had read. I showed it to him and he read on beyond the text which I had read. I did not know what followed, but it was this: *Find room among you for a man of over-delicate conscience.*[85] Alypius applied this to himself and told me so. This admonition was enough to give him strength, and without suffering the distress of hesitation he made his resolution and took this good purpose to himself. And it very well suited his moral character, which had long been far, far better than my own.

Then we went in and told my mother, who was overjoyed. And when we went on to describe how it had all happened, she was jubilant with triumph and glorified you, *who are powerful enough, and more than powerful enough, to carry out your purpose beyond all our hopes and dreams.*[86] For she saw that you had granted her far more than she used to ask in her tearful prayers and plaintive lamentations. You converted me to yourself, so that I no longer desired a wife or placed any hope in this world but stood firmly upon the rule of faith, where you had shown me to her in a dream so many years before. And you turned her sadness into rejoicing,[87] into joy far fuller than her dearest wish, far sweeter and more chaste than any she had hoped to find in children begotten of my flesh.

[83] Matt. 19.21.
[84] Rom. 13.13, 14. Saint Augustine does not quote the whole passage, which begins *"Let us pass our time honourably, as by the light of day, not in revelling and drunkenness,"* etc.
[85] Rom. 14.1.
[86] Eph. 3.20.
[87] Ps. 29.12 (30.11).

De Doctrina Christiana

De Doctrina Christiana consists of four books, the first three of which Augustine started about the same time that he began writing *Confessions*, in 396 or 397. The last book was added many years later, perhaps in 426 or 427. The work is divided into two parts, with books I–III focusing on the discovery of meaning in Scripture and Book IV focusing on teaching that meaning through allegorical expression. Although *De Doctrina Christiana* is a work of Augustine's maturity, the groundwork was laid before his conversion in Milan when he wrote *De Dialectica – On Dialectic* – a brief treatise for his son that examines ambiguity in language. We detect the influence of Stoicism and perhaps Quintilian in *De Dialectica* when Augustine notes that *Dialectica est bene disputandi scientia* – Dialectic is the science of arguing well. Successful disputation requires that the audience understand the speaker, but a significant obstacle to understanding, or "truth," is the inherent ambiguity and obscurity of words, which are signs signifying that which is perceivable through the senses or imagined in the mind on the basis of experience. When a given sign is unknown, apprehending its meaning and truth is extremely difficult because the mind cannot readily grasp the signification.

In *De Doctrina Christiana*, Augustine developed his concept of signs further, with specific reference to biblical truth. He noted in Book I that "All instruction is either about things or about signs" (I.2), and he identified "things" as a form of linguistic primitive insofar as a "thing" can "never be employed as a sign of anything else" (I.2) – that is, "things" are irreducible objects in the natural world. "Signs," on the other hand, are words, which always *can* be used to signify something else. The distinction, however, is not clear-cut, because "every sign is also a thing," but "Every thing ... is not also a sign" (I.2). The teeth in the Song of Solomon 4.2 (p. 301) are a "thing," but they simultaneously are a sign whose obscurity requires interpretation. "Things" are either for use or enjoyment, yet "if we wish to return to our Father's home, this world must be used, not enjoyed" (I.4); therefore, the only "true objects of enjoyment ... are the Father and the Son and the Holy Spirit" (I.5).

Books II and III provide a discussion of signs, which are identified as "natural" and "conventional." Natural signs lead to knowledge of something else, "as, for example, smoke when it indicates fire" (II. 2). The focus, however, is on conventional signs, because they are the principal factor in interpreting Scripture. The difficulties in understanding the Bible lie in the obscurity and ambiguity of the words, or signs, that make up the text, which is significant because, as noted previously, the language was divinely arranged to be obscure "for the purpose of subduing pride by toil" (II.6). Book II examines obscure signs and, like *De Dialectica*, notes that obscure signs are problematic owing to the fact that they deal with the unknown. Augustine argued that the key to unlocking their hidden meaning lies in the following: 1) fear of God; 2) piety; 3) knowledge of the Bible and Church doctrine; 4) resolve; 5) compassion; 6) purity of eye and heart; and 7) wisdom, which is founded in fear of God.

Book III takes up ambiguous signs. Ambiguity has several sources, such as faulty punctuation and – in a world where nearly all reading was done aloud – pronunciation. More significant is ambiguity that arises from the fact that some biblical expressions are to be understood literally whereas others are to be understood figuratively. Recognizing the difference requires great skill and diligence, but the governing principle is straightforward: Those expressions that when read literally suggest immorality or carnality must be read figuratively. Exodus 7.20, for example, which relates that Moses lifted up his staff and struck the water of the Nile, turning it to blood, is to be read literally. Genesis 19.6, on the other hand, which relates that Lot offered to give up his two daughters to a group of townsmen for sex, is to be read figuratively.

Despite Augustine's declaration to the contrary, Book IV provides the substance of Christian rhetoric, which as already noted is based on allegoresis. Augustine defends the use of rhetoric as the most effective way to counter attacks on Christianity in general and the Bible in particular. As he states in chapter 4, "It is the duty ... of the interpreter and teacher of Holy Scripture ... to teach what is right and to refute what is wrong." Although eloquence is of great importance in teaching the truth of the Scriptures, wisdom is even more important; even so, the goal is to unite eloquence and wisdom, following the stylistic model of the Gospels, especially the Pauline texts. Indeed, style on this account becomes a major feature of Christian rhetoric. Models from the classical tradition, such as Demosthenes, have no validity in this rhetoric.

Kennedy (1980) argued that *De Doctrina Christiana* should be classified as an example of "technical rhetoric" (p. 159) because it lacks any philosophical components. When located in the context of Augustine's other works, however, this assessment is difficult to support. Augustine's development of allegoresis and his application of it not only to the Bible but to life and history (as in *Confessions* and *De Civitae Dei*) are likely to strike many readers as highly philosophical, for they provide a reasonably coherent, if not rigidly systematic, framework for morality and human actions.

Reading 44

De Doctrina Christiana (On Christian Doctrine)

De Doctrina Christiana (On Christian Doctrine) (excerpt), pp. 759–64; 767–84 from Great Books, vol. 16, Saint Augustine, Encyclopaedia Britannica, 1961. Translated by J.F. Shaw.

Book IV

ARGUMENT. *Passing to the second part of his work, that which treats of expression, the author premises that it is no part of his intention to write a treatise on the laws of rhetoric. These can be learned elsewhere, and ought not to be neglected, being indeed specially necessary for the Christian teacher, whom it behoves to excel in eloquence and power of speech. After detailing with much care and minuteness the various qualities of an orator, he recommends the authors of the Holy Scriptures as the best models of eloquence, far excelling all others in the combination of eloquence with wisdom. He points out that perspicuity is the most essential quality of style, and ought to be cultivated with especial care by the teacher, as it is the main requisite for instruction, although other qualities are required for delighting and persuading the hearer. All these gifts are to be sought in earnest prayer from God, though we are not to forget to be zealous and diligent in study. He shows that there are three species of style, the subdued, the elegant, and the majestic; the first serving for instruction, the second for praise, and the third for exhortation: and of each of these he gives examples, selected both from Scripture and from early teachers of the Church, Cyprian and Ambrose. He shows that these various styles may be mingled, and when and for what purposes they are mingled; and that they all have the same end in view, to bring home the truth to the hearer, so that he may understand it, hear it with gladness, and practise it in his life. Finally, he exhorts the Christian teacher himself, pointing out the dignity and responsibility of the*

office he holds, to lead a life in harmony with his own teaching, and to show a good example to all.

Chap. 1.   This work not intended as a treatise on rhetoric

1. This work of mine, which is entitled *On Christian Doctrine*, was at the commencement divided into two parts. For, after a preface, in which I answered by anticipation those who were likely to take exception to the work, I said, "There are two things on which all interpretation of Scripture depends: the mode of ascertaining the proper meaning, and the mode of making known the meaning when it is ascertained. I shall treat first of the mode of ascertaining, next of the mode of making known, the meaning."[88] As, then, I have already said a great deal about the mode of ascertaining the meaning, and have given three books to this one part of the subject, I shall only say a few things about the mode of making known the meaning, in order if possible to bring them all within the compass of one book, and so finish the whole work in four books.

2. In the first place, then, I wish by this preamble to put a stop to the expectations of readers who may think that I am about to lay down rules of rhetoric such as I have learnt, and taught too, in the secular schools, and to warn them that they need not look for any such from me. Not that I think such rules of no use, but that whatever use they have is to be learnt elsewhere; and if any good man should happen to have leisure for learning them, he is not to ask me to teach them either in this work or any other.

[88] BK. 1, Chap. 1.

Chap. 2.   It is lawful for a Christian teacher to use the art of rhetoric

3. Now, the art of rhetoric being available for the enforcing either of truth or falsehood, who will dare to say that truth in the person of its defenders is to take its stand unarmed against falsehood? For example, that those who are trying to persuade men of what is false are to know how to introduce their subject, so as to put the hearer into a friendly, or attentive, or teachable frame of mind, while the defenders of the truth shall be ignorant of that art? That the former are to tell their falsehoods briefly, clearly, and plausibly, while the latter shall tell the truth in such a way that it is tedious to listen to, hard to understand, and, in fine, not easy to believe it? That the former are to oppose the truth and defend falsehood with sophistical arguments, while the latter shall be unable either to defend what is true, or to refute what is false? That the former, while imbuing the minds of their hearers with erroneous opinions, are by their power of speech to awe, to melt, to enliven, and to rouse them, while the latter shall in defence of the truth be sluggish, and frigid, and somnolent? Who is such a fool as to think this wisdom? Since, then, the faculty of eloquence is available for both sides, and is of very great service in the enforcing either of wrong or right, why do not good men study to engage it on the side of truth, when bad men use it to obtain the triumph of wicked and worthless causes, and to further injustice and error?

Chap. 3.   The proper age and the proper means for acquiring rhetorical skill

4. But the theories and rules on this subject (to which, when you add a tongue thoroughly skilled by exercise and habit in the use of many words and many ornaments of speech, you have what is called *eloquence* or *oratory*) may be learnt apart from these writings of mine, if a suitable space of time be set aside for the purpose at a fit and proper age. But only by those who can learn them quickly; for the masters of Roman eloquence themselves did not shrink from saying that any one who cannot learn this art quickly can never thoroughly learn it at all. Whether this be true or not, why need we inquire? For even if this art can occasionally be in the end mastered by men of

slower intellect, I do not think it of so much importance as to wish men who have arrived at mature age to spend time in learning it. It is enough that boys should give attention to it; and even of these, not all who are to be fitted for usefulness in the Church, but only those who are not yet engaged in any occupation of more urgent necessity, or which ought evidently to take precedence of it. For men of quick intellect and glowing temperament find it easier to become eloquent by reading and listening to eloquent speakers than by following rules for eloquence. And even outside the canon, which to our great advantage is fixed in a place of secure authority, there is no want of ecclesiastical writings, in reading which a man of ability will acquire a tinge of the eloquence with which they are written, even though he does not aim at this, but is solely intent on the matters treated of; especially, of course, if in addition he practise himself in writing, or dictating, and at last also in speaking, the opinions he has formed on grounds of piety and faith. If, however, such ability be wanting, the rules of rhetoric are either not understood, or if, after great labour has been spent in enforcing them, they come to be in some small measure understood, they prove of no service. For even those who have learnt them, and who speak with fluency and elegance, cannot always think of them when they are speaking so as to speak in accordance with them, unless they are discussing the rules themselves. Indeed, I think there are scarcely any who can do both things – that is, speak well, and, in order to do this, think of the rules of speaking while they are speaking. For we must be careful that what we have got to say does not escape us whilst we are thinking about saying it according to the rules of art. Nevertheless, in the speeches of eloquent men, we find rules of eloquence carried out which the speakers did not think of as aids to eloquence at the time when they were speaking, whether they had ever learnt them, or whether they had never even met with them. For it is because they are eloquent that they exemplify these rules; it is not that they use them in order to be eloquent.

5. And, therefore, as infants cannot learn to speak except by learning words and phrases from those who do speak, why should not men become eloquent without being taught any art of speech, simply by reading and learning the speeches of eloquent men, and by imitating them as far as they

can? And what do we find from the examples themselves to be the case in this respect? We know numbers who, without acquaintance with rhetorical rules, are more eloquent than many who have learnt these; but we know no one who is eloquent without having read and listened to the speeches and debates of eloquent men. For even the art of grammar, which teaches correctness of speech, need not be learnt by boys, if they have the advantage of growing up and living among men who speak correctly. For without knowing the names of any of the faults, they will, from being accustomed to correct speech, lay hold upon whatever is faulty in the speech of any one they listen to, and avoid it; just as citybred men, even when illiterate, seize upon the faults of rustics.

Chap. 4. The duty of the Christian teacher

6. It is the duty, then, of the interpreter and teacher of Holy Scripture, the defender of the true faith and the opponent of error, both to teach what is right and to refute what is wrong, and in the performance of this task to conciliate the hostile, to rouse the careless, and to tell the ignorant both what is occurring at present and what is probable in the future. But once that his hearers are friendly, attentive, and ready to learn, whether he has found them so, or has himself made them so, the remaining objects are to be carried out in whatever way the case requires. If the hearers need teaching, the matter treated of must be made fully known by means of narrative. On the other hand, to clear up points that are doubtful requires reasoning and the exhibition of proofs. If, however, the hearers require to be roused rather than instructed, in order that they may be diligent to do what they already know, and to bring their feelings into harmony with the truths they admit, greater vigour of speech is needed. Here entreaties and reproaches, exhortations and upbraidings, and all the other means of rousing the emotions, are necessary.

7. And all the methods I have mentioned are constantly used by nearly every one in cases where speech is the agency employed.

Chap. 5. Wisdom of more importance than eloquence to the Christian teacher

But as some men employ these coarsely, inelegantly, and frigidly, while others use them with acuteness, elegance, and spirit, the work that I am speaking of ought to be undertaken by one who can argue and speak with wisdom, if not with eloquence, and with profit to his hearers, even though he profit them less than he would if he could speak with eloquence too. But we must beware of the man who abounds in eloquent nonsense, and so much the more if the hearer is pleased with what is not worth listening to, and thinks that because the speaker is eloquent what he says must be true. And this opinion is held even by those who think that the art of rhetoric should be taught: for they confess that "though wisdom without eloquence is of little service to states, yet eloquence without wisdom is frequently a positive injury, and is of service never." If, then, the men who teach the principles of eloquence have been forced by truth to confess this in the very books which treat of eloquence, though they were ignorant of the true, that is, the heavenly wisdom which comes down from the Father of Lights, how much more ought we to feel it who are the sons and the ministers of this higher wisdom! Now a man speaks with more or less wisdom just as he has made more or less progress in the knowledge of Scripture; I do not mean by reading them much and committing them to memory, but by understanding them aright and carefully searching into their meaning. For there are those who read and yet neglect them; they read to remember the words, but are careless about knowing the meaning. It is plain we must set far above these the men who are not so retentive of the words, but see with the eyes of the heart into the heart of Scripture. Better than either of these, however, is the man who, when he wishes, can repeat the words, and at the same time correctly apprehends their meaning.

8. Now it is especially necessary for the man who is bound to speak wisely, even though he cannot speak eloquently, to retain in memory the words of Scripture. For the more he discerns the poverty of his own speech, the more he ought to draw on the riches of Scripture, so that what he says in his own words he may prove by the words of Scripture; and he himself, though small and weak in his own words, may gain strength and power from the confirming testimony of great men. For his proof gives pleasure when he cannot please by his mode of speech. But if a man desire to speak not only with wisdom, but with eloquence also (and assuredly he will prove of greater service if he can do both), I would rather

send him to read, and listen to, and exercise himself in imitating, eloquent men, than advise him to spend time with the teachers of rhetoric; especially if the men he reads and listens to are justly praised as having spoken, or as being accustomed to speak, not only with eloquence, but with wisdom also. For eloquent speakers are heard with pleasure; wise speakers with profit. And, therefore, Scripture does not say that the multitude of the eloquent, but "the multitude of the wise is the welfare of the world."[89] And as we must often swallow wholesome bitters, so we must always avoid unwholesome sweets. But what is better than wholesome sweetness or sweet wholesomeness? For the sweeter we try to make such things, the easier it is to make their wholesomeness serviceable. And so there are writers of the Church who have expounded the Holy Scriptures, not only with wisdom, but with eloquence as well; and there is not more time for the reading of these than is sufficient for those who are studious and at leisure to exhaust them.

Chap. 6. The sacred writers unite eloquence with wisdom

9. Here, perhaps, some one inquires whether the authors whose divinely inspired writings constitute the canon, which carries with it a most wholesome authority, are to be considered wise only, or eloquent as well. A question which to me, and to those who think with me, is very easily settled. For where I understand these writers, it seems to me not only that nothing can be wiser, but also that nothing can be more eloquent. And I venture to affirm that all who truly understand what these writers say, perceive at the same time that it could not have been properly said in any other way. For as there is a kind of eloquence that is more becoming in youth, and a kind that is more becoming in old age, and nothing can be called eloquence if it be not suitable to the person of the speaker, so there is a kind of eloquence that is becoming in men who justly claim the highest authority, and who are evidently inspired of God. With this eloquence they spoke; no other would have been suitable for them; and this itself would be unsuitable in any other, for it is in keeping with their character, while it mounts as far above that of others (not from empty inflation, but from solid merit) as it

seems to fall below them. Where, however, I do not understand these writers, though their eloquence is then less apparent, I have no doubt but that it is of the same kind as that I do understand. The very obscurity, too, of these divine and wholesome words was a necessary element in eloquence of a kind that was designed to profit our understandings, not only by the discovery of truth, but also by the exercise of their powers.

10. I could, however, if I had time, show those men who cry up their own form of language as superior to that of our authors (not because of its majesty, but because of its inflation), that all those powers and beauties of eloquence which they make their boast, are to be found in the sacred writings which God in His goodness has provided to mould our characters and to guide us from this world of wickedness to the blessed world above. But it is not the qualities which these writers have in common with the heathen orators and poets that give me such unspeakable delight in their eloquence; I am more struck with admiration at the way in which, by an eloquence peculiarly their own, they so use this eloquence of ours that it is not conspicuous either by its presence or its absence: for it did not become them either to condemn it or to make an ostentatious display of it; and if they had shunned it, they would have done the former; if they had made it prominent, they might have appeared to be doing the latter. And in those passages where the learned do note its presence, the matters spoken of are such that the words in which they are put seem not so much to be sought out by the speaker as spontaneously to suggest themselves; as if wisdom were walking out of its house, that is, the breast of the wise man, and eloquence, like an inseparable attendant, followed it without being called for.

Chap. 7. Examples of true eloquence drawn from the epistles of Paul and the prophecies of Amos

11. For who would not see what the apostle meant to say, and how wisely he has said it, in the following passage: "We glory in tribulations also: knowing that tribulation worketh patience; and patience, experience; and experience, hope: and hope maketh not ashamed; because the love of God is shed abroad in our hearts by the Holy Ghost

---

[89] Wisd. 6.24.

which is given unto us"?[90] Now were any man unlearnedly learned (if I may use the expression) to contend that the apostle had here followed the rules of rhetoric, would not every Christian, learned or unlearned, laugh at him? And yet here we find the figure which is called in Greek κλίμαξ (climax), and by some in Latin *gradatio*, for they do not care to call it *scala* (a ladder), when the words and ideas have a connection of dependency the one upon the other, as we see here that patience arises out of tribulation, experience out of patience, and hope out of experience. Another ornament, too, is found here; for after certain statements finished in a single tone of voice, which we call clauses and sections (*membra et cæsa*), but the Greeks κῶλα and κόμματα, there follows a rounded sentence (*ambitus sive circuitus*) which the Greeks call περίοδος, the clauses of which are suspended on the voice of the speaker till the whole is completed by the last clause. For of the statements which precede the period, this is the first clause, "knowing that tribulation worketh patience"; the second, "and patience, experience"; the third, "and experience, hope." Then the period which is subjoined is completed in three clauses, of which the first is, "and hope maketh not ashamed"; the second, "because the love of God is shed abroad in our hearts"; the third, "by the Holy Ghost which is given unto us." But these and other matters of the same kind are taught in the art of elocution. As then I do not affirm that the apostle was guided by the rules of eloquence, so I do not deny that his wisdom naturally produced, and was accompanied by, eloquence.

12. In the Second Epistle to the Corinthians, again, he refutes certain false apostles who had gone out from the Jews, and had been trying to injure his character; and being compelled to speak of himself, though he ascribes this as folly to himself, how wisely and how eloquently he speaks! But wisdom is his guide, eloquence his attendant; he follows the first, the second follows him, and yet he does not spurn it when it comes after him. "I say again," he says, "Let no man think me a fool: if otherwise, yet as a fool receive me, that I may boast myself a little. That which I speak, I speak it not after the Lord, but as it were foolishly, in this confidence of boasting. Seeing that many

glory after the flesh, I will glory also. For ye suffer fools gladly, seeing ye yourselves are wise. For ye suffer, if a man bring you into bondage, if a man devour you, if a man take of you, if a man exalt himself, if a man smite you on the face. I speak as concerning reproach, as though we had been weak. Howbeit, whereinsoever any is bold (I speak foolishly), I am bold also. Are they Hebrews? so am I. Are they Israelites? so am I. Are they the seed of Abraham? so am I. Are they ministers of Christ? (I speak as a fool), I am more: in labours more abundant, in stripes above measure, in prisons more frequent, in deaths oft. Of the Jews five times received I forty stripes save one, thrice was I beaten with rods, once was I stoned, thrice I suffered shipwreck, a night and a day I have been in the deep; in journeyings often, in perils of waters, in perils of robbers, in perils by mine own countrymen, in perils by the heathen, in perils in the city, in perils in the wilderness, in perils in the sea, in perils among false brethren; in weariness and painfulness, in watchings often, in hunger and thirst, in fastings often, in cold and nakedness. Besides those things which are without, that which cometh upon me daily, the care of all the churches. Who is weak, and I am not weak? who is offended, and I burn not? If I must needs glory, I will glory of the things which concern my infirmities."[91] The thoughtful and attentive perceive how much wisdom there is in these words. And even a man sound asleep must notice what a stream of eloquence flows through them.

13. Further still, the educated man observes that those sections which the Greeks call κόμματα, and the clauses and periods of which I spoke a short time ago, being intermingled in the most beautiful variety, make up the whole form and features (so to speak) of that diction by which even the unlearned are delighted and affected. For, from the place where I commenced to quote, the passage consists of periods: the first the smallest possible, consisting of two members; for a period cannot have less than two members, though it may have more: "I say again, let no man think me a fool." The next has three members: "if otherwise, yet as a fool receive me, that I may boast myself a little." The third has four members: "That which I speak, I speak it not after the Lord, but as it were foolishly, in this confidence of

---

[90] Rom. 5.3–5.
[91] II Cor. 11.16–30.

boasting." The fourth has two: "Seeing that many glory after the flesh, I will glory also." And the fifth has two: "For ye suffer fools gladly, seeing ye yourselves are wise." The sixth again has two members: "for ye suffer, if a man bring you into bondage." Then follow three sections (*cæsa*): "if a man devour you, if a man take of you, if a man exalt himself." Next three clauses (*membra*): "if a man smite you on the face. I speak as concerning reproach, as though we had been weak." Then is subjoined a period of three members: "Howbeit, whereinsoever any is bold (I speak foolishly), I am bold also." After this, certain separate sections being put in the interrogatory form, separate sections are also given as answers, three to three: "Are they Hebrews? so am I. Are they Israelites? so am I. Are they the seed of Abraham? so am I." But a fourth section being put likewise in the interrogatory form, the answer is given not in another section (*cæsum*) but in a clause (*membrum*): "Are they the ministers of Christ? (I speak as a fool.) I am more." Then the next four sections are given continuously, the interrogatory form being most elegantly suppressed: "in labours more abundant, in stripes above measure, in prisons more frequent, in deaths oft." Next is interposed a short period; for, by a suspension of the voice, "of the Jews five times" is to be marked off as constituting one member, to which is joined the second, "received I forty stripes save one." Then he returns to sections, and three are set down: "Thrice was I beaten with rods, once was I stoned, thrice I suffered shipwreck." Next comes a clause: "a night and a day I have been in the deep." Next fourteen sections burst forth with a vehemence which is most appropriate: "In journeyings often, in perils of waters, in perils of robbers, in perils by mine own countrymen, in perils by the heathen, in perils in the city, in perils in the wilderness, in perils in the sea, in perils among false brethren, in weariness and painfulness, in watchings often, in hunger and thirst, in fastings often, in cold and nakedness." After this comes in a period of three members: "Besides those things which are without, that which cometh upon me daily, the care of all the churches." And to this he adds two clauses in a tone of inquiry: "Who is weak, and I am not weak? who is offended, and I burn not?" In fine, this whole passage, as if panting for breath, winds up with a period of two members: "If I must needs glory, I will glory of the things which concern mine infirmities." And I cannot sufficiently express

how beautiful and delightful it is when after this outburst he rests himself, and gives the hearer rest, by interposing a slight narrative. For he goes on to say: "The God and Father of our Lord Jesus Christ, which is blessed for evermore, knoweth that I lie not." And then he tells, very briefly the danger he had been in, and the way he escaped it.

14. It would be tedious to pursue the matter further, or to point out the same facts in regard to other passages of Holy Scripture. Suppose I had taken the further trouble, at least in regard to the passages I have quoted from the apostle's writings, to point out figures of speech which are taught in the art of rhetoric? Is it not more likely that serious men would think I had gone too far, than that any of the studious would think I had done enough? All these things when taught by masters are reckoned of great value; great prices are paid for them, and the vendors puff them magniloquently. And I fear lest I too should smack of that puffery while thus descanting on matters of this kind. It was necessary, however, to reply to the ill-taught men who think our authors contemptible; not because they do not possess, but because they do not display, the eloquence which these men value so highly.

[...]

Chap. 9. How, and with whom, difficult passages are to be discussed

23. For there are some passages which are not understood in their proper force, or are understood with great difficulty, at whatever length, however clearly, or with whatever eloquence the speaker may expound them; and these should never be brought before the people at all, or only on rare occasions when there is some urgent reason. In books, however, which are written in such a style that, if understood, they, so to speak, draw their own readers, and if not understood, give no trouble to those who do not care to read them, and in private conversations we must not shrink from the duty of bringing the truth which we ourselves have reached within the comprehension of others, however difficult it may be to understand it and whatever labour in the way of argument it may cost us. Only two conditions are to be insisted upon, that our hearer or companion should have an earnest desire to learn the truth,

and should have capacity of mind to receive it in whatever form it may be communicated, the teacher not being so anxious about the eloquence as about the clearness of his teaching.

Chap. 10. *The necessity for perspicuity of style*

24. Now a strong desire for clearness sometimes leads to neglect of the more polished forms of speech, and indifference about what sounds well, compared with what clearly expresses and conveys the meaning intended. Whence a certain author, when dealing with speech of this kind, says that there is in it "a kind of careful negligence." Yet while taking away ornament, it does not bring in vulgarity of speech; though good teachers have, or ought to have, so great an anxiety about teaching that they will employ a word which cannot be made pure Latin without becoming obscure or ambiguous, but which when used according to the vulgar idiom is neither ambiguous nor obscure not in the way the learned, but rather in the way the unlearned employ it. For if our translators did not shrink from saying, *"Non congregabo conventicula eorum de sanguinibus,"*[92] because they felt that it was important for the sense to put a word here in the plural which in Latin is only used in the singular; why should a teacher of godliness who is addressing an unlearned audience shrink from using *ossum* instead of *os*, if he fear that the latter might be taken not as the singular of *ossa*, but as the singular of *ora*, seeing that African ears have no quick perception of the shortness or length of vowels? And what advantage is there in purity of speech which does not lead to understanding in the hearer, seeing that there is no use at all in speaking, if they do not understand us for whose sake we speak? He, therefore, who teaches will avoid all words that do not teach; and if instead of them he can find words which are at once pure and intelligible, he will take these by preference; if, however, he cannot, either because there are no such words, or because they do not at the time occur to him, he will use words that are not quite pure, if only the substance of his thought be conveyed and apprehended in its integrity.

25. And this must be insisted on as necessary to our being understood, not only in conversations, whether with one person or with several, but much more in the case of a speech delivered in public: for in conversation any one has the power of asking a question; but when all are silent that one may be heard, and all faces are turned attentively upon him, it is neither customary nor decorous for a person to ask a question about what he does not understand; and on this account the speaker ought to be especially careful to give assistance to those who cannot ask it. Now a crowd anxious for instruction generally shows by its movements if it understands what is said; and until some indication of this sort be given, the subject discussed ought to be turned over and over, and put in every shape and form and variety of expression, a thing which cannot be done by men who are repeating words prepared beforehand and committed to memory. As soon, however, as the speaker has ascertained that what he says is understood, he ought either to bring his address to a close, or pass on to another point. For if a man gives pleasure when he throws light upon points on which people wish for instruction, he becomes wearisome when he dwells at length upon things that are already well known, especially when men's expectation was fixed on having the difficulties of the passage removed. For even things that are very well known are told for the sake of the pleasure they give, if the attention be directed not to the things themselves, but to the way in which they are told. Nay, even when the style itself is already well known, if it be pleasing to the hearers, it is almost a matter of indifference whether he who speaks be a speaker or a reader. For things that are gracefully written are often not only read with delight by those who are making their first acquaintance with them, but re-read with delight by those who have already made acquaintance with them, and have not yet forgotten them; nay, both these classes will derive pleasure even from hearing another man repeat them. And if a man has forgotten anything, when he is reminded of it he is taught. But I am not now treating of the mode of giving pleasure. I am speaking of the mode in which men who desire to learn ought to be taught. And the best mode is that which secures that he who hears shall hear the truth, and that what he hears he shall understand. And when this point has been reached, no further labour need be spent on the truth itself, as

[92] "I shall not assemble their assemblies of blood," Ps. 16.4. (Vulgate)

if it required further explanation; but perhaps some trouble may be taken to enforce it so as to bring it home to the heart. If it appear right to do this, it ought to be done so moderately as not to lead to weariness and impatience.

Chap. 11.   The Christian teacher must speak clearly, but not inelegantly

26. For teaching, of course, true eloquence consists, not in making people like what they disliked, nor in making them do what they shrank from, but in making clear what was obscure; yet if this be done without grace of style, the benefit does not extend beyond the few eager students who are anxious to know whatever is to be learnt, however rude and unpolished the form in which it is put; and who, when they have succeeded in their object, find the plain truth pleasant food enough. And it is one of the distinctive features of good intellects not to love words, but the truth in words. For of what service is a golden key, if it cannot open what we want it to open? Or what objection is there to a wooden one if it can, seeing that to open what is shut is all we want? But as there is a certain analogy between learning and eating, the very food without which it is impossible to live must be flavoured to meet the tastes of the majority.

Chap. 12.   The aim of the orator, according to Cicero, is to teach, to delight, and to move. Of these, teaching is the most essential

27. Accordingly a great orator has truly said that "an eloquent man must speak so as to teach, to delight, and to persuade."[93] Then he adds: "To teach is a necessity, to delight is a beauty, to persuade is a triumph." Now of these three, the one first mentioned, the teaching, which is a matter of necessity, depends on what we say; the other two on the way we say it. He, then, who speaks with the purpose of teaching should not suppose that he has said what he has to say as long as he is not understood; for although what he has said be intelligible to himself, it is not

said at all to the man who does not understand it. If, however, he is understood, he has said his say, whatever may have been his manner of saying it. But if he wishes to delight or persuade his hearer as well, he will not accomplish that end by putting his thought in any shape no matter what, but for that purpose the style of speaking is a matter of importance. And as the hearer must be pleased in order to secure his attention, so he must be persuaded in order to move him to action. And as he is pleased if you speak with sweetness and elegance, so he is persuaded if he be drawn by your promises, and awed by your threats; if he reject what you condemn, and embrace what you commend; if he grieve when you heap up objects for grief, and rejoice when you point out an object for joy; if he pity those whom you present to him as objects of pity, and shrink from those whom you set before him as men to be feared and shunned. I need not go over all the other things that can be done by powerful eloquence to move the minds of the hearers, not telling them what they ought to do, but urging them to do what they already know ought to be done.

28. If, however, they do not yet know this, they must of course be instructed before they can be moved. And perhaps the mere knowledge of their duty will have such an effect that there will be no need to move them with greater strength of eloquence. Yet when this is needful, it ought to be done. And it is needful when people, knowing what they ought to do, do it not. Therefore, to teach is a necessity. For what men know, it is in their own hands either to do or not to do. But who would say that it is their duty to do what they do not know? On the same principle, to persuade is not a necessity: for it is not always called for; as, for example, when the hearer yields his assent to one who simply teaches or gives pleasure. For this reason also to persuade is a triumph, because it is possible that a man may be taught and delighted, and yet not give his consent. And what will be the use of gaining the first two ends if we fail in the third? Neither is it a necessity to give pleasure; for when, in the course of an address, the truth is clearly pointed out (and this is the true function of teaching), it is not the fact, nor is it the intention, that the style of speech should make the truth pleasing, or that the style

[93] Cicero, *Orator*, 21. [The reference to Cicero's *Orator* is in error. *Orator* 21 consists of Cicero's discussion of eloquence, not the aims of oratory. His discussion of aims is located at *Orator* 69. Here he states that *Probare necessitatis est, delectare suavitatis, flectere victoriae* – To prove is the first necessity, to delight is charm, to persuade is victory. Augustine is actually drawing on Quintilian, not Cicero. In *Institutio Oratoria* v. 1–3, we find: *Tria sunt item quae praestare debeat orator, ut doceat moveat delectet* – The orator must always strive to meet three aims; he must instruct, move, and charm his hearers. The difference between "proving" and "instructing" is significant. J.D.W.]

should of itself give pleasure; but the truth itself, when exhibited in its naked simplicity, gives pleasure, because it is the truth. And hence even falsities are frequently a source of pleasure when they are brought to light and exposed. It is not, of course, their falsity that gives pleasure; but as it is true that they are false, the speech which shows this to be true gives pleasure.

Chap. 13.   The hearer must be moved as well as instructed

29. But for the sake of those who are so fastidious that they do not care for truth unless it is put in the form of a pleasing discourse, no small place has been assigned in eloquence to the art of pleasing. And yet even this is not enough for those stubborn-minded men who both understand and are pleased with the teacher's discourse, without deriving any profit from it. For what does it profit a man that he both confesses the truth and praises the eloquence, if he does not yield his consent, when it is only for the sake of securing his consent that the speaker in urging the truth gives careful attention to what he says? If the truths taught are such that to believe or to know them is enough, to give one's assent implies nothing more than to confess that they are true. When, however, the truth taught is one that must be carried into practice, and that is taught for the very purpose of being practised, it is useless to be persuaded of the truth of what is said, it is useless to be pleased with the manner in which it is said, if it be not so learnt as to be practised. The eloquent divine, then, when he is urging a practical truth, must not only teach so as to give instruction, and please so as to keep up the attention, but he must also sway the mind so as to subdue the will. For if a man be not moved by the force of truth though it is demonstrated to his own confession, and clothed in beauty of style, nothing remains but to subdue him by the power of eloquence.

Chap. 14.   Beauty of diction to be in keeping with the matter

30. And so much labour has been spent by men on the beauty of expression here spoken of that not only is it not our duty to do, but it is our duty to shun and abhor, many and heinous deeds of wickedness and baseness which wicked and base men have with great eloquence recommended, not with a view to gaining assent but merely for the sake of being read with pleasure. But may God avert from His Church what the prophet Jeremiah says of the synagogue of the Jews: "A wonderful and horrible thing is committed in the land: the prophets prophesy falsely, and the priests applaud them with their hands;[94] and my people love to have it so: and what will ye do in the end thereof?"[95] O eloquence, which is the more terrible from its purity, and the more crushing from its solidity! Assuredly it is "a hammer that breaketh the rock in pieces." For to this God Himself has by the same prophet compared His own word spoken through His holy prophets.[96] God forbid, then, God forbid that with us the priest should applaud the false prophet, and that God's people should love to have it so. God forbid, I say, that with us there should be such terrible madness! For what shall we do in the end thereof? And assuredly it is preferable, even though what is said should be less intelligible, less pleasing, and less persuasive, that truth be spoken, and that what is just, not what is iniquitous, be listened to with pleasure. But this, of course, cannot be, unless what is true and just be expressed with elegance.

31. In a serious assembly, moreover, such as is spoken of when it is said, "I will praise Thee among much people,"[97] no pleasure is derived from that species of eloquence which indeed says nothing that is false, but which buries small and unimportant truths under a frothy mass of ornamental words, such as would not be graceful or dignified even if used to adorn great and fundamental truths. And something of this sort occurs in a letter of the blessed Cyprian, which, I think, came there by accident, or else was inserted designedly with this view, that posterity might see how the wholesome discipline of Christian teaching had cured him of that redundancy of language, and confined him to a more dignified and modest form of eloquence, such as we find in his subsequent letters, a style which is admired without effort, is sought after with eagerness, but is not attained without great difficulty. He says, then,

[94] "And the priests bear rule by their means." (Authorized Version)
[95] Jer. 5.30, 31 (Septuagint).
[96] Jer. 23.29.
[97] Ps. 35.18.

in one place, "Let us seek this abode: the neighbouring solitudes afford a retreat where, whilst
the spreading shoots of the vine trees, pendulous
and intertwined, creep amongst the supporting
reeds, the leafy covering has made a portico of
vine." There is wonderful fluency and exuberance of language here; but it is too florid to be
pleasing to serious minds. But people who are
fond of this style are apt to think that men who do
not use it, but employ a more chastened style, do
so because they cannot attain the former, not
because their judgment teaches them to avoid it.
Wherefore this holy man shows both that he can
speak in that style, for he has done so once, and
that he does not choose, for he never uses it again.

[…]

Chap. 16. Human directions not to be despised, though God makes the true teacher

33. Now if any one says that we need not direct
men how or what they should teach, since the
Holy Spirit makes them teachers, he may as well
say that we need not pray, since our Lord says,
"Your Father knoweth what things ye have need
of before ye ask Him",[98] or that the Apostle Paul
should not have given directions to Timothy and
Titus as to how or what they should teach others.
And these three apostolic epistles ought to be
constantly before the eyes of every one who has
obtained the position of a teacher in the Church.
In the First Epistle to Timothy do we not read:
"These things command and teach"?[99] What these
things are, has been told previously. Do we not
read there: "Rebuke not an elder, but entreat him
as a father"?[100] Is it not said in the Second Epistle:
"Hold fast the form of sound words, which thou

hast heard of me"?[101] And is he not there told:
"Study to show thyself approved unto God, a
workman that needeth not to be ashamed, rightly
dividing the word of truth"?[102] And in the same
place: "Preach the word; be instant in season, out
of season; reprove, rebuke, exhort, with all long-
suffering and doctrine."[103] And so in the Epistle to
Titus, does he not say that a bishop ought to
"hold fast the faithful word as he hath been
taught, that he may be able by sound doctrine
both to exhort and to convince the gainsayers"?[104]
There, too, he says: "But speak thou the things
which become sound doctrine: that the aged men
be sober,"[105] and so on. And there, too: "These
things speak, and exhort, and rebuke with all
authority. Let no man despise thee. Put them in
mind to be subject to principalities and powers,"[106]
and so on. What then are we to think? Does the
apostle in any way contradict himself, when,
though he says that men are made teachers by the
operation of the Holy Spirit, he yet himself gives
them directions how and what they should teach?
Or are we to understand, that though the duty of
men to teach even the teachers does not cease
when the Holy Spirit is given, yet that neither is
he who planteth anything, nor he who watereth,
but God Who giveth the increase?[107] Wherefore
though holy men be our helpers, or even holy
angels assist us, no one learns aright the things
that pertain to life with God, until God makes
him ready to learn from Himself, that God Who
is thus addressed in the psalm: "Teach me to do
Thy will; for Thou art my God."[108] And so the
same apostle says to Timothy himself, speaking,
of course, as teacher to disciple: "But continue
thou in the things which thou hast learned, and
hast been assured of, knowing of Whom thou
hast learned them."[109] For as the medicines which
men apply to the bodies of their fellowmen are of

98 Matt. 6.8.
99 I Tim. 4.11.
100 I Tim. 5.1.
101 II Tim. 1.13.
102 II Tim. 2.15.
103 II Tim. 4.2.
104 Tit. 1.9.
105 Tit. 2.1, 2.
106 Tit. 2.15; 3.1.
107 I Cor. 3.7.
108 Ps. 143.10.
109 II Tim. 3.14.

no avail except God gives them virtue (Who can heal without their aid, though they cannot without His), and yet they are applied; and if it be done from a sense of duty, it is esteemed a work of mercy or benevolence; so the aids of teaching, applied through the instrumentality of man, are of advantage to the soul only when God works to make them of advantage, Who could give the Gospel to man even without the help or agency of men.

Chap. 17. Threefold division of the various styles of speech

34. He then who, in speaking, aims at enforcing what is good, should not despise any of those three objects, either to teach, or to give pleasure, or to move, and should pray and strive, as we have said above, to be heard with intelligence, with pleasure, and with ready compliance. And when he does this with elegance and propriety, he may justly be called eloquent, even though he do not carry with him the assent of his hearer. For it is these three ends, viz., teaching, giving pleasure, and moving, that the great master of Roman eloquence himself seems to have intended that the following three directions should subserve: "He, then, shall be eloquent, who can say little things in a subdued style, moderate things in a temperate style, and great things in a majestic style": as if he had taken in also the three ends mentioned above, and had embraced the whole in one sentence thus: "He, then, shall be eloquent, who can say little things in a subdued style, in order to give instruction, moderate things in a temperate style, in order to give pleasure, and great things in a majestic style, in order to sway the mind."

Chap. 18. The Christian orator is constantly dealing with great matters

35. Now the author I have quoted could have exemplified these three directions, as laid down by himself, in regard to legal questions: he could not, however, have done so in regard to ecclesiastical questions – the only ones that an address such as I wish to give shape to is concerned with. For of legal questions those are called small which have reference to pecuniary transactions; those

great where a matter relating to man's life or liberty comes up. Cases, again, which have to do with neither of these, and where the intention is not to get the hearer to do, or to pronounce judgment upon anything, but only to give him pleasure, occupy as it were a middle place between the former two, and are on that account called middling, or moderate. For moderate things get their name from *modus* (a measure); and it is an abuse, not a proper use of the word *moderate*, to put it for *little*. In questions like ours, however, where all things, and especially those addressed to the people from the place of authority, ought to have reference to men's salvation, and that not their temporal but their eternal salvation, and where also the thing to be guarded against is eternal ruin, everything that we say is important; so much so, that even what the preacher says about pecuniary matters, whether it have reference to loss or gain, whether the amount be great or small, should not seem unimportant. For justice is never unimportant, and justice ought assuredly to be observed, even in small affairs of money, as our Lord says: "He that is faithful in that which is least, is faithful also in much."[110] That which is least, then, is very little; but to be faithful in that which is least is great. For as the nature of the circle, viz., that all lines drawn from the centre to the circumference are equal, is the same in a great disk that it is in the smallest coin; so the greatness of justice is in no degree lessened, though the matters to which justice is applied be small.

[...]

Chap. 19. The Christian teacher must use different styles on different occasions

38. And yet, while our teacher ought to speak of great matters, he ought not always to be speaking of them in a majestic tone, but in a subdued tone when he is teaching, temperately when he is giving praise or blame. When, however, something is to be done, and we are speaking to those who ought, but are not willing, to do it, then great matters must be spoken of with power, and in a manner calculated to sway the mind. And sometimes the same important matter is treated in all these ways at different times, quietly when it

[110] Luke, 16.10.

is being taught, temperately when its importance is being urged, and powerfully when we are forcing a mind that is averse to the truth to turn and embrace it. For is there anything greater than God Himself? Is nothing, then, to be learnt about Him? Or ought he who is teaching the Trinity in unity to speak of it otherwise than in the method of calm discussion, so that in regard to a subject which it is not easy to comprehend, we may understand as much as it is given us to understand? Are we in this case to seek out ornaments instead of proofs? Or is the hearer to be moved to do something instead of being instructed so that he may learn something? But when we come to praise God, either in Himself, or in His works, what a field for beauty and splendour of language opens up before man, who can task his powers to the utmost in praising Him Whom no one can adequately praise, though there is no one who does not praise Him in some measure! But if He be not worshipped, or if idols, whether they be demons or any created being whatever, be worshipped with Him or in preference to Him, then we ought to speak out with power and impressiveness, show how great a wickedness this is, and urge men to flee from it.

Chap. 20.   Examples of the various styles drawn from Scripture

39. But now to come to something more definite. We have an example of the calm, subdued style in the Apostle Paul, where he says: "Tell me, ye that desire to be under the law, do ye not hear the law? For it is written, that Abraham had two sons; the one by a bond maid, the other by a free woman. But he who was of the bond woman was born after the flesh; but he of the free woman was by promise. Which things are an allegory: for these are the two covenants; the one from the Mount Sinai, which gendereth to bondage, which is Hagar. For this Hagar is Mount Sinai in Arabia, and answereth to Jerusalem which now is, and is in bondage with her children. But Jerusalem which is above is free, which is the mother of us all",[111] and so on. And in the same way where he reasons thus: "Brethren, I speak after the manner

of men: Though it be but a man's covenant, yet if it be confirmed, no man disannulleth, or addeth thereto. Now to Abraham and his seed were the promises made. He saith not, And to seeds, as of many; but as of one, And to thy seed, which is Christ. And this I say, that the covenant, that was confirmed before of God in Christ, the law, which was four hundred and thirty years after, cannot disannul, that it should make the promise of none effect. For if the inheritance be of the law, it is no more of promise: but God gave it to Abraham by promise."[112] And because it might possibly occur to the hearer to ask, "If there is no inheritance by the law, why then was the law given?" he himself anticipates this objection and asks, "Wherefore then serveth the law?" And the answer is given: "It was added because of transgressions, till the seed should come to whom the promise was made; and it was ordained by angels in the hand of a mediator. Now a mediator is not a mediator of one; but God is one." And here an objection occurs which he himself has stated: "Is the law then against the promises of God?" He answers: "God forbid." And he also states the reason in these words: "For if there had been a law given which could have given life, verily righteousness should have been by the law. But the Scripture hath concluded all under sin, that the promise by faith of Jesus Christ might be given to them that believe."[113] It is part, then, of the duty of the teacher not only to interpret what is obscure and to unravel the difficulties of questions, but also, while doing this, to meet other questions which may chance to suggest themselves, lest these should cast doubt or discredit on what we say. If, however, the solution of these questions suggest itself as soon as the questions themselves arise, it is useless to disturb what we cannot remove. And besides, when out of one question other questions arise, and out of these again still others; if these be all discussed and solved, the reasoning is extended to such a length, that unless the memory be exceedingly powerful and active, the reasoner finds it impossible to return to the original question from which he set out. It is, however, exceedingly desirable that whatever occurs to the mind as an objection that might be urged should be stated and refuted, lest it turn up at a time when

[111] Gal. 4.21–26.
[112] Gal. 3.15–18.
[113] Gal. 3.19–22.

no one will be present to answer it, or lest, if it should occur to a man who is present but says nothing about it, it might never be thoroughly removed.

40. In the following words of the apostle we have the temperate style: "Rebuke not an elder, but entreat him as a father; and the younger men as brethren; the elder women as mothers, the younger as sisters."[114] And also in these: "I beseech you, therefore, brethren, by the mercies of God, that ye present your bodies a living sacrifice, holy, acceptable unto God, which is your reasonable service."[115] And almost the whole of this hortatory passage is in the temperate style of eloquence; and those parts of it are the most beautiful in which, as if paying what was due, things that belong to each other are gracefully brought together. For example: "Having then gifts, differing according to the grace that is given to us, whether prophecy, let us prophesy according to the proportion of faith; or ministry, let us wait on our ministering; or he that teacheth, on teaching; or he that exhorteth, on exhortation; he that giveth, let him do it with simplicity; he that ruleth, with diligence; he that showeth mercy, with cheerfulness. Let love be without dissimulation. Abhor that which is evil, cleave to that which is good. Be kindly affectioned one to another with brotherly love; in honour preferring one another; not slothful in business; fervent in spirit; serving the Lord; rejoicing in hope; patient in tribulation; continuing instant in prayer; distributing to the necessity of saints; given to hospitality. Bless them which persecute you: bless, and curse not. Rejoice with them that do rejoice, and weep with them that weep. Be of the same mind one toward another."[116] And how gracefully all this is brought to a close in a period of two members: "Mind not high things, but condescend to men of low estate!" And a little afterwards: "Render therefore to all their dues: tribute to whom tribute is due; custom to whom custom; fear to whom fear; honour to whom honour."[117] And these also, though expressed in single clauses, are terminated by a period of two members: "Owe no man anything, but to love one another." And a little farther on: "The night is far

spent, the day is at hand: let us therefore cast off the works of darkness and let us put on the armour of light. Let us walk honestly, as in the day; not in rioting and drunkenness, not in chambering and wantonness, not in strife and envying: but put ye on the Lord Jesus Christ, and make not provision for the flesh, to fulfill the lusts thereof."[118] Now if the passage were translated thus, *"et carnis providentiam ne in concupiscentiis feceritis,"* the ear would no doubt be gratified with a more harmonious ending; but our translator, with more strictness, preferred to retain even the order of the words. And how this sounds in the Greek language, in which the apostle spoke, those who are better skilled in that tongue may determine. My opinion, however, is that what has been translated to us in the same order of words does not run very harmoniously even in the original tongue.

41. And, indeed, I must confess that our authors are very defective in that grace of speech which consists in harmonious endings. Whether this be the fault of the translators, or whether, as I am more inclined to believe, the authors designedly avoided such ornaments, I dare not affirm; for I confess I do not know. This I know, however, that if any one who is skilled in this species of harmony would take the closing sentences of these writers and arrange them according to the law of harmony (which he could very easily do by changing some words for words of equivalent meaning, or by retaining the words he finds and altering their arrangement), he will learn that these divinely inspired men are not defective in any of those points which he has been taught in the schools of the grammarians and rhetoricians to consider of importance; and he will find in them many kinds of speech of great beauty – beautiful even in our language, but especially beautiful in the original – none of which can be found in those writings of which they boast so much. But care must be taken that, while adding harmony, we take away none of the weight from these divine and authoritative utterances. Now our prophets were so far from being deficient in the musical training from which this harmony we speak of is most fully learnt that Jerome, a very

[114] Tim. 5.1, 2.
[115] Rom. 12.1.
[116] Rom. 12.6–16.
[117] Rom. 13.7.
[118] Rom. 13.12–14.

learned man, describes even the metres employed by some of them, in the Hebrew language at least; though, in order to give an accurate rendering of the words, he has not preserved these in his translation. I, however (to speak of my own feeling, which is better known to me than it is to others, and than that of others is to me), while I do not in my own speech, however modestly I think it done, neglect these harmonious endings, am just as well pleased to find them in the sacred authors very rarely.

42. The majestic style of speech differs from the temperate style just spoken of, chiefly in that it is not so much decked out with verbal ornaments as exalted into vehemence by mental emotion. It uses, indeed, nearly all the ornaments that the other does; but if they do not happen to be at hand, it does not seek for them. For it is borne on by its own vehemence; and the force of the thought, not the desire for ornament, makes it seize upon any beauty of expression that comes in its way. It is enough for its object that warmth of feeling should suggest the fitting words; they need not be selected by careful elaboration of speech. If a brave man be armed with weapons adorned with gold and jewels, he works feats of valour with those arms in the heat of battle, not because they are costly, but because they are arms; and yet the same man does great execution, even when anger furnishes him with a weapon that he digs out of the ground.[119] The apostle in the following passage is urging that, for the sake of the ministry of the gospel, and sustained by the consolations of God's grace, we should bear with patience all the evils of this life. It is a great subject, and is treated with power, and the ornaments of speech are not wanting: "Behold," he says, "now is the accepted time; behold, now is the day of salvation. Giving no offence in anything, that the ministry be not blamed: but in all things approving ourselves as the ministers of God, in much patience, in afflictions, in necessities, in distresses, in strifes, in imprisonments, in tumults, in labours, in watchings, in fastings; by pureness, by knowledge, by long-suffering, by kindness, by the Holy Ghost, by love unfeigned, by the word of truth, by the power of God, by the armour of righteousness on the right hand and on the left,

by honour and dishonour, by evil report and good report: as deceivers, and yet true; as unknown, and yet well known; as dying, and, behold, we live; as chastened, and not killed; as sorrowful, yet alway rejoicing; as poor, yet making many rich; as having nothing, and yet possessing all things."[120] See him still burning: "O ye Corinthians, our mouth is opened unto you, our heart is enlarged," and so on; it would be tedious to go through it all.

43. And in the same way, writing to the Romans, he urges that the persecutions of this world should be overcome by charity, in assured reliance on the help of God. And he treats this subject with both power and beauty: "We know," he says, "that all things work together for good to them that love God, to them who are the called according to His purpose. For whom He did foreknow, He also did predestinate to be conformed to the image of His Son, that He might be the first-born among many brethren. Moreover, whom He did predestinate, them He also called; and whom He called, them He also justified; and whom He justified, them He also glorified. What shall we then say to these things? If God be for us, who can be against us? He that spared not His own Son, but delivered Him up for us all, how shall He not with Him also freely give us all things? Who shall lay anything to the charge of God's elect? It is God that justifieth; who is he that condemneth? It is Christ that died, yea, rather, that is risen again, who is even at the right hand of God, who also maketh intercession for us. Who shall separate us from the love of Christ? shall tribulation, or distress, or persecution, or famine, or nakedness, or peril, or sword? (As it is written, For Thy sake we are killed all the day long; we are accounted as sheep for the slaughter.) Nay, in all these things we are more than conquerors, through Him that loved us. For I am persuaded, that neither death, nor life, nor angels, nor principalities, nor powers, nor things present, nor things to come, nor height, nor depth, nor any other creature, shall be able to separate us from the love of God, which is in Christ Jesus our Lord."[121]

44. Again, in writing to the Galatians, although the whole epistle is written in the subdued style, except at the end, where it rises into a temperate

---

[119] Virgil, *Æneid*, BK. VII. 508.

[120] II Cor. 6.2–10.

[121] Rom. 8.28–39.

eloquence, yet he interposes one passage of so much feeling that, notwithstanding the absence of any ornaments such as appear in the passages just quoted, it cannot be called anything but powerful: "Ye observe days, and months, and times, and years. I am afraid of you, lest I have bestowed upon you labour in vain. Brethren, I beseech you, be as I am; for I am as ye are: ye have not injured me at all. Ye know how, through infirmity of the flesh, I preached the gospel unto you at the first. And my temptation which was in my flesh ye despised not, nor rejected; but received me as an angel of God, even as Christ Jesus. Where is then the blessedness ye spake of? for I bear you record, that, if it had been possible, ye would have plucked out your own eyes, and have given them to me. Am I therefore become your enemy, because I tell you the truth? They zealously affect you, but not well; yea, they would exclude you, that ye might affect them. But it is good to be zealously affected always in a good thing, and not only when I am present with you. My little children, of whom I travail in birth again until Christ be formed in you, I desire to be present with you now, and to change my voice; for I stand in doubt of you."[122] Is there anything here of contrasted words arranged antithetically, or of words rising gradually to a climax, or of sonorous clauses, and sections, and periods? Yet, notwithstanding, there is a glow of strong emotion that makes us feel the fervour of eloquence.

Chap. 21. Examples of the various styles, drawn from the teachers of the Church, especially Ambrose and Cyprian

45. But these writings of the apostles, though clear, are yet profound, and are so written that one who is not content with a superficial acquaintance, but desires to know them thoroughly, must not only read and hear them, but must have an expositor. Let us, then, study these various modes of speech as they are exemplified in the writings of men who, by reading the Scriptures, have attained to the knowledge of divine and saving truth, and have ministered it to the Church. Cyprian of blessed memory writes in the subdued style in his treatise on the sacrament of the cup. In this book he resolves the question, whether the cup of the Lord ought to contain water only, or water mingled with wine. But we must quote a passage by way of illustration. After the customary introduction, he proceeds to the discussion of the point in question. "Observe," he says, "that we are instructed, in presenting the cup, to maintain the custom handed down to us from the Lord, and to do nothing that our Lord has not first done for us: so that the cup which is offered in remembrance of Him should be mixed with wine. For, as Christ says, 'I am the true vine,'[123] it follows that the blood of Christ is wine, not water; and the cup cannot appear to contain His blood by which we are redeemed and quickened, if the wine be absent; for by the wine is the blood of Christ typified, that blood which is foreshadowed and proclaimed in all the types and declarations of Scripture. For we find that in the book of Genesis this very circumstance in regard to the sacrament is foreshadowed, and our Lord's sufferings typically set forth, in the case of Noah, when he drank wine, and was drunken, and was uncovered within his tent, and his nakedness was exposed by his second son, and was carefully hidden by his elder and his younger sons.[124] It is not necessary to mention the other circumstances in detail, as it is only necessary to observe this point, that Noah, foreshadowing the future reality, drank, not water, but wine, and thus showed forth our Lord's passion. In the same way we see the sacrament of the Lord's supper prefigured in the case of Melchizedek the priest, according to the testimony of the Holy Scriptures, where it says: 'And Melchizedek king of Salem brought forth bread and wine: and he was the priest of the most high God. And he blessed Abraham.'[125] Now, that Melchizedek was a type of Christ, the Holy Spirit declares in the Psalms, where the Father addressing the Son says, 'Thou art a priest for ever after the order of Melchizedek.'[126]" In this passage, and in all of the letter that follows, the

---

[122] Gal. 4.10–20.
[123] John, 15.1.
[124] Gen. 9.20–24.
[125] Gen. 14.18, 19.
[126] Ps. 110.4.

subdued style is maintained, as the reader may easily satisfy himself.

46. St. Ambrose also, though dealing with a question of very great importance, the equality of the Holy Spirit with the Father and the Son, employs the subdued style, because the object he has in view demands, not beauty of diction, nor the swaying of the mind by the stir of emotion, but facts and proofs. Accordingly, in the introduction to his work, we find the following passage among others: "When Gideon was startled by the message he had heard from God, that, though thousands of the people failed, yet through one man God would deliver His people from their enemies, he brought forth a kid of the goats, and by direction of the angel laid it with unleavened cakes upon a rock, and poured the broth over it; and as soon as the angel of God touched it with the end of the staff that was in his hand, there rose up fire out of the rock and consumed the offering.[127] Now this sign seems to indicate that the rock was a type of the body of Christ, for it is written, 'They drank of that spiritual rock that followed them, and that rock was Christ';[128] this, of course, referring not to Christ's divine nature, but to His flesh, whose ever-flowing fountain of blood has ever satisfied the hearts of His thirsting people. And so it was at that time declared in a mystery that the Lord Jesus, when crucified, should abolish in His flesh the sins of the whole world, and not their guilty acts merely, but the evil lusts of their hearts. For the kid's flesh refers to the guilt of the outward act, the broth to the allurement of lust within, as it is written, 'And the mixed multitude that was among them fell a lusting; and the children of Israel also wept again and said, Who shall give us flesh to eat?'[129] When the angel, then, stretched out his staff and touched the rock, and fire rose out of it, this was a sign that our Lord's flesh, filled with the Spirit of God, should burn up all the sins of the human race. Whence also the Lord says, 'I am come to send fire on the earth.'"[130] And in the same style he pursues the subject, devoting himself chiefly to proving and enforcing his point.

47. An example of the *temperate* style is the celebrated encomium on virginity from Cyprian:

"Now our discourse addresses itself to the virgins, who, as they are the objects of higher honour, are also the objects of greater care. These are the flowers on the tree of the Church, the glory and ornament of spiritual grace, the joy of honour and praise, a work unbroken and unblemished, the image of God answering to the holiness of the Lord, the brighter portion of the flock of Christ. The glorious fruitfulness of their mother the Church rejoices in them, and in them flourishes more abundantly; and in proportion as bright virginity adds to her numbers, in the same proportion does the mother's joy increase. And at another place in the end of the epistle, 'As we have borne,' he says, 'the image of the earthly, we shall also bear the image of the heavenly.'[131] Virginity bears this image, integrity bears it, holiness and truth bear it; they bear it who are mindful of the chastening of the Lord, who observe justice and piety, who are strong in faith, humble in fear, steadfast in the endurance of suffering, meek in the endurance of injury, ready to pity, of one mind and of one heart in brotherly peace. And every one of these things ought ye, holy virgins, to observe, to cherish, and fulfil, who having hearts at leisure for God and for Christ, and having chosen the greater and better part, lead and point the way to the Lord, to whom you have pledged your vows. Ye who are advanced in age, exercise control over the younger. Ye who are younger, wait upon the elders, and encourage your equals; stir up one another by mutual exhortations; provoke one another to glory by emulous examples of virtue; endure bravely, advance in spirituality, finish your course with joy; only be mindful of us when your virginity shall begin to reap its reward of honour."

48. Ambrose also uses the temperate and ornamented style when he is holding up before virgins who have made their profession a model for their imitation, and says: "She was a virgin not in body only, but also in mind; not mingling the purity of her affection with any dross of hypocrisy; serious in speech; prudent in disposition; sparing of words; delighting in study; not placing her confidence in uncertain riches, but in the prayer of the poor; diligent in labour; reverent in word; accustomed to

[127] Judges, 6.14–21.
[128] I Cor. 10.4.
[129] Num. 11.4.
[130] Luke, 12.49.
[131] I Cor. 15.49.

look to God, not man, as the guide of her conscience; injuring no one, wishing well to all; dutiful to her elders, not envious of her equals; avoiding boastfulness, following reason, loving virtue. When did she wound her parents even by a look? When did she quarrel with her neighbours? When did she spurn the humble, laugh at the weak, or shun the indigent? She is accustomed to visit only those haunts of men that pity would not blush for, nor modesty pass by. There is nothing haughty in her eyes, nothing bold in her words, nothing wanton in her gestures: her bearing is not voluptuous, nor her gait too free, nor her voice petulant; so that her outward appearance is an image of her mind, and a picture of purity. For a good house ought to be known for such at the very threshold, and show at the very entrance that there is no dark recess within, as the light of a lamp set inside sheds its radiance on the outside. Why need I detail her sparingness in food, her superabundance in duty – the one falling beneath the demands of nature, the other rising above its powers? The latter has no intervals of intermission, the former doubles the days by fasting; and when the desire for refreshment does arise, it is satisfied with food such as will support life, but not minister to appetite." Now I have cited these latter passages as examples of the temperate style, because their purpose is not to induce those who have not yet devoted themselves to take the vows of virginity, but to show of what character those who have taken vows ought to be. To prevail on any one to take a step of such a nature and of so great importance, requires that the mind should be excited and set on fire by the majestic style. Cyprian the martyr, however, did not write about the duty of taking up the profession of virginity, but about the dress and deportment of virgins. Yet that great bishop urges them to their duty even in these respects by the power of a majestic eloquence.

49. But I shall select examples of the majestic style from their treatment of a subject which both of them have touched. Both have denounced the women who colour, or rather discolour, their faces with paint. And the first, in dealing with this topic, says: "Suppose a painter should depict in colours that rival nature's the features and form and complexion of some man, and that, when the portrait had been finished with consummate art,

another painter should put his hand over it, as if to improve by his superior skill the painting already completed; surely the first artist would feel deeply insulted, and his indignation would be justly roused. Dost thou, then, think that thou wilt carry off with impunity so audacious an act of wickedness, such an insult to God the great artificer? For, granting that thou art not immodest in thy behaviour towards men, and that thou art not polluted in mind by these meretricious deceits, yet, in corrupting and violating what is God's, thou provest thyself worse than an adulteress. The fact that thou considerest thyself adorned and beautified by such arts is an impeachment of God's handiwork, and a violation of truth. Listen to the warning voice of the apostle: 'Purge out the old leaven, that ye may be a new lump, as ye are unleavened. For even Christ our passover is sacrificed for us: therefore let us keep the feast, not with old leaven, neither with the leaven of malice and wickedness; but with the unleavened bread of sincerity and truth.'[132] Now can sincerity and truth continue to exist when what is sincere is polluted, and what is true is changed by meretricious colouring and the deceptions of quackery into a lie? Thy Lord says, 'Thou canst not make one hair white or black';[133] and dost thou wish to have greater power so as to bring to nought the words of thy Lord? With rash and sacrilegious hand thou wouldst fain change the colour of thy hair: I would that, with a prophetic look to the future, thou shouldst dye it the colour of flame." It would be too long to quote all that follows.

50. Ambrose again, inveighing against such practices, says: "Hence arise these incentives to vice, that women, in their fear that they may not prove attractive to men, paint their faces with carefully chosen colours, and then from stains on their features go on to stains on their chastity. What folly it is to change the features of nature into those of a painting, and from fear of incurring their husband's disapproval, to proclaim openly that they have incurred their own! For the woman who desires to alter her natural appearance pronounces condemnation on herself; and her eager endeavours to please another prove that she has first been displeasing to herself. And what testimony to thine ugliness can

---

[132] I Cor. 5.7, 8.
[133] Matt. 5.36.

we find, O woman, that is more unquestionable than thine own, when thou art afraid to show thyself? If thou art comely why dost thou hide thy comeliness? If thou art plain, why dost thou lyingly pretend to be beautiful, when thou canst not enjoy the pleasure of the lie either in thine own consciousness or in that of another? For he loves another woman, thou desirest to please another man; and thou art angry if he love another, though he is taught adultery in thee. Thou art the evil promptress of thine own injury. For even the woman who has been the victim of a pander shrinks from acting the pander's part, and though she be vile, it is herself she sins against and not another. The crime of adultery is almost more tolerable than thine; for adultery tampers with modesty, but thou with nature." It is sufficiently clear, I think, that this eloquence calls passionately upon women to avoid tampering with their appearance by deceitful arts, and to cultivate modesty and fear. Accordingly, we notice that the style is neither subdued nor temperate, but majestic throughout. Now in these two authors whom I have selected as specimens of the rest, and in other ecclesiastical writers who both speak the truth and speak it well – speak it, that is, judiciously, pointedly, and with beauty and power of expression – many examples may be found of the three styles of speech, scattered through their various writings and discourses; and the diligent student may by assiduous reading, intermingled with practice on his own part, become thoroughly imbued with them all.

Chap. 22.   The necessity of variety in style

51. But we are not to suppose that it is against rule to mingle these various styles: on the contrary, every variety of style should be introduced so far as is consistent with good taste. For when we keep monotonously to one style, we fail to retain the hearer's attention; but when we pass from one style to another, the discourse goes off more gracefully, even though it extend to greater length. Each separate style, again, has varieties of its own which prevent the hearer's attention from cooling or becoming languid. We can bear the subdued style, however, longer without variety than the majestic style. For the mental emotion which it is necessary to stir up in order to carry the hearer's feelings with us, when once it has been sufficiently excited, the higher the pitch to which it is raised,

can be maintained the shorter time. And therefore we must be on our guard, lest, in striving to carry to a higher point the emotion we have excited, we rather lose what we have already gained. But after the interposition of matter that we have to treat in a quieter style, we can return with good effect to that which must be treated forcibly, thus making the tide of eloquence to ebb and flow like the sea. It follows from this, that the majestic style, if it is to be long continued, ought not to be unvaried, but should alternate at intervals with the other styles; the speech or writing as a whole, however, being referred to that style which is the prevailing one.

Chap. 23.   How the various styles should be mingled

52. Now it is a matter of importance to determine what style should be alternated with what other, and the places where it is necessary that any particular style should be used. In the majestic style, for instance, it is always, or almost always, desirable that the introduction should be temperate. And the speaker has it in his discretion to use the subdued style even where the majestic would be allowable, in order that the majestic when it is used may be the more majestic by comparison, and may as it were shine out with greater brilliance from the dark background. Again, whatever may be the style of the speech or writing, when knotty questions turn up for solution, accuracy of distinction is required, and this naturally demands the subdued style. And accordingly this style must be used in alternation with the other two styles whenever questions of that sort turn up; just as we must use the temperate style, no matter what may be the general tone of the discourse, whenever praise or blame is to be given without any ulterior reference to the condemnation or acquittal of any one, or to obtaining the concurrence of any one in a course of action. In the majestic style, then, and in the quiet likewise, both the other two styles occasionally find place. The temperate style, on the other hand, not indeed always, but occasionally, needs the quiet style; for example, when, as I have said, a knotty question comes up to be settled, or when some points that are susceptible of ornament are left unadorned and expressed in the quiet style, in order to give greater effect to certain exuberances (as they may be called) of ornament. But the temperate style never needs the aid of the

majestic; for its object is to gratify, never to excite, the mind.

Chap. 24. The effects produced by the majestic style

53. If frequent and vehement applause follows a speaker, we are not to suppose on that account that he is speaking in the majestic style; for this effect is often produced both by the accurate distinctions of the quiet style, and by the beauties of the temperate. The majestic style, on the other hand, frequently silences the audience by its impressiveness, but calls forth their tears. For example, when at Cæsarea in Mauritania I was dissuading the people from that civil, or worse than civil, war which they called *Caterva* (for it was not fellow-citizens merely, but neighbours, brothers, fathers and sons even, who, divided into two factions and armed with stones, fought annually at a certain season of the year for several days continuously, every one killing whomsoever he could), I strove with all the vehemence of speech that I could command to root out and drive from their hearts and lives an evil so cruel and inveterate; it was not, however, when I heard their applause, but when I saw their tears, that I thought I had produced an effect. For the applause showed that they were instructed and delighted, but the tears that they were subdued. And when I saw their tears I was confident, even before the event proved it, that this horrible and barbarous custom (which had been handed down to them from their fathers and their ancestors of generations long gone by and which like an enemy was besieging their hearts, or rather had complete possession of them) was overthrown; and immediately that my sermon was finished I called upon them with heart and voice to give praise and thanks to God. And, lo, with the blessing of Christ, it is now eight years or more since anything of the sort was attempted there. In many other cases besides I have observed that men show the effect made on them by the powerful eloquence of a wise man, not by clamorous applause so much as by groans, sometimes even by tears, finally by change of life.

54. The quiet style, too, has made a change in many; but it was to teach them what they were ignorant of, or to persuade them of what they thought incredible, not to make them do what they knew they ought to do but were unwilling to do. To break down hardness of this sort, speech needs to be vehement. Praise and censure, too, when they are eloquently expressed, even in the temperate style, produce such an effect on some, that they are not only pleased with the eloquence of the encomiums and censures, but are led to live so as themselves to deserve praise, and to avoid living so as to incur blame. But no one would say that all who are thus delighted change their habits in consequence, whereas all who are moved by the majestic style act accordingly, and all who are taught by the quiet style know or believe a truth which they were previously ignorant of.

Chap. 25. How the temperate style is to be used

55. From all this we may conclude, that the end arrived at by the two styles last mentioned is the one which it is most essential for those who aspire to speak with wisdom and eloquence to secure. On the other hand, what the temperate style properly aims at, viz., to please by beauty of expression, is not in itself an adequate end; but when what we have to say is good and useful, and when the hearers are both acquainted with it and favourably disposed towards it, so that it is not necessary either to instruct or persuade them, beauty of style may have its influence in securing their prompter compliance, or in making them adhere to it more tenaciously. For as the function of all eloquence, whichever of these three forms it may assume, is to speak persuasively, and its object is to persuade, an eloquent man will speak persuasively, whatever style he may adopt; but unless he succeeds in persuading, his eloquence has not secured its object. Now in the subdued style, he persuades his hearers that what he says is true; in the majestic style, he persuades them to do what they are aware they ought to do, but do not; in the temperate style, he persuades them that his speech is elegant and ornate. But what use is there in attaining such an object as this last? They may desire it who are vain of their eloquence and make a boast of panegyrics, and suchlike performances, where the object is not to instruct the hearer, or to persuade him to any course of action, but merely to give him pleasure. We, however, ought to make that end subordinate to another, viz., the effecting by this style of

eloquence what we aim at effecting when we use the majestic style. For we may by the use of this style persuade men to cultivate good habits and give up evil ones, if they are not so hardened as to need the vehement style; or if they have already begun a good course, we may induce them to pursue it more zealously, and to persevere in it with constancy. Accordingly, even in the temperate style we must use beauty of expression not for ostentation, but for wise ends; not contenting ourselves merely with pleasing the hearer, but rather seeking to aid him in the pursuit of the good end which we hold out before him.

Chap. 26. *In every style the orator should aim at perspicuity, beauty, and persuasiveness*

56. Now in regard to the three conditions I laid down a little while ago[134] as necessary to be fulfilled by any one who wishes to speak with wisdom and eloquence, viz. perspicuity, beauty of style, and persuasive power, we are not to understand that these three qualities attach themselves respectively to the three several styles of speech, one to each, so that perspicuity is a merit peculiar to the subdued style, beauty to the temperate, and persuasive power to the majestic. On the contrary, all speech, whatever its style, ought constantly to aim at, and as far as possible to display, all these three merits. For we do not like even what we say in the subdued style to pall upon the hearer; and therefore we would be listened to, not with intelligence merely, but with pleasure as well. Again, why do we enforce what we teach by divine testimony, except that we wish to carry the hearer with us, that is, to compel his assent by calling in the assistance of Him of Whom it is said, "Thy testimonies are very sure"?[135] And when any one narrates a story, even in the subdued style, what does he wish but to be believed? But who will listen to him if he do not arrest attention by some beauty of style? And if he be not intelligible, is it not plain that he can neither give pleasure nor enforce conviction? The subdued style, again, in its own naked simplicity, when it unravels questions of very great difficulty and throws an unexpected light upon them; when it worms out and brings to light some

very acute observations from a quarter whence nothing was expected; when it seizes upon and exposes the falsity of an opposing opinion, which seemed at its first statement to be unassailable; especially when all this is accompanied by a natural, unsought grace of expression, and by a rhythm and balance of style which is not ostentatiously obtruded, but seems rather to be called forth by the nature of the subject: this style, so used, frequently calls forth applause so great that one can hardly believe it to be the subdued style. For the fact that it comes forth without either ornament or defence, and offers battle in its own naked simplicity, does not hinder it from crushing its adversary by weight of nerve and muscle, and overwhelming and destroying the falsehood that opposes it by the mere strength of its own right arm. How explain the frequent and vehement applause that waits upon men who speak thus, except by the pleasure that truth so irresistibly established, and so victoriously defended, naturally affords? Wherefore the Christian teacher and speaker ought, when he uses the subdued style, to endeavour not only to be clear and intelligible, but to give pleasure and to bring home conviction to the hearer.

57. Eloquence of the temperate style, also, must, in the case of the Christian orator, be neither altogether without ornament, nor unsuitably adorned, nor is it to make the giving of pleasure its sole aim, which is all it professes to accomplish in the hands of others; but in its encomiums and censures it should aim at inducing the hearer to strive after or hold more firmly by what it praises, and to avoid or renounce what it condemns. On the other hand, without perspicuity this style cannot give pleasure. And so the three qualities, perspicuity, beauty, and persuasiveness, are to be sought in this style also; beauty, of course, being its primary object.

58. Again, when it becomes necessary to stir and sway the hearer's mind by the majestic style (and this is always necessary when he admits that what you say is both true and agreeable, and yet is unwilling to act accordingly), you must, of course, speak in the majestic style. But who can be moved if he does not understand what is said? and who will stay to listen if he receives no pleasure? Wherefore, in this style, too, when an obdurate

---

[134] Chaps. 15 and 17.
[135] Ps. 93.5.

heart is to be persuaded to obedience, you must speak so as to be both intelligible and pleasing, if you would be heard with a submissive mind.

Chap. 27. *The man whose life is in harmony with his teaching will teach with greater effect*

59. But whatever may be the majesty of the style, the life of the speaker will count for more in securing the hearer's compliance. The man who speaks wisely and eloquently, but lives wickedly, may, it is true, instruct many who are anxious to learn; though, as it is written, he "is unprofitable to himself."[136] Wherefore, also, the apostle says: "Whether in pretence or in truth Christ is preached."[137] Now Christ is the truth; yet we see that the truth can be preached, though not in truth – that is, what is right and true in itself may be preached by a man of perverse and deceitful mind. And thus it is that Jesus Christ is preached by those that seek their own, and not the things that are Jesus Christ's. But since true believers obey the voice, not of any man, but of the Lord Himself, Who says, "All therefore whatsoever they bid you observe, that observe and do: but do not ye after their works; for they say and do not";[138] therefore it is that men who themselves lead unprofitable lives are heard with profit by others. For though they seek their own objects, they do not dare to teach their own doctrines, sitting as they do in the high places of ecclesiastical authority, which is established on sound doctrine. Wherefore our Lord Himself, before saying what I have just quoted about men of this stamp, made this observation: "The scribes and the Pharisees sit in Moses' seat."[139] The seat they occupied, then, which was not theirs but Moses', compelled them to say what was good, though they did what was evil. And so they followed their own course in their lives, but were prevented by the seat they occupied, which belonged to another, from preaching their own doctrines.

60. Now these men do good to many by preaching what they themselves do not perform; but they would do good to very many more if they lived as they preach. For there are numbers who seek an excuse for their own evil lives in comparing the teaching with the conduct of their instructors, and who say in their hearts, or even go a little further, and say with their lips: "Why do you not do yourself what you bid me do?" And thus they cease to listen with submission to a man who does not listen to himself, and in despising the preacher they learn to despise the word that is preached. Wherefore the apostle, writing to Timothy, after telling him, "Let no man despise thy youth," adds immediately the course by which he would avoid contempt: "but be thou an example of the believers, in word, in conversation, in charity, in spirit, in faith, in purity."[140]

Chap. 28. *Truth is more important than expression. What is meant by strife about words*

61. Such a teacher as is here described may, to secure compliance, speak not only quietly and temperately, but even vehemently, without any breach of modesty, because his life protects him against contempt. For while he pursues an upright life, he takes care to maintain a good reputation as well, providing things honest in the sight of God and men,[141] fearing God, and caring for men. In his very speech even he prefers to please by matter rather than by words; thinks that a thing is well said in proportion as it is true in fact, and that a teacher should govern his words, not let the words govern him. This is what the apostle says: "Not with wisdom of words, lest the cross of Christ should be made of none effect."[142] To the same effect also is what he says to Timothy: "Charging them before the Lord that they strive not about words to no profit, but to the subverting of the hearers."[143] Now this does not mean that, when adversaries oppose the truth, we are to say nothing in defence of the truth. For where, then,

---

[136] Ecclus. 37.19.
[137] Phil. 1.18.
[138] Matt. 23.3.
[139] Matt. 23.2.
[140] I Tim. 4.12.
[141] II Cor. 8.21.
[142] I Cor. 2.17.
[143] II Tim. 2.14.

would be what he says when he is describing the sort of man a bishop ought to be: "that he may be able by sound doctrine both to exhort and convince the gainsayers"?[144] To strive about words is not to be careful about the way to overcome error by truth, but to be anxious that your mode of expression should be preferred to that of another. The man who does not strive about words, whether he speak quietly, temperately, or vehemently, uses words with no other purpose than to make the truth plain, pleasing, and effective; for not even love itself, which is the end of the commandment and the fulfilling of the law,[145] can be rightly exercised unless the objects of love are true and not false. For as a man with a comely body but an ill-conditioned mind is a more painful object than if his body too were deformed, so men who teach lies are the more pitiable if they happen to be eloquent in speech. To speak eloquently, then, and wisely as well, is just to express truths which it is expedient to teach in fit and proper words – words which in the subdued style are adequate, in the temperate, elegant, and in the majestic, forcible. But the man who cannot speak both eloquently and wisely should speak wisely without eloquence, rather than eloquently without wisdom.

Chap. 29. It is permissible for a preacher to deliver to the people what has been written by a more eloquent man than himself

If, however, he cannot do even this, let his life be such as shall not only secure a reward for himself, but afford an example to others; and let his manner of living be an eloquent sermon in itself.

62. There are, indeed, some men who have a good delivery, but cannot compose anything to deliver. Now, if such men take what has been written with wisdom and eloquence by others, and commit to memory, and deliver it to the people, they cannot be blamed, supposing them to do it without deception. For in this way many become preachers of the truth (which is certainly desirable), and yet not many teachers; for all deliver the discourse which one real teacher has composed, and there are no divisions among them. Nor are such men to be alarmed by the words of Jeremiah the prophet, through whom God denounces those who steal His words every one from his neighbour.[146] For those who steal take what does not belong to them, but the word of God belongs to all who obey it; and it is the man who speaks well, but lives badly, who really takes the words that belong to another. For the good things he says seem to be the result of his own thought, and yet they have nothing in common with his manner of life. And so God has said that they steal His words who would appear good by speaking God's words, but are in fact bad, as they follow their own ways. And if you look closely into the matter, it is not really themselves who say the good things they say. For how they can say in words what they deny in deeds? It is not for nothing that the apostle says of such men: "They profess that they know God, but in works they deny Him."[147] In one sense, then, they do say the things, and in another sense they do not say them; for both these statements must be true, both being made by Him Who is the Truth. Speaking of such men, in one place He says, "Whatsoever they bid you observe, that observe and do; but do not ye after their works"; that is to say, what ye hear from their lips, that do; what ye see in their lives, that do ye not; "for they say and do not."[148] And so, though they do not, yet they say. But in another place, upbraiding such men, He says, "O generation of vipers, how can ye, being evil, speak good things?"[149] And from this it would appear that even what they say, when they say what is good, it is not themselves who say, for in will and in deed they deny what they say. Hence it happens that a wicked man who is eloquent may compose a discourse in which the truth is set forth to be delivered by a good man who is not eloquent; and when this takes place, the former draws from himself what does not belong to him, and the latter receives

[144] Tit. 1.9.
[145] I Tim. 1.5; Rom. 13.10.
[146] Jer. 23.30.
[147] Tit. 1.16.
[148] Matt. 23.3.
[149] Matt. 12.34.

from another what really belongs to himself. But when true believers render this service to true believers, both parties speak what is their own, for God is theirs, to Whom belongs all that they say; and even those who could not compose what they say make it their own by composing their lives in harmony with it.

[...]

Chap. 31.   Apology for the length of the work

64. This book has extended to a greater length than I expected or desired. But the reader or hearer who finds pleasure in it will not think it long. He who thinks it long, but is anxious to know its contents, may read it in parts. He who does not care to be acquainted with it need not complain of its length. I, however, give thanks to God that with what little ability I possess I have in these four books striven to depict, not the sort of man I am myself (for my defects are very many), but the sort of man he ought to be who desires to labour in sound, that is, in Christian doctrine, not for his own instruction only, but for that of others also.

Sermons

Augustine used many of his sermons to dispute the heretical teachings of the Donatists and the Pelagians, but throughout all of his sermons we find him applying allegoresis to interpret and teach the Scriptures. The two selections provided here, therefore, are representative examples of Augustine's use of Christian rhetoric. It is important to note, however, that they exist as more than illustrations of free interpretation. Pinckaers (1993), for example, argued that Augustine's "Sermon on the Mount" was an important source of Christian ethics and that it provided a model for the moral Christian life. This argument is entirely congruent with Augustine's vision of Christian rhetoric's goal.

Reading 45

Our Lord's Sermon on the Mount

Our Lord's Sermon on the Mount (excerpt), excerpt from *St. Augustine: The Lord's Sermon on the Mount*, translated by J.J. Jepson. © 1948 by Joseph Plumpe and Johannes Quasten. Reprinted by permission of Paulist Press, Inc. www.paulistpress.com.

Book One: Explanation of the First Part of the Lord's Sermon on the Mount, Contained in the Fifth Chapter of Matthew

Chapter 1

The Sermon on the Mount is the perfect pattern of the Christian life. The poor in spirit.

If a person will devoutly and calmly consider the sermon which our Lord Jesus Christ spoke on the mount, as we read it in the Gospel according to Matthew, I think he will find in it, as measured by the highest norms of morality, the perfect pattern of the Christian life. We dare to promise this not without warrant: it is a conclusion based on the spoken words of the Lord Himself. For the conclusion of the sermon is so phrased as to make it apparent that it embraces all the directives we need for life. For thus He says: *Every one, therefore, that heareth these my words and doth them, I shall liken him to a wise man that built his house upon a rock: the rain fell, the floods came, the winds blew and they beat upon that house; and it fell not, for it was founded on a rock. And every one that heareth these my words and doth them not, I shall liken him to a foolish man that built his house upon the sand: the rain fell, the floods came, the winds blew and they beat upon that house; and it fell, and great was the fall thereof.*

Since, therefore, He did not say only "that heareth my words," but said this with an addition, stating: *that heareth these my words,* He sufficiently indicated, it seems to me, that these words which He spoke on the mount, so perfectly shape the life of those who wish to live according to them as deservedly to be likened to one who built upon a rock. I remark this in order to make it clear that this sermon has been made up of all the precepts by which Christian life has vitality. In the proper place there will be a fuller comment on this section.

2. Now, then, the sermon begins with these words: *But when He had seen the many crowds, He went up into a mountain, and when He was set down, His disciples came unto Him; and opening His mouth, He taught them, saying ...* (5.1 f.).

If the question is raised, what is meant by the "mountain," we can well see that it stands for the greater precepts of righteousness, the lesser ones of course being those which were given to the Jews. But here it is one and the same God who through His holy Prophets and servants, by a disposition of time that was perfectly ordered, gave the lesser precepts to a people who as yet had to be controlled by fear, and through His Son the greater ones to a people for whom it was now expedient to be free in love. In the giving of the lesser to the less and of the greater to the greater, the giving is by Him who alone knows to give to the human race the remedy suitable to the times. Nor is it surprising that the greater precepts are given on account of the kingdom of heaven and the lesser were given on account of an earthly kingdom by that one same God who made heaven and earth. Therefore, concerning this righteousness which is greater, we have the statement by the Prophet: *Thy justice is as the mountains of God;* and this illustrates well that one teacher only, one who alone is competent to teach doctrines so weighty, teaches on a mountain. Further, He teaches sitting down – which has reference to the dignity of the teaching office. *And His disciples come unto Him* that for the hearing of His words they might be the nearer even in body who were approaching moreover in soul to fulfill His precepts. *And opening His mouth He taught them, saying. ...* 5.1f. This circumlocution which runs: *And opening His mouth,* perhaps intimates by the mere

suggestion of a pause that the sermon is to be somewhat longer than usual; unless, possibly, it be not without significance that now He is said to have opened His mouth, when in the Old Law it was His wont to open the mouth of the Prophets.

3. Now, what does He say? *Blessed are the poor in spirit, for theirs is the kingdom of heaven* (3). We read in the Scriptures concerning the craving for temporal things: *All is vanity and presumption of spirit. Presumption of spirit* means boldness and haughtiness. In common parlance, too, the haughty are said to have "high spirits"; and rightly, since spirit is also called "wind." Whence it is written: *Fire, hail, snow, ice, stormy wind.* And who has not heard the haughty spoken of as "inflated," blown up, as it were, with wind? So, too, the expression of the Apostle: *Knowledge puffeth up, but charity edifieth.* For this reason *the poor in spirit* are rightly understood here as the humble and those who fear God, that is, those who do not have an inflated spirit. And there could be no more felicitous beginning of blessedness, whose ultimate goal is perfect wisdom: *The fear of the Lord is the beginning of wisdom.* Whereas, on the contrary, we have the attribution: *The beginning of all sin is pride.* Let, therefore, the haughty seek and love the kingdom of the earth; but *Blessed are the poor in spirit, for theirs is the kingdom of heaven.*

Chapter 2

The other Beatitudes

4. *Blessed are the meek, for they shall possess the land by inheritance.* The land I take in the sense of the Psalm: *Thou art my hope, my portion in the land of the living.* It stands for something solid, the stability of an undying inheritance, where the soul in a state of well-being rests as in its natural environment, as the body does on earth; and thence draws its food, as the body from the earth. This is the life and rest of the Saints. The meek are those who yield before outbursts of wickedness and do not resist evil, but overcome evil with good. Therefore let those who are not meek struggle and contend for earthly and temporal things; but *blessed are the meek, for they shall possess the land by inheritance* from which they cannot be expelled.

5. *Blessed are the mourners, for they shall be comforted* (5). Mourning is sadness for the loss of dear ones. But when people turn to God, they dismiss what they cherished as dear in this world; for they

do not find joy in those things which before rejoiced them; and until there comes about in them the love for what is eternal, they feel the sting of sadness over a number of things. They, therefore, will be comforted by the Holy Spirit, who especially for this reason is named the Paraclete, that is, the Consoler, that disregarding the temporal they may enjoy eternal happiness.

6. *Blessed are they that hunger and thirst after justice, for they shall have their fill* (6). Here He means those who love the true and unshakable good. The food with which they will be filled is the food that the Lord Himself mentions: *My meat is to do the will of my Father*, which is righteousness; and the water, of which whoso shall drink, as He Himself says, *it shall become in him a fountain of water springing up into life everlasting.*

7. *Blessed are the merciful, for mercy shall be shown them* (7). He pronounces them blessed who come to the aid of the needy, since it is paid back to them so that they are freed from distress.

8. *Blessed are the clean of heart, for they shall see God* (8). How senseless, therefore, are they who look for God with bodily eyes, since He is seen by the heart, as elsewhere it is written: *And seek Him in simplicity of heart.* For this is a clean heart, one that is a simple heart; and as the light of this world cannot be seen save with sound eyes, so God cannot be seen unless that is sound by which He can be seen.

9. *Blessed are the peacemakers, for they shall be called the children of God* (9). Perfection lies in peace, where nothing is at war; and the children of God are peaceful for the reason that no resistance to God is present, and surely children ought to bear a likeness to their father. And they are at peace with themselves who quell all the emotions of their soul and subject them to reason, that is, to the mind and spirit, and have their carnal passions well under control; these make up the kingdom of God. In this kingdom everything is in such perfect order that the noblest and most excellent elements in man control without opposition the other elements which are common to us and animals. Moreover, what is most distinguished in man – mind and reason – is subject to a higher being, which is Truth itself, the only-begotten Son of God; for it cannot control the lower unless it puts itself in subjection to its superior. And this is the peace which is given on earth to men of good will; this is the life of a man who is rounded out and perfect in wisdom. From a kingdom of this sort enjoying greatest peace and

order has been cast out the Prince of this world who lords it over the perverse and disorderly. With this peace set up and established in the soul, whatever onslaughts he who has been cast out makes against it from without, he but increases the glory which is according to God. He weakens nothing in that structure but by the very ineffectiveness of his machinations reveals what strength has grown within. Hence it follows: *Blessed are they that suffer persecution for justice' sake, for theirs is the kingdom of heaven.* (10).

Chapter 3

The Beatitudes mark the stages traversed towards perfection

10. These, then, are His maxims – eight in all. He now addresses the rest to those who were present, saying: *Blessed will ye be when they shall revile you and persecute you* (11). The earlier maxims He directed to a general audience: for He did not say, "Blessed are the poor in spirit, for *yours is the* kingdom of heaven"; but He said, *for theirs is the kingdom of heaven*; not, "Blessed are the meek, for *you* shall possess the land"; and so for the others down to the eighth, where He said: *Blessed are they that suffer persecution for justice' sake, for theirs is the kingdom of heaven.* Now, from this point He began a direct address to His audience; although what had gone before had reference also to those who made up His audience, just as what is to follow, though seemingly addressed to His immediate audience, has reference also to those who were not there and to those of a future time. Therefore we are to give good heed to the number of those maxims. For blessedness starts with humility: *Blessed are the poor in spirit*, that is, those who are not puffed up, whose soul is submissive to divine authority, who stand in dread of punishment after this life despite the seeming blessedness of their earthly life. The soul next makes itself acquainted with Sacred Scripture according to which it must show itself meek through piety, so that it may not make bold to censure what appears a stumbling block to the uninstructed and become intractable by obstinate argumentation. The soul now begins to realize what a hold the world has on it through the habits and sins of the flesh. In this third step, then, wherein is knowledge, there is grief for the loss of the highest good through clinging to the lowest.

In the fourth step there is hard work. The soul puts forth a tremendous effort to wrench itself from the pernicious delights which bind it. Here there must be hunger and thirst for righteousness, and there is great need for fortitude, for not without pain is the heart severed from its delights.

At the fifth step it is suggested to those who are continuing their energetic efforts how they may be helped to master their situation. For unless one is helped by a superior power, he is incapable of freeing himself by his own efforts from the bonds of misery which encompass him. The suggestion given is a just proposition: If one wishes to be helped by a more powerful person, let him help someone who is weaker in a field wherein he himself holds an advantage. Hence, *Blessed are the merciful, for mercy will be shown them.*

The sixth step is cleanness of heart from a good consciousness of works well done, enabling the soul to contemplate that supreme good which can be seen only by a mind that is pure and serene.

Finally, the seventh step is wisdom itself, that is, contemplation of the truth, bringing peace to the whole man and effecting a likeness to God; and of this the sum is, *Blessed are the peacemakers, for they shall be called the children of God.*

The eighth maxim returns, as it were, to the beginning, because it shows and commends what is perfect and complete. Thus, in the first and the eighth the kingdom of heaven is mentioned: *Blessed are the poor in spirit, for theirs is the kingdom of heaven*; and, *Blessed are they that suffer persecution for justice' sake, for theirs is the kingdom of heaven* – when now it is said: *Who shall separate us from the love of Christ? Shall tribulation? or distress? or persecution? or hunger? or nakedness? or danger? or the sword?*

Seven in number, therefore, are the things which lead to perfection. The eighth maxim throws light upon perfection and shows what it consists of, so that, with this maxim beginning again, so to speak, from the first, the two together may serve as steps toward the perfection of the others also.

Chapter 4

The Beatitudes and the sevenfold Gifts of the Holy Spirit. The mystical number eight.

11. To these seven steps and maxims there corresponds, so it seems to me, the sevenfold operation of the Holy Spirit spoken of by Isaias. But the prec-

edence is different: there the enumeration begins with the more excellent, here, with the more lowly. For in Isaias wisdom leads the list and the fear of the Lord brings it to a close; but *the fear of the Lord is the beginning of wisdom.* Hence, if we count them in an ascending gradation, the first in Isaias is the fear of the Lord; the second, godliness; the third, knowledge; the fourth, fortitude; the fifth, counsel; the sixth, understanding; the seventh, wisdom.

The fear of the Lord corresponds with the humble, of whom it is said in the present text: *Blessed are the poor in spirit* – that is, those not conceited, not proud; to whom the Apostle says: *Be not highminded, but fear* – that is, do not be haughty.

Godliness corresponds to the meek, for he who seeks in a godly frame of mind honors Holy Scripture and does not find fault with what as yet he does not understand, and therefore he does not oppose it – which is to be meek. Whence it is here said: *Blessed are the meek.*

Knowledge corresponds to those who mourn, who have come to learn through Scripture with what evils they are held in fetters which aforetime in their ignorance they sought as good things and useful. Of these it is here said: *Blessed are they that mourn.*

Fortitude corresponds to those who hunger and thirst, for they labor in a desire for the joy that comes from what is truly good and in an effort to stem their love for the earthly and corruptible. Hence of them it is said: *Blessed are they that hunger and thirst after justice.*

Counsel corresponds to the merciful; for this is the one means of evading burdensome evils: that we forgive as we wish to be forgiven and that we help others to the best of our ability as we hope to be helped in our need. Accordingly it is said here: *Blessed are the merciful.*

Understanding corresponds to the clean of heart – a cleansed eye, so to speak, whereby can be discerned what the bodily *eye hath not seen, nor ear heard, neither hath it entered into the heart of man*; of whom it is here said: *Blessed are the clean of heart.*

Wisdom corresponds to the peacemakers in whom everything is in order and there is no emotion to rebel against reason, but all things obey the spirit of man just as it obeys God; of whom it is here said: *Blessed are the peacemakers.*

12. Now, the one reward, which is the kingdom of heaven, is designated variously by a title congruous with the several steps.

In the first, as was fitting, there was set up the kingdom of heaven, which is the perfect and highest wisdom of the rational soul. Hence it was said: *Blessed are the poor in spirit, for theirs is the kingdom of heaven,* as if it were said: *The fear of the Lord is the beginning of wisdom.*

To the meek an inheritance was given as to those carrying out their Father's will in a dutiful spirit: *Blessed are the meek, for they shall possess the land as by inheritance.* To those who mourn, consolation, as to those who realize what they have lost and in what lowly condition they are: *Blessed are they that mourn, for they shall be comforted.* To the hungry and thirsty, abundance, like a repast for those who are at work and are energetically striving for their salvation: *Blessed are they that hunger and thirst after justice, for they shall have their fill.* To the merciful, mercy, as to those who act on the true and best counsel in order that what they do to the weaker may be accorded them by the stronger: *Blessed are the merciful, for they shall obtain mercy.* To the clean of heart, the faculty of seeing God, as to those possessing a clear-sighted eye to take in eternal realities: *Blessed are the clean of heart, for they shall see God.* To the peacemakers, the likeness of God, as to the perfectly wise and conformed to the image of God through the rebirth of the renewed man: *Blessed are the peacemakers, for they shall be called the children of God.*

And these things can be realized even in this life, as we believe the Apostles realized them. And certainly no words can express that complete transformation into the likeness of angels which is promised for the afterlife.

Blessed, therefore, *are they that suffer persecution for justice' sake, for theirs is the kingdom of heaven.* This eighth maxim, which harks back to the first, and announces the perfected man, is perhaps expressed in type in the Old Testament by circumcision on the eighth day and by the resurrection of the Lord after the Sabbath which is at once the eighth day of the week and the first; also by the celebration of the octave which we keep on occasion of the rebirth of the renewed man; and by the very name Pentecost. For to the number seven multiplied seven times – making fortynine – an eighth is added, as it were, so that we have fifty and in a way return to the beginning. It was on this day that the Holy Spirit was sent by whom we are brought into the kingdom of heaven and receive our inheritance and are consoled, are fed, and obtain mercy, and are cleansed, and made at peace; and, thus made perfect, we bear for truth and righteousness whatever annoyances we have to endure from without.

Reading 46

Sermon 95

Sermon 95, pp. 24–8 from *The Works of Saint Augustine: A Translation for the 21st Century*, translated by E. Hill (New City Press, 1992). Reproduced by permission of the Augustinian Heritage Institute, Inc.

On the Words of the Gospel, Mark 8:1–9, Where the Miracle of the Seven Loaves is Related[150]

A common larder in heaven

1. When I expound the holy scriptures to you, it's as though I were breaking bread to you. For your part, receive it hungrily, and belch out a fat praise from your hearts;[151] and those of you who are rich enough to keep excellent tables, don't be mean and lean with your works and good deeds. So what I am dishing out to you is not mine. What you eat, I eat; what you live on, I live on. We share a common larder in heaven; that, you see, is where the word of God comes from.

---

[150] Date uncertain but preached, whatever year it was, in the winter (see last section); and almost certainly at Hippo, or in one of the churches of the Hippo diocese (see note 155).

[151] Not a vulgarity in those days, as we have noted before, but an acceptable sign of appreciation from guests.

The number seven

2. The seven loaves signify the sevenfold working of the Holy Spirit;[152] the four thousand people, the Church established under the four gospels; the seven baskets of fragments, the perfection of the Church. This number, you see, stands for perfection extremely often. I mean, how come it says, *Seven times a day shall I praise you* (Ps 119:164)? Is a person going wildly astray who doesn't praise God that number of times? So what else can be the meaning of "Seven times a day shall I praise you," but "I shall never cease from praising"? You see, when he says seven times he signifies the whole of time; that's why the ages unfold in the weekly round of seven days.[153] So what else can *Seven times a day shall I praise you* mean but *His praise is always in my mouth* (Ps 34:1)?

It is because of this perfection of the number seven that John writes to seven Churches. The book of the Apocalypse is by Saint John the evangelist; he writes it to seven Churches.[154] Be true to the faith, recognize those seven baskets. You see, those scraps left over were not wasted; but because you too belong to the Church, they have of course profited you. My explaining all this to you means I am waiting on Christ. And you, when you listen quietly, are seated at the table. True, I'm sitting down in the body,[155] but in spirit I am standing up and being as attentive as I can in waiting on you – in case any of you should be put off by the dinner service, not the food. You know what God's banquet is, you have often heard about it; it's minds, not bellies that seek invitations to it.[156]

God's dinner party

3. Four thousand people were certainly given more than enough to eat from seven loaves; could anything be more wonderful? And yet it would have been incomplete unless seven baskets had also been filled with the scraps left over. What tremendous mysteries! The events took place, and the events were speaking. If you understand the things that were done, they are words. You too belong to those four thousand, because you live under the fourfold gospel.

Children and women did not belong to that number. That, after all, is what it says: *How those who ate were four thousand people, not counting children and women* (Mt 22:11).[157] As though the mindless and the effeminate were without number. However, let them too eat as well. Let them eat; perhaps the children will grow and cease to be childish; perhaps the effeminate will get a grip on themselves and be chastened. Let them eat; I'm dishing out, I'm serving up. But whoever these may be, well God inspects his own dinner party, and if they don't get a grip on themselves, well he knows how to invite them, he also knows how to put them aside.

Invitations to the banquet

4. You know this, dearly beloved; recollect the parable in the gospel, how the Lord went in to view those seated at one of his banquets. The householder who had issued the invitations, as it

---

[152] See Is 11:2–3 for the seven gifts of the Holy Spirit.

[153] But he is also alluding to the common idea that the world would last as many ages as there were days of creation; the seventh and last age being beyond the day of judgment and the end of the world in the eternal sabbath of the kingdom of God. Our weekly cycle reminds us of this – at least it reminded Augustine!

[154] See Rv 1:4. The book is not by the author of the fourth gospel, and there were many distinguished Fathers of the Church in Augustine's time and before who did not think it was.

[155] In the bishop's *cathedra* or throne, from which he normally preached. The detail indicates that he was preaching at Hippo, or at least in one of the parishes of his diocese, because if he had been preaching in the Church of another bishop, he would not have occupied the *cathedra*, but preached from one of the *ambos* or reading desks, from which the scriptures were read.

[156] He is possibly referring obliquely to the eucharist as well as to the feast of the word of God.

[157] Mark does not mention this distinction of the sexes, only Matthew. It is, however, an old manuscript, not just the Maurist editors who ascribe this sermon to Mark's gospel. Again, perhaps, we have in fact to do with a gospel harmony.

Augustine goes on to treat the exclusion of women and children from the symbolic number as itself symbolic. We mustn't suppose they are not counted among the faithful in their own right – but they stand symbolically for the "mindless and the effeminate." I doubt if by "effeminate" Augustine is referring primarily to homosexuals; simply to those persons of either sex, but chiefly men, who lack the "manly" virtues, who are cowardly, slack and self-indulgent in other words. Not very polite, making women stand for such persons; but the very word "effeminate" is essentially and inescapably sexist.

is written, *found there a man not wearing a wedding garment* (Mt 22:11). You see, the one who had issued the invitations to the wedding was that bridegroom *handsome of figure above the sons of men* (Ps 45:1). That bridegroom became ugly for the sake of his ugly bride, to make her beautiful. How did the beautiful man become ugly? If I can't prove it, I'm blaspheming.

The prophet[158] provides me with a testimonial to his beauty when he says, *handsome of figure above the sons of men*, another prophet gives me a testimonial to his deformity when he says, *We saw him, and he had no comeliness or grace; but his features were abject, his posture deformed* (Is 53:2). Hey, prophet, you that said *Handsome of figure above the sons of men*, you're being contradicted. Here's another prophet stepping out against you and saying, "You're a liar; *we saw him*. What's this the man's saying, 'Handsome of figure above the sons of men'? *We saw him having no comeliness or grace.*"

So are these two prophets quarreling in a peace corner? They were both talking about Christ, both talking about the cornerstone.[159] In a corner two walls meet and agree; if they don't agree, it's not a building but a ruin. The prophets agree with each other, don't let's leave them brawling. Instead let us get to know the reality of the peace between them; they themselves, you see, don't know how to pick a quarrel.

O Mr. Prophet, you that said, "Handsome of figure above the sons of men," where did you see him so? Answer, answer please, where did you see him? "*While he was in the form of God, he did not reckon it robbery to be equal to God.* That's where I saw him. Or do you doubt that the one who is equal to God is handsome above the sons of men?"

No, no; you've answered; let the other one answer now, who said, *We saw him, and he had no comeliness or grace.* That's what you said; say where you saw him. He makes the words of the first one his starting point; where the other fin-

ished, this one begins. Where did that one finish? *Who, while he was in the form of God, did not reckon it robbery to be equal to God.* There you have where he saw him *handsome in figure above the sons of men* now you tell us where you saw that he had no comeliness or grace. "*But he emptied himself, taking the form of a slave; made in the likeness of men, and found in condition as a man* (Phil 2:7–8). About his deformity he still has this to say: *He humbled himself, becoming obedient unto death, the death indeed of the cross.* That's where I saw him."

So they both peacefully agree, and both are pacified. What is more comely than God? What more deformed than the crucified?

The wedding garment

5. So this bridegroom, *handsome in figure above the sons of men*, who became deformed in order to make the bride beautiful, the bride who was hailed, *O gracious among women* (Sg 1:8), of whom it is said, *Who is this who comes up made white* (Sg 3:6) – made bright, that is, not daubed with false coloring;[160] so this man who issued the invitations to the wedding finds a man not wearing a wedding garment, and says to him, *Friend, why have you come in here not wearing a wedding garment? But he was speechless.* I mean, he couldn't find an answer. And the householder who had come in said, *Bind him hands and feet, and cast him forth into the outer darkness; there it will be weeping and gnashing of teeth* (Mt 22:12–13).

Such a tiny fault, such a dreadful punishment? Dreadful, surely, it is. It's called a tiny fault, not to wear a wedding garment; tiny, but not for those who understand. Would that bridegroom really have been so incensed, would he really have delivered such a judgment as to throw him on account of a wedding garment he wasn't wearing, bound hand and foot, into the outer darkness where there would be weeping and gnashing of teeth,

---

158 Augustine often calls the psalmist (whom he assumed to be David) a prophet.

159 See Ps 118:22, and the frequent quotations of it in the New Testament, for example Mk 12:10; Acts 4:11; 1 Pt 2:7.

160 He is getting in a dig at feminine cosmetics, always regarded as fair game for ancient preachers. As a matter of fact, perhaps "made white," *dealbata* in the Latin, needed some comment, because a very common meaning of the word was "whitewashed" or "plastered."

unless not wearing a wedding garment had been a very serious fault indeed?

I tell you this because it's through me you have been invited; even though it's he who invited you, he sent his invitation through me. You are all attending the party, have on the wedding garment. I will explain what it is, and if there is anyone now listening to me who doesn't have it on, let him change for the better before the householder comes to view his guests; let him accept a wedding garment and sit down at the table without the slightest anxiety.

Many in the one man thrown out

6. The truth is, dearly beloved, that that man who was cast forth doesn't just represent one person; not at all. There are many of them. Even the Lord himself who related this parable, the bridegroom himself who assembles the wedding party and gives life to the party-goers, has himself explained to us that that man does not just represent one person, but many; he does it there, in that very place, in this same parable. I won't go on long, I'll explain it straightaway, I'll break the bread right now and set it before you to eat. He says, you see, when that one who wasn't wearing a wedding garment had been thrown into the outer darkness, so he says, in an added comment, *For many are called, but few chosen* (Mt 22:14).

You've cast one forth from here, and you say, *For many are called but few chosen*? Obviously the chosen were not cast forth, and they were few, those who remained seated at table. And there were many in that one man, because that one is the single body of all bad people, the one not wearing a wedding garment.

The wedding garment is charity

7. What is the wedding garment? Let us look for it in the holy books. What is the wedding garment? Obviously it is something that the good and the bad do not have in common; let us find that, and

we have found the wedding garment. Among God's gifts what is it that the good and the bad do not have in common? That we are human beings and not animals is God's gift; but it's common to the good and the bad. That the light rises for us in the sky, that the rains fall from the clouds, springs flow, fields bear fruit, these are gifts, but common to good and bad alike.

Let's enter the wedding feast; let's leave outside those others, who didn't come when they were invited.[161] Let's just consider the guests, that is to say, Christians. Baptism is a gift of God, both good and bad have that. The sacraments of the altar are received together by the good and the bad.[162] Saul the unjust prophesied, relentlessly hostile to a holy and just man;[163] while he was persecuting him, he prophesied. And is it only the good who are said to believe? *Even the demons believe, and tremble* (Jas 2:19).

What am I to do? I have shaken everything out, I haven't yet come to that garment. I've unrolled my bundle, I've examined all or practically all its contents, I haven't yet come to that garment. There's a place in which the apostle Paul has brought me a great bundle of great matters. He explained it all before me, and I said to him, "Show me please if by chance you have discovered this wedding garment." He began to shake out the contents one by one, and to say, *If I speak with the tongues of men and of angels, if I have all knowledge, and prophecy, and all faith so as to shift mountains; if I distribute all my goods to the poor, and deliver my body to burn*. Splendid garments, but not yet that wedding one. Now produce the wedding garment for us. Why do you keep us on tenterhooks, apostle? Perhaps prophecy is the gift of God, which both good and bad do not have. *If I do not have charity*, he says, *I am nothing, it is no use to me at all* (1 Cor 13:1–3).

There's the wedding garment for you. Clothe yourselves with it, my fellow guests, companions at the feast, so that you may take your seats at the table without a shred of anxiety. Don't say, "We are too poor for getting this garment." Clothe, and you are clothed, It's winter; clothe the naked; Christ is naked, in rags; and any of you who don't

---

[161] See Mt 22:3–6.

[162] He puts "sacraments" in the plural because of the two species of bread and wine, both of which were everywhere received by all the faithful.

[163] David. The reference is to 1 Sm 19:18–24.

have a wedding garment, he will give it to you. Run to him, ask him for one. He knows how to sanctify his faithful believers, how to clothe his own who are naked.

For you to be able to have on a wedding garment, and not be afraid of the outer darkness, of chains on your limbs, on your hands and feet – don't let there be any lack of good works. If they are lacking, what are you going to do with tied hands? Where are you going to flee to on tied up feet? Hold on to that wedding garment, wear it, and take your places at table with nothing to worry about, when he comes in to take a look at you. The day of judgment will certainly come. Now we are being granted a big breathing space; any who were naked, let them some time or other get themselves that garment.

Study Questions

1   What do we learn about Libanius' personality from reading the *Autobiography*?
2   Libanius attributed his professional successes more to Fortune than to hard work, which is significantly different from modern perceptions of success. Is there such a thing as "fortune"? If so, what role does it play in our lives?
3   Libanius' *Funeral Oration over Julian* describes a philosopher-emperor who sought to preserve the old traditions. How might the world be different today if Julian had lived and enjoyed a long, successful reign?
4   Although *Oration 30* is well structured, we could say that it is rhetorically flawed. What is the nature of the flaw? What factors may have contributed to Libanius' failure to recognize that flaw?
5   What are the Gorgianic elements in Augustine's *Confessions*?
6   Libanius was only about 30 years older than Augustine yet their lives as revealed in their autobiographies were very different. What are some of the more significant differences? Some of the similarities? What does a comparison of their lives tell us about rhetoric, oratory, and culture near the end of the Empire?
7   Although in *De Doctrina Christiana* Augustine advised that interpretation must consider context, he did not always follow his own advice. What are some of the risks of interpretation without regard to context?
8   Arians and other critics of the Nicene Creed argued that the concept of the Trinity, with three manifestations of the divine rather than one God, aligned Christianity too closely with paganism, with its multiple gods. How might Augustine have responded?

Writing Topics

1   Analyze the argument of *The Silence of Socrates* in terms of Libanius' use of rhetorical proofs. Is the argument compelling?
2   Libanius did not write a *technê*, but his teaching and oratory were nevertheless governed by theory. Use his complete autobiography and his letters to identify and describe the governing theory.
3   Augustine's *Confessions* have been called an extended prayer. Identify the nature of this prayer, then examine *Confessions* in tandem with Enheduanna's poems and Sappho's *To Aphrodite*, analyzing their similarities and differences.

4   Using Homer's *Iliad*, perform a contrastive analysis of his use of allegory with Augustine's in one of his works.
5   For Augustine, biblical exegesis served as a rhetorical proof. Examine exegesis in the context of Aristotle's artificial proofs (*ethos, logos, pathos*) and its relative effectiveness in argumentation and persuasion.
6   Research the role of delivery in Christian rhetoric.

Further Reading

Augustine, *De Civitate Dei* (*City of God*).

Brown, P. (1992). *Power and persuasion in late antiquity: Towards a Christian empire*. Madison, WI: University of Wisconsin Press.

Cribiore, R. (2007). *The school of Libanius in late antique Antioch*. Princeton: Princeton University Press.

Kennedy, G. (1980). *Classical rhetoric and its Christian and secular tradition from ancient to modern times*. Chapel Hill: University of North Carolina Press.

Oakeshott, M. (1993). *Religion, politics, and the moral life*. New Haven, CT: Yale University Press.

References

Ackrill, J.L. (1972). Aristotle's definitions of psuchê. *Proceedings of the Aristotelian Society*. Reprinted in L. Barnes, M. Schofield, and R. Sorabji (Eds.), *Articles on Aristotle*, vol. 4 (pp. 65–75). London: Duckworth, 1979.

Aeschines. (1919). *Aeschines*. (C.D. Adams, Trans.). Cambridge, MA: Harvard University Press.

Anderson, G. (1993). *The second sophistic: A cultural phenomenon in the Roman empire*. London: Routledge.

Appian. (1996). *The civil wars*. (J. Carter, Trans.). New York: Penguin.

Aristides. (1997). *The complete works: Orations XVII–LII*. (C.A. Behr, Trans.). Leiden: Brill Academic Publishers.

Aristotle. (1982). *Nicomachean ethics*. (H. Racham, Trans.). Cambridge, MA: Harvard University Press.

Armstrong, D. *Horace*. New Haven, CT: Yale University Press.

Athanassiadi, P., and Frede, M. (2002). *Pagan monotheism in late antiquity*. Oxford: Oxford University Press.

Atherton, C. (1988). Hand over fist: The failure of Stoic rhetoric. *The Classical Quarterly, 38*, 392–427.

Aviles, L. (2002). Solving the freeloaders paradox: Genetic associations and frequency-dependent selection in the evolution of cooperation among nonrelatives. *Proceedings of the National Academy of Sciences, 99*, 14268–73.

Azkoul, M. (1995). St. Gregory the theologian: Poetry and faith. *Patristic and Byzantine Review, 14*, 59–68.

Barchiesi, A. (2007). Carmina: Odes and Carmen Saeculare. In S. Harrison (Ed.), *The Cambridge companion to Horace* (pp. 144–61). Cambridge: Cambridge University Press.

Barnes, T.D. (2001). *Athanasius and Constantius: Theology and politics in the Constantinian empire*. Cambrige, MA: Harvard University Press.

Bauman, R. (1992). *Women and politics in ancient Rome*. London: Routledge

Beck, F. (1964). *Greek education, 450–359 BC*. New York: Barnes and Noble.

Beloch, K.J. (1886). *Der bevölkerung der griechisch–römischen welt*. Leipzig: Duncker and Humbolt.

Bizzell, P., and Herzberg, B. (2000). *The rhetorical tradition*. Boston, MA: Bedford/St. Martin.

Bluck, R. (Ed.). (1947). *Plato's seventh and eighth letters*. Cambridge: Cambridge University Press.

Blundell, S. (1995). *Women in Ancient Greece*. Cambridge, MA: Harvard University Press.

Botsford, G.W. (2005). *The Roman assemblies from their origins to the end of the Republic*. Boston, MA Adamant Media Corporation. (Original work published 1909.)

Bowder, D. (1978). *The age of Constantine and Julian*. London: Rowman and Littlefield.

Bowersock, G. (1969). *Greek Sophists in the Roman empire*. Oxford: Oxford University Press.

Bowersock, G. (1986). From emperor to bishop: The self-conscious transformation of political power in the fourth-century AD. *Classical Philology, 81*, 298–307.

Bradbury, S. (1994). Constantine and the problem of anti-pagan legislation in the fourth century. *Classical Philology, 89*, 120–39.

Bradley, K. (1994). *Slavery and society at Rome*. Cambridge: Cambridge University Press.

Bratman, M. (1987). *Intentions, plans, and practical reason*. Cambridge, MA: Harvard University Press.

Brickhouse, T., and Smith, N.D. (1997). Socrates and the unity of virtues. *Journal of Ethics, 1*, 311–24.

Brink, C.O. (1963). *Horace on poetry. Prolegomena to the literary epistles*, vol. 1. Cambridge: Cambridge University Press.

Brink, C.O. (1971). *Horace on poetry: The Ars Poetica*. Cambridge: Cambridge University Press.

Brink, C.O. (1981). Horation poetry: Thoughts on the development of textual criticism and interpretation. *Wolfenbütteler Forschungen, 12*, 7–17.

Brittain, C. (2001). *Philo of Larissa: The last of the academic sceptics*. Oxford: Oxford University Press.

Brittain, C. (Ed. and Trans.) (2006). *Cicero: On academic skepticism*. Indianapolis: Hackett Publishing.

Brown, P. (1967). *Augustine of Hippo: A biography*. Berkeley, CA: University of California Press.

Brown, P. (1987). Late Antiquity. In P. Veyne (Ed.), *A history of private life: From pagan Rome to Byzantium*. Cambridge, MA: Harvard University Press.

Brown, P. (1992). *Power and persuasion in late antiquity: Towards a Christian empire*. Madison, WI: University of Wisconsin Press.

Brownstein, O. (1965). Plato's Phaedrus: Dialectic as the genuine art of speaking. *Quarterly Journal of Speech, 51*, 392–8.

Brunt, P.A. (1974). *Social conflict in the Roman Republic.* New York: Norton.

Brunt, P.A. (1994). The bubble of the second sophistic. *Bulletin of the Institute of Classical Studies, 39,* 25–52.

Bryant, J.M. (1986). Intellectuals and religion in ancient Greece: Notes on a Weberian theme. *The British Journal of Sociology, 37,* 269–96.

Burkert, W. (1985). *Greek religion: Archaic and classical.* (J. Raffan, Trans.) Malden, MA: Blackwell.

Burkert, W. (1987). *Ancient mystery cults.* Cambridge, MA: Harvard University Press.

Burns, T. (2003). *Rome and the barbarians, 100 BC–AD 400.* Baltimore: Johns Hopkins University Press.

Campbell, A. (1924). *Horace: A new interpretation.* London: Methuen.

Campbell, J. (1970). *The masks of god: Primitive mythology.* New York: Viking. (Original work published 1959.)

Candreva, D. (2005). *The enemies of perfection: Oakeshott, Plato, and the critique of rationalism.* Lanham, MD: Lexington Books.

Cartledge, P. (2004). *Alexander the great.* New York: Overlook Press.

Cascio, E. (1994). The size of the Roman population: Beloch and the meaning of Augustan census figures. *Journal of Roman Studies, 84,* 23–40.

Cassius Dio Cocceianus. (1917). *Roman history, V, Books 46–50.* (E. Cary, Trans.). Cambridge, MA: Harvard University Press.

Chadwick, H. (1986). *Augustine.* New York: Oxford University Press.

Cicero. (1978). *Letters to Atticus* (D.R. Shackelton Baily, Trans.). Harmondsworth, UK: Penguin Books.

Clapp, J.G. (1950). Some notes on Plato's *Protagoras. Philosophy and Phenomenological Research, 10,* 486–99.

Clarke, B. (1996). Allegory and science. *Configurations, 4,* 33–7.

Clarke, M.L. (1953). *Rhetoric at Rome: A historical survey.* New York: Routledge.

Clarke, M.L. (1967). Quintilian: A biographical sketch. *Greece and Rome, 14, 1,* 24–37.

Clarke, M.L. (1968). Cicero at school. *Greece and Rome, 15, 1,* 18–22.

Cohen, P., Morgan, J., and Pollack, M. (Eds.). (1990). *Intentions and communication.* Cambridge, MA: MIT Press.

Colby, B., and Cole, M. (1973). Culture, memory and narrative. In R. Flanegan and R. Horton (Eds.), *Modes of thought* (pp. 63–91). London: Faber and Faber.

Cole, T. (1991). *The origins of rhetoric in ancient Greece.* Baltimore: The Johns Hopkins University Press.

Condon, M. (2001). The unnamed and the defaced: The limits of rhetoric in Augustine's *Confessiones. Journal of the American Academy of Religion, 69,* 43–63.

Costa, C.D.N. (2002). *Greek fictional letters.* London: Oxford University Press.

Cowan, R. (2003). *Roman legionary, 58 BC–AD 69.* Oxford: Osprey Publishing.

Craig, C. (2004). Audience expectations, invective, and proof. In J. Powell and J. Paterson (Eds.), *Cicero the advocate* (pp. 187–213). Oxford: Oxford University Press.

Cribiore, R. (2007). *The school of Libanius in late antique Antioch.* Princeton: Princeton University Press.

Cruttwell, C.T. (2005). *The history of Roman literature from the earliest period to the death of Marcus Aurelius.* Salt Lake City, UT: Project Gutenberg Literary Archive Foundation. (Original work published 1877.)

Cumont, F. (1956). *The mysteries of Mithra.* (T.J. McCormack, Trans.). New York: Dover Publications. (Original work published 1903.)

Curd, P. (1997). *The legacy of Parmenides: Eleatic monism and later presocratic thought.* Princeton, NJ: Princeton University Press.

D'Arms, J. (1990). The Roman convivium and equality. In O. Murray (Ed.), *Sympotica: A symposium on the sympo-sion* (pp. 308–320). Oxford: Oxford University Press.

Dahlmann, H. (1953). *Varros schrift de poematis und die hellenistisch-römische poetik.* Mainz: Verlag der Akademie der Wissenschaften und der Literatur.

Deane, H. (1963). *The political and social ideas of St. Augustine.* New York: Columbia University Press.

Demosthenes. (2004). *Demosthenes I: Orations I–XVII, XX, Olynthiacs, Philippics, minor orations.* (J.H. Vince, Trans.). Cambridge, MA: Harvard University Press. (Original work published 1930.)

Den Boer, W. (1973). Aspects of religion in classical Greece. *Harvard Studies in Classical Philology, 77,* 1–21.

Depew, D., and Poulakos, T. (2004). Isocrates as civic educator. In T. Poulakos and D. Depew (Eds.), *Isocrates and civic education* (pp. 3–10). Austin, TX: University of Texas Press.

Devereux, D. (1992). The unity of virtues in Plato's *Protagoras* and *Laches. The Philosophical Review, 101,* 765–89.

Diels, H., and Kranz, W. (1951–52). *Die Fragmente der Vorsokratiker,* 6th ed., 3 vols. Berlin: Weidmann.

Dillon, G. (1981). *Constructing texts: Elements of a theory of composition and style.* Bloomington: University of Indiana Press.

DiMaio, M., and Arnold, D. (1992). *Per vim, per caedem, per bellum:* A study of murder and ecclesiastical politics in the year 337 A.D. *Byzantion, 62,* 158–211.

Diogenes Laertius. (1964). Βιοι και γνωμαι των εν φιλοσοφια ευδκιμησαυτων [The lives and sayings of eminent philosophers]. H.S. Long (Ed.). Oxford: Oxford University Press.

Dodds, E.R. (1951). *The Greeks and the irrational.* Berkeley, CA: University of California Press.

Domitius, D. (2005). Athenian imperialism and the Black Sea grain route. Retrieved June 8, 2005, from http://ancientworlds.net/aw/Article/327637.

Drake. H. (2002). *Constantine and the bishops: The politics of intolerance*. Baltimore: Johns Hopkins University Press.

Duby, G., and Perrot, M. (1992). *A history of women in the West: From ancient goddesses to Christian saints*. Cambridge, MA: The Belknap Press.

Duckworth, G. (1965). Horace's hexameters and the date of the *Ars Poetica*. *Transactions and Proceedings of the American Philological Association, 96*, 73–95.

Elmore, J. (1935). A new dating of Horace's De Arte Poetica. *Classical Philology, 30*, 1–9.

Enos, R. (1993). *Greek rhetoric before Aristotle*. Prospect Heights, IL: Waveland Press.

Enos, R. (1995). *Roman rhetoric: Revolution and the Greek influence*. Prospect Heights, IL: Waveland Press.

Enos, R. (2002). The archaeology of women in rhetoric: Rhetorical sequencing as a research method for historical scholarship. *Rhetoric Society Quarterly, 32*, 65–79.

Epictetus. (1948). *The enchiridion*. (T.W. Higginson, Trans.). New York: Liberal Arts Press.

Eusebius. (1999). *Life of Constantine*. (A. Cameron and S.G. Hall, Trans.). New York: Oxford University Press.

Everitt, A. (2001). *Cicero: The life and times of Rome's greatest politician*. New York: Random House.

Fagan, G. (1999). *Bathing in public in the Roman world*. Ann Arbor: University of Michigan Press.

Fantham, E. (1996). *Roman literary culture: From Cicero to Apuleius*. Baltimore, MD: Johns Hopkins University Press.

Fantham, E. (1997). The contexts and occasions of Roman public rhetoric. In W. Dominik (Ed.), *Roman eloquence: Rhetoric in society and literature*. London: Routledge.

Fantham, E. (2004). *The Roman world of Cicero's De Oratore*. Oxford: Oxford University Press.

Fantham, E., Foley, H.P., Kampen, N.B., Pomeroy, S.B., Shapiro, H.A. (1994). *Women in the classical world*. New York: Oxford.

Ferejohn, M. (1982). The unity of virtue and the objects of Socratic inquiry. *Journal of the History of Philosophy, 20*, 1–21.

Fernández-Lopez, J. (2003). The concept of authority in the *Institutio Oratoria*, book I. In O. Tellegen-Couperus (Ed.), *Quintilian and the law* (pp. 29–36). Leuven: Leuven University Press.

Ferri, R. (2007). The *Epistles*. In S. Harrison (Ed.), *The Cambridge Companion to Horace* (pp. 121–31). Cambridge: Cambridge University Press.

Fisher, W. (1985). The narrative paradigm: An elaboration. *Communication Monographs, 52*, 347–67.

Fleming, D. (2002). The end of composition-rhetoric. In J.D. Williams (Ed.), *Visions and revisions: Continuity and change in rhetoric and composition* (pp. 109–30). Carbondale, IL: Southern Illinois University Press.

Foerster, R. (1903–13). *Libanii opera. Vols. I–VII*. Leipzeig: B.G. Teubner.

Ford, A. (2002). *The origins of criticism: Literary culture and poetic theory in classical Greece*. Princeton: Princeton University Press.

Foucault, M. (1983). Discourse and truth: The problematization of *parrhesia*. Six lectures given by Michel Foucault at the University of California at Berkeley, Oct–Nov.

Foucault, M. (1990). *The history of sexuality: The care of the self*, vol. 3. (R. Hurley, Trans.). New York: Vintage Books.

Fraenkel, E. (1957). *Horace*. London: Oxford University Press.

Frede, M. (1992). On Aristotle's conception of soul. In M. Nussbaum and R. Rorty (Eds.), *Essays on Aristotle's De Anima* (pp. 93–107). Oxford: Clarendon Press.

Frede, M. (2002). *Pagan monotheism in late antiquity*. Oxford: Oxford University Press.

Freeman, C. (2002). *The closing of the Western mind: The rise of faith and the fall of reason*. New York: Vintage.

Freese, J.H. (1894). Introduction to Isocrates. In *Isocrates' Orations*, vol. 1. (J.H. Freese, Trans.). London: George Bell and Son. Retrieved June 19, 2006, from http://classicpersuasion.org/pw/isocrates/freese_intro.htm.

Frentz, T. (2006). Memory, myth, and rhetoric in Plato's *Phaedrus*. *Rhetoric Society Quarterly, 36*, 243–62.

Frischer, B. (1991). *Shifting paradigms: New approaches to Horace's Ars Poetica*. Atlanta: Scholars Press.

Fukuyama, F. (1999). *The great disruption: Human nature and the reconstruction of social order*. New York: The Free Press.

Gaca, K. (2003). *The making of fornication: Eros, ethics, and political reform in Greek philosophy and early Christianity*. Berkeley, CA: University of California Press.

Gagarin, M. (1969). The purpose of Plato's *Protagoras*. *Transactions and Proceedings of the American Philological Association, 100*, 133–64.

Gagarin, M. (1998). *Antiphon and Andocides*. (M. Gagarin, Trans.). Austin, TX: University of Texas Press.

Gagarin, M. (2002). *Antiphon the Athenian: Oratory, law, and justice in the age of the Sophists*. Austin, TX: University of Texas Press.

Gagarin, M., and MacDonald, D. (1998). *Antiphon and Andocides*. Austin, TX: University of Texas Press.

Gelzer, M. (1969). *The Roman nobility*. (R. Seager, Trans.). Oxford: Oxford University Press.

Gibbon, E. (1993). *The decline and fall of the Roman empire*, vol. 1. New York: Knopf. (Original work published in 1776.)

Gibson, C. (2002). *Interpreting a classic: Demosthenes and his ancient commentators*. Berkeley, CA: University of California Press.

Glenn, C. (1997). *Rhetoric retold: Regendering the tradition from antiquity through the Renaissance.* Carbondale, IL: Southern Illinois University Press.

Golden, L. (1962). Catharsis. *Transactions and Proceedings of the American Philological Association, 93,* 51–60.

Golden, L. (1992). *Aristotle on tragic and comic mimesis.* Atlanta: Scholars Press.

Goldsworthy, A. (2001). *The Punic wars.* London: Cassell and Co.

Goldsworthy, A. (2006). *Caesar: Life of a colossus.* New Haven, CT: Yale University Press.

Goody, J. (Ed.). (1968). *Literacy in traditional societies.* Cambridge: Cambridge University Press.

Goody, J. (1972, May 12). Literacy and the nonliterate. In *Times Literary Supplement.* (Reprinted in R. Disch [Ed.], *The future of literacy.* Englewood Cliffs, NJ: Prentice-Hall).

Goody, J. (1987). *The interface between the oral and the written.* Cambridge: Cambridge University Press.

Goody, J., and Watt, I. (1968). The consequences of literacy. *Comparative Studies in Society and History, 5,* 304–45.

Gotoff, H. (1993). Oratory: The art of illusion. *Harvard Studies in Classical Philology, 95,* 289–313.

Gould, J. (1980). Law, custom and myth: Aspects of the social position of women in classical Athens. *Journal of Hellenic Studies, 100,* 38–59.

Grant, M. (1992). *A social history of Greece and Rome.* New York: Scribners.

Grant, M.A., and Fiske, G. (1924). Cicero's *Orator* and Horace's *Ars Poetica. Harvard Studies in Classical Philology, 35,* 1–74.

Grassi, E. (2000). Rhetoric and philosophy. *Janus Head, 3,* 1–11. Retrieved August 9, 2006, from www.janushead. org/3-1/egrassi.cfm.

Green, P. (1990). *Alexander to Actium: The historical evolution of the Hellenistic age.* Berkeley, CA: University of California Press.

Greenberg, N. (1961). The use of poiema and poiesis. *Harvard Studies in Classical Philology, 65,* 263–89.

Greenfield, P. (1972). Oral or written language: The consequences for cognitive development in Africa, the United States and England. *Language and Speech, 15,* 169–77.

Grice, P. (1975). Logic and conversation. In P. Cole and J. Morgan, (Eds.), *Syntax and semantics,* vol 3. New York: Academic Press.

Grimaldi, W. (1972). *Studies in the philosophy of Aristotle's rhetoric.* Wiesbaden: Franz Steiner.

Gruen, E. (1995). *The last generation of the Roman Republic.* Berkeley: University of California Press.

Guthrie, W. (1977). *The Sophists.* Cambridge: Cambridge University Press. (Original work published 1969.)

Hackforth, R. (1972). *Plato's Philebus.* (R. Hackforth, Trans.). Cambridge: Cambridge University Press.

Hagendahl, H. (1967). *Augustine and the Latin classics.* Stockholm: Almquist and Wiksell.

Hall, S.G. (1992). *Doctrine and practice in the early church.* Grand Rapids, MI: William B. Eerdmans Publishing.

Halliwell, S. (1998). *Aristotle's Poetics.* Chicago: University of Chicago Press.

Hamner, D. (2004). *The God gene: How faith is hardwired into our genes.* New York: Doubleday.

Hardison, O.B., and Golden, L. (1995). *Horace for students of literature: The "Ars Poetica" and its tradition.* Gainsville, FL: University of Florida Press.

Harris, W. (2006). *Sappho: The Greek poems.* Retrieved June 1, 2006, from http://community. middlebury. edu/~harris/Sappho.pdf.

Harris, W.V. (1991). *Ancient literacy.* Cambridge, MA: Harvard University Press.

Hartelius, J. (2006). Of what use is a gold key? Unlocking discourse in rhetorical pedagogy. *Rhetoric Society Quarterly, 36,* 55–76.

Havelock, E.A. (1963). *Preface to Plato.* Cambridge, MA: Harvard University Press.

Havelock, E.A. (1957). *The liberal temper in Greek politics.* London: Cape.

Havelock, E.A. (1986). *The muse learns to write: Reflections on orality and literacy from antiquity to the present.* New Haven, CT: Yale University Press.

Havelock, E.A. (2005). *Preface to Plato: History of the Greek mind.* Cambridge, MA: Belknap Press.

Heather, P. (2006). *The fall of the Roman empire: A new history of Rome and the barbarians.* Oxford: Oxford University Press.

Hegel, F. (1956). *The philosophy of history.* (J. Sibree, Trans.). New York: Dover.

Henry, M. (1995). *Prisoner of history: Aspasia of Miletus and her biographical tradition.* New York: Oxford.

Herrick, M. (1946). *The fusion of Horatian and Aristotelian literacy criticism, 1531–1555.* Urbana, IL: University of Illinois Press.

Herrin, J. (1987). *The formation of Christendom.* Princeton: Princeton University Press.

Hesiod. (1981). *Works and days.* In H. Evelyn-White (Trans.), *Hesiod: The Homeric hymns and Homerica* (pp. 2–64). Cambridge, MA: Harvard University Press. (Original work published 1914.)

Higgins, W.E. (2005). Introduction. In L. Pernot, *Rhetoric in antiquity.* (W.E. Higgins, Trans.), (pp. ix–xiii). Washington, DC: The Catholic University of America. (Original work published in 2000.)

Hikins, J. (1981). Plato's rhetorical theory: Old perspectives on the epistemology of the new rhetoric. *Central States Speech Journal, 32,* 160–76.

Holland, T. (2003). *Rubicon: The last years of the Roman Republic.* New York: Doubleday.

Holloway, P. (1998). Paul's pointed prose: The *sententia* in Roman rhetoric and Paul. *Novum Testamentum, 40*, 32–53.

Holst-Warhaft, G. (1992). *Dangerous voices: Women's laments and Greek literature*. London: Routledge.

Homer. (1991). *The Iliad*. (R. Fagles, Trans.). New York: Penguin.

Hopkins, M.K. (1965). The age of Roman girls at marriage. *Population Studies, 18*, 309–27.

Isocrates. (1929). *Isocrates*, vol. II. (G. Norlin, Trans.). Cambridge, MA: Harvard University Press.

Jacobsen, T. (1978). *Treasures of darkness: A History of Mesopotamian Religion*. New Haven, CT: Yale University Press.

Jaeger, W. (1965). The rhetoric of Isocrates and its cultural ideal. In J. Schwartz and J. Rycenga (Eds.), *The province of rhetoric* (pp. 84–111). New York: Ronald Press.

Jaeger, W. (1976). *Paideia: The ideals of Greek culture*, 2nd edn. (G. Highet, Trans.). New York: Oxford University Press. (Original work published 1945.)

Jaffee, M.S. (2001). One god, one revelation, one people: On the symbolic structure of elective monotheism. *Journal of the American Academy of Religion, 69*, 753–76.

Janko, R. (2003). *Philodemus: the Aesthetic Works*, vol. I/1: *On Poems Book 1*. Oxford: Oxford University Press.

Jensen, C. (1923). *Philodemus über die gedichte, fünftes buch*. Berlin: Weidmann.

Jimenez, R. (2000). *Caesar against Rome: The great Roman civil war*. Westport, CT: Praeger.

Johnson, R. (1959). Isocrates' methods of teaching. *The American Journal of Philology, 80*, 25–36.

Johnson, T. (2005). *A symposion of praise: Horace returns to lyric in Odes IV*. Madison, WI: University of Wisconsin Press.

Johnson-Laird, P. (1983). *Mental models*. Cambridge, MA: Harvard University Press.

Jones, B.W. (1993). *The emperor Domitian*. London: Routledge.

Kagan, D. (2003). *The Peloponnesian war*. New York: Viking.

Kennedy, G. (1963). *The art of persuasion in Greece*. Princeton, NJ: Princeton University Press.

Kennedy, G. (1969). *Quintilian*. New York: Twayne.

Kennedy, G. (1972). *The art of rhetoric in the Roman world*. Princeton. Princeton University Press.

Kennedy, G. (1980). *Classical rhetoric and its Christian and secular tradition from ancient to modern times*. Chapel Hill: University of North Carolina Press.

Kennedy, G. (1991). *Aristotle on rhetoric: A theory of civic discourse*. New York: Oxford University Press.

Kennedy, G. (1994). *A new history of classical rhetoric*. Princeton: Princeton University Press.

Kiernan, V.G. (1999). *Horace: Poetics and politics*. New York: St. Martin's Press.

Kilpatrick, R. (1986). *The poetry of friendship: Horace Epistles I*. Edmonton: University of Alberta Press.

Kilpatrick, R. (1990). *The poetry of criticism: Horace, Epistles II and Ars Poetica*. Edmonton: University of Alberta Press.

Kimball, B.A. (1986). *Orators and philosophers: A history of the ideal liberal education*. New York: Teachers College Press.

Kinneavy, J. (2002). *Kairos* in classical and modern rhetorical theory. In P. Sipiora and J. Baumlin (Eds.), *Rhetoric and kairos: Essays in history, theory, and praxis* (pp. 58–76). Albany, NY: State University of New York Press.

Kinneavy, J., and Eskin, C. (2000). *Kairos* in Aristotle's *Rhetoric. Written Communication, 17*, 432–44.

Kirby, J. (1997). Ciceronian rhetoric: Theory and practice. In W. Dominik (Ed.), *Roman eloquence: Rhetoric in society and literature*. London: Routledge.

Kirwan, C. (1989). *Augustine*. New York: Oxford University Press.

Kousoulas, D. (1997). *The life and times of Constantine the Great: The first Christian emperor*, 2nd edn. Oxford: Routledge.

Kraut, R. (Ed.) (1997). *Plato's Republic: Critical essays*. Lanham, MD: Rowman and Littlefield.

Laird, A. (2007). The Ars Poetica. In S. Harrison (Ed.), *The Cambridge companion to Horace* (pp. 132–41). Cambridge: Cambridge University Press.

Leff, M.C. (1996). Commonplaces and argumentation in Cicero and Quintilian. *Argumentation, 10, 4*, 445–52.

Leff, M.C. (2003). Tradition and agency in humanistic rhetoric. *Philosophy and Rhetoric, 36*, 135–47.

Lelis, A., Percy, W., and Verstraete, B. (2003). *The age of marriage in ancient Rome*. Lewiston, NY: Edwin Mellen Press.

Lentz, M. (1989). *Orality and literacy in Hellenic Greece*. Carbondale, IL: Southern Illinois University Press.

Libanius. (1992). *Libanius: Autobiography and selected letters*, vols. I and II. (A.F. Norman, Ed. and Trans.). Cambridge, MA: Harvard University Press.

Long, J. (1996). *Claudian's In Eutropium: Or how, when, and why to slander a eunuch*. Chapel Hill: University of North Carolina Press.

Lunsford, A. (Ed.). (1995). *Reclaiming rhetorica: Women in the rhetorical tradition*. Pittsburgh: University of Pittsburg Press.

Luria, S. (1963). Antiphon der Sophist. *Eos, 53*, 63–7.

MacMullen, R. (1988). *Corruption and the decline of Rome*. New Haven: Yale University Press.

Maisels, C.K. (1990). *The emergence of civilization*. London: Routledge.

Mangoni, C. (1993). (Ed.). *Filodemo: Il quinto libro della Poetica*. La scuola de epicuro, vol. 14. Naples: Bibliopolis.

Mann, J.E. (2005). Of science, skepticism, and sophistry: *The pseudo-Hippocratic On the Art in its philosophical context*. Unpublished doctoral dissertation, University of Texas, Austin.

Marrou, H.I. (1938). *Saint Augustin et la fin de la cultura antique*. Paris: Boccard.

Marrou, H.I. (1982). *A history of education in antiquity*. (G. Lamb, Trans.). Madision, WI: University of Wisconsin Press. (Original work published 1948.)

Martin, T. (1996). *Ancient Greece: From prehistoric to Hellenistic times*. New Haven, CT: Yale University Press.

Martin, T. (2000). *Vox Pauli*: Augustine and the claims to speak for Paul: An exploration of rhetoric in the service of exegesis. *Journal of Early Christian Studies*, 8, 237–72.

Mayer, R. (1986). Horace's *Epistles I* and philosophy. *The American Journal of Philology*, 107, 55–73.

Mazzeo, J. (1962). St. Augustine's rhetoric of silence. *Journal of the History of Ideas*, 23, 175–96.

McBurney, J. (1936). The place of the enthymeme in rhetorical theory. *Speech Monographs*, 3, 49–74.

McComiskey, B. (1992). Disassembling Plato's critique of rhetoric in the *Gorgias* (447a–466a). *Rhetoric Review*, 11, 79–90.

McGee, M. (2006). Isocrates: A parent of rhetoric and culture studies. Retrieved July 4, 2006, from www. mcgees.net/fragments/essays/back%20burner/isocrates.html.

Meador, B. (2000). *Innana, lady of the largest heart: Poems of the Sumarian high priestess*. Austin, TX: University of Texas Press.

Millar, F. (1984). The political character of the classical Roman Republic. *The Journal of Roman Studies*, 74, 1–19.

Millar, F. (1989). Political power in mid-republican Rome: *Curia or comitium? Journal of Rhetorical Studies*, 79, 138–50.

Millar, F. (1998). *The crowd in the late Roman Republic*. Anarbor, MI: University of Michigan Press.

Mirhady, D., and Too, Y. (2000). *Isocrates I*. Austin, TX: University of Texas Press.

Misch, G. (2003). *A history of autobiography in antiquity*. (G. Misch and E.W. Dickes, Trans.). London: Routledge and Kegan Paul. (Original work published 1950.)

Mitchell, S. (2006). *History of the later Roman empire, AD 284–641*. Malden, MA: Blackwell.

Momigliano, A. (1986). The disadvantages of monotheism for a universal state. *Classical Philology*, 81, 285–97.

Morgan, G. (2006). *69 AD: The year of four emperors*. New York: Oxford University Press.

Morstein-Marx, R. (2004). *Mass oratory and political power in the late Roman republic*. Cambridge: Cambridge University Press.

Moulton, C. (1972). Antiphon the sophist, on truth. *Transactions and Proceedings of the American Philological Association*, 103, 329–66.

Mouritsen, H. (2001). *Plebs and politics in the late Roman Republic*. Cambridge: Cambridge University Press.

Muecke, F. (2007). The *Satires*. In S. Harrison (Ed.), *The Cambridge companion to Horace* (pp. 105–20). Cambridge: Cambridge University Press.

Munn, M. (2000). *The school of history: Athens in the age of Socrates*. Berkeley: University of California Press.

Nehamas, A. (1992). Pity and fear in the *Rhetoric* and *Poetics*. In A.O. Rorty (Ed.), *Essays on Aristotle's Poetics* (pp. 291–314). Princeton: Princeton University Press.

Newberg, A., D'Aquili, E., and Rause, V. (2002). *Why God won't go away: Brain science and the biology of belief*. New York: Ballantine.

Nichols, M.P. (1987). Aristotle's defense of rhetoric. *Journal of Politics*, 49, 657–77.

Nietzsche, F. (1956). *The birth of tragedy and the genealogy of morals*. (F. Golffing, Trans.). New York: Anchor Books.

Norden, E. (1905). Die composition und litteraturgattung der Horazischen Epistula ad Pisones. *Hermes*, 40, 481–528.

Norman, A.F. (1969). *Libanius: Selected orations*, vol. 1. Cambridge, MA: Harvard University Press.

Norman, A.F. (1976). *Libaniuos, Discours Moraux* [Review of a book by B. Schouler, 1973]. *The Classical Review*, 26, 23–4.

Norman, A.F. (1992). *Libanius: Autobiography and selected letters*, vol. 1. Cambridge, MA: Harvard University Press.

North, J. (1990). Politics and aristocracy in the Roman republic. *Classical Philology*, 85, 277–87.

Nussbaum, M. (2001). *The fragility of goodness*. Cambridge: Cambridge University Press.

O'Meara, J. (1990). *The young Augustine: An introduction to the Confessions of St. Augustine*. London: Longman.

Oakeshott, M. (1991). *Rationalism in politics and other essays*. Indianapolis: Liberty Press.

Oates. W.J. (1934). The population of Rome. *Classical Philology*, 29, 101–16.

Ober, J. (1989). *Mass and elite in democratic Athens: Rhetoric, ideology, and the power of the people*. Princeton, NJ: Princeton University Press.

Ober, J. (2004). I, Socrates: The performative audacity of Isocrates' *Antidosis*. In T. Poulakas and D. Depew (Eds.), *Isocrates and civic education* (pp. 21–43). Austin, TX: University of Texas Press.

Oliensis, E. (1998). *Horace and the rhetoric of authority*. Cambridge: Cambridge University Press.

Olmsted, W. (2006). *Rhetoric: An historical introduction*. Malden, MA: Blackwell Publishing.

Olney, J. (1998). *Memory and narrative: The weave of life-writing*. Chicago: University of Chicago Press.

Ong, W. (1982). *Orality and literacy: The terminologizing of the word*. London: Methuen.

Ostwald, M. (1990). *Nomos and Phusis in Athiphon's Peri Alêtheias*. Retrieved June 20, 2006, from http://repositories.cdlb.org/ucbclassics/ctm/festschrift20.

Papillion, T. (1995). Isocrates' *technê* and rhetorical pedagogy. *Rhetoric Society Quarterly, 25*, 149–63.

Parkin, T. (1992). *Demography and Roman society*. Baltimore: Johns Hopkins University Press.

Paterson, J. (2004). Self-reference in Cicero's forensic speeches. In J. Powell and J. Paterson (Eds.), *Cicero the Advocate* (pp. 79–95). Oxford: Oxford University Press.

Patterson, O. (1991). *Freedom*. New York: Basic Books.

Patton, J.H. (1977). Wisdom and eloquence: The alliance of exegesis and rhetoric in Augustine. *Central States Speech Journal, 28*, 96–105.

Pendrick, G. (1998). Plato and *phtopikh*. *Rheinisches Museum für Philologie, NF, 141*, 10–23.

Pendrick, G. (2002). *Antiphon the Sophist: The fragments*. Cambridge: Cambridge University Press.

Penner, T. (1973). The unity of virtue. *Philosophical Review, 82*, 35–68.

Perelman, C., and Olbrechts-Tyteca, L. (1969). *The new rhetoric: A treatise on argumentation*. Notre Dame, IN: University of Notre Dame Press.

Pernot, L. (1993). *La rhétorique de l'éloge dans le monde gréco-romain*. Paris: Institut d'Études Augustiniennes.

Pernot, L. (2005). *Rhetoric in antiquity*. (W.E. Higgins, Trans.). Washington, DC: Catholic University of America Press.

Petit, P. (1955). *Libanius et la vie municipale a Antioche au IV siècle après*. Paris: Geuthner.

Pinckaers, S. (1993). *Sources of Christian ethics*, 3rd edn. (M. Thomas-Noble, Trans.). Washington, DC: Catholic University of America Press.

Plutarch. (1958). *Fall of the Roman republic*. (R. Warner, Trans.). Harmondsworth, England: Penguin.

Plutarch. (1959) *Lives of the noble Greeks*. (J. Dryden, Trans., E. Fuller, Ed.). New York: Dell. (Original work published 1683.)

Pomeroy, S. (1995). *Goddesses, whores, wives, and slaves: Women in classical antiquity*. New York: Schoken Books. (Original work published 1975.)

Pontani, F.M. (1953). *Orazio: Arte poetica*. Rome: Gismondi.

Poulakos, J. (1995). *Sophistical rhetoric in classical Greece*. Columbia, SC: University of South Carolina Press.

Poulakos, T. (1997). *Speaking for the polis: Isocrates' rhetorical education*. Charleston, SC: University of South Carolina Press.

Putnam, R. (2001). *Bowling alone: The collapse and revival of American community*. New York: Touchstone/Simon and Schuster.

Putnam, R. (Ed.). (2002). *Democracies in flux: The evolution of social capital in contemporary society*. New York: Oxford University Press.

Querzoli, S. (2003). *Materia and officia* of rhetorical teaching in Book II of the *Institutio Oratoria*. In O. Tellegen-Gouperus (Ed.), *Quintilian and the law* (pp. 37–50). Leuven, Belgium: Leuven University Press.

Quintilian. *Institutio oratoria*. Retrieved January 10, 2008, from http://www. thelatinlibrary.com/quintilian.html

Raaflaub, K. (1983). Democracy, oligarchy, and the concept of the "free citizen" in late fifth-century Athens. *Political Theory, 11, 4*, 517–44.

Rawson, E. (1985). *Intellectual life in the late Roman republic*. Baltimore, MD: Johns Hopkins University Press.

Redfield, J. (1982). Notes on the Greek wedding. *Arethusa, 15*, 181–199.

Reinhardt, R. (Ed. and Trans.). *Cicero's* Topica. New York: Oxford University Press.

Richlin, A. (1997). Gender and rhetoric: Producing manhood in the schools. In W. Dominik (Ed.), *Roman eloquence: Rhetoric in society and literature*. London: Routledge.

Robb, K. (1994). *Literacy and paideia in ancient Greece*. New York: Oxford University Press.

Roberts, J. (2004). Enheduanna, Daughter of King Sargon: Princess, Poet, Priestess (2300 BC). *Transoxiana: Journal Libre de Orientales, 8*, 1–17. Retrieved April 26, 2006, from http://transoxiana.com.ar/0108/roberts-enheduanna.html.

Roberts, R. (1902). *Demetrius on style: The Greek text of Demetrius' De Elocutione*. R. Roberts (Ed. and Trans.). Cambridge: Cambridge University Press.

Rorty. R. (1984). The historiography of philosophy: Four genres. In R. Rorty, J.B. Schneewind, and Q. Skinner (Eds.), *Philosophy in History*. Cambridge: Cambridge University Press.

Rosenmeyer, P. (2006). *Ancient Greek literary letters: Selections in translation*. London: Routledge.

Rosenstein, N. (2004). *Rome at War: Farms, families, and death in the Middle Republic*. Chapel Hill: University of North Carolina Press.

Rudd, N. (1989). *Horace: Epistles Book II and Epistles to the Pisones ('Ars Poetica')*. Cambridge: Cambridge University Press.

Rudich, V. (1997). *Dissidence and literature under Nero: The price of rhetoricization*. London: Routledge.

Russell, D.A. (1967). Rhetoric and criticism. *Greece and Rome, 14*, 130–44.

Russell, D.A. (1973). Ars Poetica. In C.D.N. Costa (Ed.), *Horace* (pp. 113–34). London: Routledge and Kegan Paul.

Russell, D.A. (1983). *Greek declamation*. New York: Cambridge University Press.

Russell, D.A. (1996). Introduction. In D.A. Russell (Trans.), *Libanius: Imaginary speeches* (pp. 1–15). London: Duckworth.

Rutherford, R.B. (1995). *The art of Plato*. London: Duckworth.

Saller, R. (1987). Men's age at marriage and its consequences in the Roman family. *Classical Philology, 82*, 21–34.

Samons, L. (2004). *What's wrong with democracy? From Athenian practice to American worship*. Berkeley, CA: University of California Press.

Sardi-Mendelovici, H. (1990). Christian attitudes toward pagan monuments in late antiquity and their legacy in later Byzantine centuries. *Dumbarton Oaks Papers, 44*, 41–67.

Scaltsas, T. (1996). Biological matter and perceptual powers in Aristotle's De Anima. *Topoi, 15*, 25–37.

Scheidel, W. (2005). Marriage, families, and survival in the Roman imperial army: Demographic aspects. Retrieved on January 22, 2008, from http://www.princeton.edu/~pswpc/pdfs/scheidel/110509.pdf

Scheidel, W. (2006). Growing up fatherless in antiquity: The demographic background. Princeton/Stanford Working Papers in Classics. Retrieved on January 30, 2008, from http://www.princeton.edu/~pswpc/pdfs/scheidel/060601.pdf

Schiappa, E. (1999). *The beginnings of rhetorical theory in classical Greece*. New Haven, CT: Yale University Press.

Schiappa, E. (2003). *Protagoras and logos: A study in Greek philosophy and rhetoric*, 2nd edition. Columbia, SC: University of South Carolina Press.

Schneider, M. (1995). Sacred ambivalence: Mimetology in Aristotle, Horace, and Longinus. *Anthropoetics, 1*, 13–24. Retrieved January 27, 2007 from http://www.anthropoetics.ucla.edu/archive/anth0101.pdf

Scott, R. (1967). On viewing rhetoric as epistemic. *Central States Speech Journal, 18*, 9–17.

Scribner, S., and Cole, M. (1981). *The psychology of literacy*. Cambridge, MA: Harvard University Press.

Searle, J. (1983). *Intentionality: An essay in the philosophy of mind*. Cambridge: Cambridge University Press.

Seneca. (1974). *Controversiae*. (M. Winterbottom, Trans.). Cambridge, MA: Harvard University Press.

Sextus Empiricus. (1972). Against the schoolmasters. In R. Sprague (Ed.), *The Older Sophists* (p. 43). (G. Kennedy, Trans.). Indianapolis, IN: Hackett Publishing.

Shenk, D. (2002). Three journeys: Jesus–Constantine–Muhammad: Ethical and political foundations of "the kingdom of God." Retrieved December 14, 2006, from http://www.emu.edu/sem/churchandislam/david_shenk.pdf.

Sherman, N. (1989). *The fabric of character: Aristotle's theory of virtue*. New York: Oxford University Press.

Simonson, S. (1945). A definitive note on the enthymeme. *The American Journal of Philology, 66*, 303–06.

Sipiora, P. (2002). Introduction: The ancient concept of *kairos*. In P. Sipiora, and J. Baumlin (Eds.), *Rhetoric and kairos: Essays in history, theory, and praxis* (pp. 1–22). Albany, NY: State University of New York Press.

Sipiora, P., and Baumlin, J. (Eds.). (2002). *Rhetoric and kairos: Essays in history, theory, and praxis*. Albany, NY: State University of New York Press.

Sizgorich, T. (2007). Not easily were stones joined by the strongest bonds pulled asunder: Religious violence and imperial order in the later Roman world. *Journal of Early Christian Studies, 15*, 75–101.

Smith, J.E. (2002). Time and qualitative time. In P. Sipiora, and J. Baumlin (Eds.), *Rhetoric and kairos: Essays in history, theory, and praxis* (pp. 46–57). Albany, NY: State University of New York Press.

Sogno, C. (2006). *Q. Aurelius Symmachus: A Political Biography*. Ann Arbor: University of Michigan Press.

Solmsen, F. (1938). Cicero's first speeches: A rhetorical analysis. *Transactions and Proceedings of the American Philological Association, 69*, 542–56.

Solmsen, F. (1941). The Aristotelian tradition in ancient rhetoric. *American Journal of Philology, 62*, 35–50.

Sowell, T. (2002). *A conflict of visions: Ideological origins of political struggles*. New York: Basic Books.

Sprague, R. (2001). *The older sophists*. Columbia, SC: University of South Carolina Press. (Original work published 1972.)

Stark, R. (2003). *One true god: Historical consequences of monotheism*. Princeton: Princeton University Press.

Starnes, C. (1990). *Augustine's conversion: A guide to the argument of Confessions I–IX*. Waterloo, Ontario: Wilfrid Laurier University Press.

Stroumsa, G. (2005). *La fin du sacrifice: Les mutations religieuses de l'ntiquité tardive*. Paris: Odile Jacob.

Suetonius. (1997). *Lives of the Caesars*, Vol. II. (J. Rolfe, Trans.). Cambridge, MA: Harvard University Press. (Original work published 1914.)

Sullivan, D.L. (1992). Kairos and the rhetoric of belief. *Quarterly Journal of Speech, 78*, 317–32.

Swain, S. (1996). *Hellenism and empire: Language, classicism, and power in the Greek world AD 50–250*. Oxford: Clarendon Press.

Syme, R. (1939). *The Roman revolution*. Oxford: Oxford University Press.

Syme, R. (1960). Piso Frugi and Crassus Frugi. *Journal of Roman Studies, 50*, 12–20.

Syme, R. (1989). *The Augustan aristocracy*. London: Oxford University Press.

Symonds, J.A. (2002). *Studies of the Greek Poets*, Vol. 1. Honolulu, HI: University Press of the Pacific.

Tell, D. (2006). Beyond mnemotechnics: Confession and memory in Augustine. *Philosophy and Rhetoric, 39*, 233–53.

Tellegen-Couperus, O. (2003). Introduction. In O. Tellegen-Couperus (Ed.). *Quintilian and the law: The art of persuasion in law and politics* (pp. 11–28). Leuven, Belgium: Leuven University Press.

Teske, R.J. (2001). Augustine's philosophy of memory. In E. Stump and N. Kretzman (Eds.). *The Cambridge companion to Augustine* (pp. 148–58). Cambridge: Cambridge University Press.

Tessitore, A. (1996). *Reading Aristotle's Ethics: Virtue, rhetoric, and political philosophy*. Albany, NY: State University of New York Press.

Theodorakakou, A. (2005). Judgment in the Hellenistic doctrine of *krinomenon*. *Argumentation, 19*, 239–50.

Too, Y. (1995). *The rhetoric of identity in Isocrates: Text, power, pedagogy*. Cambridge: Cambridge University Press.

Toohey, P. (1996). *Epic lessons: An introduction to ancient didactic poetry*. London: Routledge.

Troup, C. (1999). *Temporality, eternity, and wisdom: The rhetoric of Augustine's* Confessions. Columbia, SC: University of South Carolina Press.

Untersteiner, M. (1971). *The Sophists*. (K. Freeman, Trans.). Cambridge: Cambridge University Press. (Original work published 1948.)

Untersteiner, M., and Battegazzore, A. (1962). *Sofisti, Testimonianze e frammenti IV: Antifonte, Crizia*. Florence: La Nuova Italia.

Usher, S. (1999). *Greek oratory: Tradition and originality*. New York: Oxford University Press.

van Oort, J. (1991). *Jerusalem and Babylon: A study into Augustine's City of God and the sources of his doctrine of the two cities*. New York: E.J. Brill.

Vernant, J. (1982). *The origins of Greek thought*. Ithaca, NY: Cornell University Press.

Vernesi, C., Caramelli, D., Dupanloup, I., Bertorelle, G., Lari, M., Cappellini, E., Moggi-Cecchi, J., Chiarelli, B., Castrì, L., Casoli, A., Mallegni, F., Lalueza-Fox, C., and Barbujani, G. (2004). The Etruscans: A population-genetic study. *The American Journal of Human Genetics, 74*, 694–704.

Veyne, P. (1987). The Roman empire. In P. Veyne (Ed.), *A history of private life: From pagan Rome to Byzantium*. (A. Goldhammer, Trans.). Cambridge, MA: Harvard University Press.

Villeneuve, F. (1934). *Horace epîtres*. Paris: Association Guillaume Budé.

von Heyking, J. (2001). *Augustine and politics as longing in the world*. Columbia, MO: University of Missouri Press.

Wade, A.M. (2002). *History of the Roman people*. Englewood Cliffs, NJ: Prentice Hall.

Wade, N. (2006). *Before the dawn: Recovering the lost history of our ancestors*. New York: Penguin.

Walker, J. (2000). *Rhetoric and poetics in antiquity*. New York: Oxford University Press.

Walzer, A. (2006). Moral philosophy and rhetoric in the Institutes: Quintilian on honor and expediency. *Rhetoric Society Quarterly, 36*, 263–80.

Wardy, R. (1996). *The birth of rhetoric: Gorgias, Plato and their successors*. London: Routledge.

Watson, L. (2007). The *Epodes*: Horace's Archilocus? In S. Harrison (Ed.), *The Cambridge companion to Horace* (pp. 93–104). Cambridge: Cambridge University Press.

Watson, G. (1977). Skepticism about weakness of will. *The Philosophical Review, 86*, 316–39.

Weaver, R.M. (1953). The *Phaedrus* and the nature of rhetoric. In R.M. Weaver, *The ethics of rhetoric* (pp. 3–26). Chicago: Henry Regnery.

Welch, K. (1990). Writing instruction in ancient Athens after 450 BC. In J. Murphy (Ed.), *A short history of writing instruction: From ancient Greece to twentieth-century America* (pp. 1–18). Davis, CA: Hermagoras Press.

Whately, R. (1963). *Elements of rhetoric*. D. Ehninger (Ed.). Carbondale, IL: Southern Illinois University Press.

Wheelock, F. (Ed.) (1974). *Quintilian as educator: Selections from the institutio oratoria of Marcu Favius Quintilianus*. (H. Butler, Trans.). New York: Twayne.

White, P. (1977). Horace A.P. 128–30: The Intent of the Wording. *Classical Quarterly, 27*, 191–201.

Whitmarsh, T. (2001). *Greek literature and the Roman empire: The politics of imitation*. Oxford: Oxford University Press.

Williams, S., and Friell, G. (1994). *Theodosius: The empire at bay*. New Haven, CT: Yale University Press.

Wills, G. (1999). *Saint Augustine*. New York: Viking.

Winter, B. (1997). *Philo and Paul among the Sophists*. Cambridge: Cambridge University Press.

Winterbottom, M. (1998). Quintilian the moralist. In T. Albadejo, E. del Río, and J. Caballero (Eds.), *Quintiliano: Historia y actualidad de la retórica* (pp. 317–334). Logroña: Instituto de Estudios Riojanos.

Wiseman, T. (1988). Satyrs in Rome? The background to Horace's *Ars Poetica*. *Journal of Roman Studies, 78*, 1–13.

Wolfsdorf, D. (1998). The historical reader of Plato's *Protagoras*. *The Classical Quarterly, 48*, 126–33.

Wood, N. (1974). Socrates as political partisan. *Canadian Journal of Political Science, 7*, 3–31.

Wood, N. (1988). *Cicero's social and political thought*. Berkeley: University of California Press.

Worthington, I. (1993). Once more, the client/logographos relationship. *Classical Quarterly, 43*, 67–72.

Yunis, H. (2005). Eros in Plato's *Phaedrus* and the shape of Greek rhetoric. *Arion, 13, 1*, 101–25.

Sources

The editor and publisher gratefully acknowledge the permission granted to reproduce the copyright material in this book:

R1 Excerpt from "The Second Poem – Lady of the Largest Heart," pp. 126–36 from *Inanna, Lady of the Largest Heart: Poems of the Sumerian High Priestess Enheduanna* by Betty De Shong Meador. © 2000 by Betty De Shong Meador. Reprinted by permission of the author and the University of Texas Press.

R2 Excerpt from "The Third Poem – The Exaltation of Innana," pp. 174–80 from *Inanna, Lady of the Largest Heart: Poems of the Sumerian High Priestess Enheduanna* by Betty De Shong Meador. © 2000 by Betty De Shong Meador. Reprinted by permission of the author and the University of Texas Press.

R3–R9 "With His Venom," "That Afternoon," "We Heard Them Chanting," "It's No Use," "Sleep, Darling," "I Have Had Not One Word," "Afraid," from *Sappho: A New Translation* edited and translated by M. Barnard. University of California Press, 1958. © 1958 by The Regents of the University of California, © renewed 1986 by Mary Barnard. Reprinted by permission of The University of California Press.

R10–R11 "He Seems to Me," "A Host of Horsemen," pp. 54–6 from *Greek Lyric: An Anthology in Translation*, edited and translated by Andrew M. Miller. Hackett Publishing, 1996. Reprinted by permission of Hackett Publishing Company, Inc. All rights reserved.

R12 "To Aphrodite," from *Sappho: The Greek Poems*, edited and translated by William Harris. Retrieved October 21, 2008 from http://community.middlebury.edu/~harris/sappho.html.

R13 Fragment 1, *Man Is the Measure*, p. 4 from *The Older Sophists*, edited by Rosamond Kent Sprague and translated by M. O'Brien (Hackett Publishing, 2001). Reprinted by permission of Hackett Publishing Company, Inc. All rights reserved.

R14 Fragment 2, *On the Gods*.

R15 Fragment 3, *Dissoi Logoi*.

R16 Fragment 4, *Making the Worse Appear the Better*, p. 335 reprinted by permission of the publishers and Trustees of the Loeb Classical Library from *Aristotle*, Volume XXII, Loeb Classical Library Volume 193, translated by John Henry Freese (Cambridge, MA: Harvard University Press, 1926). © 1926 by the President and Fellows of Harvard College. The Loeb Classical Library ® is a registered trademark of the President and Fellows of Harvard College.

R17 Fragment 1, *On the Nonexistent*, p. 42 from *The Older Sophists*, edited by Rosamond Kent Sprague and translated by G. Kennedy (Hackett Publishing, 2001). Reprinted by permission of Hackett Publishing Company, Inc. All rights reserved.

R18 *The Defense of Palamedes*, pp. 54–63 from *The Older Sophists*, edited by Rosamond Kent Sprague and translated by G. Kennedy (Hackett Publishing, 2001). Reprinted by permission of Hackett Publishing Company, Inc. All rights reserved.

R19 *The Encomium of Helen*, pp. 50–4 from *The Older Sophists*, edited by Rosamond Kent Sprague

Index